WORLD
CIVILIZATIONS

PHILIP LEE RALPH

ROBERT E. LERNER

STANDISH MEACHAM

EDWARD MCNALL BURNS

WORLD CIVILIZATIONS

Their History and Their Culture

VOLUME II / EIGHTH EDITION

Including material from WESTERN CIVILIZATIONS by Edward McNall Burns. Copyright 1973, 1968, 1963, 1958, 1954, 1949, 1947, 1941 and material from WESTERN CIVILIZATIONS by Edward McNall Burns, Robert E. Lerner and Standish Meacham. Copyright 1984, 1980 and material from WESTERN CIVILIZATIONS by Robert E. Lerner, Standish Meacham, and Edward McNall Burns. Copyright 1988.

Library of Congress Cataloging-in-Publication Data
Main entry under title:
World civilizations, their history and their culture / Philip Lee Ralph
... [et al.]. — 8th ed.
        p.   cm.
    Includes index.
    1. Civilization—History.   I. Ralph, Philip Lee.
CB69.W67   1991
909—dc20   90-45337
                                                                            CIP

The text of this book is composed in Bembo
Composition and manufacturing by Kingsport Press

Book design by Antonina Krass
Layout by Ben Gamit

W. W. Norton & Company Inc., 500 Fifth Avenue, New York, N.Y. 10110
W. W. Norton & Company Ltd., 10 Coptic Street, London WC1A 1PU

ISBN   0–393–95916–3

4 5 6 7 8 9 0

CONTENTS

Part Five THE FRENCH AND INDUSTRIAL
          REVOLUTIONS AND THEIR
          CONSEQUENCES

Chapter 29   NATIONALISM AND NATION-BUILDING
(1815–1870)   309

Part Six   THE WEST AT THE WORLD'S
CENTER

Chapter 30   THE PROGRESS OF INTERNATIONAL
INDUSTRIALIZATION AND COMPETITION
(1870–1914)   363

Chapter 31   THE MIDDLE CLASS CHALLENGED   393

Chapter 32   THE SEARCH FOR STABILITY (1870–
1914)   421

MAPS

XII

ILLUSTRATIONS IN COLOR

(Illustrations appear facing or following the pages indicated)

ILLUSTRATIONS IN THE TEXT

PREFACE

Edward McNall Burns observed in an earlier preface: "The time has long since passed when modern man could think of the world as consisting of Europe and the United States. Western culture is, of course, primarily a product of European origins. But it has never been that exclusively. Its original foundations were in Southwestern Asia and North Africa. These were supplemented by influences seeping in from India and eventually from China. From India and the Far East the West derived its knowledge of the zero, the compass, gunpowder, silk, cotton, and probably a large number of religious and philosophical concepts."

During the early centuries of the modern era European nations, by virtue of unprecedented advances in science and technology, spread their influence over the entire globe, with revolutionary effects upon the people of Asia and Africa. Large portions of these continents passed under Western domination but the present century has witnessed the beginning of a reversal of this trend. The political and economic ascendence that Europeans and North Americans long maintained has been eroded by the depletion of natural resources, the devastating effect of two world wars, and a frustrating competition between two superpowers striving for global hegemony. Today, as major and even minor nations of Asia enthusiastically enter the mainstream of economic development and technological progress, the West can no longer dictate their destinies, nor can it keep its own destiny separate from that of the rest of the world. The closing years of the past decade were marked by the dissolution of long-standing European and American power structures, an unforeseen development that obscured the future course of international politics, while at the same time offering hope of removing divisive ideological barriers between nations.

The mutual indebtedness of all peoples to one another for whatever progress they have made toward civilization; their increasing political, economic, and cultural interdependence; and their common responsibility for ensuring the survival of the human and all other living species have made traditional parochial curricula obsolete. The scope of education must be broadened to give students a deeper and more realistic vision of the world in which they live. Nowhere is the need more imperative than in the United States, because our nation rose to a position of leadership in the twentieth century against a background of relative isolation and because the requisites for leadership are changing in an increasingly complex world. The complexities of the present age can be successfully dealt with only by examining their roots, and these roots extend in many directions. Almost a decade ago, the president of the Association for Asian Studies reminded its members: "As Asia becomes part of our future, so it also becomes part of our past....What is needed is painful rethinking, as we assert that the histories of China and India are not an add-on in the curriculum, but a necessity." The same admonition is applicable for the histories of the countries of Latin America, Africa, and other areas too long unfamiliar. Attempts to bridge the differences that separate the world's organized communities must be based not only on a recognition of the distinctive characteristics of these communities but on an understanding of the historic forces that molded them. In the words of the late Canadian historian Herbert Norman, "History is the discipline that makes the whole world kin and is for humanity what memory is for the individual."

This work attempts to present a compact survey of the human race's struggle for civilization from early times to the present. No major area or country has been omitted. Europe, North, Central, and South America, the Commonwealth of Nations, the Middle East, Southeast Asia, Africa, India, China, and Japan have all received appropriate emphasis. Obviously, the history of none of them could be covered in full detail. The aim throughout has been to give the student both an appreciation of the distinctive achievements and limitations of the principal human societies and cultures, and an awareness of their relevance for contemporary problems. Political events are recognized as important, but the facts of political history are presented in relationship to cultural, social, and economic movements. The authors consider the effects of the Industrial Revolutions to be no less important than the Napoleonic Wars. They believe it is of greater value to understand the significance of Buddha, Confucius, Newton, Darwin, and Einstein than it is to be able to name the kings of France. In accordance with this broader conception of history, more space has been given to the teachings of John Locke, Karl Marx, and John Stuart Mill, of Mahatma Gandhi, Mao Zedong, and Leopold Senghor than to the military exploits of Gustavus Adolphus and the Duke of Wellington. If any philosophical bias underlies the narrative, it stems from the conviction that most of human progress thus far has resulted from the growth of intelligence and respect for the rights of man, and that therein lies the chief hope for a better world in the future.

The first edition of *World Civilizations* was published in 1955, the second in 1958, the third in 1964, the fourth in 1969, the fifth in 1974, the sixth in 1982, and the seventh in 1986. Each edition has included the whole of Edward McNall Burns's *Western Civilizations*, except for sections on the non-Western world, which are more fully covered in this work. The sixth, seventh, and eighth editions of *World Civilizations* incorporate *Western Civilizations* as revised for the ninth, tenth, and eleventh editions, respectively, by Robert E. Lerner of Northwestern University and Standish Meacham of University of Texas at Austin. While preserving the distinctive qualities of the Burns text, the authors of *World Civilizations*, utilizing the results of recent scholarship, have sharpened the focus on areas of greatest concern for today's students, including living conditions, the status of women, and the treatment of minority groups in human societies of the past and present. Organizational strategies and interpretive schemes have been revised where the progress of the discipline has dictated such steps. In recent editions this has resulted in dramatic reworkings of the material on the Western world in the Middle Ages and the early-modern era and in the nineteenth and early twentieth centuries. Notable features of the eighth edition are the incorporation in Part One of the exciting recent findings of paleoanthropoligists regarding the earliest human communities, a new treatment of Mesopotamia from a developmental perspective, and a fully rewritten consideration of the history of the Hebrews stressing the magnitude of their influence on subsequent thought and behavior; and, in Part Seven, a careful analysis of the complex changes within European societies and in international relations since the Second World War.

This edition of *World Civilizations* embodies extensive changes throughout. Like its three immediate predecessors it benefits substantially from the contributions of Professor Richard Hull of New York University. Updating and expanding the sections on Africa in Chapters 11, 17, 21, 30, 33 and 38, Professor Hull's narrative provides a concise and informative account of the peoples and major civilizations of the African continent and of their present state.

A fuller treatment of Latin American societies, which began with the seventh edition of *World Civilizations*, has been carried still further and includes a reinterpretation of the earliest civilizations of the New World based on recent discoveries. This edition also incorporates a thoroughly revised presentation of the civilizations of South Asia and the states of the Indian subcontinent. Chapter 5 and sections of Chapters 11, 16, 21, and 37 have been carefully reexamined, reorganized, and expanded in order to give consideration in greater depth to key topics. Current scholarship has also been drawn on to provide a fresh perspective on modern and contemporary China and the changing character of the Chinese Communist revolution. Tracing events to the Middle East crisis that began in August 1990, the text focuses on recent cataclysmic changes in Eastern Europe and the USSR. Chapters 41 and 42 analyze the implications of Mikhail Gorbachev's reversal of Soviet domestic and foreign policies, changing international power relationships, contemporary warmaking and peacemaking, the weakening of ideologies, the insistent problems of the Third World, the social and cultural impact of science and technology, and the challenge of ecology.

In conjunction with textual revisions, the maps and illustrations have received serious attention. Eight new maps have been added and the remaining maps have been amended as necessary. Fully 25 percent of the nearly 1,100 illustrations are new to this edition, having been culled from a wide range of American, Asian, and European archives. The text was the first to include color illustrations and continues to include far more color plates than any other book in the field. In this edition the text is accompanied by a thoroughly revised *Study Guide*, which includes numerous extracts from original and secondary sources, and an entirely new *Instructor's Manual*, with detailed chapter outlines, short-answer and essay questions, and extensive annotated film guides. Additional teaching aids include map transparencies and a computerized test-item file.

In preparing this edition the authors have profited from the assistance and counsel of many individuals, including not only specialists in various fields but also teachers and students who have used the text. Special acknowledgment is due to Loretta Smith (Northwestern University), Carl Petry (Northwestern University), Arelene Wolinski (San Diego Mesa College), Seymour Scheinberg (California State University at Fullerton), William Harris (Columbia University), Richard Saller (University of Chicago), James Stanely (Moody Bible College), Stephen Knoble (Moody Bible College), Richard T. Nolan (Mattatuck Community College), Stephen Ferruolo, Patricia B. Ebrey (University of Illinois), A. N. Galpern (University of Pittsburgh), Martin Katz (University of Alberta), Ronald Toby (University of Illinois), Gert Wendelborn (University of Rostock, Germany), Stephen F Dale (Ohio State University), James J. Sheehan (Stanford Unversity), Allen Cronenberg (Auburn University), James Boyden (University of Texas), Peter Hayes (Northwestern University), George Robb (Northwestern University), and Deeana Copeland.

For this edition, as for the fifth, sixth, and seventh, Robert E. Kehoe of W. W. Norton & Company has been a scrupulous editor, indispensable adviser, and faithful co-worker. His unflagging and enthusiastic devotion to the project has contributed greatly to its realization. Photo researcher Deborah Malmud was most resourceful in securing elusive illustrations, and makeup artist Ben Gamit arranged the closely coordinated illustrations and text with panache. Last but not least, I am grateful to my wife, Louise Conkling Ralph, for constructive suggestions on style and for typing the manuscript.

Philip Lee Ralph

WORLD
CIVILIZATIONS

Chapter 21

INDIA, EAST ASIA, AND AFRICA DURING THE EARLY-MODERN ERA (c. 1500–1800)

Fuji-ichi was a clever man, and his substantial fortune was amassed in his own lifetime. . . . He noted down the market ratio of copper and gold; he inquired about the current quotations of the rice brokers; he sought information from druggists' and haberdashers' assistants on the state of the market at Nagasaki; for the latest news on the prices of ginned cotton, salt, and saké, he noted the various days on which the Kyoto dealers received dispatches from the Edo branch shops. Every day a thousand things were entered in his book, and people came to Fuji-ichi if they were ever in doubt. He became a valuable asset to the citizens of Kyoto.

—I. Saikaku, *The Tycoon of All Tenants* (1688)

Between the sixteenth and the nineteenth centuries a reinvigorated Indian empire headed by a new dynasty attained the rank of a major power; China, under the last of a long series of imperial dynasties, waxed even stronger, becoming the largest and most populous country in the world; and Japan adapted her feudal institutions to the requirements of a despotic government. In both India and China, and to a lesser degree in Japan, splendor and magnificence reflected the tastes of wealthy societies and mighty rulers, as was also true in much of Europe during this same period. In the long run, however, the great Asian states found themselves at a disadvantage because they played a passive rather than an active role in the Commercial Revolution. As western European nations turned to empire building and expanded their naval forces, they established direct contacts with the coastal regions of Asia, took over the bulk of the trade between East and West, and frequently threatened the independence of non-European peoples. For several centuries the principal Eastern states were strong enough to protect themselves against the threat of aggression from the West. Faced with rigid trade restrictions in China and almost totally excluded from Japan, the seafaring Europeans

Impact of the West upon the East

turned to other quarters. In the 1570s the Spanish occupied the Philippines, subduing the native tribes and the communities of Chinese colonists in the Islands. A few years later the Dutch, through their East India Company, laid the foundations of a rich empire in Indonesia, dislodging the Portuguese who had preceded them by almost a century. The British and French somewhat belatedly turned their attention to the mainland of India, where they secured valuable trading posts in the course of the seventeenth century. During this same period the Portuguese, the British, and the Dutch established commercial enclaves on the coast of Africa.

1. INDIA UNDER THE MUGHAL DYNASTY

The rise of the Mughal Dynasty

By the end of the fifteenth century the Delhi Sultanate, which under successive Turko-Afghan dynasties had endured for three hundred years, was in a weakened condition. Early in the sixteenth century northern India fell by conquest to a new dynasty that provided more effective rule than any India had known since the reign of Harsha in the seventh century and inaugurated one of the more productive periods of Indian civilization. This dynasty, which reached its height in the seventeenth century, is known as the Mughal from the Persian term for "Mongol" (corrupted into the English "Mogul"), although it was not of Mongol origin. Its founder, Babur (1483–1530), was descended from two of the world's most renowned conquerors—the Turk Timur on his father's side and the Mongol Genghis Khan on his mother's. His own son and heir was born of a Persian mother, and later descendants mingled their blood with that of Hindu royal families.

Babur "the Tiger"

Babur was a man of tremendous energy, intelligence, and sensitivity as shown by his remarkable autobiography, but he earned the epithet "The Tiger" through his dazzling military exploits. Beginning as ruler of a tiny principality in Turkestan, Babur crossed the mountains into Afghanistan to seize Kabul. Failing in attempts to expand his kingdom in Central Asia, he turned his attention southward to the demoralized and divided Delhi Sultanate. Conveniently the viceroy of the Punjab invited Babur to help "save" him from his overlord the sultan. After defeating the sultan's army near Delhi in April 1526, Babur determined to make himself master of Hindustan. The small size of his forces relative to those opposing him was compensated for by their intense loyalty and by the fact that they possessed primitive but destructive artillery and match-fired muskets of European manufacture. The conqueror's closest brush with disaster came in 1527 when he faced the armies of a Rajput confederacy far outnumbering his own and led by a prince who had never submitted to Muslim rule. But clever strategem and reckless courage prevailed against a host divided in its loyalties. After exhorting his men to valor and vowing to abstain from wine henceforth if Allah gave him victory, Babur carried the

The Court of the Emperor Babur "the Tiger,"
Founder of the Mogul Dynasty

day. Bengal fell to him in 1529, leaving him master of most of northern
India.

The twenty-five years following Babur's death in 1530 were critical
for the fate of the dynasty. His son Humayun, able but too often
indolent, was driven out of India by Afghan generals and fled to the
court of Persia, his mother's homeland. With the help of a Persian
army Humayun recovered the Delhi throne in 1555 but he died following an accident the next year, leaving his fragile kingdom in the hands
of a thirteen-year-old son, Akbar. Fortunately for the Mughals the
lad had the protection of an able and loyal general, Bayran Khan,
who served as regent, crowned the young prince, and fought off
rival claimants until through palace intrigue he was expelled and
stabbed to death in 1561 while on pilgrimage to Mecca. The next year,
at the age of twenty, Akbar surprised the court and schemers of the
harem by taking personal command of the government.

Akbar, justifiably remembered as the "Great Mughal," was an outstanding world figure in a century that boasted several "magnificent
monarchs." By a coincidence his long reign (1556–1605) coincided
almost exactly with that of England's Elizabeth I, whose unique talents
for governance were parallel to his own. By military force Akbar
consolidated his position in northern and central India, holding Kabul

Humayun and the regency

Akbar "the great Mughal"

in the northwest and securing Gujarat on the Kathiawar peninsula, essential for commercial exports via the Arabian Sea. He extended his rule by taking Orissa on the Bay of Bengal in 1592 and Baluchistan, west of the Indus River, three years later. His forays into the Deccan won victories but few permanent conquests.

Although Akbar's reign was occupied with warfare and marked with occasional acts of cruelty, he established an effective and on the whole judicious administration. To break the opposition of the Rajput clans he coaxed one into a marriage alliance and punished any that threatened, once massacring 30,000 defenders of a captured fortress. For the separate provinces into which he divided the empire he appointed military governors with extensive powers but, unlike his predecessors, he paid them regular salaries instead of endowing them with land grants or letting them assess the people under their jurisdiction. Taxes were collected by nonmilitary officials, the revenue transmitted to the capital and thence disbursed by the central government. Provincial governors were periodically transferred from one district to another to prevent them from developing a local following that might challenge imperial authority. Akbar kept his subordinates under close observation, held them to strict accountability, and punished them for misconduct. As with most Indian regimes ancient or modern, the principal source of state revenue under the Mughals was the land tax. Akbar's assessment was comparatively light, amounting to one-third of the annual crop value of the lands actually under cultivation, and based on the average yield over a ten-year period. He had the lands surveyed to determine the value of holdings and he reduced or waived the tax in areas troubled by famine. The emperor's annual income is estimated as the equivalent of $200,000,000 and his higher officials were rewarded with very generous salaries. This was an age of autocratic rule in Europe as in Asia, with extreme disparities between the upper and lower classes. While Indian cities expanded and a substantial middle class of traders and artisans flourished, common laborers were far from prosperous and some were slaves. Rural villagers, comprising an overwhelming majority of the population, could expect only a low standard of living—but they were probably better off than they have been in modern times. Akbar's revenue system enriched the governing class but it was honestly administered and permitted the growth of a vigorous economy.

The most innovative of Akbar's policies and the key to his success was his determination to rule as an Indian sovereign rather than as a foreign conqueror. His criminal code was harsh, although not more barbarous than that of many contemporary European states. Civil law for Muslim subjects was based upon Islamic tradition and the Koran, but he permitted Hindus to settle disputes among themselves according to their own laws by the decision of village councils or Brahmanical opinion. Surpassing all of his predecessors in his efforts to conciliate his Indian subjects, Akbar abolished the special taxes

THE MUGHAL EMPIRE IN INDIA

Map labels:
(AFGHANISTAN)
CHINA
SIKHS
Lahore
PUNJAB
(PAKISTAN)
Indus R.
HIMALAYA MOUNTAINS
Delhi ★
Brahmaputra R.
RAJPUTS
Agra ★
Ganges R.
BALUCHISTAN
HINDUSTAN
(BANGLA DESH)
INDIA
GUJARAT
VINDHYA MTS.
BENGAL
Calcutta
Surat
Damão (Daman)
Diu
ORISSA
Bombay
Poona
MARATHAS
Golconda
ARABIAN SEA
DECCAN
BAY OF BENGAL
BIJAPUR
Goa
Madras
INDIAN OCEAN

Under Akbar, 1556-1605

Expansion under Shah Jahan, 1627-1658 and Aurangzeb, 1658-1707

that had been laid on non-Muslims, granted freedom of worship, and encouraged the building of Hindu temples. With an eye to political expediency he chose women of different nationalities for his harem (said to number over 5,000). His favorite wife and the mother of his successor to the throne was a Rajput princess. He employed Hindus in the military and administrative services, placing a raja in the key post of minister of finance.

Akbar's complex personality and rare combination of interests left their mark upon all aspects of his reign. He apparently suffered from epileptic attacks and occasional spells of depression, but usually displayed buoyant spirits. Endowed with a superb physique, he loved

Akbar's personality and his cultural interests

Akbar, a Contemporary Portrait.
The genius of the "Great Mu-ghal" lay in his ability to con-solidate his wide-ranging conquests through his atten-tiveness to Indian sensibilities and the creation of an adminis-trative framework that sus-tained the empire for about one hundred and fifty years.

Shah Jahan

feats of strength and dangerous exploits, sometimes risking his life in the most reckless fashion by attacking a lion singlehandedly or by riding wild elephants. In a fit of temper he could be pitilessly cruel, but he was generally fair in judgment and frequently generous to a defeated opponent. This high-strung emperor was endowed with lively intellectual curiosity and a capacious mind. He is credited with several inventions, chiefly in connection with the improvement of artillery. Although he stubbornly refused to learn to read or write, he was fond of literature and collected a huge library. A gifted musician, he not only acquired skill as a performer (especially on a type of kettle drum) but also became versed in the highly intricate theory of Hindu vocalization.

Akbar's innovative boldness led him not only to tolerate Hinduism but finally to abandon the religion of his own people. A strain of mysticism in his psyche attracted him toward Islamic Sufism, but his restless intellect kept him from finding satisfaction in any established dogma. Because he enjoyed philosophical argument he instituted a series of weekly debates among spokesmen for various religions from within and without India, and he enlivened the discussions by sharply questioning the participants. Midway through his reign, in 1581, Akbar inaugurated a religion of his own devising which he called the "Divine Faith." A synthetic monotheism affirming the virtues of wisdom, courage, chastity, and justice, it incorporated the Hindu prohibition of cow slaughter, a Parsee ceremony of fire worship, and a Christian baptismal rite. Adherents were required to perform the traditional Muslim prostration before the prophet, namely Akbar himself—whom the less sophisticated probably worshiped as God. The Divine Faith did not spread far beyond the circle of the court and disappeared soon after Akbar's lifetime. Meanwhile it alienated many orthodox Muslims who regarded the emperor as a traitor to Islam.

The most illustrious period of the dynasty was the century and a half embracing four generations of "Great Mughals." These rulers did not lack heirs, but each reign was marred by quarrels over the succession, with princes revolting against their father and joining in fratricidal strife against one another. Jahangir (1605–1627), Akbar's son and successor, probably poisoned his father. Talented, crafty, self-indulgent, and dissipated, Jahangir let the power slip into the hands of his Persian wife. The reign of her son, Shah Jahan, provided three decades of splendor (1627–1658) but at a staggering cost. Extrav-agant spending to adorn two capitals—Delhi and Agra—together with continuous wars in the Deccan and military expeditions into Central Asia and against Persia so drained the treasury that the land tax was raised to one-half the annual crop value, laying a crushing burden upon poor cultivators. Shah Jahan ended his days a prisoner of his rebellious son, Aurangzeb, who during a long reign missed an opportu-nity to restore the state to sound health.

Aurangzeb, perhaps innately the ablest of Akbar's descendants, ruled for the same number of years as his great-grandfather (1658–1707). Ambitious and energetic, he had demonstrated his capacity and gained experience in statecraft before succeeding to (and while plotting to obtain) the throne. As viceroy of the still unconquered Deccan he skillfully enticed some *sufis* and nobles in Bijapur away from their loyalty to the sultan of that rival Muslim kingdom. During the first half of his reign Aurangzeb governed prudently, adhering to the pattern established by Akbar. During the second half he depleted his resources in attempting to crush every independent state in India, whether Hindu or Muslim, and he alienated his Hindu subjects by reverting to a policy of religious persecution. Seemingly obsessed with a desire to enforce Islamic orthodoxy, he reinstituted special taxes on non-Muslims, forbade the construction of temples, and had some demolished. A man of sincere but fanatical piety, he frowned upon art as idolatrous and disparaged literature on the ground that it exalted human vanity. The royal "prayer-monger" banished music from his court and replaced the Persian solar calendar with the clumsier lunar calendar because the latter had been used by Muhammad.

The reign of Aurangzeb: A return to Islamic orthodoxy

Warring simultaneously against "idolators" within the kingdom and political adversaries without, Aurangzeb resorted to shortsighted policies that weakened the administration and jeopardized the economy. To avoid paying salaries to territorial governors as Akbar had done, he gave them grants of land, enabling unscrupulous officials to evade their responsibilities to the state and to squeeze the peasants beneath them. Aurangzeb (whose imperial name was Alamgir, "World Conqueror") spent the last twenty-six years of his life in the Deccan directing military campaigns. In 1686 his forces overthrew the long-buffeted kingdom of Bijapur and the following year absorbed the small neighboring state of Golconda. These victories were of dubious benefit because they destroyed a precarious balance of power in the Deccan, encouraging the outbreak of fresh hostilities. Although Aurangzeb's conquests extended farther into the peninsula than those of his predecessors, they could not be secured, and at the end of his reign he left the Mughals with more enemies than they had faced at the beginning.

Aurangzeb, the Last of the Great Mughals. In stark contrast to his illustrious great-grandfather, Aurangzeb sought to transform the empire into an orthodox Islamic state, and his conquests only heralded its precipitous decline.

Most intractable of the emperor's foes were the Marathas, a confederacy of Hindu tribes occupying hilly terrain in the northwestern Deccan. Some of their leaders had served with the Mughals or with Bijapur—the two rival Muslim powers between which they were wedged—but by 1662 the Marathas had established an independent kingdom of their own, dominating the western quarter of Bijapur and with Poona as its capital. Under their intrepid king Shivaji, a master of guerilla tactics, they frustrated all attempts to crush them, even when their strongholds were taken and the "mountain rat" himself was held captive for a time. The Marathas operated as a de facto state over a large section of the Deccan until late in the eighteenth century

The Marathas

The Sikhs

The evolution of the sect

when the confederacy broke into several independent principalities.

Whereas Akbar had tried to placate the Rajputs, Aurangzeb provoked them into open rebellion. Similarly he made enemies of the Sikhs of the Punjab, thus creating challenges to imperial authority in the very heart of his domain. In origin the Sikhs were a religious group with progressive and humane convictions. The sect had been founded in the fifteenth century by Nanak, a philanthropic and spiritually minded preacher whose teachings and influence have been the subject of conflicting interpretation. Recent scholars question the claim of some admirers that Nanak sought to establish a common bond between Hindus and Muslims by combining the best elements of each of the two faiths. Undoubtedly he drew much of his inspiration from contemporary Hindu beliefs and traditions, but he was a genuinely original thinker. The essence of his teaching was the brotherhood of man, the oneness of God, and the duty of acts of charity:

Make love thy mosque; sincerity thy prayer-carpet; justice thy Koran;
Modesty thy circumcision; courtesy thy Kaaba; truth thy Guru; charity thy
    creed and prayer;
The will of God thy rosary, and God will preserve thine honor, O Nanak.

Nanak rejected formal scriptures and mechanical rites, and because he repudiated caste he gained many adherents from among the depressed classes of Hindus. Although his religion contained doctrines common to Islam and Hinduism (and Christianity), the Sikhs ("disciples") became a distinctive community rather than a branch of Hinduism. Nanak was succeeded by a line of spiritual leaders or gurus, to the fourth of whom Akbar granted a site in Amritsar. Here they erected the Golden Temple, a holy of holies to the Sikhs and repository of their scriptures. While Akbar had treated the Sikhs kindly, his successor, Jahangir, executed the fifth guru for supporting the emperor's rebellious son, and Aurangzeb, unable to coerce the Sikh leader into accepting Islam, had him killed. Not surprisingly the belligerent hostility of the later Mughals goaded the Sikhs to fury. The sect which had begun as a peaceful reformist movement was gradually transformed into a military order. Its members were initiated by a rite called "Baptism of the Sword," and many of them adopted the surname Singh, meaning "Lion." While they retained an antipathy toward caste and subscribed to a strict code of personal discipline, they lost much of the generous idealism of their early leaders. Appearing sometimes as no better than brigands, they showed particular relish for slaughtering Muslims. Thus at the opening of the eighteenth century the Mughal power was menaced not only by the usual court intrigues but also by the spirited defiance of powerful Indian groups—Rajputs, Marathas, and Sikhs.

Thirty-two years after the exhausting reign of Aurangzeb the kingdom was stricken by a disaster from without. In 1739 a usurper to the throne of Persia, Nadir Shah, invaded India and sacked Delhi savagely, leaving much of the city in ruins. The empire never fully recovered from this blow, although it remained a force to reckon with and the Mughals were accorded the formal dignity of ruling sovereigns until long after the British had entrenched themselves in India.

The three centuries of Mughal rule were constructive in many respects. The Mughal administrative system proved useful to the British as they extended their jurisdiction over sections of the subcontinent. More important was the continuing evolution of cultural patterns, enriched by the addition of Persian and other Islamic strains to the Indian amalgam. The emperors were generally cosmopolitan in outlook and welcomed both commercial and cultural intercourse with foreign states. A fusion of Indian, Turkish, Arabic, and Persian was manifest in literature, the arts, and the tone of society. Literature was stimulated by royal patronage and also by the fact that several languages could be drawn upon. Both Turkish and Persian were spoken in court circles; familiarity with Arabic, the language of the Koran, was a necessity for educated Muslims, and a knowledge of the native dialects of northern India was essential for administrators. A permanent result of the intermingling between Turko-Persian and Indian cultures was the rise of a variety of speech known as Urdu ("the camp language"). While Urdu in its vocabulary includes many Persian and Arabic words and is written in Arabic script, its grammatical structure is basically the same as that of Hindi, the most prevalent Aryan vernacular of northern India. Both Urdu and Hindi came to be standard mediums of communication throughout northern India. (Urdu is now confined chiefly to Pakistan.)

While many Persian scholars and poets were attracted to the cosmopolitan Mughal court, the literary works of most enduring value were produced by Hindus, especially during the tolerant regime of Akbar. This emperor showed great interest in India's literary treasures as well as in her art and music, and he appointed a poet laureate for Hindi. He had Persian translations made from the *Vedas* and the Epics. Tulsi Das, one of India's greatest poets, lived during Akbar's reign. His principal work was an idealized and highly spiritual version of the ancient epic the *Ramayana*. This poem, which combines fine craftsmanship with a warm and fervent moral earnestness, was written in Hindi rather than in Sanskrit, although its author was a brahman.

Architecture illustrates most perfectly the interaction of Hindu and Islamic motifs. Muslim builders introduced the minaret or spire, the pointed arch, and the bulbous dome; Hindu and Jain traditions emphasized horizontal lines and elaborate ornamentation. Because Indian stonemasons and architects were frequently employed even on Muslim religious edifices, there was bound to be a fruitful interchange of ideas, and this culminated in the sixteenth and seventeenth centuries in the production of a distinctive Indo-Muslim architectural style. Some of Akbar's constructions at Agra, of durable red sandstone,

The Builders of the Mughal Empire. Left: *Akbar Inspecting the Progress of the Construction of Fatehpur Sikri in 1584.* This new city, only 26 miles from Agra, was built in honor of a Sufi saint whose promise of a male heir for Akbar had come to fruition. Described by a contemporary English traveler as larger than London, Fatehpur Sikri was abandoned five years after its completion, possibly due to the failure of its water supply. Right: *The Great Mosque at Lahore.* Built during the reign of Aurangzeb, this mosque of red sandstone with marble-covered domes shows Persian influence.

are still standing; and so is most of an entire city which he conceived and had completed at a site a few miles west of Agra and then abandoned only five years later. But Akbar's forts and government halls lacked the choice materials, the refinement, and the sensuous beauty of the buildings executed for Shah Jahan a half-century later. In place of sandstone, these employed the finest marbles, agate, turquoise, and other semiprecious stones, and were frequently decorated with inlays of gold and silver. Shah Jahan's dazzling structures, contrasting markedly with the robustness of Akbar's work, betray an excessive elegance bordering on decadence.

The public works of Shah Jahan

Shah Jahan established his chief royal residence at Delhi, where he laid out a new city and named it after himself. Both Delhi and Agra in the seventeenth century were among the world's greatest cities in respect to number of inhabitants and impressive public buildings. Agra, with a population of 600,000, was divided into separate sections for the different types of merchants and artisans and contained 70 great mosques and 800 public baths. The new Delhi was protected by walls rising 60 feet above the river. Here was constructed a huge royal palace that beggars description. It housed the famous Peacock Throne, inlaid with precious metals and jewels, the value of which has been estimated as in excess of $5,000,000. (It was seized in Nadir

Shah's raid in 1739 and carried off to Persia.) Shah Jahan's most celebrated monument is the Taj Mahal, located at Agra and designed as a mausoleum and memorial to his favorite wife (who died while bearing her fourteenth child to the emperor and while the Deccan was ravaged by famine). The Taj engaged the labor of 20,000 workmen and was some twenty years in construction. The building is a unique blend of Persian and Indian architectural elements, executed with meticulous craftsmanship. Its charm is enhanced by its setting, amid shaded walks, lakes, and gardens.

The Islamic taboos against pictorial representation were almost totally disregarded by the Mughal rulers, who were enthusiastic collectors and connoisseurs of painting. Reflecting the influence of contemporary Persian art, the most typical examples were miniatures, including landscapes and especially portraits, executed with realism and meticulous detail. Calligraphy also enjoyed the status of a fine art; many manuscripts were illuminated with pictures as in medieval Europe. Texts from the Koran were employed as decorative devices on screens and the façades of buildings in keeping with a general practice in Muslim countries. In many parts of India exacting craftsmanship and artistic standards were carried on much as they had been before the Muslim invasions. Particularly notable was the Rajput school of painting, fostered at the courts of native princes in Rajputana, more vigorous and less sensuous than the Mughal school.

In South India as in the North, reciprocal interaction between Muslim and Hindu elements stimulated creative activity. The reign of Sultan Ibrahim II of Bijapur (1580–1627) resembled that of his more famous contemporary Akbar in its encouragement of free expression and eclecticism in the arts as well as in religion. Architectural monuments from the era of this "Teacher of the World"—as the sultan's admirers

Top: *Mumtaz Mahal ("Ornament of the Palace")*. The favorite wife of Shah Jahan, who died in childbirth in 1631 at the age of 39. Bottom: *Shah Jahan (1627–1658)*. The Mughal emperor was famous for his luxurious court and his magnificent buildings.

The Taj Mahal at Agra. Built by Shah Jahan in memory of Mumtaz Mahal, it is considered one of the finest examples of Indian Muslim architecture.

The coming of the Europeans

A European Traveler in the Late Sixteenth Century. This Mughal painting shows the subject leaving his world behind for a distinctly Indian setting.

Sir Thomas Roe: "War and traffic are incompatible"

called him—are embellished with lotus stems and budding shoots, reflecting an exuberance more typically Indian than Arabic or Persian.

One aspect of the Mughal period bound to have tremendous consequences for the future of India was the impact of European traders and adventurers. Although the footholds they secured at various points on the coast were small and seemingly insignificant, they denoted the awakening of Europeans to the commercial possibilities of South and Southeast Asia. The maritime enterprise shown by Indian states in earlier times was no longer evident, and even the Mughal empire for all its splendor and formidable armies did not maintain a navy. During most of the sixteenth century the Portuguese dominated the Indian Ocean, giving them a profitable position not only in commerce but also as providers of transport for the annual Muslim pilgrimage to Mecca. The Dutch and English—budding rivals of the great Catholic powers Spain and Portugal—cooperated for several years in ousting the Portuguese from the East Indies Spice Islands, but after the Dutch demonstrated forcefully their unwillingness to share the lucrative spice trade the British were compelled to turn their attention to the Indian mainland. Here they were impeded by the Portuguese, who held several fortified ports on the Indian coast and in Ceylon. Portuguese Jesuit missionaries at the Mughal court also discouraged any cordial reception of Protestant intruders. The British East India Company, chartered by Queen Elizabeth I in 1600, failed during the first two decades of its existence to obtain trading privileges. A swashbuckling captain, William Hawkins, representing the Company, was royally entertained by the convivial emperor Jahangir, but after two frustrating years Hawkins left Agra without a treaty. The company's bargaining position improved after the British shattered a Portuguese navy and began to dominate the Arabian Sea and the Persian Gulf. Sir Thomas Roe, dispatched to Agra as ambassador by King James I, in 1619 obtained Jahangir's permission for the English to build a factory at Surat, the Mughal's principal port. Notwithstanding an increasing British presence in India, Portugal retained Goa, Damão (Daman), and Diu on the west coast until forcibly dispossessed by the government of independent India in 1961.

Sir Thomas Roe warned his countrymen to shun the Portuguese policy of seizing territory and attempting to found colonies in India. He advised them instead to seek profit "at sea and in quiet trade," remembering that "war and traffic are incompatible." For some time the British were hard pressed to keep their trade channels open, let alone found colonies. The British East India Company languished under the early Stuart monarchs, especially when King Charles I licensed a rival association to engage in the eastern trade. But the Company recovered its monopoly under the Protectorate of Oliver Cromwell—who invigorated British commerce by defeating the Dutch and negotiating a favorable treaty with the Portuguese—and after the Restoration, King Charles II issued a new charter granting the

Portuguese Goa. A map from Pedro Barreto de Resende's revised edition of Antinio Bocarto's *Curo do Estado da India Oriental,* 1646. Wrested from the Deccan state of Bijapur in 1510, Goa remained under Portuguese control for 451 years.

East India Company the right to coin money, exercise jurisdiction over Englishmen residing in its factories, and make war or peace with "non-Christian powers." During the next several decades the Company reaped profits averaging 25 percent annually. Before the close of the century it had secured three locations of strategic as well as commercial importance in widely separated regions of India: the island of Bombay off the western coast (given by Portugal in 1661 when the English King Charles II married a Portuguese princess), Madras on the southeastern coast, and Port William (Calcutta) at the mouth of the Ganges. The French, who organized their own East India Company in 1664, acquired stations in India paralleling those of the British and able to compete successfully with them. In the mid-eighteenth century it seemed that France might surpass Britain in the race for empire when the able François Dupleix, with the backing of a French fleet, captured Madras and made himself virtual ruler of the whole southeastern quarter of the peninsula. But British victories in the Seven Years War (1756–1763), fought in Europe, America, India, and on the high seas, while not immediately dispossessing the French insured England's position as the dominant European power on the subcontinent.

Sir Thomas Roe. The British royal envoy to the court of the Mughal Emperor Jahangir set the tone for the British East India Company's role on the subcontinent for more than one hundred years.

2. CHINA UNDER THE MANCHU (CH'ING) DYNASTY

*Origins of the Manchu
(Ch'ing) Dynasty*

With the disintegration of the Ming Dynasty it was China's fate to succumb once more to the rule of foreign invaders. The conquerors, who occupied Manchuria on China's northern border and from which they derived the name Manchu, were essentially the same people as the Juchên, who had divided China with the Sung emperor 500 years before. Although of nomadic origin and differing from the Chinese in language and culture, the Manchus had long admired, and, to their lasting benefit, adopted important aspects of the Ming imperial system. While sparsely inhabited northern Manchuria was still a region of hunting and herding, by the sixteenth century settled agricultural communities had been established in the south along the Liao River. Early in the seventeenth century a minor chieftain named Nurhachi (died 1636) brought several tribes under his jurisdiction, established his

The Expansion of the Manchu (Ch'ing) Empire

capital at Mukden, and assumed a dynastic name, Ch'ing (meaning "Clear" or "Pure"). Before embarking on the conquest of China the Manchus had not only proclaimed a new dynastic rule for East Asia but had also created a political structure with ministries fashioned after those of the Ming, thus marking a transition from a tribal society to a territorial state. To conquer China the Manchus had, to a significant degree, Sinicized their own institutions.

Originating in military conquest, the Ch'ing Dynasty lasted nearly 300 years, until the institution of monarchy was overthrown by revolution in 1911. Although the dynasty is dated from 1644 when Peking was taken by the Manchus, their rule was not firmly secured until nearly 40 years later because of resistance offered by Chinese loyal to the Ming. In their conquest the Manchus were heavily indebted to Chinese generals whose allegiance they had won. Pacification of the southern and southwestern regions was left to Chinese commanders who were given such broad powers that they threatened to become independent. One general set himself up as ruler of a new dynasty, but Peking's authority was assured in 1681 by victory in the "War of the Three Feudatories." Eventually the state's frontiers were extended farther than ever before in China's history. Manchuria of course was an essential part of the empire, and the peripheral regions of Korea, Burma, Nepal, and sections of Indochina were linked as tributary dependencies. Imperial forces defeated nomadic tribes in Outer Mongolia (1696) and in 1720 invaded Tibet and installed at Lhasa a Dalai Lama friendly to the Ch'ing. The island of Taiwan, which had been occupied by Dutch traders and later by an enterprising Chinese merchant family with an extensive maritime network, was in 1683 annexed as part of the mainland province of Fukien.

The Emperor K'ang Hsi Engaged in Study. His devotion to the Confucian classics and the pursuit of science contributed to K'ang Hsi's image as an enlightened monarch.

While attempting to conciliate the Chinese, the Manchu rulers were careful to preserve their own people's ethnic identity. They closed Manchuria to Chinese immigration, forbade intermarriage between Chinese and Manchu, and required Chinese males to shave their foreheads and braid their hair in a queue after the Manchu fashion as a token of submission. To guard against rebellion Manchu garrisons were stationed in the principal cities, while Chinese troops were used as auxiliaries or as a police force. Repressive measures notwithstanding, the Ch'ing emperors were determined to be accepted as legitimate rulers rather than be resented as usurpers to the throne. In the face of domestic turmoil, prolonged armed resistance, and Chinese antipathy toward invading "barbarians," they succeeded to a remarkable degree not merely in retaining authority but in revitalizing the state as well. The Ch'ing's success is explained partly by its good fortune in having nearly half of the dynasty's entire history encompassed within the administrations of two able and energetic rulers. K'ang Hsi, who reigned for sixty-one years (1661–1722) and was thus a contemporary of King Louis XIV, though less celebrated in Western annals was an abler statesman than France's famous "Sun King." While still a youth

Ch'ien Lung (1736–1796). The great Manchu emperor under whom the Ch'ing Dynasty reached its climax. (Painting on silk by a nineteenth-century artist.)

Growth and prosperity in the age of Ch'ien Lung

he crushed the rebellion of the Three Feudatories in southwest China. He not only promptly reinstated the civil service examinations but also schooled himself in the Chinese classics upon which they were based. As the Ch'ing administration developed, more than 80 percent of the lower offices came to be filled by Chinese, although they obtained a much smaller share of the higher posts. The system whereby educated Chinese were recruited for government service through the competitive state examinations resembled somewhat the Indian Civil Service developed by the British East India Company, which in the eighteenth and nineteenth centuries enlisted native talents in the service of foreign masters. Finding that some scholars, through loyalty to the Ming, refused to sit for the triennial state examinations, K'ang Hsi sought to attract them by creating new degrees to be earned through special examinations. But although his rule was vigorous and on the whole judicious, he failed to win the unquestioned allegiance of well-to-do landholding families, particularly those of the Yangtze region where China's wealth was concentrated. Routine local affairs such as the supervision of markets, charities, and waterworks were left in the hands of the local gentry, an elite group which, under the direction of an official appointed for each county, provided the central government with an able and locally respected staff of administrators. The emperor's reluctance to antagonize this influential class kept him from making a comprehensive land survey on which a realistic tax structure could have been based. Poor peasants and tenants—and also the state's revenue—suffered from the rapacity and corruption of landlords and local officials. The examination system in effect strengthened the dominance of the landed gentry in Chinese society. Although the system was theoretically based upon merit rather than birth, only candidates who had had the benefit of an education could compete successfully, and poor families could not give their sons such an education.

Under the sixty-three-year reign of K'ang Hsi's grandson Ch'ien Lung (1736–1799)—the longest reign in Chinese history—the empire's physical boundaries and its prestige reached new dimensions. A vast nomadic area in the northwest, incorporated as the "New Dominion" (Sinkiang), doubled the state's area. Although Ch'ien Lung, lacking his grandfather's acuity, was inclined to accept purely theoretical solutions to problems and although in his later years he indulged undeserving favorites, he was conscientious and diligent, and his long reign compares favorably with those of contemporary sovereigns. During the eighteenth century China was not only the largest and most populous but also one of the best-governed states in the world. The inequalities and suffering known to earlier periods were still present, but a generally high level of prosperity is evidenced by a rapid increase in China's population. Estimated at below 80 million in 1390, it grew to more than 300 million during the eighteenth century. Unevenly distributed, population was densest in the Yangtze valley and along the southeast coast, the most prosperous regions of China and those where loyalty to the Manchu regime was weakest. While agriculture remained the primary source of private wealth and of the government's tax revenues, China's southern ports had become centers of a brisk maritime commerce, bringing profits to Chinese merchants but little revenue to the government because of the absence of a central agency to regulate trade and collect customs duties. The Manchu shared the Ming prejudice against overseas voyages and forbade the building of ships large enough to engage in them. Unfortunately for the dynasty this policy placed it at an increasing disadvantage as European traders, backed by armored fleets, sought entrance into China's ports.

The growth of population, which by mid-nineteenth century had risen to about 450 million, brought severe internal problems. The lack of sufficient arable land to support such a large number of people led to the clearing and cropping of upper river valleys that had hitherto been left to nature. Soil erosion increased the danger of floods and droughts, aggravating China's agrarian problems in the modern era. The Chinese custom of dividing land equally among male heirs tended to reduce farm plots below the size necessary to support a family. At the same time the more comfortably situated landed gentry found opportunities for state employment narrowing because the government neglected to enlarge the examination system or create new posts to keep pace with population growth. When the foundations of the dynasty were being laid, the great emperor K'ang Hsi, to allay fears that private holdings might be confiscated, had decreed that tax quotas assigned to various districts should remain fixed at their existing levels. Consequently, as population increased and the country's prosperity rose the central government was denied access to an adequate share of the nation's income, while the profits of powerful provincial families expanded. The failure of the Ch'ing to develop a sound tax structure was an important cause of the dynasty's eventual decline.

Chinese society, rooted in the closely united patriarchal family, was not significantly altered under Manchu rule. Woman's position remained far inferior to man's, and her oppression may actually have become heavier. Widows were expected not to remarry and some proved their fidelity to a departed husband by committing suicide. The cruel and crippling custom of female foot-binding, which dated from the Sung Dynasty and was supposed to make a woman more attractive to a man and effectively ensure her remaining dependent upon him, became more prevalent in spite of the efforts of Ch'ing emperors to stamp it out. Not until the twentieth century was the practice completely abandoned.

The Manchu emperors, whose own religious background was one of shamanism, cultivated and exalted the Chinese state cult of Confucius, requiring temples to be maintained in every district and elevating the spirit of the ancient sage to the highest rank of official deities. Tolerant in religion, the early Ch'ing emperors were generally cordial to Christian missionaries, especially the French Jesuits, whom they

The Summer Palace of the Emperor Ch'ien Lung. This exquisite European-style summer palace just outside Peking was designed for the emperor by Jesuit architects. The palace was burned to the ground by British troops in 1860.

Intellectual activity in the Manchu era

Father Adam Schall with His Astronomical Instruments. Director of the Imperial Board of Astronomy, he wears the "mandarin square" of a Manchu civilian official.

employed at court as instructors in science, mathematics, and cartography. The emperor Ch'ien Lung patronized Jesuit painters and hired Jesuit architects to build a beautiful European-style summer palace for the imperial family.

Chinese culture of the Manchu era was characterized by refinement and fulfillment—to some extent overripeness and decadence—rather than innovation. Although the classical curriculum basic to the civil service examinations had become rigid and sterile, lively intellectual activity was displayed both by scholars and by individuals without the benefit of formal education. A thorough reexamination of the classical canon produced limited but iconoclastic textual criticism. To repair an alleged distortion of Confucian dogma under the Ming, the Neo-Confucianism of the Sung philosopher Chu Hsi was revived. "Han Learning" scholars sought to recover the unsullied wisdom of more remote antiquity. Other thinkers, disenchanted with the metaphysical idealism of Neo-Confucianism, rejected abstract speculation in favor of the study of such factual subjects as mathematics, astronomy, geography, and linguistics. Criticism was also voiced against the state examinations for their neglect of the practical and immediate.

If philosophical speculation was somewhat lacking in spontaneity, the age was one of tremendous literary productivity. Scholars who shunned the state examinations were recruited by the court to write dictionaries and encyclopedias and to compile anthologies of prose and poetry. A compilation of Chinese history and literature prepared for Ch'ien Lung filled 36,000 manuscript volumes. This emperor at the same time imposed a literary inquisition, searching libraries and private collections to remove and destroy works considered antidynastic or dangerous to authority. Creative imagination was most evident in the novel, which reached an even higher state of development than under the Ming. The best Chinese novels of this period readily bear comparison with major prose works of other nations. Satire was employed to expose social follies and political corruption; some authors dared to attack the subjection of women. *Dream of the Red Chamber,* generally regarded as China's greatest novel, was composed about the middle of Ch'ien Lung's reign. With a tragic love story as its central plot, the novel provides an exposé of the life of the rich while also probing into the nature of reality and the meaning of human existence. Some painters, bred in the Ming tradition and averse to dynastic change, portrayed a bleak and disharmonious world. One famous artist splashed the word "Dumb" on the closed door of his studio. Nevertheless, the visual arts survived and flourished under the Ch'ing. A perceptive aesthete celebrated the true painter as one who is able "to participate in the metamorphoses of the universe" and through his art evoke a mood of exaltation.

During the Manchu period Chinese civilization created a more distinct impression upon nations of the West than had ever been true before. In the eighteenth century Chinese-style gardens, pagodas, and pavilions became fashionable among the wealthy classes of western Europe. Other items borrowed from China included sedan chairs, lacquer, and incense, while the craze for Chinese porcelain reached such proportions that it had the unfortunate effect of lowering the quality of the product. In addition, largely through translations and commentaries prepared by the Jesuits, European intellectuals were introduced to Chinese thought and literature. European acquaintance with these subjects was, of course, limited and superficial, but it was sufficient to arouse admiration. Spokesmen of the Enlightenment cited fragments of Confucian texts in support of Deism and as evidence that human society could be guided by reason. Voltaire praised the emperor Ch'ien Lung as exemplifying the ideal of philosopher king.

European appraisals of the Ch'ing regime became less generous as Western maritime adventurers encountered obstacles in their efforts to open China to commercial intercourse. The overseas expansion of the Western nations during the Commercial Revolution affected China as well as India and other Eastern lands. By the early sixteenth century the Portuguese had occupied Malacca, and one of their trading vessels reached Canton in 1516. The Chinese authorities, long accustomed to peaceful commercial intercourse with Arabs and other foreigners, at first had been disposed to grant the normal privileges to the newcomers. Portuguese adventurers, however, pillaged Chinese ships engaged in trade with the Indies and raided coastal cities, looting and massacring the inhabitants. Such actions convinced the Chinese that Europeans were no better than pirates; nor was their opinion favorably revised with the arrival, a little later, of the Dutch and the English. The wanton depredations perpetrated by these early Western seafarers were responsible for the unflattering name which the Chinese came to apply to Europeans—"Ocean Devils." The government finally determined to exclude Europeans from the coastal cities but allowed the Portuguese to maintain a trading center and settlement at Macao

China under the Manchu (Ch'ing) Dynasty

A Painted Scene from The Dream of the Red Chamber. *The novel reveals much about the life of mid-Ch'ing upper-class life, its underside as well as its grandeur.*

The influx of the "Ocean Devils"

Chinoiserie. Even as the Jesuits designed Ch'ien Lung's summer palace, eighteenth-century Europeans were developing a taste for the exotic designs and benign autocracy of China. This French tapestry dating from the 1720s shows the emperor receiving tributaries in a fanciful setting.

in the far south. Established in 1557, this post has been retained by the Portuguese to the present day. As a security measure, the local officials constructed a wall blocking off the Portuguese settlement on the island of Macao and imposed rigid restrictions upon the activities of the foreigners. The trade was too profitable for the Chinese to want to abolish it altogether, and the Portuguese were soon extended the privilege of docking at Canton at prescribed times and under strict supervision.

Imperial resistance to foreign intrusion

The imperial government was inclined to resist attempts to draw it into close relationship with societies and cultures alien to Chinese traditions. In 1759 an English captain, sailing under orders of the British East India Company, was arrested and imprisoned for violating a prohibition against entering China's northern ports. The government's hostility toward any foreign intrusion into its affairs is illustrated by one item in the charges against the offending trader: He had learned the Chinese language! The military strength of the Celestial Empire during the early phase of European overseas expansion is shown in its relations with a rival land-based power. While Portuguese, Spanish, French, and British were knocking at the ports of East Asia, Tsarist Russia was pushing its eastern frontiers overland toward the Pacific and by the late seventeenth century was encroaching on the Manchurian border. Defeated by Manchu forces, the Russians signed a treaty in 1689 acknowledging China's sovereignty and fixing its northern border approximately as it has remained to the present. The day of humiliation in confrontation with Western imperialist powers was still in the distance.

The long reign of Ch'ien Lung, which marked the apex of Ch'ing grandeur, also witnessed the beginning of the dynasty's decline. In the late eighteenth century troubles, for which the government was partly to blame, multiplied. Intrigue among rival court factions sapped the administration's efficiency; the bureaucracy had grown corrupt and rapacious. Bungled military campaigns in Burma and Vietnam wasted resources and intensified popular discontent, evident in the emergence of secret societies hostile to the Ch'ing. The White Lotus, an underground organization dating from Sung times, became active in central China and in the large western province of Szechwan. Miao tribesmen staged rebellions in the southwest as did Muslims in the northwest. And the latent disaffection of the Chinese populace for Manchu rule threatened the state's vigor when it was most needed to oppose the inroads of profit-hungry Westerners.

3. JAPAN UNDER THE TOKUGAWA SHOGUNATE

The most turbulent period of Japanese feudalism was ended rather abruptly at the close of the sixteenth century when a series of military campaigns forced the daimyo (great lords) to acknowledge the authority of a single ruler. The rise of the daimyo[1] had led to the establishment of fairly effective government within their individual domains, some of which were large enough to include several of the ancient provinces. Hence, when the great lords were brought under a common central authority, the way was open for a genuine unification of the country, and Japan entered upon an era of comparative peace and stability extending to the threshold of modern times.

The establishment of a stable central government after the century of civil warfare was achieved in the space of one generation by three military heroes whose careers were marked with bloodshed, treachery, and pitiless cruelty, but whose work endured. Nobunaga, a small provincial lord who dared to challenge the great daimyo fought his way to control of the imperial city of Kyoto, where he rebuilt palaces and took the Shogun under his protection. When this official proved troublesome, Nobunaga expelled him, thus ending the Ashikaga Shogunate (1573). He moved swiftly to break the power of the great Buddhist monasteries, storming their strongholds and massacring thousands of monks, women, and children. Before his death in battle (1582) he had conquered about half of Japan's provinces.

The work of consolidation was carried forward by Nobunaga's

---

[1] See above, Vol. 1, pp. 565–66.

Hideyoshi

ablest general, Hideyoshi, who is commonly regarded as the greatest man in Japanese history. Hideyoshi was a brilliant commander, highly intelligent, and usually sound in judgment, but his fame rests equally on the fact that he is the only figure in Japan's history to rise from the lowest rank (he was a peasant's son) to ruler of the nation. By 1590 he had broken all resistance in Japan and nourished still larger ambitions. He sent an army into Korea, insulted envoys from the Ming imperial court, and launched a second ill-fated expedition with the avowed intention of conquering China.

Tokugawa Ieyasu

The third member of the triumvirate of heroes was Tokugawa Ieyasu. Once a vassal of Nobunaga, he had become the most powerful of the daimyo by the time of Hideyoshi's death in 1598. Following a decisive military victory over rebellious rivals, Ieyasu had himself appointed Shogun in 1603 (the title had been in abeyance for thirty years) and took steps to ensure that this office would remain henceforth in his family, the Tokugawa. Reaping the fruits of the labors of his two predecessors, Tokugawa Ieyasu made the Shogunate a much more efficient instrument of government than it had ever been before.

Centralization of authority

Under the Tokugawa Shogunate (1603–1867), Japan's feudal institutions remained intact, but they were systematized and made to serve the interests of a strong central government. Ieyasu founded his capital at Edo (now Tokyo), where he built a great castle surrounded with moats and an elaborate series of outer defenses. The great domains of central and eastern Japan were held by members of the Tokugawa or by men who had helped Ieyasu in his campaigns. These trusted supporters of the regime were known as "hereditary daimyo," while the lords who had acknowledged Ieyasu's supremacy only when forced to do so were called "outer daimyo." The members of both groups were hereditary vassals of the Shogun and were kept under careful surveillance lest they should try to assert their independence. The Shogun employed a corps of secret police to report any signs of disaffection throughout the country. As a special precaution he required all daimyo to maintain residences in Edo and reside there every other year, and also to leave their wives and children as hostages when they returned to their own estates. The system Ieyasu devised was so well organized and thorough that it did not depend on the personal ability of the Shogun for its operation. For the first time Japan had a durable political framework, which remained undisturbed in the hands of the Tokugawa for two and a half centuries. While the Shogunate was essentially a feudal power structure, it developed for administrative purposes a large bureaucracy of carefully recruited and competent officials.

Persistence of dual government

It should be noted that the Japanese government was still dual in form. The imperial family and a decorative court nobility continued to reside at Kyoto, while the real power was lodged in the Bakufu, the military hierarchy headed by the Shogun at Edo. The Tokugawa Shoguns cultivated the fiction that they were carrying out the will of

Left: *A Feudal Stronghold.* Hirosaki Castle, in northern Japan, was the residence of one of the "outer daimyo" during the Tokugawa Shogunate. The castle grounds are now a popular resort for cherry-blossom viewing. Right: *Five-storied Pagoda at Nikko, in Central Japan.* It was built in 1636 and dedicated to Tokugawa Ieyasu, founder of the Tokugawa Shogunate. The structure (about 100 feet high) is ornately carved, painted, and lacquered, but is given a magnificent natural setting by the surrounding forest.

a divine emperor. By emphasizing the emperor's sanctity they added an aura of invulnerability to their own position, and by keeping him in seclusion they rendered him harmless. The shadow government at Kyoto was now entirely dependent upon the Shogun even for its financial support, but it was carefully and respectfully preserved as a link with Japan's hallowed past.

The most serious problem of the early Tokugawa period concerned relations with Europeans. Before the close of the sixteenth century both the Portuguese and the Spanish were carrying on considerable trade in Japan, and the Dutch and the British secured trading posts early in the following century. Europeans had been accorded a favorable reception by the Japanese, who seemed eager to learn from them. Firearms, acquired from the Portuguese, came into use for the first time in Japan and played a part in the feudal battles of the late sixteenth century. The introduction of gunpowder had the effect temporarily of stimulating the construction of heavy stone castles by the daimyo, a practice which was carefully regulated by the Tokugawa after they had seized the Shogunate.

Along with the Western traders came missionaries, who at first

Relations with Europeans

The European Presence in Japan. Jesuit missionaries arrive with a Portuguese merchant fleet in this early seventeenth-century Japanese screen. The merchants came for profits; the Jesuits wanted souls.

The growth and suppression of Christianity

encountered little hostility. Vigorous proselyting by Portuguese Jesuits and Spanish Franciscans met with remarkable success in winning converts to the Catholic faith among all classes of the population, including some of the feudal nobles. By the early seventeenth century there were close to 300,000 Christian converts in Japan, chiefly in the south and west where the European trading centers were located. Eventually, however, the Shoguns decided that Christianity should be proscribed, not because they objected to the religion as such but because they were afraid it would divide the country and weaken their authority. They were annoyed by the bickering between rival European groups and also feared that their subjects were being enticed into allegiance to a foreign potentate, the pope. The first persecutions were mild and were directed against Japanese Christians rather than against the Europeans; but when the missionaries refused to halt their work they were severely dealt with, and many were executed. Finally, in 1637, when a peasant revolt against oppressive taxation developed into a Christian rebellion, the Shogun's forces conducted a real war against the Christian strongholds in southwestern Japan and, in spite of the most heroic resistance, wiped out the Christian communities and exterminated the religion almost completely.

Following this bloody purge, the Shoguns adopted a policy of excluding all Europeans from Japanese settlement. That they were able to enforce it shows how strong their government had become. Reluctant to cut off Western trade entirely, they made a slight exception in the case of the Dutch, who seemed to be the least dangerous politically. The Dutch were permitted to unload one ship each year at the port of Nagasaki in the extreme western corner of Japan, but only under the strictest supervision. Going even further along the line of reaction, the Shogun next forbade his Japanese subjects to visit foreign lands on pain of forfeiting all their rights and commanded that no ship should be built large enough to travel beyond the coastal waters of the island empire. But in spite of the exclusion of most Westerners, Japan was not a completely isolated nation during the Tokugawa era. The Shoguns utilized foreign policy as a means of strengthening their regime internally, and they maintained both trade and diplomatic relations with China, Korea, and the Ryukyu Islands (then an independent kingdom).

The expulsion of
Europeans and the
adoption of isolationism

The Tokugawa era gave Japan a long period of peace and orderly government and promoted the ideal of a perpetually hierarchical society. Theoretically, the social structure was arranged in accordance with the classes of China, which ranked, in order of importance: (1) scholar-officials, (2) farmers, (3) artisans, (4) merchants, and (5) soldiers, bandits, and beggars. In Japan, however, the realities of a feudalized society produced a peculiar distortion of the ideal arrangement, which was somewhat fanciful even in China. The warrior (*samurai*), who had enjoyed a position of leadership for centuries, was elevated from the lowest category to the highest. In return for the place of honor assigned to him he was expected to exhibit the qualities of the scholar also, and to a considerable extent he did. The daimyo and the samurai were no longer the uncouth, lawless ruffians of early feudal days but refined aristocrats, who cultivated literature and the arts and took pride in the rigorous discipline to which they were bred. Still, their pre-eminence had been won in the first instance by force, and their position was regarded as a hereditary right, not to be challenged by men of superior ability who had been born to a lower class. It was only in the late stage of feudalism under the Tokugawa Shogunate that separation became complete between the warrior and the laboring classes. Peasants had frequently fought in the battles of the turbulent Ashikaga period; now they were forbidden to own weapons, a right that became the prerogative of the samurai. But while the peasants were confined to their fields and paddies, their erstwhile masters, the samurai, were being removed from the land. In early feudal days the typical samurai had lived on and supervised the cultivation of his fief. Now he became a retainer, supported by revenues assigned to him by his daimyo over-lord, with whom he usually resided.

The artificiality and formal rigidity of the Tokugawa regime did not stifle economic progress. By the early eighteenth century Japan's population had reached a total of 30 million; thenceforth it increased but slightly for a century and a half. This slow rate of population growth apparently was more the result of voluntary family planning than of a scarcity of resources, although occasional famines did occur. The country as a whole was prosperous; industry and internal trade continually expanded even though foreign commerce had been curtailed. Communication was relatively easy through all parts of Japan, both by waterways and by improved highways. A brisk exchange of agricultural and manufactured goods promoted the growth of a capitalist economy. Rice merchants occupied a strategic position in the world of finance and their establishments, offering commercial credit and daily price quotations, bore some resemblance to a modern stock exchange. Cities grew in size, especially in the central area of the country. By the late eighteenth century Edo had attained a population of one million and was probably the largest city in the world at that time.

*Social stress: the samurai
and the merchants*

Economic progress, coupled with a rigid and inherently authoritarian political regime, produced severe strains within society. The position of the samurai became more and more anomalous. While they possessed a monopoly of the profession of arms, they found little opportunity to practice it because the Shogun discouraged feudal quarrels, and there were no foreign wars. Thus the samurai became, by and large, a group of respectable parasites, although many of them displayed both talent and energy. They were often employed in administrative functions by the daimyo, and sometimes took over the management of a great domain so completely that the daimyo was reduced to little more than a figurehead. On the other hand the merchants, who were ranked at the bottom of the social pyramid, steadily accumulated wealth, formed their own trade associations to replace the older and more restrictive guilds, and exerted a potent influence over the whole national economy. Inevitably they imparted a bourgeois tone to society in the bustling cities.

*Changing views of the
Japanese peasantry*

Until recently historians commonly assumed that the peasants' lot under the Tokugawa was a miserable one, but research in Japanese sources has discredited this assumption. It is true that peasant labor supported the upper classes of daimyo and samurai as well as the Shogun and his bureaucracy. It is also true that peasants endured privation and sometimes cruel treatment at the hands of their social superiors, who dismissed them contemptuously as seeds to be pressed or cattle to be driven. The outbreak of riots and actual local rebellions—in a society as disciplined as the Tokugawa—indicates the reality and the depth of popular discontent. But the evidence is undeniable that Japanese farmers and tenants shared in the country's rising prosperity. Forbidden to bear arms, they were relieved from the burden of military service, and they benefited from the two and a half centuries of almost uninterrupted peace that followed the accession of Tokugawa Ieyasu.

*Expansion of agricultural
productivity*

Japanese agriculture continued to progress. The amount of land under cultivation doubled, new crops were introduced, intensive fertilization and better tools, including a mechanical thresher, came into use, and irrigation was extended through the cooperative efforts of farm villages. A steady expansion in productivity, together with regional specialization keyed to market demands, enabled the majority of peasants to sustain a rising standard of living in spite of tax increases during the eighteenth century. But while agriculture enjoyed a flourishing condition, its rewards were not evenly distributed. A trend away from large family combinations to smaller units that could be run more efficiently widened the spread between prosperous and indigent peasants, and there was an increase in tenantry as opposed to individual farm ownership. At the same time the emergence of a mobile class of wage earners stimulated growth of village industries—processing silk, cotton, salt, tobacco, saké, and sugar cane—and provided a reserve labor force which eventually contributed to the rapid industrialization of Japan in the post-Tokugawa period.

During the Tokugawa era Japanese culture, being largely cut off from outside contacts, acquired a distinctive national character. This is not negated by the fact that intellectual circles manifested a heightened interest in Chinese philosophy. A number of Chinese scholars had fled to Japan when the Ming Dynasty was overthrown by the Manchus and, more importantly, the Shoguns encouraged study of the Confucian classics, particularly among the aristocracy, because they thought it would help to inculcate habits of discipline in their subjects. These writings, of course, had long been honored in Japan, but now they were diligently examined for the purpose of developing a native school of philosophers who, through their example and through their position as administrators, could inculcate the principles of virtue—especially obedience—among all classes of the population.

The most significant social and cultural changes were those related to the growth of large cities, such as Edo, Osaka, and Kyoto, where men of wealth were creating an atmosphere of comfort and gaiety in contrast to the restrained decorum of the feudal nobility. In these populous commercial and industrial centers the trend in art and literature and especially in the field of entertainment was toward a distinctly middle-class culture, which was sometimes gaudy but appealing in its exuberance and spontaneity. In the pleasure quarters of the cities an important figure was the geisha girl, who combined the qualities of a modern beauty queen with the talents of a nightclub entertainer. Trained in the art of conversation as well as in song and dance, she provided the sparkling companionship which men too often missed in their own homes because of the habits of docility and self-effacement that they instilled into their wives and daughters. Prostitution, also, was prevalent on a large scale in the towns, in spite of attempts by the authorities to curtail the evil. Inherently sordid as was the practice, it took on a specious refinement under the patronage of the well-do-do, and some courtesans acquired an enviable standing in the loose but highly sophisticated society which flouted established conventions. Not only merchants and businessmen but even samurai and daimyo were attracted by the gay diversions of city life, and surreptitiously exchanged the boredom of their routine existence for the delights of

The Art of Tile Making. A wood block by Hokusai (1760–1849), an artist famous for landscapes.

Woman Playing the Flute. The flutist is by Harunobu (1724–1770), earliest master of the multicolored-print technique.

a "floating world" of pleasure and uninhibited self-expression.

The dissolute society of the Tokugawa cities was by no means utterly degenerate. Some of the best creative talents in Japan catered to bourgeois appetites, just as they did in Italy during the Renaissance. Racy novels, satirizing contemporary figures and piquant with gossip, innuendo, and scandal, came into vogue. Previously art had been chiefly aristocratic and religious except for the exquisitely designed articles of ordinary household use produced by the various handicrafts. Now a type of folk art was appearing that mirrored society realistically and also was enlivened with humor and caricature. Its chief medium was the wood-block color print, which could be produced cheaply enough to reach a wide public and which has ever since been a popular art form. Another proof of the influence that urban tastes were exerting in the aesthetic sphere is seen in the evolution of the Kabuki drama. In contrast to the No, the highly stylized and austere dance-drama that had been perfected a few centuries earlier under the patronage of the aristocracy, the Kabuki offered entertainment appealing to the middle and lower classes of the towns. Although it owed something to traditional dance forms, the Kabuki drama was derived more immediately from the puppet theater and, unlike the No, it was almost entirely secular in spirit. As developed in the seventeenth and eighteenth centuries, the Kabuki drama attained a high degree of realism, with exciting plots, lively action, and effective stage devices. In the opinion of some theatrical experts, it deserves to rank as the greatest drama any civilization has ever produced.

Various forces at work in Japan tended to undermine the foundations of Tokugawa institutions in spite of their apparent durability. The partial transformation of Japan's economy from an agrarian to a mercantile basis enhanced the importance of men engaged in manufacture, trade, and transport. As a result feudalism was rendered obsolete, and the feudal classes began to feel the pinch of adversity. Although money had been in circulation for many centuries, the incomes of daimyo and of their samurai retainers were still computed in measures of rice, the chief agricultural staple. The merchants who provisioned such great cities as Edo and Osaka controlled the marketing of a large proportion of the rice crop; hence they were able to foresee fluctuations in price and sometimes even to induce fluctuations for their own benefit. Naturally, the daimyo and samurai were at a disadvantage in a period of unstable prices, because their incomes were from land rents, and because their necessities were increasingly supplied by articles that had to be purchased in the cities. Often the price of rice was considerably below the general price level; and even when it was high, the middleman appropriated most of the profit. The landed aristocrats found their real incomes diminishing while low-born traders and brokers grew richer and richer.

Inevitably, class lines began to break down, just as they did in west-

Economic changes

Kabuki Theater. Left: Famous actor Mitsugoro Bando portraying the aged warrior Ikyu in the play *Sukeroku.* Right: Kabuki actor (Matsumoto Koshiro) portrayed here as a fishmonger by Sharaku, a wood-block artist noted for his caricatures of actors (1794 or 1795).

The disruption of classes

ern Europe under similar conditions during the period of the Commercial Revolution. Wealthy Japanese merchants purchased samurai rank and title, while nobles adopted children of bourgeois families or contracted marriage alliances with this class in an effort to recoup their fortunes. Feeling honor-bound to maintain their accustomed style of living—at least in appearances—the aristocrats borrowed recklessly. As early as 1700 the indebtedness of the daimyo class was reputed to have reached a figure one hundred times greater than the total amount of money in Japan. Impoverished samurai pawned their ceremonial robes and even the swords which were their badge of rank. While townspeople in large numbers were entering the lower grades of samurai, samurai and farmers were flocking to the towns, where the more successful ones merged into the bourgeois class.

*Cultural trends generate
unrest*

The unrest generated by economic dislocation was further augmented by cultural trends in the later Tokugawa period. As a national spirit developed, it was accompanied by a renewal of interest in Japan's past. Shintoism, the ancient cult over which the imperial family presided, had been largely eclipsed by Buddhism. Gradually its popularity revived, and several new Shinto sects obtained an enthusiastic following. The study of ancient records (historical and mythological) stimulated reflection on the unique character of Japan— "founded by a heavenly ancestry, country of the gods"—and on the alleged origins of the imperial office. It directed attention to the fact that the Shogunate was a comparatively recent innovation or actually a usurpation, not an authentic part of the ancient political structure. At the same time, familiarity with China's political heritage—fostered by the vogue of Confucian scholarship which the Shoguns themselves had promoted—raised doubts among Japanese intellectuals as to the merits of a dual administrative system and of feudal institutions. Moreover, Western books and ideas were seeping into Japan through the port of Nagasaki where the Dutch were permitted a very limited trade. Even before Japan was "opened" in the nineteenth century, considerable interest had been aroused in Western guns, ships, watches, glassware, and scientific instruments. Thus Japan's insulation from the outside world was beginning to develop cracks at the same time that internal discontent had reached a dangerous point. By the opening of the nineteenth century the Shogun's position was precarious, unlikely to withstand the shock of a severe crisis, especially since other powerful families were eagerly watching for any sign of weakness on the part of the Tokugawa.

*Contributions of the
Tokugawa period*

The sweeping and revolutionary changes in Japan since the abolition of the Shogunate in 1867 have made it difficult to view the Tokugawa period with an undistorted perspective. Inward-looking, conservative, and devoted to hierarchy as it was, the Tokugawa regime went far toward unifying the nation, instilled habits of discipline, and provided a long period of security. Class structure was not so rigid as to prevent the realization of a fairly homogeneous society, especially as urban centers grew and communication improved. Education advanced significantly; by the end of the Tokugawa period about 45 percent of the male population was literate (only 15 percent of the female), a record unmatched in the rest of Asia and better than that of many countries today. Although Japan was still a predominantly agrarian society, capital techniques had been developed and applied to agriculture as well as to commerce and manufacture. Seemingly, although certainly unintentionally, the Tokugawa Shoguns had laid the foundation for Japan's transformation into a modern state.

Recently a group of Japanese historians—disillusioned with the effects of modernization and proponents of what they call "people's history"—have depicted the Tokugawa period as a kind of golden age. They claim that it contained the seeds of a freer society and even of democracy, evidenced by the growth of village cooperatives which stimulated social initiative and active participation among the peasants. They indict the imperial restoration as a "failed vision," a regretable step toward state worship, and they argue that the Tokugawa era could have provided the base for a structure different from and better than a duplication of Western industrialized society.[2]

*An unconventional
interpretation*

4. AFRICA UNDER DIVINE RULERS AND RITUAL CHIEFS

The period 1500 to 1800 marked the beginning of Africa's incorporation into the capitalist world economy. From about 1500, western Europe transformed Africa into a satellite of its own burgeoning capitalistic system. The network of international trade established by the Arabs by the thirteenth century was seized and extended by the Europeans from the opening of the sixteenth century. This maritime contact ended Africa's long isolation from the West and brought all coasts of the continent into the European commercial orbit.

*Africa as Europe's
economic satellite*

This period also witnessed the arrival of European traders and adventurers on Africa's sub-Saharan shores. A revolution in maritime and military technology enabled Europeans to navigate beyond sight of land and to conduct an efficient ocean-borne trade with swift, well-armed ships. For West Africans this provided an opportunity to expand their trade from their ancient North African markets across the Sahara to western Europe and the Americas via the Atlantic. A voluminous and highly profitable Atlantic traffic ensued with explosive force and required a concentration of territorial power in the hands of a few rulers. Instability generated by the introduction of arms trafficking and slave raiding forced weaker communities either to coalesce in self-defense or to seek the protection of larger, better organized societies

*European presence on the
coast forces a reorientation
of trade*

[2] Carol Gluck, "The People in History: Recent Trends in Japanese Historiography," *Journal of Asian Studies,* November 1978, pp. 25–50.

in neighboring areas. First coastal kingdoms, then empires, emerged in the tall forests after the 1650s in response to increasing opportunities for trade in guns, gunpowder, and exotic luxury items.

Long-distance trading networks across the Sahara, along the coasts, and through major river valleys flourished long before European contact. Canoemen traveled between the Niger Delta and the Ivory Coast and between the Gold Coast and Central Africa's Congo estuary. Small, independent fishing communities had dotted the palm-studded West and Central African coasts at least since 1300 and much earlier in East

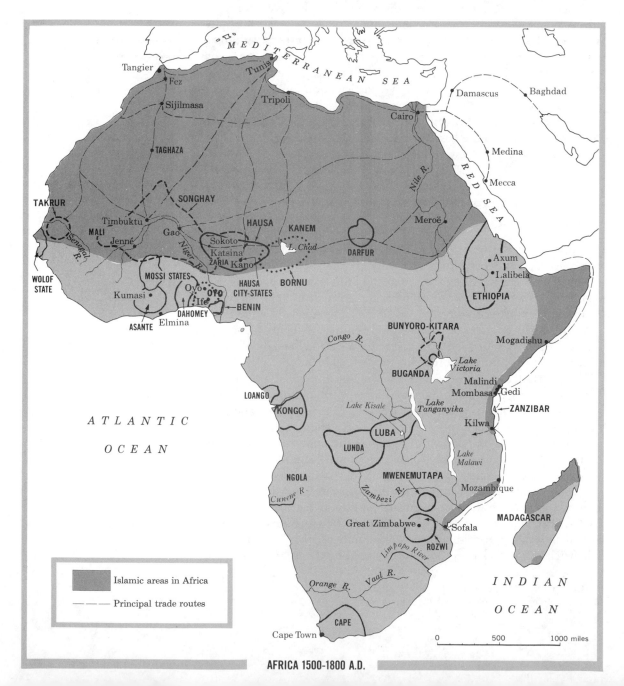

AFRICA 1500-1800 A.D.

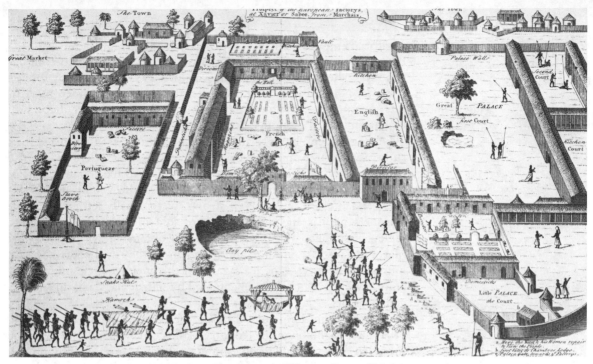

An Early Seventeenth-Century Trading Outpost on the Western Coast of Modern Nigeria. African rulers as well as Europeans actively participated in slaving and other commercial operations. They usually tried to restrict European trading activities in order to limit the European influence and to monopolize the trading relationship. Moving from left to right, note the presence of Portuguese, French, and English compounds abutting the grounds of the royal palace.

Africa. Fisherfolk exchanged ocean salt and dried fish with forest farmers for yams, goats, and cattle. For centuries, peoples of the Loango coast between the Congo river estuary and the Gabon forests produced for export fine raffia textiles, salt, and copper. By the twelfth century, cotton textiles produced in West Africa in the Hausa city-state of Kano found ready markets in Italy.

After 1500, some local industries like fishing and brewing were weakened when communities turned to less expensive European substitutes. Ultimately, European traders fostered economic rivalries and precipitated civil wars between African communities to prevent indigenous traders and chiefs from uniting. Such unity could inflate prices and weaken the European trade advantage. Nevertheless, on an individual basis, African traders sometimes proved superior to Europeans in the art of bargaining.

Impact of the European presence on trade networks

Between about 1730 and 1800 the less accessible interior states sought to extend their authority to the sea in order to trade directly with the Europeans. Seldom, however, were foreign traders permitted to operate beyond the coast. In Benin, Dahomey, and Oyo they were restricted to designated seaports and could only lease the land upon which they constructed their warehouses, fortresses, and slave markets. Some states, like Lunda, Luba, Oyo, Benin, and Asante, prospered and became

European traders restricted to the coast

*Divine kings and
territorial aggrandizement*

*The ritual of divine
kingship*

Royal Dignitary. Bronze plaque
fragment. Bini tribe, Benin.

territorial empires. Others, particularly Kongo, Ngola, and Mwene-mutapa, failed to keep the Europeans at arm's length or to comprehend fully their true motives. Their history was punctuated by foreign intrigue, political instability, and eventual collapse. Numerous African governments became so dependent on European trade that a shift in pattern spelled economic doom.

During this era, kings, claiming divine attributes, aggrandized their authority through military force. Often, neighbors were reduced to tributary status. Royal subordinates, dispatched to the conquered areas, guarded against conspiracies and assimilated the vanquished. Folkways and authority patterns, if strong, were usually left intact, while prisoners of war and dissidents were sold into slavery in order to replenish supplies of gunpowder and to obtain luxury imports that might enhance the prestige and grandeur of the royal court. Africa's human losses were America's gains in this vicious circle initiated by amoral white traffickers and facilitated by selfish black and mixed-race collaborators.

Like the divine emperors of Japan, the Obas of Benin, Asantehenes of Asante, Manikongos of Kongo, Alafins of Oyo, and other African monarchs shrouded themselves in mystery and appeared only on ceremonial occasions. Much of their time was devoted to state rituals and sacrifices to ancestral heroes. They evolved rigid codes of court etiquette and communicated with commoners only through intermediaries. Some wore finely crafted, oversized sandals to shield their feet from direct contact with the sacred earth. All of them fostered a hieratic art, aimed as exalting the sanctity of the state. To achieve this, guild artists were supported by the monarchy and forced to remain within the palace confines so that their talents would not pass to others.

These kings, their paramount chiefs, and lesser titled hereditary officials devised ingenious systems of checks and balances to prevent a concentration of power in any single office. In the Oyo empire (in western Nigeria) the Alafin served as hereditary secular leader. Yet his power had to be shared with a royally appointed nobility, which organized itself into a kind of electoral college and administrative watchdog called the Oyo *Mesi.* Its leading member, the *Bashorun,* acted as prime minister and as spokesman for most of the powerful national cults or religious orders. As a counterforce to the Oyo *Mesi,* the Alafin appointed trusted slaves, called *Ilari.* They were responsible for collecting tribute and overseeing local government. At the same time, every important town was headed by a hereditary mayor or *Oba.* Though the *Oba*'s authority derived from ancestral mandate and tradition, his powers were limited by the Ogboni Society. This organization of influential and prosperous townsfolk linked the masses of peasants, traders, and artisans to royal authority. Everyone in the Oyo empire, from the Alafin down to the poorest peasant, swore allegiance to the Oni of Ifé. Ifé was the founding city-state of the Oyo empire, the fount of Yoruba civilization; and the ancient office of Oni served as the supreme authority over spiritual matters. Power was therefore diffused throughout society. From at least the fifteenth to the late eighteenth century, the Yoruba peoples of Oyo were well served by their unwritten constitution.

In the 1790s, the authority and prestige of the Alafin's office, so vital to national solidarity, was severely diminished when its holder challenged the spiritual supremacy of the Oni of Ifé. The time-honored rules of the game eroded further when the *Bashorun,* or prime minister, tested his own strength against the Alafin's. Preoccupation with such power struggles weakened central authority and enabled the tributary states to secede. Civil war erupted, and in the mid-nineteenth century the crumbling empire fell prey to European intrigue from the south and Muslim Fulani challenges from the north.

Weakening of the central authority

Even though the Oyo empire disintegrated, its artistic and musical traditions continued to thrive. In both Oyo and neighboring Benin, guilds of Yoruba craftsmen turned out a rich variety of sculpture in brass, bronze, ivory, and wood. Metal commemorative busts and plaques, some antedating European contact by centuries, were delicate, strikingly naturalistic, and secular in intent. Companies of professional acrobats, dancers, and musicians traveled about the countryside giving performances which were sometimes critical of government practices, royal behavior, and social convention. In many ways, their programs were like an editorial column of a modern newspaper.

Belt Mask. Ivory. Bini Tribe. Benin.

Many forest states could boast of magnificent capital cities, holding sprawling palaces and temples with sunken atriums surrounded by columns. Benin City was one of the world's few urban centers to be laid out on a gridiron pattern, with broad tree-lined avenues intersecting streets at near right angles. Kumasi, the capital of Asante, was described by foreigners as Africa's garden city because of its lush flowering undergrowth set against tidy compounds with multicolored stylized façades. Slave populations tended to be concentrated around the capital cities. By 1800, slave-worked estates ringed many capitals and provided cheap food for the armies and for the urban dwellers. It was an ethnic and social apartheid, with some workers suffering varying degrees of bondage.

Capital cities

Islam experienced a revival after 1725 in the open, fertile grasslands of West Africa. Jihads, or holy wars, were declared by Muslim intellectuals and led to the establishment of numerous, mainly Fulani-led theocratic states. Islam continued to be both a factor of religious and social division and an engine of political and cultural change. The revival culminated in 1804–1810 with the Fulani conquest and consolidation of northern Nigeria's walled Hausa city-states into the sprawling caliphates of Sokoto and Gwandu. Hausa culture endured, and the Hausa language became a trade lingua franca in the major interior market towns of West Africa.

Islamic revival

It is significant that most West African forest civilizations had

*Afro-European relations
poisoned by the demands
of the slave trade*

*Demoralizing effects of the
slave and arms trade*

emerged, and in some cases reached their zenith, before European involvement. The Obaship in Benin was well established before Portuguese explorers arrived at Benin's major seaport of Gwato in 1472. Likewise, the Manikongo of Kongo ruled over an expansive domain with almost unchallenged authority before Portuguese contact a decade later. And Ifé was already recognized by the Yoruba as their major religious and cultural center.

Many African leaders received the Portuguese initially with great enthusiasm, hoping to taste the fruits of new techniques in agriculture, industry, and warfare. Before 1505 Benin and Kongo dispatched ambassadors and young intellectuals to Lisbon and the Vatican. But when America's vast resources were discovered by European explorers, it became obvious that the wealth could best be exploited by cheap labor in massive quantities. Only nearby Africa seemed to possess that necessary commodity. Thus, after about 1505, traders, missionaries, and other European visitors to Africa had different intentions from their predecessors. They came not as skilled technicians but as "advisers" who would gradually infiltrate African governments in order to better organize them for the slave trade. Thus, even though the political unification of Portugal and Spain in 1580 sacrificed African involvement to other interests, it in no way spelled an end to the Atlantic trade in humans.

Portuguese initiative in nautical science had already passed to the English, Dutch, and French—all of whom had begun to establish their own colonies of exploitation and settlement in the New World. Between 1637 and 1642 the Portuguese lost almost all their enclaves in West Africa to the Dutch. The Hollanders, unable to buy enough slaves on the West African coast, soon looked to the Ngola kingdom farther south. Only there did the Portuguese mount a successful resistance.

In the course of the seventeenth century, royally chartered companies from many European states formed monopoly enterprises and constructed warehouses and strings of stone fortresses along the West African coast. In 1672 the Royal African Company received a charter from the English crown and soon became the most active buyer of West African gold and slaves. Still, fierce competition with the Dutch in arms and munitions sales to Africans quickly led to a proliferation of deadly weapons among certain forest societies. To many African chiefs, slave raiding and trading became a painful necessity. If they refused to engage in it, the Europeans would supply arms to rivals who might in turn use them to sell their people into captivity. Dahomey and the Kongo, initially opposed to the slave trade, soon found it necessary either to play the European game or face possible economic and political ruin. Benin was one of the few African states that successfully controlled slave trading. It remained an independent political entity until the British invasion of 1897.

A number of small states were born in the seventeenth century in the Akan forest behind the Gold Coast. They were known to have supplied by that time more than 20 percent of Europe's gold reserves. Under the stimulus of the Royal African Company, this trade increased and led in the late seventeenth century to the rise of the Asante empire. The Akan peoples of Asante grew extremely powerful and wealthy by taxing trade passing through their territory en route to the coast. Between 1721 and 1750 Asante civilization reached its zenith. Asante artisans crafted earrings, anklets, pendants, and armbands from gold and bronze. On horizontal looms they wove polychromed togas of varied designs. Each pattern had a name and conveyed a symbolic meaning.

Asante civilization

The slave trade reached monumental proportions. If the relative paucity of thorough ships' records promises to keep historians from ever knowing exactly how many Africans were sold into slavery and shipped overseas, the evidence does permit educated estimates. Most scholars agree that between 1500 and 1800 nearly 11 million Africans were involuntarily exported: 7.8 million embarked on the Atlantic passage destined mainly for Brazil and the Caribbean. Another 3 million left Africa on routes across the Sahara, Red Sea, and Indian Ocean. But this was only a fraction of the total enslaved. Many served in African states, and others died defending themselves or en route to markets.

Dimensions of the slave trade

The Atlantic slave trade received a great boost after 1713 when England secured the Spanish *Asiento,* or license, to supply slaves to Spanish New World possessions. In response, the Yoruba state of Oyo expanded into a territorial empire, serving as middleman in the slave trade between the Hausaland interior and the coast. Other states exhibited a similar pattern. Immediately west of Oyo appeared the highly centralized kingdom of Dahomey. Between 1724 and 1729 Dahomey swept into the coastal Aja states and assimilated them. Unable to foster other sorts of trade with the Europeans, the Dahomeans became both suppliers and brokers in the slave trade. Oyo, fearful of this competition, diverted traffic to its own ports in 1750. To survive the consequent economic dislocation, the Dahomean government developed a state-controlled totalitarian economic and political system unparalleled in the eighteenth century. All state officials were appointed by the king, who ruled as a dictator, and a secret police was established to enforce his will. No system of checks and balances existed; only precedent and ancestral sanction guided his rule. Acting as high priest, the king dominated the major cults. He also controlled the craft guilds which produced pictorial tapestries and graceful statues to glorify royal power. A national military draft of men and women was instituted as well as a census bureau to administer it. Slave-worked plantations were established and placed under the close supervision of a minister of agriculture. Dahomey's economy was tightly regulated with central control over taxation and currency. Prices and wages, on the other hand, were set by producers' organizations. Culturally, westernization was actively discouraged by recourse to an aggressive policy of

Dahomey: example of extreme centralization

*Kongo and Ngola become
major sources for slaves
and fail to survive
European intrusions*

conquest and enforced assimilation into the traditional Fon way of life. Dahomey outlived the destructive effects of the slave trade and was able to safeguard its dynamic cultural institutions until French guns disrupted them in 1894.

Kongo and Ngola, in the savannah zone of west Central Africa, did not fare as well. After 1482 the Kongolese monarch, anxious to learn the secrets of European technology, assumed a Christian name and converted to Catholicism. But within two decades, Catholic missionaries had driven a wedge between the king and the nobility, who wished to follow the time-honored indigenous traditions. In 1556 rivalries among Portuguese advisers in the Kongo and Ngola dragged these two kingdoms into a destructive war against each other. Ngola won, but the real beneficiaries were European and mulatto slavers who reaped huge profits selling the war prisoners and refugees. Escalating demands for miners in Portuguese Brazil finally led to the total destruction of Kongo and Ngola (called Angola by the Portuguese) in 1665 and 1671 respectively. Their governments collapsed, although the Kongolese tradition of fine raffia cloth weaving remained vigorous.

*New kingdoms deeper in
the heart of central Africa*

Queen Nzinga, the former Angolan monarch, laid the foundations for a new kingdom, called Matamba, deeper in the interior. From the 1660s, Matamba became an important commercial state in Central Africa and a major broker in the growing international slave trade. Slave trading persisted and resulted in a further moral and ethical deterioration among certain segments of the population. Other African kingdoms, Lunda and Luba, arose deep in the interior, safely beyond direct Portuguese interference. Some of these highly centralized kingdoms survived into the twentieth century, but only to lose their independence to a new wave of Europeans, in search not of slaves but of copper.

*The Portuguese reaction to
Swahili civilization*

Portuguese involvement on the East African coast was equally destructive, even though it had little to do with the slave trade. In 1498 Vasco Da Gama rounded the Cape and sailed northward along the Swahili coast in search of the East Indies. He was astounded to discover a series of prosperous and highly civilized city-states with strong commercial and cultural links to Arabia, the Persian Gulf, and India. But it was distressing to him that their Sultans were fervent practitioners of Islam. It is no wonder that Da Gama had battles in three of the four city-states he visited. At Malindi his reception was cordial, only because Da Gama had sacked Malindi's commercial rival, Mombasa.

*Swahili city-states as
Portuguese tributaries*

The Portuguese were impressed by the gold and copper flowing out of Central Africa and by the extensive Indian Ocean trading network which carried the ore to distant ports. They hoped to use the Swahili city-states as a springboard to the Indies and as a source of gold for financing commercial operations in India and the Spice Islands. By 1505, after several Portuguese voyages of plunder and bombardment, the city-states were reduced to tributary status.

Portuguese in East Africa. Fort Jesus was built in 1593 at Mombasa by the Portuguese. It served as their major foothold in East Africa until 1728, when they were driven out under a combined Afro-Arab siege.

The Portuguese did not intend to govern the Swahili city-states. Rather, they attempted, with only limited success, to monopolize the Indian Ocean trade through their Viceroy at Goa on the western coast of India. After troubles with Turkish pirates and pillaging Zimba tribesmen, the Portuguese in 1593 constructed a massive stone citadel, called Fort Jesus, at Mombasa, and the malleable Sultan of Malindi was appointed to govern on their behalf. In 1622 the Portuguese were driven out of Ormuz, their strategic stronghold in the Persian Gulf, by a powerful Persian fleet. The fragility of Portuguese rule soon became evident to others. From the 1630s they had to suppress costly revolts in numerous Swahili towns. After Muscat, the gateway to the Persian Gulf, fell in 1650, the Omani Arabs emerged as a formidable naval power. In 1698 they drove the Portuguese out of Mombasa, their major port of call en route to India, and the Portuguese supremacy north of Mozambique crumbled like a house of cards. In its wake lay the ruins of a once magnificent Swahili civilization. The Omani came to East Africa as liberators, but stayed on as conquerors, practicing a kind of benign neglect which led to further cultural and economic deterioration.

Fragility of Portuguese rule

The Portuguese also failed in their attempts to control the gold and copper mines of the Zimbabwean and Katangan plateaus. After one hundred eighty years of interference in the political and religious institutions of the Mwenemutapa empire, they were forced to retreat to the Mozambique coast. Their traders and soldiers were simply no match against the more determined and better organized Shona armies. African resistance was clearly stronger than the Portuguese will to conquer. In 1798 the Portuguese attempted to link their colony in Angola with Mozambique in the hope of forging a transcontinental African empire. But malaria and the unwillingness of the crown to administer such a vast area were responsible for its failure.

Portuguese repelled

Islam in East Africa. Mombasa Mosque with minaret. Sixteenth century.

Segregation and domination in the Cape colony

History took another, more tragic, course in the extreme southwest corner of Africa. In 1652, the Netherlands East India Company established a replenishment station at the Cape's Table Bay for ships passing between western Europe and the Orient. It rapidly grew into a company-governed colony of white settlement, centered on the fort in Cape Town harbor. Almost from the start the company, anxious to avoid interracial clashes, passed decrees segregating the whites from the indigenous Khoikhoi herders. Over the next half century, the European settlers displaced and subjugated the Khoikhoi and the San, an indigenous population of Stone Age hunters and gatherers. The Khoikhoi were gradually reduced from independent cattlemen to indigent clients of the ever-expanding white stock farmers. This source of cheap labor helped to alleviate the colony's chronic shortage of manpower. By 1715, the once-proud Khoikhoi had lost nearly all their cattle and lands and had been decimated by European diseases like smallpox for which they had no natural immunity. The more primitive San were hunted down like wild game and driven into the arid north, but only after fierce guerrilla wars of resistance. By 1750 the San had been dispersed, and the Khoikhoi, literally "men of men," and their civilization had disintegrated. Khoikhoi remnants merged with Bantu-speaking slaves imported from other regions of Africa and poor whites to form a new, mixed-race population called Cape Coloreds. Though emulating European ways and adopting the evolving Afrikaans language, they were brutally discriminated against. At the same time, they refused to become part of indigenous black society, perceiving it as too primitive.

From the beginning, slave-owning became a widespread and deeply entrenched feature of Cape society. By 1800, the approximately 20,000 white settlers were outnumbered by their slaves, whom they tried to keep in tow through laws limiting their movement, employment, and ability to organize.

The company failed to control the white diaspora, and the frontier moved steadily eastward. In about 1770, the rigidly Calvinistic trek-boers, isolated from the European Enlightenment's liberal and humanitarian traditions, came up against a far more formidable competitor—the Iron-Age Bantu speakers. They, too, valued cattle and sought new pastures. But, unlike the Khoi and San, they were more socially cohesive, better organized governmentally, and greatly outnumbered the whites.

Almost immediately, Bantu-Boer relations were marked by mutual suspicion and distrust, which quickly evolved into bitterness, fear, and hate as acts of violence escalated over the struggle for land and cattle. As in the past, company efforts at racial segregation in hopes of limiting costly frontier wars failed. Some forms of frontier interracial cooperation evolved, based on mutual interests. But conflict was more common and pervasive.

Cosmopolitan Cape Town had become an internationally strategic harbor in the southern Atlantic, and in 1795 the British occupied it for fear of the French in the Napoleonic Wars. The near-bankrupt company, weakened by rebellious and independent-minded colonists, did not resist. Between 1806 and 1833 the British sought, with only limited success, to impose an Anglo-Saxon inspired color-blind legal and

The Dutch Colony of Cape Town on the Cape of Good Hope as It Appeared in a 1762 Drawing by J. Rach

The legacy of trade with the Europeans

social system on a predominantly Dutch Cape society that saw race as a key indicator of social and political status.

Viewing the collective sub-Saharan experience, African trade with the Europeans was a mixed blessing. The exchange of guns, powder, cheap manufactured textiles, and nondurable consumer goods such as alcoholic beverages for gold, ivory, pepper, and palm oil accelerated the trend in some areas toward centralization of authority and the growth of territorially based states. Certain families monopolized the trade and enriched themselves at the expense of the broad masses. Lineage structures in the areas subjected to slave raids were severely weakened socially, economically, and materially. Yet the south Atlantic trade system also led to the introduction into Africa of new food crops, including plantain from Asia, cassava from Brazil, sweet potatoes, pineapples, peanuts, and guava from other areas of the Americas, and corn from Brazil via Spain and Egypt. Increased long-distance trade also led to the wider dispersion of existing crops, such as East African coconut trees into West Africa. Thus, African diets improved, and the crops enabled societies blessed with fertile soils and reliable water supplies to sustain much higher population densities. This in turn contributed to the tendency to state creation and expansion. However, it also accelerated the process of deforestation and soil erosion. The Great Drought of 1738–1756 caused a massive decline in food output, malnutrition, and in some areas self-enslavement to avoid death from starvation.

The nature of trade with Europe

Unlike Japan, Africa's real economic growth was slowed by the exploitative, nonproductive nature of the European trade. Europeans exported items which could not be used in the production of other goods. In West Africa, guns and gunpowder by the eighteenth century had become the most important foreign trade commodity. In the two centuries after 1600, at least 20 million guns were exported to sub-Saharan Africa. Between 1796 and 1805 more than 1.6 million guns were sent to West Africa from England alone. A strong connection developed between firearms and the acquisition of slaves. The weapons were used mainly for interethnic raids and wars connected with the gathering of people for the slave markets. Wars which created many slaves for the Atlantic markets were particularly stimulated by competition among Africans for control of trade routes to the coast. Some African ethnic groups sold slaves to obtain guns to ensure their own political survival against internal rivals. In other words, slave exports were sometimes the result of politically motivated warfare rather than of pure economic incentive.

Political and social change

African contact with the Euro-American capitalist system contributed to the evolution of state formation. However, in the long run it generated political instability, bred by struggles for power and status between the old elites and the emerging military and commercial entrepreneurs. The existing bases of political and social differentiation were challenged. Greater popular involvement in warfare and in the trade in gold, slaves, and forest agricultural products enabled clever and ambitious commoners to generate independent wealth. It bred a new "bourgeoisie" of African brokers, merchants, interpreters, and caravan operators. In Asante, Oyo, Dahomey, and elsewhere the traditional royal lineages were forced to alter the hereditary political structures by incorporating ability and meritocracy into them. The rulers who failed to accommodate themselves to the changing order were faced with destructive civil wars and chronic political instability which ultimately rendered them more susceptible to European imperialist conquest in the late nineteenth century.

Yet, in spite of these disruptive influences, these three centuries witnessed an explosion in artistic endeavor and output. New, more sophisticated aesthetic standards evolved in communities exposed to international trade. There was a richer diversity in styles and an improvement in techniques. European and Islamic trade injected new designs and motifs as well as greater quantities of material, particularly metals for castings and yarns for weaving. Social and religious cults and guild associations grew in number and membership and became powerful agencies for the maintenance of traditions and for the adaptation and institutionalization of social and artistic change. Slave raiding and warfare triggered massive population migrations. This led to greater intercultural contact between refugees and indigenes and to the creation of a social climate in which people became more responsive to change and innovation.

Growth of artistic activity

This era saw the professionalization of craftspersons. In the past, most art was expressed through rock and body painting, stoneworking, and ceramics. But from the 1500s, there was dramatic growth in textile design and manufacturing, metal-casting, and mask and figurine wood sculpting. Nearly every large village could boast of guilds of weavers, cloth-dyers, spinners, and tailors. Increasing numbers of societies shifted from woven grass or bark-cloth waistbands to elaborate garments covering much more of the body. Also, greater use was made of cosmetics and scarification. Dress became a form of communication and a symbol of status and wealth.

The professionalization of the crafts

In this period, males began to exert greater social and political control through their secret societies. They also played a preponderant role in the sculptural arts, even though art was employed by both sexes in their masked festivals. Women often dictated the forms, but most of the actual carving or casting was performed by men. Pottery-making, in most cultures, remained in women's hands, though weaving was done by both sexes. However, certain types of looms were reserved for men only.

Gender roles in the arts

Royal families in the centralized states became wealthy and commissioned artisans to fashion rings, pendants, bracelets, and hairpins from gold, copper, ivory, and exotic woods. Impressive mud or reed palaces were constructed with galleries and courtyards adorned with polychromed woven, batik, or tied-and-dyed tapestries. Basic ideals

Artistic advances

Stool with Caryatid. Wood.
Luba, Congo.

of beauty were expressed through distinct symbols stamped onto cloth, molded in high relief on the façades of buildings, or shaped into fine wood or metal sculpture. Forms such as the circle, rectangle, oval, and square were brilliantly translated into artistic symbols and given deep philosophical and religious meaning. And complex notions of God and the universe were expressed in the verbal symbolism of proverbs and epic poems or in the intricate designs of royal thrones, scepters, swords, and craftsmen's tools. Over the course of these three centuries, the forest civilizations, with their unlimited supplies of timber, used a wide variety of wood as the primary art medium for sculpturing. They achieved a brilliant artistic synthesis of surrealist and expressionist, abstract and naturalistic elements. The cubist tradition itself was born not in western Europe in the early twentieth century but among artistic circles in the West African forest societies centuries before. Although Europeans robbed Africans of much of their physical and human resources, they did not succeed in weakening their artistic vitality. Indeed, the trauma of European contact seemed to propel Africans toward even greater cultural achievements.

Patterns of traditional African religion and thought also proved to be remarkably durable. Although Africans were intensely spiritual and thoughtful, no single "African" religion or philosophy evolved on a continental scale, such as we found with "Chinese" philosophy or in Hindu religion on the Indian subcontinent. Beyond Coptic Christian Ethiopia, there were no texts or written discourses of speculative and/or conceptual thought. Nevertheless, each culture possessed a collective wisdom, a set of principles or beliefs, with varying degrees of coherence, that governed human behavior. There was a considerable divergence in notions of good and evil, and in perceptions of physical and natural beauty. Different societies held to distinct moral and ethical

Reconstruction of a Kabaka's Reed Palace in Kampala, Uganda. These structures, once common to Buganda royalty, have disappeared.

African Craftsmen. Dye pits in Kano (northern Nigeria) were and still are owned by traditional craft guilds.

systems operating within their own ethos. For example, one culture might regard the birth of twins an evil omen, and the infants would be cast out. A few hundred miles away, another culture would see such an event as blessed and worthy of celebration.

Nearly all African cultures, however, shared a fundamental base for their belief systems. Over their panoplies of spirits and divinities presided a Supreme Being, a God that was viewed not as aloof but acting as an integral member of society. Africans saw the universe as a hierarchical and dialectic system of forces, each related to the other. God was the almighty creative force, the primordial artist. He was omnipresent, omnipotent, and omniscient, the ultimate judge and the great provider. Different cultures had different names for God: in Dahomey it was "Mawu," in Asante "Nyame." The Igbo called Him "Chuku." Most Africans believed that a person is born free of sin and with a benign soul that resides in the body. African societies, especially the Yoruba, placed enormous importance on achieving a dynamic harmony with God and the spirits. This was attempted through constant sacrifice, prayer, and divination. Diviners were mediums concerned with the moral order and with relations between man and the spiritual realms. Diviners were also in charge of oracles, and families consulted them on a child's birth to learn of the infant's destiny.

The dominance of a Supreme Being in African religions

Everyone was believed to be in possession of a spiritual guardian who, if well served, would preserve and enhance one's life. By the sixteenth century, many African societies had assigned names to individuals. They were loaded with meaning and symbolism. For example, a common Yoruba name for boys was Ologunna, meaning "God straightens the path." The Yoruba shared the Asante belief that every-

Belief in the individual's direct access to God

Life-size Ancestor Statues Guarding the Carved Entrance to an Important Chief's Audience Chamber in Cameroun. Ancestor veneration gave continuity to societies and enhanced the legitimacy of ruling dynasties.

one has a direct access to God, and this is expressed in the Asante maxim "No man's path crosses another's."

The veneration of ancestors

Most African cultures venerated their ancestors and looked to them for philosophical and spiritual guidance. The ancestors "owned" the land, shaped the behavioral patterns of their descendants, and provided a vital sense of continuity. To be cut off from the ancestors was, in essence, to be cut off from life itself. Some anthropologists believe that ancestor veneration stifled innovation and reform by placing taboos on thoughts or actions not attributable to societies' leading forebearers.

"Vital force"

"Essence" or "vital force" was a concept shared by many Bantu-speaking cultures. It presumed a hierarchy of forces, ranging downward from *muntu* (man, ancestors, God), *kintu* (things such as plants, animals, rocks); *hantu* (time, space), and *kuntu* (manner or modality). Every object, it was believed, possesses a certain amount of vital force. The problem is to release and then control it to one's benefit. For the Bantu and others, the earth was especially sacred. It was generally associated with the female dimension and was not to be touched by secular authorities. Thus, in many societies divine kings wore oversized sandals so as to avoid direct contact with the earth.

Clearly, between 1500 and 1800, Islam and Christianity had made significant inroads on the continent. But in very few cultures did they succeed in destroying the fundamental tenets of traditional beliefs and rituals. By 1550, classical Christianity in North Africa, Nubia, and Egypt had practically disappeared as a result of internal theological discord and the commercial challenge of Islam. In Ethiopia it remained the almost exclusive preserve of royalty and the monastic clergy. European-inspired Christianity, mainly Catholicism, was associated with post-fifteenth-century trade in slaves and arms—not education and technology—and thus failed to become deeply rooted or African-ized in the Kongo, Angola, Benin, and Mwenemutapa. Islam, on the other hand, also failed to captivate the broad masses. It remained essentially an urban-based, market-oriented faith, practiced by mal-lams (Islamic scholars), merchants, and princes. Hinduism had even less success and seldom radiated beyond the Swahili city-states of the East African coast.

The limited appeal of Christianity, Islam, and Hinduism

SELECTED READINGS

- *Items so designated are available in paperback editions.*
- Binyon, Laurence, *The Spirit of Man in Asian Art,* New York, 1935.
- Nakamura, Hajime, *Ways of Thinking of Eastern Peoples: India, China, Tibet, Japan,* Honolulu, 1964.

INDIA: *See also Readings for Chapters 5, 11, and 16*

Archer, J. C., *The Sikhs,* Princeton, 1946.
- Cole, W. O., and P. S. Sambhi, *The Sihks: Their Religious Beliefs and Prac-tices,* Boston, 1978. Based on recent scholarship.
Garratt, G. T., ed., *The Legacy of India,* Oxford, 1937.
Ikram, Mohamad, *Muslim Civilization in India,* ed. A. T. Embree, New York, 1964.
Kabir, Humayun, *The Indian Heritage,* New York, 1955.
Kulke, H., and D. Rothermund, *A History of India,* Totowa, N.J., 1986.
Moreland, W. H., and A. C. Chatterjee, *A Short History of India,* 4th ed., New York, 1957.
Prawdin, Michael, *The Builders of the Mogul Empire,* New York, 1965.
Rawlinson, H. G., *A Concise History of the Indian People,* 2d ed., New York, 1950.
- ———, *India, a Short Cultural History,* New York, 1952. An excellent interpretive study.
Smith, V. A., *Akbar the Great Mogul,* Oxford, 1917.
Spear, Percival, *India: A Modern History,* 2d ed., Ann Arbor, 1972. An excellent survey.
- ———, *The Oxford History of India, 1740–1975,* 2d ed., New York, 1979.
- Wolpert, Stanley, *A New History of India,* New York, 1977. An admirable survey, informative and well written.

CHINA: *See also Readings for Chapters 6, 11, and 16*

Blunden, C., and M. Elvin, *Cultural Atlas of China,* New York, 1983. One of the most valuable works on China available.

• Eberhard, Wolfram, *A History of China,* 4th ed., Berkeley, 1977.

• Elvin, Mark, *The Pattern of the Chinese Past,* Stanford, 1975.

• Fairbank, J. K., *The United States and China,* 4th ed., Cambridge, Mass., 1983.

Fairbank, J. K., E. O. Reischauer, and A. M. Craig, *East Asia: Tradition and Transformation,* rev. ed., Boston, 1978. A shortened edition of a major text.

• Fitzgerald, C. P., *China, a Short Cultural History,* 3d ed., New York, 1961. Unconventional in viewpoint.

Hucker, C. O., *China's Imperial Past: An Introduction to Chinese History and Culture,* Stanford, 1975. Remarkably clear, comprehensive, and readable.

• Hudson, G. F., *Europe and China: A Survey of Their Relations from the Earliest Times to 1800,* London, 1930.

• Moore, C. A., ed., *The Chinese Mina: Essentials of Chinese Philosophy and Culture,* Honolulu, 1967.

Ronan, C. A., ed., *The Shorter Science and Civilization in China,* I, New York, 1978, II, 1981. Abridgement of the first four volumes of a monumental study by Joseph Needham.

Rowbotham, A. H., *Missionary and Mandarin: The Jesuits at the Court of China,* Berkeley, 1942.

Scott, A. C., *The Classical Theater of China,* New York, 1957.

Shryock, J. K., *The Origin and Development of the State Cult of Confucius,* New York, 1932.

Sickman, L., and A. Soper, *The Art and Architecture of China,* Baltimore, 1956. Reliable, richly illustrated.

• Spence, Jonathan D., *Emperor of China: Self-Portrait of K'ang Hsi,* New York, 1975.

• _____, *The Memory Palace of Matteo Ricci,* New York, 1984. An elegant and evocative portrait of the late sixteenth and early seventeenth centuries.

_____, *The Search for Modern China,* New York, 1990.

• Sullivan, Michael, *A Short History of Chinese Art,* rev. ed., Berkeley, 1970.

Tuan Yi-fu, *China,* Chicago, 1970. An excellent cultural geography.

JAPAN: *See also Readings for Chapters 11 and 16*

Berry, Mary, *Hideyoshi,* Cambridge, Mass., 1982. A vivid and informative account.

• Brandon, J. R., W. P. Malm, and D. H. Shively, *Studies in Kabuki: Its Acting, Music, and Historical Context,* Honolulu, 1978.

Cole, Wendell, *Kyoto in the Momoyama Period,* Norman, Okla., 1967.

Dore, R. P., *Education in Tokugawa, Japan,* Berkeley, 1965.

• Duus, Peter, *Feudalism in Japan,* 2d ed. New York, 1975. A concise account of political developments through the nineteenth century.

Eliot, Charles, *Japanese Buddhism,* New York, 1959. A standard text.

Embree, J. F., *The Japanese Nation,* New York, 1945. A brilliant and well-balanced study by an anthropologist.

• Hall, J. W., *Japan: From Prehistory to Modern Times,* New York, 1971.

————, et al., *Japan before Tokugawa: Political Consolidation and Economic Growth, 1500–1650,* Princeton, 1981.

• Keene, Donald, *Japanese Literature: An Introduction for Western Readers,* New York, 1955.

• Moore, C. A., ed., *The Japanese Mind: Essentials of Japanese Philosophy and Culture,* Honolulu, 1967.

• Munsterberg, Hugo, *The Arts of Japan: An Illustrated History,* Rutland, Vt., 1957.

• Reischauer, E. O., *Japan: The Story of a Nation,* 5th ed., New York, 1974. Lucid and well organized.

Sadler, A. L., *The Maker of Modern Japan: The Life of Tokugawa Ieyasu,* London, 1937.

Sansom, G. B., *Japan, a Short Cultural History,* rev. ed., New York, 1952. A substantial but highly readable work by an eminent British scholar.

————, *The Western World and Japan,* New York, 1950.

• Smith, T. C., *The Agrarian Origins of Modern Japan,* Stanford, 1959

Toby, Ronald, *State and Diplomacy in Early Modern Japan: Asia in the Development of Tokugawa Bakufu,* Princeton, 1984.

• Warner, Langdon, *The Enduring Art of Japan,* Cambridge, Mass., 1952.

Yukio, Y., *Two Thousand Years of Japanese Art,* New York, 1958.

AFRICA: *See also Readings for Chapters 11 and 16*

Beach, David N., *The Shona and Zimbabwe 900–1850,* London, 1980.

Birmingham, David, and Phyllis M. Martin, eds., *History of Central Africa,* vol. 1, New York, 1983.

Blusse, L., and F. Gaastra, eds., *Companies and Trade: Essays on Overseas Trading Companies During the Ancien Régime,* Leiden, 1981. Examines the crucial role played by the great trading companies in opening new markets in the Asian and Atlantic worlds and as instruments of European expansion in the seventeenth and eighteenth centuries.

Curtin, Philip D., ed., *Horizon History of Africa,* New York, 1972.

• Davidson, Basil, *The African Genius,* Boston, 1969.

Egharevba, Jacob, *A Short History of Benin,* Ibadan, 1960.

Eltis, David, and James Walvin, eds., *The Abolition of the Atlantic Slave Trade: Origins and Effects in Europe, Africa and the Americas,* Madison, 1981.

Gailey, H. A., *History of Africa: From Earliest Times to 1800,* New York, 1970.

Gray, Richard, ed., *The Cambridge History of Africa,* Vol. 4: *c. 1600 to c. 1790,* Cambridge, 1975.

Hallett, Robin, *Africa to 1875,* Ann Arbor, 1970.

Hilton, Anne, *The Kingdom of Kongo,* Oxford, 1985.

Hull, Richard W., *Munyakare: African Civilization before the Batuuree,* New York, 1972.

Lovejoy, Paul E., *Transformations in Slavery,* Cambridge, 1983.

McLeod, M. D., *The Asante,* London, 1981.

Oliver, Roland, and Anthony Atmore, *The Middle Age in African History: 1400–1800,* New York, 1981.

Rawley, James A., *The Transatlantic Slave Trade,* New York, 1981.

Roberts, A., ed., *Tanzania before 1900,* Nairobi, 1968.

Smith, Robert S., *Kingdoms of the Yoruba,* London, 1969.

Vansina, Jan, *Kingdoms of the Savanna,* Madison, Wis., 1968.

India, East Asia, and Africa
During the Early-Modern Era
(c. 1500–1800)

Ade Ajayi, J. F., and Michael Crowder, eds., *Historical Atlas of Africa,* Cambridge, 1985

Davenport, T. R. H., and K. S. Hunt, eds., *The Right to the Land: Documents on Southern African History,* Capetown, 1974.

• de Bary, W. T., ed., *Sources of Chinese Tradition,* Chaps. XXII, XXIII, New York, 1960.

• ———, ed., *Sources of Indian Tradition,* "Islam in Medieval India"; "Sikhism," New York, 1958.

• ———, ed., *Sources of Japanese Tradition,* "The Tokugawa Period," New York, 1958.

Freeman-Grenville, G. S. P., ed., *The East African Coast: Select Documents from the First to the Early Nineteenth Century,* 2nd ed., London, 1975.

Gallagher, L. J. tr., *China in the Sixteenth Century. The Journals of Matthew Ricci: 1583–1610,* Milwaukee, 1942.

• Hibbett, Howard, *The Floating World in Japanese Fiction,* New York, 1959.

• Keene, Donald ed., *Anthology of Japanese Literature,* New York, 1960.

Lu, David, ed., *Sources of Japanese History,* Vol. 1, New York, 1973.

Markham, C. R., ed., *The Hawkins' Voyages,* London, 1878.

Oliver, Roland, ed., *The Middle Age of African History,* New York, 1967.

Smith, V. A., ed., *F. Bernier: Travels in the Mogul Empire* A.D. *1656–1668,* London, 1914.

Vansina, Jan, *Kingdoms of the Savanna,* Madison, Wis., 1966.

Wang, C. C., tr., *Dream of the Red Chamber,* New York, 1929.

Whiteley, W. H., compiler, *A Selection of African Prose: Traditional Oral Texts,* Oxford, 1964.

Chapter 22

THE ECONOMY AND SOCIETY OF EARLY-MODERN EUROPE

We ought to esteem and cherish those trades which we have in remote or far countries, for besides the increase in shipping and mariners thereby, the wares also sent thither and received from thence are far more profitable unto the kingdom than by our trades near at hand.

—Thomas Mun, *England's Treasure by Foreign Trade,* 1630

In nearly every state in Europe citizens are divided into the three orders of nobles, clergy, and people. . . . Even Plato, although he intended all his citizens to enjoy an equality of rights and privileges, divided them into the three orders of guardians, soldiers and labourers. All this goes to show that there never was a commonwealth, real or imaginary, even if conceived in the most popular terms, where citizens were in truth equal in all rights and privileges. Some always have more, some less than the rest.

—Jean Bodin, *Six Books of the Commonwealth,* 1570

A ny study of early-modern European society must concern itself with change, with the factors that in the two hundred years after 1600 were powerful enough to produce the political upheaval of the French Revolution and the economic stimulus for the Industrial Revolution. Unquestionably, the most profound change during that period was economic. By the latter part of the eighteenth century, the freebooting overseas expansionism that had begun in the sixteenth century with the Spanish conquistadors had ended with Europe at the center of a vast system of worldwide trade. Commerce on this increasingly global scale had given birth to institutions fashioned for its support, and had altered patterns of living among those caught up in its overpowering dynamic. Banks and joint-stock companies financed international commercial ventures. New urban workshops responded to the intensified demand for manufactured goods.

Economic change

As international banking developed into a highly sophisticated profession, its practitioners became powerful men. As urban workshops imposed new conditions and habits, the urban artisan was forced to bend uncomfortably to unfamiliar demands.

European society as a whole found bending no more comfortable. Change was imposed upon national communities which, in many cases, were still defined according to the hierarchies of the Middle Ages: landlord and peasant, nobleman and serf. Each order was expected to acknowledge its inherent obligations and responsibilities, as each was assumed to be part of an organic and divinely sanctioned communal whole. Where, within this preordained structure, was the independent commercial entrepreneur or the dispossessed laborer supposed to fit? Tension of this sort between old forms and new realities was further exacerbated by the general crisis that we analyzed in the preceding chapter. Change produced by economic expansion and dislocation occurred against the background of civil and religious turmoil that tore much of Europe to pieces in the seventeenth century, and against an equally disruptive cycle of demographic swings caused by warfare and disease, by good weather one year, bad weather—and hence famine—the next. Those were the changes closest to the lives of most Europeans, the men and women still bound to the land, for whom, as the French historian Pierre Goubert has observed, "death was at the center of life, just as the graveyard was at the center of the village." The concerns of this chapter are thus both the economic and social circumstances that represented change, and the habits and traditions that were making change complex and difficult.

1. CAPITALISM, MERCANTILISM, AND THE COMMERCIAL REVOLUTION

The early-modern world of commerce and industry was governed by the assumptions of capitalism and mercantilism. Reduced to its simplest terms, capitalism is a system of production, distribution, and exchange, in which accumulated wealth is invested by private owners for the sake of gain. Its essential features are private enterprise, competition for markets, and business for profit. Generally it involves the wage system as a method of payment of workers; that is, a mode of payment based not on the amount of wealth they create, but rather upon their willingness to compete with one another for jobs. Capitalism represented a direct challenge to the semi-static economy of the medieval guilds, in which production and trade were supposed to be conducted for the benefit of society and with only a reasonable charge for the service rendered, instead of unlimited profits. Capitalism is a system designed to encourage commercial expansion beyond the local level, on a national and international scale. Guildmasters had neither the money (capital) to support nor the knowledge to organize and direct commercial enterprises beyond their own towns. Activity on that wider scale demanded the resources and expertise of wealthy and experienced entrepreneurs. These men, who usually started as merchants operating over a wide area and ended as bankers, could afford to invest in large quantities of manufactured goods, and if necessary, to hold them unsold until they could command a high price. The capitalist entrepreneur studied patterns of international trade. He knew where markets were and how to manipulate them to his advantage.

Capitalism is a system designed to reward the individual. In contrast, mercantilist doctrine emphasized direct governmental intervention in economic policy to increase the general prosperity of the state. Mercantilism was by no means a new idea. It was in fact a variation on the medieval notion that the populace of any particular town comprised a community with a common wealth, and that the economic well-being of such communities depended on the willingness of that populace to work at whatever task God or their rulers assigned them to benefit the community as a whole. Membership in a particular order within the community ensured to men and women the privileges of that order. In the case of the poor, this meant no more than protection from unfair prices and from starvation. In return for such protection, members of the community willingly placed themselves under the regimentation that guild restrictions and town ordinances imposed.

The mercantilism of the seventeenth and eighteenth centuries translated this earlier concept of community as a privileged, but regimented, economic unit from the level of towns to the level of the entire state. This translation represented not so much a complete change as it did the extension and elaboration of theories and practices that had governed the policies of earlier rulers. The conquest and subsequent plundering of the New World by Spain was an instance of mercantilism at work on a grand scale. The Statute of Artificers, passed by the English Parliament in 1563, which established a customary "fair" wage scale applicable to all laborers, instituted economic privilege and regimentation at the national level.

Mercantile theory held that a state's power depended on its actual, calculable wealth, expressed in terms of the amount of gold and silver bullion in its possession at any given time. A state amassed bullion by ensuring itself as favorable a balance of trade as possible. Hence the degree to which a state could remain self-sufficient, importing as little as necessary while exporting as much as possible, was the clearest gauge not only of its economic prosperity but of its power. This doctrine had profound effects on state policy. First, it led to the establishment and development of overseas colonies. Colonies, mercantilists reasoned, would, as part of the national community, provide it with raw materials, including precious metals in some instances, which would otherwise have to be obtained outside the community. Second, it inspired state governments to encourage industrial production and trade, both sources of revenue which would increase the state's income. And finally, it persuaded policy-makers to discourage domestic consumption, since goods purchased on the home market reduced the goods available for export. Government policy was thus to keep wages low, so that laborers would not have money to spend for more than it took to provide them with basic food and shelter.

Mercantilism in practice

Although most western European statesmen were prepared to endorse mercantilist goals in principle, the degree to which their policies reflected those goals varied according to national circumstance. Spain, despite its insistence on closed colonial markets and its determination to amass a fortune in bullion, never succeeded in attaining the economic self-sufficiency that mercantilist theory demanded. The Spaniards therefore found it necessary to exchange their bullion for Flemish, French, and English manufactured goods which they were unable to supply to either their home market or to their colonies. Mercantilism, which appealed at least in theory to the rulers in Madrid, had little attraction for the merchants of Amsterdam. The Dutch rejected the governmental centralization implicit in the mercantilist notion of the sovereign state as an economic unit which they associated with the hated regime of Philip II of Spain. They further recognized that the United Provinces were too small to permit them to achieve economic self-sufficiency. Throughout the seventeenth and eighteenth centuries the Dutch remained dedicated in principle and practice to free trade, often investing, contrary to mercantilist doctrine, in the commercial enterprises of other countries and promoting national prosperity by encouraging the rest of Europe to rely upon Amsterdam as a hub of international finance and trade. The Dutch commitment to free trade did not extend to their colonial preserves which remained closed to their commercial rivals. It was the French and the English who combined, in differing degrees, governmental centralization and independent commercial enterprise most consistently and effectively and who became the most successful practitioners of mercantilism in early-modern Europe.

Capitalism and
mercantilism: a
commercial revolution

The goal of capitalism was a commercial system that would make individuals rich. The goal of mercantilism was a system that would make the state powerful. Though they differed as to ends, the two systems functioned compatibly together for most of the early-modern period. Together, governments and entrepreneurs designed new institutions that facilitated the expansion of global commerce during the seventeenth and eighteenth centuries and effected what has come to be called a Commercial Revolution.

Elements of the
Commercial Revolution:
(1) increased capital

Enterprise on this new scale depended on the availability of capital for investment. And that capital was generated primarily by a gradual increase in agricultural prices throughout much of the period. Had that increase been sharp, it would probably have produced enough hunger and suffering to retard rather than stimulate economic growth.

Merchants' Houses in Seventeenth-Century Amsterdam. This engraving depicts not only the opulence of middle-class life in a thriving commercial capital, but also the spirit of civic unity, expressed by the crowds gathered for a public celebration. (Several of the principal thoroughfares of Amsterdam are canals.)

Had there been no increase, however, the resulting stagnation produced by marginal profits would have proved equally detrimental to expansion. Agricultural entrepreneurs had surplus capital to invest in trade; bankers put that surplus to use to expand their commercial enterprises. Together, capitalist investors and merchants profited.

Banks played a vital role in the history of this expansion. Strong religious and moral disapproval of lending money at interest meant that banking had enjoyed a dubious reputation in the Middle Ages. Because the Church did come to allow profit-making on commercial risks, however, banks in Italy and Germany were organized under family auspices, the most notable examples being the fourteenth- and fifteenth-century operations of the Medici in Florence and the Fuggers of Augsburg. The Fuggers lent money to kings and bishops, and served as broker to the pope for the sale of indulgences. The rise of these private financial houses was followed by the establishment of government banks, reflecting the mercantilist goal of serving the monetary needs of the state. The first such institution, the Bank of Sweden, was founded in 1657. The Bank of England was established in 1694, at a time when England's emergence as a world commercial power guaranteed that institution a leading role in international finance.

The growth of banking was necessarily accompanied by the adoption of various aids to financial transactions on a large scale, further

(2) the rise of banking

*(3) expansion of credit
facilities*

*(4) changes in business
organization; the growth
of regulated companies*

Joint-stock companies

evidence of a commercial revolution. Credit facilities were extended in such a way that a merchant in Amsterdam could purchase goods from a merchant in Venice by means of a bill of exchange issued by an Amsterdam bank. The Venetian merchant would obtain his money by depositing the bill of exchange in his local bank. Later, the two banks would settle their accounts by comparing balances. Among the other facilities for the expansion of credit were the adoption of a system of payment by check in local transactions and the issuance of bank notes as a substitute for gold and silver. Both of these devices were invented by the Italians and were gradually adopted in northern Europe. The system of payment by check was particularly important in increasing the volume of trade, since the credit resources of the banks could now be expanded far beyond the actual amounts of cash in their vaults.

International commercial expansion called forth larger units of business organization. The prevailing unit of production and trade in the Middle Ages was the shop or store owned by an individual or a family. Partnerships were also quite common, in spite of the grave disadvantage of unlimited liability of each of its members for the debts of the entire firm. Obviously no one of these units was well adapted to business involving heavy risks and a huge investment of capital. The attempt to devise a more suitable business organization resulted in the formation of *regulated companies.* The regulated company was an association of merchants banded together for a common venture. Members did not pool their resources but agreed merely to cooperate for their mutual advantage and to abide by certain definite regulations. Usually the purpose of the combination was to maintain a monopoly of trade in some part of the world. Assessments were often paid by the members for the upkeep of docks and warehouses and especially for protection against "interlopers," as those traders were called who attempted to break into the monopoly. A leading example of this type of organization was an English company known as the Merchant Adventurers, established for the purpose of trade with the Netherlands and Germany.

The Commercial Revolution was facilitated in the seventeenth century when the regulated company was largely superseded by a new type of organization at once more compact and broader in scope. This was the *joint-stock company,* formed through the issuance of shares of capital to a considerable number of investors. Those who purchased the shares might or might not take part in the work of the company. Whether they did or not, they were joint owners of the business and therefore entitled to share in its profits in accordance with the amount they had invested. The joint-stock company had advantages over the partnership and the regulated company. First, it was a permanent unit, not subject to reorganization every time one of its members died or withdrew. And second, it made possible a much larger accumulation of capital, through a wide distribution of shares. Its organization

The Lyons Stock Exchange. Built in 1749, the stylish and impressive facade of the structure bespeaks the prominent role of commerce in French society.

and methods resembled to a degree those of the modern corporation. Yet the joint-stock company of the early-modern period is best understood not so much as a conscious precursor of capitalist endeavor as a pragmatic attempt at commercial expansion by both individuals and the state, its structure dictated by present opportunity and circumstance. Initially, for example, the Dutch United East India Company, one of the early joint-stock ventures, had expected to pay off its investors ten years after its founding in 1602, much as regulated companies had. Yet when that time came, the directors recognized the impossibility of the plan. By 1612, the company's assets were scattered—as ships, wharves, warehouses, and cargoes—across the globe. As a result, the directors urged those anxious to realize their profits to sell their shares on the Amsterdam exchange to other eager investors, thereby ensuring the sustained operation of their enterprise and, in the process, establishing a practice of continuous financing that was soon to become common.

While most of the early joint-stock companies were founded for commercial ventures, some were organized later in industry. A number of the outstanding trading combinations were also *chartered companies.* They held charters from the government granting a monopoly of the trade in a certain locality and conferring extensive authority over the inhabitants, and were thus an example of the way capitalist and mercantilist interests might coincide. Through a charter of this kind, the British East India Company undertook the exploitation of vast territories on the Indian subcontinent, and remained virtual ruler there until the end of the eighteenth century.

Chartered companies

A final important feature of the Commercial Revolution was the development of a more efficient money economy. Money had been used widely since the revival of trade in the eleventh century. Nevertheless, there were few coins with a value that was recognized other than locally. By 1300, the gold ducat of Venice and the gold florin of Florence had come to be accepted in Italy and also in the international markets of northern Europe. But no country could be said to have had a uniform monetary system. Coins issued by kings circulated side by side with the money of foreign states. Moreover, the types of currency were modified frequently, and the coins themselves were often debased. A common method by which kings expanded their own personal revenues was to increase the proportion of cheaper metals in the coins they minted. The growth of trade and industry in the Commercial Revolution accentuated the need for more stable and uniform monetary systems. The problem was solved by the adoption of a standard system of money by every important state to be used for all transactions within its borders. Much time elapsed, however, before the reform was complete. England began the construction of a uniform coinage during the reign of Queen Elizabeth, but the task was not finished until late in the seventeenth century. Indeed, the French did not succeed in reducing their money to its modern standard of simplicity and convenience until the early nineteenth century.

The Commercial Revolution, although it contributed to the prosperity of both individuals and states, was accompanied by serious risks and consequences occasionally disastrous to investors and to national economies. One major result of overseas expansion was the severe inflation caused by the increase in the supply of silver, which plagued Europe at the end of the sixteenth century (see Vol. I, p. 697). Price fluctuations, in turn, produced further economic instability. Businessmen were tempted to expand their enterprises too rapidly; bankers extended credit so liberally that their principal borrowers, especially noblemen, often defaulted on loans. In both Spain and Italy, failure of wages to keep pace with rising prices brought severe and continuing hardships to the lower classes. Impoverishment was rife in the cities, and bandits flourished in the rural areas. In Spain, ruined nobles found themselves compelled to join the throngs of vagrants who wandered from city to city. At the end of the fifteenth century the great Florentine bank of the Medici closed its doors. The middle of the century that followed saw numerous bankruptcies in Spain and the decline of the Fuggers in Germany, while England, Holland, and to some extent France waxed prosperous.

The period between 1540 and 1620 was characterized by an alternation of economic booms and recessions, which were followed by outbreaks of feverish speculation. These reached their climax early in the eighteenth century. The most notorious were the South Sea Bubble and the Mississippi Bubble. The former was the result of inflation of the stock of the South Sea Company in England, whose offer to assume the national debt led to unwarranted confidence in the company's future. When buoyant hopes gave way to fears, investors made frantic attempts to dispose of their shares for whatever they would bring. A crash which came in 1720 was the inevitable result.

During the years when the South Sea Bubble was being inflated in England, the French were going through a similar wave of speculative madness. In 1715 a Scotsman by the name of John Law, who had been compelled to flee from British soil for killing his rival in a love intrigue, settled in Paris, after various successful gambling adventures in other cities. He persuaded the regent of France to adopt his scheme for paying off the national debt through the issuance of paper money and to grant him the privilege of organizing the Mississippi Company for the colonization and exploitation of Louisiana. As the government loans were redeemed, those who received the money were encouraged to buy stock in the company. Soon the shares began to soar, ultimately reaching a price forty times their original value. Nearly everyone who could scrape together a bit of surplus cash rushed forward to participate in the scramble for riches. Stories were told of butchers and tailors who were supposed to have become millionaires by buying a few shares and holding them for a rise in price. But as the realization grew that the company would never be able to pay more than a nominal dividend on the stock at its inflated value, the more cautious investors began selling their holdings. The alarm spread, and soon all were as anxious to sell as they had been to buy. In 1720 the Mississippi Bubble burst in a wild panic. Thousands of people who had sold good property to buy the shares at fantastic prices were ruined.

The Mississippi Bubble

Joint-stock companies in France were more directly dependent on the state than was the case elsewhere, a reflection of French dedication to mercantilist theory. In most cases French companies were floated under governmental auspices; courtiers—and the king himself—were heavy investors. Agents of the state played a direct role in their management, sometimes to the company's ultimate disadvantage. The French East India Company, for example, was compelled by state direction to govern its colonies in accordance with the laws of Paris, a fact which, one historian has remarked, "reminds one of the complaint that French progress in the Sahara was retarded by the refusal of the camel to accommodate its habits to administrative regulations made in Paris." [1] Even though companies elsewhere were less subject to governmental regulation than they were in France, government and commerce generally worked to promote each other's interests. In time of war, governments called upon commercial capitalists to assist in the financing of their campaigns. When England went to war against France in 1689, for example, the government had no long-range borrowing mechanism available to it; during the next quarter century the merchant community, through the Bank of England, assisted the government in raising over £170 million and in stabilizing the national

The role of the state

[1] G. N. Clark, *The Seventeenth Century* (New York, 1961), p. 39.

debt at £40 million. In return, trading companies used the war to increase long-distance commercial traffic at the expense of their French enemy, and exerted powerful pressure on the government to secure treaties that would work to their advantage.

2. COLONIZATION AND OVERSEAS TRADE

Spanish colonization

The institutions of the Commercial Revolution—banks, credit facilities, joint-stock companies, monetary systems—were designed specifically to assist both capitalist entrepreneurs and mercantilist policymakers in the development and exploitation of overseas colonies and trading posts, the most visible evidence of the economic expansionism of early-modern Europe. Following the exploits of the conquistadors, the Spanish established colonial governments in Peru and in Mexico, which they controlled from Madrid in proper mercantilist fashion by a Council of the Indies. In return for a protection fee, as distinct from the royalty of one-fifth of all bullion extracted from the colonies, the Spanish navy attempted to protect treasure ships from attacks by the French, English, and Dutch. The mercantilist governments of Philip II and his successors were determined to defend their monopoly in the New World. They issued trading licenses to none but Spanish merchants; exports and imports passed only through the port of Seville (later the more navigable port of Cadiz), where they were registered at the government-operated Casa de Contratación, or customs house. In their heyday, Spanish traders circled the globe. Because of the lucrative market for silver in East Asia, they found it well worth their while to establish an outpost in far-off Manila in the Philippines, where Asian silk was exchanged for South American bullion. The silk was then shipped back to Spain by way of the Mexican ports of Acapulco and Veracruz.

*Challenges to Spanish
predominance*

Spain's predominance did not deter other countries from attempting to win a share of the treasure for themselves. Probably the boldest challengers were the English, and their leading buccaneer the "sea dog" Sir Francis Drake, who three times raided the east and west coasts of Spanish America and who, in 1587, the year before the Armada set sail on its ill-fated voyage north, "singed the beard of the Spanish king" by attacking the Spanish fleet at its anchorage in Cadiz harbor. Yet despite dashing heroics of that sort, the English could do no more than dent the Spanish trade.

English colonization

Reluctantly forsaking the search for the quick profits Spain was extracting from its colonial gold and silver mines, English colonists began to establish agricultural settlements in North America and the Caribbean basin. The first permanent, though ultimately unsuccessful, colony was established at Jamestown, in Virginia, in 1607. Over the next forty years, 80,000 English emigrants founded over twenty autonomous settlements in the New World. In this instance, however,

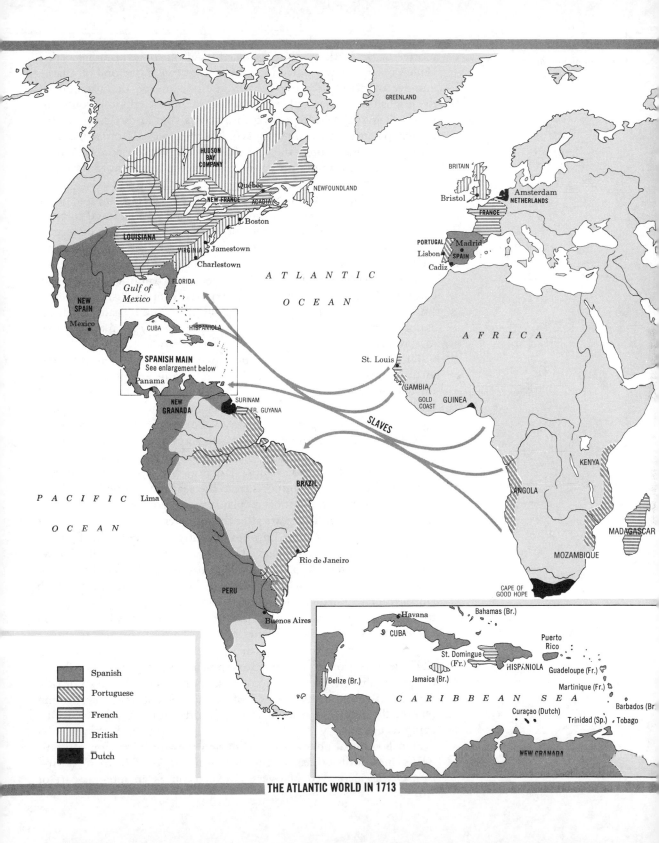

GREENLAND

BRITAIN

Bristol

Amsterdam
NETHERLANDS

FRANCE

PORTUGAL   Madrid
Lisbon   SPAIN
        Cadiz

HUDSON
BAY
COMPANY

Québec
NEW FRANCE   NEWFOUNDLAND
            ACADIA
        Boston

LOUISIANA

VIRGINIA   Jamestown
        Charlestown

FLORIDA

A T L A N T I C

O C E A N

NEW
SPAIN

Gulf of
Mexico

Mexico

CUBA   HISPANIOLA

SPANISH MAIN
See enlargement below

Panama

A F R I C A

St. Louis

GAMBIA
GOLD
COAST   GUINEA

SLAVES

NEW
GRANADA   SURINAM
        FR. GUYANA

P A C I F I C   Lima

O C E A N

BRAZIL

KENYA

ANGOLA

MADAGASCAR

MOZAMBIQUE

Rio de Janeiro

PERU

CAPE OF
GOOD HOPE

Buenos Aires

Spanish

Portuguese

French

British

Dutch

Havana   Bahamas (Br.)

CUBA

Puerto
Rico
St. Domingue
(Fr.)   HISPANIOLA   Guadeloupe (Fr.)

Belize (Br.)   Jamaica (Br.)   Martinique (Fr.)

C A R I B B E A N   S E A   Barbados (Br

Curaçao (Dutch)   Tobago
        Trinidad (Sp.)

NEW GRANADA

THE ATLANTIC WORLD IN 1713

religious freedom, rather than economic gain, was often the primary motive of the settlers. The renowned band of "pilgrim fathers" that landed on the New England shores in 1620 were but one of a large number of dissident groups that sought to escape the attempts of the English Kings, James I and Charles I, to impose religious conformity on their subjects. Religion also played a role in the efforts of the French to penetrate the hinterlands of North America. Roman Catholic missionaries, intent upon the conversion of native Americans to Christianity, joined fur traders in journeys across the continent to the Great Lakes and the Mississippi.

*The growth of English
colonial regulation*

Yet both England and France were quick to extract economic profit from their expanding colonial empires. England's agricultural colonies were producing crops in high demand throughout Europe. The success of colonial planters encouraged the governments of both Oliver Cromwell and Charles II to intervene in the management of their overseas economy. Navigation Acts, passed in 1651 and 1660, and rigorously enforced thereafter, decreed that all exports from English colonies to the mother country be carried in English ships, and forbade the direct exporting of certain "enumerated" products directly from the colonies to continental ports.

Sugar and tobacco

The most valuable of those products were sugar and tobacco. Sugar, virtually unknown in Europe earlier, had become a popular luxury by the end of the sixteenth century. Where once it had been considered no more than a medicine, one observer now noted that the wealthy were "devouring it out of gluttony." Sugarcane was raised in the West Indies after 1650 in rapidly increasing amounts. In the eighteenth century, the value of the sugar that England imported from its small island colonies there—Barbados, Jamaica, St. Kitts, and others— exceeded the value of its imports from the vast subcontinents of China and India. Although the tobacco plant was imported into Europe by the Spaniards about fifty years after the discovery of America, another half century passed before Europeans contracted the habit of smoking. At first the plant was believed to possess miraculous healing powers and was referred to as "divine tobacco" and "our holy herb nicotian." (The word "nicotine" derives from the name of the French ambassador to Portugal, Jean Nicot, who brought the tobacco plant to France.) The practice of smoking was popularized by English explorers, especially by Sir Walter Raleigh, who had learned to smoke while living among the Indians of Virginia. It spread rapidly through all classes of European society. Governments at first joined the Church in condemning the use of tobacco because of its socially and spiritually harmful effects, but by the end of the seventeenth century, having realized the profits to be made from its production, they were encouraging its use.

French colonial policy matured during the administration of Louis XIV's mercantilist finance minister, Jean Baptiste Colbert (1619–1683), who perceived of overseas expansion as an integral part of

The Dutch East India Company Warehouse and Timber Wharf at Amsterdam. The substantial warehouse, the stockpiles of lumber, and the company ship under construction in the foreground illustrate the degree to which overseas commerce could stimulate economy of the mother country.

state economic policy. He organized joint-stock companies to compete with those of the English. He encouraged the development of lucrative sugar-producing colonies in the West Indies, the largest of which was St. Dominique (present-day Haiti). France also dominated the interior of the North American continent. Frenchmen traded furs and preached Christianity to the Indians in a vast territory that stretched from Acadia and the St. Lawrence River in the northeast to Louisiana in the west. Yet the financial returns from these lands were hardly commensurate with their size. Furs, fish, and tobacco were exported to home markets, but not in sufficient amounts to match the profits from the sugar colonies of the Caribbean or from the line of trading posts the French maintained in India.

The French in America

The Dutch were even more successful than both the English and the French in establishing a flourishing commercial empire in the seventeenth century. Their joint-stock East India Company, founded in 1602, rivaled its English counterpart in Asia, gaining firm control of Sumatra, Borneo, and the Moluccas, or Spice Islands, and driving Portuguese traders from an area where they had heretofore enjoyed an undisturbed commercial dominion. The result was a Dutch monopoly in pepper, cinnamon, nutmeg, mace, and cloves. The Dutch also secured an exclusive right to trade with the Japanese, and maintained outposts in China and India as well. In the Western Hemisphere, their achievements were less spectacular. Following a series of trade wars with England, they surrendered their North American colony of New Amsterdam (subsequently renamed New York) in 1667, re-

The Dutch in the Far East

*The decline of the Spanish
and Portuguese empires*

taining Surinam, off the northern coast of South America, as well as the islands of Curacao and Tobago in the West Indies in compensation.

The fortunes of these commercial empires rose and fell in the course of the seventeenth and eighteenth centuries. The Spanish, mired in persistent economic lassitude and embroiled in a succession of expensive wars and domestic rebellions, were powerless to preserve the sanctity of their empire. Their merchant marine, once a match for cunning pirate-admirals like Drake, was by the middle of the seventeenth century unable to protect itself from attack by its more spirited commercial rivals. In a war with Spain in the 1650s, the English captured not only the island of Jamaica but treasure ships lying off the Spanish harbor of Cadiz. Further profit was obtained by bribing Spanish customs officials on a grand scale. During the second half of the century, two-thirds of the imported goods sold in Spanish colonies were smuggled in by Dutch, English, and French traders. By 1700, though Spain still possessed a colonial empire, it was one which lay at the mercy of its more dynamic rivals. Portugal, too, found it impossible to prevent foreign penetration of its colonial economies. The English worked diligently and successfully to win commercial advantages. They obtained concessions to export woolens duty-free into Portugal itself in return for similar preferential treatment for Portuguese wines. (The notorious affection of the English upper class for port wine dates from the signing of the Treaty of 1703.) English trade with the mother country led in time to English trade with the Portuguese colony of Brazil, indeed to the opening of commercial offices in Rio de Janeiro.

Dutch commerce

The Dutch, whose merchant fleet of over 16,000 vessels was the largest in Europe, were the masters of world trade throughout most of the seventeenth century. Dutch ships—about half the European total—not only sailed the high seas, but dominated the coastal carrying trade as well. To reduce the time of ocean voyages, Amsterdam shipyards developed the *fluitschip*. Longer and shallower than conventional craft, it was flat-bottomed and built of lightweight fir or pine, rather than oak. The *fluitschip* required only half the crew of regular ships, and cost half as much to build. The Dutch merchant marine ensured the position of Amsterdam as the world's premier trading center, the volume of Dutch commerce allowing Amsterdam merchants to undersell their English and French rivals. During the eighteenth century a growing Anglo-French rivalry in India stole the commercial spotlight from the Dutch spice monopoly in the Far East. The French and English East India Companies employed mercenaries to establish and expand trading areas such as Madras, Bombay, and Pondichéry. By exploiting indigenous industries, European capitalists continued to increase the flow of fine cotton textiles, tea, and spices which passed through these commercial depots on their way to Europe. The struggle for economic dominance in India was resolved in mid-century in En-

The Rewards of Commercial Exploitation. An English employee of the East India Company, enjoying his ease and his opium, as depicted by an eighteenth-century Indian artist.

gland's favor following a series of military clashes. As a sign of France's defeat, in 1769 the French East India Company was dissolved.

Despite the commercial importance of India, however, patterns of world trade came increasingly to be dominated by western routes that had developed in response to the lucrative West Indian sugar industry, and to the demand for slaves from Africa to work the plantations in the Caribbean. Here Britain, again, eventually assumed the lead. Typically, a ship might begin its voyage from New England with a consignment of rum and sail to Africa, where the rum would be exchanged for a cargo of slaves. From the west coast of Africa the ship would then cross the South Atlantic to the sugar colonies of Jamaica or Barbados, where slaves would be traded for molasses, which would make the final leg of the journey to New England, where it would be made into rum. A variant triangle might see cheap manufactured goods move from Bristol or Liverpool, in England, to Africa, where they would be traded for slaves. Those slaves would then be shipped to Virginia and exchanged for tobacco, which would be shipped to England and processed there for sale in continental markets. Other eighteenth-century trade routes were more direct: the Spanish, French, Portuguese, and Dutch all engaged in the slave trade between Africa and Central and South America; the Spanish attempted, vainly, to retain a mercantilist monopoly on direct trade between Cadiz and their South American colonies; others sailed from England, France, or North America to the Caribbean and back again. And of course trade continued to flourish between Europe and the Near and Far East. But the triangular western routes, dictated by the grim economic symbiosis of sugar and slaves, remained dominant.

Increasing dominance of western trade routes

The slave trade

The cultivation of sugar and tobacco depended on slave labor; and as demand for those products increased, so did the traffic in black slaves, without whose labor those products could not be raised or harvested. At the height of the Atlantic slave trade in the eighteenth century, somewhere between 75,000 and 90,000 blacks were shipped across the Atlantic yearly: 6 million in the eighteenth century, out of a total of over 9 million for the entire history of the trade. About 35 percent went to English and French Caribbean plantations, 5 percent (roughly 450,000) to North America, and the rest to the Portuguese colony of Brazil and to Spanish colonies in South America. Although run as a monopoly by various governments in the sixteenth and early seventeenth centuries, in its heyday the slave trade was open to private entrepreneurs, who operated ports on the West African coast. Traders exchanged cheap Indian cloth, metal goods, rum, and firearms with African slave merchants in return for their human cargo. Already disoriented and degraded by their capture at the hands of rival tribes, black men, women, and children were packed by the hundreds into the holds of slave ships for the gruesome "middle passage" across the Atlantic (so called to distinguish it from the ship's voyage from Europe to Africa, and from the slave colony back to Europe again). Shackled to the decks, without sanitary facilities, the black "cargo" suffered horribly; the mortality rate, however, remained at about 10 or 11 percent, not much higher than the rate for a normal sea voyage of one hundred days or more. Since traders had to invest as much as £10 per slave in their enterprise, they ensured that their consignment would reach its destination in good enough shape to be sold for a profit.

The ending of the trade

Not until the very end of the eighteenth century did Europeans protest this ghastly traffic. The trade was risky, dependent as it was on a good wind and fair weather, and competition was increasingly keen. Yet profits could run high, occasionally as much as 300 percent. Demand for slaves remained constant throughout the eighteenth cen-

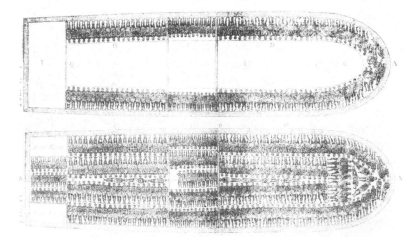

How Slaves Were Stowed Aboard Ship during the Middle Passage. Men were "housed" on the right; women on the left; children in the middle. The human cargo was jammed onto platforms six feet wide without sufficient headroom to permit an adult to sit up. This diagram is from evidence gathered by English abolitionists and depicts conditions on the Liverpool slave ship *Brookes.*

tury. By the 1780s, there were over 500,000 slaves on the largest French plantation island, St. Dominique, and 200,000 or more on the English counterpart, Jamaica. Those numbers reflected the expanding world market for slave-grown crops. As long as there was a market for the crops cultivated by slaves—as long as the economy relied to the extent it did upon slave labor—governments would remain unwilling to put an end to the system that, as one Englishman wrote in 1749, provided "an unexhaustible fund of wealth to this nation." Philosophers argued that though there was reason to rejoice that slavery had been banished from the continent of Europe (forgetting, apparently, the extent to which it continued to exist east of the Elbe in the form of serfdom), it remained a necessity in other parts of the world. Public pressure, first from Quakers and then from others motivated either by religious or humanitarian zeal, helped put an end to the trade in England in 1807, and to slavery itself in British colonies in 1833. Slavery in French colonies was abolished in 1793, but only after slaves had risen in massive revolt on St. Dominique. Elsewhere, in Latin and North America, slavery lasted well into the nineteenth century—in the United States, until the Civil War of 1861–1865.

The slave trade is an integral part of the history of the dramatic rise of English and French commerce during the eighteenth century. French colonial trade, valued at 25 million livres in 1716, rose to 263 million livres in 1789. In England, during roughly the same period, foreign trade increased in value from £10 million to £40 million, the latter amount more than twice that for France. These figures suggest the degree to which statecraft and private enterprise were bound to each other. If merchants depended on their government to provide a navy to protect and defend their overseas investments, governments depended equally on entrepreneurship, not only to generate money to build ships, but to sustain the trade upon which national power had come to rely so heavily.

The continuing rise of commerce

3. AGRICULTURE AND INDUSTRY

The pace of industrial change in early-modern Europe was not as dynamic as that of the Commercial Revolution and the expansion of overseas colonization and trade. Changes did occur, but less uniformly and dramatically than those we have been tracing. This is not surprising, since the major economic enterprise remained agricultural production, which, throughout much of the period, was generally carried on according to traditional techniques that kept the volume of production low. Yet by the end of the eighteenth century, tradition in some areas had yielded to innovation, with the result that production was increasing dramatically.

The predominance of agriculture

Most of the agricultural regions of seventeenth-century Europe consisted of open fields. In the north, these fields were usually large

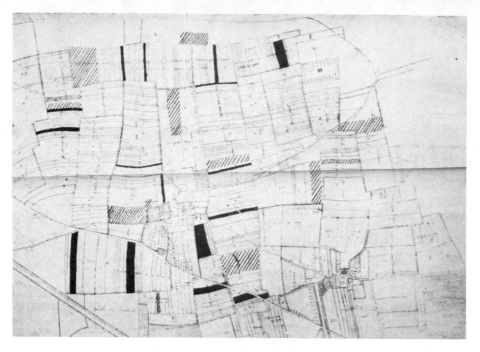

The Open-Field System in Northern France, 1738. Note the subdivision of large tracts into narrow strips, each owned by different proprietors.

The open-field system

sections of land, divided into long, narrow strips; in the south, the strips tended to reflect the more irregular shape of local landscapes. Although one or two rich aristocrats might own as much as three-fourths of the land in an open-field village, that land did not comprise one solid block. Instead it was made up of a great many plots, seldom contiguous, within the various open fields that surrounded the village. A large property owner's *desmesne* farm—which he worked with hired laborers for his own direct profit—and his tenant farms—those which he leased out to peasants—all consisted of these bits and pieces of land which lay alongside other bits and pieces that belonged to other landowners—very often small peasant proprietors. Each large open field thus resembled a patchwork quilt. Under these circumstances, in order for the fields to be cultivated with any degree of efficiency, all the "patches" had to be planted with the same crop, and sown, cultivated, and harvested together. Once the harvest was in, livestock was often turned into the fields to graze. One consequence of this practice was that crops were cut with a primitive sickle, which left more stubble for sheep and cattle, rather than with the far more efficient scythe. Inefficiency was indeed the hallmark of the open-field system, an inefficiency which those who owned large tracts of land grew more and more unwilling to tolerate. The Commercial Revolution encouraged landlords, particularly those in England and Holland, to compete for markets as capitalist agricultural entrepreneurs. In doing so, they looked for ways to improve the yield on their lands.

By the end of the eighteenth century a great many English and Dutch landlords had resolved the problem of low production by adopting a full range of innovative farming techniques, the most drastic of which was the enclosure of open fields to allow for more systematic and therefore more productive farming. "Enclosure" was the term for land reorganization within a traditional village community. The earliest enclosures in England took place in the fifteenth and sixteenth centuries and entailed the conversion of lands into fenced-off sheep meadows. Because of the great profits to be accrued from wool, some landlords converted common pastures that hitherto had supported peasant livestock into their own preserves for sheep-raising, thus threatening the livelihood of entire peasant communities. As Thomas More wrote in his *Utopia* (1516), "sheep that used to be so meek and eat so little now are becoming so greedy and wild that they devour men themselves . . . for they leave no land free for the plough."

Enclosure

Enclosure was more easily accomplished in those countries—England most notably—where the manorial emphasis had given way to a system of absolute property rights and wage labor. Where the tradition of "common" rights to grazing and foraging was strong, as in France, landlords found it far more difficult to impose a new economic order. Monarchs tended to oppose enclosure since it promised to enrich further a rival noble class. In seventeenth-century France the monarchy needed an economically stable peasantry to support its expanding tax programs, and therefore worked to secure peasants in the customary tenure of their farms. Thus defended, the peasants were able to resist effectively attempts at enclosure launched by large landholders. English property owners were more fortunate, taking advantage of the absence of royal opposition during the Cromwellian period to enclose on a broad scale.

Absolute vs. common property rights

The really dramatic enclosure movement in England took place between 1710 and 1810 when landlords began to engage in the practice of "scientific farming." They realized that by introducing new crops and farming methods they could reduce the amount of fallow lands and bring in higher yields, and thus higher profits. The most important new crops with which landowners experimented were clover, alfalfa, and related varieties of leguminous plants. These reduced fertility much less than cereal grains and helped to improve the quality of the soil by gathering nitrogen and making the ground more porous. Another new crop that had a similar effect was the turnip. The greatest propagandist for the planting of this unattractive vegetable was Viscount Charles Townshend (1674–1738), a prominent aristocrat and politician, who toward the end of his life gained the nickname of "Turnip" Townshend because of his dedication to the use of the turnip in new crop-rotation systems.

Scientific farming

Clover, alfalfa, and turnips not only helped do away with fallow lands; they also provided excellent winter food for animals, thereby aiding the production of more and better livestock. More livestock also meant more manure. Accordingly, intensive manuring became another way in which scientific farmers could eliminate the need for fallow land. Other improvements in farming methods introduced in

Improved farming techniques

the period were more intensive hoeing and weeding, and the use of the seed drill for planting grain. The latter eliminated the old wasteful method of sowing grain by hand, much of it remaining on top to be eaten by birds.

The process of enclosure

Scientific farming dictated the necessity of enclosures because the "improving" landlord needed flexibility to experiment as he wished. He could not plant one narrow open strip with turnips while peasants were continuing to rotate all the contiguous areas on the basis of the age-old three-field system. Instead, he had to organize his land into fenced-off compact plots, to leave no doubt as to which territory was his own, to maximize efficiency in experimentation, and to exclude stray grazing animals. The introduction of fodder crops such as clover eliminated the large landowner's need for common pastures, since he could now graze his livestock on his own fields. Hence, most eighteenth-century enclosures were of previously common land.

The social consequences of enclosure

Enclosure was a change that had major social consequences where it occurred. Village life under the open-field system was communal to the extent that decisions as to which crops were to be grown where and when had to be arrived at jointly. Common land afforded the poor, not only a place to tether a cow, to fish, or to gather firewood, but to breathe at least a bit of the air of social freedom. Enclosure cost villagers their modest freedoms, as well as the traditional right to help determine how the community's subsistence economy was to be managed. Cottagers (very small landholders) and squatters, who had over generations established a customary right to the use of common lands, were reduced to the rank of landless laborers.

The increasingly capitalistic basis of European agriculture

On the Continent, except for Holland, there was nothing comparable to the English advance in scientific farming. Nor, with the notable exception of Spain, was there a pronounced enclosure movement as in England and the Low Countries. Yet despite that fact, European food production became increasingly capitalistic in the seventeenth and eighteenth centuries. Landlords leased farms to tenants and reaped profits as rent. Often they allowed tenants to pay rent in the form of half their crops. This system of sharecropping was most prevalent in France, Italy, and Spain. Farther east, in Prussia, Poland, Hungary, and Russia, landowners continued to rely on unpaid serfs to till the land. Wherever the market economy replaced the economy of local self-sufficiency, it brought change in its wake.

Introduction of maize and potatoes

The eighteenth century saw the introduction of two crops from the New World, maize (Indian corn) and the potato, that eventually resulted in the provision of a more adequate diet for the poor. Since maize can only be grown in areas with substantial periods of sunny and dry weather, its cultivation spread through Italy and the southeastern part of the Continent. Whereas an average ear of grain would yield only about four seeds for every one planted, an ear of maize would yield about seventy or eighty. That made it a "miracle" crop, filling granaries where they had been almost empty before. The potato was an equally miraculous innovation for the European north. Its advantages were numerous: potatoes could be grown on the poorest, sandiest, or wettest of lands where nothing else could be raised; they could be fitted into the smallest of patches. Raising potatoes even in small patches was profitable because the yield of potatoes was extraordinarily abundant. Finally, the potato provided an inexpensive means of improving the human diet. It is rich in calories, and contains many vitamins and minerals. Northern European peasants initially resisted growing and eating potatoes. Clergymen taught them to fear the plant because it is not mentioned in the Bible. Some claimed that it transmitted leprosy. Still others insisted that it was a cause of flatulence, a property acknowledged by the French *Encyclopédie* in 1765, although the writers added: "What is a little wind to the vigorous organs of the peasants and workers?" Yet in the course of the eighteenth century the poor grew accustomed to the potato, although sometimes after considerable pressure. Frederick the Great compelled Prussian peasants to cultivate potatoes until the crop achieved acceptance and became a staple throughout much of northern Germany. By about 1800 the average north German peasant family ate potatoes as a main course at least once a day. In the same period the potato was also introduced into Ireland and England. In the 1840s, it was all that stood between millions of Irish and starvation.

The Title Page of One of Many Agricultural Tracts Available to Capitalist Farmers Interested in Improving Their Output

Agriculture was not the only commercial enterprise in early-modern rural Europe. Increasingly, manufactured goods—particularly textiles—were being produced in the countryside, as entrepreneurs battled to circumvent artisanal and guild restrictions that limited production in urban manufacturing centers. Unfettered rural industry was a response to the constantly growing demand of new markets created by the increase in regional, national, and international commerce. Entrepreneurs made use of the so-called putting-out system to address this demand and to reap large profits. Unhampered by guild regulations, which in medieval times had restricted the production and distribution of textiles to maintain price levels, merchants would buy up a stock of raw material, most often wool or flax, which they would then "put out," or supply, to rural workers for carding (combing the fibers) and spinning. Once spun, the yarn or thread was collected by the merchant and passed to rural weavers, who wove it into cloth. Collected once more, the material was processed by other workers at bleaching or dyeing shops, and collected for a final time by the entrepreneur who then either sold it to a wholesaler or directly to retail customers.

Rural manufacturing: the putting-out system

Although the putting-out phenomenon occurred throughout Europe, it was usually concentrated regionally. Most industrial areas specialized in the production of particular commodities, based on the availability of raw materials. Flanders was a producer of linens; Verviers (in present-day Belgium) of woolens; Silesia of linens and coal. As markets—regional, national, and international—developed, these rural

Regional specialization

manufacturing areas grew accordingly. Industries employed home-workers by the thousands. A large textile firm in Abbéville, France, provided work to 1,800 in central workshops but to 10,000 in their own homes. One of the largest woolen manufacturers in Linz, Austria, in 1786 was employing 35,000, of whom over 29,000 were domestic spinners.

Family production

Rural workers accepted the putting-out system as a means of staving off poverty, or possible starvation in years of particularly bad harvests. Domestic textile production involved the entire family. Even the youngest children could participate in the process of cleaning the raw wool. Older children carded. Wives and husbands spun or wove. Spinning, until the invention of the jenny at the end of the eighteenth century (see below, p. 231) was a far more time-consuming process than weaving, which had been speeded considerably by the invention of the fly-shuttle by the Englishman John Kay in the early eighteenth century, a mechanical device that automatically returned the shuttle to its starting place after it had been "thrown" across the loom.

Advantages of putting-out

In addition to providing extra income, the putting-out system brought other advantages to rural homeworkers. They could regulate the pace of their labor to some degree, and could abandon it altogether when farm work was available during the planting and harvest seasons. Their ability to work at home was not an unmixed blessing, for conditions in cottages that were wretchedly built and poorly ventilated were often exceedingly cramped and unpleasant, especially when workers were compelled to accommodate a bulky loom within their already crowded living quarters. But domestic labor, however unpleasant, was preferable in the minds of most to work away from home in a shop, where conditions might be even more oppressive under the watchful eye of an unsympathetic master. There were also advantages for the merchant-entrepreneur, who benefited not only from the absence of guild restrictions, but from the fact that none of his capital was tied up in expensive equipment. (Spinners usually owned their spinning wheels; weavers either owned or rented their looms.) Governments appreciated the advantages of the system too, viewing it as one way to alleviate the ever-present problem of rural poverty. The French abolished the traditional privileges of urban manufacturers in 1762, acknowledging by law what economic demand had long since established: the widespread practice of unrestricted rural domestic production. By that time, the putting-out system prevailed not only in northern France, but in the east and northeast of England, in Flanders, and in much of northern Germany—all areas where a mixed agricultural and manufacturing economy made economic sense to those engaged in it as entrepreneurs and producers.

Later generations, looking back nostalgically on the putting-out system, often compared it favorably to the factory system which displaced it. Life within the system's "family economy" was seldom other

Left: *"Rustic Courtship."* This detail from an etching (1785) by the English satirist Thomas Rowlandson suggests the advantages of doorstep domestic industry: natural lighting, improved ventilation, and a chance to converse with visitors. Work under these self-paced conditions, though usually long and hard, was carried on to a personal rhythm. Right: *Artisan and Family* by Gerard ter Borch. This seventeenth-century wheelwright, though a skilled artisan, is nevertheless depicted as living on the brink of poverty. Sickness, a bad harvest, unemployment—any of these might easily drive him and his family over the edge.

than hard, however. While workers could set their own pace to some extent, they remained subject to the demands of small, often inexperienced entrepreneurs who, misjudging their markets, might overload spinners and weavers with work at one moment, then abandon them for lack of orders the next. Though it often kept families from starvation, putting-out did little to mitigate the monotony and harshness of their lives. The pressures of the system are crudely if eloquently expressed in an English ballad, in which the weaver husband responds to his wife's complaint that she has no time to sit at the "bobbin wheel," what with the washing and baking and milking she must do. No matter, the husband replies. She must "stir about and get things done./ For all things must aside be laid,/ when we want help about our trade."

Textiles were not the only manufactured goods produced in the countryside. In France, for example, metal-working was as much a rural as an urban occupation, with migrant laborers providing a work force for small, self-contained shops. In various parts of Germany,

Quality of life under the family system

Roadside Inn by Thomas Rowlandson. Coaching inns brought the outside world into the lives of isolated villagers. Note the absence of any clearly defined roadway.

the same sort of unregulated domestic manufacturing base prevailed: in the Black Forest for clock making, in Thuringia for toys. English production of coal increased from 200,000 tons a year in the 1550s to more than 3 million tons by the end of the seventeenth century; that of iron, another essentially rural enterprise, grew fivefold in the same period.

Other rural manufacturing activities

Rural industry flourished despite the fact that for most of the early-modern period transportation systems remained rudimentary. In all but a very few cases, roads were little more than ill-defined tracks, full of holes as much as four feet deep, and all but impassible in the rain, when carts and carriages might stay mired in deep ruts for days. One of the few paved roads ran from Paris to Orléans, the main river port of France, but that was a notable exception. In general, no one could travel more than 12 miles an hour—"post haste" at a gallop on horseback—and speed such as that could be achieved only at the expense of fresh horses at each stage of the ride. A journey of 60 miles over good roads could be accomplished in twenty-four hours, provided that the weather was fair. To travel by coach from Paris to Lyons, a distance of approximately 250 miles, took ten days. Merchants ran great risks when they shipped perishable goods. Breakables were not expected to survive for more than 15 miles. Transportation of goods by boat along coastal routes was far more reliable than shipment overland. In 1675, English merchants calculated that it was cheaper to ship coal 300 miles by water than to send it 15 miles overland, so impassable were the roads to heavy transport. Madrid, without a river, relied upon mules and carts for its supplies. By the

Rudimentary transportation systems

mid-eighteenth century, the city required the services of over half a million mules and 150,000 carts, all forced to labor their way into town over rugged terrain. In 1698, a bronze statue of Louis XIV was sent on its way from the river port of Auxerre, southeast of Paris, to the town of Dijon. The cart in which it was dispatched was soon stuck in the mud, however, and the statute remained marooned in a wayside shed for twenty-one years, until the road was improved to the point that it could continue its belated journey.

Gradually in the eighteenth century transportation improved. The French established a Road and Bridge Corps of civil engineers, with a separate training school, in 1747. Work began in 1777 on a series of canals which eventually linked the English Channel to the Mediterranean. By the end of the century, France was spending seven million livres a year on road construction. In England, private investors, spearheaded by that inveterate canal builder the duke of Bridgewater, constructed a network of waterways and turnpikes linking provincial towns to each other and to London. With improved roads came stagecoaches, feared at first for their speed and recklessness much as automobiles were feared in the early twentieth century. People objected to being crowded into narrow carriages designed to reduce the load pulled by the team of horses. "If by chance a traveller with a big stomach or wide shoulders appears," an unhappy passenger lamented, "one has to groan or desert." Improvements such as stagecoaches and canals, much as they might increase the profits or change the pattern of life for the wealthy, meant little to the average European. Barges plied the waterways from the north to the south of France, but most men and women traveled no farther than to their neighboring market

Transportation improvements

The Duke of Bridgewater Canal

*Urban manufacturing
centers*

*Response to changing
machinery and techniques*

*Adverse reaction to new
machinery and processes*

town, on footpaths or on rutted cart tracks eight feet wide, which had served their ancestors much as they served them.

That industry flourished to the extent it did, despite the hazards and inefficiencies of transport, is a measure of the strength of Europe's ever-increasing commercial impulse. Rural "putting-out" did not prevent the growth of important urban manufacturing centers. In northern France, many of the million or so men and women employed in the textile trade lived and worked in cities such as Amiens, Lille, and Rheims. The eighteenth-century rulers of Prussia made it their policy to develop Berlin as a manufacturing center, taking advantage of an influx of French Protestants to establish the silk-weaving industry there. Even in cities, however, work was likely to be carried out in small shops, where anywhere from five to twenty journeymen labored under the supervision of a master to manufacture the particular products of their craft. Despite the fact that manufacturing was centered in homes and workshops, by 1700 these industries were increasing significantly in scale as many workshops grouped together to form a single manufacturing district. Textile industries led this trend, but it was true as well of brewing, distilling, soap and candle-making, tanning, and the manufacturing of various chemical substances for the bleaching and dying of cloth. These and other industries might often employ several thousand men and women congregated together into towns—or larger communities of several towns—all dedicated to the same occupation and production.

Techniques in some crafts remained much as they had for centuries. In others, however, inventions changed the pattern of work as well as the nature of the product. Knitting frames, simple devices to speed the manufacture of textile goods, made their appearance in England and Holland. Wire-drawing machines and slitting mills, the latter enabling nail-makers to convert iron bars into rods, spread from Germany into England. Mechanically powered saws were introduced into shipyards and elsewhere across Europe in the seventeenth century. The technique of calico printing, the application of colored designs directly to textiles, was imported from the Far East. New and more efficient printing presses appeared, first in Holland and then elsewhere. The Dutch invented a machine, called a "camel," by which the hulls of ships could be raised in the water so that they could be more easily repaired.

Innovations of this kind were not readily accepted by workers. Labor-saving machines such as mechanical saws threw men out of work. Artisans, especially those organized into guilds, were by nature· conservative, anxious to protect not only their restrictive "rights," but the secrets of their trade. Often, too, the state would intervene to block the widespread use of machines if they threatened to increase unemployment. The Dutch and some German states for example, prohibited the use of what was described as a "devilish invention," a ribbon loom capable of weaving sixteen or more ribbons at the same time. Sometimes the spread of new techniques was curtailed by states in order to protect the livelihood of powerful commercial interest groups. On behalf of both domestic textile manufacturers and importers of Indian goods, calico printing was for a time outlawed in both France and England. The cities of Paris and Lyons, and several German states banned the use of indigo dyes because they were manufactured abroad.

Changes that occurred in trade, commerce, agriculture, and industry, though large-scale phenomena, nevertheless touched individual men and women directly. Enclosure stripped away customary rights. Markets developed to receive and transmit goods from around the world altered the lives of those whose work now responded to their rhythms. An English cottager lost his family's age-old right to tether a cow on the common, now an enclosed and "scientifically" manured corn field. A linen weaver in rural Holland, whose peasant father had eked out a meager living from his subsistence farm, now supplemented his income by working for an Amsterdam entrepreneur, who paid progressively less for his food as a result of the cheap grain imported to the Low Countries across the Baltic Sea from eastern Europe. A carpenter in a Toulon shipyard lost his job when his employer purchased a mechanical saw that did the work of five men. A sailor on one of the ships built in that Toulon shipyard died at sea off the French colony of Martinique, an island of which he had never heard, at a distance so far from home as to be inconceivable to those who mourned his death when they learned of it months later. Meanwhile, in vast areas of southern and eastern Europe, men and women led lives that followed the same patterns they had for centuries, all but untouched by the changes taking place elsewhere. They clung to the life they knew, a life which, if harsh, was at least predictable.

The human implications of change

4. POPULATION PATTERNS

The patterns of life for most seventeenth-century Europeans centered on the struggle to stay alive. They lived and worked within a subsistence economy, considering themselves extremely fortunate if they could grow or earn what it took to survive. In most instances their enemy was not an invading army, but famine. At least once a decade, climatic conditions—usually a long period of summer rainfall—would produce a devastatingly bad harvest, which in turn would result in widespread malnutrition often leading to serious illness and death. A family might survive for a time by eating less; but eventually, with its meager stocks exhausted and the cost of grain high, the human costs would mount. The substitution of grass, nuts, and tree bark for grain on which the peasants depended almost entirely for nourishment was as inadequate for them as it appears pathetic to us.

The threat of famine

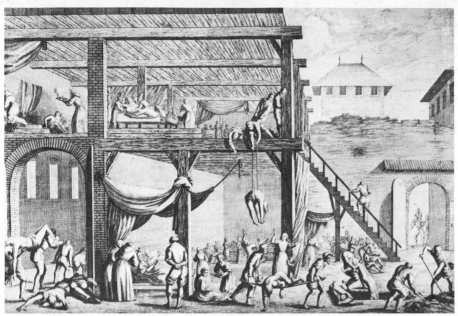

Left: *A Plague Hospital in Vienna.* The efforts to contain outbreaks of plague by gathering the sick in establishments such as this and burying the dead on the site proved unsuccessful. Right: *A Physician's Mask.* This German device containing smelling salts in its curved beak was designed to combat the plague, which physicians incorrectly believed was spread by poisonous vapors.

Population crises

Widespread crop failures occurred at fairly regular intervals—the worst in France, for example, about every thirty years (1597, 1630, 1662, 1694). They helped to produce the series of population crises that are the outstanding feature of early-modern demographic history. Poor harvests and the high prices produced by a scarcity of grain meant not only undernourishment and possible starvation, but increasing unemployment: with fewer crops to be harvested, more money was spent on food and, consequently, less on manufactured goods. The despair such conditions could easily breed would in turn contribute to a postponement of marriage and of births, and thus to a population decline. The patterns of marriages and births revealed in local parish registers indicate that throughout Europe the populations of individual communities rose and fell dramatically in rhythm with the fortunes of the harvest.

Health and sanitation

An undernourished population is a population particularly susceptible to disease. Bubonic plague had ravaged seventeenth-century Europe. Severe outbreaks occurred in Seville in 1649, in Amsterdam in 1664, and in London the following year. By 1700 it had all but disappeared; it last appeared in western Europe in a small area of southern France in 1720, though Moscow suffered an outbreak as late as 1771. Despite the gradual retreat of the plague, however, other diseases took a dreadful toll, in an age when available medical treatment was little more than crude guesswork, and in any event, beyond the reach of the poor. Epidemics of dysentery, smallpox, and typhus occurred with savage regularity. As late as 1779, over 100,000 people died of dysentery in the French province of Brittany. Most diseases attacked rich and poor impartially. Water supplies in towns and in the country were contaminated by heedless disposal of human waste and by all manner of garbage and urban filth. Bathing, feared at one time as a method of spreading disease, was by no means a weekly habit, whatever the social status of the household. Samuel Pepys, a prosperous servant of the crown in seventeenth-century London, recorded in his diary that his housemaid was in the habit of picking the lice from his scalp, that he took his first bath only after his wife had taken hers and experienced the pleasures of cleanliness, and that he had, on occasion, thought nothing of using the fireplace in his bedroom as a toilet, the maid having failed to provide him with a chamberpot. If such was Pepys's attitude toward hygiene and sanitation, imagine that of the poverty-stricken and ignorant peasant, and the threat to health implicit in such attitudes.

"Summer Amusement: Bugg Hunting." In this joking treatment of one of the facts of everyday life the bedbugs meet sudden death in a full chamber pot.

The precariousness of life helped encourage most men and women in early-modern Europe to wed much later than in traditional societies in Asia and Africa. This exceptional pattern found women marrying, on average, at twenty-five years of age, men at twenty-seven or twenty-eight, by which time they hoped to have accumulated sufficient resources to establish a household. Young couples lived on their own, and not, as in societies elsewhere, as part of "extended" families of three generations. In those extended families, a farm might pass from father to son before the death of the former. But in Europe this was not the custom. Since a son could not inherit until his father died, he was compelled to establish himself independently, and to postpone starting his own family until he had done so. Though historians have failed to find a clear explanation for this pattern of later marriages,

Implications of the European marriage pattern

Eighteenth-Century Sanitation. "Nightmen" moved through city streets after dark emptying the refuse of privies.

John Hunt

Nightman & Rubbish Carter,

At the Waggon and Horses in

Gofwell-Street, near Mount-Mill,

LONDON.

it may have resulted from a growing desire on the part of younger men and women for a higher standard of living. Late marriage helped to control the birth rate. Once married, however, a couple generally produced their first child within a year. Although subsequent children appeared with annual or biennial regularity, long periods of breast-feeding, which tends to reduce the mother's fertility, and community disapproval of extramarital sexual relations went some way toward limiting childbirth.

Population growth

Until the middle of the eighteenth century, populations continued to chart their rise and fall according to the outbreak of warfare, famine, and disease. From about 1750 on, however, there was a steady and significant population increase, with almost all countries experiencing major growth. In Russia, where territorial expansion added further to the increases, the population rate may have tripled in the second half of the eighteenth century. Gains elsewhere, while not usually as spectacular, were nevertheless significant. The population of Prussia and Spain doubled; Hungary's more than tripled; and England's population, which was about 5.5 million in 1700, reached 9 million in 1800. France, already in 1700 the most heavily populated country in Europe (about 20 million), added a further 6 million before 1790. Although reasons for the population increase remain something of a mystery, historians are inclined to agree that it was the cumulative result of a very gradual decline in the death rate, due in large measure to an equally gradual increase in the food supply. Better transportation facilitated the shipment of food over greater distances. Land clearances, particularly in England, and in Prussia and Russia, where territories were opened to colonization, provided an essential ingredient for increased production. New staples—the potato and maize—supplemented the diets of the very poor. And although evidence here is only fragmentary, it appears that whereas the climate of seventeenth-century Europe was abnormally bad, that of the succeeding hundred years was on the whole favorable.

New problems and attitudes

Population increase brought with it new problems and new attitudes. For example, the decline in the death rate among infants—along with an apparent increase in illegitimacy at the end of the eighteenth century—created a growing population of unwanted babies among the poor. Some desperate women resorted to infanticide, though since children murdered at birth died without benefit of baptism, the crime was stigmatized as especially heinous by the Church as well as by society in general. More often, babies were abandoned at the door of foundling hospitals. As an English benefactor of several such institutions, Jonas Hanway, remarked in 1766, "it is much less difficult to the human heart and the dictates of self-preservation to drop a child than to kill it." In Paris during the 1780s from seven to eight thousand children were being abandoned out of a total of thirty thousand new births. Paradoxically, some historians now argue that during this same period the decrease in infant and child mortality encouraged many parents to lavish care and affection on their offspring in a way that they had not when the repeated early deaths of their sons and daughters had taught them the futility of that emotional bond.

Although somewhere between 80 and 90 percent of the population lived in small rural communities, towns and cities were coming to play an increasingly important role in the life of early-modern Europe. One must speak of the "rise" of towns and cities with caution, however, since the pace of urbanization varied greatly across the Continent. Russia remained almost entirely rural: only 2.5 percent of its population lived in towns in 1630, and that percentage had risen by only 0.5 percent by 1774. In Holland, on the other hand, 59 percent of the population was urban centered in 1627 and 65 percent in 1795.

The "rise" of towns and cities

The total number of urban dwellers did not vary markedly after the end of the sixteenth century, when there were approximately 200 cities in Europe with a population of over 10,000. What did change between 1600 and 1800 was, first, the way in which those cities were distributed across the map, concentrated increasingly in the north and west; and second, the growing proportion of very large cities to the whole. The patterns of trade and commerce had much to do with these shifts. Cities like Hamburg in Germany, Liverpool in England, Toulon in France, and Cadiz in Spain grew by about 250 percent between 1600 and 1750. Amsterdam, the hub of early-modern international commerce, increased from 30,000 in 1530 to 115,000 in 1630 and 200,000 by 1800. Naples, the busy Mediterranean port, went from a population of 300,000 in 1600 to nearly half a million by the late eighteenth century. Where goods were traded, processed, and manufactured, fleets built and provisioned, people flocked to work. An eighteenth-century commentator noted that the laborers in Paris were "almost all foreigners"—that is, men and women born outside the city: carpenters from Savoy, water carriers from Auvergne, porters from Lyons, stonecutters from Normandy, wigmakers from Gascony, shoemakers from Lorraine.

Shifts in urban population

As some cities expanded, however, others stagnated or declined as a result of commercial changes. Norwich, in England, grew at the expense of older industrial centers on the English Channel when the manufacture of woolen goods shifted north. The population of the important German market center of Frankfurt declined during and after the period of the Thirty Years' War, when difficulties of communication and the general instability caused by frequent military campaigns diverted much of its former business to Amsterdam.

Ebb and flow of urban growth

The most spectacular urban population growth occurred in the administrative capitals of the increasingly centralized nations of Europe. By the middle of the eighteenth century, Madrid, Berlin, and St. Petersburg all had populations of over 100,000. London grew from 674,000 in 1700 to 860,000 a century later. Paris, a city of approximately 180,000 in 1600, increased to over half a million by 1800. Berlin presents a particularly interesting example of urban expansion.

Growth of administrative centers

From a population of 6,500 in 1661, it swelled to 60,000 in 1721 and 140,000 in 1783. Its increase was due in part to the fact that successive Prussian rulers undertook to improve its position as a trade center by the construction of canals that linked it with Breslau and Hamburg. Its population rose as well, however, because of the marked increase in Prussian army and bureaucratic personnel based in the capital city. Of the 140,000 citizens of Berlin in 1783, approximately 65,000 were state employees or members of their families.

5. LIFE WITHIN A SOCIETY OF ORDERS

Orders, privilege, and
freedom

Despite the economic and demographic shifts that were occurring in early-modern Europe, it remained a society ranked in traditional orders. The changes we have been concerned with occurred against the continuity of long-accepted social divisions based upon birth and occupation. As circumstances altered, the fluid patterns of economic reorganization clashed with older, rigid assumptions about the place of men and women within a pre-ordained—to many, a divinely ordained—social hierarchy. Jean Bodin, the French philosopher, wrote in 1570 that the division of the citizenry into "the three orders of nobles, clergy and people" was no more than natural. "There never was a commonwealth, real or imaginary, where citizens were in truth equal in all rights and privileges. Some always have more, some less than the rest." And some had none. Orders were demarcated by those rights and privileges. "Freedom" was understood as one such privilege, as a benefit, bestowed not upon all men and women, but upon special groups whose position "freed" them to do certain things others could not do, or freed them from the burden of doing certain things that were required of others. An English landowner was, because of the position his property conferred upon him, privileged, and therefore "free," to participate directly in the election of his government. A French nobleman was privileged, and therefore "free," to avoid the heavy burden of taxation levied upon the unprivileged orders. A German tailor who had served out his seven-year apprenticeship was free to set up his own shop for profit, something an unapprenticed man was not traditionally "at liberty" to do, no matter what his degree of skill with needle and thread. The master tailor's position conferred his freedom, just as the position of aristocrat and property owner conferred theirs.

The theater of a society of
orders

The members of the higher orders attempted at all times to live their lives in a particular style which accorded with their rank. The nobility was taught from birth to consider itself a class apart. Merchants and manufacturers were just as insistent upon maintaining the traditional marks of privilege that separated them from artisans and peasants. Sumptuary laws decreed what could be worn and by whom. An edict promulgated in the German principality of Brunswick in 1738, for

Middle-Class Fashion. In this seventeenth-century portrait of a Dutch burgo-master and his family, the patriarch and his wife are wearing the costume of an earlier generation, while the children are clothed in the current style. All display the opulence characteristic of their prosperous class.

example, forbade servant girls to use silk dress materials, to wear gold or silver ornaments, or shoes of anything but plain black leather. A similar law in the Polish city of Posen prohibited the wives of burgh-ers from wearing capes or long hair. Style was not simply a matter of current whim. It was a badge of status and was carefully adhered to as such. An aristocratic lady powdered her hair and rouged her cheeks as a sign that she was an aristocrat. Life within a society of orders demanded a certain degree of theatricality, especially from those at the top of the social hierarchy. Aristocrats "acted" their part in a calculat-edly self-conscious way. Their manner of speech, their dress, the cer-emonial sword they were privileged to wear, the title by which they were addressed, were the props of a performance which constantly emphasized the distinctions between those above and those below. Noble families lived in castles, châteaux, or country houses whose size and antiquity were a further proclamation of superiority. When they built new mansions, as the *nouveau riche* capitalist English gentry did in the eighteenth century, they made certain their elaborate houses and spacious private parks declared their newfound power. The English politician Robert Walpole had an entire village moved to improve the view from his grand new residence.

The vast majority of men and women defined and understood social hierarchy in terms of the rural communities in which they lived. At the head of those communities, in all likelihood, stood a representative of the noble elite. Aristocrats probably numbered about 3 percent of

Banquet Given in Paris by the Spanish Duke of Alva in Honor of the Prince of Asturias. The scene illustrates the ostentatious display this powerful nobleman believed suitable to his rank and fortune.

The nobility

the total population of Europe. The percentage was higher in Russia, Poland, Hungary, and Spain; lower in Germany, France, and England. Land was the hallmark of aristocratic position. And, generally speaking, the more land one possessed, the higher one stood within the aristocracy. In Hungary, five noble families owned about 14 percent of the entire country; the greatest of these, Prince Esterházy, controlled the lives of over half a million peasants. Most noblemen were not nearly so rich and powerful. Some, indeed, could rely on little more than inherited privilege to distinguish themselves from peasants.

Nobility and commerce

The pattern of noble life varied considerably from country to country. In England and Prussia, the nobility tended to reside on its estates; in south and west Germany, and in France, aristocrats were more likely to leave the management of their estates to stewards and to live at the royal court. Despite the traditional assumption that noblemen need not, and therefore must not, soil their aristocratic reputation by commercial dealing, by the end of the eighteenth century they were involving themselves in increasing numbers in a variety of entrepreneurial enterprises. Some exploited mineral deposits on their estates; others invested in overseas trade. In France, two of the four largest coal mines were owned and operated by noblemen, while the duke of Orléans was an important investor in the newly established chemical dye industry. In eastern Europe, because there were few middle-class merchants, aristocrats frequently undertook to market their agricultural produce themselves.

In no country was the aristocracy a completely closed order. Men who proved of use to the crown as administrators or lawyers, men who amassed large fortunes as a consequence of judicious—and often legally questionable—financial transactions, moved into the ranks of the nobility with increasing frequency during the late seventeenth and eighteenth century. Joseph II of Austria was making financiers into noblemen by the dozen in the late eighteenth century. In France, it was possible to attain nobility through the purchase of expensive offices from the crown. There was also a growing legal nobility of the "robe," headed by members of the thirteen provincial *parlements* whose function it was to record, and thereby sanction, the laws of the kingdom.

In time, severe tensions arose, most particularly in France but elsewhere as well, between the older nobility and those much more active and frequently more intelligent men of the new nobility. Tradition had it that noble service meant military service, that the ideal of noble honor involved heroism on the battlefield, not cunning at the law courts or conniving in palace antechambers. Hence, there was conflict over the legitimacy of those in the new noble order.

Whether recently enobled or members of one of those ancient families that existed throughout Europe and which the French called—simply and eloquently—*les grands*, most aristocrats owned large landed estates. Land ownership helped them not only to establish their position but to define it as well, by bringing them into direct relationship with the peasants and laborers who worked that land and over whose lives the aristocracy exercised dominion. The status of the peasantry varied greatly across the face of rural Europe. In the East—Russia, Poland, Hungary, and in parts of Germany beyond the Elbe—the desire for profit in agriculture and the collusion of the state with the aristocracy led to the growth of a "second serfdom," a serf system much stronger than that which had existed during the Middle Ages. In East Prussia, serfs often had to work from three to six days a week for their lord, and some had only late evening or night hours to cultivate their own lands.

Peasants throughout eastern Europe found their destinies controlled in almost all respects by their masters. Noble landlords dispensed justice in manorial courts and even ruled in cases to which they were themselves interested parties. These men were a combination of sheriff, chief magistrate, and police force in one, able to sentence their "subjects" to corporal punishment, imprisonment, exile, or in many cases death, without right of appeal. Peasants could not leave their land, marry, or learn a trade unless permitted to do so by their lord. In Russia, where half the land was owned by the state, peasants were bound to work in mines or workshops if their masters so ordered, and could be sold to private owners. Although Russian peasant serfs were said to possess a "legal personality" that distinguished them from slaves, the distinction was obscured in practice. They lived as bound to their masters as had their great-grandfathers.

Peasant obligations

In western Europe, the position of the peasantry reflected the fact that serfdom had all but disappeared by the sixteenth century. Peasants might theoretically own land, although the vast majority were either tenants or laborers. Hereditary tenure was in general more secure than in the East; peasants could dispose of their land and had legal claim to farm buildings and implements. Although far freer than their eastern European counterparts, the peasantry of western Europe still lived to a great degree under the domination of landowners. They were in many cases responsible for the payment of various dues and fees: an annual rent paid to landlords by those who might otherwise own their land outright; a special tax on recently cleared land; a fee, often as much as one-sixth of the assessed value of the land, collected by the manorial lord whenever peasant property changed hands; and charges for the use of the lord's mill, bakery, or wine press. In France, peasants were compelled to submit to the *corvée,* a requirement that they labor for several weeks a year maintaining local roads. Even access to the often questionable justice meted out in the manorial courts, which endured throughout the early-modern period in almost all of western Europe, was encumbered with fees and commissions. To many peasants, however, the most galling badge of their inferiority was their inability to hunt within the jurisdiction of their landlord's manor. The slaughter of game was a privilege reserved to the nobility, a circumstance generating sustained resentment on the part of a population that looked upon deer and pheasant not as a symbol of aristocratic status but as a necessary supplement to its meager diet. Noble landlords rarely missed an opportunity to extract all the money they could from their peasants while constantly reminding them of the degree to which their destiny was controlled by the lord of the manor.

A French Peasant . Tattered and overworked, this peasant farmer is shown feeding his livestock as the tax collector at his door relieves him of all of his profits.

Poverty and the peasantry

Despite their traditional subservience, however, western European peasants found themselves caught up directly in the process of economic change. The growth of centralized monarchies intensified the states' need for income, with the result that peasants were more burdened than ever with taxes and required services. They responded by accepting a new role as wage-earners in an expanding market economy, some as agricultural day laborers on enclosed estates, others as part of the work force in expanding rural industries. A few were genuinely independent, literate, influential members of the communities where they lived, owning not only land but considerable livestock. In France, some acted as intermediaries between their landlords, from whom they leased several large farms, and the sharecroppers who actually worked the land. Most, however, were far less fortunate. Those with claim to a small piece of property usually worked it into infertility in the course of one or two generations as they scrambled to make

Market Scene by Jean Michelin. Peasant women and children bringing produce to a nearby market town.

it produce as much as possible. Each time a peasant proprietor died, his holdings were divided among his male heirs, encouraging the sort of marginal economic existence that was the fate of most rural laborers.

Poor peasants often lived, contrary to the biblical injunction, by bread alone—two pounds a day if they were lucky, the dark dough a mixture of wheat and rye flour. Bread was supplemented by peas and beans, beer, wine, or, far less often, skimmed milk. Peasant houses usually contained no more than one or two rooms, and were constructed of wood, plastered with mud or clay. Roofs were most often thatched with straw, which was used as fertilizer when replaced, and provided fodder for animals at times of scarcity. Furnishings seldom consisted of more than a table, benches, pallets for sleeping, a few earthenware plates, and simple tools—an axe, a wooden spade, a knife.

Peasant bread and board

Wives of peasants tended livestock and vegetables, and managed the dairy, if there was one. Women went out as field workers, or worked at home at knitting, spinning, or weaving in order to augment the family income. A popular seventeenth-century poem has a laborer's wife lamenting her lot with a refrain that has echoed down the ages: ". . . my labor is hard,/ And all my pleasures are debarr'd;/ Both morning, evening, night and noon,/ I am sure a woman's work is never done."

The peasant wife

The spread of the putting-out system broke down the previously sharp demarcations between town and country, between the life lived inside a city's medieval walls and that lived outside. Suburbs merged urban and rural existence. In some, textile workers labored. In others, families of fashion took their ease, creating an environment "where

Urban living conditions

the want of London smoke is supplied by the smoke of Virginia tobacco," as one Englishman remarked wryly. Houses in areas inhabited by the wealthy were increasingly built of brick and stone, which replaced the wood, lath, and plaster of the Middle Ages. This change was a response to the constant danger of fire. The great fire of London in 1666, which destroyed three-quarters of the town—12,000 houses—was the largest of the conflagrations that swept cities with devastating regularity. Urban dwellings of the laboring poor remained firetraps. Workers' quarters were badly overcrowded; entire families lived in one-room accommodations in basements and attics that were infested with bugs and fleas.

Urban society: the bourgeoisie

Urban society was, like its rural counterpart, a society of orders. In capital cities, noble families occupied the highest social position, as they did in the countryside, living a parasitic life of conspicuous consumption at court. The majority of cities and towns were dominated by a nonnoble *bourgeoisie*. That French term originally designated a burgher or townsman who was a long-term, resident property owner or leaseholder and taxpayer. By the eighteenth century it had come to mean a townsman of some means who aspired to be recognized as a person of local importance, and evinced a willingness to work hard, whether at counting-house or government office, and a desire to live a comfortable, if by no means extravagant, existence. A bourgeois gentleman might derive his income from rents; he might, as well, be an industrialist, banker, or merchant, a professional, lawyer, or physician. If he served in the central bureaucracy, he would consider himself the social superior of those provincials whose affairs he administered. Yet he would himself be looked down upon by the aristocracy, who tended to think of the *bourgeoisie* as a class of vulgar social climbers. The French playwright Molière's comedy *The Bourgeois Gentleman* (1670) reflected this attitude, ridiculing the manners of the commercial class who were trying to ape their betters. "Bourgeois," another French writer observed, "is the insult given by noblemen to anybody they deem slow-witted or out of touch with the court." The *bourgeoisie* usually constituted about 20 to 25 percent of a town's population. As its economic elite, these men were almost always its governing elite as well. Municipal offices were considered a privilege of this order and were distributed accordingly.

Surprisingly, given the increase of commercial and industrial activity in the early-modern period, many cities witnessed a decline in the relative size of their industrial bourgeoisies. For example, Frenchmen who made their money in trade could purchase land, and by paying fees to the king, gain the right to an ennobling office. In seventeenth-century Amiens, a major textile center, the upper bourgeoisie deserted trade and derived the majority of its income from land or bonds. Where the bourgeoisie thrived, it more often than not did so as the result of a burgeoning state or regional bureaucracy.

The 'Bon Ton.' This English cartoon mocks the rage for French fashion and illustrates the affluence of a middle class able to afford the changing dictates of fashion.

Next within the urban hierarchy was a vast middle range of shop-keepers and artisans. Many of the latter continued to learn and then to practice their craft as members of guilds, which in turn contained their own particular ascending hierarchy of apprentice, journeyman, and master, thus preserving a society of orders. Throughout the early-modern period, however, commercial expansion threatened the rigid hierarchy of the guild structure. The expense and curtailed output resulting from restrictive guild practices met with serious opposition in big cities such as Paris and London, and in the industrial hinterlands of France and Germany, where expanding markets called for cheaper and more readily available goods. Journeymen tailors and shoemakers in increasing numbers set up shops without benefit of mastership and produced cheaper coats and shoes in defiance of guild regulations. In the silk workshops of Lyons, both masters and journeymen were compelled to labor without distinction of status for piece rates (wages paid per finished article, rather than per hour) set by merchandising middlemen and far below an equitable level in the opinion of the silk workers. Artisans like these, compelled to work for low wages at the behest of profiteering middlemen, grew increasingly restive. In France and Germany, journeymen's associations had originated as social and mutual-aid organizations for young men engaged in "tramp-ing" the country to gain experience in their trade. In some instances, however, these associations fostered the development of a trade con-sciousness that led to strikes and boycotts against masters and middle-men over the issues of wages and working conditions. An imperial law passed in Germany in 1731 deprived the associations of their right to organize, and required journeymen to carry a certificate of identification as testimony of their respectability during their travels.

Urban society: shopkeepers and artisans

At the bottom of urban society was a mass of semi-skilled and unskilled workers: carters and porters; stevedores and dockers; water carriers and sweepers; seamstresses, laundresses, cleaners, and domestic servants. These men and women, like their rural counterparts, lived on the margins of life, constantly battling the trade cycles, seasonal unemployment, and epidemics that threatened their ability to survive. A number existed in shanties on the edge of towns and cities. In Genoa, the homeless poor were sold as galley slaves each winter. In Venice, the poor lived on decrepit barges under the city's bridges. A French ordinance of 1669 ordered the destruction of all houses "built on poles by vagabonds and useless members of society." Deprived of the certainty of steady work, these people were prey not only to economic fluctuations and malevolent "acts of God," but to a social system that left them without any "privilege" or "freedom" whatso-ever.

Urban society: the poor

Attitudes toward poverty varied from country to country. Most localities extended the concept of orders to include the poor: "the deserving"—usually orphans, the insane, the aged, the infirm; and

Hanging Thieves. This seventeenth-century engraving is designed to teach a lesson. Troops stand by and priests administer the last rites to condemned criminals as they are executed by the dozen. "At last," the engraver's caption reads, "these infamous lost souls are hung like unhappy fruit."

"the undeserving"—able-bodied men and women who were out of work or who, even though employed, could not support themselves and their families. The authorities tended to assume in the latter case that poverty was the result of personal failings; few made a connection between general economic circumstances and the plight of the individual poor. For the deserving, private charitable organizations, such as those in France, founded by the order of St. Vincent de Paul and by the Sisters of Charity, provided assistance. For the undeserving, there was harsh treatment at the hands of the state whose concern to alleviate extreme deprivation arose more from a desire to avert public disorder than from motives of human charity. Food riots were common occurrences. In times of scarcity the French government frequently intervened to reduce the price of grain, hoping thereby to prevent an outbreak of rioting. Yet riots nevertheless occurred. When property damage resulted, the ringleaders were always severely punished, usually by hanging, The remainder of the crowd was often left untouched by the law, a fact suggesting the degree to which governments were prepared to tolerate rioting itself as a means of dealing with the chronic problem of poverty.

Poor vagrants were perceived as a serious threat to social tranquillity. They were therefore frequently rounded up at harvest time to keep them from plundering the fields. Vagrants and other chronically unemployed persons were placed in poorhouses where conditions were little better than those in prisons. Often the very young, the very old, the sick, and the insane were housed together with hardened criminals. Poor relief in England was administered parish by parish in accordance with a law passed in 1601. Relief was tied to a "law of settlement," which stipulated that paupers might receive aid only if still residing in the parish of their birth. An unemployed weaver who had migrated fifty miles in search of work could thus expect assistance only if he returned home again. In the late eighteenth century, several European countries established modest public works programs in an attempt to relieve poverty by reducing unemployment. France, for example, undertook road-building projects in the 1770s under the auspices of its progressive finance minister, Turgot. But generally speaking, indigence was perceived not as a social ill for which a remedy might be sought, but as an indelible stigma demarking the lowest of a community's social orders.

Early-modern Europe fashioned its institutions to reflect the patterns of social hierarchy. Nowhere was this more apparent than in the field of education. One barrier—a knowledge of Latin—separated aristocrats and a fair number of scholars and professionals from the commercial middle ranks; a second—the ability to read and write—separated the middle from the rest. Noblemen were generally educated by private tutors; though they might attend university for a time, they did so not in preparation for a profession but to receive further educational "finishing." Indeed during the late seventeenth and eighteenth centuries, universities more or less surrendered intellectual leadership to various academies established with royal patronage by European monarchs to enhance their own reputations as well as to encourage the advancement of science and the arts: the Royal Society of London, founded by Charles II in 1660; the French Academy of Sciences, a project upon which Louis XIV lavished a good deal of ostentatious attention; and the Berlin Royal Academy of Science and Letters, patronized by Frederick the Great of Prussia in the eighteenth century. Few noblemen had the interest or the intelligence to partici-

Education in a society of orders: the nobility

Louis XIV Visiting the French Academy of Sciences. Royal patronage sustained such academies by guaranteeing members rewards suitable to their station.

pate in the activities of these august organizations, which were not, in any case, teaching institutions. Far better suited to their needs and inclinations was "the grand tour," often of many months' duration, which led the aristocrat through the capitals of Europe, and during which he was expected to acquire a kind of international *politesse*. One observer, commenting on the habits of young English aristocrats abroad, remarked: "they game; purchase pictures, mutilated statues, and mistresses to the astonishment of all beholders."

Training for government service

Endowed, fee-charging institutions for the training of a governmental elite existed in France (the *collège*) and Spain (the *colegio mayor*) and in Germany and Austria (the *gymnasium*). Here the emphasis was by no means on "practical" subjects such as modern language or mathematics, but on the mastery of Greek and Latin translation and composition, the intellectual badge of the educated elite. An exception was the Prussian University of Halle, designed to teach a professional elite; a contemporary described that institution as teaching only what was "rational, useful, and practical."

Education for the middle orders

Male children from the middle orders destined to enter the family business or profession as a rule attended small private academies where the curriculum included the sort of "useful" instruction ignored in the *collèges* and *gymnasia*. Female children, from both the upper and middle orders, were almost invariably educated at home, receiving little more than rudimentary instruction in gentlewomanly subjects such as modern language, belles lettres, and music, if from the noble ranks, and a similar, if slightly more practical training, if from the bourgeoisie.

Education for the poor

No European country undertook the task of providing primary education to all its citizens until the mid–eighteenth century, when Frederick the Great in Prussia and the Habsburg monarchs Maria Theresa and her son Joseph II in Austria instituted systems of compulsory attendance. Available evidence suggests that their results fell far short of expectation. An early–nineteenth-century survey from the relatively enlightened Prussian province of Cleves revealed dilapidated schools, poorly attended classes, and an incompetent corps of teachers. Educational conditions were undoubtedly worse in most other European communities.

Increasing literacy

Although educational opportunities for peasants and workers remained meager by modern standards, available evidence suggests that literacy rates increased considerably in the seventeenth and eighteenth centuries; in England, from one in four males in 1600 to one in two by 1800; in France, from 29 percent of the male population in 1686 to 47 percent in 1786. Literacy among women increased as well, though their rate of increase generally lagged behind that of men: only 27 percent of the female population in France was literate in 1786. Naturally, such rates varied according to particular localities and circumstances, and from country to country. Literacy was higher in urban areas which contained a large proportion of artisans. In rural eastern Europe, literacy remained extremely low (20–30 percent) well into the nineteenth century. Notwithstanding state-directed efforts in

Prussia and Austria, the rise in literacy was largely the result of a growing determination on the part of religiously minded reformers to teach the poor to read and write as a means of encouraging obedience to divine and secular authority. A Sunday-school movement in eighteenth-century England and similar activities among the Christian Brotherhood in France are clear evidence of this trend.

Though the majority of the common people were probably no more than barely literate, they possessed a flourishing culture of their own. *Popular culture* Village life, particularly in Roman Catholic countries, centered about the church, to which men and women would go on Sundays not only to worship but to socialize. Much of the remainder of their day of rest would be devoted to participation in village games. Religion provided the opportunity for association and for a welcome break from the daily work routines. Pilgrimages, for example, to a nearby shrine would include a procession of exuberant villagers led by one of their number carrying an image of the village's patron saint and accompanied by drinking, dancing, and picnicking. In towns, Catholics joined organizations, called confraternities in France, Italy, Austria, and the Netherlands, which provided mutual aid and a set of common rituals and traditions centered upon a patron saint. Religious community was expressed as well in popular Protestant movements which arose in the eighteenth century: Pietism on the Continent and Methodism in England. Both emphasized the importance of personal salvation through faith and the potential worth of every human soul regardless of station. Both therefore appealed particularly to people whose position within the community had heretofore been presumed to be without any value. Though Methodism's founder, John Wesley (1703–1791), preached obedience to earthly authority, his willingness to rely on

Cockfight by William Hogarth. This London scene suggests the degree to which men from different social orders came together for sport, drinking, and adventure. Here a clergyman and a young gentleman consort with the London riff-raff.

*Carnival and other
amusements*

working men and women as preachers and organizers gave them a
new sense of personal importance.

While much popular culture was directly linked to religious traditions
and practices, much was now growing secular. Carnival, that vibrant
prelenten celebration indigenous not only to Mediterranean Europe
but to Germany and Austria as well, represented an opportunity for
common folk to cast aside the burdens and restraints imposed upon
their order by secular authority. Performances and processions celebrated a "world turned upside down," a theme popular throughout
much of Europe from the later Middle Ages, appealing to commoners
for a variety of ambiguous psychological reasons, but in large part,
certainly, as a way of avenging symbolically the economic and social
oppression under which they lived. For a few days, the oppressed
played the role of the oppressor and rulers were made to look like
fools and knaves. In parades, men dressed as kings walked barefoot
while peasants rode on horseback or in carriages; the poor threw
pretend money to the rich. These occasions, although emphasizing
social divisions, worked to hold communities to a common cultural
center, since both rich and poor celebrated together, as they did on
major religious holidays. Annual harvest festivals, once sponsored
by the Church, were also increasingly secular celebrations of release
from backbreaking labor, punctuated by feasting, drinking, sporting,
and lovemaking. Fairs and traveling circuses brought something of
distant places and people into lives bound to one spot. The drudgery
of everyday life was also relieved by horse races, cock fights, and
bear baiting. Taverns played an even more constant role in the daily

French Tavern. Often located outside the city limits so as to avoid the payment
of municipal taxes, taverns such as this provided a gathering place for workers
to drink, gossip, and relax after the day's labors. The tavern also served as a
convenient place for public readings and for airing common grievances.

life of the village, providing a place for men to gather over tobacco and drink to gossip and gamble.

Laboring men and women depended on an oral tradition of myth, legend, and superstition to steady their lives, and give them point and purpose. Stories in books sold at fairs by peddlers were passed on by those who could read. They told of heroes and saints, and of kings like Charlemagne whose paternal concern for his common subjects led him into battle against his selfish nobility. Belief in villains matched belief in heroes. Witchcraft, as we have seen, was a reality for much of the period to superstitious men and women. So was Satan. So was any supernatural force, whether for good or evil, which could help them make sense of a world in which they, more than any, were victims of events beyond their control.

The role of the oral tradition

Though increasingly secularized, popular customs, celebrations, and beliefs remained a stabilizing force in early-modern Europe. They were the cultural expression of that social order to which the vast majority of Europeans belonged. Popular culture in the main tended to reinforce the traditions and assumptions of order and hierarchy. As such, it helped to bind men and women to what civilization had been, as capitalism and mercantilism impelled them in the direction of what it would become.

Stability and change

SELECTED READINGS

• *Items so designated are available in paperback editions.*

• Blum, Jerome, *Lord and Peasant in Russia,* Princeton, 1961. A good study of Russian society.
• Braudel, F., *Capitalism and Material Life, 1400–1800,* London, 1973. A fascinating review of evidence pertaining to the entire world.
• _____, *The Structures of Everyday Life: The Limits of the Possible,* New York, 1981. A survey of the material conditions of life; profusely illustrated.
• Burke, Peter, *Popular Culture in Early Modern Europe,* London, 1978. Synthesizes the most recent work on the period between 1500 and 1800; fascinating.
• Chambers, J. D., and G. E. Mingay, *The Agricultural Revolution, 1750–1880,* London, 1966. Now the standard work.
• Cipolla, C. M., *Before the Industrial Revolution: European Economy and Society, 1000–1700,* 2nd ed., New York, 1980. Wide-ranging and full of deft observations.
• Curtin, Philip D., *The Atlantic Slave Trade,* Madison, Wisc., 1969. Reinterprets the character of the trade.
• Darnton, Robert, *The Great Cat Massacre and Other Episodes in French Cultural History,* New York, 1984. Fascinating explorations into early-modern French mentalities.
• _____, *The Kiss of Lamourette: Reflections in Cultural History,* New York, 1990. More striking observations on the nature of eighteenth-century French culture.
• Davis, D. B., *The Problem of Slavery in Western Culture,* Ithaca, N.Y., 1966. A brilliant analysis of Western attitudes and assumptions.
• Davis, Natalie Z., *Society and Culture in Early Modern France,* Stanford,

1975. Eight scintillating essays by a pioneer in the use of anthropological methods for the study of early-modern European history.

Forster, Robert, *The Nobility of Toulouse in the Eighteenth Century*, Baltimore, 1960. A careful analysis of the extent and nature of aristocratic power.

• Foucault, M., *The History of Sexuality: An Introduction*, Vol. 1, New York, 1978. Useful material on the early-modern period

Heckscher, E., *Mercantilism*, rev. ed., 2 vols., London, 1955. The most influential, but controversial, work on the subject.

Hufton, Olwen H., *The Poor of Eighteenth Century France*, Oxford, 1974. One of the first studies of a preindustrial "underclass."

Kaplow, Jeffry, *The Names of Kings: The Parisian Laboring Poor in the Eighteenth Century*, New York, 1972. A valuable study of the urban poor.

• Laslett, Peter, and Richard Wall, eds., *Household and Family in Past Times*, New York, 1972. A suggestive collection of essays.

Le Roy Ladurie, Emmanual, *The Peasants of Languedoc*, Urbana, Ill., 1974. A classic on peasant life and demography.

Levine, David, *Family Formation in an Age of Nascent Capitalism*, New York, 1977. A thoughtful treatment of patterns of social formation.

Lougee, Carolyn C., *Le Paradis des Femmes: Women, Salons, and Social Stratification in Seventeenth-Century France*. Princeton, 1976. Women's role in the intellectual life of the old regime.

• Miers, Suzanne, and Richard Roberts, *The Ending of Slavery in Africa*, Madison, 1988. The first comprehensive assessment of the end of slavery in Africa that explores the experiences of slaves, masters, and colonial overlords in fifteen sub-Saharan societies.

• Mousnier, R., *Peasant Uprisings in Seventeenth-Century France, Russia and China*, New York, 1970. A comparative analysis.

Parry, J. H., *Trade and Dominion: The European Overseas Empires in the Eighteenth Century*, New York, 1971. A comparative overview.

• Ranum, Orest, *Paris in the Age of Absolutism*, New York, 1968. A useful view of urban life.

Rich, E. E., and C. H. Wilson, eds., *The Cambridge Economic History of Europe*: Volume 5, *The Economic Organization of Early Modern Europe*, New York, 1977. An indispensable guide to the study of the period's economy and society.

• Stone, Lawrence, *The Family, Sex and Marriage in England, 1500–1800*, New York, 1977. An important, controversial book which argues important changes in attitudes over the course of three centuries.

• Wilson, Charles, *England's Apprenticeship, 1603–1763*, London, 1965. A reliable economic survey.

• Wrigley, E. A., *Population and History*, New York, 1969. A good introduction to family history.

SOURCE MATERIALS

Barnett, G. E., ed., *Two Tracts by Gregory King*, Baltimore, 1936. An introduction to the work of the modern world's first real statistician.

• Goubert, P., *The Ancien Régime: French Society, 1600–1750*, London, 1973. Particularly strong in its descriptions of rural life. Includes selections from illuminating documents.

Young, Arthur, *Travels in France during the Years 1787, 1788, 1789*, London, various editions. Vivid observations by an English traveler.

Chapter 23

THE AGE OF ABSOLUTISM
(1660-1789)

There are four essential characteristics or qualities of royal authority.
First, royal authority is sacred.
Second, it is paternal.
Third, it is absolute.
Fourth, it is subject to reason.

   —Jacques Bossuet, *Politics Drawn from the Very Words of Holy Scripture*

The period from the accession to personal rule of Louis XIV of France until the French Revolution is known as the age of absolutism. The label is accurate if we define absolutism as the *Absolutism defined* conscious extension of the legal and administrative power of state sovereigns over their subjects, and over the vested interests of the social and economic orders in which those subjects were ranked. The dates are suggestive in that for the period as a whole the activities of French monarchs most clearly expressed the doctrines of absolutist government. Yet both the dates and the label need to be treated with some caution. We have already noted that from about 1500 on, a general trend to make the state more powerful had manifested itself in England and on the Continent. Sixteenth-century kings saw in Protestantism a way of asserting the sovereignty of their states over the power of the papacy and the aristocracy. And political thinkers such as Jean Bodin were championing absolutist theory in their writings well before Louis XIV assumed personal rulership of France. By establishing the French monarchs as prototypical early-modern rulers, we risk ignoring other modes of centralized government instituted by the rulers of Prussia, Russia, and Austria. And we exclude the crucially important exception of England, where after 1688 absolutist tendencies gave way to oligarchy, and political power was shared among monarchy, aristocracy, and plutocracy.

The limits of absolutism

The relationship between state power and economic innovation

The term "absolutism" needs qualification. As practiced by western European eighteenth-century rulers, absolutism was not despotism. They did not understand it as a license for untrammeled and arbitrary rule, such as that practiced by Oriental potentates. Despite the best efforts of these European monarchs to consolidate their authority, they could not issue irresponsible decrees and achieve lasting compliance. Aristocrats, churchmen, merchants, and entrepreneurs remained strong enough within their respective orders to ensure that kings and queens would need to justify the actions they took. Moreover, rulers tended to respect not only the strength of their political adversaries but the processes of law; they quarreled openly and broke with tradition only under exceptional circumstances. No matter how "absolute" monarchs might wish to be, they were limited as well by rudimentary systems of transportation and communication from interfering with any degree of consistency and efficiency in the daily lives of their subjects.

Although the emphasis in this chapter is largely upon political, diplomatic, and military events, absolutism cannot be fully understood without relating it to the commercial and industrial trends we have just analyzed, Tariff legislation, industrial regulations, wars of trade, currency manipulation, tax laws—all were useful tools in the construction of a new economic order. And all were tools that could be employed only by a strongly centralized state. Governments might take active steps to manage production and exportation, as the English did when they imposed the Navigation Acts in 1660, which restricted imports to material transported on English ships or those of their country of origin, and required colonial goods to pass through English ports before being sold elsewhere. Other governments (the French, for example), in their determination to finance expanding bureaucratic and military establishments, imposed new taxes and exacted an increasingly high price for the privileges they meted out. The state's expanding financial demands placed considerable pressure on both bourgeoisie and peasantry to make more money. And the result of that pressure, in turn, was entrepreneurship and wage labor.

Bearing in mind, then, the important symbiotic relationship between state power and economic innovation, we shall, in this chapter, measure the extent of royal power throughout Europe in the late seventeenth and eighteenth centuries, examine the varieties of absolutism as instituted and practiced by different monarchs, and take note of the way in which the centralization of power contributed to the rise of an international state system.

1. THE APPEAL AND JUSTIFICATION OF ABSOLUTISM

Absolutism appealed to many Europeans for the same reason that mercantalism did. In theory and practice, it expressed a desire for an end to the constant alarms and confusions of Europe's "iron century." The French religious wars, the Thirty Years' War in Germany, and the English Civil War all had produced great turbulence. The alternative, domestic order, absolutists argued, could come only with strong, centralized government. Just as mercantilists maintained that economic stability would result from regimentation, so absolutists contended that social and political harmony would be realized when subjects recognized their duty to obey their divinely sanctioned rulers.

Absolutist monarchs insisted, in turn, upon *their* duty to teach their subjects, even against their will, how to order their domestic affairs. As Margrave Karl Friedrich, eighteenth-century ruler of the German principality of Baden, expressed it: "We must make them, whether they like it or not, into free, opulent and law-abiding citizens." Looking back to the seventeenth-century wars that had torn Europe apart, rulers can be excused for believing that absolutism's promise of stability and prosperity—"freedom and opulence"—presented an attractive as well as an imperative alternative to disorder. Louis XIV of France remembered the *Fronde* as a threat to the welfare of the nation which he had been appointed by God to rule wisely and justly. When marauding Parisians entered his bedchamber one night in 1651 to discover if he had fled the city with Mazarin, Louis saw the intrusion as a horrid affront not only to his own person, but to the state. Squabbles among the nobility and criticisms of royal policy in the Paris Parlement during his minority left him convinced that he must exercise his powers and prerogatives rigorously if France was to survive and prosper as a great European state.

In order to achieve that objective, absolutist monarchs worked to control the disposition of the state's armed forces, the administration of its legal system, and the collection and distribution of its tax revenues. This ambitious goal required an efficient bureaucracy that owed its primary allegiance not to some particular social or economic order with interests antithetical to the monarchy, but to the institution of the monarchy itself. One hallmark of absolutist policy was its determination to construct a set of institutions strong enough to withstand, if not destroy, the privileged interests that had stood in the path of royal power in the past. The Church and the nobility, the semi-autonomous regions, and the would-be independent representative bodies (the English Parliament and the French Estates-General) were all obstacles to the achievement of strong, centralized monarchical government. And the history of absolutism is, as much as anything, the history of the attempts of various rulers to bring these institutions to heel.

In those major European countries where Roman Catholicism still remained the state religion—France, Spain, and Austria—successive monarchs throughout the eighteenth century made various attempts to "nationalize" the Church and its clergy. We have already noted the way in which in the fifteenth and sixteenth centuries, popes had conceded certain powers to the temporal rulers of France and Spain. Later absolutists, building on those earlier precedents, wrested further power from the Church in Rome. Even Charles III, the devout Spanish king who ruled from 1759 to 1788, pressed successfully for a papal concordat granting the state control over ecclesiastical appointments, and established his right to sanction the proclamation of papal bulls. Powerful as the Church was, it did not rival the aristocracy as an opponent of a centralized state. Monarchs combatted the noble orders in various ways. Louis XIV controlled the ancient French aristocracy by depriving it of political power while increasing its social prestige. Peter the Great, the talented and erratic tsar of early eighteenth-century Russia, co-opted the nobility into government service. Later in the century, Catherine II struck a bargain whereby in return for the granting of vast estates and a variety of social and economic privileges such as exemption from taxation, the Russian aristocracy virtually surrendered the administrative and political power of the state into the empress's hands. In Prussia under Frederick the Great, the army was staffed by nobles: again, as in Peter's Russia, a case of co-option. Yet in late–eighteenth-century Austria, the emperor Joseph II adopted a policy of confrontation rather than accommodation, denying the nobility exemption from taxation and deliberately blurring the distinctions between nobles and commoners.

These struggles between monarchs and nobles had implications for the additional struggle between local privileges and centralized power. Absolutists in France waged constant war against the autonomy of provincial institutions, often headed by aristocrats, much as Spanish rulers in the sixteenth century had battled independent-minded nobles in Aragon and Catalonia. Prussian rulers intruded into the governance of formerly "free" cities, assuming police and revenue powers over their inhabitants. These various campaigns, constantly waged and usually successful for a time, were evidence of the nature of absolutism and of its continuing success.

Absolutism had its theoretical apologists as well as its able practitioners. In addition to the political philosophies of men such as Bodin, defenders of royal power could rely on treatises such as Bishop Jacques Bossuet's *Politics Drawn from the Very Words of Scripture* (1708), written during the reign of Louis XIV, to sustain the case for extended monarchical control. Bossuet argued that absolute government was not the same as arbitrary government, since God, in whom "all strength and all perfection were united," was united as well with the person of the king. "God is holiness itself, goodness itself, and power itself. In these things lies the majesty of God. In the image of these things lies the majesty of the prince." It followed that the king was answerable to no one but God himself, and that the king was as far above other mortals as God was above the king. "The prince, as prince, is not regarded as a private person; he is a public personage, all the state is in him. . . .

Bishop Jacques Bossuet

As all perfection and all strength are united in God, all the power of individuals is united in the Person of the prince. What grandeur that a simple man should embody so much." What grandeur indeed! Bossuet's treatise was the most explicit and extreme statement of the theory of the divine right of kings, the doctrine that James I had tried to foist upon the English. Unlikely as it may sound to modern ears, the political philosophy of Bossuet was comforting to men and women who craved peace and stability after a century or more of international and domestic turmoil, and who found themselves embarked upon bold economic adventures that required a strong and stable polity.

2. THE ABSOLUTISM OF LOUIS XIV

Examine a portrait of Louis XIV [1] (1643–1715) in court robes; it is all but impossible to discern the human being behind the façade of the absolute monarch. That façade was carefully and artfully constructed by Louis, who recognized, perhaps more clearly than any other early-modern ruler, the importance of theater as a means of establishing authority. Well into the eighteenth century, superstitious commoners continued to believe in the power of the king's magic "touch" to cure disease. Louis and his successors used such beliefs to enhance their position as divine-right rulers endowed with God-like powers and far removed from common humanity.

    The advantages of strategic theater were expressed most clearly in Louis's palace at Versailles, the town outside of Paris to which he

Absolutism as theater: Louis XIV

[1] Here, as elsewhere, dates following a ruler's name refer to dates of reign.

The Château of Versailles. Dramatically expanded by Louis XIV in the 1660s from a hunting lodge to the principal royal residence and the seat of government, the château became a monument to the international power and prestige of the Grand Monarch.

One of the 1400 Fountains in the Gardens at Versailles. The grounds as well as the palace were part of the backdrop for the theater of absolutism.

Versailles

moved his court. The building itself was a stage upon which Louis mesmerized the aristocracy into obedience by his performance of the daily rituals of absolutism. The main façade of the palace was a third of a mile in length. Inside, tapestries and paintings celebrated French military victories and royal triumphs. Outside, in gardens containing 1400 fountains, statues of Apollo, god of the sun, recalled Louis's claim to be the "Sun King" of the French. Noblemen vied to attend him when he arose from bed, ate his meals (usually stone-cold, having traveled the distance of several city blocks from royal kitchen to royal table), strolled in his gardens, or rode to the hunt. As Louis called himself the Sun King, so his court was the epicenter of his royal effulgence. Its glitter, in which France's leading aristocrats were required by their monarch to share, was deliberately manufactured so as to blind them to the possibility of disobedience to the royal will. Instead of plotting some sort of minor treason on his estate, a marquis enjoyed the pleasure of knowing that on the morrow he was to be privileged to engage the king in two or three minutes of vapid conversation as the royal party made its stately progress through the vast palace halls (whose smells were evidence of the absence of sanitation facilities and of the seamy side of absolutist grandeur).

Louis XIV on his duties

Louis understood this theater as part of his duty as sovereign, a duty which he took with utmost seriousness. Though far from brilliant, he was hard-working and conscientious. Whether or not he actually remarked "L'état, c'est moi" ("I am the State"), he believed himself

personally responsible for the well-being of his subjects. "The deference and the respect that we receive from our subjects," he wrote in a memoir he prepared for his son on the art of ruling, "are not a free gift from them but payment for the justice and the protection that they expect from us. Just as they must honor us, we must protect and defend them."

Louis defined this responsibility in absolutist terms: as a need to concentrate royal power so as to produce general domestic tranquillity. While taming the aristocracy, he conciliated the upper bourgeoisie by enlisting its members to assist him in the task of administration. He appointed them as intendants, responsible for the administration and taxation of the thirty-six *generalités* into which France was divided. Intendants never served in the regions where they were born, and were thus unconnected with the local elites over which they exercised authority. They held office at the king's pleasure, and were clearly "his" men. Other administrators, often from families newly ennobled as a result of administrative service, assisted in directing affairs of state from Versailles. These men were not actors in the theater of Louis the Sun King; they were the hard-working assistants of Louis the royal custodian of his country's welfare. Much of the time and energy of Louis's bureaucrats was expended on the collection of taxes, necessary above all in order to finance the large standing army on which France's

The administration of French absolutism: intendants and revenue

Louis XIV, the Sun King. This portrait by Rigaud illustrates the degree to which absolute monarchy was defined in terms of studied performance.

ambitious foreign policy depended. In addition to the *taille,* or land tax, which increased throughout the seventeenth century and upon which a surtax was levied as well, the government introduced a capitation tax, payable by all, and pressed hard for the collection of indirect taxes such as that on salt (the *gabelle*) and on wine and tobacco. Since the nobility was exempt from the *taille,* its burden fell most heavily on the peasantry, whose periodic local revolts Louis easily crushed.

Curbing regional opposition

Regional opposition—and indeed regionalism generally—was curtailed during Louis's reign. Although intendants and lesser administrators came from afar, did not speak the local dialect, ignored local custom, and were therefore despised, they were generally obeyed. The semi-autonomous outer provinces of Brittany, Languedoc, and Franche Comté (a part of that territory known collectively as the *pays d'état*) came to heel as central administration crippled their provincial Estates. To put an end to the power of regional *parlements* (the courts responsible for registering laws), Louis decreed that members of those bodies which vetoed legislation would be summarily exiled. The Estates-General, the national French representative assembly last summoned in 1614 during the troubled regency following the death of Henry IV, did not meet again until 1789.

Louis XIV's religious policies

Louis was equally determined, for reasons of state and of personal conscience, to impose religious unity upon the French. That task proved to be difficult and time-consuming. The Huguenots were not the only source of theological heterodoxy. Jesuits, Quietists, and Jansenists—all three claiming to represent the "true" Roman faith—battled among themselves for adherents to their particular brand of Catholicism. Jesuits served Louis's interests best, since they advocated obedience to the secular power of the French state. Quietists preached a retreat into personal mysticism. Jansenism—a movement named for its founder Cornelius Jansen, a seventeenth-century bishop of Ypres—was a French version of Calvinism which stressed the doctrine of original sin and rejected the belief in free will that was central to Jesuit teaching. Louis, adhering to the absolutist doctrine of *un roi, une loi, une foi* (one king, one law, one faith) which had served as a rallying cry for both Catholics and Protestants in France during the preceding century, took drastic steps to achieve religious conformity as part of his program of national unification. He persecuted Quietists and Jansenists, offering them the choice of recanting or of prison and exile. Against the Huguenots he waged an even sterner war. Protestant churches and schools were destroyed; Protestant families were forced to convert. In 1685, Louis revoked the Edict of Nantes, the legal foundation of the toleration Huguenots had enjoyed since 1598. French Protestants were thereafter denied civil rights, and their clergy was exiled. Thousands of religious refugees fled France for England, Holland, the Protestant states of Germany, and America, where their par-

ticular professional and artisanal skills made a significant contribution to economic prosperity. (The silk industry of Berlin and of Spitalfields, an urban quarter of London, was established by Huguenots.)

Louis's drive for unification and centralization was assisted by his ability to rely upon increased revenues to fuel the domestic and military machinery of his absolutist monarchy. Those revenues were largely the result of policies and programs initiated by Jean Baptiste Colbert (1619–1683), the country's finance minister from 1664 until his death. Colbert was an energetic and committed mercantilist who believed that until France could put its fiscal house in order it could not achieve economic greatness. Colbert assumed office at a time when France, because of costly wars, was deeply in debt. Although he could not rid the country of that burden, he did for a time establish an interest rate of no higher than 5 percent, significantly lower than those the government had been accustomed to paying, and began negotiating directly with major creditors, rather than relying, as in the past, on fee-charging middlemen. Meanwhile, he tightened the process of tax collection, hounding corrupt officials who skimmed off a share of the taxes for themselves. He eliminated wherever possible the practice of tax farming, the system whereby collection agents were permitted to withhold a certain percentage of what they gathered for themselves. When Colbert assumed office, only about 25 percent of the taxes collected throughout the kingdom was reaching the treasury. By the time he died, that figure had risen to 80 percent.

Jean Baptiste Colbert

But Colbert's efforts were not limited to managing the public debt and wringing the inefficiencies out of the tax system. During this period the state also perfected the merchandising of government positions and privileges. When new taxes were imposed and litigation resulted judges were appointed—for a price—to settle the disputes. Mayoralties were sold and guilds purchased the right to enforce trade regulations. The state extracted direct profit from every office it created and every privilege it controlled, demonstrating once again the way in which economy and politics were inextricably intertwined.

The sale of government positions and privileges

As a mercantilist, Colbert did all he could to increase the nation's income by means of protection and regimentation. Tariffs he imposed in 1667 and 1668 were designed to discourage the importation of foreign goods into France. He invested in the improvement of France's roads and waterways. And he used state money to promote the growth of national industry, and in particular the manufacture of goods such as silk, lace, tapestries, and glass, which had long been imported. Yet Colbert's efforts to achieve national economic stability and self-sufficiency could not withstand the insatiable demands of Louis XIV's increasingly expensive wars. Nor did his overseas trading companies ever achieve the stature of those of England and Holland. Unquestionably, however, France's economy was generally healthier as a result of his policies.

Colbert as mercantilist

Absolutism and national unity

Absolutism in the German states

3. ABSOLUTISM IN CENTRAL AND EASTERN EUROPE, 1660–1720

The degree of success enjoyed by Louis XIV as an absolutist monarch was in part the result of his own abilities, and of those of his advisors. Yet it was due as well to the fact that he could claim to stand as the supreme embodiment of the will of all of his people. Despite its internal division into territories and orders that continued to claim some right to independence, France was already unified before the accession of Louis XIV, and it was possessed of a sense of itself as a nation. In this, it differed from the empires, kingdoms, and principalities to the east, where rulers faced an even more formidable task than did Louis as they attempted to weld their disparately constructed monarchies into a united, centralized whole. The Thirty Years' War had delivered a final blow to the pretensions of the Holy Roman Empire, which the French philosopher Voltaire dubbed neither holy, Roman, nor an empire. Power, in varying degrees, passed to the over three hundred princes, bishops, and magistrates who governed the assorted states of Germany throughout the remainder of the seventeenth and eighteenth centuries.

Despite the minute size of their domains, many of these petty monarchs attempted to establish themselves as absolutists in miniature, building lesser versions of Louis XIV's Versailles. They remodeled cities to serve as explicit expressions of their power. Broad avenues led to monumental squares and eventually to the grand palace of the monarch. Medieval cities had masked the inequalities of the social order in their crowded, twisted streets and passageways, where social ranks often lived jumbled together in close physical proximity. Absolutist capital cities, in contrast, celebrated inequality, their planning and architecture purposely emphasizing the vast distance separating the ruler from the ruled. European absolutists followed the French example by maintaining standing armies, and paying for their expensive pretensions by tariffs and tolls that severely hampered the development of any sort of economic unity within the region as a whole. Although these rulers often prided themselves on their independence from imperial control, in many instances they were client states of France. A sizable portion of the money Louis devoted to the conduct of foreign affairs went to these German princelings. States like Saxony, Brandenburg-Prussia, and Bavaria, which were of a size to establish themselves as truly independent, were not averse to forming alliances against their own emperor.

Most notable among these middle-sized German states was Brandenburg-Prussia, whose emergence as a power of consequence during this period was the result of the single-minded determination of its rulers, principally Frederick William, elector of Brandenburg from

1640 to 1688, whose abilities have earned him the title of "Great Elector." The rise of Brandenburg-Prussia from initial insignificance, poverty, and devastation in the wake of the Thirty Years' War resulted from three basic achievements that can be credited to the Great Elector. First, he pursued an adroit foreign policy which enabled him to establish effective sovereignty over the widely dispersed and under-developed territories under his rule: Brandenburg, a large but not particularly productive territory in north-central Germany; Prussia, a duchy to the east that was dangerously exposed on three sides to Poland; and a sprinkling of tiny states—Cleves, Mark, and Ravensberg—to the west. By siding with Poland in a war against Sweden in the late 1650s, the Great Elector obtained the Polish king's surrender of nominal overlordship in East Prussia. And by some crafty diplomatic shuffling in the 1670s, he secured his western provinces from French interference by returning Pomerania, captured in a recent war, to France's Swedish allies.

Frederick William's second achievement was the establishment of a large standing army, the primary instrument of his diplomatic successes. By 1688, Brandenburg-Prussia had 30,000 troops permanently under arms. That he was able to sustain an army of this size in a state

The absolutism of Frederick William of Brandenburg

The establishment of a large standing army

Prussians Swearing Allegiance to the Great Elector at Königsberg, 1663. The occasion upon which the Prussian estates first acknowledged the overlordship of their ruler, this ceremony marked the beginning of the centralization of the Prussian state.

with comparatively limited resources was a measure of the degree to which the army more than repaid its costs. It ensured the elector and his successors of absolute political control by fostering obedience among the populace, an obedience they were prepared to observe if their lands might be spared the devastation of another Thirty Years' War.

Taxation and bureaucracy: bargaining with the Junkers

The third factor contributing to the emergence of the Great Elector's state as an international power was his imposition of an effective system of taxation and his creation of a government bureaucracy to administer it. Here he struck an important bargain with the powerful and privileged landlords (*Junkers*) without whose cooperation his programs would have had no chance of success. In return for an agreement which allowed them to reduce their peasant underlings to the status of serfs, the Junkers gave away their right to oppose a permanent tax system, provided, of course, that they were made immune from the payment of taxes themselves. (As in other European countries, taxes in Prussia fell most heavily on the peasantry.)

The Junkers and the army

Henceforth, the political privileges of the landlord class diminished; secure in their right to manage their own estates as they wished, the Junkers were content to surrender management of the Hohenzollern possessions into the hands of a centralized bureaucracy. Its most important department was a military commissariat, whose functions included not only the dispensing of army pay and matériel, but the development of industries to manufacture military equipment. Frederick William's success was due primarily to his ability to gain the active cooperation of the Junker class, something he needed even more than Louis XIV needed the support of the French nobility. Without it, Frederick William could never have hammered together his absolutist state from the disparate territories that were his political raw material. To obtain it, he used the army not only to maintain order, but as a way of co-opting Junker participation. The highest honor that could befall a Brandenburg squire was commission and promotion as a military servant of the state.

Absolutism in the Habsburg Empire

Like Brandenburg-Prussia, the Habsburg monarchy was confronted with the task of transforming three different regions into a cohesive state. In the case of Austria, this effort was complicated by the fact that these areas were ethnically and linguistically diverse: the southernmost Germanic lands that roughly comprised the present-day state of Austria; the northern Czech- (Slavic-) speaking provinces of Bohemia and Moravia; the German-speaking Silesia, inherited in 1527; and Hungary, where the Magyar population spoke a non-Slavic, Finno-Ugric language, also acquired in 1527 but largely lost to Turkish invasion just a few years afterward. For the next 150 years the Habsburgs and the Turks vied for control of Hungary. Until 1683 Turkish pashas ruled three-fourths of the Magyar kingdom, extending to within eighty miles of the Habsburg capital of Vienna. In 1683 the Turks beseiged

Vienna itself, but were repulsed by the Austrians, assisted by a mixed German and Polish army under the command of King John Sobieski of Poland. This victory was a prelude to the Habsburg reconquest of virtually all of Hungary by the end of the century.

The task of constructing an absolutist state from these extraordinarily varied territories was tackled with limited success by the seventeenth-century Habsburg emperors Ferdinand III (1637–1657) and Leopold I (1658–1705). Most of their efforts were devoted to the establishment of productive agricultural estates in Bohemia and Moravia, and to taming the independent nobility there and in Hungary. Landlords were encouraged to farm for export, and were supported in this effort by a government decree which compelled peasants to provide three days of unpaid *robot* service per week to their masters.[2] For this support, Bohemian and Moravian landed elites exchanged the political independence that had in the past expressed itself in the activities of their territorial legislative Estates.

Bargaining with Bohemia and Moravia

Habsburg rulers tried to effect this same sort of bargain in Hungary as well. But there the tradition of independence was stronger and died harder. Hungarian (or Magyar) nobles in the west claimed the right to elect their king, a right they eventually surrendered to Leopold in 1687. But the central government's attempts to further reduce the country by administering it through the army, by granting large tracts of land to German aristocrats and settlers, and by persecuting non-Catholics were an almost total failure. The result was a powerful nobility which, while it insisted upon its right to exploit its serfs as it saw fit, nevertheless remained fiercely determined to retain its traditional constitutional and religious "liberties." The Habsburg emperors could boast that they too, like absolutists elsewhere, possessed a large standing army and an educated (in this case German-speaking) bureaucracy. But the exigencies imposed by geography and ethnicity kept them at some distance from the absolutist goal of a unified, centrally controlled and administered state.

Problems with the Hungarian nobility

Undoubtedly the most dramatic episode in the history of early modern absolutist rule was the dynamic reign of Tsar Peter I of Russia (1682–1725). Peter's accomplishments alone would clearly have earned him his history-book title, Peter the Great. But his imposing height—he was nearly seven feet tall—as well as his mercurial personality—jesting one moment, raging the next—certainly helped. Peter is best remembered as the tsar whose policies brought Russia into the world of western Europe. Previously the country's rulers had set their faces firmly against the West, disdaining a civilization at odds with the Eastern Orthodox, semi-Oriental culture that was their heritage, while laboring to keep the various ethnic groups—Russians, Ukrainians, and a wide variety of nomadic tribes—within their ever-growing em-

Peter the Great. An eighteenth-century mosaic.

---

[2] The English usage of the term *robot* derives from the Czech designation of a serf.

pire from destroying not only each other but the tsarist state itself. Since 1613 Russia had been ruled by members of the Romanov dynasty, who had attempted with some success to restore political stability following the chaotic "time of troubles" that had occurred after the death of the bloodthirsty, half-mad Tsar Ivan the Terrible in 1584. Tsar Alexis I (1645–1676) took a significant step toward unification in 1654 when he secured an agreement with the Ukrainians to incorporate that portion of the Ukraine lying east of the Dneiper River into the Muscovy state. But the early Romanovs were faced with a severe threat to this unity and their rule between 1667 and 1671, when a Cossack leader (the Russian Cossacks were semi-autonomous bands of peasant cavalrymen) named Stenka Razin led much of southeastern Russia into rebellion. Stenka Razin's uprising found widespread support from hordes of serfs who had been oppressed by their masters as well as from non-Russian tribes in the lower Volga area who longed to cast off domination from Moscow. But ultimately Tsar Alexis and the Russian nobility whose interests were most at stake were able to raise an army capable of defeating Razin's zealous but disorganized bands. Before the rebellion was finally crushed, over 100,000 rebels had been slaughtered.

These campaigns were but a prelude to the deliberate and ruthless drive to absolutist power launched by Peter after he overthrew the regency of his half-sister Sophia and assumed personal control of the state in 1689. Within ten years he had scandalized aristocrats and churchmen alike by traveling to Holland and England to recruit highly skilled foreign workers and to study the craft of shipbuilding. Upon his return he distressed them still further by declaring his intention to Westernize Russia, and initiating this campaign by cutting off the "Eastern" beards and flowing sleeves of leading noblemen at court. Determined to "civilize" the nobility, he published a book of manners which forbade spitting on the floor and eating with one's fingers, and encouraged the cultivation of the art of polite conversation between the sexes.

Peter Cutting a Nobleman's Beard. In this Russian woodcut Peter the Great is portrayed as a diminutive pest.

Much as Peter wished to consider himself a westerner, his particular brand of absolutism differed from that of other contemporary monarchs. As we have seen, the autocracy imposed by Ivan III in the fifteenth century had a decidedly Eastern caste. Peter was the willing heir to much of that tradition. He considered himself above the law and thus his own absolute master to a degree that was alien to the absolutist theories and traditions of the Habsburgs and Bourbons. Autocrat of all the Russias, he ruled despotically, with a ferocious individual power that western European rulers did not possess. Armed with such arbitrary power in theory, and intent on realizing its full potential in practice, Peter set out to turn Russia to the West and to modernize his state. He would brook no opposition.

Confronted with a rebellion among the *streltsy,* the politically active, elite corps of the army who were most opposed to his innovations and

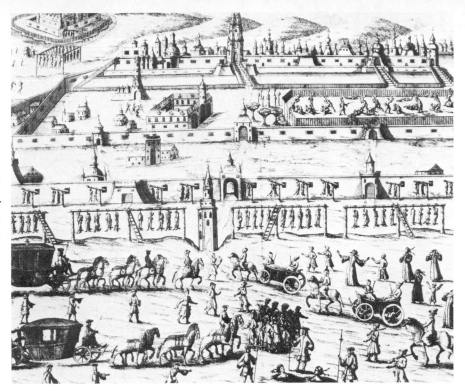

Peter the Great's Execution of the Streltsy. This contemporary print shows scores of corpses gibbeted outside the walls of the Kremlin. Peter kept the rotting bodies on display for months to discourage his subjects from opposing his efforts to Westernize Russian society.

who favored the restoration of his half-sister to the throne, Peter reacted with a savagery that astonished his contemporaries. Roughly 1200 suspected conspirators were summarily executed, many of them gibbeted outside the walls of the Kremlin, where their bodies remained for months as a graphic reminder of the fate awaiting those who would dare to challenge his absolute authority. Applying a lesson from the West, Peter proceeded to create a large standing army recruited from the ranks of the peasantry and scrupulously loyal to the tsar. One of every twenty males was conscripted for lifelong service. He financed his army, as did other absolutists, by increasing taxes, with their burden falling most heavily on the peasantry. To equip his new military force, he fostered the growth of the iron and munitions industries. Factories were built and manned by peasant laborers whose position was little better than that of slaves. Serfs were also commandeered for other public works projects, such as road and canal building, necessary for the modernization of the state.

The suppression and reconstruction of the army

In an effort to further consolidate his absolute power, he replaced the Duma—the nation's rudimentary national assembly—with a rubber-stamp senate, and appointed a procurator, dependent directly on him, to manage the affairs of the tradition-bound Russian Orthodox church, which essentially became an extension of the state. At the same time, Peter was fashioning new, larger, and more efficient administrative machinery to cope with the demands of his modernization program. Although he preferred to draw "new" men, whose

Absolutism and the new bureaucracy

The influence of foreign and domestic policy

loyalty to the tsar would be unerring, into the bureaucracy, he was compelled to rely upon the services of the aristocrat—or *boyar*—class as well, rewarding them by increasing their control over their serfs. Nevertheless, membership in his new bureaucracy did not depend on birth. One of his principal advisors, Alexander Menshikov, began his career as a cook and finished as a prince. Bureaucratic status replaced noble rank as the key to power. The administrative machinery devised by Peter furnished Russia with its ruling class for the next two hundred years.

Peter the Great's Eurocentric worldview also manifested itself in his foreign policy, as witnessed by his bold drive to gain a Russian outlet on the Baltic Sea. Previous battles with the Turks to secure a port on the Black Sea, and thus a southern passage to the West, had failed. Now he engaged in a war with Sweden's meteoric soldier-king Charles XII (1697–1718), who devoted most of his reign to campaigns in the field against the Danes, the Poles, and the Russians. By defeating Charles decisively at the battle of Poltava in 1709, Peter was able to secure his window to the West. He promptly outdid his absolutist counterparts in Europe, who had moved their courts to the outskirts of their capital cities, by moving the Russian capital from Moscow to an entirely new city on the Gulf of Finland. An army of serfs was employed to erect the baroque city of St. Petersburg

The St. Petersburg Palaces. The first of six versions of the Winter Palace here depicted (left) was erected in 1711. It quickly proved to be too modest for Peter's needs. Within a decade he had created a far more elaborate complex called Peterhof (right), complete with fountains fashioned after those of Versailles.

around a palace intended to imitate and rival Louis XIV's Versailles. It was not enough that Peter looked to the West; he wanted the Russian people to share the view.

Not surprisingly, Peter's drastic programs met with concerted resistance. Resentment smoldered under his imposing hand, even within the palace. His son Alexis, who had dared to declare himself opposed to his father's innovations, became a rallying point for the forces of resistance to the tsar and his policies, and died under torture inflicted at his father's command in 1718. Upon Peter's death in 1725, *boyar* determination to undo his reforms surfaced during the succession struggle. There followed a series of ineffective tsars, creatures of the Palace guard, thus allowing the resentful nobles to rescind many of his reforms. In 1762, the crown passed to Catherine II, a ruler whose ambitions and determination were equal to those of her august predecessor.

Peter the Great of Russia, Leopold I of Austria, Frederick William of Brandenburg-Prussia, and above all Louis XIV of France: these were the "great" seventeenth-century absolutists. Elsewhere, the fortunes of absolutism fared far less well. The ineffectual, weak-minded Spanish monarch Charles II found himself besieged by rebellions in Portugal and Sicily. In 1668, after years of fighting, he was forced to recognize Portuguese independence. In Sweden, Charles X and Charles XI managed to extend their territories at the expense of the Danes and to quell the independence of the aristocracy by confiscating their fiefdoms. During the reign of Charles XII, however, that legacy was dissipated by an adventurous but ultimately unproductive foreign policy. In Poland, the opposition of the landed gentry—or *szlachta*—to any form of centralized government produced a political stalemate that amounted to little more than anarchy. Foreign powers took advantage of this situation to intervene in Polish affairs and, in the eighteenth century, to carve up the country and distribute it among themselves.

4. THE ENGLISH EXCEPTION

But what of England, which had experienced a taste of absolutist centralization under the Tudors and early Stuarts, and indeed under Oliver Cromwell, but which possessed in its Parliament the longest tradition and most highly developed form of representative government in western Europe? England's political history in the late seventeenth century provides the most striking contrast to continental absolutism. Charles II, son of the beheaded Charles I, who returned from exile and ascended the throne in 1660, was initially welcomed by most English men and women. He pledged himself not to reign as a despot, but to respect Parliament and to observe Magna Carta and the Petition of Right, for he admitted that he was not anxious to "resume his travels." His delight in the unbuttoned moral atmosphere of his court

Charles II of England

and the culture it supported (risqué plays, dancing, and marital infidelity) mirrored a public desire to forget the restraints of the puritan past. The wits of the time suggested that Charles, "that known enemy to virginity and chastity," played his role as the father of his country to the fullest. However, as Charles's admiration of things French grew to include the absolutism of Louis XIV, he came to be regarded as a threat to more than English womanhood by a great many powerful Englishmen. However anxious to restore the monarchy, they were not about to surrender their traditional rights to another Stuart autocrat. By the late 1670s, the country found itself divided politically into those who supported the king (called by their opponents "Tories," a popular nickname for Irish Catholic bandits) and those opposed to him (called by *their* opponents "Whigs," a similar nickname for Scottish Presbyterian rebels).

As the new party labels suggest, religion remained an exceedingly divisive national issue. Charles was sympathetic to Roman Catholicism, even to the point of a deathbed conversion in 1685. He therefore opposed the stiff code of ecclesiastical regulations, known as the Clarendon Code, which had reestablished Anglicanism as the official state religion and which penalized Catholics and Protestant dissenters. In 1672, Charles suspended the Clarendon Code, although the public outcry against this action compelled him to retreat. This controversy, and rising opposition to the probable succession of Charles's ardent Roman Catholic brother James, led to a series of Whig electoral victories between 1679 and 1681. But Charles found that increased revenues, plus a secret subsidy he was receiving from Louis XIV, enabled him to govern without resort to Parliament, to which he would otherwise have had to go for money. In addition to ignoring Parliament, Charles further infuriated and alarmed Whig politicians by arranging the execution of several of their most prominent leaders on charges of treason, and by remodeling local government in such a way as to make it more dependent on royal favor. Charles died in 1685 with his power enhanced; but he left behind him a political and religious legacy that was to be the undoing of his successor.

James II was the very opposite of his brother. A zealous Catholic convert, he alienated his Tory supporters, all of whom were of course Anglicans, by dismissing them in favor of Roman Catholics, and by once again suspending the penal laws against Catholics and dissenters. His stubbornness, as one historian has remarked, made it all but impossible for him to take "yes" for an answer. Whereas Charles had been content to defeat his political enemies, James was determined to humiliate them. Like Charles, James interfered in local government, but his appointments were so personally distasteful and so mediocre as to arouse active opposition. James made no attempt to disguise his Roman Catholicism. He publicly declared his wish that all his subjects might be converted, and paraded papal legates through the streets of London. When, in June 1688, he ordered all Anglican clergymen to read his decree of toleration from their pulpits, seven bishops refused and were clapped into prison on charges of seditious libel. At their trial, however, they were declared not guilty, to the vast satisfaction of the English populace.

The trial of the bishops was one event that brought matters to a head. The other was the birth of a son to James and his second wife, the Roman Catholic daughter of the duke of Modena. This male infant, who was to be raised a Catholic, replaced James's much older Protestant daughter Mary as heir to the British throne. Despite a rumor that the baby boy was an imposter smuggled into the royal bedchamber in a warming pan, political leaders of both parties were prepared not only to believe in the legitimacy of the child but to take active steps to prevent the possibility of his succession. A delegation of Whigs and Tories crossed the Channel to Holland with an invitation to Mary's husband William of Orange, the *stadholder* or chief executive of the United Provinces and the great-grandson of William the Silent. William was asked to cross to England with an invading army to restore English religious and political freedom. As leader of a continental coalition determined to put a spoke in Louis XIV's expansionist policies, he accepted, welcoming the chance such a move represented to bring England into active opposition to the French (see below, p. 120).

The succession question

William's conquest was a bloodless coup. James fled the country, thereby allowing Parliament to declare the throne vacant and clearing the way for the accession of William and Mary as joint sovereigns of England. A Bill of Rights, passed by Parliament and accepted by the new king and queen, reaffirmed English civil liberties such as trial by jury, habeas corpus (guaranteeing the accused a speedy trial), and the right of petition and redress, and established that the monarchy was subject to the law of the land. An Act of Toleration, passed in 1689, granted dissenters the right to worship, though not the right to full political protection. In 1701, with the son of the exiled James II now reaching maturity in France, an Act of Succession ordained that the English throne was to pass first to Mary's childless sister Anne, who ruled from 1702 to 1714, and then to George, elector of the German principality of Hanover, who was the great-grandson of James I. The connection was a distant one, but the Hanoverian dynasty was Protestant, and George reputed to be a capable enough ruler. The act was further evidence of the degree to which Parliament could dictate its terms. Henceforth, all English sovereigns were to be communicants of the Church of England. If foreign born, they could not engage England in the defense of their native land, nor leave the country, without Parliamentary consent.

William III

The events of 1688 and 1689 were soon referred to by the English as "the Glorious Revolution." Glorious for the English in that it occurred without bloodshed (although James is reputed to have been suffering from a nosebleed at the moment of crisis). Glorious, too, for

A "glorious" revolution?

defenders of Parliamentary prerogative. Although William and Mary and their royal successors continued to enjoy a large measure of executive power, after 1688 no king or queen attempted to govern without Parliament, which met annually from that time on. Parliament strengthened its control over the collection and expenditure of public money. Future sovereigns were henceforth unable to conduct the country's business without recourse to the House of Commons for the funds to do so. Glorious, finally, for advocates of the civil liberties now guaranteed within the Bill of Rights.

Yet 1688 was not all glory. It was a revolution that consolidated the position of large property holders, local magnates whose political and economic power base in their rural constituencies and on their estates had been threatened by the interventions of Charles II and James II. If it was a revolution, it was one designed to restore the *status quo* on behalf of a wealthy social and economic order that would soon make itself even wealthier as it drank its fill of government patronage and war profits. And it was a revolution that brought nothing but misery to the Roman Catholic minority in Scotland, which joined with England and Wales in the union of Great Britain in 1701, and the Catholic majority in Ireland where, following the Battle of the Boyne in 1690, repressive military forces imposed the exploitive will of a self-interested Protestant minority upon the Catholic majority.

Although the "Glorious Revolution" was an expression of immediate political circumstance, it was a reflection as well of anti-absolutist theories that had risen in the late seventeenth century to challenge the ideas of writers such as Bodin, Hobbes, and Bossuet. Chief among these opponents of absolutism was the Englishman John Locke (1632–1704), whose *Two Treatises of Civil Government* (1690) was used to justify the events of the previous two years. Locke maintained that originally all humans had lived in a theoretical state of nature in which absolute freedom and equality prevailed, and in which there was no government of any kind. The only law was the law of nature, which each individual enforced for himself in order to protect his natural rights to life, liberty, and property. It was not long, however, before men began to perceive that the inconveniences of the state of nature greatly outweighed its advantages. With individuals attempting to enforce their own rights, confusion and insecurity were the unavoidable results. Accordingly, the people agreed among themselves to establish a civil society, to set up a government, and to surrender certain powers to it. But they did not make that government absolute. The only power they conferred upon it was the executive power of the law of nature. Since the state was nothing but the joint power of all the members of society, its authority could "be no more than those persons had in a state of nature before they entered into society, and gave it up to the community." All powers not expressly surrendered were reserved to the people themselves. If the government exceeded or abused the authority explicitly granted in the political contract, it

John Locke

became tyrannical; the people then had the right to dissolve it or to rebel against it and overthrow it.

Locke condemned absolutism in every form. He denounced despotic monarchy, but he was no less severe in his strictures against the absolute sovereignty of parliaments. Though he defended the supremacy of the law-making branch, with the executive primarily an agent of the legislature, he nevertheless refused to concede to the representatives of the people an unlimited power. Arguing that state government was instituted among people for the preservation of property, he denied the authority of any political agency to invade the natural rights of a single individual. The law of nature, which embodied these rights, was an automatic limitation upon every branch of the government. Locke's theoretical defense of political liberties emerged in the late eighteenth century as an important element in the intellectual background of the French Revolution. In 1688, however, it served a far less radical purpose. The landed magnates responsible for the exchange of James II for William and Mary could read Locke as an apologia for their conservative revolution. James II, rather than protecting their property and liberties, had encroached upon them; hence they had every right to overthrow the tyranny he had established and to replace it with a government that would, by ensuring their rights, defend their interests.

Locke and limited sovereignty

5. WARFARE AND DIPLOMACY: THE EMERGENCE OF A STATE SYSTEM

The rise of absolutist monarchies in the late seventeenth century resulted in the emergence of an international state system. To the extent that absolutists succeeded in attaining their goals of unification and centralization, their states took shape as individual, identifiable political and economic entities. Although the achievements of various monarchs in this regard were limited, they were significant enough to encourage diplomats to speak more commonly than in the past of the "interests" of a particular state, as if that state somehow had a corporate personality of its own, and of the way in which those interests might coincide or conflict with the interests of another state. Often the interests of a monarch might clash with those of the country over which he ruled. Bourbon kings and Habsburg emperors worried about the future of their family dynasties to the detriment of the future of France or Austria. Religion, the factor that had torn Europe apart in the preceding century, remained an international issue in 1700. But increasingly, both dynasty and religion were superseded by newer "interests"—commerce and international balance and stability. The emergence of something approaching the modern state was to result, by 1715, in a significant redefinition of the aims and calculations of diplomacy and warfare.

Emergence of state interests

The growth of diplomacy

The organization of diplomatic bureaucracies was a major accomplishment of absolutist monarchies. Had most foreign ministers and ambassadors read the Dutchman Hugo Grotius's treatise on *The Law of War and Peace* (1625), they would have agreed with him about the necessity of establishing a body of rules that would help to bring reason and order to relations between governments. In practice, of course, reason and order gave way to bribery and improvisation. Yet the rationalization of diplomatic processes and the establishment of foreign ministries and embassies in European capitals, with their growing staffs of clerks and ministers, reflected a desire to bring order out of the international chaos that had gripped Europe during its "war century." International relations in the late seventeenth century was, among other things, a history of diplomatic coalitions, an indication of the degree to which negotiation was now a weapon in the armory of the absolutist state.

The growth of professional armies

Warfare, however, continued to play an integral and almost constant role in the international arena. The armies of the period grew dramatically. When Louis XIV acceded to power in 1661, the French army numbered 20,000 men; by 1688, it stood at 290,000; by 1694, 400,000. These armies were increasingly professional organizations, controlled directly by the state, and under the command of trained officers recruited from the nobility. In Prussia, common soldiers were mostly conscripts; in other European countries they were volunteers, either native or foreign, though often "volunteers" in no more than name, having been coerced or tricked into service. Increasingly,

The Capture of Cambrai by Louis XIV in 1677. This print illustrates the tactics of siege warfare as practiced by early-modern armies. Louis is shown receiving an emissary from the city, whose walls have been breeched by siege guns.

however, enlistment was perceived by common soldiers as an avenue to a career, one which included the possibility of promotion to corporal or sergeant, and in the case of France, the promise of a small pension at the end of one's service. However recruited, common soldiers became part of an increasingly elaborate and efficient fighting force. The maneuvers of infantry, cavalry, and artillery were coordinated as never before. Soldiers were drilled with a thoroughness necessitated by tactics which depended on the accurate firepower of cannon and flintlock muskets. They were taught to stand their ground in formations of long, rigid lines in the face of direct enemy assault. They mastered the use of the bayonet (short steel spikes attached to the end of muskets, first manufactured in Bayonne, France, in the seventeenth century); the most effective procedure: stabbing the man in his left side as he raised his right arm to fire. Above all, they were made to understand the dire consequences of disobedience, breaking rank, or desertion. Soldiers were expected to obey instantly and unquestioningly. Failure to do so resulted in brutal punishment, often flogging, sometimes execution. Commissioned and noncommissioned officers carried sticks and prods with which to "encourage" correct military behavior in their men. Drill, not only on the battlefield but on the parade ground, in brilliant, elaborate uniforms and intricate formations, was designed to reduce individuals to automaton-like parts of an army whose regiments were moved across battlefields as a chess player moves pawns across the board—and with about the same concern for loss of human life.

The patterns of international relations during the period from 1660 to 1715 show European monarchs making use of the new machinery of diplomacy and warfare to resolve the conflicting interests of dynasty, stability, and commerce. At the center of that pattern, as at the center of Europe, stood Louis XIV. From 1661 until 1688, in a quest for glory, empire, and even revenge, he waged war across his northern and eastern frontiers on the pretext that the lands in question belonged both to the Bourbons and to the French by tradition, by former treaty, or by dynastic inheritance. His aggressively expansionist policies, alarming to other European rulers, led William of Orange, in 1674, to form an anti-French coalition with Austria, Spain, and various smaller German states. Yet Louis continued to push his frontiers eastward, invading territories that had been Germanic for centuries, and capturing Strassburg in 1681 and Luxembourg in 1684. Louis's seizure of Strassburg (subsequently called Strasbourg by the French), completing the conquest of the German-speaking province of Alsace begun in 1634 by Richelieu, irreversibly incorporated the seeds of a Franco-German animosity centered on this region that would bear bitter fruit in the great wars of the nineteenth and twentieth centuries. A second coalition, the so-called League of Augsburg—Holland, Austria, Sweden, and further German allies—was only somewhat more successful than the first.

The foreign policies of Louis XIV

Europe on the verge of war

These allies were concerned above all to maintain some sort of European balance of power. They feared an expansionist France would prove insatiable, as it pressed its boundaries farther and farther into Germany and the Low Countries. Louis, mistakenly expecting that William would be forced to fight an English army under James to establish his right to his new throne and would therefore be too preoccupied to devote his full attention to developments on the Continent, kept up the pressure. In September 1688 he invaded the Palatinate and occupied the city of Cologne. The following year the French armies crossed the Rhine and continued their eastward drive, burning Heidelberg and committing numerous atrocities throughout the middle Rhine area. Aroused at last to effective action, the coalition, led by William and now including in addition to its former members both England and Spain, engaged Louis in a war that was to last until 1697.

War of the League of Augsburg

The major campaigns of this War of the League of Augsburg were fought in the Low Countries. William managed to drive an army under his predecessor, James II, from Ireland in 1690; from that point on, he took command of the allied forces on the Continent. By 1694 Louis was pressed hard, not only by his allied foes, but by a succession of disastrous harvests that crippled France. Fighting remained stalemated until a treaty was signed at Ryswick in Holland which compelled Louis to return most of France's post-1679 gains, except for Alsace, and to recognize William as the rightful king of England.

The problem of the Spanish Succession

Ryswick did nothing, however, to resolve the dynastic tangle known as the Spanish Succession. Since Charles II of Spain had no direct heirs, and since he appeared to be on his deathbed in 1699, European monarchs and diplomats were obsessed by the question of who would succeed to the vast domain of the Spanish Habsburgs: not only Spain itself, but also its overseas empire, as well as the Spanish Netherlands, Naples, Sicily, and other territories in Italy. Both Louis XIV and Leopold I of Austria were married to sisters of the decrepit, unstable Charles; and both, naturally, eyed the succession to the Spanish inheritance as an exceedingly tempting dynastic plum. Yet it is a measure of the degree to which even absolutists were willing to keep their ambitions within bounds that both Leopold and Louis agreed to William's suggestion that the lion's share of the Habsburg lands should go to six-year-old Joseph Ferdinand, the prince of Bavaria, who was Charles II's grandnephew. Unfortunately, in 1699 the child died. Though the chances of war increased, William and Louis were prepared to bargain further and arranged a second treaty that divided the Spanish empire between Louis's and Leopold's heirs. Yet at the same time, Louis's diplomatic agents in Madrid persuaded Charles to sign a will in which he stipulated that the entire Spanish Habsburg inheritance should pass to Louis's grandson Philip of Anjou. This option was welcomed by many influential Spaniards, willing to endure French hegemony in return for the protection France could provide to the Spanish empire. For a time, Louis contemplated an alternative agreement which would have given France direct control of much of Italy. When Charles finally died in November 1700, Louis decided to accept the will. As if this was not enough to drive his former enemies back to war, he sent troops into the Spanish Netherlands and traders to the Spanish colonial empire, while declaring the late James II's son—the child of the warming pan myth—the legitimate king of England.

Once it was clear to the allies that Louis intended to treat Spain as if it were his own kingdom, they again united against him in the cause of balance and stability. William died in 1702, just as the War of the Spanish Succession was beginning. His position as first general of the coalition passed to two brilliant strategists, the English John Churchill, duke of Marlborough, and his Austrian counterpart, Prince Eugene of Savoy, an upper-class soldier of fortune who had been denied a commission by Louis. Under their command the allied forces engaged in battle after fierce battle in the Low Countries and Germany, including an extraordinary march deep into Bavaria, where the combined forces under Marlborough and Eugene smashed the French and their Bavarian allies decisively at Blenheim (1704). While the allies pressed France's armies on land, the English navy captured Gibraltar and the island of Minorca, thus establishing a strategic and commercial foothold in the Mediterranean, and helping to open a fourth major military theater in Spain itself.

The War of the Spanish Succession was a "professional" war that tested the highly trained armies of the combatants to the fullest. At the battle of Malplaquet in northeastern France in 1709, 80,000 French soldiers faced 110,000 allied troops. Though Marlborough and Eugene could claim to have won that battle, in that they forced the French to retreat, they suffered 24,000 casualties, twice those of the French. Neither Malplaquet nor other such victories brought the allies any closer to their final goal, which now appeared to be not the containment, but the complete destruction of the French military force. Queen Anne of England (Mary's sister and William's successor), once Marlborough's staunchest defender, grew disillusioned with the war and fired her general.

Military stalemate

More than war weariness impelled the combatants toward negotiation, however. The War of the Spanish Succession had begun as a conflict about the balance of power in Europe and the world. Yet dynastic changes had by 1711 compelled a reappraisal of allied goals. Leopold I had died in 1705. When his elder son and successor Joseph I died in 1711, the Austrian monarchy fell to Leopold's youngest son, the Archduke Charles, who had been the allies' candidate for the throne of Spain. With Charles now the Austrian and the Holy Roman Emperor as Charles VI (1711–1740), the prospect of his accession to the Spanish inheritance conjured up the ghost of Charles V and threatened to give him far too much power. International stability therefore demanded an end to hostilities and diplomatic negotiation toward a solution that would reestablish some sort of general balance.

Dynastic changes and the pursuit of peace

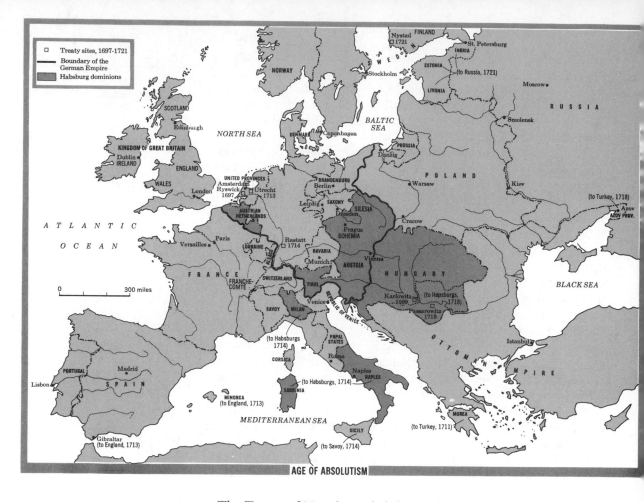

The Treaty of Utrecht

The Treaty of Utrecht settled the conflict in 1713 by redistributing territory and power in equitable portions. No one emerged a major winner or loser. Philip, Louis's grandson, remained on the throne of Spain, but Louis agreed that France and Spain would never be united under the same ruler. Austria gained territories in the Netherlands and Italy. The Dutch, victims of French aggression during the war, were guaranteed protection of their borders against future invasion. The English retained Gibraltar and Minorca, as well as territory in America: Newfoundland, Acadia, Hudson Bay, and in the Caribbean, St. Kitts. Perhaps most valuable of all, the English extracted the *asiento* from Spain which gave them the right to supply Spanish America with African slaves. The settlement reflected the degree to which new interests had superseded old. Balance of power and stability among states were the major goals of the negotiations, goals that reflected a departure from the world of seventeenth-century turmoil when religious fanaticism had been a major factor in international conflict. The eventual "winners" were undoubtedly the English, whose dynastic concerns were limited to a general acceptance of the Hanoverian settlement, and who could therefore concentrate their efforts on amassing overseas territories that would contribute to the growth of their economic prosperity and hence their international power.

6. ENLIGHTENED ABSOLUTISM AND LIMITED MONARCHY IN THE EIGHTEENTH CENTURY

Eighteenth-century absolutism was a series of variations on the dominant themes composed in the previous century by Louis XIV. That it has earned itself the historical distinction of "enlightened" absolutism suggests that those variations were of some consequence. Eighteenth-century rulers backed their sovereign claims not in the language of divine right, but in terms of their determination to act, as Frederick the Great of Prussia declared, as "first servant of the state." Enlightened rulers served their subjects by introducing reformist legislation and administration designed, at least in theory, to serve the well-being of the state community as a whole. They moved to curtail the privileges of old institutions. The Roman Catholic Church, for example, was compelled to suffer the expulsion of the Jesuits from most Catholic countries. Customary laws benefiting particular orders or interests were reformed. Serfdom was abolished or limited in some German states. Innovative policies in the areas of taxation, economic development, and education were instituted. As we shall see in Chapter 24, rational schemes of this sort reflected the spread of Enlightenment ideals as manifested in the writings of thinkers such as Beccaria, Diderot, and Voltaire. (The last was, in fact, a guest at Frederick's court for several years.) Assisting enlightened "first servants" in the implementation of these changes was a growing cadre of lesser servants: bureaucrats, often recruited from the nobility, but once recruited, expected to declare primary allegiance to their new master, the state. Despite innovation, "enlightened" absolutists continued to insist, as their predecessors had, that state sovereignty rested with the monarchy. Power remained their overriding concern, and to the extent that they combated efforts by the estates of their realms to dilute that power, they declared their descent from their seventeenth-century forebears.

Louis XIV's successors, his great-grandson Louis XV (1715–1774) and that monarch's grandson Louis XVI (1774–1792), were unable to sustain the energetic drive toward centralization that had taken place under the Sun King. Indeed, during his last years, while fighting a desperate defensive war against his allied enemies, Louis XIV had seen his own accomplishments begin to crumble under the mounting pressure of military expenses. His heir was only five years old when he assumed the throne. As he grew up, Louis XV displayed little of his great-grandfather's single-minded determination to act the role of Sun King. The heroic, baroque grandeur of the main palace at Versailles

"Enlightened" absolutism

Louis XV

Absolutism under the successors of Louis XIV

yielded to the rococo grace of the Grand and Petit Trianons, pleasure pavilions built by Louis XV in the palace gardens. Both Louis XIV and Louis XV solaced themselves with the company of mistresses. The difference in their tastes, however, is a mark of the difference in their reigns. Madame de Maintenon, the Sun King's mistress, was a stern, devout Catholic, who interested herself directly in policies of state. Madame du Pompadour, Louis XV's favorite for many years, was a stylish, witty sensualist whose legacy was the elaborate hairstyle to which she bequeathed her name.

During the minority of Louis XV, the French *parlements,* those courts of record responsible for registering and thereby legalizing royal decrees, enjoyed a resurgence of power which they retained throughout the century. No longer tame adjuncts of absolutist governmental machinery as they had been under Louis XIV, these bodies now proclaimed themselves the protectors of French "liberties." In fact they were protectors of little more than the privileges of the elite, although a growing number welcomed the *parlements'* willingness to block new taxes. In the late 1760s, hoping to emulate the success of his illustrious predecessor, and encouraged by his chancellor René Maupeou, Louis XV issued an edict effectively ending the right of *parlements* to reject decrees. Protest on the part of the magistrates resulted in their imprisonment or banishment. The *parlements* themselves were replaced by new courts charged not only with the responsibility of rubber-stamping legislation but also with administering law more justly and less expensively. When Louis XVI ascended the throne in 1774, his ministers persuaded him to reestablish the *parlements* as a sign of his willingness to conciliate his trouble-making aristocracy. This he did, with the result that government—particularly the management of finances—developed into a stalemated battle.

Stalemate was what the Prussian successors to Frederick William, the Great Elector, were determined to avoid. Absolutism, to thrive, needed to remain a dynamic force: precisely what it was in eighteenth-century Prussia. Frederick I (1688–1713), the Great Elector Frederick William's immediate successor, enhanced the appearance and cultural life of Berlin. As the Roman numeral by his name attests, he also succeeded in bargaining his support to the Austrians during the War of the Spanish Succession in return for the coveted right to style himself king.[3]

Frederick William I (1713–1740), cared little for the embellishments his father had made to the capital city. His overriding concern was the building of a first-rate army. So single-minded was his attention to the military that he came to be called "the sergeant king." Military display became an obsession. His private regiment of "Potsdam Giants" was composed exclusively of soldiers over six feet in height. The king

---

[3] The Austrian monarch was the Holy Roman Emperor and therefore had the right to create kings.

traded musicians and prize stallions for such choice specimens and delighted in marching them about his palace grounds. Frederick William I's success as the builder of a military machine can be measured in terms of numbers: 30,000 men under arms when he came to the throne; 83,000 when he died twenty-seven years later, commander of the fourth-largest army in Europe, after France, Russia, and Austria. Since he could hardly count on volunteers, most of his soldiers were conscripts, drafted from the peasantry for a period of years and required to attend annual training exercises lasting three months. Conscription was supplemented by the kidnapping of forced recruits in neighboring German lands. To finance his army, Frederick William I increased taxes and streamlined their collection through the establishment of a General Directory of War, Finance, and Domains. He instituted a system of administration by boards, hoping thereby to eliminate individual inefficiency through collective responsibility and surveillance. In addition, he created an inspectorate to uncover and report to him the mistakes and inefficiencies of his officialdom. Even then, he continued to supervise personally the implementation of state policy while shunning the luxuries of court life; for him, the "theater" of absolutism was not the palace but the office, which placed him at the helm of the state and the army. Perceiving the resources of the state to be too precious to waste, he pared costs at every turn to the point where, it was said, he had to invite himself to a nobleman's table in order to enjoy a good meal.

A hard, unimaginative man, Frederick William I had little use for his son, whose passion was not the battlefield but the flute, and who admired French culture as much as his father disdained it. Not surprisingly, young Frederick rebelled; in 1730, when he was eighteen, he ran away from court with a friend. Apprehended, the companions were returned to the king, who welcomed the fledgling prodigal with something other than a fatted calf. Before Frederick's eyes, he had the friend executed. The grisly lesson took. Thenceforward Frederick, though he never surrendered his love of music and literature, bound himself to his royal duties, living in accordance with his own image of himself as "first servant of the state," and earning himself history's title of Frederick the Great.

Frederick William I's zealous austerity and his compulsion to build an efficient army and administrative state made Prussia a lean, strong state. Frederick the Great, building on the work of his father, raised his country to the status of a major power. As soon as he became king in 1740, Frederick mobilized the army his father had never taken into battle and occupied the poorly protected Austrian province of Silesia to which Prussia had no legitimate claim. Although he had earlier vowed to make morality rather than expediency the hallmark of his reign, he seemingly had little difficulty in sacrificing his youthful idealism in the face of an opportunity to make his Prussian state a leading member of the concert of nations. The remaining forty-five years of

Frederick William I

The apprenticeship of Frederick the Great

The seizure of Silesia

Frederick the Great and Voltaire. Although Frederick offered asylum to the French *philosophe,* this "enlightened despot" did not permit his intellectual pursuits to interfere with matters of state.

his monarchy were devoted to the consolidation of this first bold stroke.

Such a daring course required some adjustments within the Prussian state. The army had to be kept at full strength, and to this end, Frederick staffed its officer corps with young noblemen. In expanding the bureaucracy, whose financial administration kept his army in the field, he relied on the nobility as well, reversing the policy of his father, who had recruited his civil servants according to merit rather than birth. But Frederick was not one to tolerate mediocrity; he fashioned the most highly professional and efficient bureaucracy in all of Europe. The degree to which both army and bureaucracy were staffed by the nobility is a measure of his determination to secure the unflagging support of the most privileged order in his realm, in order to ensure a united front against Prussia's external foes.

The Prussian army and the nobility

Frederick's domestic policies reflected that same strategy. In matters where he ran no risk of offending the aristocracy, he followed his own rationalist bent, prohibiting the torture of accused criminals, putting an end to the bribing of judges, and establishing a system of elementary schools. He promoted religious toleration, declaring that he would happily build a mosque in Berlin if he could find enough Muslims to fill it. (Yet he was strongly anti-Semitic, levying special taxes on Jews and making efforts to close the professions and the civil service to them.) On his own royal estates he was a model "enlightened" monarch. He abolished capital punishment, curtailed the forced labor services of his peasantry, and granted them long leases on the land they worked. He fostered scientific forestry and the cultivation of new crops.

Frederick the Great as an enlightened absolutist

He opened new lands in Silesia and brought in thousands of immigrants to cultivate them. When wars ruined their farms, he supplied the peasants with new livestock and tools. Yet he never attempted to extend these reforms to the estates of the Junker elite, since to have done so would have alientated that social and economic group upon which Frederick was most dependent.

Although the monarchs of eighteenth-century Austria eventually proved themselves even more willing than Frederick the Great to undertake significant social reform, the energies of Emperor Charles VI (1711–1740) were concentrated on guaranteeing the future dynastic and territorial integrity of the Habsburg lineage and domain. Without a male heir, Charles worked to secure the right of his daughter Maria Theresa to succeed him as eventual empress. By his death in 1740 Charles had managed to persuade not only his subjects but all the major European powers to accept his daughter as his royal heir—a feat known as the "pragmatic sanction." Yet his painstaking efforts were only partially successful. As we have seen, Frederick the Great used the occasion of Charles's death to sieze Silesia. The French, unable to resist the temptation to grab what they could, entered the lists in this War of the Austrian Succession against the new empress, Maria Theresa (1740–1780).

*Charles VI and the
"pragmatic sanction"*

With most of her other possessions already occupied by her enemies, Maria Theresa appealed successfully to the Hungarians for support. The empress was willing to play the role of the wronged woman when, as on this occasion, it suited her interests to do so. Hungary's vital troops combined with British financial assistance helped to enable her to battle Austria's enemies to a draw, although she never succeeded in regaining Silesia. The experience of those first few years of

*Maria Theresa: Adversity
and centralization*

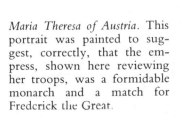

Maria Theresa of Austria. This portrait was painted to suggest, correctly, that the empress, shown here reviewing her troops, was a formidable monarch and a match for Frederick the Great.

"Enlightened" absolutism in Austria

her reign persuaded Maria Theresa, who was both capable and tenacious, to reorganize her dominions along the tightly centralized lines characteristic of absolutist Prussia and France. Ten new administrative districts were established, each with its own "war commissar" appointed by and responsible to the central administration in Vienna—an Austrian equivalent of the French intendant. Property taxes were increased to finance an expanded army, which was modernized and professionalized so as to remain on a par with the military establishments of the other great powers. Centralization, finances, army: once more those three crucial elements in the formula of absolute rule came into play.

Austrian absolutism did not stop there, however. Together Maria Theresa and her son Joseph II, with whom she ruled jointly from 1765 to 1780, and who then succeeded her for another ten years, instituted a series of social reforms which has earned them their reputation as "enlightened" absolutists. Although both mother and son were devout Roman Catholics, they moved to assert control of the Church, removing the clergy's exemption from taxation and decreeing the state's ability to block the publication of papal bulls in Austria. In 1773, following the papal suppression of the Jesuits, they used the order's assets to finance a program of state-wide primary education. Although the General Schools Ordinance of 1774 never achieved anything like a universally literate population, it did succeed in educating hundreds of thousands, and in financing not only schools for children but schools as well for those who taught the children. Joseph followed these reforms with an "Edict on Idle Institutions" in 1780, which resulted in the closing of hundreds of monastic houses, whose property went to support charitable institutions now under state control. These

Joseph II of Austria Visiting a Farm. The royal estates provided Joseph with the opportunity to experiment with agrarian reforms by raising the serfs to the status of free peasants.

reforms and others—rationalization of criminal procedures, a relaxation of censorship, and an attempt to eradicate superstition by curbing the practice of pilgrimages and celebration of saint's days—made Joseph more enemies than friends, among both the noble elite and the common people. "Enlightened" though Joseph II was, however, he nevertheless remained a staunch absolutist, as concerned with the maintenance of a strong army and an efficient bureaucracy as with the need to educate his peasantry. Joseph's brother Leopold II, who succeeded him in 1790, attempted to maintain the reformist momentum. His death two years later and the accession of his reactionary brother Francis II (1792–1835), put an end to liberalizing experiments.

Catherine the Great

Unlike Joseph II, Catherine the Great of Russia (1762–1796) felt herself compelled to curry the favor of her nobility by involving them directly in the structure of local administration, by exempting them from military service and taxation, and probably most important, by granting them absolute control over the serfs on their estates. Her policy grew out of her strong ties to powerful nobles and her involvement in the conspiracy which led to the assassination of her husband, Tsar Peter III, the last of a series of weak rulers who followed Peter the Great. Catherine was herself a German, and prided herself on her devotion to Western principles of government. Ambitious to establish a reputation as an intellectual and enlightened monarch, she corresponded with French philosophers, wrote plays, published a digest of William Blackstone's *Commentaries on the Laws of England,* and even began a history of Russia. Her contributions to social reform did not extend much beyond the founding of hospitals and orphanages, and the expression of a pious hope that someday the serfs might be liberated. Although she did summon a commission in 1767 to codify Russian law, its achievements were modest: a minor extension of religious toleration; a slight restriction of the use of torture by the state. Catherine's interest in theories of reform did, however, stimulate the development of a social conscience among certain gentry intellectuals, foreshadowing a more widespread movement in the nineteenth century.

Catherine the Great of Russia

Any plans Catherine may have had for improving the lot of the peasants, however, were abruptly cancelled after their frustration with St. Petersburg's centralization efforts erupted in a violent peasant-serf rebellion in 1773–1774. Free peasants in the Volga valley region found themselves compelled to provide labor services to nobles sent by the crown to control them, Cossacks were subjected to taxation and conscription for the first time, and factory workers and miners were pressed into service in the state's industrial enterprises. These and other disparate but dissatisfied groups, including serfs, united under the rebel banner of Emelyan Pugachev, an illiterate Cossack who claimed to be the late Tsar Peter III. The hapless Peter, who had spoken as a reformer in life, in death became a larger-than-life hero for those opposed to the determined absolutism of his successor. As Pugachev marched, he encouraged his followers to strike out not only against the empress

Emelyan Pugachev Shackled and Encaged after His Capture

but also against the nobility and the church. Over 1500 landlords and priests were murdered, and the ruling classes were terrified as the revolt spread. While Catherine's forces initially had little success against the rebel army, the threat of famine plagued Pugachev's advance and finally led to disarray among his troops. Betrayed in 1774, he was captured and taken in an iron cage to Moscow, where he was tortured and killed. Catherine responded to this uprising with further centralization and tightening of aristocratic authority over the peasantry.

The brutal suppression and punishment of the rebels reflected the ease with which the German-born Catherine took to the despotic authoritarianism that characterized Russian absolutism. She was as outsized in her tastes and personality as was Peter the Great. Her sexual appetite was voracious; her current chief officers of state as often as not were also her current lovers. But Catherine continued the work of Peter the Great in introducing Russia to Western ideas; she came to terms with the nobility in a way that brought stability to the state; and she made the country a formidable power in European affairs by extending its boundaries to include not only most of Poland but also lands on the Black Sea.

Eighteenth-century absolutist monarchs shared a desire to pursue policies that would mark their regimes as modern, befitting a world that was leaving obscurantism and fanaticism behind. They were modern, also, in their determination to press ahead with the task, begun by their seventeenth-century predecessors, of building powerful, centralized states by continuing to eliminate or harness the ancient privileges of still-powerful noble orders and provincial estates. The notion of a limited monarchy, in which power was divided between local and central authorities and shared by monarchs, nobles, and legislative assemblies, struck them as a dangerous anachronism. Yet as the century progressed, they found that conviction challenged by the emergence of England, under limited monarchy, as the world's leading commercial and naval power.

England (or Britain, as the country was called after its union with Scotland in 1707) prospered as a state in which power was divided between the king and Parliament. This division of political power was guaranteed by a constitution which, though unwritten, was grounded in common law and strengthened by precedent and by particular legal settlements such as those that had followed the restoration of the Stuarts in 1660 and the overthrow of James II in 1688. The Hanoverians George I (1714–1727) and his son George II (1727–1760) were by no means political cyphers. Though George I could not speak English, he could converse comfortably enough with his ministers in French. The first two Georges made a conscientious and generally successful effort to govern within their adopted kingdom. They appointed the chief ministers who remained responsible to them for the creation and direction of state policy. Yet because Parliament, after 1688, retained the right

George I of England

The House of Commons. Despite its architectural division into two "sides," the House was composed of men of property whose similar economic interests encouraged them to agree on political fundamentals.

to legislate, tax, and spend, its powers were far greater than those of any European parlement, estate, or diet. During the reign of the first two Hanoverians, politics was on most occasions little more than a struggle between factions within the Whig party, composed of wealthy—and in many cases newly rich—landed magnates who were making fortunes in an expanding economy based on commercial and agricultural capitalism.

The Tories, because of their previous association with the Stuarts, remained political "outs" for most of the century. To the Whigs, national politics was no longer a matter of clashing principles. Those principles had been settled—to their satisfaction—in 1688. Nor was politics a matter of legislating in the national interest. Britain was governed locally, not from the center as in an absolutist state. Aristocrats and landed gentry administered the affairs of the particular counties and parishes in which their estates lay, as lords lieutenant, as justices of the peace, as overseers of the poor, unhampered, to a degree unknown on the Continent, by legislation imposed uniformly throughout the kingdom. The quality of local government varied greatly. Some squires were as "allworthy" as Henry Fielding's fictional character of that name in the novel *Tom Jones*. Others cared for little beyond the bottle and the chase. A French traveler noted in 1747 that the country gentleman was "naturally a very dull animal" whose favorite afterdinner toast was "to all honest fox hunters in Great Britain." These men

Local government

Left: *Sir Robert Walpole with Members of His Cabinet*. Right: *Walpole as a Roman Emperor.*

Robert Walpole as chief minister

administered those general laws that did exist—the Poor Law, game laws—which were drawn in such a way as to leave their administrators wide latitude, a latitude which they exercised in order to enhance the appearance of their own local omnipotence. Thus in Britain there was no attempt to pass a law establishing a state-wide system of primary education. Centralizing legislation of that sort, the hallmark of absolutist states, was anathema to the British aristocracy and gentry. They argued that education, if it was to be provided, should be provided at their expense, in village schoolrooms by schoolmasters in their employ. Those instructors would make it their business to teach their pupils not only rudimentary reading, writing, and figuring, but the deferential behavior that bespoke the obligation of the poor to their rich benefactors. As the Church of England catechism had it, they were "to do their duty in that station of life unto which it shall please God to call them."

Politics, then, was neither first principles nor national legislation. It was "interest" and "influence," the weaving of a web of obligations into a political faction powerful enough to secure jobs and favors—a third secretaryship in the foreign office from a minister, an Act of Enclosure from Parliament. The greatest master of this game of politics was Robert Walpole (1676–1745) who was England's leading minister from the early 1720s until 1742. Walpole is sometimes called

Britain's first prime minister, a less than entirely accurate distinction, since officially that position did not exist until the nineteenth century. Prime minister or not, he wielded great political power. He took advantage of the king's frequent absences in Hanover to assert control over the day-to-day governance of the country. He ruled as chief officer of his cabinet, a small group of like-minded politicians whose collective name derived from the small room in which they met. In time the cabinet evolved into the policy-making executive arm of the British political system; Britain is governed today by cabinet and Parliament, the cabinet composed of leading politicians from the majority party in Parliament.

*Walpole and the nature of
British politics*

Walpole was a member of a Norfolk gentry family who had risen to national prominence on the fortune he amassed while serving as paymaster-general to the armed forces during the War of the Spanish Succession. Adept at bribery and corruption, he used his ability to reward his supporters with appointments to ensure himself a loyal political following. By the end of his career, grossly fat and stuffed seemingly with the profits of his years in office, he was being depicted by cartoonists and balladeers as Britain's most accomplished robber. "Little villains must submit to Fate," lamented a typical lampoon, "while great ones do enjoy the world in state." Walpole was no more corrupt, however, than the political process over which he presided. Most seats in Parliament's lower House of Commons were filled by representatives from boroughs that often had no more than two or three dozen electors. Hence it was a relatively simple task to buy votes, either directly or with promises of future favors. Walpole cemented political factions together into an alliance that survived for about twenty years. During that time, he worked to ensure domestic tranquility by refusing to press ahead with any legislation that might arouse national controversy. He withdrew what was perhaps his most innovative piece of legislation—a scheme to increase excise taxes and reduce import duties as a means of curbing smugglers—in the face of widespread popular opposition.

*George III: the battle over
prerogative*

Other Whig politicians succeeded Walpole in office in the 1740s and 1750s, but only one, William Pitt, later elevated to the House of Lords as the earl of Chatham, commanded public attention as Walpole had. George III (1760–1820), who came to the throne as a young man in 1760, resented the manner in which he believed his royal predecessors had been treated by the Whig oligarchy. Whether or not, as legend has it, his mother fired his determination with the constant injunction "George, be king!" he began his reign convinced that he must assert his rightful prerogatives. He dismissed Pitt, and attempted to impose ministers of his own choosing on Parliament. King and Parliament battled this issue of prerogative throughout the 1760s. In 1770, Lord North, an aristocrat satisfactory to the king and with a large enough following in the House of Commons to ensure some measure of stability, assumed the position of first minister. His downfall occurred a decade later, as a result of his mismanagement of the overseas war which resulted in Britain's loss of its original thirteen North American colonies. A period of political shuffling was followed by the king's appointment, at the age of twenty-three, of another William Pitt, Chatham's son, and this Pitt directed Britain's fortunes for the next twenty-five years—a political reign even longer than Walpole's. Although the period between 1760 and 1780 witnessed a struggle between crown (as the king and his political following were called) and Parliament, it was a very minor skirmish compared with the titanic constitutional struggles of the seventeenth century. Britain saw the last of absolutism in 1688. What followed was the mutual adjustment of the two formerly contending parties to a settlement both considered essentially sound.

7. WAR AND DIPLOMACY IN THE EIGHTEENTH CENTURY

Diplomacy in mid-century: the "diplomatic revolution"

The history of European diplomacy and warfare after 1715 is one in which the twin goals of international stability and economic expansion remained paramount. The fact that those objectives often conflicted with each other set off further frequent wars, in which the ever-growing standing armies of absolutist Europe were matched against each other and in which the deciding factor often turned out to be not continental military strength, but British naval power. The major conflict at mid-century, known as the Seven Years' War in Europe and the French and Indian War in North America, reflects the overlapping interests of power balance and commercial gain. In Europe, the primary concern was balance. Whereas in the past France had seemed the major threat, now Prussia loomed—at least in Austrian eyes—as a far more dangerous interloper. Under these circumstances, in 1756 the Austrian foreign minister, Prince Wenzel von Kaunitz, effected the so-called diplomatic revolution, which put an end to the enmity between France and Austria, and resulted in a formidable threat to the Prussia of Frederick the Great. Frederick, meanwhile, was taking steps to protect his flanks. While anxious not to arouse his French ally, he nevertheless signed a neutrality treaty with the British, who were concerned to secure protection for their sovereign's Hanoverian domains. The French read Frederick's act as a hostile one, and thus fell all the more readily for Kaunitz's offer of an alliance. The French indeed perceived a pressing need for trustworthy European allies, since they were already engaged in an undeclared war with England in North America. By mid-1756 Kaunitz could count France, Russia, Sweden, and several German states as likely allies against Prussia. Rather than await retribution from his enemies, Frederick invaded strategic but neutral Saxony and then Austria itself, thus once again playing the role of aggressor.

The configurations in this diplomatic gavotte are undoubtedly confusing. They are historically important, however, because they indicate the way in which the power balance was shifting, and the attempts of European states to respond to those shifts by means of new diplomatic alliances. Prussia and Britain were the volatile elements: Prussia on the Continent; Britain overseas. The war from 1756 to 1763 in Europe centered upon Frederick's attempts to prevent the dismemberment of his domain at the hands of the French-Austrian-Russian alliance. Time and again the Prussian army's superiority and Frederick's own military genius frustrated his enemies' attacks. Ultimately, Prussia's survival against these overwhelming odds—"the miracle of the House of Brandenburg"—was ensured by the death of the Tsarina Elizabeth (1741–1762), daughter of Peter the Great, and by the accession of Peter III (1762), whose admiration for Frederick was as great as was his predecessor's hostility. Peter withdrew from the war, returning the conquered provinces of East Prussia and Pomerania to his country's erstwhile enemy. The peace that followed, though it compelled Frederick to relinquish Saxony, recognized his right to retain Silesia, and hence put an end to Austria's hope of one day recapturing that rich prize.

*Shifting power balances:
the Seven Years' War*

Overseas, battles occurred not only in North America but in the West Indies and in India, where Anglo-French commercial rivalry had resulted in sporadic, fierce fighting since the 1740s. Ultimate victory would go to that power possessing a navy strong enough to keep its supply routes open—that is, to Britain. Superior naval forces resulted in victories along the North American Great Lakes, climaxing in the Battle of Québec in 1759 and the eventual surrender of all of Canada to the British. By 1762 the French sugar islands, including Martinique, Grenada, and St. Vincent, were in British hands. Across the globe in India, the defeat of the French in the Battle of Plassey in 1757 and the capture of Pondichéry four years later made Britain the dominant European presence on the subcontinent. In the Treaty of Paris in 1763 which brought the Seven Years' War to an end, France officially surrendered Canada and India to the British, thus affording them an extraordinary field for commercial exploitation.

*The British navy as key
to victory*

The success of the British in North America in the Seven Years' War was itself a major cause of the war which broke out between the mother country and her thirteen original colonies in 1775. To pay for the larger army the British now deemed necessary to protect their vastly expanded colonial possessions, they imposed unwelcome new taxes on the colonists. The North Americans protested that they were being taxed without representation. The home government responded that, like all British subjects, they were "virtually" if not actually represented by the present members of the House of Commons. Colonists thundered back that the present political system in Britain was so corrupt that no one but the Whig oligarchs could claim that their interests were being looked after.

*"Taxation without
representation . . ."*

The Battle of Québec, 1759. Most often remembered for the fact that the British and French commanders, Generals Wolfe and Montcalm, were killed on the bluffs above the St. Lawrence River (the Plains of Abraham), this battle was most notable for the success of the British amphibious assault, a measure of Britain's naval superiority.

The American Revolution

Meanwhile the British were exacting retribution for rebellious acts on the part of colonists. East India Company tea shipped to be sold in Boston at prices advantageous to the company was dumped in Boston harbor. The port of Boston was thereupon closed, and democratic government in the colony of Massachusetts curtailed. The British garrison clashed with colonial civilians. Colonial "minutemen" formed a counterforce. By the time war broke out in 1775, most Americans were prepared to sever ties with Britain and declare themselves an independent nation, which they did the following year. Fighting continued until 1781 when a British army surrendered to the colonists at Yorktown to the tune of a song entitled "A World Turned Upside Down." The French, followed by Spain and the Netherlands, determined to do everything possible to inhibit the further growth of Britain's colonial empire, had allied themselves with the newly independent United States in 1778. A peace treaty signed in Paris in 1783 recognized the sovereignty of the new state. Though the British lost direct control of their former colonies, they reestablished their trans-atlantic commercial ties with America in the 1780s. Indeed, the brisk trade in raw cotton between the slave-owning southern states and Britain made possible the industrial revolution in textiles that began in the north of England at this time, and that carried Britain to worldwide preeminence as an economic power in the first half of the nineteenth century. This ultimately profitable arrangement lay in the future.

At the time, the victory of the American colonists seemed to contemporary observers to right the world balance of commercial power, which had swung so far to the side of the British. In this instance, independence seemed designed to restore stability.

In eastern Europe, however, the very precariousness of Poland's independence posed a threat to stability and the balance of power. As an independent state, Poland functioned, at least in theory, as a buffer among the major central European powers—Russia, Austria, and Prussia. Poland was the one major central European territory whose landed elite had successfully opposed introduction of absolutist centralization and a consequent curtailment of its "liberties." The result, however, had not been anything like real independence for either the Polish nobility or the country as a whole. Aristocrats were quite prepared to accept bribes from foreign powers in return for their vote in elections for the Polish king. And their continued exercise of their constitutionally guaranteed individual veto (the "liberum veto") in the Polish Diet meant that the country remained in a perpetual state of weakness that made it fair game for the land-hungry absolutist potentates who surrounded its borders.

In 1764 Russia intervened to influence the election of King Stanislaus Poniatowski, an able enough nobleman who had been one of Catherine the Great's lovers. Thereafter Russia continued to meddle in the affairs of Poland—and of Turkey as well—often protecting both countries' Greek Orthodox Christian minority. When war finally broke out with Turkey in 1769, resulting in large Russian gains in the Balkans, Austria made known its opposition to further Russian expansion, lest it upset the existing balance of power in eastern Europe. In the end Russia was persuaded to acquire territory in Poland instead, by joining Austria and Prussia in a general partition of that country's lands. Though Maria Theresa opposed the dismemberment of Poland, she reluctantly agreed to participate in the partition in order to maintain the balance of power, an attitude which prompted a scornful Frederick the Great to remark that "She weeps, but she takes her share." According to the agreement of 1772, Poland lost about 30 percent of its kingdom and about half of its population.

Following this first partition, the Russians continued to exercise virtual control of Poland. King Stanislaus, however, took advantage of a new Russo-Turkish war in 1788 to press for a more truly independent state with a far stronger executive than had existed previously. A constitution adopted in May 1791 established just that; but this rejuvenated Polish state was to be short-lived. In January 1792, the Russo-Turkish war ended and Catherine the Great pounced. Together the Russians and Prussians took two more enormous bites out of Poland in 1793, destroying the new constitution in the process. A rebellion under the leadership of Thaddeus Kosciuszko, who had fought in America, was crushed in 1794 and 1795. A final swallow by Russia, Austria, and Prussia in 1795 left nothing of Poland at all.

*Poland and the balance of
power in eastern Europe*

*The first partition
of Poland*

*The second and third
partitions of Poland*

Dividing the Royal Cake. A contemporary cartoon showing the monarchs of Europe at work carving up a hapless Poland.

After this series of partitions of Poland, each of the major powers was a good deal fatter; but on the international scales by which such things were measured, they continued to weigh proportionately the same.

The final devouring of Poland occurred at a time when the Continent was once again engaged in a general war. Yet this most recent conflict was not just another military attempt to resolve customary disputes over commerce or problems of international stability. It was the result of violent revolution that had broken out in France in 1789, that had toppled the Bourbon dynasty there, and that threatened to do the same to other monarchs across Europe. The second and third partitions of Poland were a final bravura declaration of power by monarchs who already feared for their heads. Henceforth, neither foreign nor domestic policy would ever again be dictated as they had been in absolutist Europe by the convictions and determinations of kings and queens alone. Poland disappeared as Europe fell to pieces, as customary practice gave way to new and desperate necessity.

Though absolutism met its death in the years immediately after 1789, the relevance of its history to that of the modern world is greater than it might appear. First, centralization provided useful precedents to nineteenth-century state-builders. Modern standing armies— be they made up of soldiers or bureaucrats—are institutions whose

European upheaval

origins rest in the age of absolutism. Second, absolutism's centripetal force contributed to an economic climate that gave birth to industrial revolution. Factories built to produce military matériel, capitalist agricultural policies designed to provide food for burgeoning capital cities, increased taxes that drove peasants to seek work in rural industries: these and other programs pointed to the future. Third, in their constant struggle to curb the privileges of nobility and oligarchy, absolute monarchs played out one more act in a drama that would continue into the nineteenth century. French nobles of both sword and robe, Prussian junkers, and Russian boyars all bargained successfully to retain their rights to property and its management while surrendering to some degree their role as governors. But as long as their property rights remained secure, their power was assured. The French Revolution would curb their power for a time, but they were survivors. Their adaptability, whether as agricultural entrepreneurs or as senior servants of the state, ensured their order an important place in the world that lay beyond absolutism.

SELECTED READINGS

• *Items so designated are available in paperback editions.*

Anderson, M. S., *Historians and Eighteenth-Century Europe,* Oxford, 1979. Contains recent scholarly debate.
——, *Peter the Great,* London, 1978. A good, thorough biography.
• Avrich, Paul, *Russian Rebels, 1600–1800,* New York, 1972. A study of revolts against absolutist power.
Baxter, Stephen, *William III and the Defense of European Liberty, 1650–1702,* New York, 1965. The best study of the Dutchman who became England's king.
Bernard, Paul, *Joseph II,* New York, 1968.
• Brewer, John, *Party Ideology and Popular Politics at the Accession of George III,* Cambridge, 1976, A revisionist interpretation of political alignments and party.
Churchill, W. S., *Marlborough,* New York, 1968. An abridged edition of Churchill's magnificently written biography of his ancestor.
• Cobban, Alfred, *A History of Modern France,* New York, 1961. A survey with a point of view.
Corvisier, André, *Armies and Societies in Europe, 1494–1789,* Bloomington, Ind., 1979. Focuses on the French army.
• Dukes, Paul, *Catherine the Great and the Russian Nobility,* Cambridge, 1967. A study of the limits of absolutism.
• Dunn, Richard S., *The Age of Religious Wars, 1559–1715,* 2nd ed., New York, 1979. A detailed and up-to-date survey, useful for the history of late seventeenth- and early eighteenth-century absolutism.
Ford, Franklin, *Robe and Sword: The Regrouping of the French Aristocracy after Louis XIV,* Cambridge, Mass., 1953. An important social study of the nobility of the robe and its striving for dominance before the revolution.

- Fraser, Antonia, *Royal Charles: Charles II and the Restoration*, New York, 1979. A readable, reliable life of the king and his times.
- Goubert, Pierre, *Louis XIV and Twenty Million Frenchmen*, New York, 1972. A valuable study, the starting point for an understanding of the Sun King's reign.
- Hatton, R. H., *Europe in the Age of Louis XIV*, New York, 1969. Thoughtful interpretation of the period; excellent illustrations.
- Herr, Richard, *The Eighteenth Century Revolution in Spain*, Princeton, 1958. The best introduction to Spain in this period.
- Holborn, Hajo, *The Age of Absolutism*, New York, 1964. The best survey for Germany. Second volume of Holborn's *History of Modern Germany*.
- Krieger, Leonard, *Kings and Philosophers, 1689–1789*, New York, 1970. A thorough survey of the political and intellectual developments of this century.
- Lewis, W. H., *The Splendid Century: Life in the France of Louis XIV*, New York, 1953. A delightfully written survey.
- Palmer, R. R., *The Age of the Democratic Revolution: A Political History of Europe and America, 1760–1800*, Vol. 1, Princeton, 1964. Argues in favor of a general European aristocratic reaction prior to 1789.
  Plumb, J. H., *Sir Robert Walpole*, 2 vols., Boston, 1956, 1961. A well-written, sympathetic biography of England's leading eighteenth-century politician.
- Riasanovsky, Nicholas V., *A History of Russia*, 4th ed., Oxford, 1984. A useful introduction.
- Ritter, Gerhard, *Frederick The Great: A Historical Profile*, Berkeley, 1968. A readable biography.
- Rudé, George, *Europe in the Eighteenth Century: Aristocracy and the Bourgeois Challenge*, New York, 1972. A survey which stresses social stratification and tension.
- Speck, W. A., *Stability and Strife: England, 1714–1760*, Cambridge, Mass., 1977. A good, recent survey.
  Spielman, John P., *Leopold I of Austria*, New Brunswick, N.J., 1977. The only biography of the monarch in English.
- Wangermann, Ernst, *The Austrian Achievement, 1700–1800*, London, 1973. A suggestive introductory survey.
- Wolf, John B., *Louis XIV*, New York, 1968. The standard biography in English.
  ———, *The Emergence of the Great Powers, 1685–1715*, New York, 1951. A useful general survey of this critical period.
- Woloch, Isser, *Eighteenth Century Europe: Tradition and Progress, 1715–1789*, New York, 1982. A thoughtful, well-organized survey.

SOURCE MATERIALS

- Locke, John, *Two Treatises of Government*. (Many editions.) The argument against absolutism.
  Saint-Simon, Louis, *Historical Memoirs*. (Many editions.) A brilliant source for evidence about life at the court of Louis XIV.

Chapter 24

THE SCIENTIFIC REVOLUTION AND ENLIGHTENMENT

This is the age wherein philosophy comes in with a spring-tide. . . .
Methinks I see how all the old rubbish must be thrown away, and the
rotten buildings be overthrown, and carried away with so powerful an
inundation.

—Henry Power, *Experimental Philosophy* (1663)

Enlightenment is humanity's departure from its self-imposed immaturity. Immaturity is the inability to use one's intellect without the guidance
of others. This immaturity is self-imposed when its cause is not a lack of
intelligence but a failure of determination and courage to think without
the guidance of someone else. Dare to know! This then is the slogan of
the Enlightenment.

—Immanuel Kant, *What is Enlightenment?* (1784)

The years between roughly 1660 and 1789, which witnessed
the prevalence of absolutism in western Europe, witnessed as
well the most important mutation in all of European intellectual and cultural history to occur between the Middle Ages and the
present. Just as the sweep of fresh winds can greatly change the
weather, so in the last few decades of the seventeenth century the
sweep of new ideas led to a bracing change in Europe's "climate of
opinion." For purposes of analysis it is convenient to refer to two
phases within the larger period: the triumph of the scientific revolution in the second half of the seventeenth century and the age of
"Enlightenment" which followed for most of the eighteenth century.
But without any doubt the same intellectual winds that swept into
Europe during the later seventeenth century prevailed for well over a
hundred years. Indeed, their influence is still felt today.

How did the new intellectual climate differ from the old? Concen-
trating on essentials, three points may be stressed. First, whereas
medieval, Renaissance, and Reformation thinkers all assumed that past

New ideas: 1660–1789

knowledge was the most reliable source of wisdom, the greatest thinkers from the seventeenth century onward rejected any obeisance to ancient authority and resolved to rely on their own intellects to see where knowledge would lead them. Making their motto "dare to know," they stressed the autonomy of science and the free play of the mind in ways unheard of in the West since the golden age of Greece. Second, the new breed of thinkers believed strongly that knowledge was valueless if it could not be put to use. For a Plato, an Aristotle, or a St. Thomas Aquinas alike, the greatest wisdom was the most abstract wisdom since such wisdom helped to turn the human mind away from all earthly "corruptibility" and supposedly brought happiness by its sheer resemblance to timeless divinity. But after the change in Europe's climate of opinion in the late seventeenth century, all knowledge without practical value was belittled and thinkers from every realm of intellectual endeavor aimed directly or indirectly at achieving "the relief of man's estate." Finally, the new climate of opinion was characterized by the demystification of the universe. Up until the mid–seventeenth century, most people, learned and unlearned, assumed that the universe was driven and inhabited by occult forces that humans could barely understand and surely never control unless they were magicians. But around 1660 a mechanistic worldview swept away occultism, and pixies became consigned to the realm of children's storybooks. Thereafter nature was believed to work like the finest mechanical clock—consummately predictable and fully open to human understanding.

Why such a dramatic change in basic patterns of thought took place when it did will long remain a subject for speculation. Certainly the prior Scholastic stress on human rationality and the Renaissance reacquisition of classical Greek texts helped to bring European thought to a scientific threshold. Probably the most direct causes of the intellectual mutations, however, were the twin challenges to conventional assumptions introduced in the sixteenth century by the discovery of the New World and the realization that the earth revolves around the sun rather than vice versa, for neither the Bible nor ancient science allowed room for what one bewildered contemporary called "new islands, new lands, new seas, new peoples, and what is more, a new sky and new stars." At first many thinkers, daunted by all this novelty, experienced a sense of intellectual crisis. Some took refuge in skepticism, others in relativism, and others in a return to blind faith. Speaking for several generations, the poet John Donne lamented in 1611 that "new philosophy calls all in doubt, the element of fire is quite put out, the sun is lost, and the earth, and no man's wit can well direct him where to look for it. . . . 'tis all in pieces, all coherence gone." But just as Europe surmounted its early-modern political crisis around 1660, so did it surmount its intellectual one, above all because the last stages of a profound scientific revolution gave a new, completely convincing "coherence" to things. As Alexander Pope wrote in the early eighteenth century, almost as if in response to Donne: "Nature and Nature's Law's lay hid in night:/ God said, Let Newton Be! and all was light."

1. THE SCIENTIFIC REVOLUTION

Even though Europe did not begin to resolve its intellectual crisis until about 1660, the groundwork for that resolution was prepared earlier in the seventeenth century by four great individuals—Kepler, Galileo, Bacon, and Descartes. Kepler and Galileo—both practicing scientists—have been discussed earlier; suffice it here to say that they removed all doubts about the Copernican heliocentric theory of the solar system and helped lead the way to Sir Isaac Newton's theory of universal gravitation. As for Bacon and Descartes, their main achievements were not in the realm of original scientific discovery but rather in propagating new attitudes toward learning and the nature of the universe.

Sir Francis Bacon (1561–1626), lord chancellor of England, was also an extremely influential philosopher of science. In Bacon's view, expressed most fully in his *Novum Organum (New Instrument)* of 1620, science could not advance unless it departed entirely from the inherited errors of the past and established "progressive stages of certainty." For Bacon this meant proceeding strictly on the basis of empirical knowledge (knowledge gained solely by the senses) and by means of the "inductive method," meaning the arrival at truth by proceeding upward from particular observations to generalizations. Insisting that "the corruption of philosophy by superstition and an admixture of theology . . . does the greatest harm," and that thinking people thus should be "sober-minded, and give to faith that only which is faith's," Bacon advocated the advancement of learning as a cooperative venture proceeding by means of meticulously recorded empirical experiments. Unlike the arid speculations of the past, collective scientific research and observation would produce useful knowledge and result in bettering the human lot. Much of Bacon's ideology is vividly evoked in the cover illustration of his *Novum Organum,* wherein intrepid ships venture out beyond the Pillars of Hercules (Straits of Gibraltar) onto a fathomless sea in pursuit of unknown but great things to come.

Bacon's later contemporary, the French philosopher René Descartes (1596–1650), agreed with him on two points: that all past knowledge should be discarded, and that the worth of any idea depended on its usefulness. Yet Descartes otherwise proposed some very different approaches to science, for unlike the empiricist Bacon, Descartes was a rationalist and an apostle of mathematics. In his *Discourse on Method* (1637), Descartes explained how, during a period of solitude, he resolved to submit all inherited doctrines to a process of systematic

Title Page of Bacon's Novum Organum. Underneath the ship sailing out into the ocean is a quotation from the Book of Daniel: "Many shall venture forth and science shall be increased."

René Descartes

A Diagram Illustrating Cartesian Principles. Descartes maintained that the pineal gland, seen here at the back of the head, transmitted messages from the eyes to the muscles in purely mechanical fashion. But the pineal gland was also the link between the material body and the nonmaterial human mind. From the 1677 edition of Descartes' *De Homine.*

Descartes' influence

The English and French traditions

doubting because he knew that the "strangest or most incredible" things had previously been set down in learned books. Taking as his first rule "never to receive anything as a truth which [he] did not clearly know to be such," he found himself doubting everything until he came to the recognition that his mere process of thought proved his own existence ("I think, therefore I am"). Thereupon making rationality the point of departure for his entire philosophical enterprise, Descartes rebuilt the universe on largely speculative grounds that differed in almost every detail from the universe conceived by the Greeks, yet conformed fully to the highest principles of human rationality as expressed in the laws of mathematics. That most of his theories were not empirically verifiable did not trouble him at all, because he was confident that "natural processes almost always depend on parts so small that they utterly elude our senses."

Predictably, the details of Descartes' scientific system are now regarded as mere curiosities, but the French philosopher nonetheless was enormously influential in aiding the advance of science and in creating a new climate of opinion for several reasons. First of all, even though his systematic doubting did not succeed in establishing any solid new scientific truths, it did contribute to the discrediting of all the faulty science of the ancients. Then too, Descartes' stress on mathematics was salutary because mathematics has indeed proven to be an indispensable handmaiden to the pursuit of natural science. But undoubtedly Descartes' single most influential legacy was his philosophy of *dualism,* according to which God created only two kinds of reality—mind and matter. In Descartes' view, mind belonged to man alone, and all else was matter. Thus he insisted that all created existence beyond man—organic and inorganic alike—operated solely in terms of physical laws, or the interplay of "extension and motion." In other words, for Descartes every single entity from the solar system to the realm of animals and plants was a self-operating machine propelled by a force arising from the original motion given to the universe by God. Indeed, Descartes thought that man himself was a machine—although, in this sole exception, a machine equipped with a mind. From this it followed that the entire universe could be studied objectively, without any aid from theology or appeals to the occult. Moreover, all apparent atributes of matter, such as light, color, sound, taste, or smell, which had no "extension" were to be classified as mere subjective impressions of the human mind unfit for proper scientific analysis. Based on such assumptions the pursuit of science could be dispassionate as never before.

Roughly speaking, for about a century after the work of Bacon and Descartes the English scientific community was Baconian and the French Cartesian (a name given to followers of Descartes). This is to say that the English concentrated primarily on performing empirical experiments in many different areas of physical science leading to concrete scientific advances, whereas the French tended to remain more oriented toward mathematics and philosophical theory. Among the numerous great seventeenth-century English laboratory scientists were the physician William Harvey (1578–1657), the chemist Robert Boyle (1627–1691), and the biologist Robert Hooke (1635–1703). Pursuing the earlier work of Vesalius and Servetus, but daring, unlike them, to practice vivisection, Harvey was the first to observe and describe the circulation of the blood through the arteries and back to the heart through the veins. Similarly committed to empirical experiment, Boyle used the air pump to establish "Boyle's law"—namely, that under constant temperature the volume of a gas decreases in proportion to the pressure placed on it. Boyle also was the first chemist to distinguish between a mixture and a compound (wherein the chemical combination occurs), and accomplished much to discredit alchemy. As for Hooke, although he conducted research in astronomy and physics as well as biology, he is best known for having used the microscope to discover the cellular structure of plants. Meanwhile, in France, Descartes himself pioneered in analytical geometry, Blaise Pascal worked on probability theory and invented a calculating machine before his conversion to religion, and Pierre Gassendi (1592–1655) sought to demonstrate the truth of the atomic theory. Also within the French realm of thought was the Dutch Jew Baruch Spinoza (1632–1677), a philosopher who tried to apply geometry to ethics and believed that he advanced beyond Descartes by interpreting the universe as being composed of a single substance—simultaneously God and nature—instead of two.

The dichotomy between English Baconianism and French Cartesianism, however, breaks down when one approaches the man commonly considered to have been the greatest scientist of all time, Sir Isaac Newton (1642–1727). A highly unattractive personality in his daily conduct—being secretive, petty, and vindictive—Newton was nonetheless a towering genius who drew on both the Baconian and Cartesian heritages. For example, following Bacon, and in the sharpest opposition to Descartes, Newton refused to dismiss the phenomenon of light as a mere subjective impression of "mind." Instead, by means of laboratory experiments he demonstrated that light behaves differently when filtered through different media, and hence offered an interpretation of light as a stream of particles that solidly established optics as an empirical branch of physics. Yet, on the other hand, Newton thoroughly approved of Descartes' stress on mathematics, and once in a burst of purely theoretical inspiration discovered the infinitesimal calculus.

Sir Isaac Newton

Of course Newton's supreme accomplishment lay in his formulation of the law of universal gravitation, which, as expressed in his monumental Latin *Principia Mathematica* (*Mathematical Principles of Natural Philosophy*) of 1687, integrated Copernican astronomy with Galileo's physics. In the *Principia* Newton broached the two major scientific questions of his day: (1) What keeps the heavy earth in motion?

Newton's law of gravitation

(before Copernicus the earth had been thought immobile) and (2) Why do terrestrial bodies tend to fall to the earth's center whereas planets stay in orbital motion? (before Copernicus the planets were thought to be embedded in crystalline spheres moved by angels or "divine intelligences"). In the early seventeenth century Kepler had already suggested the possibility of mutual attractions between all bodies in the solar system that kept the earth and other planets moving, but the Cartesians attacked this explanation as being too occult since attraction over space left out the crucial Cartesian ingredient of matter. Disregarding these Cartesian doubts because he saw no alternative, Newton returned to consider Kepler's theory of mutual attractions, and uniting Baconian observations with Cartesian mathematics, arrived at a single law of universal gravitation according to which "every particle of matter in the universe attracts every other particle with a force varying inversely as the square of the distance between them and directly proportional to the product of their masses." Since this law was verified by experience in both terrestrial and celestial realms, there could be no doubt that it explained all motion. Indeed, Newton's law was so reliable that it was employed immediately to predict the ebb and flow of tides. Later, in 1846, astronomers, noting irregularities in the motion of the planet Uranus, were able to deduce on Newtonian grounds the presence of the more distant planet Neptune before Neptune was actually located with the aid of high-power telescopes.

The impact of Newton's
Principia

Historians of science consider Newton's law of gravity to be "the most stupendous single achievement of the human mind," finding that "no other work in the whole history of science equals the *Principia* either in originality and power of thought or in the majesty of its achievement." Certainly the publication of the *Principia* was the crowning event of the scientific revolution because it confirmed the most important astronomical and physical theories previously set forth by Copernicus, Kepler, and Galileo, and resolved beyond quarrel the major problems that Copernicus's heliocentric theory had created. Needless to say, scientific work did not thereafter come to a standstill. Quite to the contrary, since Newton's accomplishment proved inspirational to researchers in many other fields, scientific work advanced steadily after 1687. But a fundamental reconception of the nature of the physical universe had been made, and thinkers in all areas could proceed with their work confident that science rather than superstition was the new order of the day.

2. THE FOUNDATIONS OF THE ENLIGHTENMENT

Although the presuppositions for the Enlightenment were set by the triumph of the scientific revolution in the late seventeenth century, the Enlightenment itself was an eighteenth-century phenomenon, lasting for close to the entire century until certain basic Enlightenment postulates were challenged around 1790 by the effects of the French Revolution and the new movement of romanticism. Of course not every thinker who lived and worked in the eighteenth century was equally "enlightened." Some, such as the Italian philosopher of history G. B. Vico (1668–1744), were thoroughly opposed to everything the Enlightenment stood for, and others, most notably Jean Jacques Rousseau (1712–1778), accepted certain Enlightenment values but sharply rejected others. Moreover, patterns of Enlightenment ideology tended to vary from country to country and to change in each country over the course of the century. Yet, despite these qualifications, most thinkers of the eighteenth century definitely shared the sense of living in an exciting new intellectual environment in which "the party of humanity" would prevail over traditionalism and obscurantism by dint of an unflinching commitment to the primacy of the intellect.

The Enlightenment: the major pattern of eighteenth-century thought

Most Enlightenment thought stemmed from three basic premises: (1) the entire universe is fully intelligible and governed by natural rather than supernatural forces; (2) rigorous application of "scientific method" can answer fundamental questions in all areas of inquiry; and (3) the human race can be "educated" to achieve nearly infinite improvement. The first two of these premises were products of the scientific revolution and the third primarily an inheritance from the psychology of John Locke.

Premises of the Enlightenment

Regarding the substitution of a natural for a supernatural worldview, explanations must start with the euphoria which greeted Isaac Newton's discovery of a single law whereby all motion in the heavens and earth became intelligible and predictable. If Newton could deal so authoritatively and elegantly with motion, it seemed to follow that all nature is governed neither by mysterious divine intervention nor by caprice, but by humanly perceivable universal laws. Hence most serious thinkers from about 1690 to 1790 became inveterate opponents of belief in miracles, and considered all varieties of revealed religion to be not just irrelevant to the pursuit of science, but positively antithetical to it. This is not to say that the Enlightenment abandoned belief in the existence of God: to the contrary, only the smallest number of Enlightenment thinkers were atheists, and very few even were avowed agnostics. Rather, most adhered to a religious outlook known as *Deism* which assumed that God existed but, having once created a perfect universe, no longer took an active interest in it. Expressed in the language of the Deists themselves, God was the "divine clockmaker" who, at the beginning of time, constructed a perfect timepiece and then left it to run on with predictable regularity. Most Deists continued to attend the churches of their ancestors (either Protestant or Catholic) from time to time, but they made little secret of their doubts about the efficacy of ritual and spoke out against all forms of religious intolerance.

The rejection of supernaturalism

The Study of an Amateur Scientist. This late–seventeenth-century aristocratic dilettante collected all sorts of specimens from the natural world. The mounting of his crocodile must have offered some challenge.

Confidence in scientific method

As for the second Enlightenment premise, the accomplishments of the scientific revolution inspired a deep sense of assurance that "scientific method" was the only valid means for pursuing research in all areas of human inquiry. By scientific method Enlightenment thinkers usually meant the dispassionate, empirical observation of particular phenomena in order to arrive at general laws. Given the acknowledged triumph of Newtonian physics, it is not surprising that around 1700 western Europe was struck by a virtual mania for applying scientific method in studying all the workings of nature. Since most scientific work was still simple enough to be understood by amateurs without the benefit of years of specialized education, European aristocrats and prosperous people in all walks of life began to dabble in "research"—buying telescopes, chasing butterflies, or building home laboratories in the hope of participating in some new scientific breakthrough. Writing in 1710, the English essayist Joseph Addison satirized such pursuits by imagining a will written by one "Sir Nicholas Gimcrack," an earnest amateur who left his "recipe for preserving dead caterpillars" to his daughters, his "rat's testicles" to a "learned and worthy friend," and who disinherited his son for "having spoken disrespectfully of his little sister," whose mortal remains Sir Nicholas kept near his desk in "spirits of wine." Of course most of the aristocratic "Gimcracks" never progressed beyond pickling, but their enthusiasm for following the latest developments in scientific research led them to patronize the work of truly gifted scientists and contributed to creating an atmosphere wherein science was prized as humanity's greatest attainment.

Inevitably, in turn, such an atmosphere was conducive to an assumption which became dominant in the course of the eighteenth century—that scientific method was the only proper means for studying human affairs as well as natural phenomena. Since the world of physical nature seemed well on the way to being mastered, Enlightenment thinkers considered it mere common sense that the world of human nature could soon be mastered as well by scientific means. Thus students of religion started collecting myths from numerous different traditions, not to find any occult truth in them but to classify their common traits and learn the steps by which humanity supposedly freed itself from superstition. Similarly, historians collected evidence to learn the laws governing the rise and fall of nations, and students of politics compared governmental constitutions to arrive at an ideal and universally applicable political system. In other words, as the English poet Alexander Pope stated in his *Essay on Man* of 1733, "the science of human nature [may be] like all other sciences reduced to a few clear points," and Enlightenment thinkers became determined to learn exactly what those "few clear points" were.

The scientific method applied to human concerns

It must be stressed, however, that if most thinkers of the Enlightenment supposed that the empirical study of human conduct could reduce society's working to a few laws, most also believed that human conduct was not immutable but highly perfectible. In this they were inspired primarily by the psychology of John Locke (1632–1704), who was not only a very influential political philosopher, as we have seen, but also the formulator of an extremely influential theory of knowledge. In his *Essay Concerning Human Understanding* (1690) Locke rejected the hitherto dominant assumption that ideas are innate, maintaining instead that all knowledge originates from sense perception. According to Locke, the human mind at birth is a "blank tablet" (Latin: *tabula rasa*) upon which nothing is inscribed: not until the infant begins to experience things, that is, to perceive the external world with its senses, is anything registered on its mind. From this point of departure, Enlightenment thinkers concluded that environment determines everything. For example, in their view, if some aristocrats were any better than ordinary mortals it was not because they had inherited any special knowledge or virtues, but only because they had been better trained. It therefore followed that all people could be educated to become the equals of the most perfect aristocrats, and that there were no limits to the potentialities for universal human progress. Indeed, a few Enlightenment thinkers became so optimistic as to propose that all evil might be eradicated from the world, since whatever evil existed was not the result of some divine plan but only the product of a faulty environment that humans had created and humans could change.

John Locke's psychology and human perfectibility

3. THE WORLD OF THE PHILOSOPHES

France, the dominant country in eighteenth-century Europe, was the center of the Enlightenment movement, and thus it is customary to refer to the leading exponents of the Enlightenment, regardless of where they lived, by the French term *philosophe,* meaning philosopher. In fact the term philosophe is slightly misleading inasmuch as hardly any of the philosophes—with the exceptions, to be seen, of David Hume and Immanuel Kant—were really philosophers in the sense of being highly original abstract thinkers. Rather, most were practically oriented publicists who aimed to reform society by popularizing the new scientific interpretation of the universe and applying dispassionate "scientific method" to a host of contemporary problems. Since they sought most of all to gain converts and alter what they regarded as outmoded institutions, they shunned all forms of expression that might seem incomprehensible or abstruse, priding themselves instead on their clarity, and occasionally even expressing their ideas in the form of stories or plays rather than treatises.

By common consent the prince of the philosophes was the Frenchman born François Marie Arouet, who called himself Voltaire (1694–1778). Virtually the personification of the Enlightenment, much as Erasmus two centuries earlier had embodied Christian humanism, Voltaire commented on an enormous range of subjects in a wide variety of literary forms. Probably his greatest single accomplishment lay in championing the cause of English empiricism in previously Cartesian France. Having as a young man been exiled to England for the crime of insulting a pompous French nobleman, Voltaire returned after three years a thorough and extremely persuasive convert to the ideas of Bacon and Locke. Not only did this mean that he persuaded other French thinkers to accept Newton's empirically verifiable scientific system in place of Descartes' unverifiable one, but he also encouraged them to be less abstract and theoretical in all their intellectual inclinations and more oriented toward the solving of everyday problems. To be sure, throughout the eighteenth century France's intellectual world remained more rationalistic than England's, but Voltaire's lifelong campaign on behalf of empiricism nonetheless had a very salutary effect in making French thinkers more practically oriented than before.

Voltaire by Houdon

Continually engaged in commenting on contemporary problems himself, Voltaire was an ardent spokesman for civil liberties. In this regard his battlecry was *Écrasez l'infâme*—"crush infamy"—meaning by infamy all forms of repression, fanaticism, and bigotry. In his own words, he believed that "the individual who persecutes another because he is not of the same opinion is nothing less than a monster." Accordingly, he wrote an opponent a line which forever after has been held forth as the first principle of civil liberty: "I do not agree with a word you say, but I will defend to the death your right to say it." Of all forms of intolerance Voltaire hated religious bigotry most of all because it seemed based on silly superstitions: "the less superstition, the less fanaticism; and the less fanaticism, the less misery." In addition to attacking religious repression, Voltaire also frequently criticized the exercise of arbitrary powers by secular states. In particular, he thought that the English parliamentary system was preferable to French absolutism and that all states acted criminally when their policies resulted in senseless wars. "It is forbidden to kill," he maintained sardonically, "therefore all murderers are punished unless they kill in large numbers and to the sound of trumpets."

Although Voltaire exerted the greatest effect on his age as a propagandist for the basically optimistic Enlightenment principle that by "crushing infamy" humanity could take enormous strides forward, the only one of his works still widely read today, the satirical story *Candide* (1759), is atypically subdued. Writing not long after the disastrous Lisbon earthquake of 1755, in which over 20,000 lives were lost for no apparent reason, Voltaire drew back in this work from some of his earlier faith that mankind by its own actions could limitlessly improve itself. Lulled into false security concerning what life has in store for him by the fatuous optimism of his tutor, Dr. Pangloss, the hero of the story, Candide, journeys through the world only to experience one outrageous misfortune after another. Storms and earthquakes are bad enough, but worse still are wars and rapacity caused by uncontrollable human passions. Only in the golden never-never land of "Eldorado" (clearly a spoof of the perfect world most philosophes saw on the horizon), where there are no priests, law courts, or prisons, but unlimited wealth and a "palace of sciences . . . filled with instruments of mathematics and physics," does Candide find temporary respite from disaster. Being a naturally restless mortal, however, he quickly becomes bored with Eldorado's placid perfection and leaves for the renewed buffetings of the real world. After many more lessons in "the school of hard knocks," he finally learns one basic truth by the end of the story: settling down on a modest farm with his once-beautiful but now hideously disfigured wife, he shrugs when Dr. Pangloss repeats for the hundredth time that "this is the best of all possible worlds," and replies: "that's as may be, but we must cultivate our garden." In other words, according to Voltaire, life is not perfect and probably never will be, but humans will succeed best if they ignore vapid theorizing and buckle down to unglamorous but productive hard work.

In addition to Voltaire, the most prominent French philosophes were Montesquieu, Diderot, and Condorcet. The baron de Montesquieu (1689–1755) was primarily a political thinker. In his major work, *The Spirit of Laws* (1748), Montesquieu sought to discover the ways in which differing environments and historical and religious traditions influence governmental institutions. Finding that unalterable differences in climates and geographic terrains affect human behavior, and hence governmental forms, Montesquieu throughout much of *The Spirit of Laws* seems to be saying that external conditions force humans to behave in different ways and that there is nothing they can do about this. But ultimately he was an idealist who preferred one particular political system, the English constitution, and hoped that all nations

Candide

Montesquieu

might overcome whatever environmental handicaps they faced to imitate it. For him, the greatest strength of the English system was that it consisted of separate and balanced powers—executive, legislative, and judicial: thus it guaranteed liberty inasmuch as no absolute sovereignty was given to any single governing individual or group. This idealization of "checks and balances" subsequently influenced many other Enlightenment political theorists and played a particularly dominant role in the shaping of the United States Constitution in 1787.

Diderot and the Encyclopedia

Unlike Voltaire, who was not a very systematic thinker, and Montesquieu, who wrote in a somewhat ambiguous and primarily reflective mode, the most programmatic of the philosophes was Denis Diderot (1713–1784). As a young firebrand Diderot was clapped into solitary confinement for his attacks on religion and thereafter worked under the ever-present threat of censorship and imprisonment. Yet throughout his life he never shrank from espousing a fully materialistic philosophy or criticizing what he considered to be backwardness or tyranny wherever he found it. Although, like Voltaire, Diderot wrote on a wide range of subjects in numerous different forms, including stories and plays, he exerted his greatest influence as the organizer of and main contributor to an extremely ambitious publishing venture, the *Encyclopedia*. Conceived as a summation and means for dissemination of all the most advanced contemporary philosophical, scientific, and technical knowledge, with articles written by all the leading philosophes of the day (including Voltaire and Montesquieu), the *Encyclopedia* first appeared between 1751 and 1772 in installments totaling seventeen large volumes and eleven more of illustrative plates. Whereas modern encyclopedias serve primarily as reference works, Diderot thought of his *Encyclopedia* as a set of volumes that people would read at length rather than merely using to look up facts. Therefore he hoped that it would "change the general way of thinking." Above all, by popularizing the most recent achievements in science and technology, Diderot intended to combat "superstition" on the broadest front, aid the further advance of science, and thereby help alleviate all forms of human misery. Dedicated to the proposition that all traditional beliefs had to be reexamined "without sparing anyone's sensibilities," he certainly would have excoriated all "irrational" religious dogmas openly if left to himself. But since strict censorship made explicitly antireligious articles impossible, Diderot thumbed his nose at religion in such oblique ways as offering the laconic cross-reference for the entry on the Eucharist: "see cannibalism." Not surprisingly, gibes like this aroused storms of controversy when the early volumes of the *Encyclopedia* appeared. Nonetheless, the project was not only completed in the face of prominent opposition, but as time went on the complete work became so popular that it was reprinted several times and helped spread the ideas of the philosophes not just in France but all over Europe.

Diderot. A contemporary portrait by Van Loo.

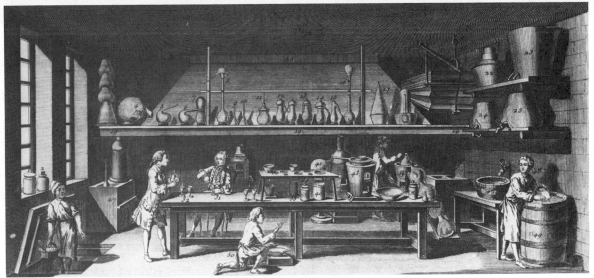

A Laboratory, from Diderot's *Encylopedia*. Each printed number refers to a detailed discussion in the text. Note the far greater stress on practical instruction here than in the illustration of the amateur scientist's study shown above, p. 148.

One of the youngest of the contributors to the *Encyclopedia,* the marquis de Condorcet (1743–1794), is customarily termed "the last of the philosophes" because his career, and the philosophes' activities in general, were cut short by the excesses of the French Revolution. In his early career Condorcet gained prominence as a brilliant mathematician, but he is best known as the most extreme Enlightenment exponent of the idea of progress. Already in the late seventeenth century, particularly as the result of the triumphs of science, several thinkers began arguing that the intellectual accomplishments of their own day were superior to any of the past and that greater intellectual progress in the future was inevitable. But since it was less clear to some that modern literature was superior to the Greek and Latin classics, around 1700 an argument raged concerning the relative claims of "ancients" and "moderns" wherein so able a critic as the English writer Jonathan Swift could regard what he called the "battle of the books" as a standoff. In the eighteenth century, however, the conviction grew that the present had advanced in all aspects of human endeavor beyond the accomplishments of any earlier time, and that the future was bound to see unlimited further progress on all fronts. Condorcet's *Outline of the Progress of the Human Mind* (1794) was the ultimate expression of this point of view. According to Condorcet, progress in the past had not been uninterrupted—the Middle Ages had been an especially retrogressive era—but, given the victories of the scientific revolution and Enlightenment, indefinite and uninterrupted progress in the future was assured. Venturing into prophecy, Condorcet confidently stated not only that "as preventive medicine improves . . . the average human

Condorcet and faith in progress

Edward Gibbon

David Hume

life-span will be increased and a more healthy and stronger physical constitution guaranteed," but that "the moment will come . . . when tyrants and slaves . . . will exist only in history or on the stage." Ironically, even while Condorcet was writing such optimistic passages he was hiding out from the agents of the French Revolution, who in fact soon counted him among the numerous victims of their "reign of terror."

Beyond France, philosophes in other countries also made significant contributions to the Enlightenment legacy. After France, the most "enlightened" country of Europe was Great Britain, where the most noteworthy philosophes were Gibbon, Hume, and Adam Smith. Edward Gibbon (1737–1794) was a man of letters and historian whose *Decline and Fall of the Roman Empire* (1776–1788) remains among the two or three most widely read history books of all time. Scintillatingly written, the *Decline and Fall* covers Roman and Byzantine history from Augustus to the fall of Constantinople in 1453. According to Gibbon, the Roman Empire was brought down by "the triumph of barbarism [i.e., the Germanic invasions] and religion [i.e., Christianity]," but the Europe of his day was no longer "threatened with a repetition of those calamities." For him the rise of Christianity was the greatest calamity because "the servile and pusillanimous reign of the monks" replaced Roman philosophy and science with a credulity which "debased and vitiated the faculties of the mind." Certainly Gibbon's antireligious bias vitiated the quality of his own work, and therefore he is read today not so much for his particular opinions as for his trenchant character portrayals and above all for his devastating wit.

The Scotsman David Hume (1711–1776), on the other hand, was a truly penetrating philosopher. Dedicated like most Enlightenment thinkers to challenging preconceived opinions, Hume pushed skepticism so far in his major work, *An Enquiry Concerning Human Understanding* (1742), that he undermined all assurance that anyone knew anything for certain. Starting with the assumption that human knowledge derives from sense data alone rather than abstract reason—that "nothing is in intellect which was not first in sense"—Hume proposed that we have no way of ascertaining whether such knowledge really corresponds to objective truths lodged in the real world. Once he arrived at such extreme skepticism, Hume also proposed a philosophy of relativistic ethics: if we know nothing for certain, then there can be no absolute moral laws, and we must decide on proper courses of action from their contexts. Yet, as skeptical as Hume was, he was by no means cynical; rather, he enthusiastically joined in Voltaire's campaign to crush "infamy," or what Hume called "stupidity, Christianity, and ignorance," on the grounds that it is preferable to voyage amidst a sea of uncertainties than to dwell in a forest of supernatural shadows.

The most practically oriented of the leading British philosophes was the Scottish economist Adam Smith, whose landmark treatise, *The Wealth of Nations* (1776), is recognized as the classic expression of "laissez-faire" economics. Strongly opposed to mercantilism—that is, any governmental intervention in economic affairs—Smith maintained that the prosperity of all could best be obtained by allowing individuals to pursue their own interests without competition from state-owned enterprises or legal restraints. The term *laissez-faire* comes from the French expression *laissez faire la nature* (let nature take its course), and Smith's advocacy of laissez-faire economic doctrine reveals how deeply indebted he was to the Enlightenment's idealization of both nature and human nature. In other words, espousing "the obvious and simple system of natural liberty," Smith believed that just as the planets revolve harmoniously in their orbits and are prevented from bumping into each other by the invisible force of gravity, so humans can act harmoniously even while pursuing their selfish economic interests if only "the invisible hand" of competitive, free-market forces is allowed to balance equitably the distribution of wealth. Ironically, although Smith thought of himself as the champion of the poor against the economic injustices inherent in state-supported mercantile privileges, his laissez-faire doctrine later became the favored theory of private industrial entrepreneurs who exploited the poor as much if not more than mercantilistic governments ever did. Nevertheless, Smith's free-market economics, as will be seen in subsequent chapters, certainly represented the wave of the future.

Elsewhere in Europe the circulation of Enlightenment ideas was by no means as widespread as in France and Britain, owing either to stiffer resistance from religious authorities, greater vigilance of state censors, or the lack of sufficient numbers of prosperous educated people to discuss and support progressive thought. Yet, aside from the Papal States, at least a few prominent philosophes flourished in virtually every country in western Europe. In Italy, for example, the Milanese jurist Cesare Beccaria (1738–1794), argued against arbitrary powers that oppressed humanity in the same spirit as the French philosophes. In his most influential writing, *On Crimes and Punishments* (1764), Beccaria attacked the prevalent view that judicial punishments should represent society's vengeance on the malefactor, asserting instead that no person has the right to punish another unless some useful purpose is served. For Beccaria, the only legitimate purpose for punishing crimes was the deterrence of other crimes. This granted, he argued for the greatest possible leniency compatible with deterrence, because enlightened humanitarianism dictated that humans should not punish other humans any more than is absolutely necessary. Above all, Beccaria eloquently opposed the death penalty, then widely inflicted throughout Europe for the most trivial offenses, on the grounds that it was no deterrent and set the bad example of public officials' pre-

Adam Smith

Cesare Beccaria

The Scientific Revolution and Enlightenment

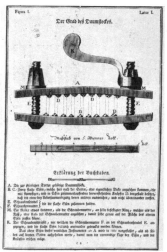

Instruments of Torture. The rack and the thumbscrew, from an official Austrian governmental handbook. Beccaria's influence helped phase out the use of such instruments by around 1800.

siding over murder rather than striving to deter it. *On Crimes and Punishments* was so favorably received that it was quickly translated into a dozen languages. Owing primarily to its influence, most European countries by around 1800 abolished torture, reserved the death penalty for capital crimes, and made imprisonment rather than any form of maiming the main form of judicial punishment.

The most representative German philosophe was the literary critic and dramatist Gotthold Lessing (1729–1781), who wrote with great eloquence of the need for tolerance. In his play *Nathan the Wise* (1779) Lessing led the audience to see that nobility of character has no relation to religious affiliations, and in his *On the Education of the Human Race* (1780) he maintained that the development of each of the world's great religions, Christianity included, was simply a step in the spiritual evolution of humanity, which would soon move beyond religion entirely toward pure rationality. The living model for Lessing's dramatic hero "Nathan the Wise" was his friend, the German Jewish sage Moses Mendelssohn (1729–1786), another philosophe who urged tolerance—in his case by writing a history of Judaism—but who also argued in favor of the immortality of the soul.

Far more difficult to classify is the greatest German philosopher of the eighteenth century—indeed one of the greatest philosophers of any nation of any time—Immanuel Kant (1724–1804). An unworldly intellectual who lived out his life far from the Enlightenment's French center of gravity in the Prussian city of Königsberg (located so far to the east that today it is part of the Soviet Union), Kant addressed his two masterworks, *The Critique of Pure Reason* (1781) and *The Critique of Practical Reason* (1790), to criticizing fashionable Enlightenment skepticism as represented most persuasively by David Hume. One of Kant's positions concerning reality and knowledge went so far against the grain of standard Enlightenment assumptions that it can hardly be called "Enlightened" at all. Namely, he maintained, in the spirit of Platonism, that the existence of a realm of absolute reality consisting of what he termed "things in themselves" cannot be doubted even though this realm remains unknowable to humans. Kant's assumption of absolute but unknowable truth, which implicitly opened philosophy to mystery, was to prove extremely attractive to his German philosophical successors in the nineteenth century, collectively known as "Idealists," but it ill accorded with his own age's stress on scientific verifiability.

In fact, however, Kant did not propose to build an action-oriented system on the basis of his assumed world of "things in themselves"; to the contrary, the bulk of his practical philosophy was more typically Enlightened. Aiming to counteract Hume's skepticism in a second way, he proposed that even though everyday knowledge begins in sense experience, the data of our senses is ordered by our rational minds in the here-and-now world of space and time in such a way as to provide us with reliable knowledge of appearances, or of what

Kant called "phenomena." In other words, Kant believed that humans could gain sufficient truth on a daily basis by a combination of sense and reason. Hence he insisted, much like Voltaire, that humans should use their learning faculties to inquire about nature, and, having done so, to improve upon it. Regarding ethics, Kant avoided the extremes of fixing upon conduct arbitrarily according to supernatural divine commandments or relativistically according to changing circumstances. Instead he maintained that if pure reason could neither prove nor disprove the existence of God, practical reason tells us that in the idea of God there exists a notion of moral perfection toward which all must strive. Thus we should always endeavor to act consistently with what Kant called the "categorical imperative": to act as if one's actions were to become a universal law of nature. Kant's principle of the categorical imperative proposed greater moral inflexibility than most philosophes thought realistic in view of the realities of everyday existence, yet it remained reconcilable with the basic Enlightenment worldview inasmuch as it rested on human rather than supernatural determinations.

Kant's practical philosophy

Immanuel Kant

In taking final stock of the Enlightenment movement, historians customarily raise two major questions. One is whether the philosophes were mere elitists who had no influence on the masses. Certainly, if one studies the sales figures of the philosophes' books or membership lists of eighteenth-century learned societies one finds that the philosophes' immediate audience consisted of aristocrats, lawyers, government officials, prosperous merchants, and a scattering of members of the higher clergy. To some degree this class bias lay beyond the philosophes' control, for many of the poorer people throughout eighteenth-century Europe remained illiterate, and most of the masses in southern and southeastern Europe—literate and illiterate alike—lived under the sway of an extremely conservative Roman Catholic hierarchy that was determined to keep them ignorant of the philosophes' ideas by means of the strictest censorship. Yet it is also true that many of the philosophes, despite their avowed commitment to clarity, wrote over the heads of most laboring people, and many did not even seek a lower-class audience because they feared that, if taken too far by the "uncouth" masses, their ideas might provoke open revolution. Typical philosophe elitism is well expressed in Gibbon's praise of imperial Roman religious policy whereby "the various modes of worship . . . were all considered by the people as equally true, by the philosopher as equally false, and by the magistrate as equally useful." Tradition also relates that whenever Voltaire discussed religion with his philosophe friends, he dismissed the servants so that they would not overhear any subversive remarks. Given this prevalent attitude, it is less surprising that Enlightenment ideas hardly percolated down to the masses than that they did have some effect on popular beliefs in France and England. For example, recent research on religious practices in southern France in the eighteenth century demonstrates

The audience of the philosophes

that from 1760 to 1790 fewer and fewer people of all classes requested that masses be said for their souls after death. Apparently, then, some servants were overhearing the philosophes' drawing-room conversations after all.

The other major question often asked about the Enlightenment is whether the philosophes were not hopelessly impractical "dreamers rather than doers." Without ignoring the clear vein of utopianism in Enlightenment thought, the answer to this must surely be no. Admittedly, most philosophes were far more optimistic about the chances of human perfectibility than most people are today, after the total wars and gas ovens of the twentieth century. Yet even the most optimistic did not expect utopian miracles to occur overnight. Rather, almost all the philosophes were committed to agitating for piecemeal social reforms which they believed would culminate, step by inevitable step, in a new world of enlightenment and virtue. Often such agitation did lead to significant changes in the conduct of practical affairs, and in at least one case, that of the American Revolution, Enlightenment ideas were the main source of inspiration for constructing a fully new political system. Moreover, sometimes even when Enlightenment propagandizing did not have any immediate practical impact, it did help to accomplish change in the future. For example, many philosophes condemned slavery on humanitarian or utilitarian grounds, thereby initiating a process of discussion that led cumulatively to the triumph of abolitionism throughout the West in the nineteenth century. In short, then, it is impossible to deny that the philosophes as a class were among the most practical-minded and influential intellectuals who ever lived.

4. THE ONWARD MARCH OF SCIENCE

Although several of the philosophes were natural scientists as well as publicists, it is preferable to treat the progress of eighteenth-century science separately because science, being highly international, is best broached by means of a topical rather than geographical method of review. The three scientific areas that witnessed the greatest progress from around the time of Newton to the end of the eighteenth century were descriptive biology, electricity, and chemistry. Regarding the first, four great pioneers in the use of newly invented high-power microscopes made enormous advances in observing small creatures and plant and cell structures during the last decades of the seventeenth century—the Italian Marcello Malpighi (1628–1694), the Englishman Robert Hooke, and two Dutchmen, Jan Swammerdam (1637–1680) and Antony van Leeuwenhoek (1632–1723). Perhaps most fundamental was the work of the last, a self-taught scientist who discovered bacteria and wrote the first description of human sperm. Building on such accomplishments as well as on numerous observations of his own, the Swedish botanist Karl von Linné (1707–1778)—commonly known by his Latinized name of Linnaeus—formulated the basic system of plant and animal classification that remains in use today. In the "Linnean Order" there are three realms—animal, vegetable, and mineral—and within the first two there are classes, "genera," and species. Furthermore, in Linnaeus's system every plant and animal is given two scientific Latin names—the first denoting the genus and the second the species. For example, robins are called *Planesticus migratorius:* the migrating species of the genus *Planesticus.*

Rivaling Linnaeus in eighteenth-century biology was the French naturalist Georges Buffon (1707–1788), whose massive *Natural History,* appearing in forty-four volumes from 1749 to 1778, was most advanced in its recognition of the close relationship between humans and other primates. Completely ignoring the biblical version of creation, yet never quite bringing himself to accept the full implications of a theory that located human origins in some form of evolution, Buffon admitted the possibility that the entire range of organic forms had descended from a single species and thus was a precursor of the evolutionism of Charles Darwin.

As opposed to developments in descriptive biology, where basic work hardly began before 1660, the "founding father" in the field of electricity was active well before the period under discussion. Around 1600 the Englishman William Gilbert discovered the magnetic properties of lodestones and introduced the word *electricity* into the language (*elektron* is the Greek word for amber, and Gilbert had observed that amber rubbed on fur will attract paper or straw). Yet because Gilbert worked before the triumph of mechanistic thought, he believed magnetism to be a purely occult force and therefore did not even dream of machines that could generate or harness electricity. Starting in the late seventeenth century, on the other hand, scientists from many different countries progressively began to master the science of electricity as we now know it. In 1672 the German Otto von Guericke published results of experiments wherein he generated electricity; in 1729 the Englishman Stephen Gray demonstrated that electricity could be conducted by means of threads and that certain other substances resisted conducting; and in 1745 a team of scientists at the Dutch University of Leyden invented a method for storing electricity in the "Leyden jar." In 1749 by using a kite-string to conduct lightning the American Benjamin Franklin charged a Leyden jar from a thunderstorm and thus was able to conclude that lightning and electricity are identical. This recognition allowed Franklin to invent the lightning rod, which saved houses from being destroyed in storms and is one of the best examples of the link between scientific theory and life-enhancing practice.

Benjamin Franklin as the God of Electricity by Benjamin West

Probably the greatest theoretical breakthrough made in the second half of the eighteenth century lay in the field of chemistry, which had been languishing for about a century after the work of Robert Boyle.

Chemistry

The reason for this delay lay mostly in the wide acceptance of errors concerning such matters as heat, flame, air, and the phenomenon of combustion. The most misleading error was the so-called phlogiston theory, based on the idea that "phlogiston" was the substance of fire— i.e., when an object burned, phlogiston was supposed to be given off. The remaining ash was said to be the "true" material. In the second half of the eighteenth century important discoveries were made which discredited this theory and cleared the way for a real understanding of basic chemical reactions. In 1766 the Englishman Henry Cavendish reported the discovery of a new kind of gas obtained by treating certain metals with sulfuric acid. He showed that this gas, now known as hydrogen, would not of itself support combustion and yet would be rapidly consumed by a fire with access to the air. In 1774 oxygen was discovered by another Englishman, the Unitarian minister Joseph Priestley. He found that a candle would burn with extraordinary vigor when placed in the new gas—a fact which indicated clearly that combustion was not caused by any mysterious principle or substance in the flame itself. A few years after this discovery, Cavendish demonstrated that air and water, long supposed to be elements, are respectively a mixture and a compound, the first being composed principally of oxygen and nitrogen and the second of oxygen and hydrogen.

Antoine Lavoisier

The final blow to the phlogiston theory was administered by the Frenchman Antoine Lavoisier (1743–1794), widely regarded as the greatest scientist of the eighteenth century, who lost his life in the French Revolution. Lavoisier proved that both combustion and respiration involve oxidation, the one being rapid and the other slow. He provided the names for oxygen and hydrogen, demonstrated that the diamond is a form of carbon, and argued that life itself is essentially a chemical process. But undoubtedly his greatest accomplishment was his discovery of the law of the conservation of mass. He found evidence that "although matter may alter its state in a series of chemical actions, it does not change in amount; the quantity of matter is the same at the end as at the beginning of every operation, and can be traced by its weight." This "law" has, of course, been modified by later discoveries regarding the structure of the atom and the conversion of some forms of matter into energy. It is hardly too much to say, however, that as a result of Lavoisier's genius chemistry became a true science.

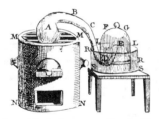

*Lavoisier's Apparatus for the De-
composition of Air*

Despite the notable scientific advances of the seventeenth and eighteenth centuries, the development of physiology and medicine progressed rather slowly during the same period for several reasons. One was the inadequate preparation of physicians, many of whom had begun their professional careers with little more training than apprenticeship under an older practitioner. Another was the common disrepute in which surgery was held as a mere trade, like that of a barber or blacksmith. Perhaps the most serious of all was the prejudice against dissection of human bodies for use in anatomical study. As late as 1750

*Comparative slowness of
medical progress*

medical schools which engaged in this practice were in danger of destruction by irate mobs. Despite these obstacles some progress was still possible. About 1670 Malpighi and Leeuwenhoek confirmed William Harvey's discovery of the circulation of the blood by observing the actual flow of blood through the network of capillaries connecting the arteries and veins. At approximately the same time an eminent physician of London, Thomas Sydenham, proposed a new theory of fever as a natural process by which diseased material is expelled from the system.

Medical progress during the eighteenth century was somewhat more rapid. Among the noteworthy achievements were the discovery of blood pressure, the founding of histology or microscopic anatomy, and the development of the autopsy as an aid to the study of disease. But the chief milestones of medical advancement in this period were the adoption of inoculation and the development of vaccination for smallpox. Knowledge of inoculation came originally from the Near East, where it had long been employed by the Muslims. Information concerning its use was relayed to England in 1717 through the letters of Lady Mary Wortley Montagu, wife of the British ambassador to Turkey. The first systematic application of the practice in the Western world, however, was due to the efforts of the American Puritan leader Cotton Mather, who implored the physicians of Boston to inoculate their patients in the hope of curbing an epidemic of smallpox which had broken out in 1721. Thereafter inoculation had some success in saving lives, but the practice understandably was widely resisted because smallpox inoculation guaranteed the patient one bout with the disfiguring disease before inducing further immunity to it. Only in 1796 did the Englishman Edward Jenner, noticing that milkmaids always seemed to have clear complexions, conclude that in contracting the virus of cowpox from their daily occupation, milkmaids gained immunity to smallpox. Hence inoculation of humans with the deadly smallpox virus appeared unnecessary, and Jenner introduced *vaccination* (from *vacca*—Latin for cow), employing the mild cowpox virus instead. Once vaccination proved both harmless and marvelously effective, the vast possibilities opened up for the elimination of contagious diseases appeared to confirm the Enlightenment belief in the ability of science to make nature's laws work for the betterment of the human condition.

*Inoculation and
vaccination*

5. CLASSICISM AND INNOVATION IN ART AND LITERATURE

Although the spirit of the scientific revolution and Enlightenment was reflected in certain great artistic monuments, there were no simple, one-to-one correspondences between intellectual and artistic trends in the late seventeenth and eighteenth centuries. Artists and writers

*Manifold influences on
artistic trends*

The Finding of Moses by Poussin. The artist has included a pyramid in the background (right) as a token of verisimilitude, but otherwise his scene appears to be set in ancient Rome. Note the stress on monumentality and perpendicular lines.

responded to a great variety of influences in addition to the new scientific view of the universe: national stylistic traditions, religious demands, differing political and sociological contexts, and, not least, the internal dynamics of artistic evolution within any given creative field. It is best, then, to look at certain major trends without forcing the explanations for them all to fit the same mold.

As we have seen earlier, the dominant style in European art between about 1600 and the early 1700s was the Baroque. But a few countries resisted the dominance of Baroque influences—particularly France, Holland, and England. The French resistance was primarily nationalistic in inspiration. Since Baroque style was closely associated with the tastes of the Spanish and Austrian Habsburgs, against whom the French were continually fighting throughout most of the seventeenth and early eighteenth centuries, it seemed inappropriate for France to admit cultural inferiority by imitating the style of its political rivals. In opposition to the exuberant Baroque, then, French artists and architects cultivated restrained classicism. Some of the best earlier examples of this are the canvases of seventeenth-century France's greatest painter, Nicolas Poussin (1594–1665), whose reposeful scenes from classical mythology, governed by the artist's programmatic commitment to "things well ordered," stand in the sharpest contrast to the swirling contortions of Poussin's Baroque contemporary, Rubens.

"Well-ordered" classicism continued to be the preferred style in France during the reign of Louis XIV (1651–1715) for three reasons. First of all, Louis in particular was determined to make sure that France cultivated its own characteristic national style for reasons of state. Second, Louis's own stylistic preferences tended toward the grand and

French classicism

See color plates facing page 166 for *Landscape with the Burial of Phocion* by Poussin sober. And third, the symmetrical qualities of classicism seemed to complement best the highly symmetrical natural order then being posited in France by Cartesian philosophers and scientists. Thus when Louis XIV decided to renovate his palace of the Louvre, the leading Baroque architect of the day, Bernini, submitted plans, but these were rejected in favor of those of a native Frenchman who emphasized severe classical monumentality. Later, when Louis erected his splendid new palace at Versailles, Baroque architectural features were introduced. Yet the Baroque of Versailles was a very restrained Baroque that emphasized massive symmetry rather than the jutting angles and startling curves favored by Bernini.

As classicism was the prevalent style in seventeenth-century French art, so too did it prevail in literature. This can be seen most clearly in the tragedies of Pierre Corneille (1606–1684) and Jean Racine (1639–1699). Both of these playwrights took as their subjects the heroes and heroines of classical mythology and history such as Medea, Pompey, Andromache, and Phaedra, and both strove as well to imitate the theoretical and structural principles of the classical Greek tragedians. Similarly, the great French writer of comedies, Jean Baptiste Molière (1622–1673), took the Roman comedies of Terence and Plautus for his models and was so committed to symmetrical formalism as to have his characters speak in rhyming couplets. Yet, unlike Corneille and Racine, Molière did set the action of his plays in the present because he believed that "the business of comedy is to represent in general all the defects of men and especially of the men of our time." Accordingly, his work was also highly satirical. In *Tartuffe,* for example, he

East Entrance of the Louvre, Paris. Built by the French architect Claude Perrault between 1667 and 1670, this facade is an excellent example of the rigorously classical style patronized by Louis XIV.

The Painter in his Studio by Vermeer. The model is posing as Clio, the muse of history, and thus stands for the timeless fame of painting. The fact that the source of light is concealed by the curtain may perhaps be bc understood to mean that the artist works essentially by the interior illumination of his mind.

pilloried religious hypocrisy, and in *The Bourgeois Gentleman* he mocked the vulgar pretentiousness of the social climber. Yet for all his satire, Molière had a measure of sympathy for the trials of human existence, rising to his greatest profundity in *The Misanthrope,* a play which pokes fun at a person who hates society but which also shows that the character has excellent reasons for his alienation. Thus mixing sympathy and occasional melancholy with wit and searing scorn, Molière was probably the most gifted European dramatic genius after Shakespeare.

In the other leading countries that resisted the Baroque, Holland and England, there can be little doubt that artistic preferences had religious as well as nationalistic causes. Since Holland and England were Protestant, they naturally preferred to limit Baroque influences emanating from Rome and the Catholic Spanish Netherlands. We have seen that the greatest seventeenth-century Dutch painter, Rembrandt, developed his own highly personal style which employed Baroque elements whenever he deemed them appropriate. Rembrandt's slightly later Dutch contemporary, Jan Vermeer (1632–1675), however, eliminated the Baroque entirely in painting the serenest realistic indoor genre scenes, as did most other seventeenth-century Dutch genre, landscape, and portrait painters. Similarly, the dominant stylistic commitment in England, after a brief flirtation with the Baroque dur-

Left: *St. Peter's Basilica with Colonnade, Rome*. Right: *St. Paul's Cathedral, London*. The sweeping colonnade in front of St. Peter's was designed by the Baroque architectural master Bernini in 1656. Such showy effects were not to the taste of the English architect Christopher Wren, who in designing St. Paul's hewed more closely to the classicism implicit in the Renaissance style of the Vatican Basilica itself. Wren's "English answer to St. Peter's," however, makes classical columns even more prominent than they were in the Vatican. Note how Wren drew inspiration from Perrault's classical Louvre facade (above, p. 163) in designing St. Paul's second-level elevation.

Chiswick House. Built near London around 1725, this country house initiated an English Palladian fad that had its echoes in Thomas Jefferson's Monticello, and later still in the Jefferson Memorial. Note how the design imitates Palladio's Villa Rotonda (Vol. 1, p. 624), just as that building itself was modeled on the Roman Pantheon (Vol. 1, p. 248).

ing the reign of the Catholic-leaning Charles I, was to a classicizing restraint. Thus the most prominent of all English architects, Christopher Wren (1632–1723), did not hesitate to borrow Baroque elements when fitting, but emphasized classicism in his columns and domes, most notably in his masterwork, St. Paul's Cathedral (built from 1675 to 1710). More classical still was the "Palladian revival" which dominated English architecture in the first half of the eighteenth century. In this period numerous country houses commissioned by the landed gentry imitated the Renaissance master Palladio's serenely classical and highly symmetrical Villa Rotonda, just as that building had imitated the Roman Pantheon. Indeed, so many English town houses built in the fashionable resort spa of Bath around 1740 imitated Palladian models that Bath was soon called, after Palladio's main area of activity, "the English Vicenza."

Parallel to the artistic classicism of Wren and the English Palladians was the literary classicism which flourished in England from about 1660 to 1760. In fact, the writers of this period expressly called themselves "Augustans." This they did for two reasons: first, the restoration of royalty in 1660 after the English Civil War seemed to presage an age of peace and civility similar to the one installed by Augustus after civil war in ancient Rome; and second, the favored poetic models of the English Augustans were the Augustan Romans—Virgil, Horace, and Ovid. Still another reason why English literary taste became resolutely classical in the later seventeenth century was that the France of Louis XIV had enormous influence in setting fashions throughout Europe, and the English did not wish to be the slightest bit out of date in following the French lead. Finally, as in France, classicism appeared to be the one available style that came closest to being dispassionately "scientific." In other words, just when the English leisured classes were celebrating the triumphs of Newtonianism and endeavoring to

The English Augustans

The Embarkation for Cythera by Watteau. This epoch-making painting broke with the severity of Poussin in favor of a greater stress on motion and lushness. No two art historians agree upon exactly what it means, but the evocation of dreamy pleasure is unmistakable.

make their own contribution to scientific advance by collecting natural specimens or gazing through telescopes, they patronized a form of writing which seemed to resemble Newtonian methods and laws in stressing simplicity, clarity, and symmetry.

Of the numerous members of the English Augustan school, the most outstanding were the prose writer Jonathan Swift (1667–1745) and the poet Alexander Pope (1688–1744). The former, a scathing satirist, was atypical of Augustan thinking in his pessimism concerning the potentialities of human nature: in Swift's masterpiece, *Gulliver's Travels,* humans at one point are dismissed as "the most pernicious race of little odious vermin that nature ever suffered to crawl upon the surface of the earth." Yet Swift's prose is fully Augustan in its economy and clarity; as opposed to earlier flowery stylists, Swift insisted on locating, as he said, "proper words in proper places." As for Pope, he was thoroughly Augustan in both style and thought—almost to a fault. A consistent exponent in highly regular rhyming verse of the naturalistic doctrines of the Enlightenment, Pope in such didactic poems as his *Essay on Man* and his *Essay on Criticism* held that humans must study and imitate nature if they were to bring any semblance of order into their affairs. Most necessary for mankind, in Pope's view, was unblinking self-knowledge, which the poet believed could be obtained entirely apart from theology or metaphysics. Summing up the secularistic spirit of his age, Pope responded to Milton's earlier poetic resolve to "justify the ways of God to man" in his most famous couplet: "Know then thyself, presume not God to scan;/ the proper study of Mankind is Man."

As impressive as numerous artistic and literary productions of French and English classicism may have been, the classical movement self-evidently was not highly innovative. Two entirely separate develop-

Jonathan Swift and Alexander Pope

Landscape with the Burial of Phocion, Nicolas Poussin (1594–1665). An outstanding example of the classical style in painting. As opposed to the Baroque stress on swirling movement, here there is practically no movement at all. Instead, nature is conceived in rigorously geometrical terms to convey a sense of permanence. Note too the presence of ancient classical buildings, making it seem as if the past is enduring. (Louvre)

A Dutch Interior, Pieter de Hooch (c. 1629–c. 1679). Seventeenth-century Dutch painters excelled at indoor genre compositions bathed in light. The restraint of the scene itself stands in contrast to the melodramatic Baroque painting in the background. (National Gallery, London)

Le Mezzetin, Antoine Watteau (1684–1721). Mezzetin was a popular character from Italian comedy. In portraying him in a relaxed pose Watteau succeeded in conveying a sense of dreamy elegance. (MMA)

The Blue Boy, Thomas Gainsborough (1727–1788). Gainsborough, eighteenth-century England's greatest portrait painter, combined Watteau's lushness with more traditional English gravity. (Huntington Library)

Madame de Pompadour, François Boucher (1703–1770). A characteristically frilly French Rococo portrait. Madame de Pompadour, King Louis XV's mistress, was a patroness of arts and letters, and for a time the virtual ruler of France. (The Wallace Collection, London)

The Stonemason's Yard, Canaletto (1697–1768). A quiet scene of everyday life, in strong contrast to the scene below. (National Gallery, London)

Marriage à la Mode, William Hogarth (1697–1764). A satirical look at the arranged marriage: the financial needs of the nobleman and the social aspirations of his middle-class counterpart dominate the negotiations. (National Gallery, London)

Sarah Siddons as the Tragic Muse, Sir Joshua Reynolds (1723–1792). Mrs. Siddons, a famous actress of the seventeenth century, is here portrayed as the Queen of Tragedy, in accordance with Reynolds's habit of depicting wealthy patrons in impressive classical poses. (Huntington Library)

Madame Recamier, Jacques Louis David (1748–1825). David was the exponent of a new classicism during and after the French Revolution. The couch, the lamp, and the costume are copied from Rome and Pompeii. (Louvre)

ments of the eighteenth century, on the other hand, emphasized greater originality—namely, the emergence of the continental Rococo style in art, and the rise of the English novel. Regarding the former, the basic explanation for the emergence of Rococo art and architecture was the sense of relaxation experienced in France at the coming of peace and at the death of Louis XIV in 1715. Whereas the prolonged War of the Spanish Succession had begun to exhaust the country, and whereas Louis in his declining years had become ever more puritanical and ever more determined to enforce his own severe tastes and standards on everyone else, around 1715 the leisured classes of the nation breathed a deep sigh of relief. This reaction, not surprisingly, resulted in an artistic pendulum swing from classical severity to a cheerful abandonment which goes by the name of Rococo style. In painting, the earliest and most gifted Rococo artist was Antoine Watteau (1684–1721), who was influenced more by the Baroque artist Rubens than by any other single source, but who replaced Rubens's massiveness with airy French elegance and grace. Watteau was admitted into the French Academy of Fine Arts in 1717 for his masterpiece, *The Embarkation for Cythera*, even though none of the members would have dreamed of admitting him two years earlier. Moreover, since the Academy had no formal classification for the *Embarkation*—which merely showed graceful people having a dreamily good time—it invented one for the purpose: "*fêtes galantes,*" best translated as stylish revels. At least Watteau's revellers were clothed, but the figures in the paintings of his Rococo successors Francois Boucher (1703–1770) and J. H. Fragonard (1732–1806) were usually half naked and displayed in postures that went well beyond sensuality in the direction of frank eroticism.

Most of the rest of Europe was too straitlaced to imitate the las-

Rococo painting

See color plates following page 166 for *Le Mezzetin* by Watteau and *Madame de Pompadour* by Boucher

A Reclining Nude by Boucher. The viewer is left to ponder the significance of the fallen flower.

French Rococo architecture

Rococo and Baroque compared

civiousness of French Rococo painting, but French Rococo architecture soon became the dominant style throughout the Continent and remained such for most of the eighteenth century. The reasons for this were, first, that the French architects who pioneered in Rococo building in the years shortly after 1715 took Baroque principles for their standards in replacing classical ones, thereby setting themselves in tune with the rest of their continental contemporaries, and second, that Rococo building design featured curvaceous elegance and thus appealed greatly to the vain European aristocrats who commissioned the major architectural projects of the day.

Perhaps the easiest way to characterize the Rococo building style is to call it the "champagne of Baroque" or "Baroque with a French accent." Both Baroque and Rococo buildings emphasize dynamic movement, but whereas Baroque style exudes force and passion, the Rococo communicates a sense of delicacy and playfulness. Most amazing to initial viewers of Rococo interiors is how light and airy they are: as opposed to Baroque interiors, which are generally sombre, Rococo ones have walls and ceilings painted in white, gold, and pink. Among the leading European Rococo buildings are the Hôtel de Soubise in Paris, the pavilion known as the Zwinger in Dresden, the jewel-box Vierzehnheiligen church in Bavaria (near Bamberg), and the Cuvilliés theater in Munich, which is still used for performances of eighteenth-century operas and plays. Although Rococo art and

Two German Rococo Interiors. The Vierzehnheiligen Church near Bamberg (left) and the Wieskirche near Munich (right) are the two foremost works of German Rococo interior decoration.

architecture unquestionably allowed great play for the imagination, from the long-term perspective of art history the Rococo style was an end rather than a beginning inasmuch as it represented the final phase of the Baroque.

In contrast, the only really new development in the artistic and literary history of the Enlightenment period that had a promising future was the emergence of the novel. In treating the rise of the novel in eighteenth-century England it must be stressed that the English novel was not invented out of nothing. To the contrary, works of prose fiction known as romances had been composed in classical antiquity and throughout western Europe from the twelfth century onward. Indeed, one European romance—Cervantes's *Don Quixote*—atypically had many of the characteristics of the modern novel. Moreover, in France, where the word *roman* means both romance and novel, prose fictions were written without interruption from the Middle Ages to the recognizably modern novels of the nineteenth-century writers Balzac and Flaubert. Nevertheless, there were such major differences between the best English prose fictions of the eighteenth century and all that came before (other than *Don Quixote*) as to make it possible to say that the modern novel was invented in eighteenth-century England.

The best way of characterizing the difference between the romance and the novel is that the former is patently a fabrication, whereas the latter (allowing a few inevitable exceptions) purports to be a reliable account of how humans behave. Assuming that a judge in a court of law were asked to accept the testimony of a romance as evidence for trying a case, he would have to throw it out and declare a mistrial because romances generally have little sense of verisimilitude, being written in an ornate style and recounting the adventures of clearly imaginary characters—usually from the mythical or semi-mythical past—who find themselves in preposterous situations. But a modern novel might stand up as excellent legal evidence, for in the novel, from the eighteenth-century English examples onward, experiences seem unique, plots and settings fully believable, and the manner of presentation dispassionately straightforward.

Two explanations may be offered for the emergence of the novel in eighteenth-century England. One is that the ideals of the Enlightenment unquestionably created the most conducive atmosphere for novel writing insofar as the "scientific," methodical study of human experience was widely regarded as the order of the day. Yet, because Enlightenment thinking predominated in France even more than in England, it remains to ask why England in particular was the modern novel's first home. The answer to this appears to relate to the distinctive nature of the English reading public. Specifically, England had a much larger nonaristocratic reading audience than France because of England's greater involvement in trade and industry; this class preferred novels to romances because novels were written in a gripping

Defoe, Richardson, and Fielding

Jane Austen and the perfection of the novel

rather than "elevated" style and the action of the novel's more prosaic characters seemed more relevant to common, nonaristocratic experience. As will also presently be seen, it was by no means irrelevant to the novelistic form in England that the majority of novel readers were not men but women.

By common consent the three most influential novelists of eighteenth-century England were Daniel Defoe (1660–1737), Samuel Richardson (1689–1761), and Henry Fielding (1707–1754). All three portrayed recognizable, nonaristocratic characters doing their best to make their way in a perilous world, unaffected by any hint of divine intervention for good or ill. In the novels of Defoe and Richardson the narrator is usually a character who participates in the action and thus knows the "truth" of one side directly, but of course cannot be expected to understand every other character's point of view. On the other hand, in Fielding's *Tom Jones* an "omnipotent narrator" stands apart from the action, and accordingly has a fuller view of it, but seems by his obtrusive presence to be creating a rather more artificial fiction.

Tom Jones is the only eighteenth-century English novel universally considered to be an enduring classic of world literature, but at the very beginning of the next century the technical achievements of Defoe, Richardson, and Fielding were consolidated by Jane Austen (1775–1817), whose *Pride and Prejudice* and *Emma* represent for many readers the heights of novelistic perfection. That a woman should emerge around 1800 as a greater writer of novels than most men was almost inevitable, above all because early-modern European fiction writing was one of the very few areas of creative expression wherein society easily tolerated female contributions. Indeed, in seventeenth-century France the most widely read authors of romances—Madeleine de Scudéry (1607–1701) and the countess de La Fayette (1634–1692)—were women, and later in England Fanny Burney (1752–1840), Ann Radcliffe (1764–1823), and Maria Edgeworth (1767–1849) all wrote novels of great popularity and considerable distinction before Jane Austen went to work. Moreover, since the English novel-reading public was predominantly female, women readers understandably were particularly interested in characteristically female problems as seen from a feminine angle, a subject matter and perspective that Jane Austen bountifully provided. But of course Austen would not rank, as she does, among the handful of greatest novelists who ever lived had she been narrowly parochial in her views and lacking in extraordinary artistic skill. Rather, men as well as women can delight in her dry, ironic wit and admire her insight into human nature. Moreover, Jane Austen's technical accomplishments may well represent novelistic skills at their pinnacle. In particular, in compromising between Defoe's and Richardson's first-person narrator and Fielding's omnipotent third-person one by the use of a third-person narrator who remains unobtrusive and pursues events primarily from the point of view of a central character, Jane Austen created a delicate balance between subjectivity and objectivity that may well never have been surpassed.

6. BAROQUE AND CLASSICAL MUSIC

The title of one of the most genial of eighteenth-century symphonic compositions, Haydn's *Surprise Symphony,* can be applied to the music of the entire age, for eighteenth-century music is continually full of surprises. Indeed, in contrast to developments in contemporary art and literature, where innovation was comparatively rare, the eighteenth century was the most fertile period of invention in all of western European musical history. Probably the major explanation for this is that early-modern composers, unlike artists and writers, did not have to concern themselves about how much they would borrow from the music of classical antiquity because the principles of ancient musical composition were virtually unknown. More free than painters and poets to strike out on their own, early-modern composers invented form after form in two successive major styles, the Baroque and the so-called classical, treating their listeners to surprise after surprise.

Innovation in Baroque and Classical music

Baroque music, like Baroque art and architecture, emerged around 1600 in Italy as an artistic expression of the Counter-Reformation. Yet from the beginning Baroque composers were perforce more inventive than their artistic counterparts, having no equivalent of columns and domes with which to work. The first important figure in the history of Baroque music was the Italian Claudio Monteverdi (1567–1643), who reacted against the highly intricate Renaissance polyphonic style of his major predecessor, Palestrina. Pursuing the Baroque goal of dramatic expressiveness, Monteverdi found that deep human emotions were difficult to convey when members of a chorus were singing against each other as they did in the music of the late Renaissance, and that dramatic intensity becomes greatest when music is combined with theater. Having no classical models to draw upon, Monteverdi thus virtually single-handedly invented a new musical form, that of opera. In addition, to lend his opera singers greater emotional power than they would have had if they had sung alone, Monteverdi wrote instrumental accompaniments so forceful that they have earned him the title of "the father of instrumentation." Since Monteverdi's new form of opera fully suited the spirit of his times, within a generation operas were performed in all the leading cities of Italy. Staged within magnificent settings, and calling upon the talents of singers, musicians, dramatists, and stage designers, opera expressed as clearly as any art form the dedication of Baroque artistic style to grandeur, drama, and display.

Claudio Monteverdi

With the notable exception of the Englishman Henry Purcell (1659–

Later Baroque music: Bach and Handel

1695), there were no enduringly great Baroque composers in the second half of the seventeenth century. Nonetheless, many imaginative musicians began to create new forms during this period, most notably the instrumental forms of the sonata and the concerto. Moreover, whatever lull there may have been in the composition of masterpieces was more than compensated for in the last phase of the Baroque era by the appearance of Bach and Handel, two of the greatest composers of all time. Born in the same year very near each other in northern Germany, Johann Sebastian Bach (1685–1750) and George Frederick Handel (1685–1759) had very different musical personalities and very different careers. Bach was an intensely pious introvert who remained in the backwaters of provincial Germany all his life and wrote music of the utmost individuality, whereas Handel was a public-pleasing cosmopolitan whose music is more accessible than Bach's in its robust affirmativeness. Despite these differences, however, both Bach and Handel were distinctly late-Baroque stylists in their commitment to writing music of the deepest expressiveness.

Bach

Anyone who has any familiarity with classical music can identify in a moment a work of Bach even if he or she has never heard it before because Bach's music is so extraordinarily individualistic. This, however, does not mean that it is in any way predictable, for part of Bach's individuality lay in his very unpredictability. Combining an uncanny imagination and capacious intellect with heroic powers of discipline and an ability to produce music of the greatest genius on demand, Bach was an extremely prolific composer in the entire gamut of contemporary forms (excluding opera), from unaccompanied instrumental pieces to enormous works for vocal soloists, chorus, and orchestra. As a church musician in Leipzig for most of his mature career, Bach's professional duty was to provide new music regularly for Sunday and holiday services. Therefore much of his work consists of religious cantatas (over two hundred surviving), motets, and passions. One might think that the mere requirement to write such music on schedule might have made it routine and lifeless, but Bach, an ardent Protestant who was entirely unaffected by the secularism of the Enlightenment, seems to have written each one of his church pieces with such fervor that the salvation of the world appears to hang on every note. Not content with expressing himself in spiritual music alone, Bach also gloried in creating joyous concertos and suites for orchestra, and succeeded in composing the purest of "pure music"— extraordinarily subtle and complex fugues for keyboard in which the capacity of the human mind for apprehending abstraction appears to approach the celestial.

Johann Sebastian Bach

Handel

Much unlike the provincial, inner-directed Bach, Handel was a man of the world who sought primarily to establish rapport with large, secular audiences. After spending his early creative years in Italy, where he mastered Italian Baroque compositional techniques, Handel established himself in London. There he tried at first to make a living by composing Italian operas, but since the highly florid Baroque operatic style proved too foreign for more staid English tastes, Handel eventually realized that he would never survive unless he turned to some more salable genre. This he found in the oratorio—a variety of music drama intended for performance in concert form. Marking a transition from the spiritual to the secular, Handel's oratorios were usually set to biblical stories but featured very worldly music, replete with ornate instrumentation and frequent flourishes of drums and trumpets. (Some music historians refer to Handel's "big bow-wow" manner.) These highly virile and heroic works succeeded in packing London's halls full of prosperous English people who interpreted the victories of the ancient Hebrews in such oratorios as *Israel in Egypt* and *Judas Maccabaeus* as implicit celebrations of England's own burgeoning national greatness. Of course Handel's music was not for one time but for all, as is demonstrated by the fact that his greatest oratorio, *The Messiah*, is sung widely throughout the English-speaking world every Christmas and its stirring "Hallelujah Chorus" certainly remains the most popular single choral piece in the entire classical repertory.

"The Charming Brute." A contemporary caricature of Handel, engraved by Joseph Groupy, 1754.

Although only a few decades separated the activity of Bach and Handel from that of their greatest eighteenth-century successors, the Austrians Franz Joseph Haydn (1732–1809) and Wolfgang Amadeus Mozart (1756–1781), the two pairs appear worlds apart because their compositional styles are utterly different. This is to say that whereas Bach and Handel were among the last and certainly the greatest composers of Baroque music, Haydn and Mozart were the leading representatives of the succeeding "classical" style. The latter term is slightly confusing because classicism in music had nothing to do with imitating music written in classical antiquity. Rather, the musical style that prevailed in Europe in the second half of the eighteenth century is called classical because it sought to imitate classical principles of order, clarity, and symmetry—in other words, to sound as a Greek temple looked. Moreover, composers of the classical school innovated in creating music that adhered rigorously to certain structural principles. For example, all classical symphonies have four movements, and all open with a first movement in "sonata form," characterized by the successive presentation of themes, development, and recapitulation. Undoubtedly the spread of the ideals of the Enlightenment influenced the development of the classical style, yet there were elements of elegant aristocratic Rococo influence at work as well, for the music of the classical era customarily has a lightness and gaiety about it that is most reminiscent of Rococo pastels.

The classical style in music

Certainly the tastes of the same European aristocrats who commissioned Rococo buildings determined the personal fortunes of most composers in the second half of the eighteenth century because these men no longer had any interest in gaining a livelihood by writing church music as Bach had done, and as yet had no large concert-hall public (Handel's London audience being exceptional). The perils of

Three Contemporary Impressions of Mozart. At the left is the child prodigy, aged seven, seated at a keyboard. The first name given as "Theoph." is not a mistake but is Greek for Mozart's real middle name, Amadeus, meaning "who loves God." The drawing of the mature Mozart in the middle is a highly idealized conception; no doubt the painting on the right comes closest to conveying what the composer really looked like.

Mozart's career

struggling for a living by composing music in the later eighteenth century can be seen best in the sad career of the sublime genius Mozart. As a phenomenal child prodigy, the young Mozart—who began composing at four, started touring Europe as a keyboard virtuoso at six, and wrote his first oratorio at eleven—was the darling of the aristocracy. The Austrian empress Maria Theresa embraced him and the pope made him "Knight of the Golden Spur." But as soon as Mozart reached puberty he was no longer a curiosity and, owing partly to his rather cantankerous personality, proved unable to gain steady employment in the service of any single wealthy aristocrat. In lieu of that, he strove to support himself as a freelance composer and keyboard performer in Vienna, but could make ends meet only with the greatest difficulty. Although he spent every year of his mature life in bountiful productivity, he had to live from hand to mouth until he died at the age of thirty-five from the effects of an undiagnosed wasting disease. Only a handful of people attended the funeral of one of the greatest creative artists of all time, and he was buried in a pauper's grave. Given these appalling circumstances, it is perfectly amazing that Mozart's music is characteristically sunny and serene. Only rarely did he write in a minor key, and even when he did so, he usually paired a melancholy work with an exuberantly joyful one, as if to demonstrate almost defiantly that the trials of his personal life had no effect on his art.

Haydn's career

Haydn's career provides an instructive contrast. Knowing much better how to take care of himself, "Papa Haydn" spent most of his life in the comfortable employment of the Esterházys, an extremely wealthy Austro-Hungarian aristocratic family that maintained its own private orchestra. But this security entailed the indignity of wearing the Esterházy livery, like any common butler. Only toward the end of his life, in 1791, did Haydn, now famous, strike out on his own by traveling to London, where for a year and a half he supported himself handsomely by writing for a paying public, as Handel once did, rather than for private patrons. The fact that London alone was able to provide opportunities for earning a commercial livelihood to two foreigners is clearly indicative of the city's unusual status in the eighteenth century as one of the few localities where there was a mass market for culture. In this regard London represented the wave of the future, for in the nineteenth century serious music would definitely leave the aristocratic salon for the urban concert hall all over Europe. It may also be noted that whereas in deeply aristocratic Austria Haydn was obliged to wear servants' livery, in London he was greeted as a creative genius—one of the earliest composers to be regarded as such even though poets and painters had been celebrated as geniuses long before. Thus Haydn's *Miracle* Symphony, written for performance in a London concert hall, is so called because during one performance a chandelier came crashing down and many would have been killed had it not been for the fact that the entire audience had moved up as close as possible to get a better view of the "genius" Haydn who was conducting.

Haydn's stay in London foreshadowed the future in still another way, for the music he wrote on that occasion was wholly secular, as opposed to the semi-religious oratorios of Handel. Indeed, the music of the entire classical era was predominantly secular, as most music would remain until the present, and this secular writing advanced primarily on three fronts—opera, chamber music, and orchestral composition. In the field of opera, an important innovator of the classical period was Christoph Willibald von Gluck (1714–1787), who emphasized the necessity for dramatic action at a time when Monteverdi's many successors had made opera much too static. But by far the greatest operatic composer of the era was Mozart, whose *Marriage of Figaro, Don Giovanni,* and *The Magic Flute* remain among the most magnificent and best loved operas of all time. As for the realm of chamber music (music written for small instrumental ensembles), the classical era was the most fertile age of chamber music origins, for the genre of the string quartet was invented at the beginning of the period and was soon brought to the fullest fruition in the quartets of both Haydn and Mozart.

Yet probably the most impressive invention of the classical era was the symphony—so to speak the novel of music—for the symphony has since proven to be the most fertile and popular of all classical musical forms. Although not the very first writer of symphonies, Haydn is nonetheless usually termed the "father of the symphony" because in over one hundred works in the symphonic form—and preeminently in his last twelve symphonies, which he composed in London—Haydn formulated the most enduring techniques of symphonic composition and demonstrated to the fullest extent the sym-

Top: *Haydn in Livery.* Bottom: *The Composer in London.* While he worked in the pay of the Esterházy family, Haydn was little more than a high-level servant. In London, on the other hand, he was portrayed as an inspired genius with a faraway look in his eye and a sheet of his own music in his hand.

phony's creative potential. Yet Mozart's three last symphonies (out of that composer's total of forty-one) are generally regarded as greater even than those of Haydn, for the grace, variety, and utter technical perfection of these works are beyond comparison. Mere words cannot do justice to any of the marvelous musical creations of the eighteenth century, yet it may confidently be stated in conclusion that if just one or two of Mozart's musical compositions had survived instead of literally hundreds, they alone would be enough to place the century among the most inspired ages in the entire history of the human creative imagination.

SELECTED READINGS

• *Items so designated are available in paperback editions.*

Baker, Keith, *Condorcet: From Natural Philosophy to Social Mathematics*, Chicago, 1975. Advances the view that Condorcet's greatest significance lies in his attempt to create a quantifiable social science rather than in his theory of historical progress.

Baumer, Franklin L., *Modern European Thought: Continuity and Change in Ideas, 1600–1950*, New York, 1977. An extraordinarily fine intellectual history, organized around major themes rather than the work of individuals.

• Becker, Carl, *The Heavenly City of the Eighteenth-Century Philosophers*, New Haven, 1932. Advances the thesis that the philosophes were just as impractical in their commitment to abstract secular rationalism as the medieval Scholastics were in their theological rationalism. Witty and stimulating but widely regarded as out of date in its views.

Briggs, Robin, *The Scientific Revolution of the Seventeenth Century*, New York, 1969. A very brief but extremely valuable survey, with a documentary appendix.

• Bronowski, J., and B. Mazlish, *The Western Intellectual Tradition*, New York, 1960. A superb, old-fashioned intellectual history which serves as an excellent complement to Baumer for the seventeenth and eighteenth centuries.

Bukofzer, M. F., *Music in the Baroque Era*, New York, 1947.

• Butterfield, H., *The Origins of Modern Science*, London, 1949. As important for its discussion of Newton's breakthrough regarding gravity and the impact of the scientific revolution on the Enlightenment as it is for its discussion of the Renaissance period.

Darnton, Robert, *The Business of Enlightenment: A Publishing History of the Encyclopédie, 1775–1800*, Cambridge, Mass., 1979. A masterful and fascinating blend of intellectual, social, and business history.

• Gay, Peter, *The Enlightenment: An Interpretation;* Vol. 1, *The Rise of Modern Paganism;* Vol. 2, *The Science of Freedom*, New York, 1966–1969. A cross between an interpretation and a survey. Emphasizes the philosophes' sense of identification with the classical world and takes a generally positive view of their accomplishments. Contains extensive annotated bibliographies.

- Hall, Alfred R., *The Scientific Revolution, 1500–1800*, 2nd. ed., Boston, 1956. The best place to look for clear accounts of specific scientific accomplishments.
- Hampson, Norman, *The Enlightenment*, Baltimore, 1968. Probably the best shorter introduction.
- Hazard, Paul, *The European Mind: The Critical Years (1680–1715)*, New Haven, 1953. A basic and indispensable account of the changing climate of opinion which preceded the Enlightenment.
- Hildesheimer, W., *Mozart*, New York, 1982. Widely regarded as the most literate and thought-provoking biography now available of any major musical figure.
- Kimball, F., *The Creation of the Rococo Decorative Style*, Philadelphia, 1943.

  Levey, Michael, *Rococo to Revolution: Major Trends in 18th Century Painting*, New York, 1966.

  Manuel, Frank E., *A Portrait of Isaac Newton*, Cambridge, Mass., 1968. A provocative psychobiography.

  Shackleton, Robert, *Montesquieu: A Critical Biography*, London, 1961. The standard work on the man and his thought.
- Shryock, Richard H., *The Development of Modern Medicine: An Interpretation of the Social and Scientific Factors Involved*, London, 1948. Fascinating reading and still the basic work on the subject.
- Summerson, John, *Architecture in Britain, 1530–1830*, 6th ed., Baltimore, 1977. The best introduction to Wren and English Palladianism.
- Wade, Ira O., *The Intellectual Development of Voltaire*, Princeton, 1969. A magnificent synthesis which stresses how Voltaire's "English experience" provided the cornerstone for all his subsequent thought.
- Waterhouse, Ellis K., *Painting in Britain, 1530–1790*, 4th ed., Baltimore, 1979. Very good on eighteenth-century developments.
- Watt, Ian, *The Rise of the Novel*, London, 1957. The basic work on the innovative qualities of the novel in eighteenth-century England.
- Westfall, R. S., *Never at Rest: A Biography of Isaac Newton*, New York, 1980. Illuminates all aspects of Newton's scientific accomplishment.

SOURCE MATERIALS

- Beccaria, Cesare, *An Essay on Crimes and Punishments, with a Commentary by M. de Voltaire*, Stanford, 1953. A reprint of the original English translation of 1767.
- Gibbon, Edward, *The Portable Gibbon: The Decline and Fall of the Roman Empire*, ed. D. A. Saunders, New York, 1952. A convenient abridgment.
- Voltaire, *The Portable Voltaire*, ed. Ben Ray Redman, New York, 1949. An excellent anthology including the complete *Candide*.

Part Five

THE FRENCH AND INDUSTRIAL REVOLUTIONS AND THEIR CONSEQUENCES

No two events more profoundly altered the shape of Western civilization than the French and Industrial Revolutions. "Modern" history begins with their occurrence. The major happenings of the nineteenth and early twentieth centuries—the spread of middle-class liberalism and economic success; the decline of the old, landed aristocracies; the growth of class consciousness among urban workers—all had their roots in these two revolutions.

The French and Industrial Revolutions took place at about the same time and affected many of the same people—though in different ways and to varying degrees. Together they resulted in the overthrow of absolutism, mercantilism, and the last vestiges of manorialism. Together they produced the theory and practice of economic individualism and political liberalism. And together they ensured the growth of class consciousness, and the culmination of those tensions between the middle and working classes that imparted new vitality to European history after 1800.

Each revolution, of course, produced results peculiarly its own. The French Revolution encouraged the growth of nationalism and its unattractive step-child, authoritarianism. The Industrial Revolution compelled the design of a new, urban social order. Yet despite their unique contributions, the two revolutions must be studied together and understood as the joint progenitors of Western history in the nineteenth and early twentieth centuries.

These great revolutions did not immediately affect the peoples of Asia, and not until the process of nation-building was completed in Europe did the Europeans subject the entire continent of Africa to their domination. But Central and South America became a theater for a series of revolutions, begun to overthrow Spanish and Portuguese colonial rule and extending through an arduous period of nation-building. Latin American political revolutions drew inspiration both from the French and especially from the North American examples. But in contrast to western Europe and the United States, the Latin American countries lacked a substantial middle class, largely because they were yet untouched by the Industrial Revolution. While nationalism flourished, liberalism and democracy languished. Consequently, the new Latin American states, rent by deep social cleavages, remained relatively unstable.

The French and Industrial Revolutions and Their Consequences

POLITICS	SCIENCE & INDUSTRY	
		1770
	James Watt's steam engine, 1763	
	Spinning jenny patented, 1770	
American War of Independence, 1775–1783		
	Beginning of factory system, 1780s	
French Revolution begins, 1789	Lavoisier discovers the indestructibility of matter, 1789	
Revolution in Haiti, 1791–1803		
France declared a republic, 1792		
Declaration of Pillnitz, 1792		
Reign of Terror, 1793–1794	Cotton gin invented, 1793	
	Edward Jenner develops smallpox vaccine, 1796	
Treaty of Campo Formio, 1797		
Napoleon, first consul of France, 1799		
Treaty of Lunéville, 1801		1800
Napoleon declared first consul for life, 1802		
Napoleon crowns himself emperor of the French, 1804		
Continental System established, 1806		
Reforms of Hardenberg and Stein, Prussia, 1808		
Latin American revolutions, 1808–1826		
Napoleon's invasion of Russia, 1812		
Congress of Vienna, 1814–1815		
Battle of Waterloo, 1815		
"Peterloo Massacre," England, 1819		
Congress of Verona, 1822	Louis Pasteur, 1822–1895	
Monroe Doctrine, 1823		
"Decembrist" Revolt, Russia, 1825	First railway, England, 1825	1825
Greek Independence, 1829		
Revolution in France, 1830		
"Young Italy," 1831		
Reform Bill of 1832, England		
Slavery abolished, British colonies, 1833		
Poor Law reform, England, 1834		
Chartist movement, England, 1838–1848		
Reign of Pedro II, Brazil, 1840–1889		
Mexican-American War, 1846–1848		
Corn Laws repealed, England, 1846		
Revolutions in Europe, 1848		
Karl Marx, *Communist Manifesto*, 1848		
Second Republic, France, 1848		
Frankfurt Assembly, Germany, 1848–1849		
Reign of Louis Napoleon, 1851–1870	Great Exhibition, London, 1851	
	Invention of the sewing machine, 1850s	

The French and Industrial Revolutions and Their Consequences (continued)

	ECONOMICS & SOCIETY	ARTS & LETTERS
1770	Jean-Jacques Rousseau, *The Social Contract*, 1762	
		Ludwig van Beethoven, 1770–1827
	Adam Smith, *Wealth of Nations*, 1776	
		Immanuel Kant, *Critique of Pure Reason*, 1781
	Jeremy Bentham, *The Principles of Morals and Legislation*, 1789	
	Utilitarianism, 1790–1870	Johann von Goethe, *Faust*, 1790–1808
	Tom Paine, *The Rights of Man*, 1791–1792	Romantic movement, 1790–1850
	Thomas Malthus, *An Essay on the Principle of Population*, 1798	William Wordsworth, *Lyrical Ballads*, 1798
1800		
		G. W. Hegel, *Phenomenology of the Spirit*, 1807
		J. G. Fichte, *Addresses to the German Nation*, 1808
	Louis Blanc, 1811–1882	
		Francisco Goya, *The Executions of the Third of May*, 1814
	Founding of Prussian Zollverein, 1818	
1825		
		Honoré de Balzac, *The Human Comedy*, 1829–1841
		Eugène Delacroix, *Liberty Leading the People*, 1830
		Realism in literature and art, 1840–1870
	Friedrich Engels, *The Condition of the Working Class*, 1844	
	John Stuart Mill, *Principles of Political Economy*, 1848	Pre-Raphaelite Brotherhood formed, 1848

POLITICS	SCIENCE & INDUSTRY

Crimean War, 1854–1856
Mexico under Emperor Maximilian, 1863–1867

Invention of the Bessemer process, 1856

Unification of Italy, 1858–1866

Charles Darwin, *Origin of Species,* 1859

Civil War, United States, 1861–1865
Otto von Bismarck's accession to power, 1862
First International, 1864

Parliamentary Reform Bill, England, 1867

Suez Canal opened, 1869
Union Pacific railroad, United States, 1869

Franco-Prussian War, 1870
War of the Pacific, 1879–1883

ECONOMICS & SOCIETY	ARTS & LETTERS
	Giuseppe Verdi, *Il Trovatore,* 1853
	Richard Wagner, *The Ring of the Nibelung,* 1854–1874
	Charles Dickens, *Hard Times,* 1854
	Gustave Flaubert, *Madame Bovary,* 1857
Emancipation of the serfs, Russia, 1861	
	Leo Tolstoy, *War and Peace,* 1866–1869
Karl Marx, *Capital,* 1867	Pope Pius IX, *Syllabus of Errors,* 1869
Emancipation of the slaves, Brazil, 1871–1888	

1850

Chapter 25

THE FRENCH REVOLUTION

Men are born, and always continue, free and equal in respect of their
rights. Civil distinctions, therefore, can be founded only on public utility.
The nation is essentially the source of all sovereignty; nor can any individual, or any body of men, be entitled to any authority which is not
expressly derived from it.

—*The Declaration of the Rights of Man and of the Citizen,* 1789

In 1789, one European out of every five lived in France. And
most Europeans, French or not, who thought beyond the boundaries of their own immediate concerns, perceived of France as
the center of European civilization. It followed, therefore, that a revolution in France would immediately command the attention of Europe,
and would from the first assume far more than mere national significance. Yet the French Revolution attracted and disturbed men and
women for reasons other than the fact that it was French. Both its
philosophical ideals and its political realities mirrored attitudes, concerns, and conflicts that had occupied the minds of Europeans for
several decades. When the revolutionaries pronounced in favor of
liberty, they spoke not only with the voice of the eighteenth-century
philosophes, but with those of the English aristocracy in 1688 and
the American revolutionaries of 1776. Absolutism was the bane of
continental noblemen, jealous to preserve their ancient freedoms from
monarchical inroads. It was also increasingly the bane of continental
entrepreneurs who had welcomed mercantilist interference on their
behalf in the past, but now found themselves chafing under absolutist
constraints to their economic independence. Across Europe, monarch,
nobility, and middle class confronted each other in uneasy hostilities
that varied in intensity, but reflected common mistrust and uncertainty.

The era of revolution

1. THE COMING OF THE REVOLUTION

Why a revolution?

Historians continue to ask why revolution broke out in France in 1789. They have provided a number of answers to a question that will probably never be wholly resolved. Those men and women involved in the struggle believed they were striking a blow against tyranny. Yet why did the government of Louis XVI appear to them to be so much more tyrannous than that of Louis XIV had seemed to their great-grandfathers?

(1) The persistence of privilege

There appear to have been several major factors that contributed to the breakdown that produced revolution. The first was the persistence of privilege, which we have seen as a continuously vexing problem for eighteenth-century absolutist monarchs. The various regions and orders continued to press for what they called their "liberties"— that is, their right to conduct their affairs without interference from the state. During the eighteenth century the efficacy of the intendant system declined in direct proportion to the crown's failure to keep the nobility isolated and impotent. By the 1780s intendants were themselves often noblemen, prepared to sacrifice state interests to those of their own privileged station.

Resurgence of the parlements

As we have noted, the *parlements,* France's powerful courts of record, had reasserted their privileged independence during the early years of the reign of Louis XV. Throughout the century they had grown increasingly insistent upon what they began to call their "constitutional" rights—in reality, their traditional habit of opposing any legislation that did not serve the interests of their aristocratic members. When Louis XVI had pressed for new taxes to be levied on the nobility as well as the rest of the community after the expensive Seven Years' War, the *parlements* successfully blocked the proposal, insisting upon their right to exemption from major national taxes. In the mid-1770s this episode was reenacted when Anne Robert Jacques Turgot (1727–1781), Louis XVI's principal financial minister, attempted to combat the government's indebtedness through a series of reforms that included the curtailing of court expenses, the abolition of the *corvée* (forced labor by the peasants on the royal roads) in favor of a small tax on landowners, and the abolition of certain guild restrictions in order to stimulate manufacturing. These innovations were steadfastly and successfully opposed by the Paris *parlement,* whose members claimed that Turgot was trampling upon ancient prerogatives and privileges— as indeed he was.

(2) Antagonisms among the social orders: the Church

This continued insistence on privilege was a symptom of the second major factor contributing to the outbreak of revolution: growing antagonism within and between the various social orders that composed French society. There was tension within the Roman Catholic church, the so-called first estate of the realm. Its rulers—bishops, archbishops, and cardinals—were in the main recruited from the aristocracy. They enjoyed large incomes, derived from property that had been willed to the Church over the centuries and that the Church successfully continued to claim was exempt from taxation by the state. In addition, the Church collected a tax—the tithe—on all land under cultivation, an average of between one-tenth and one-fifteenth of the annual harvest. Income from both property and tithe was inequitably distributed among the ranks of the clergy. The princes of the Church, along with the leading monastic orders, took the lion's shares. Parish priests received very little. This imbalance in the distribution of revenues was resented not only by the priests, but by peasant tithepayers, who hated to see their taxes spent to support a distant and haughty ecclesiastical hierarchy, rather than their own, often very deserving, local clergy.

The ranks of the aristocracy, France's second estate, were also divided. Many determined reformers were themselves noblemen, but they were nobles of the robe, men who had, often by purchase, *nobles of the robe* acquired administrative or judicial office (hence the "robe") which conferred a title of nobility, as well as the opportunity to amass a substantial fortune in land and other property. Included in this group were talented men such as the philosopher the baron de Montesquieu, the lawyer the comte de Mirabeau, and the statesman the marquis de Lafayette, who had represented France in America at the time of the Revolutionary War. Among these nobles of the robe were men who would play prominent roles in the French Revolution.

In contrast to this group stood the nobles of the sword—or *noblesse de race,* as the group enjoyed calling itself—whose titles extended back to the Middle Ages. These aristocrats regarded the nobles of the robe *nobles of the sword* as upstarts. In general, they lived at the royal court at Versailles, where they enjoyed making political mischief, leaving the management of their estates to bailiffs. In 1781, they pressed successfully for a law that restricted the sale of military commissions to men whose aristocratic lineage extended back at least four generations. If they could not prevent the general debasing of their order, they reasoned, they could at least ensure that the army remained their preserve. The tensions between the nobles of the robe and the sword kept the aristocracy fragmented and at odds with itself, and hence unable to form together into anything more than a negative and potentially destructive force.

The disdain of the *noblesse de race* for the nobility of the robe was mild compared with the contempt in which haughty aristocrats held the urban middle orders. This large group was by no means homo- *the third estate* geneous. At the top stood government officials, talented professionals, and large-scale financiers and merchants. Lesser notables were to be found throughout the ranks of the third estate. For every major entrepreneur there were scores of small-scale masters, lodged in their workshops yet removed from the artisans and laborers below them by virtue of their ownership of those shops.

Movement from the upper ranks of the third estate into the nobility

A Gentleman of the Third Estate with His Family.
A contemporary engraving which illustrates the
respectability the third estate wished to see
translated into political power.

Social mobility

had been possible in the past for wealthy, ambitious members of the
middle orders. The appointment or purchase of position—the route
favored by nobles of the robe—or the marriage of a wealthy financier's
daughter to the son of an impoverished aristocrat were the most common means of upward mobility. Yet to increasing numbers of the
urban bourgeoisie it appeared by about 1780 that the nobility of the
sword was intent upon closing off the avenue of social advancement.
Their discontent would not have been so great had their birth and
position within the third estate not excluded them from participation
in the political life of the nation. No matter how much money a
merchant, manufacturer, banker, or lawyer might acquire, he was
still excluded from political privileges. He had almost no influence
at the court; he could not hold high political office; and except in
the choice of a few petty local officers, he could not even vote. As
the middle orders achieved affluence and greater self-esteem, their
members were bound to resent such discrimination.

Not a bourgeois revolution

Powerful as this resentment was, however, it was not, as some
historians have insisted, the primary motivating force behind revolution. They have argued that a self-consciously articulate entrepreneurial
middle class, driven by a desire to achieve political power commensurate with its already established economic supremacy, made the revolution. This position overlooks the fact that though the social membrane
separating nobility from upper bourgeoisie was hardening, it was by
no means impermeable. The barrier between an aristocrat and a busi-

nessman was not as great as that between a businessman and an artisan or peasant. This theory also ignores the role played in the first phase of the revolution by noblemen such as Lafayette, and the fact that middle-class revolutionaries were far more likely to be lawyers than businessmen. Most important, such an explanation fails to account for the bitter hatred felt by rural peasants for their overlords—monarchical, aristocratic, and clerical.

We have seen how absolutist government imposed increasingly heavy financial burdens on the peasantry. Nowhere was this truer than in late-eighteenth-century France. Those peasants who owned property, as well as those who worked the land as tenant-farmers or laborers, were bound by numerous obligations: a tithe and levy on farm produce owed to the Church; fees, called *banalités,* for the use of a landlord's facilities—a mill, a wine press; fees, as well, to the nobility when land changed hands. In addition, peasants were forced to pay a disproportionate share of both direct and indirect taxes— the most onerous of which was the *gabelle* or salt tax—levied by the government. (For some time the production of salt had been a state monopoly; every individual was required to buy at least seven pounds a year from the government works. The result was a commodity whose cost was often as much as fifty or sixty times its actual value.) Further grievances stemmed from the requirement that peasants work to maintain public roads (the *corvée*) and from the hunting privileges accorded the aristocracy, which for centuries had regarded the right

Peasant obligations

Pre-Revolutionary Propaganda, 1788–1789. These prints support the popular view that the third estate was carrying the burden of national taxation on its shoulders while the privileged orders enjoyed the fruits of the peasant's labors, tax-free.

The effects of enclosure

to indulge in the diversions of the chase, to the exclusion of all others, as a distinctive badge of their order.

The vestiges of manorial custom were not the only sources of peasant discontent. During the eighteenth century they also came under pressure as a result of the increasingly frequent enclosure of what had been common land. Fields allowed to lie fallow, together with those tilled only infrequently, were considered "common," land on which all persons might graze their livestock. These common lands, particularly extensive in the west of France, were an important resource for the peasants. In addition to the right to pasturage, they enjoyed that of gathering wood and of gleaning cultivated fields following a harvest. Now the king's economic advisors declared these collective rights to be obstacles in the path of agricultural improvement. Anxious to increase their income by increasing the efficiency of their estates, the landlords attempted to enclose these common lands, thereby depriving the peasants of the open pasturage they had come to depend on.

(3) The role of ideas

A third important cause of revolution was intellectual. No event so all-encompassing occurs in an intellectual vacuum. Although ideas may not have "caused" the revolution, they played a critical role in giving shape and substance to the discontent experienced by so many, particularly among the literate middle orders. The political theories of Locke, Voltaire, Montesquieu, and Condorcet appealed to both discontented nobility and bourgeoisie: Voltaire, because of his general execration of the privileged institutions of church and absolute monarchy; Condorcet because of his belief in progress; Locke and Montesquieu because of their defense of private property and limited sovereignty. Montesquieu's ideas were especially congenial to aristocrats, who read his doctrine of checks and balances as a defense of their ancient privileges—now elevated to the status of "liberties." The *parlements* and provincial Estates, or governing assemblies, were the constituted bodies that would provide a check to royal power.

The physiocrats

The bourgeoisie also welcomed theoretical support from Enlightenment thinkers in its campaign for political recognition and against monarchical absolutism. That campaign was fueled as well by another group of libertarian thinkers, economic theoreticians called physiocrats in France, whose most influential member was Turgot, a contributor to the *Encyclopedia* as well as an experienced fiscal administrator, intendant, and royal minister. Their proposals were grounded in the ideas of the Enlightenment, particularly the notion of a universe governed by mechanistic laws. They argued that production and distribution of wealth were subject to laws as predictable and ultimately salutary as the laws of physics. Those laws would function beneficially, however, only if agriculture and trade were freed from mercantilist regulations. They urged the government to lift its controls on the price of grain, for example, which had been imposed to keep the cost of bread low, but which had not accomplished that goal. By allowing the laws of supply and demand to determine the market price, the government would encourage farmers to grow a crop that was more profitable to them, and an increase in supply would thus eventually reduce the cost to consumers.

The theories of one further thinker, Jean-Jacques Rousseau (1712–1778), played an important part in shaping the ideas and attitudes of French revolutionaries. The most significant of his writings on politics were *Discourse on the Origin of Inequality* (1753) and *Social Contract* (1762), the latter published in many editions before the revolution. Rousseau agreed with Locke that society had its origins in a state of nature. In contrast with Locke, however, he regarded the state of nature as a virtual paradise. Eventually, however, evils had arisen there, due primarily to quarrels over property rights which in turn produced social and economic inequality. To ensure general security, therefore, a civil society was established in which, according to Rousseau, individuals surrendered their rights to the community. This change was accomplished by means of a social contract, in which each person agreed to submit to the will of the majority. In the state that then emerged—characterized by small-scale institutions in Rousseau's vision—citizens were leveled by their contract into democratic equality.

Jean-Jacques Rousseau

Rousseau developed an altogether different conception of sovereignty from that of other Enlightenment political theorists. Whereas Locke and his followers had argued that only a portion of sovereign power is surrendered to the state, the rest being retained by the people themselves, Rousseau contended that sovereignty is indivisible, and that all of it became vested in the community when civil society was formed. He insisted further that individuals in becoming a party to the social contract gave up their rights and agreed to submit absolutely to the general will. The sovereign power of the state was thus subject to no theoretical limitations.

Rousseau vs. the Enlightenment

Rousseau's appeal, though great, was not so much to those men whose thoughts and actions dominated the first stage of the revolution. Although they might have agreed with Rousseau's opposition to hereditary privilege, they were, as convinced individualists, unmoved by arguments in favor of surrender to a general will. Rousseau's influence upon the revolution was greater during its second stage, when a more democratic and radical coterie emerged to lead events, first in the direction of democracy and then toward a new kind of "democratic absolutism" that accorded with Rousseau's notions of the sovereign state.

Rousseau's influence

A fourth important factor making for revolution was the continuing and deepening financial crisis of the 1770s and 1780s, brought on by years of administrative improvidence and ineptitude. This crisis was compounded by a general price rise during much of the eighteenth century, which permitted the French economy to expand by providing capital for investment, but also worked hardship on the peasantry and urban artisans and laborers, who found their purchasing power considerably reduced. Their plight deteriorated further at the end of

(4) The financial crisis

the 1780s when poor harvests encouraged landlords to extract even larger sums from their dependents in order to compensate for a sharp decline in profits, and when the high price of bread generated desperation among the urban poor. In 1788 families found themselves spending more than 50 percent of their income on bread, which comprised the bulk of their diet; the following year the figure rose to as much as 80 percent. Poor harvests contributed to a marked reduction in demand for manufactured goods; families had little money to spend for anything other than food. Peasants could no longer rely on the system of domestic industry to help them make ends meet, since they were receiving so few orders for the textiles and other articles they were accustomed to making at home. Many left the countryside for the cities, hoping to find work there, only to discover that unemployment was far worse than in rural areas. Evidence indicates that between 1787 and 1789 the unemployment rate in many parts of urban France was as high as 50 percent. The financial despair produced by this unemployment fueled resentment and turned peasants and urban workers into potential revolutionaries.

Administrative inefficiency: tax collection and dispersal

The country's financial position was further weakened by an inefficient system of tax collection and disbursal. Not only was taxation tied to differing social status, it varied as well from region to region—some areas, for example, subject to a much higher *gabelle* than others. The myriad special circumstances and exemptions that prevailed made the task of collectors all the more difficult. Those collectors were in many cases so-called tax farmers, members of a syndicate that loaned the government money in return for the right to collect taxes and to keep for itself the difference between the amounts it took in and the amounts it loaned. The system of disbursal was at least as inefficient as was revenue collection. Instead of one central agency there were several hundred private accountants, a fact which made it impossible for the government to keep accurate track of its assets and liabilities. The financial system all but broke down completely under the increased expenses brought on by French participation in the American war. The cost of servicing the national debt of four million livres in the 1780s consumed 50 percent of the nation's budget. By 1788 the chaotic financial situation, together with severe social tensions and an inept monarch, had brought absolutist France to the edge of political disaster.

(5) The character of Louis XVI

Finally, in attempting to explain the revolution, one must acknowledge the character of the monarch, Louis XVI. Faced with serious challenges to centralized power from resurgent noble elites as well as popularly based political movements in the eighteenth century, only the ablest absolutist ruler, possessing in equal measure the talents of administrative ability and personal determination and vision, could hope to rule successfully. Louis XVI possessed neither of these talents. He came to the throne in 1774 at the age of twenty, a well-intentioned but dull-witted and ineffectual monarch, far more devoted to his hobbies—hunting and lock-making—than to the business of absolutist kingship. On July 14, 1789, when mobs stormed the Bastille, he wrote in his diary "Nothing." Fortunate at the outset of his reign in that he had as his principal financial minister the extremely able Turgot, Louis lost that advantage two years after his accession when he dismissed Turgot rather than press ahead with Turgot's suggested economic reforms, which were strongly opposed by the nobility. From that time, national policy traced an unstable course, uncontrolled by the king and influenced by self-interested courtiers. As responsible as any for the king's indecisive misrule was the queen, Marie Antoinette, daughter of Austria's monarch Maria Theresa. Vain and strong-willed, fond of court entertainments and palace intrigue, she inspired the dedicated hatred of reformers, intellectuals, and the common people. Her reputation was completely dashed when it became apparent that she would even bestow her favors upon a cardinal of the church for the price of a diamond necklace. Both became the butt of jokes at court.

Louis XVI

2. THE DESTRUCTION OF THE ANCIEN RÉGIME

The French revolution thus resulted from the various factors outlined above: the continuing existence of privilege; widespread and debilitating social tensions; the spread of ideas subversive to the theory and practice of absolutism; a deepening financial crisis; and the ineptitude of Louis XVI. But the specific events of the revolution occurred in 1789 because of the inability of the king and his government to resolve the country's immediate financial crisis. When the king's principal ministers, Charles de Calonne and Loménie de Brienne, attempted in 1787 and 1788 to institute a series of financial reforms in order to stave off bankruptcy, they encountered not just opposition but entrenched aristocratic determination to extract further governmental concessions from the monarch. To meet the mounting deficit, the ministers proposed new taxes, notably a stamp duty and a direct tax on the annual produce of the soil. The king summoned an assembly of notables from among the aristocracy, in the hope of persuading the nobles to agree to his demands. Far from acquiescing, however, the nobles insisted that to institute a general tax such as the stamp duty the king would first have to call together the Estates General, representative of the three estates of the realm.

The crisis of 1789

The summoning of this body, which had not met for over a century and a half, seemed to many the only solution to France's deepening problems. No doubt most of those aristocrats who argued for its calling did so from short-sighted and selfish motives. Yet the politically conscious population as a whole agreed with the idea in an unreasonable and desperate hope that this unusual event might, because of its very strangeness, work a miracle and save the country from ruin.

FRANCE UNDER THE ANCIEN RÉGIME

The Estates General

During the period before the rise of monarchical absolutism, when the Estates General was convened more or less regularly, the representatives of each estate had met and voted as a body. Generally this meant that the first and second estates combined against the third. By the late eighteenth century the third estate had attained such importance that it was not willing to tolerate such an arrangement. Consequently its leaders demanded that the three orders should sit together and vote as individuals. More important, it insisted that the representatives of the third estate should be double the number of the first and second. Leaving this issue unresolved, Louis XVI, in the summer of 1788, yielded to popular clamor and summoned the Estates General to meet in May of the following year.

In the ensuing months the question of "doubling the third" was fiercely debated. After having opposed the reform initially, in December 1788 the king agreed to it. His unwillingness to take a strong stand from the first, and his continuing vacillation on the matter of voting procedures, cost him support he might otherwise have obtained from the bourgeoisie. Shortly after the opening of the Estates General at Versailles in May 1789, the representatives of the third estate, angered by the king's attitude, took the revolutionary step of leaving the body and declaring themselves the National Assembly. "What is the third estate?" asked the radical clergyman Abbé Emmanuel Sieyès, one of the most articulate spokesmen for a new order, in his famous pamphlet of January 1789. The answer he gave then—"everything"—was the answer the third estate itself gave when it constituted itself the National Assembly of France. Sieyès, unlike most other revolutionaries at this point, derived his argument from Rousseau, and claimed that the third estate was the nation and that as the nation it was its own sovereign. Now the middle-class lawyers and businessmen of the third estate acted on that claim. Locked out of their meeting hall on June 20, the commoners and a handful of sympathetic nobles and clergymen moved to a nearby indoor tennis court.

Here, under the leadership of the volatile, maverick aristocrat Honoré Riqueti, comte de Mirabeau, and Sieyès, they bound themselves by a solemn oath not to separate until they had drafted a constitution for France. This Oath of the Tennis Court, on June 20, 1789, was the real beginning of the French Revolution. By claiming the authority to remake the government in the name of the people, the Estates General

The National Assembly

Abbé Emmanuel Sieyès

The Tennis Court Oath by David. In the hall where royalty played a game known as *jeu de paume* (similar to tennis) leaders of the revolution swore to draft a constitution. In the center of this painting, with his arm extended, is Jean Bailly, president of the National Assembly. Seated at the table below him is Abbé Sieyès. Somewhat to the right of Sieyès, with both hands on his chest, is Robespierre. Mirabeau, with a hat in his left hand and wearing a black coat, stands somewhat farther to the right.

was not merely protesting against the rule of Louis XVI but asserting its right to act as the highest sovereign power in the nation. On June 27 the king virtually conceded this right by ordering the remaining delegates of the privileged classes to meet with the third estate as members of the National Assembly. The advocates of drastic change were inspired not only by the rhetoric of their leaders, but by the political debates which had occurred during the course of the preceding year. In preparation for the meeting of the Estates, the king had instructed local electoral assemblies to draw up *cahiers de doléances*—lists of grievances. Delegates took these instructions seriously. And the grievances they aired—financial chaos; aristocratic and clerical privileges; denial of political power to the third estate—became the basis for the radical reforms of the assembly in its initial weeks.

The course of the French Revolution was marked by three stages, the first of which extended from June 1789 to August 1792. During most of this period the destiny of France was in the hands of the National Assembly. In the main, this stage was moderate, its actions dominated by the leadership of liberal nobles and equally liberal men of the third estate. Yet three events in the summer and fall of 1789 furnished evidence that the revolution was to penetrate to the very heart of French society, ultimately touching both the urban populace and the rural peasants.

News of the events of late spring 1789 had spread quickly across France. From the very onset of debates on the nature of the political crisis, public attention was high. It was roused not merely by interest in matters of political reform, however, but also by the economic crisis that, as we have seen, brought the price of bread to astronomical heights. Belief was widespread that the aristocracy and king were together conspiring to punish an upstart third estate by encouraging scarcity and high prices. Rumors circulated in Paris during the latter days of June 1789 that the king was about to stage a reactionary coup d'état. The electors of Paris (those who had voted in the third estate) feared not only a counterrevolution but the actions of the Paris poor, who had been parading through the streets and threatening violence. These electors were workshop masters, craftspeople, shopkeepers, petty tradespeople, the men and women who would soon come to be called sans-culottes—so called because the men did not wear upper-class breeches. They formed a provisional municipal government and organized a militia of volunteers to maintain order. Determined to obtain arms, they made their way on July 14 to the Bastille, an ancient fortress where guns and ammunition were stored. Built in the Middle Ages, the Bastille had served as a prison for many years, but was no longer much used. However, it symbolized hated royal authority. When crowds demanded arms from its governor, he at first procrastinated and then, fearing a frontal assault, opened fire, killing ninety-eight of the attackers. The crowd took revenge, capturing the fortress (which contained only seven prisoners—five common criminals and

The Fall of the Bastille, July 14, 1789. A contemporary engraving celebrating the heroic actions of the citizenry of Paris.

two lunatics) and decapitating the governor. At the same time the sans-culottes were establishing a revolutionary municipal government in Paris, similar groups assumed control in other cities across France. This series of events—dramatized by the fall of the Bastille—was the first to demonstrate the commitment of the common people to revolutionary change.

The second popular revolt occurred in the countryside, where the peasants were suffering the direct effects of economic privation. They too feared a monarchical and aristocratic counterrevolution. Eager for news from Versailles, their anticipation turned to fear when they began to understand that the revolution might not address itself to their problems. Frightened and uncertain, peasants in many areas of France panicked in July and August, setting fire to manor houses and the records they contained, destroying monasteries and the residences of bishops, and murdering some of the nobles who offered resistance.

The "Great Fear"

The third instance of popular uprising, in October 1789, was also brought on by economic crisis. This time women, angered by the price of bread and fired by rumors of the king's continuing unwillingness to cooperate with the assembly, marched to Versailles on October 5 and demanded to be heard. Not satisfied with its reception by the assembly, the crowd broke through the gates to the palace, calling for the king to return to Paris. On the afternoon of the following day the king yielded. The National Guard, sympathetic to the agitators, led the crowd back to Paris, the procession headed by a soldier holding aloft a loaf of bread on his bayonet.

The "October Days"

In each of the three cases, these popular uprisings produced a decided effect on the course of political events as they were unfolding at Ver-

Achievements of the first stage: (1) the destruction of privilege

sailles. The storming of the Bastille helped persuade the king and nobles to treat the National Assembly as the legislative body of the nation. The "Great Fear" inspired an equally great consternation among the debaters in the assembly. On August 4, with one sweep, the remnants of manorialism were largely obliterated. Ecclesiastical tithes and the *corvée* were formally abolished. The hunting privileges of the nobles were ended. Exemption from taxation and monopolies of all kinds were eliminated as contrary to natural equality. While the nobles did not surrender all of their rights, the ultimate effect of these reforms of the "August Days" was to annihilate distinctions of rank and class and to make all French citizens of an equal status in the eyes of the law.

(2) the Declaration of the Rights of Man

Following the destruction of privilege the assembly turned its attention to preparing a charter of liberties. The result was the Declaration of the Rights of Man and of the Citizen, issued in September 1789. Property was declared to be a natural right as well as liberty, security, and "resistance to oppression." Freedom of speech, religious toleration, and liberty of the press were declared inviolable. All citizens were guaranteed equality of treatment in the courts. No one was to be imprisoned or otherwise punished except in accordance with due process of law. Sovereignty was affirmed to reside in the people, and officers of the government were made subject to deposition if they abused the powers conferred upon them.

(3) secularization of the Church

The king's return to Paris during the October Days confirmed the reforms already underway and guaranteed further liberalization along lines decreed by the middle-class majority in the assembly. In November 1789, the National Assembly resolved to confiscate the lands of the Church and to use them as collateral for the issue of *assignats,* or paper money, which, it was hoped, would resolve the country's inflationary economic crisis. In July of the following year the Civil Constitution of the Clergy was enacted, providing that all bishops and priests should be elected by the people and should be subject to the au-

Depart des Heroines de Paris pour Versailles le 5 Octobre 1789.

The Departure of the Women of Paris for Versailles, October 1789. Note that the contemporary caption refers to the "heroines of Paris." An early example of revolutionary propaganda.

thority of the state. Their salaries were to be paid out of the public treasury, and they were required to swear allegiance to the new legislation. The secularization of the Church also involved a partial separation from Rome. The aim of the assembly was to make the Catholic Church of France a truly national institution with no more than a nominal subjection to the papacy.

An Assignat

Response to this clerical revolution was mixed. Because the Church had enjoyed a privileged position during the Old Regime, it had earned itself the hatred of many who resented its tolerance of clerical abuses and its exploitation of vast monastic land holdings. Bishops and other members of the higher clergy had often held several ecclesiastical appointments at the same time, had paid scant attention to their duties, and had led far from spiritual lives. Exempt from taxes itself, the Church had not hesitated to extract all it could from the peasantry. And its control of the country's educational system made it a target for those men and women who, influenced by Englightenment thinkers like Voltaire, had turned against the doctrines of Roman Catholicism. On the other hand, the practice of centuries had made the parish church and priest into institutions of great local importance. Peasants found it very difficult to shed habits of deference and respect overnight. The dramatic changes embodied in the Civil Constitution of the Clergy thus encountered considerable resistance in some parts of rural France, and eventually helped to strengthen the forces of counterrevolution.

Response to secularization

Not until 1791 did the National Assembly manage to complete its primary task of drafting a new constitution for the nation. The constitution as it finally emerged gave eloquent testimony to the dominant position now held by the wealthier elements of the third estate. The government was converted into a limited monarchy, with the supreme power virtually a monopoly of the well-to-do. Although all citizens possessed the same civil rights, the vote was allowed only to those who paid a certain amount in taxes. About half the adult males in France made up this latter category of "active" citizen. Yet even their political power was curtailed, for they were to vote for electors, whose property ownership qualified them for that position. Those electors, in turn, chose department officials and delegates to the National—or, as it was henceforth to be called, Legislative—Assembly. The king was deprived of the control he had formerly exercised over the army and local governments. His ministers were forbidden to sit in the assembly, and he was shorn of all powers over the legislative process except a suspensive veto, which in fact could be overridden by the issuance of proclamations.

(4) constitution of 1791

The economic and governmental changes the National Assembly adopted were as much a reflection of the power of rich commoners as were its constitutional reforms. To raise money, it sold off Church lands, but in such large blocks that peasants seldom benefited by the sales as they had expected to. In opposition to the interests of the peasantry, the assembly proceeded with the enclosure of common

(5) economic and governmental changes

lands in order to facilitate the development of capitalist agriculture. To encourage the growth of unfettered economic enterprise, guilds and trade unions were abolished. To rid the country of authoritarian centralization and of aristocratic domination, local governments were completely restructured. France was divided into eighty-three equal departments. All towns henceforth enjoyed the same form of municipal organization. All local officials were locally elected. This reorganization and decentralization expressed a belief in the necessity of individual liberty and freedom from ancient privilege. As such these measures proclaimed, as did all the work of the assembly, that the "winners" of this first stage of the revolution were the men and women of the upper middle class.

3. A NEW STAGE: RADICAL REVOLUTION

The second stage: (1) disappointment of the common people

Their triumph did not go unchallenged, however. In the summer of 1792, the revolution entered a second stage, which saw the downfall of moderate middle-class leaders and their replacement by radical republicans claiming to rule on behalf of the common people. Three major reasons accounted for this abrupt and drastic alteration in the course of events. First, the politically literate lower classes grew disillusioned as they perceived that the revolution was not benefiting them. The uncontrolled free-enterprise economy of the government resulted in constantly fluctuating and generally rising prices. These increases particularly exasperated those elements of the Parisian population that had agitated for change in preceding years. Urban rioters demanded cheaper bread, while their spokesmen called for governmental control of the ever-growing inflation. Their leaders also articulated the frustrations of a mass of men and women who felt cheated by the constitution. Despite their major role in the creation of a new regime, they found themselves deprived of any effective voice in its operation.

(2) lack of leadership

A second major reason for the change of course was a lack of effective national leadership during the first two years of the revolution. Louis XVI remained the weak, vacillating monarch he had been prior to 1789. Though outwardly prepared to collaborate with the leaders of the assembly, he remained essentially a victim of events. He was compelled to support measures personally distasteful to him, in particular the Civil Constitution of the Clergy. He was thus sympathetic to the plottings of the queen, who was in correspondence with her brother Leopold II of Austria. Urged on by Marie Antoinette, Louis agreed to attempt an escape from France in June 1791, in hopes of rallying foreign support for counterrevolution. The members of the royal family managed to slip past their palace guards in Paris, but were apprehended near the border at Varennes and brought back to the capital. Though the Constitution of 1791 declared France a monarchy, after Varennes that declaration was more fiction than fact. From that point on, Louis was little more than a prisoner of the assembly. The leadership of that body remained in the hands of Honoré Gabriel Riquetti, comte de Mirabeau, until his death in 1791. Yet he was a less than satisfactory leader. An outstanding orator, possessed of the insight of a statesman, he was nevertheless mistrusted by many revolutionaries because of his dissolute, aristocratic youth and his notorious venality. Nor, despite his continued support of a strong constitutional monarchy, did he enjoy the confidence of the king. Even with his shortcomings, Mirabeau was the most effective leader among the moderate constitutionalists, a group that generally failed to capitalize on its opportunities.

The third major reason for the dramatic turn of affairs was the fact that after 1792 France found itself at war with much of the rest of Europe. From the outset of the revolution, men and women across Europe had been compelled, by the very intensity of events in France, to take sides in the conflict. In the years immediately after 1789, the revolution in France won the enthusiastic support of a wide range of politically committed intellectuals, businessmen, and artisans. The English poet William Wordsworth, later to become disillusioned by the subsequent course of revolutionary events, recalled the rapture of his initial mood: "Bliss was it in that dawn to be alive. . . ." His sentiments were echoed across the continent by poets and philosophers, among the latter the German Johann Gottfried von Herder, who declared the revolution the most important historical moment since the Reformation. Political societies in England proclaimed their allegiance to the principles of the new revolution, often quite incorrectly seeing it as nothing more than a French version of the far less momentous events of 1688. In the Low Countries, a "patriot" group organized strikes and plotted a revolution of its own against dominant merchant oligarchies. Political revolutionaries in western Germany and anticlericals in Italy welcomed the possibility of invasion by the French as a means of achieving radical change within their own countries.

Others opposed the course of the revolution from the start. Exiled nobles, who had fled France for the haven of sympathetic royal courts in Germany and elsewhere, did all they could to stir up counterrevolutionary sentiment. The distressed clamoring of these emigrés, along with the plight of Louis XVI and his family, aroused the sympathy, if not, at first, the active support, of European defenders of absolutism and privilege. In England the cause was strengthened by the publication in 1790 of Edmund Burke's *Reflections on the Revolution in France*. A Whig politician who had sympathized with the American revolutionaries, Burke nevertheless attacked the revolution in France as a monstrous crime against the social order. He argued that by remodeling their government as they had, the French had turned their backs on both human nature and history. Men and women were not consti-

(3) The revolution abroad

Counterrevolution: Burke

Edmund Burke

Thomas Paine

Declaration of Pillnitz

tutional abstractions, endowed with an objective set of natural rights, as the Declaration of the Rights of Man had insisted. Rights—and duties as well—were the consequence of the individual histories of the countries into which men and women were born. Those histories bound people to the past and entailed a commitment to the future, as well as the present. Hence they had no right to remake their country and its institutions without reference to the past or concern for the future, as Burke insisted the French had. Their failure to pay proper respect to tradition and custom had destroyed the precious fabric of French civilization woven by centuries of national history.

Burke's famous pamphlet, in which he painted a romantic and highly inaccurate picture of the French king and queen, helped arouse sympathy for the counterrevolutionary cause. It is questionable, however, whether that sympathy would have turned to active opposition, had not the French soon appeared as a threat to international stability and the individual ambitions of the great powers. It was that threat which led to war in 1792, and which kept the Continent in arms for a generation. This state of war had a most important impact on the formation of political and social attitudes during this period in Europe. Once a country declared war with France, its citizens could no longer espouse sympathy with the revolution without paying severe consequences. Those who continued to support the revolution, as did a good many among the artisan and small tradespeople class, were persecuted and punished for their beliefs. To be found in Britain, for example, possessing a copy of Tom Paine's revolutionary tract, *The Rights of Man* (1791–1792), a prorevolutionary response to Burke's *Reflections,* was enough to warrant imprisonment. As the moderate nature of the early revolution turned to violent extension, entrepreneurs and businessmen eagerly sought to live down their radical sentiments of a few years past. The wars against revolutionary France came to be perceived as a matter of national survival; to ensure internal security, it seemed that patriotism demanded not only a condemnation of the French but of French ideas as well.

The first European states to express public concern about events in revolutionary France were Austria and Prussia. They were not anxious to declare war; their interests at the time centered upon the division of Poland between themselves. Nevertheless, they jointly issued the Declaration of Pillnitz in August 1791, in which they avowed that the restoration of order and of the rights of the monarch of France was a matter of "common interest to all sovereigns of Europe." The leaders of the French government at this time were a moderate faction, the Girondists, so called because many of them came from the mercantile Gironde district. Afraid of losing political support in France, they pronounced the Declaration of Pillnitz a threat to national security, hoping that enthusiasm for a war would unite the French and result also in enthusiasm for their continued rule. They were aided in their scheme by the activities of monarchists, both within and outside France, whose plottings and pronouncements could be made to appear an additional threat, though to a greater extent than they actually were. On April 20, 1792, the assembly declared war against Austria and Prussia.

Almost all of the various political factions in France welcomed the war. The Girondists expected that their aggressive policy would solidify the loyalty of the people to their regime. Reactionaries hailed the intervention of Austria and Prussia as the first step in the undoing of all that had happened since 1789. Extremists hoped that initially the French would suffer reverses that would discredit the moderate Girondists and the monarchy, and thus hasten the advent of a more radical regime in France, and the triumph of people's armies and revolutionary ideals across Europe. As the radicals hoped, the forces of the French met serious reverses. By August 1792 the allied armies of Austria and Prussia had crossed the frontier and were threatening the capture of Paris. A fury of rage and despair seized the capital. The belief prevailed that the military disasters had been the result of treasonable dealings with the enemy on the part of the king and his conservative followers. On August 10 Parisian rioters, organized by their radical leadership, attacked the royal palace, slaughtering the king's guards and driving him to seek refuge in the meeting hall of the assembly. At the same time, radicals seized the municipal government in Paris, replacing it with a revolutionary Commune under their control. The Commune successfully demanded that the assembly suspend the king from his duties and hand him and his family over for imprisonment.

Response to war

From this point, the country's leadership passed into the hands of an equalitarian-minded segment of the third estate. These new leaders called themselves Jacobins, after the political club to which they belonged, whose headquarters was in Paris, but whose membership extended throughout France. Like the Girondists, the Jacobins were mostly members of the bourgeoisie, professionals and businessmen, though an increasing number of artisans joined the club as it grew. They differed from the Girondists in their political philosophy, however. Girondists were loud in their defense of liberty, by which they often meant no more than freedom to pursue their own economic interests without state regulation. Because their political base was in the provinces, they tended to mistrust Parisians and were alarmed by the extremism of the Commune. Jacobins, in contrast, were the masterminds of the Commune. They were vigorous proponents of equality. They supported the elimination of remaining civil and political distinctions, favored universal suffrage, and state programs for the maintenance of the poor. The Jacobins differed as well from the Girondists in that they were a tightly organized party. As such, again unlike the Girondists, they were able to move decisively and prepared to act ruthlessly in defense of their programs and their leadership.

Jacobins. Contemporary drawings by Heuriot.

One of the Jacobins' first actions was to call for an election by universal suffrage of delegates to a national convention, whose task would be to draft and enact a new and republican constitution. This convention became the effective governing body of the country for the next three years. It was elected in September 1792, at a time when disturbances across France reached a new height. The so-called September massacres occurred when patriotic Paris mobs, hearing a rumor that political prisoners were plotting to escape from their prisons, responded by hauling them before hastily convened tribunals and sentencing them to swift execution. Over one thousand supposed enemies of the revolution were killed in less than a week. Similar riots engulfed Lyons, Orléans, and other French cities.

When the newly elected convention met in September, its membership was far more radical than that of its predecessor, the Legislative Assembly, and its leadership was determined to demand an end to the monarchy and the death of Louis XVI. On September 21, the convention declared France a republic. In December it placed the king on trial and in January he was condemned to death by a narrow margin. The heir to the grand tradition of French absolutism met his end bravely as "Citizen Louis Capet," beheaded by the guillotine, the frightful mechanical headsman that had become the symbol of revolutionary fervor.

Meanwhile, the convention turned its attention to the enactment of further domestic reforms. Among its most significant accomplishments over the next three years were the abolition of slavery in French colonies; the prohibition of imprisonment for debt; the establishment of the metric system of weights and measures; and the repeal of primogeniture, so that property might not be inherited exclusively by the oldest son, but be divided in substantially equal portions among all immediate heirs. The convention also supplemented the decrees of the assembly in abolishing the remnants of manorialism and in providing for greater freedom of economic opportunity for the commoner. The property of enemies of the revolution was confiscated for the benefit of the government and the lower classes. Great estates were broken up and offered for sale to poorer citizens on easy terms. The indemnities hitherto promised to the nobles for the loss of their privileges were abruptly cancelled. To curb the rise in the cost of living, maximum prices for grain and other necessities were fixed by law, and merchants who profiteered at the expense of the poor were threatened with the guillotine. Still other measures of reform dealt with religion. An effort was made to abolish Christianity and to substitute the worship of Reason in its place. In accordance with this purpose a new calendar was adopted, dating the year from the birth of the republic (September 22, 1792) and dividing the months in such a way as to eliminate the Christian Sunday. Later, this cult of Reason was replaced by a Deistic religion dedicated to the worship of a Supreme Being and to a belief in the immortality of the soul. Finally, in 1794, the convention decreed simply that religion was a private matter, that church and

The Execution of Louis XVI. A revolutionary displays the king's head moments after it had been severed by the guillotine in January 1793.

state would therefore be separated, and that all beliefs not actually hostile to the government would be tolerated.

While effecting this political revolution in France, the convention's leadership at the same time accomplished an astonishingly successful reorganization of its armies. By February 1793, Britain, Holland, Spain, and Austria were in the field against the French. Britain's entrance into the war was dictated by both strategic and economic reasons. The English feared French penetration into the Low Countries directly across the Channel; they were also concerned that French expansion might pose a serious threat to Britain's own growing economic hegemony around the globe. The allied coalition ranged against France, though united only in its desire to contain this puzzling, fearsome revolutionary phenomenon, was nevertheless a formidable force. To counter it, the French organized an army that was able to win engagement after engagement during these years. In August 1793, the revolutionary government imposed a levy on the entire male population capable of bearing arms. Fourteen hastily drafted armies were flung into battle under the leadership of young and inexperienced officers. What they lacked in training and discipline, they made up for in improvised organization, mobility, flexibility, courage, and morale. (In the navy, however, where skill was of paramount importance, the revolutionary French never succeeded in matching the performance of the British.) In 1793–1794, the French armies preserved their homeland. In 1794–1795, they occupied the Low Countries, the Rhineland, parts of Spain, Switzerland, and Savoy. In 1796, they invaded and occupied key parts of Italy and broke the coalition that had arrayed itself against them.

The revolutionary wars

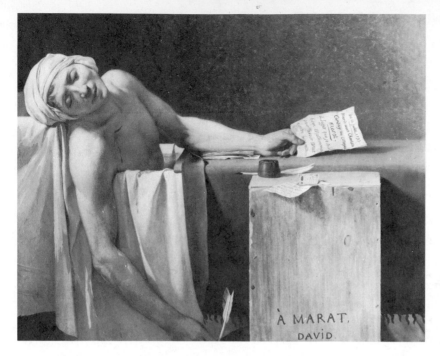

The Death of Marat. This painting by the French artist David immortalized Marat. The bloody towel, the box, and the tub were venerated as relics of the revolution.

The dictatorship of the Committee of Public Safety

These achievements were not without their price, however. To ensure their accomplishment, the rulers of France resorted to a bloody authoritarianism that has come to be known as the Terror. Although the convention succeeded in 1793 in drafting a new democratic constitution, based upon manhood suffrage, it deferred its introduction because of wartime emergency. Instead, the convention prolonged its own life year by year, and increasingly delegated its responsibilities to a group of twelve leaders known as the Committee of Public Safety. By this time the moderate Girondists had lost all influence within the convention. Complete power had passed to the Jacobins, who continued to proclaim themselves disciples of Rousseau and champions of the common man.

Foremost among the members of the Committee of Public Safety were Jean Paul Marat, Georges Jacques Danton, and Maximilien Robespierre. Jean Paul Marat (1743–1793) was educated as a physician, and by 1789 had already earned enough distinction in that profession to be awarded an honorary degree by St. Andrews University in Scotland. Almost from the beginning of the revolution he stood as a champion of the common people. He opposed nearly all of the assumptions of his more moderate colleagues in the assembly, including the idea that France should pattern its government after that of Great Britain, which he recognized to be oligarchic in form. Soon made a victim of persecution and forced to take refuge in unsanitary sewers and dungeons, he persevered in his efforts to rouse the people to a defense of their rights. His exposure to infection left him with a chronic skin affliction from which he could find relief only through frequent bathing. In 1793 he was stabbed through the heart during one of

Georges Jacques Danton

these soothing respites by Charlotte Corday, a young woman fanatically devoted to the Girondists. In contrast with Marat, Georges Jacques Danton (1759–1794) did not come into prominence until the revolution was three years old; but, like Marat, he directed his activities toward goading the masses into rebellion. Elected a member of the Committee of Public Safety in 1793, he had much to do with organizing the Terror. As time went on, however, he wearied of ruthlessness and displayed a tendency to compromise that gave his opponents in the convention their opportunity. In April 1794 Danton was sent to the guillotine. Upon mounting the scaffold he is reported to have said: "Show my head to the people; they do not see the like every day."

The most famous and perhaps the greatest of the extremist leaders was Maximilien Robespierre (1758–1794). Born of a family reputed to be of Irish descent, Robespierre was trained for the law and speedily achieved a modest success as an advocate. In 1782 he was appointed a criminal judge, but soon resigned because he could not bear to impose a sentence of death. Of a nervous and timid disposition, he was a less than able administrator, but made up for this lack of talent by fanatical devotion to principle. He adopted the belief that the philosophy of Rousseau held the one great hope of salvation for all mankind. To put this philosophy into practice he was ready to employ any means that would bring results, regardless of the cost to himself or to others. This passionate loyalty to a gospel that exalted the masses eventually won him a following. Indeed, he was so lionized by the public that he was allowed to wear the knee breeches, silk stockings, and powdered hair of the old society until the end of his life. In 1791 he was accepted as the oracle of the Jacobin Club. Later he became president of the National Convention and a member of the Committee of Public Safety. Though he had little or nothing to do with originating the Terror, he was nevertheless responsible for enlarging its scope. He came to justify ruthlessness as a necessary and therefore laudable means to revolutionary progress. In the last six weeks of his government, no fewer than 1,285 heads rolled from the scaffold in Paris.

Maximilien Robespierre

The years of the Terror were years of ruthless dictatorship in France. Pressed by foreign enemies from without, the committee faced sabotage from both the political Right and Left at home. In 1793, a royalist counterrevolution broke out in the western area of the Vendée. The peasantry there had remained generally loyal to Church and king. Government attempts to conscript troops into the revolutionary armies fanned long-smoldering resentments into open rebellion. By the summer, the peasant forces there, led by noblemen in the name of a Royal Catholic Grand Army, posed a serious threat to the convention. Meanwhile, Girondist fugitives helped fuel rebellions in the great provincial cities of Lyon, Bordeaux, and Marseilles. This harvest of the decentralizing policies of the National Assembly was bitter fruit to the

The ruthless suppression of enemies of the state

Meeting of a Revolutionary Committee of Surveillance during the Terror

committee. At the same time they met with the scornful criticism of revolutionaries even more radical than themselves. This latter group, known as the *enragés,* was led by the journalist Jacques Hébert, and threatened to topple not only the government but the country itself by its extremist crusades. Determined to stabilize France, whatever the necessary cost, the committee dispatched commissioners into the countryside to suppress the enemies of the state. During the period of the Terror, from September 1793 to July 1794, the most reliable estimates place the number of executions as high as twenty thousand in France as a whole. The victims were by no means all aristocrats. Anyone who appeared to threaten the republic, no matter what his or her social or economic position, was at risk. Far more peasants and laborers than noblemen and women were killed. Among those executed was Marie Antoinette ("The Widow Capet"). When some time later the Abbé Sieyès was asked what he had done to distinguish himself during the Terror, he responded dryly, "I lived."

Three points need to be made with regard to the Committee of Public Safety. First, it dramatically reversed the trend toward decentralization that had characterized the reforms of the assembly. In addition to dispatching its own commissioners from Paris to quell provincial insurrection, the committee published a *Bulletin des loix,* to inform all citizens what laws were to be enforced and obeyed. And it replaced local officials, some of them still royalist in sympathy, with "deputies on mission," whose task was to conscript troops and generate patriotic fervor. When these deputies appeared too eager to act independently, they were in turn replaced by "national agents," with instructions to report directly to the committee. Second, by fostering the interests of the less economically powerful the committee significantly retarded the pace of industrial transformation in France. Through

The achievements of the committee

policies which assisted the peasant, the small craftsman, and the shop-keeper to acquire property, the government during this "second" revolution encouraged the entrenchment of a class at once devoted to the principle of republicanism while unalterably opposed to a large-scale capitalist transformation of the economy of France. Third, the ruthless Terror of the committee undoubtedly achieved its end by saving France from defeat at the hands of the coalition of European states. Whether the human price extracted in return for that salvation was worth the paying is a matter historians—and indeed all thoughtful human beings—may well never finally resolve.

The Committee of Public Safety, though able to save France, could not save itself. It failed to put a stop to inflation, thereby losing the support of those commoners whose dissatisfactions had helped bring the convention to power. The long string of military victories convinced growing numbers that the committee's demands for continuing self-sacrifice, as well as its insistence upon the necessity of the Terror, were no longer justified. By July 1794, the committee was virtually without allies. On July 27 (9 Thermidor, according to the new calendar) Robespierre was shouted down by his enemies while attempting to speak on the floor of the convention. Desperate, he tried to rally loyal Jacobins to his defense and against the convention. Discovered in the thick of this plot by convention troops, Robespierre tried unsuccessfully to shoot himself. The following day, along with twenty-one fellow conspirators, he met his death as an enemy of the state on the guillotine. Now the only remaining leaders in the convention were men of moderate sympathies, who, as time went on, inclined toward increasing conservatism. Gradually, the revolution came once more to reflect the interests of the wealthier bourgeoisie. Much of the extremist work of the radicals was undone. The law of maximum prices and the law against "suspects" were both repealed. Political prisoners were freed, the Jacobins driven into hiding, and the Committee of Public Safety shorn of its absolute powers. The new situation made possible the return of priests, royalists, and other emigrés from abroad to add the weight of their influence to the conservative trend.

The third stage: the Thermidorian reaction

In 1795 the National Convention adopted a new constitution, which lent the stamp of official approval to the victory of the prosperous classes. The constitution granted suffrage to all adult male citizens who could read and write. They were permitted to vote for electors, who in turn would choose the members of the legislative body. In order to be an elector, one had to be the proprietor of a farm or other establishment with an annual income equivalent to at least one hundred days of labor. The drafters of the constitution thus ensured that the authority of the government would actually be derived from citizens of considerable wealth. Since it was not practicable to restore the monarchy, lest the old aristocracy also come back into power, executive authority was vested in a board of five men known as the Directory, chosen by the legislative body. The new constitution in-

The 1795 constitution

The Fashionable Mama, 1796. An English cartoon lampooning the new nurturing practices as well as the extreme style of dress adopted by the newly rich throughout Europe during this period.

cluded not only a bill of rights but also a declaration of the *duties* of the citizen. Conspicuous among the latter was the obligation to bear in mind that "it is upon the maintenance of property . . . that the whole social order rests."

The reign of the Directory has not enjoyed a good historical press. The collection of *nouveau riche* speculators and profiteers who rose to prominence as they labored to make a good thing for themselves out of the war was not a particularly attractive crew. They were lampooned as ostentatious and vulgar *"merveilleuses"*—outrageously overdressed men and underdressed women. But however anxious they were to live down the self-denying excesses of the past several years by self-indulgent excesses of their own, they were in no mood to see the major accomplishments of the revolution undone. They had no difficulty in disposing of threats from the Left, despite their failure to resolve that bugbear of all revolutionary governments, inflation and rising living costs. When in 1796 the radical "Gracchus" Babeuf[1] launched a campaign to abolish private property and parliamentary government, his followers were arrested, and either executed or deported.

To dispatch threats from the Right was not so easy. Elections in March 1797—the first free elections held in France as a republic—returned a large number of constitutional monarchists to the councils of government. Leading politicians, among them some who had voted for the execution of Louis XVI, took alarm. With the support of the army, the Directory in September 1797 annulled most of the election results of the previous spring. Its bold coup did little, however, to end the nation's political irresolution. Two years later, after a series of further abortive uprisings and purges, and with the country still plagued by severe inflation, the Directors were desperate. This time they called their brilliant young general, Napoleon Bonaparte (1769–1821), to their assistance.

The plight of the Directory

Bonaparte's first military victory in 1793, the recapture of Toulon from royalist and British forces, had earned him promotion from captain to brigadier general at the age of twenty-four. Though arrested as a terrorist following the fall of Robespierre, he was subsequently patronized by Viscount Paul Barras, a Directory politician. Bonaparte had gained further public fame and the gratitude of the Directory when on October 4, 1795 (13 Vendémiaire, new calendar), he had delivered the "whiff of grapeshot" that saved the convention from attack by opponents of the new constitution. Since that time he had registered a remarkable series of victories in Italy, which had resulted in Austria's withdrawal from the war. Most recently, he had attempted to defeat Britain by attacking its colonies in Egypt and the Near East. Despite initial successes on land, Bonaparte eventually found himself trapped by the British, following the defeat of the French fleet by Admiral

---

[1] Called "Gracchus" after the Roman tribune Gaius Gracchus, a hero of the people.

Horatio Nelson at Abukir Bay in 1798. A year of further fighting had brought Bonaparte no nearer decisive victory in North Africa.

It was at this point that the call came from the Directory. Bonaparte slipped away from Egypt and appeared in Paris, already having agreed to participate in a coup d'état with the leading director, that former revolutionary champion of the third estate, the Abbé Sieyès. On November 9, 1799 (18 Brumaire), Bonaparte was declared a "temporary consul." He was the answer to the prayers of the Directory: a strong, popular leader who was not a king. Sieyès, who had once declared for revolution in the name of the third estate, now declared for counterrevolution in the name of virtual dictatorship: "Confidence from below, authority from above." With those words Sieyès pronounced the end of the revolutionary period.

4. NAPOLEON AND EUROPE

Few men in Western history have compelled the attention of the world as Napoleon Bonaparte did during the fifteen years of his rule in France. And few men have succeeded as he has in continuing to live on as myth in the consciousness, not just of his own country, but of all Europe. Without doubt, part of the success of the Napoleonic myth can be credited to the fact that Napoleon never attempted to disguise his less-than-gentlemanly background. Although born in Corsica into a family that held a title of nobility from the Republic of Genoa, he cultivated the rude manners of an *arriviste,* losing his temper, cheating at cards, taking what he could get without regard to the conventions of polite society. As such, he appealed to the new citizens of a triumphantly middle-class Europe. In the minds of his admirers he would remain the "little corporal" who, without the privileges of the aristocrat, had made it to the top on his own.

The Eighteenth Brumaire. A detail from a painting by Bronchet depicting Napoleon as the man of the hour.

The character of Napoleon Bonaparte

Yet the myth was also grounded in the important fact of Bonaparte's undoubted abilities. Schooled in France and at the military academy in Paris, he possessed a mind congenial to the ideas of the Enlightenment—creative, imaginative, and ready to perceive things anew. His primary interests were history, law, and mathematics. His particular strengths as a leader lay in his ability to conceive of financial, legal, or military plans and then to master their every detail; his capacity for inspiring others, even those initially opposed to him; and his belief in himself as the destined savior of the French. That last conviction eventually became the obsession that led to Napoleon's undoing. But supreme self-confidence was just what the French government had recently lacked. Napoleon believed both in himself and in France. That latter belief was the tonic France now needed, and Napoleon proceeded to administer it in liberally revivifying doses.

His abilities

During the years from 1799 to 1804, Napoleon ruled under the title of first consul, but in reality as a dictator. Once again, France

Napoleonic reforms

(1) Centralization and finance

(2) education and law

was given a new constitution. Though the document spoke of universal male suffrage, political power was retained, by the now familiar means of indirect election, in the hands of entrepreneurs and professionals. Recognizing, however, that his regime would derive additional substance if it could be made to appear the government of the people of France, Bonaparte instituted what has since become a common authoritarian device: the plebiscite. The voters were asked to approve the new constitution and did so by the loudly proclaimed vote of 3,011,107 in favor, 1,567 opposed.

Although the constitution provided for a legislative body, that body could neither initiate nor discuss legislation. The first consul made use of a Council of State to draft his laws; but in fact the government depended on the authority of one man. Bonaparte had no desire to undo the major egalitarian reforms of the revolution. He reconfirmed the abolition of estates, privileges, and local liberties, thereby reconfirming as well the notion of a meritocracy, of "careers open to talent," dear to the hearts of the bourgeoisie. Through centralization of the administrative departments, he achieved what no recent French regime had yet achieved, an orderly and generally fair system of taxation. His plan, by prohibiting the type of exemptions formerly granted the nobility and clergy, and by centralizing collection, enabled him to budget rationally for expenditures and consequent indebtedness. In this way he reduced the inflationary spiral that had entangled so many past governments. Napoleon's willingness to proceed against the decentralizing tendencies of the earlier years of the revolution marked him as a student of the absolutist policies of the Bourbons as well as an admirer of the egalitarian reforms of his more immediate predecessors. He replaced the elected officials and local self-government instituted in 1789 with centrally appointed "prefects" and "subprefects" whose administrative duties were defined in Paris, where local government policy was made as well.

Napoleon's most significant accomplishment was his completion of the educational and legal reforms begun during the revolutionary period. He ordered the establishment of *lycées* (high schools) in every major town and a school in Paris for the training of teachers. To supplement these changes, Napoleon brought the military and technical schools under state control and founded a national university to exercise supervision over the entire system. Like almost all his reforms, this one proved of particular benefit to the middle class; so did the new legal code promulgated in 1810. The Code Napoleon, as the new body of laws was called, reflected two principles which had threaded their way through all the constitutional changes since 1789: uniformity and individualism. The code made French law uniform, declaring past customs and privileges forever abolished. By underscoring in various ways a private individual's right to property, by authorizing new methods for the drafting of contracts, leases, and stock companies, and by once again prohibiting trade unions, the code worked to the benefit of individually minded entrepreneurs and businessmen.

FRANCE: THE REVOLUTIONARY DEPARTMENTS AFTER 1789

To accomplish these reforms Napoleon called upon the most talented men available to him, regardless of their past political affiliations. He admitted back into the country emigrés of all political stripes. His two fellow consuls—joint executives, but in name only—were a regicide of the Terror and bureaucrat of the Old Regime. His minister of police had been an extreme radical republican; his minister of foreign affairs was the opportunist aristocrat Talleyrand. The work of political reconciliation was assisted by Napoleon's 1801 concordat with the pope, which reunited Church and state. Though the action disturbed former anti-Church Jacobins, Napoleon, ever the pragmatist, believed the reconciliation of Church and state necessary for reasons both of domestic harmony and of interna-

(3) reconciliation

Napoleon crowned emperor

tional solidarity. According to the terms of the concordat, the pope received the right to depose French bishops and to discipline the French clergy. At the same time, the Vatican agreed to lay to rest any claims against the expropriation of former Church lands. Hereafter, that property would remain unchallenged in the hands of its new middle-class rural and urban proprietors. In return, the clergy was guaranteed an income from the state. The concordat did nothing to revoke the principle of religious freedom established by the revolution. Although the Roman Catholic clergy received state money, so did Protestant clergy.

Napoleon's agreement won him the support of those conservatives who had feared for France's future as a godless state. To prove to the old Jacobins, in turn, that he remained a child of their revolution, he invaded the independent state of Baden in 1804 to arrest and then execute the duke of Enghien, a relative of the Bourbons, whom Napoleon falsely accused of a plot against his life. (Three years before he had deported over one hundred Jacobins on a similar charge, but with no permanent political repercussions.) The balancing act only served to increase Napoleon's general popularity. By 1802 the people of France were prepared to accept him as "consul for life." In 1804, they rejoiced when, in the cathedral of Notre Dame, in Paris, he crowned himself Emperor Napoleon I.

Across the boundaries of France, the nations of Europe had watched, some in admiration, others in horror, all in astonishment, at

Left: *Coronation of Napoleon and Josephine* by David. Napoleon crowned himself and his wife and assumed the title of Napoleon I, emperor of the French. Right: *Napoleon I* by Jean A. D. Ingres. This celebratory portrait incorporates stage props that echo the grandeur of imperial Rome, thereby suggesting the extent to which Napoleon wanted Europe to regard him as its supreme ruler.

the phenomenon that was Napoleon. They had fought France since 1792 in hopes of maintaining European stability. Now they faced the greatest threat to that stability yet to arise. The detailed history of the wars fought to contain the French is complex, and of little direct relevance to the patterns of ideas, institutions, and societies we are tracing. Suffice it to say that from 1792 until 1795 France had been at war with a coalition of European powers—principally Austria, Prussia, and Britain. In 1795, Prussia retired from the fray, financially exhausted and at odds with Austria. In 1797, the Austrians, defeated by Bonaparte in northern Italy, withdrew as well, signing the Treaty of Campo Formio, which ceded to France territories in Belgium, recognized the Cisalpine Republic which Bonaparte had established in Italy, and agreed to France's occupation of the left bank of the Rhine.

By the following year, Britain was left to fight the French alone. In 1798 it formed a second coalition against the French, this one with Russia and Austria. The results did not differ significantly from those of the first allied attempt to contain France. Russia and Austria had no success in driving the French from Italy; the French likewise failed to break Britain's advantage at sea. By 1801, the coalition was in tatters, Russia having withdrawn two years previously. The Treaty of Lunéville, signed by France and Austria, confirmed the provisions of Campo Formio; in addition the so-called Batavian, Helvetian, Cisalpine, and Ligurian republics—established by Napoleon from territories in the Low Countries, Switzerland, Italy, and Piedmont—were legitimized. The Austrians also acquiesced to a general redrawing of the map of Germany, which resulted eventually in an amalgamation of semi-independent states under French domination into the Confederation of the Rhine. The following year Britain, no longer able to fight alone, settled with the French as well, returning all the territories it had captured in overseas colonial engagements except Trinidad and Ceylon.

Under Napoleon's reign, the territories of central Europe underwent a revolution. This revolution was a thorough governmental reorganization, one which imposed the major egalitarian reforms of the French Revolution upon lands outside the borders of France, while building a French empire. Most affected were territories in Italy (the "Kingdom of Italy" as it was now called); Germany (the Confederation of the Rhine, including the newly formed Kingdom of Westphalia); Dalmatia (the Illyrian provinces); and Holland. (Belgium had been integrated directly into the empire.) Into all these territories Napoleon introduced a carefully organized, deliberate system of administration, based upon the notion of careers open to talent, equality before the law, and the abolition of ancient customs and privileges. The Napoleonic program of reform in the empire represented an application of the principles that had already transformed postrevolutionary France. Manorial courts were liquidated, and Church courts abolished. Provinces were joined into an enormous bureaucratic network

Anti-French alliances

Treaty of Lunéville

Napoleon's reforms in Europe

See color map facing page 230

that reached directly back to Paris. Laws were codified, the tax system modernized, and everywhere individuals were freed to work at whatever trade they chose. The one freedom denied throughout this new grand hegemony was that of self-government: i.e., all governmental direction emanated from Paris, and therefore from Napoleon.

The impact of these changes upon the men and women who experienced them was clearly enormous. In those principalities previously ruled by petty princelings and minor despots—the patchwork states of Germany, for example, or the repressive Kingdom of Naples— reforms that provided for more efficient, less corrupt administration, a more equitable tax structure, and an end to customary privileges were welcomed by the majority of inhabitants. Business and professional men, who had chafed against economic restrictions, were quick to appreciate the license given them to trade and practice with a new degree of freedom. Yet the Napoleonic presence was by no means an unmixed blessing. Vassal states shared the task of contributing heavily to the maintenance of the emperor's war machine. Levies of taxes and of manpower, and the burden of supporting armies of occupation in their own countries, constantly reminded Germans, Italians, and Dutch that the price of reform was high. Nor were the changes shaped to accommodate local tradition. When Napoleon received complaints that his legal code ran counter to customary practices in Holland, he haughtily retorted: "The Romans gave their laws to their allies; why should not France have hers adopted in Holland?" It was this arrogance, symbolized in the eyes of many by the self-coronation of 1804, that led the German composer Ludwig van Beethoven to revoke the dedication of his *Eroica* Symphony to Napoleon, declaring, "Now he, too, will trample on all the rights of man and indulge only his ambition."

The Continental System

Napoleon's motives in introducing radical political and administrative changes were by no means altruistic. He understood that the defense of his enormous domain depended on efficient government and the rational collection and expenditure of funds for his armies. His boldest attempt at consolidation, however, a policy forbidding the importation into the Continent of British goods, proved a failure. This "Continental System," established in 1806, was designed as a strategic measure in Napoleon's continuing economic war against Britain. Its purpose was to destroy Britain's commerce and credit—to starve it economically into surrender. The system failed for several reasons. Foremost was the fact that throughout the war Britain retained control of the seas. The British naval blockade of the Continent, implemented in 1807, served, therefore, as an effective counter to Napoleon's system. While the empire labored to transport goods and raw materials overland to avoid the British blockade, the British worked with success to develop a lively trade with South America. Internal tariffs were a second reason for the failure of the system. Napoleon was unable to persuade individual territories to join a tariff-

The Handwriting on the Wall.
This English cartoon conjures
up the biblical Feast of
Belshazzar with a vice-ridden
Paris, as the new Babylon,
doomed to destruction.
Headed by a crazed Napoleon
and a grotesque Josephine, the
banquet table offers a meal including the head of George III,
the Tower of London, and the
Bank of England.

free customs union. As a result Europe remained divided into economic
camps, fortified against each other by tariffs, and at odds with each
other as they attempted to subsist on nothing more than what the
Continent could produce and manufacture. The final reason for the
system's collapse was the fact that the Continent had more to lose
than Britain. Trade stagnated ports and manufacturing centers grum-
bled as unemployment rose.

The Continental System was Napoleon's first serious mistake.
As such it was one of the causes of his ultimate downfall. A second
cause of Napoleon's decline was his constantly growing ambition
and increasing sense of self-importance. Napoleon's goal was a united

*Reasons for Napoleon's
fall*

Europe modeled after the Roman Empire. The symbols of his empire—reflected in painting, architecture, and the design of furniture
and clothing—were deliberately Roman in origin. But Napoleon's
Rome was without question imperial, dynastic Rome. The triumphal
columns and arches he had erected to commemorate his victories recalled the ostentatious monuments of the Roman emperors. He made
his brothers and sisters the monarchs of his newly created kingdoms,
which Napoleon controlled from Paris while their mother allegedly
sat at court, anxiously wringing her hands and repeating to herself,
"If only it lasts!" He divorced his first wife, the Empress Josephine,
alleging her childlessness, and ensured himself a successor of royal
blood by marrying into the monarchically respectable house of Habsburg. Even his admirers began to question if Napoleon's empire was
not simply a larger, more efficient, and, therefore, ultimately more
dangerous absolutism than the monarchies of the eighteenth century.
War again broke out in 1805, with the Russians, Prussians, and Aus-

The Empress Josephine

Invasion of Spain

trians joining the British in an attempt to contain France. But to no avail; Napoleon's military superiority led to defeats, in turn, of all three continental allies. Ultimately only the emperor's own unwillingness to recognize that his supply of men, matériel, and good fortune was not limitless brought military defeat upon him.

In 1808, Napoleon invaded Spain as a first step toward the conquest of Portugal, which had remained a stalwart ally of the British. Napoleon was determined to bring the Iberian peninsula into the Continental System. Although he at first promised the senile Spanish king Charles IV that he would cede a part of Portugal to Spain, Napoleon proceeded to overthrow Charles and installed his brother Joseph Bonaparte on the throne. Napoleon then imposed a series of reforms upon the Spanish, similar to those he had instituted elsewhere in Europe. But he reckoned without two factors that led to the ultimate failure of his Spanish mission: the presence of British forces under Sir Arthur Wellesley (later the duke of Wellington), and the determined resistance of the Spanish people. They particularly detested Napoleon's interference in the affairs of the Church, actively opposing his ending of the Inquisition and his abolition of a number of monastic establishments. Together with the British, the Spanish maintained a concerted effort to drive Napoleon from their country, often employing guerrilla warfare to do so. Though at one point Napoleon himself took charge of his army, he could not achieve anything more than temporary victory. The campaign dragged on until 1813, when the French forces were finally driven back across the border. The Spanish campaign was the first indication that Napoleon could be beaten. As such, it helped to promote a spirit of anti-Napoleonic defiance that encouraged resistance elsewhere.

The Russsian debacle

A second stage in Napoleon's downfall began with the disruption of his alliance with Russia. As an agricultural country, Russia had suffered a severe economic crisis when it was no longer able, as a result of the Continental System, to exchange its surplus grain for British manufactures. The consequence was that Tsar Alexander began to wink at trade with Britain and to ignore or evade the protests from Paris. By 1811 Napoleon decided that he could endure this flouting of the Continental System no longer. Accordingly, he collected an army of 600,000 (only a third of whom were native Frenchmen) and set out in the spring of 1812 to punish the tsar. The project ended in disaster. The Russians refused to make a stand, drawing the French farther and farther into the heart of their country. They permitted Napoleon to occupy their ancient capital of Moscow. But on the night of his entry, a fire of suspicious origin broke out in the city, leaving little but the blackened walls of the Kremlin palaces to shelter the invading troops. Hoping that the tsar would eventually surrender, Napoleon lingered amid the ruins for more than a month, finally deciding on October 22 to begin the homeward march. The delay was a fatal blunder. Long before he had reached the border, the terrible Russian

The Retreat from Russia. In this painting by Charlet the horrors of the Russian winter can be seen.

winter was upon his troops. Swollen streams, mountainous drifts of snow, and bottomless mud slowed the retreat almost to a halt. To add to the miseries of bitter cold, disease, and starvation, mounted Cossacks rode out of the blizzard to harry the exhausted army. Each morning the miserable remnant that pushed on left behind circles of corpses around the campfires of the night before. On December 13 a few thousand broken soldiers crossed the frontier into Germany—a small fraction of what had once been proudly styled the *Grande Armée*. The lives of nearly 300,000 men had been sacrificed in Napoleon's Russian adventure.

Until the debacle of the Russian campaign, Napoleon's armies had enjoyed a striking series of victories. The Battle of Austerlitz, in December 1805, a mighty triumph for the French against the combined forces of Austria and Russia, had remained a symbol of the emperor's apparent invincibility. Subsequent victories in the following years—against the Prussians at Jena in 1806, the Russians at Friedland in 1807, and the Austrians at Wagram in 1809—increased the conviction on the part of Europe that it had no choice but to acquiesce in Napoleon's grand continental design. The great British naval victory at Trafalgar in 1805, which broke the maritime power of France, was perceived at the time by Napoleon's friends and foes alike as no more than a temporary check to his ambitions.

Napoleon's supposed invincibility

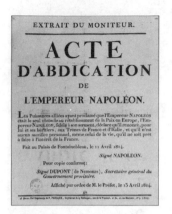

EXTRAIT DU MONITEUR.

ACTE D'ABDICATION
DE
L'EMPEREUR NAPOLÉON.

Les Puissances alliées ayant proclamé que l'Empereur NAPOLÉON était le seul obstacle au rétablissement de la Paix en Europe, l'Empereur NAPOLÉON, fidèle à son serment, déclare qu'il renonce, pour lui et ses héritiers, aux Trônes de France et d'Italie, et qu'il n'est aucun sacrifice personnel, même celui de la vie, qu'il ne soit prêt à faire à l'intérêt de la France.

Fait au Palais de Fontainebleau, le 11 Avril 1814.

Signé NAPOLÉON.

Pour copie conforme:

Signé DUPONT (de Nemours), *Secrétaire général du Gouvernement provisoire.*

Affiché par ordre de M. le Préfet, le 13 Avril 1814.

Napoleon's Abdication Proclamation, 1814

Now, however, following the retreat from Russia, the anti-Napoleonic forces took renewed hope. United by a belief that they might at last succeed in defeating the emperor, Prussia, Russia, Austria, and Britain renewed their attack. Most of the fighting during this so-called war of liberation took place in Germany. The climax of the campaign occurred in October 1813 when, at what was thereafter known as the Battle of the Nations, fought near Leipzig, the allies handed the French a resounding defeat. Meanwhile, allied armies won significant victories in the Low Countries and Italy. By the beginning of 1814, they had crossed the Rhine into France. Burdened with an inexperienced army of raw youths, Napoleon retreated to Paris, continuing, despite constant setbacks, to urge the French people to further resistance. On March 31, Tsar Alexander I of Russia and King Frederick William III of Prussia made their triumphant entry into Paris. Napoleon was forced to abdicate unconditionally, and was sent into exile on the island of Elba, off the Italian coast.

Less than a year later he once more set foot on French soil. The allies had in the interim restored the Bourbon dynasty to the throne, in the person of Louis XVIII, brother of Louis XVI.[2] Any sovereign would have suffered in the eyes of the French by comparison with Napoleon; Louis was particularly ill suited to fill a space far too great for his mediocre talents. The French rallied enthusiastically to the former emperor. By the time he reached Paris, he had generated enough support to cause Louis to flee the country. The allies, meeting in Vienna to conclude peace treaties with the French, were stunned by the news of Napoleon's return. They dispatched a hastily organized army to

Napoleon's return and final defeat

counter the emperor's typically bold offensive push into the Low Countries. There, at the battle of Waterloo, fought on June 18, 1815, Napoleon suffered defeat for the final time. Shipped off to the bleak island of St. Helena in the South Atlantic, the once-mighty emperor, now the exile Bonaparte, lived out a dreary existence writing self-serving memoirs until his death in 1821.

Napoleon's legacy

Napoleon's legacy was an impressive one. His administrative and legal reforms remained in place after his fall. The Napoleonic legal code persisted not only in France but in the Low Countries, Prussia, and various other German states. The institutions introduced during his reign—centralized bureaucracy, police and educational systems—became part of the machinery of government and society in many parts of nineteenth-century Europe.

The legacy of the revolution and the Napoleonic era

To appreciate the larger impact of the revolution and the Napoleonic era on Western civilization, one must trace the ideas and institutions it fostered as they worked their way into the history of nineteenth- and twentieth-century Europe and America. Liberty—the right to act within the world with responsibility to no one but one-

---

[2] Louis XVII, the young son of the executed king and queen, had died under mysterious circumstances in the hands of his revolutionary captors in 1795.

self—was a notion dear to those who made the French Revolution, and one which remained embodied in the reforms it produced. So was equality—the notion of rational laws applied evenhandedly to all, regardless of birth or position. National pride, the era's third legacy, was bred in the hearts of the French people as they watched their citizen armies repel attacks against their newly won freedoms. It was instilled, as well, into those whose opposition to the French made them more conscious of their own national identity. The three concepts—liberty, equality, and nationality—were now no longer merely ideas; as laws and as a new way of addressing life, they rested at the center of European reality.

5. THE VIENNA SETTLEMENT

The European powers that met at the Congress of Vienna in 1814 to draw up a permanent peace settlement for Europe labored to produce an agreement that would as nearly as possible guarantee international tranquillity. At the same time, however, they were by no means unwilling to advance the claims of their own countries to new territories, though such claims threatened conflict, or even war. Although the principal decisions of the congress were made by representatives of the major powers, it was attended by an array of dignitaries from almost all the principalities of Europe. No fewer than six monarchs attended: the tsar of Russia, the emperor of Austria, and the kings of Prussia, Denmark, Bavaria, and Württemberg. Great Britain was represented by Lord Castlereagh and the duke of Wellington. From France came the subtle intriguer Talleyrand, who had served as a bishop under Louis XVI, as foreign minister at the court of Napoleon, and who now stood ready to espouse the cause of reaction.

The dominant roles at the Congress of Vienna were played by Tsar Alexander I (1801–1825) and by the Austrian diplomat Klemens von Metternich (1773–1859).

The dynamic but baffling tsar played a leading role in the negotiations because Napoleon's defeat had left Russia the most powerful continental state. Reared at the court of Catherine the Great, he had imbibed the doctrines of Rousseau from a French Jacobin tutor, along with notions of absolutist authority from his military-minded father, Tsar Paul. In 1801 he succeeded his murdered father and for the next two decades disturbed the dreams of his fellow sovereigns by becoming the most liberal monarch in Europe. After the defeat of Napoleon in the Russian campaign, Alexander's mind turned more and more to mystical channels. He conceived of a mission to convert the rulers of all countries to the Christian ideals of justice and peace. But the chief effect of his voluble expressions of devotion to "liberty" and "enlightenment" was to frighten conservatives into suspecting a plot to extend his power over all of Europe. He was accused of intriguing

Tsar Alexander I

The Congress of Vienna

Klemens von Metternich

Barriers to French expansion

The German settlement

with Jacobins everywhere to substitute an all-powerful Russia for an all-powerful France.

The most commanding figure at the congress was Metternich, born at Coblenz in the Rhine valley, where his father was Austrian ambassador at the courts of three small German states. As a student at the University of Strassburg the young Metternich witnessed mob violence connected with the outbreak of the French Revolution, and to this he attributed his lifelong hatred of political innovation. He had been active in fomenting discord between Napoleon and Tsar Alexander, after the two became allies in 1807, and had played some part in arranging the marriage of Napoleon to the Austrian archduchess, Marie Louise. Metternich once declared himself an admirer of the spider, "always busy arranging their houses with the greatest of neatness in the world." At the Congress of Vienna, he attempted at every turn to arrange international affairs with equal neatness, to suit his own diplomatic designs. His two great obsessions were hatred of political and social change and fear of Russia. Above all, he feared revolutions inspired by the tsar for the sake of establishing Russian supremacy in Europe. For this reason he favored moderate terms for France in its hour of defeat, and was ready at one time to sponsor the restoration of Napoleon as emperor of the French under the protection and overlordship of the Habsburg monarchy.

The basic idea that guided the work of the Congress of Vienna was the principle of *legitimacy*. This principle was invented by Talleyrand as a device for protecting France against drastic punishment by its conquerors, but it was ultimately adopted by Metternich as a convenient expression of the general policy of reaction. Legitimacy meant that the dynasties of Europe that had reigned in prerevolutionary days should be restored to their thrones, and that each country should regain essentially the same territories it had held in 1789. In accordance with this principle Louis XVIII was recognized as the "legitimate" sovereign of France; the restoration of Bourbon rulers in Spain and the Two Sicilies was also confirmed. France was compelled to pay an indemnity of 700 million francs to the victorious allies, but its boundaries were to remain essentially the same as in 1789.

To ensure that the French would not soon again overrun their boundaries, however, a strong barrier was erected to contain them. The Dutch Republic, conquered by the French in 1795, was restored as the Kingdom of the Netherlands, with the house of Orange as its hereditary monarchy. To its territory was added that of Belgium, formerly the Austrian Netherlands, with the hope that this now substantial power would serve to discourage any future notions of French expansion. For the same reason the German left bank of the Rhine was ceded to Prussia, and Austria was established as a major power in northern Italy.

The principle of legitimacy was not extended to the German principalities, however. There, despite pleas from rulers of the sovereign

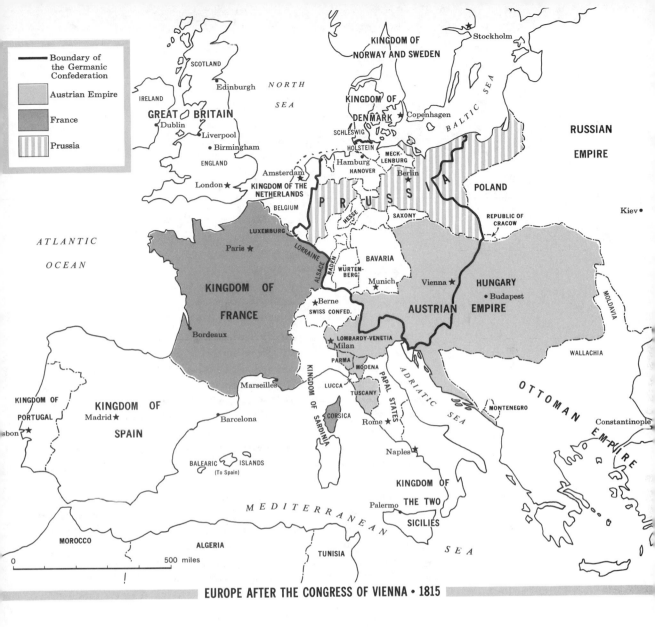

EUROPE AFTER THE CONGRESS OF VIENNA · 1815

Legend:
- Boundary of the Germanic Confederation
- Austrian Empire
- France
- Prussia

bits and pieces that had existed before 1789, the great powers agreed to retain the boundaries as redrawn by Napoleon. Fear of an aggressive Russia led the other European nations to support the maintenance—as an anti-Russian bulwark—of the Napoleonic kingdoms of Bavaria, Württemberg, and Saxony. At the same time, however, Tsar Alexander was demanding that Poland, partitioned into virtual extinction by Russia, Austria, and Prussia in the 1790s, be reconstituted a kingdom with himself as its constitutional monarch. Prussia was prepared to agree with this scheme, provided that it be allowed to swallow Saxony. National avarice for territorial expansion rapidly eclipsed legitimacy as a guiding principle in these negotiations. Metternich, hor-

"Dividing the Cake." A contemporary cartoonist's impression of the work of the congress diplomats.

rified at the double threat thus presented to Austria by Prussia and Russia, allied himself with Talleyrand and Castlereagh, both of whom secretly agreed to go to war against Russia and Prussia, if necessary, in order to prevent them from consumating their Polish-Saxon deal. A compromise was eventually reached, allowing to Russia the major part of Poland and to Prussia a part of Saxony. Britain, no less anxious than the other victorious powers to gain compensation for its long years at war, received territories principally under French dominion in South Africa and South America and the island of Ceylon, thus adding further to its commercial empire.

Triumph of the state system

Legitimacy, as expressed in the treaties that concluded the Congress of Vienna, emerged as the latter-day expression of the principles of balance and stability that had shaped diplomacy during the eighteenth century. The age of absolutism had witnessed the emergence of an international state system dedicated to those principles. By enshrining them in their settlement, the diplomats at Vienna ensured that such a state system would be part of the legacy passed to their nineteenth-century successors.

SELECTED READINGS

• *Items so designated are available in paperback editions.*

• Arendt, Hannah, *On Revolution,* New York, 1963. An analysis of the American and French Revolutions and their meaning for modern man.
• Bergeron, Louis, *France under Napoleon,* Princeton, 1981. Concentrates on the era of Napoleon rather than the man.
  Bosher, J. F., *French Finances, 1770–1790: From Business to Bureaucracy,* Cambridge, 1970. An impressive study concerned with the financial apparatus of Old Regime and revolutionary France.

- Breunig, C., *The Age of Revolution and Reaction, 1789–1850,* 2nd ed., New York, 1989. A well-written survey.
- Brinton, Crane, *Anatomy of Revolution,* rev. ed., New York, 1961. Attempts to create a general model of revolutions by comparing the English, American, French, and Russian Revolutions.
- ———, *A Decade of Revolution, 1789–1799,* New York, 1934. An excellent European survey.
- Bruun, Geoffrey, *Europe and the French Imperium, 1799–1814,* New York, 1938. Describes the impact of Napoleon upon Europe.
- Cobb, R. C., *The Police and the People: French Popular Protest, 1789–1820,* New York, 1970. A survey of peasants and sans-culottes.
- Cobban, Alfred, *The Social Interpretation of the French Revolution,* Cambridge, 1964. A penetrating critique of the radical interpretation of the revolution, more important for its questions than its conclusions.

  Egret, Jean, *The French Pre-Revolution, 1787–1788,* Chicago, 1977. Describes the collapse of the Old Regime.
- Gershoy, Leo, *The French Revolution and Napoleon,* rev. ed., New York, 1964. A good survey with annotated bibliography.

  Geyl, Pieter, *Napoleon: For and Against,* rev. ed., New Haven, 1964. The ways in which Napoleon was interpreted by French historians and political figures.

  Goodwin, Albert, *The Friends of Liberty: The English Democratic Movement in the Age of the French Revolution,* Cambridge, Mass., 1979. Detailed, subtle analysis of English reform movements.

  Greer, Donald, *The Incidence of the Terror during the French Revolution: A Statistical Interpretation,* Cambridge, Mass., 1935. An important study which reveals that the lower classes suffered most during the Terror, rather than the nobility or the clergy.
- Hampson, Norman, *A Social History of the French Revolution,* London, 1963. Deals with institutional development.
- Herold, J. Christopher, *The Age of Napoleon,* New York, 1968. A well-written popular history.
- Kissinger, Henry, *A World Restored: Metternich, Castlereagh, and the Problems of Peace, 1812–1822,* Boston, 1957. By the former U.S. secretary of state, an admirer of Metternich.
- Lefebvre, Georges, *The Coming of the French Revolution,* Princeton, 1947. An excellent study of the causes and early events of the revolution.
- ———, *The French Revolution,* 2 vols., New York, 1963–64. An impressive synthesis by the greatest modern scholar of the revolution.

  ———, *The Great Fear of 1789,* New York, 1973. The best account of the rural disturbances.

  McManners, John, *The French Revolution and the Church,* New York, 1969. Describes the impact of revolutionary anticlericalism upon the French Church.
- Markham, Felix, *Napoleon,* New York, 1966. An excellent study.
- Nicolson, Harold, *The Congress of Vienna: A Study in Allied Unity,* New York, 1946. An excellent and very readable history, written by a British diplomat.
- Palmer, R. R., *The Age of the Democratic Revolution: A Political History of Europe and America, 1760–1800,* 2 vols., Princeton, 1964. Impressive for its scope; places the French Revolution in the larger context of a worldwide revolutionary movement.

- ———, *Twelve Who Ruled,* Princeton, 1958. Excellent biographical studies of the members of the Committee of Public Safety; demonstrates that Robespierre's role has been exaggerated.
- Rudé, George, *The Crowd in the French Revolution,* Oxford, 1959. An important monograph which analyzes the composition of the crowds that participated in the great uprisings of the revolution.
- Soboul, Albert, *The Sans-Culottes: The Popular Movement and Revolutionary Government, 1793–1794,* Garden City, N.Y., 1972. An outstanding example of "history from below"; analyzes the pressures upon the convention in the year of the Terror.

  Thompson, J. M., *Napoleon Bonaparte: His Rise and Fall,* Oxford, 1958. The standard work.
- ———, *Robespierre and the French Revolution,* London, 1953. An excellent short biography.
- Tilly, Charles, *The Vendée: A Sociological Analysis of the Counter-Revolution of 1793,* Cambridge, Mass., 1964. An important economic and social analysis of the factors that led to the reaction in the Vendée.
- Tocqueville, Alexis de, *The Old Regime and French Revolution.* Originally written in 1856, this remains a classic analysis of the causes of the French Revolution.
- Williams, Gwyn A., *Artisans and Sans-Culottes,* New York, 1969. Comparative history of English and French popular movements.

SOURCE MATERIALS

- Burke, Edmund, *Reflections on the Revolution in France,* London, 1790. (Many editions). The great conservative statement against the revolution and its principles.
- Montesquieu, Baron de. *The Spirit of the Laws,* 1748. (Many editions). See especially Books I, II, III, XI.
- Paine, Thomas, *The Rights of Man,* 1791. (Many editions). Paine's eloquent response to Burke's *Reflections* resulted in his conviction for treason and banishment from England.
- Pernoud, G., and S. Flaisser, eds., *The French Revolution,* New York, 1960. Contains eyewitness reports.
- Rousseau, Jean-Jacques, *Discourse on the Origin of Inequality,* 1754. (Many editions).
- ———, *The Social Contract,* 1762. (Many editions). These two tracts provided a philosophical justification for both the American and French Revolutions.

  Sieyès, Abbé, *What Is the Third Estate?,* 1789. (Many editions). The most important political pamphlet in the decisive year 1789.

  Steward, John Hall, *A Documentary Survey of the French Revolution,* New York, 1951.

  Thompson, J. M., *French Revolution Documents, 1789–1794,* Oxford, 1948.
- Walzer, Michael, ed., *Regicide and Revolution: Speeches at the Trial of Louis XVI,* 1974. Contains a thoughtful introduction.
- Young, Arthur, *Travels in France during the Years 1787, 1788, 1789,* New York, 1972. France on the eve of revolution, as seen by a perceptive English observer.

Chapter 26

THE INDUSTRIAL REVOLUTION

Providence has assigned to man the glorious function of vastly improving
the productions of nature by judicious culture, of working them up into
objects of comfort and elegance with the least possible expenditure of
human labor—an undeniable position which forms the basis of our Factory System.

—Andrew Ure, *The Philosophy of Manufactures*

There have been many revolutions in industry during the history of Western civilization, and there will undoubtedly be
many more. Periods of rapid technological change are often
called revolutions, and justifiably so. But, historically, there is one
Industrial Revolution. Occurring during the hundred years after 1780,
it witnessed the first breakthrough from a rural, handicraft economy
to one dominated by urban, machine-driven manufacturing.

The uniqueness of the revolution

The fact that it was a European revolution was not accidental. Although in the mid-eighteenth century Europe was a continent still
predominantly agricultural, although the majority of its people remained illiterate and destined to live out impoverished lives within
sight of the place they were born—despite these conditions, which in
our eyes might make Europe appear "underdeveloped," it was of
course no such thing. European merchants and men of commerce
were established as the world's foremost manufacturers and traders.
Rulers relied upon this class of men to provide them with the wherewithal to maintain the economy of their states, both in terms of
flourishing commercial activity and of victorious armies and navies.
Those men, in turn, had for the most part extracted from their rulers
the understanding that the property they possessed, whether invested
in land, or commerce, or both, was theirs outright. That understanding, substantiated by the written contracts that were replacing
unwritten, long-acknowledged custom, helped persuade merchants,
bankers, traders, and entrepreneurs that they lived in a world that was
stable, rational, and predictable. Believing the world was so, they

Why a European revolution? (1) the commercial class

moved out into it with self-confidence and in hopes of increasing their own, and their country's, prosperity. Only in Europe does one find these presuppositions and this class of men in the eighteenth century; only through the activities of such people could the Industrial Revolution have taken place.

(2) increasing markets

These capitalists could not have prospered without an expanding market for their goods. The existence of this market explains further why it was in Europe that the Industrial Revolution took place. Ever since the beginning of the seventeenth century, overseas commercial exploration and development had been opening new territories to European trade. India, Africa, North and South America—all had been woven into the pattern of European economic expansion. The colonies and commercial dependencies took economic shape at Europe's behest. Even the new United States had not been able to declare its economic independence. Whatever commercial and industrial design Europe might devise, all would be compelled to accommodate themselves to Europe's demands.

(3) population growth

A third factor helping to ensure that the revolution would occur in Europe was the population growth that occurred throughout western Europe in the eighteenth century (see above, p. 80). Increasing populations, along with overseas expansion, provided an ever-growing market for manufactured goods. It furnished, as well, an adequate pool—eventually a surplus—of laboring men, women, and children to work in the manufacture of those goods either at home or in factories.

Qualifications to the concept of "revolution"

Two important facts have inclined historians to qualify the concept of "revolutionary" industrial change. First, the existence of a thriving commercial class, expanding markets, and increasing populations prior to the Industrial Revolution suggest that the changes we are about to analyze had important antecedents. We have already noted, for example, the manner in which the putting-out system was transforming rural areas into sizable manufacturing regions in the seventeenth and eighteenth centuries (see above, p. 71). Second, the Industrial Revolution did not take place everywhere in Europe at the same time and at the same pace. Beginning in England in the late eighteenth century, it spread gradually region by region, country by country across Europe. Unlike the French Revolution whose history can be measured by a decade, the Industrial Revolution occurred over the span of at least a century.

See color map facing page 231

1. THE INDUSTRIAL REVOLUTION IN ENGLAND

Why in England? (1) an economy of abundance

It was in England that the Industrial Revolution first took hold. England's economy had progressed further than that of any other country in the direction of abundance. In simplest terms: fewer people had to struggle just to remain alive; more people were in a position to sell a surplus of the goods they produced to an increasingly expanding market; and more people had money enough to purchase the goods that market offered. English laborers, though poorly enough paid, enjoyed a higher standard of living than their continental counterparts. They ate white bread, not brown, and meat with some regularity. Because a smaller portion of their income was spent on food, they might occasionally have some to spare for articles that were bought rather than homemade.

Further evidence of this increasing abundance was the number of bills for the enclosure of agricultural land passed by an English Parliament sympathetic to capitalism during the last half of the eighteenth century. The enclosure of fields, pasture, and waste lands into large fenced tracts of land under the private ownership and individual management of capitalist landlords meant an increased food supply to feed an increasing and increasingly urban population. Yet another sign of England's abundance was its growing supply of surplus capital, derived from investment in land or commerce, and available for further employment to finance new economic enterprises. London, already a leading center for the world's trade, served as a headquarters for the transfer of raw material, capital, and manufactured products. Portugal alone channeled as much as £50,000 in Brazilian gold per week into London. Thus English capitalists had enough money on hand to underwrite and sustain an industrial revolution.

Abundance: food and capital

But the revolution required more than money. It required habits of mind that would encourage investments in enterprises that were risky, but that represented an enormous potential for gain. In England, far more than on the Continent, the pursuit of wealth was perceived to be a worthy end in life. The aristocracy of Europe had, from the period of the Renaissance, cultivated the notion of "gentlemanly" conduct, in part to hold the line against social encroachments from below. The English aristocrats, whose privileges were meager when compared with those of continental nobles, had never ceased to respect men who made money; nor had they disdained to make whatever they could for themselves. Far more than their continental counterparts, they invested and speculated. Their scramble to enclose their lands reflected this sympathy with aggressive capitalism. Below the aristocracy, there was even less of a barrier separating the world of urban commerce from that of the rural gentry. Most of the men who pioneered as entrepreneurs in the early years of the Industrial Revolution sprang from the minor gentry or yeoman farmer class. To a degree unknown on the Continent, men from this sort of background felt themselves free to rise as high as their abilities might carry them on the social and economic ladder.

(2) climate of opinion

Eighteenth-century England was not by any means free of social snobbery: lords looked down upon bankers, as bankers looked down upon artisans. But a lord's disdain might well be tempered by the fact of his own grandfather's origins in the counting house. And the banker would gladly lend money to the artisan if convinced that the

Respect for financial success

artisan's invention might make them both a fortune. The English, as a nation, were not afraid of business. They respected the sensible, the practical, and the financially successful. Robinson Crusoe, that desert island entrepreneur, was one of their models. In the novel (1719) by Daniel Defoe, the hero had used his wits to master nature and become lord of a thriving economy. His triumph was not diminished because it was a worldly triumph; far from it. "It is our vanity which urges us on," the economist Adam Smith, defender of capitalism, declared. And thank God, Smith implied, for our blessed vanity! An individual's desire to show himself a wordly success worked to produce prosperity for the country as a whole.

(3) increasing markets.

England's eighteenth-century prosperity was based upon an expanding market for whatever goods it manufactured. The English were voracious consumers. By the mid-eighteenth century, yearly fashions were setting styles not only for the very rich but for a growing middle-class clientele as well. "Nature may be satisfied with little," one London entrepreneur declared. "But it is the wants of fashion and the desire of novelties that causes trade." The country's small size and the fact that it was an island encouraged the development of a nationwide domestic market that could respond to increasing demand. The absence of a system of internal tolls and tariffs, such as existed on the Continent, meant that goods could be moved freely to the place where they could fetch the best price. This freedom of movement was assisted by a constantly improving transportation system. Parliament in the years just before the Industrial Revolution passed acts to finance turnpike building at the rate of forty per year; the same period saw the construction of canals and the further opening up of harbors and navigable streams. Unlike the government of France, whose cumbrous mercantilist adventures as often as not thwarted economic growth, the English Parliament believed that the most effective way in which it could help businessmen was to assist them in helping themselves.

Overseas expansion

Parliament's members had every reason to promote England's economic fortunes. Some were businessmen themselves; others had invested heavily in commerce; hence their eagerness to encourage by statute the construction of canals, the establishment of banks, and the enclosure of common lands. And hence their insistence, throughout the eighteenth century, that England's foreign policy respond to its commercial needs. At the end of every major eighteenth-century war, England wrested overseas territories from its enemies. At the same time, England was penetrating hitherto unexploited territories, such as India and South America, in search of further potential markets and resources. In 1759, over one-third of all British exports went to the colonies; by 1784, if we include the newly established United States, that figure had increased to one-half. The English possessed a merchant marine capable of transporting goods across the world, and a navy practiced in the art of protecting its commercial fleets. By 1780 England's markets, together with its fleet and its established position

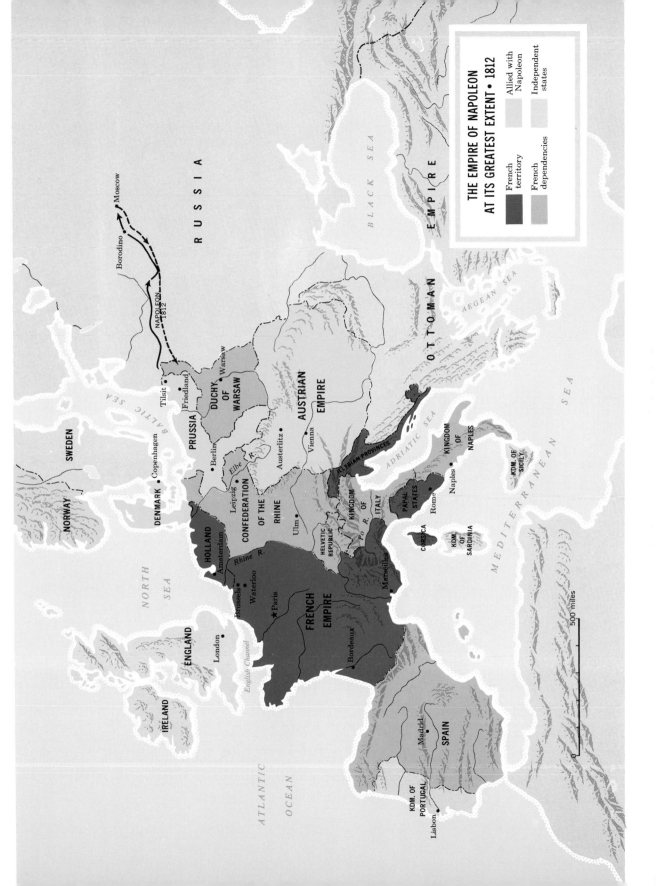

THE EMPIRE OF NAPOLEON
AT ITS GREATEST EXTENT · 1812

French territory

French dependencies

Allied with Napoleon

Independent states

NORWAY

SWEDEN

RUSSIA

BALTIC SEA

DENMARK
Copenhagen

PRUSSIA

Berlin

Tilsit

Friedland

DUCHY OF WARSAW

Warsaw

NAPOLEON 1812

Borodino

Moscow

NORTH SEA

HOLLAND
Amsterdam

Leipzig

CONFEDERATION OF THE RHINE

Elbe R.

AUSTRIAN EMPIRE

Austerlitz

Vienna

BLACK SEA

IRELAND

ENGLAND

London

English Channel

Rhine R.

Brussels
Waterloo

★ Paris

FRENCH EMPIRE

Bordeaux

Ulm

HELVETIC REPUBLIC

Po R.

KINGDOM OF ITALY

ILLYRIAN PROVINCES

ADRIATIC SEA

OTTOMAN EMPIRE

AEGEAN SEA

Marseilles

CORSICA

PAPAL STATES

Rome

KINGDOM OF NAPLES

Naples

KDM. OF SICILY

MEDITERRANEAN SEA

ATLANTIC OCEAN

KDM. OF SARDINIA

KDM. OF PORTUGAL

Lisbon

Madrid

SPAIN

500 miles

THE INDUSTRIAL REVOLUTION

Percent of population living in cities
of 100,000 or more

5% or less

6-10%

20% or more

● Iron ore deposits
● Coal and lignite deposits
☐ Centers of industry
─── Railroads in 1850

0   300 miles

RUSSIAN EMPIRE

St. Petersburg

Moscow

NORWAY

SWEDEN

Uppsala
Stockholm

DENMARK

BALTIC SEA

NORTH SEA

KINGDOM OF GREAT BRITAIN

Glasgow
Dublin
Darlington
Leeds
Liverpool
Manchester
Sheffield
Birmingham
Cardiff
London

ATLANTIC OCEAN

Amsterdam
Rotterdam
NETHERLANDS
Brussels
BELGIUM
Lille
Liège

Le Havre
Amiens
Paris
Orleans
FRANCE
Tours
Nantes
Limoges
Lyons
Avignon
Marseilles

Bremen
Hamburg
Berlin
GERMAN EMPIRE
Kassel
RUHR
Essen
Cologne
Frankfurt
SAAR
Karlsruhe
Strasbourg
Stuttgart
Mulhouse
Basel
Zurich
SWITZERLAND

Posen
SILESIA
Breslau
Dresden
Zwickau
Chemnitz
Leipzig
Nuremberg
Munich
Prague
Pilsen
Steyr
Vienna
AUSTRIAN EMPIRE
Budapest

Warsaw
Lodz
Cracow
Lemberg

ITALY EMPIRE

Turin
Milan
Florence
Livorno
Rome
Naples

Barcelona
Madrid
SPAIN
Santander
Bilbao
Gijon
Oviedo
Seville
Jerez
Granada

OTTOMAN EMPIRE

BLACK SEA

MEDITERRANEAN SEA

at the center of world trade, combined to produce a potential for expansion so great as to compel the Industrial Revolution.

English entrepreneurs and technicians responded to the compulsion by revolutionizing the production of cotton textile goods. Although fewer cotton goods were made in eighteenth-century England than woolen goods, the extent of cotton manufacture by 1760 was such as to make cotton more than an infant industry. Tariffs prohibiting the importation of East Indian cottons, imposed by Parliament to stimulate the sale of woolen goods, had instead served to spur the manufacture of domestic cotton goods. Thus the revolution, when it did occur, took place in an already well-established industry. Yet without the invention of some sort of machinery that would improve the quality and at the same time dramatically increase the quantity of spun cotton thread, the necessary breakthrough would not have come. The invention of the fly-shuttle, which greatly speeded up the process of weaving, only made the bottleneck in the prior process of spinning more apparent. The problem was solved by the invention of a series of comparatively simple mechanical devices, the most important of which was the spinning jenny, invented by James Hargreaves, a carpenter and hand-loom weaver, in 1767 (patented 1770). The spinning jenny, named after the inventor's wife, was a compound spinning wheel, capable of producing sixteen threads at once. The threads it spun were not strong enough, however, to be used for the longitudinal fibers, or warp, of cotton cloth. It was not until the invention of the water frame by Richard Arkwright, a barber, in 1769, that quantity production of both warp and woof (latitudinal fibers) became possible. This invention, along with that of the spinning

The Spinning Jenny. Invented by James Hargreaves in 1767

mule, conceived of by Samuel Crompton in 1779, and combining the features of both the jenny and the frame, solved the problems that had heretofore curtailed the output of cotton textiles. They increased the mechanical advantage over the spinning wheel enormously. From six to twenty-four times the amount of yarn could be spun on a jenny as on the wheel, by the end of the century two to three hundred times as much on the mule. Just as important, the quality of the thread improved not only in terms of strength but also of fineness.

Once these machines came into general use, the revolution proceeded apace. Cotton suited the mule and the jenny because it was a tougher thread than wool; as such cotton was a fiber that could withstand the rough treatment it received at the mechanical hands of the crude early machines. In addition, the supply of cotton was expandable in a way that the supply of wool was not. The cotton gin, invented by the American Eli Whitney in 1793, separated seeds from fiber mechanically, thereby making cotton available at a lower price. The invention kept America's slave plantations profitable, and meant that supply would meet increased demand.

Eli Whitney

The first machinery was cheap enough to allow spinners to continue to work at home. But as it increased in size, it was more and more frequently housed not in the cottages of individual spinners, but in workshops or mills located near water that could be used to power the machines. Eventually, with the further development of steam-driven equipment, the mills could be built wherever it might suit the entrepreneur—frequently in towns and cities in the north of England.

Growth of factories

The transition from home to factory industry was of course not accomplished overnight. Cotton yarn continued to be spun at home at the same time that it was being produced in mills. Eventually, however, the low cost of building and operating a large plant, plus the efficiency realized by bringing workers together under one roof, meant that larger mills more and more frequently replaced smaller workshops. By 1851, three-fifths of those employed in cotton manufacture worked in medium- to large-size mills. Weaving remained a home industry until the invention of a cheap, practical power loom convinced entrepreneurs that they could save money by moving the process from home to mill. Hand-loom weavers were probably the most obvious victims of the Industrial Revolution in England. Their unwillingness to surrender their livelihood to machinery meant that they continued to work for less and less—by 1830, no more than a pitiful six shillings a week. In 1815 they numbered about 250,000; by 1850, there remained only 40,000; by 1860, only 3,000.

The extent of the cotton trade

English cotton textiles flooded the world market from the 1780s. Here was a light material, suitable for the climates of Africa, India, and the more temperate zones of North America. Here was a material cheap enough to make it possible for millions who had never before enjoyed the comfort of washable body clothes to do so. And here was material fine enough to tempt the rich to experiment with muslins and calicos in a way they had not done before. Figures speak eloquently of the revolutionary change wrought by the expanding industry. In 1760, England exported less than £250,000 worth of cotton goods; by 1800 it was exporting over £5 million worth. In 1760, England imported 2.5 million pounds of raw cotton; in 1787, 22 million pounds; in 1837, 366 million pounds. By 1800, cotton accounted for about 5 percent of the national income of the country; by 1812, from 7 to 8 percent. By 1815, the export of cotton textiles amounted to 40 percent of the value of all domestic goods exported from Great Britain. Although the price of manufactured cotton goods fell dramatically, the market expanded so rapidly that profits continued to increase.

Unlike the changes in the textile industry, those occurring in the manufacture of iron were not great enough to warrant their being labeled revolutionary. Yet they were most significant. Britain's abundant supply of coal, combined with its advanced transportation network, allowed the English, from the middle of the eighteenth century, to substitute coal for wood in the heating of molten metal. A series of discoveries made fuel savings possible, along with a higher quality of iron and the manufacture of a greater variety of iron products. Demand rose sharply during the war years at the end of the century. It remained high as a result of calls for plant machinery, agricultural implements, and hardware; it rose dramatically with the coming of railways in the 1830s and 1840s. Britain was exporting 571,000 tons of iron in 1814; in 1852, it exported 1,036,000 tons out of a world total of almost 2,000,000—more iron than was made by all the rest of the world combined.

The need for more coal required the mining of deeper and deeper veins. In 1712, Thomas Newcomen had devised a crude but effective steam engine for pumping water from mines. Though of value to the

The iron industry

The steam engine

Aqueduct in Wales. The 124-foot-high span carried water in a 10-foot wide cast iron trough over the River Dee. Designed by Thomas Telford, this "stream in the sky" was one of the most impressive engineering feats of the early Industrial Revolution.

Old Hetton Colliery, Sunderland, England. Designed by the engineer Thomas Hair about 1840, this large mine was typical of those built to meet the increased demand for coal. Note the railways that connected the mines with the sea.

coal industry, it was of less use in other industries, since it was wasteful of both fuel and power. In 1763, James Watt, a maker of scientific instruments at the University of Glasgow, was asked to repair a model of the Newcomen engine. While engaged in this task he conceived the idea that the machine would be greatly improved if a separate chamber were added to condense the steam, so as to eliminate the necessity of cooling the cylinder. He patented his first engine incorporating this device in 1769. Watt's genius as an inventor was not matched by his business ability. He admitted that he would "rather face a loaded cannon than settle a disputed account or make a bargain." As a consequence, he fell into debt in attempting to place his machines on the market. He was rescued by Matthew Boulton, a wealthy hardware manufacturer of Birmingham. The two men formed a partnership, with Boulton providing the capital. By 1800 the firm had sold 289 engines for use in factories and mines. The steam engine replaced water as the principle motive force in industry slowly. In 1850 more than a third of the power used in woolen manufacture and an eighth of that used in cotton was still produced by water. Nevertheless, there is no question that without the steam engine there could have been no industrial expansion on the scale that we have described.

Other advances　　Other industries experienced profound changes during the hundred years of the Industrial Revolution. Many of those changes came in response to the growth of textile manufacture. The chemical industry, for example, developed new methods of dyeing and bleaching, as well as improved methods of production in the fields of soap and glassmaking. Production of goods increased across the board, as profits from the boom in manufacturing increased the demand for new and more sophisticated articles. Such trades as pottery and metalware expanded to meet demands, in the process adopting methods that in most instances reduced cost and speeded manufacture.

To understand fully the nature of the Industrial Revolution in England one must not lose sight of two important factors: the first is that dramatic as the revolution was, it happened over a period of two or three generations, at varying paces in different industries. Some men and women continued to work at home, much as their grandfathers and grandmothers had. Old tools and old methods were not immediately replaced by new ones, any more than populations fled the countryside overnight for the city. Second, the revolution was accomplished from a very limited technological and theoretical base. Except in the chemical industry, change was not the result of scientific research. It was the product of empirical experimentation—in some cases, of little more than creative tinkering. To say this is not to disparage the work of men such as Arkwright, Hargreaves, Watt, and their like. It is to suggest, however, the reason why England, without a national system of education on any level, was nonetheless able to accomplish the revolution it did. Nor are these remarks intended to belittle the magnitude of the change. What occurred in England was a revolution because of the way in which it reshaped the lives, not just of the English, but of people across the globe. By responding as it did to the demands of its apparently insatiable markets, England made a revolution every bit as profound and long-lasting as that which occurred simultaneously in France.

2. THE INDUSTRIAL REVOLUTION ON THE CONTINENT

The Industrial Revolution came in time to the Continent, but not to any important degree before about 1830. As we have seen, manufacturing in eighteenth-century France and Germany clustered in regions whose proximity to raw materials, access to markets, and traditional attachment to particular skills had resulted in their development as industrial centers. Flanders and Normandy in France, and Saxony in Germany were centers for the manufacture of woolen cloth; Switzerland, southern Germany, and Normandy, of cottons; Wallonia (the area around Liège in Belgium), the Marne valley, and Silesia in Germany, of iron. Yet for a variety of reasons, these areas failed to experience the late-eighteenth-century breakthrough that occurred in Britain. Nor were they capable at first of imitating Britain's success, once they began to perceive the great economic advantages that Britain's pronounced lead was bringing it. There were a number of reasons for the delay of continental industrialization. Whereas England's transportation system was highly developed, those of France and Germany were not. France was far larger than England, its rivers were not as easily navigable, its seaports were farther apart. Central Europe was so divided into tiny principalities, each with its own set of tolls and tariffs, as to make the transportation of raw materials or manufactured

See color map facing page 231

goods over any considerable distance impractical. Nor was France itself free of the sorts of regulations that thwarted easy shipments. In addition, the Continent was not as blessed with an abundance of raw materials as England. France, the Low Countries, and Germany imported wool. Europe lacked an abundant supply of the fuel that was the new source of industrial energy. Few major coal deposits were known to exist, while the ready availability of timber discouraged exploration that might have resulted in its discovery.

(2) lack of entrepreneurial spirit

Distances and distinctions between social and economic ranks were far greater on the Continent than in England. Money was not the social solvent in France and Germany that it was across the Channel. Before the French Revolution, continental aristocrats hesitated before investing in commercial enterprises they believed would damage their social standing. In some countries, laws prevented aristocrats from engaging in business. After the revolution, middle-class Frenchmen, though free in theory to rise as high on the social and economic ladder as they might aspire, appear largely to have remained content to make only enough money to sustain a modest-size business. The motivation of the middle class was as often social as it was economic: to ensure the continuity of a family rather than to produce increasing quantities of goods. Furthermore, capital was not as readily available on the Continent as in England. In France, again, the retarded development of agricultural capitalism, due to the tenacious economic perseverance of small peasant landholders, limited the supply of savings, both for investment in industry and for expenditure on manufactured goods. Nor was the entrepreneurial spirit that compelled Englishmen to drive competitors to the wall as highly developed in France and Germany in the years after 1815. Exhausted by the competitiveness of war, and fearful of the disruptions that war brought in its train, continental

A Swedish Mining Town, 1790

businessmen remained far more willing than the English to keep on manufacturing and selling on the same scale they always had.[1]

The Contient did not simply stand idle, however, as England assumed its industrial lead. The pace of mechanization was increasing in the 1780s. But the French Revolution and the wars that followed disrupted growth that might otherwise have taken place. Battles fought on French, German, and Italian soil destroyed factories and machinery. Although ironmaking increased to meet the demands of the wars, techniques remained what they had been. Commerce was badly hurt both by British destruction of French merchant shipping and by Napoleon's Continental System. Probably the revolutionary change most beneficial to industrial advance in Europe was the removal of previous restraints on the movement of capital and labor; for example, the abolition of trade guilds, and the reduction in the number of tariff barriers across the Continent. On balance, however, the revolutionary and Napoleonic wars clearly thwarted industrial development on the Continent, while at the same time intensifying it in England.

(3) effect of wars

A number of factors combined to produce a climate more generally conducive to industrialization on the Continent after 1815. Population continued to increase, not only throughout Europe, but in those areas now more and more dependent upon the importation of manufactured goods—Latin America, for example (see below, p. 247). European increases, which doubled the populations of most countries between 1800 and 1850, meant that the Continent would be supplied with a growing number of producers and consumers. More people did not necessarily mean further industrialization. In Ireland, for example, where other necessary factors were absent, more people meant less food. But in those countries with an already well-established commercial and industrial base—France and Germany, for example—increased population did encourage the adoption of the technologies and methods of production that had transformed Britain.

Increases after 1815;
(1) population rise

Transportation improved in western Europe both during and following the Napoleonic wars. The Austrian Empire added over 30,000 miles of roads between 1830 and 1847; Belgium almost doubled its road network in the same period; France built, in addition to roads, 2,000 miles of canals. In the United States, where industrialization was occurring at an increasingly rapid rate after 1830, road mileage jumped from 21,000 miles in 1800 to 170,000 in 1856. When these improvements were combined with the introduction of rail transport in the 1840s, the resulting increase in markets available to all Western countries encouraged them to introduce methods of manufacturing that would help meet new demands. The effect of railways on regional manufacturing, however, was not always positive. Clearly, they were a means of moving manufactured goods from a given region to more

(2) improved
transportation

[1] On this point, see David S. Landes, *The Unbound Prometheus,* pp. 132–33.

widely dispersed markets. But they also brought competition in the form of an influx of goods from outside to challenge local industries. The case of the Dijon area southeast of Paris illustrates the problem. With the coming of the railway, brewers and winegrowers there expanded their trade for a time. Eventually, however, they lost business when railways made possible the transportation of beer and wine over longer distances, from Alsace and the south of France.

(3) centralization

Governments played a more direct role in the process of industrialization on the Continent than in Britain. Napoleon's rationalization of French and imperial institutions had introduced Europe to the practice of state intervention. His legal code, which guaranteed freedom of contract and facilitated the establishment of joint-stock enterprises, encouraged other rulers to provide a similar framework for commercial expansion. In Prussia, lack of private capital necessitated state operation of a large proportion of that country's mines. In no European country but Britain would railways be built without the financial assistance of the state. In the private sector, as well, more attention was given on the Continent than in England to the need for artificial stimulation to produce industrial change. It was in Belgium that the first joint-stock investment bank—the Société Générale—was founded, an institution designed to facilitate the accumulation of ready capital for investment in industry and commerce. Europeans were also willing for the state to establish educational systems whose aim, among others, was to produce a well-trained elite capable of assisting in the development of industrial technology. What Britain had produced almost by chance, the Europeans began to reproduce by design.

(4) the lack of technicians

Until the Continent produced its own technicians it was compelled to rely on British expertise. But the pace of continental, and also American, industrialization, even after 1815, remained far slower than in Britain because of Britain's natural reluctance to see its methods of production pirated by others. British industrialists believed it their patriotic duty to prevent the exportation of their techniques, although they were more than willing to raid the Continent for technological experts: Matthew Boulton imported skilled workers from Vienna and Sweden. Continental entrepreneurs likewise argued that it was patriotism, not profit, that inspired them to compete with the British. "Our reasons for building our factory were exactly those which made you oppose it," a German firm wrote to Boulton; "that is patriotic zeal." Until 1825, British artisans were forbidden to emigrate; until 1842, much innovative machinery could not be exported. Laws did not, however, prevent the movement of creative technician-entrepreneurs and their particular skills; many Englishmen, during the first part of the nineteenth century, made fortunes as they taught others in Europe and America to do what they had taught themselves. One such man was William Cockerill, who began his career in England as a carpenter. He and his sons built cotton-spinning equipment on the Continent during the revolutionary wars. In 1817, they purchased the palace of the former bishops of Liège, converting it to a factory producing machinery and steam engines. Yet despite the presence of entrepreneurs like the Cockerills, or of continental counterparts such as the Westphalian Fritz Harkort, who built and sold steam engines across Europe in the 1820s and 1830s, the general lack of large numbers of European technicians, experts, and entrepreneurs undoubtedly hampered rapid industrial expansion in France, Germany, and elsewhere.

The growth of the textile industry in Europe was patterned by the circumstances of the Napoleonic wars. The supply of cotton to the Continent had been interrupted, thanks to the British blockade, but the military's greater demand for woolen cloth meant that expansion occurred more rapidly in the latter than in the former industry. By 1820, the spinning of wool by machine was the common practice on the Continent; weaving, however, was still accomplished largely by hand. Regional centers for the production of wool were located around Rheims and in Alsace in France; in what is now Belgium; and in Saxony and Silesia in Germany. All possessed, at least in some measure, the various elements necessary to the successful growth and development of a regional economic system: transportation, resources, markets, technology, and labor supply. Mechanization was retarded because manual labor was cheap, and by the important fact that since Britain's market was so large, continental profits too often depended upon the manufacture of some particular specialty not made in England, and therefore without broad commercial appeal. Cotton manufacture was curtailed by the same circumstances. In France, as a result, mechanization occurred first in the silk industry and those sections of the cotton industry which produced finer specialty materials—lace, for example. A tradition of prestige associated with the production of

Textiles

Silk Weavers of Lyon, 1850. The first significant working-class uprisings in nineteenth-century France occurred here in 1831 and 1834. Note the domestic character of the working conditions.

A German Textile Factory, 1848. This is an unusually large manufacturing facility for this period on the Continent.

luxury goods, dating back to the reign of Louis XIV, encouraged entrepreneurs to invest in this branch of the textile industry. They were willing to forgo mass markets in the hope that their products would not meet with British competition. France nevertheless remained the largest continental producer of cotton goods, followed by Belgium and the German territories of the Rhine valley—Saxony, Silesia, and Bavaria.

Heavy industry

In the area of heavy industry on the Continent, the picture was much the same as in textiles: i.e., gradual advances in the adoption of technological innovation against a background of more general resistance to change. Here, however, because change came later than in Britain, it coincided with an increased demand for various goods that had come into being as a result of industrialization and urbanization: iron pipe, much in use by mid-century in cities for gas, water, and drainage; metal machinery, now replacing earlier wooden prototypes. Consequently, the iron industry took the lead over textiles on the Continent, accompanied by an increase, where possible, in the production of coal. Coal was scarce, however; in the Rhineland, wood was still used to manufacture iron. The result was an unwillingness on the part of entrepreneurs to make as extensive use of the steam engine as they might have otherwise; it used too much fuel. In France, as late as 1844, hydraulic (i.e., water-driven) engines were employed far more often for the manufacture of iron than were steam engines. One further problem hampered the development of continental heavy industry during the first half of the nineteenth century. British competition forced continental machine construction firms to scramble for whatever orders they could get. This need to respond to a variety of requests meant that it was difficult for firms to specialize in a single product. The result was a lack of standardization, and continued production to order, when rationalization and specialization would have resulted in an increased volume of production.

3. THE COMING OF RAILWAYS

By about 1840, then, continental countries, and to some degree the United States, were moving gradually along the course of industrialization traced by Britain, producing far more than they had, yet nothing like as much as their spectacular pace setter. Within the next ten years, the coming of the railways was to alter that situation. Though Britain by no means lost its lead, the stimulus generally provided to Western economies by the introduction of railway systems throughout much of the world carried the Continent and America far enough and fast enough to allow them to become genuine competitors with the British.

Railways as a stimulus to the European and American economies

Railways came into being in answer to two needs. The first was the obvious desire on the part of entrepreneurs to transport their goods as quickly and cheaply as possible across long distances. Despite already mentioned improvements in transportation during the years before 1830, the movement of heavy materials, particularly coal, remained a problem. It is significant that the first modern railway was built in England in 1825 from the Durham coal field of Stockton to Darlington, near the coast. "Tramways"—parallel tracks along which

Railways as goods carriers

See color map facing page 231

The New Railway Age. Left: Stephenson's *Rocket.* A reconstruction of the railway engine built by George Stephenson in 1829. Right: "The Railway Juggernaut of 1845." A cartoon from the English humor magazine *Punch* satirizing speculation—often financially disastrous—in railway stocks.

coal carts were pulled by horses—had long been in use at pitheads to haul coal short distances. The Stockton to Darlington railway was a logical extension of this device, designed to answer the transportation needs produced by constantly expanding industrialization. The man primarily responsible for the design of the first steam railway was George Stephenson, a self-made engineer who had not learned to read until he was seventeen. He talked a group of northern England investors into the merits of steam traction and was given full liberty to carry out his plans. The locomotives on the Stockton-Darlington line traveled at fifteen miles per hour, the fastest rate at which human beings had yet moved overland.

Railways as an investment opportunity

Railways were also built in response to other than purely industrial needs: specifically, the need for capitalists to invest their money. Englishmen such as those who had made sizable fortunes in textiles, once they had paid out workers' wages and plowed back substantial capital in their factories, retained a surplus profit for which they wanted a decent yet reliable return. Railways provided them with the solution to their problem. Though by no means as reliable as had been hoped, railway investment proved capable of more than satisfying the capitalists' demands. No sooner did the first combined passenger and goods service open in 1830, on the Liverpool to Manchester line, than plans were formulated and money pledged to extend rail systems throughout Europe, the Americas, and beyond. In 1830, there were no more than a few dozen miles of railway in the world. By 1840, there were over 4,500 miles; by 1850, over 23,000. The English contractor, Thomas Brassey, the most famous, but by no means the only one of his kind, built railways in Italy, Canada, Argentina, India, and Australia.

Thomas Brassey

The railway boom accelerated industrialization generally. Not only did it increase enormously the demand for coal and for a variety of heavy manufactured goods—rails, locomotives, carriages, signals, switches; by enabling goods to move faster from factory to salesroom, railways decreased the time it took to sell those goods. Quicker sales meant, in turn, a quicker return on capital investment, money which could then be reinvested in the manufacture of more goods. Finally, by opening up the world market as it had never been before, the railway boom stimulated the production of such a quantity of material goods as to ensure the rapid completion of the West's industrialization.

Size and scope of the railway construction industry

The building of a railway line was an undertaking on a scale infinitely greater than the building of a factory. Railway construction required capital investment beyond the capacity of any single individual. In Britain, a factory might be worth anything from £20,000 to £200,000. The average cost of twenty-seven of the more important railway lines constructed between 1830 and 1853 was £2 million. The average labor force of a factory ranged from 50 to 300. The average labor force of a railway, after construction, was 2,500. Because a railway crossed the property of a large number of individual land-owners, each of whom would naturally demand as much remuneration as he thought he could get, the planning of an efficient and economical route was a tricky and time-consuming business. The entrepreneur and contractor had to concern themselves not only with the purchase of right-of-way. They also contended with problems raised by the destruction of sizable portions of already existing urban areas, to make room for stations and switching yards. And they had to select a route that would be as free as possible of the hills and valleys that would necessitate the construction of expensive tunnels, cuts, and embankments. Railway-builders ran tremendous risks. Portions of most lines were subcontracted at fixed bids to contractors of limited experience. A spate of bad weather might delay construction to the point where builders would be lucky to bring in the finished job within 25 percent of their original bid. Of the thirty major contractors on the London to Birmingham line, ten failed completely.

If the business of a contractor was marked by uncertainty, that of the construction worker was characterized by back-breaking labor. The English "navvies," who built railways not only throughout Britain but around the world, were a remarkable breed. Their name derived from "navigator," a term applied to the construction workers on England's eighteenth-century canals. The work that they accomplished was prodigious. Because there is little friction between a train's wheels and its tracks, it can transport heavy loads easily. But lack of friction ceases to be an advantage when a train has to climb or

An American Proposal for a Steam-Driven Trolley. The application of the steam engine to transportation inspired inventors to devise novel solutions to perceived problems. This particular steam engine was disguised so as not to frighten horses on crowded city streets.

The "navvies"

Construction of the London to Birmingham Railway, London, 1838. This drawing of the building of retaining walls in a new railway cut evokes the chaos created by railway construction within urban areas.

descend a grade, thereby running the risk of slippage. Hence the need for comparatively level roadbeds; and hence the need for laborers to construct those tunnels, cuts, and embankments that would keep the roadbeds level. Navvies worked in gangs, whose migrations throughout the countryside traced the course of railway development. They were a rough lot, living in temporary encampments, often with women who were not their wives. The Irish navvies were a particularly tough breed. A sign posted by local residents in Scotland in 1845 warned that if all the Irish navvies were not "off the ground and out of the country" in a week, they would be driven out "by the strength of our armes and a good pick shaft."

The magnitude of the navvies' achievement

The magnitude of the navvies' accomplishment was extraordinary. In England and in much of the rest of the world, mid–nineteenth-century railways were constructed almost entirely without the aid of machinery. An assistant engineer on the London to Birmingham line, in calculating the magnitude of that particular construction, determined that the labor involved was the equivalent of lifting 25 billion cubic feet of earth and stone one foot high. This he compared with the feat of building the Great Pyramid, a task he estimated had involved the hoisting of some 16 billion tons. But whereas the building of the pyramid had required over 200,000 men and had taken twenty years, the construction of the London to Birmingham railway was accomplished by 20,000 men in less than five years. Translated into individual terms, a navvy was expected to move an average of twenty tons of earth per day. Railways were laid upon an almost infinite base of human muscle and sweat.

Railway Navvies. Without the aid of machinery, the burden of building Britain's railways fell on the backs of men such as these.

The Dresden Railway Station. Railways had the power to alter the architecture of the city, producing new and dramatic urban spaces.

4. INDUSTRIALIZATION AFTER 1850

In the years between 1850 and 1870, Britain remained very much the industrial giant of the West. But France, Germany, Belgium, and the United States assumed the position of challengers. In the iron industry, Britain's rate of growth during these years was not as great as that of either France or Germany (5.2 percent for Britain, as against 6.7 percent for France and 10.2 percent for Germany). But in 1870 Britain was still producing half the world's pig iron; 3.5 times as much as the United States, more than 4 times as much as Germany, and more than 5 times as much as France. Although the number of cotton spindles increased from 5.5 to 11.5 million in the United States between 1852 and 1861, and by significant but not as spectacular percentages in European countries, Britain in 1861 had 31 million spindles at work in comparison with France's 5.5 million, Germany's 2 million, Switzerland's 1.3 million, and Austria's 1.8 million.

Britain still the leader

Most of the gains experienced in Europe came as a result of continuing changes in those areas we have come to recognize as important for sustained industrial growth. The improved transportation systems that resulted from the spread of railways helped encourage an increase in the free movement of goods. International monetary unions were established, and restrictions removed on international waterways such

Continuing European advance

as the Danube. The Prussian *Zollverein,* or tariff union, an organization designed to facilitate internal free trade, was established in 1818 and was extended over the next twenty years to include most of the German principalities outside Austria. Free trade went hand in hand with further removal of barriers to the freedom to enter trades and to practice business unhampered by restrictive regulation. Control of guilds and corporations over artisan production was abolished in Austria in 1859 and in most of Germany by the mid-1860s. Laws against usury, most of which had ceased to be enforced, were officially abandoned in Britain, Holland, Belgium, and in many parts of Germany. Governmental regulation of the operation of mines was surrendered by the Prussian state in the 1850s, freeing entrepreneurs to develop resources as they saw fit. The formation of investment banks proceeded apace, encouraged by an important increase in the money supply, and therefore an easing of credit, following the opening of the California gold fields in 1849.

Increased trade in raw materials

A further reason for increased European production was the growing trade in raw materials. Wool and hides imported from Australia helped diminish the consequences of the cotton shortage suffered after the outbreak of the United States Civil War and the Union blockade of the American South. Other importations—guano from the Pacific, vegetable oils from Africa, pyrites (sulfides) from Spain—stimulated the scale of food production and both altered and increased the manufacture of soap, candles, and finished textiles. Finally, discoveries of new sources of coal, particularly in the Pas-de-Calais region of France and in the Ruhr valley in Germany, had dramatic repercussions. Production of coal in France rose from 4.4 million to 13.3 million tons between 1850 and 1869; during the same years, German production increased from 4.2 million to 23.7 million tons.

The slower pace of industrialization in eastern and southern Europe

Industrialization in eastern and southern Europe after mid-century proceeded at a much slower pace than in western Europe. This was in part a result of the fact that many Eastern regions played an increasingly specialized role in the economy of the Continent, providing food and agricultural materials to the West. The constantly growing demand for agricultural products from the East resulted in the development of agriculture as a major capitalist industry there. As they rationalized their operations so as to make them more efficient and hence more profitable, entrepreneurs recognized the degree to which they were hampered by the outmoded economic practices of serfdom, a system which prevented the mobility of labor and thus the formation of an effective agricultural work force. Serfdom was abolished in most parts of eastern and southern Europe by 1850, and in Poland and Russia in the 1860s.

The fact that industry continued to take a back seat to agriculture does not mean, however, that eastern Europe was without important manufacturing regions. By the 1880s, the number of men and women employed in the cotton industry in the Austrian province of Bohemia exceeded that in Saxony. In the Czechoslovakian region, textile industries, developed in the eighteenth century, continued to thrive. By the 1830s, there were machine-powered Czech cotton mills, and iron works. In Russia, a factory industry producing coarse textiles—mostly linens—had grown up around Moscow. At mid-century, Russia was purchasing 24 percent of the total British machinery exports to mechanize its own mills. Many workers in Russian industry remained serfs until the 1860s—about 40 percent, a number of them employed in mines. Of the over 800,000 Russians engaged in manufacturing by 1860, however, most labored not in factories but in very small workshops, where average employment numbered about 40 persons.

Pockets of industrialization in the East

By 1870 Europe was by no means a fully industrialized continent. Fifty percent of France's labor force remained on farms. Agricultural laborers were the single largest occupational category in Britain during the 1860s. Great stretches of the Continent—Spain, southern Italy, eastern Europe—were almost untouched by the Industrial Revolution. And in the industrialized countries, much work was still accomplished in tiny workshops or at home. Yet if Europe was by no means wholly industrial, it was far and away the most industrially advanced portion of the globe—and not by accident. In order to maintain its position of producer to the world, Europe, and Britain particularly, made certain that no other areas stood a chance to compete. Europe used its economic and, when necessary, its military strength to ensure that the world remained divided between the producers of manufactured goods—Europe itself—and suppliers of the necessary raw materials—everyone else. Often this arrangement suited those in other parts of the world who made their money by providing the raw materials that fueled the European economy. Cotton-growers in the southern United States, sugar-growers in the Caribbean, wheat-growers in the Ukraine—all remained content with arrangements as dictated by the industrialized West. Those countries which expressed their discontent—Egypt, for example, which in the 1830s attempted to establish its own cotton textile industry—were soon put in their place by a show of force. Western Europeans, believing in their right to industrial leadership in the world, saw nothing wrong with employing soldiers, if they had to, to make others understand their destiny.

Europe's economy within the world

SELECTED READINGS

• *Items so designated are available in paperback editions.*

• Ashton, T. S., *The Industrial Revolution, 1760–1830,* London, 1948. A standard short introduction.
 Cameron, R. E., *France and the Industrial Development of Europe.* Princeton, 1968. Valuable material on the Industrial Revolution outside Britain.

Checkland, S. G., *The Rise of Industrial Society in England, 1815–1885,* New York, 1965. Emphasizes the economic organization of England.

• Deane, Phyllis, *The First Industrial Revolution,* Cambridge, 1965.

Henderson, W. O., *The Industrialization of Europe, 1780–1914,* New York, 1969

———, *The State and the Industrial Revolution in Prussia, 1740–1870,* Liverpool, 1958. A biographical approach. Good on technical education.

• Hobsbawn, Eric, *Industry and Empire: 1750 to the Present Day,* New York, 1968. A general survey of industrialization in Britain, written from a Marxist perspective.

• Landes, David S., *Revolution in Time: Clocks and the Making of the Modern World,* Cambridge, Mass., 1983. The social and economic changes wrought by the advent of cheap and accurate time-keeping.

• ———, *The Unbound Prometheus,* London, 1969. An excellent treatment of the technological innovations and economic results of the Industrial Revolution.

McManners, John, *European History: Men, Machines and Freedom,* New York, 1967.

• Mantoux, Paul, *The Industrial Revolution in the Eighteenth Century,* rev. ed., New York, 1961. The beginnings of the modern factory system in England.

Schofer, L. *The Formation of a Modern Labor Force,* Berkeley, 1975. Analyzes industrialization and its social consequences in Silesia.

• Taylor, George Rogers, *The Transportation Revolution, 1815–1860,* New York, 1968.

SOURCE MATERIALS

Dodd, George, *Days at the Factories; or the Manufacturing Industry of Great Britain Described, and Illustrated by Numerous Engravings of Machines and Processes,* Totawa, N.J., 1975. A reprint of the 1850 edition.

Mitchell, Brian R., and Phyllis Deane, *Abstract of British Historical Statistics,* Cambridge, 1962. The single best source for statistics on population, trade, manufacturing, etc.

• Smith, Adam, *An Inquiry into the Nature and Causes of the Wealth of Nations,* Chicago, 1977. Written in 1776, this revolutionary work called for the end of mercantilism.

Ward, J. T., *The Factory System, 1830–1855,* New York, 1970. Excerpts from contemporary documents describing, defending, and criticizing the factory system and industrialization.

Chapter 27

CONSEQUENCES OF INDUSTRIALIZATION: URBANIZATION AND CLASS CONSCIOUSNESS (1800–1850)

What Art was to the ancient world, Science is to the modern: The distinctive faculty. In the minds of men the useful has succeeded the beautiful. Yet rightly understood, Manchester is as great a human exploit as Athens.

—Benjamin Disraeli, *Coningsby*

The Industrial Revolution was more than an important event in the economic and technological history of the West. It helped to reshape the patterns of life for men and women, first in Britain, then in Europe and America, and eventually throughout much of the world. By increasing the scale of production, the Industrial Revolution brought about the factory system, which in turn compelled the migration of millions from the countryside and small towns into cities. Once in those cities, men and women had to learn a new way of life, and learn it quickly: how to discipline themselves to the factory whistle and survive in a slum, if they were first-generation urban workers; how to manage a work force and achieve respectable prominence for themselves in the community, if they were businessmen and their wives. One particular lesson that industrialization and urbanization taught was that of class consciousness. Men and women, to a far greater degree than heretofore, began to perceive themselves as part of a class with interests of its own, and in opposition to the interests of men and women in other classes.

Consequences of the Industrial Revolution

We shall examine this range of social and cultural changes as they occurred during the first fifty years or so of the nineteenth century, after looking briefly first at the condition of the bulk of the population, which, despite industrialization, remained on the land. Since the Industrial Revolution came first to Britain, our focus will be on that country. Yet the pattern set by the British was one that was repeated to a great extent in other European countries, as industrialization came to them in time.

1. PEOPLE ON THE LAND

Population patterns

The dramatic story of the growth of industrialization and urbanization must not be allowed to obscure the fact that, in 1850, the population of Europe was still overwhelmingly a peasant population. While in England, by 1830, a sizable minority lived in towns and cities, elsewhere society remained predominantly or overwhelmingly rural. In France and Italy, 60 percent lived in the country; in Prussia, over 70 percent; in Spain, over 90 percent; in Russia, over 95 percent. Demographic pressures, which helped produce chaos in the cities, likewise caused severe hardship in the countryside. The populations of the predominantly agricultural nations leapt forward with those that were industrializing. The population of Europe as a whole, estimated roughly at 205 million by 1800, had risen to 274 million by 1850, and to 320 million by 1870. In Britain, with its comparatively high standard of living, the numbers increased from 16 million to 27 million. Yet the rural Irish, despite their periodic famines, increased too, from 5.5 to 8 million, and the Russians from 39 to 60 million, in the same period.

Causes of continuing population expansion

The causes of this continuing population explosion remain obscure. The notion that the explanation can be traced to a desire on the part of parents in industrial counties to produce more family wage-earners is now downplayed by scholars, given the fact that increases occurred in rural regions as well. One contributing factor to this continued growth may have been a decline in the virulence of certain fatal diseases as a result of the cyclical potency of microbes. Certainly the curbing of cholera, through the adoption of sanitary reforms, and smallpox, as Edward Jenner's technique of vaccination gained gradual acceptance after 1796, help to explain the population trend. The increasing ability and desire of governments to monitor and improve the lives of their subjects had a direct effect on the decline of the death rate. At the same time the availability of less expensive foods of high nutritional value—most notably the potato— and the ability to transport foodstuffs cheaply by rail meant European populations would not suffer as much from undernourishment as in the past, and that they would thus be less susceptible to debilitating illness. Other plausible explanations suggest that the population increase was the result of rising birth rates caused by earlier marriages. As serfdom declined, peasants tended to set up households at a younger age. A relatively small expansion in the population of a region in one generation would result in a far

Interior of an English Farm Laborer's Cottage, 1846. Note the wooden crate used as an infant's cradle.

greater one in the next. As the population grew, the number of young and fertile people grew faster, thereby significantly increasing the ratio of births to total population.

Whatever the reasons for the population increase, conditions remained such as to make the life of the poorer rural inhabitants of Europe seldom more than bleak. Overpopulation brought underemployment, and hence poverty, in its train. Millions of tiny holdings produced a bare subsistence living, if that. Farmers still sowed and harvested by hand. Conditions in rural areas deteriorated sharply whenever there was a bad harvest. The average daily diet for an entire family in a "good" year might amount to no more than two or three pounds of bread—a total of about 3,000 calories. Hunger—often near-starvation—as well as epidemic disease were still common occurrences. The result was a standard of living—if one can dignify the condition with that name—that for many rural inhabitants of many areas in Europe actually declined in the first half of the nineteenth century, although not enough to reverse general population growth. Governments in some countries attempted to solve the related problems of population pressure and impoverishment by passing laws raising the age of marriage. In some of the states of southern and western Germany, as well as in Austria, men were forbidden to marry before the age of thirty, and were also required to prove their ability to support a family. Governments did their best to encourage emigration to ease the overcrowding, the majority of emigrants relocating in the Americas. Emigration from England rose from 57,000 in 1830, to 90,000 in 1840, to 280,000 in 1850. Ireland, in the early years of the nineteenth century, witnessed the departure of over 1.5 million before the great potato famine of 1846, when approximately three

Wretched rural conditions

Agricultural capitalism

out of every four acres of potatoes were blighted. After the potato famine, the flow of emigrants increased to a flood.

Even had such policies acted as an effective curb on population growth—which, in the main, they did not—they would nevertheless have failed to prevent the rural stresses that resulted from the continuing spread of agricultural capitalism. The pace of this change varied across Europe; it was furthest advanced in England and Prussia. Wherever landed proprietors determined to meet increased demand for food by farming large areas as a capital investment, they imposed a series of transformations that were bound to affect the lives of agricultural laborers. First, land must be made a negotiable commodity. It must not, therefore, be tied to ancient customs which clouded its title—as was the case, for example, with common land, to which the poor within a community might have some right of access or cultivation. Second, land must be in the hands of those with capital enough to improve it, in order to make of it a profitable investment. It must be enclosed—"regulated" was the term in Prussia—so that, as we have seen, it could be properly fertilized and drained, or, if it was grazing land, so that breeds might be scientifically improved without fear of mongrelization. Finally, a mobile force of agricultural laborers must be available to work at the capitalists' behest. They must not be "tied" to a particular piece of land, either through systems of customary rights or bondage. They must be free to go where they were told to go, to work whatever land would bring most profit to its owners.

Its results

These requirements, as they were imposed, produced dislocation and hardship. In Scotland, workers were cleared from land which they had farmed as tenants, in order to provide pasturage for the more profitable sheep. In Germany, those serfs emancipated by a reform-minded government in 1807 were compelled to forfeit somewhere between a third to a half of their land in return for their freedom; those who were able to retain small holdings were in most cases pressured to sell out to larger landholders. Not all landlords were ruthless. "Model" improvers among the wealthiest of the English landowners adjusted to capitalist competition without entirely forswearing traditional responsibilities. They built houses for tenants and laborers, and provided them with schools and churches. In eastern Europe there were among the Prussian landlords (Junkers) pietists who acknowledged obligations to their tenants as well as to the market.

*Variations in the pattern
of agricultural
development*

The speed with which agricultural change occurred in various parts of Europe depended upon the nature of particular governments. Those more sympathetic to new capitalist impulses facilitated the transfer and reorganization of land by means of enabling legislation. They encouraged the elimination of small farms and an increase in larger, more efficient units of production. In England, over half the total area of the country, excluding waste land, was composed of estates of a thousand acres or more. In Spain, the fortunes of agricultural

A Mowing Team in England, c. 1870. Roughly twenty men and boys wielding scythes were required for work that would shortly be accomplished by a single machine. The scythes, which only achieved widespread use in the nineteenth century, had replaced the sickle, a much more primitive and physically taxing tool.

capitalism fluctuated with the political tenor of successive regimes: with the coming of a liberal party to power in 1820 came a law encouraging the free transfer of land; with the restoration of absolutism in 1823 came a repeal of the law. Russia was one of the countries least affected by agricultural change in the first half of the nineteenth century. There land was worked in vast blocks; some of the largest landowners possessed over half a million acres. Until the emancipation of the serfs in the 1860s, landowners claimed the labor of dependent peasant populations for as much as several days per week.

European serfdom, which bound hundreds of thousands of men, women, and children to particular estates for generations, prohibited the use of land as a negotiable commodity and therefore prevented the development of agricultural entrepreneurship. In France, despite the fact that manorialism had been abolished by the revolution, there was no rapid movement toward large-scale capitalist farming. An army of peasant proprietors, direct beneficiaries of the Jacobins' democratic constitution, continued to work the small farms they owned. The fact that France suffered far less agricultural distress, even in the 1840s, than did other European countries, and the fact that there was less migration in France from the country to the city and overseas than there was in Germany and England, are marks of the general success of this rural lower middle class in sustaining itself on the land. Its members were content to farm in the old way, opposed agricultural innovation, and, indeed, innovation generally. Despite

The legacy of manorialism

*Rural societies and
industrialization*

Rural disturbances

*Reasons for the growth of
cities*

their veneration of the revolution, they were among the most conservative elements in European society.

Rural populations, despite their isolation from urban centers, found themselves directly affected by the events of the Industrial Revolution. Factories brought about a decline in cottage industry and a consequent loss of vital income, especially during winter months. Improved communication networks not only afforded rural populations a keener sense of events and opportunities elsewhere, but also made it possible for governments to intrude upon the lives of these men and women to a degree previously impossible. Central bureaucracies now found it easier to collect taxes from the peasantry, and to conscript its sons into their armies.

Country people responded with sporadic violence against these and other harsh intrusions upon their lives. In southern England in the late 1820s, small farmers joined forces to burn barns and hayricks in protest to the introduction of thrashing machines, a symbol of the new agricultural capitalism. They masked and otherwise disguised themselves, riding out at night under the banner of their mythical leader, "Captain Swing." Their raids were preceded by anonymous threats such as the one received by a large-scale farmer in the county of Kent: "Pull down your threshing machine or else [expect] fire without delay. We are five thousand men [a highly inflated figure] and will not be stopped." Other major rural disturbances occurred in Ireland, Silesia, and Galicia in the 1830s and 1840s, and indeed, to a lesser degree, right across Europe. In no country, however, was the agrarian population a united political force. Those who owned land, those who leased it as tenants, and those who worked it as laborers had interests as different from each other as from those of the urban populations.

2. URBANIZATION AND THE STANDARD OF LIVING

If the countryside continued to hold the bulk of Europe's population in the years between 1800 and 1850, the growth of cities nevertheless remains one of the most important facts in the social history of that period. Cities grew in size and number once the steam engine made it practical to bring together large concentrations of men, women, and children to work in factories. Steam engines freed entrepreneurs from their dependence on water power and allowed them to consolidate production in large cities. In cities, transportation was more accessible than in the countryside. Hence it was less costly to import raw materials and ship out finished goods. Workers were more readily available in cities, as well, attracted as they were in large numbers in the hope—often false—of finding steady work at higher wages than those paid agricultural laborers. Industrialization was not the only reason for the growth of cities in the early nineteenth century, however. General population growth combined with industrialization forced cities to expand at an alarming rate.

In the ten years between 1831 and 1841 London's population grew by 130,000, Manchester's by 70,000. Paris increased by 120,000 between 1841 and 1846. Vienna grew by 125,000 from 1827 to 1847, into a city of 400,000. Berlin had as large a population by 1848, having increased by 180,000 since 1815. The primary result in these and other fast-growing centers was dreadful overcrowding. Construction lagged far behind population growth. In Vienna, though population rose 42 percent during the twenty years before 1847, the increase in housing was only 11.5 percent. In many of the larger cities, old and new, working men and women lived in lodging houses, apart from families left behind in the country. The poorest workers in almost all European cities dwelt in wretched basement rooms, often without any light or drainage.

Urban population increases

With cities as overcrowded as they were, it is no wonder that they were a menace to the health of those who lived within them. The middle classes moved as far as possible from disease and factory smoke, leaving the poorest members of the community isolated and a prey to the sickness which ravaged working-class sections. Cholera, typhus, and tuberculosis were natural predators in areas without adequate sewerage facilities and fresh water, and over which smoke from factories, railroads, and domestic chimneys hung heavily. A local committee appointed to investigate conditions in the British manufacturing town of Huddersfield—not by any means the worst of that country's urban centers—reported that there were large areas without

Cities as a health menace

Women and Boys Fetching Water from a Standpipe in Fryingpan Alley, London. Not until the beginning of the twentieth century did major European cities begin to provide poorer residents with an adequate water supply.

Manchester, England at Mid-Century. This powerful photograph evokes the dreary, prison-like atmosphere of the new industrial city.

paving, sewers, or drains, "where garbage and filth of every description are left on the surface to ferment and rot; where pools of stagnant water are almost constant; where dwellings adjoining are thus necessarily caused to be of an inferior and even filthy description; thus where disease is engendered, and the health of the whole town perilled." Measures were gradually adopted by successive governments in an attempt to cure the worst of these ills, if only to prevent the spread of catastrophic epidemics. Legislation was designed to rid cities of their worst slums by tearing them down, and to improve sanitary conditions by supplying both water and drainage. Yet by 1850, these projects had only just begun. Paris, perhaps better supplied with water than any European city, had enough for no more than two baths per capita per year; in London, human waste remained uncollected in 250,000 domestic cesspools; in Manchester, fewer than a third of the dwellings were equipped with toilets of any sort.

Conditions such as these are important evidence in the debate that has occupied historians for the past several decades. The question is: Did the standard of living rise or fall in Europe during the first half century of the Industrial Revolution? One school, the "optimists," argues that workers shared in the more general increase in living standards which occurred throughout Europe from 1800 onward. A variation on this optimistic theme maintains that whatever the hardships workers were compelled to suffer during the period of intense industrialization after 1800, they represent the necessary and worthwhile price society had to pay before it could "take off" into a period of

The standard of living debate

"sustained economic growth." Sacrifices, in terms of standard of living, were required to permit accumulation of a capital base sufficient to guarantee economic expansion and an eventual level of general prosperity higher than any civilization had hitherto achieved. Other historians insist that such an analysis encourages one to ignore the evidence of physical squalor and psychological disruption that men, women, and children suffered as they provided the statistical "base" for future economic historians' abstract calculations.

The debate is hampered by an absence of reliable evidence about wage levels, hours of work, and cost of living. Some skilled workers within the new factories, along with some artisans in older trades as yet unaffected by industrialization, appear to have benefited from a slight rise in wages and a decline in living costs. But regional variables, along with a constantly fluctuating demand for labor in all countries, suggest that the more lowly paid, unskilled worker, whether in England or on the Continent, led a thoroughly precarious existence. Textile workers in England, if guaranteed something like full employment, could theoretically earn enough to support a family. Such was not the case in Switzerland, however, where similar work paid only half what was necessary, or in Saxony, where a large portion of the population was apparently dependent upon either poor relief or charity. One of the most depressing features of working-class life in these years was its instability. Economic depressions were common occurrences; when they happened, workers were laid off for weeks at a time, with no system of unemployment insurance to sustain them. Half the working population of England's industrial cities were out of work in the early 1840s. In Paris, 85,000 went on relief in 1840. One particularly hard-pressed district of Silesia reported 30,000 out of 40,000 citizens in need of relief in 1844. Nor should one overlook the plight of those whose skills had been replaced by machinery—the hand-loom

Soup Kitchen Run by Quakers, Manchester, England, 1862. Enterprises of this sort, which doled out charity "indiscriminately"—that is, without investigating the recipient's character — were condemned by many members of the middle class as encouraging the "worst" elements — idlers and loafers — among the poor.

weavers being the most notable examples. In the English manufacturing town of Bolton, a hand-loom weaver could earn no more than about three shillings per week in 1842, at a time when experts estimated it took at least twenty shillings a week to keep a family of five above the poverty line. On that kind of pay, workers were fortunate if they did not starve to death. Forced to spend something like 65 percent of their income on food, the per capita meat consumption of the average worker declined to about forty pounds per year in the early nineteenth century.

The quality of life

Such figures make the optimists' generalizations hard to countenance. Figures of whatever sort fail to take into account the stress that urban factory life imposed upon the workers. Even workers making thirty shillings a week might well wonder if they were "better off," forced as they were to come to terms with the factory disciplines and living conditions imposed upon them. Of the more than 3 million men, women, and children living in England's sixty largest towns and cities in 1850, less than half had been born there. Though most migrated but a short distance from their place of birth, the psychological distance they traveled was tremendous. These qualitative factors, admittedly difficult to assess, must be weighed along with more easily quantifiable evidence before reaching any conclusion as to the increased standard of living in early-nineteenth-century cities. Whether or not life in cities was pleasant or ghastly, however, it was, for rapidly increasing numbers, a fact of life. Once we examine that life we will better understand the full impact of industrialization and urbanization upon those who first experienced it.

3. THE LIFE OF THE URBAN MIDDLE CLASS

Isambard Kingdom Brunel. Behind him are lengths of anchor chain from the steamship *The Great Western.*

The urban middle class which emerged during this period was by no means one homogeneous unit, in terms of occupation or income. In a general category that includes merchant princes and humble shopkeepers, subdivisions are important. The middle class included families of industrialists, such as the Peels (cotton) in England and, at a later period, the Krupps (iron) in Germany. It included financiers like the internationally famed Rothschilds, and, on a descending scale of wealth and power, bankers and capitalists throughout the major money markets of Europe: London, Brussels, Paris, Berlin. It included entrepreneurs like Thomas Brassey, the British railway magnate, and John Wilkinson, the English ironmaster, who had himself buried in an iron coffin, and technicians, like the engineer Isambard Kingdom Brunel, designer of the steamship *The Great Western*. It included bureaucrats, in growing demand when governments began to regulate the pace and direction of industrialization, and to ameliorate its harshest social and economic results. It included those in the already established professions—in law particularly, as lawyers put their expertise to the service of industrialists. It included the armies of managers and clerks necessary to the continuing momentum of industrial and financial expansion, and the equally large army of merchants and shopkeepers necessary to supply the wants of an increasingly affluent urban middle-class population. Finally, it included the families of all those who lived their lives in the various subcategories we have listed.

Movement within these ranks was often possible, in the course of one or two generations. Movement from the working class into the middle class, however, was far less common. Most middle-class successes originated within the middle class itself—the children of farmers, skilled artisans, or professionals. Upward mobility was almost impossible without education; education was an expensive, if not unattainable luxury for the children of a laborer. Careers open to talents, that goal achieved by the French Revolution, frequently meant middle-class jobs for middle-class young men who could pass exams. The examination system was an important path for ascendancy within governmental bureaucracies.

Young Gentlemen, 1834. It was to models such as these that the young men of the middle class aspired.

If passage from working class to middle class was not common, neither was the equally difficult social journey from middle class to aristocratic, landed society. This was particularly the case on the Continent, where the division between noble and commoner had traditionally been most pronounced. In Britain, mobility of this sort was easier. Children from wealthy upper-middle-class families, if they were sent, as occasionally they were, to elite schools and universities, and if they left the commercial or industrial world for a career in politics, might effect the change. William Gladstone, son of a Liverpool merchant, attended the exclusive educational preserves of Eton, a private boarding school, and Oxford University, married a connection of the aristocratic Grenville family, and became prime minister of England. Yet Gladstone was an exception to the rule in Britain, and Britain was an exception to the Continent. Movement, when it occurred, generally did so in less spectacular degrees.

Movement from the middle class to the aristocracy

Nevertheless, the European middle class helped sustain itself with the belief that it was possible to get ahead by means of intelligence, pluck, and serious devotion to work. The Englishman Samuel Smiles, in his extraordinarily successful how-to-succeed book *Self Help,* preached a gospel dear to the middle class. "The spirit of self-help is the root of all genuine growth in the individual," Smiles wrote. "Exhibited in the lives of many, it constitutes the true source of national vigor and strength." Although Smiles's gospel declared that anyone willing to exert himself could rise to a position of responsibility and personal profit, however, and although some men actually did so, the notion remained no more than myth for the great majority.

Self-help

Seriousness of purpose was reflected in the middle-class devotion to the ideal of family and home. A practical importance attached to the institution of the family in those areas in England, France, and Ger-

Left: *A Salon in Vienna, 1830s*. A representation of middle-class home life on the Continent. Right: *A Victorian Family at Tea, 1860s*

Family and home

many where sons, sons-in-law, nephews, and cousins were expected to assume responsibility in family firms when it came their turn. Yet the worship of family more often ignored those practical considerations and assumed the proportions of sacred belief. Away from the business and confusion of the world, sheltered behind solid masonry and amid the solid comfort of their ornate furnishings, middle-class fathers retired each evening to enjoy the fruits of their daily labors. Inside the home, life was enclosed in a hierarchical and ritualistic system under which the husband and father was master. His wife was called his help-mate, and very occasionally within the middle class—especially in France—a wife might serve as shopkeeper or business associate with her husband. Far more frequently, however, a middle-class wife was treated by her spouse as a kind of superior servant. Her task was to keep the household functioning smoothly and harmoniously. She maintained the accounts and directed the activities of the servants—usually two or three women. Called in Victorian England the "Angel in the House," the middle-class woman was responsible for the moral education of her children. Yet she probably spent no more than two or three hours a day at most with her offspring. Until sent to school, they were placed in the custody of a nursemaid or governess. Much of a middle-class woman's day was spent in the company of other women from similar households. An elaborate set of social customs involving "calls" and "at homes" was established in European middle-class society. Women were not expected to improve their minds. They were not expected to be the intellectual companions of their husbands. Rather, they were encouraged to be dabblers, education for them usually consisting of little more beyond reading and writing, a smattering of arithmetic, geography, history, and a foreign language, embellished with lessons in drawing, painting in watercolor, singing, or piano-playing.

Queen Victoria, who ascended the British throne in 1837, labored to make her solemn—occasionally almost stolid—public image reflect the feminine middle-class virtues of moral probity and dutiful domesticity. Her court was eminently proper and preeminently bourgeois, a marked contrast to that of her uncle George IV, whose fleshly and unbuttoned ways had set the style for high life a generation before. Though possessing an imperious temper, Victoria trained herself to curb it in deference to her ministers and her public-spirited, ultra-respectable husband, Prince Albert of Saxe-Coburg. She was a successful queen because she embodied the traits dearest to the middle class, whose triumph she seemed to epitomize and whose habits of mind we have come to call Victorian.

Queen Victoria as prototype

Middle-class wives were indoctrinated to believe that they were superior to their husbands in one area only. A wife was "the better half" of a middle-class marriage because she was deemed pure—the untainted Vestal of the hearth, unsullied by cares of the world outside her home, and certainly untouched by those sexual desires which marked her husband, her natural moral inferior. A wife's charge was to encourage her husband's "higher nature." She must never respond to his sexual advances with equal passion; passion was, for her, a presumed impossibility. If she *was* passionate, and private diaries sug-

Sexuality

Prince Albert and Queen Victoria. In this photograph by Roger Fenton the royal couple is depicted not as monarch and consort but as a conventional upper-middle-class married couple.

gest, not surprisingly, that many middle-class women were, she would find it hard not to feel guilty about the pleasures she was presumed too pure to taste. Contraception, other than withdrawal, was not common practice among the middle classes. The result was that for women, sexual intercourse was directly related to the problems of frequent pregnancies. (Victoria, who had nine children, declared that childbirth was "the shadow side" of marriage.)

The middle-class wife was expected to persuade her husband to seek, through love of home and family, a substitute for the baser instincts with which nature had unhappily endowed the male. Should she fail, she must accept the fact of her "failure" as she was bound to accept the rest of her life: uncomplainingly. That she often did fail was evidenced by the brisk trade in prostitution that flourished in nineteenth-century cities. In all European cities, prostitutes solicited openly. At mid-century the number of prostitutes in Vienna was estimated to be 15,000; in Paris, where prostitution was a licensed trade, 50,000; in London, 80,000. London newspaper reports of the 1850s catalogued the vast underworld of prostitutes and their followers: those who operated out of "lodging houses" run by unsavory entrepreneurs whose names—Swindling Sal, Lushing Loo—suggest their general character; the retinue of procurers, pimps, panderers, and "fancy men" who made the lives of common prostitutes little better than slavery; the relatively few "prima donnas" who enjoyed the protection of rich, upper-middle-class lovers, who entertained lavishly and whose wealth allowed them to move on the fringes of more respectable high society. The heroines of Alexandre Dumas's novel *La Dame aux Camilles,* and of Giuseppe Verdi's opera *La Traviata*—"the lost one"—were prototypes of women of this sort.

If a middle-class wife should herself succumb to "unwomanly desires" by taking a lover, and be discovered to have done so, she could expect nothing less than complete social banishment. The law tolerated a husband's infidelity and at all times respected a husband's rights both to his wife's person and to her property. It made quick work of an "unfaithful" wife, granting to her husband whatever he might desire in terms of divorce, property, and custody, to make him amends for the personal wrongs and embarrassments he had suffered at the hands of his "unnatural" spouse.

Middle-class family rituals helped to sustain this hierarchy. Daily meals, with the father at the head of the table, were cooked and brought to each place by servants, who were a constant reminder of the family's social position. Family vacations were a particularly nineteenth-century middle-class invention. Thanks to the advent of the railways, excursions of one or two weeks to the mountains or to the seashore were available to families of even moderate means. Entrepreneurs built large, ornate hotels, adorned with imposing names—Palace, Beau Rivage, Excelsior—and attracted middle-class customers

Prostitution

Prostitution. A contemporary comment bearing the title "That girl seems to know you, George!" intimates that, as the wife surmises, the flower girl has more to sell than her posies.

The Middle Class at Leisure. The "morning lounge" at Biarritz, a French resort on the Atlantic coast.

by offering them on a grander scale exactly the same sort of comfortable and sheltered existence they enjoyed at home.

The houses and furnishings of the middle class were an expression of the material security the middle class valued. Solidly built, heavily decorated, they proclaimed the financial worth and social respectability of those who dwelt within. In provincial cities they were often free-standing "villas." In London, Paris, Berlin, or Vienna, they might be rows of five- or six-story townhouses, or large apartments. Whatever particular shape they took, they were built to last a long time. The rooms were certain to be crowded with furniture, art objects, carpets, and wall hangings. Chairs, tables, cabinets, and sofas might be of any or all periods; no matter, so long as they were adorned with their proper complement of fringe, gilt, or other ornamentation. The size of the rooms, the elegance of the furniture, the number of servants, all depended, of course, on the extent of one's income. A bank clerk did not live as elegantly as a bank director. Yet in all likelihood both lived in obedience to the same set of standards and aspirations. And that obedience helped bind them, despite the differences in their material way of life, to the same class.

The European middle class had no desire to confront the unpleasant urban by-products of its own success. Members of the middle class saw to it that they lived apart from the unpleasant sights and smells of industrialization. Their residential areas, usually built to the west of

Houses

See color plates following page 294 for *The Movings* by Boilly

Cities and the middle class

the cities, out of the path of the prevailing breeze, and therefore of industrial pollution, were havens from the congestion for which they were primarily responsible. When the members of the middle class rode into the urban centers they took care to do so over avenues lined with respectable shops, or across railway embankments that lifted them above monotonous working-class streets en route to their destination. Yet the middle class, though it turned its face from what it did not want to see, did not turn from the city. Middle-class men and women celebrated the city as their particular creation and the source of their profits. They even praised its smoke—as a sign of prosperity—so long as they did not have to breathe it night and day. For the most part, it was they who managed their city's affairs. And it was they who provided new industrial cities with their proud architectural

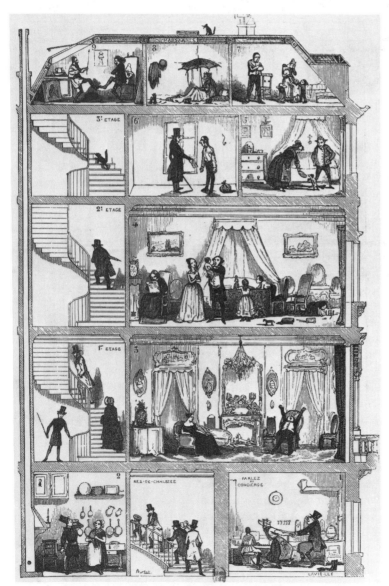

Apartment Living in Paris. This print shows that on the Continent rich and poor often lived in the same buildings, the rich on the lower floors, the poor at the top. This sort of residential mixing was unknown in Britain.

The Paris Opera. An exterior view of the Opera. Designed by Charles Garnier, it was constructed between 1861 and 1875. This grandiose display of wealth and luxury epitomized the taste of the new industrial middle class.

landmarks: city halls, stock exchanges, opera houses. These were the new cathedrals of the industrial age, proclamations of a triumphant middle class.

4. THE LIFE OF THE URBAN WORKING CLASS

Like the middle class, the working class was divided into various subgroups and categories, determined in this case by skill, wages, and workplace. The working class included skilled workers in crafts that were centuries old—glassblowing and cabinetmaking, for example. It included as well mechanics equally skilled in new industrial technology. It included the men who built textile machinery and the women and children who tended it. It included the men, women, and children who together worked in mines and quarries. And it included the countless millions who labored at unskilled jobs—dock workers, coal porters, cleaning women, and the like. The nature of workers' experiences naturally varied, depending upon where they worked, where they lived, and, above all, how much they earned. A skilled textile worker lived a life far different from that of a ditch digger, the former able to afford the food, shelter, and clothing necessary for a decent existence, the latter so busy trying to keep himself and his family alive that he would have little time to think about anything but the source of their next meal.

Ranks within the working class

Some movement from the ranks of the unskilled to the skilled was possible, if children were provided, or provided themselves, with at least a rudimentary education. Yet education was considered by many parents a luxury, especially since children could be put to work at an early age to supplement a family's meager earnings. There was movement from skilled to unskilled also, as technological change—

Social mobility

the introduction of the power loom, for example—drove highly paid workers into the ranks of the unskilled and destitute. Further variations within the working class were the result of the fact that though every year more men, women, and children were working in factories, the majority still labored either in workshops or at home. These variations mean that we cannot speak of a common European working-class experience during the years from 1800 to 1850. The life we shall be describing was most typical of English workers, during the first half century of their exposure to industrialization. Only in the years 1850–1900 did continental workers undergo this harsh process of urban acclimatization.

Housing

Life in industrial cities was, for almost all workers, uncomfortable at best and unbearably squalid at worst. Workers and their families lived in housing that failed to answer the needs of its inhabitants. In older cities single-family dwellings were broken up into apartments of often no more than one room per family. In new manufacturing centers, rows of tiny houses, located close by smoking factories, were built back-to-back, thereby eliminating any cross-ventilation or space for gardens. Whether housing was old or new, it was generally poorly built. Old buildings were allowed by landlords to fall into disrepair; new houses, constructed of cheap material, decayed quickly. Water often came from an outdoor tap, shared by several houses and adjacent to an outdoor toilet. Crowding was commonplace. Families of as many as eight lived in two or, at the most, three rooms. A newspaper account from the 1840s noted that in Leeds, a textile center in northern Britain, an "ordinary" worker's house contained no more than 150 square feet, and that in most cases those houses were "crammed almost to suffocation with human beings both day and night." When, after 1850, governments began to rid cities of some of their worst slums, many working-class men and women discovered that urban "improvement" meant relocation into dreary "model" tenements whose amenities were matched by their barracklike anonymity; or removal from one dilapidated structure to another in the wake of a clearance scheme—the nineteenth century called it "ventilation"—that replaced ancient, overcrowded housing with a more sanitary—and, for the landlord, more profitable—railway switching yard.

The life of women

The life of working-class wives and mothers was hard. Lack of cheap contraceptive devices and a belief that these devices were immoral helped to keep women pregnant through most of their childbearing years, thus endangering their general health and adding to the burden of their lives. Wives were usually handed a portion of the weekly wage packet by their husbands, and were expected to house, feed, and clothe the family on the very little they were given. Their daily life was a constant round of cooking, cleaning, shopping, and washing—in a tiny space and without enough money. Housewives could not rely, as in the country, on their own gardens to help supply them with

Nineteenth-Century Working-Class Housing. Faced with insatiable demands for urban accommodations, developers responded in a variety of ways. In Oldham (top left), a textile manufacturing center in the north of England, the answer was street after street of row houses; in Glasgow, Scotland (top right), it was multistory tenements; and in the suburbs of Paris (lower right), it was shanties. In all three settings, the result was essentially the same: a bleak existence born of overcrowding and squalor.

food. Instead, they went to markets that catered to their needs with cheap goods, often stale or nearly rotten, or dangerously adulterated. Formaldehyde was added to milk to prevent spoilage. Pounded rice was mixed into sugar. Fine brown earth was introduced into cocoa. A woman's problems were compounded, of course, when she had to work, and therefore had far less time to accomplish the household tasks she was still expected to perform.

Women were employed in growing numbers—along with children—in factories during the nineteenth century. Yet many more

A Laundress and Her Children.
Note the cramped and cluttered living quarters.

Women workers

labored at home or in small workshops—"sweatshops," as they came to be called—for wretchedly low wages based not on the hours they worked but on the amount of work they did: so much per shirt stitched or matchbox glued. By far the greatest number of unmarried working-class young women worked as domestic servants, often a lonely occupation and one that occasionally trapped female servants into undesired sexual relationships with their male employers or their sons.

Sexuality

Female sexuality within the working classes of western Europe was acknowledged in a way that it was not within the middle class. Demographic evidence reveals a sharp rise in illegitimacy between 1750 and 1850. In Frankfurt, Germany, for example, where the illegitimacy rate had been a mere 2 percent in the early 1700s, it reached 25 percent in 1850. In Bordeaux, France, in 1840, one-third of the recorded births were illegitimate. Reasons for this increase are difficult to establish. Illegitimacy in Germany may have been the result of laws forbidding the poor to marry. Certainly, increased mobility meant weaker family ties, less parental supervision, and greater opportunity for an unrestricted life. This is not to say that the majority of working-class women were sexually promiscuous. Premarital intercourse was an accepted practice in preindustrial villages, but, because of the social controls that dominated village life, it was almost always a precursor to marriage. In the far more anonymous setting of a factory town, such control often did not exist. In addition, the economic uncertainties of the early industrial age meant that a young workingman's promise of marriage based on his expectation of a job might frequently be difficult to fulfill. The same economic uncertainty led some young working-class women to a career—usually temporary—as prostitutes. The anonymity of city life encouraged prostitution. Middle-class men, prepared to postpone marriage until they could afford a house and furnishings reflecting the social position to which they aspired, turned to the sexual underworld to satisfy their desires. Class consciousness encouraged them to regard working-class women— prostitutes or not—as easy prey, possessed of coarser natures and therefore a lesser breed of womankind than the middle-class "ladies" they intended eventually to marry.

New cities could be lonely places, particularly for working-class men and women struggling to cope with an alien environment. If possible, they would live near relatives who had already made the transition and who could assist the newcomers in adjusting to their very different existence. In many cities working-class families lived in districts inhabited primarily by others working at the same trade— weavers in one place, miners in another—and in this way achieved some sense of commonality.

Adjustment to the demands of the factory was every bit as difficult for workers as was acceptance of urban living patterns. The factory system, emphasizing as it did standard rather than individual work patterns, denied skilled laborers the pride in craft that had previously been theirs. Many workers found themselves stripped of the reassuring protection of guilds and formal apprenticeships which had bound their predecessors to a particular trade or place, and which were outlawed or sharply curtailed by legislation in France, Germany, and Britain in the first half of the nineteenth century. Factory hours were long, before 1850 usually twelve to fourteen hours a day. Conditions were dirty and dangerous. Textile mills remained unventilated, so that bits of material lodged in workers' lungs. Machines were unfenced and were a particular danger to child workers, often hired, because of their supposed agility, to clean under and around the moving parts. Manufacturing processes were unhealthy. The use of poison lead in the making of glazed pottery, for example, was a constant hazard to men and women workers in that industry. Surveys by British physicians in the 1840s catalogued the toll that long factory hours and harsh working conditions were taking, particularly on young workers. Spinal curvature and other bone malformations resulted from standing hour after hour in unnatural positions at machines. Varicose veins and fallen arches were also common. One concerned doctor stated his belief that "from what I saw myself, a large mass of deformity has been produced by the factory system." And what was true of factories was true as well of mines, in which over fifty thousand children and young people were employed in Britain in 1841. Children were used to haul coal to underground tramways or shafts. The youngest were set to work—often for as long as twelve hours at a stretch—operating doors which regulated the ventilation in the mines. When they fell asleep, which, because of long hours, they frequently did, they jeopardized the safety of the entire workforce. Women—sometimes pregnant women—were employed to haul coal and perform other strenuous underground tasks. Lung diseases—popularly known as "black spit-

*Conditions in factories and
mines*

"Capital and Labour." In its earliest years, *Punch,* though primarily a humorous weekly, manifested a strong social conscience. In this 1843 cartoon, the capitalists are seen revelling in the rewards of their investments while the workers—men, women, and children—who toiled in the mines under cruel and dangerous conditions are found crippled and starving.

tle"—and eye infections, not to mention the constant danger of explosions caused by trapped gas, were constant threats to life and limb in the mines.

As upsetting as the physical working conditions was the psychological readjustment demanded of the first-generation workers in the factories. Preindustrial laborers had to work long hours and for very little monetary reward. Yet, at least to some degree, they were free to set their own hours and structure their own activities, to move from their home workshops to their small garden plots and back again as they wished. In a factory, all "hands" learned the discipline of the whistle. To function efficiently, a factory demanded that all employees begin and end work at the same time. Most workers could not tell time; fewer possessed clocks. None was accustomed to the relentless pace of the machine. In order to increase production, the factory system encouraged the breaking down of the manufacturing process into specialized steps, each with its own assigned time, an innovation that upset workers accustomed to completing a task at their own pace. The employment of women and children was a further disturbing innovation. In preindustrial communities, women and children had worked, as well as men, but more often than not, all together and at home. In factory towns women and children were frequently hired instead of

Daily routine

men: they could be paid less and were declared to be easier to manage. When this happened, the pattern of family life was severely disrupted, and a further break with tradition had to be endured. It is no wonder that workers began to see machinery itself as the tyrant that had changed their lives and bound them to a kind of industrial slavery. A radical working-class song written in Britain in the 1840s expressed the feeling: "There is a king and a ruthless king;/ Not a king of the poet's dream;/ But a tyrant fell, white slaves know well,/ And that ruthless king is steam."

Faced with a drastic reordering of their lives, working-class men and women reacted in various ways. Some sought "the shortest way out of Manchester" by taking to drink (there were 1,200 public houses in that city in 1850). Many more men and women struggled to make some sort of community out of the street where they lived or the factory where they worked. It was a long and discouraging process. Yet by mid-century their experiences were beginning to make them conscious of themselves as different from and in opposition to the middle class that was imposing a new way of life on them.

Escape

5. THE MIDDLE-CLASS WORLDVIEW

The middle class was not unaware of the many social problems it was generating as it created an industrial society. Despite its confidence that the world was progressing—and at its own behest—the middle class was beset by uncertainties. Its belief in its own undoubted abilities was shadowed by concern as to whether its particular talents might ultimately prove irrelevant to the preservation of prosperity. Self-assurance could dissolve in the face of bankruptcy, and prosperity vanish in the abyss of economic catastrophe. Those who had risen by their own exertions might fall victim to someone else's ambitions. Nor was it always a simple matter for the middle class to reconcile its own affluence with the poverty of the thousands of workers exploited under its aegis. The middle class was responsible for having wrenched European society out of old patterns of living and thrust it into new ones. To those willing to acknowledge that responsibility, the realization was enough to temper confidence with apprehension. No one was certain what the factory system and urbanization might eventually produce. Evidence drawn from the reports of various official commissions and from the intentionally lurid writings of sensational journalists suggested that city life was already spawning an underclass of men and women who preferred a life of promiscuity and criminality to one of honest toil. French novelists began to use the sewers as a metaphor to describe the general condition of urban existence for what was assumed to be a vast number of Parisians. Poverty and crime were linked together in the public—middle-class—mind, until poverty itself began to be defined as criminal. All this was part of a middle-class

Uncertainty and the need for reassurance

The Interior of the Crystal Palace. This building of iron and glass was constructed to house exhibits sent to the Exhibition of the Works of Industry of All Nations, held in London in 1851. The exhibition celebrated the triumph of middle-class industrialization.

compulsion to rationalize its own prosperity, and to legitimize its ascendancy over the urban working poor.

To assist themselves in constructing this congenial worldview, the members of the new industrial middle class made use of the theories of a number of political economists. It is important to recognize that a factory-owner or a banker was not likely to have read the works of these theorists. He might, however, have encountered popular journalistic condensations of their ideas, or have participated in discussions at which the conclusions, if not the reasoned arguments, of the economists were aired. Because those conclusions supported his own interests, he grew familiar with them, until, in time, he could talk of the ideas of these men as if they were his own.

Political economics and the worldview

We have noted already the manner in which the ideas of the economist Adam Smith sustained middle-class respect for individual enterprise. Enlightenment thought in general had extolled the virtues of individualism. John Locke, for example, celebrated the reason in men and women that allowed them to make intelligent choices based upon their own enlightened self-interest. Arguments such as these were reinforced by a second generation of economists—particularly the Englishmen Thomas Malthus (1766–1834) and David Ricardo (1772–1823)—whose writings embodied principles appealing to businessmen who desired a free hand to remake the economies of their countries. The chief elements in the theories of these economists were:

Classical economics

(1) Economic individualism. Individuals are entitled to use for their own best interests the property they have inherited or acquired by any legitimate method. People must be allowed to do what they like so

long as they do not trespass upon the equal right of others to do the same.

(2) Laissez-faire. The functions of the state should be reduced to the lowest minimum consistent with public safety. The government should shrink itself into the role of a modest policeman, preserving order and protecting property, but never interfering with the operation of economic processes.

(3) Obedience to natural law. There are immutable laws operating in the realm of economics as in every sphere of the universe. Examples are the law of supply and demand, the law of diminishing returns, and so on. These laws must be recognized and respected; failure to do so is disastrous.

(4) Freedom of contract. Individuals should be free to negotiate the best kind of contract they can obtain from any other individual. In particular, the liberty of workers and employers to bargain with each other as to wages and hours should not be hampered by laws or by the collective power of labor unions.

(5) Free competition and free trade. Competition serves to keep prices down, to eliminate inefficient producers, and to ensure the maximum production in accordance with public demand. Therefore, no monopolies should be tolerated, nor any price-fixing laws for the benefit of incompetent enterprises. Further, in order to force each country to engage in the production of those things it is best fitted to produce, all protective tariffs should be abolished. Free international trade will also help to keep prices down.

Thomas Malthus

Businessmen naturally warmed to theories so congenial to their own desires and intentions. But Malthus and Ricardo made further contributions to the middle-class worldview, based upon their perceptions of conflicting interests within society. Malthus, in his controversial *Essay on Population,* first published in 1798, argued that nature had set stubborn limits to the progress of mankind. Because of the voracity of the sexual appetite there was a natural tendency for population to increase more rapidly than the supply of food. To be sure, there were powerful checks, such as war, famine, disease, and vice; but these, when they operated effectively, further augmented the burden of human misery. It followed that poverty and pain were inescapable. Even if laws were passed distributing all wealth equally, the condition of the poor would be only temporarily improved; in a very short time they would begin to raise larger families, with the result that the eventual state of their class would be as bad as the earlier. In the second edition of his work, Malthus advocated postponement of marriage as a means of relief, but he continued to stress the danger that population would outrun any possible increase in the means of subsistence.

Malthus on population

Malthus's arguments allowed the middle class to acquiesce in the destruction of an older society which had made some attempt to care

*The application of
Malthusian doctrine*

Ricardo on wages and rent

*The uses of Ricardo's
laws*

Benthamite utilitarianism

for its poor. In England, for example, officials in rural parishes had instituted a system of doles and subsidized wages to help sustain laborers and their families when unemployed. The attempt failed to prevent distress and was met with increasing resistance by taxpayers. Now Malthus told taxpayers that schemes designed to help the poor damaged both rich and poor alike. Poor relief took money, and therefore food, from the mouths of the more productive members of society and put it into the mouths of the least productive. Malthus helped shift the responsibility for poverty from society to the individual, a shift appealing to the middle class, which wished to be freed from the burden of supporting the urban unemployed.

Malthusian assumptions played a large role in the development of the theories of the English economist Ricardo. According to Ricardo, wages seek a level which is just sufficient to enable workers "to subsist and perpetuate their race, without either increase or diminution." This Ricardo held to be an inescapable iron law. If wages should rise temporarily above the subsistence standard, men and women would be encouraged to marry earlier and produce more children, the population would increase, and the ensuing competition for jobs would quickly force the rate of pay down to its former level. Ricardo devised a law of rent as well as a law of wages. He maintained that rent is determined by the cost of production on the poorest land that must be brought under cultivation, and that, consequently, as a country's population increases and more land is cultivated, and higher rents charged for more productive land, an ever-increasing proportion of the national income is absorbed by landlords.

Here again, a theorist provided arguments useful to the middle class in its attempt to define and defend itself within a new social order. The law of wages gave employers a useful weapon to protect themselves from their workers' petitions for higher pay. The law of rent justified middle-class opposition to the continuing power of landed interests: a class which derived its income not from hard work but simply from its role as rent-collector was profiting unfairly at the expense of the rest of society and deserved to have its profit-making curtailed.

As soon as the middle class began to argue in this fashion, however, it betrayed its devotion to the doctrine of laissez-faire. Businessmen and entrepreneurs vehemently opposed to government intervention, which might deny them the chance to make as much money as they could, were nevertheless prepared to see the government step in and prevent profiteering landlords from making what *they* could from their property. How could this apparent inconsistency be justified? The answer lay in the theories of the Englishman Jeremy Bentham (1748–1832), without doubt among the most influential of middle-class apologists. Bentham, whose major work, *The Principles of Morals and Legislation,* was published in 1789, argued against the eighteenth-century notion that a satisfactory theory of social order could be grounded in a belief in the natural harmony of human interests. Men and women were basically selfish beings. To suppose that a stable and beneficent society could emerge unassisted from a company of self-interested egos was, Bentham believed, to suppose the impossible. Society, if it was to function properly, needed an organizing principle that would both acknowledge humanity's basic selfishness and at the same time compel people to sacrifice at least a portion of their own interests for the good of the majority. That principle, called utilitarianism, stated that every institution, every law, must be measured according to its social usefulness. And a socially useful law was one that produced the greatest happiness of the greatest number. If a law passed this test, it could remain on the books; if it failed, it should be abandoned forthwith, no matter how venerable. A selfish man would accept this social yardstick, realizing that in the long run he would do himself serious harm by clinging to laws that might benefit him, but produce such general unhappiness as to result in disruptions detrimental to his own interests as well as to those of others.

Jeremy Bentham

In what ways did this philosophy particularly appeal to the industrial middle classes? First, it acknowledged the importance of the individual. The interests of the community were nothing more than the sum of the interests of those selfish egos who lived within it. Each individual best understood his or her own interests, and was therefore best left free, whenever possible, to pursue those interests as he or she saw fit. Only when they conflicted with the interests—the happiness—of the greatest number were they to be curtailed. Entrepreneurs could understand this doctrine as a license to proceed with the business of industrialization, since, they argued, industrialization was so clearly producing happiness for the majority of the world's population. At the same time, Bentham's doctrines could be used to justify those changes necessary to bring an industrial world into being. Was the greatest happiness produced, English factory-owners might ask, by an antiquated electoral system that denied representation to growing industrial cities? Obviously not. Let Parliament reform itself so that the weight of the manufacturing interests could be felt in the drafting of legislation.

Utilitarianism's appeal to the middle class

Utilitarianism was thus a doctrine that could be used to cut two ways—in favor of laissez-faire; in favor of governmental intervention. And the middle class proceeded to cut both ways at once. Benthamite utilitarianism provided the theoretical basis for many of the middle-class interventionist reforms, such as a revised poor law in Britain and an expanded educational system in France, achieved between 1815 and 1848.[1] At the same time utilitarianism, combined with the theories of Malthus and Ricardo, fortified the position of those businessmen who believed that unfettered individualism had produced the triumphs of the Industrial Revolution. To restrain that individualism was to jeop-

Individualism and intervention

[1] These and other similar reforms will be discussed in the following chapter.

Belief in improvement

Auguste Comte

The Positivism of Comte

ardize the further progress of industrialization and hence the greatest happiness of the greatest number.

In arguing as it did, the middle class relied upon the conviction that industrialization and the factory system were together showering benefits on all—not just themselves. As we shall see, there were those who disagreed, who pressed, for example, for regulation of factory wages and hours. But the capitalists claimed intervention would inhibit the distribution of those benefits, and hence the proliferation of general happiness. In their support they could cite the English economist Nassau Senior, who claimed that the net profit of any industrial enterprise was derived solely from its last hour of daily operation. Reduce working hours, said Senior, and you eliminate profits, thereby compelling factories to close and workers to starve. The members of the middle class believed Senior because it was clearly in their interest to do so. They also believed him because the enterprise upon which they were embarked was so new and so uncharted that it was hard to prove him wrong. Their uncertainty led them to believe those theories that provided them with the most reassurance and encouraged them to think that what they were doing was of benefit to their fellow men.

Political economists and philosophers in France as well as in England helped provide the new middle class with a congenial worldview. Count Claude de Saint-Simon (1760–1825), while a proponent of utopian schemes for social reorganization, nevertheless preached the gospel of "industrialism" and "industrialists" (two words which he coined). Disciples of Saint-Simon were among the leading proponents in France of industrial entrepreneurship and a standardized and centralized financial system.

Far more generally influential was the Positivist philosophy of Auguste Comte (1798–1857). Comte's philosophy, like utilitarianism, insisted that all truth is derived from experience or observation of the physical world. Comte rejected metaphysics as utterly futile; no one can discover the hidden essences of things—why events happen as they do, or what is the ultimate meaning and goal of existence. All one can really know is how things happen, the laws that control their occurrence, and the relations existing between them. Positivism derived its name from the assertion that the only knowledge of any current value was "positive," or scientific, knowledge. Comte argued that humankind's ability to analyze society scientifically and to predict its future had reached a point that would soon enable Europe to achieve a "positive" society, organized not in terms of belief but in terms of facts. Such an achievement would not be a simple matter, however; "positive" attitudes and institutions could not replace those of the "metaphysical" stage through which Europe had just passed without a struggle. By dividing the history of the world into progressive stages (a "religious" stage had preceded the "metaphysical"), and by declaring that the achievement of the highest stage was not possible

without the turmoil of industrialization, Comte assured the middle
class of its leading role in the better world that was to be.

277

*Early Critics of the Middle-Class
Worldview*

6. EARLY CRITICS OF THE MIDDLE-CLASS WORLDVIEW

The middle-class worldview did not go unchallenged. Many writers
deplore the social disintegration they saw as the legacy of the Industrial
Revolution. Others criticized the materialism and hypocrisy they saw
as the hallmarks of the middle class. The Scot Thomas Carlyle (1795–
1881), though a defender of the French Revolution and a believer in
the need for a new aristocracy of industrialists ("captains of industry"),
had nothing but contempt for the theories of the utilitarians. In Carlyle's
view, they did no more than excuse the greed and acquisitiveness of
the new middle class. Equally scathing in his attacks on the middle
class was the English novelist Charles Dickens (1812–1870). In such
novels as *Oliver Twist, Hard Times,* and *Dombey and Son,* he wrote
with sympathy of the tyrannization of industrial workers by the new
rich. In France, the Abbé Felicité Lamennais (1782–1854), though
preaching respect for private property, nevertheless attacked self-interest. He argued, in his *Book of the People,* that the "little people" of
the world enjoyed far too small a share in the direction of their lives.
Honoré de Balzac (1799–1850) wrote *The Human Comedy* to expose
the stupidity, greed, and baseness of the middle class. Gustave Flaubert
(1821–1880), in his foremost novel *Madame Bovary,* depicted the banal,
and literally fatal, nature of bourgeois existence for women.

*Literary challenges to the
middle-class world view*

   One of the most trenchant critics of early industrialization was the
English philosopher and economist John Stuart Mill (1806–1873).
Mill's father had been a close disciple of Bentham, and his son began
his adult life a convinced utilitarian. A severe psychological crisis in
early manhood compelled him to modify his acceptance of classical
economic theory. First, he rejected the universality of economic laws.
Though he admitted that there are unchangeable laws governing production, he insisted that the distribution of wealth could be regulated
by society for the benefit of the majority of its members. Second,
he advocated radical departures from the doctrine of laissez-faire. He
favored legislation, under certain conditions, for shortening the working day, and he believed that the state might properly take preliminary
steps toward the redistribution of wealth by taxing inheritances and
by appropriating the unearned increment of land. In the fourth book
of his *Principles of Political Economy* he urged the abolition of the wage
system and looked forward to a society of producers' cooperatives
in which the workers would own the factories and elect the managers
to run them. On the other hand, Mill was no socialist. He distrusted
the state; his real reason for advocating producers' cooperatives was
not to exalt the power of the workers but to give them the fruits of

John Stuart Mill

The Greek Slave by Hiram Powers. The art of the bourgeoisie: titillation combined with a moral lesson.

See color plates facing page 295 for *The Gleaners* by Millet and the *Funeral at Ornans* by Courbet

their labor. In 1859 he wrote what many consider the classic defense of individual freedom, *On Liberty,* in which he attacked what he called "the tyranny of the majority." Yet his ringing defense of individualism was as much a treatise against middle-class conformism as it was against the threat of state control. "If all mankind were of one opinion," Mill wrote, "and only one person were of the contrary opinion, mankind would be no more justified in silencing that one person than he, if he had the power, would be justified in silencing mankind." Those sentiments were not the sort to appeal particularly to a society determined to define itself in accordance with rigid behavioral patterns and codes of conduct.

Artists, too, attacked the values of industrial society in their painting and sculpture. The art preferred by the European middle class in the nineteenth century was that which in some way either told a story or, better still, preached a message. Beauty was surface decoration, which could be admired for its intrinsic richness and for what it therefore declared about its owner's wealth. Or beauty was a moralism, easily understood and, if possible, reassuring. When the Great Exhibition of the Works of Industry in All Nations was held at the Crystal Palace in London in 1851 to celebrate the triumph of industrialism, one of the most popular exhibits was *The Greek Slave,* a statue by the American sculptor Hiram Powers. Depicting a young Christian woman stripped bare and standing, according to the catalogue, before the gaze of an Eastern potentate, the work allowed its Victorian male admirers a chance to relish its salaciousness, while at the same time profiting from its depiction of the woman's righteous disdain for her captor.

Some of the artists most critical of the middle class, while repudiating the artificial and decorative, nevertheless reflected the middle-class obsession with art as morality. The self-designated Pre-Raphaelite Brotherhood of English painters was a group of men and women, led by the painter-poet Dante Gabriel Rossetti (1828–1882), determined to express its disdain for contemporary values. They called themselves Pre-Raphaelites as a way of announcing their admiration for the techniques of early Renaissance artists, untainted, supposedly, by corrupted artistic taste. Yet the works of the leading members of the Brotherhood exuded a degree of sentimentality that compromised their rebel nature and rendered them conventionally pietistic and ultimately innocuous as social protest. The same can be said, to a lesser degree, of the work of the Frenchman Jean-François Millet (1814–1875). His *Man with the Hoe* is a stark, bitter statement about peasant life; his *The Angelus* softens the statement to sentiment. In both England and France, however, some of the most talented painters seriously questioned many of the values the middle class revered. Gustave Courbet (1819–1877) and Honoré Daumier (1808–1879) both expressed sympathy toward the plight of the French working class, contrasting scenes of rural and urban misfortune with unflattering caricatures of the bourgeoisie. Daumier, in particular, was a powerful satirist of social

The Angelus by Jean-François Millet. The artist's peasants accept their humble lot in this sentimental portrayal.

and political evils, ridiculing the corruption of petty officials and the hypocritical piety of the rich. There was a harsh bite to most of the work of Daumier and Courbet that proscribed sentimentalizing.

These writers and artists, while critical of the Industrial Revolution and middle-class values, proposed nothing very tangible in the way of radical reform. If they opposed the triumph of a materialistic middle class, they opposed, as well, the idea of complete democracy. Carlyle, in particular, criticized the present by comparing it with a rosy past that had never been. In this he was like one of the doughtiest critics of the new middle-class society, the Englishman William Cobbett (1763–1835). Cobbett, in his newspaper the *Political Register,* argued against industrialization itself as well as its effects. His propaganda mirrored the dilemma most critics had to face, in asking the question: Granted industrialization has brought great social and economic hardship in its train, does this mean that we should try to return to the life of preindustrial society, also often harsh, and always confining, though probably more secure?

Past or present?

For some time, a small band of thinkers had been answering that question with a resounding "no." They argued that there could be no return to old times and old ways, but that society could be at the same time both industrial and humane. These radical thinkers were often explicitly utopian. Two of the most persuasive were the Englishman Robert Owen (1771–1858) and the Frenchman Charles Fourier (1772–1837). Owen, himself the proprietor of a large cotton factory at New Lanark in Scotland, argued against the middle-class belief that the profit motive should be allowed to shape social and economic organization. Having reorganized his own mills to provide free schooling and a system of social security for his workers, he proceeded to advocate a general reorganization of society on the basis of

Utopian thinkers

The Third Class Carriage by Honoré Daumier. Daumier's realism did not mask his sympathy with the condition of the common people of France.

cooperation, with communities rewarding workers solely as a result of their actual labor. Fourier urged an even more far-reaching reconstitution, including the abolition of the wage system and the complete equality of the sexes. The numerous followers of Owen and Fourier sought escape from the confusions of the contemporary world in idealist communities founded according to the principles of their leaders. All these attempts failed after a time, victims of faulty leadership and, in the case of Fourierist communities in France, of charges of moral turpitude resulting from Fourier's revolutionary sexual doctrines.

Less utopian radical theories were proposed during the 1840s, years which witnessed recurring economic depressions and their horrifying consequences. The French politician and journalist Louis Blanc (1811–1882) stood, like many contemporary critics, against the competitiveness of the new industrial society and particularly opposed the exploitation of the working class. His solution was to campaign for universal male suffrage, which would give working-class men control of the state. Following their triumph, these workers would make the state the "banker of the poor" and institute "Associations of Production"—actually a system of workshops governed by workers—which would guarantee jobs and security for all. Once these associations became established, private enterprise would wither through competition, and with it the state, for which there would no longer be any need. As we shall see, these workshops were briefly instituted in Paris during the Revolution of 1848. Another Frenchman, Pierre Proudhon (1809–1865), condemned the profits accruing to employers at the expense of their employees. He, too, proposed new institutions, which he argued could be made to produce goods at a price fairer to the worker, a price based solely on the amount of labor devoted to the manufacture of any particular product.

Louis Blanc

The theories of the writers and thinkers whom we have been considering—both the defenders and the opponents of the middle-class industrial world—are historically important for two reasons. First, their ideas helped men and women better understand the new social order that had sprung up following the French and Industrial revolutions, and the part they might play, as members of a class, in that new order. Second, the ideas themselves helped inspire the concrete political, social, and economic changes and events that are the subject of the next two chapters.

SELECTED READINGS

• *Items so designated are available in paperback editions.*

Banks, J. A., *Prosperity and Parenthood: A Study of Family Planning among the Victorian Middle Classes,* London, 1954. Relates middle-class financial pressures to family limitation.

Bridenthal, Renate, and Claudia Koonz, eds., *Becoming Visible: Women in European History,* Boston, 1976. Essays on the slowly changing role of women in society.

Briggs, Asa, *Victorian Cities,* New York, 1963. A survey of British cities, stressing middle-class attitudes toward the new urban environment.

• Burn, W. L., *The Age of Equipoise,* London, 1964. A charming account of the mid-Victorian years.

• Chevalier, Louis, *Laboring Classes and Dangerous Classes During the First Half of the Nineteenth Century,* New York, 1973. An intriguing though controversial study of the quality of life in Paris between 1815 and 1848 which concludes that social mobility was downward and that fear of crime dominated middle-class social consciousness.

• Halévy, Elie, *The Growth of Philosophic Radicalism,* rev. ed., London, 1949. The best introduction to the thought of Malthus, Ricardo, Bentham, and their philosophical heirs.

———, *England in 1815,* London, 1949. The classic work by the greatest historian of nineteenth-century England.

• Hammond, J. L., and Barbara Hammond, *The Town Labourer, 1760–1832,* London, 1917. An impassioned account of the economic changes that affected the quality of life of the English worker.

Heilbroner, Rober L., *The Worldly Philosophers,* New York, 1967. An introduction to the thought of economic liberals.

Hobsbawn, Eric, *The Age of Capital, 1848–1875,* London, 1975. A perceptive world survey which traces the global triumph of capitalism and its impact on the working class, written from a Marxist perspective.

———, *Labouring Men: Studies in the History of Labour,* London, 1964. A series of essays on workers and the working class in England.

• Hobsbawn, Eric, and George Rudé, *Captain Swing: A Social History of the Great English Agricultural Uprising of 1830,* New York, 1975. Analyzes the formation of a rural working-class consciousness.

• Houghton, Walter, *The Victorian Frame of Mind, 1830–1870,* New Haven, 1957. An outstanding synthesis of Victorian middle-class mentality.

• Langer, William L., *Political and Social Upheaval, 1832–1852,* New York,

1969. Comprehensive survey of European history, with excellent analytical chapters and thorough bibliographies.

McLaren, Angus, *Sexuality and Social Order: The Debate over the Fertility of Women and Workers in France,* New York, 1982. Examines the relationship between private and public morality.

Manuel, Frank E., *The Prophets of Paris,* Cambridge, Mass., 1962. An entertaining introduction to the philosophers of progress, from Turgot to Comte.

• Rostow, W. W., *The Stages of Economic Growth,* rev. ed., Cambridge, 1971. A synthesis by the exponent of the "take-off" theory of economic development.

• Rudé, George, *The Crowd in History, 1730–1848,* New York, 1964. A study of popular disturbances in France and England.

• Sewell, William, *Work and Revolution in France: The Language of Labor from the Old Regime to 1848,* Cambridge, 1980. Examines the mentalities of workers' organizations.

• Taylor, A. J. *The Standard of Living in Britain in the Industrial Revolution,* New York, 1975. A good introduction to the debate on the effects of industrialization.

Tilly, Charles, and Edward Shorter, *Strikes in France, 1830–1848,* New York, 1974. A valuable study of early continental class consciousness.

Tilly, Louise, and Joan W. Scott, *Women, Work and Family,* New York, 1978. Deals with women in nineteenth-century France and England.

• Thompson, E. P., *The Making of the English Working Class,* London, 1963. Argues that the coincidence of the French and Industrial Revolutions fostered the growth of working-class consciousness. A brilliant and important work.

Walker, Mack, *German Home Towns: Community, State and General Estate, 1648–1871,* Ithaca, N.Y., 1971. Attempts to explain the absence of a strong middle class in Germany.

• Zeldin, Theodore, *France, 1848–1945,* 2 vols., Oxford, 1973–1977. A highly individualistic synthesis of French history, remarkable for its scope and insight.

SOURCE MATERIALS

• Engels, Friedrich, *The Condition of the Working Class in England,* New York, 1958. A much criticized but reliable firsthand account by the later collaborator of Marx, written in 1844. Presents a devastating portrait of living and working conditions, especially in Manchester.

• Malthus, Thomas R., *An Essay on the Principle of Population,* London, 1798 and 1803. Malthus's famous essay relating population growth and food production.

• Mayhew, Henry, *London Labor and the London Poor,* New York, 1968. A reprint of the 1851 edition; provides a fascinating view of the population and trades of London. A good factual companion to Dickens.

• Mill, John Stuart, *Autobiography,* London, 1873. The intellectual coming-of-age of one of England's major nineteenth-century figures.

• ———, *On Liberty,* London, 1859. The classic defense of individual freedom.

Owen, Robert, *A New View of Society,* London, 1813. A proposed utopian society based on cooperative villages by the founder of British socialism.

Chapter 28

THE RISE OF LIBERALISM
(1815–1870)

The general thought, the hope of France, has been order and liberty reuniting under constitutional monarchy.

—François Guizot, "Speech on the State of the Nation," 1831

The history of nineteenth-century Europe was to a great extent shaped by the interplay of the forces of liberalism and nationalism. The middle classes of France and England, where liberalism was strongest, espoused a set of doctrines reflecting their concerns and interests. Liberalism to them meant (1) an efficient government prepared to acknowledge the value of commercial and industrial development; (2) a government in which their interests would be protected by their direct representation in the legislature—in all probability, a constitutional monarchy, and most certainly not a democracy; (3) a foreign policy of peace and free trade; and (4) a belief in individualism and the doctrines of the classical economists.

The components of liberalism

Many middle-class men and women in other European countries shared these beliefs and assumptions, and worked diligently and with some success to carry through specific liberal reforms. But for them, an equally important and often more immediate objective was the achievement of some form of national unity. The middle classes in Germany, Italy, Poland, and the Austrian Empire, however dedicated they were to liberalism, believed that their chances of achieving liberal goals would be greatly enhanced if they could unify the patchwork of principalities that surrounded them into a vigorous, "modern" nation-state. In this chapter, we shall examine the phenomenon of liberalism, primarily as it affected the fortunes of England and France. In the following chapter, we shall describe the way in which liberalism combined with nationalism to reshape the history of central Europe.

The compulsion of nationalism

1. CONSERVATIVE REACTION, 1815–1830

The growth of liberalism occurred, in part, as a reaction to the conservative policies adopted by frightened governments anxious to restore domestic and international order following the Napoleonic wars. For a period of about fifteen years after 1815 the rulers of most European countries did their best to stem the advance of middle-class liberalism. In most instances, however, their repressive policies only made liberals more determined than ever to succeed. The primary concern of governments was to ensure that Europe would never again fall prey to the sort of revolutionary upheavals which it had experienced during the preceding quarter-century.

Following Napoleon's final defeat at Waterloo in 1815, the major powers reconfirmed the Vienna settlement in the hope that their efforts might result in a permanently stable "Concert of Europe." To further ensure an end to revolutionary disturbances, they formed the Quadruple Alliance—Britain, Austria, Prussia, and Russia; when France was admitted as a fifth member in 1818 it became the Quintuple Alliance. Its members pledged to cooperate in the suppression of any disturbances that might arise from attempts to overthrow legitimate governments or to alter international boundaries. At the same time, Tsar Alexander, his mystic nature now in the ascendant, persuaded the allies to join him in the declaration of another alliance—a "Holy Alliance"—dedicated to the precepts of justice, Christian charity, and peace. The only result of this second league was to confuse Europe's leaders as to Alexander's intentions. Was he a liberal—a Jacobin even, as Metternich feared—or a reliable conservative? The confusion was cleared away, as in one country after another, liberal uprisings were stifled by stern repressive policies of the allied governments, Alexander's among them.

Attacks against reactionary governments in Naples and in Spain brought the allies scurrying to a conference at Troppau in Austria in 1820. Secret brotherhoods of young liberals, many of them army officers, had spearheaded these revolts. These organizations, which originated in Italy, called themselves *Carbonari*. They were an active counterreactionary force, whose influence spread throughout Europe in the early 1820s. In both Naples and Spain, they succeeded in forcing the kings to take oaths to establish constitutions modeled on the liberal French constitution of 1789–1791. At Troppau, Austria, Prussia, and Russia reacted to these threats to international order and absolutism by pledging to come to each other's aid to suppress revolution. France and Britain declined to endorse the pledge, not so much because they opposed repression, but because they did not wish to curtail their freedom of action by binding themselves to detailed international treaties. Metternich nevertheless proceeded, with Russian and Prussian concurrence, in a repression of the *Carbonari* rebels through imprisonment or exile.

Two years later, in 1822, another congress was convened at Verona, this one to deal with the continuing liberal threat to stability in Spain, with the series of revolutions occurring in Spanish colonies in South America, and with an insurrection in the Near East. To resolve the Spanish problem, the French dispatched an army of 200,000 men to the Iberian peninsula in 1823. Without much difficulty, this force put an end to the Spanish liberals, who opposed King Ferdinand VII's attempt to undermine representative government. The French assisted Ferdinand in restoring his authority to rule as he pleased. Contrary to their experience in Spain, the defenders of the status quo were unable to succeed in stemming the move to independence and liberalism in the colonies of Central and South America. In 1823 President James Monroe of the United States issued the "Monroe Doctrine," which declared that attempts by European powers to intervene in the affairs of the New World would be looked upon as an unfriendly act by his government. Without British maritime support, the doctrine would have remained a dead letter. Britain was ready to recognize the independence of the South American republics, however, since as new countries they were prepared to trade with Britain instead of Spain. The British therefore used their navy to keep Spain from intervening to protect its vanishing empire.

*Defying the congress
system*

In the Near East, a Greek soldier, Alexander Ypsilanti, was attempting to encourage the formation of a Greek "empire," to be constructed on vaguely liberal principles. In doing so, he had engaged his band of armed followers in battles against the Turks who ruled over Greece. Though Ypsilanti was soon defeated, his movement lived on. Five years later its aims had been narrowed to the more accessible goal of an independent Greece. Supported for reasons of Mediterranean naval strategy by a joint Anglo-French-Russian naval intervention, and by a Russian invasion of the Balkans, the rebels this time succeeded. Their success signaled the extent of changes that had occurred since the Congress of Verona. No longer could Metternich and other reactionaries build alliances on the assumption that, for the powers of Europe, preservation of the status quo was the major goal. Britain, in particular, could not be relied upon. There, by the late 1820s, the liberal movement was gaining momentum fast.

Rebellion in Greece

2. LIBERAL GAINS IN WESTERN EUROPE, 1815–1832

Liberal gains in Britain came after an era of reaction that paralleled that which occurred on the Continent. The conservative Tory party had enjoyed almost unbroken political supremacy since the younger William Pitt had become first minister in 1783. Though Pitt had begun

British politics

his career as something of a reformer, the French Revolution had turned him, along with his fellow Tories, into a staunch defender of the status quo. The Tories' political opponents, the Whigs, had throughout the long years of the revolutionary and Napoleonic conflicts remained to some degree conciliatory to the French. But Whigs were as unsympathetic as Tories to democratic notions and as defensive of their rights to the full fruits of their property.

"Peterloo" and the Six Acts

Hence when rioting broke out in England after 1815 as a result of depression and consequent unemployment, there was general support among the ruling class for the repressive measures adopted by the British government. Spies were hired to ferret out evidence against popular agitators. In the industrial north, where conditions were particularly severe, radical members of the middle and working classes capitalized on the general unrest to press their demands for increased representation in Parliament. At Manchester a crowd of 80,000, demonstrating for political reform in St. Peter's Fields, was fired upon by soldiers. Eleven persons were killed and over 400 injured, including 113 women. The massacre was thereafter called "Peterloo" by British radicals: i.e., a domestic Waterloo. It was the first of several repressive measures taken by the government to stifle reform. Another was the legislation known as the Six Acts, which was passed by Parliament in 1819, and outlawed "seditious and blasphemous" literature; levied a stamp tax on newspapers; allowed the searching of houses for arms; and restricted the rights of public meeting.

The liberalizing Tories

Yet within a surprisingly short time British political leaders reversed their opposition to everything new. Instead, they displayed an ability to compromise which kept their country free from revolution. George Canning, the foreign minister, and Robert Peel, the home sec-

The Peterloo Massacre, 1819. A contemporary rendering of the shootings which condemned the "wanton and furious attack by that brutal armed force The Manchester & Cheshire Yeomanry Cavalry."

retary, son of a rich cotton manufacturer, were both sensitive to the interests of Britain's liberal-minded capitalist entrepreneurs. Under their direction, the government retreated from its commitment to the intransigent Quintuple Alliance; it was Canning who took the lead in recognizing the new South American republics. At home, these same politicians began to make order out of the inefficient tangle of British laws; for example, they abolished capital punishment for about a hundred different offenses. And Canning liberalized, though he did not abolish, the Corn Laws. These laws levied a tariff on the importation of cheap foreign grain. As such, they benefited English landlords, but hurt manufacturers, who had to pay higher wages to enable their workers to purchase more expensive bread. These "liberalizers" among the still essentially conservative Tories went so far as to abolish the laws that had kept both dissenting Protestants (members of Prostestant sects—Baptist, Congregationalist, Methodist—other than Anglican) and Roman Catholics from full participation in public political life.

What the conservatives would not do was reform the system of representation in the House of Commons, heavily weighted on the side of the landed interests. Here the Tories, the majority party in Parliament, drew the line and showed themselves still basically committed to the status quo. Yet members of the liberal middle class argued that such a reform was absolutely necessary before they could themselves play a constant and active role in shaping British policy to comply with their own interests. "Interest" was, indeed, the key word in the debate over parliamentary reform. For centuries Parliament had represented the interests of landowners, the major propertied class in England. About two-thirds of the members of the House of Commons were either directly nominated by or indirectly owed their election to the patronage of the richest landowners in the country. Many of the parliamentary electoral districts, or boroughs, which returned members to the House of Commons, were controlled by landowners who used the pressure of their local economic power—or, in many cases, outright bribery—to return candidates sympathetic to their interests. These were the "rotten" or "pocket" boroughs, so-called because they were said to be in the pockets of those men who controlled them. Those who favored the system as it was argued that it mattered little that electoral politics were corrupt, that electoral districts represented unequal numbers, or that very, very few (about one in a hundred) were enfranchised. What did matter, they claimed, was that the interests of the nation at large, which they perceived to coincide with the interests of landed property, were well looked after by a Parliament elected in this fashion.

Of course the new industrial middle class did not agree with the arguments of the landowners. They insisted, for example, that the Corn Laws did not coincide with the nation's best interest. (If they were followers of the theories of Jeremy Bentham, they might argue that the Corn Laws did not produce "the greatest happiness of the

Parliamentary reform

The middle class and reform

greatest number.") Rather, the Corn Laws worked only for the benefit of landlords, by keeping the price of grain high; and they worked to
the disinterest of everyone else. Therefore, said members of the middle class, Parliament must be reformed to represent not only landlords
but the interests of industrial England. It is important to note that the
liberal middle class was *not* arguing in favor of reform on the basis of a
belief in democracy. Some leaders within the emerging working class
did make this argument—and, as we shall see, continued to make it
after a reform bill was passed in 1832. Most of those who spoke in
favor of reform, however, declared that the middle class was capable
of representing the interests of the working class, as well as of itself, in
Parliament. Reformers took this position either because they believed
it, or because they were afraid of working-class representatives, or
because they realized that to favor direct representation for the working class would frighten the more timid reformers and hence defeat
their whole campaign.

A working-class alliance

Spurred by the example of liberal reformers on the Continent (see
below, p. 290) and by the oratory and organizational abilities of middle-class and artisan radicals at home, the movement for reform intensified after 1830. It was strong enough to topple the Tories and to
embolden the Whigs, under the leadership of Lord Grey, to make a
party issue of reform by introducing a bill to modify the ancient electoral structure of the country. The government was clearly frightened. Revolution, if it were ever to come in England, would come as
a result of the alliance now threatening between middle-class industrialists and the artisan/tradesman leadership of the new working class.
In Birmingham, a middle-class banker, Thomas Attwood, organized
a "Political Union of the Lower and Middle Classes of the People."
By July 1830, there were similar organizations in Glasgow, Manchester, Liverpool, Sheffield, Newcastle, and Coventry, some willing
to engage in bloody clashes with army units and police. Middle-class
shopkeepers declared their determination to withhold taxes and, if
necessary, to form a national guard. Plagued as well by an outbreak
of cholera, the country appeared to be on the verge of serious general
disorder, if not outright revolution. The king, William IV, wrote
worriedly to Lord Grey that "miners, manufacturers, colliers, and
labourers" appeared ready for some sort of open rebellion.[1] Sensing
the grave danger of a possible union of the working and middle classes,
the governing class once more accommodated to change, as it had in
the 1820s.

The Reform Bill of 1832

The Reform Bill of 1832, however, was not a retreat from the notion
of representation by interest. No attempt was made to create equal
electoral districts. The franchise, though increased, extended the vote
to no more than 3 percent of the total population. It was defined in

[1] Asa Briggs, *The Age of Improvement*, New York, 1959, p. 248.

terms of the amount of property owned and the length of time one had owned it. In the counties, for example, a man could vote if he paid at least ten pounds annual rental for land held on a long-term sixty-year lease. In other words, the vote was granted to the middle class, but to very few of the working class. Probably more significant than its extension of the franchise was the bill's scheme for a redistribution of seats. One hundred forty-three seats were reallocated, most of them from the rural south to the industrial north, thereby increasing representation in and around cities such as Manchester, Leeds, and Birmingham; and thereby increasing, in turn, the political power of the industrial middle classes. Though the bill was the product of change and itself brought change in its wake, it was understood as a conservative measure. It by no means destroyed the political strength of landed aristocratic interests, though it reduced that strength somewhat. And it preserved the notion of representation by interest. The liberal, industrial middle classes had been admitted into junior partnership with the landed oligarchy that had for centuries ruled Britain and was to rule it for at least one more generation.

Efforts to introduce liberal political reforms were not limited to Britain during this period. Across the world, in Russia, a group of army officers revolted, following the death of Tsar Alexander in 1825, in hopes of persuading his liberally minded brother, Constantine, to assume the throne and guarantee a constitution. In this case, however, the attempt at reform failed. Constantine was unwilling to usurp power from the rightful heir, a third brother, Nicholas. The officers, called Decembrists (because of the month of their rebellion) came from noble families and were members of elite regiments. Learned in the ways of the West, they had obtained a taste of life outside Russia during the Napoleonic wars, when they imbibed the ideas of the Enlightenment and the French Revolution. Politically, they ranged from constitutional monarchists to Jacobin republicans. Their failure was the consequence not only of repression by the tsar but also of their inability to attract mass support from rank and file peasant soldiers. Nicholas I (1825–1855) continued to rule in the severely autocratic ways Alexander had adopted toward the end of his life, creating the Third Section, a political police force, to prevent further domestic disorder. Nicholas's proclaimed goal of "Orthodoxy, Autocracy, and Nationality" meant simply that he would serve as god's lieutenant in an army in which the rest of his countrymen would labor as obedient foot soldiers. Yet even under Nicholas, perhaps Europe's most unremitting conservative, Russia evidenced signs of modernization. Bureaucracy, less dependent than in the past on the aristocracy, grew more centralized and more efficient. Laws were systematically codified in 1832. Stimulated by European demand for Russian grain, estates were reorganized for more effective production, and railways built to transport the grain to Western markets.

*Liberalism and
modernization in other
parts of the West: Russia*

France

For a time, autocracy threatened the liberal revolutionary and Napoleonic heritage in France. The upper middle class in France had remained generally content with the domestic settlement agreed upon by the major powers in 1814 and confirmed at the Congress of Vienna the following year. Louis XVIII, a clever yet self-indulgent man, had "granted" a "constitutional charter" upon his succession to the French throne. While refusing to deny himself absolute power in theory, in practice Louis XVIII had willingly enough agreed to support those principles most desired by French middle-class liberals: legal equality; careers open to talent; and a two-chamber parliamentary government, with the vote confined to property-holders. Yet by basing the franchise on age and property qualifications, which made it impossible for the vast majority of those born after 1789 to participate directly in the government of their country, Louis's charter divided France in a way that would contribute to eventual instability.

In 1824, Louis died and was succeeded by his brother Charles X (1824–1830). Charles was an honest, determined reactionary, who once declared that only he and Lafayette had not changed since 1789— Lafayette was still a liberal, Charles still a zealous monarchist. By his policies Charles immediately declared himself a foe of liberalism, modernization, and the general legacies of the revolutionary and Napoleonic eras. At his direction the French assembly voted indemnities to those aristocratic emigrés whose land had been confiscated by the state. The Church was allowed to reassert its traditionally exclusive right to teach in French classrooms. The upper middle class, strengthened by its role within the country's growing industrial economy, reacted by heading a rebellion against Charles's reactionary policies. In March 1830, members of the Chamber of Deputies, led by bankers, passed a vote of no confidence in the government. Charles dissolved the chamber, as he was constitutionally empowered to do, and called new elections for deputies. When those elections went against his candidates, Charles further retaliated by a series of ordinances, issued on his own authority, which (1) again dissolved the newly elected chamber before it had even met; (2) imposed strict censorship on the press; (3) further restricted suffrage so as to exclude the upper middle class almost completely; and (4) called for new elections.

Charles X and the threat to liberalism

The Revolution of 1830 in France

What Charles got in return for these measures was revolution. Led by republicans—workers, artisans, students, writers, and the like— Parisians took to the streets. For three days, in intense fighting behind hastily constructed barricades, they defied the army and the police, neither of which was anxious to fire into the crowds. Sensing the futility of further resistance, Charles abdicated. Those who had manned the barricades pressed for a genuine republic. But those with the power—bankers, merchants, and industrialists—wanted none of that. Instead they brought the duke of Orleans to the throne as King Louis Philippe (1830–1848) of *the French*—not of France—after extracting a promise from him to abide by the constitution of 1814 which had

The July Revolution of 1830 in Paris. Workers construct street barricades to ward off government troops.

so suited their particular liberal needs. The franchise was extended, from about 100,000 to 200,000 males. But the right to vote was still based upon property ownership. The major beneficiaries of the change were members of the middle class, those whose interests the Revolution of 1830 primarily served.

Other countries in Europe caught the revolutionary fever in the summer of 1830. As we have already noted, middle- and working-class radicals in England were inspired by the French to press their own case for liberal reform. In Belgium, an insurrection that combined elements of liberal and national sentiment put an end to the union of that country with the Dutch, instituted by the Congress of Vienna. The European powers strengthened Belgium's political structure, and hence its independence, by agreeing to the accession as king of Leopold of Saxe-Coburg, uncle of the future Queen Victoria of England. Once again, a middle class had succeeded in establishing a constitutional monarchy to its liking, congenial to its liberal and entrepreneurial goals. No such fate awaited the liberal nationalists in Poland, who moved at this time to depose their ruler, the Russian Tsar Nicholas, whose hegemony extended to Poland as a result of the Vienna settlement of 1815. Western Europe did not intervene; Russian troops crushed the Polish liberal rebels, and Poland was merged into the tsarist empire.

Liberal revolts elsewhere

Liberal forces in Spain enjoyed a greater success. There, middle-class liberalism was linked to the attempts of Queen Maria Christina, widow of King Ferdinand VII, to secure the throne for her daughter, Isabella. Though no liberal herself, the queen was prepared to court

Spain

the favor of urban middle-class elites to win her struggle against her late husband's brother, the reactionary Don Carlos. During the so-called Carlist Wars, which lasted from 1834 to 1840, liberals extracted from Isabella II (1833–1868) a constitution that ensured them a strong voice in the legislature, while restricting the franchise in such a way as to keep the more radical lower middle and artisan classes at bay. By mid-century, however, fear of these radicals led the middle class to acquiesce in a government that was nothing more or less than an authoritarian dictatorship, but that did not threaten directly their own economic interests.

3. LIBERALISM IN BRITAIN AND FRANCE, 1830–1848

Decline of aristocratic power

The Revolution of 1830 in France and the Parliamentary Reform Bill of 1832 in England represented a setback for aristocratic power in both countries. Aristocrats and their supporters did not cease overnight to play an active role in politics, however. Lord Palmerston, for example, was one of England's most influential prime ministers at mid-century and one of Europe's most authoritative arbiters. But no longer would it be possible for the legislatures of France and England to ignore the particular interests of the middle class. Henceforth representatives would include members from that class in sufficient numbers to press successfully for programs that accorded with liberal beliefs.

Liberal legislation in Britain: the new poor law

One of the major accomplishments of the first British Parliament elected after 1832 was passage of a new law governing the treatment of paupers. In accordance with the law passed in 1598 under Elizabeth I, each parish in England had been declared responsible for the maintenance of its own poor, either through accommodation in poorhouses,

An English Workhouse for the Able-Bodied Poor. This workhouse in the county of Devon was built in the late 1830s.

or through a system of doles, coupled with local public employment programs. This system, although it by no means eliminated the debilitating effects of poverty, did provide a kind of guarantee against actual starvation. But by 1830 the system had broken down. Population growth and economic depressions had produced a far larger number of underemployed men and women in Britain than had ever before existed, placing tremendous strain upon those funds, levied as taxes, which each parish used to provide relief. Industrialization also demanded that families move in search of employment from one part of the country to another; yet the law as it stood provided assistance only to those who applied in the parish of their birth. The old law did not accord with liberal notions of efficiency; the new Parliament set about to amend it. The result, drafted by Jeremy Bentham's former private secretary, Edwin Chadwick, and passed almost without dissent, clearly reflected the liberal, middle-class notion of how to achieve "the greatest happiness of the greatest number." Doles were to cease forthwith. Those who could not support themselves were to be confined in workhouses. Here conditions were to be made so severe as to all but compel inmates to depart and accept either whatever work they might find outside, no matter how poorly paid, or whatever charity their friends and relatives might be able to provide them. Parishes were to be grouped together into more efficient unions; the law was to be administered by a central board of commissioners in London. Inspiring this new legislation were the liberal belief that poverty was a person's own fault and the liberal assumption that capitalism, though unregulated, was capable of providing enough jobs for all who genuinely wanted them. Economic depressions in the early 1840s proved that latter assumption false, and wrecked the tidy schemes of the poor-law administrators. Doles were once more instituted, taxes once more increased. Yet the law's failure did not shake the liberal conviction that poverty was, in the end, an individual and not an institutional problem.

Even more symbolic of the political power of Britain's middle class than the new poor law was the repeal of the Corn Laws in 1846. The laws, even after their modification in the 1820s, continued to keep the price of bread artificially high, forcing employers, in turn, to pay wages high enough to allow workers to keep food on their tables. More than that, the Corn Laws symbolized to the middle classes the unwarranted privileges of an ancient and, to their minds, generally useless order: the landed aristocracy. The campaign to accomplish repeal was superbly orchestrated and relentless. The Anti–Corn Law League, an organization of middle-class industrialists and their supporters, held large meetings throughout the north of England, lobbied members of Parliament, and, in the end, managed to persuade Sir Robert Peel, now prime minister, of the inevitability of their goal. They were aided, as well, by the potato famine in Ireland, whose exis-

Robert Peel

Repeal of the Corn Laws

Louis Philippe

tence argued in favor of ending restrictions against the importation of cheap foodstuffs. That Peel was willing to split the Tory—or as it was now coming to be called, Conservative—party to introduce repeal suggests the power of the middle class and its belief in the gospel of free trade.

Legislation during this period reflected other middle-class concerns, and in some cases, directly conflicted with the liberal doctrine of nonintervention. Many members of the urban middle class professed devotion to the tenets of Christianity, particularly that doctrine which argued that all human beings have within themselves a soul which they must work to preserve from sin for their eternal salvation. This belief in the ability of an individual to achieve salvation, which contradicted the older Calvinist doctrine of a predestined "elect," accorded well with more general middle-class notions about the importance of individualism and the responsibility of the individual for his or her own well-being. It produced legislation such as the abolition of the slave trade in British colonies (1833), and the series of Factory Acts, which set limits on the working hours for child labor and which, in 1847, culminated in the curtailment of the workday in some trades to ten hours. Evangelicals such as William Wilberforce, who was throughout his life an eloquent spokesman for enslaved blacks, and Lord Shaftesbury, who campaigned to end the employment of women and children in mines, maintained that individual souls could not find God when imprisoned in the overworked bodies of plantation slaves or factory operatives. They were joined by others who argued, simply, that to keep people tied to their work for as long as twelve or fourteen hours a day was both inhuman and unnecessary.

The religious issue affected educational reform as well. England had no comprehensive system of state education before 1870. What state support there was came, after the 1830s, in the form of government grants to schools managed by the Church of England. Any move to increase this support, however, met with the strong opposition of middle-class dissenters, who saw it as no more than an attempt by the religious Establishment to extend its influence over the young. Middle-class liberals thus found arguments for reform confusing. The laws of classical economics clashed with other prejudices and beliefs, pulling men and women in various directions at once. Their uncertainty mirrored the extent to which no one could discern a right course in this world of new difficulties and fresh options.

The years of Louis Philippe's reign in France were not so marked as those in England with significant reforms. In the first place, France was not confronted with anything like the same degree of rapid industrialization that was compelling legislative activity on a number of fronts in England. France had nothing to compare with the problems generated by the growth of urban manufacturing centers in the north of England. Though the Chamber of Deputies contained representatives from the upper middle class, they tended to be bankers and

Apotheosis of Homer, Jean Auguste Ingres (1780–1867). Though he painted during the Romantic period, Ingres did not desert the neoclassical themes and style that dominated art during the Revolutionary and Napoleonic eras. (Louvre)

Beatrice and Dante, William Blake (1757–1827). Blake was a mystical Romantic whose work possesses a compelling uniqueness that defies exact categorization. This painting is from his series for *The Divine Comedy.* (The Tate Gallery, London)

Execution of the Rioters, Francisco Goya (1746–1828). Unlike most artists of his time, Goya dealt unflinchingly with suffering, violence, fear, and death. Depicted here is the execution of Spanish rebels by Napoleon's soldiers in 1808. This harshness caused the rebellion to spread over the whole peninsula. (Prado)

Liberty Leading the People, Eugène Delacroix (1798–1863). Delacroix was a romantic painter of dramatic and emotional scenes. In this painting he celebrates the triumph of the revolutionary principle of liberty in a tempestuous allegory. (Louvre)

The Massacre of Chios, Eugène Delacroix. Here Delacroix again puts his brush to work for the cause of liberty, eulogizing the more than 20,000 Greeks slain by the Turks during the Greek war of independence in 1822. (Louvre)

The Movings by Louis Léopold Boilly (1761–1845). Dating from 1822, this realist-allegorical painting depicts Parisians of various classes in the process of moving their household goods. By juxtaposing the buildings of contemporary Paris with the Church of Santa Maria de' Miracoli of Rome, the artist appears to suggest that for some, including the peasants in their wagon leaving the city and the corpse in the horse-drawn hearse heading for its grave, the idea of the metropolis as a place of promise and prosperity is an illusion. (Art Institute of Chicago)

The Last of England, Ford Madox Brown (1821–1893). A haunting scene of a couple emigrating from England by one of the most noted pre-Raphaelites. (The City Museum and Art Gallery, Birmingham, England)

Valley of Aosta—Snowstorm, Avalanche, and Thunderstorm, Joseph M. W. Turner (1775–1851). Turner's complete absorption in light, color, and atmosphere helped to prepare the way for the French Impressionists. (MMA)

A Woman Reading, Camille Corot (1796–1875). Corot was a Naturalist whose interest in the effects of light prefigured to a degree the work of the Impressionists. Sentimentality and a preference for scenes of innocence and simplicity distinguished him from the Realists. (MMA)

Public Notary Eltz and His Family by Ferdinand Georg Waldmüller (1793–1865). A portrait that celebrates the rise to power and influence of the bourgeois bureaucrat. (Österreichische Galerie, Vienna)

The Gleaners, Jean François Millet (1814–1875). A Realist, Millet remained fascinated with color and setting to a degree that often made his paintings something other than a record of social change. (Louvre)

Funeral at Ornans, Gustave Courbet (1819–1877). Though a less strident Realist than his contemporary Daumier, Courbet was concerned to express human nature as he found it—neither more handsome nor more ugly. This painting, in which he used men and women from his village as models, reflects his commitment to personal, as opposed to social, Realism. (Louvre)

merchants, not industrialists. Some were willing to espouse the notion of free trade, though not with the general enthusiasm of their British counterparts, whose unrivaled position as the world's leading manufacturers gave them a vested interest in that cause. Under the succession of governments dominated by France's leading politician of the period, François Guizot (1787–1874), the French expanded their educational system, thereby further underwriting their belief in the liberal doctrine of a meritocracy, or careers open to talent. A French law of 1833 provided for the establishment of elementary schools in every village. Children of indigent parents were to receive a free education; all others would pay a modest fee. In addition, larger towns were to provide training schools for trade and industry, and departments, schools for teacher training. As a result, the number of pupils in France increased from about 2 million in 1831, to about 3.25 million in 1846. Little else of lasting importance was accomplished during the regime of Louis Philippe. Guizot became more and more an apologist for the status quo. Everyone was free, he argued, to rise to the upper middle class and thus to a position of political and economic power. His advice to those who criticized his complacency was: "enrich yourselves." Politicians followed his advice, finding in schemes for the modernization of Paris and the expansion of the railway system ample opportunities for graft. Louis Philippe did little to counteract the lifelessness and corruption that characterized his regime. Although he had played a minor part in the first stage of the revolution of 1789, he was no revolutionary. He did not have the dash and glamor of a Napoleon. He was a paunchy, fussy, and undistinguished person, easily caricatured by his enemies. He appeared to most to be nothing more or less than a typically successful plutocrat. He amassed a fortune which, in characteristic bourgeois fashion, he claimed he had accumulated in order to provide for his five sons and three daughters. He enjoyed the company of bankers and businessmen, though he attempted to develop a reputation as the friend of the people. Rumor had it that when he stopped to shake hands with shopkeepers he wore a special pair of dirty gloves, which he would replace with white kid when hobnobbing with the rich. Louis Philippe was unable to rise above his stodgy public image. The German poet Heinrich Heine reported that the young people of France "yearned for great deeds and scorned the stingy small-mindedness and huckstering selfishness" that the king seemed to embody.

The slower pace of reform in France

Meanwhile radical members of the French and British lower middle and working classes who had assisted—if not propelled—the forces of liberalism to victory in 1830 and 1832 grew increasingly dissatisfied with the results of their efforts. In Britain they soon realized that the Reform Bill had done little to increase their chances for political participation. For a time they devoted their energies to the cause of trade unionism, believing that industrial, rather than political, action might bring them relief from the economic hardships they were suffering.

Growing dissatisfaction of radicals

Trade unionism

Trade union organization had been a goal of militant workers since the beginning of the century. Among the first workers' campaigns in the nineteenth century were those often-riotous revolts organized both in England and, later, on the Continent against the introduction of machinery. In some instances, factories were attacked by workers and machines smashed, in the belief that machines, by replacing skilled workers, were producing widespread unemployment. In England, the rioters were called Luddites, after "Ned Ludd," who was the mythical leader of the movement. In other instances, the hostility of trade unionists was not directed so much toward machinery as toward those workers who refused to join in unions against their masters. Yet nowhere in Europe were trade unions able to organize themselves into effective bargaining agents before 1850. They came closest in England. There, artisans and skilled workers had banded together in the mid-1820s to form both Friendly Societies, really mutual aid and insurance organizations, and cooperatives, communal stores that cut prices by eliminating the middleman between producer and consumer. By 1831, there were about 500 cooperative societies in England, with a membership of something like 20,000. These organizations encouraged the parallel growth of trade unions, which, in the early 1830s, reached the peak of their early power and effectiveness. The National Association for the Protection of Labour comprised about 150 separate local unions in the textile and mining industries of the north; the Operative Builder's Union, about 30,000 workers throughout the country. In 1834, a new and potentially far more radical organization, the Grand National Consolidated Trades Union of Great Britain and Ireland, was organized by a group of London artisans. Its leadership declared that only by bringing the country to a standstill with a general strike could workers compel the governing class to grant them a decent life. At that point, the government decided to put an end to unions. In 1834, six organizers for the Grand National were convicted of administering secret oaths (unions were not themselves illegal) and sentenced to transportation (forced emigration to penal colonies in Australia). Subsequently employers demanded that their workers sign a document pledging their refusal to join a union, thereby stifling opportunities for further organization.

Chartism

After the defeat of the Grand National, the efforts of radical democratic reformers in England turned back from trade union to political activity, centering on attempts to force further political reform upon the uninterested government through the device of the "People's Charter." This document, circulated across the country by committees of Chartists, as they were known, and signed by millions, contained six demands: universal manhood suffrage; institution of the secret ballot; abolition of property qualifications for membership in the House of Commons; annual parliamentary elections; payment of salaries to members of the House of Commons; and equal electoral districts.

The fortunes of the Chartist movement waxed and waned. In some areas its strength depended upon economic conditions: Chartism spread with unemployment and depression. There were arguments among its leaders as to both ends and means: Did Chartism imply a reorganization of industry or, instead, a return to preindustrial society? Were its goals to be accomplished by petition only, or by more violent means if necessary? The Chartist William Lovett, a cabinet-maker, for example, was as fervent a believer in self-improvement as any member of the middle class. He advocated a union of educated workers to acquire their fair share of the nation's increasing industrial bounty. The Chartist Feargus O'Connor, on the other hand, appealed to the more impoverished and desperate class of workers. He urged a rejection of industrialization, and the resettlement of the poor on agricultural allotments. These polarities and disagreements regarding the aims of the movement suggest the extent of the confusion within the working class, whose consciousness as a separate political force was only just beginning to develop. Events answered most of the Chartists' questions for them. In 1848, revolutionary outbreaks across the Continent inspired Chartist leaders to plan a major demonstration and show of force in London. A procession of 500,000 workers was called, to bear to Parliament a petition containing 6,000,000 signatures demanding the six points. Confronted, once again, with the spectre of open class conflict, special constables and contingents of the regular army were marshaled under the now-aged duke of Wellington to resist

The Great Chartist Rally of April 10, 1848. Undiscovered in the royal archives until the 1970s, this early photograph draws attention to the respectable attire of working-class radicals and to the decidedly male character of mid-century radicalism.

this threat to order. In the end, fewer than 50,000 made the march to Parliament, however. Rain, poor management, and unwillingness on the part of many to do battle with the well-armed constabulary put an end to the Chartists' campaign. Increased prosperity among skilled workers disarmed the movement after mid-century.

In France, radical agitation produced very different results. There, as well, those who had manned the barricades in 1830 soon grew disgusted with the liberalism for which they had risked their lives. In their minds they carried memories or myths of the years of the first French Republic—its domestic accomplishments, its foreign victories, if not its Reign of Terror. They were opposed to constitutional monarchy, and unenthusiastic about parliamentary government, especially by a *nouveau riche* upper middle class. They were prepared, if necessary, to use force in order to achieve their ends. Centered in an increasingly industrialized Paris, they were for the most part either writers, students, or working-class leaders. They met in secret, studied the works of the radical theorist, Gracchus Babeuf (see above, p. 210), whose socialist *Conspiracy of Equals,* written during the French Revolution, became their Bible, and succeeded in making constant trouble for the liberal, middle-class governments of Louis Philippe. Their leading spokesman was the socialist Auguste Blanqui (1805–1881). He decried the victimization of the workers by the middle class, and helped organize secret societies that were to become the instruments of eventual insurrection. Radicals waged some of their most successful campaigns in the press. Honoré Daumier's savage caricatures of Louis Philippe landed him in prison more than once. But campaigners took to the streets as well. In retaliation, the government in 1834 declared radical political organizations illegal. Rioting broke

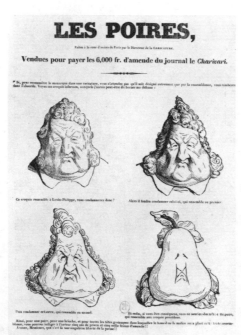

Louis Philippe in Caricature. In contrast to the portrait of Louis Philippe on page 294 as he wanted to appear, these 1833 caricatures by Charles Philipon depict the king as he increasingly appeared to his subjects and suggest the degree to which Louis Philippe failed in his attempt to celebrate the supposed virtues of the bourgeoisie.

Rue Transnomain. A drawing by Daumier to commemorate the victims of government repression in 1834.

out in Lyon and Paris in protest, where for two days government troops massacred hundreds of insurgents, and arrested some 2,000 republican leaders. In 1835, following an attempt to assassinate Louis Philippe, the government passed a censorship law, which forbade the publication of articles attempting to inspire contempt for the king and which prohibited the printing of any drawing or emblem without prior governmental approval.

These repressive measures served only to increase dissatisfaction with the regime. Guizot was advised by more progressive members of the legislature to extend the franchise to professionals whose lack of wealth now denied them the vote, but whose general adherence to the doctrines of liberalism was unquestioned. Guizot unwisely refused, thereby driving these moderates into the camp of the more radical republicans. By 1847, various elements within the opposition were disaffected enough to instigate a general campaign of agitation throughout France. At political banquets, republicans such as the poet Alphonse de Lamartine (1790–1869) and socialist republicans such as Louis Blanc (see above, p. 280) preached drastic reform, though not outright revolution. Contrary to the expressed wishes of the king, a giant protest meeting was announced for February 22, 1848. The day before, the government forbade the meeting. Rioting and barricading during the following two days ended in the abdication of Louis Philippe and increased demands for a republic.

4. THE REVOLUTION OF 1848 IN FRANCE

The February revolution in France was a catalyst which, as we shall see, helped to produce uprisings in the succeeding months throughout much of Europe. Meanwhile, in Paris, a provisional government was

A National Workshop. When few could read, newspapers were heard rather than scanned. Under government auspices, these workshops achieved a good deal less than Louis Blanc had envisioned.

Republican-socialist split: Blanc's workshops

established consisting of ten men, seven of whom, including Lamartine, were middle-of-the-road republicans; three of whom, including Blanc, were socialists. The tensions between middle-class republicans and radical socialists, which had been masked by a common disgust with the government of Louis Philippe, now emerged to shape the political events of the ensuing months in several specific ways. Blanc insisted upon the establishment of national workshops, institutions he had championed as a writer, which were to be organized by trades as producers' cooperatives, where men and women workers would be trained if necessary, put to work, and paid two francs a day when employed and a smaller stipend when unemployed. Instead, the government established what it called workshops, but what amounted to nothing more than a program of public works in and around Paris, where economic conditions had resulted in widespread unemployment. Initially, plans had called for the employment of no more than ten or twelve thousand in projects throughout the city. But with unemployment running as high as 65 percent in construction trades and 51 percent in textiles and clothing, workers began to flood into the government's so-called workshops, as many as 66,000 by April, and 120,000 by June.

Continuing agitation

Paris meanwhile attracted numbers of radical writers, organizers, and agitators. The provisional government had removed all restrictions upon the formation of political clubs and the dissemination of political literature. As a result, 170 new journals and more than 200 clubs formed within weeks; the club headed by the socialist Auguste Blanqui boasted a membership of some 3,000. Delegations claiming to represent the oppressed of all European countries—Chartists, Hungarians, Poles—moved freely about the city, attracting attention, if not devoted followings, and contributing to tension which was convincing more and more members of the middle class that stern measures were needed to forestall further insurrectionary outbreaks. This sentiment was fortified as a result of elections held at the end of April.

The provisional government had been pressured by Parisian radicals into decreeing universal manhood suffrage. Yet the election returned only a small proportion of radical socialists. The largest blocs consisted of "true," or moderate, republicans and monarchists—this latter group divided, however, between supporters of the Bourbon dynasty and the Orleanist Louis Philippe. The generally conservative tenor of the newly elected assembly strengthened the hand of those who pressed for the repression of the socialists. It also, naturally, convinced the socialists that once again, as in the 1790s, a potentially radical revolution had been betrayed by the timid, self-serving middle class.

By late spring, a majority of the assembly believed that the workshop system represented both an unbearable financial drain and a serious threat to social order. At the end of May, the workshops were closed to new enrollment as a first step toward barring membership to all who had resided for less than six months in Paris and sending all members between the ages of eighteen and twenty-five to the army. Thousands of workers lost their state-financed jobs, and with them their best chance for survival. Desperate, they and their supporters once more threw up barricades across Paris. For four days, June 23–26, they defended themselves in an ultimately hopeless military battle against armed forces recruited, in part, from willing provincials eager enough to assist in the repression of the urban working class. Whether or not the Parisian insurrectionists were fighting as members of a beleaguered class, or simply as men and women on the brink of starvation, is a matter that historians continue to debate. That they were taken seriously as a revolutionary threat can be seen by the ferocity with which they were hunted out once the street fighting had ceased. About 3,000 were killed and 12,000 more arrested, the majority of whom were deported to Algerian labor camps.

In the aftermath of the "June Days," the French government moved

The Revolution of 1848 in France. A contemporary broadside celebrating the triumph of the people.

quickly to bring order to the country. The assembly, faced with the task of drafting a republican constitution, contained a large number of men to whom the idea of a republic was anathema. Assembly members therefore arranged for the immediate election of a president. Their hope was that a strong leader might assist in bringing dissidents to heel. Four candidates stood: Lamartine, the moderate republican; General Eugène Cavaignac, who had commanded the troops in June; Alexander Ledru-Rollin, a socialist; and Louis Napoleon Bonaparte, nephew of the emperor, who polled more than twice as many votes as the other three candidates combined.

The astonishing upstart Louis Napoleon had spent most of his life in exile. Returning to France after the Revolution of 1830, he was imprisoned a few years later for attempting to provoke a local uprising. But in 1846 he escaped to England, where he was supplied with funds by both British and French reactionaries. By the summer of 1848 the situation in France was such that he knew it was safe to return. In fact, he was welcomed by members of all classes. Conservatives were looking for a savior to protect their property against the onslaughts of the radicals. Workers were beguiled by his glittering schemes for prosperity in his book, *The Extinction of Pauperism,* and by the fact that he had corresponded with Louis Blanc and with Pierre Proudhon, the anarchist. In between these two classes was a multitude of patriots and hero-worshipers to whom the name Napoleon was a symbol of glory and greatness. It was chiefly to this multitude that the nephew of the Corsican owed his astounding triumph. As one old peasant expressed it: "How could I help voting for this gentleman—I whose nose was frozen at Moscow?"

With dreams of emulating his uncle, Louis Napoleon was not long content to remain president of France. Almost from the first he used the power he already had to achieve the further power he desired. He enlisted the support of the Catholics by permitting them to regain control over the schools and by sending an expedition to Rome to restore to the pope the temporal power denied him during the revolutionary struggles of 1848. He courted the workers and the middle class by introducing old-age insurance and laws for the encouragement of business. In 1851, alleging the need for extraordinary measures to protect the rights of the masses, he proclaimed a temporary dictatorship and invited the people to grant him the power to draw up a new constitution. In the plebiscite held on December 21, 1851, he was authorized by an overwhelming majority (7,500,000 to 640,000) to proceed as he liked. The new constitution, which he put into effect in January 1852, made the president an actual dictator. After one year Louis Napoleon Bonaparte ordered another plebiscite and, with the approval of over 95 percent of the voters, assumed the title of Napoleon III, emperor of the French.[2]

[2]Napoleon I's son, Napoleon II, had died in Vienna in 1832.

AU NOM DU PEUPLE FRANÇAIS.

LE PRÉSIDENT DE LA RÉPUBLIQUE
DÉCRÈTE:

Art. 1.
L'Assemblée nationale est dissoute.

Art. 2.
Le Suffrage universel est rétabli. La loi du 31 mai est abrogée.

Art. 3.
Le Peuple français est convoqué dans ses comices à partir du 14 décembre jusqu'au 21 décembre suivant.

Art. 4.
L'état de siége est décrété dans l'étendue de la 1ᵉ division militaire.

Art. 5.
Le Conseil d'État est dissous.

Art. 6.
Le Ministre de l'intérieur est chargé de l'exécution du présent décret.

Fait au Palais de l'Élysée, le 2 décembre 1851.

LOUIS-NAPOLÉON BONAPARTE.
Le Ministre de l'Intérieur,
DE MORNY.

Napoleon III's Decree Dissolving the National Assembly

What is the significance of the French Revolution of 1848 and its political aftermath in the history of middle-class liberalism, which is our subject? Two points need particular emphasis. First, we must recognize the pivotal role of the liberal middle class. Under Louis Philippe, it increasingly perceived itself and its particular interests as neglected. Denied a direct political voice because of a severely limited franchise, it swung to the left, allying itself with radicals who, by themselves, would probably have stood no chance of permanent success. Yet no sooner had Louis Philippe abdicated than the liberal middle class began to wonder if "success" was not about to bring disaster upon its heels. And so it swung again, this time to the right, where it found itself confronting the mysterious and yet not entirely unattractive prospect of Louis Napoleon. He, in turn, was clever enough to understand this first lesson of 1848, that in France no government could survive that did not cater to the interests of the middle class. By assisting it to achieve its liberal economic goals, the emperor helped it forget just how heavily he was trampling on its political liberties.

The implications of the French Revolution of 1848

Yet 1848 proved that there was now in France another element— class consciousness may, at this point, not yet be the correct term— that governments ignored at their peril. If mid–nineteenth-century Europe saw the middle class closer than ever to the center of power, it saw the workers moving rapidly in from the edge. Their barricades could, if necessary, be destroyed, and their demands ignored, but only at an increasingly grave risk to the fabric of the state. Middle-class liberalism, if it was to thrive, would not only have to pay lip service to working-class demands, but in some measure accommodate to them as well.

5. LIBERALISM IN FRANCE AND BRITAIN AFTER 1850

Napoleon III recognized the vital role that public opinion had now assumed in the management of affairs of state. He labored hard and successfully to sell his empire to the people of France. He argued that legislative assemblies only served to divide a nation along class lines. With power residing in him, he would unite the country as it had not been for generations. The French, who craved order following their recent political misadventures, bought the program he was selling willingly enough. Napoleon III modeled his constitution upon that of his uncle. An assembly, elected by universal manhood suffrage, in fact possessed almost no power. It could do no more than approve legislation drafted at the emperor's direction by a Council of State. Elections were manipulated by the government to ensure the return of politically docile representatives. Control of finance, the army, and foreign affairs rested exclusively with the emperor. France was a democracy only in the sense that its people were periodically afforded a chance, through elections, to express their approval of Napoleon's regime.

Napoleon III

Napoleon III's constitution

In return for the gift of almost absolute power, Napoleon III gave the French what they appeared to want. For the middle class, he provided a chance to make a great deal of money. The device of the *Crédit Mobilier,* an investment banking institution, facilitated the expansion of industry by selling its shares to the public and using its income to underwrite various entrepreneurial schemes. In 1863 a limited liability law encouraged further investment by guaranteeing that stockholders could lose no more than the par value of their stock no matter how indebted the company in which they had invested. Railways, owned by the state, spread across the country, and spurred further industrial expansion. So prosperous did the French economy appear that Napoleon was prepared to follow Britain's lead in pressing for tariff-free trade between the two countries. A treaty was signed in 1860. Though funds were set aside to compensate French industries for any loss they might suffer, they were never completely expended, suggesting that French manufacturers were now well enough established to meet the threat of British competition. The apparent satisfaction of the middle class with Napoleon's regime provides a measure with which to assess the state of liberalism in France after 1850. The fact that the country no longer enjoyed a free press, that universities were politically controlled, and that political opposition was repressed seemed to matter very little to most. Liberalism, if it existed at all, existed as the freedom to have one's own economic way.

Napoleon III and the middle class

Napoleon III, though he catered to the middle class, did not fail to court the favor of the workers as well. He encouraged the establishment of hospitals and instituted a program of free medical assistance. More important, he permitted, if he did nothing to encourage, the existence of trade unions and in 1864 introduced legislation to legalize

Paris under the Second Empire. The Avenue de l'Imperatrice was designed for the enjoyment of the middle class.

strikes. Ultimately, he appealed to the workers much as he appealed to the middle class, as a glamorous, if not heroic symbol of his country's reemergence as a leading world power. The activities of his court, and of his stylish empress, Eugénie, were well publicized. The reconstruction of Paris into a city of broad boulevards and grand open spaces was calculated to provide appropriate scenery for the theater of empire—as well as to lessen the chances for successful proletarian barricade-building across narrow streets.

Grandeur, however, appeared to Napoleon III to demand an aggressive foreign policy. Although early in his regime he declared himself in favor of that central liberal tenet—international peace—he was soon at war: first against Russia in the Crimea; then in Italy; then in Mexico, where he attempted to assist in the establishment of another empire; and finally and disastrously with Prussia. The details of these adventures are part of the subject of the following chapter. It is enough at this point to remark that Napoleon III's foreign policy reflects clearly how far he—and the rest of France with him—had subordinated the liberal heritage of the first French Revolution to that of another of its legacies: national glory.

What, meanwhile, of the liberal tradition in Britain? There the course of liberalism was altered by changes occurring within the working class. Industrialization had, by this time, begun to foster and sustain a growing stratum of labor "aristocrats," men whose particular skills, and the increasing demand for them, allowed them to demand wages high enough to ensure them a fairly comfortable standard

Empress Eugénie

of living. These workers—concentrated for the most part within the building, engineering, and textile industries—turned from the tradition of militant radicalism that had characterized the so-called hungry forties. Having succeeded within the liberal economic system imposed upon Britain by the middle class, they were now prepared to accept many liberal, middle-class principles as their own. They believed in self-help, achieved by means of cooperative societies or through trade unions, whose major function was the accumulation of funds to be used as insurance against old age and unemployment. They believed in education as a tool for advancement, and patronized the Mechanics Institutes and other similar institutions either founded by them or on their behalf.

Yet the labor aristocracy, as it came to appreciate its ability to achieve a decent life for itself within the capitalist system, grew all the more dissatisfied with a political system that excluded it from any direct participation in the governmental process. Although some pressed for extension of the franchise as democrats, as many argued for it on the same grounds the middle class had used in 1832. They were responsible workers, whose loyalty to the state could not be questioned. As such, they were a bona fide "interest," as worthy of the vote and of direct representation as the middle class. They were joined in their campaign by many middle-class reformers who continued to chafe at the privileged position of national institutions that they associated with the landed society and the old order. Many middle-class men and women, for example, were dissenters from the Church of England; yet they were forced to pay taxes to support a church which was staffed, in the main, by sons of the gentry. Their sons were denied the facilities of the nation's ancient universities, Oxford and Cambridge, unless those sons subscribed to the articles of faith of the Anglican church.

Together with working-class leaders, these middle-class dissidents organized a Reform League to campaign across the country for a new reform bill and a House of Commons responsive to their interests. Though by no means revolutionary, the reformers made it clear by their actions that they were determined to press their case to the utmost. Politicians in Britain in the 1860s were confronted by a situation not unlike that which had faced Guizot in France in 1848: middle class, lower middle class, and skilled workers discontented and demanding reform. Unlike Guizot, however, the leaders of both British political parties, Conservative (formerly Tory) and Liberal (formerly Whig), were prepared to concede what they recognized it would be dangerous to withhold. Once convinced of this need, the Conservative leader of the House of Commons and future prime minister, Benjamin Disraeli, seized upon reform as an issue with which to belabor the Liberals. In 1867 he steered a bill through Parliament more far-reaching than anything proposed by his political opponents. It doubled the franchise by extending the vote to any males who paid poor rates or rent of ten pounds or more a year in urban areas (this would mean, in general, the skilled workers), and to tenants paying rent of twelve pounds or more in the counties. Seats were again redistributed as in 1832, with large northern cities gaining representation at the expense of the rural south. The "responsible" working class had been deemed worthy to participate in the affairs of state. For the next twenty years it showed its appreciation by accepting its apprentice position without demur, and by following the lead prescribed by the middle class.

The decade or so following the passage of the Reform Bill of 1867 marked the high point of British liberalism. The labor aristocracy was accommodated with an Education Act, virtually guaranteeing a primary education to all, with legalization of strikes, and with a series of measures designed to improve living conditions in the great cities; yet it was the middle class that set the governmental tone. Under Disraeli and his Liberal counterpart William Gladstone, and with the cooperation of the newly enfranchised skilled workers, Britain celebrated the triumph of the liberal principles of free trade, representative—but not democratic—government, and general prosperity.

The triumph of British liberalism

SELECTED READINGS

• *Items so designated are available in paperback editions.*

   Anderson, R. D., *Education in France, 1848–1870,* New York, 1975. Covers every level of formal education and its practical and theoretical relationship to state and society.

• Artz, Frederick B., *Reaction and Revolution, 1814–1832,* New York, 1834. A European survey, dated but still useful.

• Blake, Robert, *Disraeli,* London, 1966. A masterful biography.

• Briggs, Asa, *The Age of Improvement, 1783 to 1867.* New York, 1959. A survey of England from 1780 to 1870, particularly strong on Victorian attitudes.

• Duveau, Georges, *1848: The Making of a Revolution,* New York, 1967. Focuses on the working class during the revolution in Paris: their unity at the outset, their division in the "June Days."

   Finer, Samuel E., *The Life and Times of Edwin Chadwick,* London, 1952. An excellent biography of the great English Benthamite reformer.

   Halévy, Elie, *A History of the English People, 1905–1914,* Vols. II–IV, London, 1949–1952. The best survey of nineteenth-century England, comprehensive and analytical.

• Harrison, Royden, *Before the Socialists: Studies in Labour and Politics, 1861–1881,* London, 1965. Examines the social and political background of franchise extension in Britain.

   Johnson, Douglas, *Guizot: Aspects of French History, 1787–1874,* London, 1963. Analytical essays about the leading politician of the July monarchy.

• Kissinger, Henry, *A World Restored: Metternich, Castlereagh, and the Problem of Peace, 1812–1822,* Boston, 1957. By an admirer of Metternich.

• Langer, William L., *Political and Social Upheaval, 1832–1852,* New York, 1969. (Several chapters have been published separately under the title *The Revolutions of 1848.*) A thorough general survey.

Magnus, Philip, *Gladstone: A Biography,* London, 1955. A readable and reliable biography.

Merriman, John M., ed., *1830 in France,* New York, 1975. Recent scholarship emphasizing the nature of revolution and examining events outside of Paris.

• Pinkney, David, *Napoleon III and the Rebuilding of Paris,* Princeton, 1972. An interesting account of the creation of Modern Paris during the Second Empire.

———, *The French Revolution of 1830,* Princeton, 1972. A reinterpretation, now the best history of the revolution.

Raeff, Marc, *The Decembrist Movement,* New York, 1966. Examines the uprising; contains documents.

Roberts, David, *Victorian Origins of the British Welfare State,* New Haven, 1960. Examines various nineteenth-century reforms in England.

• Robertson, Priscilla, *Revolutions of 1848: A Social History,* Princeton, 1960. Surveys the revolutions across Europe.

de Sauvigny, G. de Bertier, *The Bourbon Restoration,* New York, 1967. An outstanding work; the best history of a neglected period.

• Stearns, Peter N., *1848: The Revolutionary Tide in Europe,* New York, 1974. Stresses the social background of the revolutions.

• Thompson, J. L. *Louis Napoleon and the Second Empire,* Oxford, 1954. A good biography. Presents Louis Napoleon as a modern Hamlet.

Woodward, E. L., *The Age of Reform,* Oxford, 1962. An excellent survey from the Oxford History of England series.

• Wright, Gordon, *France in Modern Times: 1760 to the Present,* 4th ed., New York, 1987. The best textbook on modern France.

• Zeldin, Theodore, *The Political System of Napoleon III,* New York, 1958. Examines the processes by which Napoleon maintained power as the first modern dictator.

• ———, *France, 1848–1945,* 2 vols., Oxford, 1973–77.

SOURCE MATERIALS

• Flaubert, Gustave, *L'Education Sentimentale,* London, 1961. Contains an unsympathetic but memorable portrait of the Revolution of 1848 and of the bourgeois style of life that contributed to its outbreak.

• Greville, Charles Fulke, *Memoirs,* ed. by Roger Fulford, New York, 1963. Originally published in seven volumes in 1875, these comprise the diaries of the secretary to the Privy Council for the years 1821–1861. An excellent source for the court and politics of the period.

• Price, Roger, ed., *1848 in France,* Ithaca, N.Y., 1975. An excellent collection of eyewitness accounts, annotated.

Stewart, John Hall, *The Restoration Era in France, 1814–1830,* Princeton, 1968. A brief narrative and a good collection of documents.

Chapter 29

NATIONALISM AND NATION-BUILDING (1815–1870)

The present problem, the first task . . . is simply to preserve the existence and continuance of what is German.

—Johann Fichte, *Addresses to the German Nation*

The great questions of the day will not be decided by speeches or by majority decisions—that was the mistake of 1848 and 1849—but by blood and iron.

—Otto von Bismarck, speech, 1862

I f the history of nineteenth-century Britain and France can be studied against a general background of middle-class liberalism, that of much of the rest of Europe during the same period must be understood in terms of a more complex combination of the forces of liberalism, nationalism, and nation-building. We shall define nationalism as a sentiment rooted in broad historical, geographical, linguistic, or cultural circumstances. It is characterized by a consciousness of belonging, in a group, to a tradition derived from those circumstances, which differs from the traditions of other groups. Nation-building is the political implementation of nationalism, the translation of sentiment into power.

Nationalism and nation-building defined

Men and women in Britain and France during the nineteenth century entertained national as well as liberal sentiments. When Britain's prime minister, Lord Palmerston, declared in 1850 that any British citizen, in any part of the world, had but to proclaim, like a citizen of the Roman Empire, "civis Romanus sum" ("I am a citizen of Rome") to summon up whatever force might be necessary to protect him from foreign depradations, he was echoing his countrymen's pride in the powers of their nationhood. When the French rejoiced in 1840 at the return of the Emperor Napoleon's remains from St. Helena to an elaborate shrine in Paris, they were reliving triumphs that had become

Nationalism in Britain and France

part of their nation's heritage. Palmerston's boast and Napoleon's bones were both artifacts of national traditions and sentiments bound up in the life of the English and the French.

Nineteenth-century nationalism in other areas of Europe was to be a more assertive phenomenon than it was in Britain and France, which had for centuries existed as particular geographical, cultural, and political entities. Elsewhere, common traditions and assumptions were less clearly articulated, because the political unity that might have helped define them did not exist. East Prussians or Venetians had no difficulty in perceiving of themselves as such; history had provided them with those identities. But history had not provided them, except in the most general way, with identities as Germans or Italians. They had to make a deliberate effort to think of themselves in those terms before the terms could have any political reality.

Neither nationalism nor nation-building stood in necessary opposition to liberalism. Indeed, to the extent that nationalism celebrated the achievements of a particular common people over those of a cosmopolitan aristocratic elite, it reflected liberalism's abhorrence of traditional privilege. Yet to liberalism's readiness to accept the new, nationalism responded with an appreciation, if not veneration, of the past. And to the liberals' insistence upon the value and importance of individualism, nation-builders replied that their vital task might require the sacrifice of some measure of each citizen's freedom. The success of nation-building rested upon the foundation of a general balance of international power, achieved by the European states during the half century after 1815. The emergence of new nations—a unified Italy and Germany—would require readjustments to that balance. But accommodation remained possible, with only minor skirmishes marring the stability of the settlement achieved at the Congress of Vienna.

1. ROMANTICISM AND NATIONALISM

As we noted in the preceding chapter, nationalism was in part a child of the French Revolution. It was closely related, as well, to the intellectual movement that has been called "romanticism." Romanticism was so broad and so varied that it all but defies definition, if not analysis. Perhaps as much as anything, romanticism represented a reaction against the rationalism of the eighteenth-century Enlightenment. Where the eighteenth century relied on reason, the romantics put their faith in emotion. The eighteenth century understood the mind as a blank tablet, which received knowledge from impressions imprinted upon it through the senses by the external world. Romantics also believed in the importance of sense experience. But they insisted that innate sensibility—that which constituted a person's own particular personality—was inherited, and therefore present in the mind from birth. Knowledge, then, for the romantic, was the product of both innate feelings *and* external perceptions. Romanticism thus stressed individualism, and the individual creativity that resulted from the interaction of unique personality with external experience. At the same time, by stressing the inheritance of attitudes, it also celebrated the past. And that celebration was its link with nationalism.

Romanticism and nationalism were connected by their common belief that the past should be made to function as a means of understanding the present and planning for the future. It was in Germany that this notion received its fullest airing and most enthusiastic reception. One of the earliest and most influential German romantics was Johann von Herder (1744–1803). A Protestant pastor and theologian, his interest in past cultures led him, in the 1780s, to set out his reflections in a lengthy and detailed treatise, *Ideas for a Philosophy of Human History*. Herder traced what he perceived to be the progressive development of European society from the time of the Greeks through the Renaissance. He believed that civilization was not the product of an artificial, international elite—a criticism of Enlightenment thinking—but of the genuine culture of the common people, the *Volk*. No civilization could be considered sound which did not continue to express its own unique historical character, its *Volksgeist*. Herder did not argue that one *Volksgeist* was either better or worse than any other. He insisted only that each nation must be true to its own particular heritage. He broke dramatically with the Enlightenment idea that human beings could be expected to respond to human situations in more or less the same fashion, and with the assumption that the value of history was simply to teach by example.

Johann von Herder

Herder's intellectual heirs, men like the conservative German romantics Friedrich Schlegel (1772–1829) and Friedrich von Savigny (1779–1861), condemned the implantation of democratic and liberal ideas—"foreign" to Germany—in German cultural soil. History, they argued, taught that institutions must evolve organically—a favorite word of the political romantics, and that proper laws were the product of historical growth, not simply deductions from universal first principles. This idea was not peculiar to German romantics. The English romantic poet and philosopher Samuel Taylor Coleridge (1772–1834) argued against the utilitarian state and in favor of giving that ancient institution, the national church, a larger role in the shaping of society. The French conservative Chateaubriand (1768–1848) made much the same case in his treatise, *The Genius of Christianity*, published in 1802. The past, and in particular the religious experiences of the past, are woven into the present, he declared. They cannot be unwoven without destroying the fabric of a nation's society.

The role of history and religion

The theory of the organic evolution of society and the state received its fullest exposition in the writings of the German metaphysician Georg Wilhelm Hegel (1770–1831), a professor of philosophy at the

Georg Wilhelm Hegel

Fichte

University of Berlin. Hegel wrote of history as development. Social and political institutions grew to maturity, achieved their purposes, and then gave way to others. Yet the new never entirely replaced the old, for the pattern of change was a "dialectic." When new institutions challenged established ones, there was a clash between what had been and what was becoming, producing a "synthesis," a reordering of society that retained elements from the past while adapting to the present. Hegel expected, for example, that the present disunity among the German states, which generated the idea of unity, would inevitably result in the creation of a nation-state. Hegel had no use for the theory of a state of nature, so popular with philosophers like Rousseau and Hobbes. Men and women have always lived within some society or other, Hegel argued. The institution of the state was itself a natural historic organism; only within that institution, protected by its laws and customs from personal depradations, could men and women enjoy freedom, which Hegel defined not as the absence of restraint but as the absence of social disorder.

These theories of history and of historical development articulated by the romantics relate directly to the idea of nationalism formulated during the same period. The French Revolution provided an example of what a nation could achieve. Nationhood had encouraged the French to raise themselves to the level of citizenship; it had also allowed them to sustain attacks from the rest of Europe. Applying the historical lessons of the French Revolution and the theories of romantics, Germans, in particular, were roused to a sense of their own historical destiny. The works of the philosopher J. G. Fichte (1762–1814) are an example of this reawakening. As a young professor at the University of Jena, Fichte had at first advanced a belief in the importance of an individual's inner spirit, the creator of its own moral universe. Devoid of national feeling, he welcomed the French Revolution as an emancipator of the human spirit. Yet when France conquered much of Germany, Fichte's attitude changed dramatically. He adopted Herder's notion of a *Volksgeist;* what mattered was no longer the individual spirit, but the spirit of a whole people, expressed in its customs, traditions, and history. In 1808, Fichte delivered a series of *Addresses to the German Nation,* in which he declared the existence of a German spirit to be, not just one among many such spirits, but superior to the rest. The world had not yet heard from that spirit; he predicted it soon would. Although the French military commander in Berlin, where Fichte spoke, believed the addresses to be too academic to warrant censorship, they expressed a sentiment that aided the Prussians in their conscious attempt to rally themselves and, as a political *Volk,* to drive out the French.

Nationalism, derived from romantic notions of historical development and destiny, manifested itself in a variety of ways. The brothers Grimm, editors of *Grimm's Fairy Tales* (1812), traveled across Germany to study native dialects, and collected folktales that were published as part of a national heritage. The poet Friedrich Schiller's (1759–1805) drama of *William Tell,* the Swiss hero (1804), became a rallying cry for German national consciousness. In Britain, Sir Walter Scott (1771–1832) retold in many of his novels the popular history of Scotland, while the poet William Wordsworth (1770–1850) consciously strove to express the simplicity and virtue of the English people in collections such as his *Lyrical Ballads* (1798). Throughout Europe, countries assiduously catalogued the relics of their historical past as in the society for publishing the *Monumenta Germaniae Historica* (Monuments of German History), founded in 1819; the French École des Chartes (1821); and the English Public Records Office (1838). In France, the neoclassical style, typified by the paintings of David, and used by Napoleon to exalt his image, gave way to the turbulent romanticism of painters like Eugène Delacroix, whose *Liberty Leading the People* (1830) was a proclamation not only of liberty, but of the courage of the French nation. Music, too, reflected national themes, though not until a generation or so after 1815. Many of Giuseppe Verdi's (1813–1901) operas, *Don Carlo,* for example, contained musical declarations of faith in the possibility of an Italian *risorgimento:* a resurrection of the Italian spirit. The operas of Richard Wagner (1813–1883)—in particular, those based on the German epic, *Song of the Nibelung*—managed to raise veneration for the myths of Nordic gods and goddesses to the level of pious exaltation. Architects, though they found it difficult to escape entirely from the neoclassicism of the eighteenth century, often tried to resurrect a "national" style in their designs. Sir Charles Barry, assigned the task of redesigning the British Houses of Parliament following their destruction by

Giuseppe Verdi

See color plates following page 294 for *Liberty Leading the People* and *The Massacre of Chios* by Delacroix

Houses of Parliament, London. Redesigned by Sir Charles Barry with a Gothic facade after the earlier structure was destroyed by fire.

A William Blake Etching for a Children's Book Written by Mary Wollstonecraft

See color plates following page 294 for *Beatrice and Dante* by Blake, *Execution of Rioters* by Goya, and *Valley of Aosta— Snowstorm, Avalanche, and Thunderstorm* by Turner

George Sand

fire in 1836, managed to mask a straightforward and symmetrical classical plan behind a Gothic screen, intended to acknowledge the country's debt to its own past. All this creative activity was the spontaneous result of artists' and writers' enthusiastic response to the romantic movement. Yet politicians soon perceived how historical romanticism might serve their nationalist ends. They understood how an individual work of art, whether a painting, a song, a drama, or a building, could translate into a national symbol. And they did not hesitate to assist in that translation when they deemed it useful.

Though romanticism and nationalism shared a common devotion to the past, romantics were not necessarily nationalists. Indeed, romanticism was explicitly international in its celebration of nature, and above all, of individual creativity. The romantics declared that nature was best perceived not by reason, but by the senses. And they respected those elements of nature that appeared to be the product of chance, not rational order. Whether as a single flower or a mountain range, nature was welcomed as it impressed itself directly on the senses. Men and women were declared free to interpret nature—and life as well—in terms of their individual reactions to it, not simply as it might reflect a set of general rational precepts. The English poet Percy Shelley (1792–1822), the German poet Heinrich Heine (1797–1856), the French novelist Victor Hugo (1802–1885), the Spanish painter Francisco Goya (1746–1828)—all characteristic figures of the romantic movement—expressed in their works romanticism's concern for the experiences of human individuals, a concern that transcended national boundaries. Human experience, romantics believed, was not linked to any one national tradition or *Volksgeist,* but rather to transcendent nature. The paintings of the Englishmen William Blake (1757–1827) and J. M. W. Turner (1775–1851), although they often reflect "Englishness," transcend nationalism by recording a communion with the fundamental elements of nature.

Romantics were internationalists because they enjoyed freedom from the confinement of any boundary—metaphysical or political—which tended to restrict a person's ability to realize his or her potential. In this way romanticism encouraged women to make themselves heard. The Englishwoman Mary Wollstonecraft (1759–1797), author of *A Vindication of the Rights of Woman;* Madame de Staël (1766–1817), an emigré from France to Germany during the revolutionary period, whose essay *De l'Allemagne* (On Germany) was steeped in romanticism; George Sand (1804–1876), whose novels, and whose life, proclaimed allegiance to the standards of radical individualism—these women exemplify romanticism's readiness to break with the past, and its assumptions and stereotypes, if they stood in the path of individual expression.

Romantics, as worshipers of individuality, worshiped "genius." The genius was possessed of a spirit that could not be analyzed and must be allowed to make its own rules. (It was the particular genius of an entire people, of course, that Herder extolled as the *Volksgeist*.) And the human spirit must never allow itself to be fettered by national prescriptions, any more than by social conventions, in such a way as to prevent enjoyment of its most precious possession, its freedom.

Ludwig van Beethoven

Freedom and the problem of self-recognition were major themes in the works of two of the giants of the romantic movement, the composer Ludwig van Beethoven (1770–1827) and the writer Johann Wolfgang von Goethe (1749–1832). The most remarkable quality about Beethoven's compositions is their uniqueness and individuality. In the Fifth Symphony Beethoven reaches the summit of symphonic logic, the Sixth is a glorification of nature, the Seventh a Dionysian revelry, the Eighth a genial conjuring up of the spirit of the eighteenth-century symphony. The deafness that afflicted Beethoven in his later years seems to have encouraged him in his determination to speak out through his music as one extraordinarily powerful, and at times distressed, human being. Five piano sonatas, five string quartets, the Ninth Symphony, and the great Mass, *Missa Solemnis,* constitute his final legacy. They fill the listener with awe not so much because of their unusual form or their vast proportions, but because they express boundless individual will and power.

Goethe

Goethe's dedication to the idea of individual freedom was, in part, the product of his having been born and raised in the free imperial city of Frankfurt. Frankfurt was an international center, a trading place open to intellectual winds from all quarters. Goethe was, in terms of his environment, free from the particularist, nationalist influences that directed the work of other German romantics. Goethe's own "genius" drove him first to the study of law, then medicine, then the fine arts and natural sciences. In 1775 he took up residence at the court of the young duke of Weimar. Weimar was a tiny German principality with a population of no more than half a million, another cosmopolitan community and in this respect not unlike Frankfurt. Influenced by Herder, Goethe had already published various romantically inclined works, including the immensely popular *Sorrows of Werther,* a novel expressive of Goethe's early restlessness and emotionalism. The almost excessive sensitivity characteristic of Goethe's earlier writings gave way, in his middle years, to the search for a new spirit, equally free and yet more ordered. This mode derived from his experiences in Italy and from his study of the ancient Romans and Greeks. In 1790 Goethe published the first part of his masterpiece, *Faust,* a drama in verse, which he completed a year before his death in 1832. The play, in its retelling of the German legend of the man who sold his soul to the devil in return for universal knowledge, reflects the romantic unwillingness to restrain the spirit; it also expresses Goethe's own recognition of the magnitude of humanity's daring in its desire for unlimited knowledge and its own fulfillment.

An Illustration from Goethe's Sorrows of Werther

Romanticism and nationalism bear much the same relationship to each other in the history of nineteenth-century Europe as they do in the thought of the men and women we have just surveyed. At some points, as in England, they appear to run separate courses. At others they join together, as they did in Germany, whose own history lies at the center of the history of both romanticism and nationalism.

2. NATIONALISM AND NATION-BUILDING, 1800–1848

Nationalism and reform in Prussia, 1806–1815

The humiliating French occupation of Prussia, combined with the growing sense of national destiny exemplified in Fichte's *Addresses*, resulted in a drive on the part of Prussian intellectuals and political reformers to bring their country once more to its former position among European powers. Prussia's crushing defeat by the French in 1806 had been the logical outcome of the inertia that had gripped the country during the half century or so since the aggressive achievements of Frederick the Great. Unlike the rest of the German states, however, allied directly with France in the Confederation of the Rhine, the separate kingdom of Prussia consciously avoided French "contamination," participating unwillingly in the Continental System, and otherwise holding itself aloof.

Military reforms

Its major task was to rebuild its armies, since only by that means could Prussia reassert itself against Napoleon. To that end, two generals, Gerhard von Scharnhorst and August Gneisenau, instituted changes based on an essential lesson in nation-building they had learned from the French Revolution: that men were far more effective fighters if they believed themselves to have some direct stake in the wars they fought. A reconstituted national army, eventually based upon a system of universal military service, involved the country as a whole in its own defense and grew to become a far more consciously "Prussian" force than it had been heretofore. Officers were recruited and promoted on the basis of merit, not birth, although the large majority continued to come from the Junker (aristocratic) class. This breach with tradition encouraged the Prussian middle class to take a more active and enthusiastic interest in its country's affairs. Old or inefficient officers, despite their social standing, were removed from positions of command; training at the royal cadet school in Berlin was modernized.

These reforms, which illustrate the way in which a liberal desire for modernization might combine with nationalism, paralleled similar changes instituted during the same period under the direction of Prussia's principal minister, Baron Heinrich Friedrich Karl vom Stein (1757–1831), and his successor, Prince Karl von Hardenberg (1750–1822). Stein was not himself a Prussian; he was initially less interested in achieving a Prussian nation-state than in uniting by some means

Baron Heinrich Friedrich Karl vom Stein

or other all the various principalities of Germany. He had read Hegel and Fichte, and was convinced that a state must somehow make its citizens aware of their obligations to the national interest. A sense of duty to the state could hardly be kindled, however, without first convincing men and women that loyalty meant reward as well as obligation. Stein therefore labored to dismantle the caste system which had until that time characterized Prussia, in order to permit individuals to rise within society. Stein's Municipal Ordinance of 1808 was a conscious attempt to increase the middle-class Germans' sense of them- selves as citizens—again, a goal shared by both liberals and nationalists. Cities and towns were henceforth required to elect their councilmen, while local justice and security continued to be administered by the central government in Berlin; all other matters, including finance, were left to individual communities. Education played a vital role in nation-building. Schools were ideal agencies for the dissemination of the doctrines of national duty. Recognizing this fact, the Prussian reformers expanded facilities for both primary and secondary educa- tion. The University of Berlin, founded in 1810, numbered among its faculty such ardent nationalists as Fichte and Savigny, and was the institutional embodiment of the new spirit that contributed to Prussia's eventual victory over the French.

The history of Prussia between 1815 and 1850 can most easily be understood in terms of its continuing struggle to establish itself as the leading independent national power among the thirty-nine states that comprised Germany after 1806, and as a successful rival to Austrian domination. The most important Prussian victory in this respect was the establishment of the *Zollverein,* or customs union. By the 1840s, the union included almost all of Germany except German Austria, and offered manufacturers a market of almost 34 million people. But the writings of the economist Friedrich List (1789–1846) inspired a nationalist response to the internationalism of the liberal free-trade economists. List wrote that while free trade might suit the British, it did not suit a nation such as Prussia. Economics, he argued, far from being an abstract science equally applicable everywhere, was a discipline that must be grounded in the particular national experience of individual countries. Germany's, and therefore Prussia's, experience demanded not free trade but high tariffs. Only when sheltered behind a protectionist system could Prussia build the factories and manufacture the goods that would guarantee its economic health.

The events that had altered the political shape of Britain and France in the early 1830s—revolution in the latter and liberal reforms in both—had their counterparts in Germany. Liberals had resented both Prussian nationalism and Austrian conservatism. They hoped for the achievement of both unity and freedom, avoiding the particularism that had haunted Germany's political past and the domination by either Austria or Prussia that promised to blight its future. Student societies—*Burschenschaften*—had sprung up throughout Germany following the Napoleonic wars. At an assembly in 1817 at Wartburg Castle, where Martin Luther had three hundred years before proclaimed his ninety-five theses, these modern protestants on behalf of "the holy cause of union and freedom" marched to a bonfire upon which they placed the works of reactionary writers. Repressed for a time by Metternich, the *Burschenschaften* reappeared in the late 1820s, and welcomed the 1830 revolution in France. Minor revolts occurred in Brunswick, Saxony, and Hesse-Cassel; unpopular monarchs were replaced by royal relatives more sympathetic to reform. In 1832 at an all-German festival held at Hambach, on the French border, 25,000 men and women toasted Lafayette and denounced the Holy Alliance. Once again, Metternich imposed a series of repressive reforms upon the German Confederation, which effectively stifled protest and thwarted liberal aspirations.

Prussia avoided revolution as a result of the reforms instituted a generation before by Stein and Hardenberg. In 1840 Frederick William IV succeeded to the Prussian throne. Apparently devoted to liberal principles, he relaxed censorship laws and encouraged participation in the central government by provincial diets. It soon became apparent, however, that the king was no liberal, but some sort of romantic-nationalist, and an authoritarian as well. He crushed the revolt of thousands of Silesian weavers in 1844, when they protested the importation of English yarn and cotton goods and their consequent unemployment and poverty. He further declared himself opposed to constitutionalism, that central doctrine in the liberal canon of beliefs. When Prussian liberals pressed, in 1847, for control over legislative and budgetary matters in the recently convened assembly of diets (the *Landtag*) the king saw to it that their request was denied. Frederick William then turned his attention to a scheme whereby Prussia might play a far larger role in the German Confederation. But before his plan could receive a hearing, it was overtaken by the revolutionary movement of 1848, which, as we shall see, engulfed central Europe as it had western Europe, though with different results.

National sentiment, the spirit that served to unite the Prussians, was at the same time operating to divide the heterogeneous elements within the Austrian Empire. Its people, who lived within three major geographical areas—Austria, Bohemia, and Hungary—were composed of a considerable number of different ethnic and language groups: Germans, Czechs, Magyars, Poles, Slovaks, Serbs, and Italians, to name the most prominent. In some parts of the empire, these people lived in isolation; elsewhere they dwelt in direct proximity, if not much harmony, with others. The Austrian Empire attempted to unite these groups by means of a reigning house, the Habsburgs, and a supposedly benevolent bureaucracy. These devices failed increasingly to satisfy the various groups, in whom a spirit of cultural, if not political, nationalism grew persistently stronger in the years after 1815. In the Polish territories of the empire, where the gentry had for generations been conscious of themselves as Poles, the imperial government succeeded in stifling the sentiment by playing off the serfs against their masters, encouraging a class war as a means of preventing an ethnic one. Elsewhere within the empire they were less adroit. In Hungary, nationalism expressed itself in both cultural and political forms. In 1827, a Hungarian national theater was established at Budapest. The year before, Magyar was substituted for Latin as the official language of government. A political movement, whose most formidable leader was the radical nationalist Louis Kossuth (1802–1894), was at the same time seeking independence and a parliamentary government for Hungary.

The most widespread of the eastern European cultural nationalist movements was Pan-Slavism. Slavs included Russians, Poles, Czechs, Slovaks, Slovenes, Croats, Serbs, and Bulgars. Before 1848 Pan-Slavism was an almost exclusively cultural movement, united by a generalized anti-Western sentiment, yet divided by a tendency to quarrel as to the primacy of this or that particular language or tradition. These divisions did not substantially lessen the effect of Pan-Slavism as a further problem of the Austrian Empire. The literature of the movement—for example, the historian Francis Palacky's (1798–1876) *History of the Bohemian People* and the poetry of the revolutionary Pole Adam Mickiewiez (1798–1855)—fed the desires of those who wished to rid themselves of what they considered a foreign yoke. In Russia, slavophilism had been held in check by the Western-looking Alexander I. After his death, however, the notion that the Russian people possessed its particular *Volksgeist* increased in general popularity.

Two other national movements were growing beyond infancy during the years before 1848: one in Italy, the other in Ireland. Italy, at the beginning of the nineteenth century, was a peninsula divided into a multitude of states, most of them poor and ineffectually governed. The most efficient governments in Italy after 1815 were those imposed by Austria on the northern territories of Lombardy and Venetia (see map, p. 332) and by the introverted, visionary, yet intensely reform-minded king of Sardinia, Charles Albert (1831–1849). At the opposite pole were the Kingdom of the Two Sicilies and the Papal States, governed by equally obscurantist rulers, Francis I (1825–1830), a Bourbon, and thereafter by his son, Ferdinand II (1830–1859), and Pope Gregory XVI (1831–1846). Popular uprisings in Modena, Parma, and Bologna occurred in 1830, but with no lasting consequences, either for the initiation of local liberal reforms or for the cause of unification of the various disparate states into some sort of national whole. Among the pan-Italian organizations formed in the confused period at the end of the Napoleonic wars, none was louder in its nationalist proclamations than the Italian *Carbonari*. One member

Joseph Mazzini

Nationalism in Ireland

of that group, Joseph Mazzini (1805–1872), founded a society of his own in 1831, Young Italy, which was dedicated to the cause of uniting the peninsula. In 1834, from Switzerland, Mazzini launched a totally unsuccessful verbal assault against the Kingdom of Sardinia, in the hope that the rest of Italy would join with him. Mazzini subsequently contented himself with propagandizing for the cause of Italian nationalism and republicanism, attracting a devoted following, particularly among British liberals. Liberals in Italy, however, mistrusted him. Although they too wished to see a united Italy, they were dismayed, as "good" liberals, and members of the middle class, by Mazzini's insistence upon a republic, hoping instead to merge existing principalities together into some sort of constitutional monarchy.

If Italian nationalism was primarily a middle-class liberal phenomenon at this time, the same was not true of the Irish movement to repeal the union with England. Headed by Daniel O'Connell (1775–1847), it derived its strength from the support of Irish peasants. O'Connell's remarkably successful appeal was based on the hatred all Irish felt for the English, because of the centuries of oppression Irish Catholics had suffered under English Protestant rule. Both before and after the official union of 1801, the English had imposed on the Irish a foreign rule that had brought with it little but poverty and persecution. O'Connell's campaign for the repeal of the union was grounded in the hope that he would be able to negotiate some sort of moderate agreement with the English ruling class. The desires of his followers exceeded him in being far more radical in nature. Neither the separatist hopes of O'Connell, called by the Irish the "Liberator," nor the more genuinely nationalist hopes of his followers, however, were to achieve realization. Unlike the nationalist movements of central Europe, nationalism in Ireland faced a powerful and determined adversary—England—which would for a century deny it victory.

3. NATIONALISM, LIBERALISM, AND REVOLUTION, 1848

The history of the revolutions of 1848 in central Europe can most easily be understood in terms of two major themes: the first, the struggle of various nationalities, particularly within the Austrian Empire, to assert their own autonomy; the second, the contention between the forces of liberalism and nationalism in Germany.

News of the February revolution in France traveled quickly eastward. By the end of March the Austrian Empire was split apart. Hungary, with Kossuth in the lead, severed all but the most tenuous of links with the House of Habsburg and prepared to draft its own constitution. In Vienna, workers and students imitated their counterparts in Paris, erecting barricades and invading the imperial palace. A measure of the political chaos was the fact that Metternich, veteran of

*The "March Days" in
Austria*

a score of threats to the precarious stability he had crafted, found the pressure this time too great, and fled in disguise to Britain. The feeble Habsburg emperor, Ferdinand, once he had been deserted by Metternich, yielded to nationalist demands from Bohemia and granted that kingdom its own constitution as well. To the south, Italians launched attacks against the Austrian-held territories in Milan, Naples, Venetia, and Lombardy, where the forces of the Sardinian ruler, King Charles Albert, routed the Austrians.

Yet the forces of national sentiment that had brought Austria to its knees then succeeded in allowing the empire to recoup its fortunes. The paradox of nationalism, as it manifested itself in central Europe, was that as soon as a cultural majority had declared itself an independent or semi-independent state, other cultural minorities within that new state complained bitterly about their newly institutionalized inferiority. This is precisely what happened in Bohemia. There the anti-German Czech majority refused to send delegates to an all-German assembly, which was meeting at Frankfurt to draft a German constitution. Instead, they summoned a confederation of Slavs to Prague. The delegates, most of them from within the boundaries of the old Austrian Empire, immediately recognized that the idea of a united Germany represented a far greater threat to their political and cultural autonomy than the fact of the empire ever had. The German minority in Bohemia, however, was naturally anxious to participate in discussions that might result in closer union with their ethnic counterparts. They resented the Bohemian government's refusal to do so. The resulting animosities made it all the easier for the Austrians to take advantage of a May 1848 insurrection in Prague, subdue the city, send the Slav congress packing, and reassert control in Bohemia. Although the Austrian government was at this time a liberal one, the product of the March revolution in Vienna, it was no less determined than its predecessor had been to prevent the total dismemberment of the empire, for economic as well as political reasons. Hence it was quick to restore Lombardy and Venetia to its realm when quarrels among the heretofore united Italian allies had sufficiently weakened their common stand against the Austrians.

Nationalism and counternationalism in Hungary set the stage for the final act of the restoration of Austrian hegemony. Kossuth's radical party was, above all, a Magyar nationalist party. Once in power, in early 1849 it moved the capital from Pressburg, near the Austrian border, to Budapest, and again proclaimed Magyar as the country's official language. These actions offended national minorities within Hungary, particularly the Croats, who prior to the revolution had enjoyed certain liberties under Austrian rule. The Croatians raised an insurgent army and launched a civil war. The Austrains, once more encouraging division along nationalist lines, named the Croatian rebel Josef von Jellachich their military commander against the Magyars. By this time the Viennese liberals began to recognize—too late—that

*Counternationalism as an
aid to restoration*

Civil war in Hungary

their turn might come next. They were right. Despite a second uprising in Vienna in October, the revolution was spent. Forces loyal to the emperor descended upon Vienna from Bohemia. On October 31, the liberal government capitulated.

Once the imperial government had reasserted itself, it labored to suppress nationalist impulses as thoroughly as possible. Austria's ministers recognized that, though tactically advantageous at times, nationalist movements operated generally to the detriment of the empire's political and economic unity. The emperor's chief minister, Prince Felix von Schwarzenberg, and the minister of the interior, Alexander Bach, both nation-builders, together centralized the state within one united political system. Hungary and Bohemia no longer enjoyed separate rights. Peasants of all ethnic groups, liberated from serfdom as part of the general reform movement, were permitted to retain their freedom, on the grounds of their loyalty to the empire. The law was reformed, again to achieve uniformity, and railways and roads were constructed to link the empire. Economic nationalism was encouraged through tariffs designed to exclude foreign manufactures, while a free trade area within the empire encouraged domestic industries. Having done all it could to eradicate separatist movements, the Austrian government thus moved to secure its advantage by engaging in a vigorous campaign of nation-building.

In Prussia, revolution ran a similar course. In March, King Frederick William found himself compelled to yield to demands for a popularly elected legislative assembly. When it met, the body proved particularly sympathetic to the plight of the Polish minority within Prussia, and antagonistic toward the Russians, whom radical legislators saw as the major threat to the spread of enlightened political ideas in central Europe. When the assembly's sympathy with Polish nationalism extended to the granting of self-government to Prussian Poland, however, it generated the same feelings among the German minority there that we have seen arousing minorities within the Austrian Empire. In so doing, it precipitated the same eventual results. Germans in Posen, the major city of Prussian Poland, revolted against the newly established Polish government; not surprisingly, Prussian army units on duty sided with the Germans and helped them crush the new government. Power, it now became clear, lay with the army, professionalized since the days of Gneisenau and Scharnhorst, yet still dominated by the Junkers. Against the armed authority of the military, the radical legislators of Berlin were no match; revolution ended in Prussia as quickly as it had begun.

Meanwhile, at Frankfurt, Germans engaged in the debate that provides the history of central Europe in these revolutionary years with its second theme: liberalism vs. nationalism. Delegates had been chosen from across Germany and Austria to attend the Frankfurt Assembly. They were largely from the professional classes—professors, lawyers, administrators—and generally devoted to the cause of

Procession of the German National Assembly to Its Opening Session at St. Paul's Church, Frankfurt, May 1848

middle-class liberalism. Many had assumed that their task would resemble that of the assembly that had met in 1789 to draft a constitution for the French: i.e., they would draft a constitution for a liberal, unified Germany. That former convocation, however, had been grounded in the simple but all-important fact that a French nation-state already existed. The French assembly had been elected to give the nation a new shape and new direction. But a centralized sovereign power was there to reshape; there was an authority that could be either commandeered or, if necessary, usurped. The Frankfurt Assembly, in contrast, was grounded upon nothing but its own words. It was a collection of thoughtful, well-intentioned middle-class liberals, committed to a belief that a liberal-national German state could somehow be constituted out of abstract principles.

Almost from the start, the assembly found itself tangled in the problems of nationality. Who, they asked, were the Germans? A majority of the delegates argued that they were all those who, by language, culture, or geography, felt themselves bound to the enterprise now underway at Frankfurt. The German nation that was to be constituted must include as many of those "Germans" as possible. This

Great Germans vs. Little Germans

point of view came to be known as the "Great German" position. Great Germans found themselves stymied, however, by the unwillingness of other nationalities to be included in their fold. The Czechs in Bohemia, as we have seen, wanted no part of Great Germany. In the end the Great Germans settled that the nation for which they were drafting a constitution should include, among other territories, all Austrian lands except Hungary. This decision meant that the crown of their new country might most logically be offered to the Habsburg emperor. At this point the voice of the "Little Germans" began to be heard. Prussian nationalism took precedence over German nationalism; a minority argued that Austria should be excluded altogether and the crown instead offered to King Frederick William of Prussia.

Liberalism vs. nationalism

The liberalism of the assembly was put to the test by events in Austria and Poland in the fall of 1848. When the imperial forces crushed the Czech and Hungarian rebellions, when the Prussian Junkers put an end to Polish self-government, liberals found themselves forced to cheer. They were compelled to support the suppression of minority nationalities; otherwise there would be no new Germany. But their cheers were for the forces not only of German nationalism but of antiliberal authoritarianism. The assembly's most embarrassing moment occurred when it found itself compelled to take shelter behind the Prussian army. Riots broke out in Frankfurt protesting the assembly's willingness to withdraw from a confrontation with the Danes over the future of Germans in Schleswig, a Danish province. That particular area, which many considered to be part of Germany, had been annexed by the Danes in March 1848. The Frankfurters had been unable to do more than ask the Prussians to win Schleswig back

Fighting in Frankfurt, September 18, 1848. Note the contrast between the disciplined maneuvers of the troops and the guerilla tactics of the rioting populace.

for them; and the Prussians had refused. Hence the riots; hence a second request, this time heeded, for Prussian assistance.

Reduced to the status of dependents, the Frankfurt delegates nevertheless, in the spring of 1849, produced a constitution. By this time Austria, fearing its Prussian rival, had decided to have no more to do with Frankfurt. The Little Germans thus won by default and offered their constitutional monarchy to Frederick William of Prussia. Though tempted, he turned them down, arguing that their constitution was too liberal, embodying as it did the revolutionary notion that a crown could be offered to a monarch. Frederick wanted the crown, but on his own terms. The delegates went home, disillusioned by their experience, many of them convinced that their dual goal of liberalism and nationalism was an impossible one. Some, who refused to surrender that goal, emigrated to the United States, where they believed the goal had already been achieved. Many of those who stayed behind convinced themselves that half the goal was better than none, and sacrificed their liberalism to nationalism.

The end of the assembly

Karl Marx

One German exile who took hope for the future from the events of the revolutions of 1848 was the young Karl Marx (1818–1883), whose radical ideas and activities had compelled his emigration to England. Like his friend and collaborator Friedrich Engels (1820–1895), Marx was the son of middle-class parents. After study at the university of Berlin, in 1842 he took a job as editor of the *Rhineland Gazette,* hoping to use that position to argue for the transformation of a society he was growing to despise. His radical policies soon put him at odds with his publishers, however. He moved first to Paris and then to Brussels, where he helped found the Communist League, a body whose declared aim was the overthrow of the middle class. While in Paris, Marx had renewed a former friendship with Engels. Together, during the late 1840s, they produced a theory of revolutionary change that was published by Marx at the request of the League in 1848, at the height of the struggles on the Continent, as *The Communist Manifesto.*

In the *Manifesto* Marx outlined a theory of history that owed a good deal to the German philosopher Hegel (see above, p. 311). Hegel, it will be recalled, had argued that ideas, the motive force of history, were in constant conflict with each other, and that this clash between ideas in turn would produce an eventual synthesis, representing an advance in the history of the human race. Marx adapted this particular progressive notion of history to his own uses. Whereas Hegel perceived conflict and resolution (a dialectic) in terms of ideas, Marx saw them in terms of economic forces. Society, he argued, was at any time no more than the reflection of a hierarchy of classes dictated by those who own the means of production and control the distribution of its material goods. As history had progressed, so had the means changed. Feudalism and manorialism were vanquished by capitalism. And capitalism, Marx declared, would be vanquished in

The Communist
Manifesto

turn by communism. That process, however, would first involve the concentration of capitalist economic power into the hands of fewer and fewer members of the middle class (the bourgeoisie), and the consequent opposition of an ever-increasing and ever-debased working class (the proletariat). Once the proletariat overthrew the bourgeoisie by revolution, as it was bound to do eventually, society as a whole would be emancipated. An interim period in which a "dictatorship of the proletariat" rid the world of the last vestiges of bourgeois society would be followed by an end of the dialectical process and the emergence of a truly classless civilization.

The Manifesto's *appeal*

Marx insisted that the *Manifesto* was not just another theory. His declaration that the proletariat together could consciously participate in the revolutionary process he described—could actually advance history through its own efforts—and that the revolutions of 1848 were part of that process, helps explain the document's eventual appeal. The writings of Marx and Engels did not bring about an immediate proletarian revolution. Few paid much attention to the *Manifesto* when it was published. Indeed, though the *Manifesto,* in its famous declaration, called upon the workers of the world to unite, Marx and Engels realized that this goal would not be achieved quickly. Marx and Engels, however, more than any other political thinkers of the 1830s and 1840s, provided workers with a potential sense of their worth as human beings and of their vital role in the historical process.

4. NATION-BUILDING, 1850–1870

Bismarck

The twenty years between 1850 and 1870 were years of intense nation-building in the Western world. Of the master-builders, none was more accomplished than the man who brought Germany under Prussian rule, Otto von Bismarck (1815–1898). Born into the Junker class, Bismarck had emerged during the revolutionary period of 1848 and 1849, as a defender of the monarchy. Bismarck was really neither a liberal nor a nationalist; he was before all else a Prussian. When he instituted domestic reforms, he did so not because he favored the "rights" of this or that particular group but because he thought that his policies would result in a more united, and hence more powerful, Prussia. When he maneuvered to bring other German states under Prussian domination, he did so not in conformity with a grand Germanic design but because he believed that some sort of union was almost inevitable and, if so, that it must come about at Prussia's behest. He prided himself on being a realist; and he became a first-rate practitioner of what has come to be called *Realpolitik*—the politics of what its practitioners claim to be hardheaded reality. Bismarck readily acknowledged his admiration of power. He at one point had considered a career in the military—not at all surprising considering his Junker origins. He once wrote the emperor William I that he regretted that he was compelled to serve his country from behind a desk rather than at the front. But whatever his post, he intended to command. "I want to play the tune the way it sounds good to me or not at all," he declared. "Pride, the desire to command. . . . I confess I am not free from these passions." Nor did he consider those passions unworthy of the man who was to undertake the task of shaping the fortunes of the German state.

When Bismarck came to power as minister-president of Prussia in 1862, he was confronted by a liberal parliamentary majority that, since 1859, had opposed a campaign to increase military expenditures despite pressure from the king. This majority had been produced by an electoral system that was part of the constitution granted by Frederick William to Prussia in 1850, following the collapse of the assembly. The parliament was divided into two houses, the lower one elected by universal male suffrage. Votes were apportioned according to one's ability to pay taxes, however; those few who together paid one-third of the country's taxes elected one-third of the legislators. A large landowner or industrialist exercised about a hundred times the voting power of a poor man. Contrary to the king's expectations, however, under this constitution a liberal majority was succeeding in thwarting the plans of the sovereign and his advisors. It was to break this deadlock that King William I, who succeeded his brother Frederick William in 1861, summoned Bismarck. In Bismarck the liberals more than met their match. When they refused to levy taxes, he collected them anyway, claiming that the constitution, whatever its purposes, had not been designed to subvert the state. When liberals argued that Prussia was setting a poor example for the rest of Germany, Bismarck replied that Prussia was admired not for its liberalism but for its power.

Bismarck and the liberals

Whether or not the Germans—or the rest of Europe—admired Prussia's power, they soon found themselves confronted by it. Bismarck proceeded to build a nation that in the short space of eight years came into being as the German Empire. Bismarck was assisted in his task by his readiness to take advantage of international situations as they presented themselves, without concerning himself particularly with the ideological or moral implications of his actions. He was aided as well by developments over which he had no initial control but which he was able to turn to his advantage. The first of these, the Crimean War, had occurred in 1854–1856, prior to his taking office. Russia and Turkey, perennial European squabblers, had precipitated the hostilities. Russia invaded the territories of Moldavia and Wallachia (later Rumania) in an attempt to take advantage of the continuing political rot that made the Ottoman Empire an easy prey. In 1854 France and then Britain came to the aid of the Turks by invading Russia's Crimean peninsula. These allies were soon joined by Sardinia. The quarrel had by this time enlarged to include the question of who

The Crimean War

British Encampment near Sebastopol, 1854–1855. Photograph taken by Roger Fenton. The Crimean War was the first to be reported to the world by photograph as well as by news dispatch.

was to protect the Christians in Jerusalem from the Turks; it was fueled from the start as well by Britain's continuing determination to prohibit a strong Russian presence in the Near East. The allies' eventual victory was primarily the result of a British blockade of Russia. The peace settlement was a severe setback for Russia, whose influence in the Balkans was drastically curbed. Moldavia and Wallachia were united as Rumania, which, along with Serbia, was granted power as a self-governing principality. Austrian military resources were severely taxed during the invasion and occupation of Moldavia and Wallachia. And Austria's failure to come to the aid of Russia lost her the support of that powerful erstwhile ally. It was the subsequent weakness of both Russia and Austria, the result of the Crimean War, that Bismarck used to his advantage in the 1860s.

In consolidating the German states into a union controlled by Prussia, Bismarck first moved to eliminate Austria from its commanding position in the German Confederation. As a means to this end he inflamed the long-smoldering dispute with Denmark over the possession of Schleswig and Holstein. Inhabited by Germans and Danes, these two provinces had an anomalous status. Since 1815 Holstein had been included in the German Confederation, but both were subject to the personal overlordship of the king of Denmark. When, in 1864, the Danish king attempted to annex them, Bismarck invited Austria to participate in a war against Denmark. A brief struggle followed, at the end of which the Danish ruler was compelled to renounce all his claims to Schleswig and Holstein in favor of Austria and Prussia. Then the sequel for which Bismarck had ardently hoped occurred: a quarrel between the victors over division of the spoils. The conflict that followed in 1866, known as the Seven Weeks' War, ended in

Steps to German unification: (1) weakening of Austria

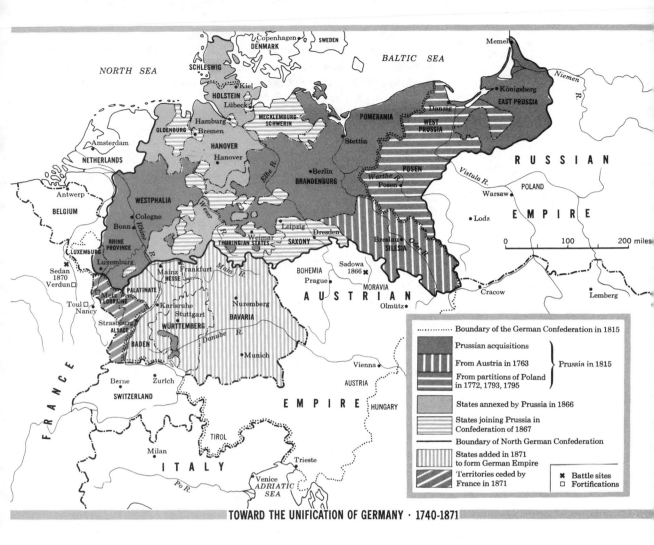

TOWARD THE UNIFICATION OF GERMANY · 1740-1871

an easy triumph for Prussia. Austria was forced to give up all claims to Schleswig and Holstein, to surrender Venetia, and to acquiesce in the dissolution of the German Confederation. Immediately following the war Bismarck proceeded to isolate Austria by uniting all of the German states north of the Main River into the North German Confederation.

To achieve the confederation Bismarck willingly turned himself into a democrat. He saw that if he was to attain his end, which was a strong union with Prussia at its head, he would need to cultivate a constituency hitherto untapped by any German politicians: the masses. He appreciated the manner by which Napoleon III had reinforced his regime through plebiscites. And Bismarck understood that the majority of Germans were not particularly enthusiastic supporters of capitalist liberals, of the bureaucracies of their own small states, or

(2) courting the masses

of the Austrian Habsburgs. The constitution he devised for his confederation provided for two chambers: the upper chamber represented the individual states within the union, though not equally; the lower chamber was elected by universal manhood suffrage. The liberal middle class, to say nothing of the Junkerdom, was astonished and dismayed, as well they might be. Bismarck's intention was to use popular support to strengthen the hand of the central government against the interests of both landlords and capitalists.

(3) the Franco-Prussian War

Bismarck's final step in the completion of German unity was the Franco-Prussian War of 1870–1871. He hoped that a conflict with France would kindle the spirit of German nationalism in Bavaria, Würtemberg, and other southern states still outside the confederation. Taking advantage of a diplomatic tempest concerning the right of the Hohenzollerns (Prussia's ruling family) to occupy the Spanish throne, Bismarck worked hard to force a Franco-German misunderstanding. King William agreed to meet with the French ambassador at the resort spa of Ems in Prussia to discuss the Spanish succession. When William telegraphed Bismarck that the demands of the French for perpetual exclusion of the Hohenzollern family from the Spanish throne had been refused, Bismarck released portions of the message to the press so as to make it appear that King William had insulted the ambassador—which he had not done. Once the garbled report of what happened at Ems was received in France, the nation reacted with a call for war. The call was echoed in Prussia, where Bismarck published evidence that he claimed proved French designs upon the Rhineland. Upon the declaration of war, the south German states rallied to Prussia's side in the belief that it was the victim of aggression. The war was quickly fought. The French were no match for Prussia's professionally trained and superbly equipped forces. Nor did other European powers come to France's assistance. Austria, the most likely candidate, remained weakened by its recent war with Prussia. The Magyars, who at this time had assumed positions of influence within the Austrian government, were quite prepared to welcome a strengthened Prussia; Prussia's growing strength in Germany would further increase Austria's weakness there. And the weaker Austria was as a German power, the stronger would be the claims of the Magyars to predominance. Once more one nationalist consciousness was grinding against another. The war began in July; it ended in September with the defeat of the French and the capture of Napoleon III himself at Sedan in France.

The German Empire

Following the collapse of the French imperial government, insurrectionary forces in Paris continued to hold out against the Germans until the winter of 1871. Bismarck meanwhile proceeded to consummate the German union toward which he had worked so assiduously. On January 18, 1871, in the great Hall of Mirrors at Versailles the German Empire was proclaimed. All those states, except Austria, which had not already been absorbed into Prussia declared their allegiance to William I, henceforth emperor or kaiser. Four months later, at Frankfurt, a treaty between the French and Germans ceded the border region of Alsace to the new empire, condemned the French to an indemnity of five billion francs, and thereby broadcast to the world the remarkable success of Bismarck's nation-building.

Events in Italy ran a course almost parallel to that which had led to the unification of Germany. Italy before 1848, it will be recalled, was a patchwork of petty states. The most important of those possessing independence were the Kingdom of Sardinia in the north, the Papal States in the central region, and the Kingdom of the Two Sicilies in the south. The former republics of Lombardy and Venetia were held by Austria, while Habsburg dependents ruled in Tuscany, Parma, and Modena. As the revolutionary fervor of 1848 swept across the peninsula, one ruler after another granted democratic reforms. Charles Albert of Sardinia outdistanced all the others by guaranteeing civil liberties and granting a parliamentary form of government. It soon became evident, however, that the Italians were as determined nationalists as they were liberals. For some years romantic patriots had been dreaming of a *Risorgimento,* which would restore the nation to the position of glorious leadership it had held in Roman times and during the Renaissance. To achieve this, it was universally agreed that Italy must be welded into a single state. But opinions differed as to the form the new government should take. Young idealists followed the leadership of Mazzini. Religious-minded patriots believed that the most practicable solution would be to federate the state of Italy under the presidency of the pope. The majority of the more moderate nationalists advocated a constitutional monarchy built upon the foundations of the Kingdom of Sardinia. The aims of this third group gradually crystallized under the leadership of a shrewd Sardinian nobleman, Count Camillo di Cavour (1810–1861). In 1850 he was appointed minister of commerce and agriculture of his native state and in 1852 prime minister.

Italian unification

The campaign for unification of the Italian peninsula began with efforts to expel the Austrians. In 1848 revolts were organized in the territories under Habsburg domination, and an army of liberation marched from Sardinia to aid the rebels; but the movement ended in failure. It was then that Cavour, as the new leader of the campaign, turned to less heroic but more practical methods. In 1858 he held a secret meeting with Napoleon III and prepared the stage for an Italian War of Liberation. Napoleon agreed to cooperate in driving the Austrians from Italy for the price of the cession of Savoy and Nice by Sardinia to France. A war with Austria was duly provoked in 1859, for a time all went well for the Franco-Italian allies. After the conquest of Lombardy, however, Napoleon III suddenly withdrew, fearful of ultimate defeat and afraid of antagonizing the Catholics in his own country by aiding the avowedly anticlerical government of Cavour. Thus deserted by its ally, Sardinia was unable to expel the Austrians from Venetia. Nevertheless, extensive gains were made; Sardinia an-

Camillo di Cavour

nexed Lombardy, and acquired by various means the duchies of Tuscany, Parma, and Modena, and the northern portion of the Papal
States. Sardinia was now more than twice its original size and by far
the most powerful state in Italy.

The second step in consolidating Italy was the conquest of the kingdom of the Two Sicilies. This kingdom was ruled by a Bourbon,
Francis II, who was thoroughly hated by his Italian subjects. In May
1860 a romantic adventurer, Giuseppe Garibaldi, set out with a regiment of one thousand "red shirts" to rescue his fellow Italians from

oppression. Within three months he had conquered the island of Sicily and had then marched to the deliverance of Naples, where the people were already in revolt. By November the whole kingdom of Francis II had fallen to Garibaldi. He at first intended to convert the territory into an independent republic but was finally persuaded to surrender it to the Kingdom of Sardinia. With most of the peninsula now united under a single rule, Victor Emmanuel II, king of Sardinia, assumed the title of king of Italy (March 17, 1861). Venetia was still in the hands of the Austrians, but in 1866, following their defeat in the Seven Weeks' War, they were forced by the Prussians to cede it to Italy. All that remained to complete the unification of Italy was the annexation of Rome. The Eternal City had resisted conquest thus far, largely because of the military protection accorded the pope by Napoleon III. But in 1870 the outbreak of the Franco-Prussian War compelled Napoleon to withdraw his troops. In September 1870 Italian soldiers occupied Rome, and in July of the following year it was made the capital of the by now united kingdom.

The occupation of Rome brought the kingdom of Italy into conflict with the papacy. During the first years of his reign, which began in 1846, Pope Pius IX instituted a series of "modern" improvements: gaslight, railways, vaccination. Yet Pius, who, like his reactionary predecessor, Gregory XVI, continued to rule over the Papal States in the manner of a secular prince, was no friend to either liberalism or nationalism. And no wonder: the movement that had brought Italian troops to Rome had from its inception expressed hostility to the Church as an impediment to unification. Following the occupation of Rome in 1870, an attempt was made to solve the problem of relations between the state and the papacy. In 1871 the Italian parliament enacted the Law of Papal Guaranties, purporting to define the status of the pope as a reigning sovereign. The reigning pontiff, Pius IX, promptly denounced this law on the ground that issues affecting the pope could be settled only by an international treaty to which he himself was a party. Whereupon he shut himself up in the Vatican and refused to have anything to do with a government that had so shamefully treated Christ's vicar on earth. His successors continued this practice of voluntary imprisonment until 1929, when a series of agreements between the Italian government and Pius XI effected settlement of the dispute.

Nation-building was the preoccupation of another major country in the first half of the nineteenth century: the United States. The history of the expansion and consolidation of this newly born country into a nation of remarkable economic potential in little over half a century can best be understood in terms of several major factors. The first is the growth of political democracy.

The United States did not begin its history as a democracy. No more than a few of the country's leaders professed genuine democratic ideals. The authors of the Constitution were not interested in the rule

Giuseppe Garibaldi

Pope Pius IX. This contemporary cartoon lampoons the pope, shown as a conniving, worldly politician hiding behind the mask of Jesus. Pius IX, though in his early years something of a liberal, took an extreme reactionary political position in the wake of the revolutionary upheaval of 1848.

Thomas Jefferson by Gilbert
Stuart

Jeffersonian principles

Jacksonian democracy

of the masses. The primary aim of the founders of the United States was to establish a *republic* that would promote stability and protect the rights of private property against the leveling tendencies of majorities. For this reason they adopted checks and balances between the branches of government, devised the Electoral College for choosing the president, created a powerful judiciary, and entrusted the selection of senators to the legislatures of the several states.

Following the establishment of a new and more firmly united government under the Constitution of 1787, democratic ideals began to win acceptance in the United States. Until 1801 the Federalists, the party of large landowners and successful merchant capitalists, held power. In 1801 the Democratic-Republicans gained control as a result of the election of Thomas Jefferson (1743–1826) to the presidency. Although this event is often referred to as the Jeffersonian Revolution, on the supposition that Jefferson was the champion of the masses and of the political power of the underprivileged, there is danger in carrying this interpretation too far. Jefferson strenuously opposed the unlimited sovereignty of the majority. His conception of an ideal political system was an aristocracy of "virtue and talent," in which respect for personal liberty would be the guiding principle.

Yet the Jeffersonian movement had a number of ultimately democratic objectives. Its leaders were vigorous opponents of special privilege, whether of birth or of wealth. They worked for the abolition of established churches. They led the campaign for the addition of a Bill of Rights to the Constitution and were almost exclusively responsible for its success. Although professing devotion to the principle of the separation of powers, they actually believed in the supremacy of the representatives of the people and viewed with abhorrence the attempts of the executive and judicial branches to increase their power.

By 1820, these notions were being expressed in more direct and forceful terms. Urban populations grew increasingly conscious of their political importance and demanded attention to their interests. The predominance of the agricultural Old South (the South of the original thirteen colonies) had declined. As a result of the Louisiana Purchase (a vast tract bought from the French in 1803) and of increased settlement in the area known as the Northwest Territory (western New York State and Ohio), a new frontier had come into existence. Life there was characterized by a rugged freedom that left little room for class distinctions. In the struggle to survive, hard work and sharp wits counted for more than birth and education. As a consequence a new democratic spirit, which eventually found its leader in Andrew Jackson (1767–1845), took shape around the principle of equality. The Jacksonian Democrats transformed the doctrines of liberalism into a more radical creed. They pronounced all (excluding slaves, American Indians, and women) politically equal, not merely in rights but in privileges. They were devoted adherents to the causes of suffrage for all white males; the election, rather than appointment, of all governmental office-holders; and the frequent rotation of men in positions of political power—a doctrine that served to put more Democratic politicians into federal office. These democratic beliefs helped encourage a spirit of unity within the United States during a period of rapid territorial expansion.

As the United States continued to acquire more territories in the West (the most notable addition resulting from the conquest of lands in the Southwest from Mexico in 1846), it not only faced the task of binding those areas and their settlers into the nation. There was, as well, the problem of assimilating the thousands of immigrants who came to America from Europe in the first half of the century. Many were Scottish and English; for them the difficulties of adjusting to a new life in a new country were generally not difficult since they spoke a common language with their fellow-citizens. For others the problems were far greater. For the Irish, who immigrated in great numbers, particularly during the 1840s, there was the fact of their alien religion, Roman Catholicism. For Germans and others from the Continent, there was the language barrier. The United States's policy toward its immigrants was directed against the creation of any foreign nationalist enclaves apart from the main body of its citizenry. Although foreign-language newspapers were tolerated, and immigrants were free to attend churches and social gatherings as they chose, English remained the language of the public schools, the police, the law courts, and the government. To hold a job, a person was almost always forced to learn at least some English. In this way, the

Immigration

"Meal Time." Between the decks on an immigrant ship to the United States in the mid–nineteenth century.

Slavery in the American South. Left: Slave pens at Pine, Birch & Co., a Virginia slave broker. Right: Cotton being prepared by slaves for the gin on a South Carolina plantation.

United States encouraged immigrants to shed their "foreign" ways and to commit themselves to their adopted nation.

(3) slavery and the South

If there were enclaves in the United States, they existed in the South, where the institution of slavery and the economic dependence of the planters upon England produced two distinct minorities, neither of which was to be assimilated without resort to war. During the nineteenth century, slavery had been abolished throughout much of the Western world, for both economic and humanitarian reasons. Southern planters continued to insist that without the slave system they would go bankrupt. To humanitarians they responded with arguments based upon theories of racial inferiority and upon their self-professed reputation as benevolent masters. The position of these Southern spokesmen grew increasingly distasteful and unconvincing to the North. As the country opened to the west, North and South engaged in a protracted tug-of-war as to which new states were to be "free" and which "slave." Northerners were motivated by more than concern for the well-being of blacks. The North was industrializing fast. Capitalists there were demanding protective tariffs to assist them in their enterprises. Southerners favored free trade, since they wished to import British goods in return for the cotton they sold to the manufacturers of Lancashire.

The American Civil War, when it came in 1861, was a war not about the issue of slavery so much as it was about preserving the union of American states and territories. President Abraham Lincoln undertook the war to defend the unity of the United States. European governments, while never recognizing the Confederacy officially, nevertheless remained sympathetic to its cause. They hoped that the fragmentation of the United States would result in the opening up of markets for their manufactured goods, much as the dissolution of the Spanish Empire had proved a boon to European commercial interests. The victory of the North in 1865, however, ensured the continued growth of the United States as a nation. The Fourteenth Amendment to the Constitution stated specifically that all were citizens of the United States, and not of an individual state or territory. In declaring that no citizen was to be deprived of life, liberty, or property without due process of law, it established that "due process" was to be defined by the national, and not the state or territorial governments.

The years following the American Civil War witnessed the binding together of the nation economically under the direction of Northern private enterprise. The symbol of the North's triumph as a nation-builder came with the driving of the final spike of the transcontinental Union Pacific railroad in 1869. Nation-building in Europe and the United States helped ensure the continuing expansion of capitalism. Liberalism had provided a general climate of opinion and a set of attitudes toward government that encouraged industrialization. Nation-building, in its turn, produced the necessary economic units—large enough to generate the wherewithal to sustain economic growth; confident enough to enter into competition with the British Goliath.

5. REVOLUTION AND NATION-BUILDING IN LATIN AMERICA

Revolutionary currents, paralleling those that brought upheavals in Europe and independence to the British colonies of North America, transformed Spanish and Portuguese colonies in the Western Hemisphere into a flock of new nations. The inhabitants of Latin America had plenty of grievances, but revolution did not occur until the upper classes—those who had suffered least from the oppressive regimes—felt strong enough to defy the royal authorities. Prosperous Creoles, or colonial whites, resented their exclusion from the highest and most lucrative positions in the government and the Church, which were reserved for Spanish-born aristocrats. They felt deprived of privileges that should rightly belong to them on the basis of their wealth and intelligence.

The Latin American revolutions were deeply indebted to contemporary developments in Europe and North America, both for their inspiration, manifestoes, and slogans, and also for material assistance. The liberal ideals of the European Enlightenment had profoundly affected the mentality of the educated minority in all the Americas. Members of this elite group became enthusiastic admirers of Voltaire,

Rousseau, and Thomas Jefferson. The North American Revolution was applauded for the principles it affirmed as well as for its success in the face of apparently overwhelming odds. A few years later the great French Revolution offered a persuasive example of the overthrow of an absolutist regime, while ensuing revolutionary and Napoleonic wars, by keeping Spain and Portugal fully occupied in Europe, provided a rare opportunity to challenge their sovereignty in the New World. Revolutionary leaders too readily imagined that the example of the newly established United States could be followed in their own countries' struggle for freedom. An Argentinian patriot worshipfully invoked the name of the "noble and grand Washington." Simón Bolívar, most famous of the revolutionary heroes, hailed the North Americans as "unique in the history of the human race."

*Differences between the
founding empires*

There were vast differences between the United States and the lands to the south, and these differences help explain why the Latin American revolutions did not fulfill the high expectations of their protagonists. Perhaps the most notable difference lay in the fact that the Latin American colonies were founded by one of the most unprogressive nations in Europe. Spain's economic system was outmoded, its government despotic and corrupt. Spanish Catholicism reeked with intolerance and superstition. The Church was used by government as an instrument of repression, and the fanaticism of the Spanish Inquisition was notorious. On the eve of the discovery of America, the most enterprising of Spain's inhabitants—the Moors and the Jews—had been driven from the country. England had the advantage of not beginning her colonization of the New World until the seventeenth century. By that time the power of her middle class was well consolidated and able to set up obstacles to despotic government. Instead of one church having a monopoly of religious authority, the Christians of England were divided into competing sects, and no one of them was strong enough to impose its will upon the others. The country, moreover, had been a haven of refuge for persecuted religionists from other nations—for the Huguenots in particular. Many of these were enterprising merchants and artisans who brought their initiative and skills with them, adding no small amount to the intellectual wealth of England. Long before the end of the seventeenth century, the "tight little island" was the most progressive nation in Europe. And while the Spanish colonists brought with them the customs and institutions of the Middle Ages, those who went out from England carried the ideas of the modern world. They believed in education, in equality of opportunity, and in the application of ambition and intelligence to the solution of human problems. These viewpoints helped immensely in promoting a free and dynamic society in North America in contrast with the static, semifeudal society of Central and South America.

Second, geographic and demographic conditions within the southern continent were in sharp contrast with those of North America. The sprawling Portuguese and Spanish empires had a heterogeneous population, and there were serious divisions within every colony. The mode of settlement in the British provinces of North America had promoted the growth of a feeling of solidarity among the colonists. The regions that became Canada and the United States comprised millions of acres of practically unoccupied land. The native peoples were so few in numbers and so widely scattered that they could easily be pushed aside or exterminated. In Latin America the Indians were more numerous, in many cases more highly civilized, and therefore more successful in resisting the encroachments of the whites. The policy of the Spaniards, moreover, was to convert the natives to Christianity, not to exterminate them. It did not seem inconsistent with this that they should also be exploited and oppressed. At the time of the revolutions the population of the Spanish colonies was 45 percent Indian, 30 percent mestizo (of mixed Indian and European descent), 20 percent white, and 5 percent black. In Brazil half the people were Negroes, a fourth were whites, and the remainder Indians and mamelucos (the Portuguese equivalent of the Spanish *mestizos*). Over the continent as a whole the nonwhites outnumbered the Caucasians 4 to 1, yet the latter fought tooth and nail to maintain a dominant position.

Third, the economic and social structure was inimical to progressive change and provided a flimsy foundation for any bold revolutionary program. Throughout Latin America the economy was still primitive. The viceroyalty of New Spain or Mexico, which included Texas, New Mexico, Arizona, and California, and was the most populous colony, produced an annual income estimated at only $20 per capita. In the rest of Latin America, excepting the region of the River Plate (Buenos Aires), the standard of living was even lower. Economic development had channeled great wealth into the hands of a few—native Spaniards and prosperous Creoles—who controlled the land and other material resources, and left the submerged classes—Indians, blacks, and, to a lesser extent, mestizos—in wretchedness. The majority lived not only in deprivation but in ignorance. Less than 10 percent enjoyed the benefits of education.

Finally, the struggle for independence in Latin America, ranging across an enormous terrain, required for its achievement not one revolutionary war but a series of armed conflicts, extending over a period of fifteen years or more. In the course of these long and bitterly fought campaigns, visions of the dawn of liberty and democratic institutions that had stirred people's imagination dimmed. And military leaders who had risen to fame and power through exploits on the battlefield exerted more influence than revolutionary idealists or political theorists.

The spark that ignited colonial unrest into actual revolution burst forth in 1808. A quarrel had developed between the weak Bourbon king of Spain, Charles IV, and his son Ferdinand. Napoleon forced both to abdicate and gave the Spanish crown to his brother Joseph. When news of these highhanded proceedings reached the colonies,

CANADA
(British)

UNITED STATES
OF AMERICA

A T L A N T I C

O C E A N

NEW

*GULF OF
MEXICO*

SPAIN

Mexico City •

CUBA
(Spain)

SAINT DOMINGUE (France)

BR.
HONDURAS

JAMAICA
(British)

SANTO DOMINGO (Spain)

CARIBBEAN SEA

P A C I F I C

Bogotá •

NEW
GRANADA

Orinoco R.

(British after 1803)

DUTCH
GUIANA

FRENCH GUIANA

Equator

0°

GALAPAGOS IS.

O C E A N

Amazon R.

B R A Z I L

A N D E S

Lima •

P E R U

M O U N T A I N S

BUENOS
AIRES
OR
LA PLATA

Rio de Janeiro •

1000

2000 miles

Santiago •

Buenos Aires •

Montevideo •
La Plata R.

P A T A G O N I A

FALKLAND
ISLANDS

CAPE HORN

Spanish

Portuguese

British

LATIN AMERICA ON THE EVE OF INDEPENDENCE ca. 1800

there was general indignation. At first the colonies vented their wrath against the French, but gradually they came to realize that here was an opportunity to get rid of all foreign oppressors. Agitation took an anti-Spanish turn and was ultimately followed by declarations of independence and revolutionary wars.

The first of the larger Spanish colonies to proclaim its independence was Venezuela. Here a revolutionary pattern had been developing for a number of years. In 1806 the impetuous Creole, Francisco de Miranda, attempted with the help of foreigners to land expeditions in his native country and wrest control of it from Spain. He obtained aid from English and American sources but failed to gain more than a temporary foothold on the territory of Venezuela. Five years later representatives from a number of provinces met in a revolutionary assembly and declared Venezuela an independent republic. Learning of the revolutionists' activities, Miranda sailed from England to enlist in the cause. Appointed commander-in-chief of the patriot armies, he launched a campaign to conquer the remainder of the country. Misfortune stalked his efforts. Reverses suffered by his armies were turned into disaster when an earthquake shook the provinces controlled by the revolutionists and snuffed out the lives of 20,000. Equal to the occasion, the Spanish government sent priests with instructions to tell the people that the catastrophe was a divine punishment for their sin of rebellion. The patriot armies disintegrated, and their commander was seized and thrown into the dungeon.

With the defeat of Miranda, the revolution in Venezuela was left to be completed by his erstwhile friend, Simón Bolívar. A wealthy Creole rancher, Bolívar had finally turned against Miranda, accusing him of deserting the revolution, and had been partly responsible for his capture by the Spaniards. A genuine patriot but egoistic and fanatical, Bolívar fought the Spanish with savage fury, and the conflict in Venezuela became a vicious civil war. When the revolutionary cause seemed hopeless, Bolívar went to Colombia and joined the rebel forces there. He returned to Venezuela in 1813 and captured Caracas. In January 1814, the Second Venezuelan Republic was proclaimed with Bolívar as its head with the title of "Liberator." In six months the new government had been crushed by the Spaniards, and its founder fled to Jamaica. He did not return for three years. In 1817 he began the rebuilding of a stronger patriot force in Venezuela, and two years later, with the help of 4,000 soldiers of fortune from Great Britain, completed a spectacular foray into Colombia. Inflicting a decisive defeat upon the Spaniards and their collaborators, he proclaimed the Republic of Colombia on August 10, 1819. Three months later a constitution was issued for the United States of Colombia, including Venezuela, with Bolívar as president. Thereafter the great Liberator devoted his efforts to freeing the remainder of the northern portion of the continent from Spanish rule. By 1821 he had liquidated the royalist forces in Venezuela. Meanwhile, his able lieutenant Antonio José de Sucre,

The revolt in Venezuela

Equestrian Statue of Simón Bolívar (1783–1830), Soldier, Statesman, and Revolutionary Leader. On Plaza Bolívar, Caracas, Venezuela.

*Temporary union of
Venezuela, Colombia,
and Ecuador*

Detail from a Painting of the Battle of Carabobo (Just West of Caracas). This battle, fought on June 24, 1821, marked Bolívar's final victory over the Spanish army in Venezuela.

had begun the liberation of Ecuador, and in 1822 won a brilliant victory against the Spaniards, which assured the independence of the country. Soon afterward Bolívar arrived in Quito and persuaded the Ecuadorean revolutionists to unite with Colombia and Venezuela in a republic of Gran Colombia.

The revolt in Argentina

Concurrently with these events in the northern areas, an independence movement was growing apace in the south. As early as 1790 businessmen in the port of Buenos Aires had developed a profitable trade with Spain and an even more profitable one with Great Britain. They longed for relief of these ventures from monopolistic restrictions imposed by the Spanish government. During the Napoleonic Wars their demands were encouraged by the British government. In 1810 a band of Creoles in Buenos Aires overthrew the vice-regal government of Joseph Bonaparte and appointed a supreme governing council to rule in the name of Ferdinand VII. While the urban Creoles were debating how far they should go in the direction of complete independence and what form of government would best suit their needs, delegates from the outlying provinces assembled at Tucumán in 1816 and declared absolute independence from the mother country. Thenceforth rivalry between the capital and the rural provinces impeded the progress of the revolution.

José San Martín

At least one native of Argentina perceived that internal squabbles would lead to nothing but ultimate defeat. This man was José San Martín, Argentina's greatest, although least-honored, national hero. He had served in the Spanish army from the age of eleven and had fought the French invaders in the Peninsular campaign. With Spain under the heel of Napoleon, he had returned to his native country. Ignoring local quarrels, he determined to give positive direction to the

Argentine revolution by attacking the royalists in Peru, their principal stronghold on the continent. He obtained an appointment as governor of the province of Cuyo, on the eastern slope of the Andes, where he planned to organize and equip an army for an incursion into Chile, which would then be used as a base for operations against Peru. In his preparations he was assisted by Bernardo O'Higgins, a Chilean revolutionary of Irish descent. By 1817 everything was ready for the daring expedition. Scrambling over the rocky slopes of the continental divide, the invaders came down into Chile, fell upon the royalists near Santiago, and won a spectacular triumph. The grateful Chileans offered San Martín a dictatorship, which he declined, insisting that it be conferred upon his Chilean collaborator O'Higgins. San Martín then turned his attention to completing plans for the attack on Peru. The expedition got under way in September 1820. Less than a year later the redoubtable patriot entered Lima, issued a declaration of independence from Spain, and vested himself with the title of "Protector" of the new Peruvian government. Although he believed that only the establishment of a monarchy could ensure stability in the turbulent country, he entertained no political ambitions for himself. Lacking Bolívar's consummate political and oratorical skills, he proved to be a reluctant and not very successful dictator, and he alienated many of his supporters. It was left to the ardent republican Bolívar—who, ironically, was more monarchic in temperament than the royalist San Martín—to complete the conquest of Peru (1824). The Liberator, received with adulation in Lima, drew up a constitution making Peru a republic but with total power lodged in a president-for-life. Shortly thereafter, the southeastern section detatched itself as a separate state and took the name Bolivia in honor of the Liberator. In 1826 Bolívar prepared for this new republic a constitution as autocratic as the one he had given Peru. His friend General de Sucre became Bolivia's first president. Meanwhile San Martín, feeling that his mission as a revolutionist had been fulfilled and embittered by his apparent rejection both by Peruvians and Argentinians, exiled himself to Europe, where he died in obscurity in 1850.

The process by which Brazil passed from colonial dependence to statehood was unique—at least in the annals of Latin America. It followed a less violent course than in most other colonies, perhaps for the reason that Brazil was more backward than the others. Two-thirds of its population were slaves. There was a very small middle class and no cities worthy of the name. Schools were few, and scarcely more than a tenth of the people could read and write. But the movement toward independence was accompanied by significant economic growth rather than debilitating conflict, and this growth continued long beyond the revolutionary period. Brazil was the only Latin American country to attain a stable independent regime as a monarchy rather than a republic. More remarkable, not only was it recognized as a legitimate monarchy before separating from Portugal, but it actually became the

José San Martín (1778–1850), a Military Genius Who Carried the Revolution from Argentina to Chile to Peru

Bernardo O'Higgins (1778–1842), Revolutionary and Supreme Director of Liberated Chile

Domestic Slavery in Nineteenth-Century Brazil

stronger of the two; and the mother country, drained by wars, seemed hardly more than an appendage of its colony.

The impetus for revolution in Brazil came from the Napoleonic Wars. When Napoleon's troops drove the Portuguese rulers from Lisbon in 1807, the Portuguese sailed to Brazil, arriving in Rio de Janeiro in March 1808. The regent, Prince John, was chagrined to find his colony so backward and launched an immediate program of reform and improvement. Most of the capital for this program was supplied by British investors. Great Britain already dominated the economy of its ally Portugal and was eager to monopolize and profit from Brazil's economic development. Prince John established schools, colleges, hospitals, a library, an art museum, and a bank. He reorganized the administration of the colony, sponsored new methods of agriculture, and abolished the restrictions on colonial manufacturing. While his wife Carlota outraged Brazilians by her unconcealed absolutist ambitions and her brazenly wanton behavior, Prince John won popular respect and affection. His position was rendered more difficult when, upon the death of his insane mother Maria I in 1816, he inherited the Portuguese throne as King John VI. Five years later, with considerable reluctance, he sailed for Portugal, leaving his eldest son Dom Pedro as regent in Brazil.

Having relinquished Brazil, John VI found himself unable to govern effectively in Portugal, where he was caught in a conflict between reactionaries and liberal constitutionalists. A key role in the unfolding Brazilian drama was played by a brilliant mineralogist, José Bonifacio, who enlisted the young regent Dom Pedro in the cause of independence. When the Lisbon authorities ordered Pedro to return to Por-

Reforms under Prince John

The reign of Pedro I

tugal to "complete his education," he refused to go. In September 1822 he declared the country independent and a month later was proclaimed emperor. In spite of its auspicious beginning, Pedro I's reign soon passed under a cloud. Pedro accepted the constitution of 1824 which made him a limited monarch, but he exiled the liberal José Bonifacio, to whom he was indebted for the throne. He wounded Brazilian national pride by failing to prevent a declaration of independence by Uruguay, which had been annexed by his father in 1816; his marital infidelities created scandal; and he stupidly drove a wedge between Brazilian and Portuguese factions by showering favors upon the latter. Finding himself criticized in the press and opposed by leading citizens and by the army, he abdicated and, in 1831, left the country. Fortunately for Brazil his son and successor, Pedro II, proved to be one of the ablest of all nineteenth-century rulers.

By 1826 all the South American countries had thrown off the yoke of European rule. Uruguay remained a province of Brazil until 1828, and Argentina was unable to solve the problem of unity between Buenos Aires and her rural provinces until 1853. Meanwhile another section of Latin America was striving for the goal of independence. This was the viceroyalty of New Spain, which included Mexico, Central America, portions of the West Indies, and the Spanish territory within the present limits of the United States. The island of Haiti was the first to raise the standard of revolt. During the eighteenth century it had become a colony of France—her most lucrative, by the way. It was a seething volcano of discontent, however. Its population had a three-class structure. At the top were a few thousand whites, mostly French planters and officials. At the bottom were 500,000 miserably exploited Negro slaves. A middle layer comprised the mulattoes, torn into mutually hostile factions and despised by both blacks and whites. In 1791 Toussaint L'Ouverture, a slave but the grandson of an African king, emerged as the leader of the Negroes. Under the influence of the French Revolutionary policy of abolishing slavery in the colonies, he led the Negroes in a prolonged revolt against their masters. With some accuracy he can be regarded as a forerunner of twentieth-century guerrilla leaders. His followers were a straggling force of irregulars, poorly armed and equipped, who followed a tactic of strike and run. In ten years they gained control of the entire island. Toussaint issued a constitution and assumed dictatorial powers.

When Napoleon had established himself as master of France, he resolved to put an end to the rule of the upstart rebel. Avowing that he would never "leave an epaulette on the shoulder of a Negro," he sent a huge expedition under the command of his brother-in-law, General Le Clerc, to overthrow Toussaint's government. Nearly two years and an act of treachery were required to accomplish the task. Informing Toussaint that he would "not find a more sincere friend than myself," Le Clerc invited the Negro to his quarters for negotia-

The revolution in Haiti

Toussaint L'Ouverture (1743–1803), Slave and Revolutionary Leader of Haiti

Haitian independence

*Father Miguel Hidalgo (1753–
1811), "the Father of Mexican
Independence." Led an Indian
Rebellion against the Creoles and
Spaniards*

tions. He then seized him and shipped him off in chains to a prison in France. Angered by this treachery, the slaves again rose in rebellion and with new and equally capable leaders soon forced the French to withdraw. In 1803 Haiti was proclaimed an independent kingdom. Unfortunately, independence brought little benefit to the Haitians, who suffered from continuous power struggles between rival factions on the island.

Scarcely anywhere in Latin America did the revolution present a more discouraging aspect than in Mexico. Here the Creoles did not constitute so powerful a class as in some parts of South America, and many feared that rebellion, by arousing the Indians and poor mestizos, might endanger their position. A revolt was finally launched in 1810, however, in the rural provinces. Its leader was a Creole priest, Father Hidalgo. The son of a poor farmer, he had obtained a good education and had become rector of the Colegio de San Nicolàs. But he was an ardent admirer of Rousseau and was reputed to have questioned the Virgin Birth and the authority of the pope. His original plan was to lead the Indians in a rebellion against the Spanish-born aristocrats, but when his scheme was exposed he turned upon the government itself. He captured the important towns of Guanajuato and Guadalajara and then advanced with 80,000 men upon Mexico City. Ultimately defeated, he was captured, condemned by the Inquisition, and shot. One of his mestizo followers, José Morelos, continued the revolution for four more years and attempted to set up an independent government. But, like Hidalgo, he eventually fell into the hands of the royalists and was condemned to death. The destinies of the revolution then passed into the hands of Augustín de Iturbide, the son of a prosperous mestizo landowner. A crafty adventurer and soldier of fortune by profession, Iturbide had hitherto fought on the side of the royalists and denounced Hidalgo's "lawless band"; but he saw a chance to further his ambitions by joining the patriots. Openly espousing independence and racial equality, he attracted formidable support and, in September 1821, entered Mexico City in triumph without fighting a battle. He induced the Mexican Congress to name him emperor of an independent Mexican empire and assumed the title of Augustín I. His harsh rule aroused opposition, and when he lost the support of the army he was forced into exile in 1823. A year later Mexico adopted a republican constitution similar to that of the United States, except that the Roman Catholic faith was made the established religion.

For half a century or, in some cases, for a whole century the new republics of Latin America wavered between anarchy and despotism. Political and social tensions were not relaxed with the coming of independence. Federalists were pitted against the advocates of a strong central government, liberal anticlericals against conservative Catholics, primitive agrarian or pastoral hinterland against the cities of the coast, and the small minority of property owners against the dispossessed majority. The revolutions had been aimed at freeing the propertied classes from outside control, not at reforming the lopsided and unjust social structure, which continued virtually unchanged under the new regimes. The plantation system of agriculture, based on slave or semiservile labor, which had become almost universal throughout Latin America, was not only oppressive but inefficient. With access to cheap labor, the landlords had little incentive to introduce improved methods of cultivation. Consequently the estates did not generate enough capital to promote industrial development. The needed capital was supplied largely by foreign investors, chiefly British at first and, later, North American. Because land constituted the main source of wealth and because its use was monopolized by a few, lower-class revolts in behalf of land redistribution occurred frequently. Such revolts, horrifying to the threatened oligarchy and frowned upon by foreign capitalists, were quickly suppressed. But as foreign banks and corporations through their investments acquired ascendancy over the economy of the fledgling states, members of the native power elite found themselves caught in a dependent relationship, more profitable perhaps but no less stringent than the one they had chafed under during the colonial era.

The numerous constitutions drawn up by Latin American nations, often imitative of the United States Constitution, did not reflect political realities and were frequently disregarded in practice. Attempts to develop democratic institutions were thwarted by the deep-seated tradition of the *caudillo*—a forceful leader who derived his power from the strength of his own personality and the loyalty of his followers rather than from any external legal code. This "strong man" cult, which gained momentum during the revolutionary wars and spawned dictatorships in their wake, has haunted the political process down to the present day. Paraguay, an extreme example, has never had an elected government. During the first century of independence more than forty chief executives came and went in Bolivia, and six Bolivian presidents were assassinated in office. Colombia's history is almost unique in that only twice during the century following independence was its government overthrown by violence. In neighboring Venezuela, revolutions occurred with such frequency as to reduce economic progress virtually to a standstill. Only the accession of a "Man on Horseback," Juan Vicente Gómez, who ruled for twenty-six years, brought a semblance of stability to the country. Numerous wars fought by the Latin American states against each other also disrupted orderly constitutional government. Brazil, Argentina, and Chile—large rival powers—tried to absorb smaller Uruguay, Paraguay, and Bolivia. Uruguay's struggle against Argentina lasted for fourteen years (1838–1852). Most famous was the War of the Pacific (1879–1883), in which Chile defeated the combined forces of Peru and Bolivia and acquired a rich nitrate-producing region by annexing three of Peru's southeastern provinces

The caudillo *tradition;*
wars and dictatorships

The gauchos of Argentina;
Manuel de Rosas

Progress in the "southern
cone"

and depriving Bolivia of its only outlet to the sea. The enmity resulting from this exchange has never entirely subsided. The bloodiest of all the wars was that of 1864–1870, in which Paraguay resisted the combined onslaughts of Brazil, Uruguay, and Argentina for six years. The Paraguayans fought almost literally to the last man. More than half of Paraguay's total population was wiped out.

Efforts to establish an effective central government in Argentina involved a long battle with the western provinces, whose inhabitants feared domination by landed and mercantile interests ruling from Buenos Aires. The great treeless plains of central Argentina and Uruguay, known as the pampas, represented a type of Wild West, the domain of the gaucho. Lord of wild horses and cattle, the gaucho was notorious for his primitive life style and also for his ruggedly independent spirit. These hardy cattlemen, sprung from a mixture of races, had established themselves on the pampas without assistance from or control by any organized government, and not before the middle of the nineteenth century were they brought within the pale of a central authority. Forced eventually to accommodate to the pressures of urban civilization, some gauchos emerged as popular heroes, exemplars of a rough frontier-type democracy. The notorious tyrant Juan Manuel de Rosas began his career as a gaucho leader who championed the cause of the provinces against the capital. But after his federalist supporters had helped him to become governor of Buenos Aires in 1829, by playing on the hatred of the masses for the upper class he kept himself in power for twenty-three years. Although he enacted some beneficial measures, he seems to have been a pathological despot who used spies, torture, and the dungeon to crush his opponents. In 1862 de Rosas was overthrown, and a year later Argentina adopted a constitution that has lasted longer than any other in Latin America.

During the course of the nineteenth century some Latin Americans made notable advances toward both political maturity and economic viability. Progress was most evident in the "southern cone," where Argentina, Chile, and Uruguay were helped by investments from abroad and also by immigration. The population of Argentina grew from 2 million in 1870 to about 4 million in 1900, and more than half of this increase was the result of immigration from Italy, Spain, France, Germany, and the British Isles. Likewise, through immigration the small state of Uruguay acquired a relatively homogeneous population, chiefly Spanish and Italian. Chile, although shaken by five revolutions within a two-year period (1827–1828), attained political stability sooner than its neighbors. A successful merchant named Diego Portales, after seizing power, gave the country a constitution in 1833, which endured until 1925. A relatively benevolent but conservative dictator, Portales guarded the interests of landowners, miners, and merchants, and he made Catholicism the state religion. Prosperity followed the exploitation of Chile's mineral resources. Silver was discovered in 1832; by

1850 Chile led the world in copper production; its nitrate production tripled between 1880 and 1890.

In bleak contrast with South America's southern cone were the Andean republics of Peru, Bolivia, and Ecuador, where a small mestizo caste held the Indian masses in subjugation. These countries remained backward politically, economically, and culturally, oppressed and terrorized by a succession of caudillos.

Two states of Latin America underwent experiences during the nineteenth century that were in a number of respects distinctive. One was Brazil, and the other was Mexico. As has already been pointed out, Brazil was exceptional in moving rapidly toward successful statehood against a primitive background and in continuing long under monarchical rule. The constitution drafted in 1824 under Pedro I remained in effect for sixty-five years. It was a moderately liberal document, guaranteeing freedom of speech, of the press, and of religion, and providing for a legislative assembly, but it left the emperor exempt from responsibility for the acts of his ministers. Pedro II, who ascended the throne when not quite fifteen years of age, reigned for forty-nine years (1840–1889). Well educated (he knew fourteen languages) and widely traveled, he was generous and tolerant by disposition, cosmopolitan and progressive in outlook, and had a more scrupulous regard for the constitution than his father had shown. Under his intelligent leadership the largest and most populous South American country, despite its still primitive plantation economy, won international respect and a good credit rating. Among Pedro II's notable accomplishments was the emancipation of the slaves, which at the beginning of his reign made up more than half of Brazil's population. It took nearly two decades (1871–1888) to complete the process, and it also brought down the wrath of plantation owners upon the emperor. When the army, which had risen in influence during the Paraguayan war of 1864–1870, threw its support to a faction demanding a republic, a bloodless coup in 1889 ended the monarchy, and the ruler who had given Brazil the best government it has ever known was driven into exile. The military chiefs promptly dissolved the Congress and in 1891 had a committee of lawyers draft a new constitution for the Republic of Brazil.

Mexico, which, like Brazil, wavered between monarchy and republic, was one of the few Latin American countries in which the mestizos and Indians played an active part in determining the course of political developments. Between 1833 and 1855 Mexico was ruled by Antonio López de Santa Anna, a cunning charlatan of Creole descent, famous in the United States for his role in the dispute over Texas and the war that followed. Although holding the title of president, he governed as a dictator with the support of a clerico-military oligarchy. Cruel, treacherous, and greedy for power, Santa Anna exemplified that *personalismo* which has been the curse of so many Latin American coun-

The backward Andean republics

Pedro II (1825–1891), Emperor of Brazil and Liberator of Slaves

Antonio López de Santa Anna (1797–1876), Mexican Caudillo Whose Unbridled Lust for Power Carried Him to the Presidency and Dictatorship

tries. After his incompetence was demonstrated by his mishandling of the Texas affair and by his conduct in the war of 1846–1848 by which Mexico lost all its North American territory to the United States, Santa Anna was finally ousted. Into the breach stepped Benito Juárez, a full-blooded Indian, who has been called the "Abraham Lincoln" of Mexico.

Born not in a log cabin but in an adobe mountain hut, he acquired a knowledge of law and managed to get himself elected governor of one of the Mexican states. Both able and just, he rapidly gained popular support. As the leading member of a coalition government, he inaugurated a program aimed at the destruction of clerical and military privilege, the separation of church and state, and the distribution of Church lands to the people. These reforms were incorporated in a new constitution adopted in 1857. Promulgation of the Constitution of 1857 was followed by a bloody civil war, the so-called War of the Reform, fought from 1858 to 1861 between liberals and clerical-conservatives. It ended in a complete victory for Juárez and his followers, with the result that more drastic anticlerical laws were enacted to supplement the provisions of the constitution. Religious orders were suppressed, Church property was nationalized, and civil marriage was established. But the triumph of the liberals did not obliterate the nation's troubles. The government was so desperate for money that it sold some of the confiscated Church lands to secular landlords. The peasants were merely transferred from one exploiter to another. The war disrupted economic conditions to such an extent that payments on foreign debts were suspended. This gave the wily Napoleon III an excuse to intervene. In 1862 he sent a French army to Vera Cruz, which finally battered its way to Mexico City and took possession of the government. Meanwhile, an assembly of Mexican conservatives went through the sham of "offering" the Mexican throne to Archduke Maximilian of Austria, who had already been selected by Napoleon III as his puppet ruler.

As emperor of Mexico, Maximilian was a pitiful failure. Although he was kindly, idealistic, and sympathetic to the plight of most of his new subjects, he was amateurish and dominated by an overly ambitious wife. He antagonized the conservatives by his acid criticisms of corruption and indifference in the Church and in the army. At the same time, the followers of Juárez had distrusted him from the beginning. The primary cause of his downfall, however, was a shift in the power struggle in Europe. The Austro-Prussian War of 1866 put Napoleon in a position where he could no longer afford to give military support to Maximilian. As a result of victory in that war, Prussia now loomed as a dangerous rival of France. Soon afterward, therefore, the French emperor withdrew his troops from Mexico. He was impelled to take this action partly, of course, by vigorous protests from the government of the United States against French violation of the Monroe Doctrine. But even without these protests, his decision could not have been long delayed.

*The War of the Reform
and the overthrow of the
republic*

Maximilian (1832–1867), Archduke of Austria and Emperor of Mexico

*The disastrous reign of
Emperor Maximilian*

In the absence of French military support, Maximilian's empire in Mexico speedily collapsed. The liberal forces of Juárez closed in upon him, and he was captured, court-martialed, and executed by a firing squad. Juárez was quickly elected president and re-elected in 1871, but death overtook him the following year. He had time to accomplish only a few of his aims for making Mexico a modern, progressive state. He drastically reduced the size of the army, eliminated waste and extravagance in the government, and initiated steps for a wide extension of public education. But the troubles of the nation were far from ended. It was impossible to repair overnight the damage caused by twenty years of civil strife. The national debt continued to increase, economic activity had shrunk, and the country seemed almost on the verge of exhaustion. In 1877 the government of Juárez's successor was overthrown, and a dictatorship was established that was destined to remain in power for more than thirty years. The new ruler was Porfirio Díaz, the son of a Creole father and an Indian mother. Originally a pupil and follower of Juárez, he repudiated his master when the latter was re-elected president in 1871. Thereafter he pursued his own ambitions and strove with an iron will to mold his country in accordance with his cherished schemes.

The return of Juárez

The regime of Díaz brought Mexico the appearance of prosperity. Foreign trade multiplied six times over, and railroad mileage increased from 400 to 16,000. Mines were brought up to unprecedented levels of production, smuggling was dramatically reduced, the national budget was balanced, and interstate tariffs were abolished to the substantial benefit of industry and commerce. Díaz was acclaimed as a great statesman by such world-renowned figures as Theodore Roosevelt and Kaiser Wilhelm II. Small wonder, for Mexico's spectacular economic growth was based on imported capital, procured through terms that mortgaged the country's natural resources to foreigners. Meanwhile, Díaz's dictatorship rode roughshod over the constitution. He manipulated the electoral machinery and ruthlessly crushed all opposition. And while the business classes luxuriated in dividends and profits, the lower classes suffered more than ever. Industrial workers and miners were exploited mercilessly. When they dared to effect organized protests or strikes, Díaz responded by sending troops to defend the investments of foreign capitalists against the workers. A limited distribution of public lands, instead of helping small farmars, swelled the estates of the rich. By the end of the Díaz regime half the population lived on the great haciendas, communally owned villages (*ejidos*) had almost disappeared, and 95 percent of rural heads of families were landless. Although slavery had been abolished, the peonage or serfdom that succeeded it was in some ways more oppressive because wages were kept down while prices rose continually. By 1911, when Díaz's government finally collapsed and the aged caudillo sailed for France, the Mexican republic was ripe for revolution to undo the evils of three decades.

The regime of Porfirio Díaz

Porfirio Díaz (1830–1915), President and Dictator of Mexico from 1877 to 1911. His oppressive regime brought economic expansion to Mexico at the cost of a deterioration of living standards for the majority of the population.

• *Items so designated are available in paperback editions.*
  Artz, Frederick B., *France under the Bourbon Restoration, 1814–1830,* New York, 1963. A basic survey with a good treatment of romanticism.
• Beales, Derek, *The Risorgimento and the Unification of Italy,* New York, 1971. Objective, concise survey of Italian unification.
• Berlin, Isaiah, *Karl Marx: His Life and Environment,* New York, 1948. The best short account.
• Binkley, Robert C., *Realism and Nationalism, 1852–1871,* New York, 1935. An excellent synthesis despite some dated passages.
• Craig, Gordon, *The Politics of the Prussian Army,* Oxford, 1964. Much more than the title implies. An excellent analysis of Prussian social structure and the role of the army in social reform and unification.
  Deak, Istvan, *The Lawful Revolution: Louis Kossuth and the Hungarians, 1848–1849,* New York, 1979.
  Epstein, Klaus, *The Genesis of German Conservatism,* Princeton, N.J., 1966. Provides excellent early-nineteenth-century background.
• Eyck, Erich, *Bismarck and the German Empire,* London, 1958. The best one-volume study of Bismarck.
  Eyck, Frank, *The Frankfurt Parliament, 1848–49,* New York, 1968. A detailed study of its composition and procedure.
  Ford, Guy Stanton, *Stein and the Era of Reform in Prussia, 1807–1815,* New York, 1922. An old but still valuable work on a leading Prussian reformer.
• Hamerow, Theodore, *Restoration, Revolution, Reaction,* Princeton, N.J., 1966. An excellent social and economic history of Germany between 1815 and 1871.
• ———, *The Social Foundations of German Unification, 1858–1871,* 2 vols., Princeton, N.J., 1972. Concentrates on economic factors which determined the solution to the unification question. An impressive synthesis.
  Hayes, C. J. H., *The Historical Evolution of Modern Nationalism,* rev. ed., New York, 1968. A valuable survey.
• Hobsbawm, Eric J., *The Age of Revolution, 1789–1848,* New York, 1962. An unrigidly Marxist interpretation, good for the entire period it covers.
• Holborn, Hajo, *History of Modern Germany,* Vols. II and III, New York, 1964. The best survey of German history in English.
• Howard, Michael, *The Franco-Prussian War,* New York, 1969. The war's effect on society.
• Kohn, Hans, *The Idea of Nationalism,* New York, 1944. A perceptive analysis.
• Krieger, Leonard, *The German Idea of Freedom,* Boston, 1957. A difficult but rewarding study of German political thought.
  Macartney, C. A., *The Hapsburg Empire, 1790–1918,* London, 1968. A worthwhile survey.
  Mack Smith, Denis, *Garibaldi: A Great Life in Brief,* New York, 1956.
  ———, *The Making of Italy, 1796–1870,* New York, 1968. A narrative with documents.
• Mehring, Franz, *Karl Marx: The Story of His Life,* New York, 1976. A good, recent life.
  Namier, Lewis B., *1848: The Revolution of the Intellectuals,* London, 1964. A controversial analysis, highly critical of the Frankfurt Assembly.

Noyes, P. H., *Organization and Revolution: Working-Class Associations in the German Revolutions of 1848–49*, Princeton, N.J., 1966. An important monograph analyzing the degree of working-class consciousness at the time of the revolution.

• Pflanze, Otto, *Bismarck and the Development of Germany, 1815–1871*, Princeton, N.J., 1963. An impressive analysis of Bismarck's aims and policies.

• Rosenberg, Hans, *Bureaucracy, Aristocracy, and Autocracy: The Prussian Experience, 1660–1815*, Cambridge, Mass., 1958. A difficult but valuable book explaining the forces that molded the modern Prussian state.

Salvemini, Gaetano, *Mazzini*, London, 1956. Biography with excerpts from Mazzini's writings.

Snyder, Louis L. *Roots of German Nationalism*, Bloomington, Ind., 1978.

• Taylor, A. J. P., *The Hapsburg Monarchy, 1809–1918*, rev. ed., London, 1965. An idiosyncratic account by an eminent historian.

LATIN AMERICA

Bailey, Helen, and A. P. Nasatir, *Latin America: The Development of Its Civilization*, 2nd ed., Englewood Cliffs, N.J., 1968.

Conrad, Robert, *Children of God's Fire: A Documentary History of Black Slavery in Brazil*, Princeton, 1983. A vivid portrayal.

• Crow, John, *The Epic of Latin America*, 3rd ed., Berkeley, 1980. Rich in detail.

Fagg, J. E., *Latin America, a General History*, 3rd ed., New York, 1977.

• Lynch, John, *The Spanish American Revolutions, 1808–1826*, 2nd ed., New York, 1986.

Slatta, Richard, *Gauchos and the Vanishing Frontier*, Lincoln, Neb., 1983.

Wilgus, A. C., ed., *South American Dictators during the First Century of Independence*, Washington, 1937.

SOURCE MATERIALS

Bismarck, Otto von, *Bismarck, the Man and the Statesman, Written and Dictated by Himself*, London, 1899. Bismarck's memoirs, written after his fall from power.

• Clausewitz, Karl von, *On War*, London, 1968. Published posthumously, this work, in reality a philosophy of war, was perceived by the Prussian military bureaucracy as a mandate for total war—for the subjugation of all interests of the state to war.

Fichte, Johann Gottlieb, *Addresses to the German Nation*, New York, 1968. Presented in 1808 while French armies occupied Prussia, these lectures helped stir a German nationalist spirit.

• Marx, Karl, and Friedrich Engels, *The Marx-Engels Reader*, 2nd ed., by R. C. Tucker, New York, 1978. Reprints the basic texts.

Schurz, Carl, *The Reminiscences of Carl Schurz*, 3 vols., New York, 1907–1908. Especially valuable is Vol. I. A young German liberal in 1848 and a delegate to the Frankfurt Assembly, Schurz spent the rest of his life as an exile in the United States.

Part Six

THE WEST AT THE WORLD'S CENTER

The years between 1870 and 1945 found the West at the center of global af-
fairs. The industrial supremacy of western Europe and the United States
gave them a combined power greater than that possessed by any nation or
empire in previous times. Yet world domination was by no means accom-
panied by any sense of general world order. The economic might of the
Western nations, while it resulted in their ability to dominate the less de-
veloped quarters of the globe, resulted, as well, in their concern lest one of
their number overpower the others. The old system of the balance of
power, designed to preserve peace by insuring that no one country achieved
overwhelming predominance at the expense of its neighbors, was strained to
the breaking point by economic rivalries that stretched around the world.
Meanwhile, tensions mounted within each nation, as landed and middle
classes, threatened by the possibility of social turmoil, tried to balance the
mounting clamor for political concessions against their desire to retain power
in their own hands. Twice during the period, in 1914 and 1939, interna-
tional and domestic pressures exploded into global wars. Those wars and
their results, generated by the rivalries and miscalculations of the Western
nations, so sapped the strength of those nations as to depose them thereafter
as the sole arbiters of the world's destinies. The nations of the East Asia,
subjected to the high tide of Western expansionism, reacted in different ways.

China, under a decrepit dynasty and exhausted by rebellion, was reduced for several decades to a condition of economic dependence, while Japan displayed new vigor when forced out of isolation. Both nations adapted elements of Western civilization to their own basic culture patterns. The great lords of Japan, in drawing up a constitution in 1889, saw fit to establish the forms of cabinet government. The leader of the Chinese Revolution of 1911 made "democracy" one of his shibboleths. But the most powerful current reaching its climax between 1870 and 1945 was undoubtedly nationalism. New states multiplied especially in Europe and in Latin America, and the peoples of the Middle East and East Asia struck out boldly for control of their own destinies. The peoples of Africa were condemned to a longer struggle for independence. Although the notorious slave trade was gradually ended, the political and technological advantages accruing to the leading Western nations were utilized by them to strengthen their hold on the resources of disunited Africa.

EAST ASIA	AFRICA	
	British occupation of Cape Colony, 1795	
	House-Canoe system in Niger Delta, c. 1800	1800
	Expansion of East African trade, 1800–1875	
	Sultan Sayyid, Zanzibar, 1805–1856	
	Sierra Leone founded, 1808	
	Liberia founded, 1821	
		1825
	British consulates in coastal states, 1830–1860	
	Exploration of interior of continent, 1830–1875	
Anglo-Chinese War (Opium War), 1839–1842		
	Decline of slave trade, 1840–1863	
Taiping Rebellion, 1851–1864		1850
Opening of Japan, 1854		
Sun Yat-sen, 1866–1925		
Meiji Restoration in Japan, 1867–1868		
	Opening of Suez Canal, 1869	
End of feudalism in Japan, 1871		
		1875
	Destruction of Zulu empire, 1879	
	British invasion of Egypt, 1882	
Adoption of constitution in Japan, 1889	Berlin West African Conference, 1884	
Sino-Japanese War, 1894–1895	Discovery of Witwatersrand gold deposit in South Africa's Transvaal, 1886	
	European Settlement of Rhodesia, 1890	
Boxer Uprising, 1900	Boer War, 1899–1902	1900
Russo-Japanese War, 1904–1905	End of involuntary servitude in sub-Saharan Africa, 1901–1910	
Revolution in China, 1911		

POLITICS	SCIENCE & INDUSTRY

1870

	First commercially practical electrical generator, 1870
	Gilcrist-Thomas steel process, 1870s
Paris Commune, 1871	
Kulturkampf, Germany, 1872	
League of Three Emperors, 1873	
Constitution for Third French Republic, 1875	Germ theory of disease, 1875
End of First International, 1876	Invention of telephone, 1876
Congress of Berlin, 1878	
Triple Alliance, 1882	
Berlin conference on imperialism, 1885	
Second International formed, 1889	
Pan-Slavism, 1890–1914	
Dreyfus affair, 1894–1899	
	Discovery of the X-ray, 1895
Spanish-American War, 1898	Marie Curie, discovery of radium, 1898
Boer War, 1899–1902	Invention of wireless telegraph, 1899

1900

V. Lenin, *What Is to Be Done?,* 1902	
	First airplane flight, 1903
Russo-Japanese War, 1904–1905	Ivan Pavlov, Nobel Prize for physiology, 1904
Revolution in Russia, 1905	Albert Einstein, development of relativity theory, 1905–1910
Triple Entente, 1907	
Bosnian Crisis, 1908	Model T Ford, 1908
Revolt of the Young Turks, 1908	
Balkan Wars, 1912–1913	
First World War, 1914–1918	
Russian Revolution, 1917	
Treaty of Versailles, 1919	
Socialist revolution, Germany, 1919	
League of Nations, 1920–1946	

1920

NEP, Russia, 1921	
Mussolini's March on Rome, 1922	
Hitler's beer-hall putsch, 1923	
New constitution, Soviet Union, 1924	
Locarno agreements, 1925	
	Discovery of viruses, sulfa drugs, and penicillin, 1930s
	World economic conference, 1933
Hitler, chancellor of Germany, 1933	
New Deal, United States, 1933–1940	

ECONOMICS & SOCIETY	ARTS & LETTERS	
	Impressionism in art, 1870–1900	*1870*
Growth of finance capitalism, 1880s Social welfare legislation, Germany, 1882–1884		
	Émile Zola, *Germinal*, 1885	
Sherman Anti-Trust Act, United States, 1890	Henrik Ibsen, *Hedda Gabler*, 1890 Paul Cézanne, *The Card Players* 1890–1892	
Meline tariff, 1892		
	George Bernard Shaw, *Plays Pleasant* and *Unpleasant*, 1898	
Women's suffrage movement, England, 1900–1914	Sigmund Freud, *The Interpretation of Dreams*, 1900	*1900*
Social welfare legislation, France, 1904; 1910	Cubism in art 1905–1930	
Social welfare legislation, England, 1906–1912		
	Marcel Proust, *Remembrance of Things Past*, 1913–1918	
	Oswald Spengler, *The Decline of the West*, 1918 Bauhaus established, 1919	
German inflation. 1920s	Writers of the "Lost Generation," 1920–1930 Surrealism and Dadaism, 1920s Ludwig Wittgenstein, *Tractatus Logico-philosophicus*, 1921 T. S. Eliot, *The Waste Land*, 1922 James Joyce, *Ulysses*, 1922	*1920*
Great Depression, 1929–1940	Neo-realism in art, 1930s	

POLITICS	SCIENCE & INDUSTRY
Italy conquers Ethiopia, 1935–1936	National rearmament programs, 1935
Rome-Berlin Axis, 1936	
Spanish Civil War, 1936–1939	
Germany annexes Austria, 1938	
Munich conference, 1938	
Nazi-Soviet pact, 1939	Discovery of atomic fission, 1939
Second World War, 1939–1941	
United States enters war, 1941	
Allied invasion of Normandy, 1944	
Bombing of Hiroshima and Nagasaki, 1945	First atomic bomb test, 1945
United Nations founded, 1946	

1940

ECONOMICS & SOCIETY	ARTS & LETTERS

J. M. Keynes, *General Theory of Employment, Interest, and Money*, 1936

Jean-Paul Sartre, *Being and Nothingness*, 1943

1940

Chapter 30

THE PROGRESS OF INTERNATIONAL INDUSTRIALIZATION AND COMPETITION (1870-1914)

We have conquered for ourselves a place in the sun. It will now be my task to see to it that this place in the sun shall remain our undisputed possession. . . .

—Kaiser William II, speech, 1901

I f most historians now speak of a second industrial revolution occurring during the years after 1870, they are quick to qualify the term. Whatever the changes in technique and in scope—and they were significant—they do not compare to those which characterized the first revolution—*the* Industrial Revolution. There is, however, good reason to distinguish a second period of industrial development and advance from the first. Successful nation-building meant that the years 1870–1914 would be characterized by sharply increased international political and economic rivalries, culminating in a scramble after imperial territories in Africa and Asia. Britain, if it did not actually surrender its industrial primacy during this period, failed to counter with any real success the energetic and determined challenges from Germany and the United States to its constantly decreasing lead. New technology, particularly in the fields of metals, chemicals, and electricity, resulted in new products. Larger populations and improving standards of living produced greater demand, which, in turn, increased the volume of production. And the need for increased production called forth significant reorganization to provide a freer supply of capital and to ensure a more efficient labor force. It is these changes that distinguish the second stage of industrialization from the first, and therefore warrant its separate treatment. Yet they must be perceived as stemming not only from those economic conditions that were the result of the first stage, but also from the more general political, social, and cultural climate whose history we have been tracing.

A second industrial revolution

In analyzing the progress of industrialization, we shall deal with changes in three major areas: in technology, in scope and scale of production, and in the reorganization of the capitalist system. Finally we shall examine the phenomenon of late–nineteenth-century imperialism, and consider the extent to which that phenomenon can be attributed to increasing economic and industrial rivalries.

1. NEW TECHNOLOGIES

Technology in steel

A most important technological change in this period resulted in the mass production of steel. The advantages of steel over iron—a result of steel's lower carbon content—are its hardness, its malleability, and its strength. Steel can keep its cutting edge, where iron cannot; it can be worked more easily than iron, which is brittle and which, if it is to be used industrially, must almost always be cast (that is, poured into molds). And steel, because of its strength in proportion to its weight and volume, makes a particularly adaptable construction material. These advantages had been recognized by craftsmen for centuries. Until steel could be produced both cheaply and in mass, however, the advantages remained more theoretical than real. Two inventions, during the earlier years of the Industrial Revolution, had reduced the price and increased the output of steel to some degree. The crucible technique, discovered in the eighteenth century in England, called for the heating of relatively small amounts of iron ore to a point at which foreign matter could be removed by skimming, the carbon content reduced, and a proper proportion of carbon distributed evenly throughout the finished product. Although individual crucibles were not large, holding on the average no more than forty-five to sixty pounds, they could be poured together to produce steel ingots of several tons. A century later, in the early 1840s, two Germans adapted the puddling process, used in the production of iron, to the manufacture of steel. While it did not produce steel as hard as that made in crucibles, it reduced its price considerably.

Bessemer, Siemens-Martin, and Gilchrist-Thomas systems

Not until the invention of the Bessemer and Siemens-Martin processes, however, could steel begin to compete with iron. In the 1850s, an Englishman, Henry Bessemer, discovered that by blowing air into and through the molten metal he could achieve a more exact degree of decarbonization in much shorter time, and with far larger quantities of ore, than was possible with either the crucible or puddling methods. Bessemer soon found, however, that his "converters" were incapable of burning off sufficient quantities of phosphorous; and phosphorous in anything but the smallest quantities made the metal unworkable. A partial solution was achieved with the introduction of nonphosphoric hematite ores. Yet this was of little long-term use in most European countries, where supplies of hematite ore were not

The Rise of the Steel Industry. Bristling with massive machinery such as this steam-hammer, the Krupp Works in Essen, Germany, was already a major force in steel production by the 1870s.

abundant. This same problem plagued the German inventors Frederick and William Siemens, whose furnace made use of waste gases to increase heat. Not until Pierre Martin, a Frenchman, discovered that the introduction of scrap iron into the mix would induce proper decarbonization, could the Siemens furnace be used to make steel commercially. And not until the late 1870s was the problem of phosphoreting solved for both the Bessemer and the Siemens-Martin processes. The solution was a simple one, discovered by two Englishmen, a clerk and a chemist: Sidney Gilchrist Thomas and his cousin Sidney Gilchrist. They introduced limestone into the molten iron to combine with the phosphorus, which was then siphoned from the mix. And they lined the converter in such a way that the slag was prevented from eating away the walls and releasing phosphorus back into the molten metal.

Together, these three processes revolutionized the production of steel. Although the use of iron did not end overnight, steel soon moved into the lead. In the British shipbuilding industry, for example, steel had overtaken iron by 1890. In part because Siemens-Martin was particularly suited to the manufacture of steel plates used in shipbuilding, that process dominated the manufacture of steel in Britain, where shipbuilding was a major industry. Bessemer steel, which could be manufactured more cheaply and in larger plants, was

Increased steel production

more commonly produced on the Continent and in America. The result was a particular increase in the production of German steel: by 1901, German converters were capable of pouring annually an average of 34,000 tons, compared to Britain's 21,750. By 1914 Germany was producing twice as much steel as Britain, and the United States twice as much as Germany.

Electricity

A second and equally important technological development resulted in the availability of electric power for industrial, commercial, and domestic use. Electricity's particular advantages result from the facts that it can be easily transmitted as energy over long distances, and that it can be converted into other forms of energy—heat and light, for example. Although electricity had, of course, been discovered prior to the first Industrial Revolution, its advantages could not have been put to general use without a series of inventions which occurred during the nineteenth century. Of these, some of the most important were the invention of the chemical battery by the Italian Alessandro Volta in 1800; of electromagnetic induction by the Englishman Michael Faraday in 1831; of the electromagnetic generator in 1866; of the first commercially practical generator of direct current in 1870; and of alternators and transformers capable of producing high-voltage alternating current in the 1880s. These inventions meant that by the end of the century it was possible to send electric current from large power stations over comparatively long distances. Electric power could be manufactured by water—hence cheaply—and delivered from its source to the place where it was needed.

New Technology: The Telephone. This 1885 photograph of a New York City telephone exchange bears witness to the transformation wrought by the dramatic expansion of the electrical industry. Note also the extent to which the position of operator has become the province of female employees.

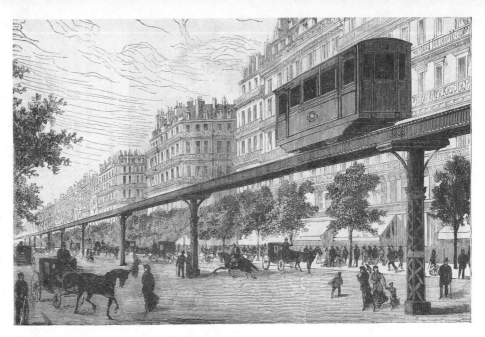

New Technology: The Elevated Train. This electric railway was erected in Paris in the 1880s.

Once it had been delivered to its destination, the power was converted and put to use in myriad ways. Households quickly became one of the major users of electrical power. The invention by Thomas Edison of the incandescent filament lamp—or light bulb—was crucial in this regard. As individual houses were electrified to receive the power that was to be transformed into light, consumer demand for electricity resulted in further expansion of the electrical industry. Demand for electrical power was increasing in the industrial sector as well. Electric motors soon began to power subways, tramways, and, eventually, long-distance railways. Electricity made possible the development of new techniques in the chemical and metallurgical industries. Most important, electricity helped to transform the work patterns of the factory. Heavy steam engines had made equipment and machinery stationery; electric motors meant that comparatively lightweight power tools could be moved—often by hand—to the site of a particular piece of work. The result was far greater flexibility in terms of factory organization. Smaller workshop industries benefited as well; they could accommodate themselves to electrically powered motors and tools in a way they could not to steam.

The uses of electricity

Steel and electricity were only two of the most important areas where technological changes were taking place. The chemical industry was significantly advanced by developments in the manufacture of alkali and organic compounds. Demand for alkali had increased with the demand for soaps and textiles, and with the changes in the manufacturing process of paper, which required large amounts of bleach. An older, more expensive and wasteful technique used extensively by the British was superseded after 1880 by a new process perfected by the Belgian Ernest Solvay. The result was, again, a rapid overtaking of

Other technological advances

The First Successful Airplane Flight

the British by the Germans in the production not only of alkalis but of sulfuric acid, a by-product recoverable in the Solvay process, and used in the manufacture of fertilizers, petroleum refining, iron, steel, and textiles. In the field of organic compounds, the impetus for further discovery came as a result of demand for synthetic dyes. Although the British and French were the first successful pioneers in this area, the Germans once more moved ahead to a commanding lead by 1900. At the turn of the century German firms controlled about 90 percent of the world market.

Improved engines

The need for more and more power to meet increasing industrial demands resulted not only in developments in the field of electricity, already noted, but in the improved design and expanded capacity of steam engines. The most noteworthy invention in this area was the steam turbine, which permitted engines to run at speeds heretofore unobtainable. Internal combustion engines made their appearance during this period as well. Their major advantage lay in their efficiency; i.e., they could be powered automatically, and did not need to be stoked by hand like steam engines. Once liquid fuels—petroleum and distilled gasoline—became available, as they did increasingly with the discovery of oil fields in Russia, Borneo, and Texas about 1900, the internal combustion engine took hold as a serious competitor to steam. By 1914 most navies had converted from coal to oil, as had domestic steamship companies. The automobile and the airplane, both still in their infancies, made little impact upon the industrial world, however, before 1914.

2. CHANGES IN SCOPE AND SCALE

These technological changes must be understood as occurring against a background of—indeed in part as a result of—a constantly growing population and a generally increased standard of living for the majority of men and women in the Western world. Between 1870 and 1914, Europe's population increased from 295 million to 450 million. This was the case despite a declining birth rate in the more industrially advanced countries of western Europe, where more and more middle- and working-class men and women were postponing marriage and limiting the number of their children, confident that those children they did have stood a fairly decent chance of survival. Population growth was primarily the result of a sharp decline in infant mortality, caused by improved sanitation and diet, and by the virtual elimination of diseases such as cholera and typhus. Increases were greatest in the areas of central and eastern Europe, where the birth rate did not drop as dramatically as in the West. Britain's population grew from 34.9 to 45.2 million between 1881 and 1911; France's from 37.4 to 39.1. But Germany's advanced during the same period from 45.2 to 64.9 million, and Russia's from 94 to an estimated 129 million.

Population increases

Declining death rates were an indicator of generally increasing prosperity. There were, of course, still a great many very poor people, both in cities and in the country: casual laborers, the unemployed, those in declining industries and trades. Those skilled workers and their families whose real incomes did rise as a result of deflation and higher wage rates did not experience anything like the rate of increase enjoyed by most of the middle class. Nor could they expect to avoid altogether the stretches of unemployment that made life so chaotic for so many of their unskilled co-workers. Yet despite these qualifications, it is fair to say that more people enjoyed a higher standard of living than ever before. And a higher standard of living produced the demand for an increase in consumer goods.

Higher living standards

Increased consumption of manufactured goods was by no means uniform; it was higher in urban and industrialized areas than in the country. But even in the country, traditional thrift was challenged as farmers and their wives journeyed by train into the cities, saw what they had not imagined they could have, and then decided they must spend their savings to have it. To accommodate the new and largely middle-class consumers, department stores and chain stores designed their products and their advertising to make shopping as easy and inviting as possible. Behind large plate-glass windows, goods were displayed attractively and temptingly; periodic sales encouraged householders to purchase "bargains"; catalogues and charge accounts made it easy for customers to spend money without leaving home. The result was an enormous increase in the volume of manufactured goods

New consumers

The Triumph of Middle-Class Consumerism. The interior of the Galeries Lafayette department store in Paris, c. 1890.

produced for this rapidly expanding consumer market. Bicycles, clocks, appliances, furnishings—these and a great many other things were being made in large quantities, and with new materials (cheap steel) and new techniques (electrical power). Many of these products were designed according to the correct assumption that women were more and more responsible for household purchases. Therefore, goods were fashioned to appeal directly to women, or to the children for whom women were responsible. The foot-powered sewing machine was a particular case in point—the first domestic appliance. Isaac Singer, the American responsible for the development of the treadle and straight needle in the 1850s, was as much an entrepreneur as an inventor. He was a pioneer in the field of advertising and promotion, encouraging purchase on the installment plan and providing courses for would-be domestic seamstresses.

Sewing machines changed far more than the sewing habits of

housewives, however. They were inexpensive, lightweight tools, easily installed and easily operated. Workshop masters could set up several, employ a handful of young women at very low wages, and make a profit turning out cheap ready-made clothing in response to increasing markets. This was just one of the ways in which the scale of manufacturing was altered during the latter part of the nineteenth century, with both demand and technology conspiring to produce the change. The sewing machine also led to the development of other new tools that helped cut costs in the clothing industry: button-holers, lace-makers, leather-stitchers. Whereas it took one cobbler ten hours to make a pair of shoes in 1850 by hand, by the end of the century it took a team of cobblers but a few hours to produce ten pairs using machinery. In metal-working, hard-edged steel allowed for the rapid cutting of patterns, which reduced price, in turn encouraging the manufacture of a variety of inexpensive metal goods—kitchenware, for example. In textiles, improved engines doubled the pace of mules and looms. In heavy industry, steam hammers performed the work of many men more precisely and with greater speed than before. New equipment of this sort was expensive. As a result, in heavy industry, it was the larger companies that prospered, and in the course of their prosperity, they grew even larger.

In all the countries of Europe, and in the United States, the pattern was one of expansion and consolidation. This was especially the case in Germany, where in the iron and steel industry nearly 75 percent

The web of industrial change

Left: *Advertisement for a German Sewing Machine*. The company proclaims the machine's versatility: unsurpassed for use in the home as well as in the workshop or factory. Right: *Sweated Industry*. This English family is "manufacturing" cheap toys at home. While the scale of some industrial enterprises increased, others remained profitable through the employment of badly paid home workers.

Industrial expansion and consolidation

Effects of increase in scale on workers: (1) relearning

(2) efficiency

of those employed worked in factories of a thousand or more, and where over 90 percent of the electrical equipment manufactured was made in factories with over fifty employees. Machinery was thus altering the scale of manufacturing in two directions at once. In the clothing industry, entrepreneurs could use inexpensive machines to make small workshops turn a profit. In steel foundries, the cost of new equipment forced small competitors to the wall, with the result that the foundries grew very much bigger.

The increase in the scale of manufacturing had important and often disturbing consequences for workers. The most obvious was the need for men and women to relearn their trades. They were compelled to adapt their older skills to the new machines. Very often this adaptation resulted in a loss of either pay or prestige, or both. Most machine work was not skilled work. A trainee could "pick up" a trade in a week or so. Workers who had prided themselves on a particular skill and had been paid according to their ability to perform it, had to face the fact that industrial change was not only forcing them to relearn, but was compelling them to tell themselves that their new "skills"—if they could be called that—did not amount to very much. For example, when the machine itself could cut metal with infinitesimal accuracy, there was far less need than there had been previously for the skills of a human "fitter." Even if workers were not forced to relearn in these ways in order to accommodate to increased scale, they often had at least to accommodate to factory reorganization and rationalization. In workplaces where the hand-carrying of materials had been a major factor in their final cost, mechanization to reduce that cost would produce a bewildering series of changes. Electric cranes, used together with huge magnets in the iron and steel industries, increased the speed with which goods could be moved, and demanded that workers defer to whatever changes their introduction might entail.

A second—and even more important—effect of the change in scale was the constant demand for further efficiency. The greater the scale of the operation, the more important it became to eliminate waste. One minute lost in the production of every ten pairs of shoes might not make much difference if only fifty pairs were produced in a day. But if hundreds were being made, it became crucial, in the eyes of management, to see that those minutes were no longer lost. In factories where capital had been spent on new machinery, the owners, conscious of the cost of their investment, increased output in order to realize a profit on that investment. In factories where older machinery was still in use, owners believed that the only way they could remain competitive with modernized operations was by extracting all they could from their less productive equipment. In both cases, workers were pressed to produce more and more. One result of this drive for efficiency was a restructuring of wage scales. Prior to this period, although there had been serious wage disputes, both management and

Technological Change and Production Speedup. An early assembly line of the Ford Motor Company, United States, 1913. Car bodies slid down the ramp and were attached to the chassis as they passed through the line below. One thousand cars were produced each day.

labor appeared content to bargain from the traditional notion of "a fair day's wage for a fair day's work." Definitions of what was fair naturally varied. But the level of individual performance was generally set by custom. What workers produced in the course of a day continued to determine what they were expected to produce. From about 1870 onward, however, expectations and procedures began to change. Periodic economic depressions in the last quarter of the nineteenth century saw profits fall before wages. This pattern caused employers to insist on greater individual productivity from their employees. It was no longer enough to work at a job with customary speed. Workers were now asked to produce as much as the owners thought they were potentially capable of producing.

But who was to determine that potential? That question plagued industrial relations during these years. Employers, who were adopting precision tools in order to increase production, grew more and more convinced that worker output could be gauged with precision as well. The foremost theoretician of worker efficiency and what was called scientific management of labor was the American Frederick W. Taylor (1865–1915). Taylor devised a three-step system whereby a worker's output could be "scientifically" measured, a system which, he argued, would provide a precise method for the determination of wage scales. First, he observed, timed, and analyzed workers' movements on the job, in order to determine how long a particular task should take. Second, he figured the labor costs of these movements. Third, he produced "norms," or general standards, which all workers were expected to maintain. These norms were invariably higher than those which had prevailed under traditional conditions.

Scientific management

Piece rates

In order to encourage workers to accept these increased standards, Taylor urged all factory-owners to adopt piece rates (i.e., payment to workers according to the specific amount produced) rather than hourly or daily wages. Payment by piece rate was already a growing practice in many European and American factories. In theory, at least, workers were not opposed to this method of payment; they reasoned that their only hope for a share in increasing output lay in their chance to be paid directly for what they made. But when they were told that their pay would not increase unless they measured up to predetermined—and, to their mind, unrealistic—norms, they objected. They argued that rates were set according to the performance of the speediest workers. Even though workers might earn more money if they agreed to the new rates, they resented the intrusion of management upon the pace of their working lives. Despite this opposition, scientific management spread throughout the industrialized West. In England, the United States, and on the Continent, particularly in the engineering trades, factory after factory subscribed to the new gospel. Where it could not entirely succeed in introducing "efficiency" on the shop floor, management proceeded to rationalize its own procedures. Accounting departments were expanded, and encouraged to attend closely to the problem of cost control in all areas of production and distribution. These reforms were no more than a reflection of the general move in the direction of greater efficiency. They were brought on by the vastly increased scale of production, the need to reduce waste wherever possible, and the desire to derive maximum profits from the elimination of unnecessary motions and unproductive habits.

3. THE NEW CAPITALISM

The growth of incorporation

Responding to the increased scope of production and to the consequent pressures for further efficiency, the institutions of capitalism began to reorganize toward the end of the nineteenth century. Hitherto, most firms had been small or at most middle-sized; now, as firms grew and their need for capital increased, they began to incorporate. Limited liability laws, enacted by most countries in the course of the century, worked to encourage this incorporation. "Limited liability" meant that an individual owning stock in a particular corporation could be held liable only for the amount of his or her shares, should that corporation bankrupt itself. Once insured in this way, many thousands of middle-class men and women considered corporate investment a safe and financially promising way of making money for themselves. A stockholding, "rentier" class emerged, brought into existence by the willingness of governments to encourage capitalism through friendly legislation, and by the desire of capitalist businessmen to expand their industrial undertakings to meet increased de-

The New York Stock Exchange, 1893

mands. More and more companies incorporated. In doing so, their management tended to be removed from the direct control of family founders or of company-based boards of directors. The influence of bankers and financiers, often situated in cities far removed from the factories they invested in, grew accordingly. These men were not investing their own money but the money of their clients; their power to stimulate or to discourage the growth of particular industries and enterprises encouraged a kind of impersonal "finance" capital.

Corporate organization on a large scale facilitated the spread of industrial unification. Some industries—steel, for example—combined vertically. Steel companies, to ensure uninterrupted production, acquired their own coal and iron mines. By doing so, they could guarantee themselves a supply of raw materials at attractive prices. Often the same steel companies would obtain control of companies whose products were made of steel: for example, shipyards or railway factories. Now they would not only possess a ready stock of raw materials but an equally ready market for their manufactured products—steel plates, steel rails, whatever they might be. Such vertical integration was only possible as a result of the money available for investment through the institutions of finance capital.

Vertical organization

A second form of corporate organization was a horizontal formation: the cartel. These were combinations of individual companies producing the same kind of goods, joined for the purpose of controlling, if not eliminating, competition. Since their products were iden-

Horizontal organization; cartels

J. P. Morgan

Opposition to cartels

Business and government

tical, an identical price could be charged. Companies involved in the production of coal and steel were especially suited to the organization of cartels because of the costs of initial capitalization. It is very expensive to build, equip, and man a steel foundry; thus there were relatively few of them. And because there were few, they were the more easily organized into a combine. Cartels were particularly strong in Germany; less so in France, where there was not as much heavy industry, where the tradition of the small family firm was particularly entrenched, and where there was longstanding opposition to competition in the form of price-cutting and general intra-industrial warfare. In Britain, though some cartels were formed, continuing subscription to the policy of free trade meant that companies would find it difficult to maintain fixed prices. How could they do so if they could not exclude, by means of a tariff, foreign competitors who wanted to undersell them? Germany had abandoned the policy of free trade in 1879; the United States, where cartels were known as trusts, did the same after the Civil War, though not all at once. Britain, however, clung to free trade until well into the twentieth century.

Defenders of the cartel argued that the elimination of competition brought more stable prices and more continuous employment. They pointed out as well that cartels almost always reduced the cost of production. Opponents questioned, however, whether those reduced costs were reflected in lower prices, or, as they charged, in higher stockholder profits. Critics of cartels were vocal in the United States, where the so-called captains of industry, most prominently the financier J. P. Morgan (1837–1913), were attacked as a new breed of feudal barons. The Sherman Anti-Trust Act was passed by Congress in 1890 to curb the practice of industrial combination. It had little effect in retarding the process, however, until the trust-busting presidency of Theodore Roosevelt (1901–1908).

Elsewhere in the West at the end of the nineteenth century, governments and big business tended to develop close working relationships contrary to the laissez-faire theories of early industrial entrepreneurs. A significant manifestation of this new partnership was the appearance of businessmen and financiers as officers of state. Joseph Chamberlain, a Birmingham manufacturer, served as Britain's colonial secretary; the German banker Bernhard Dernberg was German secretary of state for colonies; the Frenchman Charles Jonnart, president of the Suez Canal Company and the Saint-Étienne steel works, was later governor-general of Algeria; Guilio Prinetti, a north Italian industrialist, was his country's foreign minister from 1901 to 1903. The interrelationship between government and industry, like the growth of cartels and combines, was seen as a natural development in the capitalist system which, its defenders argued, was showering its benefits on all classes of society.

4. INTERNATIONAL COMPETITION: BRITAIN VS. GERMANY

Throughout the period we have been examining, Britain and Germany were locked in industrial competition. By 1914, both the United States and Germany were outproducing Britain in a number of areas. Yet the German challenge was, for the British, the more significant. Industrial competition with Germany helped reshape international political alliances at the end of the century. Britain, moving to align itself with its ancient enemy France against the Germans, found itself engaged in a contest of naval superiority with the latter, determined that in that field the British would not lose their age-old advantage to the upstart challenger.

To what degree did the Germans succeed in overtaking the British? By 1914, Britain's industrial-commercial day was by no means over. The volume of German trade at the turn of the century was no more than 60 percent as great. Because Britain was more mature industrially than Germany, the service sector of its economy was now expanding faster than its manufacturing sector. A greater proportion of the work force was involved in the business of distributing and selling goods than of making them. If Britain's output of manufactured goods did no more than double between 1870 and 1913, as compared to Germany's sixfold increase, it was in part for this reason. Nor should one suppose that all areas of German industry were functioning as efficient, modernized, and technologically advanced units. For every up-to-date chemical plant, for every thriving steel mill, there were many smaller workshops where manufacturing took place on little more than a domestic scale. Having said this, however, the fact remains that the Germans *were* a powerful threat to the British. Even before 1870, Germany had ceased to provide a ready market for British manufactures; the Germans were supplying their own needs. After 1870, Germany began to export to the rest of the world. Moving into markets that the British had considered exclusively their own, German salesmen promoted German goods in Australia, South America, China, and in Britain itself. In fields such as the manufacture of organic chemicals and electrical equipment, Germany outsold Britain across the globe.

The extent of Germany's achievement

How can Germany's success and, perhaps more important, Britain's inability to counter it be explained? To begin with, Britain was handicapped because it had been the first nation to industrialize. Because of the capital they had invested in older factories and equipment, the British were reluctant to enter new fields or to exploit new methods. For example, because the British had constructed plants to manufacture alkali by an earlier, less efficient process, they found themselves trapped into continuing to produce in that way after the Solvay process had

Reasons for Britain's lag:
(1) the problem of priority

been discovered. Rather than make the expensive switch, British manufacturers attempted to make their alkali more competitive by cutting costs and improving worker efficiency. But when further refinements were introduced in the 1890s, British output not only failed to keep pace with German and also American increases but actually decreased. The same difficulties arose with steel. Here again Britain was hampered by the problem of priority. Because the British were the first to industrialize, their manufacturing centers took shape in accordance with the scale of early– and mid–nineteenth-century production. Now there was need for large tracts of land, close to transportation, to accommodate steel mills. Because of the cramped layout of Britain's industrial cities, it could not build mills as large as those in Germany or the United States. The result was that by 1900 the largest British steel mills were no bigger than the average-sized mills in Germany. Even new plants built for other manufacturing purposes in Britain were only a third as large as those constructed by its major rival. Because German plants were big, and because, therefore, they represented a large investment of capital, those who managed them did all they could to ensure their efficient operation. They rationalized design and standardized parts to an extent the British, with their smaller plants, continued to believe unnecessary. Smaller firms tended to receive smaller and more specialized orders which did not encourage standardization. Although standardization was accomplished by 1914 in Britain in some industries—notably iron and steel—in many others it remained more the exception than the rule.

(2) *attitudes*   Britain's industrial lead, which froze its urban areas into obsolete patterns and thus prevented growth, froze British attitudes as well. Because they had come so far so fast, the British had grown complacent. Nowhere is this fact more clearly reflected than in the British attitude toward education. If the achievements of the first Industrial Revolution—for example, the steam engine, the spinning jenny—were the result of what might be called creative tinkering, those of the second revolution were the product of a close and fruitful union of pure science with technology. Achievement now depended on a generally literate workforce, a trained body of mechanics, a scientifically grounded body of technicians, and a corps of highly trained, creative scientists. Germany was producing these cadres; Britain was not. Only in 1870 was a system of public elementary education instituted in Britain, and not until ten years later was it made compulsory. In Germany, compulsory education dated from the eighteenth century. The British governing class believed the primary purpose of working-class education was control: teaching a boy or girl not only how to read and write, but to accept his or her particular place within the social structure. Though German elementary education was authoritarian in many respects as well, the fact that it had begun earlier and was directly joined to systems of secondary education encouraged

the development of abilities; it was in this respect far less wasteful than that of the British. As Britain lagged in the area of elementary education, it lagged in the development of scientific and technological laboratories and training centers. In Germany, the state established an elaborate network of such technical institutions; in Britain there were almost none before the First World War.

Complacency was the major reason for this lack. The British tended to believe, wrongly, that practical experience and on-the-job training would produce the skills necessary to keep abreast of change. In addition, the British upper middle class convinced itself that the goal of education was not the production of creative technologists but of "gentlemen." Fathers who had made their fortunes as entrepreneurs during the first Industrial Revolution sent their sons to private boarding schools and to the ancient universities of Oxford and Cambridge to receive a "gentleman's" education—training in Greek and Latin, primarily. Those sons, whose creative talents might otherwise have been channeled into science and technology, chose careers in politics, or in the imperial or domestic bureaucracies instead. The result was a severe narrowing of the pool of creative technologists and dynamic entrepreneurs. There were fewer men than in either Germany or the United States interested in organizing the increasingly large amounts of capital necessary to engage in industrial expansion. It was easier to invest money overseas than to undertake the revitalization of various enterprises at home. A suspicion of what was new, encouraged by the British tendency to rely upon practical experience of the past, prevented Britain from rising in more than a fitful way to the German challenge.

Complacency

5. INTERNATIONAL COMPETITION: IMPERIALISM

The rivalry between Britain and Germany was only the most intense aspect of international competitiveness during the last decades of the nineteenth century. As nations proceeded with the business of industrialization, their search for markets brought them into direct opposition with one another. One result was that the dogma of free trade was abandoned by all save Britain. As we have seen, the Germans rejected the policy of low tariffs in 1879. Austria and Russia had already done so. Spain instituted new scales of import duties in 1877 and again in 1891. In France, two decades of gradual abandonment were climaxed by the passage of the Méline Tariff in 1892. Although individual nations attempted to isolate themselves from each other in this way, developments in international economics mandated the continuing growth and development of an interlocking, worldwide system of manufacturing, trade, and finance. The general adoption by western Europe and the United States of the gold standard meant that the

A global economy

"Invisible" exports

Effects on Africa and Asia

currencies of the so-called civilized world could be readily exchanged with each other against the measure of a common standard—the international price of gold. Hence countries needing to import from the United States, for example, did not have to sell goods directly to that country. They could sell to South America, exchange the money they received for gold, and then buy from America.

Almost all European countries, dependent on vast supplies of raw materials to sustain their rate of industrial production, imported more than they exported. To avoid the mounting deficits that would otherwise have resulted from this practice, they relied upon "invisible" exports: i.e., shipping, insurance, and interest on money lent or invested. The extent of Britain's exports in these areas was far greater than that of any other country. London was the money market of the world, to which would-be borrowers looked for assistance before turning elsewhere. By 1914, Britain had $20 billion invested overseas, compared with the $8.7 of the French and the $6 billion of the Germans. The insurance firm of Lloyds of London served clients around the world. The British merchant fleet transported the manufactured goods and raw materials of every trading nation. It was the volume of its "invisible" exports that permitted Britain to remain faithful to the doctrine of free trade while other European nations were forced to institute tariffs.

The competition between the principal economic powers of this worldwide marketplace affected not only their relationships with each other but also with those less developed areas upon which they were increasingly dependent for both raw materials and markets. Some of those areas, such as India and China, were the seats of ancient empires. Others, such as central Africa, sheltered equally complex though less geographically expansive cultures. No matter what the nature of the indigenous civilization, the intrusion upon it of modern science and technology, systematic wage labor, financial and legal institutions caused enormous disruption. Though drawn into the world economy, these areas did not draw from it the benefits that the West did. Native industries such as Indian textile spinning and weaving stood no chance in competition with the factory-made products of Manchester. African herdsmen and hunters endured the disruption of their living habits by the activities of European ranchers and miners. Men who had made their living as boatmen and carters lost their livelihood to the railways constructed by Western nations. New jobs there might be; but they were jobs worked according to a Western style, dictated by Western economic demands, and threatened by Western economic disorders. In great measure the workers of this emerging world were assuming the role of a global unskilled working class under the hegemony of Western capitalism.

With this global background in mind, we can better understand the history of late-nineteenth-century imperialism—the subjugation by the European powers of vast tracts of land and indigenous populations, primarily on the continents of Africa and Asia. Imperialism was by no means a new phenomenon. During the eighteenth century, the French had penetrated Algeria and the British, India. In other parts of the world, where Western powers did not govern directly, they often exercised an indirect influence so powerful as to shape the policies and dictate the activities of indigenous authorities. When the West "opened" China beginning in 1834, it left the Chinese in nominal charge of their state. But it ensured that affairs would be conducted to its advantage and within its "sphere of influence." Britain added in this way to its "informal" empire, expanding into South America, Africa, and south and east Asia.

Earlier imperialism

As international rivalries increased, European powers moved with greater frequency and determination to control both the government and economy of underdeveloped nations and territories. French politicians supported imperialism as a means of restoring national prestige and honor, lost in the humiliating defeat by the Germans in the Franco-Prussian War of 1870–1871. The British, on the other hand, looked with alarm at the accelerating pace of industrialization in Germany and France and feared losing their existing and potential world markets. The Germans, recently unified in a modern nation, viewed overseas empire as a "national" possession and as a way of entering the "club" of great powers. Social Darwinists, so ubiquitous at the time, arrogantly distorted Darwinian theories of evolution and survival of the fittest in order to further rationalize the conquest of seemingly less evolved and technologically weaker societies.

European views of overseas empire

The West's stunning inventions of the late eighteenth and nineteenth centuries provided the very tools of imperialism. Metal-hulled steamships, widely used in Africa from the 1850s, provided faster, cheaper transportation and allowed for the shipment of bulk cargoes such as unprocessed crops and heavy ores. Travel time between Liverpool and Cape Town was reduced from an average of three months to three weeks. Sail power quickly lost out to steam. By the same token, river and lake steamers overcame the problem of transportation in the African interior. Submarine telegraph cables also brought Africa closer to Europe. By 1885, West and South Africa were linked to London and Paris. With the use of quinine, malaria became less threatening and Europeans were emboldened to penetrate the tropical rain forests. In military technology, the shift in Africa from muzzle-loading rifles to fast-firing breechloaders was completed by 1878. European armies gained an even greater advantage with the introduction in 1884 of the Maxim gun, a prototype of the modern machine gun, capable of firing eleven bullets a second. These and other inventions and scientific breakthroughs made imperialist conquest and resource exploitation vastly cheaper and eminently more viable.

Technology as a tool of imperialism

The scope, intensity, and long-range consequences of this so-called

Technology and Empire. A traction engine hauling an army road train in South Africa during the Boer War.

new imperialism of the late nineteenth century have generated a debate about its causes as heated as that which surrounds the first Industrial Revolution. One influential group of social critics and historians has argued that the causes were predominantly, if not exclusively, economic. As early as 1902, the English social reformer and theorist, J. A. Hobson, charged that what he called "the scramble for Africa" had occurred as a result of the economic interests of a small group of extremely rich and influential financiers throughout western Europe. Hobson declared that the colonization of Africa had produced little economic gain for the taxpayers whose countries had dispatched armies of conquest and occupation at the behest of international capitalists. Profits went only to the rich, who ventured beyond the bounds of economically stagnant western Europe in search of a higher return on their investments than could be realized at home. Hobson concluded that late–nineteenth-century imperialism was "a depraved choice of national life," appealing primarily to "the lusts of self-seeking acquisitiveness and forceful domination."

Imperialism as economics: Hobson

Hobson's analysis inspired a more influential critique of imperialism by the Russian communist and future revolutionary leader, Vladimir I. Lenin. Lenin agreed with Hobson that imperialism was an economic phenomenon. But, unlike Hobson, he saw it as an integral and inevitable phase of the capitalist system, as the title of his 1916 treatise, *Imperialism: The Last Stage of Capitalism,* explicitly declared. Capitalist competition, Lenin argued, and the consequent monopolies that it had produced, had lowered domestic profits, and thus compelled the owners of surplus capital to invest it overseas. The alternative, enlarging home markets by raising wages, would serve only to further

Lenin

decrease profits. Imperialism was thus the creature of the internal contradictions of industrial capitalism.

While most historians would agree that economic pressures were one important cause of imperialism, they have remained uncomfortable with analyses that ignore other factors they consider equally important. They remain prepared to acknowledge the role of economics when it seems to make sense to do so: in the case of Great Britain, for example, where about half its total of £4 billion in foreign investments was at work within its empire. In all western European countries, demand for raw materials made colonies a necessary investment and helped persuade governments that imperialism was a worthwhile policy. Yet the economic explanation begins to break down when one considers facts like the following: that colonial markets were generally too poor to answer the needs of European manufacturers; that Africa, the continent over which there was the greatest "scramble," was also the poorest and least profitable to investors; that only a very small portion of German capital was invested in German colonies before 1914; that only one-fifth of French capital was so invested; that, indeed, the French had more capital invested in Russia, hoping to stabilize that ally against the Germans, than in all their colonial possessions. With the decline of the Atlantic slave trade and the completion of the Suez Canal, Africa between the Sahara and the Limpopo River became increasingly marginal to the global economy. Indeed, there was little enthusiasm for territorial conquest in Africa from British, European, and American industrial and financial interests. The most ardent promoters were the journalists, missionaries, military leaders, and politicians.

*Limits to the
economic
argument*

Those in charge of the imperial building process decided policy in response to a combination of political and economic considerations, and as a corollary to the process of nation-building. National security and the preservation of a general balance of power were issues never far from the forefront of politicians' thinking and planning. Great-power interest in the eastern Mediterranean grew with the demise of the Ottoman Empire. At the Berlin Conference of 1878, France secured from Great Britain and Germany the assurance of a free hand in Tunisia as compensation for its acquiescence in British annexation of Cyprus. This understanding breathed new life into the principle that remuneration of territorial claims in one region must be compensated for by concessions elsewhere.

*Imperialism
and international
politics*

Britain's domination of Egypt in the 1880s was the result, in large measure, of its fear of what might occur in the Near East should large portions of the decaying Ottoman Empire fall into Russian hands. Britain had purchased 44 percent of the shares in the Suez Canal Company in 1875, and considered the waterway a strategic lifeline to the East. The canal had been built by the French under the direction of the engineer Ferdinand de Lesseps. Begun in 1859 and completed in 1869, it was expected to assist France in its bid for commercial

*British domination of
Egypt*

expansion to the East. Britain obtained its shares from the spendthrift khedive (viceroy) of Egypt at a time when he was threatened with bankruptcy. When, in 1882, nationalist rebels protested continuing British intervention in the internal affairs of Egypt, the British claimed they had no choice but to bombard the port of Alexandria and place the Egyptian ruler under their protection. At this point British motivation owed more to concern for the security of its economic interests in Egypt than to the danger posed to the Suez Canal by the ambitions of the French, who began expanding in West and Equatorial Africa in 1879. A continuing British presence in Egypt, and the willingness of the British government to support Egyptian claims to the Upper Nile, worried the French, who were growing to fear Britain's political domination of the entire African continent. Moving to correct what they perceived as a severe political imbalance, the French challenged the British and at Fashoda, in the Sudan, came close to war in 1898. The British called the French bluff, however, and war was averted.

Imperial policy-making

The power struggle over Suez, Egypt, and the Sudan suggests that what passed for "imperial policy" was less a matter of long-range planning than of a series of pragmatic and often spontaneous responses to particular colonial political and economic situations. Often those in charge of policy-making found themselves led beyond their original ambitions, not only by the demands of international rivalries, but by the actions of individual explorers and entrepreneurs who established claims to hitherto unknown territories which home governments then felt compelled to recognize and defend.

"The white man's burden"

Imperialism must also be understood as something more than official policy, whether carefully conceived or accidental. A French diplomat once described the dynamic English imperial adventurer Cecil Rhodes as "a force cast in an idea"; the same might be said of imperialism itself. Imperialism as an idea excited the minds of explorers like the Scottish missionary David Livingstone, who believed that his country's conquest of Africa would put an end to the East African slave trade, and "introduce the Negro family into the body of corporate nations." Rudyard Kipling, the English poet and novelist, wrote of "the white man's burden," of his mission to civilize the "half devil, half child" races that inhabited what most Europeans considered the "barbaric" and "heathen" quarters of the globe. To combat slave-trading, famine, filth, and illiteracy seemed to many a legitimate reason for invading the jungles of Africa and Asia.

Imperial propaganda

Imperialism as an idea was also of use to European governments at home. A populace could be encouraged to forget domestic hardships as it celebrated its country's triumphs overseas. Patriotism—a not always attractive corollary to nation-building—was stimulated by arguments such as that expressed by the German historian Heinrich von Treitschke in 1887: that "the colonizing impulse has become a vital question for a great nation"—the implication clearly being that a nation was not great unless it possessed colonies. Associations with a

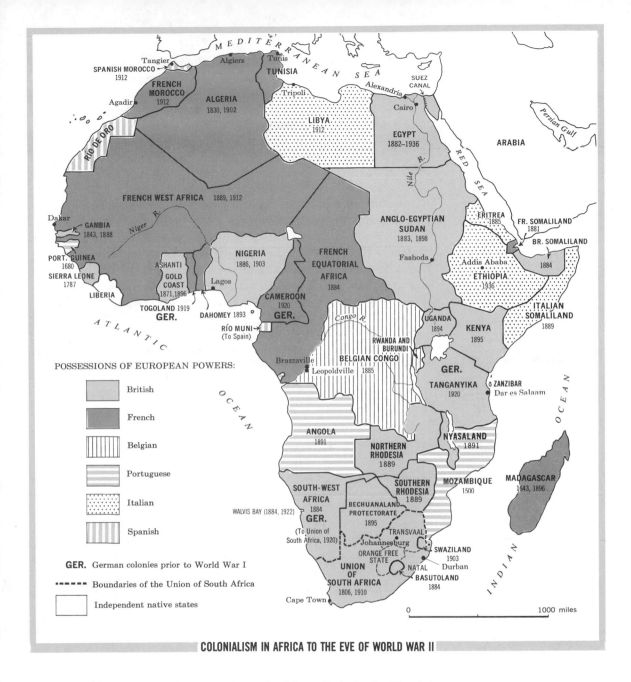

POSSESSIONS OF EUROPEAN POWERS:

- British
- French
- Belgian
- Portuguese
- Italian
- Spanish

GER. German colonies prior to World War I

‐ ‐ ‐ ‐ Boundaries of the Union of South Africa

Independent native states

0 _____ 1000 miles

COLONIALISM IN AFRICA TO THE EVE OF WORLD WAR II

semi-official standing—the Deutsche Kolonialgesellschaft, the Comité de l'Afrique Française, the Royal Colonial Institute—propagandized on behalf of empire, as did newspapers, which recognized in sensational stories of overseas conquest a means of attracting a newly literate clientele.

Imperial competition centered in Africa. In 1875, 11 percent of the continent was in European hands; by 1902, 90 percent. Germans pressed inward from the east; Frenchmen from the west. The Portu-

The colonization of
Africa

The Berlin Conference of
1885

The scramble for territory

guese schemed to connect the ancient colonies of Angola, on the west, with Mozambique, on the east. Most active among the European powers during this initial period of late–nineteenth-century colonization was a privately financed group of Belgians under the leadership of that country's king, Leopold II. In association with H. M. Stanley, a British-born naturalized American newspaperman and explorer, Leopold and a group of financiers founded the International Congo Association in 1878, which negotiated treaties with chieftains that opened the Congo River basin to commercial exploitation. The British were not fearful of Leopold's activities in the Congo because Belgium was a small, politically neutral European kingdom that espoused free trade. France, however, was a different matter. Britain challenged French claims to the mouth of the Congo River in 1882 on the grounds that it belonged to Portugal under treaties signed with Africans four centuries earlier. The British were determined to prevent France, by then a protectionist power, from gaining control over the vast Congo basin and river system.

A conference, called in Berlin in 1885 and attended by most European nations and the United States, attempted to establish ground rules for the game of imperial acquisition. The Congo was declared a Free State, under the trusteeship of Leopold (the first example of this soon-to-be-familiar device of protecting "backward" peoples). A European nation with holdings on the African coast was declared to have first rights to territory in the interior behind those coastal regions. Those rights, however, could be sustained only by what was termed "real" occupation—that is, the presence of either troops or administrators. The scramble was on! France, already advancing into the West African Sudan, accelerated its military thrust. The British, Portuguese, and Germans were more cautious and chartered private companies to hire and equip imperialist armies. But military conquest and establishment of effective administration were costly and arduous in the face of pockets of fierce African resistance. By 1897 it was clear that these companies could not advance swiftly enough, and thus the British and the French formed their own forces. Occupation was accompanied by the exploitation of native labor. Agreements reached with local chieftains, whom the Europeans courted, authorized the employment of men and women as laborers under conditions little better than slavery. Often compelled to live in compounds apart from their families, Africans were victimized by a system which rooted out prevailing custom without attempting to establish anything like a new civilization in its place. In the Congo, the Arab slave trade was suppressed, replaced by a system of forced labor. Tribal lands were confiscated and rebellions brutally crushed.

The division of the geographical spoils accelerated after 1885. The Portuguese increased their hold in Angola and Mozambique. The Italians invaded Somaliland and Eritrea. They attempted to extend their control to Ethiopia, but were repulsed by an army of 80,000 Ethiopians, the first instance of a major victory by Africans over whites. Germany came relatively late to the game. Bismarck was reluctant to engage in an enterprise which, he believed, would do little to profit the empire either politically or economically. Eventually concluding, however, that they could not afford to let other powers divide the continent among them, the Germans established colonies in German East Africa, in the Cameroons and Togo on the west coast, and in the desertlike territory of South-West Africa. The French controlled large areas in West Africa and, in the Red Sea, the port of Djibouti. It was to further their plan for an east-west link that the French risked challenging the British at Fashoda. That scheme, however, fell afoul of Britain's need to dominate Egypt, and of its plans for a north-south connection through the African continent.

The new imperialism was largely the result of the breakdown of older collaborative mechanisms among the various European powers and between them and the African states. Some African kingdoms and republics were themselves engaged in imperial expansion, notably Madagascar, Ethiopia, Matabeleland, Liberia, the Transvaal, and the Islamic empires of Samory Touré and Alhaji Umar in the West African savannah. Many of these African states mounted stiff resistance to the European imperialists, but in the end all but Ethiopia and Liberia lost their independence.

Cecil Rhodes, the British-born entrepreneur and imperial visionary, promoted the notion of a Cape Town-to-Cairo railway and telegraph network both before and after his assumption of the prime ministership of the Cape Colony in 1890. A fervent believer in the superiority of Anglo-Saxon civilization, Rhodes dreamed of creating a series of British states stretching the length of the continent that would be politically autonomous but economically and culturally bound to Great Britain and its sprawling empire. His plans were thwarted in the east by the Germans and Belgians and in the south by two independent neighboring republics, the Transvaal and the Orange Free State. Both were inhabited by Afrikaans-speaking descendants of the original Dutch, French, and German settlers in South Africa. These Boers, the Dutch word for "farmers," were so suspicious of the more secular, urban-oriented English-speaking intruders that they left the Cape Colony in the late 1830s to avoid being engulfed by them.

The British largely ignored the so-called Trekker republics until 1886, when vast quantities of gold were discovered in the Transvaal. Railway lines were extended to the gold-rich Witwatersrand, and the agrarian-minded Afrikaners welcomed foreign capital and technology. They were, however, loathe to give the English-speaking miners political power commensurate with their growing economic muscle. The British were afraid that the Transvaal would obtain an independent outlet to the sea through Mozambique or German South-West Africa. By 1889 the Transvaal was producing 25 percent of the world's annual gold output. Most of it was shipped from British-controlled seaports to London where it was used to maintain the pound Sterling as the premier currency for world trade and finance. The predominantly

Rising tensions in South
Africa culminate in the
Boer War

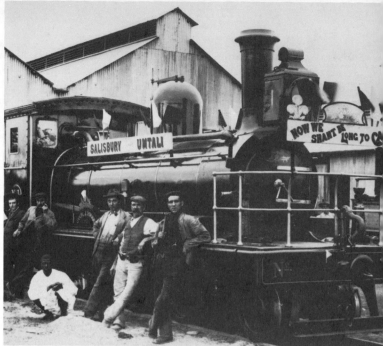

Left: *"The Rhodes Colossus."* The ambitions of Cecil Rhodes, the driving force behind British imperialism in South Africa, are satirized in this cartoon, which appeared in *Punch*. Right: *"Now We Shant Be Long to Cairo."* So read the banner across Engine No. 1 taking the first train from Umtali to Salisbury, Rhodesia, reflecting Cecil Rhodes's vision of a Capetown to Cairo railway as a symbol of British domination of the African continent.

British-owned mining companies demanded a new political order, more compatible with the needs of the extractive industries and urban industrial capitalism. Rhodes saw the Transvaal as a threat to Anglo-Saxon hegemony in southern Africa, and with the acquiescence of the British Colonial Office in London he conspired to overthrow Paul Kruger's government in Pretoria. In 1895 he dispatched a force of irregular volunteers under the command of Dr. L. S. Jameson to the Transvaal, but they were captured before they had a chance to unite with the English-speaking mining community. The abortive Jameson raid was a political fiasco, precipitating international censure of the British for harassing a peaceful and weaker neighbor. Rhodes was forced to resign as prime minister of the Cape Colony a year later. The British remained intent on bringing all of South Africa under their control, so when diplomatic pressure failed to produce the desired result war broke out in 1899. Its course, however, did not run according to British plans. The Boers proved tough fighters. It took three years to secure an armistice; it took further long months and resort to brutal policies such as detention camps and farm-burning to bring the resilient republicans to heel. The war's consequences were British loss of international prestige, and a heightening of the Anglo-German rivalry, the kaiser having publicly pronounced his sympathy with the Boer cause.

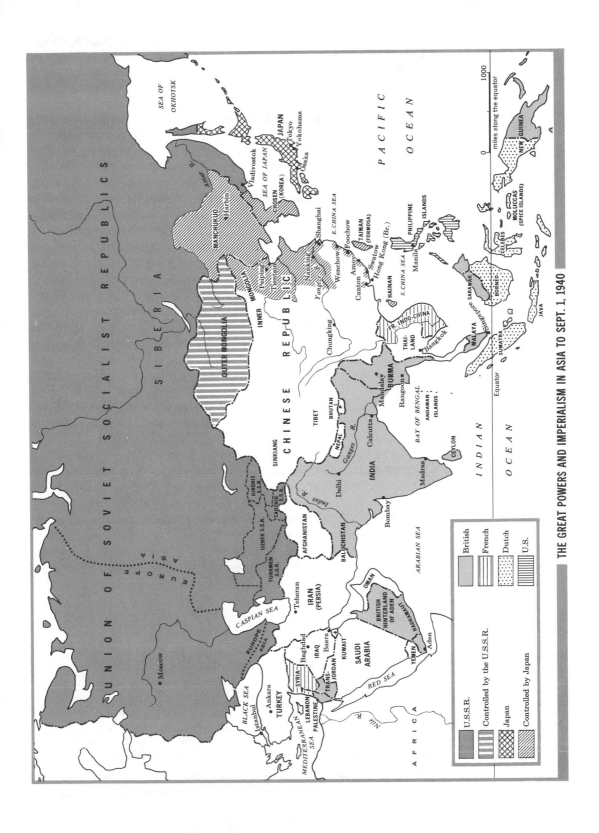

THE GREAT POWERS AND IMPERIALISM IN ASIA TO SEPT. 1, 1940

Legend:
- U.S.S.R.
- Controlled by the U.S.S.R.
- Japan
- Controlled by Japan
- British
- French
- Dutch
- U.S.

0 — 1000 miles along the equator

"The Execution of 'John Company.'" This 1857 *Punch* cartoon graphically depicts the abolition of the East India Company in the wake of the "Indian Mutiny."

British colonial rule

Imperialism elsewhere

Britain managed to increase its hold on its prize imperial possession—India—throughout the nineteenth century. The "informal" rule of the commercially motivated East India Company had proved ineffective in 1857, when native Indian troops and a large number of other disaffected elements within the subcontinent rebelled in what the British chose to call "The Indian Mutiny," but which was in fact a far more serious and deep-seated challenge to foreign control. Henceforth the British government administered the subcontinent. But at the same time, they decided to rule through the Indian upper classes, and not, as in the past, in opposition to them. Although instruction in British-sponsored schools continued in English, Indian customs were tolerated as they had not been before, and princes and their bureaucracies were incorporated as protectorates into the general scheme of government. A class of westernized, and yet devotedly Indian, civil servants and businessmen thus emerged by the end of the nineteenth century, trained by the British yet burdened by no sense of obligation to their tutors. This group provided the leadership for the nationalist movement that was to challenge British rule in India during the mid–twentieth century. Britain's aim in India was to promote order and stability. Civil servants administered justice even-handedly; they promoted improved sanitation, which, ironically, helped to increase the country's population beyond the point where it could sustain itself. The vast majority of Indians remained desperately poor, victims in many cases of the importation of cheap manufactured goods which threatened indigenous industries and testified to Britain's willingness to subordinate its colonies' economic well-being to its own.

The pattern of British imperialism differed throughout the world. In areas dominated by white settlers, home rule was introduced in hopes of preventing the sort of disaffection that had produced the American Revolution. Australia was granted self-government in the 1850s, New Zealand in 1876. In 1867, a united Dominion of Canada, with its own federal governments and legislatures, was established.

Elsewhere in the world, Western nations hastened to plant their colors upon those territories that promised rewards, either economic or strategic. Britain, France, Germany, and the Netherlands all staked claims in the East Indies, the Dutch achieving an overall hegemony there by 1900. China allowed itself to be victimized by a series of commercial treaties; among the predators was China's neighbor Japan, the only non-Western nation able to modernize in the nineteenth century. The United States played a double game. It acted as champion of the underdeveloped countries in the Western Hemisphere when they were threatened from Europe. Yet the Americans were willing, whenever it suited them, to prey on their neighbors, either "informally" or formally. When, at the end of the century, Spain's feeble hold on its Caribbean and Pacific colonies encouraged talk of rebellion, the United States stepped in to protect its investments and guarantee its maritime security. It declared and won the Spanish-American War in 1898 on trumped-up grounds. In the same year, the United States annexed

Imperialism. Left: Germans traveling in East Africa, 1907. Right: A British officer in India, c. 1900.

Puerto Rico and the Philippines, and established a "protectorate" over Cuba. When Colombia's colony, Panama, threatened to rebel in 1903, the Americans quickly backed the rebels, recognized Panama as a republic, and then proceeded to grant it protection while Americans built the Panama Canal on land leased from the new government. Intervention in Santo Domingo and in Hawaii proved that the United States was no less an imperial power than the nations of western Europe. Together, by the end of the century, those countries had succeeded in binding the world together as it had never been before. The military and economic power with which they had accomplished that achievement meant that, for the time being at any rate, they would be the world's masters.

SELECTED READINGS

• *Items so designated are available in paperback editions.*

• Ashworth, W., *A Short History of the International Economy since 1850,* rev. ed., London, 1975. A good introduction.
• Austin, Ralph, *African Economic History,* Portsmouth, N.H., 1987. The first comprehensive examination of sub-Saharan Africa's economic history, focusing on internal development and external dependency.

Barkin, Kenneth D., *The Controversy over German Industrialization, 1890–1902,* Chicago, 1970. The political and social struggles between agricultural and industrial interests.

Cameron, Rondo E., *France and the Economic Development of Europe, 1800–1914,* Princeton, 1961. Emphasizes the export of French capital and skill in the economic growth of Europe.

———, *Economics and Empire, 1830–1914,* London, 1973. Argues against the primacy of economic factors in the spread of imperialism.

• Gollwitzer, Heinz, *Europe in the Age of Imperialism, 1880–1914,* London, 1969. A brief survey with excellent illustrations.
• Headrick, Daniel R., *The Tools of Empire: Technology and European Imperialism in the Nineteenth Century,* Oxford, 1981. A study of the relationship between technological innovation and imperialism.
• Hobsbawm, Eric, *Industry and Empire: The Making of Modern English Society, 1750 to the Present Day,* New York, 1968. Emphasizes the economic background of imperialism.
• Hobson, J. A., *Imperialism: A Study,* London, 1902.
  Kieran, V. G., *Marxism and Imperialism,* New York, 1975. Argues the Marxist position effectively.
• Kindleberger, C. P., *Economic Growth in France and Britain, 1851–1950,* Cambridge, Mass., 1963. A technical account.
• Landes, David S., *The Unbound Prometheus,* London, 1969. Particularly good on the Anglo–German rivalry.
  Langer, William L., *The Diplomacy of Imperialism, 1890–1902,* New York, 1960. A thorough, standard work, useful for its analysis of the intellectual as well as political origins of imperialism.
• Lenin, Vladimir, *Imperialism: The Highest Stage of Capitalism,* 1916. (Many English editions.)
  Louis, William Roger, ed., *Imperialism: The Robinson and Gallagher Controversy,* New York, 1976. The best introduction to recent debate over the nature and causes of imperialism.
  Miller, Michael B., *The Bon Marché: Bourgeois Culture and the Department Store, 1869–1920,* Princeton, 1981. Explores the revolution in merchandising of the late nineteenth century.
  Milward, Alan S., and S. B. Saul, *The Development of the Economies of Continental Europe, 1850–1914,* Cambridge, Mass., 1977. An excellent, comprehensive text, particularly good on the smaller European nations.
  Oliver, Roland, and G. N. Sanderson, eds., *Cambridge History of Africa,* vol. 6, c. 1870 to c. 1905, Cambridge, 1985. An excellent collection of essays on the period of partition and the foundations of twentieth-century colonial rule.
  Price, Roger, *The Economic Modernization of France, 1730–1880,* New York, 1975. Rejects conventional periodizations; stresses the advent of railroads, which transformed the market structure of France.
• Reitz, Deneys, *Commando: A Boer Journal of the Boer War,* London, 1929. A superb memoir of the Boer War.
  Robinson, Ronald, and J. Gallagher, *Africa and the Victorians: The Official Mind of Imperialism,* London, 1961. Contains their famous thesis that imperialism was not deliberately pursued as a policy of state, but rather was a response to events in colonial areas.
• Shannon, Richard, *The Crisis of Imperialism, 1865–1915,* St. Albans, England, 1976. An excellent survey of the transformation of British society in the wake of modern industrialization.
  Stolper, Gustav, et al., *The German Economy, 1870 to 1940,* New York, 1967. A good introduction.

Chapter 31

THE MIDDLE CLASS CHALLENGED

The time of surprise attacks, of revolutions carried through by small conscious minorities at the head of unconscious masses, is past. Where it is a question of a complete transformation of the social organization, the masses themselves must also be in it, must themselves already have grasped what is at stake, what they are going in for, with body and soul.

—Friedrich Engels, Introduction to Karl Marx, *The Class Struggles in France, 1848–50*

Capitalism's continuing expansion encouraged middle-class men and women at the end of the nineteenth century to believe themselves the necessary key to the progress of the human race. At the same time, however, that belief was being challenged from several directions. In each case, the challenges called into question assumptions close to the core of middle-class consciousness. Socialist doctrine, which was for the first time receiving a widespread hearing, pronounced capitalism a threat, rather than a boon, to society. New scientific theories—particularly the theory of evolution—declared that the key to progress was not the well-laid schemes of humanity, but chance. Psychologists discovered the irrationality of human beings and philosophers their ultimate helplessness. Paintings, poetry, and music proclaimed an artists' revolution on behalf of the idea of art for its own sake, not for the edification of a middle-class public. Together, these various intellectual and cultural currents threatened the notion that society would most successfully advance under middle-class auspices, setting its course in accordance with middle-class moral and economic precepts, and placing its faith in a belief in the importance and inevitability of continued material progress.

The dimensions of the challenge

I. THE CHALLENGE OF SOCIALISM

Marx in England

The history of socialism in the latter half of the nineteenth century is, to a great degree, the biography of its most famous propagandist and theoretician, Karl Marx (1818–1883). Marx was both a social thinker and a political leader. At certain times theory dictated his actions; at others, political events led him to alter doctrine. But always he was at the center of the socialist movement, his moral passion, as much as his scholarly research, shaping the course of its events. The fact of his continuing influence is particularly remarkable for two reasons. First, although a German, he lived from 1849 until his death in London, an exile from the mainstream of continental socialism, in a country whose toleration of socialists was a mark of its comparative immunity from their doctrines. Second, Marx was not a leader who readily took others into his confidence. His antisocial nature was due, in part, to the poverty in which he was forced to live. He and his family were kept alive by gifts of money from his faithful friend and collaborator, Friedrich Engels, and by occasional stints as a political journalist—for a time Marx was a correspondent for the *New York Tribune*.

Capital

During the 1850s and 1860s Marx labored to produce his definitive analysis of capitalist economics, *Capital,* the first volume of which was published in 1867. The argument of *Capital* owed a great deal to that dialectical idealism and economic materialism which, as we have seen, shaped Marx's earlier thinking and writing. In *Capital* he synthesized ideas he and Engels had enunciated in their previous tracts. He described in detail the processes of production, exchange, and distribution as they operated within the capitalist system. He argued that under capitalism, workers were denied their rightful share of profits. The value of any manufactured item, Marx claimed, was determined by the amount of labor necessary to produce it. Yet workers were hired at wages whose value was far less than the value of the goods they produced. The difference between the value of workers' wages and the value of their work as sold was pocketed by members of the capitalist class, who, according to Marx, made off with far more than a justifiable portion of the sale price. This so-called labor theory of value, borrowed from a somewhat similar doctrine held by Ricardo and other classical economists, was the basis for Marx's claim that the working class was compelled to suffer under the capitalist system. Because workers were forced to sell their labor they became nothing more than commodities in the economic market.

So long as capitalists refused to pay wages more nearly equal to the labor value of their employees' work, those employees would remain exploited. Marx preached that the only class which, under capitalism, produced more wealth than it enjoyed was the working class, the proletariat. The bourgeoisie, which owned the means of production and

Karl Marx

was therefore able to appropriate that which was rightfully the workers', had a vested interest in maintaining the status quo; hence its willingness to make use of political, social, religious, and legal institutions to keep the proletariat in its place.

Marx predicted that capitalism would eventually do itself in. He argued that as time passed, market competition would compel the formation of ever-larger industrial and financial combinations. As the smaller enterpreneurial class—the petty bourgeoisie—was squeezed out by more powerful combines, its members would join with the proletariat, until society resembled a vast pyramid, with a much-enlarged proletariat at its base and an opposing force of a few powerful capitalists at its tip. At this point, Marx declared, the proletariat would rise in revolution against what was left of the bourgeoisie.

Marx as prophet

After capitalism had received its death blow at the hands of the workers, it would be followed by a socialist stage, characterized by the dictatorship of the proletariat; payment in accordance with work performed; and ownership and operation by the state of all means of production, distribution, and exchange. In time socialism would be succeeded by communism, the goal of historical evolution. Communism would bring with it a classless society. No one would live by owning, but solely by working. The state would now disappear, relegated to the museum of antiquities, "along with the bronze ax and the spinning wheel." Nothing would replace it except voluntary associations to operate the means of production and provide for social necessities. The essence of communism was payment in accordance with needs. The wage system would be abolished, and citizens would be expected to work in accordance with their abilities, entitled to receive from the total fund of wealth produced an amount in proportion to their needs.

The advent of communism

In the ten years after its publication, *Capital* was translated into English (Marx had written it in German), French, Russian, and Italian. The book's widespread appeal was the result of its compelling deterministic certainty and of its vigorous crusading temper. Though much that *Capital* predicted has failed to occur, middle- and working-class socialists reading it soon after its publication and measuring its pronouncements against the capitalistic world they knew had little difficulty in accepting Marx's reasoning. It seemed to them that he had constructed an objective science of society out of their own experiences. The book became the theoretical rallying point for a growing band of socialists who stood opposed to the world the middle class had made. For a time it breathed life into an organization of continental and British workers that had been founded in London in 1864: the International Workingmen's Association, usually referred to as the International. This body had been formed with the declared purpose of forging an international working-class alliance to overthrow capitalism and abolish private property. Marx delivered its inaugural address, in which he preached that workers must win political power

The First International

for themselves if they were ever to escape their industrial bondage. Various difficulties had prevented the formation of a radically oriented workers' organization prior to this time. There was, first of all, fear of official reprisal. Second, the irregular pace of industrialization across Europe meant that workers in one country could have little understanding of the particular plight of their fellow workers elsewhere. Finally, the period after 1850 had witnessed an increase in general prosperity which encouraged the more highly skilled—and more politically conscious—workers to forsake revolutionary goals and to pursue the more immediate end of accommodation with middle-class politicians. The German socialists' dealings with Bismarck (see below, p. 424), were a case in point. Meanwhile, however, the determination of a small band of dedicated radical socialists temporarily surmounted these problems to permit the formation of the first international workers' association.

Lassalle and Bakunin

Marx immediately assumed the direction of the International. He labored to exclude moderates from its councils and denounced the German socialists, and their leader Ferdinand Lassalle (1825–1864), for their failure to oppose Bismarck. The duty of socialists, Marx argued, was not partnership with the state, but rather its overthrow. At the same time Marx battled the doctrines of the Russian anarchist Michael Bakunin (1814–1876), who challenged the socialist notion that social evil was the product of capitalism. Bakunin argued that the state was the ultimate villain, and preached its immediate destruction through isolated acts of terrorism. He also opposed centralization within the International, urging instead a kind of federal autonomy for each national workers' group. To Marx, these individualist notions represented nothing more than reversion to a kind of primitive rebellion, heroic but ultimately fruitless. He succeeded in having Bakunin banished from the International in 1872. The International prospered for a time during the 1860s. Individual trade unions in various countries were persuaded to join in its united campaign, which preached revolution and, through the application of pressure both at the ballot box and in the factory, seemed to promise at least higher wages and shorter hours. Under Marx's direction the International was a highly organized and tightly controlled body, far more effective in this respect than any previous socialist organization.

The troubled International

Yet by 1876 it had faded from existence. Despite Marx's abilities as an authoritarian chief of staff, the International throughout its existence had to battle those same circumstances that had delayed its foundation. In addition, Marx's insistence upon control from the center thwarted a growing desire on the part of individual socialist organizations to pursue programs of immediate benefit to themselves. These factors weakened the International. What probably brought about its demise was its association with events occurring in Paris after the defeat of France by Germany in 1870 in the Franco-Prussian War.

Following the collapse of Napoleon III, a new republic, generally conservative in tone, had been established by the French. In March 1871, the government attempted to disarm the Paris National Guard, a volunteer citizen army with radical political sympathies. The guard refused to surrender, declared its autonomy, deposed officials of the new government, and proclaimed a revolutionary committee—the Commune—as the true government of France. Though this movement is commonly described as a rebellion of dangerous radicals intent upon the destruction of law and order, most of its members resembled the Jacobins of the first French Revolution and belonged largely to the lower middle class. They did not advocate the abolition of private property but rather its wider distribution. Their respect for the deposits in the Bank of France was as scrupulous as any bourgeois financier might have wished. Their most radical political action was a symbolic one: the toppling of a statue of Napoleon I in the Place Vendôme. The movement was precipitated by bitterness over the defeat of Napoleon III and exhaustion by the long siege of Paris that followed. There were fears as well that the central government would be dominated by the rural population to the disadvantage of the urban masses in the capital. After several weeks of frustrating disputation, the conflict turned into a bloody civil war. The Communards killed about sixty hostages, including the archbishop of Paris. The government numbered its victims by the thousands. The courts-martial which were set up executed twenty-six. Thousands of others were sentenced to imprisonment or banishment in New Caledonia, in the South Pacific.

While middle-class Europe reacted in horror at what it mistakenly perceived as a second Reign of Terror, Marx, in the name of the International, extolled the courage of the Communards, who, he wrote, had fought the first pitched battle in the class war he had predicted. In

A Symbol of the Paris Commune. The statue of Napoleon I in Roman garb, a symbol of imperial absolutism, is toppled from its base by the Communards.

Propaganda and the Paris Commune. This photograph, purporting to record the assassination of hostages by the radical Communards, was actually faked by their enemies in an effort to arouse anti-Communard sympathies.

a pamphlet entitled *The Civil War in France* (1871), Marx claimed that the Commune was an example of the transitional form of government through which the working class would have to pass on its way to emancipation. Yet many of the less radical members of the International were frightened and disturbed, not only by the events of the Commune itself, but by the possibility of reprisals against members of an organization that openly praised men and women who were considered by the middle class to be little more than murderers. In 1872 Marx acknowledged defeat by moving the seat of the International's council to the United States, a country far removed from the organization's affairs and from the criticisms that had begun to be heaped upon Marx for his misdirection. In 1876, the First International expired.

Although the International collapsed, socialism continued to gain ground as both a theory and a program. The German Social Democratic party was founded in 1875; a Belgian Socialist party in 1879; and in France, despite the disasters of the Commune, a Socialist party was established in 1905. In England, although socialism was much debated and discussed, no party proclaiming itself socialist emerged. When the Labour party came into being in 1901, however, various socialist societies were represented on its executive council, along with less radical, nonsocialist trade union groups. On the periphery of Europe—in Spain, Italy, and Russia—socialism made less headway. There the absence of widespread industrialization and the educational backwardness of large elements within the population retarded the development of a working-class consciousness, and of socialism as its political expression.

During the years before the First World War, socialists continuously and often bitterly debated the course they should follow as they attempted to achieve their goal of radical change. One group, led by Marx himself until his death, urged socialists to avoid collaboration with other parties to achieve such immediate ends as higher wages, shorter working hours, and unemployment insurance. These reforms, the "purists" declared, were the means by which the bourgeoisie could buy off the proletariat and hence indefinitely postpone revolution. On the other hand, "revisionists" urged their followers to take advantage of the fact that many of them now could vote for socialist candidates in elections. They argued that those candidates, if elected, could help them obtain a better life in the immediate future. Socialist theory might proclaim a worldwide struggle of the proletariat against the bourgeoisie, but was this any reason to turn one's back on a chance to make real headway through the ballot box in achieving reforms that would put a better life within reach of workers and their families?

"Purists" vs. "revisionists"

Revisionism spread despite efforts of the "purists" to put a stop to it. In Germany its most eloquent spokesman was Eduard Bernstein (1850–1932), a Social Democrat and a member of the German parliament, the Reichstag. Bernstein was among the first to question the predictions Marx had made in *Capital*. In his appropriately titled book, *Evolutionary Socialism,* published in 1899, Bernstein pointed out that for most European workers the standard of living had risen since 1850, and that the lower middle class showed no evidence that it wished to identify its interests with those of the proletariat. At the same time, increasingly wider franchises meant that workers had an excellent chance of achieving reform by means of the ballot box. The program of the future was not revolution, but democratic social reform. Bernstein's most outspoken opponent in Germany was his fellow socialist Karl Kautsky (1854–1938), an orthodox Marxist who warned that collaboration would end in the total corruption and demoralization of the proletariat. In France, the same battle was waged by the "purist" Jules Guesde, who preached that the Socialist party's primary goal should be the development of proletarian class consciousness, and Jean Jaurès, socialist leader in the Chamber of Deputies, who advocated a revisionist course. In both Germany and France, revisionists outnumbered purists by a wide margin. This was, to an even greater degree, the case in Britain. There, Fabian socialists—so named from their policy of delay, in imitation of the tactics of Fabius, a Roman general—preached what they called "the inevitability of gradualism." They believed their country would evolve toward socialism by means of parliamentary democracy. Prominent among the Fabians were the social investigators Sidney and Beatrice Webb, the novelist H. G. Wells, and the playwright George Bernard Shaw.

Revisionist gains

Jean Jaurès

The continued success of revisionism led its opponents to sharpen their attack and to advocate increasingly violent means to achieve their ends. Their campaigns, though they never managed to convince a majority of the working class, nevertheless attracted an increasing number of adherents. Some who had originally supported the revisionists grew disappointed when reforms did not come as quickly as expected. At the same time, in much of Europe, the cost of living began to rise for many workers. The comparative prosperity that some members of the working class had experienced vanished in the face of price rises that were not matched by wage increases. The result was a frustration which encouraged the adoption of a more militant stance. Germans rallied to the side of the radical socialists Rosa Luxemburg and Karl Liebknecht, while in France a new revolutionary socialist party disowned the reformist leader Alexandre Millerand after he agreed to serve as cabinet member in a nonsocialist government. The Second International, which had been founded in 1889, demanded at a conference in 1906 that affiliated parties declare their goal to be the destruction of the bourgeois order and the state that served its interests.

This militant mood encouraged acceptance of the doctrines of anarchists and syndicalists. Anarchists preached the overthrow of capitalism by violence. They differed from socialists, however, in their hatred of the machinery of the state or any government based upon coercion. Socialists argued that until the communist millennium promised by Marx, the state would remain a necessary means to the achievement of that eventual end. Anarchists worked to see the immediate abolition of a state bureaucracy which, no matter who controlled it, they believed would result in tyranny. Bakunin, whom Marx had succeeded in expelling from the First International, was anarchism's most popular propagandist. Syndicalism, like anarchism, demanded the abolition of both capitalism and the state. It resembled socialism in its demand that workers share in the ownership of the means of production. Instead of making the state the owner and operator of the means of production, however, the syndicalist would delegate these functions to syndicates of producers. The steel mills would be owned and operated by the workers in the steel industry, the coal mines by the workers in the coal industry, and so on. These associations would take the place of the state, each one governing its own members in their activities as producers.

Syndicalism received its most sympathetic hearing in France, where a General Confederation of Labour, after 1902, resolved to seek solutions to economic problems outside the legally constituted framework of French politics. The most effective spokesman for syndicalism was the Frenchman Georges Sorel (1847–1922). Sorel, in his *Reflections on Violence*, published in 1908, argued that workers should be made to believe in the possibility of a general strike by the proletariat which

Georges Sorel

The Haymarket Riots, Chicago, 1886. A contemporary illustration depicting the results of attempts to unionize workers at the McCormick Harvester works.

would result in the end of bourgeois civilization. The general strike might be nothing more than myth, Sorel acknowledged. Yet, as myth, it remained a powerful weapon in the hands of those whose goal was the destruction of society and who must not shy from the employment of violent means to achieve that end.

Socialism before the First World War, then, was not a unified force. It was divided by quarrels between purists and revisionists, and challenged by the even more radical proposals of anarchists and syndicalists. Socialists, intent on their goal of international solidarity among working classes, ignored the appeal that nationalism and imperialism might make to workers in France, Germany, and Britain. Yet despite its divisions and weaknesses, socialism appeared to the middle classes of Europe as a real threat to their continued prosperity. Capitalism had provided the machinery by which the bourgeoisie had achieved power. Socialism attacked capitalism and hence those who were its direct beneficiaries. Although most socialists disapproved of violence, violent acts were attributed by middle-class men and women to an amorphous, anticapitalist body easily labeled "socialist." Riots by trade unionists in Chicago's Haymarket Square in 1886 and in London's Trafalgar Square in 1887; the assassinations of President Sadi Carnot of France in 1894, of King Humbert of Italy in 1900, and of President William McKinley of the United States in 1901; strikes which grew in number and violence throughout Europe and America after 1900—all these events were perceived by members of the middle class as part of a larger movement whose professed goal was to tear from them their economic, political, and social security.

Socialism as a threat to the middle class

2. THE CHALLENGE OF SCIENCE AND PHILOSOPHY

Science and progress

Louis Pasteur

Marie Curie

While socialism challenged middle-class self-confidence from one quarter, science and philosophy threatened from another. The fact that science might undermine, rather than sustain, certainty was all the more difficult to comprehend, given the manner in which science and technology had together assisted in the birth and continued development of industrialization. This is not to say that science abandoned its role as an instrument for the solving of human problems and as a vital aid to continuing progress. There were striking improvements in the field of medicine, for example. The Frenchman Louis Pasteur (1822–1895) proved that all forms of life, no matter how small, are reproduced only by living beings. Hitherto, according to the theory of spontaneous generation, it had commonly been supposed that bacteria and other microscopic organisms originated from water or from other decaying vegetable and animal matter. By locating the source of bacteria, Pasteur's discovery opened the way for major improvements in the areas of public sanitation and health: among others, the process of ridding food of objectionable bacteria by sterilization—pasteurization—that was named for him. Pasteur, along with the German Robert Koch (1843–1910), also proved conclusively that germs were not, as was commonly supposed, the result but rather the cause of disease. The discovery of the X ray by the German Wilhelm von Röntgen in 1895 and of radium by the Polish scientist Marie Curie in 1898, not only altered perceptions as to the nature of energy, but suggested ways in which energy could be put to use for medical purposes. These discoveries—along with similarly important ones in the areas of cell theory, anesthetics, and antiseptics—worked to convince the educated public that science was a friend of humanity. They reinforced as well a belief in the predictability of the universe and in its essential timelessness, the sense that the passage of time brought with it no fundamental change.

Against this psychologically reassuring fortress of a harmonious universe, biological scientists hurled the bomb of evolutionary theory. We have seen that this theory was at least as old as Anaximander in the sixth century B.C., and that it was accepted by many of the great minds of antiquity. We have learned also that it was revived in the eighteenth century by the scientists Buffon and Linnaeus. But neither of these men offered much proof or explained how the process of evolution might work. The first to develop a systematic hypothesis of evolution was the French biologist, Jean Lamarck (1744–1829). The essential principle in Lamarck's hypothesis, published in 1809, was the inheritance of acquired characteristics. He maintained that an animal, subjected to a change in environment, acquired new habits, which in turn were reflected in structural changes. These acquired characteristics of body structure, he believed, were transmissible to the offspring, with the result that after a series of generations a new species of animal was eventually produced. Though Lamarck's successors found little evidence to confirm this hypothesis, it nonetheless dominated biological thought for nearly fifty years.

A much more convincing hypothesis of organic evolution was that of the English naturalist Charles Darwin (1809–1882), published in 1859. The son of a small-town physician, Darwin began the study of medicine at the University of Edinburgh, but soon withdrew and entered Cambridge to prepare for the ministry. Here he instead devoted most of his time to natural history. In 1831 Darwin obtained an appointment as naturalist without pay with a government-sponsored expedition aboard H.M.S. *Beagle,* which had been chartered for scientific exploration on a trip around the world. The voyage lasted nearly five years and gave Darwin an unparalleled opportunity to become acquainted at first hand with the manifold variations of animal life. He noted the differences between animals inhabiting islands and related species on nearby continents, and observed the resemblances between living animals and the fossilized remains of extinct species in the same locality. It was a magnificent preparation for his life's work. Upon returning from the voyage he read Malthus's essay on population, and was struck by the author's contention that throughout the world of nature many more individuals are born than can survive, and that consequently the weaker ones must perish in the struggle for food. The fruits of his observations, research, and hypothesizing were eventually published in 1859, in the *Origin of Species.*

Darwin's hypothesis was that of natural selection. He argued that it is nature, or the environment, which selects those variants among offspring that are to survive and reproduce. Darwin pointed out, first of all, that the parents of every species beget more offspring than can possibly survive. He maintained that, consequently, a struggle takes place among these offspring for food, shelter, warmth, and other conditions necessary for life. In this struggle for existence certain individuals have the advantage because of the factor of *variation,* which means that no two of the offspring are exactly alike. Some are born stronger than others; some have longer horns or sharper claws or perhaps a body coloration that enables them better to blend with their surroundings and thus to evade their enemies. It is these favored members of the species that win out in the struggle for existence and survive as the "fittest" of their generation; the others are eliminated generally before they have lived long enough to reproduce. Darwin regarded variation and natural selection as the primary factors in the origin of new species. In other words, he taught that individual plants and animals with favorable characteristics would transmit their inherited qualities to their descendants through countless generations, and that successive eliminations of the least fit would eventually produce a new species. Darwin applied his concept of evolution not only to plant and animal species but also to humans. In his second great work,

Charles Darwin

Illustrations from Darwin's First Edition of The Descent of Man. *The drawings were used to point up the similarities between a human embryo (top) and that of a dog (bottom).*

The Descent of Man (1871), he attempted to show that the human race originally sprang from some apelike ancestor, long since extinct, but probably a common forebear of the existing anthropoid apes and humans.

The Darwinian hypothesis was elaborated and improved by several later biologists. The German August Weismann (1834–1914) flatly rejected the idea that acquired characteristics could be inherited. He conducted experiments to show that body cells and reproductive cells are entirely distinct, and that there is no way in which changes in the former can affect the latter. He concluded, therefore, that the only qualities transmissible to the offspring are those that have always been present in the reproductive cells of the parents. In 1901 the Dutch botanist Hugo De Vries (1848–1935) published his celebrated mutation hypothesis, based upon Darwin's original hypothesis and, in large part, upon laws of heredity discovered by the Austrian monk Gregor Mendel (1822–1884). De Vries asserted that evolution results not from minor variations, as Darwin had assumed, but from radical differences or mutations, which appear in more or less definite ratio among the offspring. When any of these mutations are favorable to survival in a given environment, the individuals possessing them naturally emerge triumphant in the struggle for existence. Not only do their descendants inherit these qualities, but from time to time new mutants appear, some of which are even better adapted for survival than their parents. Thus in a limited number of generations a new species may be brought into existence. The mutation theory of De Vries corrected one of the chief weaknesses in the Darwinian hypothesis. The variations that Darwin assumed to be the source of evolutionary changes are so small that an incredibly long time would be necessary to produce a new species. De Vries made it possible to conceive of evolution as proceeding by sudden leaps.

Clearly, the implications of this new theory were deeply disturbing for those who had until now believed in an orderly universe, or had taken as literal the words of the Bible. For the latter the task of reconciling Darwin's account of creation with the first chapter of Genesis, though troublesome, was often not insuperable. Outside fundamentalist sects, the Bible was, at this time, perceived by growing numbers as containing a combination of myths, legends, history, and profoundly important moral truths. The work of the German theologian David Friedrich Strauss (1808–1874) and of the French historian Ernest Renan (1832–1892) had cast doubt on the historical accuracy of the Bible, and dealt with its inconsistencies. These writers had defended the intentions of the Bible's various authors, while firmly insisting upon their human fallibilities. Their searching yet nevertheless sensitive critiques helped people understand that they need not abandon their Christian faith simply because Darwin insisted that the world and all that lived within it had been created over millions of years and not in six days. Far more difficult to deal with was the notion, explicit in Darwin, that nature was not a changeless harmony, but instead a constant and apparently undirected struggle. Chance, and not order, ruled the universe. Nothing was fixed, nothing perfect; all was in a state of flux. Good and bad were defined only in terms of an ability to survive. The "best" of a species were those that triumphed over their weaker rivals. All of a sudden, the universe had become a harsh and uncompromising place, deprived of pre-Darwinian certainties; belief in a benevolent God was now much harder to sustain.

Darwin's most vigorous defender, the philosopher Thomas Henry Huxley (1825–1895), was one of those who could no longer reconcile science with a belief in God. While he did not reject the possibility of a supernatural power, Huxley averred that "there is no evidence of the existence of such a being as the God of the theologians." He pronounced Christianity to be "a compound of some of the best and some of the worst elements of Paganism and Judaism, moulded in practice by the innate character of certain people of the Western World." Huxley coined the word *agnosticism* to express his contempt for the attitude of dogmatic certainty symbolized by the beliefs of the ancient Gnostics. As propounded by Huxley, agnosticism was the doctrine that neither the existence nor the nature of God nor the ultimate character of the universe is knowable. Huxley earned himself the nickname of "Darwin's bulldog" because of his stout attacks upon orthodox Christians who refused to accept the implications of Darwinian theory. In a famous debate between Huxley and Samuel Wilberforce, the bishop of Oxford, in 1860, the bishop made the mistake of trying to turn Darwin into a joke, inquiring of the audience if anyone were willing to trace his descent from an ape, whether it was through his grandmother or grandfather. Huxley rejoined that the only ancestor of which he would feel ashamed was a man like the bishop, who so misused his talents to make light of such a serious issue. The sustained applause with which his remarks were greeted suggest the degree to which religious orthodoxy could now be safely challenged in public discussion.

Thomas Henry Huxley

The middle classes of western Europe and the United States, disoriented by the antireligious implications of evolutionary theory, received some comfort from the writings of those who adapted Darwinian thought to the analysis of society—the so-called Social Darwinists. These thinkers argued that the apparent "success" of Western civilization was the result of its special fitness. The white race, they boasted, had proved itself superior to the black; non-Jews superior to Jews; rich superior to poor; the British Empire superior to the subject territories it controlled. If nature was a matter of competition, so was society,

The Social Darwinists

Herbert Spencer

Anthropology

Friedrich Nietzsche

with the victory going to that race or nation that could demonstrate its fitness to survive by subduing others.

Though he never expressed his ideas that crudely, the English philosopher Herbert Spencer (1820–1903) extolled the virtues of competition in a way that made it easier for others to do so. Spencer grounded his philosophy upon evolutionary theory. He insisted upon the idea of evolution as a universal law. He was deeply impressed by Darwin's *Origin of Species* and enriched the hypothesis of natural selection with a phrase that has clung to it ever since—"the survival of the fittest." He contended that not only species and individuals are subject to evolutionary change, but also planets, solar systems, customs, institutions, and religious and ethical ideas. Everything in the universe completes a cycle of origin, development, decay, and extinction. When the end of the cycle has been reached, the process begins once more and is repeated eternally. As a political philosopher, Spencer was a vigorous champion of individualism. He condemned collectivism as a relic of primitive society, as a feature of the earliest stage of social evolution. Any so-called assistance individuals might receive from the state, Spencer argued, would result not only in their own degeneration, but in that of society as well.

If Social Darwinists could reassure some by implying the biological right of Western civilization to survive as the "fittest" within the contemporary world, anthropologists—pioneers in what was essentially a new scientific discipline—argued, on the contrary, that no culture could be perceived as "better" than any other. All societies were adaptations to a particular environment. Each society produced its own customs, which could not be declared "good" or "bad," but only successful or unsuccessful, according to the degree to which they helped that society survive. This notion of cultural "relativism" was a theme in the influential work of the English anthropologist Sir James Frazer (1854–1941). In his masterpiece, *The Golden Bough,* he demonstrated the relationship of Christianity to primitive practices and magical rites. Christianity was nothing more or less than one society's response to the craving for an explanation of the apparently inexplicable.

Christianity was challenged far more directly in the writings of the German philosopher Friedrich Nietzsche (1844–1900). Nietzsche was not a scientist, nor was he interested in the nature of matter or in the problem of religious truth. He was essentially a romantic poet glorifying the struggle for existence to compensate for his own life of weakness and misery. Born in 1844, the son of a Lutheran minister, he was educated in the classics at Leipzig and Bonn and at the age of twenty-five was appointed professor of philology at the University of Basel. Ten years later repeated and severe attacks of nerves forced his retirement. He spent the next decade of his life in agony, wandering from one resort to another in a fruitless quest for relief. If we can believe his own statement, each year was made up of two hundred days of pain. In 1888 he lapsed into hopeless insanity, which continued until his death in 1900.

Nietzsche's philosophy is contained in such works as *Thus Spake Zarathustra, A Genealogy of Morals,* and *The Will to Power.* His cardinal idea was the notion that natural selection should be permitted to operate unhindered in the case of human beings as it does with plants and animals. Yet he did not accept the deterministic worldview upon which the theories of Darwin—and of Marx as well—ultimately rested. He asserted the possibility of a triumph of human will over external circumstance, a triumph that he believed could eventually produce a race of supermen—not a race of physical giants but men distinguished above all for their moral courage, for their strength of character. Those who would perish in the struggle were the moral weaklings, who had neither the strength nor the courage to battle nobly for a place in the sun. Before any such process of natural selection could operate, however, religious obstacles would have to be removed. Nietzsche therefore demanded that the moral supremacy of Christianity and Judaism be overthrown. Both of these religions, he alleged, glorified the virtues of the downtrodden. They exalted into virtues qualities that ought to be considered vices—humility, nonresistance, mortification of the flesh, and pity for the weak and incompetent. The enthronement of these qualities prevented the elimination of the unfit and preserved them to pour their degenerate blood into the veins of the race.

Nietzsche's philosophy

Scientists and philosophers, as they continued to explore the various and sometimes contradictory implications of evolutionary theory, helped to undermine the comforting notion of humankind's essential superiority to the rest of the animal kingdom. The work of the Russian psychologist Ivan Pavlov (1849–1936) resulted in the discovery of the conditioned reflex. Although Pavlov experimented with animals, he insisted that his conclusions applied equally to human beings. The conditioned reflex is a form of behavior in which natural reactions are produced by an artificial stimulus. Pavlov showed that if dogs were fed immediately following the ringing of a bell, they would eventually respond to the sound of the bell alone and secrete saliva exactly as if confronted by the sight and smell of the food. This discovery suggested the conclusion that the conditioned reflex is an important element in human behavior and encouraged psychologists to center their attention upon physiological experiment as a key to understanding the mind.

Pavlov

Pavlovians inaugurated a type of physiological psychology known as behaviorism. Behaviorism is an attempt to study the human being as a purely physiological organism—to reduce all human behavior to a series of physical responses. Such concepts as *mind* and *consciousness* are dismissed as vague and meaningless terms. For the behaviorist noth-

Behaviorism

Freud and psychoanalysis

Sigmund Freud

The Protestant responses

ing is important except the reactions of muscles, nerves, glands, and visceral organs. There is no such thing as an independent psychic behavior; all that humans do is physical. Thinking is essentially a form of talking to oneself. Every complex emotion and idea is simply a group of physiological responses produced by some stimulus in the environment. Such was the mechanistic interpretation of human actions offered by followers of Pavlov.

The other important school of psychology to make its appearance after the turn of the century was psychoanalysis, founded by Sigmund Freud (1856–1939), an Austrian physician. Psychoanalysis interprets human behavior mainly in terms of the unconscious mind. Freud admitted the existence of the conscious mind (the ego), but he avowed that the unconscious (the id) is much more important in determining the actions of the individual. He considered humans as egoistic creatures propelled by basic urges of power, self-preservation, and sex. These urges are much too strong to be overcome; but inasmuch as society (the superego) has branded their unrestrained fulfillment as sinful, they are commonly driven into the unconscious, where they linger indefinitely as suppressed desires. Yet they are seldom completely submerged; they rise to the surface in dreams, or they manifest themselves in lapses of memory, in fears and obsessions, and in various forms of abnormal behavior. Freud believed that most cases of mental and nervous disorder result from violent conflicts between natural instincts and the restraints imposed by an unfortunate environment. Freud hoped that by elucidating his theory of the unconscious he could impose predictable patterns upon the irrationality that seemed to characterize so much human activity. His search for order, however, resembled that of the behaviorists by continuing to stress the extent to which men and women, like animals, were prey to drives, impulses, and reflexes over which they could exercise at best only minimal control.

Under the impact of these various scientific and philosophical challenges, the institutions responsible for the maintenance of traditional faith found themselves hard pressed. Protestantism had based its revolt against Roman Catholic orthodoxy upon the belief that men and women should seek to understand God with the aid of not much more than the Bible and a willing conscience. In consequence, Protestants had little in the way of authoritarian doctrine to support them when their faith was challenged. Some—the fundamentalists—chose to ignore the implications of scientific and philosophical inquiry altogether, and continued to believe in the literal truth of the Bible. Some were willing to agree with the school of American philosophers known as Pragmatists (Charles Pierce, William James), that if belief in a personal God produced mental peace or spiritual satisfaction, that belief must therefore be true. Truth, for the Pragmatists, was whatever provided useful, practical results. Other Protestants sought solace from religious doubt in religious activity, founding missions, and laboring among the poor. Many adherents to this "Social Gospel" were also "Modernists," determined to accept the ethical teachings of Christianity while discarding belief in miracles and the doctrines of original sin and the Incarnation.

The Roman Catholic Church was compelled by its tradition of dogmatic assertion to assist its followers in their response to the modern world. In 1864 Pope Pius IX issued a *Syllabus of Errors* condemning what he regarded as the principal religious and philosophical "errors" of the time. Among them were materialism, free thought, and "indifferentism," or the idea that one religion is as good as another. The *Syllabus* was condemned by critics as a "crusade against civilization." While heated discussions continued over the *Syllabus of Errors,* Pope Pius convoked a Church council in 1869, the first to be summoned since the Catholic Reformation. The most notable pronouncement of the Vatican Council was the dogma of papal infallibility. In the language of this dogma the pope, when he speaks *ex cathedra*—that is, in his capacity "as pastor and doctor of all Christians"—is infallible in regard to all matters of faith and morals. Though generally accepted by pious Catholics, the dogma of papal infallibility evoked a storm of protest in many circles. Governments of several Catholic countries denounced it, including France, Spain, and Italy. The death of Pius IX in 1878 and the accession of Pope Leo XIII brought a more accommodating climate to the Church. The new pope was ready to concede that there was "good" as well as "evil" in modern civilization. He added a scientific staff to the Vatican and opened archives and observatories. However, he made no concessions to "liberalism" or "anticlericalism" in the political sphere. He would go no farther than to urge capitalists and employers to be more generous in recognizing the rights of organized labor.

Pope Pius IX

The effect of various scientific and philosophical challenges upon the men and women who lived at the end of the nineteenth century cannot be measured in any exact way. Millions undoubtedly went about the business of life untroubled by the implications of evolutionary theory, content to believe as they had believed. Certainly, for most members of the middle class, the challenge of socialism was understood as "real" in a way that the challenge of science and philosophy probably was not. Socialism was a threat to livelihood. Darwinism, relativism, materialism, and behaviorism, though "in the air" and troublesome to those who breathed that air, did not impinge upon consciousness to the same degree. Men and women can postpone thoughts about their origins and ultimate destiny in a way that they cannot postpone thoughts about their daily bread. And yet the impact of the changes we have been discussing was eventually profound. Darwin's theory was not so complicated as to prevent its popularization. If educated men and women had neither the time nor inclination to read the *Origin of Species,* they read magazines and newspapers which spelled out for them its implications. Those implications in-

Pope Leo XIII

duced an uncertainty that tempered the optimism of capitalist expansion.

Schopenhauer's ideal world versus the real world

Men and women who had never read the German philosopher Arthur Schopenhauer (1788–1860) might well have agreed with his assessment of this world as one condemned to witness the devouring of the weak by the strong. Yet their commitment to the ways of the world prevented their acceptance of Schopenhauer's particular remedy: an escape into a life of personal asceticism and self-denial. Like the English poet and essayist Matthew Arnold, sensitive men and women might feel themselves trapped in a world resembling no more than "a darkling plain," where there was "neither joy, nor love, nor light, nor certitude, nor peace, nor help for pain."

3. THE CHALLENGE OF LITERATURE AND THE ARTS

Increased literacy

After 1850 a handful of artists and a greater number of writers continued to challenge the middle-class worldview, as had their predecessors, by drawing attention to the shortcomings of industrial society. As the century drew to a close, however, one of the major problems these critics now faced was the question of audience: not merely what to say, but whom to say it to. Before the middle of the eighteenth century, that audience had been primarily aristocratic. Between 1750 and 1870 it was both aristocratic and upper middle class. Now, thanks to the fact of an increasingly literate general population, the potential audience appeared to have increased enormously. In 1850 approximately half the population of Europe had been illiterate. In subsequent decades, country after country introduced state-financed elementary and secondary education—in part as an attempt to provide citizens with an opportunity for social mobility, in part as a means of control and as a preventive to the establishment of schools run by workers for workers, and in part as a measure to keep pace with changing technological knowledge. Britain instituted elementary education in 1870, Switzerland in 1874, Italy in 1877. France expanded its existing system between 1878 and 1881. After 1871 Germany instituted a state system modeled on Prussia's. By 1900, approximately 85 percent of the population in Britain, France, Belgium, the Netherlands, Scandinavia, and Germany could read. Elsewhere, however, the percentages were far lower, ranging between 30 and 60 percent.

A new journalism

In those countries where literacy rates were highest, capitalist publishers such as Alfred Harmsworth in England and William Randolph Hearst in the United States hastened to serve the new reading public. Middle-class readers had for some time been well supplied by newspapers catering to their interests and point of view. *The Times* of London had a readership of well over 50,000 by 1850; the *Presse* and *Siècle* in France, a circulation of 70,000. By 1900, however, other newspa-

The New Power of the Press. With the spread of literacy, newspapers adapted to the needs and desires of the new mass audience. Here English railway passengers scramble for the latest edition.

pers were appealing to a different mass market—the newly literate—and doing so by means of sensational journalism and spicy, easy-to-read serials.

These new developments encouraged writers and artists to distance themselves more and more from what seemed to them a vulgar, materialistic culture. They agreed with writers of the mid-century who had insisted that the purpose of art and literature was not to pander or sentimentalize. They went further, however, by declaring that art had no business preaching morality to a public that, in any event, had proved itself unwilling to heed the sermon. This generation of artists and writers argued that one did not look at a painting or read a poem to be instructed in the difference between good and evil, but to understand what was eternally true and beautiful—to appreciate art for its own sake. They were not so much interested in reaching a wider audience, whose standards of taste they generally deplored, as they were in addressing each other. This self-conscious desire not only to live apart but to think apart from society was reflected in their work. In 1850, educated men and women could read a Dickens novel or examine a Daumier print and understand it, even if they did not admire it or agree with its message. In 1900, men and women found it much harder to understand, let alone admire, a painting by Paul Cézanne or a poem by Paul Valéry. Artists and public were ceasing to speak the same language, a fact that contributed, as did the ideas of Darwin and Nietzsche, Pavlov and Freud, to the further confusion and fragmentation of Western culture.

These new perceptions of the artist's relationship to society did not surface to any measurable degree before the very end of the century. Until that time, the arts were dominated by what has come to be called *realism*. Realists were predominantly critics of contemporary society. Swayed by a fervor for social reform, they depicted the inequities of the human condition against the sordid background of industrial society. Like the romantics, the realists affirmed the possibility of human freedom, although realists emphasized more than romantics the obstacles that prevented its achievement. Realists differed most markedly from romantics in their disdain of sentiment and emotional extravagance. Adopting from natural science the idea of life as a struggle for survival, they tried to portray human existence in accordance with hard facts, often insisting that their characters were the irresponsible victims of heredity, environment, or their own animal passions.

Literary realism in France

Realism as a literary movement made its initial appearance in France. Its leading exponents included the novelists Honoré de Balzac and Gustave Flaubert,[1] whose work, as we have already noted, contained a stinging assessment of the dullness and greed of modern life. Émile Zola (1840–1902), another Frenchman, is often called a naturalist rather than a realist, to convey the idea that he was interested in an exact, scientific presentation of the facts of nature without the intrusion of personal philosophy. Naturalism was expected to dismiss moral values in a way that realism was not. Zola did have a definite moral viewpoint, however. His early years of wretched poverty imbued him with a deep sympathy for the common people and with a passion for social justice. Though he portrayed human nature as weak and prone to vice and crime, he was not without hope that a decided improvement might come from the creation of a better society. Many of his novels dealt with such social problems as alcoholism, poverty, and disease.

Realism in England

Realism in the writings of the Englishman Charles Dickens was overlaid with layers of sentimentality. Dickens was a master at depicting the evils of industrial society, but the invariable happy endings of his novels testify to his determined—and unrealistic—unwillingness to allow wrong to triumph over right. No such ambivalence marked the works of the later English novelist Thomas Hardy (1840–1928), however. In such well-known novels as *The Return of the Native, Jude the Obscure,* and *Tess of the D'Urbervilles,* he expressed his conception that humans are the playthings of an inexorable fate. The universe, though beautiful, was depicted as in no sense friendly, and the struggle of individuals with nature was a pitiable battle against almost impossible odds. If God existed, he watched with indifference while the helpless denizens of the human ant-heap crawled toward suffering and death. Yet Hardy pitied his fellow creatures, regarding them not as depraved animals but as the victims of cosmic forces beyond their control.

Realism in Germany and Scandinavia

Pity for humanity was a central theme in the work of the German Gerhard Hauptmann (1862–1946). Calling himself a naturalist, Hauptmann nevertheless reflected the realists' concern for suffering. His plays show the influence of Darwin in their emphasis upon determinism and environment. *The Weavers,* which depicts the suffering of Silesian weavers in the 1840s, is probably his most outstanding work.

---

[1] See above, p. 277.

Doubtless the most eminent playwright among realists and naturalists was the Norwegian Henrik Ibsen (1828–1906). The stark message of Ibsen's early dramas was not favorably received, and while still a young man he decided to abandon his native country. Residing first in Italy and then in Germany, he did not return permanently to Norway until 1891. His writings were characterized most of all by bitter rebellion against the tyranny and ignorance of society. In such plays as *The Wild Duck, A Doll's House, Hedda Gabler,* and *An Enemy of the People,* he satirized the conventions and institutions of respectable life, and showed, with great insight, how these oppressed women in particular. Along with his scorn for hypocrisy and social tyranny went a profound distrust of majority rule. Ibsen despised democracy as the enthronement of unprincipled leaders who would do anything for the sake of votes to perpetuate themselves in power. As one of his characters in *An Enemy of the People* says: "A minority may be right—a majority is always wrong."

The literature of the Russians, which flourished during the period of realism, includes within it themes that are both romantic and idealist as well. Russia's three outstanding novelists of the late nineteenth century were Ivan Turgenev (1818–1883), Feodor Dostoevsky (1821–1881), and Leo Tolstoy (1828–1910). They were preceded by the equally talented Alexander Pushkin (1799–1837) who, between 1820 and his death in a duel seventeen years later, established himself as one of Russia's greatest writers. Though his early work was romantic in tone, his epic verse *Eugene Onegin* demonstrated his sympathy with realistic themes.

Turgenev, who spent much of his life in France, was the first of the Russian novelists to become known to western Europe. His chief work, *Fathers and Sons,* describes in brooding terms the struggle between the older and younger generations. The hero is a nihilist (a term first used by Turgenev), who is convinced that the whole social order has nothing in it worth preserving. Dostoevsky was almost as tragic a figure as any he projected in his novels. Condemned at the age of twenty-eight on a charge of revolutionary activity, he was exiled to Siberia, where he endured four horrible years of imprisonment. His later life was harrowed by poverty, family troubles, and epileptic fits. As a novelist, he chose to explore the anguish of people driven to shameful deeds by their raw emotions and by the intolerable meanness of their lives. He was a master of psychological analysis, probing into the motives of distorted minds with an intensity that was almost morbid. At the same time he filled his novels with a broad sympathy and with a mystic conviction that humanity can be purified only through suffering. His best known works are *Crime and Punishment* and *The Brothers Karamazov.*

As an earnest champion of the simple life of the peasant, Tolstoy was somewhat less deterministic than the author of *Crime and Punishment.* Yet in *War and Peace,* a majestic epic of Russian conditions

Henrik Ibsen

Russian literature: Turgenev and Dostoevsky

Tolstoy

Leo Tolstoy in His Study Dictating to His Secretary

Victor Hugo by Auguste Rodin. The artist's realism enhances his ability to impart human character to his work.

during the period of the Napoleonic invasion, he expounds the theme that individuals are at the mercy of fate when powerful elemental forces are unleashed. His *Anna Karenina* is a study of the tragedy that lurks in the pursuit of individual desire. As Tolstoy grew older he became more and more an evangelist preaching a social gospel. In such novels as *The Kreutzer Sonata* and *Resurrection* he condemned most of the institutions of civilized society and called upon men and women to renounce selfishness and greed, to earn their living by manual toil, and to cultivate the virtues of poverty, meekness, and nonresistance. His last years were devoted to attacks upon such evils as war and capital punishment and to the defense of victims of political persecution.

The works of all these realists and naturalists, whatever their individual differences, shared two things in common: they contained vigorous moral criticism of present-day middle-class society, and they were written in direct and forceful language that the middle class could understand, if it chose to read or listen. The same can be said of realist painters such as Courbet and Daumier, discussed previously, and of the sculptor Auguste Rodin (1840–1917), whose style and message were neither difficult to comprehend nor easy to ignore. Realist artists were still anxious to address the public, if only to attack its members for their shallowness and insensitivity. The advent of the impressionist movement in painting in the 1870s marks the first significant break in this tradition. At this point artists began to turn away from the public and toward each other. The movement started in France, among a group of young artists whose work had been refused a place in the annual exhibitions of the traditionally minded French Royal Academy. They had been labeled "impressionists" in derision by critics who took them to task for painting not an object

From realism to impressionism

itself, but only their impression of that object. The name in fact suited the personal, private nature of their work. They were painting to please themselves, to realize their own potential as artists.

In a sense, impressionists were realists, for they were determined to paint only what they saw, and they were vitally interested in the scientific interpretation of nature. But impressionist technique was different from that of the older realist painters. Scenes from the world around them were not depicted as if the result of careful study. On the contrary, the works of impressionists sought to reveal immediate sense impressions, leaving it to the mind of the observer to fill in additional details. This often resulted in a type of work appearing at first glance to be nonnaturalistic. Figures were commonly distorted; a few significant details were made to represent an entire object; and dabs of primary color were placed side by side without a trace of blending. Convinced that light is the principal factor in determining the appearance of objects, the impressionists left the studio for the woods and fields in an attempt to capture the fleeting alterations of a natural scene with each transistory shift of sunlight and shadow. From science they had learned that light is composed of a fusion of primary colors visible in the spectrum. Accordingly, they decided to use these colors almost exclusively. They chose, for example, to achieve the effect of the green in nature by placing daubs of pure blue and yellow side by side, allowing the eye to mix them.

Impressionism differed from realism in one other important respect. In these new paintings artists remained detached from their subject. They did not paint to evoke pity, or to teach a lesson. They painted to proclaim the value and importance of painting *as painting*. In doing so, the artist was not deliberately setting out to exclude the viewers. It was clear, however, that the viewer must not expect to understand a painting except on the artist's terms. Probably the greatest of the impressionists were the Frenchmen Claude Monet (1840–1926) and

The Monarch of the Glen by Sir Edwin Landseer. This was the sort of conventional, easy to comprehend art that appealed to the middle class and that brought forth the revolutionary impressionist movement.

See color plates following page 422 for *Iris Beside a Pond* by Monet and *Luncheon of the Boating Party* by Renoir

Expressionism: Cézanne

See color plates following page 422 for *Montagne Sainte-Victoire with Aqueduct* and *The Card Players* by Cézanne

Auguste Renoir (1841–1919). Monet was perhaps the leading exponent of the new mode of interpreting landscapes. His paintings have little structure or design in the conventional sense; they suggest, rather than depict, the outlines of cliffs, trees, mountains, and fields. Intensely interested in the problem of light, Monet would go out at sunrise with an armful of canvases in order to paint the same subject in a dozen momentary appearances. It has been said of one of his masterpieces that "light is the only important person in the picture." Renoir's subjects include not only landscapes but portraits and scenes from contemporary life. He is famous for his pink and ivory nudes, which, as expressions of frank sexuality, represented an additional threat to middle-class sensibilities.

The freedom explicit in the work of the impressionists encouraged other painters to pursue fresh techniques and to define different goals. The expressionists turned upon the impressionists, objecting to their preoccupation with the momentary aspects of nature and their indifference to meaning. Expressionists were not arguing for a return to meaning in the sense of "message." They were instead insisting that a painting must represent the artist's particular intellect. Here again, they were making art a private matter, removing it yet another step from the public. The artist who laid the foundations of expressionism was Paul Cézanne (1839–1906), now recognized as one of the world's greatest painters. A native of southern France, Cézanne labored to express a sense of order in nature that he believed the impressionists had ignored. To achieve this end, he painted objects as a series of planes, each plane expressed in terms of a color change. While Cézanne was in this way equating form with color, he also began to reduce natural forms to their geometrical equivalents, hoping thereby to express the basic shapes of existence itself. He distorted form into geomet-

The Joy of Life, by Henri Matisse. The sensuous use of line and boldness of composition celebrate not only life but the artist's freedom to break from past convention.

Girl Before a Mirror by Pablo Picasso

rical regularity until abstraction became reality. In all this Cézanne was declaring the painter's right to recreate nature in such a way as to express an intensely personal vision.

Art as personal expression was the hallmark of two other painters in the so-called post-impressionist period, the Frenchman Paul Gauguin (1848–1903) and the Dutchman Vincent Van Gogh (1853–1890). Both, by their life as well as their art, declared war on traditional nine-teenth-century values. Dismayed by the artificiality and complexity of civilization, Gauguin fled to the South Sea Islands and spent the last decade of his life painting the hot and luscious colors of an unspoiled, primitive society. Van Gogh, whose passionate sympathy for the sufferings of his fellow humans led him to attempt the life of a minister to poor mining families and undoubtedly contributed to his eventual insanity and ultimate suicide, poured out the full intensity of his feelings in paintings such as *The Starry Night,* which seem to swirl off the canvas.

In the years between 1900 and the First World War, art underwent still further revolutionary development. Henri Matisse (1869–1954) greatly extended Cézanne's use of distortion, thereby declaring once again the painter's right to create according to an individual definition of aesthetic merit. This declaration was given its most ringing prewar endorsement by Pablo Picasso (1881–1973). Picasso, a Catalan Spaniard who came to Paris in 1903, developed a style, cubism, that takes its name from an attempt to carry Cézanne's fascination with geometrical form to its logical conclusion. Influenced both by the work of

Self-Portrait by Paul Gauguin

See color plates following page 422 for representative works by Gauguin, Matisse, Picasso, and van Gogh

Cézanne and by African sculpture, cubism results not only in distortion but in some cases in actual dismemberment. The artist may separate the various parts of a figure and rearrange them in other than their natural pattern. The purpose is to express defiance of traditional notions of form—to repudiate once and for all the conception of art as representational prettiness.

New directions in literature and music

The artistic declaration of independence from middle-class society was enunciated most dramatically by painters, but was heard also in the realms of literature and music. In France, the work of a group calling itself the symbolists, and centered upon the poetry of Paul Verlaine, Arthur Rimbaud, Stéphane Mallarmé, and Paul Valéry attempted to intensify the personal while transcending reality in a way reminiscent of the impressionists, expressionists, and cubists. In music, as well, there was a break from the romantic tradition that had dominated the nineteenth century and that had been expressed in the works of composers such as Robert Schumann (1810–1856), Felix Mendelssohn (1809–1847), and Franz Liszt (1811–1886). Already the late romantic operas of Richard Wagner had taken vast liberties with harmony and departed from stereotypical melodic patterns, producing music that was not subject to the tyranny of form but was sensitive to personal expression. Now in the works of composers such as the Austrian Richard Strauss (1864–1949) and the Frenchman Claude Debussy (1862–1918) music moved even further in the direction of the intensely personal. Strauss's opera *Der Rosenkavalier* (1911), although based externally on the conventions of late–eighteenth-century plot, is nevertheless a musical expression of the inner realities of its characters, written to express those realities more directly than heretofore. Both Strauss and Debussy were, like the impressionists, determined to convey atmosphere; Debussy's piano compositions, and his symphonic sketch, *La Mer,* are musical manifestations of the impressionists' regard for association rather than formal structure.

Self-imposed isolation

Whether in painting, in literature, or in music, artists sought to escape to a position from which they could learn and then express what was closest to their own consciousness. Their direct, calculated dismissal of conventional form and content declared their fundamental disdain for—more important, their complete lack of interest in—the problems of the world at large. Their self-imposed isolation served only to increase the general sense of a fragmented world that, despite its material prosperity, was at war with itself.

SELECTED READINGS

• *Items so designated are available in paperback editions.*

SOCIALISM
• Avineri, S., *The Social and Political Thought of Karl Marx,* London, 1968.
• Cole, G. D. H., *A History of Socialist Thought,* Vols. I–III, London, 1953–1956. A comprehensive treatment of the period 1789–1914.

- Derfler, Leslie, *Socialism since Marx: A Century of the European Left,* New York, 1973. Survey and analysis of continental socialist movements.

  Edwards, Stewart, *The Paris Commune of 1871,* London, 1971. Straightforward analysis.

  Gay, Peter, *The Dilemma of Democratic Socialism: Eduard Bernstein's Challenge to Marx,* New York, 1952. A good study of German revisionism.

  Goldberg, Harvey, *A Life of Jean Jaurès,* Madison, Wisc., 1962. A fine biography of the eminent French socialist.

- Joll, James, *The Anarchists,* London, 1964. Survey of various radical European groups.

  Lichtheim, G., *A Short History of Socialism,* New York, 1970. Provides a useful overview.

  Lidtke, Vernon, *The Outlawed Party, Social Democracy in Germany,* Charlotte, N.C. 1966. Deals with German socialists from 1878 to 1890.

- McBriar, A. M., *Fabian Socialism and English Politics, 1884–1918,* Cambridge, 1966. An extensive study of this important circle: their composition, their ideology, their methods.

  Noland, Aaron, *The Founding of the French Socialist Party, 1893–1905,* Cambridge, Mass., 1956. Primarily a narrative account of the translation of ideology into political reality.

- Schorske, Carl E., *German Social Democracy, 1905–1918,* Cambridge, Mass., 1955. A magnificent study of the problems of the Social Democrats in a time of imperialism and war.

SCIENTIFIC THOUGHT

- Butterfield, Herbert B., *The Origins of Modern Science,* rev. ed., New York, 1957. A standard survey.
- Eiseley, Loren C., *Darwin's Century: Evolution and the Men Who Discovered It,* New York, 1961. The history of evolution after Darwin.
- Gay, Peter, *Freud, Jews, and Other Germans: Masters and Victims in Modernist Culture,* New York, 1978. Essays on end-of-the-century German culture.

  Gillespie, C. C., *The Edge of Objectivity,* Princeton, 1960. A history of scientific ideas.

- Hughes, H. Stuart, *Consciousness and Society,* New York, 1958. Examines the reaction to Positivism and the growing interest in the irrational by considering the work of Freud, Max Weber, and others.
- Jones, Ernest, *The Life and Work of Sigmund Freud,* 3 vols., New York, 1953–1957. The official biography, by a close collaborator and eminent psychoanalyst.
- Rieff, P., *Freud: The Mind of the Moralist,* New York, 1959. A useful, one-volume discussion.

THE ARTS AND PHILOSOPHY

- Barzun, Jacques, *Darwin, Marx, and Wagner,* Boston, 1941. Argues that these men were not so much originators of new ideas as founders of systems that are mechanistic and pseudoscientific, and therefore threatening to the human cultural heritage.

  Kaufmann, Walter A., *Nietzsche: Philosopher, Psychologist, Anti-Christ,* Princeton, 1974. A superb intellectual biography.

Lang, Paul, *Music in Western Civilization*, New York, 1941. Useful survey and reference.

• Masur, Gerhard, *Prophets of Yesterday*, New York, 1961. A broad survey of nineteenth-century European thinkers.

Mosse, G. L., *The Culture of Western Europe: The Nineteenth and Twentieth Centuries*, Chicago, 1961. Thoughtful analysis and overview.

• Schorske, Carl, *Fin-de-Siecle Vienna: Politics and Culture*, New York, 1980. Essays on Vienna's cultural impact on the West.

• Shattuck, Roger, *The Banquet Years: The Arts in France, 1885–1918*, New York, 1958. The emergence of modernism in French art, literature, and music.

SOURCE MATERIALS

• Arnold, Matthew, *Culture and Anarchy*, New York, 1971. Originally published in 1867. A perceptive criticism of English society and a call for an authoritarian principle in an increasingly democratic society.

• Darwin, Charles, *The Descent of Man*, Cambridge, Mass., 1964. See especially Chapter XXI.

• ———, *Origin of Species*, Cambridge, Mass., 1964. See especially Chapters IX, XV.

• Edwards, Stewart, ed., *The Communards of Paris, 1871*, New York, 1976. Annotated eyewitness reports, documents, and accounts of the Paris Commune.

• Gosse, Edmund, *Father and Son*, New York, 1963. A moving autobiography by a distinguished Victorian literary critic, this work reveals the conflict between the religious fundamentalism of the father and the skepticism of the son in the wake of Darwinian theory.

Kohn, Hans, *The Mind of Russia*, New Brunswick, N.J., 1955. An edited collection of historical, literary, and philosophical works of nineteenth- and twentieth-century Russian authors, designed to reveal the conflict between traditional and Western thought in Russia.

Marx, Karl, *Capital*, intro. by G. D. H. Cole, New York, 1974. A good edition of the classic.

• Webb, Beatrice, *My Apprenticeship*, London, 1926. Beatrice Webb was one of the leading Fabian Socialists, and in this first volume of her autobiography she explains how she, as a member of one of England's wealthier families, was converted to a socialist creed.

• Zola, Émile, *L'Assommoir*, London, 1970. Written in 1877 and set in the Paris of the 1860s, this bitterly realistic novel portrays the brutalization of the French working class by the forces of industrial change, poverty, and alcohol.

Chapter 32

THE SEARCH FOR STABILITY
(1870–1914)

Ah! What a seething there has been, . . . customs worthy of the inquisition and despotism, the pleasure of a few gold-braided individuals setting their heels on the nation, and stifling its cry for truth and justice, under the mendacious and sacrilegious pretext of the interest of the State!

—Émile Zola, "J'accuse"

Between 1870 and 1914, the major powers of Europe worked to maintain both domestic and international stability. Accomplishment of this goal was facilitated by continuing industrialization. Despite periodic trade depressions, general prosperity increased for almost all classes of society at least until 1900. And prosperity, in its turn, helped to produce stability, allowing for the establishment in many countries of social welfare systems designed to benefit workers and their families, and thus to gain their political allegiance.

Continuing prosperity

At the same time, various factors operated to make the achievement of a generally stable Western world difficult, and ultimately impossible. First, the process of nation-building, which had resulted in the dramatic creation of a modern Germany and Italy, left potential conflict in its wake. Second, although the majority of citizens in most western European countries participated at least indirectly in the governance of their country and enjoyed certain guaranteed rights, heated debate continued as to the political usefulness of such arrangements. In France, monarchists threatened the republic; in Germany, democrats battled imperial and bureaucratic oligarchy; in Russia, liberals rose against tsarist autocracy. And across Europe, socialists contended against the political strength of the middle classes.

The roots of instability

Internal tension was resulting as well from shifts in class structure and class consciousness. One of the most dramatic occupational changes to occur in late-nineteenth-century Europe was the rapid growth of a lower- to middle-level, "white-collar" class of bureaucrats, employed in commerce and industry and in expanding government departments. The post office, the railways, the police, and the bureaus charged with the task of administering various social welfare and insurance programs, all demanded growing numbers of recruits. In Germany, for example, by 1914 there were over two million white-collar employees in private firms and two million lower- or middle-range civil servants. Members of this new class were particularly anxious to give sharp definition to the line separating them from skilled "labor aristocrats," who might earn as much money as they did, but whose blue collars were, in the eyes of the white-collar brigades, a badge of their inferior status. Those same "aristocrats," as we have seen, however, often found their skills made obsolete by technological change, with the result that they showed themselves more willing than in the past to make common cause with their unskilled fellow workers against the middle class.

One further important source of European instability during this period lay in the international rivalries that grew between nations as they reached out to build empires. Nations grouped into alliances, hoping that a balance between power blocs might continue to provide the international stability that Europe had enjoyed since 1815, and that had prevented general war. Instead, the alliances produced only further tensions, and ultimately general world conflict.

1. GERMANY: THE SEARCH FOR IMPERIAL UNITY

During the years immediately following the foundation of the German Empire, Bismarck was particularly anxious to achieve imperial unity under Prussian domination. In this he was aided by the economic and military predominance of the Prussian state, and by the organizational framework upon which the empire had been constructed. All powers not granted to the central government were reserved to the individual states. Each had control over its own form of government, public education, highways, police, and other local agencies. Even the enforcement of the laws was left primarily in the hands of the state governments, since the empire had no machinery for applying its laws against individuals. Despite their apparent autonomy, however, the states were in fact subordinate to the empire, and to the emperor himself, the Prussian William I. The German imperial units were once described as composed of "a lion, a half-dozen foxes, and a score of mice." The Prussian "lion" exercised authority through the person of the emperor and his chancellor. The empire was not governed by a cabinet system, in which ministers of state were responsible to a popularly elected legislature. Instead, ministers were responsible to the chancellor, and the chancellor was responsible solely to the emperor.

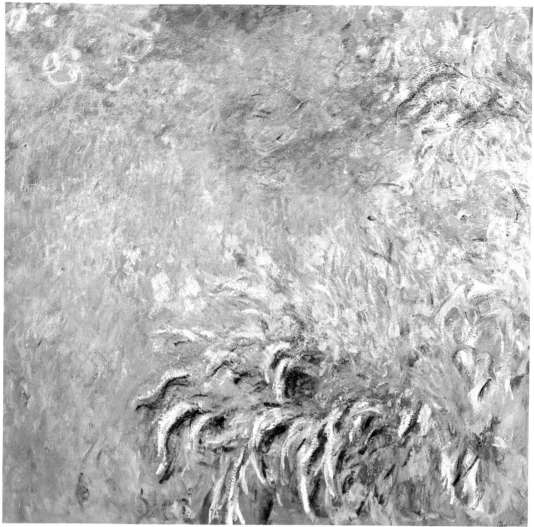

Iris beside a Pond, Claude Monet (1840–1926). Monet called some of his paintings Impressions, and the name soon came to designate a school. (Art Institute of Chicago)

Pink and Green, Edgar Degas (1834–1917). Degas was an Impressionist to the extent of his interest in fleeting motion. But as an admirer of the classicist Ingres, he emphasized line and careful composition. (MMA)

Above: *The Birth of Venus,*
Alexandre Cabanel (1823–
1889). Below: *Luncheon on the
Grass,* Edouard Manet (1823–
1883). Cabanel's painting is a
typical product of the fashionable French Salon, and was at
one time owned by Napoleon
III. It won the Salon prize in
1863 and was copied several
times by the artist (as were
other Salon paintings), emphasizing the fact that it was considered as much a piece of
"decoration" as a piece of art.
This sort of "bestseller" was
exceedingly popular with upper-middle-class collectors,
who felt no need to apolo-
gize for its semi-pornographic
nature because of its classical
subject matter. Manet's painting, done in the same year,
created an enormous furor. Its
style broke with the soft,
painterly techniques of the
Salon school; instead it was
painted with broad, flat strokes
that presaged the coming of
Impressionism. Its subject
matter caused a sensation as
well. Whereas voluptuous
classical nudes were respectable art, a painting of a young
woman seated without her
clothing at a picnic with fully
clothed gentlemen friends
conveyed a sense of serious
social impropriety to bourgeois viewers. (Louvre)

A Woman with Chrysanthemums,
Degas. In his portraits, Degas sought
to capture his subjects in familiar, informal positions. Avoiding traditional formal sittings, he frequently
brought together an assortment of
discrete observations first in his imagination, and then on canvas. When
this painting was completed in 1858 it
was a still life of flowers bearing the
imprint of Delacroix; the woman was
added in 1865. (MMA)

Luncheon of the Boating Party, Auguste Renoir (1841–1919). The
impressionists enjoyed employing
their revolutionary artistic techniques to portray the commonplace
occasions of everyday life. (Phillips
Memorial Gallery)

Montagne Sainte-Victoire with Aqueduct, Paul Cézanne (1839–1906). Cézanne's insistence upon the reduction of the landscape to patterns of form and planes of color illustrates the manner in which his genius created the vital link between impressionism and cubism. (Museum of Modern Art)

The Card Players, Cézanne. Here are exemplified Cézanne's skill in composition, his discriminating sense of color, and the sculptured qualities of solidity and depth he gave to his figures. (Stephen C. Clark)

Above: *Sunflowers in a Vase* (V. W. van Gogh); Below: *The Starry Night,* Vincent van Gogh (1853–1890). Van Gogh's compulsive style and bold technique endow his compositions with a feverish rhythm that is both compelling and disturbing. (Museum of Modern Art)

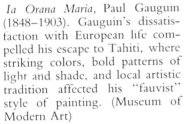

Ia Orana Maria, Paul Gauguin (1848–1903). Gauguin's dissatisfaction with European life compelled his escape to Tahiti, where striking colors, bold patterns of light and shade, and local artistic tradition affected his "fauvist" style of painting. (Museum of Modern Art)

Portrait of Gertrude Stein, Pablo Picasso (1881–1973). Picasso seems to have given this portrait of the great experimenter in poetry some elements of the distortion of form characteristic of the work of both. (Museum of Modern Art)

The Piano Lesson, Henri Matisse (1869–1954). Matisse conveyed a freshness of approach and a vitality of line and color. (Museum of Modern Art)

Three Musicians, Pablo Picasso. This painting, regarded by many as the masterpiece of Cubism, sums up the final stage of the movement. (Museum of Modern Art)

William was no mere figurehead; the emperor was vested with extensive authority over the army and navy, over foreign relations, and over the general enactment and execution of imperial laws. He had the authority to declare war if the coasts or territory of the empire were attacked. And as king of Prussia, he controlled that country's delegation in the generally conservative upper house, or Bundesrat, of the imperial parliament, commanding enough votes to veto any bill submitted. The chairman of the Bundesrat, charged with the control and supervision of the federal administration, was also the Prussian prime minister, appointed by the king of Prussia.

The parliament was no rubber stamp, however. Money for the imperial treasury had to be voted by the lower house, the Reichstag, which was elected by universal manhood suffrage, and whose membership was primarily middle class. Yet the Reichstag's powers were essentially negative. Although the parliament could veto proposals of the kaiser (emperor) and his ministers, it could not initiate legislation on its own. Hence, although Bismarck often found himself temporarily stymied by the activities of an unsympathetic legislature, he could expect, in the end, to have his way. That way was directed toward the goal of a unified Germany under Prussian domination: essentially conservative; antisocialist, though not necessarily opposed to social welfare schemes; protectionist, and thus sympathetic to the interests of German industrialists; and, in foreign affairs, anti-French, standing firm against any threat from that longtime antagonist.

William I of Germany

Bismarck's first campaign on behalf of imperial unity was launched against the Roman Catholic Church. Called the *Kulturkampf,* or "struggle for civilization," the attack was initiated, with some help from intellectual liberals, in 1872. Bismarck's motives were almost exclusively nationalistic. He perceived in some Catholic activities a threat to the power and stability of the empire he had just created. He resented, first of all, the support Catholic priests continued to give to the states'-rights movement in southern Germany and to the grievances of Alsatians and Poles. He was alarmed also by recent assertions of the authority of the pope to intervene in secular matters and by the promulgation in 1870 of the dogma of papal infallibility. For these reasons he resolved to deal such a blow to Catholic influence in Germany that it would never again be a major factor in national or local politics. His weapons were a series of laws and decrees issued between 1872 and 1875, designed to curb the independent power of the Church. Bismarck's campaign backfired, however. The Catholic Center party appealed to the electorate so effectively on behalf of the persecuted clergy, while adopting an economic policy attractive to the upper middle class, that it won fully one-quarter of the seats in the Reichstag in 1874. Recognizing that he needed Catholic support for other elements of his program, Bismarck took the occasion of the election of the more conciliatory Pope Leo XIII to make his peace with the Vatican and to negotiate an alliance of convenience with the Catholic

The Kulturkampf

Bismarck and the socialists

Center party. By 1886 almost all of his anticlerical legislation either had been permitted to lapse or had been repealed.

Having forged a new political combination in 1878, Bismarck shifted the focus of his attacks to German socialism, now perceived by him as a far more immediate threat to the empire than Catholicism. The Social Democratic party, under the reformist leadership of the politician Wilhelm Liebknecht (1829–1900), successor to Ferdinand Lassalle, was building a substantial following. Bismarck, his memory of the Paris Commune (see above, pp. 397–98) still fresh, feared socialism as anarchy, and therefore as a direct challenge to the stability and unity he was attempting to achieve within the empire. Forgetting for the moment the manner in which he had courted the socialists when he needed their support in the 1860s, Bismarck now appeared determined to extinguish them. His attack was motivated not only by his personal perception of the socialist threat but also by his continuing need to secure the favor of industrialists whom he had won to his side by his policy of protective tariffs. In 1878, two separate attempts were made by unbalanced zealots on the life of the emperor. Although neither would-be assassin had anything but the most tenuous connection with the socialists, Bismarck used their actions as an excuse to secure legislation abolishing workers' rights to meet and to publish. The legislature also agreed to a law that gave the government the right to expel socialists from major cities, as was later done in Berlin, Breslau, and Leipzig. These laws in effect dissolved the Social Democratic party until after 1890, although individual socialist candidates continued to be elected to the Reichstag.

Social welfare legislation

Bismarck was too clever a politician to suppose that he could abolish socialism solely by means of repression. He was prepared to steal at least a portion of the socialists' thunder by adopting parts of their legislative program as his own. In a speech in the Reichstag he frankly avowed his purpose of insuring the worker against sickness and old age so that "these gentlemen [the Social Democrats] will sound their bird call in vain." In addition, he had military purposes in mind. He hoped to make the German worker an effective potential soldier by safeguarding his health in some measure from the debilitating effects of factory labor. Bismarck's program of social legislation was initiated in 1883–1884 with the adoption of laws insuring workers against sickness and accidents. These acts were followed by others providing for rigid factory inspection, limiting the employment of women and children, fixing maximum hours of labor, establishing public employment agencies, and insuring workers against incapacity on account of old age. By 1890, Germany had adopted nearly all the elements, with the exception of unemployment insurance, in the matrix of social legislation that later became familiar in the majority of Western nations.

In that same year the Iron Chancellor was dismissed by the young emperor, William II (1888–1918), following the less-than-year-long reign of his father Frederick III. Bismarck's loss of power was to a degree the result of a personality clash between the two men. William's father had remarked that his son had "a tendency to overestimate himself"; his tutor noted that he "imagined he knew everything— without having learned anything." William's arrogance was encouraged by the cult of imperial family worship which had by this time become part of the patriotic creed that was imposed by the state upon its citizens. Yet the quarrel between the young kaiser and his chancellor was a matter of substance as well as personality, involving policies directed at curbing the activities and popularity of the socialists. Bismarck's dismissal came in part over William's insistence that the antisocialist legislation of the past decade had achieved very little, and his mistaken belief that socialists would respond positively to his determination to rule in his own right and to create a more unified, stable, and powerful reich. Within a few years, however, William was arguing a line that appealed to the landowners, military leaders, and industrialists, whom he continued to court throughout his reign. He wooed the landowners by embarking on a policy of agricultural protection. And he wooed the military and the industrialists with a vast program of naval rearmament. Meanwhile, despite his decision to end the ban against the Social Democrats, he did all he could to undermine their growing political strength.

State schools were instructed to teach the dangers of socialism by

William's politics

Left: *William II of Germany and Bismarck.* Right: *Dropping the Pilot.* This cartoon appeared in the British magazine *Punch* on March 29, 1890, after the inexperienced but ambitious young emperor dismissed Bismarck as chancellor and personally assumed the helm of the ship of state. Note that Bismarck appears stripped of the insignia of office.

stressing the virtues of patriotism and piety. Admission to the civil service was almost impossible unless one was an officer in the military reserve; and admission to that very influential body was not open to socialists—or to Jews. Stealing a leaf from Bismarck's text, William authorized the extension of earlier programs of social insurance, hoping to dampen enthusiasm for the Social Democrats by granting some of the reforms for which they continued to campaign. But William steadfastly refused to extend any sort of meaningful political participation beyond the powerful industrial, military, and agricultural classes. The country was administered efficiently, but not democratically. With the exception of Count Leo von Caprivi, a military officer, all his chancellors were civil servants, a fact that underscored his determination to keep the administration of the country as far removed as possible from democratic control.

Growing opposition to these policies brought the Social Democrats increasingly impressive electoral victories. In 1912 they polled a third of the votes cast, and elected 110 members—the largest single bloc— to the Reichstag. Yet they were thwarted, not only by William's determination to ignore his parliament, but by their inability to resolve the conflict within their own ranks between purist and revisionist theory (see above, pp. 399–400). The party continued to profess itself devoted to the principles of socialist purity. Yet its increasingly large following tended to push it in the direction of piecemeal reformist legislation. And even with their large bloc of Reichstag votes, the Social Democrats could not command a majority there unless they formed a coalition with center parties far less reformist—let alone revolutionary—than they were. By 1914, German politics were approaching stalemate. The country was spared a domestic constitutional crisis only by the infinitely more profound international crisis of the First World War.

2. FRANCE: THE EMBATTLED THIRD REPUBLIC

Although in 1870 France was not a newly constructed nation like the German Empire, it was a nation sorely in need of reunification and dedication to a common set of political purposes. Its history for the past century had left it torn between various factions. The conflicts it suffered after 1870 tended to be more ideological than social, a reflection not only of France's tumultuous political past, but of its comparatively slow rate of industrialization. Monarchists were divided between supporters of the Bourbon and Orleanist dynasties, their allegiance sustained by loyalties either to the descendants of Louis XVIII or of Louis Philippe. Bonapartists looked for political salvation to Napoleon III's son and heir Louis Napoleon. Republicans recalled the short-lived triumphs of their revolutionary ancestors. Socialists called down plagues on all political houses but their own. The result of this deep division was that not until 1875 did France have a constitution under which it could function.

Following the collapse of Napoleon III's empire a provisional government was organized to rule the country until a new constitution could be drafted. Elections held in 1871 for a national constituent assembly resulted in the choice of some 500 monarchists and only about 200 republicans. Conservative political sentiment was further reinforced by the events of the Paris Commune, which occurred during the period immediately following the elections. But the apparent winners, the monarchists, could not agree among themselves as to whether their king should be a Bourbon or an Orleanist. This stalemate led to the eventual passage in 1875—by one vote—of a series of constitutive laws which made France a republic. These laws established a parliament with a lower house elected by universal manhood suffrage (the Chamber of Deputies) and an upper house elected indirectly (the Senate); a cabinet of ministers presided over by a premier; and a president. Although at first the relative powers of president and premier were not clearly established, within two years the nation had declared itself in favor of a premier at the head of a government answerable to the Chamber of Deputies. An early president, Marshal Marie-Edmé MacMahon, attempted in 1877 to dismiss a premier with whom he disagreed but who was supported by a majority in the chamber. When new elections were held, MacMahon's policy was repudiated. Henceforth, premiers of the Third Republic were answerable to the chamber and not to the president, who became a figurehead. Yet the resolution of this constitutional question failed to produce political stability, since the premier had no authority to dissolve the legislature. This meant that members of the chamber could vote a premier and his fellow ministers out of office at will, with no risk of being forced to stand for reelection. If defeated on a vote, the premier and his colleagues had no alternative but to resign. The result was no fewer than fifty ministries in the years between 1870 and 1914. The Third Republic, for all its constitutional shortcomings, nevertheless managed to last until 1940—far longer than any system of French government since 1789. Its longevity was due, as much as anything, to the stability of other French institutions—the family, the law courts, and the police, for example. And its stability was attested to by the willingness of French men and women to invest their savings in state loans, rather than in industrial enterprises that appeared far less secure to them.

In the years after 1875, the republicans, who had been feared at first as dangerous radicals, proved themselves to be generally moderate. It was the discontented monarchists and authoritarian sympathizers within the army, the Roman Catholic Church, and among the families of the aristocracy who took to plotting the overthrow of duly constituted governmental authority. Much of the time of successive republican governments was taken up defending the country from these reac-

The formation of the Third Republic

Radical reactionaries

Left: *The Avenue de l'Opéra, c. 1880.* During the era of the Third Republic official Paris declared itself in favor of architecture that bespoke middle-class opulence and respectability as manifested here by the broad street lined with elegant shops and dominated by the unimpeded view of the facade of the Paris Opéra. Right: *The Rue Mouffeta, 1910.* Conditions in this working-class street remained meanwhile much as they had been throughout most of the preceding century.

tionary radicals. In the late 1880s, a general, Georges Boulanger, gathered about him a following not only of Bonapartists, monarchists, and aristocrats, but of workingmen who were disgruntled with their lot and who believed, with Boulanger, that a war of revenge against Germany would put an end to all their troubles. Thanks to the general's own indecisiveness, the threatened coup d'état came to nothing. But the attempt was a symptom of deep discontents; Boulanger appealed, like Napoleon III, to disparate groups of disenchanted citizens, promising quick, dramatic solutions to tedious problems.

The Dreyfus affair

One further symptom of the divisions that plagued the republic during the later years of the nineteenth century was the campaign of anti-Semitism that the reactionaries adopted to advance their aims. The fact that certain Jewish bankers were involved in scandalous dealings with politicians lent color to the monarchist insistence that the government was shot through with corruption and that Jews were largely to blame. An anti-Semitic journalist, Edmond Drumont, insisted that "Jews in the army" were subverting the national interest. In 1889 he and others founded the Anti-Semitic League. This ugly and heated campaign furnished the background of the famous Dreyfus affair. In 1894 a Jewish captain of artillery, Alfred Dreyfus, was accused by a clique of monarchist officers of selling military secrets to Germany. Tried by court-martial, he was convicted and sentenced for life to Devil's Island, a ghastly prison camp in the Caribbean. At first the verdict was accepted as the merited punishment of a traitor; but in 1897 Major Picquart, a new head of the Intelligence Division, announced his conclusion that the documents upon which Dreyfus had been convicted were forgeries. A movement was launched for a new trial, which the War Department promptly refused. Soon the whole nation was divided into friends and opponents of Dreyfus. On his side were the radical republicans, socialists, people of liberal and humanitarian sympathies, and such prominent literary figures as Émile Zola and Anatole France. The anti-Dreyfusards included monarchists, clerics, anti-Semites, militarists, and a considerable number of conservative workingmen. A Roman Catholic newspaper insisted that the question was not whether Dreyfus was guilty or innocent, but whether Jews and unbelievers were not the secret masters of France. Dreyfus was finally set free by executive order in 1899, and six years later was cleared of all guilt by the Supreme Court and restored to the army. He was immediately promoted to the rank of major and decorated with the emblem of the Legion of Honor.

The history of the Dreyfus affair gave the republicans the solid ground they had lacked in order to end the plottings of the radical reactionaries once and for all. The leaders of the republic chose to attack their enemies by effectively destroying the political power of the Roman Catholic Church in France. The anticlericalism expressed in this campaign was probably in part the product of a materialistic age, and of a longstanding mistrust by French republicans of the institution of the Church. Its main source, however, was the nationalism which we have already seen fueling Bismarck's *Kulturkampf*.

Anticlericalism

The great majority of the leaders of the Third Republic were hostile to the Church; and naturally so, for the Catholic hierarchy was aiding the monarchists at every turn. Clerics had conspired with monarch-

Alfred Dreyfus Leaving His Court Martial

Legislation to curb the Church

Pressure from the Left

Socialist debate

ists, militarists, and anti-Semites in attempting to discredit the republic during the Dreyfus affair. But in the end they had overreached themselves. In 1901 the government passed a series of acts prohibiting the existence of religious orders not authorized by the state, forbidding members of religious orders to teach in either public or private schools, and finally, in 1905, dissolving the union of church and state, thereby prohibiting payment of the clergy from public funds. For the first time since 1801 the adherents of all creeds were placed on an equal basis.

The republic was, during these years, pressed from the Left as well as the Right. Socialism was a political force in France, as it was in Germany. Yet the response of republicans in France to socialist pressure differed markedly from that of Bismarck. There was no antisocialist legislation. Indeed, a law was passed in 1881 abolishing "crimes of opinion," thereby extending the freedom of the press considerably. In the same year, another law authorized public meetings without prior official approval. But if there was no attempt at repression, there was little positive social reform. The largest single party in the republic, the Radicals or Radical Socialists, was really a party representing small shopkeepers and lesser propertied interests. The Radicals were willing to found and maintain a democratic compulsory educational system, but they were reluctant to respond to demands for social legislation such as had been instituted in Germany. Those laws which were passed—establishing a ten-hour workday in 1904 and old-age pensions in 1910—were passed grudgingly and only after socialist pressure. The result was a growing belief among socialists and other workers that parliamentary democracy was worthless, that progress, if it was to be made, would be made only as a result of direct industrial action: the strike.

This attitude was reinforced by the same debate—revisionism vs. purism—that we have seen dividing the Social Democrats in Germany. Purists had called it "opportunism" when the socialist Alexandre Millerand had joined the nonsocialist cabinet of Prime Minister René Waldeck-Rousseau in 1899. Millerand had insisted that his cooperation would help heal the wounds inflicted on French politics by the Dreyfus affair. His opponents charged that such collaboration was a sellout. Their successors pointed to the lack of anything more than occasional and very mild social legislation in succeeding parliaments to prove their point. In response to this growing sentiment came a wave of strikes, which swept the country for several years before 1914, including one by postal workers in 1909 and by teachers and railwaymen in 1910. The government suppressed these actions by ruthless intervention. Tension increased after 1910 during debates over the extension of military conscription from two to three years, opposed by the socialists, and over the institution of an income tax, favored by the socialists as a way of financing social programs threatened as a result of increased military spending. By 1914, the republic, though hardly

Conflicts and Contrasts in Working-Class Life. Left: In this cartoon illustrating the tension that existed throughout Europe as a result of tighter work controls a working-class French woman complains to her father that "all day long, it's against the rules to sit down." He responds: "Do as we do! Ditch them." Right: At the same time, as this scene of workers on day-holiday at Yarmouth Sands in England suggests, workers enjoyed greater opportunities for at least some leisure time than ever before. These contrasts helped to produce the class conflicts that characterized European politics before the First World War.

on the brink of revolution, remained divided and uncertain. If the threat from the radical Right had been quelled, the challenge from the Left was only just being faced.

3. GREAT BRITAIN: FROM MODERATION TO MILITANCE

During the half-century before 1914, the British prided themselves on what they believed to be a reasonable, orderly, and workable system of government. Following the passage of the Second Reform Bill in 1867, which extended suffrage to over a third of the nation's adult males, the two major political parties, Liberal and Conservative, vied with each other in adopting legislation designed to provide an increasingly larger proportion of the population the chance to lead fuller and healthier lives. Laws that recognized the legality of trade unions, allowed male religious dissenters to participate fully in the life of the ancient universities of Oxford and Cambridge, provided elementary education for the first time to all children, and facilitated the clearance and rebuilding of large urban areas, were among those placed on the

Benjamin Disraeli

William E. Gladstone Campaigning, 1885. Perhaps the first politician to make effective use of the railway in his campaigns, Gladstone took advantage of the mobility it provided to reach out to the electorate.

Gladstone and Disraeli

books during the administrations of the two leading politicians of the period, the Conservative Benjamin Disraeli (1804–1881) and the Liberal William Gladstone (1809–1898). In 1884, suffrage was once more widened, to include over three-fourths of the adult males, and to allow rural workingmen the chance to vote for the first time. Coupled with a previous act which instituted the secret ballot, this electoral reform bill brought Britain nearer to representative democracy.

Gladstone and Disraeli were remarkably different men. The former was a devout member of the Church of England, so dedicated to the cause of personal moral reform that he was willing to risk his political career by accosting prostitutes in the hope of persuading them to change their way of life. He devised his political programs—his long and ultimately unsuccessful campaign for Irish Home Rule, for example—on the basis of his moral convictions. Disraeli, on the other hand, was a pragmatist, willing to acknowledge the degree to which politics is an opportunistic game. When he became prime minister he celebrated the fact by declaring delightedly that he had at last climbed to "the top of the greasy pole." He thought Gladstone's morality a pose, and declared that he wouldn't mind the fact that his opponent had an extra ace up his sleeve, if only he didn't insist that God had put it there. Disraeli was probably correct, however, when he observed that Britain, "subject as it is to fogs and a middle class," preferred its statesmen to be properly grave. He was the exception, a converted Jew and former novelist, whose remarkably compelling political style had enabled him to overcome his unorthodox background.

Despite the personal differences between Gladstone and Disraeli, the political parties over which they presided were managed by a small ruling class of similar men drawn either from landed society or from the upper reaches of the middle class. As members of successive governmental cabinets they recognized their responsibility to Parliament and, in particular, to its lower House of Commons. It was their task, as cabinet ministers, to impose a legislative program upon the Commons. And if the House refused to agree to that program, they recognized, as well, their obligation either to resign forthwith—to make way for a cabinet of opposing party members—or to "go to the country," that is, to dissolve Parliament and order a new election to test the opinion of the voters. This system of "ministerial responsibility" meant that the cabinet retained full responsibility for the management of public affairs, subject, however, to the will of the people as represented by the House of Commons. It produced a generally stable government: although ministries had to answer to Parliament, Parliament would think twice before voting a ministry out of office when it knew that the ministry might well appeal to the voters for support in a general election. (The lack of this particular feature was what had condemned the French Third Republic to its succession of short-lived governments.) Political stability was ensured by more than the device of ministerial responsibility, however. Since both the Conservative and Liberal political leadership was drawn in large part from similar social and economic strata, there was little chance for violent change during these years. One party might espouse a particular cause—the Conservatives imperialism, the Liberals more self-government for Ireland, for example. But both parties generally agreed upon a course steered by men whose similar background and temperament promised programs that were neither radical nor reactionary. This moderation suited the electorate, which was content to defer to politicians whose leadership was secured by the undoubted fact of Britain's general prosperity.

Not everyone was content, however. Prosperity, though widespread enough, did not extend to the unskilled: dock workers, transport workers, and the like. These groups formed trade unions to press their claims. Their determination encouraged other unions to assume a more militant and demanding stance. In the 1890s this activity produced a reaction in the form of anti-trade union employers' associations and a series of legal decisions limiting the right of unions to strike. Workers, in turn, reacted by associating with middle-class socialist societies to form an independent Labour party, which was born in 1901 and five years later managed to send twenty-nine members to the House of Commons. Sensitive to this pressure from the Left, the Liberals, during their ministry, which began in 1906, passed a series of reforms they hoped would ensure a minimum standard of living for those who had heretofore known little security. Sickness, accident, old-age, and unemployment insurance schemes were adopted. A minimum wage was decreed in certain industries. Labor exchanges, designed to help unemployed men and women find new

"Ministerial responsibility"

Liberal reforms, 1906–1914

Lloyd George and Winston Churchill on Their Way to the House of Commons on Budget Day, 1910

jobs, were established. Restrictions on strikes and on the right of trade unions to raise money for political purposes were relaxed.

Lloyd George's budget

Much of this legislation was the work of David Lloyd George (1863–1945), a radical middle-class lawyer from Wales, much feared by many within the political establishment. Lloyd George was chancellor of the exchequer (finance minister) in the Liberal cabinet of Prime Minister Herbert Asquith, and together with another young Liberal, Winston Churchill (1874–1965), he hammered together legislation that was both a reflection of his own political philosophy and a practical response to the growing political power of the working class. To pay for these programs—and for a larger navy to counter the German buildup—Lloyd George proposed a budget in 1909 that included progressive income and inheritance taxes, designed to make wealthier taxpayers pay at higher rates. His proposals so enraged the aristocratic members of the House of Lords that they declared themselves prepared to throw out the budget, an action contrary to constitutional precedent. Asquith countered with a threat to create enough new peers (titled noblemen) sympathetic to the budget to ensure its passage.[1] The House of Lords eventually surrendered; the result of the crisis was an act of Parliament which provided that the House of Lords could not veto legislation passed by the House of Commons.

The rancor aroused by this constitutional conflict was intense. Self-

---

[1] In Britain the monarch had the authority to elevate an unlimited number of men to the peerage. But since the crown acts only on the advice of the prime minister, it is this official who had the actual power to create new members of the House of Lords. If necessary, he could use this power to pack the upper house with his own followers.

proclaimed defenders of the House of Lords screamed threats in a chamber unused to anything but gentlemanly debate. Angry threats were by no means confined to the Houses of Parliament during these years, however. Throughout Britain, men and women threw moderation to the winds as they disputed issues in an atmosphere little short of anarchic. The reasons for this continued agitation were various. A decline in real wages after 1900 kept the working class in a militant mood despite Liberal reforms and produced an unusually severe series of strikes in 1911 and 1912. A liberal plan to grant Home Rule (self-government) to Ireland produced not only panic in the Protestant minority counties of the north (Ulster) but arming and drilling of private militias with an intensity that seemed to forecast civil war.

Increased militance

Perhaps the most alarming—because the most unexpected—of the militant revolts that seized Britain in the years before 1914 was the campaign for women's suffrage. The middle-class women who engaged in this struggle enjoyed more freedom of opportunity than their mothers had known. Laws had been passed easing the process of divorce and permitting married women control of their own property. Some universities had started to grant degrees to women. Contraceptive devices—and feminist propaganda defending their use—had begun to result in changed attitudes toward sexuality within the middle class. Perhaps because of these gains, many women felt their lack of the vote all the more acutely. Although the movement began among middle-class women, it soon included some female members of the working class and the aristocracy. Agitation reached a peak after 1900, when militant suffragettes—under the leadership of Emmeline

Suffragettes

London Dock Strike, 1911. Police move to clear demonstrators from shops where they have taken refuge after having been fired upon.

Violent Suffragette Protest. Suffragette leader Emmeline Pankhurst is arrested during a violent demonstration at Buckingham Palace in 1911.

Pankhurst, her daughters Christabel and Sylvia, and others—resorted to violence in order to impress upon the nation the seriousness of their commitment. Women chained themselves to the visitors' gallery in the House of Commons; slashed paintings in museums; invaded that male sanctum, the golf course, and inscribed VOTES FOR WOMEN in acid on the greens; disrupted political meetings; burned politicians' houses; and smashed department store windows. The government countered violence with repression. When women, arrested for their disruptive activities, went on hunger strikes in prisons, wardens proceeded to feed them forcibly, tying them down, holding their mouths open with wooden and metal clamps, and running tubes down their throats. When hunger strikes threatened to produce deaths and thus martyrs for the cause, the government passed the constitutionally dubious Cat and Mouse Act, which sanctioned the freeing of prisoners to halt their starvation and then, once they had regained their health, authorized their rearrest. The movement was not to see the achievement of its goal until after the First World War, when reform came largely because of women's contributions to the war effort.

Whether Britain's militant mood might have led to some sort of general conflict if the war had not begun in 1914 is a question historians continue to debate. Suffice it to say that national sentiment in the last few years before the outbreak of general hostilities was far different from that of the 1870s. Britain, so confident of itself and of its moderation, was proving no less a prey to instability than other European nations.

4. RUSSIA: THE ROAD TO REVOLUTION

Reform and reaction in nineteenth-century Russia

In only one European country, Russia, did conditions pass from instability to insurrection during these prewar years. The early-twentieth-century Russian revolutionary movement had numerous forerunners. Waves of discontent broke out several times during the nineteenth century. Threatened uprisings between 1850 and 1860, partly a consequence of Russia's defeat in the Crimean War, persuaded Tsar Alexander II, who came to the throne in 1855, to liberate the serfs, to modernize the military establishment, to reform the judicial system, and to grant local self-government.

Liberation of the serfs

The law of 1861 granted legal rights to some 22 million serfs, and authorized their title to at least a portion of the land they had worked. Yet the pattern of rural life in Russia did not change drastically. Large-scale landowners managed to retain the most profitable acreage for themselves. Newly liberated serfs faced the need to pay the state for the land they held (the state, in turn, recompensing the former owners). This expense, plus the fact that peasants were often left with less than enough land to sustain themselves and their families, and without adequate pasturage, water, and forest rights, meant that they were compelled to return to work as agricultural laborers for their previous masters.

Russia: The Revolution

The military reform of 1874 was designed to broaden the ranks to include all males, not just the peasantry. Military service was now to be determined by lot. The period of active duty was reduced from twenty-five to six years. Schooling was provided for draftees and corporal punishment was abolished.

Military reform

Russia's judicial system, heretofore secret, corrupt, and tied to a rigid class system that ensured legal inequality, was reformed so as to make the courts for the first time independent of the central administration. All Russians were declared equal before the law; trial by jury was introduced for most criminal cases. Whereas formerly evidence could be presented only in written form, oral testimony was now permitted, thereby making trials far more public in character. A tiered system of courts, rising from local justices of the peace, provided the right to appeal.

Judicial innovations

The structure of local government instituted in 1861 placed responsibility in the hands of the *mir,* or village commune. Its officials regulated the assignment of land and collected taxes. They were also able to restrict the movement of residents in and out of their community, a regulation designed to ensure that peasants could not escape their obligation to pay for the land they now occupied as free men. At a higher level, district councils were authorized to administer their own courts and tax collection. In 1864, indirectly elected provincial councils—*zemstvos*—were empowered to manage local welfare and educational programs.

Local government

Though only moderately reformist, these *zemstvos* provided forums for the debate of political issues and, along with the extension of educational opportunities, encouraged middle-class Russians to suppose themselves on the way to some sort of liberalized state. The government, however, grown fearful of the path it was treading, called a halt to reform and substituted repression in its place. By 1875, censorship had been extended not only to the *zemstvos*, which were forbidden to discuss general political issues, but to the press and to schools as well. The result of suppression was, not surprisingly, further discontent and active subversion. Middle-class Russians argued privately the virtues of utopian socialism, liberal parliamentarianism, and Pan-Slavism. A growing number, calling themselves nihilists, espoused the doctrines of the anarchist Bakunin (see above, p. 396). Terrorists, believing that assassination of the tsar was the only solution to oppression, achieved their goal in 1881, when a bomb killed Alexander II.

Government repression

The most important radical political element in late-nineteenth-century Russia was a large, loosely knit group of men and women who called themselves populists. They believed that although their country must Westernize, it could not expect to do so according to examples set elsewhere. They proclaimed a new Russia, yet one based upon

Populism

the ancient institution of the village commune, which was to serve as a model for the socialist society they hoped to create. Populism sprang primarily from the middle class; a majority of its adherents were young, many of them students; and about 15 percent were women, a significantly large proportion for the period. They formed secret cadres, plotting the overthrow of tsarism by terror and insurrection. They dedicated their lives to "the people" (hence their name), attempting wherever possible to live among common laborers so as to understand and express the popular will. Populism's historical importance lies not so much in what it accomplished, which was little, but in what it promised for the future. A movement that marked the beginning of organized revolutionary agitation in Russia, it was the seedbed for thought and action that would in time produce general revolution. Populists read Marx's *Capital* before it was translated into Russian; they tested and revised his ideas and those of other major revolutionaries of the nineteenth century so as to produce a doctrine suited to Russia's particular destiny.

Autocracy and Russification

The activities of populists and anarchists, however, triggered a floodtide of reaction against the entire policy of reform. Alexander III (1881–1894), governed under the theory that Russia had nothing in common with western Europe, that its people had been nurtured on despotism and mystical piety for centuries and would be utterly lost without them. He believed that Western ideals such as rationalism and individualism would undermine the deferential faith of the Russian masses and would plunge the nation into anarchy and crime, and that in like manner, Western institutions could never bear fruit if planted in Russian soil. With these doctrines as his guiding principles, Alexander III enforced a regime of stern repression. He curtailed in

A Railroad Yard in Eastern Russia, 1896

every way possible the powers of the local assemblies, increased the authority of the secret police, and subjected villages to government by wealthy nobles selected by the state. These policies were continued, though in somewhat less rigorous form, by his son, Nicholas II (1894–1917), a much less effective ruler. Both tsars were ardent proponents of Russification, a more ruthless counterpart of similar nationalistic movements in various countries. Its purpose was to extend the language, religion, and culture of Great Russia, or Russia proper, over all of the subjects of the tsar and thereby to simplify the problem of governing them. It was aimed primarily at the Poles, Finns, and Jews, since these were the nationalities considered most dangerous to the stability of the state. Russification meant repression. The Finns were deprived of their constitution; the Poles were compelled to study their own literature in Russian translations; and high officials in the tsar's government connived at *pogroms,* i.e., wholesale massacres, against the Jews.

Despite these attempts to turn Russia's back to the West, however, the nation was being drawn more closely than it had ever been before into the European orbit. Russia was industrializing, and making use of European capital to do so. Economic policies during the 1890s, when Count Sergei Witte was the tsar's leading minister, resulted in the adoption of the gold standard, which made Russian currency easily convertible. Railways and telegraph lines were constructed; exports and imports multiplied by factors of seven and five respectively from 1880 to 1913. In addition, Russian writers and musicians contributed in a major way to the enriching of Western culture. We have already noted the singular contributions of Tolstoy, Turgenev, and Dostoevsky. The musical works of Peter Tchaikovsky (1840–1893) and Nikolai Rimsky-Korsakov (1844–1908), while expressing a peculiarly Russian temperament and tradition, were recognized as important additions to the general body of first-rate contemporary composition.

Westernization

With Westernization came the growth of a new wage-earning class. Most of Russia's workers were recruited from the countryside. We have seen that regulations made migration outside the *mir* difficult if not impossible. To live permanently in cities meant surrendering all claim to one's land. The result was that peasant factory workers lived away from their villages only temporarily, returning to attend to farming's seasonal demands. Consequently, these workers could not easily master a trade, and were forced to take unskilled jobs at extremely low wages. They lived in large barracks; they were marched to and from factories, where conditions were as unsafe and unhealthy as they had been in British factories in the early years of industrialization. An average working day in a textile mill was from twelve to fourteen hours. This sudden and extremely harsh transition from country to city living instilled deep discontent and a militant class consciousness in Russian workers.

A new working class

Worker's Quarters in St. Petersburg, c. 1900. These buildings, in which workers from the country were housed temporarily while they labored in factories, were breeding grounds for class consciousness.

Growth of political parties

The increase in class consciousness brought with it the emergence of new political parties. Middle-class businessmen and professionals combined with enterprising landowners in 1903 to form a **Constitutional Democratic party,** whose program included the creation of a nationally elected parliament or Duma to determine and carry out policies that would further the twin goals of liberalization and Westernization. Meanwhile, two essentially working-class parties, the Social Revolutionaries and the Social Democrats, began to agitate for far more radical solutions to the problems of Russian autocracy. The Social Revolutionaries concerned themselves with the onerous plight of the peasants, burdened with land purchase and high taxes. The Social Revolutionaries wanted to equalize the landholdings of peasants within their *mirs,* and to increase the power of the *mirs* in their continuing competition with large landowners. The Social Democrats were Marxists, who saw themselves as westerners and as part of the international working-class movement. In 1903 the leadership of the Social Democratic party split in an important disagreement over revolutionary strategy. One group, which achieved a temporary majority (and thus called itself the Bolsheviks—"Majority Group") favored a strongly centralized party of active revolutionaries, and opposed the notion of a postrevolutionary transitional bourgeois state, insisting instead that revolution be succeeded immediately by a socialist regime. The Mensheviks ("Minority Group"), whose position resembled that of other

European revisionist socialists, soon managed to regain control of the party. The Bolshevik splinter party remained in existence, however, under the leadership of the young, dedicated revolutionary Vladimir Ulanov (1870–1924), who wrote under the pseudonym of N. Lenin.

Lenin was a member of the middle class, his father having served as an inspector of schools and minor political functionary. He had been expelled from the University of Kazan for engaging in radical activity, following the execution of his elder brother for his involvement in a plot to assassinate Alexander III. Lenin spent three years as a political prisoner in Siberia; from 1900 until 1917 he lived as an exile in western Europe. His zeal and abilities as both a theoretician and a political activist are evidenced by the fact that he retained leadership of the Social Democrats even while residing abroad. Lenin continued to preach the gospel of Marxism and of a relentless class struggle. His treatise *What Is to Be Done?* was a stinging response to revisionists who were urging collaboration with less radical parties. Revolution was what was to be done, Lenin argued, revolution "made" as soon as possible by an elitist group of agitators working through the agency of a disciplined party. Lenin and his followers, by merging the tradition of Russian revolutionism with Western Marxism, and by endowing the result with a sense of immediate possibility, fused the Russian situation in such a way as to make eventual explosion almost inevitable.

The Young Lenin, 1897

The revolution that came in 1905, however, took even the Bolsheviks by surprise. Its unexpected occurrence was the result of a war between Russia and Japan, which broke out in 1904, and in which the Russians were soundly beaten. Both countries had conflicting interests in Manchuria and Korea; this fact was the immediate cause of the conflict. On land and sea the Japanese proved themselves the military superiors of the Russians. As dispatches continued to report the defeats of the tsar's army and navy, the Russian people were presented with dramatic evidence of the inefficiency of autocracy.

The Russo-Japanese War

Just as defeat in the Crimean War had spurred the movement for reform, so now members of the middle class who had hitherto refrained from association with the revolutionists joined in the clamor for change. Radical workers organized strikes and held demonstrations in every important city. Led by a priest, Father Gapon, a group of 200,000 workers and their families went to demonstrate their grievances at the tsar's winter palace in St. Petersburg on January 22, 1905—known ever after as Bloody Sunday. The demonstrators were met by guard troops and many of them were shot dead. By the autumn of 1905 nearly the entire urban population had enlisted in a strike of protest. Merchants closed their stores, factory-owners shut down their plants, lawyers refused to plead cases in court, even valets and cooks deserted their wealthy employers. It was soon evident to Tsar Nicholas that the government would have to yield. On October 30, he issued a manifesto, pledging guarantees of individual liberties, promising a

The Revolution of 1905

Bloody Sunday. Demonstrating workers who sought to bring their grievances to the attention of the tsar were met and gunned down by government troops, January 1905.

moderately liberal franchise for the election of a Duma, and affirming that henceforth no law would be valid unless it had the Duma's approval. This was the high-water mark of the revolutionary movement. During the next two years Nicholas issued a series of sweeping decrees which negated most of the promises made in the October Manifesto. He deprived the Duma of many of its powers, and decreed that it be elected indirectly on a class basis by a number of electoral colleges. Thereafter the legislative body contained a majority of obedient followers of the tsar.

The reasons for setback

There were several reasons for the setback to this movement for major political reform. In the first place, the army remained loyal to its commander-in-chief. Consequently, after the termination of the war with Japan in 1905, the tsar had a large body of troops that could be counted upon if necessary to decimate the ranks of the revolutionists. An even more important reason was the split in the ranks of the revolutionists themselves. After the issuance of the October Manifesto, large numbers of the bourgeoisie became frightened at threats of the radicals and declared their conviction that the revolution had gone far enough. Withdrawing their support altogether, they became known henceforth as Octobrists. The more radical merchants and professional men, organized into the Constitutional Democratic party, maintained that opposition should continue until the tsar had been forced to establish a government modeled after that of Great Britain. This fatal division rendered the middle class politically impotent. Finally, disaffection appeared within the ranks of the workers. Further attempts to employ the general strike as a weapon against the government ended in disaster.

But the Russian revolutionary movement of 1905 was not a total failure. The vengeance taken by the tsar convinced many people that their government was not a benevolent autocracy, as they had been led to believe, but a stubborn and brutal tyranny. The uprising revealed the ability of working-class leaders to control the destiny of Russia. The general strike had proved a valuable revolutionary tool, as had workers' councils, elected from the factory floor and briefly operating as the only effective government in some areas. In addition, the revolt of 1905 persuaded some of the more sagacious advisors of the tsar that last-ditch conservatism was none too safe. The result was the enactment of a number of conciliatory reforms. Among the most significant were the agrarian programs sponsored by the government's leading minister, Peter Stolypin, between 1906 and 1911. These included transfer of five million acres of royal land to the peasants for a price; the granting of permission to peasants to withdraw from the *mir* and set up as independent farmers; and cancellation of the remaining installments owed by the peasants for their land. Decrees were issued permitting the formation of labor unions, providing for a reduction of the working day (to not more than ten hours in most cases), and establishing sickness and accident insurance. Yet the hopes of some liberals that Russia was on the way to becoming a progressive nation on the Western model proved illusory. The tsar remained stubbornly autocratic. Few peasants had enough money to buy the lands offered for purchase. In view of the rising cost of living, the factory workers considered their modest gains insufficient. A new revolutionary outbreak merely awaited a convenient spark.

*Gains from the
revolutionary movement*

5. THE SEARCH FOR STABILITY ELSEWHERE IN THE WEST

Other European countries generally found it just as difficult to attain internal stability in the early twentieth century as did those whose history we have surveyed. Italy was burdened with the problems of a rapidly increasing population, the need to industrialize quickly, and a stark disparity between a relatively prosperous industrial north and an impoverished agricultural south. As the population increased, so did the stream of rural migration into cities, where there were few jobs available. In its drive to create jobs and to industrialize, the government intervened directly in the economy by placing large orders for military equipment and by undertaking an ambitious program of railway construction. By the First World War the share of industrial production in the national economy had risen to 25 percent.

Problems in Italy

These strides were largely the result of policies instituted by Giovanni Giolitti (1842–1928), who was prime minister for almost the entire period between 1900 and 1914. Yet his efforts to spur industrialization widened the division between north and south. Relying on opportunistic maneuvering which he called *trasformismo*, and which argued the pointlessness of party politics, Giolitti rewarded the support of southern politicians for his program of industrial expansion by allowing the south to remain under the domination of the great landowners, the Church, and—in Sicily—the Mafia, none of which were interested in furthering the economic well-being or political consciousness of the average citizen. Thus whereas illiteracy was reduced in northern Italy to about 11 percent, in the south it remained at 90 percent. By failing to address the desperate economic conditions in the south, *trasformismo* denied the country an opportunity to develop a much needed internal market for its goods.

Trasformismo

Hoping to gain support for his program from the socialists, Giolitti engineered passage of laws legalizing trade unions, improving factory conditions, and extending the suffrage to virtually all males over thirty. But attempts to satisfy the Left did not sit well with more conservative elements in Italian society, who remembered bread riots in Milan in 1896, the assassination of King Humbert by radicals in 1900, and widespread strikes in 1902 and 1904. Meanwhile, socialists in Italy were as divided on the matter of strategy as they were elsewhere in Europe. Reformists competed with radicals, organized into chambers of labor—local trade union councils with a revolutionary outlook—which assisted in the takeover of the Socialist party by a militant left wing in 1912.

Socialist split

Nationalist aspirations continued to be a major problem in eastern Europe. In 1867 an attempt had been made to resolve national differences in Austria by dividing the empire in two—an Austrian empire west of the river Leith, and a kingdom of Hungary to its east. Each of the two components in this so-called Dual Monarchy was to be the equal of the other, though the two were joined by the same Habsburg monarch, by several common ministries, and by a kind of superparliament. This solution failed to put an end to nationalist divisions, however.

Nationalism in Austria-Hungary

The Austrian portion of the monarchy was composed not only of a German-speaking majority, but of Czechs, Slovaks, Slovenes, and Ruthenians as well. Without concessions to these nationalities the government could expect little peace. Yet to give in to their aspirations was to antagonize the German majority, a group constantly wary of any move that appeared to threaten its predominance. During the 1890s, an attempt to pacify the Czechs by requiring all officials in areas of mixed German and Czech populations to speak both languages infuriated the Germans, who staged violent demonstrations proclaiming the superiority of their culture and forced the government to back down. Anxious to promote industrial development, the bureaucracy recognized that to introduce the requisite economic and financial

Nationalist tensions in Austria

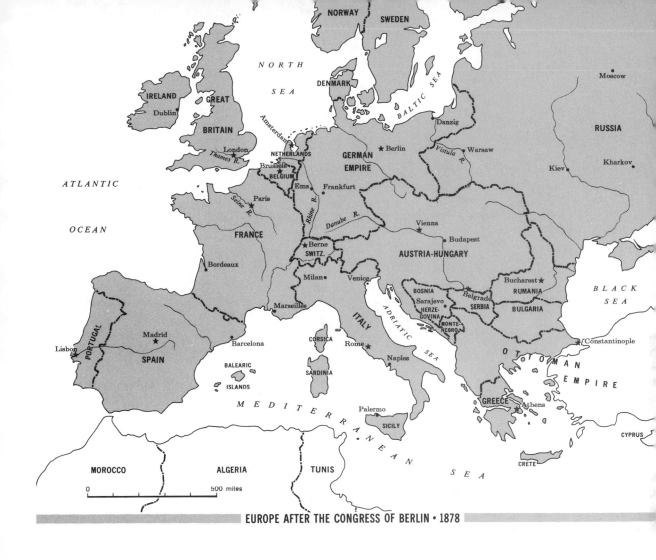

EUROPE AFTER THE CONGRESS OF BERLIN · 1878

measures, a Reichstag more sympathetic to modernization and to the needs of diverse imperial constituencies would be necessary. To that end, the Austrians introduced universal male suffrage in 1907, in the belief that newly enfranchised peasants recognized a primary allegiance to the emperor, rather than to any one particular nationality. Because the new electoral laws continued to specify quotas for each ethnic minority in the parliament, however, they strengthened the hand of the various national groups in the legislature, encouraging them to demand still further autonomy.

The major issue in the Hungarian half of the monarchy was a proposal to separate out the Hungarian regiments in the imperial army, allowing them their own insignia and requiring that they be commanded in their native language. The emperor, Francis Joseph, rejected these demands countering with a threat to introduce imperial male suffrage, a move the Magyars correctly saw as a challenge to their supremacy,

Nationalist tensions in Hungary

Vienna, 1873. Despite the fact that Vienna was the capital of an empire that straddled eastern and western Europe, it was by this date clearly a stylish and westernized metropolis.

as it had been to the Germans in Austria. The result was a standoff, part of the continuing desperate attempt on the part of the central government to play one side off against the other in order to maintain a shaky *status quo*.

In southeastern Europe nationalist agitation continued to rend the ever-disintegrating Ottoman Empire. Before 1829 the entire Balkan peninsula—bounded by the Aegean, Black, and Adriatic Seas—was controlled by the Turks. But during the next eighty-five years a gradual dismemberment of the Turkish Empire occurred. In some instances the slicing away of territories had been perpetrated by rival European powers, especially by Russia and Austria; but generally it was the result of nationalist revolts by the sultan's Christian subjects. In 1829, at the conclusion of a war between Russia and Turkey, the Ottoman Empire was compelled to acknowledge the independence of Greece and to grant autonomy to Serbia and to the provinces that later became Rumania. As the years passed, resentment against Ottoman rule spread through other Balkan territories. In 1875–1876 there were uprisings in Bosnia, Herzegovina, and Bulgaria, which the sultan suppressed with effective ferocity. Reports of atrocities against Christians gave Russia an excuse for renewal of its age-long struggle for domination of the Balkans. In this second Russo-Turkish War (1877–1878) the armies of the tsar won a smashing victory. The Treaty of San Stefano, which terminated the conflict, provided that the sultan surrender nearly all of his territory in Europe, except for a

The Ottoman Empire

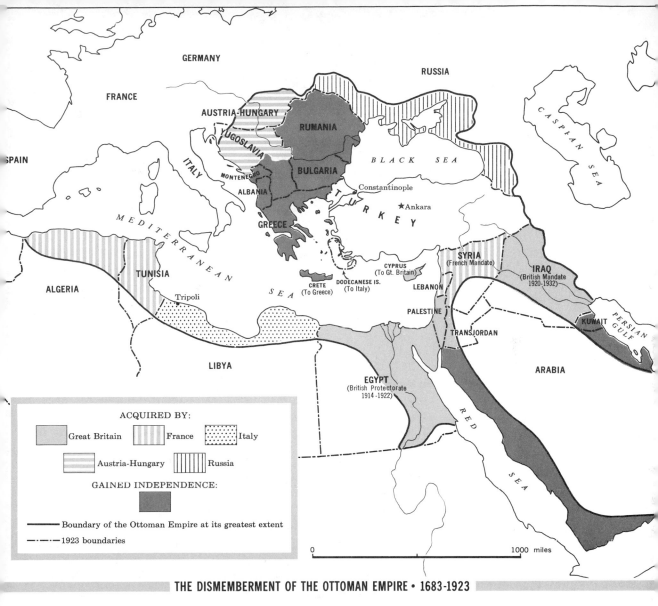

THE DISMEMBERMENT OF THE OTTOMAN EMPIRE • 1683-1923

remnant around Constantinople. But at this juncture the great powers
intervened. Austria and Great Britain, especially, were opposed to
granting Russia jurisdiction over so large a portion of the Near East.
In 1878 a congress of the great powers, meeting in Berlin, transferred
Bessarabia to Russia, Thessaly to Greece, and Bosnia and Herzegovina
to the control of Austria. Seven years later the Bulgars, who had been
granted some degree of autonomy by the Congress of Berlin, seized
the province of Eastern Rumelia from Turkey. In 1908 they established the independent Kingdom of Bulgaria.

In the very year when this last dismemberment occurred, Turkey
itself was engulfed by a tidal wave of nationalism. For some time the
more enlightened Turks had grown increasingly disgusted with the

weakness and incompetence of the sultan's government. Those who had been educated in European universities were convinced that their country should be rejuvenated by the introduction of Western ideas of science, patriotism, and democracy. Organizing themselves into a society known as the Young Turks, they forced the sultan in 1908 to establish constitutional government. The following year, in the face of a reactionary movement, they deposed the reigning sultan, Abdul Hamid II, and placed on the throne his brother, Mohammed V, as a titular sovereign. The real powers of government were now entrusted to a grand vizier and ministers responsible to an elected parliament. This revolution did not mean increased liberty for the non-Turkish inhabitants of the empire. Instead, the Young Turks launched a vigorous movement to Ottomanize all of the Christian subjects of the sultan. At the same time the disturbances preceding and accompanying the revolution opened the way for still further dismemberment. In 1908 Austria annexed the provinces of Bosnia and Herzegovina, which the Treaty of Berlin had allowed it merely to administer, and in 1911–1912 Italy entered into war with Turkey for the conquest of Tripoli.

The Young Turk revolution

Of all the major nations of the West, the United States probably underwent the least domestic turmoil during the several decades before 1914. The Civil War had exhausted the country; until the end of the century the ever-expanding frontier provided an alternative for those discontented with their present lot. Yet the United States also felt, to some degree, the pressures that made stability so hard to sustain in Europe. Though the Civil War had ended, the complex moral problem of racism remained to block all attempts to truly heal the nation. Severe economic crises, particularly an economic depression in the 1890s, accompanied by the collapse of agricultural prices and the closing of factories, caused great suffering and aroused anger at capitalist adventurers who seemed to be profiting at the expense of the country as a whole. Many grew convinced that a restricted money supply had produced the depression. Demand for the issuance of paper money and the increased coinage of silver were at the heart of the programs of the Greenback and the Populist parties, which attracted large followings, and which campaigned as well for an income tax and government ownership of railways, and telephone and telegraph lines. Socialism of a reformist brand was espoused by Eugene V. Debs (1855–1926), leader of a mildly Marxist Socialist party. It failed to appeal to the generally un–class-conscious American worker, who continued to have faith in the dream of economic mobility. More radical was the membership of the Industrial Workers of the World, a general union whose goal was to organize the unskilled and immigrant worker. Perceived as a device of foreign agitators, the IWW was repressed both by the government and by industrial management. Characteristic of the generally moderate tone of American reformism, the Progressive movement captured both the imagination and votes of a vocal minority of middle-class Americans whose hostility over

Unrest in the United States

Eugene Debs

the accumulation of private economic power and the political corruption of urban "bosses" was balanced by its belief in the democratic process and in the possibility of continuing progress. The movement, many of whose ideas were embodied in the programs of Presidents Theodore Roosevelt and Woodrow Wilson, was curtailed by the new realities that emerged with the advent of the First World War.

6. INTERNATIONAL RIVALRIES: THE ROAD TO THE FIRST WORLD WAR

Despite the domestic instabilities and uncertainties that characterized the Western world in the years before 1914, a great many men and women retained a faith in the notion of peaceful progress. There had been an absence of multinational armed conflict—with the exception of the Crimean War—for a century. European countries—even autocratic Russia—had been moving gradually toward what most agreed was the worthy goal of democracy. Indeed, instability could be understood as the result of either an overzealous or an overdelayed movement in that direction. Above all, industrialization seemed to be providing a better standard of living for all—or at least all within the Western world. There is little wonder, therefore, that men and women reacted with disbelief as they saw their world crumbling during the days of frantic diplomatic maneuvering just prior to the outbreak of war in August 1914.

The end of a century of peace

The key to an understanding of the coming of the First World War lies in an analysis of international diplomacy during the years after 1870. Europe had prided itself on the establishment of a balance of power, which had kept any one nation from assuming so predominating a position as to threaten the general peace. During his years as chancellor, Bismarck played a diplomatic variation upon this general theme, in order to ensure that France would not engage in a war of revenge against the German victors of 1870. There was little prospect that the French would attempt war singlehanded. Therefore, Bismarck determined to isolate France by attaching all of its potential allies to Germany. In 1873 he managed to form an alliance with both Austria and Russia, the so-called League of the Three Emperors, a precarious combination that soon foundered. Bismarck then cemented a new and much stronger alliance with Austria. In 1882 this partnership was expanded into a Triple Alliance with Italy. The Italians joined out of fear of the French. They resented the French occupation of Tunisia (1881), a territory which they regarded as properly theirs. Moreover, Italian politicians, still at odds with the Roman Catholic Church, feared that supporters of the papacy in France might gain the upper hand and send a French army to defend the pope. In the meantime, the Three Emperors' League had been revived. Though it lasted officially for only six years (1881–1887), Germany managed to hold the friendship of Russia until 1890, by means of a Reinsurance

The balance of power

Bismarck's diplomatic success

A diplomatic revolution

The Triple Entente

Treaty (1887) providing for the neutrality of either power if the other went to war.

Thus after more than a decade of diplomatic maneuvering, Bismarck had achieved his ambition. By 1882 France was cut off from nearly every possibility of obtaining aid from powerful friends. Austria and Italy were united with Germany in the Triple Alliance, and Russia after a three-year lapse was back once more in the Bismarckian camp. The only conceivable quarter from which help might come to the French was Great Britain; but, with respect to continental affairs, the British were maintaining a policy of "splendid isolation." Therefore, so far as the danger of a war of revenge was concerned, Germany had little to fear. Bismarck's complicated structure of alliances appeared to answer the purpose for which he claimed it had been built—to keep the peace. But the alliance system was a weapon that could cut two ways. In Bismarck's hands, it kept the peace. In hands less diplomatically capable, it might become less an asset than a liability, as was the case after 1890.

During the years between 1890 and 1907, European nations, competing across the globe for trade and territory, became more suspicious of each other. This general international insecurity produced a diplomatic revolution that obliterated Bismarck's handiwork, resulting in a new alignment that threatened the Germans. The Germans retained the support of Austria, but they lost the friendship of both Russia and Italy, while Britain abandoned its isolation to enter into agreements with Russia and France. This shift in the balance of power had fateful results. It helped convince the Germans that they were surrounded by a ring of enemies, and that consequently they must do everything in their power to retain the loyalty of Austria-Hungary.

The first of the major results of this diplomatic revolution was the formation of the Triple Entente between Russia, France, and Great Britain. William II of Germany, mistrustful of Russian ambitions in the Balkans, refused to renew the Reinsurance Treaty following Bismarck's dismissal in 1890. A growing coolness between the two countries led to Russia's political flirtation with France. Secret military conventions signed by the two countries in 1894 provided that each would come to the aid of the other in case of an attack by Germany, or by Austria or Italy supported by Germany. This Dual Alliance of Russia and France was followed by an Entente Cordiale between France and Great Britain. During the last two decades of the nineteenth century, the British and the French had been involved in frequent altercations over colonies and trade, as in the Sudan. By 1904, however, France, fearing Germany, had buried its differences with Britain and in that year signed the Entente. This was not a formal alliance but a friendly agreement, covering a variety of subjects. The final step in the formation of the Triple Entente was the conclusion of a mutual understanding between Great Britain and Russia in 1907. Again there was no formal alliance, but the ability of the two powers to reconcile their ambitions in Asia suggested a willingness to ally in case of war.

Thus by 1907 the great powers of Europe were arrayed in two opposing combinations, the Triple Alliance of Germany, Italy, and Austria-Hungary, and the Triple Entente of Britain, France, and Russia. Nevertheless, these new groupings were not without internal strains. Italy and Austria, though allied, were bitterly at odds over the disposition of territory in the Adriatic region—Trieste in particular, which the Austrians held and which the Italians claimed as *Italia Irredenta* (unredeemed Italy). The Italians had designs on portions of Africa as well. In the 1890s, under the premiership of Francesco Crispi, a hero of the Risorgimento, they had attempted to establish a protectorate over the Ethiopians, only to suffer a devastating loss at Aduwa in 1896. Now the Italians coveted Tripoli in North Africa, which they believed they might more easily obtain, over the objections of Turkey, if they supported the Moroccan claims of their French adversaries. Strains within the Entente were equally apparent. Britain viewed Russia's growing determination to control the Dardenelles as a threat to its supply routes to the East.

Strains within the two camps

The generally fragile state of international relations was certainly one of the important causes of the First World War. Yet it was by no means the only one. Recent scholars—most notably the German historian Fritz Fischer—ignited a controversy by insisting that the paramount reason was Germany's internally generated drive to power, its compulsion to aggrandize itself at the expense of the rest of Europe— not simply to achieve what the emperor had called its "place in the sun," but to see to it that the sun shone no more than fitfully on anyone else. Scholars of this persuasion, reacting to a more conventional view that has all nations sharing the blame, point to Germany's rapid commercial expansion, the growth, in particular, of its coal and steel industries, and its dockyards and overseas shipping as indications of its intentions. German capitalists financed the construction of a

German "war guilt"

The Baghdad Railroad. German and Turkish officials celebrate the launching of the enterprise.

Berlin to Baghdad railway, as part of a concerted *drang nach osten* (drive to the East). At the same time, the Germans launched a massive campaign to increase the size of their navy, a prospect particularly pleasing to the industrial bourgeoisie, who would profit directly from the new construction, and whose sons, excluded from the aristocratically based army, manned the naval officer corps. The naval buildup was accompanied by a brash and effective propaganda campaign—perhaps the first of its kind—directed by the secretary of the navy, Admiral Alfred von Tirpitz, and concerted through "navy leagues," organizations devoted to trumpeting Germany's intention of matching the strength of the British navy.

Others' responsibility

Others have taken issue with the notion that Germany faced the prospect of a preemptive war with equanimity, as it ignores the fact that many German industrialists did not want war since they had heavy investments in the economies of both Russia and France. They further argue that it is a mistake to view the problem of the war's outbreak through the single lens of Germany. They maintain that Britain's rapprochement with Russia and France, for example, reflected the demands of its own imperial policies and not simply a response to overweening German ambition.

Proliferation of "war machines"

Certainly the spirit of militarism extended beyond the borders of Germany, as all major European countries came to deploy massive "war machines." Serbia and Rumania, two very real threats to Austro-Hungarian security, possessed armies of over 400,000 each. In 1913, Russia embarked on a program of military expansion that bolstered its army by 500,000, to over 2,000,000 men, making it roughly equivalent in size to that of Germany. Nation after nation followed the German example by establishing a general staff, an institution one historian has called "the greatest military innovation of the nineteenth century." Problems of supplying and deploying mass armies had compelled governments to create a cadre of high-level planners, professional military advisors who were increasingly heeded by the civilian politicians to whom they reported. General staffs made it their particular business to deal with conscription, mobilization, the laying out of strategic railway lines—all complex technical issues demanding a high level of expertise.

Social impact of militarism

Reliance upon mass armies fostered a preoccupation with national birth rates, public health, and literacy. France regarded its declining birth rate after 1870 with alarm partly because it foretold a diminishing capacity to field a modern world-class army. If birth rates reflected a nation's long-term prospects for military manpower, the physical well-being of draft-age civilians was of immediate concern and encouraged reforms in health care and housing. A report on "physical deterioration" in Britain after the Boer War profoundly disturbed both military and civilian planners by demonstrating that in industrial cities such as Manchester as many as 8,000 out of 11,000 volunteers had been turned away by the army as unfit for military service. And, of course, with the introduction of increasingly sophisticated weaponry that required mastery of technological detail, noncommissioned officers and enlisted men could not function without the ability to read and to figure. The new armies had to be literate armies.

General European militarism was fed by notions of war as a therapeutic exercise. The French historian Ernest Renan had justified armed conflict as a condition of progress, "the sting which prevents a country from going to sleep." Middle-class citizens, anxious to prove themselves as patriotically aggressive as aristocrats, joined in the clamor to establish that the counting house was as much the seat of national fervor as the country estate. People began to speak increasingly of the "just" war. The British politician David Lloyd George praised the formation of a Balkan Alliance to fight the Turks in 1912 as "enlarging the boundaries of freedom."

*Notions of the therapeutic
value of war*

We have seen that in all the major countries of Europe clashes between the political forces of Left and Right threatened internal stability. The notion that revolution and counterrevolution were on the prowl heightened a mood that seemed to proclaim the inevitability of conflict. "Almost one might think the world wished to suffer," Winston Churchill wrote after the war was over. "Certainly men were everywhere eager to dare."

*Growing sense of the
inevitability of conflict*

Nationalism, too, fed the prevailing mood. From the beginning of the twentieth century, Serbia moved to extend its jurisdiction over all those alleged to be similar to its own citizens in race and in culture. Some of these peoples inhabited what were then the two Turkish provinces of Bosnia and Herzegovina. Others included Croatians and Slovenes in the southern provinces of Austria-Hungary. After 1908, when Austria suddenly annexed Bosnia and Herzegovina, Serbian activity was directed exclusively against the Habsburg Empire. It took the form of agitation to provoke discontent among the Slav subjects of Austria, in the hope of drawing them away and uniting the territories they inhabited with Serbia. It resulted in a series of dangerous plots against the peace and integrity of the Dual Monarchy.

Nationalism

In many of their activities the Serbian nationalists were aided and abetted by the Pan-Slavists in Russia. The Pan-Slav movement was founded upon the theory that all of the Slavs of eastern Europe constituted one cultural nation. Therefore, it was argued that Russia, as the most powerful Slavic state, should act as the protector of the smaller Slavic nations of the Balkans. Pan-Slavism was not merely the wishful sentiment of a few ardent nationalists; it was a part of the official policy of the Russian government, and went far toward explaining Russia's aggressive stand in every quarrel that arose between Serbia and Austria.

Pan-Slavism

All these factors—diplomatic instability, international militarism, domestic unrest, and nationalism—combined to produce a series of crises between 1905 and 1913. They were not so much causes as they were symptoms of international animosity. Yet each left a heritage of

Moroccan crises

The Iron Fist of the Kaiser Strikes Agadir. This British cartoon depicts the Germans' use of gunboat diplomacy in Morocco in 1911 to secure colonial concessions from the French as an overtly hostile and sinister act. In precipitating this Second Moroccan Crisis the Germans hoped to drive a wedge between Britain and France but succeeded only in driving the Entente powers closer together.

suspicion and bitterness that made war all the more probable. In some cases hostilities were averted only because one of the parties was too weak at the time to offer resistance. The result was a sense of humiliation, a smoldering resentment that was almost bound to burst into flame in the future. Two of the crises were generated by disputes over Morocco. Both Germany and France wanted to control Morocco; in 1905 and 1911 the two powers stood on the brink of war. Each time the dispute was smoothed over, but not without the usual legacy of suspicion.

In addition to the clash over Morocco, two flare-ups occurred in the Near East, the first in Bosnia in 1908. At the Congress of Berlin in 1878 the two Turkish provinces of Bosnia and Herzegovina had been placed under the administrative control of Austria, though actual sovereignty was still to be vested in the Ottoman Empire. Serbia also coveted the territories; they would double the size of its kingdom and place it within striking distance of the Adriatic. Suddenly, in October 1908, as we have seen, Austria annexed the two provinces, in flat violation of the Treaty of Berlin. The Serbs were furious and appealed to Russia. The tsar's government threatened war, until Germany addressed a sharp note to St. Petersburg announcing its firm intention to back Austria. Since Russia had not yet fully recovered from its war with Japan and was plagued by internal troubles, Russian intervention was postponed but not renounced. The Tsar's government resolved never to let itself be humiliated again.

Still more bad blood between the nations of eastern Europe was created by the Balkan Wars. In 1912 Serbia, Bulgaria, Montenegro, and Greece, with encouragement from Russia, joined in a Balkan alliance for the conquest of the Turkish province of Macedonia. The war started in October 1912; in less than two months the resistance of the Turks was shattered. Then came the problem of dividing the spoils. In secret treaties negotiated before hostilities began, Serbia had been promised Albania, in addition to a generous slice of Macedonia. But now Austria, fearful as always of any increase in Serbian power, intervened at the peace conference and obtained the establishment of Albania as an independent state. For the Serbs this was the last straw. It seemed to them that at every turn their path to western expansion was certain to be blocked by the Habsburg government. From this time on, anti-Austrian agitation in Serbia and in the neighboring province of Bosnia became ever more venomous.

It was the assassination of the Austrian Archduke Francis Ferdinand by a Serbian sympathizer on June 28, 1914, that ignited the conflict. The four-year war that ensued altered the Western world immeasurably. Yet many changes that came either during or after the First World War were the result, not of the war itself, but of pressures and forces we have seen at work during the prewar years, when European power, at its height, was challenged by forces which that power had unleashed and which it proved unable to contain.

Balkan Wars

A world at war

SELECTED READINGS

• *Items so designated are available in paperback editions.*

Barrows, Susanna, *Distorting Mirrors: Visions of the Crowd in Late Nineteenth-Century France,* New Haven, 1981. A study of crowd psychology.

• Berghahn, Victor, *Germany and the Approach of War in 1914,* New York, 1973. Examines the domestic background of German foreign policy, especially the naval program.

Blum, J., *Lord and Peasant in Russia from the Ninth to the Nineteenth Century,* Princeton, 1961. Contains a thorough discussion of emancipation.

Brogan, D. W., *France under the Republic, 1870–1930,* New York, 1940. An excellent survey, comprehensive and analytical.

• Dangerfield, George, *The Strange Death of Liberal England,* New York, 1961. Examines England's three major crises of the prewar period: women's suffrage, labor unrest, and Irish home rule.

• Emmons, Terence, *The Russian Landed Gentry and the Peasant Emancipation of 1861,* Charlotte, N.C., 1968.

• Fischer, Fritz, *Germany's Aims in the First World War,* New York, 1967. An extremely controversial study which seeks to lay major blame for the coming of the First World War on Germany.

• Haimson, L., *The Russian Marxists and the Origins of Bolshevism,* Cambridge, Mass., 1955. Analyzes the revolutionaries as part of the Russian radical tradition.

• Hale, Oron J., *The Great Illusion, 1900–1914,* New York, 1971. A general synthetic treatment of the period that is particularly concerned with mood and spirit.

Jenks, William A., *Austria under the Iron Ring, 1879–1893,* Charlottesville, Va., 1965. An examination of Austria's attempts at political and social reform, set in the context of a struggle for autonomy from German domination.

Johnson, Douglas, *France and the Dreyfus Affair,* London, 1966. A good survey, with breadth.

• Jones, Gareth Stedman, *Outcast London,* Oxford, 1971. A remarkable book which examines the breakdown in the relationship between classes in London during the latter half of the nineteenth century.

Mack Smith, Denis, *Italy: A Modern History,* rev. ed., Ann Arbor, Mich., 1969. An excellent survey.

• McManners, John, *Church and State in France, 1870–1914,* New York, 1972. Particularly good on the question of education and the final separation of church and state.

• May, Arthur J., *The Hapsburg Monarchy, 1867–1914,* Cambridge, Mass., 1951. A detailed narrative of the period.

• Mosse, W. E., *Alexander II and the Modernization of Russia,* New York, 1958. Brief but useful biography.

• Pulzer, Peter, *The Rise of Political Anti-Semitism in Germany and Austria,* New York, 1964. An excellent study of the roots of anti-Semitism and the part it played in shaping politics.

Ralston, David B., *The Army of the Republic: The Place of the Military in the Political Evolution of France, 1871–1914,* Cambridge, Mass., 1967. Useful for background to the Dreyfus affair.

Rémond, René, *The Right Wing in France: From 1815 to De Gaulle,* Philadelphia, 1969. Traces the survival of royalism and Bonapartism in French thought and politics.

Seton-Watson, Hugh, *The Russian Empire, 1801–1917,* Oxford, 1967. Standard survey.

Stavrianos, L. S., *The Balkans, 1815–1914,* New York, 1963. Surveys domestic and international affairs within the entire, troubled region.

• Taylor, A. J. P., *The Struggle for Mastery in Europe, 1848–1918,* Oxford, 1971. An excellent diplomatic history.

Thayer, John A., *Italy and the Great War: Politics and Culture, 1870–1914,* Madison, Wisc., 1964. Written to explain Italian policy and its origins in the prewar period.

Ulam, Adam, *Russia's Failed Revolutions: From the Decembrists to the Dissidents,* New York, 1981. Activities of revolutionary societies before 1917.

• Vicinus, Martha, ed., *A Widening Sphere: Changing Roles of Victorian Women,* Bloomington, Ind., 1977. Essays that trace the slow emancipation of Victorian women.

• Weber, Eugen, *Peasants into Frenchmen: The Modernization of Rural France, 1870–1914,* Stanford, 1917. Argues that the great achievement of the Third Republic was the consolidation of France, accomplished by bringing rural areas into the mainstream of modern life.

• Williams, Roger L., *The French Revolution of 1870–1871,* New York, 1969. A good narrative account.

Zelnik, R. E., *Labor and Society in Tsarist Russia: The Factory Workers of St. Petersburg, 1855–1870,* Stanford, 1971. The growth of class consciousness in Tsarist Russia.

SOURCE MATERIALS

• Childers, Erskine, *The Riddle of the Sands,* New York, 1978. A bestseller in England in 1903, this novel concerns a future war between England and Germany. Its reception gives evidence of the rise of anti-German sentiment prior to the First World War.

• Hamerow, Theodore S., ed., *The Age of Bismarck: Documents and Interpretations,* New York, 1973.

• Lenin, Nikolai, *What Is To Be Done?* London, 1918. Written in 1902, this is Lenin's most famous pamphlet. In it he called for the proletarian revolution to be led by elite cadres of bourgeois intellectuals, like himself.

• Mackenzie, Midge, ed., *Shoulder to Shoulder,* New York, 1975. A richly illustrated documentary history of the British movement for women's suffrage.

Pankhurst, Emmeline, *My Own Story,* New York, 1914. The memoirs of one of the leaders of England's militant suffragettes.

• Turgenev, Ivan, *Fathers and Sons,* New York, 1966. Turgenev's greatest novel is set in Russia in the 1860s and portrays the ideological conflict between generations at the time of the emancipation of the serfs and the rise of nihilism.

• Zola, Émile, *Germinal,* New York, 1964. Zola's realistic novel describes class conflict in France's coal-mining region.

Chapter 33

CHINA, JAPAN, AND AFRICA UNDER THE IMPACT OF THE WEST (1800-1914)

The virtue and prestige of the Celestial Dynasty having spread far and wide, the kings of the myriad nations come by land and sea with all sorts of precious things. Consequently there is nothing we lack, as your principal envoy and others have themselves observed. We have never set much store on strange or ingenious objects, nor do we need any more of your country's manufactures.

> —Edict of the Ch'ien Lung Manchu emperor to King George III of England, 1793

During the nineteenth century, for the first time in history the most advanced Western states, through the dynamic effects of the Industrial Revolution, became strong enough to alter the destinies of East Asian and African nations by direct intervention. Henceforth, the chief problems affecting these nations in this period revolved around the readjustments necessitated by Western expansion. Cultural phenomena were subordinated to political objectives, and international relations became of crucial importance. Because China, Japan, and the African states responded quite differently to the changing world conditions that confronted them, the contrasts among these countries became greater than ever before.

Increased Western intervention

1. IMPERIALISM AND REVOLUTION IN CHINA

It was unfortunate for China that intense pressure from Europeans seeking commercial intercourse came at a time when the country was afflicted with internal problems and the imperial government was beginning to show signs of decadence. The fact that the Ch'ing (Manchu) Dynasty had ruled for some 150 years, presiding over a state which, with some justification, it regarded as the center of civilization, made officials slow to realize the advantages to be gained from contacts with outsiders and left them with the comfortable assumption that the choice of granting or refusing contact would remain in their hands. Both the Manchu aristocracy and the Chinese class of scholar-officials that supported it were schooled in the tradition that trade was a contemptible business, unworthy of a gentleman's attention. The Westerners who came to China specifically for purposes of trade were looked down upon as a low order of humanity, and the power they were able to exert in enforcing their demands was slow to be recognized. The policy of the Manchu government was to avoid contamination from the Western hucksters by keeping them at a safe distance and requiring them to have relations only with Chinese merchants, not with government officials. At the same time the government expected to derive profit from levying taxes on whatever trade was permitted, and members of the bureaucracy from top to bottom also exacted commissions for extending privileges to merchants.

At the opening of the nineteenth century, although Western trade had reached fairly large proportions, it was still carried on under cumbersome restrictions which in many ways were disadvantageous to the Chinese as well as to foreigners. Aside from the Portuguese settlement at Macao, the only authorized port of exchange was Canton (by an imperial edict of 1757), at the opposite extremity of the empire from Peking, the seat of government. Silk and tea, the leading Chinese exports, had to be carried overland a distance of at least 500 miles to Canton; their transportation by boat along the coast was not permitted for fear that payment of the excise tax might be evaded. The trade at Canton was under the general supervision of a Manchu official known

"Factories" of the Foreign Powers in Canton, c. 1800. Chinese painting on glass. Western merchants were obliged to confine their activities to this prescribed area of the city. The "factories" were actually trading centers.

to foreigners as the "Hoppo" and was handled through a guild of Chinese merchants called the Co-hong. While the Co-hong merchants enjoyed a monopoly of foreign trade, they were taxed and "squeezed" by numerous officials and also were held personally responsible for the conduct of the foreigners with whom they dealt. Beginning about the middle of the eighteenth century a system of "security merchants" had been instituted, whereby every incoming foreign vessel was assigned to the supervision of a particular member of the Chinese guild during its entire stay in port. Foreign merchants were permitted to come to Canton only during the designated trading season (the winter months) and their activities were highly circumscribed. They were forbidden to bring their families or women with them, to ride in sedan chairs, or to employ Chinese servants. They were, theoretically at least, confined to the special area set aside for the "factories," and they could make no request to a government officer except through a Co-hong merchant as intermediary.

That the Canton trade was profitable both to the Chinese and to the foreigners is evidenced by the fact that it continued to grow in spite of the annoying regulations surrounding it and in spite of fluctuations in the assessments upon it. Foreigners were often kept in ignorance of the schedule of duties fixed by the Peking government. The Co-hong merchants—under pressure from the Hoppo, who in turn had to satisfy various other greedy bureaucrats and recover the expenses he had incurred in getting himself appointed to office—were inclined to charge what the traffic would bear. The foreign traders, if fleeced unduly, could of course threaten to break off intercourse altogether. Actually, remarkably stable relations were established between Chinese and foreign merchants at Canton. Large transactions were handled, sometimes on a credit basis, with only oral agreements between the two parties, and by communication through a vernacular known as "pidgin English."[1]

Methods of trade

As the volume of Western trade increased, friction was bound to arise. Two fundamentally different civilizations were coming into contact with each other. There were wide gaps between the Western and the Chinese concepts of justice and legal procedure. Westerners regarded as barbarous the Chinese view of group, rather than individual, responsibility for misbehavior and the use of torture in obtaining confessions. Consequently, misunderstandings occurred over the apprehension and punishment of criminals. Perhaps even more serious was the fact that the character of the trade began to change in a direction that was disadvantageous to China. In early days Chinese exports—tea, silk, and cotton cloth in lesser quantities—had far exceeded the value of imports into China; and the difference was made

The development of friction between Chinese and Westerners

---

[1] Some large fortunes were accumulated in the process. In 1834, one member of the Co-hong estimated his personal estate at $26,000,000. H. B. Morse and H. F. MacNair, *Far Eastern International Relations*, p. 68.

The Tribute Emissary. A Chinese view of the procession of gifts brought by Macartney to China, including the traditional objects that Europeans assumed were of interest to the Chinese emperors—astronomical and scientific instruments, elaborate clocks and other "ingenious articles" from the West.

up in silver payments to Chinese merchants. Western traders would have preferred to make the exchange in goods, but they had difficulty in discovering any appreciable Chinese demand for commodities which they could supply.

Eventually a means of altering the balance of trade was supplied by the opium trade. Opium had long been used in China as a medicine

The opium traffic

and as a drug, and the practice of smoking it was introduced along with tobacco smoking in the seventeenth century. Beginning with a decree of 1729 the emperor had attempted to suppress the practice, without success, and the importation of opium from abroad aggravated the problem. By 1829 more than 4 million pounds of opium were being shipped in annually. The importation of opium in large quantities, because it was paid for in hard currency, shifted the balance of trade to China's disadvantage. As silver flowed out of the country its value rose, creating hardship for the peasants who had to exchange their copper coins for silver in order to pay their taxes; and because the trade was illegal it brought no revenue to the state while lining the pockets of smugglers and conniving officials. When in 1834 the British East India Company was divested entirely of its trading functions and the traffic was thrown open to all comers,[2] the situation in China became more critical than ever. As British mercantile enterprise continued to expand, demand arose in England for the establishment of regular diplomatic relations with the Chinese government. An early attempt to secure this objective had failed. Lord George Macartney, dispatched in 1792 by the British East India Company on an armed naval vessel, was received courteously in Peking as a "tribute emis-

[2] See below p. 630.

sary," but his request for a permanent diplomatic residency was denied by the emperor Ch'ien Lung, who in a reply addressed to the British king affirmed: "The Celestial Empire possesses all things in prolific abundance and lacks no product within its borders. There is therefore no need to import the manufactures of outside barbarians in exchange for our own produce."[3] After considerable debate among Ch'ing officials, in which a proposal to legalize the drug was considered and rejected, the imperial government decided on a policy of strict prohibition and appointed Lin Tse-hsu, an able and experienced administrator, to enforce it. Commissioner Lin accordingly applied pressure on the Co-hong and appealed directly to the British traders. In 1839 he wrote to England's Queen Victoria urging her to prohibit the manufacture and sale of opium. Finding his efforts at persuasion unavailing, Lin finally halted all foreign commerce and blockaded ships in Canton harbor until their masters surrendered 20,000 chests of the contraband opium.

British anger over the interruption of trade, raised to the boiling point by the confiscation of the opium cargo, led to a series of incidents that culminated in the Anglo-Chinese War of 1839–1842. This conflict, which justifiably became known as the "Opium War," marked a turning point in China's international position. Although fighting was confined to the coastal regions near Canton and the lower Yangtze ports, the war served as an entering wedge for less restricted commercial intercourse and marks the beginning of the subjection of China to conditions imposed by the Western powers. By the treaty of Nanking in 1842 (supplemented the following year) the Chinese government ceded the island of Hong Kong to the British, promised an indemnity and compensation for the opium chests that had been seized, and agreed to treat Britain as a most favored nation in any future concessions that might be made. Four ports besides Canton were opened to trade, the Co-hong monopoly was abolished, and the right of residence was granted to foreigners in the treaty ports. Other nations, which had followed the course of the war with interest, were quick to follow the example of Britain in demanding treaties conferring similar privileges. A treaty negotiated by U.S. minister Caleb Cushing in 1844, besides granting the right to build hospitals, churches, and cemeteries on Chinese soil, specifically included the principle of extraterritoriality, which conceded to foreigners accused of crime the right to be tried in their own national courts rather than by Chinese tribunals. These initial treaties omitted reference to the opium traffic but provided that the Chinese tariff on exports and imports should be "uniform and moderate," a phrase interpreted as denying the Chinese government the right to raise the tariff without consent of the Western commercial powers. Thus by 1844 China was saddled with "unequal treaties," depriving her of controls over her tariffs and limiting the powers of her courts over foreigners.

[3] C. P. Fitzgerald, *China: A Short Cultural History*, 3rd Ed. pp. 357–58.

The Opium War of 1839–1842 and the "unequal treaties"

Commissioner Lin Tse-hsü. After finding the British immune to moral suasion, Lin resorted to stronger measures in the naive belief that they "dare not show any disrespect."

*Chinese Workers at a
Gold Mine in California*

*Results of the war and the
treaties*

The results of the Opium War were to intensify friction instead of removing it. Much of the fault lay with the foreigners, who took advantage of the weakness and corruption in the Chinese administration to enlarge their own interests. The privilege of extraterritoriality was abused, being extended to cover Chinese servants in the employ of foreigners, and inadequate punishment was given by the foreign powers to their own nationals who were convicted of crime. Portuguese vessels, and some others, engaged in "convoying," nominally to protect coastal shipping against piracy but actually to extort tribute from legitimate traders. Another reprehensible practice, carried on by Europeans and Americans during the middle of the century, was the recruiting of Chinese contract labor for export to plantations in the New World under conditions reminiscent of the old African slave trade. On the other hand, Westerners complained that the Chinese were evading both the spirit and the letter of the treaties. The attempt to establish foreign settlements at Canton led to rioting, because the Cantonese interpreted the treaties as granting foreigners the right of residence only outside the city walls. Less trouble was encountered in the new trading ports, where local sentiment was eager to attract commerce away from Canton now that Canton's monopoly had been broken. In Shanghai, the influx of foreigners resulted in the creating of an "International Settlement"—controlled jointly by British and Americans—and a separate French Settlement in the same city.

In all disputes with China the Western powers had the advantage of superior force, which they did not hesitate to use upon occasion. For a time, pressure was applied only locally, in the particular district where an untoward incident had occurred. In 1858, however, the British and French cooperated in large-scale hostilities against the Peking government. After negotiations at Tientsin (the port of Peking),

The war of 1858–1860

a misunderstanding arose as to the route for the foreign representatives to follow en route to Peking, whereupon the British and French forced their way up the river to the capital, drove the emperor in flight into Manchuria, and burned the beautiful summer palace of the Manchus. This war of 1858–1860 opened China more widely than ever before to Western penetration. The treaties of Tientsin and Peking added eleven ports to the list of authorized trading centers, granted foreigners the right to travel in all parts of China, and promised that Britishers would no longer be referred to in Chinese documents as "barbarians" and that official communications would henceforth be in English. At French insistence the Chinese government, compelled to acknowledge that "the Christian religion inculcates the practice of virtue," undertook to protect missionaries and their property. Evidently Christian virtue was not offended by traffic in opium, which by treaty was now legalized and subjected to a tariff.

While the Western powers were tightening their grip on China's commerce and installing their agents in its coastal cities, internal upheavals created havoc and threatened to overthrow the dynasty. The most famous of these and the most nearly successful was the Taiping Rebellion, which continued for more than a decade. Its originator was Hung Hsiu-ch'üan, a member of a non-Chinese ethnic group (Hakka) in Kwangtung province. Having thrice failed the provincial civil service examinations, Hung nourished a bitter grudge against

An Imperial Fortress Near Tientsin, 1860. Imperial resistance to European incursions continued for two years after the signing of the Treaty of Tientsin. This early "newsphoto" by Felix Beato records the damage inflicted upon imperial forces as they fell before Anglo-French assaults.

the Manchu government. Gradually his resentment became fused with a conviction that he had a divine mission to perform. He projected in his imagination an ambitious program to modernize China politically and economically, while at the same time creating an equitable but collectivist and theocratically directed society. Hung had received instruction for a short period from a Baptist missionary in Canton and, after an illness and a series of visions which he interpreted as revelations from God Almighty, he undertook to win his countrymen to the true faith. Hung's religion was largely Christian in ideology but with peculiar variations. He revered Christ as Elder Brother, and described himself as "Heavenly King and Younger Brother of Jesus." He also identified God with the ancient deity Shang Ti whom the Chinese had worshipped in preChou times, and therefore believed that in propagating his version of Christianity he was actually urging the Chinese to return to their own original faith. Taoism, Buddhism, and ancestor worship he regarded as idolatry, and his followers first attracted the attention of authorities by their zeal in desecrating temples. Eventually Hung conceived his destiny to be to lead the "Association for Worshipping God" in a movement to overthrow the Manchus and inaugurate the "Heavenly Kingdom of Great Peace." Thus the Taiping Rebellion was both an antidynastic revolt and a religious crusade.

The character of the Taiping reform program

Originating in the extreme south, the rebellion spread northward, gathering momentum as it went. By 1850 Hung had won 20,000 converts, and his forces included a women's-rights brigade. Highly emotional, ideologically radical, and utopian, the movement prefigured in some respects the twentieth-century Chinese Communist revolution. In 1853 Taiping leaders captured Nanking, which they retained as their capital for eleven years, entirely cutting off the rich Yangtze valley from the control of the Peking government, and imposing a program of radical reform. Hung's puritanical regime outlawed drugs, alcohol, prostitution, and even dancing. He introduced new examinations based on the Bible instead of the classics. He admitted women to office. The most utopian reform attempted was a law requiring the equal distribution of land among all families, removing the distinction between men and women in property rights, and providing for the storage of surplus crops in a common granary, thus creating an agrarian communism reminiscent of that developed by the Incas of South America.

Reasons for the failure of the rebellion

Although Taiping troops came within twelve miles of Tientsin in 1853 and the rebellion spread into fourteen of China's eighteen provinces, the movement finally collapsed for a variety of reasons. Hung, increasingly arbitrary and self-indulgent, quarreled with his associates. His reforms never extended beyond the regions under his control and were not fully carried out within them. While the rebels antagonized the gentry by their repudiation of Confucianism and, even more, by their threat to the property of large landowners, their idiosyncrasies alienated them from the common people and kept them from enlisting

the broad peasant support that brought the Communists to power a century later. Neither did the Taipings ally themselves with other movements opposing the dynasty. Probably the most decisive factor in their eventual defeat was the Taipings' inability to win support from the foreign powers that were involved in Chinese affairs. Some resident Protestants at first viewed the revolt with sympathy because of its associations with Christian teaching, but they soon became aware that a triumph of the Taipings would not serve the interests of Christian missionaries. Hung evidently believed that all Christians in China should accept his authority because his revelations were more recent

The role of the Western powers in the defeat of the Taiping Rebellion

The Empress Dowager T'zu Hsi. Nicknamed the "Old Buddha," she exercised de facto power over the Manchu government for forty-eight years.

The burden of weak leadership from the imperial throne

than any described in the Bible, and the rebel leaders became increasingly fanatical. The Western governments that had already successfully pressed demands upon the imperial court preferred a weak and compliant regime to one founded upon revolution.

Without formal intervention in the Taiping wars, the Western powers assisted the Manchus in suppressing the rebellion—even while the British and French were conducting their own war against the Peking authorities in 1858–1860. In view of the confused state of Chinese affairs, perhaps it is not strange that one of the military heroes in the imperial service was Frederick T. Ward, a sea captain from Salem, Massachusetts, who raised a volunteer corps for the protection of Shanghai contrary to the wishes of his own government and over the protest of British naval authorities. General Ward adopted Chinese citizenship, and, in gratitude for the exploits of his "Ever-Victorious Army," the emperor commanded that altars should be erected and perpetual sacrifices offered to his spirit. Ward's most distinguished successor was an Englishman, Major Charles ("Chinese") Gordon. Meanwhile several able Chinese, from the civilian gentry rather than from the professional military clique, had come to the rescue of the hapless Manchus and earned the major credit for suppressing the rebellion. In 1864, the combined Chinese, French, and British forces captured Nanking, the last Taiping stronghold.

The liquidation of Hung's "Heavenly Peace" movement did not bring peace even of an earthly variety to China. Muslim rebellions in the southwest and the northwest remained unsubdued until considerably later. During the thirteen years of Taiping intransigence two-thirds of the provinces had been devastated, the whole country impoverished, and probably no less than 20 million people killed by battle, massacre, and famine. The Manchu Dynasty had been saved only through the efforts of its Chinese subjects and by grace of the foreign powers. Furthermore, the injury to China's intellectual heritage through the destruction of libraries and academies in the Yangtze valley was incalculable.

The story of China from 1869 to 1911 is that of a dynasty struggling to recoup its strength while adjusting to the impact of alien forces and institutions. Lord Macartney's judgment on China, recorded in his journal in 1793 after his unsuccessful mission to Peking, was still apropos: "The empire of China is an old, crazy, first-rate man-of-war which a fortunate succession of able and vigilant officers has contrived to keep afloat for these one hundred and fifty years past," but which with lesser men at the helm would slowly drift until "dashed to pieces on the shore."[4] Although China did not lack able and intelligent individuals, their effectiveness was hampered by weak leadership from the throne. A succession of two minor heirs necessitated a regency, which placed power in the hands of a capable, strong-willed,

---

[4] Jonathan D. Spence, *The Search for Modern China*, p. 123.

extravagant, and scheming Manchu woman, the Empress Dowager, T'zu Hsi. Nicknamed the "old Buddha," she dominated the court from 1861 until her death in 1908, alternately supporting and interrupting reform programs.

Even before the crises of the nineteenth century, Confucian scholars had become critical of China's institutions, its educational system, the subjection of women, and other inequities in society. A powerful satirical novel written between 1810 and 1820 reversed the gender roles, picturing men binding their feet, piercing their ears, and performing menial tasks. The government's weakness as exposed in the Taiping Rebellion and in wars with the Western powers intensified a demand for the restructuring of institutions. Official efforts in this direction, while insufficient to save the regime, were genuine and remarkably ambitious in view of the difficulties to be overcome. A "self-strengthening" movement promoted the study of international law and of Western science and technology. The army was expanded, naval and military academies were established at Tientsin, arsenals and shipyards were constructed. Chinese students were allowed to study in France, Germany, and Great Britain. In the 1870s the government sent 120 boys to Hartford, Connecticut, where they lived with American families while attending school. Although terminated in 1881, this educational experiment demonstrated that Chinese could readily learn from Western tutors, at least in one department. Before sailing from San Francisco the Chinese boys defeated an Oakland, California, team in the great American game of baseball.

Out of the chaos of the Taiping era came a reorganization and centralization of the Chinese maritime customs service. A temporary arrangement, whereby foreigners had collected tariff duties at Shanghai while the authority of the Peking government was paralyzed, was perpetuated and extended to all the treaty ports. The higher personnel of the customs service was composed of foreigners, nominated by their consuls but appointed by Peking, with the understanding that so long as the English predominated in China's foreign trade the inspector general would always be a British subject. Thus the customs administration, while foreign staffed, was an agency of the Chinese government, maintained its headquarters at Peking, and operated as a unit regardless of provincial divisions. While the foreign inspectorate functioned efficiently, it was a reminder of the government's dependent position.

In the last quarter of the nineteenth century China's weakness was further revealed in the loss of some of its outlying possessions. By 1860 it had renounced to Russia all claims to territory beyond the Amur and the Ussuri rivers, thus allowing Russia to surround Manchuria and to control the entire Asiatic seacoast north of Korea. Through a combination of diplomatic and military pressure, culminating in a small-scale war (1884–1885), France acquired a protectorate over virtually all of Indochina except the independent state of Siam. The

The "self-strengthening" movement

The Mission School. Such schools also offered educational opportunities for the Chinese. Here a Chinese student at a mission school uses his queue to measure the radius of a circle.

A foreign-staffed customs service: efficient but dependent

Dividing the Chinese melon

The dilemma of intellectuals; K'ang Yu-wei

K'ang Yu-wei. A brilliant classical scholar, K'ang's belief that Confucianism was entirely in accord with notions of human development and progress informed his reform programs for China.

murder of a British explorer in China's southwestern province of Yunan led the British to demand, and China to yield, sovereignty over Upper Burma (1886). The Japanese government enforced a claim to suzerainty over the Ryukyu Islands (1881). Not to be outdone, the Portuguese, who had occupied Macao for 300 years, obtained its formal cession in 1887. The full measure of China's humiliation, however, followed the Sino-Japanese War of 1894–1895. Japan, only recently emerged from feudalism and isolation, gave the world a startling demonstration of China's impotence by defeating the Celestial Empire in the short space of eight months. Shortly afterward five great powers—Russia, Great Britain, France, Germany, and Japan— participated in a "battle for concessions," through which the major part of China proper was partitioned into "spheres of interest." The spheres of interest, somewhat vaguely defined and usually radiating from a leased port, theoretically did not impair China's sovereignty; but the concessions as a whole made the country an economic dependency of the great powers.

Increasing contact with the West aroused hostility against the intruders but also envy and admiration. While most of China was a land of peasants, untouched by an Industrial Revolution, the fruits of such a revolution were clearly seen in the treaty ports, where banking, commerce, and manufactures were carried on in full vigor. Antiestablishment intellectuals were ambivalent about Western institutions and their suitability for their own country. One of the ablest of these intellectuals, K'ang Yu-wei, hoped to retain the monarchy while leading it under a constitution toward enlightened goals. K'ang was a vigorous and original thinker with some very advanced ideas. He proclaimed the natural equality of men and women, and called on the world's 800 million women to work together to end their own subjugation. Willing to compromise for the present and push for modest reforms, he dreamed not only of a China able to hold its head up among other nations but of the evolution of nation-states through federations to an ultimate world union. In his utopian vision private property and the family would disappear into one "Great Community" united by a universal language and a common race. During a brief period, known as the "Hundred Days of Reform" (June to September 1898), the young emperor, under K'ang's guidance, issued a series of edicts calling for sweeping reforms in commerce, industry, and agriculture, an educational system offering Western learning and vocational training, and a modern army and navy. This innovative effort came to an unhappy end when the Empress Dowager T'zu Hsi executed a coup d'état and forced the emperor into retirement. K'ang Yu-wei escaped arrest and decapitation by fleeing the country.

Having rebuffed the liberal reformers, the Manchu court now sought to bolster its position by identifying with antiforeign movements that were gaining momentum, especially among the uneducated and disadvantaged. Several women's organizations had appeared, one of them

Boxer Uprising. German troops march into the Forbidden City of Peking after the rebels have been driven from the city.

under the name "Cooking Pan Lanterns." Most formidable was the "Society of Harmonious Fists," commonly known as the Boxers. Recruited mainly from peasants, the Boxers raised the cry "Revive the Ch'ing, destroy the foreign," and lamented in one of their songs that no rain fell from Heaven because "Churches have bottled up the sky." When in June 1900 the Empress Dowager declared war to drive foreigners into the sea, the Boxers unleashed a violent attack in Shantung and the adjacent northeastern provinces. Directed against Christians and foreigners rather than against the dynasty, the Boxer movement was at the same time an expression of bitter domestic discontent, aggravated by a severe drought in north China. Like the Taiping rebellion of a few decades before, it aroused violent emotions, especially among the youth; it was contemptuous of authority; and it inspired its followers with the simplistic belief that getting rid of the hated "devils" would bring a magical regeneration of society. In view of the fact that the movement was encouraged by the Empress Dowager and motivated by hatred of Westerners, it is surprising that the number of lives lost was not tremendous even in the critical areas.

The Boxer uprising

In other parts of China the provincial authorities, disregarding T'zu Hsi's instructions, generally tried to maintain order and protect the resident foreigners. Thus the Boxer movement was neither a revolution nor an actual war against the West; but the Western powers cooperated to stifle it with promptness and vigor, allowing their troops to indulge in wanton looting in Tientsin and in Peking, where far more damage was inflicted after the allied forces occupied the capital than while it had been held by the Boxers. Instead of abolishing the Manchu Dynasty as they might easily have done, however, the Western governments decided to shore it up, extracting certain guarantees of good behavior for the future. By the terms of settlement (the Boxer Protocol of 1901) China was assessed an indemnity equal to about twice the annual income of the empire, to be paid in gold over a forty-year period with 4 percent interest. The government was required to mete out punishments to certain of its own officials; the civil service examinations and the importation of arms were suspended temporarily; and the Western powers were granted permission to maintain military units in the Peking area.

The Manchu reform and modernization program

In a final attempt to save the dynasty and partly in response to foreign pressure, the Manchu rulers during the period 1901–1911 projected a comprehensive reform program which emphasized railroad construction, modernization of the military services, public education, and liberalization of the political structure. In 1905 the ancient civil-service examinations were formally abolished, preparatory to erecting a modern educational system. The government announced plans for a gradual transition to a constitutional regime with an elected parliament and, as a first step in this direction, established provincial assemblies in 1909. Although these assemblies were not democratically elected, they contained many individuals who, eager to speed up the process of change, spoke out so loudly that the government deemed it expedient to summon a National Assembly the following year. The National Assembly of 1910 had half its members directly appointed by the emperor's regent. Nevertheless, it proceeded to criticize the government and pressed the demand for more rapid reform.

The provinces versus the central government

The modernization process attempted by the Ch'ing in the first decade of the twentieth century eventually pitted the provinces against the central government. The initiative in developing a railway system and an efficient army was originally left to the provinces, which were expected to raise the necessary funds by stock subscriptions among the wealthy local citizens. In 1909, however, the Peking government took the whole program into its own hands, partly because it feared that decentralization was dangerous to imperial authority and partly because mismanagement and graft in the provinces were eating up the funds. The government's decision made it necessary to raise taxes and also to borrow from foreign capitalists, and angered provincial investors when they learned that their stock would not be redeemed at face value. The railroad controversy was only one among many

China's First Railway. Opposition from conservative rural interests to the first railway built near Shanghai in 1876 was so strong that the line was uprooted by provincial authorities a year later. Only when the Boxer uprising demonstrated its military value did the Manchus support railroad construction.

factors that brought antidynastic feeling to the point of open rebellion. In the fall of 1911, when outbreaks of violence occurred widely in China, a bomb explosion in Hankow touched off a general uprising in the Yangtze valley cities, during which Li Yüan-hung, commander of a rebellious imperial garrison, cast in his lot with the revolutionaries.

The revolutionary elements in China, which moved into the foreground with the impromptu insurrections of 1911, were by no means in agreement as to program or tactics. Liberal leaders, headed by K'ang Yu-wei, clung to the ideal of a limited monarchy. They would accept the continuation of the dynasty if it was willing to renounce absolutism. A more radical group wished to abolish the monarchy altogether and convert China into a republic. The prime figure among the radicals was Dr. Sun Yat-sen (1866–1925), born of a peasant family near Canton, in the province which had produced the leader of the Taipings and countless other opponents of the Manchu regime. At the invitation and expense of an elder brother, Sun had gone to Hawaii to obtain a Western education and had been converted to Christianity. After returning to China he studied medicine, chiefly with Protestant missionary physicians, and received a medical diploma at Hong Kong. He participated in an abortive revolt against the government in 1895, from which he barely escaped with his life. Thereafter Dr. Sun traveled widely, residing in the United States and visiting both England and continental Europe. During these years he had studied Western institutions, which he became convinced could be successfully adopted in China, and dedicated his energies to stirring up opposition to the Manchus among Chinese at home and abroad. In China his work was carried forward by a secret "Revolutionary

"Father of the Chinese Republic." Dr. Sun Yat-sen and his second wife, Soong Ching-ling (sister of Mme. Chiang Kai-shek).

Sun Yat-sen as radical leader

Yüan Shih-k'ai and the Revolution

Alliance," which attracted various disaffected elements in the period preceding the 1911 outbreak. Dr. Sun's leadership role was enhanced by his connection with the Soong family, several of whose members came to occupy key positions in the Chinese republic. "Charlie" Soong, an adventurous seaman-merchant and founder of the family fortune, after working for a Chinese firm in Boston, received an education in North Carolina, converted to Christianity, and became a preacher. Back in China, after producing Bibles for distribution, he turned to the manufacture of noodles and became wealthy. Dr. Sun not only was given funds secretly by the Soongs but he also married Charlie's daughter Ch'ing-ling.

Yüan Shih-k'ai, an able bureaucrat who had successfully reorganized the military forces in northern China but fallen into disfavor with the court, was recalled to service in the crisis of 1911. Keenly appraising the domestic situation, Yüan proceeded to perform a balancing act between the imperial government and the revolutionary forces. While he welcomed progressive reform, Yüan had no sympathy with demands for radical change. Yet, his demonstrated ability, which made him the Manchu's last hope, also appealed to liberals and revolutionaries, who were far from united and felt the need for an effective leader. K'ang Yu-wei's brilliant disciple Liang Ch'i-chao had declared that China would need an Oliver Cromwell to save it from chaos. Commissioned to repress the rebellion, Yüan Shih-k'ai avoided decisive battles and indicated a readiness to compromise. In November 1911 he was simultaneously elected premier by the National Assembly in Peking and appointed to the same office by the court. Meanwhile Dr. Sun's Revolutionary Alliance was gathering support in southern provinces and established a capital at Nanking in December. Dr. Sun, who had been living abroad, arrived at Shanghai on Christmas Day. After being named provisional president of the republic by the Nanking assembly, he sent Yüan Shih-k'ai a telegram offering him the presidency. Now reinforced with a triple mandate and recognizing that the revolution could not be turned back, Yüan persuaded the royal family to surrender its authority, securing for it a very generous settlement in return. On February 12, 1912, the boy emperor Henry P'u-yi abdicated, authorizing Yüan to organize a provisional republican government. The same month Dr. Sun's National Council in Nanking ratified Yüan's position as provisional president and scheduled national elections for December. The Guomindang (Kuomintang), or National People's Party, which had succeeded Dr. Sun's Revolutionary Alliance, campaigned vigorously, to the alarm of Yüan, who viewed the radical faction as visionary and dangerous to his own authority. When the parliament met in Peking in April 1913 to draw up a constitution, Yüan coerced the members into electing him president for a five-year term. He then dissolved the Guomindang and expelled its representatives from parliament which, left without a quorum, dissolved. Dr. Sun fled to Japan. From 1914 until his death two years later

Yüan Shih-k'ai ruled as a military dictator, backed by the northern army which he had organized for the imperial service and accepted as legitimate and given diplomatic recognition by the great powers. When opening parliament in 1913 Yüan, although not a Christian, had asked Protestants to pray for China in their churches, a gesture that brought warm praise from President Woodrow Wilson and his secretary of state Bryan, and prompted an American Protestant journal to liken him to Constantine the Great and Charlemagne "in subjecting pagan nations to the yoke of Christ." The Western governments, whose attitude toward the Chinese revolution had been remarkably apathetic, were on the whole favorably disposed toward Yüan and extended loans to him through an international banking group. The powers were willing to support a "strong man" in China—so long as China itself remained weak. Russian intrigue combined with Mongol nationalist sentiment to secure autonomy for Outer Mongolia; rebellion in Tibet enabled the British to extend their influence in that dependency; and the Japanese were beginning to cast covetous eyes on the Shantung Peninsula.

Although reactionary, Yüan Shih-k'ai's dictatorship at least demonstrated the fact that monarchy was thoroughly discredited in China. When Yüan committed the mistake of trying to perpetuate the power of his family by ascending the Dragon Throne as the founder of a new dynasty, he met with unexpected opposition. The great powers disapproved of his scheme, and fresh rebellions broke out in the southern provinces. The sudden death of the frustrated dictator in the summer of 1916 theoretically restored the republic under its "permanent" constitution. But a clique at Peking carried on Yüan's highhanded methods, while various provincial governors and military commanders were rendering themselves independent of any central authority. China, it seemed, had gotten rid of the Manchus only to fall prey to greedy and unprincipled warlords.

President of the Chinese Republic Yüan Shih-k'ai Flanked by His Body Guards

2. THE TRANSFORMATION OF JAPAN INTO A MODERN STATE

Japan's policy of restricted international intercourse, carefully maintained since the early seventeenth century by the Tokugawa Shoguns, was bound to give way when Western nations expanded their trading activities in East Asia. Before the middle of the nineteenth century several attempts, all unsuccessful, had been made by European powers to open Japan to trade. That the United States government finally took the initiative in forcing the issue was due partly to the fact that the British were busily engaged in China. It was also an indication that America's commerce had attained considerable proportions. Since about 1800, United States whaling and clipper ships had passed through Japanese waterways en route to China, and with the rise of

The United States and the opening of Japan

Commodore Perry and Townsend Harris

steam navigation the need for stations where ships could be refueled and provisioned became more imperative.

When Commodore Perry's "black ships" steamed into Tokyo Bay in July 1853, Perry was under instructions from Washington to secure from the Japanese government the promise of protection for shipwrecked United States seamen, permission for merchant ships to obtain repairs and fuel, and the right to trade. Perry's gunboats were sufficiently impressive to induce the Shogun to give a favorable reply when the commodore returned to Edo early the following year. However, the significance of the change in Japan's position was not apparent until a United States consul-general, Townsend Harris, after many vicissitudes negotiated a commercial treaty with the Shogun in 1858. Harris had no gunboats to back his arguments, but he skillfully used the object lesson of European aggression in China to convince the Japanese that they would be better off to yield peaceably to American demands. The Harris Treaty provided for the opening of several ports to traders and for the establishment of diplomatic intercourse, placed limitations on the Japanese tariff, and recognized the principle of extraterritoriality. Following the United States lead, other Western powers secured treaties granting them similar privileges, and it seemed that the pattern unfolding in China might be duplicated in Japan. But Japan's reaction to the Western impact resulted in a strengthening

One of Commodore Perry's Black Ships as Seen by a Japanese Artist in 1853. A source of endless fascination for the Japanese, these heavily armed iron ships embodied the industrial and technological power of the West at mid-century.

of the state, rather than its near disintegration as in the case of China. The reason for this contrast is that the Japanese, after recovering from their initial shock, succeeded in modifying their institutions to conform with Western standards without repudiating their own cultural heritage. Skillful adaptation enabled Japan to win recognition in the international community.

The first important effect of the opening of Japan was that it led to the abolition of the Shogunate, making possible a reorganization of the government along modern lines. The "outer daimyo"—especially the heads of four great domains: Choshu, Satsuma, Hizen, and Tosa—had long been awaiting an opportunity to displace the Tokugawa family from its dominant position. The action of the Shogun in yielding to the Western powers provided just such an opportunity. Before signing the treaties the Shogun had taken the unprecedented step of going to Kyoto to consult the emperor. The domain lords subsequently demanded that the emperor should be restored to his rightful position as ruler, denounced the Shogun for his weakness in submitting to the foreigners, and raised the cry that the "barbarians" must be expelled. The antiforeignism of the great daimyo was broken by direct action on the part of the "barbarians." In 1863, after an Englishman had been slain by people of the Satsuma daimyo, British vessels bombarded the domain capital. Duly impressed, the Satsuma leaders immediately voiced the desire to acquire a navy like that of Britain. The feudal lords of Choshu were similarly chastened and reoriented in their thinking in 1864 when British, French, Dutch and United States men-of-war unleashed a joint action upon Shimonoseki. In a remarkably short time the key men of the great feudal estates dropped their attitude of uncompromising hostility to the foreigners, meanwhile becoming more determined than ever to end the outmoded dual system of government.

The abolition of the Shogunate

In 1867 the Shogun was prevailed upon to surrender his prerogatives to the emperor. He had expected to be retained as generalissimo, and when he was ordered to lay down his military command also, he resisted. However, the principal daimyo, acting in concert and in the name of the emperor, quickly defeated the ex-Shogun's forces and relegated the Tokugawa family not to obscurity but to private station. Upon the abolition of the Shogunate, which had existed for almost 700 years, the imperial residence was moved from Kyoto to Edo, renamed Tokyo ("Eastern Capital"), and the old castle of the Shogun was converted into an imperial palace. This series of events constituted what is known as the Meiji Restoration.

Mutsuhito, Emperor of Japan from 1868 to 1912. Although the Meiji emperor did not wield great personal power, he did come to symbolize modernization of Japan.

It so happened that Emperor Mutsuhito, a lad of fifteen at the time of the Restoration, proved to be an extremely capable person who helped materially in the task of reorganizing Japanese institutions. The years of his reign, known as the Meiji or "Enlightened" era (1868–1912), witnessed the emergence of Japan as a modern and powerful state. Nevertheless, it would be a mistake to attribute Japan's trans-

The Meiji Restoration (1867–1868)

476

*China, Japan, and Africa under
the Impact of the West (1800–
1914)*

formation to the initiative of the emperor. As in previous periods of the country's history, effective leadership was supplied by less exalted figures, who used the throne as a symbol to promote a sentiment of national solidarity and to give the sanction of authority to their program. Quite understandably, the leaders in the political field were recruited chiefly from the ranks of feudal society, although they included some members of the old court nobility. In spite of their aristocratic backgrounds, the leaders were quick to perceive the necessity of breaking with the past if genuine progress along Western lines was to be achieved. Some of the daimyo voluntarily liquidated feudal institutions within their own jurisdiction, urging others to follow their example, and in 1871 the emperor formally abolished the whole feudal system. The hereditary fiefs reverted to the state and by authority of the emperor were divided into prefectures for administrative purposes; the peasants were made, in theory, free landowners, paying taxes instead of feudal rents. The daimyo and their samurai retainers were granted pensions (later converted into lump-sum payments) amounting to less than the revenues they had formerly claimed.

The revolution from above

The sweeping political, social, economic, and intellectual changes which took place in Japan during the Meiji era were sufficient to constitute a revolution. However, they were not the result of a mass movement or of any tumultuous upheaval from the bottom of society. The revolution was one directed and carefully controlled from above. The fact that the Tokugawa regime had already unified the country and through its discipline had instilled habits of obedience in the population facilitated the work of the Restoration leaders. The majority of the population played only a passive role in the transformation, even though they were profoundly affected by it.

*Prevailing spirit of
optimism:* Journal of the
Enlightenment

The ambitious changes and readjustments entailed by the Meiji Restoration were facilitated by a spirit of optimism that animated Japanese intellectuals during this period of transition. Optimism was indeed the prevailing mood among contemporary Western peoples, who had embraced the doctrine of progress and believed that its validity was demonstrated by their own material success and their expanding influence throughout the world. Champions of change in Japan were inclined to accept the West's appraisal of itself almost unreservedly, and they pronounced their own society barbarous or semicivilized because it lacked Western legal and educational systems, industry, technology, and science. Yet, strangely, while readily conceding Western superiority, Japanese spokesmen did not betray an inferiority complex. On the contrary, they expressed confidence that an enlightened Japan could catch up with the West and earn an honorable position among the nations of the world. A strong feeling of nationalism motivated the proponents of change as it did the conservatives who opposed change. In contrast to contemporary China, where the government floundered helplessly and reformers were driven to rebellion or despair, progressive-minded Japanese could witness with satisfaction an array of improvements instituted by their government. To promote the cause of national progress, a group of ten men, chiefly of samurai extraction but broadly educated, founded an "Enlightenment" society which met regularly for discussions, held public lectures and published a journal. Although after two years (1874–1876) the *Journal of the Enlightenment* suspended publication in the face of stringent censorship laws, its essays turned a searching spotlight on important political, economic, philosophical, moral, and scientific issues, ranging from the abolition of torture in the penal code to the protection of women's rights (stopping short of a declaration of the equality of the sexes). Even during the euphoric early years of the new regime some dissenting voices were raised. One critic, decrying an attitude of servility to the government, asserted that the Japanese had become too docile a people. What they needed to borrow from the West, he said, was not its institutions and techniques but its individualism.

Although many members of the samurai class found a good place for themselves, the abolition of feudalism exacted a real sacrifice of the samurai as a whole. The daimyo received a fairly generous financial settlement and were assigned ranks in a newly created order of nobility. But the samurai found themselves deprived of their incomes while, at the same time, the government forbade them to wear any longer the traditional two swords and ordered them to merge into the ranks of the commonalty. Smoldering discontent among the samurai broke out into open revolt in 1877, presenting the government with a test of strength which it met with complete success. The newly organized conscript army, composed of peasants with modern weapons, quickly defeated the proud samurai, and the rebellion of 1877 proved to be "the last gasp of a fast dying feudal society."

In carrying out their carefully channeled revolution, Japan's leaders made a painstaking study of the institutions of all the major Western nations and copied, with adaptations, what seemed to be the best features of each. In the political sphere, they reached the conclusion that the principles of constitutional monarchy should be introduced. A bold but somewhat ambiguous statement of policy, known as the Emperor's Charter Oath (1868), had hinted at the establishment of a deliberative assembly; but when plans for the drafting of a constitution were announced, it was made clear that any concessions would be in the nature of a gift from the throne rather than in recognition of inherent popular rights. A hand-picked commission drafted a constitution which, promulgated by the emperor in 1889, was patterned somewhat after the model of the German Imperial Constitution of 1871. It provided for a bicameral parliament or Diet, with a House of Peers (including some representatives of the wealthy taxpayers) and a House of Representatives chosen by an electorate of property owners. The Diet was assigned the normal legislative powers, except that its control over finance was limited, and the constitution included a bill of rights. In spite of some liberal features, the conservative character

The persistence of ancient traditions

Political parties

of the new government was unmistakable. So high was the property qualification for voting that only about 1 percent of the population was enfranchised. The position of the emperor was declared to be inviolable; he retained supreme command of the army and navy, directed foreign affairs, and could veto bills passed by the Diet. Notably lacking was the principle of parliamentary control over the executive; ministers were responsible not to the Diet but to the emperor. Furthermore, although there was a Cabinet of Ministers as well as a Privy Council, both these bodies were created *before* the Constitution went into effect. A peculiarity of the Japanese Cabinet (aside from the fact that it was not responsible to the Diet) was that the Army and Navy ministers could consult with the emperor directly, without the mediation of the premier.

While the Japanese constitution incorporated several important features and much of the nomenclature of Western political institutions, the government remained close to Japanese traditions in its spirit and functioning. These traditions (which had more in common with Confucianism than with Western political concepts) included such fundamental ideas as that men are by nature unequal and the inferior person should be subject to the superior, that society is more important than the individual, that government by man is better than government by law, and that the patriarchal family is the ideal pattern for the state.[4] Political reforms were considered only a means to an end, which was not necessarily to produce the greatest happiness of the greatest number but to promote the efficiency, strength, and prestige of the state. The men who, in consultation with the emperor, introduced the constitution of 1889 had no notion of relinquishing their command at the instigation of parliamentary cliques or under the pressure of public opinion. The guiding personalities were a fairly large group, numbering perhaps a hundred men, chiefly ex-daimyo and ex-samurai, who together composed a sort of oligarchy. Young men at the time of the Restoration, they retained their influence throughout the Meiji period and beyond, and eventually were referred to as the "elder statesmen" (*Genro*). Acting quietly behind the scenes, they frequently made important decisions of policy. Fortunately for Japan, these "elder statesmen" were as a whole realistic in outlook, moderate in judgment, and highminded.

In spite of the absence of democratic traditions and in spite of the authoritarian character of the Restoration government, the granting of a constitution led, almost from the outset, to a desire for further political reforms. Members of the Diet at least had the right to criticize the ministers, and voices were raised in favor of the extension of parliamentary control over the ministry. Political parties were organized, leading to a struggle in the Diet between the defenders of bureaucratic

[4] For an illuminating discussion of these concepts, see R. K. Reischauer, *Japan: Government-Politics,* chapter I.

government and the advocates of the cabinet system. The germination of political parties actually antedated the constitution. The "Liberal" party, which appeared in 1881, was primarily an outgrowth of an "association for the study of political science" founded several years earlier by Itagaki, a samurai of the Tosa domain. In 1882, Count Okuma of Hizen launched his "Progressive" party. These two "radical" aristocrats were doubtless motivated partly by resentment against the fact that their own affiliates had secured relatively few posts in the bureaucracy, most of which were filled by Choshu or Satsuma men. Nevertheless, the introduction of political parties helped to strengthen the movement for the establishment of representative government.

After the constitution went into effect, the character and the activities of political parties in Japan were peculiar and not entirely healthy. Emphasizing personalities rather than specific programs, parties came and went, fusing into one another, or changing their names in a bewildering fashion. Their effectiveness was lessened by their lack of a broad popular base, by the government's censorship of press and speech, and by the fact that when party spokesmen became too troublesome they could usually be quieted by offering them patronage or admitting them to the lower ranks of the bureaucracy. But, with all their faults, the parties provided opportunities for acquiring political experience and also forced the bureaucrats to explain and defend their policies to the public. The campaign to achieve party government— that is, to make the Cabinet responsible to the Diet—gained considerable headway on the eve of World War I and was resumed vigorously during the 1920s.

Significance of political parties

Experiments with constitutional government were only one aspect of Japan's political transformation. A modern and efficient military establishment was a prime objective that was rapidly attained, with a navy modeled after Great Britain's and an army copied from that of Germany, largely because the superiority of the latter had been strikingly demonstrated in the Franco-Prussian War. The principle of universal military service, introduced in 1873, was not a Japanese invention (although conscript peasant armies had been known to both China and Japan in ancient times and had played a part in Japan's feudal wars of the sixteenth century), but was based upon the example of modern European states. The administrative system was revised, and new judiciary and legal codes were adopted which compared favorably with those of Western countries and enabled the Japanese to claim successfully that they were not behind the West in the administration of justice. In 1894 Great Britain voluntarily surrendered extraterritorial rights in Japan, and by 1899 all the other powers had taken the same step. The abrogation of external control over the customs duties required a longer period of negotiation, but tariff autonomy was achieved in 1911. Henceforth Japan was entirely free from the humiliation of "unequal treaties."

Militarism and the abolition of foreign privileges

480

*China, Japan, and Africa under
the Impact of the West (1800–
1914)*

The growth of capitalism

The economic changes of the Meiji era were perhaps even more significant than the political. In Tokugawa feudal days Japan was far from being a purely agrarian nation, and before the Restoration of 1867 an urban economy, chiefly mercantile and capitalistic, had come into being. When the new regime undertook to strengthen the state and secure the benefits of Westernization, it launched an ambitious program for the development of industry and a modern system of communications. Because private capital was not available in sufficient quantities to do the job quickly and because of the fear that extensive borrowing from foreign investors would endanger Japan's economic independence, the government assumed the initiative in constructing railroads, telegraph and telephone lines, docks, shipyards, and even manufacturing plants, while it also aided private industry by loans and subsidies. There was no tradition of laissez faire in Japan to stand in the way of government participation in the economic sphere, and public officials were anxious to move ahead as rapidly as possible. However, many enterprises which had been fostered by the state were eventually transferred to private hands, although the state retained control of railways and communications for strategic and security reasons. Hence, in Japan, economic progress led to the growth of a capitalist class, but one which did not correspond exactly with similar classes in the Western industrial nations. The members of the new capitalist class, like the prominent political figures, were drawn largely from the old aristocracy, while not excluding men of bourgeois origin—money-lenders and rice merchants of the Tokugawa era. Daimyo now found a profitable field of investment for the funds they had received upon surrendering their feudal privileges, and the more nimble-witted of the samurai also participated in industrial development.

Manifestations of Western Influence. European-style buildings were constructed in Yokohama to house public schools, banks, and business firms that sprang up in the shadow of the flourishing silk industry.

The history of the famous house of Mitsui, which grew to be the largest combination of mercantile, financial, and industrial interests in Japan, illustrates the remarkable success of a samurai family that was shrewd enough to anticipate future developments. In early Tokugawa times the Mitsui, defying the prejudices of their class, had abandoned fighting in favor of the more solid rewards of commerce. They opened a store in Kyoto and in its management apparently anticipated the techniques of modern scientific salesmanship, displaying advertising posters and on rainy days giving away to customers paper umbrellas printed with the Mitsui trademark. Before the close of the seventeenth century, the family had established a banking house in Edo. The Mitsui heartily welcomed the opening of Japan to foreign trade, and so confident were they of the success of the Restoration that they lent large sums of money to the emperor and his entourage while the new government was in the process of formation. The Mitsui family also formed a connection with the great Choshu domain whose members filled important government posts, and thus were enabled to participate in various aspects of the economic program.[5] The Mitsubishi group of interests, which was the greatest rival of the Mitsui and, like them, developed under samurai leadership, effected a similar connection with the Satsuma group. In spite of the rapid industrialization of Japan, capitalists were relatively few, and they were generally affiliated with clan bureaucrats who dominated the government.

Mitsui and Mitsubishi

Industrial developments in Japan in the late nineteenth and early twentieth centuries differed in several respects from the typical pattern of economic change in the West. In the first place, they were so rapid that in one generation the country was producing a surplus of manufactured goods, and foreign markets had become essential to the national economy. Second, the Industrial Revolution was transported to Japan after it had already reached an advanced stage in the Western nations, and consequently characteristics of the early and late Industrial Revolutions were intermingled. The employment of women in industry at low wages, the lack of organization among the laborers or of legal safeguards to protect them, and the working conditions in factories and mines were parallel to the early stages of the Industrial Revolution in the West. On the other hand, the projection of the government into the business sphere and the appearance of finance capitalism were phenomena that were only beginning to manifest themselves in western Europe and the United States. To a considerable extent in Japan, finance capitalism preceded industrial capitalism, because there had not been time for financial reserves to accumulate from the savings effected by a gradual mechanization of industry. The wealth of the aristocracy and of merchant and banking houses—essen-

Peculiarities of Japanese capitalism

[5] O. D. Russell, *The House of Mitsui*.

Japanese Buddhists Expiate Their Sins. Japanese Buddhists, seen copying sutras in Zojoji Temple in Tokyo, reflect one of the traditional religious means of coping with the stress of modernization.

tially unproductive classes—was drawn upon to expedite industrial progress, and the fortunate members of these groups were in a position to dominate the productive enterprises of mining, manufacturing, and distribution as these grew to maturity.

Another peculiarity of Japan's industrial development was the fact that, while total production increased rapidly and some large plants were built for heavy industries, the majority of the factories remained small. Even in the 1930s, when Japan's industrial laborers numbered 6 million, almost three-fourths of them worked in small establishments employing fewer than a hundred workers and about one-half of them toiled in plants employing not more than five. The small factories, however, were usually not independent but were controlled by the great financial houses, which resembled trusts in their structure and obtained monopolies of whole fields of production. Workers in the cotton and silk textile mills, for example, might be likened to workers under the domestic system in early modern Europe, even though they tended machines instead of using hand tools. The supplying of raw materials and the distribution and sale of finished products—especially in the export trades—were handled by a few centralized organizations from which a network of controls extended over hundreds of tiny workshops scattered throughout the country. Naturally this system placed the worker at a great disadvantage, and his bargaining position was further weakened by the prevalence of an oversupply of cheap labor. In spite of the growth of huge cities, the larger part of the population remained on the land, which was insufficient in resources to support the peasant families. Hence these families were glad to supplement a meager income by letting some of their members, especially daughters, work in the shops for such wages as

The Japanese workers

they could get. Between the depressed class of small farmers and laborers and the wealthy capitalists, the gulf was as great as that which had separated the upper and lower strata of the old feudal hierarchy.

Extensive social and cultural changes also accompanied the transformation of Japan's economic and political institutions. Some of these changes were brought about deliberately by government action; others were unintended or even unwelcome. To carry out a program of Westernization a system of public education was clearly necessary. A Ministry of Education was established in 1871, careful studies were made of the procedures of Western countries, and schools were built rapidly at state expense. Japan was the first Asian nation to introduce compulsory education and did it so successfully that illiteracy almost disappeared, even among the poorest classes of society. There was also notable progress in instructional facilities at the higher level, providing boys with opportunities for technical and professional as well as academic training, and offering separate and more limited instruction for girls. The program was extremely ambitious and the curricula of the middle and higher schools were exacting. The study of Chinese classics and Confucian philosophy was retained, and to these were added—besides Japanese language, literature, and history—Western scientific and technical subjects as well as foreign languages. Notably lacking, however, was the encouragement of original thought. The system was devised to serve the ends of the government and aimed to produce a nation of loyal, efficient, and disciplined conformists. To that end, all students were required to take so-called "morals classes," which stressed patriotism. Western science and technology were appropriated without the liberal and humanistic traditions which had

Social and cultural changes

The Japanese Silk Industry. Rising demand for Japanese silk in the West spurred the importation of advanced technology in the 1870s and encouraged the expansion of the industry beyond the state-run factories into the private sector that was funded through commercial banks established by the likes of the Mitsui family.

engendered them; and investigation of the social sciences was almost entirely neglected. Thus, the emphasis was not upon the fullest development of the individual but upon enabling him to fit into a firmly fixed pattern of society without questioning it. The Ministry of Education exercised strict surveillance over teachers and texts, making the schools a powerful agency for indoctrination.

The creation of a wide reading public stimulated literary production, some of which was intended for mass circulation. Although Japanese writers were greatly influenced by contemporary Western literature, as reflected in their tendency toward realism, they were by no means mere imitators and produced literary work of great merit. Journalism became a flourishing occupation, and some newspapers of high caliber appeared. The Japanese press, however, labored under disadvantages, the most serious being the arbitrary and often erratic governmental censorship. Editors who dared to criticize officials, or who were merely unlucky enough to publish news which officials desired to keep from the public, were likely to be fined and imprisoned or to have their offices closed. It is significant that a considerable number of journalists, in spite of the risks involved, persisted in giving expression to independent and critical opinion.

In passing successfully through the difficult years of the Restoration period, the Japanese gave abundant evidence of vitality, courage, and versatility. In many fields they had come abreast of the Western nations, while they had also retained their own distinctive cultural heritage. At the same time, the accomplishments were not an unmixed good, and social problems had arisen which could not be easily solved. The most dubious aspect of Japan's condition, in spite of its mounting industrial strength, was in the economic sphere. Scientific knowledge, improved sanitation and medical facilities, and especially the impact of the Industrial Revolution induced a terrific increase in a population that had remained almost stationary for over a century. Between 1867 and 1913, the population grew from about 30 million to more than 50 million, and from this time on the rate of growth was still more rapid. There was hardly enough arable land in Japan to produce food for such large numbers, even under the most efficient methods of cultivation. While a brisk foreign trade could correct the deficiency, not only was a sufficient volume of trade difficult to maintain but the profits from manufacturing and commerce were concentrated in the hands of a small group. The standard of living of the farmers—the great majority of the population—remained almost at a standstill while the total national income was rising. With the abolition of feudalism, the peasants had become free landed proprietors, but their economic condition was not greatly improved thereby. Taxation bore far too heavily upon them; they had to compete in a cash market dominated by large landlords and industrialists; and their individual holdings were often insufficient to support a family. Many farmers had to supplement their small plots by renting additional holdings. Tenant farming in place of independent proprietorship became a striking characteristic of Japanese agriculture. The urban laborers were even worse off than the poor farmers; and Japan lacked a strong middle class to redress the balance of society. The revolutions of the Meiji era, unlike their counterparts in the Western world, were not essentially middle-class movements and had not broken the ascendancy of leaders whose ideals and outlook had been shaped in a feudal atmosphere.

The fundamental attitudes and loyalties of the old Japan passed into the new, even though they wore a somewhat different guise and were associated with more effective implements. It was not difficult for the creed of unswerving loyalty to a feudal superior to be converted into an intense patriotism, for which the emperor served as a symbol of national unity and object of common devotion. Ancient legends and the Shinto cults were refurbished to stimulate patriotic sentiments and to inspire confidence in Japan's unique destiny. As already suggested, an efficient and in many ways progressive educational system was utilized for this same end. The army, also, became an educational agency of a very potent kind. It was made up largely of literate but unsophisticated peasants, who found membership in the military establishment more rewarding financially and more gratifying to the ego than a life of grubbing on a tiny farm. The provincialism, prejudices, and legitimate resentments of the peasant rendered him susceptible to indoctrination by fanatics who preached the superiority of Japan over other nations, the infallibility of the divine emperor, and the subordination of civilians to the military. However, the influences promoting an authoritarian or militaristic regime were never unopposed. Continuous and broadening contacts with the outside world and a gradual reaction to the disturbing consequences of rapid economic change introduced a train of liberal thought, which threatened to collide with the forces of conservatism.

Japan's external relations during the Meiji era were directly related to, and appreciably affected by, internal developments. It is not strange that Japan, in the process of becoming a modern state, adopted a policy of imperialism, in view of its agility in assimilating the techniques of Western nations and also in view of the stresses created by the industrialization of the country. As time went on, however, differences of opinion appeared among Japanese statesmen, business and financial leaders, and intellectuals as to the proper course to pursue in advancing the interests of the state. Some conservative bureaucrats, generally unsympathetic to parliamentary institutions, favored an aggressive foreign policy. Others were primarily interested in building up Japan's economic and financial strength, securing foreign markets by peaceful penetration, and creating a prosperous and stable society at home. While not genuinely democratic, they at least accepted the implications of constitutional government and were anxious to win an honorable position for their country within the family of nations.

Japanese Agriculture. Above: Transplanting rice in a paddy field early in June. Below: Harvesting rice in a farm village. In the background is Mount Fuji.

A Gate of the Toshogu Shrine, Nikko National Park. Although the Japanese have adopted Western architectural styles for their public buildings, for their religious edifices they retain the native style, with its curved roofs and lavish ornamentation.

Fortunately for Japan, the moderate expansionists were fairly successful during this period in holding the militant faction in check, although not without making some concessions to them.

Japanese expansion in Eastern Asia would almost inevitably be at the expense of the decadent Chinese Empire. In 1876, the Japanese government took direct steps to end the isolation of Korea, a "hermit nation" which had been more tightly sealed against outside influences than Japan under the Tokugawa Shogunate. Copying a page from the Western book, the Japanese negotiated a treaty with the Seoul government which accorded them extraterritoriality and other rights, as well as opening Korea to commercial intercourse. The treaty also recognized Korea as an independent state, in total disregard of the fact that the Peking government considered the peninsula a tributary dependency of the Manchu Empire. Actually the Manchu officials had neglected to enforce their claims, and their belated attempt to recover their position by counterintrigue against the Japanese provoked a clash with Japan. Korea, at this time, was an ideal breeding ground for war. In spite of brilliant episodes in its past, the kingdom had degenerated into one of the most backward regions of Asia. The administration was corrupt and predatory, the peasants ignorant and wretched, and conditions in general thoroughly belied the country's poetic name—

Adventures in imperialism

Une partie de pêche.

A Cartoonist's View by George Bigot. Left: Japan and China fish for control of Korea as Russia awaits an opportunity to profit from the competition between them. Right: Japan's success against imperial China is blunted by Western imperialist powers who succumb to racist paranoia and refuse to accept Japan as an equal.

Chosen ("Land of the Morning Calm"). Japan's interest in Korea was both economic and strategic, the latter because Russia had acquired the Maritime Province on the Pacific coast directly north of the Korean border and had already attempted to intervene in Korea's troubled affairs. After a local rebellion had furnished the excuse for both China and Japan to rush troops into Korea, the Sino-Japanese War was precipitated.

It could be—and has been—argued that, beginning with its swift victory over China in 1895, Japan's policy in Asia was one of territorial aggression. In the treaty of Shimonoseki, Japan required from China not only recognition of Korean independence and the payment of an indemnity but also the cession of Taiwan, the Pescadores Islands, and the southern projection of Manchuria—the Liaotung Peninsula. Japan joined in the scramble for concessions in China, acquiring a sphere of interest in Fukien province opposite Taiwan. When harassed by the advance of Russian imperialism in Korea, Japan attacked Russia in 1904 and, after defeating its forces on land and sea, annexed the southern half of Sakhalin Island and obtained economic concessions in Manchuria. These facts, however, are only part of the story, which in its entirety indicates that the Japanese were adept in mastering the object lessons of European diplomacy and power politics. Following the Sino-Japanese War, under pressure from Russia, France, and Germany, Japan had been forced to relinquish its claim to the Liaotung Peninsula, on the ground that occupation of this region by a foreign power would threaten the safety of the Peking government. Almost immediately afterward, Russia, by a treaty of alliance with China, secured control of the very region it had denied to Japan and converted practically all Manchuria into a Russian sphere of interest. Several attempts on the part of the Japanese government to reach an accommodation with Russia in regard to Korea and Manchuria were frustrated by the recklessness and duplicity of the Tsar's agents.

Wars with China and Russia

Nevertheless, some influential Japanese considered war with Russia too dangerous an undertaking, and the government would probably not have dared to attack Russia except for the fact that the Anglo-Japanese Alliance of 1902 assured Japan of the friendly backing of the world's greatest naval power. The British welcomed Japan's accession to a position of strength as a means of checking Russian expansion in East Asia. During the Russo-Japanese War, sentiment in both Great Britain and the United States was prevailingly in favor of Japan, largely because of the devious and bullying tactics that the Russians had been pursuing. President Theodore Roosevelt's sympathy for Japan helped in terminating the hostilities, and the peace treaty was negotiated at Portsmouth, New Hampshire.

A temporary balance of power in East Asia

Japan's victory over Russia seemed for a time to restore a balance of power. Russia, shaken by the Revolution of 1905, and Japan, its financial reserves drained by the war, quickly agreed on apportioning their respective spheres in Manchuria—publicly affirming, of course, that they had no intention of violating China's territorial integrity. But the balance of power proved to be unstable. The outbreak of the European war in 1914, necessitating a "retreat of the West" from Asia, provided Japan with a golden opportunity to consolidate and extend its position.

3. AFRICA DURING THE CENTURY OF EUROPEAN IMPERIALIST EXPANSION

Free trade, abolitionist sentiment grows

By the opening of the nineteenth century, the cause for the abolition of the slave trade was winning a growing number of converts among governing circles in Denmark, England, France, and the United States. This was at a time when the overseas trade had increased more than fourfold in the last century and gave little indication of abating. Humanitarian abolitionist sentiment was strongest among the Quakers, particularly in Great Britain. And in the economic realm, a growing chorus of British merchants and industrialists questioned mercantilism and championed the doctrines of laissez faire and free trade. There was an increasing belief among plantation owners that free, paid labor was more efficient than slave labor. At the same time, sons of the Industrial Revolution were convinced that greater profits could be made from trade in tropical raw materials, especially mineral resources, needed to supply European industries. Moreover, British attitudes toward the establishment and maintenance of colonies had become increasingly negative since the fiasco of the American Revolution. In the first decade of the nineteenth century these sentiments prompted the legal banning of the slave trade. Denmark took the lead in 1805, followed by Britain and the United States in 1807. Henceforth, British naval squadrons in West African waters would protect legitimate traders and attempt to suppress the seaborne trade in slaves.

In West Africa the slave trade had contributed to the growth of autocratic, militaristic institutions in those societies that had profited from it. In some forest states, power had shifted from the elders, priests, and traditional chiefs to kings and their warrior bands. In the period 1400–1840 the internal traffic in slaves intensified, and African slavery was transformed from a marginal institution into a central feature of many societies. As early as 1650, slavery had become a key element in the social, political, and economic fabric in scattered states, particularly in West and West Central Africa, along the East African coast, and in Ethiopia. Slavery had become a distinct mode of production. In the nineteenth century, African slavery was harnessed to capitalism as the institution became internalized as a mode of agricultural production. American-styled plantations emerged in Dahomey, in the Sokoto Caliphate, and in several Swahili city-states along the East African coast. It has been argued that the transition from exporting slaves overseas to exporting agricultural commodities led to the more pervasive use of slaves within Africa itself. Indeed, by 1850, nonfree people made up near majorities of the population in numerous large market towns. Throughout the nineteenth century, the levels of enslavement for internal use remained at record highs, especially in the area between the Congo and Limpopo rivers. Thus, the end of the Atlantic and Indian Ocean slave traffic did not spell the collapse of the internal trade.

From the point of view of the missionaries and abolitionists, the productive capacities of Africans had been severely retarded by the slave trade. Therefore, it was now incumbent upon the Europeans to encourage farming, mining, and legitimate trading, and to stimulate the cultivation of cotton, tobacco, cocoa, and other cash crops which might contribute to an improvement in African living standards while also serving as a resource for European industries. Freed slaves from the ships of illegal slavers would be Westernized, Christianized, and returned to the "Dark Continent." Africa was still considered the "white man's graveyard," and humanitarians confidently assumed that repatriated blacks were better equipped to spread the fruits of Western civilization to their benighted brothers in the bush. All these assumptions, while perhaps well meaning, were deeply rooted in a cultural chauvinism dating back to the heyday of the slave trade. Yet in response to such sentiments, colonies for freed blacks were established by the British in Sierra Leone in 1808, by the Americans in Liberia in 1821, and by the French at Libreville in Gabon in 1849.

Ironically, the outlawing of the Atlantic slave trade contributed to an inflation in the price of slaves and a consequent growth in volume of the traffic. Furthermore, Eli Whitney's cotton gin, invented in 1795, created new demands for slaves on the plantations of the southern United States. The volume of trade was greater between 1810 and 1870 than in the entire seventeenth century. But major sources shifted from the Gold Coast through the Congo river to the coasts and interior of Angola and Mozambique. Brazil and Spanish Cuba became prime destinations, even though most slaves were carried in European and American–owned ships. Yet, in the final analysis, the United States absorbed less than 6 percent of the entire traffic since its inception. The growth in illicit trade led to more stringent attempts at suppression after 1820. United States participation in the antislave-trade naval squadrons propelled American legitimate merchants to Africa's shores in large numbers. Between 1850 and 1862, United States merchants, mainly from Salem, Massachusetts, dominated West African transatlantic commerce. From the late 1840s the Atlantic slave trade declined steadily. President Lincoln's Emancipation Proclamation of 1863 and recent antislaving laws in Cuba nearly brought it to an end. However, slaves continued to be shipped into Brazil until slavery as an institution was abolished in 1888. Clearly, the African slave trade was the largest involuntary migration in human history and between 650 A.D. and 1900 it may have resulted in the removal from Africa of more than 30 million people.

The emergence of a new merchant class

The slave trade and the concomitant traffic in European arms contributed to the emergence of a new class of African and mixed-race merchants in West African seaports. In their societies, power rested on personality and ability, not birth. A few of these merchants became extremely wealthy capitalists, but most of them were small-scale and undercapitalized and were edged out in the colonial era by European competition.

The House-Canoe system

The Atlantic trade after 1800 triggered unprecedented political and economic expansion in the palm-oil–rich Niger Delta. Local chiefs and affluent nonroyal enterpreneurs organized a remarkably democratic House-Canoe institution of governance, which acted as a coop-

Middlemen in the African Slave Trade. The nineteenth-century residence of a mulatto merchant who was active in the slave trade. Elmina, Gold Coast.

erative trading unit and as an institution of local government. The old hierarchical forest empires of Benin and Oyo, unable to adjust to the challenges of legitimate trade and to the rise of this dynamic merchant class, were gradually eclipsed. Asante and Dahomey, on the other hand, survived by culturally assimilating their slaves and organizing them to perform large-scale labor in Asante gold mines or on expansive plantations in Dahomey.

Former European slaving nations also had to make painful economic readjustments to the termination of the slave trade. After 1843 it was clear to the British that chartered companies lacked the financial resources to maintain the old coastal fortresses and warehouses. Reluctantly, the Crown assumed these responsibilities. The Dutch and the Danes failed to make the adjustment to the changing nature of trade and transferred their coastal installations to the British in 1850 and 1872 respectively. British treaties with African potentates, aimed initially at restricting the slave trade, gave way in the 1830s to treaties calling for the protection of European commercial interests through the establishment of consulates. British consuls would be responsible for ensuring the free flow of goods from the interior to European warehouses in coastal ports. Because the British treasury, bending to popular opinion at home, refused to undertake the costs of maintaining such enclaves, the consuls had to finance them by levying duties. Beginning in the 1860s, ambitious consuls, on their own initiative, did not hesitate to dispatch military expeditions to inland kingdoms to punish chiefs if they hindered the free flow of trade.

African and European responses to the abolition of the slave trade

Such interference in the affairs of African governments created a vicious cycle of political disintegration. Recalcitrant chiefs, humiliated and intimidated by the superior firepower of European weapons, lost their ability to hold distant provinces together. In Oyo in the 1860s and in Asante after 1874, this condition released centrifugal tendencies and contributed to a breakdown of law, order, and security. Oyo's economy, crippled from the decline of the Atlantic slave trade, was further weakened by the rise of a coastal trade in palm oil. As inland states, Benin and Oyo found it impossible to compete effectively with African trading houses located among the oil-rich estuaries of the Niger Delta. From 1821 to 1893 the Oyo empire in particular was torn first by a breakdown in the constitution, then by a destructive Fulani invasion that left its magnificent capital in ruins, and finally by civil war. By 1865 refugees from the countryside had begun to stream into stockaded villages like Ibadan, which swelled into sprawling cities. The Yoruba became an urbanized people almost overnight, and leadership passed into the hands of professional military men who could offer protection.

Political disintegration

Once the British had thrown their weight onto the balance of African rivalries, it became a matter of prestige and commitment for them to remain in Africa. In the Niger Delta in 1854 they exiled the powerful African trader king, Dappa Pepple, for cornering the lucrative

A British Colonial Officer on Tour in His Administrative District, a wood carving from Nigeria. During the colonial era African artists portrayed their European overlords in traditional African styles of sculpture, often highlighting their seemingly eccentric characteristics. The Europeans thought they were being caricatured while the Africans were depicting the world as they saw it.

British interference in
Nigerian trade and politics

palm-oil trade to the detriment of British nationals. In 1861 they established a consulate at Lagos, thus opening a hundred-year chapter of direct interference in Nigerian trade and politics. In 1874 they bombarded the capital of Asante in order to punish the king for closing trade routes to the coast. And after 1874 they squelched an experiment by the Fante people in nation building along Western democratic lines by declaring their territory a "Gold Coast Colony." Likewise, ambitious French governors in Senegal had, since 1854, become involved in the internal affairs of inland Muslim states.

Local initiatives and anti-
imperialist sentiment in
Europe

Significantly, these militant gestures were usually initiated not by home governments but rather by men in the field—governors, consuls, and sometimes traders. Before 1875, European powers rarely manifested an impulse to territorial empire in Africa. Nor had any of them formulated a coherent or consistent colonial African policy. The tide of public opinion, especially in Great Britain, ran against imperialist ventures, largely because they were so costly. Other than officials and entrepreneurs, those who came to Africa were usually scientists, privately financed and interested in resolving botanical, ethnographic or geographical questions; or they were missionaries and physicians like David Livingstone, who sought to root out domestic slavery and the internal slave trade, introduce modern medical practice, and further Christian proselytization.

The demystification of
Africa

By 1875 the major geographical mysteries had been solved: the course of the Niger River (1830), the source of the Nile (1862), Mounts Kilimanjaro and Kenya (1848 and 1849, respectively) and the vast river system of the upper Congo Basin (1860s). European explorers had also made direct contact with the major inland empires: Asante (1817),

Sokoto Caliphate (1824), Bunyoro (1872). By the 1850s quinine proved to be an effective drug for mitigating the effects of the hitherto deadly malaria. European probes into the interior now became more frequent and less costly in human lives. Fear of malaria had previously discouraged the white man from penetrating the tropical rain forest.

Like West Africa, East Africa during the first three quarters of the nineteenth century witnessed a dramatic revival of trade, particularly in slaves, cloves, and ivory. By 1800 Africans in what are today Kenya and Tanzania had begun to organize long-distance caravans and trading networks. Previously, items passed haphazardly from community to community before reaching their destination. Criteria for leadership among these small-scale societies now changed from skills in hunting and expertise in rain making to ability in organizing trade, negotiating business deals, and accumulating European manufactured weapons.

The Omani Arabs, preoccupied with internal strife in southern Arabia for a century, were reunited by 1805 and determined to reassert their authority over the East African coastal towns. Under the cunning leadership of Sultan Sayyid Said, Omani hegemony was restored and the capital was transferred from Muscat in Oman to the fertile and picturesque island of Zanzibar, some twenty miles off the East African coast. On Zanzibar, Sultan Said stimulated the growth of a vast plantation economy, built upon the cultivation of cloves and coconuts and worked by African slaves imported from the mainland. Indians were attracted to the island to serve as financial advisers and moneylenders to Arab and Swahili caravan operators.

Slaves were readily available in the 1840s because of a severe social and demographic upheaval in what are known today as Tanzania, Malawi, and northern Mozambique. Thousands of warrior bands of

The expansion of East African trade brings social, political, economic reorientations

Sayyid Said and the reassertion of Omani hegemony

Indian Financiers in Zanzibar. An Indian merchant's house in Zanzibar.

Panorama of the Island Town of Zanzibar. Zanzibar, one of the oldest Swahili city-states, may have been flourishing as early as the first century A.D. In the fifteenth century it was minting its own coinage and trading actively with

Ngoni streamed into the region from South Africa. They descended upon the local populations, which had no tradition of fighting and were therefore defenseless. Entire communities were often sold into bondage to Arab, Swahili, and other African slavers.

The East African ivory and slave trade

East Africa by mid-century had become the world's most important source of ivory and the major area for illicit slaving. Dispossessed captives were forced to carry huge quantities of elephant and rhinoceros tusks to the coast. The ivory was shipped to Britain and India while the slaves were sold either to Arab plantation owners on Zanzibar, to French planters on the nearby sugar-producing islands of Mauritius and Réunion, or to sheikhs in Arabia.

New East African trading networks

By the 1870s numerous East African individuals and communities had established their own trading networks and armed themselves to protect their economic spheres. The He-he, taking advantage of an unprecedented growth in the European arms traffic after the Franco-Prussian War, became highly organized warriors. Entrepreneurs like Tippu Tip and Mirambo forged their own extensive trading operations and successfully competed with the Arabs for inland resources. However, the Arabs enjoyed the financial backing of Zanzibar as well as commercial connections with Indian and Arabian overseas markets.

In 1843 Arab traders were received at the court of the king of Buganda

cities of the Persian Gulf and beyond. By the nineteenth century there was a significant Western presence. Note that the Sultan's palace, arsenal, and battery are flanked by European and American consulates.

on the northwest shore of Lake Victoria. Within another decade they extended their operations west of Lakes Victoria and Tanganyika. They were not interested in the propagation of Islam nor in territorial conquest; their sole concern was for trade. And for that reason they often found a warm reception among East African chiefs, who sought arms and imported luxury items in order to boost their own prestige.

Arab penetration

While the East African interior sank into a condition of almost complete social disintegration, Sayyid Said continued to build a vast commercial empire in the western Indian Ocean. Nearly every important coastal town from Mombasa in Kenya to the Mozambique border fell under Said's commercial sway. Not since the fifteenth century had the Swahili city-states enjoyed such prosperity. But it was a false wealth, based on exploitation of the interior. Fortunes were made in Zanzibar on slaves, cloves, and ivory; and the economic stability and security provided by Sultan Said attracted seafarers from Britain, Germany, France, and the United States. While these nations established consulates at Zanzibar, only the British one survived beyond 1850. Indeed, after the opening of the Suez Canal in 1869, the western Indian Ocean, particularly Zanzibar, became strategically more important to British interests in India than it had ever been before.

Growing British influence over the Zanzibar Sultanate

Since 1822, the British had forced on Sultan Said a series of ordi-

nances restricting his slave-trading activities. In return, the British navy would protect the Sultan's legitimate trade and government from foreign interference. Sayyid Said struck an excellent bargain and kept it until his death in 1856, after more than half a century in power. After his demise, the British quickly split his domain into two parts, Muscat and Zanzibar, with separate sultans over each. Henceforth, ambitious British consuls in Zanzibar used the pretense of slave-trade suppression as a cloak for the expansion of their own control over the Sultanate.

In the 1870s Zanzibar became a springboard for European missionary activity on the mainland. British, German, and French missionaries, Catholic and Protestant, followed the trails blazed only decades earlier by the caravan drivers. They found the interior of Tanzania in social and political chaos. The fabric of civilization had been almost totally destroyed. Yet along the western shores of Lake Victoria, the highly centralized kingdom of Buganda had begun to emerge as the most powerful state in East Africa. Its king, or *kabaka,* was both respected and feared by Europeans and Africans alike. Buganda itself had recently passed from a feudal to a bureaucratic stage of development and was in the process of undertaking an imperialistic policy of territorial expansion.

The nineteenth century in South Africa opened with a change of European rule at the Cape from the Netherlands East India Company to the British Crown. The Netherlands East India Company had established a refreshment station at Table Bay in 1652 for their ships sailing between the Netherlands and Java. By 1750 it had swelled into a large company colony, consisting not only of Dutch settlers and company employees but also of French Huguenots and Germans. Some merged into the indigenous African population to form a distinct racial group called the "Cape Colored." However, the majority of these predominantly Calvinistic settlers remained racially aloof and clung dogmatically to a fundamentalist interpretation of the Bible. Their religion became a justification for racial separation. Far removed from the European Enlightenment and liberal currents, they remained intensely provincial in outlook. The majority were illiterate farmers and cattlemen whose only socially cohesive force was the Dutch Reformed Church and its preachers, or *predikants.* As strong individualists, these frontiersmen resented the authority of company rule, emanating from distant Cape Town.

In 1795 the British temporarily occupied the Cape to prevent it from falling into the hands of Napoleon's navy. The Netherlands had already been overrun by the French and were in no position to assume responsibilities for the nearly bankrupt Netherlands East India Company. British occupation became permanent after 1806. Following the Napoleonic wars, Britain enjoyed mastery of the world's major sea lanes. The Cape Colony was thus taken primarily for its strategic importance in relation to India. Table Bay, at the foot of the African continent, offered one of the finest harbors en route to the Orient.

Britain's attempt to anglicize the Cape Colony met with fierce resistance from the predominantly Dutch settlers. The settlers hated the liberal, cosmopolitan, nonracial attitudes of these newcomers, many of whom were Anglican missionaries. They also resented the substitution of English for Afrikaans as the offical language and the introduction of British-staffed circuit courts, with judges who allowed slaves to testify against their masters. In 1834 the institution of slavery was abolished and Africans were henceforth equal to Europeans before the law.

Dutch settlers' resistance to Anglicization

The following year, several thousand Dutch settlers, called Boers, reacted to these ordinances by migrating en masse across the Orange River onto the high grassy plains known as the veld. This "Great Trek" culminated in the establishment of a series of autonomous racist republics. However, the so-called Promised Land had been inhabited by politically segmented but culturally related Bantu societies for nearly six hundred years. Their small, defenseless communities were no match for well-armed, determined foreigners. And indeed these Bantu peoples were caught amid three converging imperialistic thrusts backed by the force of arms: mixed-race groups seeking slaves to sell to white farmers in the Cape, Portuguese from Mozambique demanding slaves to work on Brazilian sugar plantations, and bands of Zulus and Boers each looking to secure new lands for their livestock and expanding families.

The Great Trek and the indigenous Bantu societies

British policy toward the Boers and Bantu had always been one of vacillation. In 1848 the British crushed the new Boer republics, only to restore their independence less than a decade later. Their policy

British vacillation

The Zulu City of Umgungundhlovu. All Zulu royal cities followed a consistent elliptical design. These were essentially predatory cities, which thrived not on market or craft activity, but on pillage of the surrounding countryside. At its zenith, Umgungundhlovu contained over 1,700 dwellings, capable of accommodating twenty soldiers in each. This city was burned to the ground by Boer commandos in 1838.

The African diaspora

regarding the Bantu swung from noninterference and racial separation to paternalistic cooperation and integration. The only constant elements in their policy were the prevention of Boer access to the sea and the minimization of Bantu-Boer conflicts.

Clashes between Zulu and Boer east of the Orange River brought havoc to the local Sotho, Nguni, and Ndebele populations and forced them to disperse in all directions. Some refugees coalesced and organized centralized kingdoms in parts of what are today Lesotho, Swaziland, Botswana, Zambia, and Zimbabwe. Others, like the Nguni, became warriors in self-defense against Zulu imperialism and moved northward across the Zambezi River into Tanzania. There these roving bands of Ngoni (as they were called in East Africa) caused the same kind of social disruption that had been inflicted upon them by the Zulu and Boers only decades earlier in their former South African homelands. In 1879, in a gesture of conciliation to the Boers, the British defeated the highly disciplined though ill-equipped Zulu and shattered their proud empire into thirteen weak chieftaincies. The Zulu empire ceased to exist, but Zulu nationalism and culture continued to flourish.

The new Ethiopian empire

Of the hundreds of African states, only Ethiopia and Liberia succeeded in withstanding the European imperialist conquest. Ethiopia survived largely because of its modernization programs. Since the 1850s it had begun to emerge from nearly four centuries of isolation. By 1855 a young warrior from the Shoa kingdom had gained control over the nearly independent kingdoms of Gondar, Gojjam, and Tigre, and in so doing had reunited them into an Ethiopian empire. Taking the title of Emperor Theodore II, he laid the foundations of a modern state through administrative reforms and through the creation of a modern national army. For the first time, an effort was made to bring the clergy's extensive feudal estates under government control and to weaken the provincial nobility by establishing districts under Theodore's own appointed governors.

Ethiopian expansion and modernization

Theodore's work was extended under Emperor Menelik II (1889–1913), who with Italian firearms launched an era of imperial expansion. By the turn of the century, he had through war and diplomacy conquered the Galla in the north, the Gurage and Kaffa in the south, the Muslim state of Harar and Somali-occupied Ogaden in the east, and Wallage in the west. At the Battle of Adowa in 1896 Menelik's 100,000-strong army defeated the invading Italians and saved Ethiopia from European conquest. From his new capital of Addis Ababa in the Abyssinian highlands, he employed European technocrats to construct highways and bridges, hospitals and schools, a postal and telegraphic network, a modern banking system, and a more efficient civil service.

Socially, however, Ethiopia remained an essentially feudal state, with most fertile lands held by the royal families and the hierarchy within the Coptic Christian Church. The peasants had little incentive to develop, and consequently food production remained stagnant under archaic methods of farming. Political institutions also failed to become more democratic, and power remained firmly in the hands of conservative aristocratic elites until the Marxist military coup in 1974. But even then, power simply shifted from a civilian dictatorship to a military dictatorship that confiscated all Church lands and collectivized agriculture.

Liberia, independent since 1847, also attempted to modernize, using the United States as a model. But faced with chronic economic stagnation, soaring debts, and gradual frontier encroachments by the British and French, the Liberians turned for survival to the United States in 1912. Though the nation became an economic dependency of American corporate and financial institutions, it was able to maintain its political sovereignty. This was largely due to solidarity among the Americo-Liberian ruling elites, whose ancestors had returned to Africa from America. Unfortunately, power was not shared equally with the indigenous Africans who were in the overwhelming majority. From the start, Liberia was a pigmentocracy under which skin color was an index of social and political status. This did not begin to change fundamentally until the military coup of 1980 that toppled the Americo-Liberian power structure.

The colonial era, which lasted roughly from 1875 to 1975, resulted in the full integration of Africa into the world economic system. Many African food farmers and hunters were transformed into producers of cash crops and miners of precious ores, both destined for export to processing plants in western Europe and North America. This process entailed a dramatic increase in seasonal migration, which removed men from their farms and families and weakened social structures. From the less fertile West African savanna, blacks migrated to cash-crop farms and plantations in the coastal belt, while in south-central Africa they sought wage employment in the mines of South Africa's Witwatersrand and Northern Rhodesia's copperbelt. Rural self-sufficiency was seriously undermined in the process.

All forms of traditional slavery were abolished. Slavery was replaced in French and Portuguese Africa by forced labor, which was often more brutal and inhumane. Moreover, slavery's abolition could not erase deep-rooted African prejudices against the descendants of slaves.

Free Africans lost control over the use and distribution of the land everywhere. In Kenya, Southern Rhodesia, and South Africa, they were herded into less fertile Native Reserves, where the soil was rapidly depleted through overuse and erosion. These overcrowded Native Reserves became reservoirs of cheap labor for European-owned farms and mines. The transfer of control over land and labor from the traditional elders, chiefs, and homestead heads to the colonial authorities altered fundamental social and political relationships. Moreover, the transition from polygyny to monogamy contributed to a narrowing of kinship relationships from the extended to nuclear family. This

500

*China, Japan, and Africa under
the Impact of the West (1800–
1914)*

profoundly affected socialization practices and traditional support networks.

To raise revenue, colonial governments gave concessions of mineral and agriculturally rich land to private companies. Most of these concerns were dominated by British, South African, and, later, American capital. Such concessions were most common in the French and Belgian Congo, Gabon, the German Cameroons and Togoland, Portuguese Angola, Southern Rhodesia, and Swaziland. Though the colonial powers espoused concepts of freehold land and representative government at home, in Africa they nationalized vast tracts of land and denied the franchise to all but a handful of Westernized elites. Prices were controlled, and overseas trade was monopolized through government marketing boards.

The social and economic roles of women were transformed in the colonial era. In non-Islamic rural areas women, who did most of the farming, lost power over production with the transfer of land from lineage ownership to individual male heads-of-household. The introduction of male-oriented cash-crop marketing organizations further eroded their position. In West African towns, on the other hand, some women benefited from new opportunities in local trading and in the retailing of goods imported from overseas. Other women who migrated to urban areas lost the support of their families and became prostitutes to survive.

Western medicine and substantial improvements in health care dramatically lowered infant mortality rates. But a higher incidence of respiratory, digestive, and venereal diseases kept life expectancy rates relatively low. Nevertheless, the colonial era witnessed an unprecedented population explosion. But with colonial emphasis on cash-crop production for export, staple food production failed to keep pace with population growth. By the mid-1920s, many governments were importing food from other parts of their empire, from Dutch Indonesia, or from North America.

The colonial era was accompanied by a vast expansion of transportation and communications networks and a return to more peaceful and secure conditions. This situation contributed to the explosive growth of Christianity and Islam.

Christian missionary stations provided health care and Western education, and were especially attractive to former slaves and outcasts seeking upward economic and social mobility. In return, missionaries demanded a radical reorientation in world view and life style. Ancestor veneration declined, along with the rich sculptural arts that sustained it. Polygyny was discouraged, and greater emphasis was placed on the individual as opposed to the group. Africans were baptized with Christian names that bore no relation to their former lives, and converts were expected to dress in Western attire and to master the language of their colonial overlords. As early as the late nineteenth century, growing numbers of African Christians broke from the culturally chauvinistic domination of the European-based churches and formed their own independent organizations. The new entities constituted a synthesis of Christian doctrine and varying degrees of indigenous cosmology and ritual.

Islam, for centuries confined largely to the market towns of the West African Sudan and the East African coast, now penetrated the rural areas. Islam seemed more tolerant than Christianity of indigenous social and cultural institutions. Like traditional African faiths, Islam was concerned with communal practices and spiritual divining. It tolerated spirit cults and ancestor veneration as vital to the maintenance of kinship structure and extended-family welfare. However, Muslims discouraged the representational arts and gave more attention to textiles, jewelry, leather-working, and music. Islam provided women even less scope for ritual participation and religious leadership than either Christianity or the traditional religions. Like Christianity, Islam favored patrilineal succession and inheritance. Both faiths imbued Africans with radical new conceptions of time and its measurement. Astronomically based calculations of time were more precise than those geared to seasons and provided for a more efficient ordering of human activity.

The impact of Islam

SELECTED READINGS

• *Items so designated are available in paperback editions.*

CHINA (*See also Readings for Chapter 21*)

Bays, D. H., *China Enters the Twentieth Century: Chang Chih-tung and the Issues of a New Age, 1895–1909,* Ann Arbor, 1978.

Ch'ên, Jerome, *Yuan Shih-k'ai,* 2d ed., Stanford, 1972.

• Chesneaux, Jean, *Peasant Revolts in China: 1840–1949,* New York, 1973.

Collis, Maurice, *Foreign Mud,* London, 1964. An account of life among the English merchants at Canton.

• Fairbank, J. K., *The United States and China,* 4th ed., Cambridge, Mass., 1979. Brief but perceptive.

Fleming, Peter, *The Siege of Peking,* New York, 1959. The Boxer uprising and its suppression.

• Franke, Wolfgang, *A Century of Chinese Revolution 1851–1949,* New York, 1971.

Gaster, Michael, *Chinese Intellectuals and the Revolution of 1911,* Seattle, 1969.

Hsü, C. Y., *The Rise of Modern China,* 2d ed., New York, 1975. Especially good on the nineteenth century.

• Levenson, J. R., *Confucian China and Its Modern Fate: A Trilogy,* Berkeley, 1968.

• Michael, Franz, *The Taiping Rebellion: History,* Seattle, 1972.

• Schiffrin, H. Z., *Sun Yat-sen and the Origins of the Chinese Revolution,* Berkeley, 1968.

• Spence, Jonathan, *The Search for Modern China,* New York, 1990. A masterly treatment of the last 400 years of China's history; comprehensive, clear, and judicious.

• Tan, C. C., *The Boxer Catastrophe,* New York, 1955.

Wakeman, Frederic, *Strangers at the Gate: Social Disorder in South China, 1839–1861*, Berkeley, 1966.

Yeng, S. Y., *The Taiping Rebellion and the Western Powers*, New York, 1971. Comprehensive and informative.

JAPAN (*See also Readings for Chapter 21*)

Allen, G. C., *A Short Economic History of Modern Japan, 1867–1937*, rev. ed., New York, 1963.

Barr, Pat, *The Coming of the Barbarians: The Opening of Japan to the West, 1853–1870*, New York, 1967.

Beckmann, G. M., *The Making of the Meiji Constitution: The Oligarchs and the Constitutional Development of Japan, 1868–1891*, Lawrence, Kan., 1957.

Borton, Hugh, *Japan's Modern Century*, 2d ed., New York, 1970.

Craig, A. M., *Chōshū in the Meiji Restoration*, Cambridge, Mass., 1961.

• Gluck, Carol N., *Japan's Modern Myths: Ideology in the Late Meiji Period*, Princeton, 1988.

Huber, Thomas, *The Revolutionary Origins of Modern Japan*, Stanford, 1981. Presents an unconventional view of the Meiji Restoration, downplaying the influence of the West.

Jansen, M. B., *Sakamoto Ryōma and the Meiji Restoration*, Princeton, 1961. A penetrating study of the conflict and confusion in Japanese politics at the end of the Tokugawa period.

• Lockwood, W. W., *The Economic Development of Japan, 1868–1938*, Princeton, 1954.

Reischauer, R. K., *Japan. Government-Politics*, New York, 1939.

Roberts, J. G., *Mitsui: Three Centuries of Japanese Business*, New York, 1974. Carries the story through the American occupation.

Russell, O. D., *The House of Mitsui*, Boston, 1939.

• Storry, Richard, *A History of Modern Japan*, Baltimore, 1960.

Walworth, Arthur, *Black Ships off Japan*, New York, 1946.

AFRICA (*See also Readings for Chapter 21*)

Anstey, Roger, *The Atlantic Slave Trade and British Abolition, 1760–1810*, London, 1975.

Baumgart, Winfried, *Imperialism: The Idea and Reality of British and French Colonial Expansion, 1880–1914*, Oxford, 1982. A brilliant study of British and French motives and the interaction of politics and economics in imperialist expansion.

Boahen, Adu, *African Perspectives on Colonialism*, Baltimore, 1987. A highly readable account of colonialism in Africa by a prominent Ghanian historian.

Bravman, René, *African Islam*, Washington, D.C., 1987.

Curtin, Philip D., *The Image of Africa*, Madison, Wis., 1964.

• Davenport, T. R. H., *South Africa: A Modern History*, rev. ed., Houndmills, U.K., 1987. Meticulously researched, balanced, and thorough account of South African history with emphasis on political history.

• Davidson, Basil, *The African Slave Trade*, Boston, 1961.

Donham, Donald, and Wendy James, *The Southern Marches of Imperial Ethiopia*, Cambridge, 1986.

Duignan, Peter, and L. H. Gann, eds., *Colonialism in Africa, 1860–1960,* London, 1975.

———, *The United States and Africa: A History,* Cambridge, 1984.

• Fage, J. D., *A History of West Africa,* New York, 1969.

Flint, John, ed., *The Cambridge History of Africa,* Vol. 5, *c. 1790 to c. 1870,* Cambridge, 1976.

Forde, D., and P. M. Kaberry, eds., *West African Kingdoms in the Nineteenth Century,* New York, 1967.

Guy, Jeff, *The Destruction of the Zulu Kingdom,* Johannesburg, 1979. A neo-Marxist interpretation by a highly respected African scholar.

Hargreaves, John D., *West Africa Partitioned,* vol. II, London, 1985.

Hartwig, G. W., and K. O. Patterson, *Disease in African History: An Introductory Survey and Case Studies,* Durham, N.C., 1978.

Hull, Richard, *Southern Africa: Civilizations in Turmoil,* New York, 1981.

Inikori, J. E., ed., *Forced Migration: The Impact of the Export Slave Trade on African Societies,* New York, 1982.

Konczacki, Z. A., and J. M. Konczacki, eds., *The Economic History of Tropical Africa,* Vol. 1, *The Pre-Colonial Period,* London, 1977

Liebenow, J. Gus, *Liberia: The Quest for Democracy,* Bloomington, In., 1987. A balanced, up-to-date, study of the political and economic history of Liberia with special attention devoted to the Republic's relations with the United States.

Manning, Patrick, *Slavery, Colonialism, and Economic Growth in Dahomey, 1640–1960,* Cambridge, 1982.

Miers, Suzanne, *Britain and the Ending of the Slave Trade,* London, 1975.

Miers, Suzanne, and Igor Kopytoff, eds., *Slavery in Africa: Historical and Anthropological Perspectives,* Madison, Wis., 1977.

Munro, J. Forbes, *Africa and the International Economy, 1800–1960,* London, 1976.

Ogot, B. A., and J. A. Kieran, eds., *Zamani: A Survey of East African History,* New York, 1969.

Penrose, E. F., ed., *European Imperialism and the Partition of Africa,* London, 1975.

Pope-Hennessy, John, *A Study of the Atlantic Slave Traders: Sins of the Fathers,* New York, 1969.

Roberts, A. D., ed., *The Cambridge History of Africa,* vol. 7, 1905 to 1940, Cambridge, 1986.

Rotberg, Robert I., *The Founder: Cecil Rhodes and the Pursuit of Power,* New York, 1988. A readable and penetrating psychobiography.

Wilson, Henry S., *The Imperial Experience in Sub-Saharan Africa since 1870,* London, 1977.

SOURCE MATERIALS

Braisted, W. R., tr., *Meiroku Zasshi: Journal of the Japanese Enlightenment,* Cambridge, Mass., 1976.

Crowder, M., and J. F. Ade Ajayi, eds., *History of West Africa,* Vol. I, New York, 1972.

Curtin, Philip D., ed., *Africa Remembered,* Madison, 1967.

• de Bary, W. T., ed., *Sources of Chinese Tradition,* Chaps. XXIV, XXV, XXVI, New York, 1960.
• ———, ed., *Sources of Japanese Tradition,* Chaps. XXIV, XXV, New York, 1958.
• Michael, Franz, *The Taiping Rebellion: Its Sources, Interpretations, and Influences.*
  The Complete Journal of Townsend Harris, New York, 1930.
• Teng Ssu-yü, and J. K. Fairbank, *China's Response to the West: A Documentary Survey,* 2 vols., Cambridge, Mass., 1954.
  Toson, S., *The Broken Commandment,* tr. K. Strong, Tokyo, 1974. A major novel of the Meiji period.
  Waley, Arthur, tr., *The Opium War through Chinese Eyes,* London, 1958.

Chapter 34

THE FIRST WORLD WAR

Nevertheless, except you share
With them in hell the sorrowful dark of hell,
Whose world is but the trembling of a flare,
And heaven but as the highway for a shell,

You shall not hear their mirth:
You shall not think them well content
By any jest of mine. These men are worth
Your tears. You are not worth their merriment.

—Wilfred Owen, "Apologia Pro Poemate Meo"

The war that broke out in 1914 was not really the "first world war." The wars against Napoleon at the beginning of the nineteenth century had extended beyond the European continent. Yet the war that took place between 1914 and 1918 had an impact that far exceeded any ever fought before. It quickly became a "people's war," to which civilians as well as soldiers and sailors were directly and totally committed. It bore fruit in revolution, and sowed the seeds of new and even more deadly conflicts in the future. It set the pattern for an age of violence that has continued through most of the twentieth century.

The world at war

1. PRELUDE TO WAR

The assassination of the Austrian archduke was the immediate cause of the First World War. Francis Ferdinand was soon to become emperor of Austria-Hungary. The reigning monarch, Francis Joseph, had reached his eighty-fourth year, and his death was expected momentarily. The murder of the heir to the throne was therefore considered in a very real sense as an attack upon the state. The actual murderer of Francis

The assassination of Francis Ferdinand

The Assassination at Sarajevo. Left: The Archduke Francis Ferdinand greets Bosnian notables a few hours before his death. Right: The police seize Princip after he had killed the heir to the Habsburg monarchy.

Ferdinand was a Bosnian student, Gavrilo Princip, the tool of Serbian nationalists. The murder, though committed in Sarajevo, the capital of Bosnia, was the result of a plot hatched in Belgrade, the Serbian capital. The conspirators were members of a secret society officially known as Union or Death, but commonly called the Black Hand. Their opposition to Francis Ferdinand stemmed from his support for a plan which would have resulted in the reorganization of the Habsburg Empire. This plan, designated as *trialism,* entailed changing the Dual Monarchy into a triple monarchy. In addition to German Austria and Magyar Hungary, already virtually autonomous, there was to be a third semi-independent region to accommodate the Slavs. Serbian national extremists opposed this scheme, fearing that if it were put into effect, their Slovene and Croatian kinsmen would be content to remain under Habsburg rule. They therefore determined to assassinate Francis Ferdinand before he could become emperor and press ahead with his reform.

The Austrians were immediately convinced that the Serbian government was behind this violent act. Austria waited for more than three weeks before acting on its suspicions and seizing the opportunity to extract a high price from Serbia for its transgressions. The delay was due in part to Austria's inability to decide how to proceed and in part to its unwillingness to mobilize its forces until after the harvest. On July 23 the Austrian government dispatched a severe ultimatum

See color map of Europe on the Eve of the First World War following page 550

Austrian ultimatum to Serbia

to the Serbians consisting of eleven demands: among them Serbia was to suppress anti-Austrian newspapers; to crush secret patriotic societies; to eliminate from the government and from the army all persons guilty of anti-Austrian propaganda; and to accept the collaboration of Austrian officials in stamping out the subversive movement against the Habsburg Empire. Two days later the Serbian government transmitted its reply. Of the total of eleven demands, only one was emphatically refused, and five were accepted without reservations. The Austrians, however, pronounced the Serbian reply unsatisfactory, severed diplomatic relations, and mobilized parts of their army. The Serbs themselves had been under no illusions about pleasing Austria, since, three hours before transmitting their reply, they had issued an order to mobilize their troops.

The Austrian intransigence vis-à-vis the Serbian response was actually the culmination of a belligerence that had been growing among European nations prior to the events that followed the assassination. As early as July 18 Sergei Sazonov, the Russian foreign minister, warned Austria that Russia would not tolerate any effort to humiliate Serbia. On July 24 Sazonov informed the German ambassador: "I do not hate Austria; I despise her. Austria is seeking a pretext to gobble up Serbia; but in that case Russia will make war on Austria." Russia had the support of France; on the twentieth of July, Raymond Poincaré, president of France, paid a visit to St. Petersburg to strengthen the Russian resolve to "be firm" and to avoid any compromise that might result in a loss of prestige for the Triple Entente. He warned the Austrian ambassador that "Serbia has very warm friends in the Russian people. And Russia has an ally, France."

The attitude of Germany in these critical days was ambiguous. Al-

Nicholas II and Raymond Poincaré, the President of the French Republic, in St. Petersburg on July 23, 1914

though the kaiser was shocked and infuriated by the assassination, his government did not make any threats until after the actions of Russia gave cause for alarm. Yet both William II and the chancellor, Theobald von Bethmann Hollweg, adopted the premise that stern punishment must be meted out to Serbia without delay. They hoped in this way to confront the other powers with an accomplished fact. The kaiser declared on June 30: "Now or never! Matters must be cleared up with the Serbs, *and that soon.*" On July 6 Bethmann Hollweg gave a commitment to the Austrian foreign minister which was interpreted by the latter as a blank check. The Austrian government was informed that the emperor would "stand true by Austria's side in accordance with his treaty obligations and old friendship." The Germans apparently hoped that by taking quick punitive action against Serbia, the Austrians would be able to counter a very real Serbian threat before Russia and its allies could recover from the shock of the assassination and mobilize either diplomatically or militarily.

Austria declared war against Serbia on July 28, 1914. For a fleeting, anxious moment there was a possibility that the conflict might be contained. But it was quickly transformed into a war of larger scope by the action of Russia. On July 24 the Russian government decided to respond to any Austrian military initiative against Serbia with a partial mobilization. By July 30, however, Sazonov and a prowar military clique persuaded Tsar Nicholas II to issue an order mobilizing all troops, not only against Austria but against Germany as well, on the grounds that such a vast country as Russia would require considerable time to get its military machine into operation.

There was now no drawing back from the abyss. The Germans were alarmed by Russian preparations for war. The latest action by the tsar's government made the situation far more critical, since in German military circles, and also in French and Russian, general mobilization meant war. Upon learning that the tsar's decree had gone into effect, William II's government sent an ultimatum to St. Petersburg demanding that mobilization cease within twelve hours. On the afternoon of August 1, the German ambassador requested an interview with the Russian foreign minister. He appealed to Sazonov for a favorable answer to the German ultimatum. Sazonov replied that mobilization could not be halted, but that Russia was willing to continue negotiations. The ambassador repeated his question a second and a third time, emphasizing the terrible consequences of a negative answer. Sazonov finally replied: "I have no other answer to give you." The ambassador then handed the foreign minister a declaration of war and, bursting into tears, left the room. In the meantime, the kaiser's ministers had also dispatched an ultimatum to France demanding that its leaders make known their intentions. Premier René Viviani replied on August 1 that France would act "in accordance with her interests," and immediately ordered a general mobilization of the army. On August 3 Germany declared war upon France.

August 1, 1914. A German officer reads the declaration of war in the streets of Berlin.

These grim timetables had doomed the efforts of Britain's foreign secretary, Sir Edward Grey, to convene a conference to settle the Austro-Serbian dispute. Perhaps if Britain had declared its readiness to go to war on the side of France and Russia earlier, that declaration would have compelled Germany and Austria to draw back. Yet Grey was not certain enough of his country's willingness to fight to make such a commitment. Although military conversations between the British and French had bound the former to an expeditionary force on French soil in case of war, the British public did not know this. Opinion was divided: Conservatives generally favored war; the Liberals, still in power, disagreed among themselves; Labour was opposed.

The British position

Fortunately for Grey and the prime minister, Herbert Asquith, both of whom wanted a British declaration of war, Germany's invasion of neutral Belgium brought together parliamentary and public support for intervention. In 1839, along with the other great powers, Britain had signed a treaty guaranteeing the neutrality of Belgium. Moreover, it had been British policy for a century or more to try to prevent domination of the Low Countries, lying directly across the Channel, by any powerful continental nation. The Germans planned to attack France through Belgium. Accordingly, they demanded of the Belgian government permission to send troops across its territory, promising to respect the independence of the nation and to pay for any damage

Britain enters the war

to property. When Belgium refused, the kaiser's legions began pouring across the frontier. The British foreign secretary immediately went before Parliament and urged that his country rally to the defense of international law and to the protection of small nations. The next day, August 4, 1914, the cabinet sent an ultimatum to Berlin demanding that Germany respect Belgian neutrality, and that the Germans give a satisfactory reply by midnight. The kaiser's ministers offered no answer save military necessity, arguing that it was a matter of life and death for Germany that its soldiers reach France by the quickest route. As the clock struck twelve, Great Britain and Germany were at war.

The conflagration spreads

Other nations were quickly drawn into the struggle. On August 7 the Montenegrins joined with their kinsmen, the Serbs, in fighting Austria. Two weeks later the Japanese declared war upon Germany, partly because of their alliance with Great Britain, but mainly for the purpose of conquering German possessions in the Far East. On August 1 Turkey negotiated an alliance with Germany, and in October began the bombardment of Russian ports on the Black Sea. Italy, though still technically a member of the Triple Alliance, proclaimed neutrality. The Italians insisted that the Germans were not fighting a defensive war, and that consequently they were not bound to go to their aid. Italy remained neutral until May 1915, when it entered the war on the side of the Triple Entente.

Diplomacy and the question of guilt

The diplomatic maneuvers during the five weeks that followed the assassination at Sarajevo have probably best been characterized as "a tragedy of miscalculation." Because the war brought such disaster in its train, debate about immediate responsibility for its outbreak has been continual and often acrimonious. The eventual victors—Britain, France, the United States, and their allies—insisted at the war's end that Germany assume that responsibility, and wrote German war "guilt" into the postwar settlement. Historians during the 1920s and 1930s challenged that harsh assessment, arguing instead that all the major European nations—and the alliance systems they had constructed—had driven the world into conflict in those fatal weeks during the summer of 1914. More recently, Fritz Fischer has insisted that William II and Bethmann Hollweg did everything they could to encourage the Austrians to go to war against Serbia, knowing that such a war would almost certainly engage the Russians on the side of the Serbians and the French on the side of the Russians. Undoubtedly there were those in positions of power in Germany arguing that war was inevitable, that to wait until Russia had fully recovered from its war with Japan, and until France's armies had been strengthened by its three-year conscription law, was to invite defeat. Better to do battle now, from a position of strength. It is now clear that Bethmann Hollweg, had, indeed, succumbed to such fatalism by July 1914.

2. THE ORDEAL OF BATTLE

Because the war soon demanded the wholehearted support of entire civilian populations, national leaders felt compelled to depict it as a noble conflict rather than a widespread quarrel between imperialist powers or the unexpected outcome of nationalist jealousies. The socialist Second International had declared that workers should respond to a call to arms with a general strike. Although none of the European socialist parties heeded that call, governments continued to fear subversion of the war effort from "below," and attempted to head off any such movement by ceaseless appeals to patriotism. Propaganda became as important a weapon as the machine gun. The task of the Allies was at first made easier by Germany's treatment of the neutral Belgians: their execution of civilian hostages, destruction of the ancient library at Louvain, and massacre of over six hundred civilians at Dinant.

A "patriotic" war

On August 6, 1914, Prime Minister Asquith declared that Britain had entered the conflict to vindicate "the principle that smaller nationalities are not to be crushed by the arbitrary will of a strong and overmastering Power." Across the Channel, President Poincaré was assuring his fellow citizens that France had no other purpose than to stand "before the universe for Liberty, Justice and Reason." Later, as a consequence of the writings of individuals such as H. G. Wells and Gilbert Murray, and the pronouncements of the American president, Woodrow Wilson, the crusade of the Entente powers became a war to redeem mankind from the curse of militarism. In the opposing camp, the subordinates of the kaiser were doing all in their power to justify Germany's military efforts. The struggle against the Entente powers was represented to the German people as a crusade on behalf of a superior *Kultur* and as a battle to protect the fatherland against the wicked encirclement policy of the Entente nations. German socialist politicians were persuaded to vote for the war on the grounds that a German war with Russia would help liberate the Russian people from the tsarist yoke.

Propaganda efforts

British Propaganda Poster. During the war governments, confronted with the bitter fruit of prewar militarism and nationalist rivalry, resorted to using any image that seemed likely to stir the passions of their populations against their foes.

The First World War fooled military experts who believed it would end quickly. Open warfare soon disappeared from the Western Front— the battle line that stretched across France from Switzerland to the North Sea, where the fighting was concentrated for four years. Germany's initially successful advance into France followed war plans drawn up by General Alfred von Schlieffen and adopted in 1905. Schlieffen's strategy called for Austria to hold against the Russians while Germany dealt a quick blow to the French, knocking them out of the war. Germany was then to turn, with Austria, to the major task of defeating the Russians. Contrary to expectation, however, the advance to the west, which brought German troops to within thirty miles of Paris, was halted. A series of flanking maneuvers by both sides ended in the extension of the battle lines in a vast network of trenches. Attacks to dislodge the enemy from their positions on the line failed to achieve more than very limited gains. Protected by barbed wire and machine guns—both making their first major appearance in a European war—defenders had the advantage. The one weapon with the potential to break the stalemate, the tank, was not introduced into battle until 1916, and then with such reluctance by tradition-bound commanders that its half-hearted employment made almost no difference. Airplanes were used almost exclusively for reconnaissance, though occasional "dog-fights" did occur between German and Allied pilots. The Germans sent Zeppelins to raid London, but they did little significant damage. Commanding officers continued to believe that the war would have to be won on the ground. Only by battering their enemies first with artillery and then with thousands of men armed with rifles, grenades, and bayonets, did they believe they could achieve the always-elusive "breakthrough." On more than one occasion those in charge of the war attempted to end the stalemate by opening military fronts in other areas of the world. In 1915, Britain and France attempted a landing at Gallipoli, in Asia Minor, in the hope of driving Turkey from the war. The campaign was a disaster for the Entente powers, however, failing, as did others, to refocus the fighting or to free it from the immobility of the trenches.

War of attrition

Life for the common soldier on the Western Front alternated between the daily boredom and extreme unpleasantness of weeks spent in muddy and vermin-ridden trench communities, and the occasional and horrifying experience of battle, a nightmare not only of artillery,

Life in the trenches

Trench Warfare. After the first few battles, the war on the Western Front settled into static or position warfare. During the four-year period, veritable cities of mud, stone, and timber sprang up behind the trenches.

Inside the British Trenches during the Battle of the Somme, 1916

machine guns, and barbed wire, but of exploding bullets, liquid fire, and poison gas. Morale among most troops remained remarkably steady, given the dreadful conditions in the trenches and the endless series of battles fought without significant gain to either side. Mutinies did occur among French troops in 1917, when soldiers moved forward in attack bleating like sheep, their pathetic way of protesting their commanders' continued willingness to lead them like lambs to the slaughter.

By 1916 the war, which appeared to have settled into an interminable stalemate, had extracted a fearful cost. Over 600,000 were killed and wounded when the Germans unsuccessfully besieged the French stronghold of Verdun, near France's eastern border, in the spring of that year. The Germans acknowledged that their aim was not so much to take the fortified city, which they knew the French would defend with desperation, but to "bleed France white of all able-bodied men"; yet the Germans lost as many men as the French. In August 1916 the British launched an enormous attack along the Somme River to ease the pressure on Verdun. Lasting from July to October, the battle cost the Germans 500,000, the British 400,000, and the French 200,000 in return for an Allied advance of seven miles across the front. On the first day of fighting alone, over 57,000 British troops were killed or wounded. Meanwhile, conditions within Germany worsened, as an Allied blockade slowly reduced the country's raw materials and food supply.

The enormous human cost

In time such losses fueled an unsuccessful move on the part of a minority on both sides to press for a negotiated peace. But in the minds of those who were making decisions, both military and civil-

Changes in leadership

ian, the immediate effect of the carnage was to reinforce determination to press ahead for total victory. This intransigence led, in turn, to changes in leadership. In Britain, the ineffectual prime minister Asquith was replaced by Lloyd George, a buccaneer politician who, if he had little new to propose, nevertheless projected a properly fervent public image. In France, the following year, Georges Clemenceau assumed the premiership, again with a mandate to counter a growing defeatist attitude within the military high command. And in Germany, control continued to pass into the hands of Generals Paul von Hindenburg and Erich Ludendorff, the men responsible as well for the overall military strategy of the Central Powers.

The expansion of the conflict

As the conflict dragged on, other countries were drawn into the war. Italy was bribed by the Allies with a promise of Austrian territories and a generous slice of the eastern shore of the Adriatic. Bulgaria joined the Central Powers in September 1915, and Rumania sided with the Allies a year later. It was the intervention of the United States on the Allied side, however, in April 1917, that tipped the balance. The United States entered the war vowing, in the words of its president, Woodrow Wilson, to "make the world safe for democracy," to banish autocracy and militarism, and to establish a league or society of nations in place of the old diplomatic maneuvering. Undoubtedly the primary reason for the American decision to enter the war, though, was the government's concern to maintain the international balance of power. For years it had been a cardinal doctrine in American diplomatic and military circles that the security of the United States depended upon a balance of forces in Europe. So long as Great Britain was strong enough to prevent any one nation from achieving suprem-

Wartime Leaders. Left: Allied Generals Haig and Joffre, and Prime Minister Lloyd George discuss strategy. Right: Reviewing a map are Hindenburg, William II, and Ludendorff, members of the German high command.

The Lusitania *Leaving New York Harbor*. In May 1915 the *Lusitania* was torpedoed and sunk by a German U-boat. Among the 1,200 people drowned were 119 Americans. The disaster was one step in the chain of events which led to the entry of the United States into the war on the side of Britain and France.

acy in Europe, the United States was safe. American officials had grown so accustomed to thinking of the British navy as the shield of American security that they found it difficult to contemplate any different situation. Germany, however, presented not merely a challenge to British naval supremacy; it threatened to starve the British nation into surrender and to establish a hegemony over all of Europe.

Submarine warfare

The direct cause of United States participation in the First World War was the U-boat, or submarine, warfare of the Germans. Once it became clear that the war would be one of attrition, the Germans recognized that unless they could break the Entente's stranglehold on their shipping, they would be defeated. In February 1915, the kaiser's government announced that neutral vessels headed for British ports would be torpedoed without warning. President Wilson replied by declaring that the United States would hold Germany to a "strict accountability" if any harm should come to American lives or property. The warning caused Germany to discontinue the campaign, but only temporarily. The Germans were convinced that the U-boat was one of their most valuable weapons, and they considered themselves justified in using it against the British blockade. They also believed, correctly, that the British were receiving war matériel clandestinely shipped aboard passenger ships from the United States, and continued to sink them, thus appearing to violate United States neutrality. When the kaiser's ministers announced that, on February 1, 1917, they would launch a campaign of unrestricted submarine warfare, Wilson cut off diplomatic relations with the Berlin government. On April 2 he went before Congress and requested and received a declaration of war.

The success of the Atlantic convoys

The immediate result of U.S. entry was an increase in the amount of war matériel and food—later, in the number of troops—shipped unmolested in armed convoys across the Atlantic. New ship construction overcame earlier losses; submarine warfare, Germany's most effective weapon against the Allies, had been neutralized.

3. REVOLUTION IN THE MIDST OF WAR

Gregory Rasputin

In the midst of world war came revolution. Russia, already severely weakened by internal conflicts before 1914, found itself unable to sustain the additional burden of continuous warfare. In a nation ruled as autocratically as was Russia, a successful war effort depended greatly on the determination and talents of its ruler, the tsar. Nicholas II was, by nature, irresolute and weak. His limited capabilities were further undermined by the irrationality of his wife, Alexandra, a religious fanatic, and of her spiritual mentor, the monk Rasputin. The latter had gained the tsarina's sympathy by his ability to alleviate the sufferings of her hemophiliac son, and used his influence over her to shape policy to his own self-aggrandizing ends. Russia's armies proved incapable of sustained success in the field. Although they managed to advance against the Austrians into Galicia in the south, they suffered two stunning defeats in 1914, at Tannenberg and the Masurian lakes in the north, losing almost 250,000 men in the process. In some instances soldiers were sent to the front without rifles; their clothing supplies were inadequate. Medical facilities were scarce. The railway system broke down, producing a shortage of food not only in the army but in cities as well. By the end of 1916, Russia's power to resist had all but collapsed.

The March 1917 revolution

The revolution in Russia followed a pattern of successive radicalization not unlike that of the French Revolution. It began in March 1917 with the forced abdication of the tsar. For this the immediate cause was disgust with the conduct of the war. The Russians had

Tsar Nicholas II and His Family on the Eve of the Revolution

Scenes from the Russian Revolution. Top left: Mass demonstration sponsored by the First All-Russian Congress of Soviets in which Bolshevik banners far outnumber the rest, spring 1917. Top right: Street fighting in Petrograd, summer 1917. Bottom right: Russian soldiers join the Bolsheviks in front of the Winter Palace, fall 1917.

attempted a major offensive in the summer of 1916, to coincide with the campaign along the Somme in the west. The offensive, though initially successful, turned into a humiliating retreat, however, thanks to transportation breakdowns and a lack of ammunition. In addition to military disasters, inflation and consequent high prices, and shortages of food and fuel had produced a rebellious urban population. Demands for a popularly elected, broad-based government were met by the tsar's determination to retain power in his own hands until bread riots in Petrograd precipitated the abdication. (The city had abandoned its supposedly Germanic name of St. Petersburg at the beginning of the war.) Troops summoned to quell the fighting broke ranks and joined the protesters, further evidence of the collapse of both civilian and military order. With the overthrow of the tsar, the authority of the government passed into the hands of a provisional ministry organized by leaders in the Duma in conjunction with representatives of workers in Petrograd, calling themselves a *soviet* or government council. With the exception of Alexander Kerensky (1881–1970), who was a member of a moderately socialist political group, nearly all of the ministers were middle-of-the-road bourgeois liberals. Their hope was to transform the Russian autocracy into a constitutional monarchy modeled after that of Great Britain. In accordance with this aim, they issued a proclamation of civil liberties, released thousands of prisoners, and made plans for the election of a constituent assembly.

The Kerensky government

The increasingly powerful soviets of workers and soldiers pressed for social reform, the redistribution of land, and a negotiated settlement with the Central Powers. Yet ministers of the provisional government insisted that demands for domestic change must be subordinated to the war effort, which they defined in terms of previously declared imperialistic aims. They argued that basic governmental and economic reform should await the convening of the constituent assembly. Because the provisional ministers could not govern without the cooperation of the soviets, Kerensky, vice-president of the Petrograd soviet by the summer of 1917, became prime minister. He organized a government which managed to retain power for several months. Meanwhile, opposition to the growing radicalization of the ministry—reflected in Kerensky's elevation—encouraged conservatives and liberals to make common cause, and to mount a military action led by General Lavr Kornilov, the commander-in-chief of the army, against the government. The attempted coup was crushed. Yet

Kerensky (second from right) and His Aides in the Winter Palace. This is the last known photograph of Kerensky in Petrograd.

Kerensky's own position had been undermined, his enemies on the Left arguing that Kornilov's ability to mount a counterrevolutionary effort was a sign of Kerensky's ineffectual leadership and willingness to compromise revolutionary aims.

On April 3, 1917, Lenin, who had been living in exile in Switzerland, was smuggled into Russia by the Germans, who recognized his potential as a revolutionary, and hence his value to them as a troublemaker. They correctly reasoned that his opposition to Russia's participation in the war would further weaken their enemy to the east. Throughout the spring and summer of 1917, while Kerensky was struggling to hold his government together, Lenin led the Bolsheviks on a bolder course which shunned all collaboration with the bourgeoisie and condemned their war policies. He soon became the leader of a vast popular uprising of workers, soldiers, and peasants; the Bolsheviks at this time clearly spoke to the people's needs as no other party did. Lenin, determined to sieze power from Kerensky, after Kornilov's failure waited on the advice of his fellow Bolsheviks until the convening of the All-Russian Congress of Soviets on November 7. The preceding day, a coup d'état, centered in Petrograd and directed by Lenin's ally Leon Trotsky (1879–1940), succeeded in overturning the provisional government.

Lenin and the Bolsheviks

Lenin immediately proceeded to issue decrees that would give substance to the Bolsheviks' slogan of "Peace, Bread, and Land." The "People's Commissars" (ministers) ordered the partition of land and its distribution to peasants, without compensation to former owners; nationalized banks, confiscating private accounts in the process; handed factory control over to workers; and began to negotiate a treaty with the Germans. The resulting agreement, signed at Brest-Litovsk in March 1918, surrendered Poland, Finland, and the Ukraine to the Germans. The treaty aroused the fury of Lenin's political enemies, both moderates and reactionaries, who were still a force to be reckoned with and who were prepared to plunge Russia into civil war rather than accept the revolution.

Revolutionary changes

Yet another outbreak of revolution in this period was the so-called Easter Rebellion in Ireland. At the beginning of the world war, Irish nationalists, who resented the rule of their country by the British, were ripe for revolt. They had been promised self-rule on the eve of the war, but the British later reneged on the grounds that a national emergency must take preeminence over everything else. This greatly angered the Roman Catholic majority of southern Ireland. They scheduled Easter Monday, 1916, as a day for revolt. British forces quelled the uprising, but not until a hundred people had been killed. Sporadic outbreaks kept the island in turmoil for years thereafter, but were finally brought to a temporary end by an agreement constituting southern Ireland as a free republic. The northern counties, or the province of Ulster, were to continue subject to the British crown.

The Easter Rebellion in Ireland

Strife in Ireland, 1916. British troops raiding the office of a Dublin printer who supported the rebellion.

4. ARMISTICE AND PEACE

Peace proposals

While the fighting raged on for four years, various attempts were made to bring about peace negotiations. In the spring of 1917, Dutch and Scandinavian socialists summoned an international socialist conference to meet at Stockholm to draft plans to end the fighting which would be acceptable to all the belligerents. The Petrograd soviet embraced the idea and on May 15 issued an appeal to socialists of all nations to send delegates to the conference and to induce their governments to agree to a peace "without annexations and indemnities, on the basis of the self-determination of peoples." The socialist parties in all the principal countries on both sides of the war accepted this formula and were eager to send delegates to the conference, but when the British and French governments refused to permit any of their subjects to attend, the project was abandoned. The rulers of the Entente states did not reject these proposals because they emanated from socialists. Indeed, a similar formula suggested by the pope was just as emphatically rejected. Nowhere was there a disposition to take peace proposals seriously. Woodrow Wilson, as spokesman for the Allies, declared that negotiation of peace under any conditions was impossible so long as Germany was ruled by the kaiser. The Central Powers regarded the general import of the papal suggestions with favor, but they refused to commit themselves on indemnities and restorations, especially the restoration of Belgium.

The Fourteen Points

The best known of all the peace proposals was President Wilson's program of Fourteen Points, which he incorporated in an address to Congress on January 8, 1918. Summarized as briefly as possible, this program included: (1) "open covenants openly arrived at," i.e., the abolition of secret diplomacy; (2) freedom of the seas; (3) removal of economic barriers between nations; (4) reduction of national armaments "to the lowest point consistent with safety"; (5) impartial adjustment of colonial claims, with consideration for the interests of the peoples involved; (6) evacuation of Russia by foreign armies; (7) restoration of the independence of Belgium; (8) restoration of Alsace and Lorraine to France; (9) a readjustment of Italian frontiers "along clearly recognizable lines of nationality"; (10) autonomous development for the peoples of Austria-Hungary; (11) restoration of Rumania, Serbia, and Montenegro, with access to the sea for Serbia; (12) autonomous development for the peoples of Turkey, with the straits from the Black Sea to the Mediterranean "permanently opened"; (13) an independent Poland, "inhabited by indisputably Polish populations," and with access to the sea; (14) establishment of a League of Nations. On several other occasions Wilson reiterated in public addresses that his program would be the basis of the peace for which he would work. Thousands of copies of the Fourteen Points were scattered by Allied planes over the German trenches and behind the lines, in an effort to convince both soldiers and civilians that the Entente nations were striving for a just and durable peace.

With Russia now no longer a combattant, Germany appeared to have gained an advantage that would almost guarantee ultimate victory. Yet by the late spring of 1918 the Germans were suffering acutely, not only because of the continued effectiveness of the Allied blockade, but because of a growing domestic conflict over war aims. German socialists attacked expansionist goals—control of the steel- and coal-producing areas of Belgium and of the agricultural regions in eastern Europe—which conservatives continued to urge and which the government endorsed. Socialists were alarmed as well by the reactionary administration imposed upon the territories taken from Russia at Brest-Litovsk. By the fall of 1918, Germany was a country on the verge of civil war.

Domestic conflict in Germany

German Supplies Moving toward the Somme during the Last German Offensive in 1918

Meanwhile, fighting continued as it had for four years on the Western Front. A great offensive launched by the British, French, and United States forces in July dealt one shattering blow after another to the German battalions and forced them back almost to the Belgian frontier. By the end of September the cause of the Central Powers appeared hopeless. Bulgaria withdrew from the war on September 30. Early in October the new chancellor of Germany, the liberal Prince Max of Baden, appealed to President Wilson for a negotiated peace on the basis of the Fourteen Points. But the fighting went on, Wilson now demanding that Germany agree to depose the kaiser. Germany's remaining allies tottered on the verge of collapse. Turkey surrendered at the end of October. The Habsburg Empire was cracked open by rebellions on the part of the empire's subject nationalities. A German-Austrian offensive in Italy in October 1917 had gained them a major victory at Caporetto, where Italian military police were ordered to shoot their own soldiers, if necessary, to stem the retreat. Yet a year later, the Italians responded to a similar attack with a counteroffensive that cost Austria the city of Trieste and 300,000 prisoners. On November 3 Emperor Charles, who had succeeded Francis Joseph in 1916, signed an armistice which took Austria out of the war.

Germany was now left with the impossible task of carrying on the struggle alone. The morale of its troops was rapidly breaking. The blockade was causing such a shortage of food that there was real danger of starvation. Revolutionary tremors that had been felt for sometime swelled into an earthquake. On November 8 a republic was proclaimed in Bavaria. The next day nearly all of Germany was in the throes of revolution. A decree was published in Berlin announcing the kaiser's abdication, and early the next morning he was moved across the frontier into Holland. In the meantime, the government of the nation had passed into the hands of a provisional council headed by Friedrich Ebert, leader of the socialists in the Reichstag. Ebert and his colleagues immediately took steps to conclude negotiations for an armistice. The terms as now laid down by the Entente powers provided for acceptance of the Fourteen Points with three amendments. First, the item on freedom of the seas was to be stricken (in accordance with the request of the British). Second, restoration of invaded areas was to be interpreted in such a way as to include reparations, that is, payment to the victors to compensate them for their losses. Third, the demand for autonomy for the subject peoples of Austria-Hungary was to be changed to a demand for independence. In addition, troops of the Entente nations were to occupy cities in the Rhine valley; the blockade was to be continued in force; and Germany was to hand over 5,000 locomotives, 150,000 railway cars, and 5,000 trucks, all in good condition. The Germans could do nothing but accept these terms. At five o'clock in the morning of November 11, two delegates of the defeated nation met with the commander of the Entente armies, Marshal Foch, in the dark Compiègne forest and signed the papers officially ending the war. Six hours later the order "cease fire" was given to the troops. That night thousands of people danced through the streets of London, Paris, and Rome in the same delirium of excitement with which they had greeted the declarations of war four years before.

The peace concluded at the various conferences in 1919 and 1920 more closely resembled a sentence from a court than a negotiated settlement. Propaganda had encouraged victorious soldiers and civilians to suppose that their sacrifices to the war effort would be compensated for by payments extracted from the "wicked" Germans. The British prime minister, David Lloyd George, campaigned during the election of 1918 on the slogan "Hang the Kaiser!", while one of his partisans demanded "Squeeze the German lemon until the pips squeak!" In all the Allied countries nationalism and democracy combined to make compromise impossible and to reassert the claim that the war was a crusade of good against evil. The peace settlement drafted by the victors inevitably reflected these feelings.

A harsh peace

The conference convoked in Paris[1] to draft a peace with Germany was technically in session from January until June of 1919, but only six plenary meetings were held. All of the important business of the conference was transacted by small committees. At first a Council of Ten was made up of the president and secretary of state of the United States, and the premiers and foreign ministers of Great Britain, France, Italy, and Japan. By the middle of March this body had been found too unwieldy and was reduced to the Council of Four, consisting of the American president and the English, Italian, and French premiers. A month later the Council of Four became the Council of Three when Premier Vittorio Orlando withdrew from the conference in a huff because Wilson refused to give Italy all it demanded.

The Paris Conference

The final character of the Treaty of Versailles was determined almost entirely by the so-called Big Three—Wilson, Lloyd George, and Clemenceau. These men were as different in personality as any three rulers who have ever come together for a common purpose. Wilson was an inflexible idealist, accustomed to dictating to subordinates and convinced that the hosts of righteousness were on his side. When confronted with unpleasant realities, such as secret treaties among the Entente governments for division of the spoils, he had a habit of dismissing them as unimportant and eventually forgetting that he had ever heard of them. Though he knew little of the devious maneuvers of European diplomacy, his unbending temperament made it difficult for him to take advice or to adjust his views to those of his colleagues. Lloyd George, the canny Welshman, possessed cleverness and Celtic humor that enabled him to succeed, on occasions, where Wilson failed;

The Big Three: Wilson, Clemenceau, and Lloyd George

[1] The conference did most of its work in Paris. The treaty of peace with Germany, however, takes its name from Versailles, the suburb of Paris in which it was signed.

The Council of Four. Meeting to draft a peace treaty in Paris were Orlando of Italy, Lloyd George of Britain, Clemenceau of France, and Wilson of the United States.

but he was above all a politician—shifty, and not particularly sympathetic to particular European problems such as nationalism.

The third member of the great triumvirate was the aged and cynical French premier, Georges Clemenceau. Born in 1841, Clemenceau had been a journalist in the United States just after the Civil War. Later he had won his nickname of "the Tiger" as a relentless foe of clericals and monarchists. He had fought for the republic during the stormy days of the Boulangist episode, the Dreyfus affair, and the struggle for separation of church and state. Twice in his lifetime he had seen France invaded and its existence gravely imperiled. Now the tables were turned, and the French, he believed, should take full advantage of their opportunity. Only by keeping a strict control over a prostrate Germany could the security of France be preserved.

Emasculating the Fourteen Points

From the beginning a number of embarrassing problems confronted the chief architects of the Versailles treaty. The most important was what to do about the Fourteen Points. There could be no doubt that they had been the basis of the German surrender on November 11. It was beyond question also that Wilson had represented them as the Entente program for a permanent peace. Consequently there was every reason for the peoples of the world to expect that the Fourteen Points would be the model for the Versailles settlement—subject only to the three amendments made before the armistice was signed. In actuality, however, no one among the highest dignitaries at the conference, with the exception of Wilson himself, gave more than lip service to the Fourteen Points. In the end, the American president was able to salvage, in unmodified form, only four parts of his famous program: point seven, requiring the restoration of Belgium; point eight, demanding the return of Alsace and Lorraine to France; point ten, providing for independence for the peoples of Austria-Hungary; and the final provision calling for a League of Nations. The others were ignored or modified to such an extent as to change their original meanings.

By the end of April 1919 the terms of the Versailles treaty were ready for submission to the enemy, and Germany was ordered to send delegates to receive them. On April 29, a delegation headed by Count von Brockdorff-Rantzau, foreign minister of the provisional republic, arrived in Versailles. When Brockdorff-Rantzau protested that the terms were too harsh, he was informed by Clemenceau that Germany would have three weeks to decide whether or not to sign. Eventually the time had to be extended, for the heads of the German government resigned their positions rather than accept the treaty. Their attitude was summed up by Chancellor Philip Scheidemann in the pointed statement: "What hand would not wither that sought to lay itself and us in those chains?" The Big Three now made a few minor adjustments, mainly at the insistence of Lloyd George, and Germany was notified that seven o'clock on the evening of June 23 must bring either acceptance or invasion. Shortly after five a new government of the provisional republic announced that it would yield to "overwhelming force" and accede to the victors' terms. On June 28, the fifth anniversary of the murder of the Austrian archduke, representatives of the German and Allied governments assembled in the Hall of Mirrors at Versailles and affixed their signatures to the treaty.

Germany sentenced

Crowds Greet President Wilson in Paris after the War. Despite public demonstrations of this sort, Wilson's attempt to shape the peace was a failure.

The provisions of the Treaty of Versailles can be outlined briefly. Germany was required to surrender Alsace and Lorraine to France, northern Schleswig to Denmark, and most of Posen and West Prussia to Poland. The coal mines of the Saar Basin were to be ceded to France, to be exploited by the French for fifteen years. At the end of this time the German government would be permitted to buy them back. The Saar territory itself was to be administered by the League of Nations until 1935, when a plebiscite would be held to determine whether it should remain under the league, be returned to Germany, or be awarded to France. Germany's province of East Prussia was cut off from the rest of its territory, and the port of Danzig, almost wholly German, was subjected to the political control of the League of Nations and the economic domination of Poland. Germany was disarmed, surrendering all its submarines and navy of surface vessels, with the exception of six small battleships, six light cruisers, six destroyers, and twelve torpedo boats. The Germans were forbidden to possess an air force, and their army was limited to 100,000 officers and men, to be recruited by voluntary enlistment. To make sure that Germany would not launch any new attack upon France or Belgium, it was forbidden to keep soldiers or maintain fortifications in the Rhine valley. Last, Germany and its allies were held responsible for all the loss and damage suffered by the Entente governments and their citizens, "as a consequence of the war imposed upon them by the aggression of Germany and her allies." This was the so-called war-guilt provision of the treaty (Article 231), and also the basis for German reparations. The exact amount that Germany should pay was left to a Reparations Commission. In 1921 the total was set at $33 billion.

For the most part, the Treaty of Versailles applied only to Germany. Separate pacts were drawn up to settle accounts with Germany's allies—Austria-Hungary, Bulgaria, and Turkey. The final form of these treaties was determined primarily by a Council of Five, composed of Clemenceau as chairman and one delegate each from the United States, Great Britain, France, and Italy. The treaties reflected a desire on the part of their drafters to recognize the principle of national self-determination. The experience of the prewar years convinced diplomats that they must draw national boundaries to conform as closely as possible to the ethnic, linguistic, and historical traditions of the people they were to contain. Yet practical, political difficulties made such divisions impossible.

*The treaty with Austria:
the compromising of
national self-determination*

The settlement with Austria, completed in September 1919, was known as the Treaty of St. Germain. Austria was required to recognize the independence of Hungary, Czechoslovakia, Yugoslavia, and Poland, and to cede to them large portions of its territory. In addition, Austria had to surrender Trieste, the south Tyrol, and the Istrian peninsula to Italy. Altogether the Austrian portion of the Dual Monarchy was deprived of three-fourths of its area and three-fourths of its people. Contrary to the principles of self-determination, in several of the territories surrendered the inhabitants were largely German-speaking—for example, in the Tyrol, and the region of the Sudeten mountains awarded to Czechoslovakia. The Austrian nation itself was reduced to a small, land-locked state, with nearly one-third of its population concentrated in the city of Vienna.

The second of the treaties with lesser belligerents was that with Bulgaria, which was signed in November 1919 and called the Treaty of Neuilly. Bulgaria was forced to give up nearly all of the territory it had gained since the First Balkan War. Land was ceded to Rumania, to the new kingdom of Yugoslavia, and to Greece. Here again, self-determination was compromised. All of these regions were inhabited by large Bulgarian minorities. Since Hungary was now an independent state, it was necessary that a separate treaty be imposed upon it. This was the Treaty of the Trianon Palace, signed in June 1920. It required that Slovakia be ceded to Czechoslovakia, Transylvania to Rumania, and Croatia-Slovenia to Yugoslavia. Nowhere was the principle of self-determination of peoples more flagrantly violated. Numerous sections of Transylvania had populations that were more than half Hungarian. Included in the region of Slovakia were not only Slovaks but almost a million Magyars and about 500,000 Ruthenians. As a consequence, a fanatical irredentist movement flourished in Hungary after the war, directed toward the recovery of these lost provinces. The Treaty of the Trianon Palace slashed the area of Hungary from 125,000 square miles to 35,000, and its population from 22 million to 8 million.

The treaties with Bulgaria and Hungary

The settlement with Turkey was a product of unusual circumstances. The secret treaties had contemplated the transfer of Constantinople and Armenia to Russia and the division of most of the remainder of Turkey between Britain and France. But Russia's withdrawal from the war after the Bolshevik Revolution, together with insistence by Italy and Greece upon fulfillment of promises made to them, necessitated considerable revision of the original scheme. Finally, in August 1920, a treaty was signed at Sèvres, near Paris, and submitted to the government of the sultan. It provided that Armenia be organized as a Christian republic; that most of Turkey in Europe be given to Greece; that Palestine and Mesopotamia become British "mandates," i.e., to remain under League of Nations control but to be administered by Britain; that Syria become a mandate of France; and that southern Anatolia be set apart as a sphere of influence for Italy. About all that would be left of the Ottoman Empire would be the city of Constantinople and the northern and central portions of Asia Minor. The decrepit government of the sultan, overawed by Allied military forces, agreed to accept this treaty. But a revolutionary government of Turkish nationalists, which had been organized at Ankara under the leadership of Mustapha Kemal (later called Atatürk), deter-

The Treaties of Sèvres and Lausanne with Turkey

ICELAND
(Denmark)

FAEROES
(Denmark)

SHETLANDS

ORKNEYS

HEBRIDES

SCOTLAND

GREAT BRITAIN

IRELAND

Dublin

ENGLAND

London

ATLANTIC

OCEAN

English Channel

NORTH

SEA

NORWAY

SWEDEN

Christiania

Stockholm

Skagerrak

Kattegat

DENMARK

Copenhagen

GOTLAND

ÖLAND

BALTIC

SEA

GULF OF BOTHNIA

FINLAND

Helsingfors

Leningrad

G. of Finland

Tallinn

ESTONIA

Riga

LATVIA

LITHUANIA

Kaunas

E. PRUSSIA
(Germany)

Danzig

Brest-Litovsk

Warsaw

POLAND

Berlin

GERMANY

Rhine

NETHERLANDS

Amsterdam

Brussels

BELG.

LUXEMBURG

R.

Paris

LORRAINE

ALSACE

Berne

SWITZ.

FRANCE

BAY OF
BISCAY

Danube R.

Prague

CZECHOSLOVAKIA

Vienna

AUSTRIA

Budapest

HUNGARY

RUMANIA

Bucharest

YUGOSLAVIA

Belgrade

SERBIA

Sofia

BUL-

MONTENEGRO

Tirana

ALBANIA

GREECE

Aegean

ADRIATIC SEA

ITALY

Rome

CORSICA
(France)

SARDINIA
(Italy)

BALEARIC IS.
(Spain)

PORTUGAL

Lisbon

Madrid

SPAIN

Strait of
Gibraltar

Tangier

SP. MOROCCO

Rabat

MOROCCO

Algiers

ALGERIA

Tunis

TUNISIA

M E D I T E R R A N E A N

SICILY
(Italy)

MALTA
(Gt. Britain)

CRETE
(Greece)

Athens

Tripoli

LIBYA

0

1000 miles

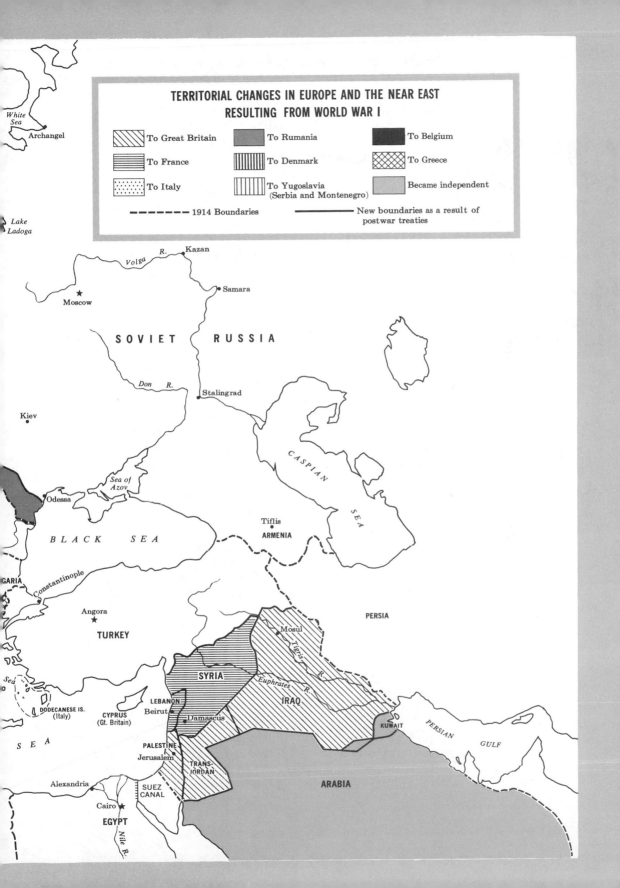

TERRITORIAL CHANGES IN EUROPE AND THE NEAR EAST
RESULTING FROM WORLD WAR I

Kemal Atatürk

The League of Nations

Successes and failures of the league

mined to prevent acceptance of the settlement of Sèvres. The forces of Kemal obliterated the republic of Armenia, frightened the Italians into withdrawing from Anatolia, and conquered most of the territory in Europe which had been given to Greece. At last, in November 1922, they occupied Constantinople, deposed the sultan, and proclaimed Turkey a republic. The Allies now consented to a revision of the peace. A new treaty was concluded at Lausanne in Switzerland in 1923, which permitted the Turks to retain practically all of the territory they had conquered. Though much reduced in size compared with the old Ottoman Empire, the Turkish republic still had an area of about 300,000 square miles and a population of 13 million.

Incorporated in each of the five treaties which liquidated the war with the Central Powers was the Covenant of the League of Nations. The establishment of a league in which the states of the world, both great and small, would cooperate for the preservation of peace had long been the cherished dream of President Wilson. Indeed, that had been one of his chief reasons for taking the United States into the war. He believed that the defeat of Germany would mean the deathblow of militarism, and that the road would thenceforth be clear for setting up the control of international relations by a community of nations instead of by the cumbersome and ineffective balance of power. But to get the league accepted he found himself compelled to make numerous compromises. He permitted his original idea of providing for a reduction of armaments "to the lowest point consistent with domestic safety" to be changed into the altogether different phrasing of "consistent with national safety." To induce the Japanese to accept the league he allowed them to keep former German concessions in China. To please the French, he sanctioned the exclusion of both Germany and Russia from his proposed federation, despite his long insistence that it should be a league of *all* nations. These handicaps were serious enough. But the league received an even more deadly blow when it was repudiated by the very nation whose president had proposed it.

Established under such unfavorable auspices, the league never achieved the aims of its founder. In only a few cases did it succeed in allaying the threat of war, and in each of these the parties to the dispute were small nations. But in every dispute involving one or more major powers, the league failed. It did nothing about the seizure of Vilna by Poland in 1920, because Lithuania, the victimized nation, was friendless, while Poland had the powerful backing of France. When, in 1923, war threatened between Italy and Greece, the Italians refused to submit to the intervention of the league, and the dispute was settled by direct mediation of Great Britain and France. Thereafter, in every great crisis the league was either defied or ignored. Its authority was flouted by Japan in seizing Manchuria in 1931 and by Italy in conquering Ethiopia in 1936. By September 1938, when the Czechoslovakian crisis arose, the prestige of the league had sunk so low that scarcely anyone thought of appealing to it. Yet the league justified its existence in other, less spectacular, ways. It reduced the international opium traffic and aided poor and backward countries in controlling the spread of disease. Its agencies collected invaluable statistics on labor and business conditions throughout the world. It conducted plebiscites in disputed areas, supervised the administration of internationalized cities, helped find homes for racial and political refugees, and made a notable beginning in codifying international law. Such achievements may well be regarded as providing a substantial groundwork for a later effort at international organization, the United Nations, formed after the Second World War.

The league, with all its failings, was seen as the one promising result of the war that many soon recognized as a hideously wasteful carnage. The price would have been enormous even if all the results which were supposed to flow from an Entente victory had really been achieved. Altogether 8.5 million men died and more than twice that number were wounded. The total casualties—killed, wounded, and missing— numbered over 37 million. Germany lost 6 million and France almost as many, a larger proportion, indeed, of its total population. But despite these appalling losses, almost nothing was gained. The war which was to "end all wars" sowed the seeds of a new and more terrible conflict in the future. The autocracy of the kaiser was destroyed, but the ground was prepared for new despotisms. The First World War did nothing to abate either militarism or nationalism. Twenty years after the fighting had ended, there were nearly twice as many men under arms as in 1913; and national and ethnic rivalries and hatreds were as deeply ingrained as ever.

A war of waste

If the war failed to make the world less of an armed camp, it nevertheless altered it drastically in other ways. In the first place, it strengthened a belief in the efficacy of central planning and coordination. To sustain the war effort, the governments of all the major belligerents were forced to manage their economies by regulating industrial output, exercising a close control over imports and exports, and making the most effective use of manpower—both civilian and military. Second, the war upset the world trade balance. With few manufactured goods coming from Europe, Japanese, Indian, and South American capitalists were free to develop industries in their own countries. When the war was over, Europe found it had lost many of its previously guaranteed markets, and that it had become a debtor to the United States which, throughout the war, had lent large sums to the Allies. Third, while war was altering the patterns of world trade, it was also producing worldwide inflation. To finance their fighting, governments resorted to policies of deficit financing (spending above their income) and increased paper money which, with the shortage of goods, inflated their price. Inflation hit hardest at the middle class, those men and women who had lived on their income from invested

Changes brought by the war

Women at Work. The all-out war effort combined with a manpower shortage at home brought women into factories across Europe in unparalleled numbers. On the left, men and women work side-by-side in a British shell factory. At the right, women toil in a German gun factory.

money, and now saw that money worth far less than it once had been. Fourth, the war, while it brought hardships to most, brought freedom to many. Women were emancipated by their governments' need for them in factories and on farms. The contribution of women to the war effort undoubtedly explains the granting of female suffrage in both Great Britain and the United States in 1918 and 1920. Finally, despite this legacy of liberation, the war's most permanent contribution to the spirit of the postwar years was disillusion—particularly within the middle classes. A generation of men had been sacrificed— "lost"—to no apparent end. Many of those left alive were sickened by the useless slaughter, to which they knew they had contributed and for which they believed they must share at least part of the guilt. They were disgusted by the greedy abandonment of principles by the politicians at Versailles. Hatred and mistrust of the "old men" who had dragged the world into an unnecessary conflict, who had then mismanaged its direction with such ghastly results, and who had betrayed the cause of international peace for national gain soured the minds of many younger men and women in the postwar period. The British poet Edmund Blunden expressed this profound disillusionment when he took as the title for a poem, written to celebrate New Year's Day 1921, the biblical verse: "The dog is turned to his own vomit again, and the sow that was washed to her wallowing in the mire."

SELECTED READINGS

• *Items so designated are available in paperback editions.*

THE WORLD WAR AND THE PEACE SETTLEMENT

Albertini, Luigi, *The Origins of the War of 1914*, 3 vols., New York, 1952–1957. An exhaustive, valuable study.

Albrecht-Carré, Rene, ed., *The Meaning of the First World War*, Englewood Cliffs, N.J., 1965. The war's consequences for both soldiers and civilians.

• Balfour, Michael, *The Kaiser and His Times*, London, 1964. An excellent biography of William II.

• Falls, Cyril, *The Great War*, New York, 1961. A military history.

Feldman, Gerald D., *Army, Industry, and Labor in Germany, 1914–1918*, Princeton, 1966. The effect of war on the domestic economy.

• Ferro, Marc, *The Great War, 1914–1918*, London, 1973. Social and economic developments receive particular treatment.

Fischer, Fritz, *War of Illusions*, New York, 1975. Deals with Germany within the context of internal social and economic trends. See also his *Germany's Aims in the First World War*, mentioned in the preceding chapter.

• Fussell, Paul, *The Great War and Modern Memory*, New York, 1975. A brilliant examination of British intellectuals' attitudes toward the war.

• Hardach, Gerd, *The First World War, 1914–1918*, Berkeley, 1977. An excellent economic history of the war.

Horne, Alastair, *The Price of Glory: Verdun, 1916*, New York, 1963.

Lafore, Laurence D., *The Long Fuse: An Interpretation of the Origins of World War I*, Philadelphia, 1971. Argues that the war was the result of obsolete institutions and ideas.

Laqueur, Walter, and G. L. Mosse, eds., *1914: The Coming of the First World War*, New York, 1969. An excellent series of essays by modern scholars.

• Marwick, Arthur, *The Deluge: British Society and the First World War*, Boston, 1965. The war's impact on the home front.

Mayer, Arno, *Politics and Diplomacy of Peacemaking: Containment and Counterrevolution at Versailles, 1918–1919*, New York, 1967. Emphasizes the role of the Russian Revolution in the peacemaking process.

• Moorehead, Alan, *Gallipoli*, London, 1956. A study of the British campaign.

Nicolson, Harold, *Peacemaking, 1919*, Boston, 1933. Written by a participant, provides a good account of the atmosphere of Versailles.

• Steiner, Zara S., *Britain and the Origins of the First World War*, New York, 1977. Argues that external rather than internal strains brought Britain into the war.

• Taylor, A. J. P., *English History, 1914–1945*, New York, 1965. An excellent treatment of the war and its impact on British society.

• Turner, L. C. F., *Origins of the First World War*, New York, 1970. Stresses Russia's role in the prewar diplomatic situation.

• Tuchman, Barbara, *The Guns of August*, New York, 1962. A popular account of the outbreak of war.

• Wheeler-Bennett, J. W., *Brest-Litovsk: The Forgotten Peace, March 1918*, London, 1939. An excellent study of personalities involved in the Russo-German peace treaty.

Williams, John, *The Home Fronts: Britain, France and Germany, 1914–1918*, London, 1972. A survey of life away from the battlefield and the impact of the war on domestic life.

• Wohl, Robert, *The Generation of 1914*, Cambridge, Mass., 1979. Uses generational analysis to explain attitudes toward the war.

Zeeman, Z. A. B., *The Break-up of the Hapsburg Empire, 1914–1918*, New York, 1961.

THE RUSSIAN REVOLUTION

• Deutscher, Isaac, *The Prophet Armed: Trotsky*, New York, 1954. The first volume of a magnificent biography of Trotsky; covers the years 1879–1921.

Ferro, Marc. *October 1917: A Social History of the Russian Revolution*, London, 1980. A compelling if idiosyncratic analysis.

• Fitzpatrick, Sheila. *The Russian Revolution*, Oxford, 1982.

Keep, John L. H., *The Russian Revolution*, New York, 1977.

Pares, Bernard, *A History of Russia*, rev. ed., New York, 1953. A useful, straightforward survey.

• Pipes, Richard, *The Formation of the Soviet Union*, New York, 1964. A solid, reliable study.

• Rabinowitch, Alexander, *The Bolsheviks Come to Power*, New York, 1976. A well-researched and carefully documented account.

Ulam, Adam, *The Bolsheviks*, New York, 1965. Analysis of both ideas and events.

• Wolfe, Bertram D., *Three Who Made a Revolution*, rev. ed., New York, 1964. A study of Lenin, Trotsky, and Stalin.

SOURCE MATERIALS

Carnegie Foundation, Endowment for International Peace, *The Treaties of Peace, 1919–1923*, 2 vols., New York, 1924.

Gooch, G. P., and H. Temperley, eds., *British Documents on the Origins of the War, 1898–1914*, London, 1927.

Keynes, John Maynard, *The Economic Consequences of the Peace*, London, 1919. A contemporary attack upon the peace settlement, particularly the reparations agreements, by the brilliant economist who served on the British delegation to the peace conference.

• Owen, Wilfred, *Collected Poems*, London, 1963. Moving evidence of the horror of life at the front by Britain's most talented war poet.

• Reed, John, *Ten Days That Shook the World*, New York, 1919. (Many editions.) A contemporary account by a sympathetic American journalist of the Bolshevik revolution.

• Remarque, Erich Maria, *All Quiet on the Western Front*, 1929. (Many editions.) A famous novel describing the war on the Western Front.

Chapter 35

THE WEST BETWEEN THE WARS

Democracy of the West today is the forerunner of Marxism, which would
be inconceivable without it. It is democracy alone which furnishes this
universal plague with the soil in which it spreads. In parliamentarianism,
its outward form of expression, democracy created a monstrosity of filth
and fire. . . .

—Adolf Hitler, *Mein Kampf*

A mong the claims made by the Allied Powers during the First
World War was that an Allied victory would make the world
"safe for democracy." The boast was grounded in a belief in
the inevitability of progress, fostered by a century of growing material
prosperity and by a habit of mind that found it all but impossible to
equate the events of history with something other than the "advance"
of civilization. The history of Europe in the 1920s and 1930s, however, would make it increasingly difficult for men and women to
believe in progress as they had, or to assume that war might prove of
ultimate benefit to mankind. These were decades of disillusionment
and desperation, a circumstance brought about not only by the war
itself but by the events that followed in the wake of war. Rather
than encourage the growth of democracy, those events were often
the direct cause of its decline and fall. A number of Western nations
remained democracies—Great Britain, France, and the United States
being the most notable cases—yet they nevertheless experienced the
same pressures and strains which in other countries resulted in the
demise of democracy altogether.

Although the reasons for the decline of democracy in the West varied according to particular national circumstances, its failure can be
attributed to several major causes. First, class conflict increased in many
countries during the interwar years. The real issue in most parts of
continental Europe was whether control of the government and economic system would continue in the possession of aristocracies,
industrialists, and financiers, or some combination of these elements.

Decline of democracy

Reasons for the decline

None of them were willing to surrender more than a fraction of their considerable power to the less privileged majorities which, at great sacrifice, had made major contributions to the war effort. The common people expected and had been promised that those contributions would be rewarded by greater attention to their political rights and economic needs. When they were ignored, they were naturally embittered, and hence prey to the blandishments of political extremists. Second, economic conditions worked against the establishment of stable democracies. The creation of new nations encouraged debilitating economic rivalries. War had disoriented the world's economy, leaving in its wake first inflation and then depression. Finally, nationalist sentiment encouraged discontent among minorities in the newly established states of central Europe. Countries weakened by conflicts between national minorities were an unlikely proving ground for democracy, a political system that functions best in an atmosphere of unified national purpose.

Rise of totalitarianism

The political history of the interwar years must be understood not only in terms of the decline of democracy, however, but also against the background of the rise of the totalitarian state. Totalitarianism, whatever it promised, preached the destruction of the political systems that had failed to grapple successfully with the problems of class conflict, economic chaos, and nationalism. Although there were significant differences between the communism of the Soviet Union under Joseph Stalin, the fascism of Italy under Benito Mussolini, and the National Socialism—or, as it was called, Nazism—of Germany under Adolf Hitler, all three systems can be defined as totalitarian.

Totalitarianism defined

These systems demanded the total subordination of individuals and classes to the greater good of the state as defined and directed by an all-powerful single political party. To this end, violent force, intimidation, and propaganda were employed to divert men and women from the pursuit of their individual interests, to deny them their freedom as citizens, and to compel them to labor on behalf of goals defined as useful to the nation. Churches, trade unions, even parliamentary government were either subverted or suppressed completely. The state, through the party, imposed its will on the total life of society.

Its ideology and appeal

Totalitarian governments framed their programs in ideology. In the case of Soviet Russia, the ideology was a nationalistic version of Marxist socialism. In the case of Italy and Germany, it was a peculiar concoction of nineteenth-century nationalism and socialism. These ideologies proclaimed the necessity of revolutionary change and encouraged belief in the ability of the party and its leader to effect that change. They thus appealed to those who saw themselves dispossessed by the system as it was, or as it had become, and who believed that nothing but desperate measures would suffice to bring society to rights. During the interwar years the ranks of those people in Europe were legion.

1. THE RISE OF TOTALITARIANISM IN COMMUNIST RUSSIA

Soon after the 1917 revolution in Russia, the country's desperate plight—a result of wartime devastation and tsarist corruption and mismanagement—compelled the Bolshevik leaders to exercise bold and often ruthless leadership. During this traumatic period, Lenin showed himself as capable a revolutionary administrator and politician as he had been a strategist. He commanded the respect and loyalty of his fellow Bolshevik ministers. His dedication to his own theory of revolution and his readiness to apply that theory with a ruthless disregard for human lives, if necessary, was combined with a willingness to heed the opinions of his close adherents. He welcomed free discussion during the decision-making process. Once a decision had been reached, however, discussion gave way to unquestioning implementation. Lenin won the confidence of the Russian people by speaking frankly to them of the dangers and difficulties inherent in a revolution as bold and all-consuming as theirs was. He was what he appeared to be: a selfless man, unwilling to claim special privileges for himself, wholly dedicated to the revolution which he had done so much to bring about. He cared nothing for luxury or personal glory, living an almost monklike existence in two rooms in the Kremlin, and dressing little better than an ordinary worker.

Lenin's ablest and most prominent lieutenant was Leon Trotsky (1879–1940). Originally named Lev Bronstein, Trotsky was born of middle-class Jewish parents in the Ukraine. Before the revolution he had refused to identify himself with any particular faction, preferring to remain an independent Marxist. For his part in the revolutionary movement of 1905 he was exiled to Siberia; he escaped, and for some

Lenin Speaking to Crowds in Moscow. To the right of the platform, in uniform, is Trotsky.

years led a roving existence in various European capitals. He was expelled from Paris in 1916 for pacifist activity and took refuge in the United States. Upon learning of the overthrow of the tsar, he attempted to return to Russia. Captured by British agents at Halifax, Nova Scotia, he was eventually released through the intervention of Kerensky. He arrived in Russia in April 1917 and immediately began plotting the overthrow of the provisional government and later of Kerensky himself. He became commissar of foreign affairs in the government headed by Lenin, and later, commissar of war.

The civil war

Scarcely had the Bolsheviks concluded the war with the Central Powers than they were confronted with a desperate civil war at home. Landlords and capitalists did not take kindly to the loss of their property. The result was a prolonged and bloody combat between the Reds, or Bolsheviks, and the Whites, including not only reactionary tsarists but also disaffected liberals, Social Revolutionaries, Mensheviks, and peasants. The Whites were assisted for a time by expeditionary forces of British, French, American, and Japanese troops—hoping to defeat the Bolsheviks in order to bring Russia back into the war against Germany—and later by the armies of the newly created republic of Poland. Under the direction of Trotsky, who appealed to the Russian people both in the name of revolution and the fatherland, the Red army was mobilized to a degree that allowed it to withstand both the foreign invaders and the Russian insurgents. By 1922, the Bolsheviks had managed to stabilize their boundaries, although to do so they were forced to cede former Russian territory to the Finns, to the Baltic states of Latvia and Estonia, to Poland, and to Rumania. Internally, a civil war between the Whites and the Reds resulted in the death of 100,000 victims on both sides. Whites murdered a number of communist leaders, and wounded Lenin himself. The Red secret police shot thousands as suspects and hostages. The tsar and tsarina and

See color map of the Soviet Union following page 550

The Red Army, 1919. This scene near the southern front was the celebration of the victory over the counterrevolutionary forces.

their children were executed by local Bolsheviks in July 1918 as White forces advanced on the town of Ekaterinburg, where the family was held prisoner. That same year "enemies of the state" were hunted down in large numbers following the attempted assassination of Lenin. The terror abated when the regime had satisfied itself that it had destroyed its internal opposition.

The civil war was accompanied by an appalling economic breakdown. In 1920 total industrial production was only 13 percent of what it had been in 1913. To alleviate the shortage of goods, the government abolished the payment of wages and distributed supplies among urban workers in proportion to their need. All private trade was prohibited; everything produced by the peasants above what they required to subsist was requisitioned by the state. This system was an expedient to crush bourgeois opposition to the revolutionay regime and to obtain as much food as possible for the army in the field. In 1921 it was superseded by the New Economic Policy (NEP), which Lenin described as "one step backward in order to take two steps forward." The NEP authorized private manufacturing and private trade on a small scale, reintroduced the payment of wages, and permitted peasants to sell their grain in the open market. In 1924 a constitution was adopted, replacing imperial Russia with the Union of Soviet Socialist Republics. The union represented an attempt to unite the various nationalities and territories that had constituted the old empire. Each separate republic was, in theory, granted certain autonomous rights. In fact, government remained centralized in the hands of a few leaders. Further, central authority was maintained by means of the one legal political party—the Communist party—whose Central Committee was the directing force behind both politics and government, and whose organizational apparatus reached out into all areas of the vast country.

*Economic and
constitutional changes*

The philosophy of Bolshevism, now known as communism, was developed primarily by Lenin during these years. It was proclaimed not as a new body of thought, but as a strict interpretation of Marx's writings. Nevertheless, from the beginning it departed at several important points from Marx's teachings. These changes were the necessary result of the fact that Marx had expected revolution to occur first in highly industrialized countries, whereas it had in fact broken out and succeeded in one of the least industralized nations in Europe. Marx had assumed that a capitalist stage must prepare the way for socialism; Lenin denied that this was necessary, insisting rather that Russia could leap directly from a feudal to a socialist economy. In the second place, Lenin emphasized the revolutionary character of socialism much more than did its original founder. Marx did believe that in most cases revolution would be necessary, but he was inclined to deplore the fact rather than to welcome it. Finally, communism differed from Marxism in its conception of proletarian rule. When Marx spoke of the "dictatorship of the proletariat," he meant by this a dic-

The tenets of communism

Left: *Lenin's Casket Is Carried through the Streets of Moscow*. It was not known with certainty until 1956 that, prior to his death, Lenin had discredited Stalin. Right: *Lenin and Stalin*. Under Stalin this picture was used to show his close relationship with Lenin. In fact, the photograph has been doctored.

tatorship of the whole working class over the remnants of the bourgeoisie. Within the ranks of this class, democratic forms would prevail. Lenin, however, was persuaded by the desperate circumstances attendant upon the birth of the Soviet Union to proclaim the need for a dictatorship by the party elite, wielding supremacy not only over the bourgeoisie but over the bulk of the proletarians themselves.

The death of Lenin in January 1924 precipitated a struggle among various factions to inherit his mantle of power. Outside of Russia it was generally assumed that Trotsky would succeed the fallen leader. But the fiery commander of the Red army had a formidable rival in the tough and mysterious Joseph Stalin (1879–1953). The son of a peasant shoemaker in the province of Georgia, Stalin received part of his education in a theological seminary. Expelled at the age of seventeen for "lack of religious vocation," he thereafter dedicated his career to revolutionary activity.

In 1922 Stalin assumed the secretary-generalship of the Communist party which, in the years that followed, became the heart of the government. Theoretically, Soviet Russia was ruled by a Central Executive Committee, which in turn represented local, provincial, and regional Councils of Workers and Peasants. Because the Central Executive did not remain in continuous session, however, power increasingly fell into the hands of that body responsible for day-to-day operations and decisions: the Council of the People's Commissars—that is, the various departmental ministers. These commissars were nominated by, and were themselves members of, the Communist

The struggles between Trotsky and Stalin

Stalin and the party

party. In his position as the party's secretary-general, Stalin was ultimately able to control nominations to the Council of Commissars, and thus to fill the government with party members loyal to him.

The battle over Lenin's succession was not simply a struggle for personal power; fundamental issues of political policy were also involved. Trotsky maintained that socialism in Russia could never be entirely successful until capitalism was overthrown in surrounding countries. Therefore, he insisted upon a continuous crusade for world revolution. Stalin was willing to abandon the program of world revolution, for the time being, in order to concentrate on building socialism in Russia itself. His essentially nationalistic strategy had triumphed by the end of the decade. Stalin's rivals—most notably Trotsky—were officially disgraced. In 1927 Trotsky was expelled from the Communist party, and two years later he was driven from the country. In 1940 he was murdered in Mexico City by Stalinist agents. Others, including Gregory Zinovier and Lev Kamenev, were convicted of crimes against the state in public trials and executed in the 1930s. Lenin did not hold either Stalin or Trotsky in lofty esteem. In a "testament" to the Council written shortly before his death, he criticized Trotsky for "far-reaching self-confidence" and for being too preoccupied with administrative detail. But he dealt far less gently with Stalin, condemning him as "too rough" and "capricious" and urging that the commissars remove him from his position at the head of the party.

Once Stalin consolidated his power, he reinforced the role of the party as a state within a state, with its own bureaucrats—the *apparatchiki*—assuming ever-increasing influence in the administration of the country and in the determination of its fortunes. He insisted that Russia's first priority was economic well-being. His major reform was the introduction of the so-called Five-Year Plan, based on the conviction that the Soviet Union had to take drastic steps to industrialize and thereby achieve economic parity among the nations of the world. The plan instituted an elaborate system of priorities. It decreed how much of each major industrial and agricultural commodity the nation should produce, the wages workers should receive, and the prices that should be charged for goods sold at home and abroad. The first plan, instituted in 1928, was succeeded by others during the 1930s. In some areas goals were met, in a few they were exceeded, in some they fell short. One of the major results of the Five-Year Plans was the creation of an extensive state bureaucracy, charged with the task of organization and supervision at all levels.

Included in the first plan was a program for agricultural collectivization. The scheme was designed to bring rural farms together into larger units of several thousand acres, under the communal proprietorship of peasants. Only with this sort of reorganization, Russia's rulers declared, could the new and expensive processes of mechanization be introduced, and the country's agricultural yield thereby increased. Not surprisingly, the argument failed to win the support of the more

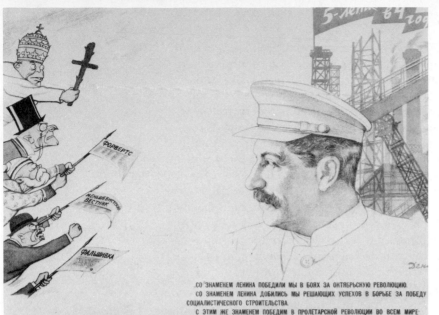

.CO ЗНАМЕНЕМ ЛЕНИНА ПОБЕДИЛИ МЫ В БОЯХ ЗА ОКТЯБРЬСКУЮ РЕВОЛЮЦИЮ.
CO ЗНАМЕНЕМ ЛЕНИНА ДОБИЛИСЬ МЫ РЕШАЮЩИХ УСПЕХОВ В БОРЬБЕ ЗА ПОБЕДУ
СОЦИАЛИСТИЧЕСКОГО СТРОИТЕЛЬСТВА.
С ЭТИМ ЖЕ ЗНАМЕНЕМ ПОБЕДИМ В ПРОЛЕТАРСКОЙ РЕВОЛЮЦИИ ВО ВСЕМ МИРЕ·
(С т в л / к к. Политический отчет ЦК XVI съезду ВКП(б).)

"The Five-Year Plan in Four Years." Stalin faces down reactionary capitalist enemies in this Soviet propaganda poster of the 1930s.

prosperous farmers—the kulaks—who had been allowed to retain ownership of their land. Their opposition led to another terror, made all the more deadly by a famine which occurred in southeastern Russia in 1932. The kulaks were liquidated, either killed or transported to distant labor camps: the rural bourgeoisie was eliminated, to be replaced by a rural proletariat. Collectivization was an accomplished fact by 1939. To a vast number of Russians it represented a revolution far more immediate than that of 1917. Twenty million people were moved off the land, which, once it had been reorganized into larger units, and production had been mechanized, required fewer laborers. They were sent to cities, where most went to work in factories. Although agricultural output did not increase during the early years of collectivization, the scheme was nevertheless of benefit to the government. By controlling production, the central bureaucracy was able to regulate the distribution of agricultural products, allocating them for export, where necessary, to pay for the importation of much-needed industrial machinery.

As part of Stalin's campaign to put the interests of Russia ahead of those of international communism, the Bolshevik regime adopted a new and more conservative foreign policy during the 1930s. Its international goals contradicted the militant socialist internationalism of the 1920s. Lenin had supported revolutionary leftist movements in Europe, sending money and lending moral support to the radical German Marxists Karl Liebknecht and Rosa Luxemburg in 1919, and to the short-lived Soviet regime of the Bolshevik Béla Kun in Hungary in the same year. Shortly thereafter, the Third International—later called the Comintern—was formed. It declared its allegiance to inter-

The Third International

national communism; its policy was to oppose cooperation or collaboration with the capitalist governments of the West and to work for their overthrow.

With Stalin's suppression of the internationalism advocated by Lenin and Trotsky, however, came a change in tactics and the revival of an interest in playing the game of power politics. The Russian army was more than doubled in size and was reorganized in accordance with the western European model. Patriotism, which strict Marxists despised as a form of capitalist propaganda, was exalted into a Soviet virtue, a symptom of totalitarianism. When Germany once again appeared to threaten Russian security, as it did in the 1930s, the Soviet leadership looked abroad for allies. Along with their efforts to build up a great army and to make their own country self-sufficient, they adopted a policy of cooperation with the western European powers. In 1934 they entered the League of Nations, and in 1934 they ratified a military alliance with France. *Stalinist conservatism*

In June 1936, the Soviets adopted a new constitution, some of whose provisions suggested the possibility of a more liberal regime. Power continued to reside in a governing body (the Presidium) and an administrative agency (the Council of Ministers), both of which were chosen by a two-chamber parliament, the Supreme Soviet, which was elected, in turn, by universal suffrage. This pyramidal structure was not unlike that which it superseded and which, because of the dominant position of the Communist party, had resulted in the concentration of power in the person of Stalin. Now, however, the constitution provided citizens with a bill of rights guaranteeing freedom of speech, of assembly, and of religion. In addition, they were promised the right to employment, the right to leisure, and the right to maintenance at the expense of the state in case of old age or disability. *The constitution of 1936*

These guarantees meant very little, however, so long as all aspects of life in the Soviet Union continued to be dominated by the Communist party, whose membership of about 1 million in 1930 was but a small fraction of the total population of 150 million. That the new "bill of rights" was a sham was quickly proved by a series of purges which began shortly after the constitution was adopted. In August 1936, the first of several "show trials" occurred, at which persons alleged to be "Trotskyites" and spies were publicly condemned and either imprisoned, executed, or exiled to Siberia. Although the accused for the most part confessed to their "crimes," those confessions were obtained by physical and psychological torture. *The purge trials*

Stalin's victims were people at all levels who had opposed his personal rule, men such as Nikolai Bukharin, editor of the newspaper *Izvestia,* who had spoken out against the elimination of the kulaks; Karl Radek, a leading political theorist; and a number of "old" Bolsheviks, who had been unwilling to acquiesce in Stalin's refusal to debate policy, who had opposed his increasingly nationalistic foreign *Stalin's victims* policy, or who had hoped that revolution did not mean the complete suppression of personal liberty. The purges were the result of Stalin's own psychological instability and pathological distrust. They were as well, however, the logical result of totalitarianism's inability to tolerate any dissent whatsoever. Whatever their cause, the purges took a toll of almost nine million imprisoned, banished, or killed.

The results of the Soviet revolution were profound. No other regime in the history of western Europe had ever attempted to reorder completely the politics, economy, and society of a vast nation as the Russians had in the short space of twenty years. By 1939 private manufacturing and trade had been almost entirely abolished. Factories, mines, railroads, and public utilities were exclusively owned by the state. Stores were either government enterprises or cooperatives in which consumers owned shares. Agriculture had been almost completely socialized. At the same time, the nation had been industrialized. By 1932 over 70 percent of Russia's national product was industrial in origin. In the area of social reform, illiteracy was reduced from at least 50 percent to about 20 percent, and higher education was made available to increasingly large numbers. Government assistance for working mothers and free hospitalization did a great deal to raise the national standard of health.

Revolutionary accomplishments

But, as we have seen, those achievements were purchased at a very high price. In addition to the liquidation of millions of kulaks and political dissidents and the internment of millions of others in slave-labor camps, the Russian people were subjected to an unrelenting campaign of indoctrination that encompassed every aspect of their lives. Subtle forms of persecution were implemented to discourage religious orthodoxy while the nation's youth were inculcated with the new Soviet ideals of steadfast loyalty to the Soviet state and unquestioning obedience to the Communist party. Over time, experiments in the arts and literature, which had been promoted during the early years of the revolution under Lenin, gave way to the culture of totalitarian bureaucracy. The composers Sergei Prokofiev and Dimitri Shostakovich, the poet Vladimir Mayakovsky, the writer Maxim Gorky and his protégé Isaac Babel, the filmmaker Sergei Eisenstein, and other creative men and women flourished in the Soviet Union during the 1920s. Although most of them continued to work through the following decade and after, those who remained in official favor were compelled to compromise their art to conform to the increasingly totalitarian dictates of Stalin's Russia.

The price of revolution

Education became a tool of the revolution, much as violence and intimidation had. Control of the minds of the populace was regarded as a prerequisite to building a new society in which individual interests would be sacrificed to those of the state. After two decades of revolutionary change, the Stalinist regime had fastened upon the Russian people a tyranny as heavy as any imposed by the tsars.

2. THE EMERGENCE OF TOTALITARIAN FASCISM IN ITALY

That Italy turned to totalitarianism may at first seem surprising, in view of the fact that the Italians emerged as victors after the First World War. Yet Italy's difficulties were rooted in longstanding problems that the war had done little to resolve. Italy continued to be divided into two sharply contrasting halves: a relatively prosperous industrialized north, and a wretchedly poor agrarian south. In addition to the problems the country faced as a result of that unhealthy economic split, it was also the victim of an unrequited imperialist impulse which had existed since the 1890s. Its unsuccessful attempts to establish itself as a power in North Africa had left the country with a sense of frustration and humiliation. Before the war, the ruling class was held in public contempt by a younger generation anxious to cleanse the nation of rulers widely perceived to be at once cynical and corrupt, vaccilating and defeatist.

Italy's long-term problems

But the establishment of a dictatorship in Italy would never have been possible without the demoralizing and humiliating effects of the First World War. The chief business of the Italian armies had been to keep the Austrians occupied on the Southern Front while the British, French, and Americans hammered Germany into submission along the battle lines in the west. To accomplish this assignment, Italy had mobilized more than 5,500,000 men; of these nearly 700,000 were killed. The direct financial cost of Italian participation in the struggle was over $15 billion. These sacrifices were no greater than those made by the British and the French; but Italy was a poor country. Moreover, in the division of the spoils after the fighting, the Italians got less than they expected. While Italy did receive most of the Austrian territories promised in the secret treaties, the Italians maintained that these were inadequate rewards for their sacrifices and for their valuable contribution to an Entente victory. At first the nationalists vented their spleen for the "humiliation of Versailles" upon President Wilson, but after a short time they returned to castigating their own rulers. They alleged Premier Orlando had been so cravenly weak and inept that he and those who governed with him had allowed their country to be cheated of its just deserts.

The demoralizing and humiliating effects of the war

The war contributed to the revolutionary mood in a multitude of other ways. It resulted in inflation of the currency, with consequent high prices, speculation, and profiteering. Normally wages would have risen also, but the postwar labor market was glutted by the return to civilian life of millions of soldiers. Furthermore, business was demoralized, owing to extensive and frequent strikes and to the closing of foreign markets. In the minds of the upper and middle classes the most ominous consequence of the war was the growth of socialism. As

Inflation, radicalism, and economic chaos

hardship and chaos increased, the Italian socialists embraced a philosophy akin to Bolshevism. They voted as a party to join the Third International. In the elections of November 1919, they won about a third of the seats in the Chamber of Deputies. During the following winter socialist workers took over about a hundred factories and attempted to run them for the benefit of the workers. Radicalism also spread through rural areas, where so-called Red Leagues organized to break up large estates and to force landlords to reduce their rents. Two large political parties with mass appeal, the Socialists and the Catholic People's party, drained strength from other parties of the Center and moderate Left. Neither preached revolution; yet both urged far-reaching social and economic reforms. Industrialists and landowners were badly frightened and were therefore ready to accept totalitarianism as a less dangerous form of radicalism that might save at least part of their property from confiscation.

The career of Mussolini

How much the Fascist movement depended for its success upon the leadership of Benito Mussolini is difficult to say. Mussolini was born in 1883, the son of a socialist blacksmith. His mother was a schoolteacher, and in deference to her wishes he eventually became a teacher. But he was restless and dissatisfied, soon leaving Italy for further study in Switzerland. Here he gave part of his time to his books and the rest to writing articles for socialist newspapers. He was eventually expelled from the country for fomenting strikes. Returning to Italy, he became a journalist, and eventually editor of *Avanti,* the leading socialist daily. His ideas in the years before the war were a contradictory mixture of radicalisms. He professed to be a Marxist socialist, but he mingled his socialism with doctrines of corporatism, adapted from the French syndicalists.

Mussolini's contradictory ideas

Mussolini in fact believed in no particular set of doctrines. No man with a definite philosophy could have reversed himself so often. When war broke out in August 1914, Mussolini insisted that Italy should remain neutral. He had scarcely adopted this position when he began urging participation on the Entente side. Deprived of his position as editor of *Avanti,* he founded a new paper, *Il Popolo d'Italia,* and dedicated its columns to arousing enthusiasm for war. He regarded the decision of the government the following spring to go in on the side of the Entente allies as a personal victory.

The evolution of fascism

The word *fascism* derives from the Latin *fasces,* the ax surrounded by a bundle of sticks representing the authority of the Roman state; the Italian *fascio* means group or band. *Fasci* were organized as early as October 1914, as units of agitation to drive Italy into the war. Their members were young idealists, fanatical nationalists, and frustrated white-collar workers. The original platform of the Fascist party was drafted by Mussolini in 1919. It was a surprisingly radical document, which demanded universal suffrage, abolition of the conservative Senate, the establishment by law of an eight-hour day, a heavy capital levy, a heavy tax on inheritances, confiscation of 85 percent of war profits, acceptance of the League of Nations, and "opposition to all imperialisms." This platform was accepted more or less officially by the movement until May 1920, when it was supplanted by another of a more conservative character. Indeed, the new program omitted all reference to economic reform. On neither of these platforms did the fascists achieve much political success.

The fascists made up for their initial lack of numbers by disciplined aggressiveness and strong determination. As the old regime crumbled, they prepared to take over the government. In September 1922, Mussolini began to talk openly of revolution. On October 28 an army of about 50,000 fascist militia, in blackshirted uniforms, marched into Rome and occupied the capital. The premier resigned, and the following day the king, Victor Emmanuel III, invited Mussolini to form a cabinet. Without firing a shot the blackshirts had gained control of the Italian government. The explanation of their success is to be found not in the strength of fascism, but in the chaos created by the war and in the weakness and irresolution of the old ruling classes. By the end of the next three years Mussolini's revolution was virtually complete.

The march on Rome

Italian fascism embodied a variety of doctrines that were an expression of its totalitarian nature:

(1) Statism. The state was declared to incorporate every interest and every loyalty of its members. There was to be "nothing above the state, nothing outside the state, nothing against the state."

Major doctrines of fascism

(2) Nationalism. Nationhood was the highest form of society. It had a life and a soul of its own apart from the lives and souls of the individuals who composed it. Yet there could be no real harmony of

Left: *Mussolini Reviews a Fascist Youth Parade.* Totalitarianism demanded the capture of youthful minds. Right: *Mussolini Addressing a Crowd of his Followers from the Balcony of the Palazzo Venezia in Rome.*

interests between two or more distinct nations. Hence internationalism was a perversion of human progress.

(3) Militarism. Strife was the origin of all things. Nations which did not expand would eventually wither and die. War exalted and ennobled man and regenerated sluggish and decadent peoples.

Declaring his allegiance to these principles, Mussolini began to rebuild Italy in accordance with them. He abolished the cabinet system and all but extinguished the powers of the Parliament. In characteristic totalitarian fashion, he made the Fascist party an integral part of the Italian constitution. The king was compelled to select a prime minister from a list compiled by the party's Great Council. Voters, as well, were left with no real choice; they were forced to select their candidates from lists prepared by the party. Within a few years, there were no other political parties left in Italy. Mussolini assumed the dual position of prime minister and party leader *(duce)*. A potent and effective mechanism of political discipline was the party's militia, which Mussolini used to eliminate his enemies by violent means. Police supervision, censorship of the press and of academic life—the hallmarks of totalitarian regimes—were soon fastened upon the Italian people by the party.

Mussolini's fascist state

Mussolini reorganized the economy while preaching the end of class conflict as fascist doctrine. He secured worker support by instituting massive public works and building projects, along with state-sponsored programs of library-building, vacations, and social security. He won further popular acclaim when, in 1929, he settled Italy's sixty-year-old conflict with the Roman Catholic Church by a treaty granting independence to the papal residence in the Vatican City and establishing Roman Catholicism as the official religion of the nation's schools.

His bid for worker support

At the same time that Mussolini was attempting to pacify the Italian working class, he was pulling the teeth of the country's labor movement. The Italian economy was placed under the management of twenty-two corporations, each responsible for a major industrial enterprise. In each corporation were representatives of trade unions, whose members were organized by the Fascist party, the employers, and the government. Together, the members of these corporations were given the task of determining working conditions, wages, and prices. In fact, however, the decisions of these bodies were closely managed by the government and favored the position of management.

Corporatism

Although Mussolini's fascism was totalitarian in nature, it did not revolutionize government, economy, and society as did Soviet communism. Party officers exercised a degree of political supervision over bureaucrats, yet did not infiltrate the bureaucracy in significant numbers. Party and state were kept apart in Italy as they were not in the Soviet Union. Mussolini remained on friendly terms with the wealthy industrialists and bankers who had assisted his rise to power, insuring that whatever he might proclaim about the distinctions between fascism

Differences between Italian and Soviet totalitarianism

and capitalism, the economy of Italy would remain dependent upon private enterprise. Further evidence of Mussolini's conservatism was his concordat with the Church—this despite his earlier declarations of allegiance to atheism.

The Italian dictator enjoyed boasting that fascism had pulled the country back from economic chaos. The economy did improve some-what—along with the economies of other European countries—in the late 1920s, yet fascism did little to lessen Italy's plight during the years of worldwide depression which occurred in the 1930s. Al-though he managed to make his country appear more efficient—his admirers often bragged that he had at last "made the trains run on time"—Mussolini failed to solve its major problems, particularly those of the peasantry, whose standard of living remained desperately low. Mussolini's fascism was little more than illusion. It is a measure of the Italians' disgust with their past leaders that they were so ready to be taken in by him.

Its failure

3. THE RISE OF NAZI GERMANY

Germany succumbed to totalitarianism later than Italy. For a brief period following the First World War, events seemed to be moving the country to the Left. Most of the leading politicians in the imme-diate post-armistice government were socialists, members of the Social Democratic party. Their reformist policies, which had seemed radical enough to many prior to the war, now appeared too mild to a group of extreme Marxists who had been encouraged by the revolution in Russia. Calling themselves Spartacists,[1] and led by the able Rosa Luxemburg and Karl Liebknecht, they attempted an uprising in 1919 designed to bring the proletarian revolution to Germany. Despite assistance from the Russian Bolsheviks, the rebellion was crushed; Liebknecht and Luxemburg were killed by soldiers while being taken to prison. In engineering the Spartacists' defeat, the German govern-ment had recourse to private vigilante groups headed by disillusioned former army officers, men whose true sympathies lay no more with democratic socialism than with Russian communism, and whose dis-content would soon focus on the government they had helped to sal-vage.

Germany: the Spartacists

With the Spartacist revolt only just behind them, the leaders of a co-alition of socialists, Catholic centrists, and liberal democrats in 1919 drafted a constitution for the new German republic reflecting a gener-ally progressive political and social philosophy. It provided for uni-versal suffrage, for women as well as men; the cabinet system of gov-ernment; and for a bill of rights, guaranteeing not only civil liberties but the right of the citizen to employment, to an education, and to

The Weimar Republic

[1] After the Roman, Spartacus, who led a slave revolt.

Left: *Karl Liebknecht and Rosa Luxemburg*. Right: *The German Election of 1919.* Here women line up to vote for the first time.

protection against the hazards of an industrial society. But the republic established under this constitution was beset with troubles from the start. Reactionaries and other extremists plotted against it. Moreover, the German people had had little experience with democratic government. The Weimar Republic (named for the city where its constitution was drafted) did not spring from the desires of a majority of the nation. It was born of change forced upon Germany in its hour of defeat. Its instability made it a likely victim of the forces it was desperately attempting to tame.

Causes of German totalitarianism: (1) defeat in war

Various factors led to the eventual triumph of German totalitarianism. First was the sense of humiliation arising from defeat in the war. Between 1871 and 1914 Germany had risen to lofty heights of political and cultural prestige. German universities, science, philosophy, and music were known and admired all over the world. The country had likewise attained a remarkable prosperity, by 1914 surpassing Britain and the United States in several fields of industrial production. Then came the defeat of 1918, with Germany left to the mercy of its powerful enemies. It was too much for the German people to understand. They found it difficult to believe that their invincible armies had really been worsted in battle. Quickly the legend grew that the nation had been "stabbed in the back" by socialists and Jews in the government. Though there was no truth in this charge, it helped to salve the wounded pride of German patriots. Those in search of a scapegoat also blamed the laxity and irresponsibility that appeared to distinguish the republican regime. It was alleged that Berlin had displaced Paris

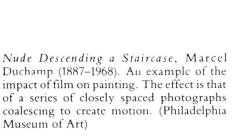

Panel (3), Wassily Kandinsky (1866–1944). The Expressionist painters carried their explorations of the psychological properties of color and line to the point where subject matter was deemed unnecessary and even undesirable. (Museum of Modern Art)

Nude Descending a Staircase, Marcel Duchamp (1887–1968). An example of the impact of film on painting. The effect is that of a series of closely spaced photographs coalescing to create motion. (Philadelphia Museum of Art)

The Funeral Procession, George Grosz (1893–1959). Painted in the late stages of the First World War, this portrayal of a funeral procession gone mad shows death triumphant as humanity is swept into a hell of its own making. The work expressed an anger and a loathing felt by an entire generation. (Reproduced by Permission of the Estate of George Grosz, Princeton, New Jersey)

The Table, Georges Braque (1881–1963). An example of later Cubism showing the predominance of cur- vilinear form and line instead of geometric structure. (Museum of Modern Art)

I and the Village, Marc Chagall (1889–   ). The subject refers to the artist's childhood and youth in Vitebsk, Russia. The profile on the right is probably that of the artist himself. (Museum of Modern Art)

The Persistence of Memory, Sal- vador Dali (1904–   ). The Spaniard Dali is the outstand- ing representative of the Sur- realist school. Many objects in his paintings are Freudian images. (Museum of Modern Art)

Barricade, José Clemente Orozco (1883–1949). The Mexican muralist Orozco was one of the most celebrated of contemporary painters with a social message. His themes were revolutionary fervor, satire of aristocracy and the Church, and deification of the common man. (Museum of Modern Art)

Around the Fish, Paul Klee (1879–1940). Klee is recognized as the most subtle humorist of twentieth-century art. The central motif of a fish on a platter suggests a banquet, but many of the surrounding objects appear to be products of fantasy. (Museum of Modern Art

Mystery and Melancholy of a Street, Giorgio de Chirico (1888–1978). Employing perspective to fashion familiar components into dreamscapes fraught with anxiety and loneliness, de Chirico had a profound effect on the surrealists. (Lee Boltin)

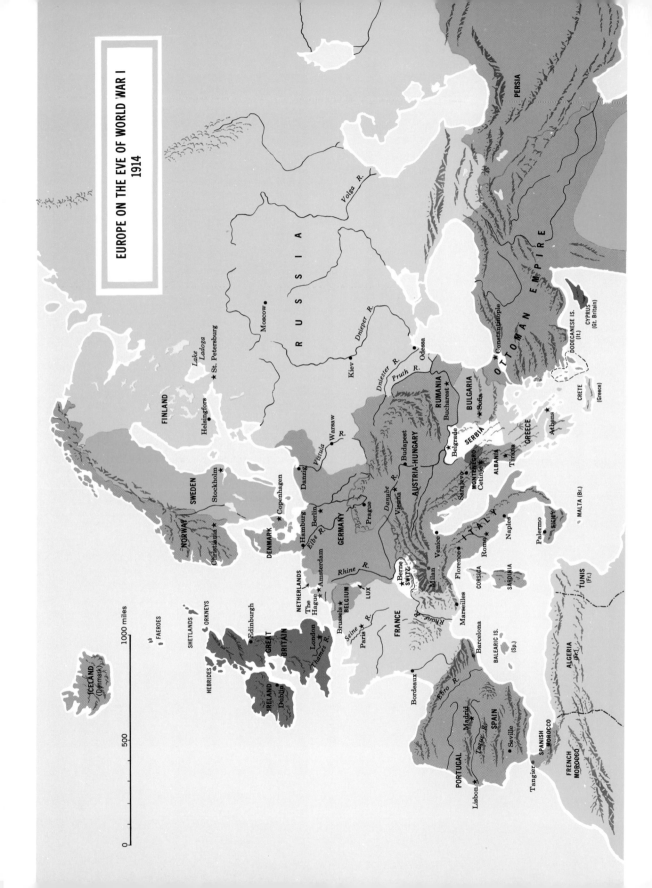

EUROPE ON THE EVE OF WORLD WAR I
1914

ICELAND
(Denmark)

FAEROES

SHETLANDS

ORKNEYS

HEBRIDES

Edinburgh

IRELAND

Dublin

GREAT
BRITAIN

London
Thames R.

NETHERLANDS

The Hague

Brussels

BELGIUM

LUX.

Amsterdam

Hamburg

Berlin

Elbe R.

GERMANY

Prague

Rhine R.

Seine R.

Paris

FRANCE

Berne

SWITZ.

Rhône R.

Bordeaux

Marseilles

CORSICA

SARDINIA

Barcelona

BALEARIC IS.
(Sp.)

Ebro R.

SPAIN

Madrid

Seville

Tagus R.

PORTUGAL

Lisbon

Tangier

SPANISH
MOROCCO

FRENCH
MOROCCO

ALGERIA
(Fr.)

TUNIS
(Fr.)

NORWAY

Christiania

SWEDEN

Stockholm

DENMARK

Copenhagen

Danzig

Vistula

FINLAND

Helsingfors

Lake
Ladoga

St. Petersburg

Moscow

RUSSIA

Volga R.

Dnieper R.

Kiev

Warsaw

R.

AUSTRIA-HUNGARY

Vienna

Budapest

Danube R.

Venice

Milan

ITALY

Florence

Rome

Naples

SICILY

Palermo

MALTA (Br.)

Sarajevo

Belgrade

SERBIA

MONTENEGRO

Cetinje

ALBANIA

Tirana

GREECE

Athens

Dniester R.

Pruth R.

Odessa

RUMANIA

Bucharest

BULGARIA

Sofia

OTTOMAN EMPIRE

Constantinople

PERSIA

DODECANESE IS.
(It.)

CYPRUS
(Gt. Britain)

CRETE
(Greece)

0   500   1000 miles

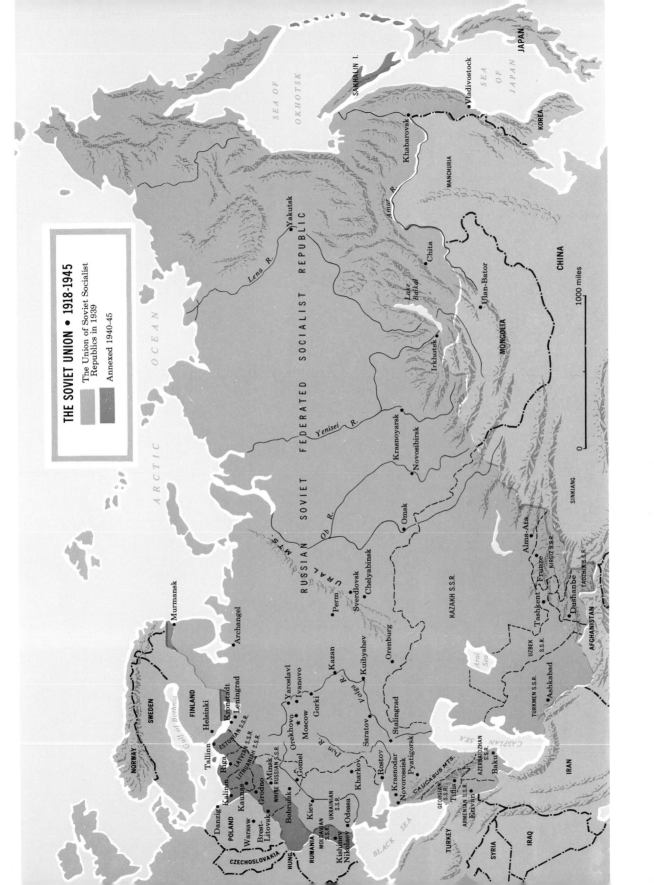

THE SOVIET UNION • 1918-1945

The Union of Soviet Socialist
Republics in 1939

Annexed 1940-45

JAPAN

SEA OF OKHOTSK

SAKHALIN I.

Vladivostock

SEA OF JAPAN

KOREA

Khabarovsk

MANCHURIA

Amur R.

Chita

CHINA

Yakutsk

Lena R.

Lake Baikal

Irkutsk

Ulan-Bator

1000 miles

S O V I E T   F E D E R A T E D   S O C I A L I S T   R E P U B L I C

MONGOLIA

Krasnoyarsk

Novosibirsk

Yenisei R.

SINKIANG

Omsk

Ob R.

ARCTIC OCEAN

R U S S I A N

Alma-Ata

KIRGIZ S.S.R.

Frunze

TADZHIK S.S.R.

U R A L   M T S.

KAZAKH S.S.R.

Tashkent

Dushanbe

AFGHANISTAN

Murmansk

Archangel

Perm

Sverdlovsk

Chelyabinsk

UZBEK S.S.R.

Ashkhabad

TURKMEN S.S.R.

Orenburg

Aral Sea

SWEDEN

FINLAND

Gulf of Bothnia

Helsinki

Kronstadt

Leningrad

Kazan

Volga R.

Kuibyshev

CASPIAN SEA

NORWAY

Tallinn

ESTONIAN S.S.R.

Riga

Kalinin

LATVIAN S.S.R.

LITHUANIAN S.S.R.

Kaunas

Yaroslavl

Ivanovo

Moscow

Gorki

Orekhovo

Saratov

Stalingrad

IRAN

Danzig

POLAND

Warsaw

Brest-Litovsk

Grodno

Bobruisk

Minsk

WHITE RUSSIAN S.S.R.

Gomel

Kiev

Don R.

Kharkov

Rostov

Krasnodar

Pyatigorsk

Novorossisk

Baku

AZERBAIDZHAN S.S.R.

CAUCASUS MTS.

CZECHOSLOVAKIA

HUNG.

RUMANIA

MOLDAVIAN S.S.R.

UKRAINIAN S.S.R.

Kishinev

Nikolaev

Odessa

BLACK SEA

Tiflis

GEORGIAN S.S.R.

ARMENIAN S.S.R.

Erivan

TURKEY

SYRIA

IRAQ

EUROPE ON THE EVE OF WORLD WAR II
Sept. 1, 1939

as the most frivolous and decadent city of Europe. What the country seemed to need was authoritative leadership to spearhead a campaign to regain the world's respect.

The sense of humiliation was increased by two of the provisions imposed on the Germans in the Versailles treaty. First, Germany was compelled to reduce its army to 100,000 men, a requirement that produced bitter discontent among the politically powerful corps of officers that remained at the head of its ranks. Second, the enormous burden of reparations payments continued to arouse the anger of the Germans. Opponents of the reparations settlement urged an obstructionist policy of nonpayment, arguing that the sum of $33 billion demanded would doom the German economy for the foreseeable future. German politicians of all persuasions agreed that the sum was impossibly large. Yet Weimar's foreign minister in the early 1920s, Walter Rathenau, opposed the obstructionists, and attempted to reach a compromise with the former Allied powers. Rathenau's assassination in 1922, by a secret organization of obstructionist army officers, produced a reaction that led to the German government's refusal to make further payments. The result was French occupation of the Ruhr valley in early 1923, in a fruitless attempt to compel German miners there to produce for France. The ensuing stalemate, which lasted for several months, was ended by the German chancellor, Gustav Stresemann, who recognized the futility of obstructionist tactics. His success in persuading the Germans to accept his point of view was aided by an international agreement to renegotiate reparations under the guidance of a committee of experts headed by the American Charles G. Dawes. Crisis was temporarily averted, but the psychological wounds caused by the reparations controversy did not heal.

Another major reason for totalitarianism's appeal in Germany was the inflation the country suffered in the 1920s. The German government increased the supply of money in the early 1920s in a desperate effort to finance social welfare programs in the face of rising unemployment and to buy gold with which to make reparations payments. The result was a period of wild inflation, particularly demoralizing to the middle class. Salaries could not keep up with the vast increase in the cost of living. Farmers were angered by the collapse of agricultural prices and by their burden of debts and taxes. University students saw little prospect of gaining a place in already overcrowded professions. Those who existed on fixed incomes—pensioners, stockholders—saw their security vanish. As they lost their faith in the ability of the government to come to their aid, these men and women began, as well, to lose whatever faith they may have had in the republic. The middle class, traumatized by inflation, continued its search for a government that promised attention to its needs and sympathy with its problems. That search intensified with the advent of the Great Depression of 1929. As we shall see, the depression was a major

*The treaty
as humiliation*

Inflation and the German Mark. As German inflation gained momentum and the value of the mark plummeted, every imaginable kind of container was pressed into service to transport money from place to place.

(2) economics

*The early career of Hitler;
the early days of the Nazi
party*

disaster for most of the world. In few countries, however, were its effects more keenly felt than in Germany. Six million workers were unemployed. Once again the middle class saw its savings vanish.

For a brief period in the late 1920s, however, it had appeared that the German economy, and the Weimar Republic with it, might recover. Borrowed money meant that the country was able to make its reparations payments, scaled down in accordance with the Dawes Committee recommendations, and to earn money abroad with cheaply priced exports. Building programs, sponsored by socialist municipal governments in large cities such as Frankfurt, Düsseldorf, and Berlin—schools, hospitals, and low-cost worker housing—suggested that the country was both politically and economically healthier than it actually was. In fact the Dawes Plan, by stressing the need for immediate increases in production, ensured that the economy would remain in the hands of the country's leading industrialists whose tendency to overcapitalize their enterprises impaired their ability to cut costs once the Depression struck. These were very conservative men, some of whom sympathized with the restoration of a more authoritarian form of government than Weimar represented. They were allied with equally conservative landowners, bound together by their mutual desire for a protective economic policy that would stimulate the sale of domestically produced goods and foodstuffs. These conservative forces were augmented by the army and civil service, staffed with men opposed to the traditions of parliamentary democracy and international cooperation embodied in the republic.

By the end of the decade, party politics had polarized much as they had in Italy. The moderate parties attracted diminishing support while candidates for the Communist party on the Left and the monarchist German People's party on the Right were enjoying increased success. In 1932 discontent with the republic manifested itself in the national elections, which resulted in the continued presidency of the war hero Marshall von Hindenburg. What was significant, however, was not Hindenburg's return to power, but the fact that the Communists polled about five million votes, and that the candidate of the radical Right, Adolf Hitler, received over eleven million votes, more than one-third of those cast. The Weimar Republic was doomed. And Hitler was its logical nemesis.

Hitler was born in 1889, the son of a petty customs official in the Austrian civil service. Hitler's early life was unhappy and maladjusted. Rebellious and undisciplined from childhood, he seems always to have been burdened with a sense of frustration. He was a failure in school, decided that he would become an artist, and went to Vienna in 1909, hoping to enter the Academy. But he failed the required examinations. After squandering not one, but two good-sized inheritances, he eked out a dismal existence as a casual laborer and a painter of watercolors during his last eighteen months in Vienna. Meanwhile he developed violent political prejudices. He became an ardent admirer of certain vociferously anti-Semitic politicians in Vienna; and since he associated Judaism with Marxism, he learned to hate that philosophy as well. When war broke out, Hitler was living in Munich. Though an Austrian citizen, he immediately enlisted in the German army. Following the war, he joined with other disaffected Germans to denounce the Weimar Republic, choosing as the vehicle to express his alienation the newly formed National Socialist Workers' Party.[2] Originally a party of the Left, addressing itself primarily to working-class discontents, the Nazis under Hitler's direction in the mid-twenties broadened their appeal to attract disaffected members of the middle class as well. Nazism's doctrines derived in large part from a rambling treatise by Hitler entitled *Mein Kampf* (My Struggle), which he wrote while in prison following an attempt by the Nazis' private army to stage a "putsch," or sudden overthrow of the government, in Munich in 1923. In *Mein Kampf*, Hitler expressed his hatred of Jews and communists, his sense of Germany's betrayal by its enemies, and his belief that only with strong leadership could the country regain its rightful place within the European concert of nations.

One Step Away from Power. President Hindenburg followed by Hitler.

Hitler's message appealed to an ever-growing number of his disillusioned and economically threatened countrymen and women. In the election of 1928 the Nazis won 12 seats in the Reichstag. In 1930 they won 107 seats, their popular vote increasing from 800,000 to 6,500,000. During the summer of 1932 the parliamentary system broke down. No chancellor could retain a majority in the Reichstag; the Nazis declined to support any cabinet not headed by Hitler, and the communists refused to collaborate with the socialists. In January 1933, a group of reactionaries prevailed upon President Hindenburg to designate Hitler as chancellor, in the mistaken belief that they could control him. It was arranged that there should be only three Nazis in the cabinet, and that Franz von Papen, a Catholic aristocrat, should hold the position of vice-chancellor. The sponsors of this plan failed to appreciate the tremendous popularity of the Nazi movement, however. Hitler was not slow to make the most of his new opportunity. He persuaded Hindenburg to dissolve the Reichstag and to order a new election on March 5. When the new Reichstag assembled, it voted to confer upon Hitler practically unlimited powers. Soon afterward the flag of the Weimar Republic was lowered and replaced by the swastika banner of the National Socialists. The new Germany was proclaimed to be the Third Reich, the successor of the Hohenstaufen Empire of the Middle Ages and of the Hohenzollern Empire of the kaisers.

An Anti-Nazi Poster Employed by the Social Democrats in 1932

During the next few months, other sweeping changes converted Germany from Bismark's federalized state into a highly centralized totalitarian regime. As both chancellor and leader of the Nazi party, Hitler was in a unique position to put the powers of the state to the

---

[2] The name of the party was soon abbreviated in popular usage to Nazi.

Nazi rule

purposes of the party. To this end, all other political parties were declared illegal. Nazi party luminaries were appointed heads of various government departments, and party *gauleiters,* or regional directors, assumed administrative responsibility throughout the country. Hitler made use of paramilitary Nazi "storm troopers" (the S.A.) to maintain discipline within the party and to impose order on the populace through calculated intimidation and violence. Not even the S.A. itself was immune to the imperatives of totalitarian terror: when the aspirations of the S.A. leadership to supplant the established army hierarchy threatened to undermine Hitler's support within the military at a critical moment, he unleashed a bloody purge in which more than a thousand high-ranking S.A. officials were summarily executed. Hitler and his associates would brook no interference with their plans to achieve absolute power. During the late 1930s, a second paramilitary organization, the *Schutzstaffel* (bodyguard) or S.S. became the most dreaded arm of Nazi oppression and terror. Headed by the fanatical Heinrich Himmler, who answered to Hitler himself, the S.S. exercised sovereign power over the lives of all Germans, arresting, detaining, imprisoning, and murdering any who appeared to stand in the path of Nazi domination.

Nazi ideology and ruralism

Although Germany was one of the most highly industrialized countries in the world, National Socialist ideology had a peculiar peasant flavor. The key to Nazi theory was contained in the phrase *Blut und Boden* (blood and soil). The word *soil* reflected not only a deep reverence for the homeland but an abiding affection for the peasants, who were said to embody the finest qualities of the German race. This high

The Nazi Party Congress in Nuremberg, 1934. The Nazis were masters of the use of humanity *en masse* as propaganda. Hitler stands at attention in the center.

Nazism and the Rural Myth. Left and center: During the 1930s the Nazi artist W. Willrich painted sober, healthy peasant-types, the ideal Hitler professed to admire and to cultivate. Right: To stress the rural strength of Aryan Germany, Hitler appeared in lederhosen in the 1920s.

regard for country folk came partly, no doubt, from the fact that they had the highest birth rate of the nation's citizens and therefore were most valuable for military reasons. It was explainable also by the reaction of the Nazi leaders against everything that the city stood for—not only intellectualism and radicalism but high finance and the complicated problems of industrial society.

Despite these sentiments, however, the Nazis did little to restructure the economy of Germany. Although they came to power promising to tax chain stores heavily so as to benefit the small shopkeeper, they succumbed to pressure from bankers to mitigate those plans. Indeed, they encouraged heavy industry as part of their program of rearmament, forming what amounted to partnerships with such giants as I. G. Farben, the chemical concern, which worked closely with the government on the development of synthetic fuels. Like other Western nations, the Germans battled unemployment with large state-financed construction projects: highways, public housing, and reforestation. Late in the decade, rearmament and a substantial increase in the size of the military establishment all but ended the German unemployment problem—much as the same policies and programs were ending it elsewhere.

Germany's social structure remained relatively untouched by Nazi

Rearmament and pro-industrial economic policy

rule. Government policy encouraged women to withdraw from the labor force, both to ease unemployment and to conform to Nazi notions of a woman's proper role. "Can woman," one propagandist asked, "conceive of anything more beautiful than to sit with her husband in her cozy home and listen inwardly to the loom of time weaving the weft and warp of motherhood . . .?" Like Mussolini, Hitler moved to abolish class conflict by robbing working-class institutions of their power. He outlawed trade unions and strikes, froze wages, and organized workers and employers into a National Labor Front, while at the same time increasing workers' welfare benefits. Class distinctions were to some degree blurred by the regime's insistence on infusing a new national "spirit" into the entire society. Organizations like the Hitler Youth, a sinister variant on the Boy Scout movement, and National Labor Service, which drafted students and others for a term to work on various state-sponsored building and reclamation projects, cut across, but did not abolish, class lines.

For the National Socialists, the great social dividing line was race. In this Nazism differed from other forms of totalitarianism, particularly in its single-minded persecution of the Jews. Anti-Semitism is a centuries-old phenomenon. It had manifested itself in nineteenth-century Europe: in the Russian pogroms; in the Dreyfus affair in France; and in the politics of Germany, where in 1893 sixteen avowed anti-Semites were elected to the Reichstag, and the Conservative Party made anti-Semitism part of its official program. Jews were a threat to those who feared urbanization and reform. The majority of Jews lived in cities, where they had advanced themselves in business and finance. They were in the forefront of scientific, cultural, and political innovation. Sigmund Freud was a Jew, as, of course, was Karl Marx. By attacking Jews, Anti-Semites could as well attack the modern institutions which they despised and which they associated with a "conspiracy" to deprive civilization of its reassuring base in tradition and authority. They perverted evolutionary theory to suit their arguments. Jews were declared "outsiders," without roots in any particular national culture, and therefore destructive of the racial "purity" necessary for the survival of the race. "The Jews are our national misfortune," the German historian Heinrich von Treitschke wrote in 1879. By that he meant that they were an alien force, subversive to the future of a triumphant German reich.

Hitler was a fanatical believer in the anti-Semitic dogmas of the Right. The Nazis argued that the so-called Aryan race, which was supposed to include the Nordics as its most perfect specimens, was the only one ever to have made any notable contributions to human progress. They contended further that the accomplishments and mental qualities of a people were determined by blood. Thus the achievements of the Jew forever remained Jewish, no matter how long he or she might live in a Western country. It followed that no Jewish science or Jewish literature or Jewish music could ever truly represent the

German nation. A series of laws passed in 1935 deprived Jews and people of Jewish blood of their German citizenship, and prohibited marriage between Jews and other Germans. Eventually, millions of Jews were rounded up, tortured, and murdered in concentration camps. Other representatives of "imperfect" racial and social groups—homosexuals, gypsies, and anti-Nazi intellectuals—met a similar fate. The extremism of Hitler's anti-Semitic campaigns underscores the fact that National Socialism was more fanatical than Italian fascism. It was a new religion, not only in its dogmatism and its ritual, but in its fierce intolerance and its zeal for expansion.

If Nazism was a form of perverted religion, Hitler was its high priest. His appeal was based in part on his ability to give the German people what they wanted: jobs for workers, a productive economy for industrialists, a bulwark against communism for the still-influential Junker class. But more important, he preached what the German people wished to hear. His power lay not so much in the programs he championed, many of which were ill-thought out or contradictory, but in his talent for responding to the sentiments of his fellow-Germans, and for turning those sentiments into holy writ. As one of his early followers remarked: "Hitler responds to the vibrations of the human heart with the delicacy of a seismograph. . . . His words go like an arrow to their target; he touches each private wound on the raw, liberating the mass unconscious, expressing its innermost aspirations, telling it what it most wants to hear." That so many wanted most to listen to the poisonous dogmas of Adolf Hitler is a depressing commentary on the state of the Western world in the 1930s.

The power of Adolf Hitler

The significance of German and Italian totalitarianism remains a subject of controversy among students of modern history. Some argue that it reflected the enthronement of force by capitalists in an effort to save their dying system from destruction. And it is true that the success of both movements in gaining control of the government depended on support from great landowners and captains of industry. Others explain German and Italian totalitarianism as a reaction of debtors against creditors, of farmers against bankers and manufacturers, and of small businessmen against high finance and monopolistic practices. Still others interpret it as a reaction to communist threat, a reversion to primitivism, a result of the despair of the masses, a protest against the weaknesses of democracy, or a supreme manifestation of nationalism. Undoubtedly it was all of these things combined. One further argument holds that fascism and Nazism were extreme expressions of tendencies prevalent in all industrialized countries. If official policies in most Western countries in the 1930s took on more and more of an authoritarian semblance—a tightly controlled economy, limitation of production to maintain prices, and expansion of armaments to promote prosperity—it was because nearly all nations in that period were beset with similar problems and, in varying degrees, frightened of their implications.

The significance of German and Italian totalitarianism

4. THE DEMOCRACIES BETWEEN THE WARS

The histories of the three major Western democracies—Great Britain, France, and the United States—run roughly parallel during the years after the First World War. In all three countries there was an attempt by governments to trust to policies and assumptions that had prevailed before the war. The French, not surprisingly, continued to fear Germany and to take whatever steps they could to keep their traditional enemy as weak as possible. Under the leadership of the moderate conservative, Raymond Poincaré, who held office from 1922 to 1924, and again from 1926 to 1929, the French pursued a policy of deflation, which attempted to keep the price of manufactured goods low, by restraining wages. This policy pleased businessmen, but was hard on the working class. Edouard Herriot, a Radical Socialist who served as premier from 1924 to 1926 was, despite his party's name, a spokesman for the small businessman, farmer, and lower middle class. Herriot declared himself in favor of social reform, but refused to raise taxes in order to pay for it. Class conflict lay close to the surface of French national affairs throughout the 1920s. While industries prospered, employers rejected trade unionists' demands to bargain collectively. A period of major strikes immediately after the war was followed by a sharp decline in union activity. Workers remained dissatisfied, even after the government passed a modified social insurance program in 1930, insuring against sickness, old age, and death.

Class conflict flared in Britain as well. Anxious to regain its now irretrievably lost position as the major industrial and financial power in the world, Britain, like France, pursued a policy of deflation, designed to lower the price of manufactured goods and thus make them more attractive on the world market. The result was a reduction in wages which undermined the standard of living of many British workers. Their resentment helped to elect a Labour party government in 1924

Labor Troubles in Britain. Mounted police escorting delivery wagons through a mob of angry strikers during the general strike of 1926.

Left: *U.S. Farmers on Their Way West in the 1930s.* Forced from their land by depression debts and by drought, thousands of farmers and their families headed to California, Oregon, and Washington in search of employment. Right: *The Stock Market Crash, October 24, 1929.* Crowds milling outside the New York Stock Exchange on the day of the big crash.

and 1929. But its minority position in Parliament left it little chance to accomplish much of consequence, even had its leader, Prime Minister J. Ramsay MacDonald, been a more adventurous socialist than he was. In 1926 British trade unions grew increasingly militant because of the particularly distressing wage levels in the coal mining industry, and because the Conservative government, returned to power under Stanley Baldwin in 1925, refused to be deflected from its deflationary stance. The unions staged a nationwide general strike which, though it failed as an industrial strategy, turned the middle class more than ever against the workers.

The United States was undoubtedly the most impregnable fortress of conservative power among the democracies. The presidents elected during the 1920s—Warren G. Harding, Calvin Coolidge, and Herbert Hoover—upheld a social philosophy formulated by the barons of big business in the nineteenth century, and the Supreme Court used its power of judicial review to nullify progressive legislation enacted by state governments and occasionally by Congress.

Conservatism in the U.S.

The course of Western history was dramatically altered by the advent of worldwide depression in 1929. We have already seen the way in which depression contributed to the rise of Nazism. But all countries were forced to come to terms with the economic and social devastation it produced. The Great Depression had its roots in a general agricultural slump in the 1920s, the result of increased postwar production which drove down the price of grain and other commodities to the point of bankrupting farmers, though not far enough to benefit

The Great Depression

Léon Blum

the urban poor. To chronic agricultural distress was added the financial crisis that began with the collapse of prices on the New York Stock Exchange in 1929. With a drop in the value of stocks, banks found themselves short of capital and forced to close. International investors called in their debts. Industries, unable to sell their products, stopped manufacturing and started laying off workers. Unemployment further contracted markets—fewer people had money with which to buy goods or services—and that contraction led to more unemployment.

The results of the depression took varied forms throughout the West. In 1931 Great Britain abandoned the gold standard; the government of the United States followed suit in 1933. By no longer pegging their currencies to the price of gold, these countries hoped to make money cheaper, and thus more available for programs of public and private economic recovery. This action was the forerunner of a broad program of currency management, which became an important element in a general policy of economic nationalism. As early as 1932 Great Britain abandoned its time-honored policy of free trade. Protective tariffs were raised in some instances as high as 100 percent.

Domestically, Britain moved cautiously to alleviate the effects of the depression. A national government, which came to power in 1931 with a ministry composed of members from the Conservative, Liberal, and Labour parties, was reluctant to spend beyond its income, as it would have to in order to underwrite effective programs of public assistance. Of the European democracies, France adopted the most advanced set of policies to combat the inequalities and distress that followed in the wake of the depression. In 1936, responding to a threat from ultraconservatives to overthrow the republic, a Popular Front government, under the leadership of the socialist Léon Blum (1872–1950), was formed by the Radical, Radical Socialist, and Communist parties, and lasted for two years. The Popular Front nationalized the munitions industry and reorganized the Bank of France so as to deprive the 200 largest stockholders of their monopolistic control over credit. In addition, it decreed a forty-hour week for all urban workers and initiated a program of public works. For the benefit of the farmers it established a wheat office to fix the price and regulate the distribution of grain. Although the threat from the political Right was for a time quelled by the Popular Front, conservatives were generally uncooperative and unimpressed by its attempts to ameliorate the conditions of the French working class. The anti-Semitism that had appeared at the time of the Dreyfus affair resurfaced; Blum was both a socialist and a Jew. Businessmen saw him as the forerunner of a French Lenin, and were heard to opine, "better Hitler than Blum." They got their wish before the decade was out.

The most dramatic changes in policy occurred not in Europe but in the United States. The explanation was twofold. The United States had clung longer to the economic philosophy of the nineteenth century. Prior to the depression the business classes had adhered firmly to the dogma of freedom of contract and insisted upon their right to form monopolies and to use the government as their agent in frustrating the demands of both workers and consumers. The depression in the United States was also more severe than in the European democracies. Industrial production shrank by about two-thirds. The structure of agricultural prices and of common stocks collapsed. Thousands of banks were forced to close their doors. Unemployment rose to one-third of the total labor force. An attempt to alleviate distress was contained in a program of reform and reconstruction known as the New Deal. The chief architect and motivator of this program was Franklin D. Roosevelt (1882–1945), who succeeded Herbert Hoover in the presidency on March 4, 1933.

The aim of the New Deal was to preserve the capitalist system, by managing the economy and undertaking programs of relief and public works to increase mass purchasing power. Although the New Deal did assist in the recovery both of individual citizens and of the country, through programs of currency management and social security, it left the crucial problem of unemployment unsolved. In 1939, after six years of the New Deal, the United States still had more than nine million jobless workers—a figure which exceeded the combined unemployment of the rest of the world. Ironically, only the outbreak of a new world war could provide the full recovery that the New Deal had failed to assure, by directing millions from the labor market into the army and by creating jobs in the countless factories that turned to the manufacture of war matériel.

Its achievements

5. INTELLECTUAL AND CULTURAL TRENDS IN THE INTERWAR YEARS

The First World War, which proved so disillusioning to so many, and the generally dispiriting political events which followed in its train, made it difficult to hold fast to any notion of a purposeful universe. Philosophers, to a greater degree than their predecessors, declared that there was little point in attempting to discover answers to questions about the nature of ultimate reality. These antimetaphysicians broke dramatically with the philosophers of the past century, who had grounded their speculations in a belief in progress and in a search for all-encompassing explanations of human behavior. Probably the most influential of these new thinkers was the Viennese Ludwig Wittgenstein (1889–1951), founder, with the Englishman Bertrand Russell (1872–1970), of the school of Logical Positivism. Developed further by the so-called Vienna Circle, whose leader was Rudolf Carnap, Logical Positivism emerged as an uncompromisingly scientific philosophy. It is not concerned with values or ideals except to the extent that they may be demonstrable by mathematics or physics. In general,

Bertrand Russell

the Logical Positivists reject as "meaningless" everything that cannot be reduced to a "one-to-one correspondence" with something in the physical universe. They reduce philosophy to a mere instrument for the discovery of truth in harmony with the facts of the physical environment. They divest it almost entirely of its traditional content and use it as a medium for answering questions and solving problems. They are concerned especially to attack political theory, regarding that subject as particularly burdened with unproved assumptions and questionable dogmas.

Religion as a cultural force

Sociologists reinforced philosophers in denying the value of metaphysics. One of the most important was the German Max Weber (1864–1920), who, in his book *The Protestant Ethic and the Spirit of Capitalism* (1905), argued that religion must be understood as a cultural force, in this case assisting directly in the spread of capitalism. By making work a cardinal virtue and idleness a supreme vice, Protestantism had encouraged the work ethic, which, in turn, had fueled the energies of early capitalist entrepreneurs. When he turned to a study of the contemporary world, Weber concluded that societies would inevitably fall more and more under the sway of ever-expanding and potentially totalitarian bureaucracies. Recognizing the extent to which such a development might threaten human freedom, Weber posited the notion of "charismatic" leadership as a means of escaping the deadening tyranny of state control. A term derived from the Greek word for gift, "charisma" was, according to Weber, an almost magic quality which could induce hero worship and which, if properly directed by its possessor, might produce an authority to challenge bureaucracy. Weber himself recognized the dangers as well as the attractions of charismatic authority, dangers which the careers of Stalin, Hitler, and Mussolini soon made all too apparent. Another thinker who treated religion as a powerful social and psychological force, rather than as a branch of metaphysics, was the Swiss psychologist Carl Jung (1875–1961). Originally a student and disciple of Freud, Jung broke with his intellectual mentor by proclaiming the existence of a force behind individual id, ego, and superego: the "collective unconscious." Jung's literary background and his personal penchant for mysticism helped persuade him of the enduring psychological and therapeutic value of myth and religion, something Freud refused to acknowledge.

Antirationalist and antidemocratic philosophies

The writings of some philosophers during the interwar years not only reflected a sense of crisis and despair but, because of the influence of those works, contributed to it as well. Foremost among these were the Italian Vilfredo Pareto (1848–1923) and the German Oswald Spengler (1880–1936), who agreed in their contempt for the masses, in their belief that democracy was impossible, in their anti-intellectual viewpoint, and in their admiration for strong and aggressive leaders. Spengler was, in many respects, more extreme than Pareto. In his *Decline of the West,* completed in 1918, and even more in his later writings, he gave vent to attitudes that reflect the extent to which totalitarianism might appeal to an "anti-intellectual" intellectual. In his *Hour of Decision,* published in 1933, he fulminated against democracy, pacifism, internationalism, the lower classes, and nonwhite peoples. He sang the praises of those "who feel themselves born and called to be masters," of "healthy instincts, race, the will to possession and power." Spengler despised the analytical reasoning of urban intellectuals and called upon men to admire the "deep wisdom of old peasant families." Human beings, he maintained, are "beasts of prey," and those who deny this conclusion are simply "beasts of prey with broken teeth."

Further confusion and uncertainty were encouraged by the pioneering work of the German physicist Albert Einstein (1879–1955), whose theorizing and experiments were revolutionizing the way in which men and women perceived the universe. In 1905 Einstein began to challenge not merely the older conceptions of matter but practically the entire structure of traditional physics. The doctrine for which he is most noted is his principle of relativity. During the greater part of the nineteenth century, physicists had assumed that space and motion were absolute. Space was supposed to be filled with an intangible substance known as *ether,* which provided the medium for the undulations of light. But experiments performed by English and American physicists near the end of the century exploded the ether hypothesis. Einstein then set to work to reconstruct the scheme of the universe in accordance with a different pattern. He maintained that space and motion, instead of being absolute, are relative to each other. Objects have not merely three dimensions but four. To the familiar length, breadth, and thickness, Einstein added a new dimension of *time* and represented all four as fused in a synthesis which he called the *space-time continuum.* In this way he sought to explain the idea that mass is dependent upon motion. Bodies traveling at high velocity have proportions of extension and mass different from those they would have at rest. Einstein also posited the conception of a finite universe—that is, finite in space. The region of matter does not extend into infinity; the universe has limits. While these are by no means definite boundaries, there is at least a region beyond which nothing exists. Space curves back upon itself so as to make of the universe a gigantic sphere within which are contained galaxies, solar systems, stars, and planets.

The Einstein theories had a major influence in precipitating another revolutionary development in physics: the splitting of the atom to release the energy contained within it. As early as 1905 Einstein became convinced of the equivalence of mass and energy and worked out a formula for the conversion of one into the other, which he expressed as $E = mc^2$. E represents the energy in ergs, m the mass in grams, and c the velocity of light in centimeters per second. In other words, the amount of energy locked within the atom is equal to the mass multiplied by the square of the velocity of light. But no practical application of this formula was possible until after the discovery of the neutron by the Englishman Sir James Chadwick in 1932. Since

Einstein's theories

Albert Einstein

*Releasing the energy
within the atom*

the neutron carries no charge of electricity, it is an ideal weapon for bombarding the atom. It is neither repulsed by the positively charged protons nor absorbed by the negatively charged electrons. Moreover, in the process of bombardment it produces more neutrons, which hit other atoms and cause them in turn to split and create neutrons. In this way the original reaction is repeated in an almost unending series.

Laying the groundwork for the atomic bomb

In 1939 two German physicists, Otto Hahn and Fritz Strassman, succeeded in splitting atoms of uranium by bombarding them with neutrons. The initial reaction produced a chain of reactions, in much the same way that a fire burning at the edge of a piece of paper raises the temperature of adjoining portions of the paper high enough to cause them to ignite. Scientists in Germany, Great Britain, and the United States were spurred on by governments anxious to make use of these discoveries for military purposes during the Second World War. The first use made of the knowledge of atomic fission was in the preparation of an atomic bomb—a device that would further heighten and perpetuate the anxieties of the era.

Literary disillusion

Literary movements during the interwar period showed tendencies similar to those in philosophy. Like the philosophers, the major novelists, poets, and dramatists were disillusioned by the brute facts of world war and by the failure of victory to fulfill its promises. Many were profoundly affected also by revolutionary developments in science, such as the theories of Einstein, and especially by the probings of the new science of psychoanalysis into the hidden secrets of the mind. Much of the literature of the interwar period reflected themes of frustration, cynicism, and disenchantment. The general mood of the era was expressed individually by different writers; for example, by the early novels of the American Ernest Hemingway (1899–1961), by the poetry of the Anglo-American T. S. Eliot (1888–1965), and by the plays of the German Bertolt Brecht (1898–1956). In *The Sun Also Rises,* Hemingway gave the public a powerful description of the essential tragedy of the so-called lost generation and set a pattern that other writers, like the American F. Scott Fitzgerald, were soon to follow. In his poem *The Waste Land* (1922), T. S. Eliot presented a philosophy that was close to despair. Once you are born, he seemed to be saying, life is a living death, to be endured as boredom and frustration. Brecht, in plays written to be performed before the proletarian patrons of cabarets, proclaimed the corruption of the bourgeois state and the pointlessness of war.

T. S. Eliot

The works of many writers in the interwar period reflected to an increasing extent the isolation of self-conscious intellectuals and the constricting of their audience that characterized the years before the First World War. While Brecht carried his revolutionary messages into the streets of Berlin, others wrote primarily for each other or for the small elite group who could understand what they were saying. Eliot crammed his poetry with esoteric allusions. The Irishman James Joyce (1882–1941), whose ability to enter his characters' minds and to reproduce their "stream-of-consciousness" on paper made him a writer of the very first order, nevertheless wrote with a complexity that only few could appreciate. The same was true, though to a lesser extent, of the novels of the Frenchman Marcel Proust (1871–1922) and the Englishwoman Virginia Woolf (1882–1941). In her novels and essays, Woolf was, as well, an eloquent and biting critic of the ruling class of Britain, focusing in part on the enforced oppression of women even in that class.

Virginia Woolf

The depression of the 1930s forced a reexamination of the methods and purposes of literature. In the midst of economic stagnation and threats of totalitarianism and war, literature was politicized. Authors came to believe that their work must indict meanness, cruelty, and barbarism, and point the way to a more just society, that it should also be a literature addressed not to fellow intellectuals, but to common men and women. The American John Steinbeck (1902–1968), in *The Grapes of Wrath,* depicted the sorry plight of impoverished farmers fleeing from the "dust bowl" to California only to find that all the land had been monopolized by companies that exploited their workers. Pervading the novels of the Frenchman André Malraux (1901–1976) was the strong suggestion that the human struggle against tyranny and injustice is that which gives meaning and value to life. Young British writers such as W. H. Auden, Stephen Spender, and Christopher Isherwood declared, as communist sympathizers, that artists had an obligation to politicize their art for the benefit of the revolution. They rejected the pessimism of their immediate literary forebears for the optimism of political commitment to a common cause.

Influence of the depression

In this they differed radically from their French contemporary, Jean-Paul Sartre (1905–1980), whose pessimistic philosophy of Existentialism was receiving its first hearing at this time. Sartre was a teacher of philosophy in a Paris *lycée* and subsequently a leader of the French Resistance movement against the Germans during the Second World War. His philosophy takes its name from its doctrine that the *existence* of human beings as free individuals is the fundamental fact of life. But this freedom is of no help to humanity; instead it is a source of anguish and terror. Realizing, however vaguely, that they are free agents, morally responsible for all their acts, individuals feel themselves strangers in an alien world. They can have no confidence in a benevolent God or in a universe guided by purpose, for, according to Sartre, all such ideas have been reduced to fictions by modern science. The only way of escape from despair is the path of "involvement," or active participation in human affairs. It should be noted that in addition to the atheistic Existentialism of Sartre, there was also a prior Christian version, which had its origin in the teachings of Søren Kierkegaard (1813–1855), a Danish theologian of the mid–nineteenth cen-

Jean-Paul Sartre

George Orwell

John Maynard Keynes

tury. Like its atheistic counterpart, Christian Existentialism also teaches that the chief cause of human agony and terror is freedom, but it finds the source of its freedom in original sin.

Another writer who refused to allow himself the luxury of political optimism was the Englishman George Orwell (1903–1950). Although sympathetic to the cause of international socialism, Orwell continued to insist that all political movements were to some degree corrupted. He urged writers to recognize a duty to write only on the basis of what they had themselves experienced. Above all, writers should never simply parrot party propaganda. Orwell's last two novels, *Animal Farm* and *1984,* written during and immediately after the Second World War, are powerful expressions of his mistrust of political regimes—whether of the Left or the Right—that profess democracy but in fact destroy human freedom.

Optimism during the 1930s was generally the property of those writers who were prepared to advocate a violent change in the social order, most notably men and women sympathetic to the doctrines of communism and the achievements of Soviet Russia. An exception to this rule was the British economist John Maynard Keynes (1883–1946), who argued that capitalism could be made to work if governments would play a part in its management, and whose theories helped shape the economic policies of the New Deal. Keynes had served as an economic advisor to the British government during the 1919 treaty-making at Paris. He was disgusted with the harsh terms imposed upon the Germans, recognizing that they would serve only to keep alive the hatreds and uncertainties that breed war. Keynes believed that capitalism with its inner faults corrected could provide a just and efficient economy. First, Keynes abandoned the sacred cow of balanced budgets. He did not advocate continuous deficit financing. He would have the government deliberately operate in the red whenever private investment was too scanty to provide for the economic needs of the country. When depression gave way to recovery, private financing could take the place of deficit spending for most purposes. He favored the accumulation and investment of large amounts of venture capital, which he declared to be the only socially productive form of capital. Finally, Keynes recommended monetary control as a means of promoting prosperity and full employment. He would establish what is commonly called a "managed currency," regulating its value by a process of contraction or expansion in accordance with the needs of the economy. Prosperity would thus be assured in terms of the condition of the home market, and no nation would be tempted to "beggar its neighbor" in the foolish pursuit of a favorable balance of trade.

Trends in art tended to parallel those in literature. For much of the period, visual artists continued to explore aesthetic frontiers far removed from the conventional taste of average men and women. Picasso followed his particular genius as it led him further into cubist

John Maynard Keynes

variations and inventions. So did others, such as the Frenchman Fernand Léger (1881–1955), who combined devotion to cubist principles and a fascination with the artifacts of industrial civilization. A group more advanced, perhaps, than the cubists, the expressionists argued that since color and line express inherent psychological qualities which can be represented without reference to subject matter, a painting need not have a "subject" at all. The Russian Wassily Kandinsky (1866–1944) carried the logic of this position to its conclusion by calling his untitled paintings "improvisations," and insisting that they meant nothing. A second group of expressionists rejected intellectuality for what they called "objectivity," by which they meant a candid appraisal of the state of the human mind. Their analysis took the form of an attack upon the greed and decadence of postwar Europe. Chief among this group was the German George Grosz (1893–1959), whose cruel, satiric line has been likened to a "razor lancing a carbuncle." Another school expressed its disgust with the world by declaring that there was in fact no such thing as aesthetic principle, since aesthetic principle was based on reason and the world had conclusively proved by fighting itself to death that reason did not exist. Calling themselves dada-ists (after a name picked at random, allegedly, from the dictionary) these artists, led by the Frenchman Marcel Duchamp (1887–1968), the German Max Ernst (1891–1976), and the Alsatian Jean Hans Arp (1887–1966), concocted "fabrications" from cutouts and juxtapositions of wood, glass, and metal, and gave them bizarre names: *The Bride stripped bare by her Bachelors, even* (Duchamp), for example. These works were declared by critics, however, to belie their professed meaninglessness, to be, in fact, expressions of the subconscious. Such certainly were the paintings of the surrealists, artists such

Trends in art

See color plates following page 550 for representative works by Kandinsky, Grosz, Duchamp, de Chirico, Dali, and Orozco

Big Julie by Fernand Léger. Note the artist's fascination with industrial shapes and images.

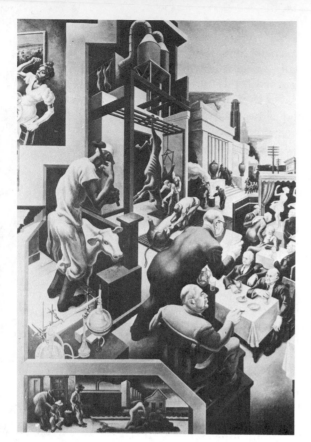

Left: *Mural of Kansas City, Missouri* by Thomas Hart Benton. The mural protests the corruption of American politics and the Depression misery and degradation of farm workers and industrial laborers. The man in the armchair is the political boss of Kansas City in the 1930s, Tom Pendergast. Right: *"Tie Yourself to the Fatherland, Dear Fatherland"* by George Grosz. Grosz's attacks on unfeeling capitalism during the Weimar years undoubtedly served to weaken the political center during the 1930s.

as the Italian Giorgio de Chirico (1888–1978) and the Spaniard Salvador Dali (1904–1989), whose explorations of the interior of the mind produced irrational, fantastic, and generally melancholy images.

Art as social commentary

For a time in the 1930s artists, like writers, responded to the sense of international crisis by painting to express their pain and outrage directly to a mass audience. Among the chief representatives of the new movement were the Mexicans Diego Rivera and Jose Clemente Orozco, and the Americans Thomas Hart Benton, Reginald Marsh, and Edward Hopper. The fundamental aim of these artists was to depict the social conditions of the modern world and to present in graphic detail the hopes and struggles of peasants and workers. While they scarcely adhered to the conventions of the past, there was nothing unintelligible about their work; it was intended to be art that anyone could understand. Much of it bore the sting or thrust of social satire. Orozco, in particular, delighted in pillorying the hypocrisy of the Church and the greed and cruelty of plutocrats and plunderers.

Music, along with the rest of the arts, continued its movement away from nineteenth-century form and intentions. Impressionists, such as Debussy, were succeeded by expressionists, whose work is concerned more with form than with sensuous effects and tends toward abstraction. Expressionism, more radical and more influential than impressionism, comprises two main schools: atonality, founded by the

Viennese Arnold Schoenberg (1874–1951), and polytonality, best typified by the Russian Igor Stravinsky (1882–1971). Atonality abolishes key. In this type of music, dissonances are the rule rather than the exception, and the melodic line commonly alternates between chromatic manipulation and strange unsingable leaps. In short, the ordinary principles of composition are reversed. The atonalists attempt, with some success, to let musical sound become a vehicle for expressing the inner meaning and elemental structure of things.

Polytonality is essentially a radical kind of counterpoint, deriving its inspiration partly from baroque practices of counterpoint that were placed in the service of new ideas. However, it does not simply interweave independent melodies which together form concord, but undertakes to combine separate keys and unrelated harmonic systems, with results that are highly discordant. While the atonalists have retained elements of romanticism, the polytonalists have tried to resurrect the architectural qualities of pure form, movement, and rhythm, stripping away all sentimentality and sensuous connotations.

Architects during this period were also intent upon denying sentimentality. Between 1880 and 1890 designers in Europe and America announced that the prevailing styles of building construction were out of harmony with the facts of modern civilization, and declared as well their intention of restoring that harmony. The chief pioneers of this "functionalism" were Otto Wagner (1841–1918) in Germany and Louis Sullivan (1856–1924) and Frank Lloyd Wright (1869–1959) in the United States. The basic principle of functionalism is the idea that the appearance of a building should proclaim its actual use and purpose. There must be no addition of friezes, columns, tracery, or battlements merely because some people consider such ornaments beautiful. True beauty consists in an honest adaptation of materials to the purpose they are intended to serve. Functionalism also embodies the notion that architecture should express either directly or symbolically the distinguishing features of contemporary culture. Ornamentation must therefore be restricted to such elements as will reflect an age of science

Igor Stravinsky

Development of functional architecture

Taliesin East by Frank Lloyd Wright. A famous example of the functional style, with the pattern of the house conforming to the natural surroundings.

Contrasting Architectural Styles in Germany between the Wars. Left: The Bauhaus by Walter Gropius. This school in Dessau, Germany, is a starkly functional prototype of the interwar "international style." Right: The Chancellery in Berlin by Albert Speer. Note the massive qualities of the Nazi state style.

and machines. A leading European practitioner of functionalism was the German, Walter Gropius (1883–1969), who in 1919 established a school—the *Bauhaus*—in Dessau to serve as a center for the theory and practice of modern architecture. Gropius and his followers declared that their style of design, which in time came to be called "international," was the only one which permitted an honest application of new material—chromium, glass, steel, and concrete.

The arts under Hitler

Gropius was one of the multitude of German intellectuals—both Jewish and non-Jewish—to leave their country after Hitler's rise to power. Totalitarianism had its own cultural aesthetic. Functionalism, which celebrated the qualities of material, line, and proportion, had no place in a totalitarian regime, where the arts were obliged to advertise the virtues of the state, its tradition, and the aspirations of its people. Instead of Gropius, Hitler had Albert Speer, an architect of unimpressive talents, who produced for him grandiose designs whose vacuous pretentiousness was an unconscious parody of Nazi ideology. Atonality in music was banished along with functionalism in architecture, to be replaced by a state-sponsored revival of the mystical and heroic nationalism of Wagner.

Art was an important part of the new and cultural arm of totalitarianism: propaganda, the practice of indoctrinating populations to believe only what governments wished them to believe. It mattered not at all that belief was based on falsehood, as in the "superiority of the Aryan race," for example. If it served the interest of the state, it was disseminated as truth. Never before had so many of the world's people been able to read. Nineteenth- and twentieth-century governments had encouraged literacy, fearing an ignorant working class as a revolutionary threat. Now totalitarian regimes used education unashamedly as a means of propagating a party line. "All effective propaganda has to limit itself to a very few points and to use them like slogans," Hitler wrote in *Mein Kampf.* "It has to confine itself to little and to repeat this eternally." Books critical of the state were banned, their places on school and library shelves taken by others specifically written to glorify the present leadership. Youth programs instructed children in the virtues of discipline and loyalty to the state. Mass gymnastic displays suggested the ease with which well-trained bodies could be made to respond to the military needs of the nation. Propagandizing was made more effective by the advent of mass-circulation publishing, the radio, and the motion picture. Newspapers which printed only what the state wanted printed reached a wider audience than ever before. Party political broadcasts, beamed into homes or blared through loudspeakers in town squares, by their constant repetitiveness made people begin to accept—if not believe—what they knew to be untrue. Films could transform German youths into Aryan gods and goddesses, as they could Russian collective farms into a worker's paradise. Sergei Eisenstein (1898–1948), the Russian director, rewrote Russian history on film to serve the ends of the Soviet state. Hitler commissioned the filmmaker Leni Riefenstahl to record a political rally staged by herself and Speer. The film, entitled *Triumph of the Will,* was a visual hymn to the Nordic race and the Nazi regime. (And the comedian Charlie Chaplin riposted in his celebrated lampoon, *The Great Dictator,* an enormously successful parody of totalitarian pomposities.)

Propaganda

In Western democracies, although the media were not manipulated by the state as they were elsewhere, their effectiveness as propagandizers was nevertheless recognized and exploited. Advertising became an industry when manufacturers realized the mass markets that newspapers, magazines, and radio represented. Much that was printed and aired was trivialized by writers and editors who feared that serious or difficult material would antagonize the readers or listeners upon whom they depended for their livelihood. This is not to say that the new media were uniformly banal, or that artists and performers were unable to use them to make thoughtful protests. The film version of Steinbeck's *Grapes of Wrath,* directed by John Ford, though an exception to the normal run of escapist Hollywood comedies and adventures, was perhaps as stinging an indictment of capitalism as the novel, and it reached far more people. During these years popular culture, whatever else it was, remained a powerful and alarming new fact of life:

*The media in the
democracies*

powerful in terms of its vast audience; alarming because of its particular applicability as a means of controlling the minds of men and women.

SELECTED READINGS

• *Items so designated are available in paperback editions.*

GENERAL

Carsten, F. L., *Revolution in Central Europe, 1918–1919*, London, 1972. A useful treatment of the postwar revolts.

• Collaer, P., *A History of Modern Music*, Cleveland, Ohio, 1961. Useful introduction.

• Galbraith, John Kenneth, *The Great Crash, 1929*, Boston, 1955. An entertaining and informative account by the celebrated economist.

• Gamow, George, *Thirty Years That Shook Physics*, Mineola, N.Y., 1966. An erudite yet readable account.

• Hamilton, George Heard, *Painting and Sculpture in Europe, 1880–1940*, Baltimore, 1967. An excellent survey.

• Hartnack, Justus, *Wittgenstein and Modern Philosophy*, Garden City, N.Y., 1965. Clear introduction to a difficult subject.

• Hitchcock, H.R., *Architecture: 19th and 20th Centuries*, London, 1958. Thorough and well-written survey.

• Kahler, Erich, *The Tower and the Abyss*, New York, 1957. A survey of the arts in the context of contemporary culture.

• Kindleberger, C. P., *The World in Depression, 1929–1939*, Berkeley, 1973. A first-rate study of the worldwide aspects of the slump.

Laqueur, W., and G. L. Mosse, eds., *the Left-Wing Intellectuals between the Wars, 1919–1939*, New York, 1966. Recent essays by modern historians.

Masur, Gerhard, *Prophets of Yesterday*, New York, 1961. A useful intellectual history of the interwar period.

Mosse, George L., *The Naturalization of the Masses: Political Symbolism and Mass Movements in Germany from the Napoleonic Wars through the Third Reich*, New York, 1975. Attempts to trace the roots of Nazism in naturalist movements.

• Payne, Stanley G., *Fascism: A Comparative Approach toward a Definition*, Madison, Wisc., 1980. A review of various European fascist movements, written with balance and careful thought.

• Rothschild, Joseph, *East Central Europe between the Two World Wars*, Seattle, 1975. An authoritative survey; does not include Austria.

Shapiro, Theda, *Painters and Politics: The European Avant-Garde and Society, 1900–1925*, New York, 1976. An analysis of the political and social attitudes of a revolutionary generation in the arts.

• Sontag, Raymond V., *A Broken World, 1919–1939*, New York, 1971. A fine detailed survey of interwar Europe.

THE SOVIET UNION

Carr, E. H., *The Russian Revolution: From Lenin to Stalin*, New York, 1979. A distillation from his ten-volume *History of Soviet Russia*. A fine starting point for the general reader.

Conquest, Robert, *The Great Terror*, New York, 1968. An analysis of the Stalin purges.

• Daniels, Robert V., *The Conscience of the Revolution*, Cambridge, Mass., 1960. Discusses the opposition to Bolshevism in the 1920s.

• Deutscher, Isaac, *The Prophet Armed*, London, 1954; *The Prophet Unarmed*, London, 1959; *The Prophet Outcast*, London, 1963. A superb, three-volume biography of Leon Trotsky.

• Fitzpatrick, Sheila, ed., *Cultural Revolution in Russia, 1928–1931*, Bloomington, Ind., 1978. A first-rate analysis of the cultural effect of Bolshevik rule.

• Tucker, Robert C., *Stalin as Revolutionary, 1879–1929: A Study in History and Personality*, New York, 1973. An excellent account of Stalin's rise to power, and of the change from revolution to dictatorship in Russia.

GERMANY AND ITALY

• Bracher, Karl Dietrich, *The German Dictatorship: The Origins, Structure, and Effects of National Socialism*, New York, 1970. A penetrating and exhaustive study of the Nazi state by a political scientist.

• Bullock, Alan, *Hitler: A Study in Tyranny*, rev. ed., New York, 1971. The standard biography.

• Eyck, Erich, *History of the Weimar Republic*, 2 vols., Cambridge, Mass., 1962. A sympathetic account by a prominent German liberal.

• Gay, Peter, *Weimar Culture: The Outsider as Insider*, New York, 1970. Examines the failure of commitment to the Weimar Republic by German intellectuals.

• Hale, Oron J., *The Captive Press in the Third Reich*, Princeton, 1964. Examines the manner in which totalitarianism invades journalism.

Lyttelton, Adrian, *The Seizure of Power: Fascism in Italy, 1919–1929*, London, 1973. An excellent introduction.

Mack Smith, Denis, *Mussolini's Roman Empire*, New York, 1976. An able treatment of Italian fascism by the foremost English scholar of Italy.

• Nolte, Ernst, *The Three Faces of Fascism*, New York, 1966. A difficult but rewarding study of Germany, Italy, and France, from a philosophical perspective.

Rogger, Hans, and Eugen Weber, eds., *The European Right: A Historical Profile*, 1965. A country-by-country survey.

• Schoenbaum, David, *Hitler's Social Revolution: Class and Status in Nazi Germany, 1933–39*, Garden City, N.Y., 1966. Hitler's impact upon the various social and economic classes in Germany.

• Stern, Fritz, *The Politics of Cultural Despair: A Study in the Rise of Germanic Ideology*, Berkeley, 1961. Assesses the way in which cultural beliefs influence politics.

• Zeman, Z. A. B., *Nazi Propaganda*, New York, 1973. Examines an important bulwark of the authoritarian state.

THE DEMOCRACIES

Bullock, Alan, *The Life and Times of Ernest Bevin: Trade Union Leader, 1881–1940*, London, 1960. An excellent study of the British trade unionist and the political and social history of Britain between the wars.

• Burns, James M., *Roosevelt: The Lion and the Fox*, New York, 1956. A readable analysis.

Colton, Joel, *Léon Blum: Humanist in Politics,* New York, 1966. A first-rate biography that illuminates the history of the Popular Front.

• Graves, Robert, and Alan Hodge, *The Long Weekend: A Social History of Great Britain, 1918–1939,* London, 1940. A striking portrait of England in the interwar years.

• Greene, Nathanael, *From Versailles to Vichy: The Third Republic, 1919–1940,* Arlington Heights, Ill., 1970. Valuable survey.

Harrod, R. F., *The Life of John Maynard Keynes,* New York, 1951. A solid biography by an admirer of Keynes.

Hughes, H. Stuart, *The Obstructed Path: French Social Thought in the Years of Desperation, 1930–1960,* New York, 1968. Detailed analysis of major French thinkers.

• Leuchtenburg, W. E., *Franklin Roosevelt and the New Deal, 1932–1940,* New York, 1964. A good introduction.

• Mowat, Charles L., *Britain between the Wars, 1918–1940,* Chicago, 1955. A detailed political and social history, especially valuable for its extensive bibliographical footnotes.

• Taylor, A. J. P., *English History, 1914–1945,* New York, 1965. The best survey of the period; witty, provocative, insightful.

Weber, Eugen, *Action Française: Royalism and Reaction in Twentieth Century France,* Stanford, 1962. The best study of this protofascist movement.

SOURCE MATERIALS

Cole, G. D. H., and M. I. Cole, *The Condition of Britain,* London, 1937. A contemporary analysis by English socialists.

• Ehrenburg, Ilya, *Memoirs, 1921–1941,* New York, 1964. The intellectual at work within the Stalinist regime.

• Greene, Nathanael, comp., *European Socialism Since World War I,* Chicago, 1971. A collection of contemporary accounts.

Gruber, H., *International Communism in the Era of Lenin: A Documentary History,* Greenwich, Conn., 1967. A very useful collection of primary materials.

• Hitler, Adolf, *Mein Kampf,* New York, 1962. Hitler's autobiography, written in 1925. Contains his version of history and his vision for the future. Especially important for his insight into the nature of the masses and the use of propaganda.

Noakes, Jeremy, and Geoffrey Pridham, *Documents on Nazism, 1919–1945,* New York, 1975. An excellent sourcebook; comprehensive and annotated.

• Orwell, George, *The Road to Wigan Pier,* New York, 1972. Vivid description of Britain's interwar poverty and class system by an independently minded socialist.

• Silone, Ignazio, *Bread and Wine,* rev. ed., tr. H. Ferguson, New York, 1965. A moving account of the effects of Italian fascism.

• Speer, Albert, *Inside the Third Reich,* New York, 1964. The self-serving but informative memoirs of one of the leaders of Nazi Germany.

Tucker, Robert C., ed., *The Great Purge Trial,* New York, 1965. An annotated edition of the transcript of one of the Soviet "show-trials" that so puzzled Western observers.

Chapter 36

THE SECOND WORLD WAR

The President [Roosevelt] and the Prime Minister [Churchill], after a complete survey of the world situation, are more than ever determined that peace can come to the world only by a total elimination of German and Japanese war power. This involves the simple formula of placing the objective of this war in terms of an unconditional surrender by Germany, Italy, and Japan.

—Franklin D. Roosevelt, Casablanca, January 24, 1943

In September 1939, Europe was drawn again into a general war. The peace of 1919–1920 proved to be no more than an armistice; once more millions of people were locked in a conflict whose devastation surpassed any that had occurred heretofore. As had happened in 1914–1918, the new struggle soon became worldwide. Although the Second World War was not merely a continuation of, or a sequel to, the First, the similarity in causes and characteristics was more than superficial. Both were precipitated by threats to the balance of power, and both were conflicts between peoples, entire nations, rather than between governments. On the other hand, there were notable differences between the two conflicts. The methods of warfare in the Second World War had little in common with those of the earlier conflict. Trench warfare was superseded by bombing and by sudden aerial (Blitzkrieg) attacks, with highly mobile armies, on both civilian populations and military installations. Because so many were now vulnerable to the ravages of warfare, the distinction between those on the battlefield and those at home was more completely obliterated in the second war than it had been in the first. Finally, this war was not greeted with the almost universal, naïve enthusiasm that had marked the outbreak of the other. Men and women still remembered the horrors of the First World War. They entered the Second with determination, but also with a keener appreciation of the frightful devastation that war could bring than their predecessors had possessed.

A comparison of the two world wars

1. THE CAUSES OF THE WAR

The causes of the Second World War related to the failure of the peace terms of 1919–1920. Those terms, while understandable in view of the passions and hatreds engendered by the First World War, created almost as many problems as they solved. By yielding to the demands of the victors for annexation of territory and the creation of satellite states, the peacemakers sowed new seeds of bitterness and conflict. By proclaiming the principle of self-determination while acquiescing in the distribution of national minorities behind alien frontiers, the treaties raised expectations while at the same time frustrating them. Perhaps most important, by imposing harsh terms on Germany, the treaty-makers gave the Germans what seemed to many to be legitimate grievances, by depriving them of their rightful share of international power and saddling them with the entire burden of war "guilt."

Power politics were a second cause of war. Although Woodrow Wilson and other sponsors of the League of Nations had acclaimed the league as a means of eliminating power struggles, it did nothing of the sort. It merely substituted a new and more precarious balance for the old. The signatures on the peace treaties had scarcely dried when the victors began the construction of new alliances to maintain their supremacy. A neutralized zone consisting of the Baltic states, Poland, and Rumania was created as a buffer against Soviet Russia. A "Little Entente" composed of Czechoslovakia, Yugoslavia, and Rumania was established to prevent a revival of Austrian power. These combinations, together with a Franco-Belgian alliance and a Franco-Polish alliance, would also serve to isolate Germany. Even the league itself was fundamentally an alliance of the victors against the vanquished. That there would be fears and anxieties over a disturbance of the new power arrangement was natural. The first sign of such a disturbance appeared in 1922 when Germany and Russia negotiated the Treaty of Rapallo. Though disguised as a mere trade agreement, it opened the way for political and, according to some accounts, even military collaboration between the two states.

Diplomats made various attempts to preserve or restore international amity during the 1920s and 1930s. Some saw in disarmament the most promising means of achieving their purpose. Accordingly, a succession of conferences was called in the hope of at least limiting a race to rearm. In 1925 representatives of the chief European powers met at Locarno and acted on the suggestion of the German and French foreign ministers, Gustav Stresemann and Aristide Briand, that Germany and France pledge themselves to respect the Rhine frontiers as established in the Versailles treaty. They agreed also that they would never go to war against each other except in "legitimate defense." More widely celebrated than the Locarno Agreements was the Pact of Paris, or Kellogg-Briand Pact of 1928. Its purpose was to outlaw war as an international crime. Eventually, nearly all the nations of the world

Members of the Council of the League of Nations. In the front row, from the right, are Chamberlain of Britain, Vandervelde of Belgium, Stresemann of Germany, and Briand of France.

signed this agreement renouncing war as "an instrument of national policy" and providing that the settlement of international disputes "of whatever nature or of whatever origin" should never be sought "except by peaceful means." Neither the Locarno Agreements nor the Pact of Paris was much more than a pious gesture. The signatory nations adopted them with so many reservations and exceptions in favor of "vital interests" that they could never be effective instruments for preserving peace. Had the League of Nations been better organized, it might have relieved some of the tensions and prevented clashes between nations still unwilling to relinquish their absolute sovereignty. Yet it was not a league of all nations, since both Germany and Russia were excluded for much of the interwar period.

Economic conditions were a third important cause of the outbreak of war. The huge reparations imposed upon the Germans, and the French occupation of much of Germany's industrial heartland, helped, as we have seen, to retard Germany's economic recovery and bring on the debilitating inflation of the 1920s. The depression of the 1930s contributed to the coming of the war in several ways. It intensified economic nationalism. Baffled by problems of unemployment and business stagnation, governments resorted to high tariffs in an attempt to preserve the home market for their own producers. The depression was also responsible for a marked increase in armaments production, which was seen as a means of reducing unemployment. Despite the misgivings of some within the governments of Britain and France, Germany was allowed to rearm. Armaments expansion, on a large scale, was first undertaken by Germany about 1935, with the result that unemployment was substantially reduced and business boomed. Other nations followed the German example, not simply as a way of boosting their economies, but in response to Nazi military power. The depression helped as well to produce a new wave of militant expansionism directed toward the conquest of neighboring territories

Economic conditions

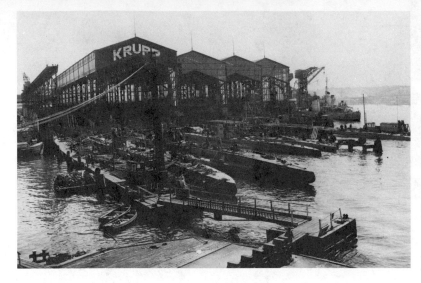

The Krupp Shipworks in Germany. Seen here are German submarines in the final stages of assembly.

as a means of solving economic problems. Japan took the lead in 1931 with the invasion of Manchuria. The decline of Japanese exports of raw silk and cotton cloth meant that the nation as a consequence was unable to pay for needed imports of coal, iron, and other minerals. Japanese militarists were thus furnished with a convenient pretext for seizing Manchuria, where supplies of these commodities could then be purchased for Japanese currency. Mussolini, in part to distract the Italians from the domestic problems brought on by economic depression, invaded and annexed Ethiopia in 1936. Finally, the depression was primarily responsible for the triumph of Nazism, whose expansionist policies contributed directly to the outbreak of war.

Nationalism

Nationalism was a further cause of the general discontent that helped increase the chances for world war. In eastern Europe, national and ethnic minorities remained alienated from the sovereign states into which the treaty-makers had placed them. This was particularly the case of the Sudetenland Germans, who had been included in the newly created state of Czechoslovakia. That country could in fact boast no national majority, including as it did Czechs, Slovaks, Poles, Ruthenians, and Hungarians, as well as Germans. Although it possessed an enlightened policy of minority self-government, the patchwork state of Czechoslovakia remained unstable. And its instability was to prove a key factor as the tensions mounted in the late 1930s.

Appeasement

A final cause of war was the policy of "appeasement" which was pursued by the Western democracies in the face of German, Italian, and Japanese aggression. The appeasers' strategy was grounded in three commonly held assumptions. The first was that the outbreak of another war was unthinkable. With the memory of the slaughter of 1914–1918 fresh in their minds, many in the West embraced pacifism, or at any rate adopted an attitude that kept them from realistically addressing the implications of Nazi and fascist policies and programs. Second, many in Britain and the United States argued that Germany had been mistreated in the Versailles treaty, that the Germans had legitimate grievances which should be acknowledged and resolved. Finally, the appeasers were, for the most part, staunch anti-Communists. They believed that by assisting Germany to regain its former military and economic power, they were constructing a bulwark to halt the westward advance of Soviet communism. When Japan invaded Manchuria, the West refused to impose sanctions against the Japanese through the League of Nations, arguing that Japan, too, could serve as a counterweight to Russia.

Hitler took advantage of this generally tolerant attitude to advance the expansionist ambitions of Germany. As the country rearmed, Hitler played upon his people's sense of shame and betrayal, proclaiming their right to regain their former power within the world. In 1933, he removed Germany from the League of Nations—and thus from any obligation to adhere to its declarations. In 1935 Hitler tore up the disarmament provisions of the Treaty of Versailles, announcing the revival of conscription and the return to universal military training. In 1936 he repudiated the Locarno Agreements and invaded the Rhineland. Britain and France did nothing to stop him, as they had done nothing to prevent Mussolini's invasion and conquest of Ethiopia the previous year. Hitler's move tipped the balance of power in Germany's favor. While the Rhineland remained demilitarized and German industry in the Ruhr valley unprotected, France had held the upper hand. Now it no longer did so.

Hitler's aggressive moves

In 1936 civil war broke out in Spain; a series of weak republican governments had proved unable to prevent the country's political disintegration. Although they had signed a pact of nonintervention with the other Western powers, Hitler and Mussolini both sent troops and equipment to assist the forces of the rebel fascist commander, Fran-

The Spanish Civil War

Guernica by Pablo Picasso. This painting, a protest against the bombing of an undefended city during the Spanish Civil War, has come to be recognized as one of the century's most profound antiwar statements.

The Munich Conference, 1938. Left: Prime Minister Chamberlain of Britain and Hitler during the Munich conference. Right: Chamberlain addressing a crowd on his return from the Munich conference.

cisco Franco. Russia countered with aid to the Communist troops serving under the banner of the Spanish republic. Again, Britain and France failed to act decisively. The Spanish Civil War lasted three years, with the forces of the fascists finally victorious over those of the republicans. The conflict engaged the commitment of many young European and American leftists and intellectuals, who saw it as a test of the West's determination to resist totalitarianism. The fighting was brutal; aerial bombardment of civilians and troops was employed for the first time on a large scale. Because of this, the Spanish war has often been seen as a "dress rehearsal" for the much larger struggle that was shortly to follow. The war also served to confirm Hitler's belief that if Britain, France, and Russia did decide to attempt to contain fascism, they would have a difficult time concerting their policies— another reason, indeed, why Britain and France did remain content to do nothing.

Munich and after

In March of 1938, Hitler annexed Austria, declaring it his intention to bring all Germans into his Reich. Once more, there was no official reaction from the West. Hitler's next target was the Sudetenland in Czechoslovakia. With Austria now a part of Germany, Czechoslovakia was almost entirely surrounded by its hostile expansionist neighbor. Hitler declared that the Sudetenland was a natural part of the Reich and that he intended to occupy it. The British prime minister, Neville Chamberlain, determined to negotiate, but on Hitler's terms. On September 28, Hitler agreed to meet with Chamberlain, Premier Édouard Daladier of France, and Mussolini in a four-power conference in Munich. The result was another capitulation by France and Britain. Ignoring the vital interests of a nation whose territory the Versailles treaty had guaranteed, the four negotiators bargained away a major slice of Czechoslovakia, while that country's representatives were left to await their fate outside the conference room. Chamberlain returned to England proclaiming "peace in our time." Hitler soon proved that fatuous boast untrue. In March 1939 he invaded what was left of Czechoslovakia and established a puppet regime in its capital, Prague. This action convinced British public opinion of the foolhardiness of appeasement. Chamberlain, compelled to shift his policies dramatically, guaranteed the sovereignty of the two states now directly in Hitler's path: Poland and Rumania. France followed suit.

See color map of Europe on the Eve of the Second World War facing page 551

Meanwhile, the appeasement policies of Britain and France had fueled Stalin's fears that the timid Western democracies might strike a bargain with Germany at Soviet expense by diverting Nazi expansion eastward. This, combined with the suspicion that they might make unreliable allies, convinced Stalin that he must look elsewhere for security. Tempted by the traditional Russian desire for territory in Poland, and promised a share of both Poland and the Baltic states by Hitler, Stalin signed a pact with the Nazis in August 1939. In going to Munich, Britain and France had put their interests first; Russia would now look after its own.

Nazi-Soviet pact

2. THE OUTBREAK OF HOSTILITIES

Following the extinction of Czechoslovakia, and despite Chamberlain's guarantee, Hitler demanded the abolition of the Polish Corridor, a narrow strip of territory connecting Poland with the Baltic Sea. The corridor contained a large German population, which Hitler declared must be reunited with the Fatherland. Judging Britain and France by past performance he believed their pledges to Poland worthless. With the Soviets now in his camp, he expected that Poland would quickly

Beginning of the war

The Beginning of the Second World War. A long line of German tanks crossing into Poland.

The blitzkrieg

capitulate, and that the Western allies would back down once more as they had done at Munich. When Poland stood firm, Hitler attacked. On September 1, 1939, German tanks crossed the Polish border. Britain and France sent a joint warning to Germany to cease its aggression. There was no reply; on September 3, Britain and France declared war against Germany.

The conflict with Poland proved to be a brief encounter. In less than three weeks the Polish armies had been routed, Warsaw had been captured, and the chiefs of the Polish government had fled to Rumania. For some months after that the war resolved itself into a kind of siege, a "phony war" or "sitzkrieg," as it was sometimes called. Such fighting as did occur was largely confined to submarine warfare, aerial raids on naval bases, and occasional battles between naval vessels. In the spring of 1940 the sitzkrieg was suddenly transformed into a blitzkrieg, or "lightning war." The Germans struck blows at Norway, Denmark, Belgium, the Netherlands, and France, conquering them in short order, and driving the British and French forces back against the English Channel at Dunkirk in Belgium. Despite heavy German air attacks, the British were able to evacuate over 300,000 troops, many of them in commercial and pleasure boats which had been pressed into emergency service. Northern France, including Paris, was occupied by the Germans. In the south, a puppet government loyal to the Germans was established at Vichy under the leadership of the aged First World War hero, Marshal Henri-Philippe Pétain.

Before launching an invasion across the Channel, the Nazis decided to attempt the reduction of Britain's military strength and civilian will

Left: *London during the Blitz.* This picture conveys a vivid impression of the agony which the British capital suffered during the Battle of Britain, which lasted from August 1940 to June 1941. Behind the tumbling ruins brought down by firebombs is St. Paul's Cathedral. Right: *French Refugees Driven from Their Homes during the Early Years of the Nazi Occupation.*

by air raids. From August 1940 to June 1941, in the so-called Battle of Britain, thousands of planes smashed at British ports, industrial centers, and air defenses throughout the country. Despite the fact that whole sections of cities were laid in ruins and more than 40,000 civilians killed, the British held firm. Winston Churchill had by this time succeeded Neville Chamberlain as prime minister of Britain. A maverick Conservative, who had served in Britain's First World War government as a Liberal, Churchill was not trusted by his party's leadership, particularly since he had been one of the few who had spoken out in favor of British rearmament during the years of appeasement. Now that his warnings had proved true, he was given direction of the war as head of a national government composed of ministers from the Conservative, Liberal, and Labour parties. Churchill, an exceedingly compelling orator, used the radio to persuade his countrymen and women—and the rest of the free world—that Britain must not, and would not, surrender to the Nazis. His friendship with President Roosevelt, and the latter's conviction that the United States must come to Britain's aid, resulted in the shipment of military equipment and ships to the British under the Lend-Lease Act passed by the U.S. Congress in 1941.

The Battle of Britain

Meanwhile, Germany moved eastward into the Balkans, subduing the Rumanians, Hungarians, Bulgarians, and Yugoslavs. The Italians, less successful in their campaigns in Greece and North Africa, required German assistance to accomplish their missions. Scornful of Mussolini's military inadequacies, Churchill called him Hitler's "jackal." Frustrated in his attempt to subjugate Britain, Hitler broke with his erstwhile ally Russia, and turned eastward, on June 22, 1941, with a massive invasion. Before the end of the year his armies had smashed their way to the gates of Moscow but never actually succeeded in capturing it. The defense of Moscow by the Russian armies marked one of the war's important early turning points.

The German invasion of Russia

The war was converted into a global conflict when Japan struck at Pearl Harbor on December 7 of the same year. The Japanese had been involved in a costly war with China since 1937. To wage it successfully they needed the oil, rubber, and extensive food resources of the Netherlands Indies, the Malay Peninsula, and Southeast Asia. They had allied with Germany in 1940. (Germany, Italy, and Japan were together known as the Axis powers, a name derived from the Rome-Berlin diplomatic axis formed in the 1930s.) Now, before attacking south, they considered it necessary to secure their position to the rear by crushing American naval and air power on the base of Pearl Harbor. The next day the United States Congress recognized a state of war with Japan, and on December 11 Germany and its allies declared war upon the United States.

Pearl Harbor

In the course of the next two and a half years, events turned slowly but inexorably against the forces of Germany, Italy, and Japan. Churchill and Roosevelt, meeting shortly after the United States's entry

Pearl Harbor, December 7, 1941. This photo shows American battleships sunk at their moorings, following the Japanese raid on what President Franklin D. Roosevelt declared was "the day that will live in infamy."

A German V-2 Rocket. Used in the later years of the war, it was the forerunner of the early space launch vehicles.

The battle of Stalingrad

into the war, agreed that victory in the West would be their first priority. As an initial step toward that goal, the British succeeded in turning the North African advance of Germany's brilliant tank commander, General Erwin Rommel, who had driven the British back across the Sahara to the Egyptian border. That victory was the prelude to a joint Anglo-American invasion of North Africa in November 1942. The success of this first major combined Allied offensive led in turn to further Mediterranean campaigns in the next year, first in Sicily and then in Italy. Mussolini's government was overthrown, and his successors sued for peace. The Germans, however, sent troops into Italy and resurrected Mussolini as the ruler of a puppet state in the north, where he remained a virtual prisoner of the Nazis until his death at the hands of his countrymen at the time of the general defeat of the Axis powers in Europe. Despite Allied attempts to break the German grip on the peninsula, the Nazi forces continued to hold central and northern Italy until the spring of 1945.

In eastern Europe, meanwhile, the Germans had continued to press the war against the Russians, turning in 1942 to the south and the rich agricultural and industrial areas of the Ukraine, the Donets Basin, and the Caucasus oilfields. The German advance was stopped at Stalingrad, in a military struggle of great strategic and symbolic importance for both sides. The battle saw 300,000 Germans for a time in control of the city, then enclosed by the counterattacking Russians in a pincers movement, and eventually, by the time of their surrender, reduced to fewer than half their original number. The loss of the battle of Stalingrad compelled the Germans to undertake a general retreat. By the spring of 1943, they were no further east than they had been the previous year.

Stalin continued to pressure his allies to open a second front in the west to relieve the concerted Nazi drive against Russia. The North African and Italian campaigns were a response to that plea. But not until June 1944 did Allied troops invade France. On June 6 (D–Day) a massive invasion force landed on the Normandy coast. Air superiority, plus a tremendous buildup of matériel and manpower, produced a series of successful advances and the liberation of Paris on August 25. Despite a final German assault in December 1944, the Allied armies penetrated deep into Germany itself by the early spring of 1945.

The D-Day invasion

At the same time, Soviet troops were approaching from the east. On April 21, 1945, they hammered their way into the suburbs of Berlin. During the next ten days a savage battle raged amid the ruins and heaps of rubble. On May 2 the heart of the city was captured, and the Soviet red banner flew from the Brandenburg Gate. A few hours earlier Adolf Hitler killed himself in the bomb-proof shelter of the Chancellery. On May 8 representatives of the German High Command signed a document of unconditional surrender.

End of the war in Europe

The war in the Pacific came to an end four months later. Important victories won by the United States Navy against the Japanese at the battles of the Coral Sea and Midway in the spring of 1942 forestalled Japanese attempts to capture Australia and the Hawaiian Islands so as to deprive the United States of advance bases for a counteroffensive against Japan. Final Allied victory followed further naval battles, island assaults, and land battles in Southeast Asia. In June 1945, the island of Okinawa was taken, after eighty-two days of desperate fighting. The American forces now had a foothold less than 500 miles from the Japanese homeland. The government in Tokyo was anticipating

The Pacific war

Left: *D-Day.* Cargo ships are seen pouring supplies ashore during the invasion of France. Balloon barrages float overhead to protect the ships from low-flying enemy planes. Right: *Signing the German Surrender, May 7, 1945*

The atomic bomb

Total war

an invasion and calling upon its citizens for supreme endeavors to meet the crisis.

On July 26 the heads of the United States, British, and Chinese governments issued a joint proclamation calling upon Japan to surrender or be destroyed. In the absence of a reply the United States resolved to make use of a new and revolutionary weapon to end the war quickly. This was the atomic bomb, which could destroy entire cities and their inhabitants, a weapon developed in secrecy in the United States by scientists from Europe and America, some of whom were exiles from Nazi or fascist oppression.

Many high military and naval officers contended that use of the bomb was not necessary, on the assumption that Japan was already beaten. Harry Truman, who had succeeded Roosevelt following the latter's death in April 1945, decided otherwise. On August 6, a single atomic bomb was dropped on Hiroshima, completely obliterating about 60 percent of the city. Three days later a second bomb was dropped, this time on Nagasaki. President Truman warned that the United States would continue to use the atom bomb as long as might be necessary to bring Japan to its knees. On August 14, Tokyo transmitted to Washington an unconditional acceptance of Allied demands.

To an even greater extent than was the case in the First World War, total populations were mobilized as part of the war effort. Governments imposed the rationing of food and clothing and the regulation of manpower. Production quotas demanded that factories produce around the clock. In Russia, all men between the ages of sixteen and fifty-five and all women between the ages of sixteen and forty-five were pressed into service, either in the armed forces or on the home

View of Hiroshima after the First Atom Bomb Was Dropped, August 6, 1945. This photo, taken one month later, shows the utter devastation of the city. Only a few steel and concrete buildings remained intact.

front. The Germans destroyed much of Russia's industrial plant and existing war matériel in the early months of the war—over 90 percent of Russia's tanks, for example. To produce what was necessary, factories were rebuilt in the security of the Ural mountain region, and whole populations moved there to work in them.

In countries conquered and occupied by the Germans and Italians, the Axis powers installed administrations willing to follow their commands without question. (Vidkun Quisling, the Norwegian Nazi leader, made his name synonymous with the word "traitor.") Life for civilians was harsh at best. Rations in occupied France, for example, were less than half the amount considered to be a healthy minimum. There and elsewhere, Resistance movements emerged, composed of men and women of various political persuasions united in their determination to assist the Allies in driving the Axis powers from their native lands. By transmitting intelligence reports, aiding prisoners to escape, distributing newspapers to counter official propaganda, and undertaking acts of direct sabotage to military and industrial targets, these groups helped the Allied cause immeasurably. The success of the Normandy invasion was in part the result of information concerning German military emplacements sent to Britain by the French Resistance.

The Resistance

The war brought devastation in the form of street fighting and air bombardment to most of the major urban centers of Europe. The Allies proved to be fully as ruthless and even more efficient than the Axis powers in this regard. After some debate, British and American strategists abandoned pinpoint bombing in favor of the nighttime aerial bombardment of entire cities. The result was the deliberate firebombing of civilian populations, climaxing in Europe in early 1945 with the brutal obliteration of Dresden, a German city without significant industry and filled with refugees. These attacks were equaled by the German bombing of French, Belgian, Dutch, Russian, and British cities and civilian populations. Such raids were, of course, dwarfed by the United States's atomic bomb attacks on the Japanese cities of Hiroshima and Nagasaki.

The war's devastation of cities

Ghastly as was the destruction meted out by the armed forces to each other and to civilians, none of it matched in premeditated, obscene horror the systematic persecution by the Nazis of whole Jewish populations, not only in Germany itself, but in occupied countries as well. When Allied armies opened the concentration camps in Germany and elsewhere in what had been German-occupied Europe, they found the starved, diseased, and brutalized survivors of the ghastly experience of Nazi persecutions that cost six million prisoners their lives. Most of the men, women, and children who had been imprisoned, tortured, and killed were Jews, although Poles, Russians, Gypsies, homosexuals, and other "traitors" to the Reich had been incarcerated, used for forced labor, and executed also.

The concentration camps

German Civilians Compelled to View the Bodies of Concentration Camp Victims at the Landesburg Camp in 1945 as an American army Officer Lectures Them on the Horrors of the Nazis' "Final Solution"

3. THE PEACE SETTLEMENT

Postwar plans

During the war the Allied leaders had come together on several occasions to discuss war aims and postwar goals. The public rhetoric of government propaganda spoke of the need for a world without conflict and of the right of all people to political self-determination, objectives expressed in the "Atlantic Charter" issued by Roosevelt and Churchill in August 1941, and in a declaration signed by twenty-six nations, including Britain, the United States, the Soviet Union, and China, the following year. Yet those worthy goals, like most of Wilson's Fourteen Points, fell eventual victim to the realities of international politics.

Allied conflicts

Stalin, Churchill, and Roosevelt convened in two conferences that were of major importance in determining the shape and political complexion of postwar Europe. In both cases, tensions between the three major participants were to some degree glossed over in their desire to present a united front to the world. Yet those tensions were real. The focus of disagreement was central Europe, and particularly the future of Germany and Poland. Stalin insisted that Russia retain the Polish territory annexed in 1939 at the time of the Nazi-Soviet pact, an expression of his understandable desire to build a bulwark against any future German aggression, and a reflection of his unwillingness to see postwar Western influence extended too far in Russia's direction. His memories of Anglo-American participation in the attempt by White Russians to overthrow the newly created communist regime in 1919 were matched by American perceptions of the Soviet Union as an expansionist and politically alien and dangerous regime. All three leaders were also confronted by conflicting plots and aspirations on the part of governments-in-exile from Nazi-occupied countries, and of extra-governmental Resistance groups—often led by Communists—whose struggles to retain or to assume leadership in their homelands were exceeded only by their determination to oust the Germans.

When the three leaders met in Teheran in December 1943, they managed to put forward a declaration of unified purpose only by postponing the really knotty problems that confronted them. The invasion of France was agreed to for the following year; Stalin undertook to enter the war against Japan following the defeat of Germany. But on the question of Poland, only the most tentative agreement was reached regarding boundary lines, and the nature of the postwar Polish government was left for further negotiation.

The Teheran conference

By the time Stalin, Churchill, and Roosevelt met again, in February 1945 at Yalta, the military situation favored Russia's position. Soviet troops had occupied Poland the previous spring; they now held part of Czechoslovakia as well, and were poised to invade Germany. Once more the matter of Poland's future arose, as well as that of the composition of postwar regimes. A general declaration outlined plans for Russian expansion westward into Poland, and the compensation of Poland with territory taken from the Germans. As to Poland's government, though communiqués spoke of the need for free elections there and elsewhere among the occupied countries, the fact remained that the Soviets had already established a communist government in Warsaw, and were unlikely to tolerate its replacement by an anti-communist faction still in London, whatever the results of an election. Yalta produced accord on several important issues: the establish-

The Yalta conference

The Yalta Conference. Churchill, Molotov, Secretary of State Stettinius, at the left, and Stalin, in the center, with glasses raised in a toast. Roosevelt is also to Stalin's left.

The Potsdam conference

ment of a United Nations organization to keep the peace; the terms for Russian entry into the Japanese war; the positioning of zones of Allied occupation in Germany and Austria; and agreement in principle to a policy of German reparation payments—though in goods and equipment rather than in gold, as had been the case after the First World War.

Little more than two months after Germany's surrender, the Allies met again, this time at Potsdam, a suburb of Berlin and the former residence of Prussian kings. Roosevelt had died the previous spring; his place at the conference was taken by his successor, President Harry Truman. Churchill represented Britain until replaced, as the result of elections at home, by the new prime minister and Labour party leader, Clement Attlee. Stalin remained to negotiate for the Soviets. As at past conferences, less was settled than was allowed to remain unresolved. Peace treaties were to be prepared with the "recognized democratic governments" of previously occupied lands. Yet the question as to whether those governments set up by the Soviets in Poland and—by this time—elsewhere in eastern Europe were truly democratic was not settled. Polish boundaries were redrawn to conform to the general agreement reached at Yalta. An inter-Allied war tribunal was established to try major Nazi leaders for "war crimes." In November 1945, the trials began in Nuremberg, Germany. The following September, eighteen of the twenty-two defendants were found guilty and received sentences ranging from ten-years' imprisonment to death.

The Potsdam conference was shadowed by the East-West conflict that had darkened all the wartime meetings and was to do the same to

The Potsdam Conference. Churchill, a cigar in his mouth, is seated in the back to the left; Stalin is at the right; Truman is seated with his back to the camera.

international politics in the immediate postwar years. The division of Germany into four occupied zones—American, British, French, and Soviet—and the agreement to structure reparations payments on the basis of those zones rather than on a united Germany, forecast the unwillingness of either the Soviet Union or the Western powers to trust each other, or to tolerate the extension of the other's influence in that country which, though devastated, still remained vital to the security and peace of Europe as a whole.

The treaty with Japan, though it too produced disagreement between Russia and the West, did not reflect conflicts as immediate as those that characterized the European negotiations. The treaty deprived the Japanese of all the territory they had acquired since 1854—their entire overseas empire. They surrendered the southern half of Sakhalin Island and the Kuril Islands to Soviet Russia, and the Bonins and Ryukyus to control by the United States. They also renounced all rights to Formosa, which was left in an undefined status. They yielded as well to the United States the right to continue maintaining military installations in Japan until the latter was able to defend itself. The treaty went into effect in April 1952 despite opposition from the Russians, who feared a United States military presence in the Far East.

As in the case of the Versailles treaty one of the most significant elements in the settlements was their provision for an international organization. The old League of Nations had failed to avert the outbreak of war in 1939, and in April 1946 it was formally dissolved. Yet Allied statesmen continued to recognize the need for some international organization. In February 1945, they agreed at Yalta that a conference to respond to that need should be convoked the following April. Despite the sudden death of Roosevelt two weeks earlier, the conference met as scheduled. A charter was adopted on June 26, providing for a world organization to be known as the United Nations and to be founded upon the principle of "the sovereign equality of all peace-loving states." Its important agencies were to be (1) a General Assembly composed of representatives of all the member states; (2) a Security Council composed of reresentatives of the United States, Great Britain, the Soviet Union, the Republic of China, and France, with permanent seats, and of six other states chosen by the General Assembly to fill the nonpermanent seats; (3) a Secretariat consisting of a secretary-general and a staff of subordinates; (4) an Economic and Social Council composed of eighteen members chosen by the General Assembly; (5) a Trusteeship Council, and (6) an International Court of Justice.

Although the United Nations has failed to live up to the hopes of its founders, it continues to function as the world's longest lived international assembly of nations. By far the most important functions of the new organization were assigned by the charter to the Security Council. This agency has the "primary responsibility for the maintenance of international peace and security." It has authority to investigate any dispute between nations, to recommend methods for settlement, and, if necessary to preserve the peace, to employ diplomatic or economic measures against an aggressor. If, in its judgment, these have proved, or are likely to prove, inadequate, it may "take such action by air, naval, or land forces" as may be required to maintain or restore international order. The member states are required by the charter to make available to the Security Council, on its call, armed forces for the maintenance of peace.

The veto power of the Big Five

The Security Council was so organized as to give almost a monopoly of authority to its permanent members, since no action of any kind could be taken without the unanimous consent of Great Britain, France, the United States, the Republic of China, the Soviet Union, and two other members besides. This absolute veto given to each of the principal states, instead of bolstering the peace of the world, crippled the council and rendered it helpless in the face of emergencies.

Other agencies of the U.N.

The remaining agencies of the U.N. were given a wide variety of functions. The Secretariat, composed of a secretary-general and a numerous staff, is chiefly an administrative authority. Its duties, though, are by no means routine, for the secretary-general may bring to the attention of the Security Council any matter which, in his opinion, threatens international peace. The functions of the Economic and Social Council are the most varied of all. Composed of eighteen members elected by the General Assembly, it has authority to initiate studies and make recommendations with respect to international social, economic, health, educational, cultural, and related matters, and may perform services within such fields at the request of U.N. members.

Record of the U.N.

During its first three decades the work of various U.N. agencies helped the organization achieve a modestly impressive record of accomplishment. But against its successes must be recorded major failures as well. The U.N. was unable to establish control of nuclear weapons. And it was powerless in the face of any determined effort by a major power to have its own way, as in the case of the Soviet suppression of a revolt in Hungary in 1956; or the massive intervention by the United States in Vietnam in the 1960s and early 1970s. If the United Nations acted upon occasion to defuse potentially explosive world situations, it failed to achieve the lofty peacemaking and peacekeeping goals set for it by its founders.

SELECTED READINGS

• *Items so designated are available in paperback editions.*

• Carr, E. H., *The Twenty-Years' Crisis, 1919–1939,* London, 1942. Stimulating, though somewhat dogmatic.
• Carr, Raymond, *The Spanish Tragedy: The Civil War in Perspective,* London, 1977. A thoughtful introduction to the Spanish Civil War and the evolution of Franco's Spain.

Collins, Larry, and Dominique, LaPierre, *Is Paris Burning?*, New York, 1965. A highly readable account of the liberation of Paris.

• Dawidowicz, Lucy S., *The War Against the Jews, 1933–1945*, New York, 1975. A full account of the Holocaust.

• Divine, Robert A., *Roosevelt and World War II*, Baltimore, 1969. A diplomatic history.

• Feis, Herbert, *Churchill-Roosevelt-Stalin: The War They Waged and the Peace They Sought*, Princeton, 1957. A standard survey.

Géraud, André, *The Gravediggers of France*, Garden City, N.Y., 1944. A critical and impassioned account of the fall of France.

Gilbert, Martin, and R. Gott, *The Appeasers*, Boston, 1963. Excellent study of British pro-German sentiment in the 1930s.

Holborn, Hajo, *The Political Collapse of Europe*, New York, 1951. Examines Europe's position in light of the rise of Russia and the United States as superpowers.

• Jackson, Gabriel, *The Spanish Republic and the Civil War, 1931–1939*, Princeton, 1965. A solid, useful account.

Michel, Henri, *The Shadow War: The European Resistance,1939–1945*, New York, 1972. Thoroughly researched and compelling reading.

• Milward, Alan S., *War, Economy, and Society, 1939–1945*, Berkeley, 1977. Analyzes the impact of the war on the world economy and the ways in which economic resources of the belligerents determined strategies.

• Paxton, Robert O., *Vichy France: Old Guard and New Order, 1940–1944*, New York, 1972. A bitter account.

• Taylor, A. J. P., *The Origins of the Second World War*, New York, 1962. A controversial but provocative attempt to prove that Hitler did not want a world war.

Thomas, Hugh, *The Spanish Civil War*, New York, 1961. A thorough and balanced account.

Wheeler, Bennett, J. W., *Munich: Prologue to Tragedy*, London, 1966. A sensitive treatment of prewar diplomatic negotiations, outdated to some extent, but still evocative.

• Wright, Gordon, *The Ordeal of Total War, 1939–1945*, New York, 1968. Particularly good on the domestic response to war and the mobilization of the resources of the modern state.

SOURCE MATERIALS

• Bloch, Marc, *Strange Defeat: A Statement of Evidence Written in 1940*, London, 1949. An analysis of the fall of France, written by one of France's greatest historians, who later died fighting for the Resistance.

• Churchill, Winston S., *The Second World War*, 6 vols., London, 1948–1954. The war as Churchill saw it and as he wanted history to see it. Especially useful is the first volume on the 1930s, *The Gathering Storm*.

• De Gaulle, Charles, *The Complete War Memoirs*, New York, 1964. De Gaulle's apologia.

• Hershey, John, *Hiroshima*, New York, 1946. A moving account of the aftermath of the U.S. atomic bombing written very soon after the event.

Noakes, Jeremy, and Geoffrey Pridham, *Documents on Nazism, 1919–1945*, New York, 1975. A helpful collection.

Part Seven

THE EMERGENCE OF
WORLD CIVILIZATION

Western civilization, as we have described and analyzed it, no longer exists today. Instead, we speak in terms of a world civilization, one that owes much of its history and many of its most perplexing problems to the West, but one which is no longer shaped by those few nations that for so many centuries dominated the globe.

The great powers of the nineteenth century—Britain, France, and Germany—are powers now only insofar as they have agreed to pool their interests in an all-European Common Market. The mid–twentieth century superpowers, the United States and the Soviet Union, after two decades of confrontation, have begun to understand the limitations of their power and to adjust their expectations accordingly. Power, and with it the attention of the world, is shifting from the West to the emerging nations of Africa, the Middle East, Asia, and Latin America. Their vast natural resources are affording many of them the chance to play the old Western game of power politics, and in a world arena wider than ever before. The equally vast dimensions of their internal problems—economic, racial, nutritional, and political—suggest that their solution will have to be worldwide as well. We are all, as the American designer Buckminster Fuller has said, partners for better or worse on "spaceship earth."

The Emergence of World Civilization

POLITICS	SCIENCE & INDUSTRY

1945

Truman Doctrine, 1947
Communist regimes established in eastern Europe,
    1947–1948
Marshall Plan, 1948
Division of Germany, 1949
NATO, 1949

                                                Hydrogen bomb, 1952

Death of Stalin, 1953   Discovery of polio vaccine, 1953
                                                Discovery of DNA, 1953
Hungarian revolt, 1956

                                                Sputnik launched, 1957

1960

Berlin wall, 1961

Cuban missile crisis, 1962
Assassination of John F. Kennedy, 1963
War in Vietnam, 1964–1975 (U.S. phase)
Assassination of Malcolm X, 1965

Assassination of Martin Luther King, Jr., 1968

1970   Manned U.S. spacecraft lands on moon, 1969
                                                Advent of automation, 1970s

First SALT agreements signed, 1972

U.S. rejection of Salt II agreement, 1981

Solidarity movement in Poland, 1982–
1985   *Perestroika* and *Glasnost* in the Soviet Union, 1986–

Soviet-American short-and medium-range nuclear
    missile agreement, 1987

The collapse of communist regimes in eastern
    Europe, 1989–1990

Reunification of Germany, 1990

ECONOMICS & SOCIETY	ARTS & LETTERS

Richard Wright, *Native Son,* 1940
Abstract expressionism in art, mid-1940s
Albert Camus, *The Plague,* 1947

1945

Simone de Beauvoir, *The Second Sex,* 1949–1950

Samuel Beckett, *Waiting for Godot,* 1952

European Common Market established, 1958

Boris Pasternak, *Doctor Zhivago,* 1957

Lorraine Hansberry, *A Raisin in the Sun,* 1959
"Pop" art, 1960s

1960

Black civil rights movement, United States, 1960–1968
Frantz Fanon, *Wretched of the Earth,* 1961
Youth "revolution," 1960s
Women's liberation movement, 1960s–1970s

François Truffaut, *Jules et Jim,* 1961

James Baldwin, *The Fire Next Time,* 1963

Arthur Penn, *Bonnie and Clyde,* 1967

1970

Worldwide inflation and unemployment, late 1970s and early 1980s

Arthur Penn, *Bonnie and Clyde,* 1972
Alexsandr Solzhenitsyn, *The Gulag Archipelago,* 1973

1985

The Emergence of World Civilization (continued)

THE AMERICAS	INDIA AND THE MIDDLE EAST

1850

Great Indian Mutiny, 1857–1858

Mahatma Gandhi, 1869–1948

Organization of Indian National Congress, 1885
Jawaharlal Nehru, 1889–1964

1900

Organization of Australian Commonwealth, 1901

Madero Revolution in Mexico, 1911

New Constitution in Mexico, 1917

Amritsar Massacre (India), 1919
Intensification of Indian nationalism, 1919–1947
Republic of Turkey proclaimed, 1923
Mustafa Kemal Atatürk, president of Turkey,
   1922–1938

Perón regime in Argentina, 1946–1955

Independence of India and Pakistan, 1947
State of Israel proclaimed, 1948
Egypt becomes a republic, 1952–1953
Suez crisis, 1956

1950

Establishment of Castro regime in Cuba, 1959
Second Turkish Republic, 1961

Military dictatorship in Brazil, 1964–1985

Separatist movement in Quebec, 1967–

Indira Gandhi prime minister of India, 1966–
   1977; 1980–1984
Six-Day War, 1967

Military dictatorship in Chile, 1973–1990
ASEAN, 1967
India-Pakistan war, 1971
Republic of Bangladesh, 1972

Panama Canal treaties, 1977
"Yom Kippur War," 1973
Revolutions in Nicaragua and El Salvador, 1979
Egyptian-Israeli peace treaty, 1979
Falkland Islands War, 1982
Revolution in Iran, deposing the Shah, 1979
Soviet military intervention in Afghanistan,
   1979–1989
Iraq-Iran war, 1980–1988
War in Lebanon, 1982–1985

1985

Elective revolutions, 1989–90

Iraqi invasion of Kuwait, 1990

U.S. invasion of Panama, 1989

Persian Gulf war, 1991–

EAST ASIA	AFRICA	
		1850
Taiping Rebellion, 1852–1864		
Opening of Japan, 1854		
Sun Yat-sen, 1866–1925		
Meiji Restoration in Japan, 1867–1868	Opening of Suez Canal, 1869	
	Destruction of Zulu empire, 1879	
Adoption of constitution in Japan, 1889		
Sino-Japanese War, 1894–1895	Boer War, 1899–1902	1900
Boxer Uprising, 1900		
Russo-Japanese War, 1904–1905	Union of South Africa, 1909	
Revolution in China, 1911		
Dictatorship of Yüan Shih-k'ai, 1914–1916		
Era of warlords in China, 1916–1928		
Nationalist regime in China, 1928–1949		
Triumph of militarists in Japan, 1936		
War in Far East, 1937–1945		
Vietnam War, French phase, 1947–1954		
Communist regime in China, 1949–	Apartheid policy in South Africa, 1948–	
Independence of Indonesia, 1949	Independence of Libya, 1949	1950
Korean War, 1950–1953	Mau Mau revolts in Kenya, 1952–1958	
Bandung Conference, 1955	Algerian war of independence, 1954–1962	
	Conflict in the Congo, 1960	
Vietnam War, American phase, 1963–1975	Organization of African Unity, 1963–	
Great Proletarian Cultural Revolution in China, 1966–1969	Civil war in Nigeria, 1967–1970	
	Guerrilla war in Rhodesia, 1972–1980	
Death of Mao Tse-tung, 1976		
Democracy movement, in China, 1978–		
Vietnam-Cambodia war, 1978–1979		
Chinese invasion of Vietnam, 1979		
	Rhodesia becomes independent state of Zimbabwe, 1980	1985
	AIDS epidemic in Africa, 1980s	
Death of Emperor Hirohito, 1989	Independence of Namibia, 1989	
Suppression of the, Democracy movement, 1989	South African government opens dialogue with the African National Congress, 1990	

Chapter 37

THE COMMONWEALTH OF NATIONS

We are fortunate to witness the emergence of the Republic of India and our successors may well envy us this day, but fortune is a hostage which has to be zealously guarded by our own good work and which has a tendency to slip away if we slacken in our efforts or if we look in wrong directions.

—Jawaharlal Nehru, 1951

One of the most significant developments in the history of democracy in the modern world has been the evolution of the Commonwealth of Nations. Originally called the British Commonwealth of Nations, it now includes a number of states which repudiate any suggestion of allegiance to Britain. All members of the Commonwealth are self-governing, but many of them recognize the British monarch, represented by a governor-general, as their head of state. This group includes—in addition to the United Kingdom—the large Dominions of Canada, Australia, and New Zealand, and such small ones as Barbados, Jamaica, Malta, Mauritius, Sierra Leone, and Trinidad and Tobago. Political changes within the last few years have resulted in the creation within the Commonwealth of many republics, with no ties to the British Crown. The most conspicuous example is India, but the Commonwealth embraces more than a dozen republics, ranging in size from medium to tiny: Bangladesh, Botswana, Cyprus, Sri Lanka (Ceylon), Fiji, Gambia, Ghana, Guyana, Kenya, Malawi, Malaysia, Nigeria, Singapore, Tanzania, Uganda, and Zambia. The little African state of Lesotho (an enclave within the Republic of South Africa) has the distinction of being a separate kingdom within the Commonwealth, under the headship of its Paramount Chief. Evidently the only requisite for membership in the Commonwealth is the desire to belong. Because members may secede at any time and new states may join, the Commonwealth is an evolving organization. Ire-

The Commonwealth defined

land withdrew in 1949 and South Africa in 1961. Pakistan—shaken by a disastrous war with India and angered by the recognition accorded to Bangladesh—terminated its membership in the Commonwealth in 1972. The newly independent Republic of Bangladesh joined the next year. The status of Rhodesia was in dispute for fifteen years following a declaration of independence in 1965 by Ian Smith, leader of Rhodesia's white minority. Britain is no longer the focal point of the Commonwealth, whose membership is spread around the globe. Since 1965 the organization has had its own Secretariat headed by a secretary-general. In recent years the area of most active political change has been the Caribbean, where all of Britain's former colonies are preparing for, or have already achieved, independence. The dozen or so ministates resulting from this movement seek economic aid outside the Commonwealth and also wish to establish closer ties with their non-English-speaking neighbors. Dominica, a tiny island of the Lesser Antilles, which progressed from an "associated state" to an independent republic in 1978, elected to remain in the Commonwealth but also planned to join the Organization of American States and other international organizations. Jamaica (which retains as nominal head of state a governor-general appointed by the British Crown rather than an elected president), under Prime Minister Michael Manley (1972–1980), experimented with close ties to Castro's Cuba. Since the United States treats the area as subject to its jurisdiction, such ties are fraught with danger for these tiny states, as Grenada discovered in 1983 when U.S. military forces invaded the island and overthrew its socialist revolutionary government.

The history of the United Kingdom and of the principal African states is discussed elsewhere. The purpose of this chapter is to give an account of the major Asian republics that rose within the Commonwealth and of the self-governing dominions settled primarily by emigrants from Britain.[1]

The growth of the Commonwealth

The Commonwealth of Nations as an association of independent or virtually independent states has a history of about a century. At an Imperial Conference in 1887, attended by prime ministers of the principal British possessions, suggestions were made that the colonies furthest advanced ought to have the right to participate in the government of the Empire. The idea was revived at subsequent Imperial Conferences, in 1897, in 1902, and in 1907. It was not, however, until World War I that the proposal gave much promise of becoming a reality. The free and liberal assistance given to the mother country by the dominions in that struggle fortified their claims not only to a direct

[1] The Commonwealth of Nations must be distinguished clearly from the British Empire. The latter consists of two parts: the independent empire and the dependent empire. The independent empire includes those members of the Commonwealth of Nations which still render some tenuous allegiance to Great Britain. The dependent empire comprises a diminishing number of colonies ruled directly from London.

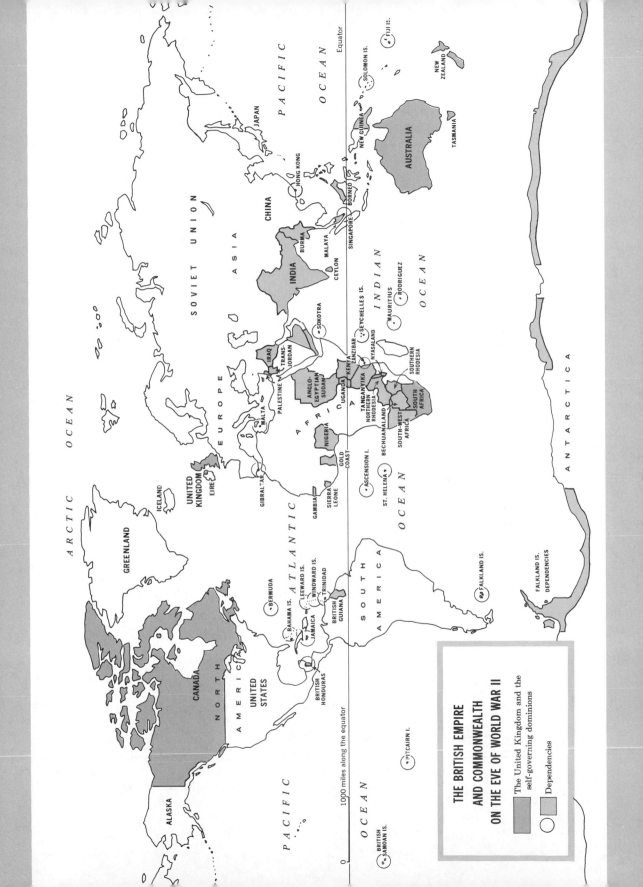

THE BRITISH EMPIRE
AND COMMONWEALTH
ON THE EVE OF WORLD WAR II

The United Kingdom and the
self-governing dominions

Dependencies

voice in imperial affairs but to a more definite recognition of their own independence. The Imperial Conference of 1921 agreed that the events of the war had clearly established the right of the self-governing dominions to be considered coequals with the mother country in foreign affairs. The Conference of 1926 adopted a report prepared by Arthur James Balfour, former prime minister of Great Britain. The report described the self-governing areas under the British flag (including the United Kingdom) as "autonomous communities within the British Empire, equal in status, in no way subordinate one to another in any aspect of their domestic or external affairs, though united by a common allegiance to the crown, and freely associated as members of the British Commonwealth of Nations." In 1931 the substance of the Balfour Report was enacted by Parliament in a memorable law known as the Statute of Westminster.

The Statute of Westminster

Since the enactment of the Statute of Westminster the several states of the Commonwealth of Nations have functioned as practically independent republics. No longer may any law passed by a dominion parliament be disallowed by the Parliament in London or vetoed by the British Cabinet, and no law of the British Parliament may be applied to any dominion unless its government specifically requests that this be done. The prime minister of each dominion has an equal right with the prime minister of Britain to "advise" the queen directly. The queen herself serves as a mere symbol of the unity of the Commonwealth. Although she is represented in each dominion (but not in the Republics) by a governor-general, the latter has no real authority. His primary function is to receive the resignation of an outgoing prime minister and to designate the leader of the opposition party as his successor. This involves no more freedom of choice than is exercised by the monarch herself when the head of the British Cabinet loses the support of the majority in the House of Commons and gives way to the leader of Her Majesty's Loyal Opposition.

Deficiencies and advantages of the Commonwealth

The Commonwealth is no longer the boon to Great Britain that it formerly was. Even those members that acknowledge allegiance to the British monarch have shown an increasing spirit of economic independence and indifference to the welfare of the United Kingdom. It has been said that most of the Old World members are about as beneficial to the former mother country as "poor relations on pay day." Though they continue to look for generous contributions of British aid, they show little disposition to confer any benefits in return. Ghana, for example, grants no preference to British goods. While Australian industrial products enter New Zealand duty free, British goods are subject to tariffs. Air India not only competes with British Airways, but equips its fleet with commercial airliners purchased from the United States. In 1965 Britain had a total trade deficit with the Commonwealth nations of over $1 billion. Whether or not advantageous to Great Britain, the Commonwealth is of benefit to the world, if only by proving that a group of independent nations (some fifty in all), differing in race, origin, power, and economic status, can maintain a sense of common interest and share responsibilities. Also it has served as a laboratory for the development and testing of democratic institutions.

I. THE DOMINION OF CANADA

Canadian history illustrates dramatically the evolution of the concept of the Commonwealth, its operating principles, and its inherent problems. At the same time, it provides a striking example of the successful building of a nation out of diverse elements and under the stress of conflicting interests and loyalties. Beginning as a French colony, Canada incorporated the British legal and parliamentary systems, and kept a balance between these two distinct traditions while accommodating to pressure from the powerful republican neighbor to the south. And emerging as a fully independent but faithful member of the Commonwealth, Canada has played a constructive role in the wider community of nations.

Canada: nation-building within the Commonwealth

The recorded history of Canada dates from 1608 when Samuel Champlain, a French naval officer with an interest in the fur trade, founded a settlement at Québec. For thirty years thereafter he continued his activities in the St. Lawrence valley, staking claims for the French king as far west as Lake Huron. Later in the seventeenth century the French government granted monopolies to trading companies to colonize and develop "New France." Although the companies ultimately failed, they did establish a few forts and trading posts and brought over a few thousand of their countrymen as permanent settlers. Finally, Jesuit missionaries contributed their part toward opening up the country and enlarging knowledge of its resources and attractions. By the middle of the eighteenth century the population of Canada included about 70,000 Frenchmen.

The founding of Canada

France lost Canada to Great Britain in the French and Indian War, but for some years thereafter the British continued to assume that their newly acquired possession would remain French. When the British Parliament passed the Québec Act in 1774 to correct certain defects in the organization of the Empire, Canada was not given a representative assembly, since it was taken for granted that the people could neither understand nor be loyal to British institutions. But after the American War for Independence so many Loyalist refugees from the United States, together with immigrants from Great Britain, settled in Ontario that William Pitt thought it advisable to have Parliament enact a law in 1791 separating Upper Canada (Ontario), which was almost entirely British, from Lower Canada (Québec), which was overwhelmingly French, and providing for an elective assembly in each of the two

Troubles between French and British Canada

provinces. The scheme ended in failure. The French and British distrusted each other, and conflicts soon arose between the elective assemblies and the royal governors sent out from London. In 1837 the antagonism flared into an open rebellion. Although quickly suppressed, it called attention to Canada's grievances and impressed upon the British government the necessity of doing something about them. Lord Durham was appointed high commissioner to investigate conditions in Canada, and his report, published after his return to England, was destined to become famous in the history of dominion government.

The beginning of responsible government

The Durham Report enunciated two principles, which may be regarded as the cornerstone of the dominion system. First, its author declared that colonies already possessing representative institutions should be granted "responsible government." This meant that they should be permitted to manage their local affairs through cabinets or ministries responsible to their own legislatures. In the second place, Lord Durham urged the principle that similar colonies in the same geographic area should be federated into one large unit. Applying this to Canada, he pleaded for the unification of the British and French portions into a single dominion. In accordance with this recommendation Upper and Lower Canada were presently united. In 1847 Lord Durham's son-in-law, Lord Elgin, became governor of Canada and put into effect the principle of choosing his cabinet from the party that controlled a majority of seats in the assembly. He allowed it to be inferred that the cabinet would remain in office only so long as it received the support of the majority party. In addition he signed bills sponsored by the cabinet, despite the fact that they conflicted with the interests of the mother country. By these means he conferred upon Canada for all practical purposes a system of responsible government similar to that of Great Britain.

Establishment of the Dominion of Canada

But the dominion government as we now know it dates only from 1867. In that year the hitherto separate colonies of New Brunswick and Nova Scotia united with Québec and Ontario to form a confederation under the name of the Dominion of Canada. A frame of government was provided for them by the British North America Act passed by the London Parliament in the same year. This act embodied a constitution which the Canadians themselves had adopted in 1864. It established a federal system with a division of powers between the central government and the governments of the provinces. All powers not delegated to the governments of the provinces were declared to be reserved to the central government, with its capital at Ottawa in Ontario Province. This departure from the federal pattern in the United States (which proved in practice to carry little weight) was inspired in part by the fact that the claims of the seceding southern states to full sovereignty had helped to bring on the American War between the States.

The Fathers of Confederation. Painting by R. Harris. The constitution that established the confederation was based on the British system of parliamentary government. The British system had to be adapted to satisfy the need for a federal rather than a unitary structure, and the framers of the constitution and the confederation inevitably looked to the Constitution of the United States for guidance. The result was a uniquely Canadian achievement designed to address Canada's particular requirements.

The British North America Act confirmed the principle of responsible government. A governor-general, appointed technically by the king but actually by the British Cabinet, was made the nominal head of the Dominion. The real power over local affairs was placed in the hands of a Dominion cabinet, nominally appointed by the governor-general but actually responsible to the lower house of the legislature for its official acts and its tenure of office. Legislative power was vested in a parliament of two houses, a Senate appointed by the governor-general for life, and a House of Commons elected by the people. Except for the fact that cabinet responsibility was to be enforced by the House of Commons exclusively and that money bills must originate therein, both houses were given equal powers. In practice, however, the Senate has retired into a kind of dignified obsolescence, performing no functions except those of an unambitious revising chamber. The Canadian constitution also provided for responsible government in the provinces. The nominal head of each province is a lieutenant-governor appointed by the Dominion cabinet. The effective authority is exercised by a cabinet responsible to the provincial legislature. Except in Québec the legislative bodies in the provinces have only one house.

One difficulty immediately confronting the new Dominion was the

The British North America Act

*Relations with the United
States: Treaty of
Washington*

hostility of the United States. Citizens of the northern states were angered by the sympathy that Canadians as well as the British had shown for the Confederate cause during the Civil War, and some expansionists believed that the whole North American continent should eventually fall to the United States. Tension eased after the Treaty of Washington was signed by the United States and British governments in 1871. The treaty upheld the principle of the arbitration of disputes; the United States disavowed any intention of altering the political divisions of the continent; and the British withdrew their troops from Canada. The Canadian prime minister participated in the negotiations and, although the treaty was at first unpopular in Canada, it was accepted by the Canadian parliament. This successful diplomatic engagement marked the beginning of closer relations with the United States. The process of nation-building in the Dominion continued in anything but a state of isolation. Canadians, in addition to domestic disputes, were caught in the pull of competing international currents. They were bound by ties of loyalty to Britain and the empire, but a growing feeling of North American solidarity impelled them toward genuine independence. At the same time, their economy was becoming geared to that of the United States, and Ottawa sometimes sided with Washington rather than with London on issues of mutual concern. There have been disagreements and occasional moments of severe friction between the United States and Canada, but the development of reciprocal relations between the two countries undoubtedly contributed to the evolution of the Commonwealth as a voluntary association of free nations. While retaining sentimental and symbolic links with the British crown, the Dominion accepted closer ties with the North American republic than had ever existed before between two independent states.

Growth of the Dominion

Since 1867 the growth of Canada has roughly paralleled that of the United States. When the British North America Act was passed, Canada had a population of 3½ million. By 1985 it had grown to 25 million. During the same period the population of the United States increased from 38 million to 196 million. The growth in area of the Dominion of Canada was equally phenomenal. In 1869 the province of Manitoba was carved out of territory purchased from the Hudson's Bay Company. In 1871–1873 British Columbia and Prince Edward Island were added to the Dominion. By 1905 the completion of the Canadian Pacific Railway made possible the creation of two new prairie provinces, Alberta and Saskatchewan. Not until 1949 did the island of Newfoundland join the Confederation as its tenth province. The growth of Canada cannot be measured in terms of area and population alone. The latter half of the nineteenth century and the early years of the twentieth witnessed the establishment of a sound banking and currency system, a civil service, and a protective tariff for the benefit of Canadian industry. Marked progress occurred also in the exploitation

The Completion of the Main Line of the Canadian Pacific Railway, November 7, 1885. The completion of the trunk line of the Canadian Pacific served to unify Canada by providing a reliable and efficient means of transportation and communication that spanned the continent.

of mineral and forest resources. Canada became the chief supplier of nickel, asbestos, cobalt, and wood pulp to the United States.

In its progress toward national maturity, Canada has sought to mold a multitude of immigrants into a cohesive but pluralistic state. With the opening up of the West, thousands of Ruthenians, Russians, Poles, Scandinavians, and Germans flooded the prairie provinces. Between 1903 and 1914 nearly 2.7 million such immigrants made their way into Canada. As late as 1941 more than 40 percent of the population of the prairie provinces was of central or east European origin. But by far the largest minority population was the French Canadian, concentrated heavily in the province of Québec. French had been the primary language of Québec for three and a half centuries, and most French Canadians are descended from people who reached North America before 1750. After joining the Confederation, the province retained its own institutions, differing in many respects from those of English-speaking Canada. The law courts operate under an adaptation of the Napoleonic Code rather than the English common law. The Catholic Church, to which the great majority of citizens adhere, has performed many functions elsewhere left to government, including the supervision of education. Proud of their cultural heritage, Québecers regarded themselves as a distinctive society, if not a separate nation. Fearful of domination by the English-speaking majority and unable to exert much influence on the policies of the central government, they fortified their independent spirit by an increase in numbers—the "revenge of the

Linguistic minorities

nursery." Until well into the twentieth century French Canadians had one of the highest birth rates in the world, and today they constitute more than 25 percent of Canada's total population of 25 million. Since 1954, however, their birth rate has been declining, and Québec now has the lowest rate of population increase in the Dominion. A growing disadvantage in numbers strengthened the French Canadians' determination to resist assimilation.

In the twentieth century Canada's economic growth was accompanied by increasing participation in international affairs. In 1909 the government added to its executive branch a Department of External Affairs. That same year a treaty with the United States established an International Joint Commission, composed of three Americans and three Canadians, with power to issue binding decisions regarding water use and also to arbitrate any other controversy referred to it with the consent of both countries. The Boundary Waters Treaty of 1909, both durable and flexible, has proved highly successful although it has not been able to resolve every problem concerning the use and abuse of water in the Great Lakes area.

Boundary Waters Treaty of 1909

It is generally asserted that Canada achieved maturity as a nation during the First World War. Although interested but little in the tortuous diplomacy leading up to the conflict, the Ottawa government accepted Britain's's declaration as an automatic commitment for the whole Empire. The Dominion pledged itself to unlimited support and made sacrifices proportionately equal to those of the mother country itself. Out of a population of only 9 million at the time, 600,000 joined the armed forces, and more than 50,000 gave up their lives on the fighting front. Proud of their efforts in what was generally regarded as a noble cause, Canadians lost their sense of colonial inferiority and came forth as leading champions of Western ideals of democracy and peace. After 1917 the Canadian prime minister sat in the Imperial War Cabinet as an equal of the prime minister of Great Britain in formulating policy. When the war ended, Canada demanded and received a seat at the Peace Conference and subsequently was admitted to the League of Nations. In the years that followed, the Dominion asserted its independence in foreign policy by refusing to accept commitments under treaties negotiated by the British without Canadian participation. Nevertheless, when the Second World War broke out, Canada plunged into the fray with hardly a moment's hesitation. The threat to the survival of Britain was almost universally regarded as a threat to the interests of Canada. Although the Dominion might legally have remained neutral, it pledged its wealth and the lives of its youth in the same unstinted measure that had characterized its action in the First World War.

Effects of world wars in welding Canada into a nation

By the end of the Second World War, Canada, with a greatly strengthened economy, had won a prominent place on the international scene. The Dominion made loans to Great Britain and played a

International relations

significant role in the development of the United Nations and in the establishment of NATO. A contribution of incalculable value to the work of the United Nations Organization resulted from Canadian initiative during the Suez crisis of 1956, provoked by a joint attack on Egypt by Israeli, French, and British forces. The Liberal ministry then in office in Canada sided with the United States in condemning British action, and Lester Pearson, secretary of state for external affairs, skirting the deadlocked Security Council, persuaded the Assembly to create a United Nations Emergency Force to police a cease-fire in the area of hostilities. On many subsequent occasions the UNEF has proved its usefulness.

Canadians gradually discovered that larger world responsibilities entailed greater burdens. The geographic position of their country was a source of uneasiness. It had the misfortune to lie directly athwart the air routes between Russia and the United States. As the Cold War between the two giants waxed in intensity, Canada had reason to fear that the United States might attempt to dictate an increasing number of its military and economic policies. A network of "early warning" radar fences stretching across Canada was constructed as a joint enterprise. In 1957 the two governments established an integrated North American Air Defense Command (NORAD), jointly controlled but located at Colorado Springs and with an American in command. After long and bitter debate, climaxed by a parliamentary election won by the Liberals in 1963, Canada agreed to accept nuclear warheads in its defense installations.

While the Dominion faced new problems in the wake of the Second World War, it continued to wrestle with old ones. As a nation Canada was still underpopulated. With an area almost equal to that of Europe, it had fewer inhabitants than New York State. Forty-five percent of its people dwelt in the St. Lawrence valley in an area covering but 2 percent of the country. The Yukon and Northwest territories, equal in size to half of the United States, contained only 14,000 inhabitants. At least 50 percent of the land of the Dominion remained unsuitable for agriculture or for almost any other occupation except fur trading and mining. Worse still, the population was sharply divided on the basis of sectional and ethnic interests. Ontario was dominated by industrial and financial ambitions, which gave to the province a conservative outlook in economic affairs and at the same time a determination to achieve independence from British and American influences. The prairie provinces, inhabited largely by immigrants from the United States and from Continental European countries, were the stronghold of agrarian collectivism and of radical innovations for currency inflation and cheap credit. French Canada, embraced by the province of Québec, continued its devotion to the culture and religion of its ancestors and its resistance to domination from Ottawa. In recent decades the most pressing issues faced by Canadians fall roughly into three

The Parti Québecois

Pierre Trudeau, Prime Minister of Canada, 1968–1979 and 1980–1984

Reform program and the separatist issue in Québec

categories: economic policy, both domestic and relative to the United States; separatism, especially as it affects the status of Québec; and revision of the constitution.

For all but nine months out of a sixteen-year period (1968–1984) the brilliant, colorful, and controversial Pierre Trudeau held the office of prime minister as leader of the Liberal party. His first challenge came from Québec, where long-rankling discontent found expression in a political party founded by René Lévesque in 1967. The *Parti Québecois* set as its goal the separation of Québec from the Canadian federation. The separatist party won a sizable majority in the provincial legislature in the election of 1976, making Lévesque Québec's premier and the question of separation a foremost national issue. Trudeau, himself a bilingual French Canadian, sympathized with the grievances of the French-speaking *Québecois,* who comprised five-sixths of the province's 6 million inhabitants. In 1969 he had secured passage of the Official Languages Act, which required the use of both French and English in all public announcements and throughout the civil service. But a year later, after terrorists murdered a Québec cabinet minister, he invoked the repressive War Measures Act. Hoping to unify the nation more closely by expanding the role of the central government, Trudeau adamantly opposed any threat of secession.

In Québec, the coming to power of Lévesque's party turned the tables on the English-speaking minority, which had dominated provincial politics and economy to an extent far out of proportion to its numbers. Smarting with resentment against the discrimination that the French population had long endured, the *Parti Québecois* enacted legislation to break the monopoly of the Anglo-Saxon Protestant ("WASP") elite, promoted the ascendancy of French culture, and seemed determined to banish the English language from the province almost completely. English-speaking people began to emigrate, and several large business firms moved their headquarters to Ontario or the United States. But in spite of the popularity of some of its reforms, the *Parti Québecois* won only limited support for its proposal to separate Québec from the rest of Canada. A referendum in the spring of 1980 indicated that two-thirds of Québec's voters opposed separation. By 1984, with a worsening economy which brought high unemployment and a wave of strikes, the strength of the *Parti Québecois* had seriously eroded.

If not an open threat of secession, disaffection bordering on revolt festered during Trudeau's administration in the western provinces. This large, thinly populated area, once the domain of cattle and wheat, had undergone rapid development with the exploitation of its huge reserves of oil and gas. Calgary, the center of Alberta's oil industry, grew from a frontier settlement to a booming metropolis. By 1980 Alberta was producing 90 percent of Canada's oil, and the four western provinces collectively accounted for half of the gross national product. Their inhabitants wanted to let the price of oil rise to the world market level, and they demanded a greater voice in the allocation of revenues. Trudeau held oil prices down to benefit consumers and, through taxation, diverted a generous share of the profits to projects intended to benefit the nation as a whole. With a distrust of eastern monied interests similar to that shown by western sections of the United States from time to time, western Canadians resisted what they regarded as encroachment by the central government upon their affairs. The bilingual requirement imposed by the Official Languages Act aroused resentment. In Alberta, Germans and Ukrainians far outnumbered speakers of French, and they objected to being confronted with a "foreign" language.

Unbowed before the storms of sectional conflict, Trudeau tackled the prickly task of changing the constitution, which by 1979 had become a heated issue. What Trudeau proposed was to "patriate" the constitution—that is, to replace the British North America Act, under which the Dominion had formally been governed for more than a century, with a new document to be created and amended in Canada. When the Dominion was first established under the British North America Act, by Canadian request the amendment process had been left with the British Parliament. The British North America Act had been amended a score of times but always at Canada's request and with the assent of all the provinces. Although there was no question as to Canada's independence, Trudeau considered it a matter of national pride to bring the constitution home. He also wanted to include a bill of rights, an amending formula, and a clearer definition of the relation between the provinces and the central government. When a constitutional conference of provincial prime ministers in 1980 became hopelessly deadlocked, Trudeau resolved to have the Canadian parliament, which his party controlled, draft a constitution and submit it to Westminster for ratification. This proposal raised a storm of controversy in Canada and embarrassed the British government as members of Parliament found themselves besieged by lobbyists for various factions. One member is reported to have remarked: "We want to give the Canadians what they want, but who are the Canadians?" Forced by provincial pressures to compromise some of his objectives, Trudeau secured an agreement acceptable to most of the provinces.

Trudeau's drive to "patriate" the constitution

The new constitution (the Canada Act), signed in Ottawa by Queen Elizabeth II in April 1982, is necessarily flexible and vague. Flexibility is inherent in the British political tradition and consistent with Canadian experience and practice. Previously no amendments had been made to the British North America Act without the consent of all the provinces. Henceforth it may be possible for one province to reject an amendment adopted by the Confederation or for the Canadian parliament to pass a law conflicting with the constitution. The relationship between the several parts of the state has never been clearly resolved, and, fortunately, no attempt has been made to resolve it by resort to mass violence. In some respects the provinces are more autonomous

Canada's new constitution

Queen Elizabeth II Signing the Canada Act in a Ceremony in Ottawa on April 17, 1982. Prime Minister Pierre Trudeau is seated on the Queen's right.

than is typical of a federal structure, as is illustrated by their veto power over amendments to the constitution. During the Great Depression of the 1930s, which was felt very severely in Canada, the central and provincial governments alike tried to evade responsibility for alleviating the crisis, but reluctance on the part of the provinces to entrust Ottawa with greater authority contributed to the lack of effective action. No equivalent of President Franklin Roosevelt's New Deal was seen in Canada. Major social legislation at the national level began only with the Second World War, but in recent decades the central government has been a more active participant in the economic sphere and in welfare programs than has the powerful government of the United States.

Difficulties in defining the Canadian national identity

Conflicting sectional interests, disaffection between the English- and French-speaking populations, a secessionist faction in Québec, and divergent interpretations of the constitution have made it difficult for Canadians to define their national identity, or even to be certain that they have one. The character and destiny of their country were ambiguous from the beginning (the name *Canada* is derived from an Indian word meaning "the village"). Immigration since the Second World War has further confused the picture. Since 1980 70 percent of the immigrants have come from non-European countries, chiefly Hong Kong, Vietnam, India, and Pakistan, and these elements have not been readily assimilated. An act of the Ottawa parliament in 1988 declared Canada to be "multicultural," and prescribed equal treatment for all racial groups and the preservation and enhancement of minority languages. Lacking enforcement provisions, the law has brought little or no benefit to minorities subject to discrimination. Canada, no less than its neighbor to the south, can be charged with mistreatment of its aboriginal inhabitants, exhibitions of racism, callous treatment of refugees seeking political asylum, and occasional abuses of human rights and civil liberties.

Canada's close association with the United States has both stimulated and threatened its quest for national identity. The degree of interdependence between the economies of the two countries is remarkable. Between 1930 and 1950 Canada's exports to the United States tripled, while imports from the States more than quadrupled. American sales to Canada exceeded those to all of Europe and Latin America combined. Although Ottawa in 1976 established a contractual link with the European Common Market and entered into trade negotiations with Japan, trade with the United States increased even further. Beginning in 1968 the balance of Canadian-American trade shifted in Canada's favor, and Canada now has heavy capital investments in the United States. But increasing integration of the two economies was bound to challenge the independence of Canadians. With investments of some $35 billion, by 1970 United States capital controlled the greater part of Canada's rubber and petroleum industries and about 45 percent of total manufacturing and mining capacity. The western oil boom, stimulated by still more American financing, forged commercial links extending from Calgary to Houston. By 1980 seventeen top petroleum companies, accounting for 72 percent of all oil and gas sales, were run by foreign interests, chiefly American. Not surprisingly, some businessmen complained that Canada was becoming a "branch-plant economy." In the fall of 1980 Trudeau's government took a number of controversial steps designed to reduce foreign control of mineral and energy resources.

After a long political career, Prime Minister Trudeau retired from office in June 1984. In the September elections the Liberal party, which had held office for forty-two of the last fifty years, was defeated in a landslide by the Progressive Conservative party headed by Brian Mulroney, a bilingual Irishman. Facing a large budget deficit and an unemployment rate of 11 percent, Mulroney sought to stimulate the economy and promote capital growth by encouraging American investment without restrictions, thus reversing the policy of economic nationalism pursued by Trudeau during the 1970s. Early in 1988 Prime Minister Mulroney and President Ronald Reagan signed the U.S.-Canada Free Trade Agreement, which by the following year would remove almost all trade barriers between the two countries. This proposal provoked stormy debate in Canada. Some Canadians feared that free trade would lead to the complete absorption of their economy into the much larger one of the United States, reducing the Dominion to the status of a "fifty-first state." ("We like you, look like you, talk like you, but don't want to be you" was an expressed or implied Canadian sentiment.) Because of popular protest and because the Canadian Senate—controlled by the Liberal party—took the unusual step of rejecting the treaty, Mulroney was forced to call a general election on the issue. During the campaign his Liberal opponent accused him of having sold out to the United States, and the fear was expressed that even Canada's government-supported health-care system would be jeopardized. The Free Trade Agreement, however, had the backing

Prime Minister Brian Mulroney of Canada and President George Bush of the United States Conferring on Issues of Mutual Interest

of the business community, and political opposition was divided between the Liberal party and the New Democratic (socialist) party. In the November election, although the Conservatives lost some seats in the House of Commons, Mulroney secured the victory he needed.

Conflict rooted in ethnic, cultural, and regional differences

Ethnic, cultural, and regional differences still cast a shadow over Canada's national destiny. In Québec, which refused to ratify the 1982 constitution, the secessionist movement regained momentum in the late 1980s. In 1987 an accord accepting Québec's demand for recognition as a "distinct society" in Canada was signed by the prime minister and ten provincial premiers and promptly ratified by the Québec National Assembly. This accord would have become law if unanimously ratified within the three year period specified by the constitution, but the deadline (June 23, 1990) passed with two provinces (Manitoba and Newfoundland) withholding approval. The failure of these protracted negotiations left a wake of bitterness on all sides and left unresolved the question of whether and under what conditions Québec, Canada's second wealthiest province with one-quarter of the country's population, would remain within the federation. Meanwhile, both the Québec and national governments were facing a confrontation with aboriginal minorities—Inuits and Mohawk Indians—who claimed they had been illegally dispossessed of their lands.

Promise for the future

With full allowance for Canada's difficulties, there is little doubt that its future holds bright promise. Canada is one of the world's most richly endowed countries in natural resources. With a population hardly more than one-tenth that of the United States, the Dominion's foreign trade is almost one-third as large. Canada leads the world in the production of asbestos, nickel, platinum, zinc, and wood pulp. The nation ranks second in the production of aluminum, cobalt, and uranium, third in the production of gold and titanium, and fourth in the production of wheat. Extensive deposits of iron ore have been discovered in Labrador. A gigantic hydroelectric project begun in 1971 in the James Bay region of Québec is exporting power to Vermont and New York, and is expected to furnish half of Québec's electricity by 1990. Since 1960 Canada has expanded trade with and contributed financial aid to African Commonwealth nations. It could benefit substantially by serving the "front-line" African states as a link to the outside world if tight sanctions were imposed upon South Africa.

2. THE COMMONWEALTH OF AUSTRALIA

Australia: The people and the land

Australia, an island continent, has an area about the size of the United States minus Hawaii and Alaska and nearly twenty-five times that of the British Isles. Its human habitation began some 50,000 years ago with a mixture of races, predominantly black, coming probably from the Indonesian Archipelago. For millennia these aborigines, organized in several hundred communities, lived as nomads and skillful

Left: *The Landing of Captain Cook at Botany Bay, 1770.* This painting, by E. Phillips Fox, depicts the first landing by Englishmen on the east coast of the Australian continent. Right: *Commissioner Hardy Collecting License Fees in the Victoria Gold Fields in the 1850s.* Diggers scatter in order to evade paying the fees.

hunters. Although their technical achievements were modest, they created remarkably complex symbolic paintings which have recently won high acclaim from art critics. Near the end of the eighteenth century the aborigines' hunting grounds, which had sustained them and which they revered as sacred, began to be lost to white settlers who used them for cattle and sheep grazing. Driven into barren foothills and ravaged by unfamiliar diseases contracted by contact with the aliens, the indigenous populations and their culture declined rapidly. Not until some 200 years later were serious attempts made to recognize and protect the rights of the aborigines.

Australia began its recorded history under inauspicious circumstances. Discovered by the Dutch in the seventeenth century and rediscovered and claimed for England by Captain James Cook in 1770, it was too remote from the homeland to offer attractions for settlement. When the American Revolution eliminated the thirteen colonies in the Western Hemisphere as dumping grounds for British convicts, the government in London turned to Australia. The first convict ship sailed for the island continent in 1787, and Australia remained a penal colony for more than fifty years. Under England's then-harsh penal code many men and women were sentenced to deportation for what would now be considered minor offenses, such as hunting partridges on some noble's estate. But whether hardened criminals or petty thieves, the convicts faced a cruel fate in their land of exile. The story of conditions in the prison camps is so appalling that the Australians as well as the British have tended to blot it from memory. A common form of punishment was beating with a cat-o'-nine tails until the flesh was torn open. Women prisoners were degraded and sexually exploited. A contemporary Australian author claims that con-

Australia as a penal colony

ditions in the worst prisons foreshadowed the horrors of twentieth-century concentration camps.[2]

Convict labor and sheep ranching

Gradually a few adventurous free citizens filtered into the colony to establish sheep ranches or "stations." Convicts were released to them as shepherds with the provision that after the expiration of their terms of sentence they would continue to live in Australia. By the time the British government abandoned its policy of deportation in the mid-nineteenth century, 162,000 convicts had been brought over. Their gradual release from imprisonment provided a supply of cheap labor for the ranches. By 1830 the wool industry had become the backbone of the Australian economy.

The discovery of gold

In 1848 the trend of Australian development was abruptly changed by the discovery of gold in New South Wales and Victoria. Fortune hunters and adventurers from all over the world followed the magic lure of the yellow metal. Between 1850 and 1860 the population of the continent almost trebled. Inevitably more people came than could find a livelihood in prospecting and mining. When the excitement died away, and the hills and streams no longer yielded gold in easy abundance, the problem arose of what to do with the surplus population. The logical solution seemed to be to encourage them to become farmers. Efforts to establish themselves in this occupation involved a desperate struggle. Scanty rainfall, inadequate transportation facilities, and refusal of the wool growers to "unlock" their vast estates dogged the footsteps of all but the most fortunate farmers with disaster. Not until the building of railways to the ports, the perfection of dry-farming techniques, the development of suitable strains of wheat, and the improvement of chemical fertilizers was agriculture in Australia placed on a sound foundation.

Effect of the gold rushes: (1) the White Australia policy

A considerable number of the basic political and social policies of Australia as a nation can be traced to the gold rushes of the 1850s and their aftermath. First was the White Australia policy, designed to exclude black, brown, and yellow races from settlement on the continent. In the 1850s thousands of Chinese poured into Victoria and New South Wales and threatened the wage scales and living standards of the white miners. Rapidly the Australians became obsessed with the idea that their country was a "white island in a vast colored ocean." Having already expropriated and partially exterminated the indigenous black population, they pointed to the hundreds of millions of dark-skinned inhabitants of India, the Netherlands Indies, China, and Japan as a flood tide which would overwhelm them unless they built dikes in the form of rigid exclusion laws. Even the tropical regions of northern Australia were to be kept uncontaminated by Oriental labor.[3] The White Australia policy was motivated both by

[2] Robert Hughes, *The Fatal Shore*, New York, 1986.

[3] It is an ironical fact, however, that in the nineteenth century thousands of Melanesians and Polynesians were brought in from the Pacific islands and shamelessly exploited. They were deported in 1906.

feelings of race superiority and by fear of economic competition.

A second policy resulting from the gold rushes of the nineteenth century was to foster the growth of a manufacturing industry through the use of protective tariffs. Originally adopted by the colony of Victoria in the 1860s, tariffs were later extended to the Commonwealth as a whole. Their use was motivated in part at least by the need for domestic industry to absorb the surplus miners. A third policy was the adoption of heavy governmental borrowing for the construction of public works. Obviously, the need for public-works construction could be justified for many reasons: to provide irrigation projects for the benefit of farmers in arid regions; to speed up the development of transportation facilities; to furnish employment opportunities for the influx of immigrants brought in by the discovery of gold.

(2) protective tariffs and government borrowing

The Australian Commonwealth as an organized state did not come into existence until 1901. Prior to that time the continent was divided into separate colonies, most of which had split off from the original colony of New South Wales. Movements to federate them made slow progress, mainly because the weak feared domination by the strong and prosperous. But such fears did not prevent a rapid growth of local democracy. By 1850 each of the colonies had its legislative council as a check upon the governor, and had obtained the right to alter its own constitution. Soon afterward the eastern colonies achieved responsible government. Universal manhood suffrage was introduced in South Australia in 1855, in Victoria in 1857, and in New South Wales a year later. About the same time the secret ballot was adopted in Victoria, South Australia, New South Wales, and Queensland. Before 1900 two colonies had begun payment of salaries to members of their legislatures, and several had given women the privilege of voting.

The growth of democracy in the Australian states

The stage was eventually reached where the arguments for federation outweighed the objections. Foremost among them was the need for a common defense against the militant imperialism of the Great Powers. Important also was the growing inconvenience of tariffs levied by the various colonies against each other. The first step for a union of the continent was taken in 1885 with the establishment of the Australian Federal Council. Possessing only legislative power with no executive or financial authority, this agency was reduced to impotence by the noncooperation of New South Wales. Its chief significance lay in the renewed impetus it gave to the demand for effective union. In 1897–1898 a series of conferences resulted in the drafting of a plan of federation which in 1901 was approved by the British parliament and became the Constitution of the Commonwealth of Australia. The Commonwealth was organized as a federal union comprising the six states of New South Wales, Victoria, Queensland, South Australia, Western Australia, and Tasmania. The capital was temporarily established at Melbourne, but the constitution contained a provision that a permanent capital should be built in the state of New South Wales, not less than 100 miles from Sydney. In the course of a decade

Establishment of Commonwealth of Australia

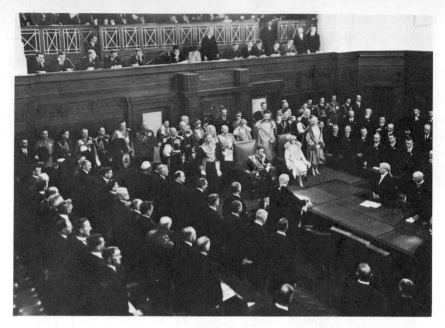

Establishment of the Seat of Government at Canberra. The Duke and Duchess of York in the Senate at the official opening of the Federal Parliament House in Canberra on May 9, 1927. The Duke reads King George V's commission for the establishment of the seat of government at Canberra.

the government invited city planners from all over the world to submit blueprints for a garden municipality to be known as Canberra. The award was given to Walter Griffin of Chicago, a brilliant architect and associate of Frank Lloyd Wright. Profuse plantings of trees and shrubs made the garden city a reality by the time the Commonwealth seat of government was transferred to Canberra in 1927, even though the Australian parliament refused to appropriate sufficient funds for the series of public buildings envisioned by Griffin.

The government of Australia

The government of Australia resembles that of the United States in some respects but, like Canada's, incorporates the British principle of making the cabinet responsible to the legislature. Because of the spirit of independence existing within the states of Australia and their distrust of one another, the constitution delegated only specified powers to the government of the Commonwealth, reserving all nondelegated powers to the states. The Australian parliament consists of two houses, a Senate and a House of Representatives. The former is composed of six members from each state, elected directly by the people for six years. Membership in the House is proportionate to population. Like several other members of the Commonwealth, Australia has a governor-general representing the British Crown, but his powers are insignificant. As in all of the dominions, executive authority as well as the primary control over legislation is vested in the cabinet headed by the prime minister. Curiously, both in Canada and in Australia the disposition of power between the federal government and political subdivisions has in recent years shifted in opposite directions. While Canada's provinces have become less amenable to direction from Ottowa, in Australia the balance of power has been shifting from the states to the Commonwealth, illustrated by the enactment of sorely needed measures to promote conservation and protect the environment, and by the reservation of tracts of land for the exclusive use of the aborigines.

Australia moved rapidly ahead of Great Britain in democratic political reform. The Chartist program of the 1830s, rejected in Britain, was carried by its exponents to New South Wales and by the 1860s had been almost completely enacted in the Australian states. Without the restriction of an established church or a landed aristocracy the legislatures adopted such reforms as universal adult suffrage, a secret ballot, payment of members of parliament, and also factory acts to protect the health and safety of workers.

Australia, together with New Zealand, pioneered to a limited extent in the field of social legislation. A flock of reforms enacted toward the end of the nineteenth century, partly in response to a severe depression in 1896, largely duplicated the pattern of Great Britain and Germany. Principal examples are the minimum wage, old-age pensions, widows' allowances, unemployment and health insurance, state hospitals, primary education, and child subsidies. A bonus is paid for every infant born in Australia, and an endowment is provided for every child under sixteen. A National Health System furnishes free drugs, subsidizes hospital and medical expenses, and provides pensions for the blind and victims of tuberculosis. One other element of Australian collectivism, however, has had no counterpart in the mother country. This is a system of compulsory arbitration and wage fixing, designed to maintain industrial peace and safeguard standards of living for industrial workers. In sharp contrast with the attitude of organized labor in most countries, Australian workers have accepted, and for the most part actually welcomed, compulsory arbitration. They regard it as a means to security and as a source of strength for the labor movement, since it tends to bring more members into the union.

One of the most interesting facts of Australian history is the extent to which the country has pursued a policy of social and economic planning. Even during the nineteenth century when the mother country was worshiping the slogans of free competition and free trade, Australia was steadily enlarging the sphere of governmental action to promote social cohesion and maintain a high standard of living. The reasons for this policy are numerous and varied. Geography alone provides a large part of the explanation. One-third of the continent has an average annual rainfall of less than 10 inches, and most of the remainder has less than 20. But even these averages do not reflect the poor distribution of the rain that does fall. In many areas the precipitation may be concentrated within a short period of the year, with months or years of subsequent drought. As a result, only about 8 percent of the total area can be utilized for farming or orchard purposes. About 40 percent is waste, and 50 percent is used for pasture. Under such conditions, it has been impossible for Australia to develop into a nation of independent proprietors cultivating small plots as family farms. In the pasture areas rainfall is so scanty or unreliable that sheep and cattle must be grazed over thousands of acres. This has necessitated the development of vast estates or pastoral "stations" established by owners with considerable capital. They provide employment for what is essentially an agricultural proletariat: shepherds, shearers, and "boundary riders," who have no hope of ever becoming proprietors. Conscious of their grievances, they have been drawn into militant trade unions. Unionism in Australia has surpassed in strength that of most other countries. A limited supply of labor—a scarcity that occasionally induced the state governments to encourage European immigration—helped to strengthen the movement. Trade unions that struggled for old-age pensions and minimum wages have been consistent supporters of government intervention in economic affairs.

Protectionism and government ownership

One of the earliest forms of government intervention in Australia was control of international trade. The methods employed have included tariffs, bounties, quotas, and marketing restrictions. A second form of government intervention is public ownership of a wide variety of economic enterprises. Ventures brought under government ownership include railways, shipping lines, power plants, hotels, banks, insurance companies, lumber mills, and coal mines. Because of the federal structure of the government, most such enterprises are conducted by the states rather than by the Commonwealth. Government ownership in Australia is the result in part of the strong influence that labor wields in both state and national politics, but organized labor has not been the only force supporting state ownership. The geography of Australia has impelled many capitalists and landowners to look with favor upon government operation of railways and public utilities, at least. Railroads were needed to bring out the grain, wool, meat, and minerals. With few private corporations bold enough to incur the risks involved, there was no alternative but for governments to shoulder the burden. As a consequence, in these and in some other lines, public ownership of economic ventures has been welcomed as an aid and support of private business.

Australia and the Post–World War Two World

During the first one and one half centuries of its existence as a commonwealth Australia, like Canada, retained close ties with the mother country, as illustrated by a marked preference for British immigrants over those from any other country. The Second World War marked the beginning of a shift in Australia's international position, both political and economic. Shocked by the discovery that Britain could no longer protect them from attack, Australians welcomed a defensive alliance with the United States. Meanwhile economic changes throughout the world forced Australia to find new trade patterns. Per capita income in the Commonwealth—the world's highest in the 1880s—declined steadily until by 1982 it had fallen to sixteenth place. Great Britain's entry into the European Common Market, together with protectionist policies in other industrialized countries, restricted the export of Australian raw materials. The United States displaced Great Britain as Australia's source of imports and capital, and Japan displaced Britain as the main outlet for wool, grain, and minerals. By 1971 30 percent of the Commonwealth's exports went to Japan, and more than 60 percent of its mineral exports. For coking coal the figure was close to 100 percent; and while Australians had become Japan's chief supplier of raw materials other than oil, they might also expect to develop a profitable market in China, especially for their wheat.

Another significant change since the Second World War has been in the extent and character of immigration. Since 1945 an influx of more than three million people increased Australia's population by nearly 25 percent. In spite of the government's wishes, Asian immigrants—especially Indochinese—began to outnumber Europeans. By 1970 one-fourth of those admitted were Asians, and more than 60 percent by 1983. It is evident that, in spite of opposition in some quarters, the White Australia policy has finally come to an end.

Immigration and Australia

Australia has been affected internally as well as externally by being drawn into the orbit of the United States. Some observers, noting a trend toward the Americanization of Australian culture and society, profess to see similarities in basic personality traits between the two peoples: American frontier-bred individualism is likened to the rugged independent spirit of Australians toughened by life in "the Bush." In spite of borrowing in both directions, however, Australia's culture is not likely to become a carbon copy of the American. Vigorous productivity in drama, literature, and the arts in recent decades indicates that the Australians, while moving away from their British heritage, are fully capable of finding their own national identity.

Australian culture and the U.S. connection

Since the Second World War Australia has faithfully followed the United States' lead in foreign policy. In 1951 the Commonwealth government joined a mutual-defense alliance (ANZUS) with New Zealand and the United States. In 1966 the prime minister, endorsing American intervention in Vietnam, declared, "Wherever the United States is resisting aggression . . . we will go a-waltzing Matilda with you," and promised that Australia would go "all the way with LBJ." (President Lyndon B. Johnson on a visit to Canberra in October 1966 expressed his gratitude by pronouncing Australia to be like Texas.)

ANZUS and U.S. policy

During the past three decades, except for a brief interlude in 1972–1975, Australian politics was dominated by a coalition of two parties, the Liberal party and the Country party, each of which was actually conservative. A split in the ranks of the Labor party and apprehension over national security, aggravated by the Cold War, helped give the conservatives their long tenure of power. During this era the government sent troops to fight in Korea and in Vietnam, and permitted the United States to install defense bases and electronic communications stations on Australian soil. Growing dissatisfaction with these commitments, together with inflation and the threat of rising unemployment, undermined the popularity of the conservative administration of Prime Minister William McMahon. The national election of December 1972

The Labor Ministry of Gough Whitlam

E. Gough Whitlam, Prime Minister of Australia, 1972–1975. Whitlam's removal from office by the governor-general precipitated a constitutional crisis and created uneasiness concerning the U.S.–Australia relationship.

The return of Labor and the problems of minority policies

returned the Labor party to office with a majority in the House of Representatives, and the new prime minister, Gough Whitlam, embarked on an active policy in both domestic and external affairs. He introduced new social-welfare measures, including free university education and the promise—long overdue—of humane treatment of the aborigines who had been oppressed, neglected, and forced to live in the desolate "Outback" or in city slums. While not repudiating the tripartite security treaty which bound Australia and New Zealand to the United States, Whitlam sought a more independent role for his country. He withdrew Australian troops from the Vietnam War, of which he had long been a critic, ended the military draft, and normalized relations with North Vietnam, North Korea, and the People's Republic of China.

The Labor government under Whitlam's innovative leadership lasted only three years. The high cost of his welfare measures aroused resentment, particularly in business circles. The government faced a projected $4-billion deficit, the inflation rate was 14 percent, and unemployment was nearly 5 percent, a high figure for Australia. The abrupt demise of the Whitlam ministry was attended by a constitutional crisis. In October 1975 the Australian Senate, where the conservatives had a majority, for the first time in the Commonwealth's history, refused to pass the government's budget bill. Then the governor-general took the unprecedented and perhaps unconstitutional step of dismissing the prime minister. The governor-general's "coup" was greeted with public consternation. Labor staged strikes and mass rallies in protest. Some voices demanded a new constitution to clarify the relationship between prime minister and ceremonial head of state. Rumors of outside interference circulated, fueled by the knowledge that the U.S. government regarded Whitlam as a threat to its security interests. Nevertheless, in the national election of 1975 the conservative coalition of Liberal and Country parties won by a landslide. The new prime minister, Malcolm Frazer, a wealthy farmer, promised to combat inflation, cut welfare spending, and restore business confidence.

After more than seven years of rule by the conservative Liberal-Country coalition, the Labor party returned to power in the spring of 1983 under its vivacious leader Robert Hawke. Labor had promised to reexamine the joint U.S.–Australia communications posts, but Hawke, after assuming office, seemed disinclined to jeopardize relations with the United States. An abiding domestic problem was the plight of the indigenous black population, intensified by the fact that an influx of Asian immigrants was introducing new minority groups. Largely unemployed, the aborigines show the demoralizing effects of cultural uprooting and economic deprivation. Their life expectancy is twenty years below the average for the population. Belatedly the nation has acknowledged the injustice of its historic racial policy. Prime Minister Hawke proposed a "treaty" to assist in the recovery of the rights of aborigines, and the Minister for Aboriginal Affairs suggested the creation of separate parliaments for blacks. Meanwhile the aborigines (numbering only about 250,000) are divided over the conflicting goals of assimilation into white society or revitalizing their ancient but sorely eroded culture.

3. THE DOMINION OF NEW ZEALAND

Located about 1,100 miles southeast of Australia, New Zealand was also discovered by the Dutch but explored and claimed for the British by Captain James Cook. At the time of discovery (1769) it was inhabited exclusively by Maoris, an intelligent but warlike people of Polynesian stock. For three-quarters of a century thereafter the only white settlers were missionaries, who labored with modest success to convert the Maoris to Christianity. In 1840 the first boatload of British colonists entered the harbor of what is now Wellington. They had been sent out by the New Zealand Company, founded by Edward Gibbon Wakefield, leader of the new British school of systematic colonizers. While completing a prison term for abducting a schoolgirl heiress, Wakefield came to the conclusion that Britain would be engulfed by civil war unless new economic opportunities could be found for the distressed population of its industrial cities. Caught in the maelstrom of depression and unemployment, workers by the thousands were turning to Chartism and sundry varieties of socialism. A conflict with the privileged classes was inevitable. Eventually Wakefield hit upon the idea that colonization would banish the specter of civil war. The company he founded would transport selected colonists to New Zealand. They would be provided with land at prices sufficiently high to prevent easy acquisition. Only the more prosperous and enterprising colonists would attain the status of owners. The others would have to content themselves for years with jobs as farm laborers. In time they too would buy land, and the proceeds from the sale would be used to finance further immigration.

Discovery and settlement

Wakefield's scheme attracted so much attention that the British government decided to take action. A governor was appointed, and the islands were formally annexed to the British Empire. The announced purpose was to protect the Maoris against unscrupulous white settlers. A week after the first colonists landed at Wellington the newly appointed governor arrived. He proceeded to negotiate a treaty with the native chiefs recognizing the sovereignty of the British Crown over all New Zealand. In return the British guaranteed to the Maoris full possession of their lands, "except as the Crown might wish to purchase them," and granted to the natives the rights and privileges of British subjects. Perhaps it was well that the government acted as it did, for a broadening stream of colonists continued to flow to the islands. By 1856 New Zealand had a white population of 45,000.

Annexation to the British Empire

In 1852 the British government endowed New Zealand with a

constitution. It conferred the executive power upon a governor-general representing the king, and acting with the advice of an Executive Council. Legislative authority was vested in a House of Representatives elected by the people and a Legislative Council appointed by the governor-general. In 1856 the Executive Council was formally recognized as a cabinet, exercising its functions under the principle of responsible government, and in 1951 the appointive upper house was abolished. Other steps in the direction of political democracy came easily. In 1879 universal manhood suffrage was adopted, and a few years later plural voting was abolished. In 1893 New Zealand led the Commonwealth of Nations in bestowing the suffrage upon women in national elections.

Economic reform followed in the wake of political democracy. When the Liberals came into power in 1891 they dedicated their efforts to making New Zealand a nation of small, independent farmers and herdsmen. Measures were adopted to break up large holdings, the formation of which had previously been encouraged by the sale of Maori lands to wealthy individuals. To combat the power of the big landowners required the support not only of landless agriculturists but also of workers in the cities. The Liberals therefore espoused a program of combined agrarian and labor reform which won the allegiance of both classes. The agrarian measures took the form primarily of special taxes on land held for speculative purposes and limitation of the size of holdings in the future. For the benefit of the workers the Liberals provided old-age pensions, factory inspection, regulation of working hours, and compulsory arbitration of industrial disputes. The accession of the Labor party to power in 1935 brought an extension of these measures, with increased benefits to the urban workers.

New Zealand has followed policies of collectivization quite similar to those of Australia. The reasons also have been similar. Lacking the capital to take advantage of new inventions, especially the railroad and the telegraph, the Dominion turned to foreign sources. Money proved to be more easily obtainable when the government itself was the borrower. Moreover, there was a deeply rooted fear among the colonists themselves of private monopoly. The beginning of collectivism occurred about 1870, when the Dominion government entered the London capital market for funds to construct roads, trunk railways, and telegraph lines. About the same time a state life-insurance system was established, and later state fire and accident insurance. A few coal mines also were added to the list of public enterprises, and finally a Bank of New Zealand. Important as a principle of collectivization has been the use of state-owned enterprises for "yardstick" purposes. Government purchase of coal mines, for example, was dictated by the theory that private companies needed the restraint of state competition to keep them from charging excessive prices.

The construction of a welfare state coincided with several years of prosperity, during which New Zealand enjoyed a comfortable position within the Commonwealth and increasingly close relations with the United States. Economic reverses following the Second World War brought changes both domestically and in external relations. The oil crisis of the 1970s struck at the same time as Great Britain's entry into the European Common Market, a step depriving the dominions of their privileged trade position. New Zealand's exports to the British Isles dropped from 70 percent (1950) to 9 percent (1988). Britain's "offshore farm" was forced to seek new markets in the Middle East and, with greater success, in Japan. In a time of rising inflation New Zealanders found that higher taxes were required to pay for the state-administered benefits they were accustomed to. Fifty years after its first accession to power the Labor party sharply altered its direction under David Lange, who became prime minister in 1984. Externally Lange reversed the policy of close support of the United States; domestically he attempted to shift the country from a socialist to a market economy, abolishing tariffs, reducing subsidies, slashing income-tax rates, and selling state-operated enterprises. Such departures—paralleling the conservative current in Britain, the United States, and elsewhere but an abrupt break with New Zealand traditions—became unpopular when they failed to restore prosperity or reduce unemployment while creating alarming disparities in income distribution within a society that had prided itself on equality. By contrast, general public support greeted Lange's decidedly anti-Conservative foreign policy, dramatized by his barring of U.S. nuclear-armed vessels from New Zealand harbors, a move that caused the canceling of joint naval exercises in February 1985. The Washington administration retaliated by refusing to share intelligence information, excluding New Zealand from ANZUS meetings, and snubbing the prime minister when he visited Washington in April 1989. Undaunted, the Dominion parliament in 1987 passed a Nuclear Free Zone Disarmament and Arms Control Act. The new Labor leader, Geoffrey Palmer, who became prime minister in August 1989, while not repudiating Lange's antinuclear stance, sought to improve relations with the United States. The government's exclusion of nuclear cargoes reflected uneasiness over the military ties that placed both New Zealand and Australia in the path of a potential holocaust and also the determination of a tiny nation—with a population about the size of that of Philadelphia—to assert its own identity.

Geographically, New Zealand has a wide margin of superiority over Australia. Although a mountainous region, with peaks that rise to 12,000 feet, extends the entire length of the southern island, there are no deserts and few areas unsuited to agriculture or grazing. Almost everywhere rainfall is adequate and permits an intensive use of the land. North Island, which contains over 60 percent of the population, has an average of about 50 inches of rain annually. Throughout the Dominion temperatures fluctuate within a comparatively narrow range. Extremes of over 100 degrees or below zero have never been

Dramatic policy revision at home and abroad

David Lange, Prime Minister of New Zealand, 1984–1989. The Labor prime minister set New Zealand on a new independent course in the international arena.

Comparison of New Zealand and Australia

recorded, and in both islands 75 degrees is considered unpleasantly high and 40 degrees uncomfortably low. Such favorable geographic conditions have given to New Zealand a character quite different from that of Australia. For one thing, the distribution of population is much more even. Instead of a few large cities along the seacoast and an almost unoccupied hinterland, there are hundreds of towns of moderate size and only a few cities exceeding 100,000. The mean density of population is slightly over 15 persons per square mile compared with 2 for Australia. Geography, more than anything else, has made New Zealand a democracy of small, independent agrarians.

New Zealand: Independent in international affairs but British at its core

New Zealanders, like Australians, have felt an increasing American influence, especially noticeable in popular culture. For example, by 1986 more than 40 percent of the New Zealand Broadcasting Corporation's television programs were of American origin. But accusations that New Zealand as well as Australia are allowing their culture to be vulgarized through the indiscriminate adoption of Americanisms would seem overdrawn. Although New Zealand has shown a determination to chart its own course in international relations, it seeks to preserve its traditional British character. Early immigrants brought with them not merely the social customs and political institutions, but also the flowers, trees, and birds of their native Britain. New Zealand was populated in considerable measure by people coming from landless and unemployed elements of Britain, by people of liberal and even radical tendencies who were often infected with Chartism and even traces of socialism, and, as a consequence, by people who developed institutions of political and economic democracy surpassing those of the mother country.

Troubles in paradise

Despite its hospitable environment and natural beauty, New Zealand is not the trouble-free paradise pictured by some entranced visitors. It has begun to experience problems, especially economic ones, shared by most of the rest of the world. The country has rich pastoral resources, but its exports of high-quality butter, lamb, and wool have not earned enough to prevent an adverse trade balance, and the national debt has grown at a formidable rate. Another source of anxiety is an influx of immigrants from South and Southeast Asia—Chinese, Indians, Vietnamese, Cambodians, and Polynesians—changing a reputedly homogeneous and equalitarian society into a multiethnic and stratified one. The native Maoris, who had lived in relative harmony with the white community for more than a century, have begun to press for greater rights.

4. INDIA UNDER COMPANY AND CROWN

A British aristocrat and Convervative member of Parliament, who died only fifteen years before India achieved independence, once declared, "We did not conquer India for the benefit of the Indians. . . .

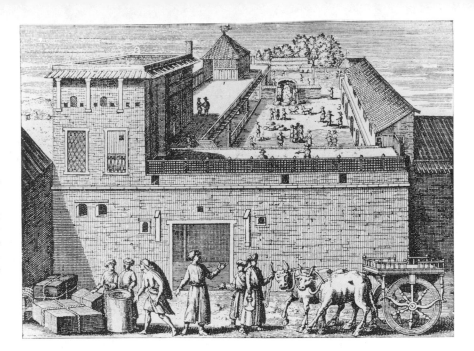

The Modest Beginning of British Rule in India. An early "factory" or trading station, with a walled enclosure containing a warehouse, promenade area, and church. From a copper engraving.

We conquered India by the sword and by the sword we shall hold it. We hold it as the finest outlet for British goods."[4]

From the beginning and throughout its course the history of British India is marked by paradox and contradictions. Britain's original contacts with India were incidental to efforts to obtain and market luxury products from the islands of eastern Asia—the fabulous "Indies." In securing outposts on the subcontinent of India in the seventeenth century, the British had no intention either of colonizing or of ruling territories. Their chief motive was trade, not primarily the export of European goods but the import of silks, jewels, and other precious commodities from India. Gradually and quite unsystematically, trading posts were transformed into centers of political administration. The absorption of native states, even though it ultimately involved large-scale military operations, was initiated not by the British government but by the British East India Company—a privately owned joint-stock corporation chartered by the crown and only belatedly subjected to effective control by Parliament.

The unanticipated assumption by the East India Company of sovereignty over territories penetrated by its agents created a need for efficient administration, a need that was not met promptly or adequately. In the early days Company agents had been selected without regard to their knowledge of Indian affairs (proficiency in Latin and Greek literature was considered much more important), and most of the agents did not remain in India long enough to become well acquainted with the country or its people. There was little uniformity in the administration of the separate British holdings, although the acquisition

India as a British market

Trading centers transformed into centers of political administration

The British East India Company as sovereign

[4] William Joynson-Hicks. Quoted in R. Palme Dutt, *The Problem of India*, p. 112.

Tipu's Tiger. Wooden model of a tiger mauling a British East India Company officer. This monstrosity (fitted inside with a bellows and miniature organ pipes to simulate groans) was made for Sultan Tipu, ruler of Mysore. Tipu was defeated and killed by Governor Wellesley's troops in 1799.

of the great province of Bengal (by Robert Clive, in 1757) made Calcutta eventually the Company's most important center of administration. Furthermore, the governing body of the Company, the Court of Directors in London, was so far away that its members could not be adequately informed as to what was going on in India. The governors, sent out as servants of the Company, in practice often modified or even formulated its policies. They negotiated treaties with native rulers, fought wars, and annexed territories.

Changes in the status of the Company

An act of Parliament in 1814, which renewed the Company's charter for twenty years, threw open the commerce of India to all British subjects but allowed the Company to retain its monopoly in China and East Asia. By 1834 free-trade sentiment had become so influential in England that the Charter Act of that year deprived the Company of all its trading privileges, except for the shipment of opium to China. Since it had originally been founded for the purpose of engaging in trade and had now lost that function altogether, the British East India Company might logically have expired in 1834. Instead of doing so, it was permitted to continue administering patronage in the British portions of India, serving as a governmental agency although ultimately subject to parliamentary check. Furthermore, to satisfy the English stockholders, dividends of the Company were fixed by law at 10½ percent annually, to be derived no longer from the profits of commerce but levied as a permanent charge upon the revenues of India.

Expansion and conquest

British territorial expansion inevitably led to conflicts with states beyond the Indian borders. Two Burmese wars made possible the annexation of Lower Burma (1852) and gave the British control of the Bay of Bengal. Less fortunate for the British was their intervention in the independent state of Afghanistan in 1838–1839. Out of an invading force of 16,000 troops only one man escaped death or capture. But this fiasco was a prelude to the conquest and annexation of the Indian state of Sind. The British had used neutral Sind as a military base during the Afghan war, and shortly thereafter, without the formality of a declaration of war, dispatched troops to depose the ruling princes. After two wars against the strong Sikh kingdom in the northwest of India, the governor-general, acting on his own responsibility, annexed the Punjab in 1849. Within the span of a century and through physical conquest of only portions of India, including the seacoasts, the British had established a strategic ring encircling the subcontinent. Thereafter, by befriending or intimidating the independent states of the interior (numbering more than 500), they were able to maintain their paramount position. For another 100 years British India remained the richest prize of empire—the "jewel in the crown."

Because of widely differing conditions in the sections of India occupied by the British, administrative systems imposed by the Company varied from province to province. In Bengal a "permanent land settlement" made with the *zamindars*—local landlords and revenue collectors—locked in at a set figure the government's annual land revenue, allowing the *zamindars* to profit excessively from any rise in agricultural productivity. In most of northern, southern, and western India, tax settlements were made directly with peasants or with peasant associations, and provided for periodic land surveys and reassessment. In every case the land tax became the most important source of government revenue under the Company and later under the crown, producing more than half of total receipts by the mid-nineteenth century.

Diverse administrative systems and the land tax

Shortly after the midpoint of the nineteenth century a military uprising known to the British as the Great Mutiny presented a serious challenge to the British presence in India. The uprising was the culmination of resentment engendered by highhanded acts of the governor-general—notably the annexation of several hitherto independent Indian states—and a series of governmental decisions reflecting incredible insensitivity to the feelings of the subject population. Ill-founded but inflammatory rumors spread the fear that European missionaries were conspiring with the government to coerce both Hindus and Muslims to convert to Christianity. The rebellion, which began on May 9, 1857, with sepoy troops (Indian mercenaries) stationed near Delhi, caught the British completely by surprise. These indigenous recruits, greatly outnumbering their British officers, had been so carefully selected, drilled, and imbued with pride in their regiments that the Company relied on them to fight its wars, complacently assuming that they would remain loyal even in the face of mistreatment or insult. There was a rude awakening as rebel forces advanced to Delhi and within a few weeks seized control of most of the Gangetic Plain, India's heartland. The Anglo-Indian war, which necessitated the dispatching of British regular troops, was fierce and bitter, marked by atrocities on both sides. In revenge for the slaughter of English prisoners

The Anglo-Indian war of 1857–58

at Cawnpore, British troops wiped out entire villages and executed captives by shooting them from the mouth of a cannon. Not until the latter part of 1858 was the rebellion crushed and British authority restored. In spite of its intensity, the fighting was confined largely to the northern parts of British India, and most of the independent princes remained neutral, if only because they respected the superiority of British arms.

Disunity and the collapse of the rebellion

Although the armed struggle of 1857–1858 was more than a mutiny, it was less than a revolution or a national war of independence. Rebel leaders were divided in their objectives. A Muslim faction, dreaming of restoring the great Mughal empire, actually placed on the throne at Delhi the dynastic heir—an old man with little stomach for the role thrust upon him (he was later exiled and his sons butchered). One Hindu group sought to restore a Maratha principality. Leaders of the various factions were united only in their resentment toward or hatred of the British. Sikhs from the Punjab—seemingly more quick to forgive the British for annexing their kingdom than to forgive the Bengal sepoys for helping in the conquest—fought with the British during the closing stages of the war and provided valuable military support in future conflicts. The collapse of the rebellion of 1857–1858 marked the end of any lingering dynastic ambitions that might challenge British rule, but victory came at an enormous price. It had left a wall of fear and hatred between British and Indians and destroyed bridges of communication capable of promoting mutual understanding. bridges that would be difficult to restore.

An important result of the mutiny was the termination of the East India Company and the transfer of full responsibility for the govern-

View of Lucknow (North Central India) in the Wake of Heavy Fighting between Indian Mutineers and British Forces in 1858. Lucknow, Cawnpore, and Delhi were the three main centers of the Great Mutiny, 1857–1858

ment of India to the British crown and parliament.[5] The Government of India Act of 1858 created a secretary of state for India with an advisory council to assist him and bestowed upon the governor-general the title of viceroy. There was no immediate change in the details of the administrative system, but a royal proclamation issued by Queen Victoria offered conciliatory assurances in regard to religious toleration, material improvements, and the admission of native Indians to government service.

After 1858, in contrast to the earlier period, the policy of the British government in India was one of caution and conservatism. To minimize the danger of rebellion in the future, the bulk of the people were disarmed and the army was reorganized. The recruited troops were grouped in accordance with sectarian, tribal, or local divisions so that there would be little feeling of common interest among the different units. Although Europeans formed a minority of the military personnel, they monopolized the ranks of commissioned officers and retained possession of the heavy artillery. At the same time the government sought to avoid antagonizing any powerful element or prejudice within the population. Notably, the British authorities refrained from further territorial aggression. By treaties with the remaining native princes, the British government guaranteed to these rulers their hereditary rights and possessions but required them to relinquish all control over external affairs. Henceforth a clear division was maintained between the five or six hundred native states and the British provinces. The states ranged in size from Hyderabad—with an area almost equal to that of Great Britain—to tiny principalities, and included altogether about 40 percent of the land area of India. A few of the rulers were more progressive than the British, but most of them were uninspiring survivals from an age of despotism, quite content to enjoy the protection of the "paramount" power, Great Britain.

While the government sought to preserve the status quo, changes were taking place within Indian society, stimulated by the British presence. Many Christian missionaries decried the poverty, ignorance, and suffering afflicting the lives of the lower classes. Recognition of the necessity for reform, together with fear that missionary activity might endanger the Hindu religion prompted educated upper-class Hindus to organize societies dedicated to change. Most influential of these was the Brahmo Samaj, a monotheistic sect founded in 1828 by Ram Mohan Roy of Calcutta. Roy visualized religion as a constructive social force. He affirmed that Christ's teachings, which he regarded as "better adapted toward the use of rational beings than any other"— were latent in the Hindu heritage and that a purified Hinduism could be an instrument for elevating the condition of society. Other Hindu

Raja Ram Mohan Roy (1770–1833). Dubbed "the Founder of Modern India" by his countrymen, the founder of Brahmo Samaj defied Hindu orthodoxy in the cause of social reform and promoted constructive British-Indian intercourse.

---

[5] The Company stockholders were still treated with tender consideration. The guaranteed annual dividends of 10½ percent continued to be paid until 1874, at which time the stock was redeemed by a government purchase in the amount of £12,000,000.

organizations, reactionary in outlook, sought to preserve traditional beliefs and institutions. The government, fearful of being accused of interfering with religion, made little attempt to promote social reform, although it had outlawed the cruel custom of widow burning (suttee) as early as 1829.

In the area of education the British government did acknowledge a responsibility. By the late eighteenth century a number of European scholars had mastered Sanskrit and incidentally had made the exciting discovery that the languages of northern India—ancient and modern— were branches of one great family of languages embracing Persian, classical Greek and Latin, and most of the modern European tongues. In 1784 Sir William Jones, a linguistic genius and admirer of India's cultural heritage, founded the Asiatic Society of Bengal, which began the translation of Sanskrit classics into English. Conceivably, a system of popular education employing the vernacular languages could have been devised with the twin aims of combating illiteracy and making contemporary generations more fully cognizant of their country's history and literature. But the liberal utilitarian school of thought that was gaining ascendancy in England in the early nineteenth century impelled the government in a different direction from that marked out by the "Orientalists." James Mill (died 1836), an administrator of India House in London, firmly believed that instruction in English, natural science, and the principles of democratic government was essential in order to bring India into the family of progressive societies. Mill's associate, Lord Macaulay, the famous essayist and historian, condemned Hindu literature as nothing but "false history, false astronomy, false metaphysics, false religion." In 1833 the government announced its decision to devote all educational funds henceforth to instruction solely in the English language.

Although the British made no effort to develop a comprehensive program of public education, by establishing a number of universities they were able to create an elite class of English-speaking and Western-oriented Indians. Contrary to the optimistic hope of James Mill, the result was not a step toward a democratic society. Intellectually alienated from their own people, university graduates could find only limited opportunities to employ their talents. If they were accepted for government service it was at the lowest level. Typically, the English conception of an educated Indian was not that of an emancipated working partner but of a faithful, efficient, and subservient *babu* (clerk). The British were slow to realize the paradoxical situation they were creating by exposing their Indian subjects to a history and literature illuminated by a struggle for freedom, individual dignity, and self-government. The attempt to "raise a race of administrators on the language of revolt" was bound eventually to undermine the foundations of an authoritarian alien rule.

Initially Indian Muslims, resentful of the conquests that had swept away Muslim sovereignties, stayed aloof from contact with the British.

Shunning the opportunity offered for acquiring secular Western-style learning, they consequently lagged far behind Hindus in securing government posts. A leader of a movement to reverse this situation was Sayyid Ahmad Khan. Born to a family with ties to the Mughal court at Delhi, Sayyid early realized the necessity for his coreligionists to accommodate themselves both to British rule and to the impact of Western culture. In 1875, over the objections of conservative Muslims, he founded Aligarh University, offering a broad curriculum embracing Western learning. In contrast to the government schools, Aligarh sought to combine secular scientific education with the Islamic religious heritage. In the wake of the "Aligarh Movement" an elite class of educated Muslims arose. This was, on the whole, more inclined than its Hindu counterpart to support the British government in times of crisis.

The Muslim response to the British presence: the "Aligarh Movement"

Sayyid Ahmad Kahn (1817–1898). A Muslim counterpart to the Hindu Roy, Sayyid Ahmad Kahn established the Aligarh movement in an effort to ensure that his Islamic Indian world would come to terms with Western civilization while maintaining its own vitality.

The physical changes effected in India during the last century of British occupation were enormous. Modern communications were introduced, including a network of railroads rising from 34 miles of track in 1854 to 35,000 miles sixty years later. Irrigation works were constructed sufficient to provide for thirty million acres of land. The curbing of internal warfare, together with better sanitation and medical facilities provided by the British, stimulated a phenomenal expansion of population. The number of people rose from 150 million in 1850 to 250 million in 1881. By 1921 it exceeded 300 million, and another 50 million was added by 1945.

Almost all the improvements, however, had their darker side. The rapid increase in population depressed the living conditions of large numbers of the people, and the problem of an adequate food supply was never solved. Severe famines had been known in India long before the British arrived, but some of the worst occurred during the period of British control. Ironically, the proclamation of Queen Victoria as empress of India in 1877 coincided with the greatest famine in India's history, which took a toll of 5 million lives. It is estimated that between 1877 and 1900 no fewer than 15 million people died of famine. A basic cause of these disasters was the fact that a majority of the population lived close to the starvation level even in normal times and had no savings and no reserves of physical stamina to carry them through an emergency.

Although British rule did not introduce poverty into India, it did little to alleviate it. Excessive taxation had been known before, but in contrast to the situation under earlier empires, much of the revenue raised was drained out of India—in salaries to the higher administrative officials and to European army officers, in dividends to the East India Company stockholders, and in interest on the public debt, most of which was held by Englishmen. Not only did taxation bear too heavily upon the poorest classes but only a small fraction of the government's budget was allotted to relief, social welfare, or education. The major portion was expended on the police, the courts, and especially the

Inequities in the system of taxation

Indian army, a professional body which was sometimes used in imperial wars outside of India—in Afghanistan, Burma, or China. In spite of the introduction of sanitation measures, the Indian death rate remained appallingly high, augmented by such diseases as cholera, malaria, and bubonic plague, which can be controlled by modern medical science and have been almost eliminated in Western countries.

Other evils of economic policy

One aspect of British rule in India open to criticism was its economic policy. In the early days of the East India Company there had been a great demand for Indian handmade goods of superior quality, especially silks, cottons, and muslins, which were generally paid for in specie. With the coming of the Industrial Revolution in England, the character of its Asian commerce changed. The British became interested in India as a source of raw materials and, even more, as a market for manufactured goods. The Indians were forced to accept "free trade" as applied to British manufactures but were effectively denied the right to export their own manufactures either to England or other countries. An inevitable result of this policy was the decline of village handicrafts which had for centuries constituted a vital element in the whole Indian economy. During the period of British rule, in spite of the growth of some large cities, the proportion of India's population dependent on the land for sustenance actually increased, until by the opening of the twentieth century it constituted more than 80 percent of the total. Excessive ruralization, small tenant holdings, oppressive taxes, and the unchecked extortions of moneylenders go far to explain why India remained a land of poverty and famine. The introduction of factory industries in the late nineteenth century offered a new source of employment, but only for a tiny fraction of the population. An oversupply of labor kept wages extremely low, and the sordid conditions of English mill towns during the early Industrial Revolution were repeated and far exceeded in India.

The Indian Civil Service

Indian response to the British presence was ambivalent and varied. In the course of the nineteenth century a curious love-hate relationship developed between the two peoples. Beginning in the 1880s Indians were allowed to compete in examinations for the selection of civil servants, but the examinations were held in London and few Indians could afford the expense of travel. Because the supply of university graduates greatly exceeded the demand for personnel, an attitude of subservience was engendered in those lucky enough to find employment. The Indian Civil Service, because of the efficiency, integrity, and loyalty of its members, became a source of pride to the British, who rightly regarded it as a bulwark of their authority. At the same time it was producing a corps of trained and experienced administrators which, although obedient to a foreign master, had closer ties to the subject peoples.

Perversely, while association between British and Indians was becoming closer and more extensive, the British attitude of superiority seemed to stiffen. In contrast to the early days of conquest when

The Great Durbar at Delhi, 1903. This spectacular coronation celebration in honor of Great Britain's King Edward VII was designed by Lord Curzon as a visible sign of an ideal pattern of empire.

English adventurers often fraternized with, intermarried with, and admired the arts of the local inhabitants, after the Mutiny of 1857 British residents generally held themselves aloof from such social contacts. They barred Indians from their clubs and subjected them to various humiliations. Resident British families, isolating themselves from their surroundings, affected an imperial life-style requiring gentlemen to dress formally for dinner and ladies to stifle themselves in the many-layered garments decreed by Victorian fashion. Undoubtedly the resurgence of European imperialism in the late nineteenth century contributed to this attitude of disdainful hauteur. In the renewed struggle for colonies during the 1870s and 1880s Great Britain again acquired the lion's share, and many Englishmen saw this as a proof of divine favor and England's unique destiny. Pseudo-Darwinian doctrines, proclaiming the superiority of master races, were used to rationalize the conquest of "backward" regions. Eloquent spokesmen called upon Britain to shoulder the "white man's burden," to rule over and thus bring enlightenment to "lesser breeds without the law."

The resurgence of the imperialistic impulse and the cult of British superiority

In the closing stages of the era of British occupation, British objectives for India were at cross-purposes. While the government acknowledged its role as the preparation of India for eventual self-rule, most Britishers wished to retain the fruits of empire. The ultimate paradox lay in the fact that the country that had given the world the finest example of progress from absolutism to democracy had also emerged as the giant of imperialism. History provides no clearer illustration of the incompatibility of imperialism with the goals of democracy.

The paradox of democracy and imperialism

The resentment harbored by subjection to foreign rule, combined with a growing awareness of the possibility for change, eventually gave rise to a nationalist movement in India. With the possible exception of the era of the Maurya dynasty in the third century B.C., India had never been unified politically, not even under the powerful Mughal empire of the sixteenth and seventeenth centuries, and it lacked both a homogeneous population and a common culture. Deep social cleavages presented formidable obstacles to the cultivation of a common allegiance or a sense of national identity. Differences in language, ethical and cultural tradition, and especially religion, together with the deeply rooted caste system separated communities rather than creating bonds between them. The concept of the nation-state was of European origin, and a relatively recent phenomenon even among Europeans. To Indian Muslims it posed special problems. The Islamic political ideal was not a territorial state but a community of true believers, wherever located, directed by the custodians of the sacred law. In strict theory the faithful Muslim was enjoined to flee from the jurisdiction of an infidel ruler, although in India obviously an accommodation had been reached. In fact, as a political movement led by Hindus gained momentum Muslims tended to look to the British Raj for protection, although many individuals joined with Hindus in the struggle for independence. Considering the obstacles in its path, nationalism might never have progressed far had not British rule given it impetus and the framework within which it could develop.

The genesis of a political movement embracing the idea of nationalism is customarily dated from the founding of the Indian National Congress in 1885. Not the first organization attempting to unite broad segments of the population, it eventually eclipsed the others and absorbed most of them. Ironically, the organization that finally led the struggle for independence from British rule was founded by an Englishman, Allan O. Hume, a retired senior officer of the Indian Civil Service, who served as General Secretary of the Congress during the first twenty-one years of its existence. More progressive in his views than most contemporary English liberals, Hume looked forward to India eventually becoming a self-governing dominion like Canada.

During its early years the Indian National Congress scarcely deserved its name. Composed of a handful of European and Indian intellectuals, it lacked a national constituency, did not legislate or formulate a program of action, and gave little intimation of the powerful political force it was to become. The original members were an educated elite drawn mainly from the wealthy landowning class. With the rise of large-scale industry in the late nineteenth century some bourgeois capitalists were attracted to membership, giving Congress the backing of two powerful interest groups—agricultural and industrial—a combination capable of influencing public policy. But while gaining sufficient confidence to address the government, Congress scrupulously avoided any demand for social reform, lest it alienate the classes from which it drew its support.

The First Meeting of the India National Congress, December 1885, in Bombay. This initial session was attended by seventy-three men, including several Englishmen, representing every province of British India. Welcomed by British colonial officials at its inception, the Congress was to become the main instrument of the movement for independence.

Failure of the Congress to deal with the problems of poverty and social injustice led to tension between "moderates" and "extremists" and threatened to split the organization. Far from being revolutionaries, the "extremists" sought change within the existing political framework rather than its overthrow. Nevertheless, their relatively mild demands were sufficiently alarming to authorities to cause some of them to be imprisoned or deported. High-handed actions of the viceroy, Lord Curzon, who in 1905 partitioned the great province of Bengal (an act reversed a decade later), fueled the passions of the progressive or radical Congress faction. By the opening of the twentieth century Congress leaders, though still hopeful of cooperation with the British Raj, freely criticized public policy and to some extent assumed the role of a loyal opposition.

Tensions within an increasingly assertive Congress

British response to growing unrest in the country and growing assertiveness by the Indian National Congress oscillated between conciliatory gestures and repression. Successive acts of Parliament authorized the viceroy and the provincial governors to appoint Indian members to their councils, and following a reform act of 1909 the Indian representatives were made elective, but by an extremely limited franchise which embodied the principle of separate electorates for Muslims and Hindus.

The British response

During the First World War the professed aims of Britain and her

Indian support of Britain in the First World War

allies kindled the hope of constitutional change among Indian national-ists. India made substantial contributions to the war effort, furnishing troops and vast supplies of raw materials, foodstuffs, and even manufac-tures as cotton, jute, and steel production was intensified. The coopera-tive attitude of Britain's Indian subjects reflected the belief that a British victory would bring benefits to the world's colonial areas and generous political reforms in India. In 1917 Edwin Montagu, secretary of state for India, announced in the House of Commons that England's policy toward India was "the increasing association of Indians in every branch of the administration and the gradual development of self-governing institutions with a view to . . . responsible government as an integral part of the British Empire."

Disillusionment in postwar India; the Government of India Act of 1919

Although the close of the war found India in a state of high expecta-tion, the prevailing mood quickly changed to disappointment. The period was one of widespread suffering, caused by inflated prices, a severe famine, and the ravages of disease, including an influenza epi-demic that wiped out thirteen million people in 1918–1919. The politi-cal reforms embodied in the Government of India Act of 1919 fell far short of responsible government. The franchise was still restricted to a tiny minority of property owners numbering about 3 percent of the population of British India, and the electorate was further divided by granting separate representation not only to religious communities but also to landowners and other special-interest groups.

British repression: the Amritsar Massacre

Disappointment with the Act of 1919 swelled to anger as the govern-ment adopted a policy of harsh repression to forestall any popular uprising. The climax of this punitive policy was the Amritsar Massacre of April 13, 1919. Brigadier-General Dyer, sent to Amritsar in the Punjab to halt rioting, ordered his troops to fire into an unarmed crowd trapped in an enclosure to which he barred the exit. Almost four hundred people were killed and more than a thousand wounded. Though Dyer was subsequently relieved of his command he received no other punishment and English admirers raised a purse in his behalf. The shock of this cold-blooded butchery and the indulgent attitude of the government toward those responsible for it turned into enemies many former supporters of Britain, including the poet and educator Rabindranath Tagore, who returned the commission of knighthood with which he had been honored.

A more aggressive Indian National Congress; the Nehrus and Mohandas K. Gandhi

While the government's policy stiffened, it met a more aggressive challenge from the Indian National Congress, which now numbered among its members several leaders of broad and progressive outlook. Among these were Motilal Nehru and his son Jawaharlal, who risked their freedom and their comfortable position as members of a wealthy and influential brahman family to further the nationalist cause. Jawahar-lal (1889–1964), destined to become the first prime minister of inde-pendent India, had been educated in the best English schools, held a degree from Cambridge University, and reflected the impact of West-ern culture both in his personal tastes and in his political and social

Leaders of Indian Nationalism—Nehru and Gandhi. Gandhi was assassinated in 1948. Nehru served as Prime Minister of India from 1947 to his death in 1964.

goals. Most important of all from the standpoint of making the Congress a potent force, it had developed a disciplined structure, promotional techniques, and a vastly increased membership. The person most responsible for transforming the Congress from an elitist organization to one with a mass following was Mohandas K. Gandhi.

Gandhi was born in 1869 in a small native state on the western coast of India. He came from a middle-class family which had supplied prime ministers to the prince, and his mother, a pious Hindu, endeavored to instill in him fidelity to the traditions of their caste. His family sent him to England to study law, and after his return home he was offered a position with an Indian firm in South Africa, where he spent some twenty years and had a successful legal practice. His chief interest in South Africa, however, became a deep concern for the unfair treatment to which his countrymen were subjected in that color-conscious region. At the risk of his life and in disregard of insults and humiliation, he campaigned continually against economic and social discrimination, encouraging the timid Indian laborers to organize and calling upon the government to remove flagrant injustices.

Gandhi's experience in South Africa was of basic importance for his career as a nationalist leader. First, he worked with Hindus and Muslims drawn from different regions of India and predominantly from the lower strata of society. Second, in his contest with the government he developed a unique philosophy of social conflict and a technique for resolving it which he named *satyagraha*. More than "nonviolent resistance," by *satyagraha* ("soul-force" or "truth-force") Gandhi meant active and open resistance to evil and injustice without resort

The emergence of Gandhi

Gandhi's social philosophy

to violence, while at the same time attempting both to perfect one's own self-control and to convert the opponent to the cause of justice. Gandhi's philosophy and prescription for action were grounded in religious concepts, including emphatically those of Christianity. He also drew inspiration from the Russian Leo Tolstoy, the Englishman John Ruskin, and the American Henry David Thoreau. His invocation of religious teachings, the ascetic life-style he adopted, and his work for social betterment among poor Indian villagers caused him to be hailed as Mahatma ("great soul"), a title that he decried and tried to avoid. His distinct innovation lay in his attempt to make lofty moral principles work in the arena of politics, an arena more typically guided by the precepts of Machiavelli. And though this frail, saintly figure— contemptuously dismissed by Winston Churchill as "a half-naked fakir"—may have dreamed an impossible dream, he was able not only to arouse the populace but also to dominate the Congress, parley with viceroys, and bring consternation to bureaucrats in Whitehall.

The beginning of Hindu-Muslim cooperation

Upon Gandhi's return to India in 1914 he endorsed and urged support of Britain's military struggle, but the disappointing constitution of 1919 and the shocking Amritsar Massacre convinced him of the need to oppose the government. If India was to offer effective opposition it was essential for Hindus and Muslims to join together in a common effort. The prospect of cooperation between the two rival communities had brightened during the War of 1914–1918 as the British and their allies proceeded to overthrow the Ottoman Sultan-Caliph, theoretical head of all Islam. Grateful for Hindu support on the Khalifat (Caliphate) issue, many Muslims joined the Congress, and in the Lucknow Pact of 1916 Congress and Muslim leaders pledged mutual cooperation in the task of securing justice for India. Unfortunately, the spirit of unity was soon dispelled by mutual distrust.

Congress and the noncooperation movement of 1920–1922

Under the leadership of Gandhi, Congress in 1920 voted to launch a noncooperation program, calling for the boycott of government councils, courts, and educational institutions. The campaign, which Gandhi ended abruptly in 1922, was weakened by the lack of Muslim support and by division among the Hindu leaders, who feared that a popular uprising might jeopardize property interests. Though failing to alter government policy, the spectacle of thousands of unlettered humble folk courageously facing police attacks and imprisonment demonstrated the potential of *satyagraha* as a social and political weapon.

The objectives of Gandhi's domestic Constructive Program

The Noncooperation movement of 1920–1922 ended with Gandhi in prison. When released two years later, he withdrew temporarily from an active role in the Congress and during the later 1920s devoted himself to a domestic Constructive Program aiming to combat illiteracy and improve living conditions in the peasant villages where more than three-fourths of the people lived. Gandhi made himself the champion of the Untouchables, whom he called *Harijan,* or "children of God." His campaign on their behalf illustrates his tactic of relating an ideal goal to immediate and practical objectives. Full social acceptance of Untouchables was a necessary act of justice; but Gandhi also perceived that only by breaking the taboo against handling dirt and filth—traditionally the exclusive responsibility of the despised lowest class—could hygienic habits be instilled among the general population. Besides promoting better methods of land cultivation, Gandhi's Constructive Program included the ambitious goal of rehabilitating the ancient village economy which had long been in decay. To this end he urged the development of subsidiary industries, especially hand spinning and weaving. Whether traversing the countryside or spending quiet days in his *ashram* (disciplined community), established in one of the poorest regions of central India, Gandhi continued his "experiments with truth" (the title of his autobiography), searching for a key to a just and free society. In defining national goals he insisted on two basic principles: (1) the unity of Hindus and Muslims with full acceptance and respect on both sides, and (2) adherence to nonviolence as the only path to Indian autonomy or independence. Looking to the more distant future he asserted that Hinduism, of which he considered himself an adherent, must wipe out the stain of untouchability or itself disappear. Gandhi's social and economic views were simplistic and somewhat self-contradictory. In contrast to Nehru and many of his other close associates he rejected most of Western civilization as too materialistic. Although he adopted an ascetic life-style and championed the downtrodden, especially the Untouchables, he relied heavily on the wealthy for financial support. Rejecting the Marxist dogma of class conflict he called upon capitalists and landlords to hold their property as a trust and dedicate it to improving the well-being of the less fortunate—a proposal overly dependent on the benevolence of those best able but least inclined to implement it. For Gandhi India's independence meant freedom not only from foreign rule but also from foreign institutions and ideologies. His ideal was a nation of peaceful, autonomous, and largely self-sufficient villages—a Utopian anarchism. Not surprisingly, the Utopian vision receded as India drew closer to the achievement of statehood.

Returning to the political scene in 1930, Gandhi was again authorized by the Congress to launch a nonviolent, civil-disobedience campaign. Shrewdly he chose to defy the government's monopoly of salt manufacture and salt tax, which fell most heavily upon the poorest families. Passing through village after village he led a large body of followers on a "march to the sea," where they evaporated pans of seawater to make salt, thus breaking the law by a seemingly innocent act. While disregarding the moral challenge presented by defiance of the salt tax and the boycott of state liquor shops, and while paying no heed to defiant resolutions issuing from the Congress, the government attempted to negotiate with carefully selected individuals. In 1931 Gandhi was invited to attend as India's sole representative the second of three Round Table Conferences held in London. The conferences accomplished little except to reveal how wide was the gulf separating not only Indians and British but also the several Indian communities and factions.

The civil disobedience campaign of 1930

The Round Table Conference on the Indian Constitution in Session in London, 1931. Gandhi, the sole delegate from the Indian National Congress, sits at the chairman's left.

The Government of India Act of 1935

Reluctantly confronting the necessity of constitutional change, the British Cabinet in 1927 appointed a commission to formulate recommendations. Composed solely of members of the British parliament, the commission provoked angry protests in India. After several years of wrangling among Conservative and Liberal politicians, the British government enacted a new constitution for India, the Government of India Act of 1935—the longest statute in British history and one of the least memorable. The 1935 Act enlarged the franchise modestly in British India but pushed the device of separate electorates to excess. It granted provincial legislatures the right to manage internal affairs but subject to "discretionary powers" retained by the governors. Because it was weighted heavily on the side of property owners and because it envisioned an Indian federation in which the princely states would share power, it appeared designed as a bulwark of empire rather than a step toward genuine self-government.

The Muslim League; Mohammad Ali Jinnah

The new constitution was denounced by practically all articulate groups in India. The Indian National Congress nevertheless decided to test it by running candidates for office, and in the election of 1937 gained working majorities in seven of the eleven British provinces. Although the next two years witnessed the unprecedented spectacle of British bureaucrats executing the orders of Indian ministers, the brief episode of responsible parliamentary government was not wholly auspicious. The Congress ministries made no attempt to introduce social or economic reforms. They dealt severely with their critics, even invoking against them repressive measures established by the British. Still more damaging to the prospect of national unity, the strength and confidence displayed by the Congress ministries heightened fear among Muslims that, if India became independent, they might be subjected to the tyranny of a dominant Hindu majority.

A separate organization for Muslims, the Muslim League, for many years following its founding in 1905 had had few members and little influence. Gradually as communal tension increased, the Muslim League became a political party, claiming to speak for all Indian Muslims and capable of challenging the Indian National Congress. The individual most responsible for effecting this transformation was Mohammad Ali Jinnah (1887–1948). Jinnah came from a family of relatively recent converts to Islam, and his wife was a Parsee. A successful lawyer, Western educated, he was, in contrast to his opposite number, Gandhi, thoroughly secular in temperament. It is somewhat ironic that he became the head of a militant Islamic movement. Jinnah started his political career as a nationalist Muslim, an active member of the Indian National Congress, but he broke away during the 1920s to champion Muslim interests, asserting that these interests could be protected only by giving Muslims autonomy in any future political arrangement. As the goal of independence approached realization he advanced the claim that Indian Muslims constituted not merely a religious community but a distinct nation.

Mohammad Ali Jinnah

Muhammad Ali Jinnah, President of the Muslim League

The Second World War, like the First, focused attention upon the question of India's future. But in contrast to the situation during the earlier conflict, Indian nationalists were unwilling to rely on vague promises of reform in the future, and the British no longer held an unassailable position. The Congress declared that India would fight only as a free nation and demanded self-government with permission to draw up a new constitution. British officials refused to grant any immediate concessions, promising only to reconsider the 1935 constitution after the war and seemed unconcerned when the Congress provincial ministries resigned in protest and Gandhi launched a symbolic but ineffectual civil-disobedience campaign. Indian public opinion generally supported the war against the Axis powers, and India made very substantial contributions in troops and supplies to the Allied cause. It was not anything that Indians said or did but what the Japanese were doing that induced the government to reverse its stand. As Japanese armies swept across southeast Asia, occupied Burma, and threatened the borders of India, the London government saw the need to ensure closer collaboration. In March 1942 Sir Stafford Cripps, known as a friend to India, was dispatched to negotiate with the Congress leaders but under instructions that were restrictive and ambiguous. The mission was basically a public-relations ploy, and the "Cripps Offer" was rejected by the Congress. Nevertheless it put Great Britain on record as pledging dominion status or independence for India.

The Second World War and the "Cripps Offer"

Political developments in London at the close of the war facilitated the honoring of the pledge wrung from a reluctant Tory government. A Labour cabinet under Clement Attlee replaced the Churchill minis-

*The dilemma posed by the
Hindu-Muslim division
and the partition of India*

try, and in March 1946 Attlee announced that the choice of dominion status or complete independence would be India's alone. He sent a cabinet mission to work with Indian leaders in arranging the transfer of authority, and the deadline of June 1948 which Attlee set for Britain's departure from India was actually met almost a year sooner.

Although its final stages make the liquidation of the British Raj appear abrupt, it was in reality a process of gradual transition. not the product of climactic change or revolution. During the century preceding independence the relationship between India and Britain had been shifting dramatically. As India developed industry, increased exports, and established trade with other parts of the world, it became less valuable to Britain economically. For many years India's dependence on British imports had enabled Britain to redress the deficit in its trade with other countries. By the end of the Second World War positions were almost reversed. Britain drew so heavily upon Indian raw materials and manufactures that by 1946 it had contracted a debt in India of 1⅓ billion pounds sterling. Paralleling economic change, the long British rule had laid the political basis for an independent Indian nation. In spite of animosities and apparently contradictory goals, British and Indians had worked side by side to build a viable political structure for the subcontinent. Transfer of power was largely imperceptible but continuous. The Indian Civil Service became Indianized in personnel; so did the army, the police, even the courts and the higher professions. At the time of independence Indians could conceive of no other administrative system than the one they had learned from the British, and they continued it with only minor changes.

In the hour of Britain's departure the chief obstacle in the way of a united independent state was the debilitating conflict disrupting Indian society. The Indian National Congress, composed mostly of Hindus, claimed to represent a majority of the population, but the Muslim League had strengthened its position during the war by supporting the government while the Congress adopted a policy of noncooperation. In May 1946 the British cabinet mission presented a plan for a federation of three largely autonomous regions—one Hindu and two Muslim—with safeguards to protect minorities. This proposal, seeming to offer a reasonable compromise, was tentatively accepted by Congress and the League, but later each body rejected it, and when a constituent assembly met in December 1946 to draft a constitution the Muslim League refused to participate. Muslims under Jinnah were now demanding the right to form a separate state—Pakistan. Their claim was arguably consonant with Islamic tradition, but only recently had it been put forth as a political objective. Blame for failure to prevent the unfortunate partition of the subcontinent has been directed against all the parties involved—the Muslims, the Hindus, and the British, who, after a cautious and dilatory policy of some ninety years, seemed suddenly in a hurry to leave. It is probable that tempers had

Riot in Calcutta, 1946. A dead Hindu surrounded by Muslims armed with lathis. Such scenes were not uncommon on the eve of Indian independence, when extreme tension developed between Hindu and Muslim segments of the population.

become too inflamed to permit agreement on any form of political union. Seeing no other alternative, the new viceroy, Lord Mountbatten, prepared to transfer British sovereignty in India to two separate governments, a delicate and difficult operation. Not only were the Hindu and Muslim provinces separated, but three provinces—Bengal, the Punjab, and Assam—had to be split in order to prevent large Hindu minorities from being assigned to Pakistan. Although Pakistan did not include all the areas demanded by the Muslim League, the division was accepted by both sides in the controversy. Indian independence was formally granted by act of Parliament in July 1947, and in August all authority was surrendered to the two new dominions.

The official formalities inaugurating two new states were relatively painless; far more traumatic was the experience of people forced to accommodate to a drastically altered political pattern. Even before partition was completed, refugees began to stream across the new borders—Hindus and Sikhs fleeing from Muslim domination and Muslims fearing Hindu persecution. More than ten million people were involved in the mass exodus during the latter part of 1947, and the governments could not prevent the outrages committed by frenzied fanatics on both sides. The worst violence occurred in the Punjab, India's richest province, which had once been a Sikh kingdom embrac-

Violence in the wake of independence

ing most of the territory now assigned to Pakistan. The Sikhs, concentrated in the eastern half of the province, would probably have preferred to form an independent state, but India gave no support to such a proposal and Pakistan would have blocked it by force. When the western Punjab was assigned to Pakistan and the eastern half to India, the border became a slaughtering ground as Sikhs and Muslims murdered one another, taking a toll of half a million lives and leaving two million refugees.

The assassination and legacy of Gandhi

Gandhi's final service to India was an attempt to halt communal strife. By appealing to Hindus and threatening to fast he stopped riots in Calcutta. At Delhi early in 1948 he began a fast that ended when key spokesmen for the Congress pledged protection for the lives and property of Muslims. On January 30, on his way to evening prayers, Gandhi was shot and killed by a member of a chauvinistic Hindu society. The labors of the man who had contributed more than any other individual to India's struggle for freedom were not crowned with complete success. Independence had finally come, without revolution but not without violence. The opportunity for Hindu-Muslim unity, which Gandhi had made a cardinal objective, seemed to be lost forever. And while the Mahatma was venerated as a martyr and commemorated with a lavish tomb, his ethical code did not become the national norm or the determinant of state policy. Despite failures, however, Gandhi remains one of the outstanding personalities of the twentieth century. His influence has outlasted his lifetime and has been felt in lands far from his native India—as reflected in opposition to apartheid in South Africa and in Martin Luther King's nonviolent crusade for civil rights in the United States in the 1960s.

5. INDEPENDENT INDIA, PAKISTAN, AND BANGLADESH

Division and hostility on the Indian subcontinent

It was a tragic circumstance that the Indian struggle for independence should conclude with the country divided and in an atmosphere of hostility. The partition of India, from the standpoints of geography and economics, was highly artificial. Pakistan included the areas producing jute, cotton, and rice. India, with an insufficient food supply, had the factories needed to process Pakistan's raw materials. Important canals and river systems were bisected by the political boundaries. Nor did partition solve the minority problem. Approximately 15 percent of Pakistan's inhabitants are non-Muslims, chiefly Hindus. The Republic of India has a Muslim minority of approximately 11 percent.

The princely states; the Kashmir conflict

An immediate source of controversy between India and Pakistan was the disposition of the princely states. Since the states were no longer protected by the British Raj, it was assumed that they would voluntarily join either India or Pakistan. Most of them did so, the greater number of course going to India. The Indian government forcibly deposed the ruler of Hyderabad, claiming to act on behalf

Republic of India Declared. Prime Minister Jawaharlal Nehru moves the resolution for an independent sovereign republic before the constituent assembly in New Delhi in 1950.

of his Hindu subjects, and assumed the administration of this large Deccan state. But toward Kashmir, with a population predominantly Muslim, the New Delhi government applied a different logic, asserting that the ruling prince had the legal right to transfer sovereignty to India. The maharaja had hoped to remain independent, but when he appealed for help against invading Muslim tribesmen India demanded accession as the price of military aid. Invading troops from India and Pakistan clashed in Kashmir and a cease-fire agreement, arranged through a U.N. commission in 1949, left the principality divided into two parts, occupied respectively by Pakistan and India, with the larger under Indian control. This partition frustrated but could not extinguish an independence movement that persisted among the Kashmiri. Hostility between India and Pakistan, exacerbated by the Kashmir dispute, erupted into three full-scale wars during the first forty years following the end of British rule.

India retained the status of a dominion only until 1950, when a new constitution made it an independent republic, replacing the governor-general by an elected president and severing all ties with the British crown. Nevertheless, India voluntarily remained within the Commonwealth of Nations (with the term "British" deleted) and thus became the first completely independent republic to hold membership in the association. The constitution provides for an independent judiciary and a president chosen by an electoral college, but follows the English system of parliamentary government, with the chief power vested in a prime minister responsible to the lower house of the central legislature. The subordinate states, with unicameral legislatures, have the same type of ministerial government. Both the state and national legislative bodies are elected by universal adult suffrage for five-year terms. The constitution includes a comprehensive bill of rights, outlaw-

The Republic of India

*Obstacles to Indian unity:
linguistic differences*

...we must be cautious—some rich nations are jealous of the progress we have made....

A Political Cartoonist's Scathing Critique of Nehru's "politics of accommodation"

*The Five-Year Plans;
population increase and
unrelenting poverty*

ing untouchability and discrimination based on caste, and providing for legal equality of the sexes. Although federal in structure, the government has been handicapped by a distribution of power between the center and the states which is both rigid and ambiguous. The constitution gives the president power to suspend a state government in an emergency, and this power has frequently been invoked, but some very critical areas of jurisdiction are reposed in the states, including education, agriculture, and taxes on land.

Many difficulties confronted the Republic of India from the very beginning. The absorption of more than 500 princely states into the new political structure, a formidable task in itself, was handled with relative dispatch. Other problems proved more obstinate, revealing dangerous sectional and social cleavages. One of them had to do with linguistic rivalries. In the interest of promoting national unity, the government announced that Hindi, the principal tongue of northern India but spoken by only about one-third of the total population, was to become the official language of the country by 1965. Resistance on the part of other regional linguistic groups proved so strong, however, that on the date when the change was to go into effect, in January 1965, bloody riots broke out in the south, two cabinet ministers resigned, and the government felt constrained to announce that English would remain an "associate official language" as long as non-Hindi-speaking Indians desired.

The independent states of India and Pakistan were bequeathed many things of value by the British: the rudiments of parliamentary government, trained civil servants, an excellent network of railroads, the nuclei of effective military forces, and an educated elite versed in Western institutions and practices. The new states also inherited the unsolved problems of the era of colonial rule, chief of which is backwardness and crushing poverty of most of the population. Nature has not condemned India to be a land of poverty forever. The country holds extensive resources—the world's largest iron-ore reserves (estimated at nearly 22 billion tons), manganese, and other valuable minerals; substantial deposits of coal and probably of oil; and great potential for hydroelectric development.

The National Congress party, under Nehru's guidance, announced two developmental goals: (1) the expansion of basic and heavy industries, and (2) land reform and the reorganization of agriculture on a cooperative basis. Substantial progress was made toward the first of these goals, almost none toward the second. The Indian government created a Planning Commission and launched a series of Five-Year Plans, beginning in 1951. In many fields impressive results were achieved. Food production grew by almost 90 percent; power generation increased sevenfold in less than a decade; irrigation facilities doubled. By 1970 India was exporting heavy machinery and manufacturing 85,000 motor vehicles a year. Two nuclear power plants were in operation by August 1972. But although improvements in agriculture advanced to the point of making India self-sufficient in basic foodstuffs, its population grew too rapidly to allow any surplus, and poor distribution left many people inadequately provided for. By 1970 India's population was increasing at the rate of 13 million each year. From a figure of 342 million in 1947 it had risen to 810 million in 1989 and was expected to pass the one billion mark by the year 2000, perhaps displacing China as the world's most populous nation. Widely publicized campaigns in support of birth control have failed to check the rate of increase, and poverty has kept pace with population growth. It is estimated that if the present ratio continues, by the end of this century India will have 472 million at the lowest poverty level—a number exceeding the total population at the time of independence in 1947. To solve the problem of rural poverty would require the transfer of land ownership from a small minority of landlords and wealthy peasants to the great body of cultivators, either in the form of family holdings or as shares in agricultural cooperatives, for which a precedent has been cited in the self-governing rural villages of antiquity. That such a radical structural transformation is possible is shown by the examples of China, Taiwan, and North Korea, countries with differing ideologies but coercive governments. Nehru and his associates hoped to accomplish the necessary change without coercion, but they lacked the means or the determination to succeed. In the face of stout resistance from entrenched interests—wealthy proprietors who controlled local cooperatives and dominated the state legislatures—they succumbed to a "politics of accommodation." A long array of proposals, commissions, agencies, and legislation has failed

Building of the Tunga-bhadra Dam in Southern India. This dam, intended to provide irrigation for over 1 million acres, was one of more than eighty major water and power projects initiated during the first two decades after independence.

INDIA TODAY

to free India's rural population—"the vast continent of silence"—from degrading poverty, ignorance, and superstition.

Within the framework of democratic institutions India, during its first thirty years of independence, operated under what was in effect a one-party system. The Congress party, instead of dissolving as Gandhi had recommended, dominated all branches of the government, and Jawaharlal Nehru served continuously as prime minister until his death in May 1964. This long tenure of power was not an unmixed

Preponderance of the Congress party under Nehru

blessing either for the party or for the country. Once the focal point of an indomitable struggle for freedom, the Congress developed into an Establishment, entrenched behind its monopoly of patronage and the administrative services (vastly larger than the old British Indian civil service), and its vigor and integrity became corroded. Even the luster of Nehru—generally revered as a revolutionary hero and Gandhi's heir—dimmed in later years. Endowed with qualities of mind and heart that entitle him to high rank among popular leaders of this century, Nehru was not entirely successful as a statesman. His own idealism was unquestionable but fuzzy in application, his policies vacillating and impulsive. As an avowed enemy of colonialism, in 1961 he authorized the forcible occupation of Goa, Diu, and Damão (Daman), the last remnants of Portugal's empire on the subcontinent; but the next year he blundered into a border clash with Communist China with humiliating results. In the long controversy with Pakistan over Kashmir he was both unyielding and inconsistent. Although publicly admitting the right of the Kashmiris to determine their own destiny, he deposed and imprisoned without trial Sheikh Muhammad Abdullah, the premier of Kashmir, when Abdullah advocated independence for the country. Nehru appeared blind to the corruption and incompetence of his trusted associates, and he neglected to press for the reform program that he himself recognized as essential to India's welfare. His chief asset as a leader was his personality, which combined intellectual faculties of a high order with a charisma that won and held the allegiance even of the unlettered masses.

Nehru's death left the party with no leader of sufficient stature to hold its dissident factions together; rivalries broke out into the open, while India's internal condition deteriorated. In 1966 the party chiefs picked as prime minister Nehru's daughter, Mrs. Indira Gandhi, hoping that the prestige of the family name would restore public confidence. Threatened by opposition from elements of both the extreme right and the extreme left, the Congress party in 1969 split into two factions, and a struggle for power ensued between established leaders of the "old Congress" and Mrs. Gandhi's "new Congress party." Squarely accepting the challenge, she took the bold step of calling for general elections in March 1971—a year ahead of schedule—and she campaigned throughout the country, sometimes making fourteen speeches in a single day. The result was a personal triumph for Indira Gandhi and a sweeping victory for her party, which won a two-thirds majority in the national legislature (Lok Sabha).

Difficulties following Nehru's death; Indira Gandhi's new Congress party

Emboldened by the popular enthusiasm she had aroused—the "Indira wave," which reached its apogee with India's smashing defeat of Pakistan in the brief December war—Mrs. Gandhi became increasingly arbitrary and inflexible. She blamed her political opponents for the failure of the economy to improve, while her own administration was, like its predecessors, inefficient and tainted with corruption. As discontent grew she attempted to quiet it by spectacular diversions.

A period of personal rule

In May 1974 her government announced it had exploded a 10-kiloton nuclear device—proof of technological progress but alarming to neighboring countries despite assurances of "purely peaceful" intent. A year later she annexed the tiny protectorate of Sikkim after Indian troops, on the pretext of quelling a rebellion, arrested the monarch.

A crisis in the summer of 1975 led to a coup—not against the government, but by Mrs. Gandhi against the constitution and the political opposition. On June 12 a state court pronounced her guilty of illegal campaign practices. Instead of resigning the prime ministership, she ordered wholesale arrests of political opponents of all shades of opinion, including members of her own party. The nature of her crackdown was dramatized by the night arrest of "the People's Hero," ailing seventy-two-year-old socialist Jayaprakash Narayan. On June 26 Mrs. Gandhi had the president of India proclaim a state of national emergency. Then she induced a compliant parliament to amend the constitution to free the executive from any restraint by the judiciary, suspended civil liberties, and imposed a rigid censorship.

Indira Gandhi's "emergency" rule of twenty-one months yielded a few positive results—slum clearance in Delhi, a burst of productivity in the industrial sector, a temporary halt to inflation, and some efforts at land redistribution—but her campaign pledge to abolish poverty and promote "internal democracy" proved an empty promise. She seemed bent upon perpetuating her personal authority, not by broadening its base of support but by isolating every potential rival, thus further weakening the Congress party. Resentment against the emergency government was intensified by an insensitive sterilization campaign that created a strong backlash. Mrs. Gandhi's son Sanjay, who with no official position attained the prominence of an heir apparent, provoked a storm when he subjected seven million men to vasectomies with or without their consent. The incidence of Mrs. Gandhi's "emergency" rule is significant for several reasons. First, it showed a woman rising to the top in a male-dominated society; second, it embodied a constitutional crisis; third and most important, it marked a test of dictatorship and its rejection, even by the prime minister herself. When a general election in March 1977, held after a year's postponement, went against Mrs. Gandhi, to the surprise of many she stepped down from office and the emergency rule ended. Ironically the succeeding administration—a shaky coalition of diverse elements—showed itself so incapable of effective government that Indira's star began to rise again. She regained a seat in parliament in November 1978. Fourteen months later, backed by a two-thirds majority in the Lok Sabha, she became prime minister for a second time.

Indira Gandhi Campaigning on the Eve of Her Return to Power in Early 1980

Although enthusiasm greeted Mrs. Gandhi's return to power in 1980, sectional, social, and communal conflicts intensified, exacting a death toll reminiscent of the one that had accompanied partition in 1947. Strikes and rioting in Assam disrupted oil production. The immigration of several million Bangladeshi Muslims into West Bengal angered the Hindu inhabitants, and attempts to enroll the newcomers as voters in the state election in February 1983 unleashed a storm. Thousands of rampaging Hindu students massacred the residents of fifty villages, leaving 4,000 rotting corpses in their wake. The severest crisis confronting the government stemmed from disaffection among the Sikhs, whose nationalist aspirations had been thwarted in 1947 when the Punjab was divided between India and Pakistan. In 1966 Indian Punjab had been split again to give separate statehood to the Hindi-speaking southeastern portion, which became Haryana. Both the Sikhs and the Hindus of Haryana claimed the beautiful city of Chandigarh as their capital. Punjab, India's richest agricultural region, reduced to a fraction of its original size, was kept in turmoil by the agitation of Sikh nationalists demanding autonomy or even complete independence from the central government. The leader of an extreme faction set up his headquarters in the Sikh Golden Temple in Amritsar, converting this revered shrine into a fortress. With lamentable indecision Mrs. Gandhi neither negotiated nor interfered, until in June 1984 she suddenly ordered army troops to storm the Golden Temple, giving Amritsar, site of the notorious 1919 massacre, another horror to remember, this time the shedding of Indian blood by Indians. Unwittingly, Mrs. Gandhi had signed her own death warrant. On October 31, 1984, as she walked from her home in Delhi toward her office, she was gunned down by two Sikh officers of her trusted bodyguard. In a frenzy of retaliation following this act of terrorism thousands of innocent Sikhs were murdered by Hindu mobs.

The shock of the prime minister's assassination rallied public support for the government and facilitated the acceptance of Rajiv Gandhi,

The Sikh Golden Temple in Amritsar (Northern India). The scene of a bloody battle between Sikh extremists and Indian troops dispatched by Prime Minister Indira Gandhi in June 1984, the Golden Temple is shown here on October 1, 1984, as Indian soldiers occupy it once again in the wake of renewed Sikh demonstrations at the site. Mrs. Gandhi was assassinated by members of the sect several weeks later.

Rajiv Gandhi, Prime Minister of India, 1984–1989. Elevated to office in the wake of his mother's assassination, the inexperienced Rajiv Gandhi was unable to overcome the entrenched interests and divisions within Indian society.

Repudiation of the Congress party

Changing economic and military agendas

Indira Gandhi's surviving son, as her successor. Following the death in an airplane crash of her younger and favored son, the egotistical, abrasive Sanjay, Mrs. Gandhi had plucked Rajiv from his job as an Air India pilot and inducted him into politics. Although relatively inexperienced he made a good impression during the crisis that followed his mother's assassination, promising swift prosecution of the guilty while pleading for restraint on the part of all religious communities. In national elections held in February 1985 Rajiv Gandhi, the new prime minister, surpassed the records of both his mother and grandfather by winning more than half of the popular vote. The popular mandate for a continuation of the Nehru political dynasty brought India's basic problems no closer to solution. Unschooled in politics and indecisive, Rajiv was unable to end the conflict between Sikhs and Hindus. Acts of terrorism in the Punjab took a thousand lives in 1987 alone, and the violence continued. Though he had pledged to seek détente with Pakistan, Rajiv blundered into a confrontation that brought the two countries to the brink of war. His efforts to stimulate the economy were frustrated by the resistance of business leaders to sorely needed tax reform, and his administration was tainted with corruption.

Following a general election in November 1989 in which the Congress party lost its majority in the Lok Sabha, Rajiv Gandhi resigned from office. The repudiation of his leadership and of his party reflected general dissatisfaction with government at both state and national levels rather than the endorsement of a clear-cut alternative program. A five-party National Front coalition which formed a government headed by V. P. Singh—a former Congress party member and cabinet minister—was internally divided as to objectives. The new prime minister was no more successful than his predecessor in ending sectional and communal conflicts. Tension between India and Pakistan mounted in 1990 as agitation for independence reached fever pitch among Kashmiri Muslims. Indian troops fired on demonstrators in the capital city of Srinagar, Delhi and Islamabad exchanged recriminations, and both governments moved troops into the area.

A shift toward a free-market economy, begun by Rajiv Gandhi, was carried further under the Singh ministry, which relinquished state control over many enterprises and encouraged foreign capital investment to speed the growth of heavy industry. During the past decade the government appears to have abandoned its original goal of building a socialist society in favor of making India a major industrial power, a goal toward which it has taken impressive strides. India now has one of the largest pools of scientific manpower, including theoretical scientists, engineers, and doctors, and is a leading exporter of pharmaceuticals. India also has a multibillion-dollar military research program and has added a nuclear-powered submarine to its growing navy.

Although 36 percent of India's population lives below the official poverty line, the scourge of famine has been banished and some steps are being taken toward conserving and protecting the land. A reforestation program begun in West Bengal enables low caste and tribal inhabitants of a barren region to supplement their meager agricultural incomes while improving the environment. The southwestern state of Kerala, with a history of radical activism, has pioneered in efforts to eradicate poverty, setting an example that other Indian states might benefit from following. A reform measure begun in Kerala in 1969 gave land ownership to 1½ million tenants. Providing rural villages with access to transportation, health care, education, and basic commodities at low prices has reduced infant mortality in Kerala to a rate one-third that for the whole of India and has raised adult literacy to about twice the national percentage.

Reform programs: poverty and the environment

India's reputation as "the world's largest participatory democracy" is justified in terms of formal political and legal structure and the electoral process. But India is an aggregate of separate communities with structures and traditions more hierarchical than democratic. Just as Indian philosophy and religion embrace almost every conceivable strain of thought, so Indian society exhibits every variety of the human condition from the most deprived and primitive to the most privileged and sophisticated. Some tribal groups, still unassimilated, are employed as seasonal migrant laborers, depressing the wage scale in the areas affected. Poverty is the lot of the majority of inhabitants both rural and urban. Caste is still a decisive factor, and the constitutional outlawing of untouchability has not significantly improved the condition of the Harijans, who suffer from discrimination, segregation, and physical abuse. In 1956 several hundred thousand untouchables in the state of Maharashtra converted en masse to Buddhism in protest against their treatment in the Hindu community. Some three-fourths of India's population is still illiterate, and in isolated sections of the country social and religious life has hardly changed since medieval or even earlier times. In villages of central India, for example, elaborate purification rites are required to remove the pollution attributed to birth and death, sorcerers are more frequently consulted than brahmans, and smallpox is attributed to possession by a goddess. Social reform legislation has remained a dead letter. A 1978 law prohibits the marriage of women below the age of eighteen, yet the marriage of children, even infants, persists. It was reported that more than 40,000 child weddings took place in Rajasthan during the days of the full-moon cycle in early May 1989. The degradation of women is shockingly illustrated by instances of "bride burning"—capital punishment inflicted by the husband or his family because the wife failed to bring a sufficient dowry to the marriage. A persistent obstacle to the development of homogeneous democratic society is the ideological divergence among communal groups. A section of the criminal code requiring an ex-husband to contribute financial support to his divorced wife was so strongly resented by Muslims that they were exempted from it in 1986 on the plea that this provision conflicted with Islamic

Enduring problems of contemporary India

law. Although polygamy is legal for Muslims and illegal for Hindus, a study in 1975 revealed that its incidence was almost exactly the same in each community (between 6 and 7 percent). Even progressive and democratically oriented Muslims find it difficult to reconcile their support of a secular nationalist state with loyalty to Islamic law and tradition. Considering the difficulties to be overcome, if India eventually succeeds in bringing its diverse elements into a harmonious commonwealth it will set an example that the rest of the world might well emulate.

The route taken by Burma

However short it may have fallen of the ideal democratic goal, the Republic of India has a far better record in this respect than its Asian neighbors. A striking contrast is presented by Burma (Myanmar), which won independence from the British Empire at the same time as India. Like India, endowed with rich natural resources and encompassing many divergent ethnic groups, Burma unlike India is underpopulated. With resources adequate to support a stable and prosperous society, the country has languished under a military dictatorship during the past three decades. Ne Win, an associate of the respected Aung San—leader of Burma's independence struggle, who was assassinated in 1947—seized power by a military coup in 1962. While he stifled political freedom Ne Win also crippled the economy in an attempt to create a state socialism. Under army rule Burma's mainly peasant but highly literate population remained poor, and the country, torn by civil war, was kept isolated from the world community. That liberal aspirations could not be extinguished was vividly demonstrated in the late summer of 1988 when antigovernment demonstrations erupted in most of the cities. Townspeople and students, led by Buddhist monks, held the city of Mandalay for five weeks in defiance of the military. Although the uprising was finally suppressed and hundreds of protesters were executed, Ne Win's dictatorship had received a severe jolt. Buddhist monks, whose national order (*Sangha*) had long served as a prop for monarchy, feeling their autonomy threatened under Ne Win cultivated popular support. Aung San Sun Kyi, daughter of the founding father of modern Burma, returned from her home in Britain to lead her National League for Democracy to compete in elections the army had promised to hold. Although the election in May 1990 gave a clear victory to the League for Democracy, the army refused to relinquish power or to release from house arrest the League's intrepid leader, Aung San Sun Kyi.

Pakistan's internal divisions

The problems confronting Pakistan have been similar to India's and even more acute. Pakistan began not as a nation but as a collection of heterogeneous racial and linguistic communities dominated by the Urdu-speaking Punjabis. The country's west and east wings—separated geographically by 1,000 miles—were equally far apart in terms of economics, language, and cultural traditions, with religion serving as the only common bond. Separatist movements within a state which was itself the fruit of separatism threatened to disrupt it and finally succeeded, with the secession of East Pakistan in 1971. Industrial development in West Pakistan, impressive during the 1960s, rested on the exploitation of the eastern wing, which the government treated like a colony. East Pakistan, formerly East Bengal and now Bangladesh, with only one-sixth of the nation's area contained more than half of the population. Its jute industry earned most of Pakistan's foreign exchange, but the larger share of this was diverted to development in the west, and the disparity in per-capita income between the two sections increased steadily. Economic oppression—coupled with political discrimination, social neglect, and undisguised contempt for Bengalis—prepared the ground for revolt. In more prosperous West Pakistan as in the rest of the subcontinent, income distribution was extremely unequal, and industrial progress came largely at the expense of the peasants, whose wages or profits from agriculture were kept low to stimulate investment in manufactures. Economic growth also depended upon heavy doses of foreign aid, especially economic and military aid from the United States. Most of Pakistan's wealth remained concentrated in a plutocracy of "twenty-two families" that controlled 65 percent of industry and 80 percent of banking assets as well as the best farmland.

Political democracy has been almost nonexistent in Pakistan, where the creation of any kind of viable government proved an arduous task. Two successive constituent assemblies struggled with the drafting of a constitution. Declared in effect in March 1956, it defined Pakistan as an "Islamic republic" under a president who was required to be a Muslim. Elections were never held under this constitution. Following a coup in October 1958 Pakistan remained under military rule, except for a six-year interlude, until November 1988. The first dictator was General Muhammed Ayub Khan, who built a new capital, Islamabad, near the northwest frontier and was hailed in some quarters as a second Atatürk but whose rule ended in corruption, oppression, and bloody rioting. Ayub's successor in 1969, General Yahya Khan, promised to establish a parliamentary democracy, but by duplicity and abuse provoked a civil war. Elections held in December 1970 brought a resounding victory to East Pakistan's Sheikh Mujibur Rhaman, leader of a party demanding regional autonomy. Instead of allowing Mujibur to assume the premiership as he had promised, Yahya Khan secretly flew troops to the east and imprisoned the sheikh.

Legacy of military dictatorship

The murderous events in East Bengal from March to December 1971, resulting in a full-scale war between India and Pakistan, were among the most horrible in a century of unprecedented horrors. Atrocities may have been initiated by the Bengalis, and were perpetrated by them on the Bihari minority after the war had ended; but the most revolting excesses were committed by government troops. West Pakistani soldiers, who began their attack by shooting helpless university students, raped some 200,000 women and slaughtered whole communities of civilians. Their program of genocide was apparently

The India-Pakistan war of 1971

Victims of the Indian-Pakistani War of 1971. Left: Refugees from East Bengal seeking sanctuary in India. Right: Prime Minister Indira Gandhi of India visiting a refugee camp in West Bengal, offering reassurance to homeless East Bengalis.

aimed at exterminating every potential leader among the population they despised as rebels and racial inferiors. The government of India admitted 10 million refugees into West Bengal, assisted East Pakistan guerrillas, and early in December entered the war as an active belligerent. The brief combat, conducted on western and eastern fronts, demonstrated India's decisive military superiority over its rival, whose forces surrendered on December 16.

Zulfikar Ali Bhutto and the Pakistan People's party

After his humiliating defeat Yahya Khan resigned the presidency in December 1971. For the first time in thirteen years Pakistan gained a civilian head of state when Zulfikar Ali Bhutto took the oath of office as president and immediately assumed most of the other important cabinet posts as well. A graduate of the University of California and of Oxford, Bhutto was a colorful figure, with a talent for arousing mass enthusiasm. He chose as motto for his Pakistan People's party, "Islam is our faith, democracy is our policy, socialism is our economy, all power to the people." His six-year rule did little credit to these ideals. It followed the familiar path of corruption and tyranny, marked by arrests, kidnapping, and torture of opponents. Elections held in March 1977 were so obviously rigged in Bhutto's favor that they provoked widespread rioting, and in July the army removed Bhutto in a coup led by the chief of staff, General Muhammad Zia ul-Haq, who imposed a second era of military rule. In response to popular clamor, Zia ul-Haq had the deposed president brought to trial, sentenced to death, and hanged in April 1979. To his dedicated followers, who hailed him as a "Martyr King," Bhutto's grave became a shrine. Although Zia had promised to hold elections within three months of his accession to power, he postponed them indefinitely and governed by martial law.

With more political agility than his predecessors, General Zia by balancing competing factions against one another managed to retain power until his death eleven years later. He proceeded cautiously in his announced program of Islamicizing the state, a move viewed with misgivings by the Shiite minority. In firm control of the army, Zia strengthened his position by exploiting Pakistan's military alliance with the United States. U.S. aid of more than $3 billion, supplemented by an annual remittance of $3 million from Pakistani workers in the Gulf oil fields, was a key factor in bolstering a shaky economy. Although Zia claimed to be laying the foundation of an Islamic republic, his authority was grounded in martial law. Arbitrary arrests, torture, and similar violations of human rights characterized his dictatorship. Pakistan's women suffered most of all under religiously sanctioned oppression. General Zia's death in a mysterious airplane explosion in August 1988 opened the way for a return to civilian parliamentary government. Prominent among several candidates contending for office was the daughter of Zulfikar Ali Bhutto.

General Zia ul Haq, President of Pakistan, 1978–1988. Zia believed that Pakistan had to be transformed into an Islamic state in order to achieve national unity.

Benazir Bhutto, a beautiful thirty-five-year-old graduate of Radcliffe and Oxford, had lived in exile after several years' imprisonment, but returned home to lead what remained of her father's People's party in opposition to Zia's rule. After a vigorous campaign and to the surprise of many observers Benazir was chosen prime minister as a result of the November 1988 elections, becoming the first woman in modern times to head a Muslim state. Her father had proclaimed a socialist program for the benefit of the masses while remaining dependent on the support of rich landowners. Benazir by contrast opted for an open-market economy and sought foreign investments, while also promising to redistribute ten million acres of state land. The road to economic improvement, if any could be found, was bound to be rough. Pakistan's population had swelled from 60 million in 1971 to 105 million by 1988. The literacy rate for men was 36 percent, for women 15 percent. In addition to a depressed economy, persistent domestic problems included corruption in the administration, violent intra-Muslim clashes in Ms. Bhutto's native province of Sind, and the continuing standoff with India over Kashmir. With dwindling popular support and under pressure from the army, which had not willingly accepted civilian rule, Benazir Bhutto was dismissed from office by presidential decree early in August 1990. New elections were scheduled for October.

Benazir Bhutto, Prime Minister of Pakistan, 1988–1990. The first woman leader of a modern Islamic state was removed unilaterally by Pakistan's president amid disputed charges of widespread corruption. Her efforts to regain the office in the November 1990 elections failed.

Bangladesh ("Bengal nation"), born from the ashes of victory in 1971, remains in the most precarious position of all Asian states. More than 100 million people are crowded into an area smaller than

Sheikh Mujibur Rahman, Prime Minister of Bangladesh, 1971–1975. The charismatic Sheikh was committed to forging a secular state in an overwhelmingly Muslim society at a time when Islamic fundamentalism was on the rise.

Indian foreign policy

the state of Wisconsin. The ratio of persons to acreage of cultivated land has increased fourfold since the beginning of the century and may be eight times as great by its close. Occupying a region buffeted by typhoons and tornadoes, it suffers alternately from droughts and floods that take an annual toll of thousands of lives. That the nation manages to survive is a testimony to the durability of the human spirit. On achieving independence Bangladesh faced the additional problem of repairing the ravages of war (which took 3 million lives), finding food and shelter for returning refugees, disarming guerrilla bands, and creating a government out of chaos. Sheikh Mujibur Rahman, given a hero's welcome when he returned to Dacca in 1972 after nine months in West Pakistan jails, set up a provisional government that promised to create "a secular, democratic, socialist state" but which soon became autocratic and corrupt. In 1975 Mujibur was brutally murdered in a coup led by young military officers. This was the first of eighteen attempted or successful coups that mark Bangladesh's brief political history. Two of its nine presidents have been assassinated. Lieutenant-General Hussain Ershad, upon coming to power by a coup in March 1984, established an appearance of stability sufficient to keep a current of foreign aid flowing.

The annual $2 billion in aid supplied to Bangladesh by foreign governments and humanitarian organizations has not been managed well enough to bring appreciable relief. More promising, although limited in scope, are grass-roots efforts to assist determined individuals to escape from the poverty trap. Noteworthy is the Village Bank begun in 1983 by Muhammad Yunus, a university-trained economist who discarded textbook theories to bring help directly where it was most needed. Yunus' corps of "bicycle bankers," making small loans to villagers with no collateral other than their promise, by 1989 had found half a million borrowers. The Village Bank, while enabling thousands of the poorest villagers, especially women, to augment their incomes dramatically, also has a remarkably low record of default.

In international relations the republics of India and Pakistan have generally pursued separate paths. Jawaharlal Nehru initially favored a policy of nonalignment, stemming from a distaste for military alliances and from a desire to cultivate a spirit of friendship with other Asian countries, including the Communist. Sino-Indian relations, which had been marked by expressions of cordiality on both sides, suffered a rude shock following China's provocative action in Tibet. The New Delhi government gave asylum to the Dalai Lama, who escaped from his country while Chinese troops were suppressing a Tibetan rebellion in 1959. A brief border war between India and China in 1962, in which ill-equipped Indian troops were abruptly routed, induced the government to upgrade and expand its military forces, which proved more effective in a three-weeks' war against Pakistan in 1965. These summer hostilities, provoked by friction over

Kashmir, drew India away from the United States and into the orbit of the Soviet Union, with whom the Delhi government signed a twenty-year treaty of friendship and cooperation in August 1971. India relied on Moscow's backing during the two-weeks' war with Pakistan the following December, when both China and the United States supported Pakistan and refused to denounce the brutalities committed by Pakistani troops in East Bengal. If the conflict over Bangladesh was something less than the "holy war for democracy and human rights" acclaimed by a Calcutta journalist, India's smashing victory at least heightened national self-confidence. India had attained an identity—not as the exemplar of nonviolence that Gandhi envisioned—but as a military power.

Pakistan, partly from fear of its more powerful neighbor, readily entered into alliances, with results that proved disillusioning. While India was pursuing the path of neutralism, Pakistan became a member both of SEATO and of CENTO as a dutiful ally of the United States. Under a military-aid pact of 1954, the United States agreed to provide supersonic aircraft and other modern weapons, and in turn received permission to use Pakistan territory for strategic intelligence activities. This military partnership intensified India's mistrust and hostility but did nothing to mitigate Pakistan's disastrous defeat in the Bangladesh war. In 1972 President Bhutto announced his country's withdrawal from the Commonwealth of Nations and also from SEATO. A factor contributing further to Pakistan's isolation was the discovery that its government had for some time been secretly developing atomic weapons—the "Islamic bomb"—to offset India's nuclear capacity. In recent years Pakistan has cultivated ties with conservative Muslim states of the Persian Gulf area by lending them troops and laborers. When Russian forces invaded Afghanistan in September 1979 to install a Soviet puppet in Kabul, Western powers and China turned hopefully to Islamabad as a possible buffer against Russian expansion. The United States offered Zia military aid and advisers. Pakistan became the sanctuary for thousands of refugees from the war in neighboring Afghanistan and a staging area for guerrilla attacks on Soviet troops. The USSR's agreement in April 1988 to withdraw from Afghanistan raised questions as to the future of the refugees and of Pakistan's international position. The removal of Russian soldiers from Pakistan's doorstep and the restoration of civilian government in Islamabad did not end the internal threat posed by disaffected ethnic elements within Pakistan. Baluchi and Pushtuns, inhabiting both sides of the Pakistan-Afghanistan border and the Northwest Frontier, entertain their own nationalist aspirations. Armed groups in Sind protest Punjabi dominance. The demand for autonomy or independence has been a recurrent theme in Baluchistan, where President Bhutto fought a four-year war against insurgents.

Changes in Pakistan's foreign policy

Pakistani President Zulfikar Ali Bhutto and Indian Prime Minister Indira Gandhi in Pursuit of Peace. During this 1972 summit conference the two leaders agreed to demilitarize their common borders and to seek peaceful solutions to all problems.

• Items so designated are available in paperback editions.

THE COMMONWEALTH

Bercuson, David, *Canada and the Birth of Israel: A Study in Canadian Foreign Policy,* Toronto, 1985. Highly critical.

Bothwell, Robert, I. Drummond, and J. English, *Canada since 1945: Power, Politics, and Provincialism.* Buffalo, 1982. A vivid account.

Cameron, Roderick, *Australia: History and Horizons,* New York, 1971.

Craig, Gerald, *The United States and Canada,* Cambridge, Mass., 1968. Clear and informative.

Doran, Charles, *Forgotten Partnership: U.S.-Canada Relations Today,* Baltimore, 1983.

Fitzpatrick, Brian, *The Australian People, 1788–1945,* Melbourne, 1946. An analytical and revealing account.

• Graubard, Stephen, ed., *Australia: Terra Incognita?,* Cambridge, Mass., 1985. Illuminating essays by two English, one American, and fourteen Australian authors.

• Hughes, Robert, *The Fatal Shore,* New York, 1986. Depicts the degrading aspects of colonization by transportation in Australia.

Lipson, Leslie, *The Politics of Equality: New Zealand's Adventures in Democracy,* Chicago, 1948.

MacInnes, Colin, *Australia and New Zealand,* New York, 1966.

McIntyre, W. D., *The Commonwealth of Nations: Origins and Impact, 1969–1971,* Minneapolis, 1977.

McWhinney, Edward, *Canada and the Constitution, 1979–1982: Patriation and the Charter of Rights.* Buffalo, 1982. Criticizes the excessive influence of the provincial premiers.

• Siegfried, André, *The Race Question in Canada,* New York, 1907. A perceptive study.

Wase, Mason, *The French Canadians,* New York, 1955.

INDIA, PAKISTAN, AND BANGLADESH *(See also Readings for Chapter 21)*

Azad, M. A. K., *India Wins Freedom: An Autobiographical Narrative,* New York, 1960. A close friend of Nehru and minister in his first cabinet faults Nehru for reversing his support of the Cabinet Mission plan.

Babb, Lawrence, *The Divine Hierarchy: Popular Hinduism in Central India,* New York, 1975.

Bhatia, Krishan, *Indira: A Biography of Prime Minister Gandhi,* New York, 1974.

————., *The Ordeal of Nationhood: A Social Study of India since Independence, 1947–1970,* New York, 1971. Informed and objective account of India's problems.

• Bondurant, Joan, *Conquest of Violence: The Gandhian Philosophy of Conflict,* rev. ed., Berkeley, 1967. An excellent analysis.

Brecher, Michael, *Nehru: A Political Biography,* New York, 1959.

• Brown, Judith, *Modern India: The Origins of an Asian Democracy,* New York, 1985. An admirable study incorporating recent research.

Dutt, R. P., *The Problem of India*, New York, 1943. Examines the sources of Indian nationalism.

Edwardes, Michael, *Nehru: A Political Biography*, New York, 1972.

Embree, A. T., *India's Search for National Identity*, New York, 1972. An analysis of Indian nationalism to 1947.

• Erikson, E. H., *Gandhi's Truth: On the Origins of Militant Nonviolence*, New York, 1969.

Fischer, Louis, *The Life of Mahatma Gandhi*, New York, 1950. An admirable biography.

Frankel, Francine, *India's Green Revolution: Economic Gains and Political Costs*, Princeton, 1971. A significant and challenging study.

• _____, *India's Political Economy, 1947–1977; The Gradual Revolution*, Princeton, 1979.

Gopal, Sarvepalli, *Jawaharlal Nehru: A Biography* (vol. 3, 1956–1964), Cambridge, Mass., 1984.

Hardgrave, R. L., Jr., *India: Government and Politics in a Developing Nation*, New York, 1970. Well balanced and clear.

• Iyer, R. N., *The Moral and Political Thought of Mahatma Gandhi*, New York, 1973. A stimulating analysis.

Kothari, Rajni, *Politics in India*, Boston, 1970. Throws light on relationship between caste and politics.

Malik, Hefeez, *Moslem Nationalism in India and Pakistan*, Washington, 1963.

Mehta, Ved, *Mahatma Gandhi and His Apostles*, New York, 1977. Emphasizes India's failure to realize Gandhi's ideals.

Moore, R. J., *Churchill, Cripps, and India 1939–1945*, New York, 1979. Attributes the partition of India to the failure of the Cripps mission of 1942.

• Nehru, Jawaharlal, *The Discovery of India*, New York, 1946.

• Palmer, N. D., *The Indian Political System*, Boston, 1961.

Roberts, P. E., *History of British India under the Company and the Crown*, 3rd ed., New York, 1952. An excellent political text.

Rudolph, Lloyd, and Susanne Rudolph, *Gandhi: The Traditional Roots of Charisma*, Chicago, 1983. An illuminating essay.

Sayeed, K. B., *Pakistan: The Formative Phase, 1857–1948*, 2d ed., New York, 1968.

Siddiqui, Kalim, *Conflict, Crisis, and War in Pakistan*, New York, 1972. An indictment of Pakistan's civilian and military elites.

Singh, Anita, *The Origins of the Partition of India, 1936–1947*, New York, 1987. A careful analysis of the Muslim political community.

• Suntharalingam, R., *Indian Nationalism: An Historical Analysis*, New Delhi, 1983. Comprehensive and remarkably objective.

von Vorys, Karl, *Political Development in Pakistan*, Princeton, 1965. Pessimistic.

Wolpert, Stanley, *Jinnah of Pakistan*, New York, 1984.

• Woodruff, Philip, *The Men Who Ruled India*, 2 vols., New York, 1954.

SOURCE MATERIALS

Birla, G. D., *In the Shadow of the Mahatma: A Personal Memoir*, Bombay, 1953. Selections from Gandhi's correspondence, interviews, and conversations.

• Bohm, Robert, *Notes on India,* Boston, 1982. A collection of personal interviews presenting a disturbing portrait.

Chakravarty, A., ed., *A Tagore Reader,* New York, 1961.

• Gandhi, M. K., *The Story of My Experiments with Truth,* Boston, 1957. Autobiography.

• Jack, H. A., ed., *The Gandhi Reader: A Source Book of His Life and Writings,* Bloomington, Ind., 1956.

Narayan, Jayaprakash, *Prison Dairy,* ed. A. B. Shah, Seattle, 1978. Secret diary of Mrs. Gandhi's most famous prisoner.

• Nehru, Jawaharlal, *Toward Freedom,* New York 1951. Autobiography.

———, *Independence and After* (speeches, 1946–1949), New York, 1950.

———, *Jawaharlal Nehru's Speeches, 1949–1953,* Delhi, 1954.

Philips, C. H., *The Evolution of India and Pakistan, 1858 to 1947: Select Documents,* New York, 1962.

Russell, W. H., *My India Mutiny Diary,* London, 1957. Contemporary account by the London *Times* correspondent.

Tagore, Rabindranath, *My Reminiscences,* New York, 1917.

Chapter 38

THE MIDDLE EAST AND AFRICA

All secular power, no matter what form it takes, is the work of Satan.
It is our duty to stop it in its tracks and to combat its effects. . . . It is
not only our duty in Iran, but it is also the duty of all the Muslims of
the world, to carry the revolutionary Islamic policy to its final victory.

—Ayatollah Ruholla Khomeini, *Islamic Government*

1. THE MIDDLE EAST

Few areas of the earth have witnessed more turbulence and rapidity
of change than have the countries of the Middle East in recent
times. The pattern of their history has been much the same.
Before the First World War most of them stagnated and slumbered
under the rule of the Ottoman Turks. With the breakup of the Ottoman
Empire they saw visions of independence and a chance to throw off
all traces of foreign domination. Nationalist movements sprang up
to prod governments into vigorous action. In many instances they
gained control of governments, often in defiance of the religious authorities. They proceeded then with attempts to launch programs of
modernization, for building highways, railroads, and schools, subsidiz-
ing industries, and sponsoring scientific agriculture and land reform.
The problems they encountered, however, in the form of ignorance,
corruption, vested interests, and foreign meddling were often too
great to be overcome. To this day illiteracy, disease, and high death
rates persist in many parts of the Middle East, and poverty is all but
universal.

The pattern of Middle Eastern history

A survey of the Middle East may properly begin with Turkey,
since it ranks first in population and since nearly the whole region at
one time was subject to Turkish rule. We have already seen that the
dismemberment of the Ottoman Empire began as early as 1829 when
the Sultan's government was forced to acknowledge the independence
of Greece. Thenceforth one after another of the European provinces

Establishment of the Turkish republic

broke away. By 1914 Turkey in Europe had been reduced to nothing but Istanbul (Constantinople) and a corner of eastern Thrace. But Turkey in Asia still included a vast area from the western border of Persia to the Mediterranean Sea. At the end of World War I, the Turkish government, which had fought on the losing side, accepted a treaty depriving the empire of virtually everything except Istanbul and the northern and central portions of Asia Minor. But before this treaty could be put into effect a group of nationalists, under the leadership of Mustafa Kemal, reconquered much of the lost territory. In 1922 they marched on Istanbul, deposed the Sultan, and in 1923 proclaimed Turkey a republic. The Allies, in the meantime, consented to the making of a new treaty at Lausanne, Switzerland, which permitted the Turks to retain practically all the lands they had reconquered. The new state included Anatolia, Armenia, and eastern Thrace, but none of the outlying territories of Mesopotamia, Arabia, Palestine, or Syria.

Mustafa Kemal: political and educational reforms

For two decades the history of the Turkish republic was almost synonymous with the personal history of Mustafa Kemal. Kemal had played a minor part in the "Young Turk" Revolution of 1908. That reform movement had resulted not in the hoped-for constitutional regime but in a virtual military dictatorship. Now it was Kemal's imagination and determination that moved the country forward toward a modern, progressive state. His reform program was aided by Westernizing trends that had already laid the foundations for a national system of public education and had begun the emancipation of women. While Kemal guaranteed religious toleration, his decree abolishing the Caliphate declared that the antiquated religious courts and codes must be replaced by "modern scientific civil codes," and that the schools of the mosques must give way to government schools, which all children between the ages of six and sixteen would be required to attend. But before much progress could be made in educational reform, it was deemed necessary to adopt a new system of writing. The Turkish language was still written in Arabic script, which Kemal regarded as an impossible medium for the expression of Western ideas. In 1928 he had a commission prepare an alphabet using the Roman letters, and this was done so successfully that modern Turkish spelling is consistently phonetic. When he had taught himself the new alphabet, Kemal proceeded to teach others, traveling throughout the country with his blackboard, lecturing audiences on how the characters should be formed. Soon he issued a decree forbidding the holding of public office by anyone who was not adept in the new writing.

Social and economic reforms

The achievements of Kemal also included a social and economic revolution. He issued decrees abolishing the fez, discouraging polygamy, and encouraging women to appear unveiled and both sexes to wear Western clothes. He established schools for girls and made women eligible for business careers and for the professions. In 1929 he gave women the suffrage in local elections and five years later in national

Mustafa Kemal Atatürk. One of Kemal Atatürk's reforms was the adoption of the Roman alphabet in place of the Arabic. Here he is seen instructing his people in the use of the new letters.

elections. Although the traditions of a patriarchal society die hard and equality of the sexes has not yet been attained, the initiative shown by Turkish women under the republic, not only in entering occupations and professions previously reserved for men but in rising to positions of leadership, makes Turkey unique among Muslim countries and an example for others as well. Equally significant were Kemal's economic reforms. He endowed agricultural colleges, established model farms, and founded banks to lend money to farmers. He freed the peasant from the tithe and set up agencies to distribute seed and farm machinery to almost anyone who could offer a guaranty to use them effectively. Although he undoubtedly had the power to do so, he refrained from instituting measures of forced collectivization such as those of the Russians. He chose rather to adhere to the tradition of Muhammad in encouraging small holdings, in helping the farmer to buy his land, and in teaching him to work it profitably. At the same time he recognized the importance of promoting industrialization. He therefore built thousands of miles of railways and established state monopolies for the manufacture of tobacco, matches, munitions, salt, alcohol, and sugar. Despite the fact that Turkey has abundant resources of coal, iron, copper, and petroleum, and is the world's largest producer of chrome, three-fourths of its 55 million inhabitants still derive their living from agriculture.

Mustafa Kemal, known to posterity as Atatürk ("Father of the Turks"), governed Turkey from 1922 until his death in 1938. Venerated as the liberator of his people and founder of their nation, he has remained a controversial but enduringly fascinating figure both because of his accomplishments and because of his complex personality. Legally his position was that of an elective president chosen by the Assembly for a four-year term and indefinitely re-eligible, but he himself was president of the Assembly and, except for a brief period in 1930, he permitted no opposition party to exist. Yet if he ruled as a dictator it was not in the pattern of Mussolini or Hitler, both of whom he despised. The constitution that he established outlawed political activity advocating either a Marxist or a religious regime. His avowed objective was the creation of a strong secular republic, democratic in structure but emphasizing national sovereignty rather than individual rights. This ideal could be obtained, he believed, only after the citizens had developed a sense of responsibility and liberated themselves from prejudices of the past. He had full confidence in his ability to lead in the right direction: his famous speech to the nation in 1927 lasted six days. A soldier by profession, Atatürk set the example of subordinating the military to civilian authority, and to his credit he did not involve his country in war after independence had been won. Neither did he attempt to exterminate ethnic minorities, although he suppressed a revolt of the Kurds in 1930 with merciless severity, executing twenty-nine of the leaders. His ardent nationalism did not inculcate racism. He offered asylum to Jewish intellectuals from Hitler's Germany and he suppressed anti-Semitic propaganda in Turkey.

The character of Kemal's regime

Under Kemal Atatürk's successors, Ismet Inönü and Celal Bayar, Turkey took steps toward supplanting its benevolent dictatorship with a democratic republic. But after the Second World War, severe economic difficulties, resulting mainly from extravagant spending and inflation, led the government to impose restrictions. Freedom of the press was abolished, and members of parliament opposing the government were arrested. Successive student demonstrations against these repressive measures triggered a revolt in 1960 by army officers, who seized control and established a provisional government. Nearly 600 members of the previous regime were tried on charges of corruption and subversion of the Constitution. Of those convicted by the court, three were executed, including the deposed prime minister Adnan Menderes. In 1961 a new constitution was adopted proclaiming the Second Turkish Republic. It provided for a president elected by a Grand National Assembly (parliament) for a seven-year term and ineligible for re-election, and for a prime minister designated by the president on the basis of party representation in the parliament. It included also guarantees of civil liberties, clauses for the protection of workers' rights, and safeguards against abuse of executive power.

Revolution of 1960; The Second Turkish Republic

Sporadic progress toward modernizing Turkey's economy was impeded by major obstacles. The great bulk of the population was rural, illiterate, and poor. The novel experiment of parliamentary government was exploited by demagogues and stymied by the bickering of rival politicians. Ideological cleavages surfaced, pitting leftist reformers

Social unrest and political division

against conservatives and secularists against the defenders of Islamic tradition. After strikes, riots, and political assassinations had produced an atmosphere of terror, in March 1971 the military forces imposed martial law, and for twenty-nine months a "government of national union" ruled, backed by the army. When civilian government was reinstated no party was able to win a majority in the Assembly. Atatürk's Republican Peoples party was now divided and, like its conservative rival the Justice party, felt compelled to woo support from Islamic fundamentalists.

A severe social and political crisis reached its climax in the late 1970s, a decade marked by turmoil approaching civil war or anarchy and raising questions as to whether Atatürk's dream of a progressive secular republic could be realized. After a burst of prosperity in the early 1970s the national economy seemed to be sinking beneath the weight of trade deficits, uncontrolled inflation, and an unemployment figure nearing 40 percent. Industry was operating at about half its capacity, and by 1979 there were shortages of most basic commodities, including foodstuffs. Meanwhile, unchecked violence throughout the country took a toll of thousands of lives. In September 1980 the army high command, in an almost bloodless but decisive coup, suspended parliamentary government for the third time in the history of the republic. Although the generals promised to honor the tradition of return to civilian rule after social disorder had been curbed, they arrested more than one hundred persons and imposed martial law. A new constitution, drafted by the military and approved by popular vote in 1982, preserved the forms of democracy with an elective parliament and a prime minister but retained General Kenan Evren, leader of the 1980 coup, as president for a seven-year term with almost unlimited power. Turgut Özal, an economist who had served with the World Bank, was named deputy prime minister and charged with reviving the economy.

The coup of 1980

The authoritarian regime of the 1980s succeeded in giving Turkey the appearance of stability and in promoting unprecedented economic growth. Özal stimulated industrial expansion by terminating state monopolies and subsidies, encouraging private initiative, and attracting foreign capital. The country's annual growth rate averaged about 8 percent, and before the end of the decade the government had paid off enough of its foreign debt to earn a good credit rating. While inflation remained close to an annual rate of 75 percent, domestic oil production boomed, roads were improved, two great bridges spanned the Bosporus to connect Europe and Asia, and luxury hotels sprang up to make it easy for tourists to enjoy Turkey's unmatched archeological treasures and magnificent seacoast. The reverse side of this attractive picture was a brutal repression that muzzled the press, purged universities and labor unions, and silenced every critic of the government. Some 45,000 political prisoners were incarcerated and many were cruelly tortured, prompting the comment that the army had "stopped

An authoritarian regime

terrorism in the streets and brought it into the police station." The junta's extreme sensitivity to the threat of subversion is illustrated by its attack on the Turkish Peace Association, an organization of intellectuals opposed to nuclear war. Twenty-three members of this society were arrested, including university professors, a career diplomat, and the presidents of the Turkish medical and bar associations.

Improved democratic prospects

Despite the spasm of repression, prospects for Turkey's democratic progress have brightened. Martial law was lifted in 1987. Having dissolved all political parties at the time of the coup, the government subsequently allowed new ones to form and campaign. Özal's centrist Motherland party ran ahead of the junta's own slate in 1983 and in the election of 1987 secured a substantial majority of parliamentary seats. In the next general election, scheduled for 1992, it undoubtedly will face competition both from the right and from the left.

Internal problems: the economy, the Kurds, and religion

Turkey, still a poor country in spite of remarkable economic progress, faces the domestic problems common to developing nations. Its population, already 55 million, will soon equal or surpass that of a major European power, but per capita gross national product is only one-tenth that of France, while Turkey's infant mortality rate is ten times as great. One internal problem stems from the disaffection of the Kurds, a minority people suffering periodic persecution in Turkey, Syria, Iraq, and Iran. The Ankara government seems determined to obliterate the distinctive Kurdish language and traditions, officially classifying Kurds as "mountain Turks." Even more potentially explosive is the tension between secularists and traditionalists who, in the name of democracy, demand an expanding role for religious foundations. Courses in Islamic doctrine have been made mandatory in state schools, and private Islamic secondary schools are flourishing.

Turkey's international position

In some respects Turkey is unique among Third World nations. Although overwhelmingly Muslim, the Turks do not share close ties with or hold deep affection for their Arab neighbors. Turkey was the first—and for three decades the only—Muslim state to recognize Israel. Wedged between two superpowers' competing spheres of influence, Turkey's precarious international position is of great strategic importance. More than willing to develop ties with the United States, the Turks could not afford to antagonize Soviet Russia, whose proffered financial aid they sorely needed. Washington welcomed the Ankara government into the North Atlantic Treaty Organization, established a number of military bases and electronic listening posts within Anatolia, and considered the Turks, with their 600,000-man army, a key NATO partner. A Turkish invasion of Cyprus and occupation of the whole northern half of the island in 1979—which so angered the Greek government that it threatened to withdraw from NATO—led to the temporary suspension of U.S. arms sales to Turkey. But since the coup of 1980 American military aid has substantially increased.

Evidence of Turkey's orientation toward the West is its application for membership in the European Economic Community (Common Market), a request thus far denied. Reluctance of the EEC members to admit Turkey is explained partly by doubt as to Turkey's economic stability although Portugal, almost as undeveloped as Turkey, was recently admitted to the EEC. Other negative factors are a fear that Turkey's population, expanding at the rate of 2½ percent annually, might overwhelm other regions if complete freedom of movement were granted; cool relations between Greece and Turkey; Ankara's poor human-rights record; and probably the unacknowledged but still lingering distrust of Muslims by Christians. The Turks have contributed substantially to western Europe's economic growth, particularly Germany's, by providing a large supply of unskilled and therefore cheap labor, recruited chiefly from illiterate Anatolian peasants. Regrettably, the practice of employing "guest laborers," while economically beneficial, has incited recrimination and feelings of hostility rather than promoting mutual respect.

Obstacles to EEC membership

Equal to Turkey in population, and perhaps on its way to becoming first in that category among nations of the Middle East, is the Arab Republic of Egypt. Although technically a part of the Ottoman Empire until 1914, Egypt was for all practical purposes a dependency of Great Britain after 1882. The British kept up the pretense of acknowledging the sovereignty of the Khedive and his overlord the Sultan, but when Turkey joined the Central Powers in 1914 the London government issued a proclamation that Egypt would henceforth constitute a protectorate of the British Empire. When the war ended, the London authorities refused to allow Egypt to send a delegation to Paris to lay its case before the peace conference. The upshot was the emergence of an Egyptian nationalist movement known as the *Wafd*. The name means literally "delegation," and the movement had been

The beginning of nationalism in Egypt; the rise of the Wafd

Suez Canal at the Onset of the First World War. Britain's concern for the Suez Canal as a lifeline to the empire was one of the primary factors behind the establishment of a protectorate over Egypt in 1914 and the "reservations" linked to the proclamation of independence in 1922.

Abolition of the British protectorate

The revival of nationalism after the Second World War

Gamal Abdul Nasser, Dynamic Arab Nationalist and President of Egypt, 1956–1970

organized originally to present Egypt's demands and grievances at the peace conference. When the British attempted suppression and deported its leader to Malta, the *Wafd* came forth with an insistence upon nothing less than complete independence.

Following a campaign of sabotage and terrorism waged by the *Wafd*, the British decided to abolish the protectorate and in 1922 proclaimed Egypt an independent and sovereign state. But "independence" was made subject to four reservations, to be left absolutely to the discretion of the British pending adjustment by mutual agreement. The first was the protection of the Suez Canal and other vital links in the lifeline of the British Empire. The second was the defense of Egypt itself against foreign encroachments or interference. The third was the protection of foreign interests and minorities in Egypt. The fourth was the maintenance of the dependent status of the Sudan under the joint rule of Britain and Egypt. For the next three decades the history of Egypt was largely occupied by controversy and conflict over these four points or reservations.

Although the majority of Egyptians resented the attempts of the British to keep the country in a state of vassalage, they were alarmed by Mussolini's invasion of Ethiopia in 1935, and in 1936 accepted an Anglo-Egyptian Treaty of Friendship and Alliance. Egypt agreed to coordinate its foreign policy with that of Britain in return for British assistance in gaining admission to the League of Nations. Before all the terms of the Anglo-Egyptian Treaty could be put into effect, the Second World War broke out. The British were reluctant to take any steps that might threaten their communications with the East, and the Egyptians did not press the issue of the removal of British troops from their soil. But when the war ended, the flames of nationalist aspirations were kindled anew. The Egyptians now demanded that the British withdraw entirely from both the Suez Canal area and the Sudan. In 1951 the Egyptian government announced that it was abrogating the Treaty of 1936 and also the condominium or joint rule in the Sudan. In July 1954 Britain agreed to the removal of all British troops from Egyptian territory.

In July 1952, Major General Muhammad Naguib seized control of the Egyptian government and the army. The pleasure-loving King Farouk I, alleged to be subservient to the British, was deposed. A year later Egypt was proclaimed a republic, with General Naguib as its first president and premier. The new ruler announced a program of sweeping economic and social reforms, but before it could be fully effected, conflict developed within the military junta that had overthrown the monarchy. Naguib's rival, Lieutenant-Colonel Gamal Abdul Nasser, secured the office of premier, and in June 1956, in a carefully managed election in which he was the only candidate, Nasser was chosen president. In the same election the Egyptian voters adopted a new constitution proclaiming the country an Islamic-Arab state with a democratic form of government.

Aswan High Dam. The dam was designed to serve a twofold purpose: to facilitate the irrigation of vast areas of arid land and to generate electrical power.

Although Nasser was a charismatic figure who won acclaim from fellow Arabs, his policies were of dubious benefit for Egypt. To hasten transition from an agricultural base to an industrial one he nationalized most industries, banks, and the communications system, a step that produced a large state bureaucracy but little economic growth. He also sought to increase agricultural productivity by desert reclamation projects, most of which were unsuccessful. Hailed as a step toward "Arab socialism," his reform measures hardly touched the problems of poverty, illiteracy, and extreme inequalities in Egyptian society. Ruling as a military dictator, he seemed to be laying the foundations of a police state rather than a welfare state. Nasser's most ambitious domestic project was the construction of the Aswan High Dam, a gigantic reservoir to back up the waters of the Upper Nile and provide irrigation for 2 million acres of arable land. To finance this enterprise required foreign capital, most of which was eventually supplied by the Soviet Union. When the United States and Great Britain withdrew their offers of a loan, an angry Nasser retaliated by expropriating the owners of the Suez Canal, who were chiefly British and French, and declared that he would use the revenues of the canal to build the dam. After months of fruitless negotiation, the British and French encouraged an invasion of Egyptian territory by the Republic of Israel. The Israelis had plenty of grievances, since they had been the victims of border raids from the Sinai Peninsula for many years. The invasion began on October 29, 1956, and the British and French intervened soon afterward. The affair precipitated a crisis which threatened for a time to engulf the world. The Soviet rulers warned Israel that its

Nasser, Suez, and Arab-Israeli War

Sadat and the Nasser legacy

Sadat's Middle East peace initiative

very existence was in danger and darkly hinted their intention of joining forces with Egypt. The United Nations finally arranged a cease-fire, and in March 1957 the Nasser government reopened the canal, under its own terms of national ownership, to all users except Israel. Nasser formed alliances with Jordan and Syria and vowed that Israel must be wiped from the map. In 1967, when he closed Aqaba, Israel's only direct outlet to the Red Sea, the Israelis responded with a lightning war against Egypt and its Arab allies. The Egyptian and Syrian forces were routed in six days, and the Syrians accepted a cease-fire a short time later, leaving Israel in occupation of the Gaza Strip and Sinai peninsula and the West Bank of the Jordan River. Although he was not solely to blame, Nasser's foreign policy ended in disaster. While aggravating Israeli-Arab hostility, he failed to realize his ambition of uniting the several Arab states under the banner of Arab nationalism. Conflicting ideologies and objectives kept them apart except for temporary alliances.

Following Nasser's death in 1970 Anwar Sadat, a relatively obscure member of the group that had overthrown the monarchy in 1952, became president of Egypt. With little political experience but a flair for showmanship (his youthful ambition had been to become an actor), Sadat was confronted by pressing domestic and foreign problems bequeathed by Nasser. He announced an "open door" economic policy, hoping to attract investment capital. This resulted in an influx of foreign consumer goods rather than solid industrial growth, keeping Egypt heavily dependent on outside sources for basic necessities. A new constitution, enacted in 1971, incorporated democratic features, but political power remained with the one and only legal party, the Arab Socialist Union, which had become bureaucratic and corrupt.

Sadat's most distinctive contribution was the reversal of his predecessor's foreign policy. He had inherited the quarrel with Israel, which in October 1973 erupted into open conflict once more when Egypt and Syria launched a surprise offensive in the Sinai and Golan Heights areas, respectively. Seventeen days of fierce fighting—ended under joint pressure from the United States and the USSR—brought little change except to show that Israel's preponderant military advantage had begun to erode. At this juncture Sadat, at the risk of sacrificing leadership of the Arab world, resolved to end the state of war with Israel which exacted a tremendous economic price and continually posed the threat of a general conflagration. Piecemeal agreements, negotiated with the help of United States Secretary of State Henry Kissinger in 1974 and 1975, provided for mutual disengagement in the Suez Canal area and the return of Sinai oilfields to Egyptian control. In June 1975 the canal—closed since 1967—was reopened to merchant ships of all nations, including Israel. Seizing an even bolder initiative, President Sadat—after requesting an invitation—in November 1977 became the first Arab leader to pay an official visit to the state of Israel, where he met an enthusiastic reception in Tel

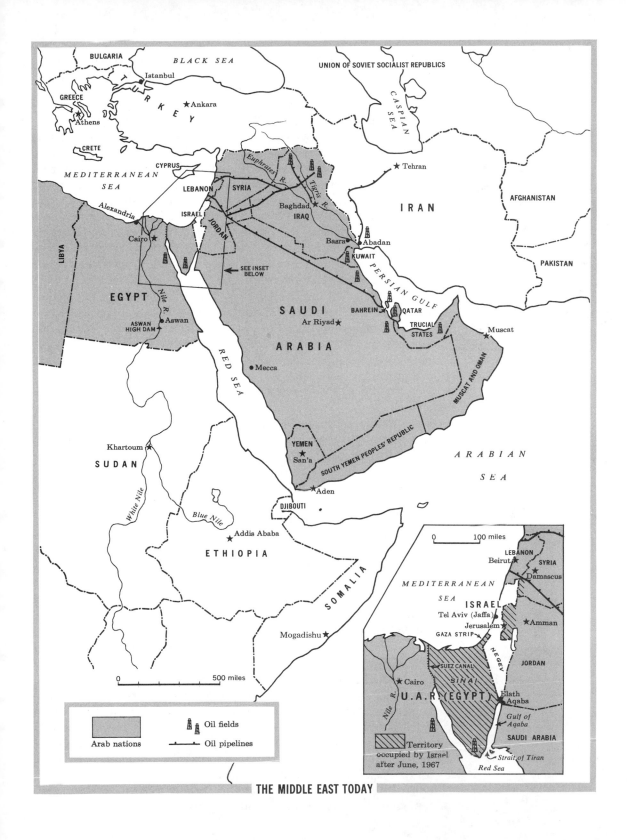

THE MIDDLE EAST TODAY

President Anwar Sadat of Egypt Addressing the Israeli Knesset in 1977

The political skills of Hosni Mubarak

Mubarak and the Muslim Brotherhood

Aviv and Jerusalem. This surprisingly auspicious weekend visit resolved none of the difficulties between the two states but it opened the door to improved relations. In his speech before the Israeli parliament (Knesset) Sadat affirmed Israel's right to exist, but at the same time he called unequivocally for withdrawal from all occupied Arab lands, for Arab access to the holy city of Jerusalem, and for the creation of an independent Palestinian state. Not until March 1979, after many months of negotiation, was an Egyptian-Israeli peace treaty signed, and it left important issues unresolved, particularly the exact nature of the "full autonomy" promised to the Palestinians, and the status of the city of Jerusalem—sacred to the adherents of three religions but which the Israelis had vowed to retain as their nation's capital.

While rapprochement with Israel was a constructive and statesmanlike move, it brought Egypt no reward beyond diplomatic support and increased financial and military aid from the United States. Hoping that Egypt would displace Israel as America's partner in the Middle East, Sadat had gambled and lost. Meanwhile Egypt faced isolation in the Islamic community. Sixteen Arab states, the Palestinian Liberation Organization, and Iran severed diplomatic relations with Cairo. In October 1981 President Sadat was assassinated by Egyptian Islamic fundamentalists.

Sadat's successor as president was Hosni Mubarak, commander-in-chief of the Egyptian army during the October 1973 war with Israel. Without the panache that had made his two predecessors celebrities, Mubarak showed promise of providing more stable leadership than either of them, while also moving in a democratic direction. Although he maintained rigid restrictions on political activity, he released political prisoners and allowed the press greater freedom than it had ever before enjoyed in the country's history. By this time an extra-legal but potent organization known as the Muslim Brotherhood had won support among an overwhelming majority of Egyptian Muslims. Founded in 1928, the Muslim Brotherhood embodied resistance to British colonial rule and provided effective fighters in the wars against Israel. Aiming to transform the state in the direction of conformity with Islamic law, its leaders declared their goal to be compatible with both modernization and democratic institutions. They are represented in parliament and in the leading professions, operate businesses, banks, and an extensive network of social-service agencies. Without granting it official recognition, the government not only tolerates the Brotherhood but actually cooperates with it in restraining extremist factions prone to violence. Some progressive leaders of the Brotherhood assert that the Coptic Christians—a minority of some nine million that has suffered persecution—could be accommodated harmoniously within a reformed Islamic state. Mubarak's skill in balancing the army against emerging political parties—and in tolerating popular pressure for the Islamization of institutions while suppressing radical fundamentalists—has won general support. In October 1987 he was reelected to a second presidential term with few dissenting votes.

President Hosni Mubarak of Egypt and Yasir Arafat of the Palestine Liberation Organization. Mubarak has plied his political skills in the larger Middle Eastern arena as well. Here he is seen with Yasir Arafat trying to mediate a dispute between King Hussein of Jordan and the PLO.

Egypt's most intractable problems are economic and demographic. Population doubled in the three decades following 1937. Impoverished or landless peasants pouring into the cities have made Egypt the most urbanized of Arab countries. Cairo, with two million inhabitants in 1952, had nine million twenty-five years later. Housing was so scarce that as many as ten people slept in a single room, and squatters improvised quarters in Cairo's cemeteries. While population expands relentlessly, soil fertility has begun to decline—the result of salinization from excessive irrigation and the encroachment of the desert—leading to a reduction in crop production of 18 percent annually. One of the world's oldest and choicest agricultural regions, which until past the middle of the twentieth century was self-sufficient in foodstuffs, has become a food-importing area. This deficiency, coupled with attempts to industrialize, necessitated heavy borrowing. In twelve years Egypt's foreign debt increased more than eight-fold to $44 billion in 1988. The country does have economic assets—tolls on Suez Canal traffic and substantial petroleum reserves, the export of which could provide revenue to stimulate industrial development if it does not have to be sacrificed to pay for food imports. While the Aswan High Dam has fallen short of solving the agricultural problem, the power potential of the dam, which supplies 40 percent of Egypt's electricity, is threatened by droughts and by competition for the waters of the Upper Nile, vital to several African states. Ethiopia, which controls the Blue Nile tributary, has refused to sign any joint agreement on water regulation. In 1985 Egypt's foreign minister warned: "The next war in our region will be over the waters of the Nile, not over politics."

The country known as Israel was the latest of five small Middle Eastern states to arise on lands taken from the Turks in 1918 and given to Britain and France to administer as mandates under the League of Nations. Palestine, which went to Britain, had a population about

Egypt's economic and demographic problems

70 percent Arab and 30 percent Jewish and Christian. In accepting the mandate for Palestine the British government, in conformity with the Balfour Declaration of 1917, promised to establish a Jewish homeland and also "to secure the preservation of an Arab National Home and to apprentice the people of Palestine as a whole in the art of self-government." Such was Britain's promise; but a curious thing happened on the way to its fulfillment. In 1921 Winston Churchill, the British colonial secretary, turned over the administration of the land east of the Jordan River to Abdullah, son of Sharif Hussein of Mecca, to whom the British were indebted for help in the war against Turkey. Abdullah, who had already sent a private army into Transjordan, installed himself as ruler, taking the title of king in 1946. In 1950 he renamed his country the Hashemite Kingdom of Jordan. Abdullah's brother Faisal, also in quest of a kingdom but driven out of Syria by the French, with British support acquired Iraq. Thus, by his decision regarding eastern Palestine, which he claimed to have made "one Sunday afternoon in Jerusalem," Churchill reduced the mandate to one-fourth of its original size. Meanwhile, Zionists in Britain and the United States were encouraging Jewish immigration into the promised national home.

In spite of its restricted size, for ten years Palestine prospered as never before in its history. Factories were built, land was relcaimed, irrigation works were constructed, the Jordan River was harnessed for electric power, and unemployment disappeared from the face of the land. Except for rioting in Jaffa in 1921, no incident of violence occurred to disturb the general tranquillity. The aspect of the country was so peaceful that in 1926 the British reduced their armed forces to a single RAF squadron and two companies with armored cars.

By 1929, however, evidences of disharmony had begun to appear in the land that was holy to three great religions. The prosperous and well-educated Jews were arousing the envy and fears of the Arabs by their high standard of living and their more strenuous competition. Their purchases of land, in many cases from absentee owners, had resulted in the displacement of thousands of Arab cultivators and had thrown them into the cities at a time when the Great Depression was beginning to make unemployment a serious problem. But the major cause of Arab foreboding was the steady increase in the Jewish population. The opportunity to emigrate to Palestine had offered a greater temptation than the Arabs had expected. As a consequence, some of them foresaw a relentless advance and expansion of Europeans and Americans, backed by foreign capital and flaunting a culture that was alien to the ways of the Arab majority. In 1929, 1930, and 1931 armed attacks were waged upon Jewish settlements followed by terrorist murders.

But these episodes paled into insignificance when compared with the bloody violence that followed. When the mandate was established, no one could have foreseen the desperate plight that was to overtake

Immigration to Palestine. Left: British soldiers guard the shore as a ship loaded with unauthorized refugees attempts to land in 1947. Right: A view of the unbearably crowded conditions aboard ships bringing refugees to Palestine.

the European Jews with the accession of the Nazis to power in Germany. As news of the persecutions spread, it was inevitable that pressure should be brought upon the British government to relax the barriers against immigration into Palestine. During the period 1933–1935 the admission of more than 130,000 Jewish immigrants was authorized, and uncounted thousands more came in illicitly. From this time on Palestine was a seething caldron of violence and warfare. The Arabs rose in open rebellion against the mandate. Organized terrorism swept the country. Guerrilla attacks in the rural areas and looting, burning, and sabotage in the towns and cities kept the whole population in turmoil. By 1938 Britain had 20,000 troops in Palestine, and even these were unable to maintain order.

Rebellion of the Arabs against the mandate

The early years of the Second World War were characterized by relative quiet in Palestine, but trouble broke out anew when a conference of American Zionists at the Biltmore Hotel in New York, in May 1942, adopted the so-called Biltmore Program, demanding the establishment of a Jewish state and a Jewish army in Palestine. Soon afterward both Jews and Arabs prepared for war to the hilt. Fanatical Zionists, as well as Arabs, resorted to the use of terrorist methods. Illegal military organizations sprang up on both sides and devoted their energies to raiding, burning, and assassination.

The Biltmore Program

In April 1947 the British government referred the Palestine problem to the United Nations and announced that a year later it would terminate the mandate and withdraw all its troops from the country. A United Nations proposal to split the region between Jews and Arabs

*Termination of the
mandate and establishment
of the State of Israel*

was unacceptable to the Arabs, but on May 15, 1948, the day the British mandate came to an end, a Jewish provisional government proclaimed the establishment of an independent State of Israel. Elections were held for a Constituent Assembly, which met in February of the following year and adopted a temporary constitution for a democratic republic. Its chief features were a weak president, a strong cabinet, and a powerful parliament. The constitution also provided for proportional representation, a unicameral parliament, and universal suffrage for Jews and Arabs alike. A unique element in the system was the close association of religion with the state. Marriage and divorce were placed under the exclusive jurisdiction of religious courts—Jewish, Christian, or Muslim as the affiliation of the parties might require.

Meanwhile, from the day of proclaimed independence until the spring of 1949, Israel and its Arab neighbor countries were at war. United Nations efforts brought about truces several times; Israel and Egypt signed a general armistice agreement in February 1949; Jordan and Syria also signed armistices in April. Israeli forces had captured some of the land assigned to the Arabs, but Egypt held the Gaza Strip and Jordan retained the West Bank, which it annexed in 1950. The status at the cease-fire was regarded as a victory for Israel and a defeat for the Arab powers; neither, however, accepted it as final. Violent incidents continued to occur, including retaliatory massacres.

Despite troubles with the Arabs, Israel strengthened its economy, and many new industries were created. Large sums of money flowed into the country as a result of West German restitution for the outrages of Nazism. Agriculture advanced to a stage sufficient to supply the needs of the home market while export crops such as olives, melons, and citrus fruits were rapidly developed. Land under cultivation more than doubled between 1955 and 1967. The index of industrial production increased from 100 in 1963 to 185 in 1969. The nation had seven universities, two with more than 10,000 students each. Total enrollment in all state schools had increased from 130,000 in 1948 to approximately 800,000 in 1970.

Yet the fate of Israel was not a happy one. The state was born in strife and during the first twenty-five years of its existence fought four wars with its Arab neighbor states. In the face of adversity Israel managed not only to endure but to grow in strength—a testimony to the resourcefulness and determination of its citizens but also owing to massive economic and military aid from the United States (currently $3 billion a year). Obsession with the problem of security has exacted a heavy economic and psychological toll. Between 1967 and 1975 defense spending rose to become the highest in the world in proportion to population. While purchasing U.S. weapons, Israel became an exporter of arms to some fifty other countries. Between 1975 and 1982 its arms sales doubled, reaching an annual figure of $1 billion, amounting to nearly 20 percent of the nation's industrial exports. At the same time the expanding military establishment affected government policies and the character of national life.

Until 1977 the government of Israel was controlled by the Labor party, secular in outlook and committed to a program of democratic socialism. In the election of May 1977 the Labor party was defeated and replaced by the Likud bloc, which drew much of its support from extreme nationalists opposed to any compromise with Israel's enemies. The areas seized by Israel in the 1967 war, which more than doubled the state's size and brought 1½ million Palestinians under its jurisdiction, were regarded by the extremists not as occupied Arab lands but as part of "Eretz Yisrael"—the ancient homeland assigned to the Jews by God—which it was their right and duty to preserve. Menachem Begin, the new prime minister, was a veteran of the struggle for independence and known as a hard-liner. Nevertheless, he agreed to exploratory talks with President Sadat of Egypt and accepted the invitation to a summit meeting at Camp David, Maryland, where President Jimmy Carter's patience and persistence bore fruit in the signing of a basic agreement. The Camp David Accords of September 1978 bound Sadat and Begin to take positive steps toward peace in the Middle East. But the formidable difficulties remaining were scarcely lessened by the Egyptian-Israeli treaty signed the following March. Palestinians feared that they would never be granted the autonomy called for in the Camp David accords, much less be permitted to form an independent state, which was their ultimate goal. This fear was intensified as Jewish settlements were planted in the occupied territories, frequently on lands expropriated from Arabs, adding 60,-000 Jews by the late 1980s. Gradually the Palestine Liberation Organization gained recognition as the leading champion of the Palestinian cause. Throughout its beleaguered history the PLO was alternately in and out of favor with Arab states and repeatedly forced to shift

The Camp David Accords

On the Path to Peace in the Middle East. From left to right, Egyptian President Anwar Sadat, U.S. President Jimmy Carter, and Israeli Prime Minister Menachem Begin shake hands at the announcement of the Camp David accord which laid the groundwork for a peace treaty between Egypt and Israel.

its headquarters. Although its reputation was clouded by repeated acts of violence, under the nimble leadership of Yasir Arafat it gradually came to embrace a policy of moderation in pursuing the goal of an independent state, and was denounced by Arab extremists as too willing to compromise with Israel. Nevertheless the Israeli government refused to meet with PLO representatives.

Exasperated by the depredations of terrorists stationed in southern Lebanon, the Israel government in June 1982 embarked on a punitive expedition that turned into the longest and most costly war of Israel's brief history. The objective announced by Begin's defense minister, Ariel Sharon, was to create a 40-kilometer buffer zone to protect Israel's northern border, but Sharon's real ambitions went much further. He hoped to destroy the Palestine Liberation Organization, establish a pro-Israel regime in Lebanon, and, by a smashing military victory, stifle opposition to the retention and settlement of the lands already occupied. The invasion of heavily armed Israeli troops into Lebanon, already wracked by civil war, unleashed a murderous free-for-all that tore the tiny country apart. Lebanese factions with long-standing rivalries and their own private militias fought one another. Syria (of which Lebanon had been a part until separated under the French mandate) intervened as a counterpoise to Israel and to safeguard its water rights. Israeli forces carried the battle into the city of Beirut, reducing much of this "Paris of the Middle East" to rubble. Among many horrifying incidents, the most shocking was the massacre of hundreds of Muslim civilians in two refugee camps, an act of butchery carried out in September 1982 by Israel's erstwhile ally, the Christian Phalangist militia. Although Sharon succeeded in driving a greatly weakened PLO out of Lebanon, he could not extinguish Arab nationalism; nor was he able to win a political victory or establish a stable government in Lebanon.

*Divisive effects of the
Lebanon war and the resort
to a coalition government*

The war in Lebanon, with a cost in human suffering beyond calculation, divided the Israeli people much as Vietnam had divided Americans. Soldiers who had fought bravely to defend Israel's borders refused to serve in an "imperialist" war. Public resentment over a failed military policy was heightened by the threat of economic collapse. During the last seven years of Likud-bloc rule, inflation had risen from an annual rate of 40 percent to 400 percent. The government was running a $30-billion deficit, and the nation's foreign debt was one of the largest in the world per capita. Elections for the Knesset in July 1984 produced a stalemate between the two major parties, necessitating the formation of a coalition National Unity government. Elections in November 1988 failed to break the deadlock but doubled the representation in the Knesset of four religious parties, each of which had a narrow constituency but which together held a balance of power between Labor and Likud.

For two decades the chief obstacle to a durable peace in the Middle East was the refusal of the Arabs to accept the legitimacy of the state of Israel. In the 1980s, after Israel had amply demonstrated its military capacity, the chief obstacle seemed to lie in the uncertain fate of the Palestinian refugees under Israeli control. In Gaza many still lived in camps that had been erected by a UN agency in 1948 as temporary shelters without sanitary facilities. Unemployment was high, especially in Gaza, even though the occupied regions supplied day laborers for Israeli industries. Inhabitants of the West Bank included many well-educated and influential leaders of the Arab community— intellectuals who chafed under military rule. The government's policy of establishing new Jewish settlements recruited largely from Israeli elements most hostile toward Arabs heightened Palestinian resentment. At the close of the year 1987 a resistance movement, initiated by Palestinian women and known as the *Intifada* (uprising), broke out into the open. The defense minister declared that he would meet the uprising with "force, might, and beatings." In reprisal for isolated acts of violence and to discourage verbal abuse and rock throwing, soldiers teargassed a peaceful procession of women, fired on unarmed demonstrators, and bulldozed entire villages. Five hundred Palestinians were killed and more than 20,000 were arrested. All Palestinian schools were closed and the teaching of children at home was made a criminal offense. While external pressure mounted against the government's repressive tactics, small but vigorous peace groups within Israel called for reconciliation between Jews and Arabs, conducted workshops in conflict resolution, and advocated a policy of "trading land for peace." Although Israeli officials refused to meet with any Palestinian leaders except those of their own choosing, the U.S. government, reversing

Obstacles to peace: the Palestinian refugees

The Faces of Conflict in Contemporary Israel. Left: Palestinian protesters on the West Bank burn the Israeli flag to punctuate their demand for an independent Palestinian state. Right: An ultra-orthodox Jew carries on a heated debate with an Israeli peace activist carrying a placard which reads "*Sharon* Get Your Hands Off J'slem."

its earlier stand, briefly pursued a series of talks with PLO representatives. By the summer of 1990 the National Unity coalition had foundered on the Palestinian issue. After parliamentary elections once again failed to give Labor a commanding majority, a ministry was formed by the Likud bloc allied with several rightist religious factions. This ongoing refusal of the Israeli electorate to give either Labor or Likud a mandate relegated Israel to a condition of political impotence in which the prospect for the peaceful resolution of the Palestinian dilemma seemed more remote than ever.

The changing character of Israeli society

During the first thirty years of Israel's existence as a state, the character of the nation changed considerably. Many early Zionists had visualized Israel as a haven for small farmers or a community of agricultural cooperatives. By the mid-1970s it had become a land of teeming cities, with a society 80 percent urban. A potential internal problem centered on the Israeli citizens of Arab descent, who were subjected to the strain of conflicting loyalties in times of controversy between Israel and Arab states. Theoretically equal under the law, Israeli Arabs were discriminated against in practice, and most of them lived in exclusively Arab villages in northern Israel. With the world's highest birth rate, their numbers more than quadrupled, constituting 17 percent of Israel's total population by 1987. Another factor affecting the character of society was a change in the pattern of immigration—a decline in the influx of Western Jews and an increase in those coming from Arabic and North African countries. By 1977 the Sephardic or "Oriental" elements outnumbered those of Western European or American origin (called Ashkenazi), but they suffered some of the same disadvantages as the Israeli Arabs. They resented the fact that their cultural traditions and contributions were ignored in defining Israel's goals and national character. Even Judaism was becoming a divisive force in Israel. The Jewish population was roughly 80 percent "secular" and 20 percent Orthodox, yet neither Reformed nor Conservative Judaism was tolerated. Orthodox fundamentalists were demanding strict prohibition of activities on the Sabbath and occasionally resorted to violence to impose it. The more extreme among them seemed determined to convert the most progressive and democratic state in the Middle East into a theocracy.

The formation of Saudi Arabia

In contrast to the successor states of the defunct Ottoman Empire, the origins of the Kingdom of Saudi Arabia can be dated from the mid-eighteenth century, when the Arabian House of Saud formed an advantageous alliance with an ascetic Islamic reformer. By the early twentieth century the Saud family ruled a large area in the interior of the Arabian Peninsula, known as the Nejd, with its capital in Riyadh. To the west lay the rival kingdom of the Hejaz, ruled by the Hashemite family under Sharif Hussein, "Protector of the Holy Cities of Mecca and Medina." (He was the father of Abdullah and Faisal, who later became kings of Jordan and Iraq, respectively.) Abdul ibn-Saud (1880–1953), after defeating and driving out Sharif Hussein, in January 1926 had himself proclaimed King of the Hejaz in the great Mosque of

A Meeting of the Arab Kings. In the wake of a war on the Nejd-Iraq border, King Faisal of Iraq (seated fourth from the left) and King Abdul ibn-Saud of Saudi Arabia (seated fifth from the left) negotiated a lasting peace under British auspices in 1930.

Mecca. Soon afterward he united the two kingdoms of Hejaz and Nejd into a theocratic state which he named Saudi Arabia.

Saudi Arabia is as large as the United States east of the Mississippi River, but it is almost 100-percent desert. Not a single river or lake exists to relieve the monotonous aridity, and to this day it is inhabited by fewer than 13 million people. Ibn-Saud was shrewd enough to realize that the Muslim world could not hold its own against Western encroachments without adopting Western improvements. Accordingly, he allowed a few railways to be built and imported motor vehicles for his own court and for the transportation of pilgrims to the Holy Cities, and he instituted plans for free education. By far the greatest impetus was the discovery, in the 1930s, that eastern Arabia contained undreamed of riches in the form of petroleum deposits, amounting to the world's largest known reserves. King ibn-Saud granted concessions for the exploitation of this wealth to the Arabian-American Oil Company (ARAMCO), owned jointly by Texaco and the Standard Oil Company of California. Royalties paid by ARAMCO provided the funds for electrification of cities and the construction of highways, railroads, and airports, to say nothing of aid to agriculture, education, and public health.

Saudi oil and ARAMCO

Abdul ibn-Saud's son and heir, a wildly reckless spendthrift, was deposed by the royal family in 1964 and replaced by his half brother Faisal. King Faisal, who also retained the prime ministership, proved to be an enlightened and able statesman. He abolished slavery in his kingdom, opened public schools for girls, and won wide respect.

Yamani and OPEC

Sheikh Ahmed Zaki Yamani, Oil Minister of Saudi Arabia, at an OPEC Conference outside Algiers in March 1975

His success owed much to the loyal service of Sheikh Ahmed Zaki Yamani. Western-educated (New York University, Columbia, Harvard), brilliant, and level-headed, Yamani had been appointed minister of petroleum and mineral resources in 1962, before Faisal's accession to the throne. Sheikh Yamani negotiated agreements with ARAMCO providing for the gradual transfer of ownership to Saudi Arabia, directed similar negotiations with Western oil companies for other Arab states, and initiated the formation of the Organization of Petroleum Exporting Countries (OPEC). In April 1978 King Faisal was assassinated by a member of his own family. After the brief reign of Faisal's sickly brother Khalid, in 1982 the throne passed to Crown Prince Fahd, the eleventh of ibn-Saud's numerous sons.

Saudi Arabia affords a striking illustration of how the impact of advanced technology and an expanding market can telescope centuries and divergent cultures. The government is an absolute monarchy, with power exercised by the king but residing in about 3,000 princes of the Saudi royal household. Abject poverty is still prevalent outside the few rapidly modernizing cities. Society for the most part is bound by the rigid restrictions of Muslim traditionalism, seen typically in the banning of alcoholic beverages and in the seclusion of women.

A Saudi Arabian Oil Refinery and Storage Tanks. Saudi oil production reached a high of 10.5 million barrels per day in early 1981 as the government sought to make up the shortfall created by the Iran-Iraq war that began in late 1980, to force the OPEC nations to devise a unified policy, and to forestall the onset of a worldwide economic crisis. Only their first objective was realized. As a worldwide recession took hold, demand for oil dropped off sharply and with it the price and OPEC's influence. By 1986 Saudi Arabia was producing less than 3 million barrels of oil per day and trying to cope with the effects of more than a $90 billion drop in income from five years earlier. Saudi production and the price of oil rose again in 1990 in response to the Iraqi invasion of Kuwait and a United Nations–sanctioned economic embargo of Iraq, but the benefits were offset by fears of a major armed conflict that threatened to consume the entire Persian Gulf region.

But the citizens, with no elections and no parliament to represent them, nevertheless enjoy welfare benefits that might be envied by socialist democracies: free medical service, free education through the university level, subsidies to farmers, and loans to homeowners. The wealth accruing to Saudi Arabia as the world's largest oil-exporting country has enabled it to finance ambitious domestic projects and also to contribute subsidies to Egypt, Jordan, Syria, and the PLO.

Modernization

Saudi wealth was greatly enhanced when the 1973–1974 Arab oil embargo against the Western powers sent oil prices skyrocketing from less than $6 per barrel to over $46 by the end of the decade. In the early 1980s a glut of oil on the world market, traceable in part to the economic impact of the earlier Arab oil embargo, brought a sharp decline in price. OPEC members other than Saudi Arabia repeatedly broke their pledge to reduce production, eventually forcing the Riyadh government to expand its own output and thus further lowering the price. The price of oil bottomed out at $9 per barrel in 1986. By 1988 Saudi Arabia's liquid capital assets had shrunk to $65 billion—half of what they had been eight years earlier—necessitating budget reduction and the curtailment of social services. However, the regime's stability did not appear to be in doubt. The price of oil recovered to $20 per barrel by the summer of 1990 when the Iraqi invasion and annexation of Kuwait threw the entire Persian Gulf region into crisis and triggered a new wave of volatility in the international oil market (see below, p. 695).

The triumph of Iranian nationalism under Riza Khan

The easternmost of the states commonly regarded as making up the Middle East is Iran, known throughout most of its long history by the name of Persia. In the limited world view of the ancient Greeks and Romans, Persia represented Asia as opposed to Europe—the luxurious and despotic Orient. For many centuries Persia under successive dynasties was the seat of a powerful empire—a match for Rome and its successor Byzantium, and, after the rise of Islam, a Muslim power rivaling the empire of the Ottomans. But by the twentieth century the country had lapsed into a backward condition, and its government was weak. Rich in resources but steeped in languor, Persia was a constant temptation to ambitious imperialists. In 1907 Great Britain and Russia signed an agreement providing for the division of the country into spheres of influence. The northern sphere was assigned to Russia and the southern to Great Britain. A middle zone was to be left, temporarily at least, under the control of the native shah. The overthrow of the tsar in 1917 filled the minds of British imperialists with hopes that all Persia might be theirs. By 1919 Lord Curzon had extorted from the Shah an agreement transferring to Great Britain political and military control of the entire country. But the plans of the British were frustrated by Riza Khan, a young army officer who forced the Shah to appoint him minister of war and commander-in-chief of the army. In 1923 he became premier and two years later Shah with the title Riza Pahlavi. In 1932 he canceled the concession of the powerful Anglo-Persian Oil Company and obtained a new contract with terms more advantageous to his own government. In 1935 he changed the name of his country from Persia to Iran, or land of the Aryans.

The Second World War brought almost as much turmoil and anguish to Iran as if it had been one of the belligerents. Accused of Nazi sympathies, Riza Shah in 1941 was forced to abdicate and was succeeded on the throne by his son Muhammad Riza Pahlavi. Because of its strategic importance, Iran's territory was occupied by the British, Russians, and Americans under pledges to respect its sovereignty and independence and to render economic assistance during and after the war. Despite these pledges, unrest and inflation plagued the country. An internal political conflict led to the temporary expulsion of the Shah. Premier Muhammad Mossadegh, a nationalist leader, precipitated an international crisis in 1951 when he secured authorization from parliament to nationalize the petroleum industry. Western opposition to any assertion of economic independence by an underdeveloped semicolonial country was complicated by Anglo-American rivalry. Averse to prolonged negotiation, the United States government cut off aid to Teheran and persuaded the British to join in enforcing a boycott which denied Iran access to oil tankers and oil markets. The consequent shutdown of the huge Anglo-Iranian refinery at Abadan brought the Iranian government to the point of bankruptcy. In August 1953 a CIA-directed coup overthrew the government, replacing Mossadegh with a former Nazi collaborator and restoring the Shah to his throne. Under a new agreement, 40 percent of Iran's petroleum industry was allotted to five American companies.

Muhammad Riza Pahlavi's reign, spanning nearly four decades, brought his country considerable material progress, an overblown military establishment, brutal repression, and finally a revolution that shook society to its roots. During the 1960s Iran achieved an annual economic growth rate of 9 percent and doubled the gross national product. Revenues from oil, the chief natural resource, made possible highway construction, power-generating dams, and the beginnings of a system of public education. But the Shah's much advertised reform program did little to alleviate the poverty of the majority of his subjects. In 1979 three out of five rural families owned either no land or practically none, and millions of uprooted agricultural workers had drifted to the cities in search of work. One-tenth of the population controlled half of the wealth. Social services were inadequate and inferior. Sixty percent of the adult population was illiterate.

While indulging in the trappings of absolute monarchy—exemplified by five palaces maintained for the royal family, and by a multi-million-dollar extravaganza at Persepolis in 1971 to celebrate the 2,500th anniversary of Persian monarchy—the Shah hoped to modernize the nation. Seemingly equating modernization with militarization, between 1959 and 1978 he spent $36 billion on arms, about half of them purchased from the United States. In order to pay for sophisticated planes, missiles, and supporting equipment, he raised the price of oil—contributing to the upward surge that quadrupled oil prices in 1974. Expansion of land, air, and naval forces made Iran the strongest military power in the Persian Gulf area.

Disregarding a 1906 constitution that guaranteed basic rights to the citizens, the Shah, however, suppressed all political parties except one of his own invention and forbade any opposition to his rule. Commander-in-chief of the armed forces, he bolstered his position by keeping an imperial guard and, especially, through the notorious SAVAK, a secret police force employing terror and various forms of torture. While repression did not prevent eventual revolution, it eliminated much of the potential leadership needed for reconstruction after the advent of revolution.

Muhammad Riza Pahlavi, Shah of Iran

Latent opposition to the Shah's rule had long rankled among Muslim religious leaders, the *mullahs,* both because their influence had been curtailed and because some aspects of modernization were repugnant to them. Intellectuals were alienated by government repression and corruption. Disaffection spread throughout the Iranian population in the late 1970s when an economic slump halted industrial projects and rising unemployment was accompanied by a 50-percent rate of inflation. January 1978 inaugurated a year of riots and bloody clashes. Crowds of millions demonstrated in the streets; some 8,000 people were killed as the police cracked down on protesters. In September the Shah imposed martial law and appointed a military governor, confident that, with the army behind him, he could weather the storm. But strikes in the oil fields and violent eruptions led by university students paralyzed the government and brought the economy to a standstill. When it became evident that the army was not without sympathy for the revolutionaries, the Shah was forced to vacate his throne. On January 16, 1979, he left Iran by plane "on a vacation," and a Revolutionary Council was installed in his place. Revolutionary courts sentenced and executed hundreds of the Shah's former supporters, including nearly a third of the military high command.

Revolution: expulsion of the Shah

The Shah's abrupt capitulation left the country in a divided and chaotic state. Western governments had been strangely blind to the nearly universal hatred which Iranians bore toward their ruler. Having praised the Shah as a staunch ally, commanding "an island of stability in one of the most troubled areas of the world," American officials were unprepared to deal effectively with his successors.

Washington's failure to anticipate the revolution

Beyond expulsion of the Shah, the objectives of the popular revolution that swept Iran were not entirely clear. The key revolutionary figure and soon the wielder of absolute power was a seventy-eight-year-old Islamic theologian, the Ayatollah Ruholla Khomeini. A lifelong enemy of the Pahlavi dynasty, Khomeini had been exiled in 1964, sought refuge in Iraq and later in Paris, and in the French capital gathered around him the nucleus of a revolutionary government. A man of great energy and passionate convictions, Khomeini was

Ideology of the Revolutionary regime

The Ayatollah Ruholla Khomeini of Iran

Confrontation with the United States; war with Iraq

idolized upon his re-entry into Iran on February 1 and, with the assistance of a Revolutionary Council, issued decrees for the nation. Before long, every secular or moderate leader was eliminated, and Khomeini drafted a new constitution designed to remake society in rigid conformity with Islamic law and Shiite tradition. The constitution provided for a popularly elected president but made all officials subject to supervision and removal by the religious authorities. Although SAVAK was abolished, a special police force was created to ferret out any opposition and enforce behavioral codes. Women lost what few rights they had ever possessed. Reduced in the eyes of the law to chattels of their husbands, they were forbidden to appear in public unless concealed by the veil and tentlike *chador*. Khomeini suppressed dissidents as ruthlessly as had the Shah; it appeared that a secular tyranny had been replaced by an equally cruel one grounded in religious fanaticism. The Ayatollah viewed himself not simply as Iran's leader but as the precursor of an "Islamic world order." An adherent of the "Twelvers" Shiite tradition, he looked forward to the coming of a Twelfth Imam or Messiah (*Mahdi*), who would usher in a "world government of God." He rejected both the concept of the nation-state and the present international system, which he viewed with stark simplicity as a dualistic struggle between good and evil forces. To him the United States represented "Great Satan," the Soviet Union "Lesser Satan"—which together oppressed the world's peoples and must be opposed with physical and moral force. He saw it as his mission to prepare the way for the world's salvation by calling on people everywhere to establish "true Islamic" governments. Never before, not even among the most fervent Communist ideologues, had the doctrine of exporting revolution been given such intense expression as by Ruholla Khomeini.

Khomeini's defiant international stance was soon put to the test. In dealing with "Great Satan" he was able to capitalize on anti-American sentiment, provoked by the close ties that had existed between Washington and the Shah's government and aggravated when the ailing exiled monarch was admitted to an American hospital for treatment. In reprisal a group of militants seized the United States embassy in Teheran in November 1979 and held fifty-two hostages captive for 444 days. Their release was obtained only after long, repeatedly stalemated, and humiliating negotiations. A more severe test came in September 1980 when Iraq, a neighbor with whom Iran had long-standing disputes, launched a military attack. The Iraqis, repudiating a 1975 agreement made with the Shah, hoped to gain control of the Shatt-al-Arab—the 100-mile-long terminus of the great Tigris-Euphrates river system emptying into the Persian Gulf. The Baghdad government also feared the spread of Islamic fundamentalism and revolutionary fervor, which might infect Iraq's substantial Shiite population.

The eight-year Iran-Iraq war proved to be the longest, bloodiest,

Iranian Demonstrators Outside the U.S. Embassy in Teheran, November 25, 1979. Militants, bearing portraits of Ayatollah Khomeini and cardboard effigies of President Jimmy Carter, protested the American role in Iranian affairs during the previous 26 years while 52 American hostages were held in the embassy.

and costliest in the modern history of the Middle East. Iraq had counted on a quick victory because of its superior striking power, but this advantage was countered by Iran's large population and its leaders' willingness to sacrifice wave after wave of the nation's youth as "martyrs" in a holy war. The Baghdad government could neither win the war nor end it because Khomeini demanded as a precondition for peace negotiations the ousting of Iraq's president, Saddam Hussein.

The Baath party which seized power in Iraq in 1968 had been carrying out a secular, socialist revolution before the outbreak of the war with Iran. While imposing a military dictatorship, the revolutionary leaders strengthened Iraq's economy and initiated a land-redistribution program for the benefit of the cultivators. Huge oil reserves—largest among the Arab states except for Saudi Arabia and carefully managed—gave Iraq an advantageous position in foreign trade and its people a relatively high standard of living. Upon a population comprising both Shiite and Sunnite Muslims as well as Christians, the secular rulers imposed religious toleration and decreed equality of the sexes, granting women the right of divorce and making their forced marriage a criminal offense. Meanwhile, Iraq's military establishment was steadily expanding in order to displace Iran as the strongest power in the Persian Gulf. Saddam Hussein, who in 1979 replaced the ailing President Bakr as head of the Revolutionary Command and president, asserted that Iraq's political struggle was a revolution against imperialism, and he called upon other Arabs to join him in creating a new power on the world scene. This ambitious goal was shelved during the exhausting war with Iran which reduced Iraq from a capital-surplus nation to a debtor nation.

Iraq's bid for Arab leadership

Arms sales and scandal

In addition to the suffering the Iran-Iraq war inflicted upon civilian populations of the Gulf region, it carried the continual risk of igniting a wider conflagration. While fully aware of the danger, nations that were capable of exerting pressure upon the belligerents but were profiting from arms sales to them did little to force an end to the conflict. A U.S. naval force dispatched to the Persian Gulf to protect neutral shipping ignored the depredations inflicted by Iraq. Yet the Washington administration, which had excoriated Iran as the fountainhead of terrorism, secretly offered to supply Iran with high-tech missiles in return for help in securing the release of American hostages held by terrorists. When it became public knowledge, the abortive arms-for-hostages deal—complicated by the intention to divert profits from the arms sale to the "Contra" forces attempting to overthrow the government of Nicaragua—caught the Reagan administration in a scandal reminiscent of "Watergate" under President Nixon. The initiative for terminating the war came primarily from the United Nations, whose secretary-general's persistent efforts finally persuaded Security Council members to pass a resolution in July 1987 calling for a cease-fire and threatening an arms embargo for noncompliance. Early the following year the cease-fire was accepted by both Baghdad and Teheran.

The cooling of Iran's messianic ardor

The heavy cost of the war and its long duration inevitably tempered the messianic fervor of the Khomeini regime. Remarkably, the struggle did not exhaust Iran's resources. Annual expenditures were kept somewhat lower than they had been under the Shah—an indication of the extravagance in which the monarchy had indulged. Moreover, the revolutionary government invested heavily in rural development and in school buildings, roads, clinics, and small-scale industry. Midway through the war Teheran softened its attitude toward the neighboring Gulf monarchies, no longer denouncing them as "greedy pigs." Although Atatürk's Turkey was the antithesis of the true Islamic state, Iran and Turkey remained on friendly terms and were joined by Pakistan in an economic association. After the death of the aged Khomeini in the early summer of 1989 the speaker of the parliament, Hojatolislam Hashemi Rafsanjani, while expressing loyalty to the Ayatollah's principles, undertook to mend Iran's diplomatic fences.

Hussein and the Iraqi national will

Without having achieved his objectives in the war with Iran, nor even a peace treaty, Saddam Hussein interpreted his escape from defeat as a victory and resumed his program of industrial and military growth. He expanded exports to pay off war debts, rebuilt ravaged cities on a lavish scale, and publicized his leadership role by displaying his picture everywhere, seeking respect not as a Muslim or even as an Arab but as the embodiment of a strong national will. To instill a sense of destiny among Iraqis he appealed to antiquity, restoring the ancient city of Babylon. Eulogists likened him to the Babylonian lawgiver Hammurabi.

In early August 1990 Saddam Hussein, without warning but with massive force, invaded the tiny neighboring state of Kuwait, deposed the royal family, and showed every intention of retaining this oil-rich strip of desert at the head of the Persian Gulf. More than provoking a Middle East crisis, Hussein's aggressive action conjured up the fear that the end of the Cold War would merely mark the beginning of new regional wars carrying the risk of world conflagration. The Iraqi invasion was condemned by the United Nations' Security Council and vehemently denounced by the United States where energy conservation had never been seriously undertaken and the prospect of skyrocketing oil prices threatened to rock an already sluggish economy. The rulers of Saudi Arabia, fearing that they might be the next victims of an expansionist Iraq, welcomed Washington's prompt offer of military protection provided it could be cloaked in the garb of a multinational effort with a substantial Arab component. American initiative secured wide support for a boycott of Iraq-Kuwait exports and imports. Finally, in addition to courting international censure, Hussein had divided the Arab nations by attacking one of them. Egypt, a major power in the Middle East, headed the Arab opposition. Nevertheless, in spite of the odds against him, Hussein held some high cards. The ace up his sleeve was his claim to be the champion of have-not Third World peoples exploited by imperialist masters shielded and dominated by the United States. With some justification he could charge that Kuwait and the Gulf emirates, while providing cheap fuel for the industrial nations, had brought enormous wealth to an elite few without helping other Arabs beyond employing them for hard labor at minimal wages. Saddam's rhetoric was geared less toward converting governments than toward subverting them by issuing a call to revolution to the impoverished masses of the Middle East.

Ambiguities in the Arab position were sharply illustrated by the dilemma facing the state of Jordan, whose King Hussein, with ties to the West, denounced the occupation of Kuwait and agreed to join the UN-sponsored blockade. However, to close the Jordanian port of Aqaba, as was requested, would not only invite retaliation from Saddam Hussein but would also cripple Jordan's economy. Meanwhile, many of King Hussein's subjects expressed an eagerness to fight with the Iraqi strongman against "imperialists." Palestinians also, resenting the American failure to pressure Israel on their behalf, looked toward Saddam as a possible deliverer. Anticipating the impact of the trade embargo, President Hussein offered to formalize peace with Iran on Iran's terms, renouncing rights to the Shatt-al-Arab waterway, for which he had begun the war ten years earlier.

The ideological bases of the confrontation in the Gulf were weak on both sides. For such a secular figure as Saddam Hussein to claim he was waging a holy war on behalf of Islam was bizarre, especially with Muslims divided against Muslims. By the same token, while the United States and its allies were on firm moral ground in condemning an act of aggression, in defending absolute monarchies with semifeudal societies they could not credibly define their role as opposing communism or upholding democracy. Basically, the contest was over power, prestige, and petroleum.

The invasion of Kuwait and the response of the international community

President Saddam Hussein of Iraq. Casting himself as the heir of Hammurabi, who styled himself "King of the Four Quarters of the World," Hussein ruthlessly pursued a vision of Iraq as a great power.

Ambiguity in the Arab World

A contest over power, prestige, and petroleum

The Iraqi Threat to Stability in the Middle East: The Case of Jordan. Left: In the wake of the Iraqi invasion and occupation of Kuwait, thousands of Asian refugees fled from Kuwait to Jordan where they were stranded in tent cities. Added to the existing Palestinian refugee problem, this latest wave of displaced people placed an enormous burden on Jordan's fragile economy. Right: Large numbers of Jordanians and Palestinians rallied to Saddam Hussein's call for a "holy war" to free Arab soil of Western imperialists and their agents. Caught between Iraq and an international force led by a U.S. army of over 400,000 men and women, the government of King Hussein of Jordan faced the specter of revolution.

War in the Persian Gulf

Although internationally supported sanctions—the most stringent ever imposed on any country—cut off all of Iraq's exports and most of its imports, the Bush administration, unwilling to wait out the slow course of economic strangulation, pressed for and obtained a United Nations Security Council resolution authorizing the use of "all means necessary" against Saddam Hussein if he did not withdraw from Kuwait by January 15, 1991. Within hours after this deadline the United States with allied support began an aerial attack with hi-tech weaponry previously unknown to warfare. Six weeks of unremitting bombardment inflicted such heavy casualties—military and civilian—and so devastated Iraq's basic utilities and infrastructure that the subsequent ground assault met with little resistance and within days forced Saddam to sue for a ceasefire. Defeated by external enemies he now faced rebellion by Kurds from the north and Shiites to the south. But if victory for the coalition came more swiftly than anticipated it found the victors unsure of their objectives. President Bush, who had urged the Iraqis to overthrow Saddam, now feared the consequences of Iraq's dismemberment and forbade US troops to aid the rebels. Israel, having yielded to American pressure not to retaliate against Iraqi missile attacks, opposed a conference on the Palestinian issue and at the end of March the "New World Order" of Bush's aspiration appeared remote.

The Middle East has been in ferment ever since the Second World War. Lands that had cradled Western civilization and nurtured ancient empires were subjected to more rapid change than ever before in their long history. In a region where abject poverty is the lot of the majority of the population, the discovery of enormous stores of petroleum—totaling two-thirds of the world's proven reserves—has brought wealth and clout to desert monarchies and small Gulf sheikdoms. Their strategic importance was demonstrated dramatically in the mid-1970s when they precipitated a crisis in the industrialized world by imposing an embargo on oil shipments from the Arab states and Iran, bringing a nine-fold increase in the price of this essential commodity. But OPEC failed to become an effective cartel; its share of world oil production fell from 50 percent in 1979 to 28 percent in 1985. Unity in any sphere is a quality conspicuously lacking in the Middle East. An Arab League, formed in 1945 with Egypt, Saudi Arabia, Jordan, Iraq, Syria, Lebanon, and Yemen as the original members, failed to resolve internal differences. Egypt, the League's military right arm, was expelled in 1979 in retaliation for Anwar Sadat's rapprochement with Israel and became temporarily a pariah in the eyes of fellow Arabs. The long-standing quarrel between Jews and Arabs and the problem of the Palestinians in the occupied territories are complicated by other explosive forces, including the ambitions of ethnic minorities: Kurds in Turkey, Iran, and Iraq; Baluchi in Iran, Afghanistan, and Pakistan. The rising level of armaments, including highly sophisticated weapons from the United States, the Soviet Union, West Germany, and France among others, has made regional conflicts increasingly lethal and threatening to world peace.

Recent international developments offered hope that the peoples of the Middle East could escape from the trap of their dismal modern history. The Iran-Iraq war ended without spreading an epidemic of revolutions. Defrosting the Cold War has facilitated diplomatic initiatives. Under the leadership of Mikhail Gorbachev, beginning in 1985 the Soviet Union switched its foreign policy from confrontation to conciliation, seeking not only to renew ties with the Arab states but also to establish ties with Israel, and making overtures to Iran. Furthermore, the United Nations, understaffed and underfunded but tireless in offering its services, promises to be a more dynamic and effective instrument for peace in a post-Cold War environment in which the strategic interests of the superpowers no longer automatically dictate obstructionist behavior. But the Gulf war that began in January 1991, even if it eliminated Saddam Hussein, by fueling local rivalries and inflaming Arab animosity against the West, could jeopardize for decades the prospect of a stable and peaceful Middle East.

2. THE REPUBLIC OF SOUTH AFRICA

Perhaps in no other African state have the problems of national building, tribalism, and racial cooperation proved more difficult than in

President Paul Kruger of the Transvaal

The Boer War (1899–1902)

Prime Minister Cecil Rhodes of the Cape Colony

the Republic of South Africa. Conflicts between Boer, Bantu, and Briton have punctuated the history of South Africa for generations. Each group almost fanatically adheres to its own traditions and conceptions of how society should be organized.

Before the 1870s Great Britain had followed a colonial policy of benign neglect toward South Africa. The interior, long considered barren in natural resources, was of little importance to the British. Indeed, their prime concern lay in protecting the vital sea route to India by controlling the strategically important harbors along the South African coast. But in 1867 diamonds were discovered at Kimberley, and nineteen years later the fabulous gold fields of the Witwaterstrand became a mecca for prospectors and adventurers from all over the world. Between 1872 and 1902 the white population of South Africa quadrupled. Congested cities such as Johannesburg and Bloemfontein mushroomed on the veldt. The simple pastoral economy of the old-fashioned Boers had come to an end.

The discovery of diamonds and gold multiplied the political difficulties of the Boer republics. British and other foreigners swarmed in such numbers that they threatened to overwhelm the white Afrikaner settlers. The latter retaliated by branding the immigrants as outlanders and denying them political privileges except under the most rigorous conditions. The suffrage was refused, the press censored, and public meetings practically forbidden. In desperation the British organized a conspiracy to overthrow the most obstinate of the Boer governments, that of Paul Kruger, president of the Transvaal. Ammunition was collected, with the connivance of Cecil Rhodes, prime minister of the Cape Colony; and on December 29, 1895, 600 Britons and their armed retainers, under the leadership of Rhodes's friend, Dr. Leander Jameson, raided the Transvaal. The invaders were quickly surrounded and captured, but their act greatly magnified the tension between British and Boers. The Afrikaner governments increased the restrictions against foreigners and accumulated arms in preparation for a showdown. In October 1899, war broke out between these republics and the predominantly British colonies.

The Boer War dragged its length through three bloody years. Not until Britain sent sizable reinforcements under the leadership of its best generals was it able to snatch victory from the jaws of defeat. Finally, outnumbered seven to one, the Boers yielded and signed the Treaty of Vereeniging. In return for submitting to British rule, they were exempted from indemnities, promised representative institutions at an early date, and permitted to retain their own language in the courts and schools. The British government provided $15,000,000 to accelerate the process of reconstruction. It was one of the most generous peace settlements in history. At this time the victorious British were in the position to impose on South Africa a universal, nonracial franchise. Tragically, the plight of the African majority was ignored. The question of racial justice was avoided in the name of Boer-British reconciliation.

In 1910 Cape Colony, Natal, the Orange Free State, and the Transvaal were merged into the Union of South Africa. This was a self-governing dominion within the British Empire, alongside the dominions of Canada, New Zealand, and Australia. The National Convention that drafted the Constitution provided for a unitary instead of a federal state. The reasons were several. The need for railway construction and for solving the problems of a large black population seemed to demand unification. More important was the fact that the two white nationalities did not occupy separate provinces as in Canada. In most states the rural population was Afrikaner or Boer, the urban population British. In some additional respects also the government of South Africa differed from that of the other dominions. The Cabinet did not stand or fall as a unit, but, theoretically at least, disagreements were permitted among the members. Its control over the upper house of parliament was more effective. In case of a conflict between the Cabinet and the Assembly, or lower house, both houses might be dissolved and their members compelled to stand for re-election. South Africa had a much more conservative attitude toward the suffrage than did the other dominions. Universal manhood suffrage for whites was not adopted until 1930. Woman suffrage was also adopted in the same year, but in the face of stiff opposition. The minister of justice, for example, declared that the female franchise conflicted "with the intentions that the Creator had for women." As for the Africans, who constituted more than 75 percent of the population, all were disfranchised except in the southernmost Cape Province, where Negro and Asian citizens voted under limited conditions.

The franchise was an especially passionate issue among blacks. Organized African political activity emerged in the late nineteenth century under the moderate leadership of Western-educated middle-class black professionals and clergymen. They were seeking a nonracial franchise and an end to racial discrimination. The Bambata Rebellion of 1906, in which over four thousand Africans died, was the last armed resistance against white supremacy by traditional African leaders. The new elites abhorred violent resistance and sought inspiration in the ideas of passive resistance developed by a local Indian attorney, Mahatma Gandhi. Africans were excluded from deliberations on the new constitution of 1910, and two years later they formed their own political party, the African National Congress. White politicians shrugged off their demands for equality and in 1936 passed a law barring any chance for blacks to directly elect representatives to parliament. Fears of being outvoted by the numerically superior black population were thus assuaged. But nonwhite frustration and anger were fueled, and youths became increasingly impatient with the moderate tactics of the older leadership.

The sharpest controversies in South African politics since the formation of the Union have been those relating to nationality and race. Although the British made repeated efforts at reconciliation following the Boer War, the old hatreds died hard. In 1912 a faction of extremist

General James B. M. Hertzog, Leader of the Afrikaner Nationalist Party and Prime Minister, 1924–1939

General Jan Christiaan Smuts, Spokesman of South African Moderates and Prime Minister, 1919–1924 and 1939–1948

Boers broke away from their kinsmen and formed the Nationalist party. Under the leadership of General Hertzog, they strove to preserve the cultural independence of the Afrikaners and to tolerate no fusion with the British. They resented British aggressiveness and regarded it as synonymous with an imperialism which threatened to obliterate the customs and institutions of their revered ancestors. They eventually came to advocate the severance of all ties with the British and the transformation of the Dominion into an Afrikaner republic. Anti-Semitism also emerged as a cardinal policy in the minds of the most fanatical. The finance capitalists who controlled the gold and diamond mines of the Rand[1] were alleged to be mostly Jews who were lightly taxed by the British-dominated government. By 1938 the Nationalists seemed almost as greatly disturbed by the "Jewish Menace" as they were by the "Black Peril" and were demanding the exclusion of all Jewish immigrants.

The two world wars of 1914 and 1939 contributed to the strength of the Nationalist movement. The followers of General Hertzog were determined that South Africa should not be dragged into war at the behest of the London government. The right to remain neutral they considered an indispensable badge of their nation's sovereignty. In 1914 some of them organized a rebellion as an armed protest against enslavement to British objectives. But the policy of their opponent, General Jan Christiaan Smuts, prevailed, and South Africa contributed its share toward winning the war. Eight years after the Armistice the Nationalists, supported by Labor, gained control of the government, but with a watered-down program that did not demand complete independence. When Britain again went to war in 1939, the South African government split. Six Cabinet ministers supported the war, five opposed. In the Assembly the vote was 80 in favor of the war to 67 against. It was obvious that the termination of hostilities would leave the country torn asunder and that the difficulties and tensions growing out of the war would widen the cleavage still further. Military production brought thousands of Africans into the towns and created fears of Communist uprisings or some other form of social revolution. In the official census of 1946, blacks for the first time in history outnumbered whites in the urban areas. Following this, the government-appointed Fagan Commission held that the incorporation of blacks in the nation's economic system is an irrevocable reality and that the Africans' progressive integration into the whites' political system should be accepted as a logical consequence. The commission maintained that the permanence of an urban black labor force could neither be denied nor reversed and that total segregation was impossible.

---

[1] The Rand, or Witwaterstand, is a sixty-mile ridge which constitutes a watershed between the Vaal and Limpopo rivers.

As an Afrikaner party of the extreme right, the Nationalists played upon the fears engendered by the Fagan Commission and in the 1948 elections they gained control of parliament. The Nationalists not only espoused the idea of an independent republic purged of British influence but demanded a policy of apartheid, or strict legal separation of the races. South Africa would be a republic founded upon the ideals of Paul Kruger, not upon those of Cecil Rhodes or Jan Smuts.

In the decade ahead, the Nationalist-dominated parliament passed a long series of segregationist legislation, affecting every aspect of life. In effect, this legislation was a more precise and comprehensive elaboration of segregationist laws passed in the early 1920s, when the English-speaking population was politically dominant. The Prohibition of Mixed Marriages Act (1949) made interracial marriages illegal. In 1950, the Population Registration Act provided for the classification of the population into whites, coloreds (people of mixed race and Indians), and Bantu. The Group Areas Act, passed in the same year, called for the division of the nation into separate areas according to race and tribe. Apartheid in the realm of land ownership was already enshrined in the Native Land Act of 1913, which was aimed at regulating the purchase, ownership, and occupation of land outside urban areas on a racial basis. Only 13 percent of South Africa's total land area was reserved for Africans, even though they made up more than 80 percent of the population. Attempts to control the movement of Africans from place to place, particularly from rural to urban areas, date back to 1760 with the first pass law. Civil and political rights have always been withheld from urban Africans on the pretext that they are "temporary sojourners" with a permanent residence in some far-off tribal reserve. The Reservation of Separate Amenities Act (1953) provided for the segregation of public amenities, including parks and transportation terminals. In the same year, the Native Labour Act redefined the term "employee" to exclude all blacks, thereby disenfranchising their unions and forbidding strikes. African trade unions, while not prohibited, were denied recognition and severely circumscribed. The Industrial Conciliation Act of 1956 and subsequent amendments banned racially mixed labor unions and provided that certain jobs or occupations be reserved for whites only. A series of Bantu Education Acts brought schools under central government control and extended segregation to university education. Moreover, a constitutional amendment disenfranchised coloreds, who had been voting in Cape province since the 1850s. Opposition to these and the plethora of other apartheid laws was stifled through the Suppression of Communism Act (1950), an omnibus law which empowered the government to ban any organization or person suspected of "communism" or of endangering the security of the state. In an attempt to control the rising tide of African nationalism by fostering tribalism at the expense of pan-Africanism, the government passed the Promotion of Bantu Self-Government Act (1959). In classical divide-and-

The Pass System in South Africa. Among the restrictions imposed upon blacks was the requirement that they carry passports at all times. The pass system, or influx control, remained in effect until 1985. Here a policeman and an interpreter check the papers of an African bound for Johannesburg.

rule fashion, it envisioned the consolidation of the 260 scattered native reserves into a series of "independent" Bantu states, or Bantustans, each with its own tribal identity.

Reactions to segregationist laws

African, colored, and Asian reactions to these and the many other segregationist laws, including the pass laws, were manifested in a number of futile passive-resistance and defiance campaigns between 1952 and 1956. Their failure led to a rift within the African National Congress (founded in 1912); and in 1959 a radical, racially exclusive group split off under the leadership of Robert Sobukwe and took the name of Pan-Africanist Congress. The white political spectrum had also become more polarized. The United party, mainly English-speaking, over the years had steadily lost ground in parliament to the Afrikaner-dominated Nationalists. In 1959 a small group of anti-apartheid white liberals broke from the United party and formed the Progressive party. Over the next decade and a half they held a single seat in the Assembly.

Sharpeville and its aftermath

In 1960 African resistance to apartheid culminated in a passive demonstration at Sharpeville. The South African police panicked in the face of the large, angry gathering and killed sixty-seven peaceful black demonstrators. This flagrant act of repression spurred the leadership of the African National Congress, including Nelson Mandela, to adopt a more radical and violent strategy. Following the Sharpeville massacre a state of emergency was declared, the African National Congress and the Pan-Africanist Congress were banned, and their leaders who escaped arrest either fled the country or went underground to engage in terrorist activity. Whites, growing ever more fearful of the "black menace," responded in the 1960s with legislation further eroding the personal liberties of nonwhites. The General Law Amendment

Act of 1963 empowered police to arrest and detain people indefinitely without trial or access to legal counsel. A Publications Control Board, created in the same year, imposed censorship over literature and films. Throughout the 1960s police raids resulted in the arrest and imprisonment of militants. Mandela was sentenced to life imprisonment in 1964 for conspiring to overthrow the white-dominated government.

In 1961 Prime Minister Hendrik Verwoerd took steps toward implementing these ideals when he ordered the withdrawal of South Africa from the Commonwealth of Nations and proclaimed the country an independent republic. It was clear that the ultimate objective was an Afrikaner nation thoroughly purged of British influences. Verwoerd was assassinated in 1966 and was succeeded by John B. Vorster. In the following year, a severe Terrorism Act was passed, presuming the guilt of everyone accused of terrorism until proven innocent. Two years later, the Bureau of State Security (BOSS) was created to suppress radical movements.

The Terrorism Act and the Bureau of State Security

South Africa's economy boomed in the early 1970s, benefiting most racial and ethnic groups. White feelings of security were sufficiently restored for the Vorster government to embark on a futile policy of rapprochement with black African nations to the north. It also moved quickly to devolve more autonomy on the newly created Bantu states within South Africa. In late 1976, the Transkei became the first Bantu homeland to receive its nominal independence. Economic prosperity led to a shortage of white skilled labor, and as a consequence the job reservation act was eased to enable blacks to move into positions formerly reserved for whites. These moves failed to assuage African nationalism. In 1972 the moderate Black Peoples' Convention was formed, along with the black South African Students' Movement. This reawakening of black consciousness, led by a new and more militant generation of youths, was further stimulated by the articulate speeches of Chief Mangosuthu Buthelezi of the KwaZulu homeland. However, by 1984 Buthelezi was unable to extend his own leadership beyond the Zulu ethnic group.

The abortive policy of rapprochement with black African nations and the reawakening of black consciousness

Among white Afrikaners, two schools of thought emerged: the enlightened, or verlighte, and the narrow-minded, or the verkrampte. The verlightes demanded an easing of the rigid apartheid laws, especially in the areas of sports and culture. But they were not prepared to grant the principle of "one man one vote."

Two schools of Afrikaner thought

The rising sentiment for liberalizing race relations within South Africa and pursuing improved relations with neighboring black African states subsided almost as quickly as it had begun. In 1975 Portugal, in a surprising about-face, gave independence to Mozambique and Angola, two close neighbors of South Africa. This rekindled the revolution of rising political expectations among South Africa's blacks, coloreds, and Asians. Moreover, in the same year, the nation began to slide into an economic recession, after enjoying a steady annual growth rate of more than 5 percent since 1933. Whites again became

The death of détente and the renewal of suppression

Police Action in Johannesburg. In downtown Johannesburg the authorities disperse a group of black and white demonstrators who were protesting police actions in the huge Soweto ghetto. Over 1,000 blacks were killed by police in Soweto in June 1976.

fearful of a loss of status; and this fear was exacerbated by the installation of Marxist, militantly anti–South African governments in Mozambique and Angola. South African military intervention in the Angolan civil war in 1975–1976 drew world-wide condemnation and killed Vorster's détente program with black Africa. African student militancy, inspired by such intellectuals as Steve Biko, grew rapidly after a 1974 pro-Mozambique student rally. Feelings exploded in violent riots in June 1976 in Soweto, a sprawling ghetto of nearly 3 million Africans not far from downtown Johannesburg. More than a thousand black youths were killed by the South African police and many more were imprisoned. An intensification of the suppression and liquidation of black opposition came to world attention in September 1977 with the police killing of the jailed Steve Biko, president of the Black Peoples' Convention. Racial tension was mounting and the major African newspaper, the *World,* was banned and its editor detained.

As world opinion turned against South Africa, the white pendulum swung further to the right. English-speaking and Afrikaans-speaking whites began to close political ranks. The opposition United party disintegrated, with most of its members joining the Nationalist party but a few joining with the Progressives to form the Progressive Federal party. In the November 1977 elections the Nationalist party gained vast new strength, winning 134 of 165 seats in the all-white National Assembly. South Africa was moving toward a one-party state. When Pieter W. Botha became prime minister in October 1978, racial and ethnic relations among the nation's 4.3 million whites, 2.4 million

The resurgence of the Nationalist party

coloreds, 765,000 Asians, and 19 million blacks were deteriorating steadily. The South African government was becoming increasingly isolated from the world community of nations.

In the early 1980s the government pursued a dual and often contradictory race policy of institutional liberalization in the social and economic realms and more severe repression in the political realm. Urban black elites were given a greater degree of political autonomy in the segregated ethnic townships. African trade unions were officially recognized and given the right to bargain collectively, and a wide range of public facilities were desegregated. Also, government spending on black education and health increased dramatically, as did average wages for workers in mining and industry. On the other hand, the government tightened influx controls on blacks moving from the rural to urban areas. By 1984, nearly 3 million Africans had been deprived of their citizenship and rusticated to one of the six poverty-stricken and overcrowded ethnic homelands. Moreover, key black trade-union officials were arrested in the face of the growing size, power, and militancy of organized labor.

In 1984 a new constitution was promulgated, conferring near-dictatorial powers on the executive president, P. W. Botha. A tricameral legislature was also created, providing separate chambers for whites, coloreds, and Asians. Blacks, totally excluded from the new arrangement, became more violent and united in their opposition. Sporadic riots in the urban ghettos were quickly followed by the nation's first massive work stoppage. For the first time the government called on the national army to suppress the growing resistance—a sign of both the gravity of the situation and the growing power of the military leadership within the Botha regime. Violence continued to escalate in the black townships and black local government began to collapse. In mid-1985 President Botha declared a State of Emergency in most of the country. A year earlier, South Africa tried to reduce external threats and African National Congress supply bases by forcing nonaggression pacts on its neighbors Mozambique and Swaziland. They also refused to accept the United Nations independence formula for Namibia, a territory held by South Africa since the early 1920s, until November 1988. These events transpired at a time when all of southern Africa was suffering from severe economic recession and drought-related food shortages.

In a near repeat of the dark days of Sharpeville and Soweto, capital began to stream out of the country. Foreign investors and creditors became nervous in the face of escalating violence in the sprawling black ghettos and wondered if this might be the twilight of white rule and capitalism in South Africa. Crisis struck in August 1985 when key American banks refused to renew their loans. By then, South Africa's external debts had reached an unprecedented $25 billion. As government repression grew in response to the gathering storm, new pressures from anti-apartheid groups in the United States led to a dramatic change of mood in Congress. The Reagan administration's

Pieter W. Botha, President of the Republic of South Africa from 1984 to 1989 and Prime Minister from 1978 to 1984

The constitution of 1984 and the rising tide of violence

The flight of capital and the credit crisis

mild package of sanctions was matched by the passage in Congress of a bill calling for a broad range of restrictions on American trade and investment. Rising disinvestment and divestment pressures from a broad spectrum of Americans and Europeans led to a growing exodus of mainly British and American banks and corporations from South Africa. The rate of new investment fell precipitously. By early 1986, the South African economy had reached its lowest point since the 1930s.

Political movement

Frustrated opponents of apartheid became more politicized and moved leftward. From mid-1986 the United Democratic Front (UDF), a loose coalition of organizations formed in 1983 to oppose the constitutional changes, began to draw closer to the exiled African National Congress. They were joined by the mammoth Congress of South African Trade Unions (COSATU), which was successfully staging massive consumer boycotts, work-stayaways, and strikes in the vital mining and transport sectors. At the other end of the political and racial spectrum, frustrated, fearful, and extremist Afrikaner elements in the ruling National party gravitated toward the recently formed Conservative party. Some moved even further to the right, into the extra-parliamentary neo-fascist Afrikaner Resistance Movement. The Botha regime, worried over the erosion of its Afrikaner constituency, stalled their pragmatic reformist programs while seeking to draw moderate English-speaking whites into the party fold. In the May 1987 elections, the Conservative party, which had peeled off from the National party in 1982, won enough parliamentary seats to oust the liberal Progressive Federal party as the official opposition. Meanwhile, the multiracial though overwhelmingly African UDF, COSATU, and other black militant groups steadily gained in numbers and in organizational strength. Many large local and foreign corporations also began to open a dialogue with the ANC and to urge the Botha regime to resume its reformist course.

Intensification of government repression

The South African government intensified its repression of nearly all extraparliamentary opposition, including the press. The State of Emergency remained in force, enabling the police, military, and security forces to harass and detain key leaders. In early 1988 new curbs were placed on COSATU and numerous other organizations in an effort to depoliticize them. The government also fostered division within the black community by supporting conservative, ethnically based groups such as the Zulu's "Inkatha." Since mid-1987 hundreds of Africans in Natal province were killed in sporadic fighting between Inkatha and the remnants of the UDF. Throughout the nation key leaders of black anti-government organizations were arrested, detained, or fled into exile. The mass turmoil in the black townships subsided though acts of sabotage and labor unrest became chronic. By 1989, the country had become deeply polarized racially, ethnically, and ideologically. Buffeted by pressures from within and without, the regime drew itself into the proverbial bunker from whence it promised to become virtually impossible to take constructive action.

Fearing that South Africa was fast approaching an all consuming conflagration, cooler heads in the white and black communities had begun to think and talk about a multiracial future. When a stroke in the spring of 1989 forced P. W. Botha to loosen his grip on the reins of power, reform-minded elements within the National party led by education minister F. W. de Klerk wrested control of the party apparatus from him and ultimately the presidency. While still a subordinate of President Botha, de Klerk met with President Kenneth Kaunda of Zambia, a constant critic of South African racial policy, to reassure the nation's external critics of the party's intentions.

National party candidates ran in the September 1989 "whites only" parliamentary elections on a platform of "evolutionary change." Despite a net loss of nearly 25 percent of the National party's parliamentary seats to the far-right Conservative party and the more liberal Democratic party, de Klerk boldly interpreted the election results as a resounding mandate to pursue a negotiated political settlement with the nation's black population—one that would extend full political rights to the black majority without jeopardizing the interests of the white minority. Blacks took to the streets to protest their exclusion from participation in the election. Negotiations with the black community moved swiftly to capture the attention of the ANC and to forestall international demands for more stringent economic sanctions even as de Klerk exercised great care to avoid alienating the white population whose support was essential to the success of any negotiated settlement. Eight prominent black opposition leaders were released from jail within weeks of the election—and the president followed the example of his predecessor by holding direct and indirect discussions with the jailed ANC leader and national hero Nelson Mandela.

Reformers ascendant in the National party

The mandate to pursue a negotiated political settlement

President F. W. de Klerk of the Republic of South Africa and Nelson Mandela, Deputy President of the African National Congress as They Meet in May 1990 to Open Negotiations on the Future of South Africa

*The release of Nelson
Mandela and the
legalization of the ANC*

In February 1990 President de Klerk shocked the world with his announcement of the release of Mandela from prison after a 27½-year internment, the lifting of bans against numerous anti-apartheid opposition organizations including the African National Congress and the Pan Africanist Congress, and the release of about 120 other political prisoners. Mandela struck the new leadership of the National party as the essential element in the process—the only black South African of sufficient stature in both the black and white communities whose vision of the future, understanding of the past, and sensitivity to the concerns of all groups lent credibility to a process that might otherwise have been dismissed as an act of political chicanery.

*The quest for a multiracial
society*

The ensuing discussions focused on establishing the groundwork for negotiating a new constitution. For the government the essential precondition was that the ANC renounce the use of violence in pursuit of their goals. In its turn the ANC insisted on an unconditional amnesty for all political prisoners and exiles and an end to the State of Emergency decree under which the government had ruled since 1985. Even as de Klerk and Mandela took each other's measure in negotiations, they had to cope with knotty problems: de Klerk struggling to ensure the primacy of civilian leadership in the government against the considerable power of the military and police and to keep the conservative wing of his party from deserting him; Mandela striving to unify the disparate forces within the ANC as well as achieving understandings with other opposition groups including the conservative Inkatha with whom the ANC had been fighting continually since 1987. The ongoing black-against-black violence between the ANC and Inkatha long fostered by white extremists in and out of government escalated in the summer of 1990. In spite of the obstacles, the preconditions for meaningful negotiation of a new constitution were within reach by summer's end. The prospects for establishing an equitable multiracial society in South Africa seemed brighter than at any time in the twentieth century.

3. THE UPSURGE OF AFRICA

*Early African nationalism
and pan-Africanism*

Modern African nationalism and pan-African sentiment are not post–World War II phenomena. Their roots go back to 1847 with the establishment of the independent Republic of Liberia. Liberia was the first independent state in Africa to support Western-style institutions and to prove that black men were capable of governing themselves along so-called modern lines. Edward Blyden, a leading Liberian intellectual (born in the West Indies), called in the 1860s for racial integrity and solidarity and coined the phrase "Africa for Africans." He exhorted black men to preserve the African essence of their civilizations and to resist Westernization at the hands of European imperialists. Indigenous, Western-educated intellectuals on the Gold Coast (now Ghana) and Nigeria were to take up this call in the two decades prior to the First World War. Nevertheless, these protonationalists represented but a thin veneer and were predominantly drawn from among second sons of wealthy traditional nobility. Many of them were torn between their rich African heritage and that of Western civilization and found it difficult to identify with their peasant brethren in the bush. They were willing to work within the colonial framework and to pursue a moderate, gradualist course. After World War II, these early elites were eclipsed by impatient youthful nonaristocratic intellectuals who returned to Africa after many years abroad. Armed with the techniques of political party organization, they reached out to the masses, particularly the urban unemployed.

Colonial resistance assumed a far more militant posture after the Second World War as African nationalism spread. It was characterized by labor strikes and agitation in colonial legislatures. Africans took advantage of the extension of the franchise in the English and French colonies by forming mass political parties. Although the most effectively organized resistance was directed against Great Britain and France, Belgium, Italy, and Portugal were also targets. The first of the former colonies to gain independence was Libya. Taken by Italy from Turkey in 1912, Libya passed under the control of the United Nations at the end of the Second World War. In 1949 the U.N. recognized the Libyan demand for freedom, and two years later independence was formally proclaimed. This was followed by the British withdrawal from Egypt in 1954 and Tunisian independence in 1956.

The spread of colonial resistance

The most violent of the colonial revolts in northern Africa occurred in Algeria. Algeria had been a part of the French Empire since the middle years of the nineteenth century. The French poured millions of dollars of capital into their colony, and thousands of French nationals came there to settle. Many people of other nationalities, especially Spaniards, also emigrated to Algeria, with the result that by 1960 the European inhabitants numbered about 1 million in a total population of 10,300,000. These Europeans, inaccurately referred to as the "French" population, monopolized not only the government positions but also the best economic opportunities in industry, agriculture, trade, and finance. The Arab and Berber inhabitants were chiefly peasants and laborers, though some, of course, maintained their own shops in the *casbah,* or native quarter, of each of the large cities. In 1954 Arab and Berber (Muslim) nationalists rose in revolt when their demand for equal status with the European population was denied by the French government. The revolt continued its bloody course for seven years. It was complicated by the fact that many of the European settlers (*colons*) hated the government in Paris almost as much as they did the Algerian nationalists. They were determined to keep Algeria "French" and feared a sell-out by President Charles de Gaulle that would make the former colony independent and subject the *colons* to the rule of the Arab and Berber majority. In April 1961, the announce-

The war in Algeria

Anti-Imperialist Revolt in Algeria, 1960. At Dar-es-Saada, Muslims take furniture from the homes of Europeans and burn it in the streets.

ment of a plan by de Gaulle to negotiate a settlement in Algeria that would pave the way for eventual independence led to a revolt in the territory by four French generals. They seized government buildings, arrested loyal French officials, and threatened to invade France. De Gaulle proclaimed a state of emergency and ordered a total blockade of Algeria. In the face of such determined opposition the revolt collapsed. The war of the nationalists, however, continued for another year. On a promise of immediate self-government and eventual independence the nationalists laid down their arms in March 1962. Three months later Algeria entered the ranks of independent states and was admitted to the United Nations. The war had cost the lives of about 40,000 soldiers and civilians and had left a heritage of bitterness that would probably linger for years.

Nkrumah and Ghanaian independence

If any one country could be considered the leader of the African colonial revolt in sub-Saharan Africa, it was Ghana, formerly called the Gold Coast, a colony of Great Britain. In 1954 Britain granted self-government, independence in 1957, and in 1960 Ghana became a republic. Leadership of the Ghana independence movement was at that time supplied by Kwame Nkrumah. The son of an illiterate goldsmith, he obtained an education in the United States and in England. He returned to his homeland in 1948 and became a nationalist agitator. Though he classified himself as a Marxist, he denied being a Communist. Yet he admired Lenin and generally looked to eastern-bloc countries for support of his policies rather than to London or Washington. Apparently the key to his thinking was opposition to neocolonialism, manifested by Great Power economic domination of internal African economies. He regaled his followers with stories of a Golden Age in Africa, whose cultural center was in Timbuktu, with a great university manned by distinguished scholars. For a time Nkrumah ruled benevolently even after converting the nation into a one-party state. He established hospitals and schools and raised the literacy standards. Accused of extravagance and corruption, he was deposed by a revolt of army officers in 1966. He was driven from his homeland and forced to take refuge in Guinea where he died in 1972. Nevertheless, Nkrumah's writings on neocolonialism and his pan-African ideas are still widely read by African intellectuals. The Organization of African Unity, established in 1963, owed much to Nkrumah's statesmanship but fell short of his dream of a United States of Africa under a single government. Nationalism proved to be a stronger force than pan-Africanism.

Kwame Nkrumah (Center, Seated) and Members of His Government in Ghana

The most violent of the revolts in Central Africa occurred in the Belgian Congo, now called Zaire. Fearing an outbreak of violence among its disaffected colonial subjects, Belgium, in 1960, granted them independence. This was the signal for the beginning of a series of rebellions and assassinations that raged for more than five years. A chief cause of the flaming disorders centered in the southeastern province of Katanga. Here were located rich copper resources controlled by Belgian capitalists. At one time the copper mines of Katanga had produced revenues sufficient to defray one-half the costs of the colonial government. In July 1960, Katanga seceded and attempted to gain control of the entire country. In the revolt several former premiers and other high officers were murdered. The U.N. Security Council sent a contingent to guard against revival of civil war. Strongman rule was revived by President Mobutu, placed in power by the United States' Central Intelligence Agency, and a degree of stability was ultimately restored.

The revolt in the Congo

In many colonies there was at least the illusion of stability and peace. Nigeria, the Ivory Coast, and Senegal are good examples. Some authorities held that British and French colonial administrations were wiser than that of most other European empires. Whereas the Portuguese and Belgians withheld self-government as long as they could, and then granted it suddenly, the British and French brought their colonies to independence more gradually. Many local leaders were trained in administration and knew how to deal with intricate problems before they actually arose. Yet even in resource-rich Nigeria the familiar charges of corruption and inefficiency led to the murder of the premier and the overthrow of the government in 1966. After more assassinations a military government seized control. Within a year the Eastern Region seceded and proclaimed itself the Republic of Biafra. Civil war followed and harassed the country for three years. The total of casualties was enormous. More than 1 million people lost their lives. Thousands were killed in battle, but many more died of starvation. The rebels capitulated in 1970. From every standpoint the war was a tragedy. The crisis in Nigeria illustrated vividly the enormous problems confronting Africa in its search for a more equitable distribution of power and opportunity among disparate ethnic and religious groups. National unity would prove elusive as Africa gained its independence.

Civil War in Nigeria

MEDITERRANEAN SEA

TUNISIA
MOROCCO
CAPE VERDE
ALGERIA
LIBYA
SAHARAWI ARAB
D.R.
EGYPT
RED
SEA
MAURITANIA
MALI
NIGER
CHAD
SUDAN
SENEGAL
GAMBIA
BURKINA
FASO
GUINEA
NIGERIA
ETHIOPIA
SIERRA LEONE
IVORY
COAST
GHANA
CENTRAL AFRICAN
REPUBLIC
LIBERIA
TOGO BENIN
CAMEROON
SOMALIA
EQUATORIAL
GUINEA
UGANDA
KENYA
GABON
CONGO REPUBLIC
ZAIRE
RWANDA
BURUNDI
SAO TOMÉ
AND PRINCIPE
ATLANTIC
CABINDA
(Angola)
SEYCHELLES
ZANZIBAR
TANZANIA
OCEAN
COMORO IS.
ANGOLA
MALAWI
ZAMBIA
MALAGASY
REPUBLIC
ZIMBABWE
MOZAMBIQUE
MAURITIUS
WALVIS BAY
(South Africa)
NAMIBIA
BOTSWANA
INDIAN
SWAZILAND
OCEAN
REPUBLIC
OF
SOUTH AFRICA
LESOTHO

Independent before 1945

Independent after 1945

0   1000 miles

THE NEW AFRICA·1990

4. INDEPENDENT AFRICA IN TRANSITION

By 1990, Africa boasted of over fifty politically independent countries
exhibiting an enormous variety of distinct languages, religions, ethnic
groupings, and cultures. Since the onset of the independence era in

the 1950s, most of these countries have undergone substantial transformations in political and military leadership. Whereas urban protest generally radicalized and popularized nationalist movements in the immediate postwar years, the effects were short-lived. Radical trade unionists, intellectuals, and other revolutionary leaders seldom went on to assume positions of real authority. Instead, power passed to the traditional elites or to those who had collaborated with the departing colonial regimes. The new leaders tended not to articulate any plans for structural transformations and those who did were unable to translate their ideology into practical application.

In the 1960s power became personalized rather than institutionalized nearly everywhere in Africa. Many heads of government whose charisma carried them to positions of power during the struggle for liberation attempted to maintain their status and influence by developing a cult of personality reminiscent of traditional rulers of the precolonial era. This resulted in institutional fragility and encouraged leaders to pursue extra-constitutional strategies to remain in power. Elections were either canceled or rigged and opposition parties were banned and their leaders assassinated, detained, or driven into exile. Patronage politics replaced popular politics and the state bureaucracies became bloated and parasitic. The colonial legacy of force, coercion, and promotion of self-interest by state functionaries carried over into the era of independence contributing to a decline in representative government, an erosion of civil and human rights, and growing press censorship. Labor unions shrank in size and influence everywhere but in South Africa. Since 1963 nearly three-quarters of the independent countries of Africa have experienced at least one military coup. Some countries, notably Nigeria, have alternated continually between civilian and military governance.

Following independence, African governments experienced great difficulty in maintaining national unity. During the struggle for liberation it was relatively easy to mobilize the entire population against colonial oppression. However, the task of achieving a common national purpose, or ideology, proved far more difficult once the symbol of oppression had been removed. Long-standing ethnic and regional antagonisms and rivalries, some rooted in the precolonial past, resurfaced. National boundaries, hastily and arbitrarily drawn by Europeans at the height of the imperialist scramble for territory in the late nineteenth century, often divided people belonging to the same cultural or ethnic group. Moreover, during the colonial era some ethnic groups were favored over others and became disproportionately prosperous or better educated. After independence, these entities generated their own subnationalism to protect their privileged status. This resulted in bitter secessionist movements and/or bloody civil wars in Nigeria between the government and the secessionist state of Biafra; in the Sudan and Chad between a Muslim north and a Christian/animist south; in Ethiopia between the Marxist central government and the Islamic Eritreans;

Changes in political and military leadership

The personalization of power and institutional weakness

Internal conflict in the independent African states

Civil War in Chad. Chad has been in the throes of internal strife, born of ethnic, religious, and regional disputes, for fully thirty years with light-skinned Muslim Arabs from the north at odds with dark-skinned, Christian sub-Saharan Africans from the south. Here the commander-in-chief of the Popular Liberation Front conducts a political meeting in a military camp.

in Zaire between the central government and the mineral-rich province of Shaba; in Angola and Zimbabwe between the government and ethnically and regionally based revolutionary movements that had participated in the struggle for independence but not in the subsequent regime; and in Liberia between ethnic groups, informed by a history of resentment between descendants of American slaves who ruled until 1980 and indigenous Africans. None of these breakaway resistance movements has succeeded, but they have left a legacy of tension, suspicion, and chronic violence. The conflict in Liberia resulted in the total collapse of governmental authority. These internal conflicts stem more from differences of religion and culture than of ideology, and they are animated by support from neighbors or non-African powers.

The Organization of African Unity

The goal of pan-African unity has been equally elusive. Nearly all African countries belong to the Organization of African Unity (O.A.U.), though few of them fully adhere to its stated principles. The O.A.U. is often slow to act on inter-African crises, and by 1984 most member states were in considerable arrears in their dues. Consequently, the organization is financially crippled. Over the years since its founding in 1963, deep divisions and power blocs have emerged within the organization over such issues as the wars in Chad and the Western Sahara, the invasions of Shaba in Zaire, and the turmoil in Uganda. In 1984, Morocco severed its ties to the O.A.U. after the group recognized the independence of a former Spanish colony occupied by Morocco.

Since independence, all efforts to form bi- or trilateral political unions but one have failed. Stillborn were the Ghana-Guinea-Mali Union and the East African Federation. Tanganyika and Zanzibar joined to form the United Republic of Tanzania, but the union has been extremely tenuous. Far more successful have been efforts at creating regional economic groupings. The sixteen-nation Economic Community of West African States (ECOWAS) became operational in 1978, and a year later the nine-nation Southern African Development Coordination Conference (SADCC) was formed. SADCC has contributed to improved cooperation in areas of communication, transportation, and agricultural research, and to a reduction of members' economic dependence on South Africa. Related to SADCC is the Preferential Trade Area (PTA), which became effective in 1984. It includes eighteen countries of eastern and southern Africa and strives to enhance regional trade by reducing customs barriers.

The checkered career of intra-African cooperation

Former French colonies remained closely linked to France through a common currency zone, trade preferences, and defense treaties. However, for years the nations of former French Equatorial Africa have adhered to the Union Douanière et Economique de l'Afrique Centrale. The most serious obstacles to any kind of cooperation have been the strength of African nationalism, rivalries among heads of state for leadership in the organizations, and differing national ideologies or approaches to development.

The limits of cooperation among the former French colonies

Indeed, after independence a considerable divergence had emerged among the various countries in terms of government structure and strategies for economic and political growth. Ethiopia, Angola, and Mozambique became intensely ideological and pursued Marxist-Leninist strategies. Tanzania, Zimbabwe, and Zambia practiced a form of socialism modeled after Scandinavian countries. And Nigeria, Kenya, Ivory Coast, Gabon, and Cameroon had no formal ideology and favored indigenous capitalism and private Western investment. Clearly, no one model of development prevailed. As in the precolonial era, there was a wide variety of political and economic systems.

In the 1960s and early 1970s, most African states became progressively socialistic and began to intervene in the economy on a massive scale, often in reaction to the perceived depredations of colonial capitalism. They attempted to reduce foreign ownership of major corporations and to speed the Africanization of corporate management by decree. In the process, indigenous forms of capitalism were also weakened. In those states that were most committed to a socialist path to economic development, government adopted policies favoring state farms, industries, and marketing boards at the expense of small, independent entrepreneurs, whose productivity declined steadily. Yet most of the state-sponsored corporations were inefficiently managed and became financial liabilities. President Julius Nyerere of Tanzania in the early 1970s attempted to develop his own brand of African socialism by forcing independent farming families into government-sponsored communes, called *ujamaa* (family) villages. The financially strapped government was unable to provide either the materials or the managerial expertise needed to ensure their viability. Families became frustrated and disillusioned, and without incentives, many were

President Julius Nyerere of Tanzania. Nyerere, accompanied by a group of officials from the People's Republic of China, lays the foundation stone of the New Chinese-Tanzanian Friendship Textile Mill in Dar es Salaam in 1966.

*Urbanization and the crisis
of African political
economy*

less productive than when they worked their own farms. Instead of becoming more self-reliant, Tanzania had to rely more than ever on food imports.

As urbanization accelerated in a broad range of new African nations, political power became concentrated in the cities, leading to policies that favored urban over rural areas. Urban-biased subsidies, price-fixing, and overvalued currency exchange rates led to cheaper luxury imports but lower producer prices for agricultural goods. Again the incentive for small-scale peasant farmers was reduced and agricultural output fell as more farmers migrated to increasingly congested cities. This often necessitated the importation of food to replace local staples. Vast sums were borrowed from the international financial community to pay for imports and to stimulate industrialization. Inflated exchange rates also hurt export profitability and discouraged investment in export industries. Price controls discouraged domestic production and contributed to smuggling. There was a great expansion of economic activities beyond state control. A second, or parallel, economy developed and deprived the state of enormous amounts of revenue. Although Africa had achieved its political freedom by 1970, it had begun to lose its economic independence and its ability to generate its own wealth. From the mid-1970s to the mid-1980s, almost every sub-Saharan economy declined in virtually every measurable way.

Economic decline swept across Africa after the global escalation of petroleum prices in 1973 and the attendant inflation in prices for Western technology, seed, and fertilizer. During the same period world prices collapsed for agricultural commodities and metals, major African exports and sources of foreign exchange. It became increasingly difficult for African nations to meet their heavy debt obligations to Western financial institutions. The crisis was compounded by drought, beginning in 1973 along the southern fringe of the Sahara and spreading after 1980 to nearly every region of Africa. As domestic agriculture stagnated, millions suffered hardships so severe that unprecedented numbers of Africans became refugees (estimates range as high as one-in-four for the continent as a whole). Conditions were most desperate in Ethiopia, Sudan, and Mozambique where starvation was a common cause of death. This occurred as population growth rates soared uncontrollably, from 2.3 percent per year in 1960 to 3.1 percent by the mid 1980s. Children under fifteen years of age, a tiny minority a century ago, now represent more than 50 percent of the population.

The failure of political leadership, the worsening terms of trade, and the high cost of debt service imposed serious constraints on growth and led to a crisis of confidence in the international financial and commercial communities. The development crisis deepened in the early 1980s in the face of continued weakening commodity prices on world markets, falling export earnings, accelerating inflation, and rising costs of essential imports. These factors, combined with soaring debt service expenditures left most African countries with insufficient foreign exchange to finance trade and to sustain economic growth. By 1987, Africa's total foreign debt had climbed to $218 billion, or three times the continent's annual export earnings. Moreover, private banks and other creditors, already forced to forgive or reschedule African debts, were reluctant to lend more to countries struggling to implement reforms and to resuscitate their faltering economies. Western disengagement from Africa's economic life was compounded by the flight of domestic capital as well. Consequently, African governments, in desperate need of fresh capital, sought to increase their exports while dramatically reducing imports of new machinery and spare parts needed to boost productive capacity. A few national governments also had to cope with such natural disasters as drought, famine, locust infestations, and costly civil strife.

Africa's debt crisis was reflected in declining real growth rates, rising urban youth unemployment and crime, diminishing purchasing power of consumers, and deteriorating infrastructure. Accompanying budget deficits forced governments to reduce spending and to slash development plans. These austerity programs required massive retrenchments in oversized, inefficient bureaucracies, salary freezes, and politically destabilizing cutbacks in social services as well as reductions in state subsidies of consumer staples. Governments were also forced to sell off, reduce, or terminate state-owned corporations. At the same time, local currencies were devalued in a desperate effort to attract foreign investment and to make their exports more competitive in world markets.

Austerity programs

Such draconian measures angered populations already suffering from a decade-long decline in real per capita income and lower standards

The Refugee Problem. A starving child crying at a feeding center in a village in southern Ethiopia. Due to overpopulation, a number of African nations are facing serious problems which manifest themselves in the form of food shortages, inadequate housing, poor health and educational services, and high unemployment rates.

of living. These actions brought to an abrupt end the postwar revolution of rising expectations and spurred social unrest. In an effort to control the attendant turmoil, numerous governments became more authoritarian, placing new restrictions on civil liberties, censoring the press, punishing dissident students, and clamping down on trade unions.

The revision of political and of economic strategies

Nevertheless, the crisis has gradually injected a new element of realism in governing circles. As the tide of political liberalization arose in East Asia, East Europe, and Latin America, and as independent Africa's founding generation retired from public life, most African states were susceptible to challenges to the single party system. Even President Robert Mugabe of Zimbabwe, a longtime champion of single-party rule, opened the door to multiparty participation in the nation's political life. Demands for constitutional reform gained momentum in Zimbabwe, Kenya, and the Ivory Coast. The Namibian Constitution of 1989 set a new standard for democratic development in Africa. Furthermore, regimes have begun to liberalize and diversify their overregulated economies, opening them to market forces and free enterprise. The emphasis is now being placed on self-sufficiency, import substitution, and peasant food production. An unprecedented effort is under way to improve the quality and efficiency rather than the quantity of government services. Economic necessity and the demands of creditors have compelled even the more ideological and socialistic countries, particularly Tanzania, Mozambique, Angola, and the Congo, to reduce the role of the state in the economy and to postpone or abandon their ambitious state-directed plans in favor of a more pragmatic course. To compensate for the decline in support from private sources, the World Bank and other public agencies have stepped up their loans for infrastructure development and to indigenous private entrepreneurs.

New developments in agriculture

By 1990 there were signs that Africa was in the early stages of a green revolution. New crop hybrids and drought-resistant seed varieties, better use of fertilizers, and more effective techniques for controlling soil erosion have raised agricultural output in dozens of countries. Zimbabwe, under a nominally Marxist regime, has achieved remarkable success in regenerating peasant farming while providing incentives for white commercial farmers as well. Continued development and dissemination of such agricultural improvements promise to enhance Africa's ability to feed itself, with all the attendant consequences for the continent's economic viability, quality of life, and public health.

The AIDS crisis

Africa achieved significant breakthroughs in public health during the 1970s and early 1980s. River blindness was virtually eradicated and the impact of malaria and dysentery was reduced dramatically. Tragically these encouraging signs have been dwarfed by the devastating impact of AIDS (Acquired Immune Deficiency Syndrome) on the African scene in the 1980s. A web of unique medical, cultural, and economic factors—including long-neglected epidemics of sexually transmitted diseases, traditional family rituals, and large migrant labor forces—made Africa especially susceptible to the spread of AIDS through the heterosexual population. By 1989 the World Health Organization conservatively estimated that in excess of five million adults and half a million children in Africa were infected with the deadly AIDS virus. AIDS threatens to be the scourge of the 1990s as the death toll rises and as the full social and economic impact of the epidemic is felt.

In other realms, Africa made considerable progress. After independence, most countries devoted great sums of money and energy toward eliminating illiteracy. Primary education was greatly expanded, and today literacy rates have risen dramatically, from an African average of 4 percent in 1950 to 22 percent by 1984 and exceeding 50 percent in nearly a dozen countries. The position of women has also greatly improved. Higher education, once restricted almost entirely to men, is now open to women. They are consequently moving rapidly into the professions and rising to positions of leadership in Africa's political and commercial life. The dramatic advances made by women in these areas is traceable in part to Africa's increasing success in divorcing itself from the male bias of colonial education and agricultural extension services. With a renewed recognition of the importance of women in agricultural development came enhanced status and influence and a broadening of opportunities.

Educational progress and the position of women

Religion and philosophy have also made impressive strides. Africans are succeeding in naturalizing the Christian Church, its teachings, leadership, and liturgy. Under African leadership, Christian doctrine has become more adaptable, accommodating itself to Marxist political leadership and ideology. However, the role of Christianity in secular education has diminished as governments attempt to extend their control over questions of curriculum and to assume greater fiscal responsibility for educational development. Thus, Christianity is spreading somewhat less rapidly than it was during the colonial era, but the Church itself is more vital and dynamic in terms of innovation and reform.

Islam, on the other hand, has experienced far greater numerical growth and wider geographical distribution. A number of African heads of state are practicing Muslims and give cultural encouragement to the established Islamic orders. However, militant Islamic fundamentalism has grown like a brushfire among the uprooted urban unemployed in the seething ghettos of West Africa's savanna region. These movements tend to be youthful, anti-Western, ultraconservative, and anti-intellectual. Governments view them with alarm, and in the early 1980s the Nigerian regime brutally suppressed two Maitaitsine sect revolts in key northern cities.

A new development is the emergence and maturation of secular African philosophy as an intellectual discipline. Before the era of independence, traditional African philosophies were analyzed and written

Leopold Sedar Senghor, President of Senegal from 1960 to 1981. A prominent nationalist in the 1950s and the pre-eminent leader of his nation to and in independence, he is perhaps best known as the founder of an intellectual movement called Négritude.

down by foreign Christian theologians and social anthropologists. Attempts at developing a new, modern African philosophy were made primarily by the more intellectual nationalist leaders, especially Kwame Nkrumah, J. B. Danquah, Leopold Senghor, and Julius Nyerere. They sought to restore the dignity of African culture. The Négritude movement in French-speaking colonies in Africa and the West Indies attempted to rediscover a proud past in order to build pride and confidence in their own present. By the 1950s, nationalists in all Africa were seeking to reaffirm their identity by divorcing themselves from European cultural influences and exploring those cultural traits that seemed uniquely African. Some philosophers described this as the search for a distinctly "African personality." Pan-Africanism, culturally rooted in nineteenth-century America where the quest was for a global "Negro" unity, became Africa-centered after the Second World War. For Nkrumah it implied a political United States of Africa. But to the Francophone leaders it meant focusing on building cultural unity and economic integration.

The continent is also experiencing a literary transformation. African writers are moving away from themes concerning tensions between generations and between traditional and nontraditional beliefs. In the process, African literature is becoming less culture-specific and more universal in the questions it addresses. Its tone has become less stridently anti-imperialist. Négritude seemed less and less relevant to authors such as 1986 Nobel Prize winner Wole Soyinka who dryly noted that "a tiger does not need to proclaim his tigritude." Recent work suggests a move toward introspection and national self-appraisal and self-criticism extending to bold attacks on government leadership.

Africa remains a deeply spiritual and philosophical continent. There may never be a universal "African" philosophy, religion, or ideology. However, efforts are continuing to graft the best in African institutions onto the best and most appropriate models found in other cultures. Africa's greatest legacy to world civilizations could very well be the creation of a viable cultural synthesis that in itself could serve as a model to others.

SELECTED READINGS

• *Items so designated are available in paperback editions.*

THE MIDDLE EAST

Ahmed, J. M., *The Intellectual Origins of Egyptian Nationalism,* New York, 1960. Informative and well-documented account.
• American Friends Service Committee, *A Compassionate Peace: A Future for the Middle East,* New York, 1981. An examination of the problems and proposals for their solution.
Bose, T. C., *The Superpowers and the Middle East,* New York, 1972.

Halpern, Manfred, *The Politics of Social Change in the Middle East and North Africa*, Princeton, 1967.

Issawi, Charles, *Egypt in Revolution: An Economic Analysis*, New York, 1963.

• Keddie, Nikki R., *Roots of Revolution: An Interpretive History of Modern Iran*, Cambridge, 1981.

• Laqueur, Jacques, *The Struggle for the Middle East,* Baltimore, 1972.

• Lewis, Bernard, *the Emergence of Modern Turkey*, 2d ed., New York, 1968.

• _____, *Semites and Anti-Semites,* New York, 1986. A leading scholar of the Middle East explores the development of anti-Semitism in the Islamic world.

Lewis, Geoffrey, *Turkey*, 3d ed., London, 1965.

• Prittie, Terence, *Israel: Miracle in the Desert,* rev. ed., Baltimore, 1968.

Quandt, W. B., F. Jabber, and A. M. Lesch, *The Politics of Palestinian Nationalism*, Berkeley, 1973.

• Rodinson, Maxime, *Israel and the Arabs,* Baltimore, 1970.

Rubin, Barry, *Paved with Good Intentions: The American Experience and Iran,* New York, 1980. Reliable account of U.S.-Iranian diplomacy.

• _____, *The Arab States and the Palestine Conflict,* Syracuse, 1981. Covers the period from the late nineteenth century to 1948.

Saadawi, Nawal, *The Hidden Face of Eve: Women in the Arab World,* Boston, 1982. An exposition of the subjection of women.

Stone, I. F., *Underground to Palestine,* New York, 1979. Account of a secret voyage through the British blockade in 1946.

• Vatikiotis, P. J., *The History of Egypt: From Muhammad Ali to Sadat,* 2d ed., Baltimore, 1980.

• Waterbury, John, *The Egypt of Nasser and Sadat: The Political Economy of Two Regimes,* Princeton, 1983. A perceptive analysis.

• Wilber, D. N., *Iran Past and Present,* 7th ed., Princeton, 1975.

AFRICA

Bates, Robert H., *Essays on the Political Economy of Rural Africa,* Cambridge, 1983. An excellent study of the problems of food production in contemporary Africa.

Baynham, Simon, *Military Power and Politics in Black Africa,* New York, 1986. A reliable survey of military rule in Africa and of the interrelationships between military and civilian elites.

• Berg, Robert J., and Jennifer S. Whitaker, eds., *Strategies for African Development*, Berkeley, 1986. A thought-provoking analysis of the key development problems and proposed strategies for their resolution.

Birmingham, David, and Phyllis M. Martin, eds., *History of Central Africa,* vol. II, London, 1983.

Brain, Robert, *Art and Society in Africa,* London, 1981.

Clark, M. K., *Algeria in Turmoil,* New York, 1959.

Coetzee, J. M., *Waiting for the Barbarians,* London, 1980. A searing critique of South Africa by a brilliant Afrikaner novelist.

• Fieldhouse, D. K., *Black Africa, 1945–1980: Economic Decolonization and Arrested Development,* London, 1986. A well-balanced and candid assessment of the process of decolonization by a leading authority.

• Geiss, Imanuel, *The Pan-African Movement,* New York, 1974.

Gifford, Prosser, and William Roger Louis, eds., *Decolonization and African Independence, 1960–1980*, New Haven, 1987. A comprehensive and critical analysis of decolonization and the rise of African nationalism by the leading scholars in the field.

• Harrison, Paul, *the Greening of Africa: Breaking Through in the Battle for Land and Food,* New York, 1987. An incisive survey of the roots of Africa's agrarian crisis, from debts to deforestation, and new approaches and technologies that are helping to boost food production.

Iliffe, John, *The African Poor: A History,* Cambridge, 1987. A peerless examination of poverty in Africa in the twentieth century.

Kalu, O. U., ed., *The History of Christianity in West Africa,* London, 1980.

Kennedy, Paul, *African Capitalism: The Struggle for Ascendancy,* Cambridge, 1988. A reasoned examination of the problems African governments and entrepreneurs face in developing a strong pirvate sector.

Nattrass, Jill, *The South African Economy: Its Growth and Change,* Cape Town, 1981.

• Ngugi wa Thiong'o, *Decolonizing the Mind,* London, 1986. A call by one of Africa's foremost writers for the pursuit of indigenous themes.

O'Connor, Anthony, *The African City,* London, 1983. Explores the various characteristics of tropical African cities in the postcolonial era.

Palmer, Robin, and Neil Parsons, eds., *The Roots of Rural Poverty in Central and South Africa,* Berkeley, 1977. It argues that certain key elements of precapitalist systems were deliberately allowed to survive under capitalism in the colonial and postcolonial periods in order to keep wages depressed. The essays are scholarly, readable, generally neo-Marxist in approach.

Robertson, Claire, and Iris Berger, eds., *Women and Class in Africa,* New York, 1986. Splendid essays focusing on the inherent tensions between women's class interests and gender solidarity.

Rodney, Walter, *How Europe Underdeveloped Africa,* London, 1972. A neo-Marxist critique of colonialism and neocolonialism.

Thompson, Leonard, and Andrew Prior, *South African Politics,* London, 1982. An excellent, well-balanced survey of contemporary South Africa.

Tordoff, William, *Government and Politics in Africa,* Bloomington, 1984. Highly readable, wide-ranging, and up-to-date.

SOURCE MATERIALS

Africa South of the Sahara, London, annual. The most useful and accurate country-by-country reference work on Africa.

Ben-Gurion, David. *Israel: A Personal History,* New York, 1971.

Berkes, Niyazi, *Turkish Nationalism and Western Civilization,* tr. Z. Gökalp, London, 1959.

Brookes, Edgar H., *Apartheid: A Documentary Study,* London, 1968.

Edib, Halide, *Memoirs,* London, 1926.

Horrell, Muriel, comp., *A Survey of Race Relations in South Africa, 1977,* Johannesburg, 1978.

Hyden, Goran, *Beyond Ujamaa in Tanzania: Underdevelopment and the Uncaptured Peasantry,* London, 1980.

Langley, J. Ayo, ed., *Ideologies of Liberation in Black Africa, 1856–1970: Documents,* London, 1979.

Meir, Golda, *My Life,* New York, 1975.

Weizmann, Chaim, *Trial and Error,* New York, 1949.

Chapter 39

ERUPTION IN EAST ASIA

Countries want independence, nations want liberation, and people want revolution.

—Premier Zhou Enlai

Japan is the only major power that can afford no enemies.

—Marius S. Jansen, *Japan and Its World*

The contemporary era of the countries of East Asia began under the stimulation provided by the impact of Western explorers and merchants. By the middle of the twentieth century profound changes had taken place not only within these countries but also in their relationship to the West. No longer merely peripheral to the main fields of interest of the Western nations, they had become in some measure the pivotal center of world affairs. Japan seized upon a large empire in Asia and the Pacific, which it retained until defeated in a long struggle against the most powerful of the Western states. China, after almost disintegrating and after passing through a cycle of revolution, emerged with radically altered institutions but, once again, as one of the strongest states of Asia. Moreover, China for the first time in its history was in a position to assume a major role in world politics.

The new East Asia

I. NATIONALISM AND COMMUNISM IN CHINA

The overthrow of the Manchu (Ch'ing) Dynasty, accomplished with comparatively little effort in 1911, marked the beginning in China of a long period of instability and disorder that has witnessed a wide displacement of China's traditional institutions and culture. Perhaps never before in the country's history has there occurred such a transformation as during its modern revolutionary era. The Chinese Revolution falls roughly into four overlapping stages: (1) the pseudo-republic of

Stages of the Chinese Revolution

Yüan Shih-k'ai, 1912–1916; (2) the rule of warlords and the weakening of the central government, 1916–1928; (3) the Nationalist revolution, 1923–1949; and (4) the Communist revolution, which gained momentum in the 1930s and, after a military triumph in 1949, brought fundamental external and internal changes to China. The second period, almost purely negative, was the natural result of the turmoil that had accompanied the downfall of the Manchu Dynasty. The third and fourth stages had some objectives in common and were combined for a time, although they finally came to be directly opposed to each other.

The rise of the warlords

Yüan Shih-k'ai, the first president of the Republic, who tried unsuccessfully to restore the monarchy, maintained at least a semblance of unity in the state. After his death in 1916, much of China passed under the rule of independent military commanders, although a group at Peking preserved the fiction of a republican government. Some of these militarists had been officials under the Manchus; others were ex-soldiers or ex-bandits who had collected an army and taken over the administration of one or more provinces. Most of them were extortionate, and the common people of China suffered deplorably from their tyranny. China's participation in World War I at a time when the central government was unable even to put its own house in order was a factor contributing to internal confusion. At the urging of the Allied powers, the Peking government declared war on Germany in 1917, hoping to gain advantages at the peace settlement. During the war, however, Japan seized the opportunity to "assist" its weak ally, selling war materials and extending loans to China and securing economic concessions within the country. At the Paris Peace Conference the requests of the Chinese delegation were almost completely disregarded, and Japan refused to restore the Shantung Peninsula, which it had taken over from Germany. The shabby treatment of China by its allies the great powers provoked a storm of resentment among Chinese intellectuals and patriots. The "May Fourth Movement," named after a demonstration by Chinese students in Peking's Tiananmen Square on that day in 1919, followed by clashes with police and an anti-Japanese boycott, became a benchmark in the revolutionary struggle.

The Guomindang

The third stage of the Revolution is associated with the personality and program of Sun Yat-sen. Dr. Sun's part in the inauguration of the Republic in 1912 had been a brief one, but after returning to Canton, where his following was strongest, he directed a barrage of criticism against the Peking military government. The rise of warlords was not confined to the north, and Sun actually was dependent for support upon militarists in control of the Kwangtung-Kwangsi area. His party, the Guomindang (Kuomintang),[1] was a small faction, and its

[1] In keeping with the designation of *pinyin* as the official romanization system of the People's Republic of China in place of the older Wade-Giles system, *pinyin* is

Demonstration in Tiananmen Square, Peking, 1919. Thousands of students and other concerned citizens gathered on May 4, 1919, to protest the inequities perpetrated at the Versailles peace conference and the corruption of Chinese society and culture.

professed principles of parliamentary democracy seemed utterly unrealistic in a "phantom Republic" ravaged by irresponsible military bands. But with remarkable swiftness the Guomindang changed into a dynamic organization capable of making a bid for control of the state. The initiative and organizing skill for accomplishing this transformation were largely supplied from outside China, by agents of the revolutionary Communist regime in Russia.

Understandably, the Bolshevik leaders, faced with the task of consolidating their power in Russia and confronted by the hostility of the great powers, were eager to win support in revolutionary China. Rebuffed by the Peking government, they turned to Dr. Sun in Canton. The Third (Communist) International had organized a Far Eastern division and established at Moscow a university named after Sun Yat-sen to train Chinese revolutionaries, some of whom joined the Communist party. Although Dr. Sun rejected communism, he had hoped for the support of Western nations and welcomed the offer of Russian cooperation. In 1923 Sun and the Russian emissaries arrived at a working agreement which provided for Russian assistance and for the admission of Chinese Communists to the Guomindang but left Sun the undisputed head of the Guomindang party. Acknowledging that China's immediate task was to achieve national unity and free

Russian aid to the Guomindang under Dr. Sun

used in this chapter for most personal names and terms. The Wade-Giles spellings appear in parentheses at the point of first use. Place names continue to be expressed in their Wade-Giles renditions for clarity's sake.

Dr. Sun Yat-sen Surrounded by His Military Staff

itself from the yoke of foreign imperialism, the Soviet government sent military and political advisers to Canton.

Consolidation of power by the Guomindang at Canton

During the Moscow-Canton entente of 1923–1927, the Chinese nationalist movement acquired a disciplined leadership, clear-cut objectives, and considerable popular support. A general dissatisfaction with the dreary and corrupt rule of the military cliques, the humiliation of China at the Paris Peace Conference, and the entrenched position of the great powers in their spheres of interest all helped to intensify nationalist sentiment. Disillusionment following the war stimulated a spirit of revolt among young intellectuals and among the lower classes, as evidenced by the growth of labor unions in the Yangtze valley industrial cities, peasant movements, youth movements, and movements for the emancipation of women. The various dissident elements needed only effective leadership to be enlisted in a campaign for the regeneration and strengthening of China under a truly national government. Soviet advisers taught Sun Yat-sen and his associates how to supply this leadership. Guided by a seasoned revolutionary who, under the name of Michael Borodin, had worked as an agitator in Turkey and Mexico, the Guomindang was revamped on the model of the Russian Communist party. On the propaganda front, posters, pictures, and slogans dramatized the Guomindang program, which was to unseat the warlords, introduce honest and democratic government, stamp out the opium habit, and promote other reforms.

Character of the Canton government

By 1925 Canton had become the center of a small but effective government, which collected taxes, regulated commerce, and was developing its own "new model" army, officered by men trained at the Whampoa Academy (near Canton) under supervision of European military experts, and indoctrinated with loyalty to Sun Yat-sen and to his party. This Canton government was actually a Soviet regime without being Communist. Controlled by the high command of the Guomindang, it provided the first example of a party dictatorship in China. Although the Canton government showed vigor, it was not recognized by foreign powers, not even by Soviet Russia. Russia maintained correct relations with the Peking government, and restored some Russian concessions to its jurisdiction after Peking recognized the Soviet Union in 1924. At the same time, Russian agents were assisting Sun Yat-sen's group in preparations to overthrow the Peking regime.

Dr. Sun did not live to see the phenomenal success of the organization that he had founded, but he left a body of doctrines as a heritage of the Guomindang party. His most important writings were put together rather hastily during the period of Communist-Guomindang collaboration and partly at the urging of Borodin, who recognized their value for propaganda purposes. The gist of Sun's program and political philosophy is contained in the famous *San Min Chu I* ("Three Principles of the People"), which became a sort of Bible for the Guomindang. The Three Principles, usually translated as "Nationalism," "Democracy," and "Livelihood," have been likened to Abraham Lincoln's "government of the people, by the people, and for the people"; but there is considerable difference between the American and the Chinese interpretations of the terms. By nationalism Sun meant, first, the freeing of China from foreign interference and, second, the development of loyalty among the people to the state instead of to the family or the province. In his second principle, Sun was concerned with popular sovereignty and the ideal of representative government. Recognizing that people are unequal in capacity, he believed that the chief political problem, in both China and the West, was to discover how popular sovereignty could be combined with direction by experts. The principle of livelihood referred to the necessity for material progress and also to social reform, rejecting Marxism but failing to outline any specific program. Sun's ideas as a whole were neither very original nor very radical nor even very clear. Democracy apppeared in his conception as a rather remote goal, to be attained at the end of the revolutionary struggle. The three stages of revolution, according to Sun, would be (1) the military stage, necessary to establish order; (2) the "tutelage" stage, devoted to training the people and with power restricted to the revolutionary leaders (the Guomindang party); and (3) the constitutional stage, embodying representative popular government.

Late in 1924 Dr. Sun journeyed to Peking at the invitation of one of the northern warlords, but he was already suffering from liver cancer and died the following March. Although his career had been a succession of failures, when removed from the scene he acquired legendary stature and was revered by his followers as Father of the Revolution. "Sunyatsenism" proved to be a far more potent force than Dr. Sun had ever been. He left behind him a legacy of hope,

The doctrines of Sun Yat-sen

A 1925 Poster Deploring the Treatment of Chinese Patriotism at the Hands of Warlords and Foreign Imperialists

The death and veneration of Dr. Sun

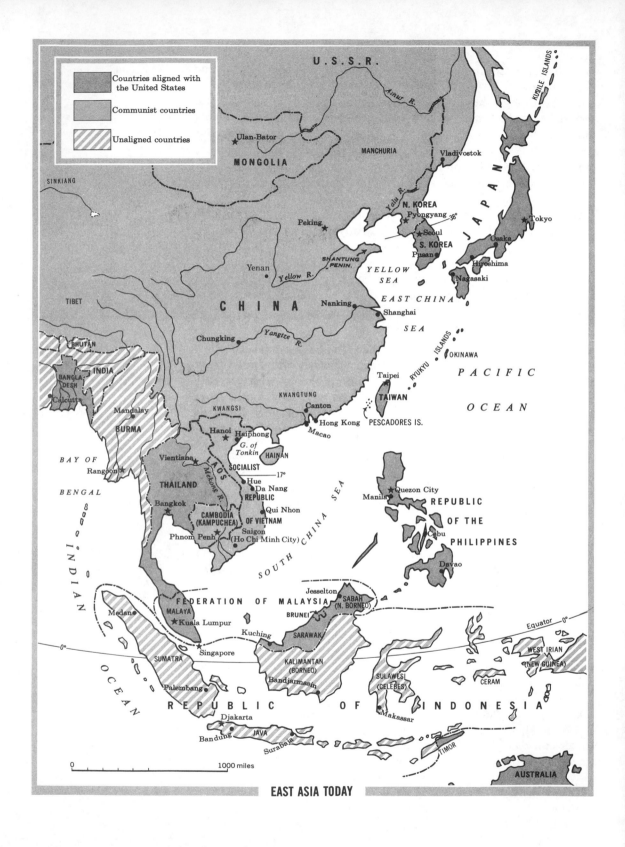

EAST ASIA TODAY

Legend:
- Countries aligned with the United States
- Communist countries
- Unaligned countries

U.S.S.R.

KURILE ISLANDS

Ulan-Bator

MONGOLIA

MANCHURIA

Vladivostok

SINKIANG

Amur R.

JAPAN

Yalu R.

N. KOREA

Pyongyang 38°

Peking

Seoul

S. KOREA

Pusan

Osaka

Tokyo

Hiroshima

Nagasaki

Yenan

Yellow R.

SHANTUNG PENIN.

YELLOW SEA

TIBET

CHINA

Nanking

Shanghai

EAST CHINA SEA

RYUKYU ISLANDS

OKINAWA

BHUTAN

BANGLA-DESH

INDIA

Calcutta

Mandalay

BURMA

Chungking

Yangtze R.

KWANGTUNG

Canton

Hong Kong

Macao

PESCADORES IS.

Taipei

TAIWAN

PACIFIC OCEAN

BAY OF BENGAL

Rangoon

Hanoi Haiphong

KWANGSI

G. of Tonkin

HAINAN

SOCIALIST

17°

Hue

Da Nang

REPUBLIC

Vientiane

LAOS

Mekong R.

THAILAND

Bangkok

CAMBODIA (KAMPUCHEA)

Phnom Penh

Saigon (Ho Chi Minh City)

Qui Nhon

OF VIETNAM

SOUTH CHINA SEA

Manila

Quezon City

REPUBLIC

OF THE

PHILIPPINES

Cebu

Davao

INDIAN

OCEAN

Medan

FEDERATION OF MALAYSIA

MALAYA

Kuala Lumpur

Kuching

Singapore

SUMATRA

Palembang

Jesselton

SABAH (N. BORNEO)

BRUNEI

SARAWAK

KALIMANTAN (BORNEO)

Bandjarmasin

Equator 0°

WEST IRIAN (NEW GUINEA)

SULAWESI (CELEBES)

CERAM

Makassar

REPUBLIC OF INDONESIA

0°

Djakarta

Bandung

JAVA

Surabaja

TIMOR

AUSTRALIA

0 ——— 1000 miles

and he had stirred the imagination of Chinese all over the world with the vision of a strong and free China under a republican constitution which would combine the best thought of ancient sages with modern scientific techniques. By the Guomindang, his writings and speeches were treasured as unalloyed wisdom, while their vagueness made it possible to invoke the master's authority for contradictory policies.

By 1926, when the Canton government had become strong enough to challenge the northern militarists, the Nationalist revolution entered its active phase. Guomindang forces under command of the young general Chiang Kai-shek (1888–1975) swept rapidly northward into the Yangtze valley and in less than six months overran half the provinces of China. The success of this "punitive expedition," however, brought to the surface a dissension that had been stirring for some time within the party. A conservative faction distrusted the Communist connection and wanted to oust Communists entirely. The radical wing, hoping to base the organization upon the support of the peasant and working classes, stressed the desirability of a concrete reform program and of continued association with the Russian advisers.

Although the radical faction held the ascendancy temporarily, prospects for success were dubious. The Chinese Communists at this time numbered only about 50,000. While there were plenty of discontented peasants and a Chinese Federation of Labor claimed 2½ million members, these groups were not capable of dislodging the landed gentry and industrialists from their entrenched positions or of overthrowing the northern military regimes. The Guomindang army, swelled by defectors from disintegrating warlord forces, was not the spearhead of reform, especially under the command of Chiang Kai-shek. While he professed to uphold the ideals of the revolution, Chiang detested the Communists and hoped to win support from the propertied classes. A significant omen for the future was Chiang's behavior after his troops in March 1927 occupied the key city of Shanghai, where organized workers had staged a general strike. Praising the unions for their courage, Chiang secretly negotiated with the Shanghai Chamber of Commerce, business and financial leaders of the foreign concessions, and members of a notorious underworld gang. On April 12 he launched an assault upon the union headquarters, inflicting heavy casualties. Still posing as a revolutionary, Chiang extorted contributions from Shanghai businessmen for the support of his troops.

The Soviet-Guomindang alliance ended in 1927 with total defeat of the radical faction. In April one of the northern warlords had raided the Russian embassy in Peking, claiming to have unearthed a Soviet plot, and he arrested a number of Chinese who had taken refuge there. By mid-summer Borodin and the other Russian advisers were dismissed; trade unionists and radicals were disciplined or driven out of the party, and some party members went into voluntary exile in

Division within the Guomindang

Dr. Sun Yat-sen (Seated) and Chiang Kai-shek

The termination of the Soviet-Guomindang alliance

Russia. In supporting the Moscow-Canton entente of 1923–1927, the Soviet leaders, hoping for the speedy coming of world revolution, had gambled and lost. But they had provided the spark without which the Guomindang might never have been fired into action.

Under a cloud for his high-handed actions in Shanghai, Chiang Kai-shek temporarily relinquished his posts. In August he visited Charlie Soong's widow then living in Japan and won her consent to his marriage to the Soongs' youngest daughter, even though the general already had a wife. The match earned support for Chiang in the United States where Soong Mei-Ling, a 1917 Wellesley College graduate and a Christian, was widely admired. Furthermore it made Chiang brother-in-law to Sun Yat-sen's widow. (Though not a Christian, Chiang promised "to study Christianity.") Reappointed commander-in-chief of the Guomindang army in 1928, Chiang henceforth dominated the party, purged of its radical elements. Seemingly united under conservative leadership, the Nationalists resumed the campaign to extend their authority nationwide. Meeting little resistance, Guomindang forces advanced through the territories of discredited military dictators and before the close of 1928 occupied Peking, which they renamed Pei-p'ing ("Northern Peace").

They established their own capital at Nanking, the city where Sun Yat-sen had been proclaimed president of the Republic in 1911. The task of national reconstruction confronting the Guomindang leaders was a far more difficult undertaking than the seizure of power had been. Even the maintenance of power was not easy, as remnants of the warlord regimes lingered on in various parts of China. The northward advance of Nationalist troops had been blocked in Shantung province by the Japanese who, anxious to protect their sphere of influence in Manchuria, had eliminated a powerful Chinese warlord based in Manchuria by blowing up his train while he was en route to Mukden. The warlord's son, Zhang Xueliang (Chang Hsüeh-liang), prudently promised the Japanese to maintain the autonomy of Manchuria, but the "Young Marshal," as he was called, accepted an appointment from the Nanking government, raised the Nationalist flag at Mukden, and worked against further Japanese encroachment. Although Guomindang supremacy, where it existed, depended on military support, the party claimed that it had completed the first, or military, stage of Dr. Sun's formula of revolution and had inaugurated the second stage—that of political "tutelage." In spite of its anti-Communist orientation, the structure both of the Guomindang and of the government which it set up at Nanking followed closely the Soviet pattern. The party was a hierarchy, reaching from the smallest units, or cells, through district and provincial bodies up to the Central Executive Committee at the top. The president of the National Government and the members of his Council of State were selected by the Central Executive Committee of the Guomindang, of which the key member was Chiang Kai-shek. At the central, provincial, and local levels the government embodied, not democracy, but a party dictatorship.

Manchurian Warlord Zhang Zuolin (center) and His Son, the "Young Marshall" Zhang Xueliang (left)

While progress undoubtedly occurred during the era of Nationalist rule, the defects of the regime became more and more apparent. The Guomindang when in power neglected to carry out the promises embodied in Sun Yat-sen's "Principle of Livelihood," intended to relieve the lot of poor peasants and laborers. Instead of promoting democracy, Chiang Kai-shek and his associates evidenced admiration for the totalitarian regimes of Germany and Italy. Chiang's government welcomed Italian help in developing airports, planes, and trained pilots, and his admirers compared his role to that of Mussolini, who allegedly had rescued Italy from chaos following the First World War. In command of a one-party government and eager to perpetuate its own authority, the Guomindang employed coercive methods not only against radicals but against anyone who opposed it. Victims of political assassination included the head of a League for the Protection of Civil Rights. A secret-police force was disguised under the title of "Bureau of Investigation and Statistics." A tightly disciplined Youth Corps, ironically named *San Min Chu I* after Sun's "Three Principles," indoctrinated party recruits. In effect the Nationalist regime seemed to be preparing the Chinese people less for democracy than for a permanent condition of tutelage.

The downfall of the Guomindang in China, after a rule of twenty years was caused by three factors: (1) failure of the Guomindang regime to solve the problems of Chinese society; (2) unrelenting opposition from the Chinese Communists, who ultimately set up a rival government; and (3) the long war beginning with the Japanese invasion of 1937, which drained the country's resources, demoralized the people, and promoted the chaotic conditions so favorable to the spread of communism. The struggle against the Communists began almost as soon as the Guomindang had established its government at Nanking and was a continuous process even during the most successful years of the Nationalist period. Following the rupture with the Guomindang in 1926, the Communist party had been driven underground but extended its activities in both rural and urban areas of central and southern China, and established several small governments in the form of soviet republics. Almost annihilated by Guomindang forces in a series of military campaigns, the Communist leaders turned the desperate struggle to their advantage by inciting revolutionary aspirations among the depressed peasantry and by developing the technique of guerrilla warfare into a fine art. Mao Zedong (Mao Tse-tung) was the key personality behind both of these policies.

The son of a relatively well-to-do peasant, Mao Zedong (1893–1976) as a youth had rebelled against landlordism and the tyranny of parental authority. One of a dozen men who founded the Chinese Communist party in 1921, he became a deputy member of the Central Executive Committee of the Guomindang and was entrusted by the Communists with the task of peasant organization. A report prepared for the Chinese Communist party in 1927 on peasant revolutionary activity in Hunan (south central China) provides the clue to Mao's

A Young Mao Zedong. A photograph taken in 1923 when Mao was still a leader of the radical left opposition within the Guomindang.

strategy of revolution and is prophetic of his ultimate program for China. Already he was instigating direct action among the lowliest tenants: (1) forming village cooperative associations; (2) smashing temples and burning the wooden idols for fuel; (3) intimidating and assaulting "bad gentry." "A revolution is not the same as inviting people to dinner," he wrote. "A rural revolution is a revolution by which the peasantry overthrows the authority of the feudal landlord class. . . . several hundred million peasants will rise like a tornado or tempest, a force so extraordinarily swift and violent that no power, however great, will be able to suppress it." In sharp disagreement with both the Chinese and Russian party leaders, Mao was convinced that whoever won the peasants would win China.

The "Long March" to Yenan

Threatened with extinction by Chiang's superior troops, the Chinese Communists conceived and executed the famous "Long March" of October 1934 to October 1935—a mass migration across 6,000 miles of difficult terrain and one of the most amazing exploits in military history. To execute one river crossing in wild mountain country twenty men armed with grenades crawled, hand over hand, one hundred yards along the chain of a suspension bridge while exposed to enemy fire, and then routed the defenders on the other side. Of the 80,000 men who slipped through Chiang's lines in southwestern China, not more than 9,000 reached Yenan, in northern Shensi province, which was to be the Communists' headquarters until their final victory in the civil war. Shattering as the experience had been, it served to weld the survivors into a solid group of tested loyalty and toughness, relying upon their own tenacity and ingenuity. At the end of the campaign Mao Zedong, originally the deputy of Zhou Enlai (Chou En-lai) in

The Luding Bridge. In May 1935 Communist forces seized this chain suspension bridge, 270 miles northwest of Chunking in Szechuan province, in one of the most daring exploits of the 370-day Long March.

coordinating the Long March, had become accepted as the head of the Chinese Communist party and its policy director. Observing that it was "the first of its kind in the annals of history," Mao called the Long March a "manifesto, a propaganda force, a seeding machine." The Yenan years were crucial for the history of the CCP, which by 1937 had only 40,000 members. Poor in resources and isolated from the rest of China, the party looked to Moscow for guidance but the Bolsheviks sent conflicting signals and no assistance. Mao relied upon his tactic of "retreat in order to advance" and his ability to sustain and renew his forces directly from the countryside while the cities and economic apparatus of the state remained hostile. Gradually the Communist region of the northwest acquired the attributes of a separate state, with a fluid political structure and well-organized military units. In expanding the area of their influence, the Communists' chief asset was their introduction of reforms which the Nanking government had promised but never fulfilled. By forcing rent reductions, establishing land banks and cooperatives, building irrigation works, and educating peasants in better methods of cultivation and crop control they competed successfully with the Guomindang regime for popular favor. The Communists also strengthened their position by calling for national resistance against Japanese aggression, to which Chiang Kai-shek, intent upon crushing communism, had offered only halfhearted opposition.

The Nanking government's seeming indifference to Japanese aggression while it relentlessly pursued Chinese Communists stirred public resentment. A popular novel, *Cat Country,* written after the Japanese attack on Shanghai in 1932, depicted China as a nation of cats, remaining helpless before an invasion by small animals and finally tearing one another to pieces. In response to Stalin's line calling for "popular fronts" to combat imperialism and fascism, the Chinese Communists offered to cooperate with Nanking in the struggle against Japan, but the offer was refused by Chiang Kai-shek. In December 1936 troops of the "Young Marshall" Zhang of Manchuria stormed Chiang's field headquarters, killed his bodyguards, and kidnapped the generalissimo, found hiding in a cave. Zhang publicly demanded an end to the civil war, release of political prisoners, and the convening of a freely chosen national assembly. Two weeks of delicate negotiations among Chiang, Zhang, and the Communist leaders ended with the release of Chiang, unharmed, on Christmas Day. Back in Nanking he was greeted as a hero by his coterie while Zhang's reward for his bold initiative was trial by court martial and a sentence to ten years' imprisonment. The agreement between the CCP and the Guomindang for joint action, obtained under duress, was a shaky one with mistrust on both sides. The Guomindang rejected the Communists' offer to transfer their troops to Chiang's command in return for their full acceptance as partners in a nationwide struggle. Nevertheless Japanese militarists, alarmed at the prospect of facing a united China, goaded their govern-

The creation of a fragile united front against the Japanese

Chiang Kai-shek in June 1935 as He Single-mindedly Sought to Deliver a Death Blow to the Long March Forces

Japanese Troops Enter Peking in July 1937 at the Beginning of the Eight-Year War with China

ment into launching an attack in the Peking area on July 7, 1937. This was the beginning of a fateful conflict that soon expanded into the Second World War.

Japanese forces, infuriated by the stubborn courage shown by less well equipped Chinese and shocked by the discovery that what the imperial government called the "China Incident" was nothing less than a full-scale war, attacked savagely. In Nanking beginning in December 1937 Japanese troops engaged in a seven-week rampage of looting, rape, and murder. More than 40,000 soldiers and civilians were killed in Nanking and 20,000 girls and women were raped. In an effort to halt the Japanese advance Chiang Kai-shek blew up dikes, diverting the course of the Yellow River to the south of Shantung province. The consequent flooding destroyed over 4,000 villages in north China but did not stem the tide of invasion. The formidable Japanese military machine, although unable to conquer all of China, occupied the coastal cities, organized regional puppet governments, and by the end of 1937 forced the Nationalists to move their capital far inland to Chungking in Szechuan province.

During the period of the united front, which theoretically lasted throughout the war, the CCP under Mao's direction refrained from wholesale expropriation of property, but in the regions under its control it reduced land rents, introduced more equitable tax structures, and weeded out corruption. It also provided practical education combined with political indoctrination in rural villages, thus developing strong ties with the peasants. Meanwhile CCP military units fought more effectively against the Japanese than did those of the Guomindang. Communist guerrillas penetrating behind Japanese lines and sabotaging installations gradually secured control of much of northern China. On the other hand, after the United States entered the war against Japan in 1941 and began to supply Chungking with substantial military aid, the Nationalist government contributed little to the war effort. Chiang Kai-shek, unsure of the loyalty of his own staff and determined to hoard his military resources for a final reckoning with the Communists, had severely strained the united front as early as January 1941 when he attacked and killed 3,000 of the Communist troops that had been left behind in central China during the Long March. Subsequently Chiang sealed off the Shensi "Border Region" government, stationing an army of one-half million in the northwest to maintain a blockade. Efforts by the United States government over a two-year period (1945–1947) to bridge the gap between the two rival Chinese power centers foundered on Chiang Kai-shek's unwillingness to compromise, although after a meeting with Mao in Chungking he did agree to the convening of a political consultative conference. That conference, bringing together representatives of the Guomindang, the CCP, and several independent organizations including a Youth Party and a Democratic League, called for a constitution embodying the cabinet system of government, but the delegates' proposal was sabotaged by the Guomindang Central Committee. The Nationalists then convened their own assembly to draft a constitution and in 1948 reelected Chiang Kai-shek president.

After Japan's surrender China's internal conflict flared into open civil war. Initially the Nationalists seemed to have a decided advantage because of their greater numbers and the aid they continued to receive from the Washington government, which blamed the Communists for its failed efforts at reconciliation. Guomindang forces assisted by an American airlift occupied the principal cities, where China's wealth was concentrated. Holding much of the countryside, the Communists had also secured bases in northern Manchuria, and they seized stores of Japanese arms and ammunition conveniently left behind by Russian troops withdrawing from Manchuria. Chiang made the strategic mistake of trying to dislodge the Communists from their northern stronghold before he had consolidated his own position in central China. Far more serious was his failure to win the confidence of the civilian population. Instead of trying to bring relief to the common people who had suffered throughout the war, the Guomindang by its chaotic, oppressive, and corrupt administration made conditions even worse. While a skyrocketing inflation was paralyzing the economy, party officials built fortunes on graft and speculation. The callous and arrogant behavior of Chiang Kai-shek's government in the hour of victory against Japan made it easy for the Communists to pose as the saviors of a revolution that the Guomindang had betrayed. While the Nationalists were belatedly drafting a democratic constitution for China they were rapidly being dispossessed from the country by the advance of Communist armies. So low had the prestige of the Guomindang party

Civil War; the retreat of the Nationalists

Mao Zedong Declaring the Founding of the People's Republic of China before 300,000 People in Tiananmen Square in Peking on October 1, 1949

fallen that it could summon very little assistance in its hour of peril. In 1949 the southerly retreat of Nationalist forces turned into a rout that ended with all the mainland in the hands of the Communists. By 1950 the jurisdiction of President Chiang's government was confined to the island of Taiwan. As if to document their claim to be the legitimate rulers of mainland China, the fleeing Nationalists carried with them or shipped in advance crates of Ch'ing Dynasty archives and priceless works of art. Accompanied by 300,000 troops, they were able to impose their rule upon the reluctant Taiwanese, many of whom were executed.

After their victory over the Nationalists, the Communist leaders moved rapidly to secure their hold upon the vast territory of China. In October 1949 they proclaimed the People's Republic of China with its capital in Peking. In 1954 they enacted a constitution for the People's Republic, which, like the constitution of Soviet Russia, combined the language and forms of parliamentary democracy with the principle of domination by the Communist party. Nominally, supreme authority was vested in an All-China People's Congress, charged with enacting laws and electing major officials. The constitution contained a Bill of Rights covering the whole field of individual liberties, but it left the application of these rights very tentative by giving the government power to punish "traitors, counterrevolutionaries, and bureaucratic capitalists."

The accession of the Chinese Communists to power was followed by sweeping economic, social, and cultural changes which transformed the country and its people in fundamental ways. The Chinese Revolution, one of the most far-reaching in history and in some ways unique, was stamped by the dominating personality of Party Chairman Mao Zedong, who adapted theoretical Marxism to immediate problems and blended it with elements of China's traditional culture pattern. Educated in the Chinese classics, Mao was also deeply influenced by his study of Western philosophy and politics. His view of history, though simplistic, was less rigidly deterministic than in most communist ideologies. While stressing the role of material forces, he emphasized the importance of human will in shaping the course of events, asserting that "human knowledge and the capability to transform nature have no limit." Invoking China's "glorious revolutionary tradition," he paid tribute to some pre-Communist reformers and to Sun Yat-sen, whose widow—Chiang Kai-shek's sister-in-law—became an honorary vice-chairman of the People's Republic. The Marxist dogma of class struggle Mao identified with recurring unsuccessful peasant uprisings, including the nineteenth-century Taiping rebellion. The Chinese Communist revolution was the first successful one to be founded on peasant support and directed by a leader from the peasant class. In this respect it contrasts with the revolution of Lenin and Stalin, which entailed expropriation and forcible suppression of the peasants. No less than the Soviet revolution, it aimed at creating

Unique features of the Communist revolution

a new society, but, again in contrast with the Russian example, this radical objective was pursued for nearly thirty years—until Mao's death in 1976.

The Communist regime in China claimed to have achieved a coalition of classes, namely peasants, workers, petty bourgeoisie, and "national bourgeoisie." The inclusion of the last two classes marked a departure from orthodox Marxism and an attempt to win the support of financial and industrial elements whose cooperation was essential to bolstering the economy. Businessmen who qualified as "Communist" or "national" capitalists by being willing to work with the new government were allowed to retain their properties temporarily, but they were gradually expropriated through the assessment of heavy fines, and in 1955 all industries were nationalized. The Central Committee of the Communist party or Chairman Mao himself determined public policies, the permissible limits of debate, and the operation of organs of government, in keeping with the principles of a "People's Democratic Dictatorship."

The economic transformation of China since 1949, although in part merely a continuation of a process begun under the Nationalist regime, is impressive when viewed against the previous retarded condition of the country. The Communist leaders, following the Soviet example, made the development of heavy industry a high priority. The savings necessary for capital investment were extracted from the peasants—not by their liquidation as in Stalin's Russia but by requiring them to sell one-fourth of their produce to the state at low prices. To expand the agricultural base the acreage of irrigated land was more than doubled between 1949 and 1969. The same period witnessed a vigorous reforestation program, but an attempt to end the danger of flooding in the Yellow River basin by a system of dams and reservoirs proved unsuccessful. With Soviet technical assistance the People's Republic proceeded to exploit China's mineral resources, which as geological surveys revealed were much larger than had been previously estimated. By 1977 China's oil production equaled that of Indonesia. In coal deposits China ranks third among the world's countries and also has large known reserves of natural gas as well as adequate supplies of manganese, tungsten, antimony, tin, copper, and aluminum. In recent years the Chinese have supplemented their energy sources by building 7 million small biogas plants which, at low cost, convert animal and vegetable waste into methane gas and fertilizer. By 1960 China's furnaces were producing almost as much steel as was made in France, and the output of electric power had been increased ten times. Railroad mileage doubled. Chinese factories eventually were producing cars, trucks, jet planes, even electronic, surgical, and scientific instruments.

More profound than the changes in the scope and tempo of industrialization has been the agrarian revolution, which passed through several successive stages. The first phase of land reform was simply expropria-

A People's Court in Action.
Here a peasant accuses a landlord before a People's Court.
During the initial stage of land
reform as many as one million
landlords are believed to have
been killed.

tion of the landlords, many of whom were killed. Then, the newly
created peasant proprietors were urged to form cooperatives, pooling
the resources of one or more villages. The next step was a drive for
collective farms, communally owned and directed by party members
or supporters. This was accomplished with remarkable swiftness between 1955 and 1957, by which time more than 90 percent of the
family holdings had been collectivized. Although Chinese farmers
undoubtedly "volunteered" to join cooperatives because they were
given little choice, the government relied primarily upon psychological
and social pressure, employing what Mao has described as "persuasive
reasoning." The Communist leaders, obsessed with ideology, constantly sought to combine economic development with changes in
thought patterns and social behavior. Since the task is inherently difficult and the leaders disagreed on tactics, official policies frequently
shifted in a confusing manner. The relaxation of tension known as
the "Soviet thaw" under Khrushchev had its parallel in China. Hoping
to enlist the support of intellectuals, Chairman Mao in a speech in
May 1956 called for "letting a hundred flowers bloom" and "a hundred
schools of thought contend." But when the popular response revealed
widespread dissatisfaction and Peking students covered "Democracy
Wall" with posters demanding more freedom, the party launched a
corrective campaign that ruined the careers of 300,000 intellectuals
branded as "rightists." Mao's dogged pursuit of ideological goals more
than once threatened to jeopardize the positive gains of the revolution.
The so called "Great Leap Forward" launched in 1958 ordered the
merging of rural cooperatives and collective farms into large communes which embodied the principle of ownership by the whole people
rather than by a single community. The purpose of the communes

was to provide a mobile labor force to implement an overly ambitious program of rapid industrialization and to increase food production. Although it added irrigation projects and in a search for uranium for atomic-bomb production discovered new mineral resources, the "Great Leap" proved to be a disaster. The callousness and ineptitude of local directors and the ravages of a prolonged drought brought food shortages, demoralized labor, and drained industrial capital. A famine took 20 million lives between 1959 and 1962. Forced to revise its tactics drastically, the government in 1962 announced its intention to give agriculture top priority for the immediate future. The communes were reduced in size, a degree of ownership and management was restored to local production teams, and farmers were permitted to cultivate small private plots and sell on the open market.

During the turmoil of the failed "Great Leap Forward" Mao relinquished the office of state chairman and, continuing as party chairman, worked quietly to consolidate his support among the rank and file. His ally in this endeavor was Lin Biao (Lin Piao), defense minister and chairman of the People's Liberation Army, who shared Mao's extreme radicalism and injected it into the army, temporarily abolishing all ranks and titles. In 1963 Lin published *Quotations from Chairman Mao,* the "little red book" that served as a powerful propaganda device within the army and throughout the population. In 1965 when Mao felt strong enough to make another attempt to create a radically egalitarian society, he initiated the "Great Proletarian Cultural Revolution," a crusade that kept China in a frenzy for years and was not finally laid to rest until after Mao's death. Rooted in disagreement among party leaders as to both ends and means, the Cultural Revolution unloosed a power struggle between pragmatists bent on strengthening China economically and militarily under the unrelenting vigilance of

The "Great Proletarian Cultural Revolution"

A Red Guard Demonstration in Peking. Middle-school students display their solidarity with the Cultural Revolution by waving copies of the book of quotations from Chairman Mao. The slogan painted on the wall proclaims: "We are not only able to destroy the old world, we are able to build a new world instead—Mao Zedong."

A "Political Pickpocket." The Red Guard parades an official wearing a cap as a mark of public shame through the streets of Peking in January 1967.

the party and a faction headed by Mao that made transforming society its highest priority, for which it was willing to sacrifice efficiency and discipline. Mao chastised Soviet leaders for stopping short of the goal of a classless society, and he denounced as "revisionists" all those within his own party who showed signs of succumbing to the fleshpots of capitalism. He feared that the prospect of material success had brought a relaxation of effort, which China could ill afford in view of its unrealized potential and weak military posture. He viewed with misgivings the tendency of a bureaucracy to grow rigid and complacent, producing a managerial elite more "expert" than "red." As early as 1958 he had expounded his theory of "continuing revolution": "Our revolutions are like battles. After a victory we must at once put forward a new task. In this way cadres and the masses. . . . will forever be filled with revolutionary fervor."

With the onset of the Cultural Revolution scores of officials were arrested, demoted, or forced to make public confession of such crimes as "hedonism," "revisionism," "antiparty activity," or "taking the road to capitalism." The purge numbered high personnel among its targets, including Liu Shaoqi (Liu Shao-ch'i), president of the Republic since 1959 and long regarded as Mao's heir apparent. As the stepped-up purification campaign met with stubborn resistance, Mao turned to the nation's youth, exhorting them to undertake their own Long March and to "learn revolution-making by making revolution." He closed the schools and urged students to organize themselves into units of Red Guards (formally inaugurated at Peking in August 1966) and devote their energies to ferreting out enemies of the revolution. China was treated to the unprecedented spectacle of mobs of teenage youths denouncing their elders, smashing ancient monuments, invading private homes, and noisily demanding unswerving devotion to the thought of Mao Zedong, which now called for the abolition of

The Revolutionary Leadership of the People's Republic of China. From the left: Liu Shaoqi, chief theorist of the party and heir apparent to Mao; Mao Zedong; Peng Zhen, Mayor of Peking (1951–66); Zhu De, Commander-in-Chief of the PLA; and Premier Zhou Enlai. Liu Shaoqi was purged from the party during the Cultural Revolution as a "capitalist roader" and Peng Zhen was severely criticized and demoted.

all private property from the peasants' tiny plots to the interest on bank deposits. Mao encouraged the formation of Revolutionary Committees combining party and nonparty members, and put them in charge of factories, local and provincial governments; in 1967 the Ministry of Foreign Affairs in Peking was taken over by radicals. He hoped to replace the Soviet-style dual system of state and party structures that was developing in China with a flexible but unified system.

The attempt to achieve such radical goals generated a condition of chaos bordering on anarchy. Strikes in major industrial centers, disruption of the transport system, and widespread disorders in rural areas placed China's economic gains in jeopardy. Millions of city dwellers were relocated in the countryside to purify themselves by association with the peasants. Thousands of intellectuals were beaten to death or died of injuries inflicted upon them. Many committed suicide. Valuable libraries were destroyed; artistic and literary expression was shackled. The fanatical Jiang Qing (Chiang Ch'ing), a former actress and Mao's third wife, as cultural inquisitor converted the Chinese stage into a crude propaganda medium. While suffering from self-inflicted wounds China also found herself isolated diplomatically, even in the Communist world.

When revolutionary violence finally led to the outbreak of civil war in some provinces, Mao and Zhou Enlai called upon the People's Liberation Army (which had protected vital installations throughout the upheaval) to restore order, and the party line shifted to a denunciation of extremists. Mao's desire to curtail the role of the PLA now that it had served his purpose partly explains the sudden fall from grace of Lin Biao, recently acclaimed as Mao's "closest comrade" and designated successor. Accused of plotting to assassinate Mao, Lin and his wife fled from China and died in a plane crash in Mongolia in September 1971.

Although costly to life and property and leaving deep scars on the nation's psyche, the Cultural Revolution was not the total catastrophe envisioned by some critics. In the midst of the domestic crisis Chinese physicists succeeded in producing a hydrogen bomb (in 1967) far earlier than Western experts had thought possible. Economic progress resumed in the 1970s and diplomatic ties were restored. And while Mao had failed to achieve the complete leveling he had striven for, Chinese society—for centuries one of the most stable in the world—had been profoundly altered.

One formidable problem, independent of ideological controversy, facing the government of the People's Republic was how to nourish a large and continually expanding population. Despite vigorous campaigns to restrict the birth rate—by providing contraceptives and family-planning courses, encouraging late marriages, and even ordering couples to limit the number of children they had to one—the population reached the 1 billion mark by 1982. Although less than 15 percent

The high cost of the Cultural Revolution

Chairman Mao Zedong. Shown here with his then "closest comrade" Marshal Lin Biao (Defense Minister and Vice Chairman of the Republic who was purged in 1971). Premier Zhou Enlai stands behind them.

of China's land is cultivated, some 80 percent of its people are rural dwellers. China is still poor in comparison with advanced Western countries or Japan. Annual per capita income may not exceed that of India, but instead of being concentrated at the top it has become more evenly distributed, making the majority of the Chinese people better off in basic material necessities than they had been for many centuries. Improved standards of hygiene and sanitation, expanded medical facilities, and educational campaigns succeeded in stamping out opium addiction, curtailing prostitution, and raising the level of public health. By supplementing a scarce supply of skilled professionals with semiskilled trainees, the government was able to provide child day-care centers, hospitals, and mobile clinics employing both up-to-date Western and traditional Chinese medicine and techniques. Low rents, free medical service, and disability and retirement pensions compensated for the low wages of industrial workers.

The impact of Mao's vision on individual freedom

Uprooting the institutions of a landlord-bourgeois regime exacted a heavy price in terms of individual freedom. While party leaders did not hesitate to use physical force, "reform through labor" was a more typical technique applied to recalcitrants, and the whole citizen body was exposed to political indoctrination through the communication media, entirely government controlled. Mao Zedong believed it possible to remake human nature, producing a "new man" who would instinctively put the interests of society foremost, and he hoped to create a direct working relationship between party chiefs and the masses, eliminating middle levels of authority. This utopian objective did not prevent the rise of a bureaucratic managerial class legitimatized by a twentieth-century version of the ancient imperial formula: a benevolent government wielding absolute power over an obedient population under the "Mandate of Heaven."

Changes in the family; partial emancipation of women

Prominent among social changes effected by the Communist Revolution was the replacement of the centuries-old patriarchal family structure with the independent nuclear family as the basic social unit, making possible greater social mobility. A related reform, which has been embraced in theory but realized only partially in practice, is the emancipation of women. Pre-Communist and early Communist reformers, including Mao Zedong, excoriated the subjection and mistreatment of women in traditional society, and the party made the establishment of equality between the sexes one of its primary goals. But deeply rooted customs, reinforced by religious beliefs, have proved resistant to such a fundamental change even when enacted into law. Peasants feared that women's emancipation would rob them of their wives' services, and party leaders shrank from antagonizing the class from which they drew their main support. A much heralded marriage law of 1950 gave wives as well as husbands the right to divorce a mate. Within a year nearly a million women had availed themselves of the opportunity—impressive evidence of a lack of domestic tranquillity. Chinese women have been liberated en masse to enter the labor force,

Women at a Commune Stack Their Rifles While They Labor in the Fields, 1958

and many talented and courageous females contributed to the success of the revolution, even holding responsible positions. But most leadership slots are reserved for men, the husband's job rather than the wife's usually determines a couple's place of residence, and a son is generally more desired than a daughter. Legislative enactments have failed to stamp out the practices of wife beating, forced marriage, and the sale of brides.

The transformation of Chinese culture under the Communist regime, while extensive and innovative, in some areas represented the completion of programs initiated in earlier periods. A "literary revolution" of the 1920s had made vernacular speech an accepted vehicle for modern authors in place of the difficult, archaic language of Chinese literary classics. Linguistic reform under the Communists involved simplification of written characters and adoption of an allegedly more nearly phonetic system of transliteration into languages using the Roman alphabet called *pinyin,* in place of the older "Wade-Giles" system. In *pinyin,* for example, Peking is written "Beijing" and Nanking "Nanjing." A drastic reordering of the economic and political order had long been called for by liberal intellectuals, who scathingly attacked its injustices. Writing in the early 1920s, a famous novelist and essayist, Lu Xun (Lu Hsün) condemned Chinese civilization as "cannibalistic"—"a feast of human flesh prepared for the rich and mighty." But as the Communist party gained custody of revolutionary forces, it discouraged free individual expression, whether critical of the old order or not.

During the Cultural Revolution, while Western art, literature, and music were denounced as polluting, China's own cultural heritage

Cultural transformation

was also repudiated. Mao attacked Confucius as a reactionary defender of a slave-owning aristocracy, and he praised the Legalist scholars who had supported the tyrannical Ch'in emperor. Education inevitably was buffeted by shifting revolutionary currents. Mao Zedong renounced completely the classical Chinese tradition of a scholarly elite drawn from the gentry. He stressed the need to combine theory with practice, instituted "half-study, half-work" programs, and sent youths from city classrooms out into the fields to work with and learn from the peasants. The regular schools, closed during the Cultural Revolution, were not restored to normal operation until after Mao's death. About 25 percent of the population is still illiterate.

China's foreign relations

The rapid unification of China under a totalitarian regime has drastically altered the power relationships in Asia. With a large army at their disposal, the Communists reestablished Chinese jurisdiction over important areas that had been lost during the decline of the Manchu Dynasty. Although Mongolia became a separate republic with ties to the Soviet Union, the Chinese retained Sinkiang in the far west, and installed their forces in Tibet. And while augmenting China's national prestige they posed as the champions of Asian peoples against Western imperialism, assisting revolutionary movements against the British in Malaya and against the French in Indochina.

Hostility of the United States; the "containment" policy

At the outset the greatest external threat to the Communist regime seemed to lie with the United States, which had supported Chiang Kai-shek throughout the war and financed his military establishment of 600,000 troops on the island of Taiwan—within 100 miles of the mainland. The Korean War (1950–1953), frustrating to Americans and costing the Chinese nearly a million casualties, intensified hostility on both sides. An anticommunist crusade, led by the demagogic senator Joseph McCarthy of Wisconsin, purged the U.S. State Department of its best-informed Asia specialists. Stung by charges that liberals and crypto-Communists had "lost China" for the United States, successive Washington administrations withheld diplomatic recognition from the People's Republic, blocked its admission to the United Nations, embargoed American trade with the mainland, and installed a ring of military bases around East Asia. Through its "containment" policy, implemented by a network of defensive alliances, the United States sought to isolate China, and effectively isolated its own citizens from contact with an important area of the world.

The Sino-Soviet rift and its significance

The simultaneous isolation of China and Russia—as the Cold War alienated the USSR from its erstwhile Western allies—at first strengthened the fraternal and ideological bonds between the two large Communist states. In 1950 their representatives signed a thirty-year treaty of "friendship, alliance, and mutual assistance," which invalidated the 1945 treaty between the USSR and the Chinese Nationalists. The preamble of China's 1954 Constitution reaffirmed "indestructible friendship" with the Soviet Union. China relied heavily upon Russia for technical assistance in economic development. The late 1950s, however, evidenced disaffection between the two Communist giants. Differences led swiftly to deterioration in both diplomatic and economic relations. The Chinese resented the Russians' failure to fulfill their aid agreements, including the promise of help in developing atomic weapons. Other factors were the inevitable rivalries of great-power politics and conflicting national territorial ambitions. The Chinese hinted at the eventual rectification of their frontiers at Russia's expense, and both China and the Soviet Union deployed large numbers of troops along their 5,000-mile common border from Central Asia to Manchuria. In 1969 violent clashes occurred between Russian and Chinese troops in Sinkiang in the far west and along the Ussuri River in the northeast. The most fundamental source of disagreement between the two countries was ideological. Chinese Communists accused the Russians of abandoning the cause of world revolution against imperialism and condemned Khrushchev's policy of peaceful coexistence. The breach between Peking and Moscow reflected the differences in outlook between the heirs of an old revolution and the directors of one still comparatively young. In Mao Zedong's view Soviet Russia, now a have nation, had succumbed to revisionism and was taking the primrose path to accommodation with the capitalist powers for the sake of security and the grantification of consumer demands.

Mao Zedong and his comrades strove to avoid close dependence on any other state, Communist or not. (Russian assistance during the 1950s was chiefly in the form of loans and these were repaid.) The break with the Soviets in the early 1960s and the internal turmoil that followed a few years later made China's isolation almost complete. But with the return to more moderate policies in the 1970's the Peking government restored ruptured diplomatic relations and proceeded to win recognition from a rapidly growing number of states. The end of China's isolation was dramatically illustrated in 1971 by rapprochement with the United States and by China's admission to the United Nations and the transfer of a permanent seat in the Security Council from the Chinese Nationalists to the People's Republic.

The end of China's isolation

Ironically, the American president who renewed ties with China had built a political career on strident anticommunism. President Richard Nixon's decision to cultivate cordial relations with his inveterate ideological enemies was prompted partly by the promise of new trade opportunities and partly by the hope of gaining an advantage in dealing with the Soviets by drawing closer to their repudiated ally. In any case it was no longer possible to ignore the People's Republic, which had become a military power equipped with nuclear bombs and missiles. Summit meetings in 1972 did not produce formal diplomatic recognition, but a joint communiqué issued at Shanghai on February 28 pledged the two countries to work toward the normalization of relations and the relaxation of tensions in Asia, including Indochina. One crucial question remained unresolved: the Chinese stipulated that "the liberation of Taiwan is China's internal affair"; the Americans

The changing course of Sino-American relations

Generalissimo Chiang Kai-shek

affirmed "interest in a peaceful settlement of the Taiwan question by the Chinese themselves," and the "ultimate objective of the withdrawal of all United States forces and military installations from Taiwan."

The subject of Taiwan is a story in itself, which cannot be detailed here. Ever since 1949 when Chiang Kai-shek and his defeated forces retreated to the island, it had been a thorn in the side of the Peking government and the chief source of friction with the United States, which retained its alliance with Chiang Kai-shek, recognized his government at Taipei as the "Republic of China," supplied him with arms and money, and threatened to "unleash" his forces to reconquer the mainland. On one point the Communists and the Nationalists agreed—that Taiwan was an integral part of China. They disagreed as to whether it was a severed head or a severed foot. In an atmosphere of international tension, Taiwan's economy thrived. The Nationalists had imposed themselves upon the Taiwanese by force; their rule was an extension of the party dictatorship they had developed at Nanking. But while Chiang Kai-shek had botched the governance of China, he scored a major success in Taiwan. Helped by United States investments and by World Bank credits, the Nationalists' republic sustained a high rate of economic growth. Between 1952 and 1978 the gross national product increased nearly twentyfold and per capita annual income rose from $148 to $1,304, bringing Taiwan to third rank in that category (after Japan and Singapore) among East Asian countries. While the native Taiwanese—about 85 percent of the island's 17 million inhabitants—were given very limited political rights and held under martial law, they benefited from land reform that increased peasant proprietorship and shared in the material progress of both agriculture and industry. Wealth is fairly evenly distributed, and while women have achieved less freedom than their sisters in the People's Republic, the Taiwanese are far better off in material goods than are the mainland Chinese. With sizable military forces as well as a bustling and technologically advanced economy, Taiwan has many characteristics of an independent middle-class power. Yet political independence (which native Taiwanese might prefer) is out of the question because of the

Taiwan under the Nationalist regime

fixed policies of both the Taipei and Peking governments. In spite of official hostility between Peking and Taipei their societies are mutually affected by expanding economic intercourse, while social tension in Taiwan has also begun to relax. Chiang Kai-shek's son, Chiang Ching-kuo, served as president with a Taiwanese vice president, Lee Teng-hui. Lee, who succeeded to higher office at Chiang's death in 1988 and was also elected chairman of the Guomindang, permitted visits to the People's Republic. Several Taiwanese business firms have established subsidiaries on the mainland to take advantage of a cheap labor supply.

In December 1978 President Carter abruptly announced his intention to break diplomatic relations and abrogate the 1954 mutual defense treaty with the Taiwan regime, and the following March he restored normal diplomatic relations with Peking. The initial shock of this policy reversal was softened somewhat when Congress passed the Taiwan Relations Act in April 1979. The act stipulated that any attempt to determine the future of Taiwan by other than peaceful means would be regarded as "of grave concern to the United States." The diplomatic break had no adverse effect on the island's economy. During the first four months of 1979 Taiwan's foreign trade rose 36 percent over the same period of the preceding year, and trade with the United States increased by more than 20 percent. At an annual figure of close to $10 billion, United States trade with Taiwan was ten times as great as with the mainland.

During the decade of the 1980s China's revolutionary leaders sought to make the country a full participant in the community of nations while also promoting its internal development. Changes in foreign policy involved some deviation from the prescriptions of Mao. According to the "Three World Thesis"—attributed to Mao but in reality one of Zhou Enlai's contributions—the two superpowers constitute the first world, other advanced industrial nations of East and West the second, and underdeveloped ex-colonial nations the third. While claiming affiliation with the last group the Chinese began avidly to cultivate relations with the second, not only as an aspect of their rivalry with the USSR but also in order to speed industrial progress.

The agenda formulated by the CCP for economic development specified as objectives "four modernizations," namely agriculture, industry, the military, and science and technology. Unresolved internal conflicts simmering during Mao Zedong's fading years portended grave difficulties in the course projected. Premier Zhou Enlai died in January 1976. A man of sterling character and superb diplomatic skill, Zhou, though less revered than Mao, was more genuinely loved by the Chinese people, and his death occasioned widespread mourning. The following April a demonstration in Tiananmen Square honoring Zhou, viewed by Mao as an expression of political dissent, was suppressed by police and Zhou's protégé Deng Xiaoping (Teng Hsiao-p'ing), who had delivered the eulogy at the premier's funeral, was dismissed from office. Hua Guofeng (Hua Kuo-feng), groomed by Mao to maintain the radical line, acceded to power in October 1976 as chairman of the party and of the Military Affairs Commission; but Hua had to face his rivals without further support from Mao, who had died the month before and lay entombed in Tiananmen Square. Gradually Deng Xiaoping's faction eclipsed Hua Guofeng, who relinquished the party chairmanship in 1981 and faded into the background.

The ascendancy of the pragmatist Deng, twice purged by Mao, seemed to signal a shift from ideology to efficiency, practical reform, and relaxation of the Maoist vendetta against deviationists. Deng's closest associates were Hu Yaobang (Hu Yao-pang), secretary of the Academy of Sciences, and Zhao Ziyang (Chao Tzu-yang), who had

The U.S. break with Taiwan and restoration of diplomatic relations with China

China's new strategies for internal and external development

Deng Xiaoping. Having resigned the vice premiership, the vice chairmanship of the party, and, in 1987, his seat on the central committee of the party, Deng retained the chairmanship of the Military Affairs Commission through which he retained ultimate control of the People's Liberation Army and his status as China's preeminent leader.

748

Eruption in East Asia

Jiang Qing on Trial. Arrested shortly after the death of her husband, Mao Zedong, in 1976, Jiang Qing and the other members of the Gang of Four were accused of "persecuting to death" 34,800 people and framing and persecuting nearly 730,000 others during the Cultural Revolution.

The status of Hong Kong

The implications of China's efforts to foster rapid economic growth

restored agricultural productivity in Szechuan province after the ravages of the Cultural Revolution. Public resentment against the reign of terror that had shaken society erupted in mass demonstrations encouraged by Deng. Heroes of the Cultural Revolution were vilified and its victims rehabilitated (a posthumous award in some cases). Liu Shaoqi, the ousted president of the Republic, who had died in 1969 but whose wife and children had suffered persecution for a decade, was now acclaimed for his "boundless rectitude" and "awe-inspiring righteousness." By making Liu—who was safely dead—a symbol of proletarian rectitude, the new leaders hoped to strengthen their own position and enhance the prestige of the party bureaucracy.

In a sensational sixty-seven-day public trial ending on January 25, 1981, ten defendants were accused of having killed 34,000 people during the Cultural Revolution, of torturing or persecuting hundreds of thousands, and of plotting to poison Zhou and eliminate Mao. Pilloried as the archvillain was none other than the widow of Mao, the feared and hated Jiang Qing, acknowledged leader of the notorious "gang of four," which had become a scapegoat for the excesses and failures of the Cultural Revolution. Jiang's scornful and defiant outbursts against her accusers and judges injected a note of excitement into an otherwise dismal, and apparently well-coached, performance. She was given a suspended death sentence, commuted two years later to life imprisonment. To distance themselves from the Cultural Revolution without repudiating its author, the new leaders in 1981 published an official evaluation of Mao Zedong. Admitting that the "Great Helmsman" had made mistakes 30 percent of the time, it affirmed that his errors were "secondary" and his merit "primary."

Deng and his associates set as their goals internal order, efficient management, and rapid economic development, to achieve which they sought to improve relations with foreign countries. An agreement negotiated with Great Britain in 1984 specified that when British treaty rights in Hong Kong expired in 1997 and the island reverted to China it would be treated as a "special administrative region" for fifty years, retaining its capitalist economy and British law during that period. This promise did not dispel the worries of Hong Kong's inhabitants, many of whom sought residence elsewhere.

To spur the economy's rapid growth the CCP relaxed controls, giving wider scope to individual initiative. In 1985 the communes were dismantled and peasants permitted to negotiate contracts with the state and sell surplus produce for cash. Newspaper headlines exhorted: "Strive to become rich." In 1984 a plaque was awarded to the first millionaire in Communist history, a peasant. Such a drastic shift in the party line caused considerable confusion within a population drilled in the belief that China could advance only through its own efforts and that private gain must be sacrificed to the general good. Now party spokesmen declared that "the proletariat can and must learn from the bourgeoisie," called upon capitalist nations for technological help, opened the country to tourists, and began cautiously to accept foreign investments and credits. Loosening economic restrictions brought new problems. Agricultural output declined as the communes were broken into small private plots, making the use of machinery impractical, and many farmers switched from grain to more profitable cash crops like sugar and tobacco. Peasants owning their own land wanted sons to help work it, inhibiting the enforcement of the one-child-per-family law. Youths who had been sent down to the countryside during the Cultural Revolution drifted back into the cities in search of employment that was unavailable. The influx of foreign capital was not sufficient to fuel rapid industrial expansion. While the number of people continued to increase and poverty remained the lot of most, a few were able to reap large fortunes by exploiting the new opportunities for individual enterprise. The government itself set an unsavory example as corruption spread throughout the CCP. Most threatening of all to the regime was a mounting demand for political reform kindled by liberalization of the economy.

In December 1978 a student wall poster acclaimed democracy as a "fifth modernization." The author of the poster, Wei Jingshen (Wei Ching-shen), who had once been a Red Guard and still retained faith in socialism, declared democracy to be a necessary condition for its fulfillment. When demonstrations followed in Tiananmen Square the government arrested their leaders, including Wei Jingshen who was sentenced to fifteen years in prison. Deng Xiaoping, who less than three years before had been punished for instigating a demonstration, now was meting out the punishment, inspiring the caustic comment of an anonymous writer who jeered at officials "frightened out of their wits" by "a few lines of writing, a few shouts." As intellectuals within and without the party voiced demands for an open society and the discarding of inflexible dogma, government policy swung back and forth between progress and retreat. The trend toward a free-market economy continued, evidenced by a proposal to transfer the railways to private corporations. The People's Liberation Army,

Economic liberalization and the rise of the pro-democracy movement

The PRC Leadership Presides over the Official Memorial Service for Hu Yaobang, April 22, 1989. The speaker is President Yang Shangkun, and to the right of him are Chinese Communist Party Secretary-General Zhao Ziyang, Deng Xiaoping, and Premier Li Peng. The memorials honoring Hu afforded students the opportunity to call for an end to corruption in government and for greater democratic participation.

Demonstrations and Disaster in Tiananmen Square, Peking, May 21–June 4, 1989.
Bottom left: A Peking University student leader addresses demonstrators in the
shadow of the Forbidden City. Top left: Over a million demonstrators defied
martial law to keep government troops from entering the heart of the city. Top
right: PLA troops killed over 700 demonstrators in Peking after receiving the
order to crush the demonstrations.

*Tiananmen Square and the
suppression of the pro-
democracy movement*

reduced in size and given permission to engage in the international
arms traffic, sold "silkworm" missiles to Iran and Iraq. But economic
experiments did not improve the condition of poor families harassed
by an inflation rate that reached 20 percent in 1988, and food shortages
necessitated the rationing of basic commodities. Mass demonstrations
late in 1986 in Peking, Tientsin, Nanking, and Shanghai—where
30,000 students marched—foreshadowed the climactic eruption in
the capital three years later.

In the spring of 1989 Tiananmen Square, flanked by Mao's portrait
and the Gate of Heavenly Peace, became a gigantic rostrum for advocates of democracy. Vociferous but peacefully demonstrating crowds
led by students swelled to more than a million during May. Three
thousand students went on a hunger strike to protest the government's
indifference to their petitions. In the midst of the turmoil Soviet party
chairman Mikhail Gorbachev visited Peking on a mission related to
efforts of the two Communist states to repair the rupture between
them. The timing embarrassed the Chinese authorities because at the
moment when Gorbachev was opening freedom's door in eastern
Europe they were slamming it shut in eastern Asia. After declaring
martial law Deng Xiaoping and Premier Li Peng (Li P'eng) surrounded
the city with seasoned troops under orders to suppress the demonstration, which they did with lethal force, killing hundreds and wound-
ing thousands. Following the massacre of June 4 the government
arrested leaders of the pro-democracy movement, executed many,

and tried to retrieve for punishment those who were hiding or had fled abroad. Although world public opinion was shocked by this indiscriminate and brutal action, its perpetrators calculated, correctly, that they ran little risk of interference or reprisal from foreign governments. Britain and the United States while applauding the dawn of political freedom in eastern Europe seemed remarkably unconcerned with its suppression in China, where beleaguered students had paid tribute to the great Western democracy by erecting a replica of the Statue of Liberty in Tiananmen Square. Scorning Gorbachev's reforms in the Soviet Union as well as Western-style democracy, the Peking government continued to persecute dissenters, tightened party discipline, and announced plans to reduce higher education and expand it at the elementary level to equip the young with basic skills and inoculate them against the virus of rebellion.

As the aging Deng Xiaoping showed the colors of an uncompromising conservative he appeared to repeat the behavior of his old adversary Mao Zedong, who in the course of inciting and then checking a popular uprising had sacrificed his comrades Liu Shaoqi and Lin Biao. Similarly Deng discarded the two men who had risen to power with him. Hu Yaobang, opposed to the infringement of party dogma upon the freedom of scientific research, resigned under pressure in January 1987. Party Secretary Zhao Ziyang, who preferred talking with students to shooting them, was replaced by hard-liners in 1989. As China moved toward the twenty-first century it seemed to have discarded, along with its static and semifeudal past, the vision of a free society. Whether the long and tortuous Chinese revolution had finally come to an end in a stultifying despotism, or whether an energized but cowed population might break the barriers and, with the help of returning exiles, resume the task of building a social order combining socialism with democracy only the future could show.

The ascendency of the hardliners

2. THE CLIMAX OF IMPERIALISM AND THE BEGINNING OF A NEW ERA IN JAPAN

In the early twentieth century, while China was in the throes of revolutionary struggle, Japan was enjoying relative stability and increasing prosperity. The transformations that characterized the Meiji Restoration had been accomplished without seriously disturbing the structure of Japanese society. Before 1914 Japan had enlarged its territories, acquired the basis for a strong industrial economy, and finally found itself in a position to seek hegemony in East Asia.

The Japanese government entered the war against Germany in 1914, nominally out of regard for the Anglo-Japanese alliance but actually from a desire to secure Kiaochow Bay and the German concessions in the Shantung Peninsula. The Japanese also seized the German outposts in the Pacific north of the equator—the Marshall, Caroline, and Mariana Islands—acting upon the opportunities presented by Chi-

Results of participation in the First World War

na's weakness and by the involvement of the Western powers in the titanic struggle in Europe.

The success of Japan's policy of exerting diplomatic and economic pressure was demonstrated at the Peace Conference of 1919. The Chinese delegation naturally demanded the restoration of Shantung, a request entirely consonant with Wilsonian principles. The Japanese refused to comply, and Wilson did not press the matter vigorously, partly because another Japanese objective of a less questionable character had been defeated. The Japanese had asked for a declaration endorsing the principle of "the equality of nations and the just treatment of their nationals." The fear that such a declaration would conflict with the policy of limiting Oriental immigration led the Americans and British to oppose it when the matter was put to a vote in the League of Nations Commission. At the same time they yielded to Japan on the Shantung question and also allowed Japan to retain, as mandates under the League of Nations, the North Pacific islands taken from Germany.

In spite of having plucked the fruits of imperialism, Japan after the First World War seemed to be moving in a liberal direction, both in domestic affairs and in international relations. The antiwar sentiment prevalent for a short time in much of the Western world was manifest, to a lesser degree, in Japan and provoked a revulsion against military leadership. Japan had been associated with the foremost Western democracies during the war, was one of the "Big Five" at the Paris Peace Conference, and—in contrast to Wilson's own United States—signed the Versailles Treaty and joined the League of Nations. Twice before in their history the Japanese had revealed a capacity for adopting what seemed to be the most effective and up-to-date institutions in the world as they knew it, and many of their leaders were persuaded that democracy was essential for progress in the twentieth century. Japanese statesmen were impressed by the fact that autocratic and militaristic Germany had been defeated and autocratic Russia had collapsed in revolution, while the apparently weaker democratic nations had been victorious. And, although few of these statesmen were convinced democrats in the full sense of the term, they were at least desirous of retaining the good will of the democratic powers which seemed to be in command of the world's destiny at the moment.

During much of the 1920s Japan's international policy was on the whole conciliatory, as illustrated by the Washington Conference of 1921–1922, which produced a Naval Arms Limitation Agreement, a Nine-Power "Open Door" Treaty concerning China, and a Four-Power Pacific Pact. The Japanese accepted a limitation of Japan's battleship tonnage to a figure three-fifths that of the United States and of Britain, and agreed to terminate their alliance of twenty years' standing with Great Britain. The Four-Power Pact which replaced the alliance was based on nothing more substantial than the promise of friendly consultation on problems of the Pacific and pledges to maintain the status quo in regard to fortifications in this area. The Nine-Power Treaty, affirming the principle of the Open Door, actually restored nothing to China, but the Japanese delegates, in private conferences with the Chinese, promised that their government would withdraw its troops from Shantung and return the administration of the province to China, leaving Japanese interests represented only in the form of private capital investments. This action was carried out as promised before the close of 1922. Many Japanese businessmen were convinced that the cultivation of friendly relations with the sprawling mainland state would pay far bigger dividends than would the seizure of territory by force and at the risk of inviting a boycott of Japanese trade. A Japanese scholar, writing in 1930, rejoiced that he had lived to see his country join the ranks of the great powers and work with them "to maintain the peace of the world."

Promising as the liberal-democratic trends in Japan were, they did not become vigorous enough to extinguish deeply entrenched reactionary forces which eventually led the country to disaster. The failure of the liberal elements must be attributed in part to external factors. The disillusionment and cynicism that became general in the postwar years throughout the West had their counterpart in Japan. The trends of international politics did not indicate a substantial gain for democratic processes. The rise of fascism in Europe demonstrated a powerful movement in the opposite direction. Almost everywhere, virulent nationalism seemed to be in the ascendancy, obscuring the hope of a cooperative world order. With democracy on the defensive or in retreat in the countries of the West, where it was indigenous, it could scarcely be expected to triumph easily in such a nation as Japan, where it was a recent innovation with no cultural or institutional roots.

The counterinfluence of nationalism

The sensibilities of the Japanese were irritated by the discrimination they encountered in the form of tariffs and immigration laws. In 1924 the United States Congress passed an Oriental Exclusion law, placing Asians in a category inferior to that of the most backward Europeans. The United States was not alone in such a policy, and many Japanese began to feel that the great white nations were determined never to treat them as equals. The high tariff policies of the United States and other Western powers were another disturbing factor, producing psychological as well as economic repercussions. By 1930 the larger share of Japan's foreign trade, both export and import, was with the United States, with a trade balance decidedly favorable to the latter country. Protectionists in the United States alleged that American standards were threatened by competition from "cheap" Japanese labor. Yet the chief Japanese import was raw cotton and Japan's leading export to the United States was raw silk, an item hardly competitive with American industry.

Discriminatory polices of Western nations

In the last analysis, the defeat of liberal forces was due to deficiencies in the structure of Japanese society and in the economic system. The fundamental problem of creating a stable economy and satisfactory living standards for the majority of the people was never solved, and the problem became steadily more acute as the population continued to increase at the rate of 1 million a year. In spite of the expansion of commerce and manufacture, Japan's per capita income by 1928 was equal only to about one-eighth of that of the United States. Japan's prosperity, such as it was, depended upon participation in a world market that was subjected to more and more intense competition. Foreign trade received a severe blow when the price of silk, the country's leading export, declined about 75 percent between 1925 and 1934. To compensate for the collapse of the silk market, Japanese manufacturers stepped up the production of cotton cloth, but in this field they were bucking old and strongly established competitors. The Great Depression struck Japan just when the country seemed to be pulling out of a slump. Between 1929 and 1931 Japan's foreign commerce fell off by one-half, while rural and industrial indebtedness swelled to a figure in excess of the national income.

The highly inequitable distribution of wealth within Japan made for an artificial stratification of classes and interests that was unfavorable to the development of a democratic society. The middle class was too small and insecure to be a very effective liberal force. The great body of farmers and laborers had been ushered out of the discipline of Tokugawa feudalism into the discipline of an efficient centralized bureaucracy, without ever being emancipated from their traditions of docility and the acceptance of direction from above. Aspects of a feudal mentality persisted within the nation after feudalism had been replaced by a modern capitalist order. Industry, commerce, and finance were concentrated in the hands of a few huge trusts, known collectively as the Zaibatsu, each controlled by a closely integrated family group and almost beyond the reach of public supervision. The Zaibatsu not only dominated the economic picture but also were affiliated with bureaucrats in the government and deeply influenced political parties.

The flimsy foundations of Japanese liberalism are revealed in the history and character of political parties during the 1920s and early 1930s, when two competing parties had risen to prominence. The Seiyukai was a descendant of the old Liberal party of Itagaki, but it exemplified a metamorphosis of liberalism into something almost its opposite. Itagaki's party, largely agrarian from the beginning, had passed under the domination of great landlords in place of the small tenants. To this conservative agrarian element was added the leading representative of big business, the house of Mitsui. Thus the Seiyukai constituted an alliance of landlords, monopoly capitalists, and bureaucrats, and it had connections also with the armed services. While the party favored constitutional methods, it was extremely conservative on domestic issues and rabidly expansionist on foreign policy, advocating forceful measures to improve Japan's economic position.

755

*The Climax of Imperialism and
the Beginning of a New Era in
Japan*

In 1927 an opposition party to the Seiyukai was formed, incorporating remnants of the old Progressive party of Count Okuma. This new party, the Minseito, was backed primarily by industrial rather than agrarian interests, and favored policies conducive to the health of the business community, including social-welfare measures to relieve working-class discontent. But while it was progressive in comparison with the Seiyukai, it could hardly be considered truly liberal in composition or principles. It was supported by one of the great Zaibatsu houses (the Mitsubishi) and was as intensely nationalistic as the Seiyukai, differing from the latter chiefly on the question of which methods would best advance the country's interests.

The Minseito

A hopeful interlude, of brief duration, began when a Minseito cabinet came into office in 1929 and attempted to reverse the "strong" policy of the previous ministry, which had thrown troops into Shantung province as the Chinese Nationalist forces advanced toward Peking. The impact of the world depression upon Japan's economy, however, jeopardized the position of the moderate Minseito cabinet, and the assassination of the premier by a fanatic not only weakened the cabinet but also gave ominous warning of the length to which intransigent nationalist groups would go in promoting their own cause. Then, in September 1931, the Japanese army stationed in Manchuria took matters into its own hands by attacking Chinese troops. By the following February, Manchuria had become the "independent" state of Manchukuo under Japanese auspices, and in 1933 Japan, branded publicly as an aggressor, defiantly withdrew from the League of Nations.

*The failure of moderation;
the Manchuria incident*

Throughout the 1930s liberal elements in Japan never entirely abandoned their struggle to hold back the tide of militant nationalism. But when the issues became international, as in the struggle over Manchuria and, later, in the war against China, patriotic sentiments blunted the edge of popular opposition. The only groups strong enough to challenge the militarists were the financial and business interests, and

*The omnipotence of
nationalism*

*Japanese Troops in the Walled
City of Mukden, Manchukuo
(Manchuria)*

these were easily seduced by the promise of profits in the offing. Most of the business leaders had come to regard expansion as essential to Japan's economy. They hoped it could be carried out peacefully and painlessly, but they had helped to build, and had profited from building, a war machine that would be extremely difficult to hold within bounds.

Of course, the primary center of aggressive truculence lay in the military services themselves, particularly the army. As previously pointed out, the Japanese army was composed largely of peasants, an unfortunate class, whose legitimate discontents were, under skillful direction, sublimated into an unreasoned and frenzied patriotism. After the Meiji period the army officers also were drawn chiefly from small towns and rural communities, and they lacked the temperate and relatively broad-minded attitude that had distinguished the samurai leaders. Gradually a "young officer" group developed an ideology of its own, which began to permeate the rank and file. Idealists in the worst sense of the term, these soldier fanatics preached absolute loyalty to the emperor and affirmed that Japan, of divine origin and superior to other nations, had the right to extend its rule over other parts of the world. At the same time, reflecting their peasant affinities, they demanded agrarian reforms or even nationalization of the land and castigated both capitalists and politicians as selfish and corrupt. Their program, a medley of radical and reactionary principles, aimed to make Japan an invincible state, solidly unified under the imperial will, which they claimed to represent most faithfully. Although it has been likened to fascism, the "Imperial Way" proclaimed by the ultranationalists undoubtedly had more in common with the ancient Japanese concepts of the state as a patriarchal society and of the superiority of government by men to government by law.

The creation of the puppet state of Manchukuo in 1932 and its development under Japanese management did not yield the substantial benefits to Japan's economy that had been anticipated. To exploit the coal, iron, and oil resources of Manchuria required an extensive outlay of capital, and Japanese capital was not readily forthcoming, partly because of the fear that industry in Manchukuo would compete with Japan's and partly because of the rigid governmental controls imposed upon capital and industry in the puppet state. As plans matured for making Manchuria not simply a source of raw materials for Japan but a center of heavy industry for Asia, it became apparent that the assurance of access to a wide market area was imperative. Hence, Japanese expansionists attempted to convert China's northeastern provinces into an "autonomous" region, linked economically with Manchukuo. Finally they enlarged their objectives to encompass the creation of a "Greater East Asia Co-Prosperity Sphere." Instead of alleviating Japan's economy, this aggressive imperialistic policy saddled it with additional burdens, entailing larger and larger expenditures for arma-

The Beginning of the Occupation in Japan. American troops entering Tokyo September 8, 1945. The devastating effects of the bombing raids are plainly evident.

ments in support of a program that had no foreseeable limits and was bound to meet with resistance at every point.

The role of Japan in the Second World War, into which its conflict with China was merged, is discussed elsewhere in this volume. Japan's surrender in 1945 was the prelude to a new phase of history, in many ways different from anything experienced in the past. Never before had the Japanese nation been defeated in war and never before had the country been occupied by a foreign power. The occupation of a conquered country was also a new experience for the United States. An international tribunal, established in Tokyo to try Japanese "war criminals," imposed sentences of life imprisonment upon ten of the defendants and the death penalty upon seven others, including the wartime prime minister General Hideki Tojo, who was hanged.

For six and a half years, authority in Japan was nominally held by the Far Eastern Commission in Washington and the advisory Allied Council for Japan in Tokyo. Actually it was held by General Douglas MacArthur as Supreme Commander for the Allied Powers (SCAP) under orders from Washington. From beginning to end the Japanese Occupation was an undertaking and a responsibility of the United States. Military rule was indirect, however, and was exercised through the regular Japanese government, which had not disintegrated with Japan's military defeat. The emperor accepted the surrender terms, called upon his subjects to cooperate with the occupying forces, and served as the connecting link between the old order and the new. In spite of the relative unimportance of the emperor politi-

The defeat of Japan in the Second World War

The American Occupation

Destruction of Japanese Naval Weapons. Miniature submarines at the naval base at Kure are being destroyed. In its new constitution, Japan renounced the right to make war.

cally in modern times, his role was of great value psychologically in providing a symbol of continuity when so much of the past seemed to have been destroyed forever.

The Japanese response to the Occupation

Japan's military defeat and subsequent occupation by the conqueror's troops marked the third time in the country's history that it was subjected to strong doses of foreign influence. Unlike the earlier occasions, the Japanese were not acting voluntarily. But although forced to accept changes, they again succeeded to a remarkable degree in adapting these to their own social and cultural traditions and in using them to promote renewed growth and fresh achievements.

The Constitution of 1946

One of the first major tasks of the Occupation authorities was to furnish Japan with a new constitution grounded in democratic principles. A draft prepared by a group of Japanese consultants was replaced by an American document, which was approved by the emperor and formally promulgated by him in the Diet in November 1946. It went into effect in May of the following year. Breaking cleanly with tradition and with the Constitution of 1889, it declared that sovereignty lay with the Japanese people and left the emperor with only formal powers like those of the British monarch. The new Constitution contained an elaborate Bill of Rights, in which to the normal civil liberties were added such benefits as the right to work and to bargain collectively, social equality, and equality of the sexes. Universal adult suffrage was established, with a bicameral Diet, and a cabinet responsible to the House of Representatives. The Constitution also incorporated the American principles of separation of church and state and judicial review of acts of the legislature. Particularly arresting was Article 9, which declared that "the Japanese people forever renounce war as a sovereign right of the nation" and that "land, sea, and air forces, as well as other war potential, will never be maintained." Its highly utopian flavor made the new Constitution one of the most remarkable documents of its kind ever issued. If its principles could have been carried into active and complete realization, they would have made Japan a more advanced democratic nation than the United States.

While introducing political changes the Occupation authorities projected a far-reaching reform program. In conformity with the policy of demilitarization, an extensive purge was conducted to remove from office and from teaching positions all persons suspected of ultranationalist proclivities. A direct attack was launched against the Zaibatsu groups with the passage of an Antimonopoly Law and the creation of a Fair Trade Commission. Pursuant to the liberal economic provisions of the new Constitution, labor organizations were encouraged. Between 1945 and 1950 membership in labor unions increased from 5,000 to more than 6,000,000 and the government enacted a comprehensive labor welfare code. Perhaps most significant among the reforms was that which dealt with the long-neglected problem of land ownership. An agrarian law of 1946, providing for government purchase of tracts from absentee landlords and for the sale of these tracts to tenant farmers at moderate prices, led to a sweeping transformation of agricultural land ownership.

The character of the Occupation and its accompanying reforms were clearly stamped with the complex personality of General MacArthur. Filled with a strong sense of mission that sometimes made him arrogant, he was nevertheless capable of sound judgment, and he strove vigorously and sincerely to promote what he believed to be Japan's long-range best interests. He successfully opposed demands to abolish the imperial office, realizing its value both as a symbolic link to the past and as a vehicle for legitimatizing institutional reforms. Honored as a military hero in America, MacArthur came to be looked upon almost as a demigod in Japan. His policies, however, were sometimes impractical and even contradictory. He insisted on the disestablishment of Shinto as a state religion to further the objective of complete religious freedom, yet he entertained hopes of converting the Japanese to Christianity. The purge directed against militarists and ultranationalists caught some liberals whose only fault seemed to be their adherence to ideals boldly announced in the new Constitution. Labor was prodded into organizing and collective bargaining, but strikes were restricted by the Occupation government. MacArthur took particular pride in his campaign to promote free enterprise by breaking up the huge Zaibatsu combinations. The ultimate results of this trust-busting program could hardly have been foreseen and were considerably different from what MacArthur intended. The efficient organizational structures that Mitsui and Mitsubishi had developed were, with their dissolution, replaced by a rigid bureaucracy created by the Occupation to enforce competition and

The reform program

Occupation policies

control foreign trade. Clumsily and inflexibly managed, it temporarily disrupted the economy and hampered recovery. But the precedent of a centralized bureaucracy, remaining as a legacy of the Occupation, eventually proved useful in speeding Japan's economic growth. The Japanese government, which before the war had exercised relatively weak control over the private sector, at the end of the Occupation stepped into SCAP's role as chief economic planner and director. Although the great trusts were not formally reconstituted, Japan acquired a centrally guided rather than a laissez-faire economy. Beginning in 1948, the economic restraints imposed by SCAP were gradually relaxed. Occupation policy, reflecting the pressures of global power politics, shifted from reform to retrenchment and recovery. The program of decentralizing industry halted with the realization that if Japan's industrial strength were preserved it could be an asset to the West in the Cold War with the Communist powers. A recent study has shown that some American planners even contemplated the revival of a Japanese co-prosperity sphere, dominating the economy of East Asia. The venerated statesman George Kennan predicted that Japan, the "natural workshop of the Far East," would need to reopen "some sort of empire toward the South."[2] State Department officials, viewing Japan's recovery as an aspect of U.S. global strategy, did not foresee the time when the conquered nation would loom as America's most formidable rival.

The peace treaty

A peace treaty between the United States and Japan negotiated at San Francisco in September 1951, and ratified the following April, was also signed by forty-eight other countries, not including the Soviet Union, which remained technically in a state of war with Japan until 1956. The settlement, while it ended the Occupation and restored formal independence to Japan, was very drastic territorially, reducing Japan to the area it had held at the time of Commodore Perry's visit in 1853, although its population was now three times as great. The peace treaty, supplemented by a security treaty, acknowledged Japan's right to arm for "self-defense" and authorized the stationing of foreign troops (meaning American) in Japan for the defense of the country. That the United States regarded even a disarmed Japan as strategically important was evident from the beginning. General MacArthur had portentously described Japan as "the westernmost outpost of our defenses" and boasted that "the Pacific has become an Anglo-Saxon lake."

Political trends in postwar Japan: The Liberal Democratic party

Encouraged by a democratic constitution, numerous political parties sprang into being, but the persisting tradition of loyalty to personalities, kinship groups, or local interests made it difficult to establish them on a nationwide basis with broad popular support. In 1955 two major organizations, successors respectively of prewar Seiyukai and Minseito,

---

[2] W. S. Borden, *The Pacific Alliance: United States Foreign Economic Policy and Japanese Trade Recovery, 1947–1955.*

merged to form the Liberal Democratic party (LDP), which has held a predominant position ever since. In spite of its name the party is conservative, and its continual success reflects the conservative bias of the majority of voters. Deriving support from the business community, old-line bureaucrats, rural constituents—which are overrepresented in the Diet—and civil service officials, the LDP has operated as a coalition of factions without a clear program or well-organized and active membership. In power for three and a half decades, the party became in effect the Japanese establishment, nourishing the country's expanding economy and maintaining its ties with the United States.

The leading political rival of the LDP is the Japanese Socialist Party, which in 1955 won a third of the seats in the lower house of Parliament but failed to repeat this performance. Groups challenging the dominant party have diverged widely in aims, and opposition parties have been plagued by factional disputes. A small Japanese Communist party, aligned neither with Moscow nor Peking, sought to woo the electorate with such innocuous slogans as "Cover drainage ditches" and "Build more day nurseries." At the extreme right the Clean Government party, political arm of a militant Buddhist sect, has appealed primarily to middle- and lower-income groups.

The opposition

To what extent political democracy has taken root in Japan is a matter for debate. The Constitution, organs of government, judicial and electoral processes clearly meet democratic standards. The press is free and of high caliber. At the same time, Japanese political habits and psychology carry overtones of an earlier tradition. The tenacity of local loyalties and personality cults—a preference for government "by men" rather than "by law"—has prevented the rise of national parties with clearly defined policies, or even the development of a national political consciousness. Without presenting a distinctive platform on which to stand or fall the LDP has been able to keep the reins of office by balancing the claims of competing groups. Minorities and opposition parties, in spite of their poor showing at the polls, are not without political input. Their pressure is sometimes reflected in initiatives of the ruling party, which respects the Japanese fondness for reaching a consensus acceptable to all rather than a victory for one contestant.

Extent of democracy

During the past twenty years the Liberal Democratic party has been badly shaken by the exposure of corruption, illegal practices such as vote buying, and scandals involving high government officials. In 1974 Prime Minister Kakuei Tanaka was forced to resign and subsequently was tried and sentenced to a fine and a four-year prison term for accepting a large bribe from the Lockheed Corporation. In successive national elections the LDP lost ground, both to the Socialists on the Left and to Komeito (Clean Government party) on the Right, but by forming temporary alliances managed to retain control of the government. The office of prime minister passed to Yasukiro Naka-

Kakuei Tanaka, Prime Minister of Japan, 1974–1977

Yasukiro Nakasone, twice Prime Minister of Japan during the 1970s and 1980s

Japan's economic recovery and expansion

sone, a wily LDP politician nicknamed "Mr. Swivel Chair" and also called "the Japanese Reagan" because of his effective use of television to enhance his image. An ultraconservative, Nakasone had advocated revising the Constitution to elevate the position of the emperor and strengthening Japan's military forces. Disturbing to many observers was the fact that Nakasone owed his leadership position largely to the "shadow Shogun" Tanaka, who even from his prison cell commanded a large band of loyal followers within the party. Nakasone's popularity, at its height in the spring of 1985, when he was serving a second term as prime minister, declined sharply thereafter and the LDP dropped plans to nominate him for a third term. There was evidence of growing apathy among the general body of voters, who allowed the LDP to win by default, unpersuaded that any available opposition group would do any better. The factor probably most responsible for the LDP's seemingly unshakable position was the economic recovery and expansion that accompanied its tenure of office.

The economic difficulties confronting Japan immediately after its surrender seemed practically insurmountable. Before the close of hostilities almost one-third of the homes in Japan's urban areas were destroyed by air attacks, and the direct economic loss caused by the war was staggering. Japan was shorn of its empire, industrial production had fallen 80 percent below the 1937 level, foreign trade stood at zero, and the country depended upon imports even for foodstuffs. Viewed against this dismal background, Japan's economic recovery and advance have been spectacular. By 1953 the index of production was 50 percent above the level of the mid-1930s, and it continued upward, with textiles, metal goods, and machinery leading the way. During the 1950s economic productivity doubled; in the next decade it overtook that of England, France, and West Germany to become the third largest in the world. By the late 1970s Japan's gross national product was more than half that of the United States. A remarkable aspect of this economic expansion was that Japan both competed successfully in long-established industries and also pioneered in new fields. It became the world's largest shipbuilder, exported steel, light and heavy machinery, and gained a commanding position in such areas as chemicals, synthetics, optics, electronics, and computer technology. Japan now produces more than half of the world's semiconductors and an even larger percentage of its data-storing microchips. The Japanese outpaced most Western nations in the development of mass-transit facilities, especially railways, famous in recent years for their "bullet trains." By the 1980s they were exporting prefabricated houses, producing artificial seafood and computer-controlled sailing ships, and carrying on advanced research in biotechnology, robotics, and artificial intelligence. Contributing significantly to the country's strong economic position are its financial resources. The surplus capital accruing from industrial expansion and technological innovation has made Japan a creditor nation, with large investments in developed and developing countries. The world's ten largest banks are Japanese.

Electronics Industry of Japan. Mass-production lines of television sets at the Matsushita Electrical Industrial Company plant in Ibaragi. Better than 90 percent of Japanese families own television sets. The Japanese electronics industry has also become a major factor in the American market for such products.

Several factors explain Japan's seemingly miraculous rise from a condition of prostration to one of dizzying prosperity. First, in spite of devastating losses from the war, the Japanese retained their technical proficiency, labor force, and traditions of hard work. A determination to recover lost ground and to overtake and surpass the West became a national obsession, eliciting self-sacrifice and mitigating disputes between management and underpaid labor. Employees of large corporations served them with a loyalty like that of the old feudal samurai to his lord. Statistics reporting the growth of the GNP were scanned with the avidity devoted in more leisurely societies to the sports pages. Postwar Japan achieved an extremely high ratio of savings to earnings, in some years amounting to 30 percent. A second factor helping to stimulate recovery was American financial aid, not only during the Occupation but especially by the purchase of goods and services for the Korean conflict. The stimulating impact of the war boom was reflected dramatically in the Tokyo stock market. A third factor was the initiative of the government in stimulating and guiding the growth of an essentially private-enterprise economy. The government encouraged capital investment by incentive tax and loan policies, operated an Economic Planning Agency to compile data and predict market trends, and through a Ministry of International Trade and Industry took the lead in directing industrial development. Japanese economic policy successfully combines governmental guidance with private ownership and initiative. The most important asset of all was—paradoxi-

Explanation of Japan's rise to prosperity

cally—the defeat and elimination of Japan's military establishment, which had systematically drained the country's resources. During a crucial period Japan enjoyed the distinction of being the only great industrial nation operating on a peace economy instead of a war economy. This unique advantage began to disappear, however, as the nation approached the stature of an industrial giant. Before 1982 Japan's military expenditures were kept within 1 percent of the GNP, but since that year they have expanded at an annual rate of about 6 percent, not counting appropriations to the Maritime Safety Agency for the upkeep of harbors and infrastructure. Viewing Japan as a vital link in the chain of defense for the Western Pacific, the Washington government applied increasing pressure on its ally to assume a larger role in making the area impregnable—presumably against a Soviet attack. Pressure was most successful during the Nakasone-Reagan administrations in Tokyo and Washington, respectively, when the U.S. secretary of defense and the head of Japan's Defense Agency established a first-name relationship and consulted frequently. The Japanese government permitted Nipponese firms to negotiate contracts with the Pentagon for Strategic Defense Initiative (SDI "Star Wars") research and increased its financial support for U.S. troops stationed in the Islands. Joint military exercises employing land, sea, and air units were conducted on Japanese soil. Prime Minister Nakasone pronounced his country an "unsinkable aircraft carrier" for American forces. Opinion polls have repeatedly shown that the Japanese public overwhelmingly opposes rearmament, and the unpopularity of the Defense Force has made recruiting difficult. The Japanese Veterans Against War, organized early in 1988, seeks liaison with similar organizations in other countries working for disarmament. With Japan now ranking among the world's foremost military powers and carrying an annual defense budget exceeding Great Britain's, its "peace constitution" seems to have become a dead letter.

Pollution in Industrial Japan. Kawasaki is a heavily industrialized city in the Tokyo-Yokohama Industrial Zone. The works of numerous heavy and chemical industry companies are located here.

765

*The Climax of Imperialism and
the Beginning of a New Era in
Japan*

Japanese society has been profoundly affected by the tremendous expansion of the nation's economy. A continual rise in the standard of living has made Japan's the highest in Asia and brought it close to that of western Europe. By 1970, 90 percent of the families possessed an electric refrigerator, washing machine, and television set. Increasing inflation and a decline in the rate of industrial growth that accompanied the world recession of 1974–1976 forced a lowering of expectations and a reassessment of goals. Far from solving all of Japan's problems, prosperity augmented some of them. A staggering rate of population increase, which brought the total to 117 million by 1982, has been almost halted, as it has in China. Japanese society is shifting from an agricultural to an industrial base. The proportion of the rural work force actually engaged in farming has declined by 47 percent, while the average rural income from farming has declined even more. At the same time, many new industrial plants have been opened in rural areas, where site costs and wages are lower and the environment more attractive. Kyushu, the southernmost island and formerly a center for beef and oranges, has become "Silicon Island," producing 40 percent of Japan's integrated circuits. About half of the nation's inhabitants are concentrated on 2 percent of the land, the bulk of them in an urban belt stretching from Tokyo to Osaka. Tokyo, with some 9 million people, became the largest city in the world—until it yielded this dubious honor to Shanghai. With population density in urban areas three times as great as in the United States, Japan faces major problems of urban congestion and air and water pollution.

*The problems of Japan's
changing society*

While industrial progress has created large fortunes, it has done little to raise wages in the small shops and home factories that still employ a majority of the working force. Although Japan's GNP is the third largest in the world, the nation ranks only sixteenth in per capita income. An efficient health-care system with emphasis on preventive medicine has put Japan ahead of the United States in life expectancy and in the reduction of infant mortality and deaths from heart disease; but there is an unmet demand for better roads, sewers, environmental protection, and housing. Most residents of Tokyo live in tiny two-room apartments. One precarious element in Japan's situation is its dependence on external markets. Japan is the world's largest importer of oil, coal, iron ore, lead, copper, zinc, lumber, wood, cotton, and many other raw materials. It must also import about half of its food. America supplies its feed grains with the exception of rice, which is protected from foreign competition. The Japanese depend on foreign fuels for 85 percent of their energy supply, 60 percent of which is provided by Persian Gulf oil. The development of nuclear power to the point where, by 1976, Japan ranked fourth in nuclear-produced kilowatts of electricity, has encountered popular resistance because of the hazards involved in this technology. One of Japan's thirty-three nuclear reactors is of the same type as Chernobyl's in the USSR, where in 1986 a malfunction caused incalculable radiation damage. A source of concern

*Japan's lagging standard of
living and dependence on
external markets*

*Innovation blended with
tradition; persistence of
inequalities*

is the disposal of spent nuclear fuel, currently shipped abroad to have plutonium extracted and reshipped to Japan for fast-breeder reactors scheduled to be operational in 1992. In exploiting solar energy Japan has forged ahead, equipping more than 2 million houses with solar water heaters, in comparison with some 30,000 in the United States.

Japanese society, like politics and the economy, is a blend of innovation and tradition. In income distribution and in providing opportunities for advancement it has become more equalitarian than most societies. Recent polls disclosed that 90 percent of the Japanese regard themselves as "middle class." The old feudal class structure has disappeared along with titles of nobility, and pedigrees are no longer important. But to a considerable extent society is still hierarchical, with status dependent not upon birth but upon identification with a group, rank in an organization, or, especially, educational credentials. Japan is one of the most literate and most educated nations in the world, its people benefiting from superior instructional standards in the lower and middle schools. Higher education is expensive and deficient in breadth and flexibility, but a degree from a prestigious institution, especially Tokyo University (whose students come from families with incomes that are twice the national average), is normally a stepping stone to a leadership career in business or politics. The persistence of paternalistic and patriarchal traditions, while tending to inhibit the development of individuality, offers the individual a degree of security lacking in less closely organized societies. The preservation of social harmony is valued above the attainment of abstract justice, and litigation is infrequent. Japan has only one-twentieth as many lawyers per capita as the United States. The country's modern industrial growth was aided by a climate of cooperation between labor unions and management and by the loyalty of employees, who regarded their job as a lifetime commitment. There are signs, however, that this familial and mutually binding pattern is breaking down as economic recessions and technological advances make it impossible to retain all workers and as an increasing proportion of the population moves into the over-working-age bracket. There is now a shortage of young workers while many older ones cannot find employment. There are also unfortunate exceptions to the laudable ideal of equality of opportunity and merit as a determinant of status. About 2 percent of the population, known as *burakumin* or "hamlet people" and possibly a carryover from feudal times, are treated as outcasts. Physically indistinguishable from other Japanese and equal before the law, they are generally socially ostracized. Another exception to the homogeneity of Japanese society is the failure to assimilate a resident Korean minority of some 600,000. Some 24,000 Ainu survive on the northern island of Hokkaido, a region ill suited to agriculture but which was opened for industrial development during the Meiji era with disturbing effects upon a society of hunters and fishermen. A Brotherhood Association, which has demanded legislation to restore native land rights, in 1990 opposed a proposal to construct a dam that would, if completed, flood a large valley sacred to the Ainu.

The most conspicuous failure in the implementation of the democratic ideal in Japan is seen in the inferior position of women. Judgments differ as to the status of Japanese women both in earlier times and today. A recently published study of a section of Kyushu in the mid-1930s reports a surprising degree of female independence and initiative in this rural area. The village women, largely uneducated, tradition-bound, and burdened with heavy labor, are portrayed as able to manage their own affairs to a great extent, even following their inclinations in regard to marriage, divorce, and remarriage.[3] The rapid industrialization of Japan after the Second World War created new employment opportunities for women but in some respects increased their dependence. Women have not been accepted readily in positions of leadership, and they are still exploited economically and in family relationships. In 1972, although 57 percent of all factory workers were women, their average wage was less than half that of male workers. Regarded as temporary employees, they are not permitted to share in the benefits extended to labor by management. While the claim of one critic that Japanese women "are virtually as fully oppressed as they have been since the victory of the warrior culture in the Kamakura period of the twelfth century" is an exaggeration, it is doubtless true that they "continue as unrecognized and undervalued servants of Japan's prosperity."[4] A considerable number of women gained seats in the upper house of parliament when, in the July 1989 election the LDP lost its majority in that chamber to the Socialist party, chaired by a woman, Takako Doi. Ms. Doi has attacked the Imperial Household Law barring women from the throne, calling the exclusion rule a violation of the traditions of a nation that has had ten empresses, one as recently as the eighteenth century.

Since the Second World War Japan's foreign policy has been conditioned by two main factors: a struggle for economic recovery and ascendancy, and a close relationship with the United States. Striving to dispel the hostility and distrust remaining as a legacy from its imperialist era, Japan made generous reparations settlements with the small states of Southeast Asia that its armies had overrun, and contributed substantially to various development programs. When the Asian Development Bank was inaugurated in 1966, a Japanese became the first president of this regional organization. Most of Japan's foreign aid has been in the form of loans, under terms profitable to Japanese investors and traders. Japan's successful penetration of the market in Indonesia, Malaysia, Singapore, the Philippines, and Thailand aroused resentment throughout Southeast Asia. The image of the "ugly American" gave way to one inspired by Japanese businessmen, bankers,

[3] Robert Smith and Ella Wiswell, *The Women of Suye Mura.*
[4] Joan Mellen, *The Waves at Genji's Door: Japan through the Cinema*, p. 27.

and technicians, disparagingly referred to as "honorary whites" or "Yellow Yankees." But it is doubtful that Japan, through economic superiority, will dominate Southeast Asia completely, partly because the Japanese are sensitive to accusations of neocolonialism and, more importantly, because the Southeast Asian market is not adequate to fulfill their needs. To reap full benefit from their specialized and advanced technology they must have access to high-income areas, such as Australia, western Europe, and North America. In 1965 Japan's share of the Asian market was only 17 percent. It will undoubtedly grow larger, especially as Chinese-Japanese trade increases. Meanwhile the Japanese are seeking other areas for investment and are already active in Latin America.

Relations with the Soviet Union

Japan found it more difficult to reach an understanding with the Soviet Union than with any other of its former enemies. An agreement signed by the two countries in October 1956 restored diplomatic relations and paved the way for Japan's entrance into the United Nations, but it was not a formal treaty of peace. There have been frequent disputes—over Japanese prisoners of war never accounted for by Russia, fishing rights, and Japanese claims in the Kuril Islands, all of which are held by Russia. Russian attempts, beginning in the early 1970s, to enlist Japan's help in developing Siberian reserves of oil and gas have not met with much success.

Japanese-American relations

The American presence continued to be felt in Japan by virtue of the Security Treaty of 1951, which pledged the two countries to mutual consultation and allowed the United States to retain military bases in Japan. Successive Japanese administrations followed Washington's lead in international diplomacy so dutifully that some critics accused the foreign ministry of being "the Asian Department of the United States State Department." Popular resentment provoked riotous demonstrations against renewal of the Security Treaty in 1960 and again in 1970, and escalation of the war in Indochina further intensified anti-American feeling. Friction between Japan and the United States, never severe enough to invalidate the relationship, was alleviated by the return to Japanese sovereignty, in 1968 and 1972 respectively, of the Bonin and the Ryukyu Islands, which had been heavily fortified and used as bomber bases in the Korean and Vietnam wars. The terms of the transfer agreement called for the removal of nuclear weapons but left the United States the right to continue to use the bases.

The "Nixon shock"

President Nixon's announcement in the summer of 1971 of his intention to visit Peking the following year surprised and angered the Japanese. Washington had pressured them into close ties with the Nationalist regime in Taiwan and had stressed the necessity of joint action in dealing with mainland China, yet had not consulted with nor informed them in advance of the United States' dramatic reversal of policy. Beyond suffering a temporary loss of face, the Japanese now felt impelled to mend their own diplomatic fences. In September 1972 Prime Minister Tanaka made his pilgrimage to a summit meeting in Peking, offered an apology to the Chinese people for Japan's past misconduct, and—in advance of the United States— established full diplomatic relations between Japan and the People's Republic of China. The Zhou-Tanaka joint statement issued in Peking was a masterpiece of diplomatic finesse and graceful ambiguity which laid a basis for "peace and friendship" without a formal peace treaty and with important issues left unresolved. Japan recognized that Taiwan "ought to" belong to China, withdrew its ambassador from Taipei, but replaced its embassy there with unofficial liaison offices which effectively served the same purposes. (The United States adopted a similar procedure half a dozen years later.)

Japan's foreign relations have inevitably been affected by the recurring crises of the 1970s. Closely following the "Nixon shock" was the "oil shock" of 1974, the quadrupling of oil prices by OPEC. It struck no nation more severely than Japan, totally dependent on outside sources for this essential commodity. The recession following the oil crisis slowed the economic growth rate, brought the threat of unemployment—negligible heretofore—and caused the Japanese to reexamine national priorities and to question whether the "miracle of Japan" was reality or illusion. A factor hampering economic recovery was, ironically, the strength of the yen in comparison with the dollar and other depreciating Western currencies. The yen's high valuation made goods produced in Japan expensive (although products were exported at lower than the domestic prices), and the Japanese found they were being undersold by such Asian competitors as South Korea, Taiwan, and Hong Kong. Many small firms were forced out of business; in 1977 more than 18,000 bankruptcies were reported in Japan. To alleviate the situation the government sought to expand the market for exports and investments in less developed areas. In February 1978 Japan signed a $20-billion eight-year trade agreement with China, followed six months later by a formal peace treaty with the People's Republic.

The "oil shock" and its consequences

In seeking new economic opportunities the Japanese have also been mindful of political and strategic factors, realizing that a major conflict in East Asia would place them in grave jeopardy. The nation that for centuries remained in almost complete isolation is today one of the least isolated, dependent for its survival upon reciprocal relations with many other countries.

From isolation to interdependence

Significant changes in the semipartnership between the United States and Japan resulted from the latter's growing economic strength, which stimulated dissatisfaction with a condition of dependence. The balance of trade between the two countries shifted in Japan's favor, by 1976 yielding an annual surplus of $5 billion and, by 1989, of $49 billion. Moreover, as the islanders gained preeminence in specialized and sophisticated technologies, the United States in its trade with them played a "colonial" role, providing grains, lumber, cotton, and other raw materials in exchange for steel, machinery, cameras, watches, electronic components for radio and television, and innumerable other manufac-

Changes in the relationship

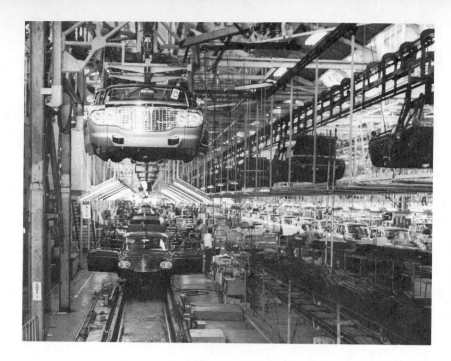

Automobile Assembly Line, Toyota Motor Company. In 1980 the Japanese automobile industry became the largest in the world.

tures ranging from pianos to barber chairs. American automobile sales in Japan matched only a small fraction of Japanese car sales in the United States. A continual trade deficit, bringing the prospect of falling profits and rising unemployment, worried United States manufacturers. The president of Zenith Radio Corporation warned that the American consumer-electronics industry faced a threat "every bit as real as the threat of extinction faced by the coyotes, the bald eagles, the seals, the alligators, and the rattlesnakes." There has been lively, sometimes heated, debate in both countries over trade policies and their effect. Restrictions on imports, bureaucratic regulations, and subsidies to domestic producers that make the Japanese market hard to penetrate were countered in the United States by quotas on Japanese products and by demands for protective legislation. While agreeing to remove some restrictions the Japanese argued persuasively that their success in marketing reflected the high quality of their manufactures and a scrupulous attention to customer demand. The Japanese invest far more in industrial research and development than Americans, keeping them in the forefront of technological advance. Their productivity is increasing three times as fast as the Americans', but a 38 percent improvement in U.S. factory production in 1989 suggests that competition with the Japanese is healthy rather than ruinous. Acknowledging the need to reduce its large trade surplus, Japan in recent years has moved cautiously toward an open-market economy, transferring the railway and telegraph systems to private ownership and attempting to stimulate domestic consumption by expanding imports, which have risen more than 50 percent since 1984. Americans, accustomed to a long period of ascendancy in world affairs, are understandably perturbed at seeing a nation they flattened in defeat forty-five years ago now threatening to eclipse their own economy. A Tokyo professor of international affairs predicted that a "Confucian cultural zone"—including South Korea, Taiwan, and Singapore as well as Japan—by combining Confucian ethics with free-market principles would dominate the twenty-first century. Notwithstanding rivalry and disagreements Japan and the United States are destined to remain trading partners, to their mutual advantage. The huge American public debt is currently underwritten by Japan. In 1986 in addition to investments in American real estate, hotels, and commercial enterprises, the Japanese devoted more than a third of their $90 billion trade surplus to purchasing U.S. bonds and Treasury notes. Whether such support will continue may depend upon efforts by the Washington government, not yet apparent, to reduce the federal deficit.

The Japanese government, like most of its contemporaries, has not sufficiently addressed the problems inherent in highly industrialized societies. While wealth in terms of the GNP has steadily increased, disparities in income have grown wider. An egregious example of government partiality to a special interest group is that of the rice farmers. Rice production in Japan is six times more expensive than for that of California's best quality, but high tariffs and subsidies to the Japanese producers keep the price artificially high in Japan, constituting a tax on all consumers. Also, reserving acreage for inefficient rice cultivation has greatly inflated real estate values, making home ownership impossible for most workers. While watching their manufactures flood markets the world over, undercutting the price of items produced locally, the Japanese find they can hardly afford to live in their own country, where the overall cost of living rose more than 600 percent between 1960 and 1980 and the average family must spend 30 percent of its income on food. They see the profits accruing from a favorable foreign trade balance used to keep the U.S. government solvent while little is done to protect the environment or improve services in overcrowded cities, 40 percent of whose buildings are not connected to public sewer systems.

Governmental inattention to the social and environmental costs of rapid industrial growth

The contrast between events in China and in Japan during the year 1989–1990 shows vividly how two states geographically close can be far apart in terms of social and political maturity. In China the revolutionary uprising of an oppressed population was brutally suppressed. In Japan public discontent brought a flurry of electoral activity, followed by business as usual. Dissatisfaction with LDP administrations had been growing in Japan for some time. When the government in response to U.S. demands reduced the subsidies to rice farmers it angered a major voting bloc. Incidents of official corruption and a revelation that large corporations were underpaying their taxes provoked widespread resentment, reflected in the LDP's loss to the Socialists in elections for the upper house of the Diet in July 1989. The Socialists had attracted support by denouncing corruption and a highly

The political implications

unpopular consumption tax recently imposed. Their victory by no means signaled a radical departure in national policy. Posing as champions of free enterprise against the advocates of big government, the LDP swept the February 1990 elections for members of the lower house, ensuring their retention of power. In these lackluster campaigns, neither party rose above ideological rhetoric to formulate programs for meeting such pressing needs as welfare services for the elderly, adequate housing, and recreational facilities.

SELECTED READINGS (*See also Readings for Chapters 21 and 33*)

• Items so designated are available in paperback editions.

CHINA

• Barnett, A. Doak, *China and the Major Powers in East Asia,* Washington, D.C., 1977. A careful study of international relations.

Bianco, Lucien, *Origins of the Chinese Revolution, 1915–1949,* tr. Muriel Bell, Stanford, 1971. A brilliant interpretive summary.

Bonavia, David, *Verdict in Peking: The Trial of the Gang of Four,* New York, 1984.

Brugger, Bill, *Contemporary China,* New York, 1977. An impressive historical interpretation of the period 1942–1973.

• Ch'en, Jerome, *Mao and the Chinese Revolution,* New York, 1965.

• Clubb, O. E. *Twentieth-Century China,* 3d ed., New York, 1978. One of the best surveys of modern Chinese history.

Davies, J. P., Jr., *Dragon by the Tail: American, British, Japanese, and Russian Encounters with China and One Another,* New York, 1972. An American diplomat's jolting account of bungling and intrigue.

• Dirlik, Arif, *The Origins of Chinese Communism,* New York, 1989.

• Floyd, David, *Mao against Khrushchev: A Short History of the Sino-Soviet Conflict,* New York, 1964. A readable account.

Gittings, John, *The World and China, 1922–1972,* New York, 1974. Informative for Sino-Soviet relations.

Hamrin, Carol, *China and the Challenge of the Future: Changing Political Patterns,* Boulder, Col., 1989.

Hsiung, J. C., *Ideology and Practice: The Evolution of Chinese Communism,* New York, 1970. Valuable for an understanding of the Cultural Revolution.

• Isaacs, H. R., *The Tragedy of the Chinese Revolution,* Stanford, 1964.

Jacobs, Daniel, *Borodin: Stalin's Man in China,* Cambridge, Mass., 1981.

• Johnson, Kay Ann, *Women, the Family and Peasant Revolution in China,* Chicago, 1983.

• Milton, David, and Nancy Milton, *The Wind Will Not Subside: Years in Revolutionary China—1964–1969.* New York, 1976. Vivid account of the Cultural Revolution.

• Schwarcz, Vera, *The Chinese Enlightenment: Intellectuals and the Legacy of the May Fourth Movement of 1919,* Berkeley, 1986.

Selden, Mark, *The Yenan Way in Revolutionary China,* Cambridge, Mass., 1971. Scholarly treatment of the "Border Region," 1935–1947.

- Shabad, Theodore, *China's Changing Man: National and Regional Development, 1949–71,* rev. ed., New York, 1972. A valuable reference work.

  Sharmon, Lyon, *Sun Yat-sen: His Life and Its Meaning,* New York, 1934. A critical biography.
- Snow, Edgar, *Red Star over China,* New York, 1938. A classic account of the Communists' early years of struggle.
- Spence, Jonathan, *The Gate of Heavenly Peace: The Chinese and Their Revolution, 1895–1980,* New York, 1981. A penetrating account of the contributions and frustrations of China's intellectuals.
- ———, *The Search for Modern China,* New York, 1990. A masterly treatment of the last 400 years of China's history; comprehensive, clear, and judicious.
- Tuchman, Barbara, *Stilwell and the American Experience in China, 1911–1945,* New York, 1972.

  Wilbur, C. M., *Sun Yat-sen: Frustrated Patriot,* New York, 1976. Provides fresh insights.

  ———, ed., *Mao Tse-tung in the Scales of History,* New York, 1977. Ten essays of high quality.

JAPAN

- Benedict, Ruth, *The Chrysanthemum and the Sword,* New York, 1967. A classic analysis of prewar Japanese society.

  Blaker, Michael, *Japanese International Negotiating Style,* New York, 1977. A study of diplomacy between 1895 and Pearl Harbor.

  Borden, W. S., *The Pacific Alliance: United States Foreign Economic Policy and Japanese Trade Recovery, 1947–1955,* Madison, Wis., 1984.

  Butow, R. J. C., *Japan's Decision to Surrender,* Stanford, 1954.

  ———, *Tojo and the Coming of the War,* Princeton, 1961.

  Emmerson, J. K., *Arms, Yen and Power: The Japanese Dilemma,* New York, 1971. Balanced, informative, optimistic.

  Fukutake Tadashi, *The Japanese Social Structure: Its Evolution in the Modern Century,* New York, 1982. Stresses the imbalance between economic and social development.
- Ishida Takeshi, *Japanese Society,* New York, 1971.

  Jansen, Marius, *Japan and Its World: Two Centuries of Change,* Princeton, 1980. Brief and insightful.
- Mellen Joan, *The Waves of Genji's Door: Japan through the Cinema,* New York, 1976. Provides a feminist critique of Japanese character and society.

  Minear, R. H., *Victors' Justice: The Tokyo War Crimes Trial,* Princeton, 1972. Challenges the moral and legal validity of the trials.

  Morris, Ivan, *Nationalism and the Right Wing in Japan: A Study of Post-War Trends,* London, 1960. A clear and forceful study.
- Nakane Chie, *Japanese Society,* Berkeley, 1972. A social anthropologist's analysis.
- Reischauer, E. O., *The Japanese,* Cambridge, Mass., 1977. A highly informative survey by an eminent scholar.

  ———, *The United States and Japan,* 3d ed., New York, 1965.
- Robins-Mowry, Dorothy, *The Hidden Sun: Women of Modern Japan,* Boulder, Col., 1983.

- Smith, R. J., and Ella Wiswell, *The Women of Suye Mura,* Chicago, 1982. An eyewitness account of village life in the 1930s.

  Thayer, N. B., *How the Conservatives Rule Japan,* Princeton, 1969.

  Tsuneishi, W. M., *Japanese Political Style: An Introduction to the Government and Politics of Modern Japan,* New York, 1966. An excellent brief study.
- Van Alstyne, Richard W., *The United States and East Asia,* New York, 1973.

  Vogel, E. F., *Japan As Number One: Lessons for America,* Cambridge, Mass., 1979.
- Wray, Harry, and Hilary Conroy, eds., *Japan Examined: Perspectives on Modern Japanese History,* Honolulu, 1983.

  Yanaga Chitoshi, *Big Business in Japanese Politics,* New Haven, 1968.

  Yoshitsu, Michael, *Japan and the San Francisco Peace Settlement,* New York, 1983. Highly informative.

SOURCE MATERIALS

- Aoki, M. Y., and M. B. Dardess, *As the Japanese See It: Past and Present,* Honolulu, 1981.
- Binyan, Liu, *People or Monsters? and Other Stories and Reportage from China after Mao,* Bloomington, Ind., 1983.

  Bodde, Derk, *Peking Diary, 1948–1949: A Year of Revolution,* New York, 1967.
- Brandt, C., B. F. Schwartz, and J. K. Fairbank, *A Documentary History of Chinese Communism,* London, 1952.
- Chai, Winberg, ed., *The Essential Works of Chinese Communism,* New York, 1969.

  Chiang Kai-shek, *China's Destiny,* New York, 1947.
- de Bary, W. T., ed., *Sources of Chinese Tradition,* Chaps. XXVII, XXVIII, XXIX, New York, 1960.
- ———, ed., *Sources of Japanese Tradition,* Chaps. XXVI, XXVII, XXVIII, XXIX, New York, 1958.
- Gao Yuan, *Born Red: A Chronicle of the Cultural Revolution,* Stanford, 1987.

  Grew, Ambassador Joseph C., *Ten Years in Japan,* New York, 1944.
- Lin, N. T., tr., *In Quest: Poems of Chou En-lai,* Cambridge, Mass., 1979.
- Minear, R. H., ed., *Through Japanese Eyes,* 2 vols., New York, 1974. Selections from the period of the Pacific War to the 1970s.
- Schram, Stuart, ed., *Chairman Mao Talks to the People: Talks and Letters, 1956–1971,* New York, 1975.

  Schwarcz, Vera, *Long Road Home: A China Journal,* New Haven, 1984.
- Starr, J. B., *Continuing the Revolution: The Political Thought of Mao,* Princeton, 1979.

Chapter 40

PROGRESS, POVERTY, AND REVOLUTION IN LATIN AMERICA

What is the oligarchy? It consists of the great landowners—the *"latifundistas"*—their political and military henchmen, and their financial allies (the bankers and the capitalists, in the old sense of the word). . . . The oligarchs form a true caste, with aristocratic impulses, racist attitudes, and a profound contempt for their own countries.

—Victor Alba, *Alliance without Allies: The Mythology of Progress in Latin America*

I brought food to the hungry, and people called me a saint.
I asked why people were hungry, and people called me a communist.

—Dom Helder Camara, Brazilian archbishop

L atin America comprises an area more than twice the size of the United States. Its terrain is more varied than that of the North American republic and large portions are barren or inaccessible, but it is rich in natural resources. It has the potential to support a populous and vigorous civilization, but this potential has been imperfectly realized. In the course of a tortuous and often violent history, Latin American societies and cultures have been deformed and partially immobilized by the unrelenting pressure of contradictory forces.

Unrealized potential

1. THE CONFLICT OF SOCIETIES AND CULTURES IN THE NINETEENTH CENTURY

As related in Chapter 29, the revolutions that established independent states in Latin America left economic and political power concentrated in the hands of a small minority of property owners. Constitutions,

*Obstacles to democratic
progress*

Material progress

though usually patterned after that of the United States, served to legitimize the dominance of the upper and middle classes rather than to open a path toward democratic progress. The political philosophy of the constitution makers, borrowed from the European Enlightenment, was abstract, theoretical, and essentially meaningless for states with populations still largely uneducated and impoverished. Political leaders sincerely devoted to justice and liberty tended to identify these ideals with the interests of their own class.

The concept of progress, so prominent in European and North American mentality in the nineteenth century, also took strong hold among Latin Americans. On the face of it their record during the nineteenth century was one of substantial progress. The clearest example is in population, which tripled between 1800 and 1900, reaching about 60 million by the latter date. The increase was partly due to European immigration, which contributed significantly to national development in Argentina, Uruguay, and Chile. In contrast to Canada and the United States, however, where a stream of European immigrants into frontier regions served as a democratizing force, the Europeans who settled in Latin America, whether as poor laborers or prosperous entrepreneurs, reinforced the aristocratic character of society. Statistics testify to substantial economic advance. Electricity was introduced, steamships plied the waterways, telegraph lines and railroads were built, linking interior regions to the coast and promoting the growth of large cities. The expansion of commerce was spectacular, especially in the latter half of the century. Argentine exports multiplied sevenfold between 1853 and 1873 and doubled again by 1893. By 1900 Argentina was shipping 2,250,000 tons of wheat abroad annually. Mexico's exports quadru-

*Agriculture in Argentina.
A harvesting scene at the
end of the nineteenth
century. The nation's
booming wheat industry
contributed substantially
to its prosperity early in
the twentieth century.*

777

*The Conflict of Societies and
Cultures in the Nineteenth
Century*

pled in the last three decades of the century, and Brazil's foreign trade increased in like proportions. The smaller states also experienced a comparable growth. The benefits of economic expansion, however, were very unevenly distributed. Railroad lines primarily expedited the movement of exports rather than improving internal communication. They encroached on farm and pasture land, and their construction necessitated tax increases. The emphasis upon production for export made agriculture less diversified and less devoted to producing food for the needs of local populations. By adopting a one-crop economy, nations made themselves dependent on the vagaries of external market forces beyond their control. Even the industrial development of the last quarter of the century increased dependency because manufactured items were chiefly for the wealthy and the machines to produce them were imported. The main beneficiaries of the vaunted material progress were European and North American capitalists who marketed Latin American products, acquired extensive ownership of lands, mines, banks, and industries, and profited from loans made to the governments.

To a large extent the changes affecting Latin America in the nineteenth century represented the triumph of a program imposed by an elite minority upon a reluctant and tenaciously resisting population. The Spanish colonial regime, although exploitative and oppressive, had not sought to destroy Indian customs and institutions entirely. Under Madrid's domination and the mantle of Christianity, the Indians had kept intact much of their traditions and folkways. But the leaders of the newly independent states were less tolerant of indigenous cultures than the imperial Spanish had been. Eager to break with the colonial past, they embraced the creed of extreme individualism that was exciting contemporary Europeans and which bred contempt for the more helpless members of society. Proponents of Social Darwinism and similar perversions of the evolutionary theory classified races on a scale like that later adopted by Hitler's Nazis. In spite of their own Iberian descent, they scorned the Spanish and Portuguese as decadent—weakened by their partial Indianization—and lauded the "superior" races of northern Europe and North America. Indians and Africans were dismissed as inferior and "backward"; whites were hailed as the chosen custodians of civilization.

*Antipathy toward
indigenous cultures; racist
doctrines*

Emboldened by racist doctrines, the dominant minorities undertook not only to appropriate the Indians' land but to destroy their culture and—in some cases—to exterminate the people as well. In Argentina a campaign to occupy the pampas, where gauchos and "mongrel races" had had a relatively free reign, almost reached the point of genocide, climaxed by the "Conquest of the Desert" (1879–1880), a massacre of Indians by the army. This bloody campaign was defended as a struggle for civilization against "nests of land pirates," renegades, and "barbarians."

Destruction of the Indians

CANADA

UNITED STATES
OF AMERICA

ATLANTIC OCEAN

GULF OF MEXICO

Nassau
BAHAMAS
(Brit.)

Havana

MEXICO
(1821)

Mexico City ★

CUBA
(1898)

HAITI (1804)
DOMINICAN REP. (1844)

San Juan

JAMAICA
(1962)
Port au Prince

Santo
Domingo

PUERTO RICO (U.S.)

BARBADOS (1967)

CARIBBEAN SEA

TRINIDAD AND
TOBAGO (1962)

Port of Spain

Caracas

VENEZUELA
(1811)

Georgetown
Paramaribo

Orinoco R.

GUIANA (1966)

SURINAM (Du.)

FRENCH GUIANA
Cayenne

Bogotá

COLOMBIA
(1821)

R.

SEE INSET
BELOW

CENTRAL AMERICA

PACIFIC

Equator

OCEAN

GALAPAGOS IS.
(Ecuador)

Quito

ECUADOR (1822)

Amazon R.

PERU
(1821)

ANDES MTS.

Lima

BOLIVIA
(1825)

★ La Paz

Sucre ★

BRAZIL (1822)

★ Brasília

PARAGUAY
(1811)

★ Asunción

Rio de Janeiro

CHILE
(1818)

ANDES MOUNTAINS

0   1000   2000 miles

Santiago ★

Buenos Aires ★

ARGENTINA
(1816)

URUGUAY (1828)
★ Montevideo

La Plata R.

FALKLAND ISLANDS
(Br.)

*CAPE
HORN*

Dates indicate year
of independence

CENTRAL AMERICA

JAMAICA
(1962)

Kingston

★ Belize
BRITISH HONDURAS

GUATEMALA
(1821)

*CARIBBEAN
SEA*

HONDURAS (1821)

Guatemala ★

Tegucigalpa

Salvador ★

EL SALVADOR
(1821)

NICARAGUA
(1821)

Managua

San José ★

COSTA RICA
(1821)

PANAMA
CANAL

Panama

PANAMA (1903)

PACIFIC OCEAN

LATIN AMERICA TODAY

In Central and South America as well as in North America some intelligent and compassionate whites spoke out against the depredations being committed. An academic conference in Guatemala City in 1893 asserted that the Indian was capable of being assimilated and imbued with the idea of progress through education. A few dissenting voices flatly rejected the goal of Europeanization. The Argentinian Juan Bautista Alberdi, writing in the 1850s, attacked the prevailing view that regarded the countryside as barbaric. He found the "educated barbarism" of the city to be "a thousand times more disastrous for true civilization than that of all the savages of the American hinterlands." Silvio Romero, who published a monumental *History of Brazilian Literature* in 1888, was another intellectual who turned conventional beliefs upside down. Asserting that Brazil was the product of the joint efforts of Indians, Europeans, and Africans, he advocated an intermingling of the several stocks to produce a fine and vigorous race. But the majority of writers, popular or academic, bolstered the belief that progress was synonymous with industrialization, urbanization, and Europeanization.

Defenders of the Indians

During the first half of the nineteenth century a genuine folk culture continued to thrive in rural villages isolated from the centers of government. These small communities and their way of life were, for a time, protected by local caudillos who, although generally described as tyrants, were closely identified with the traditions and sentiments of the people over whom they wielded authority. Defenders of the life style of the Indian rural communities stoutly resisted the drive for modernization that climaxed in the latter half of the century. The result was a confrontation comparable to that provoked by the Spanish conquests of the early sixteenth century.

Indian folk culture protected by caudillos

In Guatemala the modernization process was blocked for a generation under the presidency of Rafael Carrera (1838–1865). The Indians, not only deprived of their lands but also forced to build roads and pay heavy taxes, had revolted in 1837, bringing Carrera to power. Of mestizo blood and a respecter of native culture, Carrera enacted measures to benefit the Indians, who constituted three-fourths of Guatemala's population. He restored their lands, reduced taxes, and undertook to provide basic education throughout the country. While not opposed to progress, he believed it should come gradually and without entering the trap of dependency upon foreign capitalists. During his rule Guatemala provided Latin America with a unique example of the conquered race holding a dominant position. Unfortunately, after Carrera's death in 1865 his program was quickly reversed. Railroads financed and owned by foreigners were built to facilitate the export of coffee; haciendas absorbed the lands of Indian farmers, and the dispossessed farmers were again reduced to the status of wage laborers.

Guatemala under President Carrera

In the closing decades of the century Mexico was the scene of repeated uprisings led by defenders of native rights. Longest and most violent

The Mayas of Yucatán

*Paraguay under Francia
and the Lópezes*

was the so-called Caste War in Yucatán, where Mayan corn culture was threatened by the expansion of sugar plantations owned by whites and mestizos, who claimed to be advancing "the holy cause of order, humanity, and civilization." Beginning about 1850, the conflict lasted into the twentieth century. For fifty years the Mayan rebels of Yucatán governed themselves, while preserving a pre-Columbian type of village and family organization and a distinctive culture blending Mayan and Spanish elements. By 1900 soil exhaustion and epidemics of disease had weakened the Mayan communities, and under the tyrannical Porfirio Díaz their independence was ended.

Indian rebellions occurred in Ecuador and Peru, and slave uprisings in Brazil before the abolition of slavery in 1888. By far the most successful resistance to the process of forced Europeanization took place in Paraguay between 1819 and 1870, led by three successive caudillos who are customarily faulted as tyrants but who demonstrated a more realistic perception of the condition and needs of their country than did their critics. José Francia (1814–1840) enacted reforms anticipating in several respects the program of Mexican revolutionaries of the twentieth century. In firm control of the economy, Francia nationalized the Roman Catholic Church, confiscating its lands and those of great private estates, rented portions to small farmers, and made the country self-sufficient in food. Francia's successors, Antonio López and Antonio's son Solano López, demonstrated clearly that the protection of native agriculture was by no means incompatible with material progress. The Lópezes built railroads and telegraph lines, developed a modern steam-operated navy, and established an iron foundry, all without resorting to foreign loans. Unfortunately, these remarkable accomplishments, which might have served as an example for others to follow, were jeopardized by the hostility of Paraguay's neighbors— hostility aggravated by the truculent and defiant attitude of López. On the pretext of checking a threat to their own territories, Argentina and Brazil, after inducing Uruguay to join them, launched a war of attrition that lasted for six years (1864–1870), ending only when 90 percent of Paraguay's adult male population had been killed. Although the victors claimed they were bringing civilization to barbarians, an English newspaper, the *Manchester Guardian,* pronounced a different verdict. The war, it reported, "had overturned the only South American state wherein the native Indian race showed any present likelihood of attaining or recovering such strength or organization as to fit it for the task of government." During a five-year period of military occupation, Paraguay's popular institutions were dismantled, foreign capital poured in, and great estates reappeared as speculators snapped up lands at bargain prices. Thus stricken, Paraguay entered the twentieth century as one of the most backward and impoverished of Latin American states.

2. TWENTIETH-CENTURY PROGRESS AND POVERTY IN MEXICO AND SOUTH AMERICA

Mexico alone among the larger Latin American states experienced a genuine revolution—social and economic as well as political. Mexico's liberating revolution began in 1910–1911 with the overthrow of the dictatorship of Porfirio Díaz, consumed the following decade, and has never been formally ended. The struggle to liquidate the legacy of dictatorship was intensely violent, taking some two million lives between 1910 and 1917. Ousting Díaz did not break the power of the entrenched oligarchy nor bring unanimity to reforming liberals. The ensuing rivalry among various aspiring leaders was watched with more than casual interest by major powers, especially the United States, which by 1910 had placed 40 percent of its total overseas investments in Mexico. Without directly opposing the revolution, the Washington government hoped to manage it and to that end played one faction against another. Francisco Madero, the liberal *hacendado* (estate owner) who had succeeded Díaz, was driven from office in 1913 by Victoriano Huerta, an unsavory throwback to the old order who executed his predecessor. President Woodrow Wilson withheld recognition of Huerta on the grounds that he had usurped office unconstitutionally, although an equally cogent reason was Huerta's offer of oil concessions to the British. When the revolution was rekindled in Mexico by Huerta's misrule, President Wilson first favored the charismatic guerrilla fighter Francisco "Pancho" Villa but switched support to his rival, Venustiano Carranza, and in 1916 sent an expeditionary force across the border in pursuit of the elusive Villa. Carranza, who, after becoming president with U.S. backing, soon fell out of favor both with the United States and with his own people, was forced from office in 1920. Seemingly the revolution had ended in failure, but such was not the case. During Carranza's brief administration a constitutional convention had drafted a reformist, democratic charter, which was enacted in May 1917.

Victoriano Huerta, President of Mexico, 1913–1914

The Constitution of 1917, which embodied promise rather than fulfillment, had several objectives in line with the revolutionary ideals of those who had been struggling to remake the country ever since the end of the Díaz regime: (1) to democratize the government; (2) to reduce the influence of the Church; and (3) to give to the nation control over its economic resources and to provide for the masses a more equitable share of the wealth they produced. In pursuance of the first, the Constitution bestowed the suffrage upon all male citizens twenty-one years of age and over and subjected the powers of the president to a measure of control by Congress. In keeping with the second, freedom of religion was guaranteed, the Church was forbidden to conduct primary schools, and the state legislatures were empowered to limit the number of priests in each district. But the most significant

Left: *U.S. Infantry Troops Encamped at San Antonio, Texas, in 1911.* President Woodrow Wilson dispatched troops to the border as a precautionary measure when Mexico was shaken by revolution. Right: *Pancho Villa (left) and General John J. Pershing of the United States Army.* In 1916 Pershing commanded the United States expeditionary force sent to Mexico to apprehend Villa.

provisions of the Constitution were probably those dealing with economic reform. Peonage was abolished. An eight-hour day with one day's rest in seven was proclaimed the standard for industrial workers. The right to strike was recognized, and the government was given the authority to provide for social insurance. Mineral resources were declared to be the property of the nation. No foreigners were to be granted concessions to develop them unless they agreed to be treated as Mexican citizens. Private property of any kind might be expropriated by the government after the payment of just compensation.

The Mexican revolution, whose ambitious goals have been only partially achieved, embodied a social pact theoretically uniting the state, peasants, labor, and business. The task of democratizing society and removing its inequities demanded not only the cooperation of these four elements but resolute executive leadership and a sweeping legislative program as well—a combination easier to imagine than to realize. The most vigorous attempt to implement the revolutionary program came under the presidency of Lázaro Cárdenas (1934–1940), who was affectionately nicknamed Tato ("Daddy"). While the Great Depression was driving some highly developed countries toward fascism, Cárdenas sought to strengthen democracy by making it operative in society and the economy. In an attempt to revive the tradition of cooperative farm communities (*ejidos*) he distributed land to 800,000 peasants, about one-third of the rural population, with the provision

Cárdenas and the challenge of democratizing Mexican society

that the land must be worked, not rented for profit. Besides land redistribution his reform program advanced primary education and included legislation to protect industrial laborers. During his administration 3,000 trade unions combined to form the Federation of Mexican Workers (CTM). When U.S. oil companies refused to submit a labor dispute to arbitration, Cárdenas, following the constitution's mandate, nationalized the oil fields, infuriating the foreign owners, who pressed the U.S. Congress to take retaliatory action. Fortunately, President Franklin D. Roosevelt, adhering to his Good Neighbor policy, offered long-term credits to enable the Mexican government to compensate U.S. companies. The Mexican good will gained by this conciliatory action was an asset more valuable than oil revenues.

Beginning in 1940 the Mexican government concentrated on industrial development with impressive results. For three decades manufacturing expanded at an annual rate averaging 8 percent, setting the pace for what was hailed as an economic miracle. But the construction of factories and communication and energy networks depended on foreign investment capital and mortgaged much of the economy to transnational corporations. While the cost of living rose, wages were kept low to stimulate exports, and the government neglected the rural *ejido* program instituted by Cárdenas. The political side of the miracle was the ascendancy of a propertied elite and a conservative shift in the dominant party, which in 1946 changed its name to Institutional Revolutionary Party. As a firmly established institution the PRI controlled local and national offices, handpicked presidential candidates, and won every election. The Federation of Mexican Workers, as a partner of the state, became bureaucratized and, like the political organs, infected with corruption. Despite almost uninterrupted economic growth the republic was not as stable as it appeared on the surface. Social unrest was held in check partly by minor concessions and cosmetic reforms but also by using police and the army to break strikes and silence dissenters of every class. One of the most flagrant examples of brutal repression, but by no means the only one, occurred in the heart of Mexico City in October 1968, a week before the Olympic Games were to open there. Several hundred students who had gathered at the university stadium for a mass protest were killed by government troops at the order of President Díaz Ordaz.

The tensions within Mexican society and the economy's vulnerability became apparent in a series of crises during the 1970s and 1980s. Ill-advised government expenditures and continued borrowing, while failing to relieve unemployment or halt spiraling inflation, quadrupled the national debt. In 1976, the economy gained a reprieve from imminent collapse with the discovery of enormous supplies of oil and gas off the western shore of the Gulf of Mexico, constituting one of the world's largest reserves of these prized fuels. Inspired by visions of wealth, the government embarked on a spending spree, building refining and manufacturing plants and laying out new cities in the oil regions. These ambitious projects were financed by heavy borrowing

Political and social realities in the face of industrial development

Lázaro "Tato" Cárdenas as President of Mexico, 1934–1940, with His Family. One of the ablest of Mexico's presidents, he nationalized oil fields and distributed millions of acres of land to the peasants.

Oil and the national debt

from foreign banks. A state-owned oil company, PEMEX, was inefficiently managed and soon, like the government itself, honeycombed with corruption. Unfortunately for Mexico the oil boom collapsed as suddenly as it had begun. As the price of oil dropped, Mexico lost two-thirds of its exports. In 1982, when the government was unable to make interest payments to its creditors, $80 billion in foreign loans had to be rescheduled to prevent the failure of American banks, some of which had lent one-half of their total assets to Mexico.

Two-thirds of Mexico's people have become urban dwellers, largely because increasing rural poverty has driven them to the cities in search of work. Mexico City, with its surrounding slums and 18 million inhabitants, became the world's largest city and one of the most congested, inadequately serviced, and heavily polluted. More than half of Mexico's eighty million people suffer from malnutrition, and the same number are less than fully employed. Potentially a prosperous country, Mexico has one of the world's most inequitable distributions of wealth. Ten percent of the households receive almost 40 percent of the total income, while the poorest one-tenth earn less than 1 percent.

While Mexican society—almost 90 percent literate—has remained relatively calm in the face of widespread deprivation, economic crises, and earthquakes that leveled much of Mexico City in 1985 with a loss of more than ten thousand lives, social unrest is evident in grass-roots movements. Among these are "Christian Base" communities dedicated to human rights, a Mexican housewives' association, and a national coalition to coordinate urban reform groups. Resentment over electoral fraud has finally begun to erode the PRI's monopoly of power. The presidential election of July 1988 aroused unprecedented excitement because of a challenge to the establishment by a progressive political movement ("Democratic Current") led by Cuauhtémoc Cárdenas, son of Mexico's great reforming president (his given name is that of the last Aztec emperor). Although the PRI candidate was declared the winner, the government acknowledged that Cárdenas had captured 35 percent of the popular vote. The incoming president, Carlos Salinas, soon gave encouraging evidence that his pledge of honest government and electoral reform was not an idle promise.

Of all Latin American countries Mexico is the most important for the United States, to which it is linked both by geography and by economic ties. Sending 60 percent of its exports to its northern neighbor, Mexico is the United States' third largest trading partner and its leading source of foreign oil. Mexico's $100-billion national debt, second largest in the Third World, is of crucial concern to American investors, who have financed much of it. Because Mexico cannot provide employment for more than half of the 100 million workers that enter the job market each year, immigration to the United States is bound to continue. Mexican workers in this country—2½ million in 1980—may, it is predicted, reach 6 or 7 million by 2,000 A.D., effecting an unanticipated reoccupation of lands owned by the migrants' forefathers 150 years earlier.

Brazil, the largest country in Latin America, with an area almost equal to that of the United States, in the course of the twentieth century became so highly industrialized that it attained the status of a major power rather than a Third World nation. Yet it exhibits dramatically the problems and contradictions common to all of Latin America. Its pyramidal social structure allots half the nation's income to 1 percent of the population. According to a 1985 report, 65 percent of Brazil's 45 million people—three-fourths of whom are city dwellers—suffer from malnutrition. The infant mortality rate is one of the highest in Latin America. Industrial and commercial expansion has turned Rio de Janeiro and São Paulo into glittering metropolises, but the influx of destitute country folk has ringed their suburbs with ghastly slums. The height of wealth coexists with the depths of poverty; the height of fashion, sophistication, and innovative enterprise with the remnants of a semifeudal culture.

For several decades Brazil made halting and interrupted progress toward political democracy. Constitutional changes adopted in 1934 provided for the secret ballot and the enfranchisement of both men and women, though a literacy qualification debarred many from voting. Getúlio Vargas twice held the presidency for a total period of eighteen years—1930–1945 and 1951–1954. He ruled as a dictator when in office, imposing press censorship and disbanding political parties, but also strengthening the authority of the central government over the several states. Following the dismissal of Vargas by the army in 1954, a bitter struggle ensued between his followers and their opponents.

In spite of factional wrangling, the later 1950s showed stirrings of progress in Brazil. President Juscelino Kubitschek planned an ambitious program of economic development, but because he avoided tax increases, his policy of government spending was highly inflationary. At the same time, volunteer reformers, supported by trade unions, political radicals, a Catholic Action Movement, and even some bishops of the Church hierarchy, brought help to the depressed rural area of northeastern Brazil, organizing peasant cooperatives, starting schools and health clinics, and offering technical assistance. Such radical activity at the grass roots, added to the mild reformism of the government, was too much for the oligarchy that controlled most of the land and the army. Kubitschek's successors had been no more successful than he in stabilizing the economy, and on March 31, 1964, President João Goulart, a leader of the Labor party, was overthrown by a coup d'état. A military dictatorship held Brazil in its grip for twenty-one years.

In the 1960s the country seemed to be caught in the surge of an economic boom. A resplendent new capital, Brasília, was constructed deep in the interior, and São Paulo on the coast grew from a sleepy

The promise and problems of Brazil

President Getulio Vargas of Brazil

Progress in the 1950s

Specious prosperity under a military dictatorship

provincial town to become the largest industrial city in the Southern Hemisphere. Proponents of a trans-Amazonian highway boasted that the gigantic project would be visible to the naked eye from the moon. Industry expanded and diversified, to free the economy from dependence upon its single staple, coffee. Manufactures—including shipbuilding, automobiles, steel products, and precision instruments—increased sufficiently to contribute 20 percent of Brazil's exports. By 1971 the overall annual growth rate approached 11 percent. Prosperity, however, was obtained at the risk of eventual disaster. The increasingly industrialized economy depended precariously on outside support—chiefly from the United States, Canada, Japan, and West Germany—for 40 percent of capital investment and 60 percent of foreign trade. During the mid-1970s the growth rate slumped to below 5 percent, and there were signs that the "economic miracle" was coming to an end. Because imports supplied 80 percent of its oil, Brazil was badly jolted by the sharp rise in the price of petroleum products while the price of its agricultural exports was declining. Rather than attempting to rehabilitate agriculture, the government continued to promote industrial expansion, encouraged by the discovery of one of the world's largest reserves of iron ore. By 1984 iron ore rivaled coffee and soybeans as a leading export, with manufactures not far behind. The armaments industry expanded to the point of freeing Brazil from dependence upon the United States for weaponry. Brazil became a supplier of goods to Third World countries, increasing its trade with black African states sixfold between 1970 and 1980.

The social impact of repressive rule and rapid industrialization

The combination of repressive rule and a drive for rapid industrialization put a heavy strain on an already unbalanced society. While national income rose substantially, the real wages of workers declined, one-fifth of them were unemployed, and the annual inflation rate exceeded 200 percent. A severe drought in the dirt-poor region of the northeast—an area as large as France and Spain together—brought 2 million people to the verge of starvation. Nor had any of the newly acquired wealth been devoted to improving social services or health care.

Return to civilian rule

The military junta that governed for twenty-one years broke with Brazil's tradition of moderation, not only by halting the democratic process but also by suppressing every vestige of civil liberty, imposing tight censorship, incarcerating citizens without trial, and torturing suspected opponents of the regime. Rural workers, lawyers, priests, and nuns were among those murdered. After a bleak decade the repression gradually relaxed. A congress with limited responsibility was elected in 1978, and some political exiles were granted amnesty. In a 1985 presidential election, general rejoicing greeted the choice (by an electoral college rather than direct popular vote) of Tancredo Neves, a respected politician who had served as prime minister under Goulart before the 1964 coup. Unfortunately, Neves died on the day before his scheduled inauguration, and the presidency passed to his running mate José Sarney, an inexperienced politician whose publicly expressed

Modern Brazil. Left: A slum on the outskirts of Rio de Janeiro contrasts sharply with Brasília, Brazil's capital, on the right.

doubts as to his capacity for the office were well founded. The problems bequeathed by two decades of military dictatorship would have taxed leadership of the highest caliber; lacking such, the economy continued to deteriorate while social unrest intensified. In 1982, with inflation nearing a monthly rate of 100 percent, the government issued a new currency, replacing the old at a ratio of one to one thousand. The foreign debt grew to $120 billion by the late 1980s, largest among the world's developing countries. Pressure from the debt, coupled with the diversion of funds to support an overblown government bureaucracy, produced a skyrocketing inflation approaching 1,800 percent for 1989 that robbed working people of their means of livelihood. Dissatisfaction with the government was reflected in victories scored by leftist candidates in municipal elections in the fall of 1988; a fifty-three-year-old woman of Marxist pursuasion was chosen mayor of the great city San Paôlo. As Brazil's economic condition worsened and public outrage swelled in the ensuing months, the Sarney government shook the international community by suspending interest payments on its foreign debt.

In national elections in November 1989 Fernando Collor de Mello, a brash, energetic forty-year-old political conservative dubbed "Indiana Jones" by the Brazilian press, rode a pledge to create and maintain a healthy market economy to a resounding majority victory in a field

Collor's strong economic medicine

Brazil's development program and the threat of environmental catastrophe

Argentina's natural advantages

of twenty-two candidates. The day after his inauguration in March 1990 Collor froze bank accounts and investment funds, effectively removing 80 percent of the nation's money supply from circulation. He quickly moved to implement wage and price controls, cut government spending, privatize state-owned businesses, eliminate commodity subsidies, impose new taxes, and encourage foreign investment in an effort to rein in inflation and spur sustainable economic growth. These stringent measures met with broad public support.

One aspect of Brazil's development program of crucial importance not only to Latin America but also to the world community is the threatened destruction of the Amazon Basin rain forest, constituting approximately one-third of the earth's remaining tropical forests. Besides nurturing thousands of plant and animal species found nowhere else on the planet, this vast region, called "the lungs of the world," plays an essential role in replacing the atmosphere's oxygen and in combating the "greenhouse effect." The Amazon Basin also contains valuable timber and mineral resources, the systematic exploitation of which began with the industrialization campaign of the 1970s and 1980s. Logging, road building, and surface mining have proceeded so rapidly that, if allowed to continue at the present rate, will completely destroy the Amazon forest within seventy years. The clearing of land for farming and cattle ranching also jeopardizes the habitat and livelihood of Brazil's indigenous Indian societies, which by subsistence agriculture and small-scale rubber harvesting have sustained their communities for hundreds of years without harming the environment. In October 1988 a group of Kayapo warriors, resolutely nonviolent but painted and decked in full war regalia, invaded the sanctity of a courtroom to demand official recognition of Indian rights. When international lending agencies withheld loans intended to finance hydroelectric and other construction projects, the Brazilian government belatedly responded to the pleas of conservationists. Early in 1989 President Sarney announced a new program to halt deforestation in the Amazon and Atlantic forest areas.

Argentina has the natural endowment to enable it to become a rich country. Besides extensive agricultural and pastoral lands, it holds valuable mineral resources as well as waterways suitable for developing hydroelectric power, and it is virtually self-sufficient in oil and natural gas. Within an area considerably larger than that of Mexico dwell less than half as many people. Argentina's population is singularly homogeneous, partly because of an influx of European immigrants and partly because most of the Indians have been driven out or exterminated. Argentine society, 80 percent urban, has one of the highest literacy rates in Latin America. During the First and Second World Wars the country profited from high prices paid for its beef and grain. With Buenos Aires serving as the financial capital of the southern continent, Argentina was the undisputed leader of all the Latin American states. But whereas at the opening of the twentieth century Argentinians enjoyed a standard of living comparable to that of North Americans, as the century neared its close the country tottered on the verge of bankruptcy. Years of social strife, reckless waste of resources, governmental mismanagement, and the ravages of military dictatorship had reduced Argentina to the status of a debt-ridden Third World nation.

In contrast to its large rival Brazil, Argentina's history has been marked by violence, instability, and authoritarianism, making progress toward democracy extremely difficult. Universal manhood suffrage and the secret ballot were adopted in 1912, but voting has typically been manipulated by powerful cliques for their own advantage. Since 1930 only one president has completed his mandated term of office. The deep-seated animosities which jeopardize stability and democratic progress can be traced in part to rapid industrialization and to the fierce antagonism between urban and rural classes. More than 50 percent of the population is employed in industry, and a wide gulf separates the interests and attitudes of Buenos Aires—where a third of the population is concentrated—from those of the outlying provinces. A second and related source of conflict has been the role of the trade unions. Originating under the leadership of Spanish and Italian immigrants tinged with syndicalist ideology, they developed a strong sense of labor solidarity and militancy. A national confederation of organized workers (CGT), eventually encompassing half of the labor force, became a power within the state, alternately supporting and combating the recurring military dictatorships. Still another factor tending to foster autocratic government has been an intense national pride, which has made Argentinians not only resentful of outside interference—especially from the United States—but somewhat contemptuous of other Latin Americans.

Much of Argentine political history in the twentieth century has revolved around a small number of dominating personalities. One such was Hipólita Irigoyen, who inspired fanatical loyalty among his followers and was elected president in 1916 for a six-year term and again in 1928. His popularity stemmed partly from the fact that he managed to keep Argentina neutral during the First World War and later gained for her a place of recognition in world affairs. But he ruled as an autocrat, enforcing a vicious antistrike policy against labor, and, during his second term, permitting widespread corruption. He was overthrown by a revolution in 1930 engineered by conservatives and high-ranking officers of the armed forces. With the outbreak of the Second World War a sinister fascist movement began to develop in Argentina. Sympathy with the Axis, based in part upon fear of communism, was widely prevalent. Large numbers of the business classes were of German or Italian extraction, and many army officers were German trained. The nation was already in the throes of economic crises, the government was almost bankrupt, and inflation and overcrowding in the cities inflicted cruel hardships on people with meager

General Juan Perón, Shown with His Wife Eva Duarte, at the Height of His Power in 1952. The glamorous Eva, who won popular adulation by administering charity to the poor, was dying of cancer.

resources. The official policy of paying low wages as a means of boosting exports created a surly, rebellious class of workers ready to follow any demagogue who promised to better their condition. The man who stepped into this role was General Juan D. Perón. Leader of a movement to force the resignation of the incumbent president, he ran for the office himself in 1946. By promising wage increases, rent controls, and partitioning of great estates, he won enough support among the *descamisados* ("shirtless ones") in addition to that of the military and business elements to ensure his election. By recruiting peasants he enlarged the trade unions and made them his power base, using them to intimidate the industrial oligarchy and to hold the military in check. His colorful personality and bold, unscrupulous actions attracted a devoted mass following, but his methods of governing resembled the familiar pattern of fascist dictatorship—censorship, saber rattling, antiforeignism, and economic nationalism.

Perón ousted

Perón antagonized the Catholics by legalizing divorce and by attempting the separation of church and state. And while he did little for the peasants, he incurred the enmity of the middle class by conferring expensive benefits upon his followers in the General Confederation of Labor and by expanding the national debt. Though a revolt which broke out in June 1955 was suppressed, it flared up again in September. The rebels won the support of the navy and finally threatened to bombard the city of Buenos Aires if Perón did not surrender. A military junta persuaded him to relinquish his rule and go into exile. He fled to Paraguay and later found refuge in Madrid. In May 1956 the constitution was restored and the great liberal newspaper *La Prensa* was given back to its rightful owners.

The restoration of constitutional government proved to be short-lived and did not end the threat to democracy in Argentina. It was impossible to eradicate overnight the influence of 2 million *peronistas* who longed for a revival of the dictatorship that had conferred favors upon the working classes. It was also impossible to suppress the ambitions of the generals and colonels, who demanded strong government until Perónism and communism could be completely eliminated as effective instruments of class legislation. In 1962 and again in 1966 the army removed an elected president from office. Meanwhile economic ills remained, dating from the depression of the 1930s as well as from the Perón regime—a foreign-trade deficit, chronic unemployment, a mountain of public debt, and a steadily advancing cost of living. The military junta that seized power in 1966 dissolved all political parties, purged the universities, and tightened control over the trade unions, but it was unable to resolve the economic crises. Seven years later a brief experiment with civilian rule failed dismally. The still popular General Perón, invited to return from exile, scored a victory for his nominee in the presidential election of March 1973, but within a three-year span the chief executive office passed from the elected incumbent to Perón himself and after his death in 1974 to his widow, Isabelle Perón, a former cabaret dancer. Her disastrous administration of twenty months witnessed the spread of corruption throughout the bureaucracy, black marketing, debasement of the currency, and the world's highest rate of inflation, bringing the government to the brink of ruin. She was deposed by a smoothly executed coup in March 1976, and a junta, headed by General Jorge Videla, acceded to power.

The military junta that ruled Argentina for seven years after the overthrow of Señora Perón checked the imminent collapse of the economy, but without remedying its basic defects and at the expense of every trace of freedom. The junta seized control of the powerful CGT and froze wages, but not prices, which, after a temporary check to inflation, continued to rise. The generals vowed to exterminate the guerrilla terrorist bands that had shaken the country over a period of many years. Identifying as a terrorist "anyone who spreads ideas contrary to Western and Christian civilization," the military government unleashed a terror of its own, employing more than a dozen different agencies to stifle dissidents by fright, torture, and executions. Security forces raided homes by night, dropped bodies from helicopters into the South Atlantic, and destroyed the evidence of their depredations. Amnesty International estimated that within two years some 20,000 people had disappeared, while thousands more were held in official prisons or secret detention camps. One victim who managed to survive the "dirty war" was the courageous journalist Jacobo Timmerman, who, after twenty-nine months of imprisonment and torture, was permitted to emigrate to Israel. Paradoxically, while the junta was lending its agents to help repressive governments in Bolivia and Guatemala combat alleged communist subversives, it was cultivating

The Falkland Islands war; fall of the junta

closer ties with communist Russia, which welcomed Argentine grain during President Jimmy Carter's embargo of American shipments. In return, Russia supplied Argentina with high technology. Meanwhile, Argentina's generals were raiding their own country's crippled economy.

As popular revulsion mounted against the generals, they attempted to win public approval by embarking on a military adventure. Its failure brought about their downfall. The Falkland Islands (Malvinas), lying 400 miles east of the southern tip of Argentina, had been regarded by Argentinians as rightfully their property ever since the islands were seized by the British in 1833. Repeated attempts to negotiate a transfer of sovereignty of the islands had failed. In deciding upon a forceful seizure the Argentine military apparently believed that Britain would expend little effort to defend a tiny possession of dubious value 8,000 miles from home and also that the Washington government, whose attitude toward them had changed from coldness to cordiality with the accession of President Ronald Reagan, would raise no objections—two serious miscalculations. Argentine forces that invaded the Falklands in April 1982 were forced to surrender in June. The seventy-four-day war, which cost $2.6 billion and a thousand lives, earned no merit points either for Great Britain or for Argentina, but it had the salutary effect of undermining the credibility of a government that had deluded its people with the promise of an easy victory. In a presidential election held in October 1983—to the chagrin of the *peronistas,* who had expected to return to power—52 percent of the popular

War in the Falkland Islands. Left: Argentine prisoners under British marine guard as the Argentine forces surrendered in June 1982. Right: Graves of British officers and soldiers who fell during the seventy-four-day war for control of the Falkland Islands.

President Raúl Alfonsín of Argentina Receiving the Mothers of Dissidents Who "Disappeared" under the Previous Regime. These women urged Mr. Alfonsín to take meaningful action to locate their sons and to punish the military officers responsible for their abduction and possible deaths.

vote was garnered by the moderate reformist Civic Union party, headed by Raúl Alfonsín.

Alfonsín immediately promised the trial and punishment of officers guilty of atrocities, but the promise was difficult to fulfill because much evidence had been destroyed, some suspects had fled the country, and Alfonsín wished to preserve the morale of the armed forces while reforming them. When military courts refused to proceed with the trials as ordered, the civilian courts took action. Although most of the agents employed in administering the terror escaped prosecution, two of the nine junta members were sentenced to life imprisonment and three others to lesser terms—the first time in Latin American history that military criminals had been punished by a civilian government. Alfonsín's presidential term, viewed with sullen resentment by the army, was also marred by his inability to rescue the sinking economy. Inflation multiplied at such a rate that the value of money evaporated faster than notes could be printed, and in 1985 the government replaced the worthless currency with a new issue. The national debt, which had grown from $8 billion to $45 billion under the military junta, rose to $60 billion in 1988 when the government stopped making interest payments on the long-term portion of the foreign debt. Two army mutinies in 1987 were easily suppressed, but food riots also broke out. In July 1989, with inflation racing toward a total of 3,700 percent for the year and five months before the expiration of his term, Alfonsín resigned the presidency in favor of the newly elected Carlos Saúl Menem, the ex-governor of a province and head of Perón's Justicialista party. Menem, asserting that his party had matured since its early flamboyant days, called upon all citizens to prepare for therapeutic measures of austerity.

In seeking an explanation of Argentina's economic decline, it could be argued that prosperity came too easily. In contrast to the Japanese, for example, who worked hard to rebuild their nation after the Pacific

The Alfonsín administration: military reform and economic decline

The roots of Argentina's problems

war, white settlers in the Argentine seemed to have wealth presented to them on a silver platter. Many came from comfortable circumstances in Europe and were accustomed to enjoying the benefits of other people's labor. Rapid exploitation of the great pasturelands of the interior—at the expense of Indians and ruggedly independent gauchos—created the impression of an inexhaustible natural bounty. This attitude was encouraged by a paternalistic government that granted favors to special-interest groups and, to cushion unemployment, maintained inefficiently operated state-owned enterprises that ran up large deficits. While the government sank deeper into debt, its citizens indulged in tax evasion on a notorious scale. During the critical 1980s wealthy Argentinians transferred their assets to foreign banks, creating a capital flow approaching the size of the national debt. As elsewhere in Latin America, an excessive portion of land and income in Argentina is controlled by a small oligarchy. A crowning threat both to a sound economy and to democratic progress resides in the Argentine military establishment, which is dominated by an entrenched aristocracy and—except for a temporary and uneasy alliance with labor under Perón—has supported the oligarchy. During the junta era of the late 1970s the military not only controlled the state but also filled government offices with its own personnel (meanwhile reducing Argentina's per capita income from fifteenth place among nations to thirty-seventh). The officers never expressed regret for their reign of terror; neither have the secret intelligence agencies they employed against civilians been dismantled.

Chile's mineral resources

Chile, occupying a long strip of the continent between Argentina and the Pacific Ocean, has natural advantages similar to those of its larger neighbor and, until recently, has had a less turbulent history. Its population is small and, like those of Argentina and Uruguay, homogeneous, predominantly of European origin. With a limited amount of arable land, Chile's economic development has been linked to the exploitation of its minerals: silver, gold, nitrates, and, in the most recent period, copper, which by 1980 accounted for 80 percent of Chile's foreign trade. Concentration on the export of minerals brought the economy increasingly under foreign control as British and North American capitalists acquired ownership of the mines, provided shipping facilities, and smelted most of the ore in their own foundries. It also inhibited diversification of the economy and diverted attention from the needs of agriculture.

Stability in spite of inequality

From the beginning of its independence in 1818, Chile had been remarkably free from internal upheavals. As in most parts of the continent, the economy was dominated by large landowners and foreign investors, while peasants and industrial workers—together constituting 70 percent of the population—were almost propertyless. As late as 1968, 2.6 percent of the people received nearly 50 percent of the national income. Eight percent of the farms held more than two-thirds of all cultivated land, and poor tenants *(inquilinos)* on great haciendas commonly lived in one-room huts with only straw mats to sleep on. Yet Chile had a middle class and an urban working class, both of which carried weight, and the political structure seemed relatively stable, committed to democratic principles and—with a few brief interruptions—controlled by civilians. Following the authoritarian presidency of Major Carlos Ibáñez in 1925–1931, constitutional rule continued unbroken for four decades. In 1973 it was destroyed in a blood bath accompanying a military coup instigated by ultraconservatives and foreign conspirators.

The administration of Eduardo Frei, who as head of the Christian Democratic party was elected president in 1964, secured agreements for a gradual transfer of the copper mines from foreign to national ownership but made little progress with the basic problem of land ownership. The presidential election of September 1970 was watched with great concern abroad, especially in the United States, where the recent announcement of Chile's intent to nationalize the huge Anaconda Copper Company's holdings had alarmed business circles. Anxiety was heightened when the 1970 election, with 86 percent of the registered voters participating, brought Salvador Allende Gossens into office at the head of a Popular Unity coalition of Socialists, Communists, and other left-wing groups. A long-time member of the Chilean Socialist party, Allende sought radical changes but was determined to achieve them by democratic methods. His government broke the control of monopolies, enacted a substantial program of agrarian reform, improved health care sufficiently to cut the infant mortality rate in half, and brought relief to the workers by reducing unemployment. His determination to pursue a "Chilean way to socialism"— democratic and nonviolent—aroused the fears of both native and foreign business interests, who resolved to fight him with all the resources they could command. There are conflicting accounts and interpretations of the events that led to Allende's downfall. He himself was partly to blame. By pushing a nationalization program too rapidly, he undermined confidence in the economy. His policies were bound to alienate conservative business interests, and he lacked the personal charisma to enable him to lead a successful revolution against them. Finally, he made the fatal, though perhaps inevitable, mistake of antagonizing the armed forces. Several factors contributed to a deepening economic crisis. The United States demanded immediate payment of loans that were nearing maturity, ended all except military-aid grants, and exerted pressure on private banks and international lending agencies to cut off fresh credits to the Allende government. A heavy blow was inflicted by a drop in the price of copper, Chile's leading export. With falling revenues and inflation out of hand, the country appeared to be headed for an economic breakdown—attributed by critics to Allende's ineptitude and Marxist ideology—but to a considerable extent deliberately engineered by Chilean far-right elements, with the support of multinational corporations and the United States govern-

Allende and the "Chilean way to socialism"

Salvadore Allende, President of Chile, 1970–1973

*Forceful overthrow of
democratic government in
Chile*

ment. The CIA, at the urging of the International Telephone & Tele-graph Company, had tried to prevent Allende's installation as president in 1970. Failing in this the CIA secretly spent some $8 million in an attempt to "destabilize" the Chilean government.

In spite of a well-financed scare-and-smear campaign, the congressional elections of March 1973 gave Allende's Popular Unity coalition almost 44 percent of the vote, actually increasing its representation in the legislature although not to the point of holding a majority. Infuriated by this popular vote of confidence in the president, his opponents resorted to extreme measures. After several abortive attempts to incite a popular uprising against the government, the military high command mobilized a force of 100,000 men and on September 11, 1973, launched attacks on key centers throughout the country. The operation was less a coup d'état than an undeclared civil war, though such an uneven contest that there could be little doubt as to the outcome. Although disorganized and poorly armed, civilian resistance proved much stiffer than had been expected. A small band led by Allende defended the Presidential Palace for five hours against tanks and aerial bombardment. Allende was machine-gunned by his captors (who announced his death as suicide) and the slaughter continued for weeks. Some 15,000 civilians were killed outright; thousands more were imprisoned, tortured, or exiled.

Rule of the junta

The overthrow of one of the few constitutional democracies in Latin America transferred power to a four-man junta headed by General Augusto Pinochet Ugarte, who liked to compare himself to Spain's Generalissimo Franco and who vowed to replace discredited "liberal democracy" with something more suitable to the times. Secret police caused people to disappear without a trace and abused prisoners in torture chambers bearing such sardonic titles as "Discothèque" and "Palace of Laughter." An International Commission of Jurists estimated that during the first eighteen months after the military takeover 95,000 persons—about 1 percent of the population—were arrested for at least a twenty-four-hour period. The terror that drove many Chileans into exile pursued them beyond the state's border. In September 1976 Orlando Letelier, formerly Allende's ambassador to the United States and an outspoken critic of the junta, was murdered on a street in Washington, D.C., by Pinochet's agents. Despite U.S. protests, Letelier's assassins were never brought to trial.

In the face of internal resistance and the opprobrium of the world community General Pinochet's dictatorship proved remarkably durable. Opposition in the form of strikes, boycotts, demonstrations, and satirical plays daringly performed by a theatrical troupe on the streets of Santiago were ineffective against a regime backed by the army and the ever-present *carabineros* (armed police) and which did not hesitate to employ kidnapping, torture, and assassination. Although sympathy and support from U.S. officials had helped Pinochet seize power, he showed no inclination to accept direction from Washington. When

General Augusto Pinochet, Dictator of Chile, Watching a Military Parade on the Tenth Anniversary of the 1973 Coup That Brought Him to Power

Down with the Junta. In one of a constant stream of demonstrations against the military government in Chile in July 1983, students at the University of Santiago protest the ruthless suppression of civil liberties and the continued imprisonment of thousands of citizens who dared to speak out against the government.

the U.S. Congress cut off military aid in 1976, private banks continued to offer financial assistance to the junta. The U.S. military command maintained liaison with its Chilean counterpart, and joint naval exercises between the two countries continued.

General Pinochet described Chile under his rule as an island of peace in a troubled world and boasted that he had laid a sound economic base for future development. After an industrial slump in the late 1970s, the economy did show signs of growth. Wages were kept low enough to stimulate exports, the investment of foreign capital was encouraged, and inflation was held to the comparatively low figure of 20 percent. The nation's capital was kept clean and its streets policed against petty crime, attractive shopping malls were built, and modern subway trains ran to fashionable suburbs. But residents of the slums fringing Santiago and other cities were worse off than before because the government had terminated social-welfare programs. Schools were closing, sewer ditches were left uncovered, and the gulf between rich and poor widened.

Pinochet's "Island of Peace"

A constitution enacted in 1980 provided for a Congress with limited authority, made the military a partner in government, and vested almost complete power in the president. As mandated by this constitution, a plebiscite was held in October 1988 giving citizens the limited choice of expressing their approval or disapproval of Pinochet's presidency. In spite of his attempt to identify the opposition with a communist conspiracy and his charge that the nation's choice was between "me or chaos," the No votes prevailed. This rebuff of Pinochet's regime opened the door for a presidential election in December 1989 when centrist Christian Democratic party leader Patricio Aylwin led

The Constitution of 1980 and the dawn of the post-Pinochet era

a coalition of seventeen opposition groups to victory against Pinochet's hand-picked candidate. Even as President Aylwin assumed office in March 1990 amid promises to restore democracy and to pursue the truth about the repression of the Pinochet era, General Pinochet reiterated his intention to remain commander-in-chief of the armed forces. Meanwhile, these forces are shielded by a 1978 amnesty law absolving military personnel of criminal liability for earlier human-rights violations and constitutional restraints against removing sitting commanders of the armed forces for eight years. Faced with disunity in the ranks of labor, the fragility of his governing coalition, and the specter of Pinochet leading a coup against him, President Aylwin will be obliged to tread lightly in his efforts to effect significant change in Chile.

*Peru: the failed reform
programs of leftist military
dictatorships*

Peru, with a population largely Indian and one of the lowest standards of living in Latin America, is not condemned by nature to be a land of poverty. The country has ample natural resources, including copper and other ores, hydroelectric potential, and probably large oil fields. Wealth, both industrial and agricultural, is concentrated in the cities and fertile slopes of the Pacific coast, while poverty is almost universal in the sierra and jungle regions of the interior. During the last three decades Peru's leaders have tried without marked success to promote economic and social development. President Fernando Belaúnde Terry, elected in 1983, promised reform for the benefit of poor Indians but accomplished little. In 1968 he was removed from office by a military coup and for the next twelve years Peru remained under a military dictatorship which, in contrast to the usual pattern, sprang from the left side of the political spectrum. General Jean Velásco Alvarado appropriated several million acres of land for redistribution, set up workers' cooperatives, extended educational opportunities for both men and women, and nationalized large foreign properties. Because of cool relations with the United States, Peru turned to the Soviet Union for its chief source of arms. Velásco's welfare measures entailed heavy expenditures which the anticipated oil revenues were insufficient to meet. When another general replaced Velásco in 1975 the reform program was halted, while the economy deteriorated alarmingly. Admitting failure, the military returned the government to civilian control in 1980 and Fernando Belaúnde, whom they had ousted twelve years before, was reelected to the presidency. Abandoning his plans for social reform, Belaúnde bent every effort to attract foreign investments—with little success—while he spent freely and pushed the country more deeply into debt.

*Promise confounded by
monumental problems*

Hopes for greater social stability and democratic progress in Peru revived with the election in 1985 of Alan Garcia Perez, charismatic thirty-six-year old leader of the American Popular Revolutionary Alliance (APRA), who enunciated a threefold policy of anti-imperialism, nonalignment, and support for Latin American unity. Eyed with skepticism in conservative circles abroad, he aroused enthusiasm among

Peruvians and attracted attention throughout Latin America, but the problems confronting him were monumental. A weakening of exports resulting from a decline in the price of oil and minerals, deficits incurred by poorly managed state-owned enterprises, and long continued borrowing from abroad had crippled the economy, and pressure from creditors demanding interest payments threatened to devastate it.

The task of restructuring Peru's grossly inequitable society was made more difficult by a violent underground revolutionary movement known as *Sendero Luminoso* ("Shining Path"). Professing a radical post-Marxist, even post-Maoist, ideology, its leaders considered themselves the "fourth sword" of world revolution. Starting from a base south of Lima they spread terror throughout the country, committing acts of sabotage and executing alleged enemies. Belaúnde's attempts to suppress Shining Path by direct military attack failed, while he rode roughshod over due process of law. Because the guerrillas had won some support among the rural poor, President Garcia hoped to reduce their influence by introducing measures to relieve poverty. With the country in the midst of a depression and an inflation rate approaching 2,800 percent in 1989, the prospects did not seem bright. Meanwhile the Shining Path had secured a base in the northeastern valleys where poor *campesinos,* turning to coca planting in response to the insatiable North American demand for cocaine, were invading the Amazon rain forests. By 1989 more than half a million acres of this irreplaceable resource had been destroyed, imperiling national parks and the future of agriculture.

President Alberto Fujimori of Peru. Fujimori inspired a dream of a Japanese-style economic miracle in Peru.

Peruvians registered their unwillingness to return to business as usual with the election to the presidency in June 1990 of the politically obscure Alberto Fujimori, an agronomist born of Japanese immigrants, on a platform extolling "Work, Honesty, and Technology" and evoking the Japanese economic miracle. Calling for a revival of the rural economy through crop substitution and construction of roads and railways with U.S. assistance as a means of diminishing the appeal of the "Shining Path" and the economic viability of coca production, Fujimori noted that "people have the right to rebel in the face of social injustice. You can't allow the suffocation of a people by social structures." He presented himself as a political outsider who would reform Peru's notoriously corrupt and inefficient public sector amid a new wave of hope.

The destinies of the smaller states of South America have followed varying courses. Uruguay, one of the three states occupying the relatively prosperous Southern Cone, in the early twentieth century acquired a reputation as a showcase of democracy. Impetus to political and social progress was given by José Batlle y Ordóñez, one of the ablest statesmen in Latin American history, who served as president of Uruguay from 1903 to 1907 and again from 1911 to 1915. A thoroughgoing democrat who approached the question of social change pragmatically rather than from ideological commitment, Batlle firmly believed that almost all problems could be solved by legislation and free elections. A reform program that identified Uruguay as a welfare state began during his second administration and included the eight-hour day, regulation of working conditions, workmen's compensation, old-age pensions, and the protection of labor unions. At the same time, the government began to acquire some industries and entered the insurance field. A new constitution, drafted in convention and ratified by plebiscite, was adopted in 1919. Modeled partly after that of Switzerland, the Constitution of 1919 provided for the separation of church and state, universal manhood suffrage, and the secret ballot. Two years later the vote was extended to women. Unfortunately, the reforms begun by Batlle and continued by his immediate successors, while benefiting urban workers, did little to improve the lot of poor peasants and rural laborers. Insisting that Uruguay had no pressing agrarian problem, Batlle took no action to break the land monopoly of great estate owners.

*From democracy to
dictatorship*

For several decades—interrupted by the Great Depression and a brief dictatorship—Uruguay enjoyed relative prosperity. By mid-century, however, the country was suffering from economic decline, attributable partly to falling prices for its exports of wool, meat, and hides, but partly to such internal factors as a narrow concentration of wealth, inefficiency in both agriculture and industry, and bureaucratic waste in government. Demoralized by uncontrolled inflation, Uruguay was torn by strikes and riots and terrorized by bands of desperate guerrillas. Yielding to pressure from the army, President Juan Bordaberry in June 1973 dissolved Congress and announced that he would govern by decree. His coup was accompanied by wholesale arrests. Subsequently, the constitution was suspended, parliament replaced by a National Security Council, political parties and trade unions suppressed, and censorship imposed. The military removed President Bordaberry in 1976 and, following a gruesome pattern of intimidation and torture, set a new record for political imprisonment. By the end of 1975, 2 percent of the population was under detention. Uruguay—a state once hailed as the "Switzerland of South America" and a model democracy—had become one of the worst offenders against human rights. The Organization of American States condemned the excesses of the regime, and the United States suspended aid. Faced with accelerating internal opposition and a rapidly deteriorating economy, the of the regime, and the United States suspended aid. Faced with accelerating internal opposition and a rapidly deteriorating economy, the generals returned power to an elected civilian government in 1985. The army, however, refused to allow its officers to be brought to trial for offenses committed during military rule. Under pressure the Uruguayan Congress in 1986 enacted an amnesty law protecting members of the security forces from prosecution—a measure that the defense minister claimed was necessary for "the future's calm and the army's dignity."

Uruguay's slightly larger neighbor, Paraguay, has a markedly different and more somber history. This country has never known democratic government, but it achieved the doubtful distinction of having the longest-tenured head of state in Latin America. General Alfredo Stroessner seized power by a coup in May 1954 and held it for more than thirty-four years. Conforming more to the pattern of a fascist dictator than of a traditional caudillo, Stroessner covered his tyranny with a gloss of legality by invoking periodically an article of the 1967 constitution that allowed for the declaration of a state of emergency and the suspension of civil rights. Paraguay's record of abuse, arbitrary arrest, and torture is one of the worst in the hemisphere. Agrarian leagues, labor unions, and other protesting groups were all brutally suppressed. Under President Stroessner the Paraguayan institutional environment, assisted by credits from international lending agencies, was profitable for the military, the Stroessner family, and a few international corporations, but quite the opposite for the poverty-stricken Indians who make up a majority of the population and own very little of the land on which they toil. Early in February 1989 when the seventy-six-year-old dictator was in failing health, he was deposed and exiled by a bloodletting coup led by General Andres Rodriguez, who was overwhelmingly endorsed as president in national elections three months later. Although human rights advocates rejoiced at Stroessner's departure, the coup was directly related to a power struggle within the military command. General Rodriguez's promise to respect human rights and promote democracy had to be weighed against his record of long and close association with the dictator (whose son had married Rodriguez's daughter), of sharing in the profits of corruption, and of suspected association with the international drug traffic.

Bolivia, with sharply contrasting geographical features ranging from snow-crowned Andean peaks to the Amazon jungle, and equally widely separated social strata, could be viewed as a working model of the problems and frustrations confronting Latin American nations. Possessing abundant resources of silver, gold, natural gas, and probably oil, Bolivia is among the poorest of Latin American states. A tremendous gulf separates an affluent class of whites and mestizos from the Indian two-thirds of the population, which exists below what would normally be considered the poverty level. Most Bolivians are undernourished throughout their life span, which averages forty-seven years. Workers in the mines usually die after seven years of labor.

Bolivia's record of political instability is unmatched. Repeatedly the army has disrupted attempts to establish democratic institutions, but attempts continue in spite of the lack of foundations on which to build. Bolivia's coups are numbered in the hundreds; five occurred during

Paraguay's legacy of dictatorship

General Alfredo Stroessner, Dictator of Paraguay since 1954. His long tenure in power has been marked by cruelty and corruption.

Bolivia: a nation of sharp contrasts

Democracy thwarted by coups and military dictatorship

the period 1978–1980, frustrating a determined effort to form a democratic government under civilian control. A brief but heroic role was played by a grandmother in her fifties, Lydia Gueiler Tejada. Selected as provisional president after a general strike had forced a power-hungry colonel to leave the country, she managed to keep the generals in their barracks long enough to carry out plans for a free general election, held in June 1980. But when the voters chose as president an elder statesman responsible for popular reforms passed during his tenure of office in the 1950s, the military, led by General Luis García Metza, struck swiftly, arresting Gueiler and her cabinet and preventing the newly elected president from taking office. General Metza claimed that his action was essential to protect democracy against the threat of communism. The real enemies of democracy were not communism, nonexistent as a political force in Bolivia, but the oligarchy and the officers who reaped millions from their control of an illegal but flourishing traffic in cocaine. The July 1980 coup had been planned in Buenos Aires and assisted by General Jorge Videla, dictator of Argentina. Videla declared that an elected government in Bolivia posed "a high degree of risk because of the possibility that such a government would promote ideas contrary to our way of life and the permanence of military government." After eighteen years under the military, Bolivia returned to civilian rule following an election of 1982. Subsequently the government sought U.S. assistance in helping to eradicate the coca plantations that were preempting the nation's agricultural resources.

Phenomenal increase in population

During the past century Latin America has undergone major changes. Foremost is a phenomenal increase in population. Around 1800, Central and South America had a population of about 17 million; by 1900 this had grown to 70 million and by 1985 to 405 million. The population of Brazil more than trebled between 1900 and 1960. Argentina surpassed even this ratio, with a growth in numbers from 4,200,000 in 1900 to 20 million sixty years later. The number of Mexicans rose from 20 million in 1940 to 47 million in 1968 and over 80 million by 1989. With an average annual growth rate of about 3 percent, the Latin American countries seem destined to double their present population by the year 2025 when, according to predictions, it would total 779 million. Nearly everywhere population was beginning to exert terrific pressure upon available resources. Since 1950 there has been a steady migration of people from rural districts to the cities, but the expansion of industry and commerce has been too limited to absorb displaced peasants into profitable employment.

Defects in Latin American economies

Economic defects in Latin American economies are easier to spot than to remedy; examples are a highly inequitable distribution of income, failure to develop agriculture to its full potential, dependence on a few staple crops for export—among them coca leaves, most deleterious of all. Roughly 10 percent of the people still own all productive land. Industrialization, while impressive in many areas, has added its own problems and has failed to raise living standards for the majority, even in countries that no longer allow profits to be siphoned off by foreign corporations. In Mexico, for example, the average city worker—if he is lucky enough to have a job—earns the equivalent of $100 a month, the country laborer less than $25 a month. The professions, government positions, and the officer ranks of the army are monopolized by a landlord class, together with its allies in banking and industry. Central to Latin American economic problems is the heavy indebtedness of its governments. During the nineteenth century a large influx of foreign capital was matched by an influx of goods from the United States and other developed countries, a process that created the appearance of prosperity without promoting the growth of self-sustaining local economies. Eventually the cost of servicing the debts exceeded the borrowers' capacity to pay, necessitating further borrowing. In 1983 almost two thirds of the value of all Latin American exports for that year would have been required to meet debt charges if the charges had actually been met. Mexico, Brazil, and Argentina—the three largest debtors—were saved from imminent default in 1982 by a "rescheduling" of debt payments. Such an arrangement can avert a crisis but does not remove its causes. And when the International Monetary Fund extends a new loan, to protect creditors if often requires the debtor nation to adopt an austerity program that reduces the living standards of its people.

Recent decades have yielded both turmoil and encouraging signs, not least in several of the smaller countries. In Venezuela the exploitation of vast petroleum reserves has transformed an agricultural society into an urban and increasingly industrialized one. Although oil revenues, which accounted for most of the state's income, were spent so extravagantly in the 1970s that the government went heavily into debt, they have given Venezuela the highest standard of living in Latin America. After the overthrow of a military dictator, Marcos Pérez Jiménez in 1950, the nation gained political stature as a durable democracy. Since 1973 a two-party system has functioned successfully.

Venezuela's success

Even the largely undeveloped coffee-and-banana republics of Colombia and Ecuador, with their subjugated Indian populations, have begun to be stirred by the winds of change. Ecuador has long been dominated by a Spanish landed aristocracy constituting 5 percent of the population and by foreign corporations—Pepsi Cola, General Electric, and United Fruit—with poverty so extreme among Indians that 70 percent of the children die before the age of three. The year 1972 saw the fifth and final exit from Ecuador's presidential seat of the colorful but worthless dictator Velasco Ibarra, whose exemplification of the cult of *personalismo* was summed up in his boast "Give me a balcony, and Ecuador is mine!" This small and most densely populated of South American countries has benefited from recent discoveries of oil, which produced a burst of economic growth in the 1970s but brought no appreciable improvement in the lot of rural or industrial

*Ecuador; decline of
military governments*

workers. The tiny country suffered from a severe earthquake in 1986. Colombia, frequently cited as an outstanding example of a stable Latin American democracy, actually has one of the world's most violent societies. Kidnappings, murders, and other terrorist acts perpetrated by guerrillas, vigilante groups, and the military—producing 15,000 homicides in 1986 alone—have kept the country in a state of turmoil and constantly threaten the survival of civilian authority. Despite the joint efforts of the Washington and Bogota governments, Colombia has become the chief center of cocaine manufacture, processing the coca paste imported from Bolivia and Peru. The drug cartel, well financed and heavily armed, openly defies the civilian authorities. Although it would be rash to assume that the age of dictators is past, there is reassurance in noting that by 1990 governments at least nominally civilian had been installed in more than three-fourths of the independent republics of South America, leaving military dictatorships in only two—Paraguay and Surinam (the former Dutch Guiana).

3. CRISIS AND REVOLUTION

The Cuban revolution

Continuous postponement of the drastic reforms necessary to bring twentieth-century Latin American societies to a condition of robust health has planted the seeds of revolution. Before the middle of the present century Mexico was the only country where revolution had borne fruit, but since the Second World War it has taken root in small states of the West Indies and Central America. Cuba was the first of these countries to be radically transformed by a revolutionary process. Freed from Spanish rule in 1898, Cuba became nominally independent but actually a semicolony of the United States. By treaty and by a clause inserted in the Cuban Constitution of 1901, the United States was given the right to intervene in the internal affairs of the new republic, and did so several times before the so-called Platt Amendment was revoked in 1934 under President Franklin Roosevelt's Good Neighbor Policy. The United States, however, retained a naval base at Guantánamo Bay. A rising spirit of nationalism, resentment against a narrow concentration of wealth, and the weakness of a two-crop economy left the country a prey to disorder. Events reached a crisis during the world depression of the 1930s. In 1936 a ruthless army sergeant, Fulgencio Batista, with aid from the United States and the support of the army, gained control of the government and maintained a dictatorial rule until 1959. In that year he was overthrown by a coterie of young revolutionists under the leadership of Fidel Castro. Castro's program was essentially a patchwork and his followers a motley assortment. Some were anti-Communists, some were democratic socialists, and several had definite commitments to communism. Calling their bid for power the Twenty-sixth of July Movement because it had been launched on July 26, 1953, Castro and his comrades

Fidel Castro

eventually demanded a complete revolution in Cuba. They would obliterate all traces of United States imperialism, expropriating American owners of banks, industries, and hotels. They would nationalize these properties and some others in order to provide jobs for the unemployed. They proposed also an extensive land reform for the benefit of the peasants. As the movement extended its power over the country and gained full control in 1959, it took on a more radical character. In 1961 Castro announced himself "a Marxist-Leninist."

Following their dramatic victory in 1959 the revolutionaries faced difficult years as they attempted to transform Cuba's social and economic base while struggling to survive and to win international recognition. Alarmed at the prospect of profit losses to investors if foreign holdings were nationalized, the United States severed relations with Cuba in 1961, later persuaded the Organization of American States to expel Cuba from membership, and imposed a trade embargo. Unable to isolate the wayward island republic completely, the Washington government in April 1961 planned and assisted an invasion of Cuba by embittered Cuban exiles. An attempted landing at the Bay of Pigs was a total failure. Stung by this rebuff the Kennedy administration permitted anti-Castro saboteurs and terrorists to operate out of Miami and urged the CIA to "get rid of" Castro. A Senate investigating committee later reported that between 1961 and 1963 eight separate assassination plots against the Cuban president had been considered. The threat of invasion or subversion from the Colossus of the North forced Castro to seek allies outside the Western Hemisphere and, ultimately, to become dependent on the Soviet Union for financial, military, and diplomatic support.

Years of crisis

The Cuba of Fidel Castro presents strange contradictions. The revolution bettered living conditions for classes that had always been impoverished, making Cuba a greatly admired welfare-state model for Third World countries. It has lifted the country out of the stagnation that paralyzes most Latin American societies. Improved sanitation, hygiene, medical and hospital facilities, and an adequate supply of physicians raised the level of public health, as evidenced by a decline in deaths from tuberculosis, malaria, typhoid, and polio. Life expectancy, which was fifty-four years in 1959, has risen to seventy-four years for men and seventy-six for women. The infant mortality rate is the lowest in Latin America. Women, given legal equality with men, have advanced in all the professions; 52 percent of the physicians are women. Beaches and resorts have been opened to the public. The provision of education through the ninth grade has almost eliminated illiteracy. But the shift from a semicolonial dependency of the United States to membership in what until recently was perceived as the Soviet bloc has not enabled Cuba to realize its economic potential. The island possesses enough fertile land to make it a prosperous agricultural country, but it has remained dependent on a few exports, such as nickel and especially sugar, and the price of these declined sharply

Cuba: land of contradictions

in the 1970s. There are shortages of many commodities; even necessities are rationed. Belying Castro's boast that by 1980 every family would own a house or an apartment and that every farmer would have an air-conditioned tractor, plans for industrial development have been drastically curtailed. Aside from serious blunders in economic planning, the picture is shadowed by the suppression of personal freedom, censorship, and constant indoctrination—"government by oratory." By 1960 Castro was holding more political prisoners than had been jailed by Batista. Over 700,000 Cubans have left the country and other hundreds of thousands undoubtedly would do so if they could.

*The regime as a reflection
of Castro's personality*

The strong and weak points of the regime reflect the complex personality of its leader, viewed by some as a tyrannical despot and by others as the greatest figure in Latin American history since Simón Bolívar. A man of charisma, courage, and drive but essentially an improviser, Castro drifted from one ideological position to another. Renouncing at the outset the repression inherent in Communist models in Eastern Europe and China, he promised that his revolution would create a society of equality, social justice, and intellectual freedom. During the 1960s he attracted so many poets, artists, and intellectuals of all types from Europe and America that Havana became the literary capital of the Spanish-speaking world. But the Soviet-patterned Cuban Communist party, adopted as an insurance policy against the real or imagined threat of attack from without, inhibited democratic tendencies. Increasingly rigid and bureaucratic, the party became institutionalized and—ironically—more resistent to reform than its Russian counterpart, which in the late 1980s under Mikhail Gorbachev began to break the rigid mold imposed by Stalin and Brezhnev. The recent dissolution of communist regimes in eastern Europe, the prospect of a reduction in Soviet financial aid, and a stiffening of U.S. anti-Cuban policy have induced speculation as to whether the Castro regime can long survive. Dedicated anti-Castro Cubans living in Miami proclaimed the imminent fall of the dictator and even began to prepare for their own early return to the liberated island. But it is unlikely that the scenario unfolding in eastern Europe and the USSR will be duplicated in the Caribbean communist republic—not because Castro disapproves of the anti-Marxist reforms but because Cuba's revolutionary heritage is very different from that of the eastern European countries where communism was imposed from without and against the national will. The Cuban brand of communism was homegrown and developed as part of a drive to win independence from foreign control. And despite frustration and failed promises, Castro still commands the loyalty of the majority of his people. *Fidelismo,* more than socialism or communism, has become a national creed.

Although the USSR has kept Cuba in line by absorbing half its sugar crop and providing free military assistance, the relationship has been an uneasy one. In 1962 when the Soviets installed missile bases in Cuba with weapons aimed at the United States, a confrontation between the two superpowers was ended with removal of the missiles, but only by direct exchanges between Washington and Moscow and after President Kennedy had imposed an embargo against Soviet supply vessels in Caribbean waters. Cubans resented the fact that they had not been consulted during the crisis even though the nuclear war so narrowly averted would have begun on their soil. The Havana government has sent technicians, military instructors, and soldiers to several fledgling African states. Two thousand Cubans lost their lives defending the Angolan government against rebel and invading South African forces. Having demonstrated that a small nation of ten million people on Uncle Sam's doorstep could make itself independent of its mighty neighbor, Castro sought to restore ties with the United States, with little success. American animosity was reinforced when, with Castro's permission, beginning in the spring of 1979 a flood of Cuban immigrants crowded into vessels of every description and descended upon the Florida coast. Of the 125,000 who came to American shores in 1979–1980 a small number were mental patients or criminals. Although rebuffed by successive Washington administrations, Castro's Cuba has established diplomatic ties with fifteen states of the Western Hemisphere, including Canada, now an important trade partner. An active leader in the nonaligned movement, Castro called for cooperation between capitalist and socialist countries to raise the economic level of developing nations.

Central America, long one of the most depressed regions in the Western Hemisphere and therefore a likely breeding ground for rev-

Cuba's relations with the world

The Cuban "Boatlift." Between 800 and 900 Cuban refugees crammed on board the ocean-going tug *Dr. Daniels* on this day in early 1980 for the perilous trip from Cuba to Key West, Florida. Thousands of Cubans seized the opportunity to leave Cuba on any boat that would take them to the United States. The Cuban government sought to use this embarrassing situation to rid itself of individuals it identified as "undesirables."

Factors impeding
revolution in Central
America

olution, was too compartmentalized politically to enable its inhabitants to unite in a common struggle. An area nearly a third smaller than the state of Texas (to which it was once joined, together with Mexico, under Spanish colonial rule) is divided into six independent states, differing widely from one another. At one extreme is Costa Rica, with a homogeneous population and democratic, pacific traditions; at the other extreme is Guatemala, with a two-tiered society dominated by the military. Because of Central America's political weakness and its accessibility, its economies were easily invaded and dominated by large trading companies which, in return for grants of land and other concessions, helped keep the oligarchs in power. At the same time, a potential challenge to the establishments was rising from within the Catholic Church, an institution that traditionally had been a bulwark of the status quo. Increasing numbers of the clergy were embracing a "liberation theology" that called upon the Church to champion the rights and alleviate the suffering of the poor and downtrodden. In Central and South America hundreds of priests, nuns, and even bishops sacrificed their lives in opposing tyrannical regimes. In El Salvador, Jesuits had been denounced as "agents of international communism." Protestants, fewer in number, were also joining Catholics in support of change.

Economic growth and
population increase in
Central America

Following the Second World War, prosperity seemed to be coming to the Central American states. During the 1950s and 1960s the annual rate of growth averaged above 5 percent, and per capita income rose accordingly. But this phenomenon was largely the result of heavy investment in key export commodities such as sugar, coffee, bananas, and cotton, with capital funneled through U.S. aid programs. And while it promoted the growth of a small middle class, it further enriched the oligarchies and left the lot of the common people unchanged. Meanwhile within a thirty-year period the population of the area nearly tripled, rising from 8.6 million to 23 million. Between 1960 and 1989 El Salvador's population grew from 2.5 million to about 5.6 million. In the late 1970s a jump in oil prices coupled with a collapse in the price of agricultural exports brought a severe recession and widespread unemployment. As suffering increased among peasants and workers and no redress was offered, sporadic outbreaks of violence occurred. Worried heads of government readied troops for counter-guerrilla duty and began to ship large sums of money to the safety of foreign banks.

The fall of the Somoza
regime

That protest could reach the stage of popular revolution in the face of severe repression was convincingly demonstrated in 1979 when a ragged band of guerrillas toppled Nicaragua's Anastasio Somoza, one of the most notorious dictators in Latin America. Somoza's father, commanding a national guard trained by United States Marines, had made himself president of Nicaragua in 1937, and his family henceforth treated the country as its private possession, acquiring ownership of practically the whole economy while forcibly stifling opposition.

The Nicaraguan Revolution. Sandanista commandos and elated citizens celebrate the fall of the Somoza government by toppling a huge statue of Anastasio Somoza Garcia, the father of the ousted president, in Managua, the nation's capital.

Somoza's corruption and insatiable greed eventually lost him support of the business community, but effective resistance awaited the rise of the Sandinista National Liberation Front (named after a guerrilla leader who had been treacherously murdered by the elder Somoza) from the ranks of the dispossessed. In August 1978 twenty-five Sandinista commandos stormed the national palace, seized 1,500 hostages, and held them for ransom. By the following July the rebels had enlisted support throughout the country and, after forcing Somoza to flee to Miami, they set up a National Reconstruction Government. Somoza, invited to Paraguay by his friend General Stroessner, indulged his excessive appetites in Asunción until he was assassinated in September 1980.

The victorious Sandinistas installed a junta headed by Daniel Ortega Saavedra as president and representing a coalition of four political parties covering a wide spectrum of the population. Four priests served in the new government, and half of the Nicaraguan Catholic clergy supported the revolution. Sandinismo, the ideology underlying the Nicaraguan revolution, is unique in that it combines elements of nationalism, democratic socialism, Marxism, and Christianity. In embracing the message of "liberation theology" it attracted the poor but alienated Pope John Paul II and conservative clerics. Undertaking to rehabilitate the economy—depleted by Somoza, who had emptied the treasury and left a large foreign debt, and now shattered by war—the junta pursued a program of social, economic, and educational reform. With the help of Cubans and other foreign volunteers they were able to reduce illiteracy from 50 percent to 12 percent within two years.

The Sandinista regime

By 1983 the number of students in Nicaragua's national university had grown from 5,000 to 30,000. Day-care centers were established, free medical service provided, and lands confiscated from the Somoza family distributed to farmers. The economy remained mixed, with only 25 percent of industry state owned. Popular support of the revolutionary regime was demonstrated in a general election held in 1984, in which Sandinista candidates won 65 percent of the votes.

The Latin American policy
of the Reagan
administration

It was the Nicaraguan revolution's misfortune to coincide with the advent of a Washington administration steeped in a Cold War ideology that viewed every popular uprising not as "the struggle of poor and oppressed people to live better" (Mexican President López Portillo's words) but as an incident in a global East-West confrontation fomented by the Soviets, directed by Cuba, and endangering the security of both hemispheres. President Ronald Reagan's Latin American policy, never clearly defined, seemed to rest on three propositions: (1) Central America and the Caribbean Basin, constituting the "back yard" of the United States, were subject to its hegemony; (2) any revolutionary movement that challenged the status quo could not be tolerated; (3) United States interests in the region would take precedence over treaties, conventions, and international law. That gunboat diplomacy could be an instrument of this policy was joltingly demonstrated in October 1983, when the administration sent a large force to attack the tiny Caribbean island of Grenada in order to obliterate a Marxist government that had ties with Cuba. The invasion of Grenada, condemned by most Latin American democracies and by several NATO allies, including Great Britain, heightened an already existent fear of precipitate American action in the future. The CIA's covert activities had included the mining of Nicaragua's harbors, an undeclared act of war that endangered the ships of neutral nations. When Nicaragua sued for damages in the World Court, the United States refused to acknowledge the court's jurisdiction.

The CIA, the contras, and
the battle against the
Sandinistas

Labeling the Sandinista regime a ruthless communist dictatorship (although the proportion of private property in Nicaragua now surpassed that of most Latin American countries), the Reagan Administration sought by rhetoric, economic strangulation, and brute force to overthrow it. A 10,000-strong army of contras (counterrevolutionaries), organized by the CIA and funded from time to time by the U.S. Congress, was stationed in southern Honduras on the Nicaraguan border. Recruited partly from Nicaraguans disillusioned with Sandinista policies and partly from Latin American expatriates in Miami, the contras were led by former officers of Somoza's National Guard. Too weak to engage the Nicaraguan army in pitched battle, they ravaged the countryside destroying crops, schools, and other essential facilities. The drain of the war upon an economy flattened to begin with led the government to curtail social services, intensify restrictive security measures, and, as in the case of Cuba, depend upon the Soviet bloc for survival. Meanwhile at a cost of more than $3 billion in

U.S. aid, Honduras was converted into a military base, without appreciable benefit to the economy of this most backward and poverty-stricken of Central American countries.

Impetus toward ending the war in Nicaragua came from neighboring Latin American states, first in the 1983 Contadora proposal of the foreign ministers of Colombia, Mexico, Panama, and Venezuela, and, more boldly, in a plan presented in 1987 by Costa Rican President Oscar Arias Sanchez, for which he was awarded the Nobel Peace Prize. The Arias formula called for withdrawal of foreign troops, disarming and repatriation of rebel forces, democratization of institutions in Nicaragua, and international monitoring to ensure compliance with its terms. Despite opposition from the Washington administration the plan was approved in August 1987 by the presidents of Costa Rica, Guatemala, Honduras, El Salvador, and Nicaragua, who called upon the United Nations and the Organization of American States to implement it. Two years later the Sandinista government signed an accord with seventeen Nicaraguan opposition parties guaranteeing free and open elections at the local and national levels in February 1990.

The Contadora and Arias peace plans

In those elections—the fairest and most carefully monitored in Latin American history—the Sandinistas lost to the National Opposition Union (UNO), a patchwork coalition of parties ranging from Communists to ultra-Rightists and led by Violeta Barrios de Chamorro, the widow of revered newspaper publisher Pedro Joaquín Chamorro Cardenal, whose assassination in 1978 triggered the anti-Somoza uprising that became the Sandinista revolution. Although Mrs. Chamorro's election to the presidency was pronounced a victory for democracy, it by no means assured the realization of that goal. The lack of a national consensus was evident in the wide diversity within UNO and in the fact that some members of the Chamorro family still sup-

Chamorro's electoral victory over the Sandinistas

Violetta de Chamorro's Inauguration. Former President Danial Ortega adjusts the sash of Chamorro moments before her installation as president of Nicaragua in April 1990. The participation of the leader of the defeated Sandinista government in the proceedings had great symbolic value as Mrs. Chamorro set out to unify the country.

ported the Sandinistas. (Violeta herself had once been a member of the ruling Sandinista junta.) Recognizing the fragility of her new governing coalition in the face of the beleaguered and distrustful contras and a stunned and well-armed Sandinista opposition, President Chamorro took the extraordinary step of inviting General Humberto Ortega Saavedra, the Sandinista defense minister and brother of the former president, to assume command of Nicaragua's military forces under her government in the interest of healing the wounds incurred during Nicaragua's ten-year civil war. Upon Mrs. Chamorro's inauguration, the United States restored full diplomatic relations with Nicaragua, lifted its trade embargo, and prepared to extend economic assistance to the new government.

El Salvador: from revolt to civil war

Like tinder awaiting the match, the ingredients for revolution were present in other Central American countries. Guatemala, where fewer than 5 percent of the population owns 80 percent of the land and where an alliance between the military and oligarchy had crushed every resistance movement, installed a civilian government in 1986. The new president promised land redistribution but with little likelihood of success. Nor was he able to restrain the extra-legal death squads. In tiny El Salvador a coup led by younger army officers in October 1979 expelled the country's hard-line dictator. The course of the Salvadoran revolution has been almost the reverse of the Nicaraguan upheaval. A joint military-civilian junta that came to power with the coup began by announcing a far-reaching reform program for El Salvador, including nationalization of banks and land redistribution. Opposition from large landowners and conservative business interests crippled the reform process and infuriated the radical left, resulting in rapidly escalating outbreaks of violence. The ruling junta allied itself more and more closely with the conservative faction, tolerating right-wing death squads that kidnapped, tortured, and executed their opponents. Battle lines were drawn between the Democratic Revolutionary Front, formed by representatives of some 150 organizations, and the National Guard, a force trained in the same school as Somoza's and fully as brutal. In 1980 the death toll approached or exceeded 10,000, and an equal number of families fled from their homes. In March, Archbishop Oscar Romero, who had protested the shipment of U.S. arms to El Salvador, was assassinated. The following December four American missionary women were murdered in the countryside. In January 1981 two American labor advisers and the head of El Salvador's Agrarian Reform Institute were killed. The United States gave the junta increasing military aid, theoretically contingent upon an improved human-rights record but which continued although no ranking officer was successfully prosecuted. A presidential election in May 1984 was hailed as a victory for democracy when it was won by José Napoleon Duarte, a Christian Democrat who had been chosen twelve years earlier but kept out of office by the military. But Duarte was unable to muster majority support in

José Napoleon Duarte, Hailed as Victor in El Salvador's Presidential Election of May 1984. His Christian Democratic party did not win a majority in the legislature until the following year.

The Terror in El Salvador. Left: A demonstration to commemorate the fifth anniversary of the assassination of Archbishop Oscar Romero, March 25, 1985. Right: A Salvadoran mother identifies the remains of her son who was a death squad victim six years earlier. A total of 70,000 people died in the civil war in El Salvador.

the assembly or to control the expanding army. Exhausted and dying of cancer, in March 1989 he lost by a landslide to the presidential candidate of the National Republican Alliance (ARENA), a militant nationalist party dedicated to "total war" against the insurgents and dominated by Major Roberto D'Aubuisson, notorious for his association with death squads. Unable to destroy the guerrilla forces and sensing that the Revolutionary Front still commanded popular support, the government sought to silence or eliminate every agency—including the Christian clergy—that offered relief to the urban or rural poor. In November 1989 six Jesuit priests, faculty members of a San Salvador university, with their cook and her daughter were dragged from their beds and shot. Although President Alfredo Cristiani admitted that army personnel had perpetrated these murders, the guilty officers have not yet been prosecuted nor was U.S. aid to the regime suspended. With no end in sight, the civil war has deepened the tragedy of a nation immured in poverty. Contained within an area the size of Vermont, El Salvador's population of more than five million exceeds in density that of India, and from soil erosion, deforestation, and the depletion of water supplies the country has lost two-thirds of its cropland during the last forty years. While the United States poured upwards of one million dollars a day into El Salvador during the 1980s, the war took 70,000 lives and made hundreds of thousands homeless refugees.

Relations with the United States have always been of crucial importance to Latin Americans. During their struggles for independence and

The role of the United
States: the Monroe
Doctrine and intervention

throughout the early nineteenth century, they looked to the United States for example and leadership and, in spite of the great differences between the two societies, regarded North Americans with admiration and genuine affection. The Monroe Doctrine of 1823—which flatly stated the opposition of the United States to the erection of any new, or the expansion of any old, colonial regime in the Americas—was generally welcomed as an omen of good will. In reality, the Monroe Doctrine has been applied very selectively. The United States showed no concern when the British took the Falkland Islands from Argentina in 1833, nor when they occupied a slice of Honduras two years later. Without U.S. protest the French bombarded the city of Vera Cruz in 1838, and France, Spain, Germany, and Britain each intervened in Haiti between 1869 and 1877. The Monroe Doctrine was cited in repudiating the rule of Emperor Maximilian in Mexico in 1867, but on very rare occasions has it been invoked by the United States against a European power. Toward the end of the nineteenth century Latin Americans began to feel that whatever protection they received stemmed from the inclination of the stronger power to look upon them as part of its own sphere of interest. Beginning with the Spanish–American War of 1898, the United States intervened frequently in Latin American affairs, sometimes to the detriment of progressive forces. A flagrant example is that of Guatemala, where by mid-century the United Fruit Company had become the largest landowner and also controlled the railroads and a shipping port. When President Jacobo Arbenz proposed to expropriate uncultivated portions of large estates with compensation to the owners—a land reform less radical than that of Mexico—he was denounced as a communist. Prodded by the United Fruit Company, the CIA plotted an invasion, launched from Honduras, which overthrew Arbenz in 1954 and installed one of the conspirators in his place. Since the 1954 coup Guatemala has been ruled by dictators, with attendant violence that has taken the lives of more than 40,000 people. In 1965, four years after the Dominican Republic was freed from the oppressive rule of General Rafael Trujillo by the tyrant's assassination, President Lyndon Johnson induced the Organization of American States to join in a military expedition to the island republic which prevented the duly elected president, Juan Bosch, from taking office. Bosch, a liberal intellectual, was considered unacceptable because some of his supporters were Communists. Not before 1978 was there a peaceful transfer of power between two constitutionally elected Dominican governments. Ironically, on that occasion it was the threat of U.S. interference that prevented a coup.

While urging Latin Americans to hasten their progress toward democracy, the United States has maintained cordial relationships with some highly authoritarian regimes that left vested interests undisturbed. An example is the Republic of Haiti, which shares with the Dominican Republic the island once known as Hispaniola—"the pearl of the Antilles." Generously endowed by nature, Haiti after centuries of defores-

U.S. support of authoritar-
ian regimes: the example
of Haiti

tation, topsoil erosion, relentless population pressure, and misrule has become the poorest state in Latin America, with three-fourths of its children undernourished, an infant mortality rate more than ten times that of the United States, and a population 80 percent illiterate. From 1945 until 1986 Haiti was ruled by the Duvalier family—"Papa Doc" François and "Baby Doc" Jean-Claude—under an exploitative dictatorship that terrorized the population with a private police force outnumbering the regular army. Long supported by the United States because of its anticommunist stand and the favorable terms offered to foreign investors, the Duvalier regime was ousted by a coup, with Washington's assistance, in February 1986. Although Duvalier's departure was greeted with popular rejoicing, his successor was a military junta composed of members schooled in his methods. In the next four-and-one-half years the government would turn over four more times. Only in the late spring of 1990 was a government initiated by election.

Latin Americans have usually responded warmly to friendly overtures, and they are willing to forget past injuries. Mexicans did not long nourish a grudge over the loss of Texas and California. Franklin Roosevelt's Good Neighbor Policy, though not always observed, won gratitude south of the border. President John F. Kennedy's much advertised Alliance for Progress of the 1960s produced such material benefits as new school buildings but was largely a misdirected effort. Marred by a contempt for native institutions and by the assumption that economic development must follow the pattern of Europe and the United States, its effect was to entrench the position of the upper and middle classes rather than improve the conditions of the urban and rural poor. President Jimmy Carter's administration, coming during the high tide of military dictatorships in South America, brought a ray of hope to oppressed people by championing the cause of human rights. Though his administration could not unseat dictators, it was able to nudge them by suspending U.S. aid; in the Dominican Republic in 1978 it thwarted a contemplated military coup. A significant example of the rewards of patient diplomacy during the Carter administration was the settling of a long and bitter dispute over the Panama Canal. Under United States control since 1903, the canal had declined in both economic and strategic importance. The surrounding zone, however, held fourteen military bases, used by the U.S. Southern Command and by the School of the Americas, which trained counterinsurgency forces for Latin American military governments. In September 1977 President Carter and General Omar Torrijos Herrera of Panama signed treaties providing for United States withdrawal from the zone, the gradual phasing-out of the military bases, and the transfer of canal operation to Panama by the end of the century. In their first free election in nearly a decade, Panamanians ratified the treaties by plebiscite in October 1977, and relations with the United States grew more cordial.

Successful U.S. diplomacy: the Panama Canal treaties

Failed U.S. diplomacy: the invasion of Panama

The tone of U.S.-Panamanian relations changed dramatically under the next Washington administration, which attempted to remove Torrijos's successor, General Manuel Antonio Noriega. Noriega, while making Panama a key link in the international drug traffic, had at the same time served the CIA in intelligence operations and in supplying contra forces. When he stopped cooperating in U.S. efforts to destabilize the Sandinista government in Nicaragua, the Reagan Administration pronounced him an enemy and called for his trial in a U.S. court on charges of drug trafficking. Noriega's corrupt and unsavory dealings had brought him into disrepute throughout Latin America, but his defiant stand under siege by the northern colossus made him something of a hero. Although diplomatic and economic pressure alone could not dislodge Noriega, it did paralyze tiny Panama's economy, overwhelmingly dependent on servicing transnational corporations and banks. Embarrassed by its failure to respond effectively to an attempted military coup against Noriega in October 1989 as well as by the fallout from the long-term U.S. support of his activities, the Bush administration organized and executed a massive invasion of Panama in December 1989, employing paratroops, tanks, attack helicopters, and the previously untested Stealth bomber. After American forces had broken into and searched the Nicaraguan embassy and harassed the Vatican embassy where Noriega had taken refuge, the general surrendered and was whisked off to the United States to stand trial on drug-related charges. The victors of an election that had been held in May 1989 and immediately voided by Noriega were installed under the supervision of U.S. military occupation forces to form a democratic government and to resuscitate Panama's devastated economy. Casualties among military personnel during the brief engagement had been remarkably light—twenty American and fifty Panamanian soldiers killed. The number of civilian lives lost, eventually reported by military authorities as around two hundred, evidently exceeded this figure many times over as whole sections of Panama City were reduced to rubble. While many Panamanians welcomed the Americans as deliverers, the invasion, which violated the provisions of several hemispheric treaties including the Panama Canal Treaty of 1977, was condemned by every member of the Organization of American States except the United States and El Salvador.

New signs of independence in Latin America

Signs of growing independence among Latin American countries—not always welcomed by North Americans—may be an augury of beneficial change. The initiative taken by five Central American states—later supported by Peru, Brazil, Argentina, and Uruguay—to end the war in Nicaragua without the lead and even against the will of the United States is a significant example. Spontaneous regional efforts have begun to bypass the Organization of American States, which for many years was hardly more than an adjunct of the U.S. State Department. Exemplifying a new type of leadership is Carlos Andrés Pérez of Venezuela who, after a rocky term of office in the

1970s, was reelected president in December 1988 on a boldly populist platform. Aspiring to the role of a Simón Bolívar, Pérez called for concerted Latin American action to secure debt-repayment terms that would free debtor nations from the "economic totalitarianism" of the International Monetary Fund (IMF).

The destinies of the two American continents are bound to be drawn more closely together. Willing or not, the United States is absorbing Latin American peoples and their cultures. The largest stream of immigration is now from Mexico and the Caribbean Basin. By 1980 the Hispanic community accounted for nearly 15 percent of the United States population, and the numbers will continue to increase.

SELECTED READINGS (See also Selected Readings for Chapter 29)

- *Items so designated are available in paperback editions.*
  Arciniegas, Germán, *Latin America: A Cultural History,* New York, 1967.
  Berryman, Philip, *The Religious Roots of Rebellion: Christians in Central American Revolutions,* Maryknoll, N.Y., 1984.
- Boorstein, Edward, *Allende's Chile: An Inside View,* New York, 1977. By Allende's economic adviser.
  Britton, J. A., *Carleton Beals: A Radical Journalist in Latin America,* Albuquerque, 1987.
- Burns, E. B., *The Poverty of Progress: Latin America in the Nineteenth Century,* Berkeley, 1980.
  Crassweller, R. D., *Perón and the Enigmas of Argentina,* New York, 1987. A vivid and generally sympathetic portrait.
- Cumberland, C. C., *The Meaning of the Mexican Revolution,* New York, 1967.
  DeVylder, Stefan, *Allende's Chile: The Political Economy of the Rise and Fall of the Unidad Popular,* New York, 1976.
- Dobyns, H. F., and P. L. Doughty, *Peru: A Cultural History,* New York, 1977.
  Draper, Theorore, *Castroism, Theory and Practice,* New York, 1965. Highly critical.
  Fiechter, G. A., *Brazil since 1964: Modernization under a Military Regime,* tr. Alan Braley, New York, 1975. A judicious account by a Swiss author.
- González Casanova, Pablo, *Democracy in Mexico,* 2d ed., tr. Danielle Salti, New York, 1972. A brief study by a distinguished Mexican scholar.
- Hodges, D. C., *Intellectual Foundations of the Nicaraguan Revolution,* Austin, Texas, 1986. An analysis of the ideology of *Sandinismo.*
- LaFeber, Walter, *Inevitable Revolution: The U.S. in Central America,* New York, 1983.
- Levine, D. H., *Religion and Politics in Latin America: The Catholic Church in Venezuela and Colombia,* Princeton, 1981.
- Lombardi, J. V., *The Search for Order, the Dream of Progress,* New York, 1982. A stimulating account of the rapid urbanization of Venezuelan society.

MacEoin, Gary, *Revolution Next Door: Latin America in the 1970s,* New York, 1971. A profoundly disturbing view of Latin American realities.

NACLA (North American Congress on Latin America), *Report on the Americas,* New York. Comprehensive, documented, in-depth coverage of current developments, published bimonthly.

Page, J. A., *Perón: A Biography,* New York, 1983.

• ——, and P. H. Smith, *Modern Latin America,* New York, 1984.

Rotberg, R. I., with C. K. Clague, *Haiti: The Politics of Squalor,* Boston, 1971.

• Skidmore, T. E., *Politics in Brazil, 1930–1964: An Experiment in Democracy,* New York, 1969.

• Smith, P. H., *The Church and Politics in Chile: Challenges to Modern Catholicism,* Princeton, 1982. Examines the relationship of the Church to reform movements and to Marxism.

• ——, *Labyrinths of Power: Political Recruitment in Twentieth-Century Mexico,* Princeton, 1979. A careful analysis of the Mexican political power structure.

• Smith, W. S., *The Closest of Enemies,* New York, 1987. The record of a perceptive U.S. diplomat in Cuba.

Thomas, Hugh, *Cuba: The Pursuit of Freedom,* New York, 1971. A monumental, well-documented history of Cuba from 1762 to 1970.

Vásquez, Josefina, and Lorenzo, Meyer, *The United States and Mexico,* Chicago, 1985. Gives the Mexican perspective.

Weinstein, Martin, *Uruguay: The Politics of Failure,* Westport, Conn., 1975. A compact, informative analysis.

• Wiarda, H. J., and M. J. Kryzanek, *The Dominican Republic: A Caribbean Crucible,* Boulder, Colorado, 1982. Views the Dominican Republic as a microcosm of change in the Third World.

SOURCE MATERIALS

• *Amnesty International Report: 1984,* London, 1984.

Hanke, Lewis, *Latin America, a Historical Reader,* Boston, 1974.

• Timmerman, Jacobo, *Prisoner without a Name, Cell without a Number,* New York, 1981.

Chapter 41

NEW POWER RELATIONSHIPS AND A CHANGING WORLD ORDER

Not only the West but also the East is becoming aware of the importance
of all-European cooperation. Slowly, and it is to be hoped not too late,
it will become clear that the cooperation and unification of Europe is
not directed against anyone. In a dangerous epoch and in a strife-divided
world it could, rather, be an example of how nations and states, regardless
of different kinds of governmental and social systems, can achieve prosperity and security by peacefully working together.

—Willy Brandt, *A Peace Policy for Europe*

In April 1945 European men and women, surveying the devastation
that their countries had brought down upon each other during
the past six years, found it all but impossible to imagine their
continent arising from the ashes of total conflict. As in the First World
War, both victors and vanquished had endured punishing destruction.
Between 1914 and 1918, 8 million had died. Now the total was
four times as great. Although France and Britain had suffered fewer
casualties in the Second than in the First World War, loss of life
elsewhere had been cataclysmic. Poland's population was reduced by
20 percent (in part as a consequence of the Nazis' ruthless destruction
of the Jews); losses in the Soviet Union were close to 15 million; in
Germany, they were 5 million.

The costs of war

Across Europe, cities lay in ruins. Hitler had boasted in 1935 that
in ten years Berlin would be transformed so that no one could recognize
it. His prophecy came true, though in a grisly fashion he had not
intended. Industrial and commercial centers in France, the Low Countries, Italy, and in the wasted territories of central Europe and Russia
were largely rubble. Housing was scarce everywhere—in some areas
it was practically nonexistent. Six million houses had been destroyed
in German-occupied Soviet Russia; 93 percent of the homes in Düsseldorf, Germany, were deemed uninhabitable. Food remained in danger-

The extent of the destruction

Berlin, 1945. The rubble from which the German "miracle" was created.

ously short supply, a consequence of the violation of agricultural lands
and people, the lack of farm machinery and fertilizer, and a severe
drought in the summer of 1945. A year later, about 100 million
people in Europe still existed on less than 1,500 calories per day—
not enough to sustain working adults in a healthy state. Food rationing
remained a dreary fact of life everywhere, for without it a large portion
of the Continent's population would have starved to death. The food
shortage was intensified by a general breakdown of transportation
and communication. In the British and American zones of Germany
740 out of 958 major bridges had been destroyed. France had suffered
the loss of about two-thirds of its railway stock and its merchant
fleet. Canals had been bombed; harbors were choked with scuttled
warships. During the winter of 1945–1946, many regions had little
or no fuel for heat and what coal there was (less than half the prewar
supply) could not be transported to those areas most in need of it.

No wonder Europeans were initially dazed by the trauma they
had inflicted upon themselves. The wonder, indeed, was that the period
of trauma lasted such a relatively short time. Ten years later, Europe
had been transformed—though not restored. Two all-important
changes had occurred by then. The first, reflecting an altered balance
of international power, resulted in a dividend continent, the East under
the control of the Soviet Union, the West dominated by the military
and diplomatic presence of the United States. The second change, a
consequence of human determination and favorable economic trends,
produced in the West a buoyant, lively, and creative civilization, more

Ten years later

expansive and up-to-date than even the most optimistic forecaster might have deemed possible in 1945.

The war had been as traumatic and devastating an experience for the peoples of Asia as for the Europeans. China was convulsed with civil war while simultaneously suffering a Japanese military invasion. Japan's armies occupied most of Southeast Asia, toppling the outposts of European imperialism and thereby inadvertently contributing to national independence movements. The war ended with most of Asia in turmoil and imperial Japan not only defeated but seemingly prostrate in the wake of the atomic bombing of Hiroshima and Nagasaki. Nevertheless, Asian nations both old and new showed the same vigor as the Europeans in making rapid recovery. Moreover, not only China and Japan but even smaller Asian countries began to play an important role internationally.

The impact of the war in Asia

1. FOUR DECADES OF SOVIET-AMERICAN RIVALRY

During the decade after the Second World War the world of nations assumed a bipolar character, in large measure the result of mutual mistrust and increasing hostility between the Soviet Union and the United States. The war had left these two nations the most powerful on earth. Germany, Italy, and Japan were destined for a time to play a subordinate international role as a consequence of their defeat. Britain and France possessed neither populations nor resources great enough to qualify as "superpowers." China, the remaining major victor in the conflict, was soon thereafter overwhelmed by a revolution that turned that nation in upon itself. Hence the dominance of the United States and the Soviet Union, both vying for world supremacy and both striving to draw the states of Europe into their orbits.

A bipolar world

The Soviet Union had insisted during the negotiations at Teheran and Yalta that it had a legitimate claim to hegemony over eastern Europe, a claim that Western leaders willingly acknowledged. When visiting Moscow in 1944, Churchill and Stalin had bargained like two Old World power brokers over the fate of several supposedly free nations. Churchill proposed a 90 percent preponderance of Soviet influence in Rumania, countered by 90 percent for the West in Greece; Yugoslavia, 50–50; and so on. Stalin, however, increasingly mistrustful of Western leadership, believed that bargains with the West, no matter how attractive they might appear on paper, were really worth little. "Churchill," he remarked, "is the kind who, if you don't watch him, will slip a kopek out of your pocket. . . . Roosevelt . . . dips in his hands only for bigger coins." Stalin's authoritarian domestic regime was motivated by a siege mentality that saw almost everyone as an enemy or, at best, a threat. Not surprisingly, his foreign policy was dictated by that same state of mind.

Yet Stalin's anti-Western policy was based upon more than personal

Winston Churchill Denounces Soviet Tyranny. In a speech at Fulton, Missouri, in March 1946, Churchill coined the phrase "iron curtain" to characterize the Soviets' partitioning of eastern from western Europe.

The United States after the war

paranoia. It was a reflection of traditional fears that had characterized Russia's attitudes toward its European neighbors for centuries, of ambivalences toward Western ways that had marked the regime of Peter the Great, for example, at the beginning of the eighteenth century, and of Alexander III at the end of the nineteenth. Stalin's mistrust of the United States in particular stemmed as well from the prewar years when the Americans had never hesitated to express their antagonism to Stalinist communism. U.S. mistrust was matched by escalating fear on the part of Russia's leaders of American-inspired military and economic encirclement.

From the standpoint of economic power, the United States far outdistanced the other nations of the world. Since 1939 Americans had doubled their national income and quadrupled their savings. Though they constituted only 7 percent of the world's population, they enjoyed over 30 percent of the world's estimated income. For the first time in its history the United States was in a position to be the economic and military arbiter of at least half the earth. The United States controlled both the Atlantic and Pacific Oceans, policed the Mediterranean, and shaped the development of international policy in western Europe. And until 1949, America had a monopoly of death-dealing atomic weapons.

Russia's strengths and weaknesses

Soviet Russia emerged from the Second World War as the second-strongest power on earth. Though its navy was small, its land army and possibly its air force by 1948 were the largest in the world. Soviet population was climbing rapidly toward 200 million, and this in spite of the loss of 7 million soldiers and about 8 million civilians during the war. In mineral wealth and petroleum resources Russia's position compared favorably with that of the richest countries. On the other hand, its industrial machine had been badly crippled by the war. No fewer than 1,700 Russian cities and towns had been totally destroyed along with 40,000 miles of railway and 31,000 factories. Stalin declared in 1946 that it would probably require at least six years to repair the damage and rebuild the devastated areas.

The Soviet Union in eastern Europe

In part because of the need to recoup their enormous industrial losses, the Soviets were particularly determined to maintain political, economic, and military control of those countries in eastern Europe which they had liberated from Nazi control. The Russians employed diplomatic pressure, political infiltration, and military terrorism to establish "people's republics" in eastern Europe sympathetic to the Soviet regime. In country after country the process repeated itself: at first, all-party coalition governments from which only fascists were excluded; then further coalitions, in which communists predominated; and finally, one-party states. By 1948, governments that owed allegiance to Moscow were established in Poland, Hungary, Rumania, Bulgaria, and Czechoslovakia. The nations of eastern Europe did not all succumb without a struggle. Greece, which the Russians wished to include within their sphere of influence, was torn by civil war

See color map of Europe facing page 871

until 1949, when with Western aid its monarchy was restored. A direct challenge to the Yalta guarantee of free, democratic elections occurred in Czechoslovakia, where in 1948 the Soviets crushed the coalition government of liberal leaders Eduard Beneš and Jan Masaryk.

The most important check the Soviets received at this time to their campaign for eastern European hegemony also occurred in 1948, when the Yugoslavian government of the wartime hero Marshal Tito declared its independence of Moscow and its determination to steer a course unallied to either East or West. Tito, the only satellite communist leader who had risen to power on his own and not as a Soviet puppet, possessed political authority rooted within his own country that secured his position from reprisals once he had established Yugoslavia's freedom from Soviet hegemony. Events in Czechoslovakia and Yugoslavia inspired a series of Soviet-directed purges within the political hierarchies of the various satellite governments, a measure of the degree to which Stalin remained prey to the fear of opposition.

The United States countered these moves with massive programs of economic and military aid to western Europe. In 1947, President Truman proclaimed the Truman Doctrine, which provided assistance programs to prevent further communist infiltration into the governments of Greece and Turkey. The following year, the Marshall Plan, named for Secretary of State George Marshall who first proposed it, provided funds for the reconstruction of western European industry. The plan was notable in two respects: first, it represented an attempt by the United States to restore the strength of its most serious economic competitors, and of its former enemy Germany, in the belief that an economically independent Europe would be less likely to fall prey to Soviet domination. Second, it relied upon a willingness on the part of the western European nations to coordinate their economic efforts, substituting, at least to some degree, cooperation for competition.

At the same time, the United States moved to shore up the military defenses of the West. In April 1949, a group of representatives of North Atlantic states together with Canada and the United States signed an agreement providing for the establishment of the North Atlantic Treaty Organization (NATO). Subsequently Greece, Turkey, and West Germany were added as members. The treaty declared that an armed attack against any one of the signatory parties would be regarded as an attack against all, and that they would combine their armed strength to whatever extent necessary to repel the aggressor. The joint military command, or NATO army, established in 1950, was increased from thirty to fifty divisions in 1953, with a rearmed West Germany contributing twelve of the divisions.

The Russians reacted with understandable alarm to the determination of the United States to strengthen western Europe economically and militarily. They organized an international political arm, the Cominform, responsible for the coordination of worldwide communist policy

Crises in Berlin. Left: The Berlin Airlift, 1948. For fifteen months the United States, Britain, and France airlifted over two million tons of supplies into West Berlin, around which the Russians had imposed a land blockade. Right: The Berlin Wall, 1961. Thirteen years after the blockade, the East German government constructed a wall between East and West Berlin to stop the flow of escapees to the West.

and programs. In addition the Soviets rejected an original offer of Marshall Plan aid, and instead organized an eastern European counterpart for economic recovery, the Council for Mutual Economic Assistance. They responded to NATO with the establishment of military alliances, confirmed by the Warsaw Pact of 1955. This agreement set up a joint armed forces command among its signatories, and more important, authorized the continued stationing of Russian troops in Albania, Czechoslovakia, Hungary, Poland, Rumania, and the eastern portion of Germany, which had remained under Soviet domination since the end of the war.

Focus on Germany

Germany was, in fact, the focal point of East-West tensions during these years. After the war, the Russians had continued to insist on $10 billion worth of reparations from Germany in the form of industrial production. Although the Soviets' desperate economic condition and fear of a revived Germany played a role in this posture, Britain and the United States read this demand as a reflection of a Soviet desire to keep Germany weak and therefore susceptible to political instability—specifically, to the spread of communism.

By 1946 the joint administration of Germany by the four former

Allied powers had collapsed. The Soviet Union remained in control of its satellite, which eventually became the nominally independent German Democratic Republic (East Germany), while the Western powers continued to support the industrial recovery of the area under their control—in its turn to emerge as the Federal Republic of Germany (West Germany). A crisis arose in 1948 when, in retaliation for the reunification of the western zones of control under one authority, the Russians closed down road and rail access from the west to Berlin. Berlin, though within the territory of East Germany, was administered by all four powers. The Western powers countered with an airlift of food and other necessary supplies which prevented the collapse of the city into Soviet hands. After almost a year the Russians lifted the blockade. For many years to come, however, Berlin was to remain one of the hottest spots in the ongoing "Cold War," as it came to be called, between Russia and the West. The city symbolized opposition to a divided Germany, as well as the determination of the Western powers to ensure that nation's economic recovery.

The Berlin blockade

The most serious clash between communist and noncommunist forces in the first postwar decade occurred not in Europe but in Korea. At the close of the Second World War, U.S. troops remained in the peninsula south of the thirty-eighth parallel and Russian troops were stationed in the north. Japan had signed treaties providing that Korea, under Japanese rule since 1910, would become an independent and united country, and a United Nations–sponsored plan called for holding free nationwide elections. The U.S. government, which previously had shown little interest in Korea, now viewed it as vital to the policy of containing Soviet Russia. President Harry Truman believed that South Koreans were eager for democracy and that a pro-American state created for them would soon attract the northerners also. Actually there were points of dissension among the peoples of the peninsula, and intervention by the two superpowers turned a potential civil war into a major international conflict. To counter American moves in the south the Russians established a communist republic in the north which, with Soviet prompting, sent troops across the thirty-eighth parallel to invade the south in June 1950. By taking advantage of a temporary Russian boycott of the United Nations, the United States was able to secure U.N. approval of a counterattack with forces predominantly American and commanded by General Douglas MacArthur. The war was fought savagely, with tremendous destruction of lives and property, and it came close to turning into a third world war in November 1950 when the People's Republic of China sent troops to help the North Koreans and General MacArthur contemplated using atomic weapons against them, a proposal rejected by President Truman, who recalled the general from his command. After dragging on for three years the stalemated war ended with a truce but no peace treaty in June 1953, leaving the country artificially divided and temporarily ruined.

The Korean Conflict

*The Cold War: U.S.
attitudes*

Russian attitudes

Stalinism

After Stalin

The tensions that produced the Cold War were the result of a set of misconceptions on both sides. Americans, who had been persuaded by wartime government propaganda to admire the Russians as stalwart anti-fascists, were naïvely disillusioned when they discovered that their erstwhile allies were in fact not democrats. Concerned about the economic weakness throughout postwar western Europe, U.S. leaders allowed themselves to believe that the Russians were hatching a vast plan to take advantage of that weakness by establishing communist regimes throughout the West, as they had in the East.

Scholars have recently argued convincingly that there was no grand Soviet strategy of this sort. The Russians were not willing to undertake any such campaign, primarily because they were economically and militarily incapable of doing so. However, since the Soviets had long feared encirclement by hostile capitalist powers, they saw the Truman and Marshall programs as a direct form of neoimperialism, an American plot to subject western Europe to the economic hegemony of the United States. Stalin found it useful to orchestrate his propaganda to this theme. As a result of wartime destruction, he needed to convince the Russian people that they must undergo a further series of rugged Five-Year Plans stressing the production of heavy industrial materials rather than consumer goods. He could demand sacrifices more convincingly if he could point to an international anti-Russian conspiracy.

Stalin himself remained deeply suspicious, not only of the West, but of any power or personality perceived by him as a threat to his dictatorial rule. He convened neither Central Committee nor party congress. He relied on a shrinking number of political henchmen to carry out the business of government, among them: Vyacheslav Molotov, the Soviet foreign minister; Lavrenty Beria, head of the powerful secret police; and Andrei Zhdanov, secretary of the party central committee. The latter was charged with the task of devising a new communist gospel, one prescribed by Stalin, which tended to ignore the earlier doctrines of Marx, Engels, and Lenin, and amounted to little more than an apologia for Stalin's repressive personal despotism. Party propaganda preached Soviet superiority to the West. Writers and artists were attacked for imitating their Western counterparts. Economists were taken to task for suggesting that European industry might succeed in recovering from the damages it had sustained. In the realm of science, accepted genetic theory was supplanted by that of the Russian Trofim Lysenko, whose work implied the inheritance of acquired characteristics; Einstein was vilified; and Freud was pronounced a decadent charlatan.

Only with Stalin's death in 1953 did this relentless barrage of anti-Western propaganda begin to abate somewhat. Although relations between East and West remained wary, tensions eased considerably during the late 1950s and 1960s. The United States, it is true, continued to adhere to a policy of Soviet "containment," seeking as allies those most willing to oppose by military force, if necessary, the spread of international communism. By the mid-1950s, however, western European nations had begun to wonder whether U.S. intervention in their affairs might not, in fact, represent as much an American power play as an attempt to protect the West from Soviet aggression. American claims to the role of "protector of the free world" began to sound hollow, particularly after U.S. Secretary of State John Foster Dulles negotiated a diplomatic and military understanding with the aging Spanish dictator Francisco Franco in 1955.

In the Soviet Union, a change of direction was signaled by the accession to power in that same year of Nikita Khrushchev (1894–1971). Khrushchev possessed a kind of earthy directness which, despite his hostility to the West, nevertheless helped for a time to ease tensions. Abandoning the seclusion of the Kremlin, where Stalin had immured himself, he traveled throughout the world. On visits to the United States in 1958 and 1960 he traded quips with Iowa farmers and was entertained at Disneyland. Attending a meeting of the United Nations in New York, he underscored his disagreement with the speaker by banging his desk with his shoe.

As testimony to his desire to reduce international conflict, Khrushchev soon agreed to the first of a series of summit meetings with the leaders of Britain, France, and the United States. This new Soviet determination to lower international tensions grew out of Khrushchev's need to consolidate his regime at home and to prevent the threatened crumbling of the communist bloc in eastern Europe. The harsh demands of the Stalin regime had generated discontent among the Russian people. Dissenters, their voices no longer silenced by the Stalinist police, began to demand a shift from the production of heavy machinery and armaments to the manufacture of consumer goods, and, in the arts, a return to at least a measure of intellectual freedom of expression. Their voices were heard in essays and in novels such as Ilya Ehrenburg's *The Thaw* (1954), which contributed its name to the period. The Russian leadership followed a tricky and not always successful line, on the one hand denouncing the excesses of the Stalinist regime and the "cult of personality" that Stalin had imposed upon his nation; on the other, as Stalin's heirs, loosening only partially their grip on the lives of their countrymen and women. When, in 1956, Khrushchev delivered a secret speech to the Communist party's twentieth congress on the crimes of the Stalin regime, he did so by describing Stalin himself as a bungler and, ultimately, a madman, but at the same time by defending the system of government that Stalin had created.

Meanwhile, throughout the other communist states, growing resentment of Soviet demands for rapid industrialization and collectivization generated arguments for an easing of the restrictions that Stalinism had imposed. In response to these pressures the Soviet leaders altered their economic goals and began preaching that there was more than one road to socialism. The Soviet Union's new posture toward its

Nikita Khrushchev, Premier (1958–1964) and First Secretary of the Communist Party (1956–1964) of the Soviet Union, Addressing the United Nations in 1958

Khrushchev's goals and policies

Challenges in eastern Europe: Poland and Hungary

client states in eastern Europe received its severest test in 1956 when
Poland and Hungary demanded greater autonomy in the management
of their domestic affairs. In Poland, the government at first responded
to major strikes with military repression and then with a promise of
liberalization. The anti-Stalinist Polish leader Wladyslaw Gomulka
was able to win Soviet permission for his country to pursue its own
"ways of socialist development" by pledging Poland's continued loyalty to the terms of the Warsaw Pact. Events in Hungary produced
a different result. There, protests against Stalinist policies developed
into a much broader anti-communist struggle. If the Russians were
prepared to entertain a liberalization of domestic policy, they would
not tolerate a repudiation of the Warsaw Pact. On November 4, 1956,
Russian troops occupied Budapest; leaders of the Hungarian liberation
were taken prisoner and executed.

Despite these events, Khrushchev did not abandon his policy of
"peaceful coexistence" with the West. Though he did not renounce
his ultimate belief in the triumph of communism, he argued that
victory could be achieved by other than military means. Yet Soviet
leaders remained unyielding in their determination to reduce any possible German military threat to eastern Europe. They continued to
nurture the fear that Germany might launch a new war, abetted by
its capitalist allies. For this reason, they staunchly opposed the reunification of the country. In 1961 the East German government built a
high wall separating the two sectors of Berlin in order to cut off the
escape of thousands of East Germans to West Berlin and thence to
western Germany. The wall remained as a symbol of Soviet determination to prevent the formation of a united Germany.

Khruschchev eventually fell prey to political rivals and was deposed

The limits of coexistence:
The Berlin Wall

*The Occupation of Czech-
oslovakia.* In 1968 the
liberalized regime of
Alexander Dubček was
suppressed by the Sovi-
ets. The violent re-
sponse by the citizens
was put down by mili-
tary force.

in 1964, with the reins of Soviet power passing to Alexei Kosygin (1904–1980) as premier and Leonid Brezhnev (1906–1982) as secretary of the Communist party. The Soviets continued to hold the governments of eastern Europe in check. In 1968 they sent troops into Czechoslovakia after the leadership there had attempted to meet criticisms by decentralizing the administration, democratizing the Communist party, and permitting a brief flowering of intellectual life.

The Czech revolt of 1968

Throughout the 1960s and 1970s, politicians in western Europe responded in various ways to the fact of their divided continent. Following the events in Hungary and Czechoslovakia, leaders of Communist parties in France, Italy, and elsewhere recognized a need to separate themselves from Moscow's repressive line if they were to retain credibility with their memberships or attain political power. In 1975 the word "Eurocommunism" appeared for the first time in print. Eurocommunists declared their independence of Soviet foreign policy, while proclaiming their continuing adherence to the principles first espoused by Marx and Engels. The practice of yielding to Moscow on matters of foreign policy, so characteristic of western European Communist parties from the 1920s to the 1950s, was henceforth abandoned. "We, the communists of today," the Spanish leader Santiago Carillo remarked, "have no international discipline imposed upon us. What unites us today are the bonds of affinity, based on the theory of scientific socialism." Eurocommunists showed a new interest in participating as partners in coalition governments with noncommunist parties of the Left which they had heretofore shunned. In a joint statement in 1975, the French and Italian communists proclaimed that "socialism is democracy realized in the most complete manner, and the prerequisite in achieving this goal is a continuous democratization of economic, political and social life." The political division of Europe into Eastern and Western camps had compelled Western communists to cut their close ties to the Soviet Union. Moscow had been to them what Rome was to Catholic Christendom, Carillo declared. No longer, however. The great divide had fragmented an international movement into a collection of polycentric political entities.

Eurocommunism and independence from Soviet policy

Tensions between East and West, which eased during the 1960s and 1970s, arose once more in the next decade, in response to the Soviet Union's meddling in Poland's internal affairs. In 1980, calling their movement "Solidarity," Polish workers had organized strikes which brought the government of the country to a standstill. The strikers were objecting to working conditions imposed by the government to combat a severe economic crisis which had produced high prices. Again the Russians assisted a puppet military regime in reimposing authoritarian rule. Though the Soviet Union did not intervene directly, the implied threat that it might do so, reinforced by the presence of increasing numbers of Russian troops near the Polish border, reemphasized Soviet unwillingness to permit its eastern European neighbors autonomy over their internal affairs.

The "Solidarity" movement and the renewal of East-West tensions

Defiance in Poland. Thousands of striking workers take part in religious services in the Lenin Shipyards in Gdansk on August 24, 1980. This was the scene of the first in a series of strikes that paralyzed an already troubled economic and political system and challenged Soviet domination of Polish governmental policy.

Gorbachev, the new self-criticism and bureaucratic resistance

With the accession to the party leadership of Mikhail Gorbachev in 1985, Soviet policy began to make a dramatic break with the patterns of past leadership. In his mid-fifties, Gorbachev was significantly younger than his immediate predecessors and therefore, perhaps, less prey to the habits of mind that had shaped Soviet domestic and foreign affairs. Frankly critical of aspects of repressive communist society and its sluggish economy, Gorbachev did not hesitate to voice those criticisms openly. He proclaimed a policy of freeing domestic dissidents, and he allowed those released to engage in political activity. He expressed a more tolerant attitude than past Soviet leaders toward deviant political behavior within the satellite states. And he advocated a degree of economic reorganization in the face of the Soviet Union's continuingly disappointing industrial performance.

Gorbachev and the revision of Soviet foreign policy

The most startling policy change inaugurated by Gorbachev was in the Soviet Union's foreign relations. He stressed the theme of a common European home to which the USSR as well as noncommunist states belonged. Abandoning Russia's traditional stance of confrontation with the West, he offered cooperation with the United States and its allies. He persuaded President Ronald Reagan—who had branded the Soviet Union as the "Evil Empire"—to meet with him and accept a treaty calling for the mutual removal of short- and intermediate-range missiles from European soil. As a step toward the reduction of armaments in the late 1980s he ordered a unilateral cutback of Soviet military forces and the withdrawal of 5,000 tanks from Europe, signaling his belief that the Cold War was obsolete and forcing a reappraisal of power relationships both within and outside Europe.

Gorbachev's policies of *glasnost* ("openness") and *perestroika* ("restructuring") marked an extraordinary turning point in the history of the Soviet Union. During 1989, the country experienced its first competitive elections and witnessed the convening of its first working parliament in seventy years. In February 1990 Gorbachev persuaded the Communist party leadership to accept a multi-party political system. A month later, following a close vote of approval by the Congress of People's Deputies, he assumed new powers as president, enabling him to propose legislation, negotiate treaties, veto bills, and appoint ministers. These new powers reflected the increased role of the presidency at a time when the chairmanship of the Communist party, a position still held by Gorbachev, was waning.

Mikhail Gorbachev, General Secretary of the Central Committee of the Communist Party of the Soviet Union, 1985– and President, 1990–

These sweeping changes have not yet solved the Soviet Union's economic problems, nor have they visibly improved the country's standard of living. In a poll published in early 1990, nearly half of those questioned replied that daily existence was harsher than in 1985. An unrealistic price structure that bears little relation to costs and is wasteful of resources has been only partially reformed. Food rationing continues and housing is scarce.

An equal threat to Soviet stability lies in the increasing unwillingness of several of the nation's fifteen disparate republics to remain yoked to a central state. Lenin once referred to the tsarist empire as a "prison of nations," that is, a collection of varied national entities bound against their will to an imperialist overlord. The government of the USSR under Stalin and his successors ensured the continuing close confinement of republics as different from one another—and as independently nationalistic—as Georgia, Armenia, Azerbaijan, Uzbekistan, Moldavia, and the Ukraine in the south and Lithuania, Latvia, and Estonia in the north. *Perestroika* has now encouraged ethnic and generational independence movements in Georgia and Azerbaijan. In the latter case, unrest required the dispatch of 17,000 Soviet troops to restore order in 1989, after Azerbaijani Muslims rioted in support of links with fundamentalist Iran. The most serious challenge to Soviet central authority arose in Lithuania, where in March 1990 a freely elected parliament—the first in fifty years—voted to sever ties with Moscow. Gorbachev responded to this evidence of serious destabilization by seeking power to suspend the republic's legislature. While refraining from military action he applied economic pressure to induce Lithuania to revoke or at least delay its declaration of independence.

More dramatic than events within the Soviet Union has been the rapid collapse of the communist-controlled governments of eastern Europe, and with that collapse the virtual disappearance of Stalin's "iron curtain." In Poland, following further demonstrations by Solidarity supporters, the Communist party agreed in March 1989 to relinquish its constitutionally guaranteed monopoly of power. After

President Václav Havel of Czechoslovakia. An acclaimed writer, Havel was interned in 1979 as a dissident for his outspoken liberal views. In 1989 he was elected president in the first popular election since the 1930s.

national elections were held, a coalition government was eventually formed under the prime ministership of Solidarity editor Tadeusz Mazowieki. In December 1990 Lech Walesa, leader of Solidarity from its earliest days, was elected president of the republic by an overwhelming majority. Czechoslovak demonstrations in late 1988, marking the twentieth anniversary of the 1968 uprising and subsequent Soviet invasion, lit another fuse that eventually resulted in the explosion of communist rule. A year later the reform movement "Civic Forum" inspired a general strike which led to the collapse of the ruling government and the eventual elevation to the presidency of Václav Havel, a playwright and former political prisoner. At the same time, Alexander Dubček, leader of the abortive reform movement of 1968, was named leader of the new Federal Assembly. Elsewhere in eastern Europe events followed much the same pattern. By spring 1990 noncommunist politicians were either in power or in a position to challenge entrenched regimes in Bulgaria, Hungary, and Rumania. Only in the last-named country was the change accompanied by violence. There the despotic ruler Nicolae Ceausescu was executed along with his wife, after they had been driven from power by a "National Salvation Front" coalition.

Most astonishing was the rapidity of changes in East Germany. Increasingly effective demonstrations in 1989, protesting the inability of East Germans to move freely outside their country, were symptomatic of the degree to which the government under President Erich Honecker was losing control of events. When Gorbachev visited East Berlin in October 1989 to speak at the celebrations marking the fortieth

The dismantling of the Berlin Wall

Berlin Reborn. Left: A protester assaults the Berlin Wall with a sledge hammer under the gaze of East German border guards in November 1989. Right: At this December 1989 celebration of the removal of barriers between East and West Berlin, school children from both East and West raise their flags.

anniversary of the founding of the German Democratic Republic (East Germany), he warned Honecker that reforms were essential to the survival of his government. As more and more East Germans fled to the West across the border between Hungary and Austria, the Honecker government faltered at first and then announced the action that more than any other signaled the end of the European postwar era: the dismantling of the Berlin Wall. Honecker was deposed and arrested for corruption and abuse of office, his government replaced by a reformist coalition which promised free elections for spring 1990.

As celebrants poured jubilantly across the now-open border between East and West, politicians on both sides pondered with some apprehension a world that in so short a time had changed so completely. For over forty years government leaders had accustomed themselves to geopolitical habits of mind dictated by the so-called Cold War. Now the war appeared to be over, and with it the assumptions that had grown into apparent certainties. One of the most ingrained of those assumptions was that Germany would remain divided. Yet by March 1990 politicians from both German republics, led by West German chancellor Helmut Kohl, were prepared to declare that a reunited Germany was only a matter of time. The time came more quickly than anyone anticipated. Supported by both Washington and Moscow—as Gorbachev in discarding Soviet Cold War strategy even agreed to let Germany remain a member of NATO—reunification was formally consummated on October 3, 1990. General elections in December gave a resounding victory in both sections to Chancellor Kohl's conservative Christian Democratic party. Though a dramatic achievement, reunification brought formidable problems, such as reviving East Germany's crippled economy and determining the future direction of foreign policy. That the new Germany would be Europe's economic and political leader was beyond question.

2. EUROPEAN ECONOMIC RENAISSANCE AND MOVEMENT TOWARD INTEGRATION

Western Europeans, who likened their successful postwar economic recovery to a "miracle," ignored the degree to which human agencies and predictable economic forces precipitated the change. First, the war had encouraged a variety of technological innovations with direct and important peacetime applications: improved communications (the invention of radar, for example), the manufacture of synthetic materials, the increasing use of aluminum and alloy steels, and advances in the techniques of prefabrication. Secondly, nations had added significantly to the sum of their productive capital during the war. In Britain the total was in excess of one and one-half billion pounds and it was even greater in West Germany. Despite the apparent wartime devastation, capital invested in plants that were easily impaired but difficult to destroy completely survived to sustain a postwar boom. This boom

The prospect of a new European political reality and a united Germany

Chancellor Helmut Kohl of the Federal Republic of Germany. As chancellor of West Germany Kohl successfully orchestrated the union of East and West Germany in October 1990.

was fueled by a third set of factors: the continued buoyancy of consumer demand and the consequent high level of employment throughout the 1950s and 1960s. These in turn encouraged continued capital investment and technological innovation. Finally, brisk foreign demand for goods convinced Europeans of the need to remove obstacles to international trade and payments. This fortuitous combination of circumstances made possible a remarkable period of dynamic economic growth.

*Movement toward
"mixed" economies*

Governments resorted to a variety of devices to encourage economic expansion: West Germany provided tax breaks to encourage business investment; Britain and Italy offered investment allowances to their steel and petroleum industries. Virtually all of western Europe experimented with the nationalization of industry and services in an effort to enhance efficiency and productivity. The result was a series of "mixed" economies combining public and private ownership. France, Britain, Italy, and Austria took the lead in the move toward state-controlled enterprise. In France, where public ownership was already well advanced in the 1930s, railways, electricity and gas, banking, radio and television, and a large segment of the automobile industry were brought under state management. In Britain, the list was equally long: coal and utilities; road, railroad, and air transport; and banking. Though nationalization was less common in West Germany, the railway system—state-owned since the late nineteenth century; some electrical, chemical, and metallurgical concerns; and the Volkswagen company—the remains of Hitler's attempt to produce a "people's car"— were all in state hands, though the latter was largely returned to the private sector in 1963.

Economic growth rates

These government policies and programs contributed to astonishing growth rates. Between 1945 and 1963 the average yearly growth of Gross Domestic Product (Gross National Product minus income received from abroad) in West Germany was 7.6 percent; in Austria, 5.8 percent; in Italy, 6 percent; in Holland, 4.7 percent; and so on. This was a remarkable reversal of the economic patterns of an interwar period which had been beset by slack demand, overproduction, and insufficient investment. In the face of reconstruction and recovery, production facilities were hard pressed to keep up with soaring demand.

West German resurgence

West Germany's recovery was particularly noteworthy. Production increased sixfold between 1948 and 1964. Unemployment fell to record lows, reaching 0.4 percent in 1965, when there were six jobs for every unemployed person. Though prices rose initially, their subsequent leveling off provided an opportunity for most citizens to participate in a domestic buying spree that caused production to soar. In the 1950s, an average of half a million housing units were constructed annually to accommodate both those whose homes had been destroyed and an influx of new resident-refugees from East Germany and eastern Europe, and transient workers from Italy, Spain, Greece, and elsewhere who were attracted by West Germany's labor demands.

The reasons for this remarkable economic renaissance were diverse.

Certainly the presence of an army of highly skilled workers and a long tradition of industrial know-how counted for much. Other factors included: (1) the split from East Germany, which meant that the powerful and generally reactionary Junker class was no longer able to brake progress as it had since the mid-nineteenth century; (2) the crippling of much of Germany's industrial plant, entailing the opportunity to incorporate up-to-date equipment and techniques into rebuilt factories; and (3) the fact that initially West Germany was expressly forbidden by the occupying powers to spend money on defense.

In France the major problem following the war centered on a perceived need to modernize the nation's industries, many of which remained small family enterprises resistant to technological change. Under the direction of a minister for planning, Jean Monnet, a special office—the General Commissariat for Planning—was established to initiate and execute a program for national economic recovery. Using money provided by the Marshall Plan, the French government played a direct and active role in the revival and reform, contributing not only capital but expert advice, and facilitating shifts in the national labor pool to place workers where they were most needed. The plan gave priority to basic industries, with the result that the amount of electricity produced doubled, the steel industry was thoroughly modernized, and the French railway system became the fastest and most efficient on the Continent. Other sectors of the economy tended to stagnate, however, while agriculture remained in the hands of a peasant class loathe to avail itself of government incentives intended to foster productivity through mechanization. Nevertheless, the French Gross National Product increased at the very creditable rate of about 5 percent per year in the 1950s.

Italy's industrial "miracle" was even more impressive than that of

Explanations for West Germany's economic renaissance

France's program of national economic recovery

An Italian Washing-Machine Factory. Consumer goods once considered luxuries became commonly accepted necessities in postwar Europe.

West Germany and France, given the woeful state of the nation's economy immediately following the war. Stimulated by infusions of capital from the government and from the Marshall Plan, Italian companies soon began to compete with other European international giants as the products of Olivetti, Fiat, and Pirelli became familiar in households across the world to an extent that no Italian goods had in the past. Electric power production—particularly important in Italy because of its lack of coal—had by 1953 increased 100 percent over that in 1938. By 1954 real wages were 50 percent higher than they had been in 1938. Yet Italy's success was marred by the enduring poverty of the country's southern regions, where illiteracy remained high and land continued to be held by a few rich families.

Elsewhere on the Continent, nations with little in common in terms of political traditions or industrial patterns all shared in the general prosperity. Spain's economy changed markedly in the late 1950s, when a combination of rising foreign investment and the lifting of government controls spurred higher levels of production. Tourism was for Spain, as for all European countries, an increasingly important industry. Seventeen million visitors came to Spain in 1966, making it second only to Italy as a tourist attraction. Holland, Belgium, Austria, Greece, and the Scandinavian countries all enjoyed booms in the late 1950s. Though each country succeeded in increasing its GNP significantly, however, there remained marked differences in the levels of prosperity across the Continent. The per capita GNP in Sweden, for example, was almost ten times that of Turkey.

Britain throughout remained a special case. Although it shared in the economic prosperity of the postwar years, it did so to a lesser extent than other European countries. Britain was burdened with obsolete factories and techniques, the legacy of its early industrialization. It was plagued as well by a series of balance-of-payments crises precipitated by an inability to sell more goods abroad than it imported. Industrial leadership suffered from an entrepreneurial failure of nerve. Neither government nor private investors were willing to gamble on the future of British industry in the way their continental counterparts did. Because shipbuilders refused to invest in new productive capacity, for example, tonnage built fell from 1.2 million in 1949 to 1 million in 1965, while in the same period it increased in Japan from 0.1 to 5 million. Finally, the country's worldwide defense commitments, its unwillingness to surrender its obligations to colonies and former colonies overseas, its position as an island dependent to a great degree upon imports in order to survive—in short its history and its geography—all helped dictate its economic position in the postwar world.

The western European renaissance was achieved by more than the efforts of individual nations. From the late 1940s on, they took steps to bind themselves together as an effective economic third force between the superpowers. In 1951 a European coal and steel community

Heating Fuel Shortage in Great Britain. This scene of British householders queuing for coal during the severely cold winter of 1948 provides a measure of the degree to which "winners" as well as "losers" suffered in the immediate aftermath of the Second World War.

was created, which placed the management of those industries in France, West Germany, Belgium, Holland and Luxembourg (a small principality lying between the Low Countries and France) under a joint High Authority. Consisting of representative experts from each of the participating countries, the Authority possessed the power to regulate prices, to increase or limit production, and to impose administrative fees. Britain declared itself unwilling to participate, fearing the effects of European economic union on its declining coal industry and on its relationship with long-time trading partners such as Australia, New Zealand, and Canada.

During the mid-1950s, further steps toward supernational economic integration were taken—the establishment of EURATOM, for example, a research organization in the field of nuclear development—culminating in 1957 with the founding of the European Economic Community, or Common Market. The EEC declared its goals to be the abolition of all trade barriers between the initial six members: France, West Germany, Italy, Belgium, Holland, and Luxembourg. In addition, the organization pledged itself to common external tariffs, the free movement of labor and capital, and the establishment of uniform wage structures and social security systems, so as to foster similar working conditions throughout the EEC. A commission with headquarters in Brussels was charged with the administration of this ambitious program.

Despite inevitable difficulties, particularly in the area of agricultural policy and prices, the European Economic Community was a remarkable success. By 1963, it had become the world's largest importer. Its steel production was second only to that of the United States, and total industrial production was over 70 percent higher than it had been in 1950. Even critics who complained about constant interference of EEC "Eurocrats"—over 3,000 in Brussels by 1962—conceded that centralized European planning and decision-making had brought the Continent extraordinary and unheralded prosperity. In addition, the Common Market operated increasingly as a semiautonomous political unit. In 1972 citizens of member nations voted directly for representatives to an EEC parliament, and its court of justice has ruled on a variety of different issues, both economic and social. Special aid programs to developing countries in Asia and Africa suggest that the EEC is a force to reckon with beyond the realm of economics and beyond the border of Europe.

Behind the drive for economic growth in western Europe lay the determination of individual men and women to improve their standard of living and quality of life. To this end, they demanded more from their governments in the form of social services. Governments, in turn, relied on their generally robust economies to provide for their citizens to a greater degree than ever before. State welfare programs had, of course, existed throughout the twentieth century, their roots extending back to the insurance schemes for old age, sickness, and invalidity introduced by Bismarck in Germany in the late 1880s. Post-war western Europe saw the expansion of such programs based on assumptions of state support that were hardly less compelling than the obligation to keep the peace, nowhere stated more clearly than in the preamble of the French constitution: "The nation guarantees the condition necessary for the development of the individual and the family. It guarantees every individual . . . the protection of health, material security, rest and leisure." A survey in 1957 found that public expenditure on health, pensions, family allowances and assistance, but excluding housing and education, accounted for 20.8 percent of the national income in West Germany, 18.9 percent in France, and 12.1 percent in Britain. In Sweden, money spent on social services was six times higher in 1957 than in 1930; in Italy, it was fourteen times higher.

The economic condition of eastern Europe

Economic recovery and development in eastern Europe, although substantial, did not equal that of the western states of the continent, partly because the Soviet Union required its satellites to design their economic policies to serve other than their own national interests. Regulations governing the eastern equivalent of the Common Market, the Council of Mutual Economic Assistance (COMECON), ensured that Russia could sell its exports at prices well above the world level while other members were compelled to trade with the Soviet Union to their disadvantage. During the late 1970s the eastern European nations encountered severe financial difficulties arising from their indebtedness to western nations from whom they had borrowed heavily to promote industrial growth. By 1980 Poland's hard currency indebtedness to western countries, for example, was almost four times as great as its annual exports. The solution to this problem attempted in Poland and elsewhere was to cut back on production for domestic consumption in order to increase exports, a policy that encountered strong popular opposition. The result of further cuts, therefore, was a degree of discontent that in Poland contributed significantly to the Solidarity movement of 1980. In spite of divisive ideologies and mutual suspicion, economic forces were able to pierce the "iron curtain" separating the two halves of the continent. Poland and Hungary, in particular, developed economic connections with the West, primarily with France and West Germany. By the 1970s commerce outside the Soviet bloc accounted for about 30 percent of eastern Europe's volume of trade.

Brandt and West German Ostpolitik

The noncommunist politician most effective in bridging the gap between East and West was Willy Brandt, chancellor of West Germany in the early 1970s. Brandt, in his youth an outspoken enemy of Hitler, had fled Germany in the 1930s to Norway, where he joined the anti-Nazi resistance movement in the Second World War. His wartime record increased his credibility with eastern Europeans, who, if they were not pleased to be subject to the Soviet Union, had as much historical reason to fear Germany as they did Russia. Brandt recognized the need to accept the division of Germany into two nations. Accordingly his government initiated a policy to regularize relations with West Germany's eastern neighbors (*Ostpolitik*). A complex series of diplomatic negotiations with the Soviet Union, East Germany, and Poland resulted in treaties that established East and West Germany as separate states within one nation, guaranteed unimpeded Western access to Berlin, and recognized Poland's claim to a western frontier along the Oder and Neisse Rivers as established originally after the Second World War.

Whatever modification of their condition of dependency eastern European countries achieved during the era of the Cold War was insignificant in comparison to the cataclysmic changes that marked the closing years of the 1980s. People of the former Soviet satellites were quick to take advantage of Gorbachev's willingness to loosen their ties with Moscow. But along with feelings of relief and jubilation came uncertainty as to the future and formidable problems in the way of any progress toward a democratic political order and an economy free from state or party domination. The demand of Germans for the reunification of their country was loud and clear, but many East Germans feared unemployment would follow the demise of state-guaranteed jobs, and West Germans faced the prospect of a decline in prosperity from assimilation with their poorer neighbor. A more serious problem was the question of the orientation of a united German state. The United States and its allies insisted that it must remain a member of NATO, a proposal that for the Soviets raised the specter of an industrial giant that would not only dominate the European economy but also might again threaten the peace. The liberalizing eastern European states were burdened with flattened economies that perhaps could be revitalized only by a new Marshall Plan, and they were wracked by internal conflicts among ethnic and religious groups whose aspirations had been held in check under totalitarian rule. But if the prospect for the immediate future was chaos, old barriers had been broken and the way had been opened for a closer integration of the peoples of Europe—eastern and western—than had been known since the days of the Roman Empire.

West German Chancellor Willy Brandt in Poland, 1970. This widely distributed photograph of Brandt kneeling before a memorial to Jewish victims of the Nazi Holocaust in Warsaw signalled both his determination to make amends for past German war crimes and to ease animosities between East and West.

3. IMPERIAL DECLINE AND EMERGENCE OF THE THIRD WORLD

Following the end of the Second World War came the dissolution of several European colonial empires and the consequent emergence of newly independent states in Africa and Asia, adding members to what began to be called the "Third World," as distinguished from the two superpowers and other advanced industrialized nations.

The most radical change affecting both the Third World and established power relationships was the Chinese Revolution, described in

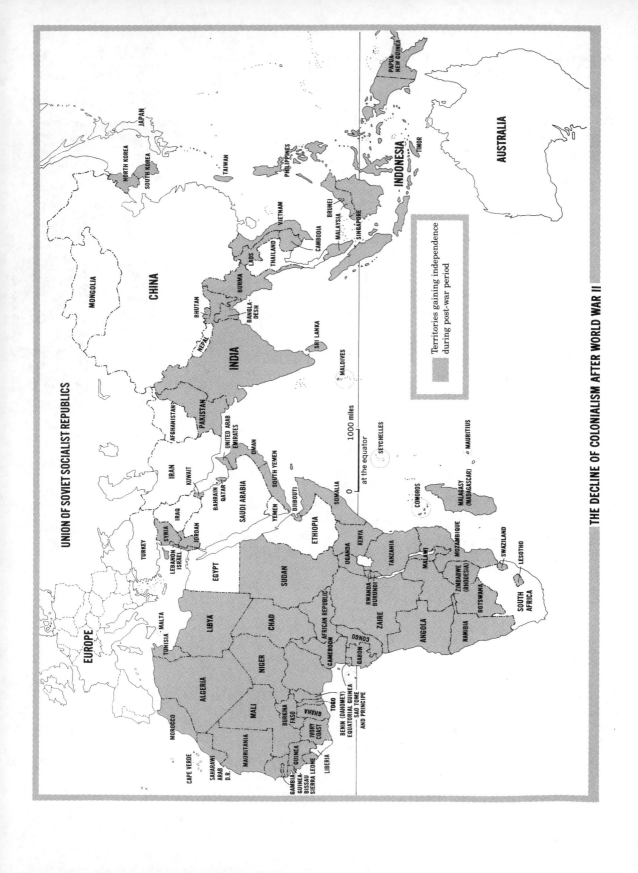

THE DECLINE OF COLONIALISM AFTER WORLD WAR II

Territories gaining independence
during post-war period

Chapter 39. Of comparable importance was the emergence of independent states in the Indian subcontinent, revolutionary upheavals in the Middle East, and the rise of black Africa (discussed in Chapters 37 and 38, respectively). Great Britain, having surrendered India and Burma, was further constrained to give up most of the remaining portions of its empire. Over a period of years Britain liberated Ceylon (Sri Lanka), Malaysia, Mauritius, Fiji, Singapore, and Nauru, among others, together with the Caribbean colonies of Guyana, Trinidad and Tobago, Jamaica, and Antigua, and significant territories in sub-Saharan Africa as well. The years following the Second World War also witnessed the liquidation of Dutch and French colonial empires in Southeast Asia.

Indonesia, known for more than two centuries as the Netherlands Indies, was the most valuable jewel of the Dutch imperial crown. Indeed, it was one of the richest countries in the world in natural resources. When Japan extended its aggressions to Southeast Asia in 1941, the empire of the Dutch was a prize conquest. But toward the end of the war, nationalists, under the leadership of Achmed Sukarno, a one-time architect and flamboyant politician, rebelled and proclaimed an independent republic. Although the Dutch attempted for four years to regain their sovereignty, the opposition of the indigenous population proved too strong. In 1949 the kingdom of the Netherlands recognized the independence of its former colony.

Under the colorful but erratic President Sukarno, the Republic of Indonesia assumed an aggressive role in Asian politics, but his reckless policies brought both economic disaster and internal discord. With encouragement from China, and to some extent from Sukarno, communist influence increased, and the Indonesian Communist party for a few years was the third largest in the world. An abortive coup in September 1965, attributed to the Communists, led to the imposition of a military regime which stripped Sukarno of his power. The Indonesian Communist party was shattered but at the price of a reign of terror lasting several months and a bloodbath that took the lives of at least half a million people. General T. N. J. Suharto, who replaced Sukarno as president, has maintained a tight dictatorship. Calling his regime a "guided democracy," he allowed a People's House of Representatives to meet, but directly appointed 60 percent of the members. Although the Indonesians had won their independence, they did not grant the same privilege to the inhabitants of the eastern half of the island of Timor, which had been a Portuguese colony. When East Timor repudiated Portuguese rule in 1975, it was overrun by Suharto's army and annexed to the Republic of Indonesia. A savage war and consequent epidemics of disease have not entirely broken resistance in East Timor. General Suharto, while ruthlessly stifling internal dissent and incarcerating thousands of political prisoners, projected an ambitious program of industrial development. The nation of 190 million, fifth largest in the world, comprises some 300 ethnic groups and as

Ho Chi Minh

many languages. It is also one of the world's poorest nations, with a per capita income of about $560 a year. But the sprawling island republic has the potential to become prosperous, owing to the strong demand for its exports—petroleum and natural gas, coal, rubber, palm oil, tin, and coffee.

France after the Second World War faced almost simultaneous revolts in two of its richest colonies, Algeria and Indochina. Indochina had been a casualty of Japanese conquests, and after the defeat of Japan in 1945 France sought to recover its lost empire in the Far East. These efforts ended in failure, however. The French were immediately confronted by a rebellion of Vietnamese nationalists under the leadership of Ho Chi Minh (1890–1969). The rebels resorted to guerrilla warfare and inflicted such costly defeats upon the French that the latter decided to abandon the struggle. An agreement was signed at Geneva in 1954 providing for the division of Vietnam into two zones, pending elections to determine the future government of the entire country. Ho Chi Minh became president of North Vietnam and established his capital at Hanoi. His followers, who came to be called Viet Cong, were numerous in both halves of the country. Had elections been held as provided by the Geneva Agreement, Ho Chi Minh would probably have been elected president of all of Vietnam. But the government of South Vietnam, backed by the United States, refused to permit elections to be held.

From this point on, involvement by the United States in the Vietnamese civil war steadily increased. President Kennedy was convinced that the Chinese Communist juggernaut would soon roll over all of Southeast Asia. The first victims would be Vietnam, Laos, Cambodia, Malaysia, and Singapore. Then would come Thailand, Burma, and India. How far Kennedy would have gone in his crusade against communism had he escaped assassination in 1963 is impossible to say with certainty. Kennedy's successor, Lyndon B. Johnson (1908–1973), hoped that a relatively small force of perhaps 100,000 men would be sufficient to defeat the Viet Cong and drive them back into their own country. Little consideration was given to the fact that these forces were solidly entrenched in both states of Vietnam, and that they had been waging a bitter national struggle for upwards of eighteen years. They had succeeded in driving out the French in 1954 and were not likely to surrender to a new invader, as they conceived the Americans to be. The Viet Cong and the North Vietnam regulars, though less well-equipped, nevertheless fought the South Vietnamese and their American allies to a standstill on several occasions. During the Tet offensive of 1968 they came close to capturing Saigon, the South Vietnamese capital.

Exasperated by failure to win an easy victory in South Vietnam, the American civilian and military chiefs determined upon aerial bombing. Alleging—without verification—that North Vietnamese ships had attacked American naval vessels in the Tonkin Gulf, President

War in Vietnam. Confronted with a new kind of warfare, the American military sought to adapt its methods to the Vietnamese situation.

Johnson obtained from Congress authorization to use whatever measures necessary to repel communist aggression. Soon afterward American bombers unloaded their first cargoes upon towns and villages occupied by the North Vietnamese and the Viet Cong. When increasingly devastating aerial raids failed to crush the insurgent forces, the only answer of those responsible for strategy in Washington and Saigon seemed to be "Cover up the failure by escalating the war." As the struggle entered its fifth year, with no end in sight, disillusionment spread throughout the United States. Criticism of President Johnson was so harsh in 1968 that he was forced to abandon his plans to run for a second term. *President Johnson escalates the war*

Under Johnson's successor, Richard M. Nixon, while ground troops were being withdrawn from Vietnam, in May 1970 the United States invaded Cambodia and a few months later the kingdom of Laos. In April 1972, the North Vietnamese, with massive aid from Russia and China, launched a powerful counteroffensive with the apparent objective of conquering South Vietnam and driving all foreign armies out of the country. A number of South Vietnamese strongholds were captured and the offensive seemed more dangerous than the famous Tet offensive of 1968. Nixon countered with increased bombing of North Vietnam's factories and railroads and by mining its harbors, including savage raids while negotiations were under way in December 1972. A cease-fire, early in 1973, did no more than postpone the inevitable. Two years later, South Vietnam fell to the Viet Cong and the North Vietnamese. *The Nixon policies*

The aftermath of the Indochina war bore little resemblance to what either United States planners or their revolutionary adversaries had intended. Expulsion of the foreign invaders led not to peace, but to desperate internal struggles and renewed warfare. In Cambodia the *Disastrous effects of the war in Indochina*

Pol Pot of Kampuchea

Communist Khmer Rouge, which had overthrown a U.S.-backed general, proclaimed the new state of Kampuchea in January 1976 and instituted a reign of terror that came close to a policy of genocide. The paranoid leader Pol Pot, in his determination to create an agrarian society more radically equalitarian than that of China, liquidated the bourgeoisie and intellectuals, including technicians and doctors, and forced entire city populations to move to the country. Khmer Rouge zealots abolished currency, private property, and private households, and were responsible for the death of some 2 million Cambodians. The Communist rulers of the Socialist Republic of Vietnam (SRV), whose forces had borne the brunt of the fighting, appeared more conciliatory than the fanatics of Kampuchea and placed a high priority on rebuilding Vietnam's economy. The task of reconstruction was staggering, with industry destroyed, per capita annual income only $150 and declining, and foreign aid not readily forthcoming.

The conflicts in Indochina of the late 1970s and beyond, although aggravated by great power rivalry, stemmed basically from the resurgence of centuries-old ethnic and national rivalries that had been temporarily suppressed by the common effort against French and American imperialism. Both Thailand and Vietnam aspired to dominance in the area, forcing the smaller states of Laos and Cambodia to serve as pawns or buffers between them. A Communist regime installed in Laos in 1975 was held closely aligned with Vietnam, but antagonisms rankled between Vietnamese and Cambodians, and Pol Pot, with only a shaky hold over his own Kampuchea, staged military incursions into Vietnam. Relations between Vietnam and China had never been cordial, even while they were nominally allied. The Chinese viewed Vietnamese with the same disdain the Vietnamese felt toward Cambodians, and the Vietnamese remembered their long struggle to win independence from imperial China. When Peking terminated its aid program with Hanoi, the SRV was forced to look for support elsewhere. Rebuffed by the United States, the Vietnamese yielded to Russian pressure to sign a Treaty of Friendship and Cooperation with the Soviet Union in March 1978.

War between Vietnam and Kampuchea was preceded by Khmer Rouge raids into Vietnam and punitive strikes by Vietnamese troops deep into Cambodia. Unable to induce Pol Pot to accept a demilitarized zone, Hanoi opened a full-scale assault in December 1978 and toppled the Khmer Rouge government the following month. The war threatened to destroy what little was left of Cambodia. After the fall of Phnom Penh, the capital, fighting continued between the new Vietnamese-backed regime and various guerrilla groups, including one headed by Cambodia's exiled ruler, Prince Norodom Sihanouk, and one—with considerable military strength—the remnant of Pol Pot's Khmer Rouge. Thousands of sick, wounded, and starving refugees swarmed to the Thai border. International relief agencies, attempting to avert famine, were frustrated by the dictates of competing political authorities. The war put a heavy strain on Vietnam's stunted economy. Finally, Vietnam's Cambodian adventure provoked an attack by the People's Republic of China. The Chinese felt it necessary to support Pol Pot—in spite of his unsavory reputation—because his was the only regime in Indochina aligned with Peking and because its destruction would remove a check on Vietnam's expansionist ambitions. The Chinese invasion of Vietnam, which began on February 17, 1979, and lasted only seventeen days, destroyed bridges, utilities, mining operations, and thousands of homes, without producing any discernible advantage for either side to offset the heavy losses. The Vietnamese continued to occupy the greater part of Cambodia and, utilizing emergency supplies donated by private relief agencies, began to revive the economy. Because Hanoi refused to withdraw its troops as long as China was helping the Khmer Rouge, the United States and its allies continued to support the Khmer Rouge's dubious claim to represent Kampuchea in the United Nations General Assembly.

After a ten-year occupation the Vietnamese withdrew from Cambodia late in 1989, leaving the country with a reviving economy and with the Buddhist religion reinstated. Vietnam's economy, pulverized at the end of the French and American wars, had suffered further from the drain of fighting in Cambodia and from the restrictive regulations imposed by the ruling Communist party. Significant policy changes, beginning in 1986 and inspired partly by Gorbachev's reforms in the USSR, aimed at speeding economic growth by giving scope to private initiative and by offering liberal terms to foreign investors. With Washington refusing requests for aid, the Vietnamese hoped to attract capital from Europe and Japan. Meanwhile the civil war continued in Cambodia, where among the rebel forces the Khmer Rouge posed the greatest threat not only to the Vietnamese-backed government at Phnom Penh but to the survival of the Cambodian nation.

*Postwar Vietnam and
Cambodia*

The Flight from Cambodia. Thousands of Cambodian refugees fled the fighting between the Pol Pot regime and the Vietnamese army. Here civilians, wearing traditional Khmer head scarves, are streaming across the border into Thailand. On this day alone (April 27, 1979) some 12,000 sought refuge in Thailand, where the facilities for caring for them were woefully inadequate.

The diminishing global
reach of the United States
and the Soviet Union

4. THE COURSE AND CONSEQUENCES OF THE STRUGGLE FOR WORLD DOMINATION

During the Cold War era the dominance of the superpowers, though threatening to reduce lesser states to helplessness, was more apparent than real and rested upon fragile foundations. The global reach of both the United States and the USSR, formidable in the years immediately following the Second World War, steadily declined thereafter. American strategists for years conjured the specter of a monolithic communism bent on world domination. When the rupture of the Sino-Soviet alliance in 1960 dispelled this specter they branded China as the instigator of insurgency in Southeast Asia, even though the Vietnamese steadfastly opposed China's encroachment and fought a war to halt it soon after the withdrawal of American troops. Peking's efforts to manipulate Indonesia through the Indonesian Communist party collapsed when the party was liquidated in a bloody uprising in 1965. After a fifty-year occupation of Tibet the People's Republic of China has failed to break the resistance of its inhabitants. The USSR, alternately wooed and rebuffed by Arab nations of the Middle East, struggled to gain footholds among the new African states, with mixed results. Recent events in eastern Europe and within Russia have revealed startlingly the inherent weakness of what had long loomed as the West's bête noire. Obviously the iron rule of the Communist party had been unable to fuse the vast regions under Soviet control into a nation-state, and the loosening of imperial bonds threatened its dissolution. Policy reversals also point less dramatically but unmistakably to the decline of the American empire. After pouring billions of dollars into the shah's Iran to make it a Middle East bastion for the West, Washington's influence collapsed in 1979 when that country was shaken by an anti-Western Islamic revolution, and Americans could only watch helplessly as their nationals, seized as hostages by militant revolutionaries, were imprisoned for fourteen months. Once the most powerful voice in the United Nations the United States can no longer shape its policies, nor can it dictate to the Organization of American States in its own hemisphere.

The Great Power rivalry
in the Third World: (1) the
U.S. legacy in Korea and
Indochina

The transformation of European colonies in Africa and Asia into independent states, most of them poor and torn by domestic strife, posed a challenge to the superpowers. In competing for influence the two rivals frequently drew Third World countries into political and ideological conflicts that ran the risk of igniting a world conflagration and ended without victory for either side. The Korean War of 1950–1953 left the peninsula divided between a Soviet-aligned Democratic People's Republic of Korea in the north with Pyongyang as its capital and a U.S.-aligned Republic of Korea with Seoul as its capital in the south. Both have been police states, and mutual hostility has forced each to maintain an army of half a million troops. The United States, resolved to keep South Korea within its alliance system, supplied military and economic aid in spite of flagrant violations of human rights by successive Seoul governments dominated by the military. Although in recent years the prospects for a democratic future under civilian rule in South Korea have brightened, popular discontent persists, evident especially in a demand for reunification of the two Koreas, a demand opposed both by Seoul and Washington. The United States' fifteen-year struggle in Vietnam, Laos, and Cambodia, which cost over $150 billion and the loss of 58,000 American lives, brought not the defeat of communism but the overthrow of every U.S.-sponsored government in Indochina except Thailand, which had remained neutral.

The USSR under Leonid Brezhnev, as if to prove that it had learned nothing from the experience of the French and Americans in Vietnam, attempted to compel obedience from Afghanistan, a Middle Eastern country bordering on Russia where a pro-Soviet regime had been installed in April 1978. Weary of the stubborn resistance offered by the Muslim population of Afghanistan, the Soviets attacked in strength in December 1979 and installed a compliant puppet as prime minister in Kabul. While Russian troops policed the cities, Afghan tribesmen inflamed the countryside with guerrilla attacks from their mountain strongholds, inaugurating a long and ruinous civil war. Ten years later, following skillful and patient negotiations by a United Nations diplomat and the accession to power of Mikhail Gorbachev, a force of 100,000 troops that had proved themselves unable to quell persistent opposition to the invasion was withdrawn. Contrary to expectations, when Russian troops left the country Kabul did not fall to the guerrilla forces which, sharply divided in ideology, fell to fighting among themselves. The Afghan war, ending with no definitive settlement, had proved costly not only to the Soviets but also to the United

*(2) Soviet entanglement in
Afghanistan*

The Soviet Withdrawal from Afghanistan. Here a Soviet tank, part of one of the last Soviet military units to leave Afghanistan, prepares to make the river crossing to the USSR in February 1989.

States and Pakistan, each of which had aided the Mujahideen insurgents throughout the struggle.

Unavoidably subject to pressure from the major powers, the emergent Third World states have resisted interference in their internal affairs and, while favoring a policy of nonalignment with great-power blocs, have made limited progress toward combining for mutual security. Of several attempts to promote solidarity among nations of the Third World—beginning with the Asian-African Conference of twenty-nine states held at Bandung, Indonesia, in 1955—the most promising to date is the Association of Southeast Asian Nations (ASEAN) established in 1967 by Indonesia, Singapore, Malaysia, Thailand, and the Philippines (and joined by Brunei when that state achieved independence in 1985). There are wide differences in culture, religion, and economic condition among the members of the association. Indonesia, though presently poor, ranks first in size, population, and natural resources. The island of Singapore, by comparison, is a thriving port and financial center. Each of the ASEAN states is anticommunist but most have repressive governments, and they have experienced social upheavals, coups, or revolutions. Thailand, nominally a monarchy but long under army rule, has for more than a year sustained a democratically elected civilian government, while the army, with personal ties to its Burmese drug-trafficking counterpart, remains a potential challenge.

The extremely unstable Republic of the Philippines is perhaps the most volatile of the ASEAN members. Annexed by the United States after the Spanish-American War of 1898, following the Second World War it was given independence and a constitutional government democratic in form, but the economy and best farmlands remained in the grip of rival oligarchic clans. The Islands were plunged into civil war by Muslims revolting against rule by Christians and by armed guerrillas, including Marxists, who demanded a redistribution of lands. Although the civil war officially ended in 1954, the guerrilla insurgency has continued in one fashion or another to the present day. The populace suffered severely during the twenty-year rule of President Ferdinand Marcos and his extravagant wife Imelda. The poverty rate rose from 28 percent of the population to 70 percent; the nation's external debt came to exceed $25 billion; and while virtually bankrupting the country the Marcoses accumulated a private fortune approaching $20 billion. Finally, when the president attempted to extend his dictatorship by a fraudulent election, he was overthrown in a courageous "people's revolution" that the army refused to suppress and that brought to the presidency the charismatic Corazon Aquino, whose husband had been murdered at Marcos's orders. Caught off guard by Marcos's sudden fall, in February 1986 the United States flew him by helicopter to Hawaii, providing "a chauffeur service for failed dictators." Although Marcos had long been treated as a close ally because of his anticommunist stand and his acceptance of U.S. bases in the Philippines, the Washington administration hailed the change as a triumph

*Instability in the
Philippines*

*President Corazon Aquino of the
Philippines.* The widow of a prominent opposition leader assassinated by agents of the Marcos regime, she succeeded the discredited Ferdinand Marcos as president.

for democracy and promised Mrs. Aquino support. Faced with the almost impossible task of alleviating poverty without infuriating the wealthy, and attempting to govern in the face of repeated coup attempts by factions of the military, she needed all the help she could find.

ASEAN's declared intent was to promote mutual economic growth and cooperation, social progress, and cultural development, but collective action has been confined chiefly to joint security efforts. Generally supportive of U.S. policy in the area, the association condemned Vietnam's occupation of Cambodia while ignoring China's support of the Khmer Rouge, and it has rejected Vietnam's application for membership in ASEAN. Nevertheless the memory of Chinese aggression in Southeast Asia runs deep, and China is viewed by some as a bigger threat than any posed by the USSR. If Vietnam should be permitted to join, drawing together communist and noncommunist states and reconciling such longstanding rivals as Vietnam and Thailand, ASEAN could become a positive force for stability in Indochina.

*ASEAN: mutual security
ascendent*

The failure of the world's greatest constellations of power to achieve their goals suggests that in an era of highly advanced technology power becomes subject to the law of diminishing returns. Its expansion eventually makes it self-defeating. This was illustrated in the Korean War of 1950–1953 when the United States government refused to permit General MacArthur to invade China or to deploy nuclear weapons as he had requested, for fear that such moves might provoke a world war. This policy puzzled and angered many Americans accustomed to the concept of all-out war and unconditional surrender. Especially galling to them was the fact that President Truman saw fit to fire General MacArthur, hero of the Pacific war against Japan and now commander of the United Nations forces, because MacArthur

*The limits of power: (1)
the impotence of nuclear
weapons*

United Nations General Assembly Session on the Cuban Missile Build-Up, October 25, 1962. U.S. ambassador Adlai Stevenson (seated at the far right) presents aerial photos of launching sites under construction in Cuba. This episode dramatically illustrated the limits within which both the United States and the Soviet Union were compelled to operate.

was opposed to fighting a limited war. Similarly, in the Cuban missile crisis of 1962 the United States and the Soviet Union were forced to ask themselves how much they were willing to risk in order to protect their own strategic interests. President Kennedy and Chairman Khrushchev found it necessary to compromise—the Soviets removing missiles from Cuba, the United States lifting the blockade and promising not to invade Cuba—to avert a nuclear holocaust.

*(2) fragile alliances and
reluctant allies*

The limits of power are also illustrated in the instability of alliances and the impossibility of forcing compliance from one's own allies. Unable to secure reliable partners in the Middle East or Africa, the USSR in the late 1980s faced the loss of control over its eastern European client states. The United States, while shoring up NATO, had very limited success in building alliances elsewhere. For a couple of decades it relied upon a Southeast Asia Defense Treaty (SEATO) negotiated in 1954 and designed as a counterpart to NATO in an overall program for containing communism. The organization, only three of whose eight members were Asian states (Thailand, Pakistan, and the Philippines), was neither popular nor effective. By 1967 France had virtually withdrawn; Pakistan left in 1972. Five years later what remained of SEATO was quietly laid to rest with a brief ceremony in Bangkok. The Southeast Asian states, disinclined to revive the Cold War, looked upon ASEAN as an association more suitable to promoting their common interests.

Alliances reexamined

The retreat of communism in eastern Europe, the lessening of tension between Russia and the Western powers, and the rising popular demand for a reduction of military forces raised questions as to whether alliances could any longer serve the interests of peace or security. With members of the Warsaw Pact demanding the withdrawal of Russian troops from their territories, why did western Europe any longer need NATO for its protection?

*The challenge of a new
Europe and a changing
world order*

Institutions tend to outlive their usefulness, and deeply ingrained habits of thought are hard to uproot. An ideal replacement for the outmoded system of alliances would seem to be a world federation empowered to restrain abuses of power by any of its members. But the grudging support given to the United Nations leads one to wonder whether sovereign states are yet prepared to make the sacrifices necessary for the success of such an organization. To deal effectively with the problems created by the emergence of a new Europe and a changing world order will require farsighted and innovative leadership able to withstand pressure from vested interests resistant to change. The easing of East-West tensions did not bring universal agreement that the Cold War was over or assurance that a "peace dividend" would be forthcoming. Mikhail Gorbachev, after withdrawing Soviet troops from Afghanistan, stated publicly that Russian intervention had been not only a mistake but immoral—a salutary confession on the part of a head of state not yet duplicated by his Western counterpart. While the Berlin Wall—grim symbol of the "iron curtain" separating East and

West—was being dismantled and its pieces sold as souvenirs, the twenty-foot-high and ten-foot-thick concrete wall erected by the United States in 1976–1979 along the thirty-eighth parallel in Korea showed no sign of crumbling.

SELECTED READINGS

• *Items so designated are available in paperback editions.*

Amter, Joseph, *Vietnam Verdict: A Citizen's History,* New York, 1964.

Ardagh, John, *The New French Revolution,* New York, 1969. The social impact of economic change.

• Aron, Raymond, *The Imperial Republic: The United States and the World, 1945–1973,* Lanham, Md., 1974. World analysis by a leading French political theorist.

Ash, Timothy, *The Polish Revolution: Solidarity,* New York, 1983. The best account.

• Beer, Samuel, *Britain Against Itself,* New York, 1982. A clear-headed analysis of the reasons for British decline.

Black, C. E., *The Dynamics of Modernization: A Study in Comparative History,* New York, 1966. Includes material on non-Western countries as well.

• Brzezinski, Z., *The Soviet Bloc: Unity and Conflict,* rev. and enl. ed., Cambridge, Mass., 1967. Eastern European politics analyzed by a former U.S. National Security Advisor.

Cady, J. F., *Southeast Asia: Its Historical Development,* New York, 1964.

Chaliand, Gérard, *Revolution in the Third World: Myths and Prospects,* New York, 1977. Gloomy but insightful.

• Crouzet, Maurice, *The European Renaissance Since 1945,* New York, 1971. Optimistic appraisal of Europe's postwar recovery.

• Dahrendorf, Ralf, *Society and Democracy in Germany,* New York, 1971. The extent of the change from fascism to democracy.

• DePorte, A. W., *Europe Between the Superpowers: The Enduring Balance,* New Haven, 1979.

• Fitzgerald, Frances, *Fire in the Lake: The Vietnamese and the Americans in Vietnam,* Boston, 1972. A detailed and moving account.

• Gaddis, John, *The United States and the Origins of the Cold War, 1942–1947,* New York, 1972. Focuses on the United States. A balanced account.

Hough, Jerry, and Merle Fainsod, *How the Soviet Union Is Governed,* Cambridge, Mass., 1979.

Kolko, Gabriel, *The Politics of War: The World and United States Foreign Policy, 1943–1945,* New York, 1969. Argues that the blame for the Cold War rests with the Western Allies.

• Kornai, János, *The Road to a Free Economy,* New York, 1990. A penetrating analysis of the challenges confronting eastern European states as they strive to transform their planned economies into market-driven economies.

• LaFeber, Walter, *America, Russia and the Cold War,* 5th ed., New York, 1985. Another revisionist treatment.

• Laqueur, Walter, *Europe Since Hitler,* rev. ed., New York, 1982. A useful, thorough survey.

• Leslie, R. F., et al., *The History of Poland Since 1863*, New York, 1981. Useful background for current events.

Matray, James, *The Reluctant Crusade: American Foreign Policy in Korea, 1941–1950*, Honolulu, 1985.

Mayne, Richard, *The Recovery of Europe, 1945–1973*, Garden City, N.Y., 1973. Another reliable account.

Mowat, R. C., *Creating the European Community*, New York, 1973. A diplomatic historian's account of the merging of Europe's economic fortunes.

Mozingo, David, *China's Policy toward Indonesia, 1949–1967*, Ithaca, N.Y., 1976.

Parker, Geoffrey, *The Logic of Unity*, 3rd ed., London, 1981. Another study of the forces working for and against European community.

• Patti, A. L. A., *Why Vietnam? Prelude to America's Albatross*, Berkeley, 1980. A favorable account of Ho Chih Minh by a former OSS officer.

Póstan, M. M., *An Economic History of Western Europe, 1945–1964*, London, 1967. A lively account of a lively period.

• Sampson, Anthony, *The Changing Anatomy of Britain*, New York, 1982. A sharp critical dissection of British society.

Sandusky, Michael, *America's Parallel*, Alexandria Va., 1983. Criticizes the U.S. decision to divide Korea at the thirty-eighth parallel.

• Ulam, Adam, *Expansion and Coexistence: Soviet Foreign Policy, 1917–1973*, 2nd ed., New York, 1974.

• Williams, Lea E., *Southeast Asia: A History*, New York, 1976. From the fifteenth to the late twentieth century.

• Worsley, Peter, *The Third World*, 2nd ed., Chicago, 1970.

SOURCE MATERIALS

Adenauer, Konrad, *Memoirs, 1945–1953*, Chicago, 1966. Adenauer served as chancellor of the Federal Republic of Germany from 1949 to 1963 and sought both American support and the reunification of dismembered Germany.

• Barnes, Thomas G., and Gerald D. Feldman, eds., *Breakdown and Rebirth: 1914 to the Present*, Boston, 1972. An excellent documentary collection of contemporary history, primarily European.

• Caputo, Philip, *A Rumor of War*, New York, 1977. The best memoir of the American experience in the Vietnam war.

De Gaulle, Charles, *Memoirs of Hope: Renewal and Endeavor*, New York, 1971.

Kennan, George F., *Memoirs, 1925–1950*, New York, 1967. Kennan, a career diplomat, was America's leading expert on Russia and instrumental in the formation of the containment policy.

• Servan-Schreiber, J. J., *The American Challenge*, New York, 1968. A Frenchman's assessment of the impact of American economy and technology on Europe.

Chapter 42

PROBLEMS OF WORLD CIVILIZATION

The nuclear accident at Chernobyl is a tragedy for those killed or injured by the fire and for the many more who must live with the fear that exposure to radiation may cause cancer and genetic defects in the future. Nevertheless we should remember that the danger from this accident is negligible compared with what would happen in a nuclear war.

—George Rathjens and Jerome Grossman, Council for a Livable World,
1986

Are we willing to pay the price of the redemption of the Earth in terms of a revolution in values, in lifestyles, in economic and political goals, and even in the nature of the science and technology we practice? The stage is set. Whether the play can be performed before the theater burns down remains to be seen.

—Charles Birch, University of Sydney

The writing of a final chapter in a textbook of this sort is a difficult task. It demands not only an instant analysis of contemporary society but also an attempt to discern in present events patterns that will continue to be of some consequence five to ten years hence. In other words, the authors are called upon to pick historical winners, to decide not what *has* mattered, which is difficult enough, but what *will* matter. Historians, whose job it is to acknowledge the way in which human idiosyncrasies make prediction a tricky business, are particularly loath to single out this movement or that trend and to pronounce it "significant" in terms of the future. We shall therefore content ourselves with a discussion of some of the trends and most serious problems confronting society since the 1970s, calling attention at the outset to the fact that the problems are rooted in historical developments.

The present as history

1. WAR MAKING AND PEACE MAKING IN THE NUCLEAR AGE

Since the Second World War human societies have lived under the threat of annihilation by thermonuclear weapons tested with awesome results upon two Japanese cities in 1945. While these weapons surpassed in destructive power anything previously known, their production and possession was defended as a guarantee of peace. Nations, it was argued, were secure beneath the "nuclear umbrella" because the indiscriminate destruction the devices were capable of inflicting would deter every government from using them. Conventional wisdom credited America's massive nuclear arsenal—matched step by step with that of the Soviets—with preventing a major war for more than forty years. This assumption overlooks the fact that the age of nuclear weapons had engendered an arms race of unprecedented proportions, led by the United States and the USSR, but eventually joined almost universally. Neither of the leading antagonists ever felt secure enough to halt the development of more and more sophisticated weapons, ensuring that if an all-out war did come its devastation would far surpass anything previously conceivable. Even if governments exercised restraint, the complexity of offensive and defensive devices multiplied the chances of their accidental discharge. On numerous occasions automatically signaled warnings of an impending attack have been detected as false barely in time to forestall the launching of retaliatory missiles. Meanwhile it has proved impossible to prevent the spread of nuclear technology to countries eager to acquire it, shattering the dream of a "nuclear club" restricted to the U.S., the USSR, Britain, and France. Gradually it became evident that midget states, or even private groups of terrorists, might acquire atomic weapons for the purpose of blackmailing or destroying an enemy. Besides threatening a nuclear doomsday the steadily expanding manufacture of armaments produced huge stockpiles of highly toxic radioactive waste. Recent investigations revealed that the U.S. Department of Energy had neglected to monitor weapons-producing plants whose operation was imperiling the health of hundreds of American communities. While the manufacture of substances that will retain their toxicity for thousands of years continues, no reliable plan for disposing of or storing these wastes has yet been devised.

If a nuclear holocaust has thus far been avoided and Europe has preserved an armed truce, the period since the Second World War has nevertheless been one of almost continual warfare. The superpowers, careful to avoid direct hostilities with each other, armed client states and used them as proxies in fighting their battles—discovering, however, that they could not always control their clients' actions. An assumption that the nuclear arsenals would not be unlocked encouraged small states to engage in warfare without fear of starting a world conflagration in which they themselves would perish. Equipped with the means of destroying the world, the superpowers were unable to police it or effectively to restrain their own dependents. Several of the wars fought since 1945 should by any rational standard be classified as major. Both the Korean and the Vietnam conflicts foreshadowed the possibility of the total destruction of a country by the technology of nonnuclear "conventional" warfare. In Korea some four million people, mostly civilians, were killed. The total U.S. bomb tonnage dropped over Indochina (an area about the size of Texas) was more than three times as much as that released by Americans over enemy territory during the Second World War. In Vietnam, besides those killed and wounded, at least eight million people were turned into homeless refugees. Crops were destroyed and farmlands ravaged. Exposure to the highly toxic defoliant Agent Orange—sprayed on forests over a nine-year period—may have inflicted permanent genetic damage upon human survivors. The strife-torn character of the past half century is engraved on its roster of lethal engagements ranging from major clashes in Korea, Indochina, India, Afghanistan, and the Middle East to "low-intensity conflict" against insurgents in Latin America.

National governments have devoted far less effort and resources to peacemaking or to removing the causes of war than they have expended in the opposite direction. According to a reliable estimate, by 1987 the world was spending 2,900 times as much on national military forces as on international peacekeeping activities. Besides disarmament initiatives emanating from the United Nations, diplomats of the superpowers repeatedly sought agreements to brake the acceleration of the arms race and maintain an equilibrium between the arsenals of the two rivals. The modest objective of negotiators was "arms control" rather than arms reduction. In 1962 Chairman Khrushchev and President Kennedy signed a treaty renouncing the testing of nuclear devices in the atmosphere; underground testing, however, continued. Talks initiated during the period of détente under Presidents Richard Nixon and Gerald Ford in the 1970s produced a Strategic Arms Limitation Treaty (SALT I) intended to forestall a first-strike capacity on either side. The United States refused to ratify its successor, SALT II, following the Soviet invasion of Afghanistan in 1979. President Ronald Reagan, who took office in 1981, denounced the SALT negotiations during his campaign and subsequently pressed for drastic increases in his military budgets for sophisticated weapons, even as he proclaimed his devotion to the cause of disarmament. Publicly committed to missile deployment and to an elaborate and astronomically expensive space-based system (SDI, popularly known as "Star Wars"), his administration at first gave a mixed response to the bold initiatives of the new Soviet leader Mikhail Gorbachev. In December 1987, despite continuing disagreement on other issues, Gorbachev and Reagan signed a treaty in Washington eliminating all short- and medium-range nuclear missiles from the European arsenals of both East and West. Under President George Bush, who succeeded Reagan in 1989, relations

*Periodic progress toward
peace*

President Ronald Reagan of the United States and President Mikhail Gorbachev of the Soviet Union at a Summit Meeting on Arms Control in December 1987

between Washington and the Soviet leader warmed to the point of cordiality. Gorbachev was given a hero's welcome when he came to the United States for a summit meeting in the spring of 1990, which augurs well for the prospect of early agreements to reduce both strategic and conventional land-based forces and to eliminate stockpiles of chemical weapons. Even under favorable conditions, however, significant progress toward disarmament will be difficult. Talks on the limitation of nuclear-equipped naval forces have not yet begun.

2. POLITICAL AND SOCIAL CHANGE WITHIN THE INDUSTRIALIZED NATIONS

The high cost of military "supremacy": (1) the United States

During the first three-quarters of the twentieth century the international political trend was toward a contraction in the number of major powers, culminating after the Second World War in a concentration of power in two competing centers. A reversal of this trend began as the growth of vigorous economies in widely scattered states, including those temporarily shattered by military defeat, challenged the dominant position of the two superpowers. In competing for supremacy both the Soviet Union and the United States wasted resources in wars fought or subsidized by them and in fueling an arms race that distorted and impaired their own economies. The cost to the United States of its military buildup during the 1970s and 1980s exceeded $4 trillion. The growth of the federal deficit—unchecked since its unprecedented expansion during the Reagan administrations—at its present pace will reach $4.5 trillion by 1995, bringing interest payments alone to $335 billion a year. At mid-century the world's largest creditor nation, the United States has become the one most heavily in debt. While pouring huge sums into the development of new weapons and the "modernizing" of old ones, U.S. executives and legislators neglected to address basic social needs, allowing the quality of life for millions of citizens to deteriorate. Programs to assist poor families, protect children, improve health care, and promote education were cut back drastically. Within a decade the number of hungry children in America increased by two million, bringing the total to 20 percent of the child population. More than one-seventh of the nation's population was living below the official poverty level. For young families the proportion was more than 20 percent. The upkeep of bridges and highways was so underfunded that, according to a General Accounting Office estimate, it would require $500 billion to renovate this vital infrastructure. Meanwhile, insufficient investment in research to improve manufacturing productivity cost Americans their once-dominant position in world markets. Instead of a surplus the United States now runs an annual trade deficit exceeding $100 billion. In the year 1987 it reached $160 billion. A continuing decline in factory jobs since 1979 forced many workers to seek lower-paid employment in "service" industries. In terms of buying power the income of the average American worker declined more than 10 percent during the past decade. In the mid-1970s the United States ranked thirteenth in the number of teachers per school-age population; seventeenth, just below Poland, in the ratio of physicians to population; seventeenth, tied with East Germany, in the infant mortality rate; and twentieth in life expectancy. Although the U.S. economy—still the world's largest—is not in imminent danger of collapse, it is clear that changes in national priorities are needed if America is to retain its position as a world leader or to restore the health of its society.

Excessive military spending exacted an even heavier price from the Soviet Union than from the United States. Nikita Khrushchev once boasted that the Soviets' expanding economy would surpass and "bury" those of the West. But in spite of its large labor force, vast territory, and abundant resources, communist Russia failed to keep pace with the countries of western Europe in productivity. Fifty years after the revolution of 1917 the Soviet Union ranked twentieth in a list of 130 countries in per capita income. Agriculture was too inefficient to free the Soviets from the need to import foodstuffs, and they required foreign capital to implement plans for developing the oil and gas deposits of Siberia. In addition to a parasitical defense establishment, Russia's economy was strangled by rigid centralization and a cumbersome and corruptible bureaucracy that discouraged innovation. Gorbachev's reform program of the late 1980s exposed the decrepitude of the party-dominated economic structure and the enormity of the task of reshaping it. His policy of *glasnost,* inviting open discussion, led to a rising chorus of complaints over shortages of consumer goods and a malfunctioning transportation system. Attempts to move toward a free-market economy, without relinquishing price controls needed to check inflation, caused confusion and anger. Ironically, while Gorbachev was winning acclaim throughout the West as a statesman of first rank, at home he was being assailed by radicals who wanted more rapid reform, by conservatives who wanted none, and by a public at last permitted to air its grievances. Some foreign observers were predicting that not only would Gorbachev soon be overthrown but also that the Soviet Union would disintegrate. Regardless of Gorbachev's fate—and thus far no leader with his consummate political agility has appeared—there is little likelihood of Soviet Russia's demise, even if some non-Russian republics secede. The economy is stronger than it appears on the surface. During the grim years of party domination resourceful citizens devised means of circumventing the system, resorting to barter and the private exchange of skilled services for commodities, creating a "second economy" that accounts for more than 10 percent of the Soviet gross domestic product. In spite of the confusion and controversy erupting under Gorbachev the Soviet GNP has grown at a rate between 1.5 and 3 percent annually. The grain harvest in 1989 exceeded the previous year's by 26 million

(2) *The Soviet Union*

tons. Production of consumer goods was up by 10 percent, industrial production by 14 percent. The Soviet economy, still the second largest in the world, almost certainly will not collapse, but Russia—in the throes of reorganization and in need of foreign capital and trade concessions—cannot pose a threat of hegemony to Europe or Asia in the foreseeable future.

Centralization, ideology, and social welfare

Two political trends discernible during the later twentieth century are the greater concentration of authority within the state and the decline of ideology as a policy determinant. The first of these was to some extent induced by the ascendancy of the superpowers. The second has accompanied their subsiding influence. A strengthening of executive authority can be noted among states both old and new, socialist and capitalist, democracies and dictatorships. Accelerated by a search for security in an insecure world, this trend also reflected the felt need for governmental action to cope with the problems confronting society at the close of the Second World War. In almost all countries, successive administrations either initiated or expanded social-welfare programs, ensuring that entire populations would receive protection from the depredations of unemployment, sickness, and old age. Building upon the examples set by Germany and Britain before the First World War, Western nations instituted increasingly comprehensive national programs for health and social security. Socialist and Third World countries likewise moved, in some cases with remarkable speed, to alleviate the problems and disabilities of people who for generations had been denied the chance of a healthy and secure existence.

Reasons for the increased government planning

This movement to expand social-welfare systems resulted in an increased tendency on the part of governments to manage and control their citizenry. Programs of social insurance were designed to benefit and hence to regulate the lives of all classes of men and women, not just the destitute. New agencies, staffed by armies of newly recruited bureaucrats, imposed rules while they dispensed assistance to a clientele that grew to include the entire citizenry. As government planning became more sophisticated this increasingly large and powerful class of technocrats argued that decisions could only be based on expert knowledge that lay beyond the reach of elected representatives. The European Economic Community, whose headquarters was a bureaucratic hive staffed by thousands of supranational civil servants, seemed to critics in the 1980s a particularly potent breeder of a protechnocratic, antidemocratic attitude toward representative government.

The reaction against centralization

While beneficial in many respects, the centralization of power in the executive and consequent decline of legislative authority carries risks, notably a greater likelihood that civil liberties may be curtailed. Also, the enlargement of the sphere of governmental action in traditionally democratic states, together with the discovery that even powerful governments cannot prevent economic crises or heal all social ills, eventually led to disenchantment with government-directed programs, and a call for less interference in the private sector. During the mid-1970s a reaction of some magnitude occurred in several Western countries against the notion that governments should manage the lives of their citizens to the extent they were. Social reform, critics said, has cost too much, and has not really achieved what it was supposed to. There is still poverty and misery. Admit that they will always exist, these people argued, and moderate your goals accordingly; in the process, put an end to big government. This viewpoint was occasionally translated into political victory. The socialist government of Sweden, in power for decades, was succeeded by a conservative one. Margaret Thatcher, arch-conservative leader of Britain's Tory party, became the first woman prime minister of that country in 1979, as well as the first woman head of state of a Western nation, on a platform which blamed her country's economic decline in the 1970s on the fact that the government had overextended itself. In the United States, Ronald Reagan was elected president in 1980 after promising to undo much of the social legislation passed in the 1960s and early 1970s. As president, he continued to blame the country's economic problems—inflation, flagging production, unemployment—on the willingness of past administrations to spend borrowed money on programs in the areas of housing, education, and family assistance. (Reagan remained willing, however, to spend vast sums on armaments.)

The conservative wave ascendant during the 1970s and 1980s, while affecting policies and priorities, has not checked the continuing concentration of power. The effective site of power is not always in elected officials, not always visible. Agencies appointed by the executive and not directly accountable to the legislature, notably those engaged in espionage, may play a role in shaping foreign policy. Such nongovernmental entities as transnational corporations learn to operate within, and sometimes to manipulate, the political process. As long ago as the late 1950s President Dwight Eisenhower warned in his farewell presidential address of the growing might of what he called "the military-industrial complex." That his concern was justified was confirmed in the late 1960s and early 1970s, when the United States was at war in Vietnam. Evidence subsequently published showed that the democratically elected Congress was misled by President Lyndon Johnson and his advisors into believing that hostile North Vietnamese attacks on American ships had compelled U.S. intervention, whereas the attacks had instead been "manufactured" to allow the government to pursue its own aggressive policies. Concern about the arrogance of governmental power reached its peak in the United States during the Watergate investigations leading to the resignation of President Richard Nixon in 1974, when it was learned that Nixon had authorized domestic spying in the name of national security but without proper regard for the constitutional rights of American citizens. Following that dramatic episode came revelations about the role played in secret by the U.S. Central Intelligence Agency in subverting

Margaret Thatcher, Prime Minister of Great Britain from 1979 to 1990

President Nixon Resigns. Here Nixon bids his last farewell to the White House in the wake of his resignation.

leftist Third World governments, along with the intervention of giant multinational corporations and the CIA together in assisting to overthrow a democratically elected socialist government in Chile. Although Congress enacted legislation intended to hold the CIA and other intelligence agencies to strict accountability, they seemed as unrestrained as ever when the Reagan administration conducted military operations in Central America. The violation of treaties and of national and international law by agents of the executive branch during the 1980s far exceeded Richard Nixon's transgressions, but—although these actions were exposed in congressional hearings and a few individuals were indicted—no attempt was made to impeach the chief executive. Popular acceptance of a strong presidency is illustrated by the fact that the invasions of Grenada under President Reagan in 1983 and of Panama under President Bush in 1989—both in violation of signed treaties—were generally approved by members of Congress and the public.

It is too early to predict what effect the popular upheavals in eastern Europe and the USSR will have upon the evolution of political institutions. Concentration of power, which for the Russian Communist party was an article of faith, reached its climax in the terrifying dictatorship of Josef Stalin. Contemporary efforts to democratize the Communist party and the state may be expected to effect a significant decentralization of authority. After five years of struggle, however, Gorbachev became convinced that to carry out his reforms he would need to consolidate political power in his own hands. Avoiding the risk of defeat in a popular referendum, he persuaded the newly established Congress of People's Deputies to elect him to the office of president.

Efforts to democratize the Communist party and the Soviet state

Although competing ideologies still attract fervent supporters, doctrinaire programs designed as governmental policy guides have given way under the pressure of events. After the Second World War socialists throughout western Europe, recognizing the political popularity of economic prosperity, toned down their rhetoric and their demands, speaking far less about the inevitability of class war and more often about the contribution workers were making to the European postwar renaissance. A program adopted by the German Social Democrats in 1959, for example, abandoned orthodox Marxism by declaring the need to leave economic planning as much as possible to individual enterprise rather than in the hands of the state. Euro-communists collaborated with noncommunist reformers in France, Italy, and Spain.

The waning of ideology in the face of economic realities

Governments resorted to a variety of devices to encourage economic expansion. Virtually all of western Europe experimented with the nationalization of industry and services in an effort to enhance efficiency and productivity. The result was a series of mixed economies combining public and private ownership. In the United States where in contrast to other industrialized nations there was no national health insurance system and socialism was a pejorative term, beginning with the New Deal of the 1930s an increasing governmental regulation of industry,

The quest for economic expansion

finance, and agriculture was accepted as necessary to protect the public, especially its weaker members, from exploitation. In the 1980s the United States experienced an attempted return to the halcyon days of laissez-faire when the Reagan administration deactivated federal regulatory agencies. The results of this "revolution against big government" were, among others, an increase in occupational hazards in the workplace, pollution of the environment by toxic wastes from unsupervised nuclear weapons plants, and a spree of speculative investment by savings-and-loan institutions that culminated in the greatest financial scandal in American history, with a cost to generations of taxpayers as yet undetermined but certain to exceed $300 billion.

While the disintegration of communist regimes in eastern Europe and Russia provides the most dramatic examples of the withering of ideologies, the notion that it also represents the vindication of capitalism is naive. Some Western enthusiasts, hailing the victory of capitalism over its archrival, declared that human history had finally come to an end—an apocalyptic pronouncement reminiscent of ancient Zoroastrian eschatology, which envisioned the triumph of Light over Darkness in the world's final days. The peoples of eastern Europe in repudiating discredited political and economic institutions were not necessarily abandoning the ideals that had been entrusted to and betrayed by the managers of these institutions. Nor were contemporary capitalist states perfect models for the newly liberated societies to emulate.

*Western misperceptions of
the collapse of communist
regimes in eastern Europe*

Social tensions, inherent in every community, during the past half century in Europe and America produced movements that may be considered revolutionary. The traditional class struggle between proletariat and bourgeoisie, central to Marxist thought, became blurred as periods of prosperity lifted many workers into the middle class and as the multiplication of managerial and service roles made it difficult to identify a distinctly bourgeois sector. Labor unions remained generally stronger in western European nations than in the United States, which clung to the tradition that it has no permanent labor class. Here, however, inequity in the distribution of wealth was growing wider. A restructuring of the federal tax code in the 1980s, shifting a larger proportion of the burden to the lower-income groups, abetted this trend. In 1986 the wealthiest one-fifth of American families were receiving nearly 44 percent of the national income, while twice as many families earned barely more than 15 percent. Some social critics warned that American society, despite its great productive capacity, was breeding a permanent underclass, typified by the unemployed and often homeless inhabitants of crime- and drug-ridden urban slums.

*The blurring of the
traditional class struggle in
the West*

The years from 1965 to 1972 were marked by widespread protests and upheaval among youth in Europe and the United States. Young people had, of course, revolted in previous generations—indeed, revolt has always been considered a prerogative of youth. The Russian revolution of 1917 and the Nazi movement of the 1930s were both instances

Student Uprising at the University of Paris, May 1968. Following demonstrations calling for sweeping reforms at the university, French students took to the streets to make their case more forcefully and violently at the barricades.

in point. Yet in those cases, leadership had come from an older generation. Now it was to come from men and women in their twenties. The most serious outbreak of student unrest in Europe occurred in Paris in the spring of 1968. Inspired in part by the role youths had played in the revolt against Soviet oppression in Czechoslovakia that same year, French students at the University of Paris demanded reforms that would modernize their university. Confrontation with authorities precipitated riots, which in turn brought police interference. Sympathy with the students' cause expanded to encompass opposition to de Gaulle's regime, leading to massive trade union strikes. By mid-May 10 million French workers had walked off their jobs. The government was able to satisfy the strikers by acquiescing to wage increases, thereby isolating the students, who grudgingly agreed to resume university life. Young people across Europe staged protests as well. Students in Berlin rioted at the appearance there of the shah of Iran and against newspapers critical of the revolt of the young. In Italy, undergraduates staged a lengthy series of riots to draw attention to university overcrowding. And in the United States, serious protests against the Vietnam War continued into the early 1970s.

More significant and less ephemeral than the revolt of youth were efforts on behalf of ethnic minorities and women—two groups almost universally subject to discrimination. Women, like young people, began to assert themselves during the 1960s and 1970s. As was the case with the youth rebellion, the women's movement was first directed from within the middle class. By the mid-seventies the movement had spread worldwide, including the Third World nations, and was no longer limited to the middle class. Many of the early activists within the movement had been part of the youth rebellion during

The women's movement

its most intense phase in the sixties. Their activism, in part, stemmed from a realization that even in a radical political atmosphere, women were relegated to second place. Women's position within society had changed dramatically since the nineteenth century. The assumption that the middle-class woman's place was in the home had been challenged by the ever-increasing demand for women workers and by the need experienced by more and more women to hold a job—either for financial reasons or because housework was for a growing number an unfulfilling occupation. The increased availability and social acceptance of birth-control devices meant that women were having fewer children, and that they could begin to exercise more control over the pattern of their lives.

Yet society seemed loath to acknowledge the implication of these changes: that women are equal to men. Women were paid less than men for similar work. Women with qualifications no different from men were turned down because of their gender when they applied for jobs. Women with excellent employment records were forced to rely on their husbands to establish credit. Political action helped alleviate some of these inequities in the late 1960s and the 1970s. The U.S. government instituted programs of "affirmative action" which mandated the hiring of qualified women as well as members of racial minority groups. In Britain an Equal Pay Act, passed in the late 1960s, established that wages for women should be equal to those of men holding the same job. In France, a ministry for the status of women was created in the mid-1970s.

Women's political action

The campaign for equality did not meet with universal approval, however. A particularly volatile subject was a woman's right to an abortion. Feminists argued that women must enjoy the freedom to plan for their future unencumbered by the responsibilities of motherhood if they choose, and that their bodies are theirs to govern. Their opponents, which included members of the so-called right-to-life movement, countered with the argument that abortion encouraged

The issue of abortion

Vietnam Protest, 1971. Veterans of the U.S. Armed Forces march on the Capitol to protest continued U.S. involvement in the war in Vietnam.

The Women's Movement in France. French women demand equal pay for equal work.

sexual irresponsibility; some declared that abortion is the equivalent of murder. By the mid-1980s, however, despite the failure in the United States of passage of a constitutional Equal Rights Amendment, the campaigners for women's equality had a good many successes to their credit.

The Third World and racial conflict

The liberation of colonial peoples in the decades following the Second World War heightened racial consciousness and racial conflict, not only in Africa and Asia but in the West as well. Newly independent black nations, on guard against real or perceived threats of neocolonialism, remained understandably sensitive to the fact of their economic dependence upon the predominantly white nations of Western Europe and America. Black and Asian immigration into those nations produced tension and frequent violence. And indigenous black populations in the West, particularly in the United States, derived a sense of both their present social and economic inferiority and their potential strength as a political force from the independence movements occurring elsewhere in the world.

U.S. blacks after the Civil War

The growth of insurgency among American blacks paralleled the rise of black nations in Africa and the Caribbean. Through most of the years from the Civil War to 1900, black people were condemned, in the North as well as the South, to a subordinate role within a predominantly white culture. Black political consciousness and black leaders were not unknown before the turn of the century: Harriet Tubman, Sojourner Truth, Frederick Douglass, Nat Turner, and others, were eloquent and powerful spokespeople and activists. But with the twentieth century came a massive emigration of blacks from the

South to the North. Although the North shared most of the attitudes of the South, there were more opportunities for blacks in the industrial cities than in the primarily agrarian South. Many thousands of black people emigrated to the North during the years of the First World War, when the lack of white labor created a need for their services.

In 1910 the National Association for the Advancement of Colored People was founded and contributed to the growing awareness among black people that they were an oppressed group and that this should be changed. The work of the NAACP was supplemented in 1911 with the founding of the National League on Urban Conditions Among Negroes (later known as the National Urban League). The work of black leaders of this time—for example, Ida Wells-Barnett (1862–1931), A. Philip Randolph (1889–1979), W. E. B. Du Bois (1868–1963), Mary McLeod Bethune (1875–1955)—who were visible and vocal opponents of lynching, promoters of educational opportunities for blacks, and of the organization of blacks into labor unions, kept the movement for equality alive.

The Second World War saw another influx of blacks into northern cities and intensified their drive for dignity and independence. The Congress of Racial Equality (CORE) was founded by James Farmer in 1942. By 1960 CORE had combined its efforts with those of other political and civil rights organizations seeking the same goals. Together they helped to promote "freedom rides" on behalf of civil rights and boycotts directed at private businesses and public services that discriminated against blacks in the South. The leader of these protests, and the undoubted leader of the black movement in the United States in the 1960s, was Martin Luther King, Jr. (1929–1968), a Baptist minister. Like Farmer, King embraced the Gandhian philosophy of nonviolence. His personal participation in countless demonstrations, his willingness to go to jail for a cause that he believed to be just, and his ability as an orator to arouse both blacks and whites with his message led to his position as the most highly regarded—and widely feared—defender of black rights. His career was ended by assassination in 1968.

The goal of King and of organizations like CORE was a fully integrated nation. That of other charismatic black leaders was complete independence from white society. Marcus Garvey (1887–1940), a native of Jamaica who lived in the black New York City ghetto of Harlem, emphasized the African origins of black Americans. He claimed that his people were the descendants of the "greatest and proudest race who ever peopled the earth." In his campaign for black separatism he generated a movement of black emigration from America to Africa. Another black separatist was Malcolm X (1925–1965), who assumed the "X" after having discarded his "white" surname. For most of his adult life a spokesman for the Black Muslim movement, Malcolm X urged blacks to renew their commitment to their own heritage—the Muslim religion, for example—and to establish black

Early twentieth-century civil rights movements

Martin Luther King, Jr., American Civil Rights Activist

Black independence: Garvey and Malcolm X

British Police Arrest a Black Rioter in the London Suburb of Brixton, 1981. Deteriorating relations between police and black residents, along with high unemployment, were cited as causes of the violence.

Blacks in the 1970s and 1980s

businesses as a way of maintaining economic and psychological distance from white domination. Like King, he was assassinated, in 1965 while addressing a rally in Harlem.

Civil rights laws enacted under the administration of President Lyndon B. Johnson (1908–1973) in the 1960s brought American blacks some measure of equality with regard to voting rights—and, to a much lesser degree, school desegregation. In other areas, such as housing and job opportunities, blacks continue to suffer disadvantage and discrimination, as a result of white racism, which lies beneath arguments that blacks should be satisfied with the gains they have made, and the general recalcitrance of administrations following Johnson's domestically innovative one. These problems are not confined to the United States. In Great Britain, for example, where there has been a large immigration of blacks from former colonies, extreme discrimination in jobs and housing menaces the chances for early or satisfactory integration. Because most black workers are "last hired, first fired," they are particular victims of Britain's rising unemployment. In the summer of 1981 and again in 1985 black frustrations resulted in serious rioting in London and other British cities. Disturbances broke out again in the United States in 1982 in Miami, where an influx of Latin American refugees, most of them Cuban, had created further tensions. Response to these outbreaks followed the pattern established in the 1960s: immediate concern and investigation, but little else, particularly in terms of solving the problems of economic inequality. In the United States the poverty rate among blacks is still three times that for whites.

Many Third World countries are rich in natural resources. Nations in the Middle East, Venezuela and Mexico in Latin America, and Nigeria in Africa possess oil in quantities sufficient to make every move vitally important to energy-consuming states. Other African nations, Zaire and Angola, for example, contain valuable mineral deposits. Some small states that gained independence after the Second World War have industrialized to the point of competing successfully for a share in world markets. Developments in both North and South Korea show that it is possible for small countries, even in the wake of war's devastation, to rise above the low economic level that afflicts most of the Third World. In both Koreas a program of land distribution to small farmers created a strong agricultural base, a prerequisite for high productivity which has likewise been achieved in China and Taiwan but not yet in India or Latin America. South Korea, with the benefit of U.S. financial assistance, sustained an average annual growth rate of 7 percent between 1960 and 1986, raising its per capita yearly income from $100 to $2,180. No longer a purely agrarian society, the Republic of Korea now ranks near the top in such fields as shipbuilding (second to Japan), electronics, steel, and automobile manufacture.

Population is both a liability and an asset in the Third World. The people of China, by their sheer numbers, constitute an implicit threat to the balance of power. The people of India, again by their numbers, represent a threat to the stability of their own country and hence to all Asia. While ranging in income levels from the fabulously wealthy Persian Gulf oil emirates to the semitribal peasant communities of Africa, a majority of the Third World nations are desperately poor. The most destitute of all, such as Bangladesh, are sometimes referred to as the Fourth World. During the decade of the 1980s, despite improvement in China and India, poverty increased drastically in other parts of Asia, in sub-Sahara Africa, and in Latin America. A United Nations Food and Agricultural Organization report disclosed that a billion people—one-fifth of the earth's inhabitants—exist in absolute poverty.

Since 1950 per capita income in the wealthy nations has nearly tripled in real terms while remaining almost stationary throughout the Third World, continually widening the gap between the rich countries and the poor to the detriment of both. As ideologies fade and superpower rivalry subsides, the most critical confrontation may prove to be between the industrially advanced "have" nations and the dispossessed—a confrontation sometimes phrased as "North" versus "South." Economists stress the need to narrow the gap. This can be done effectively only by utilizing the resources of the developing countries to raise the economic level of their own societies. Too often these resources have been transferred out of their place of origin through trade and loan arrangements. Aid to the Third World, never excessively generous, has been designed largely to benefit the donor's economy or to further strategic objectives by strengthening an ally. For example, U.S. aid funds to Israel in 1988 were equal to $631 for every Israeli, while the sub-Sahara African countries received less than $2 per capita in U.S. assistance. By the 1980s the indebtedness of Third World countries had increased to the point that interest payments exceeded all that was received in financial aid—presenting the depressing spectacle of a "Marshall Plan in reverse." When the debt incurred by developing countries reaches unmanageable proportions the possibility of default sends jitters through creditor nations, not only because bankers might lose their investments but also because thousands of workers might lose their jobs if buying power dries up in the debtor countries.

The potential dangers of Western patterns of development

Attempts on the part of Third World nations to catch up with the West by following Western patterns of "development" may actually have worsened their condition by inducing them to abandon agricultural practices that sustained their societies for centuries. Encouraged to increase income by exporting the raw materials desired by industrialized states, they switch from diversified to one-crop agriculture and too rapidly deplete mineral and forest resources. Tragically, in many regions the opium poppy or the cocaine-yielding coca plant has replaced nutritional crops that no longer command a high enough price in world markets to make them profitable exports.

The militarization of Third World societies

Every war fought since 1945 has directly involved one or more Third World nations. Incessant immersion in armed conflict has not only taken a heavy toll in lives and property but has induced these countries to militarize their own societies. Much of the aid supplied by donor countries has gone to national military establishments. Since the mid-1960s three-fourths of all arms sales have been to Third or Fourth World nations, some of which cannot feed or house their own people. During the last twenty years the number of armored vehicles in Third World states quadrupled. Their total defense budgets are seven times as great as they were in 1960. Though bruised by the arms race, many Third World countries joined it, eventually aspiring to possess thermonuclear and chemical weapons.

Problems in the making?

The deep-seated problems of Third World nations are rapidly becoming problems for all of humanity. Almost every part of the Third and Fourth Worlds is a potential trouble spot. Prosperous states, disappointed with results of the aid they have given to developing nations, may be reluctant to continue it, especially while the eastern European countries are in need of help to revive their economies. At the same time the military establishments in prosperous states, sensing an end to the Cold War and needing to target a new enemy, may look to the vast populations with unfulfilled expectations as potential antagonists. A conference attended by fifteen Latin American and U.S. military commanders in Argentina in March 1987 defined the threat to national security as "Amero-communism," exemplified by the growth of labor unions, peasant associations, and popular movements demanding reform. The conferees branded as agitators of an international communist plot such institutions as the Ford Foundation, the American Association of Jurists, and the Latin American Council of Churches. Under the administration of President George Bush the United States has begun to deploy military forces in joint efforts with Latin American governments to suppress the drug traffic. Because some Latin American army officers have working relationships with drug lords, and because in both Colombia and Peru the "drug war" is to some extent a civil war between the oligarchy and the *campesinos,* U.S. intervention could escalate into another Nicaragua or Vietnam.

4. INTELLECTUAL AND CULTURAL PATTERNS

Intellectual life in the West after 1945, patterned broadly as it had been in the interwar years, was too diverse to be comprehended within any single category. While many creative thinkers grappled with the problems of our era, either directly or obliquely—suggesting ways of dealing with them or finding them beyond hope of solution— others experimented with new and seemingly obscure modes of expression. The gulf remained wide between the avant-garde and the generally educated public—now far larger than ever before, thanks to burgeoning universities. If attendance at museums increased—as it did dramatically—more often than not it was because people were attracted by exhibits of treasures from the distant past—from King Tutankhamen's tomb or from the Renaissance collections of the Vatican Museum. Audiences who welcomed a chance to hear the works of long-dead composers—Mozart and Verdi—sung by internationally acclaimed "stars"—the soprano Maria Callas, the tenor Luciano Pavarotti—rejected as pointless the puzzling works of composers such as John Cage, whose "silent sonata" entitled "4.33" consisted of a pianist seated at the piano for precisely four minutes, thirty-three seconds, but who never once actually struck a note. Intellectuals, on the other hand, railed against the increasing vapidity of mass culture and in particular of television, the "idiot box" that by 1965 had found its way into 62 million homes in the United States, 13 million in Britain, 10 million in West Germany, 5 million each in France and Italy. They also objected to the promotion of art and music as big business, with jam-packed "blockbuster" art exhibits attended by tens of thousands and opera tickets sold at prices approaching $100 apiece.

Growing gulf between avant-garde and the educated laymen

Despite this continuing alienation, the work of many of the West's leading writers did reflect the dilemmas of the human condition that prevailed throughout the years after 1945. During the immediate postwar period novelists concerned themselves with the horrors of war

Postwar literature

and of the totalitarian systems that had spawned the conflict of the 1940s. The Americans James Jones (1921–1977) and Norman Mailer (1923–   ), in *From Here to Eternity* and *The Naked and the Dead,* portrayed the coarseness and cruelty of military life with ruthless realism. The German Günter Grass's (1927–   ) first and probably most important novel, *The Tin Drum,* depicted the vicious and politically diseased life of Nazi Germany in the 1930s. In France Jean-Paul Sartre (1905–1980), as a result of his own and his country's wartime experiences, recommitted himself in his novels, plays, and other writings to a life of active political involvement as a Marxist. Whereas he had previously defined hell in terms of individual hostilities, he now defined it in terms of class inequality. Unlike Sartre, his compatriot Albert Camus (1913–1960) was unable to construct a secular faith from his own perceptions of the world and its apparent absurdities. Though idealist enough to participate in the French resistance movement against the German occupation in the Second World War, and though proclaiming the virtues of rebellion, Camus remained tortured in novels such as *The Fall, The Plague,* and *The Rebel* by the problem of humanity's responsibility for its own miserable dilemma and by the limitations placed upon the ability of men and women to help each other.

Shifting focus on Marx in the West

Marxism continued to attract European intellectuals, both as a recipe for changing the world and as a way of explaining it. Historians, economists, and sociologists focused their attention more frequently on the writings of the younger Marx, less on his economic theories, more on his perceptions of alienation and class consciousness. The writings of the Italian Antonio Gramsci (1891–1937) and the Hungarian Georg Lukacs (1885–1971), both concerned with these particular matters, attracted widespread attention. Claude Lévi-Strauss (1908–   ), a French sociologist who considers himself a Marxist in contemporary matters, nevertheless applied a different model than Marx's essentially idealist and value-laden dialectic to the study of society. A leading exponent of the so-called structuralist school, Lévi-Strauss subjected all elements of the primitive societies he studied—kinship, rituals, and traditions—to analysis in terms of thought structures, which though unconscious, were nevertheless said to possess an objective reality. He argued that his method proved the intrinsic value of every society and that there was rationality where many had previously seen only the irrational or the absurd.

The fate of Marx within the Soviet Union

It is worth noting that these reinterpretations of Marx came from outside the Soviet Union. Inside, genuine philosophical debate has been repressed by the government, although nothing like the grisly purges of the 1930s has occurred since the Stalin era. Soviet thinkers, while paying lip service to Marxism's past achievements, kept their innermost thoughts to themselves. With the coming of *glasnost* in the 1980s, they began to denounce the repression under which they had suffered and to participate in the process of political change.

Four Darks in Red, Mark Rothko (1903–1970). Oil on canvas. Rothko became obsessed with the need to reduce both color and form, achieving thereby a kind of gloomy mysticism. (The Whitney Museum of American Art)

Summer Rental No. 2, Robert Rauschenberg (born 1925). Oil on canvas. Rauschenberg experiments with problems of dimensionality and painterly technique as he strives to achieve a total harmony out of disparate elements. (Collection Whitney Museum of American Art). Gift of the Friends of the Whitney Museum of American Art.

Three Flags, Jasper Johns (born 1930). Encaustic on canvas. Painted with absolute objectivity Johns' objects, in this case three American flags, cease to be mere reproductions and take on distinctive identities of their own. (The Whitney Museum of American Art)

Woman with Dog, Duane Hansen (born 1925). Polyvinyl, polychromed in oil, life size. Hansen recreates the human artifacts of Middle-American culture as symbols of a hollow society. (Collection Whitney Museum of American Art). Gift of Frances and Sydney Lewis.

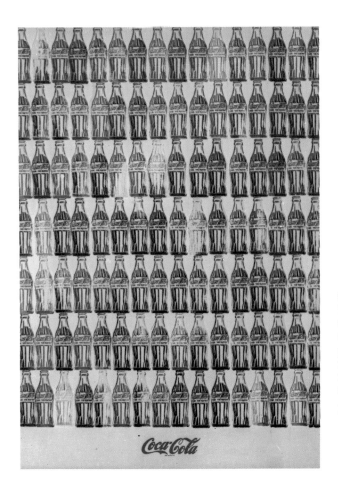

Green Coca Cola Bottles, Andy Warhol (born 1931). Oil on canvas. Warhol, who stands as the high priest of the "pop art" movement in the public imagination, turns mass production into art. Here he takes a commercial product and presents it in row after row, much as it might appear on a grocery store shelf. (Collection Whitney Museum of American Art). Gift of the Friends of the Whitney Museum of American Art.

Gran Cairo, Frank Stella (born 1936). Synthetic polymer paint on canvas. The artist employs absolute symmetry and a rectilinear pattern with compelling effect. (Collection Whitney Museum of American Art). Gift of the Friends of the Whitney Museum of American Art.

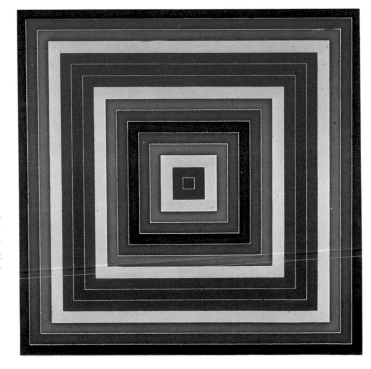

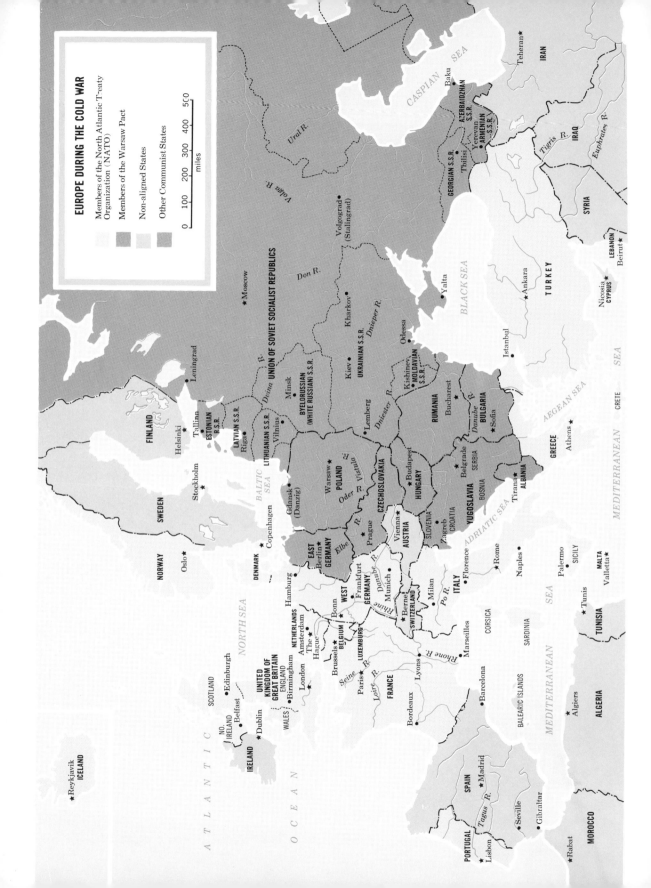

EUROPE DURING THE COLD WAR

Members of the North Atlantic Treaty
Organization (NATO)

Members of the Warsaw Pact

Non-aligned States

Other Communist States

0   100   200   300   400   500
miles

ICELAND ★Reykjavik

IRELAND ★Dublin
NO. IRELAND ●Belfast
SCOTLAND ●Edinburgh
WALES
UNITED KINGDOM OF GREAT BRITAIN
ENGLAND ●Birmingham
London ★

NETHERLANDS Amsterdam ★
The Hague ★
BELGIUM Brussels ★
LUXEMBURG ★

FRANCE Paris ★
Bordeaux ●
Lyons ●
Marseilles ●

PORTUGAL Lisbon ★
SPAIN Madrid ★
Barcelona ●
Seville ●
Gibraltar ●

MOROCCO Rabat ★

Algiers ●
ALGERIA

Tunis ★
TUNISIA

BALEARIC ISLANDS
SARDINIA
CORSICA

ITALY Rome ★
Florence ●
Milan ●
Naples ●
Palermo ●
SICILY
MALTA Valletta ★

SWITZERLAND Berne ★
AUSTRIA Vienna ★

WEST GERMANY Bonn ★
Hamburg ●
Frankfurt ●
Munich ●

EAST GERMANY Berlin ★

DENMARK Copenhagen ★

NORWAY Oslo ★
SWEDEN Stockholm ★

FINLAND Helsinki ★

POLAND Warsaw ★
Gdansk (Danzig) ●

CZECHOSLOVAKIA Prague ★

HUNGARY Budapest ★

YUGOSLAVIA Belgrade ★
SLOVENIA
CROATIA Zagreb ★
BOSNIA
SERBIA

ALBANIA Tirana ★

RUMANIA Bucharest ★

BULGARIA Sofia ★

GREECE Athens ★

TURKEY Ankara ★
Istanbul ●

CYPRUS Nicosia ★
CRETE

ESTONIAN R.S.R. Tallinn ●
LATVIAN S.S.R. Riga ●
LITHUANIAN S.S.R. Vilnius ●
●Leningrad
Moscow ★

UNION OF SOVIET SOCIALIST REPUBLICS

Minsk ●
BYELORUSSIAN (WHITE RUSSIAN) S.S.R.

Lemberg ●
Kiev ●
Kharkov ●
UKRAINIAN S.S.R.

Odessa ●

Kishinev ●
MOLDAVIAN S.S.R.

Volgograd (Stalingrad) ●

Yalta ●

Baku ●
AZERBAIDZHAN S.S.R.
Tbilisi ●
GEORGIAN S.S.R.
Yerevan ●
ARMENIAN S.S.R.

Teheran ★
IRAN

IRAQ

Tigris R.
Euphrates R.

SYRIA

LEBANON Beirut ★

Ural R.
Volga R.
Don R.
Dnieper R.
Dniester R.
Duna R.
Oder R.
Vistula R.
Elbe R.
Danube R.
Rhine R.
Po R.
Rhône R.
Seine R.
Loire R.
Tagus R.

ATLANTIC OCEAN
NORTH SEA
BALTIC SEA
BLACK SEA
CASPIAN SEA
AEGEAN SEA
ADRIATIC SEA
MEDITERRANEAN SEA

The specific issues that drove men and women in western Europe and America to committed action in the mid-1960s compelled writers to take sides as well. Günter Grass, in *Local Anaesthetic*, published in 1970, was only one of many who wrote of student unrest and political involvement. Women authors described not only the general loneliness of the human condition, but the particular plight of women trapped in a world not of their own making. The Frenchwoman Simone de Beauvoir (1908–1986) in *The Second Sex*, a germinal study of the female condition, denounced the male middle class for turning not only workers but also its own women into objects for its own ends. American writers like Germaine Greer, Tillie Olsen, and the philosopher Mary Daly helped define the politics and culture of the women's movement.

Simone de Beauvoir

The theme of individual alienation and helplessness, a reflection of the problems arising from the growth of state power, was one to which writers addressed themselves with increasing frequency in the 1960s and 1970s. The Russian Boris Pasternak (1890–1960), in his novel *Dr. Zhivago*, indicted the Soviet campaign to shape all its citizens to the same mold. His countryman Aleksandr Solzhenitsyn (1918–) attacked the brutal methods employed by the Soviet Union in its rapid climb to world power. His *Gulag Archipelago*, published in 1973, is a fictionalized account of the fate of those whose willingness to stand in the way of Soviet "progress" sentenced them to life in Siberian labor camps. Although both Pasternak and Solzhenitsyn were awarded the Nobel Prize for literature, the former in 1958 and the latter in 1970, their works were condemned by the Soviet government and Solzhenitsyn was sent into exile. Herbert Marcuse, (1898–1979), an American, charged that authoritarianism was just as much a fact of life under capitalism as under communism. He argued that industrial capitalism had produced a "one-dimensional" society, in which the interests of individual citizens had been ruthlessly subordinated to those of the powerful corporate interests which were the true governors of the world.

Boris Pasternak

Some authors, although they agreed with indictments of contemporary civilization, believed the human condition too hopeless to warrant direct attack. They expressed their despair by escaping into the absurd and fantastic. In the plays of Samuel Beckett (1906–1986), an Irishman who wrote in French, and of the Englishman Harold Pinter (1930–), nothing happens. Characters speak in the banalities that have become the hallmark of modern times. Words which are meaningless when spoken by human beings nevertheless take on a logic of their own; yet they explain nothing. Other authors, less willing, perhaps, to attempt to make a statement out of nothingness, have invaded the realms of hallucination, science fiction, and fantasy. The novels of the Americans William Burroughs and Kurt Vonnegut convey their readers from interior fantasizing to outer space. Significantly one of the most popular books among the youth of the sixties and seventies

Aleksandr Solzhenitsyn

Film

Fine arts

See color plates
following page 870 for
representative works by
Rothko, Rauschenberg,
Johns, Hansen, and
Stella

was *The Lord of the Rings,* a pseudo-saga set in the fantasy world of "Middle Earth," written before the Second World War by the Englishman J. R. R. Tolkien.

Filmmakers, in the decades after the Second World War, made films which mirrored the problems and concerns of society, with a depth and artistic integrity seldom attempted or achieved previously. The Swede Ingmar Bergman, the Frenchmen Jean-Luc Godard and François Truffaut, the Italians Frederico Fellini and Michelangelo Antonioni, to name but a few of the most gifted directors, dealt in their films with the same themes that marked the literature of the period: loneliness, war, oppression, and corruption. One important factor facilitating the achievement of artistic quality was the general willingness on the part of censors—state or industry sponsored—to reflect public taste by permitting filmmakers great license in the handling of themes such as racism, violence, and sexuality. While there is no question that this relaxation led to exploitation, it cleared the way for extraordinarily powerful film statements, such as the American Arthur Penn's *Bonnie and Clyde* (1967) and the Italian Bernardo Bertolucci's *Last Tango in Paris* (1972), shocking declarations about humanity made possible by explicit depictions of violence and sex. Several powerful American films depicted the senseless brutality of the Vietnam war. Film, while gaining a general maturity it had heretofore lacked, did not desert its role as entertainment. The international popularity of the British rock-and-roll group, the Beatles, was translated, for example, into equally successful films—charming, slapstick escapism which nevertheless proclaimed the emancipation of youth from the confining formalities and conventions of their elders.

Unlike writers or filmmakers, the majority of postwar artists did not use their work as a vehicle to express either ideological commitment or a concern for the human situation. Following trends established by the impressionists and cubists, they spoke neither about the world nor to the world, but instead to each other and to the extremely small coterie of initiates who understood their artistic language. Foremost among the postwar schools of art was abstract expressionism, whose chief exponents were the American painters Jackson Pollock (1912–1956), Willem de Kooning (1904–   ), and Franz Kline (1910–1962). Their interests lay in further experimentation with the relationship between color, texture, and surface, to the total exclusion of "meaning" or "message" in the traditional sense. Jasper John's painting of the American flag demanded that the viewer see it not as *a* painting—that is, something to be interpreted—but instead as painting, the treatment of canvas with paint. Robert Rauschenberg, in revolt against the abstract expressionists, exhibited blank white panels, insisting that by so doing he was pressing art to the ultimate question of a choice of medium. Painters fought the notion that their work in some way expressed disgust with an empty civilization. "My paintings are based on the fact that only what can be seen is there," declared the American Frank Stella, who painted stripes on irregularly shaped

Composition (1955) by Willem de Kooning. A work representative of the abstract expressionists' desire to explore the varieties of light, texture, and surface.

canvases. "Pop" art, a phenomenon of the late sixties which took as its subject everyday objects such as soup cans and comic-strip heroes, was likewise, according to its practitioners, not a protest against the banality of industrialism but another experiment in abstractions.

Even the remote and yet extraordinarily compelling abstractions of Mark Rothko (1903–1970), glowing or somber rectangles of color imposed upon other rectangles, were said by the artist himself to represent "nothing but content—no associations, only sensation." Only with the coming, in the 1970s, of the so-called hyper-realists, artists such as the American Duane Hansen, who recreates his invariably depressing human subjects in plastic down to the last eyelash, can we perhaps say that some artists are making a statement not only about technique but about what they perceive as the vacuity of life. Most artists, however, remained uninterested in commenting directly upon the elements of alienation, pain, and despair that were a part of Western life in the forty years after the Second World War or upon the generally positive, productive nature of society during that same exciting, if ultimately disappointing, period.

Divorce of visual arts from social commentary

5. THE PROBLEMS OF ECOLOGY AND POPULATION

Pessimism about the human condition in the 1980s stemmed from more than the problems of the present. It derived as well from a

The meaning of ecology

Assaults upon nature

fear about the future, the future of the earth's human beings, of the earth itself, and of what is termed its ecology. The word *ecology* is often used to refer to human beings and their environment, but its meaning is much broader than that. Ecologists think of humans as related to a vast chain of life which extends through mammals, amphibians, invertebrates, and the simplest microorganisms, either plants or animals. In popular usage ecology may be synonymous with pollution problems. Again this is an oversimplification. The causes and prevention of pollution make up important elements in the study of ecology, but they are not its whole subject. Equally important is the use of our environment in ways that will safeguard the heritage of fertile soil, pure air, fresh water, and forests for those who come after us.

Ecological violations consist not merely of poisoning the atmosphere and contaminating oceans, rivers, and lakes by dumping wastes into them, but of any assault upon them that makes them less valuable for human survival. The excessive construction of dams, for example, causes the silting of rivers and the accumulating of nitrates at a faster rate than the surrounding soil can absorb. The use of insecticides, especially those containing DDT, may result in upsetting the balance of nature. An example in the recent history of Malaysia illustrates such an occurrence. The Malaysian government resorted to extensive spraying of remote areas with DDT in the hope of stamping out malaria-carrying mosquitoes. The DDT killed the mosquitoes but also poisoned the flourishing cockroaches. The cockroaches in turn were eaten by the village cats. The cats died of the DDT poison. The net result was a multiplication of rats formerly kept from a population explosion by their natural enemies, the cats. So badly disturbed was the balance of nature that a fresh supply of cats had to be airlifted from other regions. Other assaults upon the balance of nature have been even more serious. The Aswan High Dam of Egypt, undoubtedly valuable for increasing the water supply of that country, has at the same time cut down the flow of algal nutrients to the Mediterranean, with damaging effects on the fishing industry of various countries. From the ecological standpoint the rapid development of industry in modern times is an almost unmitigated disaster. For thousands of years the human race introduced into the environment no more waste substances than could easily be absorbed by the environment. But modern technology has introduced a variety of wastes never abundant before. Among them are carbon monoxide, carbon dioxide, sulfur dioxide, and nitrogen oxide, carried in the atmosphere as poisonous gases. Besides a host of synthetic products that are not biodegradable, nature has been inundated with toxins from pesticides, wastes from nuclear reactors and weapons plants, and the fallout of nuclear testing. Some 150 million Americans live in cities where the air they breathe is dangerous to their health. As the nature and gravity of these problems become apparent, governments are pressured to take preventive and

Disaster at the Chernobyl Nuclear Power Station, May 1986. The explosion at this Soviet nuclear power facility (the white arrow indicates the damaged unit surrounded by debris) near Kiev produced radioactive fallout that killed and injured numerous people close to the site, and threatened the health of thousands more as it spread across Europe. This accident fueled the continuing debate on the safety of nuclear power plants not only in the Soviet Union but around the earth.

remedial action. In late 1982 the United States government was actually compelled to purchase the entire town of Times Beach, Missouri, where a pesticide had been sprayed (with permanently damaging effects to the health of its citizens), before it could proceed with a detoxification program. In 1986, a nuclear power station at Chernobyl, near Kiev in the Soviet Union, exploded, producing highly dangerous radioactive fallout not only in the vicinity of the accident but, because of prevailing winds, across the continent of Europe. Affected countries protested, while citizens increased the pressure on their governments to curtail the manufacture of such lethal industrial and military by-products.

The ecological problem is caused not simply by the dumping of harmful and nondegradable products. It is also the result of wastage of land as our most valuable natural resource. In many parts of the world rivers run brown because they are filled with earth washed from the fields bordering them. Each year 24 billion tons of earth's topsoil are lost, largely through erosion. Forests are disappearing, not only from overcutting but from the effects of "acid rain" produced by the millions of tons of sulfur dioxide spewed into the air by utilities and other soft-coal–burning plants.

Ecology and the population explosion

Of increasing concern in recent years is the prospect of a gradual warming of the earth's climate from emissions that trap heat currents within the atmosphere. This is the so-called greenhouse effect, which could eventually melt the polar icecaps. In May 1990 a panel of thirty-nine nations concluded that, if the warming trend is not checked, rising sea levels will inundate Bangladesh, the Netherlands, and numerous other coastal areas and islands. This slow but detectable climatic

Global warming

change is directly linked to the accumulation of carbon dioxide gas. Some 5.6 billion tons of CO_2 are discharged into the atmosphere every year as a result of the burning of fossil fuels and of the annual destruction of more than forty million acres of tropical forest. A parallel hazard lies in the depletion of the ozone layer through chemical reaction with chlorofluorocarbons (CFCs), used in aerosol sprays and in refrigerants. Destruction of the ozone would expose living creatures to damaging radiation from the sun's ultraviolet rays.

Strategies for slowing or reversing ecological deterioration

Although the rate of ecological deterioration is justifiably alarming, the process can probably be reversed if governments, with popular support and the cooperation of industry, are willing to take the steps—not all of them costly—already identified by environmentalists as essential. Carbon dioxide emissions could be cut almost in half through energy conservation practices alone. Mass-transit systems could reduce the need for automobiles, and these could be powered with nonpolluting fuels. Fully insulating homes and water heaters and replacing incandescent with fluorescent lighting could reduce the consumption of electricity by at least one-third. The sun, wind, and tides are vast renewable and nonpolluting sources of energy that have barely begun to be tapped. Among many recently reported inventions are air conditioners and refrigerators that use no CFCs and "super-windows" that collect solar heat in winter and deflect the sun's rays in summer. Racing against time, several governments have initiated bold programs to help save the environment. Norway and the Netherlands led the way by imposing restrictions on automotive and industrial emissions. Great Britain and West Germany are contemplating similar action. Australia, where eighteen species of mammals and one hundred of flowering plants suffered extinction during the past two centuries, proposes to plant a billion trees during the decade of the 1990s.

Ecology and the population explosion

A close link exists between the problems of ecology and the population explosion that is occurring throughout the world. Indeed, if population had not increased alarmingly in recent years, the problems of ecology might well have passed unnoticed. For example, New York City on the eve of the Civil War had a total population of 700,000. The area was not essentially smaller than it is now. Yet the inhabitants of the five boroughs constituting the city have multiplied ten times over. The example of New York City can be duplicated in many other overcrowded areas, not only in America but especially in Asia. Calcutta now has a population of 10.5 million, compared with 3 million in 1961. Tokyo has grown from 9 million to over 14 million in little more than twenty years. The total population of the earth at the beginning of the Christian era was about 250 million. More than sixteen centuries passed before another quarter-billion had been added to that total. Not until 1860 did the population of the globe approximate 1 billion. From then on the increase was vastly more rapid. The sixth half-billion, added about 1960, required scarcely more than ten years. By 1990 the earth's population had surpassed 5 billion.

Industrial Pollution. This photo shows steel mills in Westfalenhuette, West Germany. While polluting gases and particular matter are released into the air, industrial wastes, both thermal and chemical, are released into nearby waters.

What have been the causes of this demographic revolution that overturned the ancient balance between births and deaths that long kept the population on a stationary or slowly rising level? Fundamentally, what has happened has been the achievement of a twentieth-century death rate alongside a medieval birthrate. Infant mortality rates have markedly declined, except in the Third World, where 40,000 infants die each year from malnutrition and infectious diseases. Deaths of mothers in childbirth have also diminished. The great plagues, such as cholera, typhus, and tuberculosis, take a much smaller toll than they did in earlier centuries. Wars and famines still number their victims by the millions, yet such factors are insufficient to counteract an uncurbed rate of reproduction. Though the practice of contraception has been approved by the governments of such nations as India, China, and Japan, only in the last decade have the effects of that policy been noticeable. In some countries poverty, religion, and ignorance have made the widespread use of contraceptives difficult. Leaders in Third World countries charge that attempts by Western powers to encourage them to limit population growth, either by contraceptive devices or by sterilization, is a not-so-subtle form of genocide.

The effects of the demographic revolution have been most conspicuous in the underdeveloped nations of Central and South America, Africa, and Asia. Whereas the population of the world as a whole will double, at present rates of increase, in thirty-five years, that of Central and South America will multiply twofold in only twenty-

Causes of the demographic revolution

Its uneven effects

six years. An outstanding example is that of Brazil. In 1900 its population was estimated to be 17 million. By 1975 this total had grown to 98 million, and by 1986 to 143 million, a more than eightfold increase in less than one hundred years. The population of Asia (excluding the USSR) grew from 813 million in 1900 to approximately 2.9 billion in 1986—approximately 60 percent of the world's population. A situation in which the poorest nations are also the most overpopulated does not augur well for the future of world stability.

6. THE ACHIEVEMENTS AND LIMITATIONS OF SCIENCE AND TECHNOLOGY

Science and technology: cause and cure of the world's problems

For solutions to many of these problems, men and women have, paradoxically, turned to those agencies responsible, in many cases, for the creation of the problems: science and technology. Scientists and technicians invented and perfected the internal combustion engine and the chemical DDT. Now other scientists and technicians are seeking ways to combat their deleterious effects. Scientific research has been responsible for the medical advances which have helped to produce worldwide population increase. No one would argue, of course, that the research should not have taken place, or that the continuing battle against disease is not one of humanity's most worthwhile engagements. Most would agree, however, that science must move as quickly as possible to come up with a safe and simple method of controlling birth, as it continues to fight to prolong life.

The discovery of viruses; DNA

The achievements of science in the field of health during the past half-century have been truly remarkable. Two discoveries of great importance have enabled scientists to understand more clearly the ways in which the human body receives and transmits disease. The discovery of viruses was the result of experimentation conducted chiefly by the American biochemist Wendell Stanley in the 1930s. Viruses are microscopic organisms which show signs of life—including the ability to reproduce—only when existing inside living cells. They are the cause of many human diseases, including measles, poliomyelitis (infantile paralysis), and rabies. Not until the nature of viruses was understood could scientists begin to develop means of treating and preventing the virus-produced illnesses in human beings. A second most important discovery that has increased our understanding of human life occurred in 1953, when the Englishman F. H. C. Crick and the American James D. Watson further unlocked the mysteries of genetic inheritance that had been explored by Gregor Mendel at the end of the nineteenth century. Crick and Watson successfully analyzed deoxyribonucleic acid, or DNA, the chemical molecular structure that occurs in the nuclei of gene cells. They discovered that DNA is composed of smaller molecules of four different kinds, linked together in spiral chains. The arrangement of these molecules in each

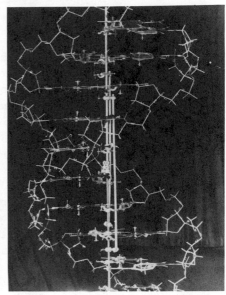

The Decoding of DNA. Left: F. H. C. Crick and James D. Watson discuss their efforts to analyze the molecular structure of DNA. Right: A model of the molecular structure of DNA. The dual spiral chains are called a double helix.

cell forms a distinct chemical message which determines the character of the genes and therefore of the human organism of which they are a part. The knowledge gained through analysis of DNA has enabled scientists and doctors to understand the causes of hereditary disease and also, by altering a patient's body chemistry, to prevent it. Despite the great benefits that have resulted from this recent discovery, scientists and others have warned that an understanding of the workings of DNA could lead to dangerous tampering with the genetic processes, as, for example, in attempts to produce artificially a breed of more "perfect" human beings.

Experimentation based upon a fuller understanding of the causes of disease has led to the discovery of new medicines to treat it. In 1935 the German Gerhard Domagk discovered the first of the sulfa drugs, which he called sulfanilamide. Soon others were added to the list. Each was found to be marvelously effective in curing or checking such diseases as rheumatic fever, gonorrhea, scarlet fever, and meningitis. About 1930, the Englishman Sir Alexander Fleming discovered the first of the antibiotics, penicillin. Antibiotics are chemical agents produced by living organisms and possessing the power to check or kill bacteria. Many have their origin in molds, fungi, algae, and in simple organisms living in the soil. Penicillin was eventually found to be a drug that could produce spectacular results in the treatment of pneumonia, syphilis, peritonitis, tetanus, and numerous other maladies hitherto frequently fatal. Scientists used knowledge obtained through the analysis of DNA to strengthen the cultures used to develop penicillin. In the 1940s the second most famous of the antibiotics—

Medical advances: sulfa drugs, antibiotics, tranquilizers

Dr. Jonas Salk in His Laboratory

The First Lunar Landing. Astronaut Edwin E. Aldrin, Jr., is photographed walking near the lunar module of Apollo 11. Astronaut Neil Armstrong, who took the picture, and part of the lunar module are reflected in Aldrin's face plate.

streptomycin—was discovered by the American Dr. Selman W. Waksman. Streptomycin seems to hold its greatest promise in the treatment of tuberculosis, though it has been used for numerous other infections that do not yield to penicillin.

As important as the discovery of new drugs to treat disease has been the development of new means of preventing it. Sir Edward Jenner discovered the first successful vaccine, used to prevent smallpox, in 1796. But not until the 1950s were vaccines found that could protect from diseases such as mumps, measles, and cholera. One of the most exciting breakthroughs occurred with the development of an inoculation against poliomyelitis by the American Dr. Jonas Salk, in 1953. Still to be discovered are effective agents for the successful treatment of two of the world's most deadly killers, heart disease and cancer, and of a recent and potentially more dangerous worldwide plague Anti-Immune Deficiency Syndrome (AIDS), a virus that attacks the body's immune system, thus making it prey to any number of deadly diseases and infections. Unlike the victims of heart disease and cancer, no AIDS patient has ever been cured.

Few would today oppose continued campaigns by scientists intent upon eradicating disease. Governments have found it increasingly difficult, however, to justify the spending of vast sums of public money on programs designed to facilitate the exploration of outer space. From their inception, these "experiments" have resembled international competitions between the United States and the Soviet Union as much as they have scientific and technological investigations. On October 4, 1957, the government of the Soviet Union rocketed the first artificial satellite into space at a speed of about 18,000 miles an hour. Though it weighed nearly 200 pounds, it was propelled upward higher than 500 miles. This Russian achievement gave the English language a new word—Sputnik, the Russian for satellite or fellow traveler. In April 1961, the Russians succeeded in sending the first man into orbit around the earth. Meanwhile, scientists and military specialists in the United States had been competing to match the Soviets' achievements. After a number of successes with animals and "uninhabited" capsules, and the suborbital journey of a manned capsule, they launched the first American manned spaceship into orbit around the earth on February 20, 1962. Their successes were climaxed in July 1969 when Neil Armstrong, a civilian astronaut, left his lunar landing module and became the first man on the moon's surface. These voyages and those that followed were hailed as events of capital importance. They did promise an extension of our knowledge of outer space and could doubtless prepare the way for exploration of the moon and eventually of distant planets. But by the mid-1970s, both the United States and the Soviet Union had drastically cut back their space programs in response to demands on their economies from other quarters. A space "shuttle" and laboratory, plus continuing experiments of a minor nature, kept the programs alive, despite an accident in 1986 that killed all the crew members of a U.S. space shuttle. But the value of these devices was being questioned, in view of the billions required to keep them operational.

Undoubtedly it was in the area of nuclear science that the largest and most troubling questions arose as to the capabilities, limitations, and implications of science and technology. Even more disturbing than the results of the nuclear bombs dropped on Japan at the end of the Second World War were the first tests of a hydrogen bomb by the U.S. Atomic Energy commission in November 1952. The tests were conducted at Eniwetok Atoll in the South Pacific; an entire island disappeared after burning brightly for several hours. The hydrogen bomb, or H-bomb, is based upon fusion of hydrogen atoms, a process which requires the enormous heat generated by the splitting of uranium atoms to start the reaction. The fusion results in the creation of a new element, helium, which actually weighs less than the sum of the hydrogen atoms. The "free" energy left over provides the tremendous explosive power of the H-bomb. The force of hydrogen bombs is measured in *megatons,* each of which represents 1,000,000 tons of TNT. Thus a 5-megaton H-bomb would equal 250 times the power of the A-bombs dropped on Hiroshima and Nagasaki.

Clearly the scientists had, at the behest of their government, unleashed a weapon of devastating proportions upon the world. By the 1970s, not only the United States, but the Soviet Union, China, Britain, France, India, Israel, and other nations either possessed atomic weapons or were in the process of developing the technology to do so. Science was once and for all proved to be something other than "pure," that is, without practical and political implications. The appli-

*Proliferation of nuclear
weapons*

*The uses of atomic energy;
electronics*

An H-Bomb Mushrooms. The cloud spreads into a huge mushroom following a 1952 explosion of a hydrogen bomb in the Marshall Islands of the Pacific. The photo was taken 50 miles from the detonation site at about 12,000 feet. The cloud rose to 40,000 feet two minutes after the explosion. Ten minutes later the cloud stem had pushed about 25 miles. The mushroom portion went up to 10 miles and spread 100 miles.

cation of its discoveries had become a burdensome fact of life for humanity the world over.

Governments experimented with schemes to harness nuclear energy for peaceful purposes. Some progress has been made in the development of atomic power as an alternative source of domestic and industrial fuel. But the dangers of radiation as a byproduct suggest that this scheme may prove of limited value. During the late 1970s, when the West's supplies of oil were threatened, heated debate continued between advocates of further construction of atomic power plants and those who argued in favor of other energy forms—among them solar—as safer and cheaper alternatives. Meanwhile, technologists working for private industry made use of discoveries in atomic physics to pioneer the field of electronics. Electronics derives from that branch of physics which deals with the behavior and effects of electrons, or negatively charged constituents within the atom. Electronic devices have multiplied in staggering profusion since the Second World War. Among them are devices to measure the trajectory of missiles, to give warnings of approaching missiles or aircraft, to make possible "blind" landings of airplanes, to store and release electrical signals, to amplify and regulate the transmission of light and sound images, and to provide the power for photoelectric cells that open doors, and operate various automatic machines. The spacecraft industry, which has made possible the exploration of outer space, is closely dependent upon electronics.

The use of electronic devices for radio reception led to initial progress in automation. Automation should not be confused with mechanization, though it may be considered the logical extension of that process. More correctly, automation means a close integration of four elements: (1) a processing system; (2) a mechanical handling system; (3) sensing equipment; and (4) a control system. Though all of these elements are necessary, the last two are the most significant. Sensing equipment performs a function similar to that of the human senses. It observes and measures what is happening and sends the information thus gained to the control unit. It employs such devices as photoelectric cells, infrared cells, high-frequency devices, and devices making use of X rays, isotopes, and resonance. It operates without fatigue and much faster and more accurately than do the human senses. Moreover, its observations can be made in places unsafe for, or inaccessible to, human beings. A control system receives information from a sensing element, compares this information with that required by the "program," and then makes the necessary adjustments. This series of operations is continuous, so that a desired state is constantly maintained without any human intervention, except for that initially involved in "programming." This revolution has been greatly extended by the invention of lasers. A laser is a device for amplifying the focus and intensity of light. High-energy atoms are stimulated by light to amplify a beam of light. Lasers have demonstrated their value recently in medicine. They have been used effectively in arresting hemorrhaging in the retina in eye afflictions. Through automation, expensive and complicated machines are constantly taking the place of much human labor. Data-processing machines and electronic computers are employed to control switching operations in railroad yards, to operate assembly lines, to operate machines that control other machines, and even to maintain blood pressure during critical operations in hospitals.

Electronic inventions have proved no more an unmixed blessing than have the other discoveries and developments of scientists and technicians. One obvious problem generated by devices that can do the work of humans is that they put humans out of work. Technological unemployment has become an important problem for the modern world. Though new industries absorbed many workers, others were bound to be displaced by automation. While the demand for skilled labor remained high, the so-called entry jobs performed by the unskilled were fast disappearing. They were being eliminated not by computers so much as by fork-lift trucks and motorized conveyors and sweepers. Mechanization of agriculture also eliminated thousands of jobs for unskilled and uneducated workers.

Technological unemployment

Science and technology provide no panaceas for the problems of the world. If those problems are to be solved, men and women, not machines, will have to do the work. They will be better equipped to do so if they possess some sense of their own past. The lesson of history is not that it repeats itself. The lesson is, rather, that the present can be clearly perceived, and the future intelligently planned for, only when those responsible for the world's destiny understand the workings of human nature. And for knowledge of that extraordinarily complicated and fascinating mechanism, there is no better source than history.

Science, technology, and an understanding of human nature

SELECTED READINGS

• *Items so designated are available in paperback editions.*

Barr, A. H., Jr., *What Is Modern Painting?* New York, 1966. Especially useful for beginning students of art history.
• Bell, Daniel, *The End of Ideology: On the Exhaustion of Political Ideas in the Fifties,* Glencoe, Ill., 1960. Major spokesman for the point of view expressed in the title.
Cornish, Edward, *The Study of the Future: An Introduction to the Art and Science of Understanding and Shaping Tomorrow's World,* Washington, D.C., 1977. An introduction to the world of the "futurists."
• Erlich, Paul, *The Population Bomb,* New York, 1968. Discusses the threat of overpopulation.
• Falk, Richard, *A Study of Future Worlds,* New York, 1975.
• Fanon, Frantz, *The Wretched of the Earth,* New York, 1968. An extraordinary and brilliant delineation of the oppression of Third World peoples.

• Galbraith, John Kenneth, *The New Industrial State,* Boston, 1967. A penetrating analysis of the changes in capitalism wrought by advanced technology.

• Gamow, George, *Thirty Years That Shook Physics,* New York, 1966. A lucid account by a physicist.

• Harrington, Michael, *The Other America: Poverty in the United States,* New York, 1962. An influential polemic of the early 1960s.

Heilbroner, Robert L., *An Inquiry into the Human Prospect,* New York, 1974, 1980. Optimistic assessment of the durability of Western cultural values.

Infeld, Leopold, *Albert Einstein: His Work and Its Influence on Our World,* New York, 1950. A general introduction.

• Marcuse, Herbert, *Counterrevolution and Revolt,* Boston, 1972.

Myrdal, Gunnar, *Against the Stream: Critical Essays on Economics,* New York, 1972. Offers pertinent comments on problems of the Third World.

———, *The Challenge of World Poverty: A World Anti-Poverty Program in Outline,* New York, 1970.

• Popper, Karl, *The Open Society and Its Enemies,* rev. ed., London, 1962. A vigorous comparison of the totalitarian and democratic philosophies by a libertarian.

• Rich, Adrienne, *On Lies, Secrets, and Silence,* New York, 1979. Essays by a leading feminist thinker.

Rosenberg, Harold, *The Anxious Object: Art Today and Its Significance,* New York, 1964. Written by a leading apologist for contemporary art trends.

Servan-Schreiber, J. J., *The World Challenge,* New York, 1981. Analyzes problems of distribution of world resources.

• Solzhenitsyn, Aleksandr, *The Gulag Archipelago, 1918–1956,* New York, 1974–1975. An account of prison camps during the Stalinist era by the exiled Russian novelist.

• Sullerot, E., *Women, Society, and Change,* New York, 1971. A good introduction to the recent history of changing roles for women.

• Toffler, Alan, *Future Shock,* New York, 1971. An extended essay on the consequences of rapid change in modern industrial society.

• Worldwatch Institute, *State of the World, 1990,* New York, 1990. Fact-packed examination of environmental problems and the requisites for building a sustainable society.

RULERS OF PRINCIPAL STATES SINCE 700 A.D.

The Carolingian Dynasty

Pepin, Mayor of the Palace, 714
Charles Martel, Mayor of the Palace, 715–741
Pepin I, Mayor of the Palace, 741; King, 751–768
Charlemagne, King, 768–814; Emperor, 800–814
Louis the Pious, Emperor, 814–840

West Francia

Charles the Bald, King, 840–877; Emperor, 875
Louis II, King, 877–879
Louis III, King, 879–882
Carloman, King, 879–884

Middle Kingdoms

Lothair, Emperor, 840–855
Louis (Italy), Emperor, 855–875
Charles (Provence), King, 855–863
Lothair II (Lorraine), King, 855–869

East Francia

Ludwig, King, 840–876
Carloman, King, 876–880
Ludwig, King, 876–882
Charles the Fat, Emperor, 876–887

Holy Roman Emperors

Saxon Dynasty

Otto I, 962–973
Otto II, 973–983
Otto III, 983–1002
Henry II, 1002–1024

Franconian Dynasty

Conrad II, 1024–1039
Henry III, 1039–1056
Henry IV, 1056–1106
Henry V, 1106–1125
Lothair II (of Saxony), King, 1125–1133; Emperor, 1133–1137

Hohenstaufen Dynasty

Conrad III, 1138–1152
Frederick I (Barbarossa), 1152–1190
Henry VI, 1190–1197
Philip of Swabia, 1198–1208 ⎱ Rivals
Otto IV (Welf), 1198–1215 ⎰
Frederick II, 1220–1250
Conrad IV, 1250–1254

Interregnum, 1254–1273

Emperors from Various Dynasties
Rudolf I (Hapsburg), 1273–1291

Adolf (Nassau), 1292–1298
Albert I (Hapsburg), 1298–1308
Henry VII (Luxemburg), 1308–1313
Ludwig IV (Wittelsbach), 1314–1347
Charles IV (Luxemburg), 1347–1378
Wenceslas (Luxemburg), 1378–1400
Rupert (Wittelsbach), 1400–1410
Sigismund (Luxemburg), 1410–1437

Hapsburg Dynasty

Albert II, 1438–1439
Frederick III, 1440–1493
Maximilian I, 1493–1519
Charles V, 1519–1556
Ferdinand I, 1556–1564
Maximilian II, 1564–1576
Rudolf II, 1576–1612
Matthias, 1612–1619
Ferdinand II, 1619–1637
Ferdinand III, 1637–1657
Leopold I, 1658–1705
Joseph I, 1705–1711
Charles VI, 1711–1740
Charles VII (not a Hapsburg), 1742–1745
Francis I, 1745–1765
Joseph II, 1765–1790
Leopold II, 1790–1792
Francis II, 1792–1806

Rulers of France from Hugh Capet

Capetian Kings

Hugh Capet, 987–996
Robert II, 996–1031
Henry I, 1031–1060
Philip I, 1060–1108
Louis VI, 1108–1137
Louis VII, 1137–1180
Philip II (Augustus), 1180–1223
Louis VIII, 1223–1226
Louis IX, 1226–1270
Philip III, 1270–1285
Philip IV, 1285–1314
Louis X, 1314–1316
Philip V, 1316–1322
Charles IV, 1322–1328

House of Valois

Philip VI, 1328–1350
John, 1350–1364
Charles V, 1364–1380
Charles VI, 1380–1422
Charles VII, 1422–1461
Louis XI, 1461–1483
Charles VIII, 1483–1498
Louis XII, 1498–1515
Francis I, 1515–1547

Bourbon Dynasty

Henry IV, 1589–1610
Henry II, 1547–1559
Francis II, 1559–1560
Charles IX, 1560–1574
Henry III, 1574–1589

Louis XIII, 1610–1643
Louis XIV, 1643–1715
Louis XV, 1715–1774
Louis XVI, 1774–1792

After 1792

First Republic, 1792–1799
Napoleon Bonaparte, First Consul, 1799–1804
Napoleon I, Emperor, 1804–1814
Louis XVIII (Bourbon dynasty), 1814–1824
Charles X (Bourbon dynasty), 1824–1830
Louis Philippe, 1830–1848
Second Republic, 1848–1852
Napoleon III, Emperor, 1852–1870
Third Republic, 1870–1940
Pétain regime, 1940–1944
Provisional government, 1944–1946
Fourth Republic, 1946–1958
Fifth Republic, 1958–

Rulers of England

Anglo-Savon Kings

Egbert, 802–839
Ethelwulf, 839–858
Ethelbald, 858–860
Ethelbert, 860–866
Ethelred, 866–871
Alfred the Great, 871–900
Edward the Elder, 900–924
Ethelstan, 924–940
Edmund I, 940–946
Edred, 946–955
Edwy, 955–959
Edgar, 959–975
Edward the Martyr, 975–978
Ethelred the Unready, 978–1016
Canute, 1016–1035 (Danish Nationality)
Harold I, 1035–1040

Hardicanute, 1040–1042
Edward the Confessor, 1042–1066
Harold II, 1066

Anglo-Norman Kings

William I (the Conqueror), 1066–1087
William II, 1087–1100
Henry I, 1100–1135
Stephen, 1135–1154

Angevin Kings

Henry II, 1154–1189
Richard I, 1189–1199
John, 1199–1216
Henry III, 1216–1272
Edward I, 1272–1307
Edward II, 1307–1327

Edward III, 1327–1377
Richard II, 1377–1399

House of Lancaster

Henry IV, 1399–1413
Henry V, 1413–1422
Henry VI, 1422–1461

House of York

Edward IV, 1461–1483
Edward V, 1483
Richard III, 1483–1485

Tudor Sovereigns

Henry VII, 1485–1509
Henry VIII, 1509–1547
Edward VI, 1547–1553
Mary, 1553–1558
Elizabeth I, 1558–1603

Stuart Kings

James I, 1603–1625
Charles I, 1625–1649

Commonwealth and Protectorate, 1649–1659

Later Stuart Monarchs

Charles II, 1660–1685
James II, 1685–1688
William III and Mary II, 1689–1694
William III alone, 1694–1702
Anne, 1702–1714

House of Hanover

George I, 1714–1727
George II, 1727–1760
George III, 1760–1820
George IV, 1820–1830
William IV, 1830–1837
Victoria, 1837–1901

House of Saxe-Coburg-Gotha

Edward VII, 1901–1910
George V, 1910–1917

House of Windsor

George V, 1917–1936
Edward VIII, 1936
George VI, 1936–1952
Elizabeth II, 1952–

Prominent Popes

Silvester I, 314–335
Leo I, 440–461
Gelasius I, 492–496
Gregory I, 590–604
Nicholas I, 858–867
Silvester II, 999–1003
Leo IX, 1049–1054
Nicholas II, 1058–1061
Gregory VII, 1073–1085
Urban II, 1088–1099
Paschal II, 1099–1118
Alexander III, 1159–1181
Innocent III, 1198–1216
Gregory IX, 1227–1241
Boniface VIII, 1294–1303
John XXII, 1316–1334
Nicholas V, 1447–1455
Pius II, 1458–1464
Alexander VI, 1492–1503

Julius II, 1503–1513
Leo X, 1513–1521
Adrian VI, 1522–1523
Clement VII, 1523–1534
Paul III, 1534–1549
Paul IV, 1555–1559
Gregory XIII, 1572–1585
Gregory XVI, 1831–1846
Pius IX, 1846–1878
Leo XIII, 1878–1903
Pius X, 1903–1914
Benedict XV, 1914–1922
Pius XI, 1922–1939
Pius XII, 1939–1958
John XXIII, 1958–1963
Paul VI, 1963–1978
John Paul I, 1978
John Paul II, 1978–

Rulers of Austria and Austria-Hungary

*Maximilian I (Archduke), 1493–1519
*Charles I (Charles V in the Holy Roman Empire), 1519–1556
*Ferdinand I, 1556–1564
*Maximilian II, 1564–1576
*Rudolph II, 1576–1612
*Matthias, 1612–1619
*Ferdinand II, 1619–1637
*Ferdinand III, 1637–1657
*Leopold I, 1658–1705
*Joseph I, 1705–1711
*Charles VI, 1711–1740
Maria Theresa, 1740–1780

* Also bore title of Holy Roman Emperor.

*Joseph II, 1780–1790
*Leopold II, 1790–1792
*Francis II, 1792–1835 (Emperor of Austria as Francis I after 1804)
Ferdinand I, 1835–1848
Francis Joseph, 1848–1916 (after 1867 Emperor of Austria and King of Hungary)
Charles I, 1916–1918 (Emperor of Austria and King of Hungary)
Republic of Austria, 1918–1938 (dictatorship after 1934)
Republic restored, under Allied occupation, 1945–1956
Free Republic, 1956–

Rulers of Prussia and Germany

*Frederick I, 1701–1713
*Frederick William I, 1713–1740
*Frederick II (the Great), 1740–1786
*Frederick William II, 1786–1797
*Frederick William III, 1797–1840
*Frederick William IV, 1840–1861
*William I, 1861–1888 (German Emperor after 1871)
Frederick III, 1888
William II, 1888–1918

*Kings of Prussia.

Weimar Republic, 1918–1933
Third Reich (Nazi Dictatorship), 1933–1945
Allied occupation, 1945–1952
Division into Federal Republic of Germany in west and German Democratic Republic in east, 1949–1990
Reunification of Federal Republic of Germany and German Democratic Republic as Federal Republic of Germany, 1990–

Rulers of Russia

Ivan III, 1462–1505
Basil III, 1505–1533
Ivan IV, 1533–1584
Theodore I, 1584–1598
Boris Godunov, 1598–1605
Theodore II, 1605
Basil IV, 1606–1610
Michael, 1613–1645
Alexius, 1645 1676
Theodore III, 1676–1682
Ivan V and Peter I, 1682–1689
Peter I (the Great), 1689–1725
Catherine I, 1725–1727

Peter II, 1727–1730
Anna, 1730–1740
Ivan VI, 1740–1741
Elizabeth, 1741–1762
Peter III, 1762
Catherine II (the Great), 1762–1796
Paul, 1796–1801
Alexander I, 1801–1825
Nicholas I, 1825–1855
Alexander II, 1855–1881
Alexander III, 1881–1894
Nicholas II, 1894–1917
Soviet Republic, 1917–

Rulers of Italy

Victor Emmanuel II, 1861–1878
Humbert I, 1878–1900
Victor Emmanuel III, 1900–1946
Fascist Dictatorship, 1922–1943
   (maintained in northern Italy until 1945)

Humbert II, May 9–June 13, 1946
Republic, 1946–

Rulers of Spain

Ferdinand { and Isabella, 1479–1504
and Philip I, 1504–1506
and Charles I, 1506–1516 }

Charles I (Holy Roman Emperor Charles V),
   1516–1556
Philip II, 1556–1598
Philip III, 1598–1621
Philip IV, 1621–1665
Charles II, 1665–1700
Philip V, 1700–1746
Ferdinand VI, 1746–1759
Charles III, 1759–1788

Charles IV, 1788–1808
Ferdinand VII, 1808
Joseph Bonaparte, 1808–1813
Ferdinand VII (restored), 1814–1833
Isabella II, 1833–1868
Republic, 1868–1870
Amadeo, 1870–1873
Republic, 1873–1874
Alfonso XII, 1874–1885
Alfonso XIII, 1886–1931
Republic, 1931–1939
Fascist Dictatorship, 1939–1975
Juan Carlos I, 1975–

Principal Rulers of India

Chandragupta (Maurya Dynasty), c. 332–298 B.C.
Asoka (Maurya Dynasty), c. 273–232 B.C.
Vikramaditya (Gupta Dynasty), 375–413 A.D.
Harsha (Vardhana Dynasty), 606–648
Babur (Mogul Dynasty), 1526–1530
Akbar (Mogul Dynasty), 1556–1605
Jahangir (Mogul Dynasty), 1605–1627
Shah Jahan (Mogul Dynasty), 1627–1658

Aurangzeb (Mogul Dynasty), 1658–1707
Regime of British East India Company, 1757–1858
British *raj*, 1858–1947
Division into self-governing dominions of India and
   Pakistan, 1947
Republic of India, 1950–
Republic of Pakistan, 1956–
Republic of Bangladesh, 1971–

Dynasties of China

Hsia, c. 2205–1766 B.C. (?)
Shang (Yin), c. 1766 (?)–1100 B.C.
Chou, c. 1100–256 B.C.
Ch'in, 221–207 B.C.
Han (Former), 206 B.C.–8 A.D.
Interregnum (Wang Mang, usurper), 8–23 A.D.
Han (Later), 25–220
Wei, 220–265
Tsin (Chin), 265–420
Southern Dynasties: Sung (Liu Sung), Ch'i, Liang,
   Ch'eñ, 420–589

Northern Dynasties: Northern Wei, Western Wei,
   Eastern Wei, Northern Ch'i, Northern Chou, 386–
   581
Sui, 589–618
T'ang, 618–907
Five Dynasties: Later Liang, Later T'ang, Later Tsin,
   Later Han, Later Chou, 907–960
Sung, 960–1279
Yüan (Mongol), 1279–1368
Ming, 1368–1644
Ch'ing (Manchu) Dynasty, 1644–1912

Periods of Chinese Rule

Chinese Republic, 1912–1949

Communist Regime, 1949–

Periods of Japanese Rule

Legendary Period, c. 660 B.C. –530 A.D.
Foundation Period, 530–709 A.D.
Taika (Great Reform) Period, 645–654
Nara Period, 710–793
Heian Period, 794–1192
Kamakura Period, 1192–1333
Namboku-cho ("Northern and Southern Dynasties") Period, 1336–1392

Muromachi (Ashikaga) Period, 1392–1568
Sengoku ("Country at War") Period, c. 1500–1600
Sengoku Period, c. 1500–1600
Edo (Tokugawa) Period, 1603–1867
Meiji Period (Mutsuhito), 1868–1912
Taisho Period (Yoshihito), 1912–1926
Showa Period (Hirohito), 1926–1989
Heisei Period (Akihito), 1989–

Rulers of Principal African States

Ewuare the Great, Oba of Benin, 1440–1473
Muhammad Runfa, King of Kano, 1463–1499
Afonso I, King of Kongo, 1506–1543
Ibrahim Maje, King of Katsina, 1549–1567
Idris Alooma, Mai of Bornu, 1569–ca. 1619
Osei Tutu, King of Asante, ca. 1670–1717
Agaja, King of Dahomey, 1708–1740
Sayyid Said, ruler of Zanzibar and Muscat, 1804–1856
Shaka, King of the Zulu, 1818–1828
Moshesh, King of Basutoland, 1824–1868
Menelik, King of Shoa, 1865–1889; Emperor of Ethiopia, 1889–1913
Haile Selassie, Emperor of Ethiopia, 1930–1974
H. F. Verwoerd, Prime Minister of South Africa, 1958–1966
Gamal Abdul Nasser, President of Egypt, 1956–1970

Leopold Sedar Senghor, President of Senegal, 1960–1980
Felix Houphouet-Boigny, President of the Ivory Coast, 1960–
Kwame Nkrumah, President of Ghana, 1960–1966
Julius K. Nyerere, President of Tanzania, 1962–1985
Kenneth D. Kaunda, President of Zambia, 1964
Jomo Kenyatta, President of Kenya, 1964–1978
Sese Seko Mobutu, President of Zaire, 1965–
Houari Boumedienne, head of Algeria, 1965–1978
Anwar el Sadat, President of Egypt, 1970–1981
Agostinho Neto, President of Angola, 1975–1979
Olusegun Obasanjo, head of Nigeria, 1975–1979
P. W. Botha, Prime Minister of South Africa, 1978–1984
Robert Mugabe, Prime Minister of Zimbabwe, 1980–
Hosni Mubarak, President of Egypt, 1981–
P. W. Botha, President of South Africa, 1984–1989
F. W. de Klerk, President of South Africa, 1989–

Index